OTHER BOOKS BY DANNY PEARY

WE PLAYED
THE GAME

WE PLAYED THE GAME

65 PLAYERS REMEMBER

BASEBALL'S GREATEST ERA,

1947–1964

EDITED BY

DANNY PEARY

WITH AN INTRODUCTION BY
LAWRENCE S. RITTER

NEW YORK

THE AUTHOR WISHES TO THANK THE FOLLOWING TEAMS AND PLAYERS FOR GRACIOUSLY PROVIDING PERMISSION TO USE PHOTOGRAPHS: THE BALTIMORE ORIOLES, THE BOSTON RED SOX, THE CHICAGO WHITE SOX, THE DETROIT TIGERS, JOHN BERARDINO, EDDIE JOOST, AL KOZAR, BOB CAIN, RALPH KINER, JOHNNY KLIPPSTEIN, HANK SAUER, DON NEWCOMBE, TOM CHENEY, JIM BROSNAN, BILLY MORAN, BOB TURLEY, MINNIE MINOSO, HAL WOODESHICK, AND THE BASEBALL HALL OF FAME.

BOOK DESIGN BY KATHY KIKKERT

LIBRARY OF CONGRESS CATALOGING-IN-PUBLICATION DATA
WE PLAYED THE GAME: 65 PLAYERS REMEMBER
BASEBALL'S GREATEST ERA, 1947–1964/
EDITED BY DANNY PEARY; INTRODUCTION BY LAWRENCE S. RITTER. —
1ST ED.
P.   CM.
INCLUDES INDEX.
ISBN 0-7868-8091-0
1. BASEBALL PLAYERS—UNITED STATES—BIOGRAPHY.   2. BASEBALL—
UNITED STATES—HISTORY—20TH CENTURY.   PEARY, DANNY, 1949–
GV865.A1W4   1994
796.357'0973'09045—DC20   93-26497
CIP

FIRST PAPERBACK EDITION
10 9 8 7 6 5 4 3 2 1

To my brother, Gerry, who sparked
my interest in baseball;
my parents, Joe and Laura,
who never even knew the definition
of a home run but provided a cheery home
for two baseball-obsessed sons;
and my wife, Suzanne,
who keeps hot chocolate in the cupboard,
Popsicles in the freezer,
and a baseball game on the TV set.
And to the 65 special players
in this book, the longtime fans who
remember them, and the young fans
who want to learn all about them.

ACKNOWLEDGMENTS

In my preface, I refer to this book as ''a two-year labor of love.'' But I must say that my love for the project remained intact only because ''my'' two years of labor was shared and made easier by a number of talented individuals. Books can be lonely and frustrating endeavors, but I was helped every step of the way. Foremost I want to thank my editor Judith Riven for helping shape the manuscript, for the three o'clock lunches, and for the countless and necessary encouraging phone calls that revived me at the computer. I am also eternally grateful to Hyperion publisher Bob Miller and Tim Onosko for helping me conceive this project and sending me out on the road. And I am equally appreciative of Hyperion's Brian DeFiore for giving me confidence that the book would meet its planned publication date despite a hectic, seemingly impossible schedule, and then shepherding it through to completion. He was helped in his deadline busting by his crack assistant Catherine Rezza, Hyperion's production editor, Angela Palmisono, designer Kathy Kikkert, and copy editor Elaine Chubb, who humbled me with her baseball knowledge (and caught where I typed in the name of movie actress Bebe Daniels instead of Pittsburgh pitcher Bennie Daniels). I applaud the efforts of all of them, as well as those of Vicki Di Stasio and Henry Price, who made several saves along the way, at Hyperion for making my dream project come to fruition.

I thank Lawrence S. Ritter both for his introduction and for serving as my mentor before and after each of my trips to secure interviews. I am most grateful to my longtime friend and agent Chris Tomasino, and Robert L. Rosen, Suzanne Maroon, Lisa Laskowitz, and Jonathan Diamond. I thank my research assistants Cliff Lauder and Paul Brenner. I acknowledge everyone at the National Baseball Hall of Fame Library, especially Milo Stewart, Jr. (who supplied me with the great majority of the photos in this book), Jeff Stevens, Jr., Robert Browning, Christopher Schroeder, Patricia Kelly, and Virginia Reinholdt. I thank Gabe Schecter, Timothy Rogers, and Dan Heaton for their assistance in Cooperstown. Around the country I was helped by such gracious individuals as Randy Shandobil, Jeanie Dooha, Mikael Dooha, Totte Gardeman, Jesse Gardeman, Bob Nowacki, Julie Weiss, Barbara Haynes, Carol Summers, Susan Rabinovitz, Curren Warf, Michael Lepie, Jenny Hurwitz, John Wasylik, Esther Rae, Marty Appel, Merilyn Kozar, Pamela Jameson, Roy Campanella II, Jackie Cheney, Tom Mortenson, Jeannie Sauer, Patti Latman, Dana Nowel, Barb Kozuh, Margot De Maestri, Linda Kaplan, Debbie Matson, Elinor Nauen, Donna Villani, Tricia Katz, Joy Grant, the staff at Broglio's in Cleveland, and the staff of Dick Groat's Champion Lakes Golf Club outside Pittsburgh. Old friends and new friends.

Of course I am grateful beyond words to the 65 players who were included in this book for agreeing to be interviewed and, in many cases, allowing this stranger into their homes or offices. I didn't take them for granted because there were a few other former players I contacted along the way who weren't so accommodating. I also thank those players (and their wives) who went through the added trouble of sending me photographs. And I thank the publicity departments of the major league teams for supplying additional photographs.

ACKNOWLEDGMENTS

I definitely must recognize singers Patty Loveless, Nanci Griffith, Merle Haggard, Alan Jackson, Emmylou Harris, Cyndi Lauper, Suzy Bogguss, Lorrie Morgan, Mary Chapin-Carpenter, Carlene Carter, Pam Tillis, Ricky Skaggs, Tish Hinojosa, Jane Wiedlin, the McGarrigle Sisters, Michelle Shocked, Dolly Parton, Trisha Yearwood, Ralph Stanley, and Kathy Mattea for providing super background music for hours at a time in my office and, especially, out on some endless roads. They were great company.

I thank my parents, Joseph and Laura Peary, and my brother, Gerald Peary. Last but never least, my wife, Suzanne, and daughter, Zoë, deserve my most sincere gratitude for, among many positive things, never asking, ''Aren't you through with that book yet?'' Now they can ask.

INTRODUCTION

You don't have to read very far into Danny Peary's marvelous chronological oral history of baseball from 1947 to 1964 to realize why the game today is a far cry from the one that captivated postwar America half a century ago. There were no designated hitters back then, no artificial turf, no indoor baseball, no quarrelsome players' strikes and/or owners' lockouts, and no spoiled multimillionaires with .240 batting averages. Nor were there any playoffs to cheapen the World Series or "wild cards" to demean the integrity of the regular season.

In the forties and fifties, we sat in the afternoon sunshine and watched the likes of Joseph Paul DiMaggio, Ted Williams, Stan the Man, and Rapid Robert Feller— all of whom, by the way, spent their entire careers with one team—and with role models like them, it was no wonder just about all the sports idols of kids growing up were baseball players. Nowadays, teenagers' heroes are less likely to wear spikes than cleats or (very expensive) sneakers. We used to be familiar with the players' bios, not their contracts; we memorized their stats, not their salaries; and our sports pages in the newspapers were distinguishable from the business sections.

Cynics might say that ballplayers were always motivated (along with everyone else) by the Almighty Dollar. But I discovered differently when I interviewed players from the turn of the century and shortly thereafter for my book *The Glory of Their Times*. And the interviews in *We Played the Game* affirm that the players hadn't changed in this respect until at least the early sixties when, as Hal Woodeshick laments, a new breed of ballplayer emerged.

Professional athletes always had to earn a living, of course, to provide for themselves and their families, and they were never about to take less than they could get. But with rare exceptions the 65 players in this book, from Hall of Famers to bench warmers, played mostly for the sheer love of the game—and the thrill of being one of only 400 major leaguers in the world—in a day when salaries were artificially depressed by the notorious reserve clause that hog-tied every player to one team for the duration of his career. (In the forties and fifties, an average big leaguer earned about the same as a factory foreman or a mid-level corporate executive.) Almost every player interviewed admits he felt grossly underpaid and underappreciated by management, yet felt incredibly lucky just the same.

"I had dreamed of playing in the majors since I was a little kid," recalls Bill Rigney about his rookie season with the Giants. "I had such love for the game and couldn't let myself think what I might do if I failed and had to do something other than play professional baseball."

The most socially significant event that occurred during the era covered in this book was undoubtedly the historic breaking of the color line by Jackie Robinson. Since the 1880s club owners had abided by an unwritten "gentlemen's agreement" to keep the game lily-white by excluding black players. In 1947 Brooklyn Dodgers part-owner and general manager Branch Rickey became a traitor to his class when he broke the owners' pact by signing Robinson to a Brooklyn contract.

Today, close to a third of major league ballplayers are black, but not in 1947. With discriminatory racial laws still on the books in the South, Robinson could not eat in the same restaurants as his teammates during spring training or stay at the same hotels. Once the season started, a barrage of insults was directed at him from fans and opposing dugouts. As soon as his signing became public, four Brooklyn regulars asked Rickey to be traded. A group of St. Louis Cardinals let it be known that they would go on strike rather than take the field against the Dodgers.

The rebellion was promptly crushed by National League president Ford Frick with a blunt ultimatum: ''I do not care if half the league strikes,'' he declared. ''Those who do will encounter quick retribution. All will be suspended even if it wrecks the National League for five years. This is the United States of America and one citizen has as much right to play as another.''

The pronouncement had such a sobering effect that the worst was soon over. Four more black players were signed by big league teams during the 1947 season, including Larry Doby—the first in the American League—by the Cleveland Indians. Among others, Roy Campanella joined the Dodgers in 1948, Don Newcombe, the Dodgers in 1949, Sam Jethroe, the Boston Braves in 1950, and Willie Mays, the Giants in 1951. The New York Yankees acquired their first black player, Elston Howard, in 1955. When the Boston Red Sox at long last obtained Pumpsie Green, in 1959, it meant that every major league team finally had at least one black player.

Jackie Robinson died in 1972 at the relatively young age of 53. The following pages contain many reminiscences about him. One of my favorites, by Ralph Kiner, deals strictly with his talent: ''I knew Jackie Robinson slightly from California,'' said Kiner, ''because I had played softball against him. I knew of him when he went to UCLA, where he was an unbelievable football player, great basketball player, and fantastic track star. Baseball was his worst sport!''

As anyone who lived through the era knows well, the years from 1947 through 1964 were dominated by the mighty New York Yankees. In those 18 years the Yankees won the American League pennant 15 times: in 1947, 1949 through 1953, 1955 through 1958, and 1960 through 1964. Eleven times they won the World Series as well, defeating the Dodgers (and Jackie Robinson) in 1947, 1949, 1952, 1953, and 1956. Casey Stengel

managed the Yankees to a record 10 American League pennants and 7 World Championships in 12 years. It is hard to believe that over 30 years have passed since Casey piloted the Yankees, especially since the recollections about him in this book by former Yankees and opposing players are so vivid. There is a fascinating diversity of opinion about this colorful and controversial figure—some players sing his praises while others think him overrated or still bear grudges.

Stengel was unceremoniously released five days after the 1960 World Series, a Series the Yankees lost by the narrowest of margins when Pittsburgh second baseman Bill Mazeroski dramatically homered in the bottom of the ninth inning of the seventh game.

''I've been fired because of my age,'' Stengel said at the time. ''I'll never make the mistake of being seventy again.''

It doesn't take an advanced degree from an Ivy League college to figure out that multiyear dynasties like the Yankees and Dodgers of the late forties, fifties, and early sixties can never be duplicated. Now it is impossible to keep a winning team in one uniform for more than a season or two. In 1975 arbitrator Peter Seitz ruled that the reserve clause, which had governed baseball labor-management relations for a hundred years, was no longer enforceable. Thus dawned free agency for players, which, along with television, revolutionized the financial structure of the sport. Individual players can now market their services to the highest bidder, so that it is no longer economically feasible to hold the nucleus of a winning team together for very long.

For better and for worse, the time span from 1947 to 1964 also witnessed the first franchise transfers in half a century. Since 1903 all major league cities had been concentrated on the East Coast or in the nearby Midwest, within overnight railroad distance from each other. St. Louis was the farthest west, less than a third of the way across the country from the East Coast. But when regular transcontinental airplane service began, in the 1940s, it was only a matter of time before teams would become more widely scattered geographically.

The first franchise shift in 50 years occurred in 1953, when the Boston Braves moved to Milwaukee and became the Milwaukee Braves. In 1954 the St. Louis Browns turned into the Baltimore Orioles; in 1955 the Philadelphia Athletics transferred to Kansas City; and in 1958 the New York Giants moved to San Francisco and the Dodgers deserted Brooklyn for Los Angeles. In addition, in 1961 the American League added the Los Angeles Angels and the "new" Washington Senators (the "old" Senators had fled to Minneapolis), and in 1962 the National League expanded by adding the Houston Colt .45s and the New York Mets (managed by none other than 72-year-old Casey Stengel).

Of all the transfers, the abandonment of Brooklyn by the Dodgers caused the most anguish. I remember it well because although I was a Giants fan I had gone to Boys High in Brooklyn and spent many of my happiest teenage years hanging around Ebbets Field. The community had taken the ballclub to its bosom and the ethnically diverse, racially mixed metropolis was united by love for its team. Why did the Dodgers leave? Both fans and players were puzzled. It wasn't for lack of attendance, which is what drove the Braves out of Boston, the Browns out of St. Louis, the Giants out of New York, and the A's out of Philadelphia. The Dodgers were quite profitable in Brooklyn. They moved simply because owner Walter O'Malley—Branch Rickey had been eased out in 1950—figured that profits would be even greater in Los Angeles. The residents of Los Angeles surely deserved major league baseball, but why they should have obtained it at the expense of Brooklyn was never satisfactorily explained.

Ballplayers are an unsentimental lot, and few of them expressed regret at leaving the cities (and disillusioned fans) they had represented. But there are welcome exceptions. "I loved playing ball in New York," Giants pitcher Johnny Antonelli tells Danny Peary. "Leaving New York was sad. I thought that New York City deserved major league teams in both leagues, and I couldn't believe both the Dodgers and Giants would leave. I just couldn't believe it. It was such a letdown."

Ebbets Field, home of the Dodgers since 1913, was razed in 1960. When demolition was about to begin, a number of ex-Dodgers stood at attention as Lucy Monroe sang the National Anthem, just as she had at the start of so many Brooklyn home games. This storied site is now occupied by a high-rise apartment complex. The only consolation is that the Jackie Robinson Intermediate School stands nearby, a reminder of what took place in Brooklyn when major league baseball was truly something special.

"The best thing about baseball today," someone recently said, "is its yesterdays." Danny Peary's *We Played the Game* tells you why.

—Lawrence S. Ritter

PREFACE

We Played the Game is a two-year labor of love, a fantasy-fulfilling endeavor for which I traveled across the country in search of my childhood baseball idols. My intention was both to obtain personal histories of the individual players—those colorful stars, everyday players, and bench warmers who brightened my youth—and to allow their combined words to help re-create that splendid, singular baseball era (1947 to 1964) I was fortunate enough to be born into and become obsessed with as a youngster.

I am extremely gratified that the introduction of this book was contributed by Lawrence S. Ritter, because the inspiration for my project was *The Glory of Their Times,* a classic collection of interviews with ballplayers from the early twentieth century to World War II, whom Mr. Ritter tracked down. In the mid-'60s, Mr. Ritter brought to every fan's attention that along America's highways and byways, in towns and cities, in suburbs and farm country, there reside former major league baseball players. It's a wonderful truth that wasn't so obvious to those of us who always thought baseball players were bigger-than-life figures. It meant that while my childhood cowboy heroes holstered their guns and rode off into the sunset, my baseball heroes simply put away their bats, balls, and gloves and settled down, usually near their birthplaces or where they played ball. Significantly, like the ballplayers Mr. Ritter spoke to, these ex-players retained vivid (though often contradictory) memories of their playing days and were willing to take me back to that glorious time when they played the game.

As did Mr. Ritter three decades before, I took several journeys across present-day America to find the past. More than fifty of my sixty-five interviews were done in person. As was Mr. Ritter, I was a stranger to the ballplayers I sought, having previously known only Vic Power, my favorite player from 1954 to 1965, and Tim McCarver. (All interview material in *We Played the Game* is original except for a portion of the Power material that I included in an earlier book.) When Mr. Ritter tracked down his subjects it was like Stanley searching for Livingstone in uncharted Africa, since back then most surviving old-time ballplayers had been neglectfully allowed to drift into obscurity. My much different problem was that by the 1990s autograph seekers had located and hounded all former players. My letters asking for interviews were routinely placed unopened on piles of autograph requests. It turned out that more than half of the interviews I was granted came about while I was already on the road, through direct calls to players from motel rooms or diners saying that I was in their town or would soon be driving through. For instance, at one point, I called Art Fowler from a phone booth at a lonely crossroads in northwestern South Carolina, deciding that if he didn't pick up the phone and grant this intruder an interview I would head either into Georgia or go back up to North Carolina in search of players.

I interviewed Fowler during the course of a wild, endless, and definitely surreal night at his hangouts in Spartanburg: a busy bar, a busier country-music club, and the busiest all-night breakfast spot in town. That was probably the strangest interview experience. He was wary at first, but since I'd also grown up in nearby

Columbia, we became fast friends and he assured me that he'd come to my rescue if anyone jumped on me.

There were other interviews that were equally rewarding. In Florida, I finally met the very first baseball player I was conscious of as a child, Jim Fridley, who was the lone big leaguer from my birthplace of Philippi, West Virginia. In California, I spent a surprisingly relaxing hour with Don Newcombe, a pitcher who awed me as a kid. I met a reticent and nervous Al Kozar at his lakeside cabin in Highlands, North Carolina—America's leaf capital—where, at his wife's urging, he granted me his first real interview ever and relaxed enough to speak for four hours and establish his place in baseball history. I spent a few hours with Gene Woodling on his Ohio farm. The next day, Frank Baumholtz took me to dinner in his favorite restaurant outside of Cleveland. I took Ryne Duren out for lunch and ice tea in Wisconsin. At a McDonald's in Atlanta, I split the check with Rube Walker, at what was likely the last interview he granted before his death. I visited Dick Groat at his golf course near Pittsburgh. I spent several hours with a trim, forthright Pedro Ramos—who was working as a college pitching coach—at a small ballpark in Miami. I met up with Chico Carrasquel at Comiskey Park, Bill Rigney at Oakland-Alameda Stadium, and Ralph Kiner at Shea Stadium. I visited with players in numerous restaurants, offices, apartments, and houses (with trophy rooms if I was lucky), often located not more than a few miles from where they grew up.

The era of which we spoke began in 1947, when the Yankees won the first of an incredible fifteen pennants in eighteen years, Jackie Robinson broke the color barrier, the pension plan was initiated, and baseball truly returned to form—and even improved—after the war and one year of adjustment. The era ended for some in 1957 when the Dodgers and Giants broke hearts and created football fans by heading for the West Coast. But for me it actually culminated in 1964, when the Yankees won that fifteenth pennant, the final ingredient that tied baseball of the new money-oriented expansion era to baseball of the postwar period.

On one level baseball during this era seemed simple, innocent, and peaceful. The old parks stood proudly, the grass was green and real, most games were played in the sunshine, and they even played baseball in Washington, D.C. Most catchers were chubby, most first basemen were clunky, most second basemen were short, most shortstops were swift, and most third basemen were solid as rocks. Right fielders had rockets for arms, center fielders could run like the wind, and left fielders (with Gene Woodling being an exception) were usually in the lineup because of their bats. Yogi supposedly read comics and chugged Yoo Hoo, and the equally popular Campy smiled infectiously and proved his words about having to be a boy at heart to play this man's game; Mantle hit moonshots; Willie let his hat fly off; Snider became royalty; Ted and Stan the Man got hits every time up; DiMaggio exhibited class and Bob Feller threw gas; Bob Lemon, Robin Roberts, and Warren Spahn won and won; little Eddie Gaedel walked into folklore; Big Klu flexed his muscles; Aaron had grace and Clemente had style; Ernie smiled through the losses; Brooks demonstrated a Hoover at third base; Maris passed Ruth, Wills passed Cobb; Minoso got clunked; Koufax dominated; Drysdale and Gibson intimidated; and on and on. The umps got booed; managers got fired and were recycled elsewhere; teams stayed intact year after year; and the Yankees won too many pennants for those of us who weren't their fans. (No, the Yankees weren't, literally or figuratively, the only game in town.)

But even we kids knew that beneath the calm surface there continued to be racial tension and exploitation of players by the omnipotent and callous owners and general managers. When Walter O'Malley and Horace Stoneham took the Dodgers and Giants west, abandoning their loyal fans, all of us were shocked and forever jaded by their shameless willingness to reveal what all but the most naive among us suspected: that baseball was a business first, a sport second.

I wanted to know how former players, the best witnesses, remembered this era. The sixty-five players in this book speak candidly about their lives on and off the field, telling what it was like to be a major league ballplayer at this time and to play for specific teams during a time when the Yankees were so dominant and the New York teams got most of the media attention. With exceptions like the Cardinals of the late '40s and early '50s, the Phillies in 1961 and 1962, the Braves, Tigers, and Dodgers in 1964, and the Athletics from 1960 to 1964, the various teams are represented year by year by at least one of my subjects. They cover everything from their diamond highlights to their relationships with teammates, managers, general managers, and owners, and from their day-to-day activities to ''Ball Four'' topics. Of course, inaccuracies (which I ask my readers to call my attention to) are bound to creep in when we rely on memories that go back as much as fifty years. However, I was surprised at how much my subjects remembered of their playing days. Indeed, as an editor I helped out the players mostly in regard to scores and statistics, which tended to get jumbled with the passage of time.

Their eyes would twinkle when they spoke of certain people and incidents. But the kindly grandfather image would disappear when they touched on less cheerful topics, perhaps remembering an ugly pitcher-batter confrontation or an unsuccessful salary negotiation, which nearly all the players endured. Those eyes would narrow menacingly, their strong fists would clinch, and their arm muscles would ripple. They could be imposing at 60 or 70, so I could tell how formidable they were in their playing prime. Most definitely, these men were of a different, much harder breed than the athletes who followed. As a group, they represented the last in the tradition of the hard-nosed, fundamentally sound, underpaid yet dedicated ballplayers that Lawrence Ritter interviewed for his book.

As do most of the players who played between 1947 and 1964, I believe that this was baseball's greatest era. It was an improvement over the past simply because the best black and white players now shared the field and because there was so much competition for so few jobs. I think there were an extraordinary number of great and colorful players, men who not only had talent but—in contrast to today's players—also knew how to play the game down to its most subtle aspects. I also think that the escalating, increasingly visible and infuriating prob-

lems in baseball that Mr. Ritter refers to in his introduction actually made the game even more interesting (at least for the fans who didn't quit the game entirely when their favorite team deserted them). Most of all, what made it so appealing was the amazing bond between the underpaid players and their fans, a connection that was heightened by the advent of television, the influence of newspapers and radio, and the popularity of the new lines of baseball cards. We felt we knew these often-beleaguered players and that they needed our encouragement to succeed. Such partnerships could never form in subsequent years once rich, elitist players became motivated by high salaries rather than cheers, and willingly left their teams and fans behind for high-priced free-agent contracts.

I think all of us who were fans between 1947 and 1964 assumed that our beloved players felt as we did about baseball and played it out of passion rather than for profit. That benign suspicion is supported throughout this book. I believe *We Played the Game* rewards us for having been such devoted baseball fans by presenting us with the words that confirm our lifelong gut feelings about the character of our favorite ballplayers. Dick Ellsworth's words have impact: ''All the players just loved the game of baseball, and we couldn't wait to get to the ballpark. We wanted to play and were very protective of the uniforms that we wore. We weren't critical of how they fit or how we looked in them—we were just appreciative and proud to wear them. That may sound corny, but that's how we felt in our hearts.''

They weren't perfect, but they *were* worthy of all the admiration and affection we felt for them. It's good to know that they didn't betray our trust.

—Danny Peary

THE PLAYERS

JOHNNY ANTONELLI (b. 1930, New York) was a left-handed pitcher for the Boston Braves (1948–50), Milwaukee Braves (1953), New York Giants (1954–57), San Francisco Giants (1958–60), Cleveland Indians (1961), and Milwaukee Braves (1961). Having signed a huge bonus contract out of high school, he twice won over 20 games, was the National League ERA leader in 1954, led the league in shutouts 3 times, and made 5 All-Star teams.

FRANK BAUMHOLTZ (b. Ohio) was a left-handed hitting outfielder for the Cincinnati Reds (1947–49), Chicago Cubs (1949, 1950–55), and Philadelphia Phillies (1956–57). Also a professional basketball player, he hit .290 lifetime, twice batting over .300—he finished second in the 1952 batting race—and led the National League in pinch hits in 1955 and 1956.

JOHN BERARDINO (b. 1917, California) was a right-handed hitting infielder for the St. Louis Browns (1939–42, 1946–47, 1951), Cleveland Indians (1948–50, 1952), and Pittsburgh Pirates (1950, 1952). An actor in the off-season, he had the dubious distinction of playing on both the world championship Indians team in 1948 and two of the worst postwar franchises, the Browns and Pirates.

EWELL BLACKWELL (b. 1922, California) was a right-handed pitcher for the Cincinnati Reds (1942, 1946–52), New York Yankees (1952–53), and Kansas City Athletics (1955). Called "The Whip" because of his intimidating side-armed delivery, he led the National League in shutouts in 1946, and in wins—including 16 in succession and a no-hitter—complete games, and strikeouts in 1947, and pitched in the All-Star Game from 1946 to 1951.

ED BOUCHEE (b. 1933, Montana) was a left-handed hitting first baseman for the Philadelphia Phillies (1956–60), Chicago Cubs (1960–61), and New York Mets (1962). He made the All-Rookie team in 1957 when he batted .293 with 35 doubles, 8 triples, and 17 home runs.

JIM BROSNAN (b. 1929, Ohio) was a right-handed pitcher for the Chicago Cubs (1954, 1956–58), St. Louis Cardinals (1958–59), Cincinnati Reds (1959–53), and Chicago White Sox (1963). One of baseball's best relievers from 1960 to 1962, when his effective slider helped him win 21 games and saved 41, "the Professor" also had time to write two controversial, first-person bestsellers, *The Long Season* and *Pennant Race*.

BOB BUHL (b. 1928, Michigan) was a right-handed pitcher for the Milwaukee Braves (1953–62), Chicago Cubs (1962–66), and Philadelphia Phillies (1966–67). Although he could never help himself with the bat—baseball's worst hitting pitcher went 0 for 70 in 1962—he threw hard enough to win in double figures 10 times, went 72–35 between 1956 and 1960, and was the best pitcher in the league against the Dodgers.

LEW BURDETTE (b. 1926, West Virginia) was a right-handed pitcher for the New York Yankees (1950), Boston Braves (1951–52), Milwaukee Braves (1953–63), St. Louis Cardinals (1963–64), Chicago Cubs (1964–65), Philadelphia Phillies (1965), and California Angels (1966–67). He pitched a no-hitter against the Cubs in 1960, beat the Yankees 3 straight times when he was voted MVP of the 1957 World Series, pitched 33 shutouts, started between 32 and 39 games for 8 consecutive years, and won in double figures for 10 consecutive seasons, twice winning 20 games.

BOB CAIN (b. 1924, Kansas) was a left-handed pitcher for the Chicago White Sox (1949–51), Detroit Tigers (1951), and St. Louis Browns (1952–53). He outdueled Bob Feller, 1–0, in baseball's only double 1-hitter, and was the pitcher who walked midget Eddie Gaedel in baseball's most famous stunt.

CHICO CARRASQUEL (b. 1926, Venezuela) was a right-handed hitting shortstop for the Chicago White Sox (1950–55), Cleveland Indians (1956–58), Kansas City Athletics (1958), and Baltimore Orioles (1959). A record-breaking fielder and solid hitter, he had a 24-game hit-streak as a rookie and made 4 All-Star teams.

TOM CHENEY (b. 1934, Georgia) was a right-handed pitcher for the St Louis Cardinals (1957, 1959), Pittsburgh Pirates (1960–61), and Washington Senators (1961–64, 1966). Although 8 of his 13 complete games and 19 victories were shutouts, he gave up 1 run in his greatest effort, a 16-inning 2–1 victory over Baltimore on September 12, 1962, in which he struck out a major-league-record 21 batters.

JOE DE MAESTRI (b. 1928, California) was a right-handed hitting shortstop for the Chicago White Sox (1951), St. Louis Browns (1952), Philadelphia Athletics (1953–54), Kansas City Athletics (1955–59), and New York Yankees (1960–61). A fixture with the Athletics, he was best known for his fielding but went 6 for 6 in a game in 1955.

RYNE DUREN (b. 1929, Wisconsin) was a right-handed pitcher for the Baltimore Orioles (1954), Kansas City Athletics (1957), New York Yankees (1958–61), Los Angeles Angels (1961–62), Philadelphia Phillies (1963–64), Cincinnati Reds (1964), Philadelphia Phillies (1965), and Washington Senators (1965). His poor eyesight, alcoholism, and 100 mph combined to make him one of baseball's most imposing and successful relievers, beginning with the Yankees in 1958, when he won 6 games and led the American league with 20 saves, and 1959, when he saved 14 games and had a 1.88 ERA.

DICK ELLSWORTH (b. 1940, Wyoming) was a left-handed pitcher for the Chicago Cubs (1958–66), Philadelphia Phillies (1967), Boston Red Sox (1968–69), Cleveland Indians (1969–70), and Milwaukee Brewers (1970). A one-time high school star, he won 22 games in 1963, made the All-Star team in 1964, and threw over 200 innings from 1962 to 1966.

DEL ENNIS (b. 1925, Pennsylvania) was a right-handed hitting outfielder for the Philadelphia Phillies (1946–56), St. Louis Cardinals (1957–58), Cincinnati Reds (1959), and Chicago White Sox (1959). Although he batted .300 three times, he was best known for his outstanding run production, hitting over 20 homers 9 times, and driving in over 100 runs 7 times.

ELROY FACE (b. 1928, New York) was a right-handed pitcher for the Pittsburgh Pirates (1953, 1955–68), Detroit Tigers (1968), and Montreal Expos (1969). Employing a lethal forkball, he was his era's greatest reliever, making over 50 appearances in 11 seasons, leading the National League in saves 3 times, setting a league record with 574 career games finished, and setting a major league record with 18 relief wins in 1959, losing only once that year.

ART FOWLER (b. 1922, South Carolina) was a right-handed pitcher for the Cincinnati Reds (1954–57), Los Angeles Dodgers (1959), and Los Angeles Angels (1961–64). A tireless arm and pinpoint control allowed him to make the majors at the age of 31, after 10 years in the minors, to start and relieve at that level until he turned 41, and pitch again in the minors until he was 48—before becoming Billy Martin's most reliable pitching coach.

HERSHELL FREEMAN (b. 1928, Alabama) was a right-handed pitcher for the Boston Red Sox (1952–53, 1955), Cincinnati Reds (1955–58), and Chicago Cubs (1958). As the Reds' relief ace in 1956, he had 18 saves and 14 victories, including 3 in a 24-hour period.

JIM FRIDLEY (b. 1924, West Virginia) was a right-handed hitting outfielder for the Cleveland Indians (1952), Baltimore Orioles (1954), and Cincinnati Reds (1958). Big and powerful, he won his first big league game with a home run and later set a rookie record with 6 hits in a game.

JIM "MUDCAT" GRANT (b. 1935, Florida) was a right-handed pitcher for the Cleveland Indians (1958–64), Minnesota Twins (1964–67), Los Angeles Dodgers (1968), Montreal Expos (1969), St. Louis Cardinals (1969), Oakland Athletics (1970), Pittsburgh Pirates (1970–71), and Oakland Athletics (1971). With Cleveland, he became the first successful black starting pitcher in the American League and with Minnesota in 1965, he won 21 games.

PUMPSIE GREEN (b. 1933, California) was a switch-hitting infielder with the Boston Red Sox (1959–62) and New York Mets (1963). A former Pacific Coast League player, he was the first black on Boston, the last major league team to integrate.

DICK GROAT (b. 1930, Pennsylvania) was a right-handed hitting shortstop for the Pittsburgh Pirates (1952, 1955–62), St. Louis Cardinals (1963–65), Philadelphia Phillies (1966–67), and San Francisco Giants (1967). An All-American and pro basketball player, he developed into baseball's best hit-and-run man, had 201 hits and a league-leading 43 doubles in 1963, and batted over .300 four times, including a league-leading .325 in 1960, when he was the National League's MVP.

FRED HATFIELD (b. 1925, Alabama) was a left-handed hitting infielder for the Boston Red Sox (1950–52), Detroit Tigers (1952–56), Chicago White Sox (1956–58), Cleveland Indians (1958), and Cincinnati Reds (1958). A descendant of the feuding Hatfields, he was best known for his fielding, but he batted .294 as a part-time player in 1954.

RANDY JACKSON (b. 1950, Arkansas) was a right-handed hitting third baseman with the Chicago Cubs (1950–55), Brooklyn Dodgers (1956–57), Los Angeles Dodgers (1958), Cleveland Indians (1958–59), and Chicago Cubs (1959). ''Handsome Ransom'' was a solid fielder and belted 59 homers from 1953 to 1955, twice making the All-Star team.

BILLY JOHNSON (b. 1918, New Jersey) was a right-handed hitting third baseman for the New York Yankees (1943, 1946–51) and St. Louis Cardinals (1951–53). A seasonal fielding leader in both the American and National Leagues, he twice drove in over 90 runs, had 8 runs and a record 3 triples in the 7-game 1947 World Series, and tied a World Series career record with 4 triples.

EDDIE JOOST (b. 1916, California) was a right-handed hitting shortstop for the Cincinnati Reds (1936–42), Boston Braves (1943–45), Philadelphia Athletics (1947–54), and Boston Red Sox (1955). A 2-time American League All-Star after a mediocre National League career, the 1954 player-manager of the Athletics walked over 100 times each year from 1947 to 1952, twice had over 20 homers, and led the American League shortstops in several fielding categories, including putouts for a record-tying 4 years in a row.

JOHN ''SPIDER'' JORGENSEN (b. 1919, California) was a left-handed hitting third baseman for the Brooklyn Dodgers (1947–50) and New York Giants (1950–51). After a fine rookie season in which he broke in with his minor-league teammate, Jackie Robinson, he became the rare player to be managed by Leo Durocher on both the Dodgers and Giants.

GEORGE KELL (b. 1922, Arkansas) was a right-handed hitting third baseman with the Philadelphia Athletics (1943–46), Detroit Tigers (1946–52), Boston Red Sox (1952–54), Chicago White Sox (1954–56), and Baltimore Orioles (1956–57). A future Hall of Famer, who was the best player to develop during the war years, he made 10 All-Star teams, led third basemen in fielding 7 times, batted over .300 9 times, led the league with a .343 average in 1949, and in 1950 led the league with 218 hits and 56 doubles.

HARMON KILLEBREW (b. 1936, Idaho) was a right-handed hitting third baseman, first baseman, and outfielder for the Washington Senators (1954–60), Minnesota Twins (1961–74), and Kansas City Royals (1975). The 1969 American League MVP, an 11-year All-Star, and a future Hall of Famer, the gentlemanly ''Killer'' won 3 RBI and 6 homer titles, slamming more than 40 homers 8 times and a career total of 573, fifth highest in major league history.

RALPH KINER (b. 1922, New Mexico) was a right-handed hitting outfielder for the Pittsburgh Pirates (1946–53), Chicago Cubs (1953–54), and Cleveland Indians (1955). The greatest slugger of the postwar years and a future Hall of Famer, he won National League homer titles his first 7 seasons and twice topped 50 homers, drove in 100 runs six times, led the league three times in slugging percentage, homered on eight successive Sundays, twice homered in four successive at-bats, and had the second highest home run frequency in baseball history.

JOHNNY KLIPPSTEIN (b. 1927, Washington, D.C.) was a right-handed pitcher for the Chicago Cubs (1950–54), Cincinnati Reds (1955–58), Los Angeles Dodgers (1958–59), Cleveland Indians (1960), Washington Senators (1961), Cincinnati Reds (1962), Philadelphia Phillies (1963–64), Minnesota Twins (1964–66), and Detroit Tigers (1967). Exclusively a reliever in the second half of his long career, he won a total of 101 games and saved 66, including a league-leading 14 in 1960.

AL KOZAR (b. 1921, Pennsylvania) was a right-handed hitting second baseman with the Washington Senators (1948–50) and Chicago White Sox (1950). He had a promising rookie campaign and capped his 1949 season by scoring the run that ultimately cost the Red Sox the pennant.

JIM LANDIS (b. 1934, California) was a right-handed hitting outfielder for the Chicago White Sox (1957–64), Kansas City Athletics (1965), Cleveland Indians (1966), Houston Astros (1967), Detroit Tigers (1967), and Boston Red Sox (1967). A speedy Gold Glove–winning center fielder, he was also a strong clutch hitter who hit 22 homers and drove in 85 runs in 1961.

BARRY LATMAN (b. 1936, California) was a right-handed pitcher for the Chicago White Sox (1957–59), Cleveland Indians (1960–63), Los Angeles Angels (1964), California Angels (1965), and Houston Astros (1966–67). A hard thrower who struck out 133 batters in 149.1 innings in 1963, he was selected to the All-Star team in 1961 when he went 13–5.

FRANK MALZONE (b. 1930, New York) was a right-handed hitting third baseman for the Boston Red Sox (1955–65) and California Angels (1966). A mainstay on the Red Sox, he batted over .290 3 times, had at least 15 homers and 87 RBIs 5 times each, played over 150 games 7 straight years, won 3 consecutive Gold Gloves, and tied an American League record by leading third basemen in double plays 5 straight years.

TIM MCCARVER (b. 1941, Tennessee) was a left-handed hitting catcher for the St. Louis Cardinals (1959–69),

Philadelphia Phillies (1970–72), Montreal Expos (1972), St. Louis Cardinals (1973–74), Boston Red Sox (1974–75), Philadelphia Phillies (1975–80). A 4-decade major leaguer, he caught 2 no-hitters, helped develop pitching greats Bob Gibson and Steve Carlton, was the only catcher to lead his league in triples, with 13 in 1966, hit a key 3-run homer in the 1964 World Series, and was second in the NL MVP balloting in 1967.

MINNIE MINOSO (b. 1922, Havana, Cuba) was an outfielder for the Cleveland Indians (1949, 1951), Chicago White Sox (1951–57), Cleveland Indians (1958–59), Chicago White Sox (1960–61), St. Louis Cardinals (1962), Washington Senators (1963), Chicago White Sox (1964, 1976, 1980). A 6-decade professional player, the ageless, enormously popular Negro League veteran led the league 3 times each in stolen bases and triples, led the league in hits at the age of 37, scored and drove in 100 runs 4 times each, had 4 20-homer seasons, batted over .300 8 times, was hit by the pitch a then-record 189 times, won 3 Gold Gloves, and had 6 All-Star seasons.

BILLY MORAN (b. 1933, Alabama) was a second baseman-shortstop with the Cleveland Indians (1958–59), Los Angeles Angels (1961–64), and Cleveland Indians (1964–65). He led the American League second basemen in most fielding categories in 1962 and 1963, and made the All-Star team in 1962 when he batted .282, with 25 doubles, 17 homers, 90 runs, and 74 RBIs.

BILL MONBOUQUETTE (b. 1936, Massachusetts) was a right-handed pitcher for the Boston Red Sox (1958–65), Detroit Tigers (1966–67), New York Yankees (1967–68), and San Francisco Giants (1968). A four-time All Star, he struck out 17 Senators in a 1961 game and no-hit the White Sox in 1962.

LES MOSS (b. 1925, Oklahoma) was a right-handed hitting catcher for the St. Louis Browns (1946–51), Boston Red Sox (1951), St. Louis Browns (1952–53), Baltimore Orioles (1954–55), Chicago White Sox (1955–58). A power-hitting part-time catcher who would eventually coach and manage in the big leagues, he had the distinction of catching Satchel Paige and Bobo Holloman when he threw a fluke no-hitter in 1953.

DON NEWCOMBE (b. 1926, New Jersey) was a right-handed pitcher for the Brooklyn Dodgers (1949–51, 1954–57), Los Angeles Dodgers (1958), Cincinnati Reds (1958–60), and Cleveland Indians (1960). The majors' first black All-Star pitcher, the tall, imposing hard-throwing ex-Negro Leaguer won 20 games 3 times, and became the only player to be given the Rookie of the Year, MVP, and Cy Young awards, winning the last two trophies—he was the majors' first Cy Young winner—when he went 27–7 in 1956.

BILLY O'DELL (b. 1933, South Carolina) was a left-handed pitcher for the Baltimore Orioles (1954, 1956–59), San Francisco Giants (1960–64), Milwaukee Braves (1965), Atlanta Braves (1966), and Pittsburgh Pirates (1966–67). A high school sensation, "Digger" had 105 victories and a low 3.29 ERA in his career, winning as many as 19 games as a starter and twice leading the National League in victories by a reliever.

JIM O'TOOLE (b. 1937, Illinois) was a left-handed pitcher with the Cincinnati Reds (1958–66) and Chicago White Sox (1967). One of the most dependable hurlers of the early sixties, he was 69–43 from 1961 to 1964, with 14 shutouts and an ERA ranging from 2.66 to 3.50.

GARY PETERS (b. 1937, Pennsylvania) was a left-handed pitcher for the Chicago White Sox (1959–69) and Boston Red Sox (1970–72). A ground-ball pitcher, he won 19 games and had a league-leading 2.33 ERA when he was Rookie of the Year, tied for the league-lead with 20 victories in 1964, and had a league-leading 1.98 ERA in 1966.

BILLY PIERCE (b. 1927, Michigan) was a left-handed pitcher for the Detroit Tigers (1945, 1948), Chicago White Sox (1949–61), and San Francisco Giants (1962–64). A crafty, hard-throwing former prep star who became a 7-time All-Star and long-time ace of the White Sox, he won 211 games, including 38 shutouts—in 1958, he had a perfect game for 8.2 innings—won 20 games twice, had the fifties' only sub-2.00 ERA in 1957 with a sterling 1.97, and capped his career with the Giants in 1962 by going 16–6 with 13 straight wins at Candlestick Park, the last being a 3-hit World Series victory.

VIC POWER (b. 1931, Arecibo, Puerto Rico) was a right-handed hitting first baseman-infielder-outfielder for the Philadelphia Athletics (1954), Kansas City Athletics (1955–58), Cleveland Indians (1958–61), Minnesota Twins (1962–64), Los Angeles Angels (1964), Philadelphia Phillies (1964), and California Angels (1965). One of the era's most colorful players, he was a 4-year All-Star and the first All-Star from Puerto Rico, batted over .300 3 times, tied a major league record in 1958 by stealing home twice in a game against Detroit, and won 7 consecutive Gold Gloves at first base, where he caught everything one-handed.

PEDRO RAMOS (b. 1935, Pinar del Rio, Cuba) was a right-handed pitcher for the Washington Senators (1955–60), Minnesota Twins (1961), Cleveland Indians (1962–64), New York Yankees (1964–66), Philadelphia Phillies (1967), Pittsburgh Pirates (1969), Cincinnati Reds (1969), and Washington Senators (1970). Playing on bad teams resulted in his leading the league in losses 4 straight years, yet he won in double figures 6 consecutive seasons, twice led the league in starts, helped the Yankees win the 1964 pennant with one win and 8 saves down the stretch, hit 15 lifetime homers, and utilized his great speed to pinch run and win side bets racing against other players.

BILL RIGNEY (b. 1918, California) was a right-handed hitting infielder for the New York Giants (1946–53). A future major league manager, he played his entire 8-year career with the Giants, initially as a leadoff hitter—he had 24 doubles and 17 homers in 1947—and then a valuable bench player for his mentor, Leo Durocher.

BROOKS ROBINSON (b. 1937, Arkansas) was a right-handed hitting third baseman for the Baltimore Orioles (1955–77). A future Hall of Famer, he hadn't any special natural talent but he was a hard-worker who became the greatest third baseman of the era, winning 16 consecutive Gold Gloves, having 6 20-homer and 14 20-double seasons, starting in the All-Star game from 1960 to 1975, and being voted the AL MVP in 1964 and the World Series MVP in 1970.

ED ROEBUCK (b. 1931, Pennsylvania) was a right-handed pitcher for the Brooklyn Dodgers (1955–57), Los Angeles Dodgers (1958, 1960–63), Washington Senators (1963–64), and Philadelphia Phillies (1964–66). The last Brooklyn Dodger to win a game, he relieved in 459 of his 460 major league games after spending years in the minors as a starter, and achieved an impressive .627 winning percentage and 62 saves.

JOHNNY SAIN (b. 1917, Arkansas) was a right-handed pitcher for the Boston Braves (1942, 1946–51), New York Yankees (1951), and Kansas City Royals (1955). A future pitching coach, he was a workhorse for the postwar Boston Braves who started between 34 and 39 games every year from 1946 to 1950, winning 20 games in 4 of those 5 years—and bested Bob Feller 1–0 in the 1948 World Series opener—and finished his career as a reliever for the Yankees, saving a league-leading 22 games in 1954.

HANK SAUER (b. 1917, Pennsylvania) was a right-handed hitting outfielder for the Cincinnati Reds (1941–42, 1945, 1948–49), Chicago Cubs (1949–55), St. Louis Cardinals (1956), New York Giants (1957), and San Francisco Giants (1958–59). One of the most popular players ever on the Cubs, he topped 97 RBIs 5 times, topped 30 homers 6 times in 7 years, including his 1952 NL MVP season, and became the first batter to twice hit 3 homers in a game off the same pitcher, victimizing the Phillies' Curt Simmons in 1950 and 1952.

DICK SCHOFIELD (b. 1935, Illinois) was a switch-hitting shortstop for the St. Louis Cardinals (1953–58), Pittsburgh Pirates (1958–65), San Francisco Giants (1965–66), New York Yankees (1966), Los Angeles Dodgers (1966–67),

St. Louis Cardinals (1968), Boston Red Sox (1969–70), St. Louis Cardinals (1971), and Milwaukee Brewers (1971). A standout defensive player who was a starter in only 3 of 19 big league seasons after signing a bonus contract, he is best remembered for batting .406 in the Pirates' 1960 September pennant drive while filling in for injured batting champion Dick Groat.

ANDY SEMINICK (b. 1920, West Virginia) was a right-handed hitting catcher for the Philadelphia Phillies (1943–51), Cincinnati Reds (1952–55), and Philadelphia Phillies (1955–57). A tough player who caught in the World Series despite a broken ankle, he had back-to-back 24-homer seasons and hit 2 of the record-tying 5 homers which the Phillies hit in one inning against the Reds in 1949.

AL SMITH (b. 1928, Missouri) was a right-handed hitting outfielder-third baseman for the Cleveland Indians (1953–57), Chicago White Sox (1958–62), Baltimore Orioles (1963), Cleveland Indians (1964), and Boston Red Sox (1964). A Negro League veteran, he led the American League with 123 runs scored in 1955, twice topped .300, had double figures in home runs in 10 consecutive seasons, was a 2-year All-Star, and hit the White Sox pennant-winning homer in 1959.

FRANK THOMAS (b. 1929, Pennsylvania) was a right-handed hitting outfielder-third baseman-first baseman for the Pittsburgh Pirates (1951–58), Cincinnati Reds (1959), Chicago Cubs (1960–61), Milwaukee Braves (1961), New York Mets (1962–64), Philadelphia Phillies (1964–65), Houston Astros (1965), Milwaukee Braves (1965), and Chicago Cubs (1966). A 3-time All-Star who slammed over 20 homers 9 times, he is equally remembered for being Ralph Kiner's successor as the Pirates' top slugger, for being the first slugger on the original New York Mets, and for having had the uncanny ability to catch fastballs barehanded on the sidelines.

BOB TURLEY (b. 1930, Illinois) was a right-handed pitcher for the St. Louis Browns (1951, 1953), Baltimore Orioles (1954), New York Yankees (1955–63), Los Angeles Angels (1963), and Boston Red Sox (1963). A strikeout king with the Baltimore Orioles in 1954, he won the major league Cy Young award when he won a league-leading 21 games for the Yankees in 1958, and went on to win Games 5 and 7 of the World Series against the Braves.

COOT VEAL (1932, Georgia) was a right-handed hitting shortstop for the Detroit Tigers (1958–60), Washington Senators (1961), Pittsburgh Pirates (1962), and Detroit Tigers (1963). Although never given the opportunity to fulfill the promise he showed when he made the *Sporting News* All-Rookie team in 1958, he gained distinction by being the first batter for the expansion Washington Senators.

BEN WADE (b. 1922, North Carolina) was a right-handed pitcher for the Chicago Cubs (1948), Brooklyn Dodgers (1952–54), St. Louis Cardinals (1954), and Pittsburgh Pirates (1955). With Don Newcombe in the service, Wade won 11 games as a starter to help the Dodgers win the 1952 pennant, and then relieved in 1953, finishing every inning in which he pitched.

ALBERT "RUBE" WALKER (b. 1926, North Carolina) was a left-handed hitting catcher for the Chicago Cubs (1948–51), Brooklyn Dodgers (1951–57), and Los Angeles Dodgers (1958). A future manager, he was Roy Campanella's backup receiver his entire time in Brooklyn and replaced the injured starter in the last 2 games of the 1951 playoffs, hitting 2 homers in the second game.

STAN WILLIAMS (b. 1936, New Hampshire) was a right-handed pitcher for the Los Angeles Dodgers (1958–62), New York Yankees (1963–64), Cleveland Indians (1965–69), Minnesota Twins (1970–71), St. Louis Cardinals (1971), and Boston Red Sox (1972). A future pitching coach, he was a 6′4″ high-and-inside flamethrower who won 43 games as a Dodgers starter from 1960–62, striking out 205 batters in 1961, was 13–11 with a 2.50 ERA as a starter and reliever for the 1968 Indians, and went 10–1 with 15 saves and a 1.99 ERA as a reliever for the Twins in 1970.

BILLY WILSON (b. 1928, Nebraska) was a right-handed hitting outfielder for the Chicago White Sox (1950, 1953–54), Philadelphia Athletics (1954), and Kansas City Athletics (1955). Once a high-priced rookie, he hit 32 homers in 631 at-bats in 1954 and 1955, including the first ever hit by the Kansas City Athletics.

HAL WOODESHICK (b. 1932, Pennsylvania) was a left-handed pitcher for the Detroit Tigers (1956), Cleveland Indians (1958), Washington Senators (1959–60), Washington Senators (1960), Detroit Tigers (1961), Houston Colt .45s (1962–64), Houston Astros (1965), and St. Louis Cardinals (1965–67). After bouncing around several organizations, he developed a slider and became the ace reliever at Houston, winning 11 games, saving 10 others and having a 1.97 ERA in his 1963 All-Star season, and leading the league with 23 saves in 1964.

GENE WOODLING (b. 1922, Ohio) was a left-handed hitting outfielder for the Cleveland Indians (1943, 1946), Pittsburgh Pirates (1947), New York Yankees (1949–54), Baltimore Orioles (1955), Cleveland Indians (1955–57), Baltimore Orioles (1958–60), Washington Senators (1961–62), and New York Mets (1962). A tough ballplayer and players-pension negotiator, he played all his 1796 major league games in the outfield, excelling defensively and batting over .300 5 times, as well as hitting .318 with 3 homers and 21 runs scored in 5 World Series.

GUS ZERNIAL (b. 1923, Texas) was a right-handed hitting outfielder for the Chicago White Sox (1949–51), Philadelphia Athletics (1951–54), Kansas City Athletics (1955–57), and Detroit Tigers (1958–59). The Athletics top slugger during their last years in Philadelphia and first years in Kansas City, "Ozark Ike" drove in over 100 runs in 1951, 1952, and 1953, and had 7 seasons in which he hit at least 27 home runs.

WE PLAYED
THE GAME

PRELUDE

"AFTER WORLD WAR II, AGING COST SEVERAL PLAYERS THEIR CAREERS, SO A LOT OF US CHEATED ON OUR AGES. I WAS BORN IN 1921, BUT MY BASEBALL RECORD ALWAYS HAD IT AT 1922. I WAS LUCKY BECAUSE I STILL HAD A FEW YEARS LEFT AND WASN'T RUSTY."

AL KOZAR

"THEY WERE AFRAID OF US ROOKIES TAKING AWAY THEIR JOBS. ONE SMART-ALECKY GUY CALLED TO ME IN THE BATTING CAGE, "GET OUT OF THERE, BUSH BASTARD!" I HAD THE BAT IN MY HAND AND TOLD HIM TO COME GET ME OUT. I HAD JAPANESE SHELLS COMING AT ME DURING THE WAR, SO THAT WASN'T GOING TO BOTHER ME."

FRANK BAUMHOLTZ

THE WAR ENDS

RALPH KINER:

When I got out of the navy after the war ended in 1945, I just wanted to play baseball. I had the opportunity to stay in the reserve program, along with most of the guys I flew with, but I wanted no part of it. It felt wonderful to be free of the service and back home. The war had been so catastrophic that all of us who went through it, either overseas or on the home front, were greatly affected by it. There was immediate jubilation in the country and the attitude was "Gee, I'm alive and let's enjoy life and make the best of it." It was great to be a ballplayer because that was one of the ways you could make a good living at the time. Remember that prior to the war we also had suffered through a Depression, when nobody had anything. Everyone was so eager to

The Pirates' Ralph Kiner won the homer title as a rookie in 1947 and went on to become the top slugger of the postwar era, slamming round-trippers at a frequency second only to Babe Ruth in baseball history.

play, break with the past, and make a little money that the 16 training camps were packed in 1946, and there was tremendous competition between returning vets, rookies, and players from the war years for the 400 major league jobs.

When I arrived in San Bernardino, I hadn't yet played for the Pirates. But I had been to three of their training camps after Hollis "Sloppy" Thurston signed me in 1940, upon my graduation from high school in Alhambra. I was given $3,000, which was the largest bonus ever given out in southern California—it was a good sum of money considering that my mother, who raised me, was making only about $125 a month as an office nurse for an insurance and trust company. Because of their large investment, the Pirates watched over me in the minors and really hoped I would reach the majors. However, I wasn't scheduled to make the Pirates in 1946, at the age of 23. Pittsburgh earmarked me for Hollywood in the Pacific Coast League. But I had a terrific spring with about 12 or 13 homers, and they kept me.

FRANK BAUMHOLTZ:

In September of 1941, a month before my 23rd birthday, I had enlisted in the navy, intending to get my one year of conscription out of the way so I could pursue my career in the Reds farm system and play basketball. World War II broke out on December 7 and I ended up spending four and a half years in the service. At the end of the war, I was captain of a ship that protected troops landing on the beaches. When the Japanese surrendered, I was told to take a group of ships to Japan for two years. Fortunately, I found out I had enough points to get out of the service, and two days later I was on my way home to Ohio. I had been an All-American basketball player at Ohio University, and soon after I got back, I was recruited by the Youngstown Bears of the National Basketball League. Del Rice, who was a catcher on the Cardinals, and Chuck Connors, who was the property of the Dodgers, were also in the NBL, playing for the champion Rochester Royals. I made the All-Pro 10.

During that winter I wrote a letter to Warren Giles, the general manager of the Reds, and asked my baseball status. He said I was still the property of the Reds and instructed me to report to spring training in 1946. So I

had to leave the Bears with 13 games left on the schedule and go to the Reds' training camp in Tampa, Florida. The Red Sox were in Sarasota, Washington was in Orlando, the Cardinals were in St. Petersburg, and other teams had camps in Florida, so I played against many great players I had only heard about. I was witnessing the transformation of baseball as it moved into the postwar era. For a lot of returning veterans, it wasn't easy getting back into the swing. Many players discovered that the years had taken a toll on their skills and bodies.

EWELL BLACKWELL:

I was in the army three years, three months, three days. I'd had my basic training in Texas and then Hank Gowdy, the old catcher, who was a Cincinnati coach, got me transferred to Fort Benning, Georgia. I played a lot of baseball there and then went overseas in 1945, and played more ball. I got to spring training in 1946 on the day the Reds broke camp and went north. My major league experience was only 2 games in 1942 with the Reds, but I knew I was going to make the team because I had gotten stronger and improved in the army, pitching 6 no-hitters. The Reds knew I was ready. They left me and a veteran pitcher, Gene Thompson, who was having arm trouble and would end up on the Giants, down in Plant City to get back into shape with the minor league teams still in training camp.

SPIDER JORGENSEN:

If the war had lasted another year, I probably would have made a career of the army. At 28 or 29, I would have been too old to begin a major league career. From 1942 to 1945 I was stationed in Washington, Idaho, Arizona, and, mostly, El Paso, Texas, where I played ball with the camp team and in a professional league on Sundays. Fortunately, I played enough so that my skills hadn't deteriorated. I had just been a farmhand before the war, so I wasn't surprised that the Dodgers didn't keep in touch with me. But when I got out I was told to go to a tryout camp in Sanford, Florida, which Dodgers owner Branch Rickey was holding about a month before the regular spring training. The Dodgers had a lot of farm teams, and everyone in the system who was coming back from the service was there, between 400 and 500 players. We had a 6-team league among us—we all wore the same uniforms, but we were called the Reds, Blues, Grays, Whites, etc. The players who had lost their skills were culled out, and by the time regular spring training came around, half the players were gone. I was assigned to the Montreal Royals, the Dodgers' AAA club.

AL KOZAR:

Back in 1942, when I played second base for Scranton, a Red Sox Class A team, they'd stop games late at night and there would be speeches about the war. I had an appointment to meet a navy officer to get me into the navy, but once he gave me the papers to fill out, I chickened out. However, when I went home to McKees Rocks, Pennsylvania, after the season, there was a letter that said: "The Army Wants You." So I had to go to Pittsburgh, and in three days I was bending over and in the army. I went into the engineers, eventually becoming a sergeant. One day I was taken to Memphis, where a colonel was getting together a ballclub of pros, managed by Phillies pitcher Hugh Mulcahy, who was the first major leaguer to enter the service. This was Eighth Army headquarters. We all roomed together, away from the other soldiers. I drove a jeep in a motor pool and played ball every day. What a deal! It probably saved my life, because my outfit went over to Germany and was almost entirely wiped out. Eventually, we were sent to Leyte in the Philippines, New Guinea—where we played ball against Phil Rizzuto's Seabees—and Yokohama and Tokyo after the surrender. The Red Sox weren't in touch with me during the war, but I knew I was going back to baseball. Mulcahy would tell interviewers, "After the war is over, watch this guy, Al Kozar. He'll be sure to make the big leagues."

After World War II, aging cost several players their careers, so a lot of us cheated on our ages. I was born in 1921, but my baseball record always had it at 1922. I was lucky because I still had a few years left and wasn't rusty. Some players who were over 30 learned baseball was a young man's game. It was tougher than before the war. Players came back from the service and competed with youngsters and those who had taken their places during their absence. The Red Sox were loaded with players throughout their system. When I came back, I

hoped to move up to Louisville, the Red Sox Triple A team, but they were filled up there, so I had to try to win my job back at Scranton. Our shortstop had to beat out 30 competitors for the job, and I had to beat out 17 at second base.

BILL RIGNEY:

During the war, I was in the navy air corps and was living at home in Oakland. In 1944, when I was 26, my father handed me a newspaper and said, "Here's your Christmas present." I read that the New York Giants had acquired my contract from the Oakland Oaks of the Pacific Coast League. I was actually swapped for Dolph Camilli, who came to manage Oakland, and $30,000. It was like heaven had come early. I had dreamed of playing in the majors since I was a little kid who played ball with my dad and watched him and my uncles play semipro ball for the Rigney Tile Company. The Giants had been my favorite team all my life, and I had even been scouted by them in the 1930s when I played sandlot ball in the Bay Area.

I went to spring training in Miami with the Giants in 1946. We stayed at the Venetian Hotel in Biscayne Bay. I put on the Giants' uniform and was so excited. There were 96 players in camp. The Giants had finished last in both 1944 and 1945, so they were giving everybody a chance to make the club. I played in the morning and never got to know the afternoon players. But I could see that there was a tough breed of player emerging. Some of these guys had come out of the army with a Silver Star for bravery, and 75 percent had seen some part of the service. But their army records weren't going to help them make the majors. I was so intent on making my own mark as a rookie that I didn't pay attention to the sad situation of some players who weren't able to make it back after the layoff. I was married and had a baby and another on the way, so I was focused on myself. The Giants' shortstops were Buddy Kerr and Dick Bartell, who began his career in 1927. Bartell and I knew that if I made the team, he would be let go. Yet he took me aside and worked with me. He taught me some of the amenities, and how the game was played in the majors, where you had to be much quicker. I never forgot his generosity. I made the club and he became a coach.

After losing three of his prime baseball years while in the service, infielder John Berardino returned to the St. Louis Browns and had a solid season in 1946, his final year as a full-time player.

JOHN BERARDINO:

I had played for the St. Louis Browns from 1939 until I joined the navy early in the 1942 season. I was stationed in the States part of the time and ended up in Pearl Harbor. I played some baseball there and listened to the 1944 World Series, in which the Cardinals beat the Browns. I hadn't heard much from the Browns during the war but thought they'd send me some money from the team's Series share. I got something in the mail from them, but when I opened it, all I found was a deck of monogrammed baseball cards. I got so mad that I threw those damned things away. Who knew anything about memorabilia in those days?

The government guaranteed that players would get their jobs back when they returned from the service, so when I went to the Browns' camp in 1946 I wasn't worried about making the team. But I could see that the caliber of play was extremely high and that I would have to produce to prolong my career. I was concerned because I had suffered a back injury at Pearl Harbor for which I would need a lot of therapy.

LES MOSS:

In 1941 the Browns had signed me off a sandlot team in Tulsa, Oklahoma, at the age of 16. After a year in D ball and another in Double A, I became a merchant seaman, spending thirty-three months in the South Pacific and North Atlantic before the war ended. I attended the Browns' spring training camp in California in 1946, but after a week I realized I wasn't going to make the club. I needed more time because I hadn't played at all in the service.

So I went to the Browns' minor league camp in San Antonio. This was a six-week tryout for the Browns' Triple A and Double A teams and maybe for a couple of lower farm clubs. We had two fields and 300 ballplayers. There were ballplayers all over the place. There were many guys coming back from the service, and some of them had been over there three to five years. There were some pretty rough cookies. Every time you turned around, there was a fight going on. We had a morning workout and afternoon workout on each field, with split teams and rotating players. We were told apart by numbers. It was a mess. They weeded them out fast. Some of the vets couldn't do it anymore. I made the Triple A Toledo club.

JOHNNY SAIN:

It was a fantastic feeling returning to baseball after the war. When I joined the navy flying program in 1942, after one year with the Boston Braves, I was 25, and when I got out I was already 28, which was pretty late to get started. The Braves trained in Fort Lauderdale, and there were so many people in camp that they didn't have a hotel big enough for the team and we were scattered all over town. Fortunately, Billy Southworth, who had just come over from the Cardinals to manage the Braves, had kept up with me. I had played ball with Ted Williams in the navy, and Ted had said some complimentary things to Billy and the Boston writers about me. So I had a little inside track on making the team. I knew I had improved but had no idea what I was capable of doing. The writers were focused on a kid pitcher who was setting the world on fire. Southworth had a meeting in which he said, "That youngster may not be here opening day and Sain is going to win 20 games for us." That let me know that I was going to have an opportunity to pitch that year in the majors.

DEL ENNIS:

I had enlisted in the navy because everybody was getting drafted into the army back in 1943. So I spent three years in the South Pacific. When I went in, I had only played part of a season at Trenton in the Interstate League. Their scout, Jocko Collins, came to Philadelphia to see a pitcher on my high school team but when I hit 3 homers and drove in about 15 runs in one game he signed me instead. I batted over .400 with Trenton and had just signed a contract with the Philadelphia Phillies when I entered the service. I never played for them, but when I went overseas I had ''Phillies'' written on all my belongings and my records stated I was on their inactive roster. That's why I was recruited to play in a league for major leaguers in Guam and Hawaii. I played with Phil Rizzuto, Virgil Trucks, Billy Herman, Bill Dickey, and all of those guys who were my idols. I became a better hitter in the service and the Yankees offered me $2,500 to sign with them. The Cubs offered me $10,000! Those offers made me realize I had real talent, but I belonged to the Phillies.

When I returned from the service, the Phillies put me on the National League waivers list. They had no idea how good I was. All the major leaguers I'd played with told their owners to claim me. When other teams started claiming me, Phillies manager Ben Chapman decided to keep me and play me for thirty days to see why I was in such demand.

GENE WOODLING:

When I got out of the navy, I returned to the Cleveland Indians. They had signed me when I was 17 in 1940, although when growing up in East Akron, Ohio, I played a total of only 9 high school games and no sandlot or semipro ball. Swimming was my sport and I didn't like baseball. When Bill Bradley came to my door I thought he was just someone who wanted me to play baseball in the summer in Akron. I didn't know he was an Indians scout and was reluctant to talk to him. Then he signed me to a contract, and for the rest of my life I'd look back and think how lucky I was. I wouldn't waste the opportunity to get out of my poor, tough environment. I made $80 a month my first year, which was double what I made during the offseason at Goodyear Tire Company. I played in the minors at several levels before Cleveland called me up for a short time in 1943. I

was looking forward to rejoining them when the war ended. There were many people in camp, but I had the talent to be a starting outfielder.

EDDIE JOOST:

In 1944 I was informed that I was going to be drafted. So I voluntarily retired from the Boston Braves and went to work in a meat-packing plant for a full year. I then took my physical. The doctor told me that since the war was about to end and I had two children, he'd given me a six-month deferment. Otherwise I'd have gone to Germany for four years as part of the occupation forces. He said that if I had been trying to beat the draft, he'd have enlisted me.

In 1945 I went back and played briefly with the Braves. One day Billy Jurges of the Giants slid into me at third and broke my wrist. After an operation I asked John Quinn, the Braves GM, if I could go home before the final road trip because I was unable to play. He said he'd see me the next spring. No sooner had I gotten back to California when I got a letter from the Braves saying, ''You are hereby suspended without pay for the rest of the season for jumping the ballclub without permission.'' I was livid. I called Judge Landis immediately. He said, ''We'll get together. If they're wrong, they will pay for it.'' Unfortunately, Landis became ill and a guy named O'Connor took over his Commissioner duties. During the winter I got a note from him saying that I had no recourse.

So in 1946, I was blacklisted in major league baseball—not only because of what had happened with Quinn but because I had the reputation for not getting along with managers from incidents I'd had with Bill McKechnie in Cincinnati and Casey Stengel in Boston. I had gone through a lot since I was a rookie back in 1936, and knew a whole lot more about the system than most players. I had learned that players were at the mercy of management. If they wanted to downgrade you, they could. If they wanted to send you to another team or just get rid of you so you wouldn't play with anyone else, they had ways to do it.

So here I was, after 8 years with the Reds and Braves, accepting an offer to play with the Rochester Red Wings in Triple A ball. Joe Ziegler, the general manager, had bought my contract from Quinn and offered to make me the highest-paid player in the league. I had known Joe a long time, and he told me that there was no way I'd get back into the majors because there was collusion between owners. Either my career was over or I'd go to Rochester. Burleigh Grimes, the old spitballer, was the manager and a nice guy. He told me he didn't believe what he heard about me and promised I'd play shortstop for him every day. That was good to hear.

GEORGE KELL:

I never went into the service. The day I was called, they took about 50 guys down to the recruitment center on a bus and rejected almost all of us. I was turned down because of a bad knee, but they just weren't taking anybody at that time. When I was called up a second time, the war was winding down, so they didn't take me again. The first time I was eager to go—I was just a gung-ho kid and my brother was in—but the second time I was pretty much established in baseball and didn't want to go anymore.

I became the regular third baseman with the Philadelphia Athletics in 1944 only because the war was going on. That's being honest. I had jumped from Class B all the way to the majors, so I got my training in the majors, getting better all the time. I felt privileged to play in the big leagues. This had been my ambition since I was a four-year-old in Swifton, Arkansas. I knew I was lucky to have been in the right place at the right time. Some players would say that when the war ended and the players came back from the army a lot of us would be demoted. Well, I thought those guys would have to beat me out of my job.

DON NEWCOMBE:

Even before I was a teenager, my father started taking my three brothers and me to Rupert Stadium in Newark, where for 25 cents we sat in the left-field bleachers and watched either the Eagles of the Negro Leagues or the Bears, the Yankees' Triple A team. I loved the Bears and Bob Seeds was my favorite player, but when I dreamed of someday playing at Rupert Stadium my mind-set was that I might play in the Negro Leagues. When I joined the Newark Eagles in the Negro Leagues in 1944, I believed I had reached the pinnacle. I had played integrated baseball in school and in sandlot games, but the only integrated professional games I had seen were exhibitions that pitted black all-star teams against white all-star teams. I hadn't thought it would go any further than that. Then, when I was 18, Lennie Pearson and pitcher Terris McDuffie told me there were whispers that the major leagues would soon integrate.

I had first heard the name Jackie Robinson in 1945 when he came to Newark with the Kansas City Monarchs to play against the Eagles. I don't remember if I spoke to him, but I remember him playing shortstop. I was more aware of Satchel Paige, who pitched for the Monarchs. If you were black and a baseball fan, then you knew about Satchel Paige. He was a legend. Our owner, Ethel Manley, was going to set up a promotion whereby youth was going to challenge old age and I was going to pitch against Paige. That was exciting because I had seen Paige pitch to Roy Campanella, Larry Doby, and other Eagles stars in previous years. Unfortunately, we got rained out.

That year, McDuffie, Robinson, and Marvin Williams were given a superficial tryout with the Boston Red Sox. McDuffie got to throw only 5 or 10 pitches, and Robinson and Williams got about that many swings, and then they were told the Red Sox would get back to them. They never heard from the Red Sox. Boston knew it wasn't going to sign any of these black players, although they had the talent to play on any major league team. They lied because they wanted to stop the noise. But the seed had been planted. That tryout got a lot of publicity from black newspaper writers like Sam Lacy, Wendell Smith, Joe Bostic, and Billy Rowe, who had traveled to Boston.

In 1945 there was an all-star game at Ebbets Field in which I was on a team with Roy Campanella, Monte Irvin, and Lennie Pearson that played against white major league stars like Eddie Stanky, Ralph Branca, Clyde Kluttz, and Virgil Trucks. I started that game, but I hurt my elbow in the third inning. I went into the clubhouse and was feeling sorry for myself when a white man with a big hat walked in. He introduced himself as Clyde Sukeforth. I didn't know who he was. He said he was a scout for the Brooklyn Dodgers and he wanted to set up a meeting between Branch Rickey and me the next day. I didn't even know who Branch Rickey was. He told me that Rickey, who was the majority owner of the Dodgers, had an idea to have a Negro League team called the Brooklyn Brown Dodgers play in Ebbets

Field when the white Dodgers were on the road and was talking to players who might be on that team. I told him I was interested.

The next day, when I was going into Mr. Rickey's office, Roy Campanella was coming out. He told me he had just signed a contract to play with the Brooklyn Brown Dodgers. I went in and met Branch Rickey, who was seated behind his desk. He was a big man with a cigar. He asked if I had a contract with the Newark Eagles. I said that I didn't. Before I knew it, I signed a contract with Mr. Rickey and was given a $1,000 check, which Rickey's assistant, Spencer Harris, went downstairs and cashed for me. He brought me back a stack of $10 and $20 bills. I had never seen that much money in my life. At Newark I got $175 a month in 1944 and $350 a month in 1945.

I went home and gave some money to my mother and some to my wife. And I waited for the Dodgers to contact me. A month or two went by. My wife and I went to Newark to a movie and afterward I saw the New York *Daily News* with the headline: JACKIE ROBINSON SIGNED BY MONTREAL ROYALS. I wondered who the hell the Montreal Royals were. I read the paper and learned they were a Dodgers' Triple A farm team. I said to my wife, "Maybe now there is a chance for me to play in the major leagues."

The next week I got a call from Clyde Sukeforth, who told me to return to Brooklyn for another meeting. I went back to Rickey's office and Roy was there again. Roy already knew what was going on, but couldn't say anything because Mr. Rickey wanted to tell me. Mr. Rickey informed me that he really didn't want Roy and me to play for any Brooklyn Brown Dodgers, but wanted us to play for Danville, Illinois, the Dodgers' Class A team. However, the president of the league had called and said, "If you send those niggers out here, we're going to close the league down." Rickey was very despondent because he didn't want to sign us unless he could place us with a Dodgers' minor league team. The only team left was Nashua, New Hampshire, in Class B, which played all its games in New England. Their general manager was Buzzy Bavasi and the manager was Walter Alston. While I sat there, Rickey called up Bavasi and asked if he'd take two black players. Buzzy's one question was "Can they play baseball?" He was willing to take us. That's when Roy and I found

out we were going to be part of the Brooklyn Dodgers' system!

THE GAME RESUMES

GEORGE KELL:

I was overwhelmed by the change that I saw in baseball in 1946. In the American League alone, such stars as Ted Williams, Bob Feller, Joe DiMaggio, and all the great Yankees came home. Hank Greenberg and a few others had returned during the 1945 season—Hank won the pennant for Detroit with a grand slam on the last day—but now they got to play in earnest against stronger competition—Hank would lead the league in homers and RBIs in 1946. The change I witnessed had mostly to do with talent, but it also had to do with attitude, as the fans began to flock back to the parks as if to say, "We've all been through this terrible war and now here's baseball, the one great constant in our lives." Everyone was happy that the great game had survived.

Players came from all over. Many had grown up in the Depression, many had been to war, which had been the equivalent of a college education to a lot of young, poor, rural boys. Having gone through that, it was no big deal moving to Detroit, New York, Chicago, or Philadelphia. They weren't as overwhelmed by the city as they might have been earlier in life. It was a more mature group than had gone off to war. There was still a rough element in baseball and a few old-timers who sharpened their spikes before a game, but overall the players weren't as wild a breed as the players of the past. Connie Mack, the longtime manager and owner of the Philadelphia Athletics, told me that in the twenties and thirties they had trouble finding hotels to take in the teams because of the character of the ballplayers. He said that one of the changes he liked best was that there were now more mature, college and professional-type players than there had been. "The hotels," he told me, "now clamor for our business."

Many wartime players lost their jobs, but I kept mine. However, I was traded to the Tigers on May 18, 1946, for outfielder Barney McCosky, a lifetime .300 hitter who was struggling since his return from the service. When you're a 23-year-old kid who is traded, you naturally feel rejected, but Mr. Mack explained to me very carefully and honestly, "George, you're going to be a good ballplayer and make a lot of money. I'm trading you to a ballclub that can pay you more than we can afford." Detroit was known for high salaries. Hank Greenberg was probably the highest-priced player in baseball when he went into the service, making something like $55,000.

A lot of people from my native Arkansas migrated to Detroit to work in the automobile factories, especially during the war. So I had a lot of friends in Detroit when my wife and I moved there. But being a young, married ballplayer with a small child was very, very hard. My son had been born in Philadelphia in September 1945. I don't think my wife fully understood what she was getting into. We were high school sweethearts and had married right after graduation. She didn't know that we'd be traveling all over the country or that I'd be gone from home for long periods of time. To get some stability, we built a house back home in Swifton, Arkansas, in 1946 so that we could go back every off-season.

One of the few players to wear glasses, infielder Bill Rigney would provide spirit, leadership, and a rough-and-tumble style of play to the Giants from 1946 to 1953.

BILL RIGNEY:

Jorge Pasquel and his brother formed the Mexican League in 1946 and were offering major leaguers a lot of money to defect, thousands more than they were making in the majors. Stan Musial even considered leaving the Cardinals. The Giants held a meeting and our manager Mel Ott asked, "Is anyone here going to Mexico?" Babe Young, an outfielder–first baseman, said we all should have raised our hands because we'd have gotten better contracts. As it was, we lost Sal Maglie, who had shown great promise as a rookie pitcher in 1945, outfielder Danny Gardella, second baseman George Hausmann, and a couple of other guys. They went down there, though our new Commissioner, Happy Chandler, threatened them with permanent banishment. (Gardella would later sue major league baseball for reinstatement after the Mexican League folded.)

The rest of us headed north. John McGraw had started a tradition: anytime the Giants would open a season in New York, they'd play the Cadets at West Point the day before. After barnstorming up the coast playing Cleveland in exhibition games, we went to West Point. Then we came down to New York City.

I'd never been to New York, I'd never been to a major league ballpark, I'd never seen the Polo Grounds. We got in at ten o'clock at night. We carried our own bags in those days, and I walked up those steps and into the Giants' clubhouse. It was a marvelous clubhouse: you walked down the steps and there was one big room and down six more steps and there were all the lockers. The trainer's room was there and the showers were upstairs; the manager's office was on the first deck. I looked for my locker and there it was next to the locker of Johnny Mize. I put my stuff down and said to myself, "Christy Mathewson, Bill Terry, John McGraw, Mel Ott, Travis Jackson, and all the other great Giants of the past dressed right here." Both clubhouses were in center field, and I walked down the twenty steps onto the field. The night lights were on. I saw that the Polo Grounds was built like a horseshoe with home plate in the middle. I remember the chill I got thinking, "Tomorrow you're going to be the shortstop in front of 45,000." I wondered what I was doing there. I wondered if I could handle it.

The next day I was introduced and ran onto the diamond in front of all those fans. I prayed that a ball would be hit to me quickly so I could calm down. And the Phillies' little shortstop, Skeeter Newsome, hit the ball through the box. I picked it up one-handed and threw him out. The crowd cheered. And I said, "Oh boy, this is going to be all right." The first time I batted, Oscar Judd threw me a screwball on a 3–2 pitch and struck me out. A 3–2 screwball? I said, "This is the major leagues." Later I solved him for two hits, we beat the Phils 8–2, and Bill Voiselle got the victory.

Mel Ott was our manager and leader, but there were players I'd go to if I needed help. I got to know Babe Young and pitcher "Prince" Hal Schumacher really well. They were at the tail ends of their careers. Red Kress, a coach I had known from the Bay Area, helped me if I had a problem. But mostly you made your own way, especially on a last-place team.

That first year I lived in the Bronx, on 183rd Street. My wife was pregnant, and the apartment we rented was on the top floor and had no air conditioning. We just about died. I was under a lot of pressure to succeed. I wanted to raise a family and support them by being a ballplayer. I had such love for the game and couldn't let myself think what I might do if I failed and had to do something other than play professional baseball. It was my life. But after I batted .236, I told my wife that I didn't think that was good enough for the Giants to ask me back.

JOHN BERARDINO:
Despite my troubled back, I had a fairly good year with the Browns in 1946, hitting in 22 straight games at one point. For the first time since my rookie 1939 season, I played second instead of short—Vern Stephens had taken over there during the war years—and it was an easier position. I was in the starting lineup 143 times, every game at second. This was the last time in my career that I'd play over 90 games.

LES MOSS:
At Toledo, I played with Pete Gray, the one-armed outfielder who had been called up to the Browns during the war. In one doubleheader, I went 0 for 8 and he went 6 for 8. He was one of a kind. He had just one arm but could hit the ball out of parks, could bunt as good as any man who ever lived, could steal bases, and could play the outfield. His only problem was hitting a changeup—

they'd get him out in front and he couldn't hold back. Pete was strong but he was a quiet guy. He was supposed to be grumpy but I never saw it—he wasn't sensitive about his arm. We got along great and had a lot of fun. He loved to play poker, but I had to shuffle for him.

I caught 121 games and hit over .300, so at the end of the year the Browns brought me up for four or five weeks. The manager, Zack Taylor, was a catcher, so he worked with me and I did quite well defensively, as well as with the bat. It was an exciting time.

EWELL BLACKWELL:
I joined the Reds in Cincinnati just before the season opened. Paul Derringer had retired after the 1945 season and I took his spot in the rotation. I went just 9–13 but had a league-leading 6 shutouts and a 2.45 ERA. If you gave up 2 runs on the Reds you'd have to forfeit because we were last in the league in runs scored and batting average.

EDDIE JOOST:
I had a great year with Rochester in 1946. I batted .280, hit 22 home runs, and drove in over 100 runs. Judge Ruther, a Cubs' scout, started following me around, telling me the Cubs were interested in signing me despite my reputation. One day he told me that if they didn't follow his recommendation to sign me the next day, he would immediately resign. They didn't sign me, and he quit.

DEL ENNIS:
Everything seemed so enormous to me, coming out of the navy and going right to the big leagues and playing in my hometown for what had been my favorite team growing up. But I tried not to give too much thought to anything because I had just 30 days to make good with the Phillies.

It made it easier that I played in Philadelphia because I was born there in 1925 and grew up in the boroughs—Crescentville, Lawndale, Oxford, and Jenkintown, where I eventually settled. My parents were there, and for 50 years my father worked for Stetson Hats at Fifth and Montgomery—he was a hatter, not a batter. I had been going to Shibe Park since my father took me there as a kid. Coming home each night gave me stability.

When we played in New York, I would even take the train home between games. On the road, my roommate was Jimmy Wasdell, only I didn't get to know him because he never stayed in the room.

Chapman played me every day to see if what he had heard about me was true. I batted behind Ron Northey, who could throw BBs from the outfield. Ron, third baseman Jim Tabor, and most of the guys were jokers, but they could play. I played left field and hit pretty good for a 20–21-year-old, batting .313, driving in over 70 runs, and getting 30 doubles and 17 homers to lead the team and set a club rookie record. I could run pretty fast, so I also got a few triples and stolen bases. I was the first player to be selected Rookie of the Year by the *Sporting News*. I got a raise.

JOHNNY SAIN:

I had made $600 a month in 1942, $4,200 for the baseball year. When I got out of the service four years later, the Braves sent me the same contract although the value of a dollar had gone down. It was like being hit in the face with a wet towel. I didn't know if I could live on that, so I wrote back asking for $800 a month if I was with the club past the cutdown date. So they agreed. I pitched Opening Day and won 3 games by cutdown day, so I made the team and was offered a new contract. I wanted $6,500 for the year. They ended up giving me $500 under the table and signing me to the $800-a-month contract, for a total of $6,100.

On July 12, in Cincinnati, I beat the Reds 1–0. I missed a perfect game by one hit, when Grady Hatton's pop fly fell between three of our players, who each said later that they could have caught it. Our GM, John Quinn—he was the son of Bob Quinn, who owned the Braves in 1942 when I was a rookie—called me up in the hotel and said, ''That's what we want!'' I said, ''Good, I'll be in to see you as soon as we get back to Boston.'' So I went to see him and he said, ''Now, what do you want?'' I said, ''$6,500—just what I had asked for.'' So they gave me more money under the table. His idea was to keep my salary at $800 a month in case I stumbled.

But I didn't stumble. I was one of the few players who returned from the service and did extremely well immediately. Even Joe DiMaggio had trouble adjusting.

Arguably the most successful pitcher of the postwar era, the Boston Braves' Johnny Sain would win 20 games four times between 1946 and 1950 and combine with Warren Spahn to form the best righty-lefty duo in baseball.

I pitched 265 innings and led the league with 24 complete games in 34 starts and posted a 2.21 ERA, which would be the best of my career. And like Billy Southworth predicted, I won 20 games, which was second in the league to the 21 wins by Howie Pollet of the Cardinals.

I had no idea what I should ask for the next year, so I asked advice from some of the Braves' veteran pitchers, Mort Cooper, Si Johnson, and Bill Lee. They suggested $18,000. Lou Perini, the Braves' owner, and Quinn wanted to sign me before the annual New York writers' dinner, so they agreed.

After the season I barnstormed with Bob Feller's major league all-star team. We played against Satchel Paige's black all-stars. Both Feller and Paige had DC-3s, and we played on both coasts and up to Vancouver—32 games in about 30 days. We played in New Haven in the afternoon and Yankee Stadium at night. We ate a lot of cheese sandwiches. It was interesting meeting and competing with a lot of the black players for the first time.

SPIDER JORGENSEN:

I played at Montreal for Clay Hopper. This was Jackie Robinson's first year in the Dodgers' system, so we got a lot of attention and drew large crowds. The fans got somewhat unruly when we went to Syracuse—where someone threw a black cat on the field—and Baltimore, but for the most part it was calm and incident-free. We had a very good team with Robinson leading the league in hitting and such players as Herman Franks, Dixie Howell, Marv Rackley, and Al Campanis, who was a pretty good shortstop. We ran away with the league title and then beat Louisville in the Little World Series. I hit over .300 all season but then pooped out and finished at .297.

FRANK BAUMHOLTZ:

I made the Reds in spring training by playing a lot, but for the first six months of the season I didn't play an inning. Our manager, Bill McKechnie, didn't seem interested in young players. It was no fun sitting on the bench. There were a couple of guys who came back from the war and found out they were just bench warmers. They were afraid of us rookies taking away their jobs. One smart-alecky guy called to me in the batting cage, "Get out of there, bush bastard!" I had the bat in my hand and told him to come get me out. I had Japanese shells coming at me during the war, so that wasn't going to bother me. He later became a good friend of mine.

After 6 weeks, I was demoted to Columbia, South Carolina, in the Sally League. Ted Kluszewski, the big football player from the University of Indiana, was there. I hit .343 and he hit higher. After the baseball season, I averaged 14 points a game for the Cleveland Rebels in the initial season of the Basketball Association of America, the predecessor of the NBA.

RALPH KINER:

When I arrived in Pittsburgh for the first time, it was about ten in the morning but it was like night because of the pollution from the coal. It was eerie and depressing. Later I saw Forbes Field for the first time and discov-

ered it was 365 feet down the left-field line and 457 feet in left center. I was quite discouraged about my prospects for hitting home runs.

The players after the war did have some things in common with those from before the war. For instance, they always had on dirty, ill-fitting uniforms and always wanted to play—at least on teams other than the Pirates. Pittsburgh was a really bad team and most of the guys were crazy and cared only about gambling and running around spending money. They were a card-playing, heavy-drinking, all-fun-and-games bunch. It wasn't a good situation for a rookie.

I was never told that I had to hit home runs to play in the majors. I wasn't trying for homers but just wanted to hit well enough to earn playing time. My first base hit was a single off Johnny Beazley in St. Louis. To me, that was the most important non-homer of my career.

I wasn't the typical shy rookie because I had been in the war and nothing fazed me. Which was good because major league baseball turned out to be harder than I expected. I felt I was in a bit over my head that first year. I batted only .247 and led the league in strikeouts. But I did beat out Johnny Mize for the National League home run title with 23 to his 22. I was lucky to win—Mize missed over 50 games with a broken arm. I didn't realize that would mean so much, but I was the first Pirates homer champ since 1906 and tied Johnny Rizzo's team record. Frankie Frisch was the Pirates' manager until the end of the season, and he helped me get a raise by going to the owner on my behalf. I was lucky because managers also could tell owners not to give raises.

I wasn't involved in the formation of baseball's pension plan in 1946. I stayed out of all arguments and negotiations at the advice of catcher Al Lopez, who was the elder statesman on the team and a highly intelligent guy. But I knew what was going on. There was a Boston attorney named Bob Murphy who was trying to organize ballplayers into a labor organization he called the American Baseball Guild. He picked Pittsburgh as the team to begin with because the city was highly unionized. The team held meetings and made an effort to gain representation with the owners. It was divisive and ugly. There was one incident when union people beat up a couple of our players in a parking lot. In the middle of the season there was a strike situation in which we voted whether or not to play a game against the Giants. The majority voted not to play, but we needed a two-thirds majority. If we hadn't played, the Pirates would have fielded another team and we would have been locked out. Once that fell through, Bob Murphy fell by the wayside. However, as a result of players like Danny Gardello, Sal Maglie, Vern Stephens, Max Lanier, and Lou Klein taking the big money offered by the Pasquel brothers to join the Mexican League, those who stayed behind thought they were entitled to a pension plan and minimum salary. Marty Marion of the Cardinals, Dixie Walker of the Dodgers, and Johnny Murphy of the Yankees were the guys who represented the players in dealing with the owners and general managers. They established a $5,000-a-year minimum wage, got spring training expenses—which we called ''Murphy money''—and brought about the first pension plan, which would begin officially on April 1, 1947. The players and owners would put in initial money—the owners put up about $1 million—and add money annually, and the pension would get funding from yearly World Series and All-Star Game proceeds. After retirement, 5-year veterans would get $50 a month and 10-year veterans would get $100 a month. It was a case of the players taking over and getting a lot of things without creating a union. At least we didn't call ourselves a union, because many players were afraid of that name. We had a difficult time getting individual players to even consider that they might have to strike, and that they would be backed by the other players if they did. At that time, we wouldn't have succeeded with a strike because we weren't well enough organized.

GENE WOODLING:

There was a great deal of talk about the pension plan. I was with the Indians, and my teammate Bob Feller helped initiate the fight for the pension plan. (He's why it would later be operated out of Cleveland.) He was never given credit for what he did, but he was about the only big league ballplayer who stuck his neck out. Johnny Murphy did a good job, too. The pension plan would go into effect on April 1, but we put up the money in 1946. With one or two exceptions, every player and coach put up $300 apiece, and that was a lot

of money for us making just $2,500 a year. I know I couldn't really afford it. This money started the plan, and after that we would give a portion of our paychecks—amounting to $2 a day—and a certain percentage of All-Star Game and World Series money would go into the fund. We knew we were doing something for our future, but nobody forecast that it would become such an important part of baseball and develop as it would.

I played for the Indians and in the minors in 1946. In my minor league years, my averages were like .398, .344, and .386, but now that I came to the big leagues, I was told I couldn't hit. In December they would trade me to Pittsburgh for Al Lopez.

DON NEWCOMBE:

In 1946 Roy Campanella and I rode the train with our wives up to Nashua, New Hampshire. We checked into a Howard Johnson's motel outside of town. There was snow on the ground and it was cold. We were building log fires and going into the restaurant to eat fried clams. We waited for the Nashua team to come back from spring training—they were delayed when their bus broke down. We hadn't met the players or anyone else and I was concerned about our reception. Roy was the steadying hand all the time. He was a grown man who had been all over the United States, Puerto Rico, Mexico. He was my father figure, and anything he did, I followed. It would be that way all through the majors.

I'll never forget when Roy and I finally walked into the clubhouse. Walter Alston, who was the player-manager, was leaning back on his chair. He was a huge, strong man. And a nice man. He welcomed us to the team. We then met the players, who also made us feel welcome. Everyone was schooled by Branch Rickey, Clyde Sukeforth, Buzzy Bavasi, and Walt Alston. They had told the white players that we were going to be members of the team. We had no problems with anybody. On the contrary—we had guys standing up for us there.

It wasn't as difficult playing in New Hampshire as it was for Jackie on Montreal. What nerve he had to go to Daytona Beach, Florida, for the first day of spring training with Montreal, knowing that the sheriff was there with the intention of locking him up. And then he had to play in Syracuse and Buffalo, New York, and Baltimore, Maryland, where they had a lot of crackers who didn't want to see a black face on that field. There was almost a riot in Baltimore. But we had some incidents, too. Sal Yvars threw dirt in Roy's face. He knew Roy couldn't defend himself. Roy told him, "If you do that again, I'm going to break your arm for you." He never did it again. Yvars always denied that he did it, but neither Roy nor I ever forgot it.

Alston was a first baseman and pretty good right-handed hitter. He was trying to catch a pop fly between home and first base and Yvars hit him and almost broke his back. Walter couldn't play anymore after that. Yvars was a dirty goddamn baseball player then and when he got to the New York Giants. I never forgot and tried to bust his ass many times when he came to the plate. He knew what I was doing. That was then—Sal changed, as did a whole lot of other players. But at the time, look what was going on: blacks were coming in to take jobs away from white boys. Even when we got to the Dodgers the same thing went on.

In 1946, when Roy and I were on Nashua, John Wright, a black pitcher, joined Jackie at Montreal to become the second black to reach that high a level. He didn't last long, however, so the Dodgers brought in Roy Partlow, a good left-hander from the Philadelphia Stars of the Negro Leagues. It was apparent that the Dodgers were signing blacks and then using a stair-step procedure for getting them to the majors. They hoped that the animosity would be swept away by 1949 or 1950. So Jackie was going to be first, pitcher Dan Bankhead was going to be second, Roy was going to be third. Whoever came after them would be determined by talent. According to Buzzy Bavasi, I was the man they were after to integrate baseball, but they thought I was too young and brash. They knew I could throw a fastball as hard as any human being ever threw it, but when I was in the minors, I dared hit white boys with it.

NATIONAL
LEAGUE
1947

"IF THE WIND WOULD BE BLOWING

OUT, MIZE WOULD LIE BACK IN BED

AND PUFF THAT CIGAR AND SAY,

'ROOMIE, I'M GOING TO HIT ONE OR

TWO TODAY.' AND HE WOULD. IF

THE WIND WAS BLOWING IN, HE'D

COME BACK TO THE BED AND PUT

OUT HIS CIGAR AND JUST LIE

THERE."

BILL RIGNEY

BOSTON BRAVES

JOHNNY SAIN:

On April 15, 1947, the Braves opened the season in front of 26,623 fans in Brooklyn and I became the first pitcher to face Jackie Robinson. We knew he was going to play although they hadn't announced it, which may be why there were over 6,000 empty seats at Ebbets Field. I was going to pitch Opening Day for the second straight year and was pretty excited. I didn't care who I pitched against and was concentrating on what I did against all the Dodgers, not on an event that would go down in history. There were no incidents or mischief during the game, which is why nobody would remember who pitched to Robinson. He played first base and batted second. In his first at-bat in the first inning, I threw him a low curveball and he grounded to Dick Culler at short. He went 0 for 3, but reached on an error on a sacrifice bunt and then scored. I lost that game 5–3. Joe Hatten started for Brooklyn.

Most of the Braves didn't think Robinson entering the majors was a big deal. There were a few people who may have tried to hurt him, but rookies of all colors got harsh treatment. He was a black and a rookie, so he was bound to be in a tough situation. Robinson quickly proved to everybody that he was an outstanding player who could do many things. I know he gave me a lot of trouble on the base paths. At that time I had trouble holding men on base, and he and Pee Wee Reese stole second on me quite easily.

The Dodgers were the best team in the National League in 1947. But the Dodgers had the Giants, and our chief rivals were the St. Louis Cardinals. I didn't like pitching in either of their parks. Ebbets Field was more legitimate before the war. Right field was close, but it was a long ways to center and left until they put box seats out there and made it into a bandbox. There was also a short right field in Sportsman's Park in St. Louis, but what really made it difficult there was the heat and humidity. When I'd walk off the field, my shoes were soaked with perspiration and my eyeballs were sunk back in my head.

I perspired an awful lot no matter where I pitched. Between innings I'd cool my blood by sticking my hand in an ice bucket with ammonia water. At times I took an ice pack and put it on my stomach. Our uniforms were wool, and if they weren't big enough, they would bind you so you couldn't stretch. That's why we wore baggy uniforms. They weren't that uncomfortable except if we played in 100-degree temperatures in St. Louis. (Later, they came out with polyester uniforms that would stretch a bit, and one year they would even have satin uniforms.)

Weather-wise, I was so fortunate pitching in Boston, where there were cool days and nights. I also liked Braves Field. It was an old-fashioned park with a one-deck grandstand and had a capacity of about 40,000. Like Fenway, it had a high wall in left, but was more of a legitimate park, and I liked it much better. The offices were above the gates and there were stairs leading upward. That's why I came up with my saying about negotiating for a better salary: "Climb the golden stairs." I'd walk to the park from Coolidge Corner, taking Beacon to Commonwealth Avenue, where Braves Field was built in 1915. It was near Fenway, which contributed to our little rivalry. We also had good attendance in those days and good, loyal fans who were aware of our longer history.

I was friendly with all my teammates, especially Warren Spahn, first baseman Earl Torgeson, and utility player Sibby Sisti. But I didn't socialize with them. I was a loner off the field and didn't go out to dinner with this one or that one. I enjoyed eating but not dining out. I was conscientious about what I ate, particularly at breakfast, and I knew I could get as good a meal in a diner or the hotel as in an expensive restaurant. I didn't know the best restaurants in New York, Philadelphia, or other cities. Anyway, the $6-a-day meal money wouldn't buy you much in New York. In New York, our traveling secretary would give us $18 for three days, but instead of going out, I'd pocket that money and sign the check in the hotel restaurant and it would be billed to the Braves. And I didn't go drinking with anyone. If we had a game the next afternoon, I probably wouldn't even go to a movie at night. Instead I'd put that dollar in my pocket and go to bed early. So I'd resent it when our clubhouse man, Shorty Young, would wake me up by knocking on doors at the midnight curfew.

I held on to my money. I never had anything growing up in Havana, Arkansas—my dad was a mechanic but during the Depression his customers couldn't pay their bills. My desire was to come out of baseball with as much money as I could. That made it difficult for my wife. We got married in 1945 and it was always hard for her. The game itself was an outlet for the players, but the wives didn't have outlets. They had to move from one place to another and worry about schools, finances, and whether their husbands were about to lose their jobs. It was an unstable life. I didn't know if I was going to play one year, two years, three years, four years. . . . I didn't know. I just knew I had a lot of responsibility toward my wife and my folks in Arkansas.

The Braves had improved since 1946. At third base we had Bob Elliott, who was a great player. He was called "Mr. Team" because when the Braves acquired him from Pittsburgh at the end of the 1946 season, they traded a bunch of players for him. That nickname was appropriate because Elliott provided a lot of leadership. He batted well over .300, slugged over 20 homers, and drove in over 100 runs. That's why he was voted the league's Most Valuable Player.

Earl Torgeson was a really bear-down, hard-nosed, intelligent rookie. He was 6′3″ and weighed about 180 pounds, yet he was quick around first base and fast on the base paths, stealing a fair number of bases. Earl stepped in as a 23-year-old and did a good job for us. After Elliott, he was our best power hitter.

We picked up Bill Voiselle from the Giants during the 1946 season, and he became the fourth starter behind me, Spahn, and Red Barrett. He was a tall right-hander who threw a wicked fastball. We kidded him that he had three pitches: hard, harder, and harder. He was an aggressive type. Bill was the only pitcher whose uniform number was the name of his hometown: he wore 96 because he came from Ninety Six, South Carolina.

Like me, Warren Spahn pitched briefly for the Braves in 1942, but didn't get much work until he returned from the service in 1946. He was already 25 when he got his first win, a late start for someone who would win 363 games. In 1947 Warren came into his own as a great pitcher, winning 21 games and leading the league in earned run average. It was his first of the thirteen 20-win seasons he'd achieve by 1963, and of 4 he'd have in Boston by 1952. I went 21–12, with a 3.53 ERA, pitching 266 innings and completing 22 of 35 starts. Spahn and I would be the most effective lefty-righty combination in the majors through 1950.

We were both workhorses but we had different styles. Batters didn't mind hitting against Spahn because he couldn't throw sidearm and his delivery and rhythm were the same on every pitch, straight up and over, every time. But he had uncanny control and painted the corners. Also, Spahn being left-handed, his ball moved naturally. He had all the pitches and then added a screwball. He also had a very good pickoff move, which I didn't have yet. My speed was just above average. My hard curve was my best pitch, my out pitch. Then I threw a screwball and changed speeds and motion. I was an unorthodox, deceptive pitcher who kept batters off stride by throwing a variation of breaking balls, using different speeds, and using different deliveries and points of release. We played the other seven teams so often that batters could familiarize themselves with each pitcher—that's why I developed an unpredictable style. The batters that gave me the most trouble were those that would wait, but my motion was so quick it was hard to wait on me. I might give up 8 to 10 hits and keep the other team under 2 runs. I didn't give up many extra-base hits. Spahn might allow fewer hits yet give up the same number of runs. Spahn and I both worked on getting hitters out without necessarily overpowering them with fastballs. We learned so much from each other.

I figured that Ewell Blackwell and I were considered the best pitchers in the league at this time. Blackwell was more of a superstar because he was a power pitcher, but we were pretty even when we matched up. I was the only National Leaguer to have won 20 games in both 1946 and 1947. In 1947 he won 22 games and no-hit us in Crosley Field. Bama Rowell was our last hitter and Blackwell struck him out. Rowell came back to the dugout with a big smile on his face and said, ''That ball *riz!*'' Blackwell was considered the toughest pitcher on right-handed batters because he threw sidearm. I know I didn't wear him out when I faced him at the plate, but I was a very good-hitting pitcher—in 1947 I batted .346, going 37 for 107—and I don't remember him striking me out.

Although I didn't frighten batters like Blackwell did, they didn't like facing me because, as Billy Southworth said, it looked like I was mad at everybody. There was no place for foolishness during a game and I never showed any emotions.

Southworth gave me the confidence to become a good pitcher, and I respected him for that. Still, everyone thought I got along with him worse than I did, including him. Billy even asked my roommate, Si Johnson, ''Why doesn't that guy like me?'' I think he would have liked me to chat with him more, but I wasn't like that with any manager—I just did what they asked. You have a tendency to second-guess whoever is in charge, so little things would come up and you'd wonder if Billy was doing a good job. But the only thing he ever did that I resented was bringing in Johnny Beazley, Ernie White, and Mort Cooper. They had pitched for him at St. Louis on those pennant-winning teams during the war, but they couldn't throw anymore. They were his friends and he wanted them to hang around when he was doing too much drinking. Billy's drinking began when his son, who was in the service, crashed his plane at an airport and was killed. Billy would go out to that airport and just sit for hours. It was real sad.

ST. LOUIS CARDINALS

JOHNNY SAIN (BRAVES):

The Cardinals were a rough-and-tumble team. They were always ready to give you a battle. They had a great infield with Stan Musial, the best hitter in the league, at first, Red Schoendienst at second, Marty Marion at short, and Whitey Kurowski at third, and such veteran outfielders as Terry Moore, Enos Slaughter, and even Joe Medwick. Some of those guys were throwbacks to the Gashouse Gang. They hustled all the time—remember Slaughter winning the 1946 World Series against Boston by racing home from first base on Harry Walker's short hit and a slow relay. They also had a strong staff with pitchers like Murry Dickson, Harry Brecheen, Howie Pollet, Red Munger, and Al Brazle. They were a tough, experienced team and, after finishing at the top in 1946, were second in 1947, 5 games in back of Brooklyn and 3 games ahead of us.

SPIDER JORGENSEN (DODGERS):

The Dodgers and Cardinals had developed a strong rivalry, especially in 1946, when the Cardinals beat Brooklyn in a playoff to win the National League title. It was tougher playing them than the Yankees in the World Series. They never let up, never gave up. They played hard. Slaughter would slide with his spikes high. You had to watch him. Our teams didn't have many brawls, but we didn't let them get away with anything.

JOHNNY KLIPPSTEIN:

My dad was a 30-year army man and for a time was stationed at Walter Reed hospital in Washington, D.C., where I was born in 1927. My mother lived in Silver Springs, Maryland, and that's where I grew up. I was a Senators fan and would listen to Arch McDonald's tickertape broadcasts, in which he'd strike gongs every time the batter passed a base. I played pickup ball as a kid and one year of American Legion, which is where I learned I had pitching talent.

When I was 15, my mother and I rode a bus to visit relatives in Appleton, Wisconsin, where the Cardinals were holding a three-day tryout camp. I arrived with a softball glove and softball hat and looked like a dope. They started out with 300 ballplayers, and finally three of us were informed that we would be hearing from them in the spring. My mother was reluctant to let me leave home at the age of 16, but my parents finally agreed to let me go. So in 1944 I signed a contract with the Cardinals, and after my junior year I played professional ball in Allentown, Pennsylvania. That was Class B and I was getting $150 a month. All the guys were between 18 and 21 and I felt they were old enough to be my father. The first time I went to the mound, I was so scared that my knees shook. I struck out 5 out of 9 guys and no one hit the ball out of the infield. Unfortuantely, the next 5 times out, everybody either got a hit off me or walked. So I was sent to Ohio to play Class D ball and had a pretty good year. Then I finished my senior year in high school and returned to Allentown.

I turned 18 in October of 1945 and volunteered immediately for the army so I would have to serve only a year and miss only one baseball season. The next month I went into the army. Brigadier General Helmick at Fort Meade put out a direct order that all the baseball players in camp wouldn't be shipped overseas for the occupation. I played about 90 games of army ball in 1946.

In 1947 I returned to the Cardinals system and was sent to Columbus in Triple A. There was no way I was ready. They demoted me to Omaha in the Western League, which was Class A. We didn't have a ballpark, so we'd take a train to Council Bluffs, Iowa, to play. We were managed by Ollie Vanek, who was given some of the credit for signing Stan Musial. We were playing in Sioux City and they had gotten 2 scratch hits off me when Ollie sent up another pitcher to hit for me. The next day, instead of asking why I was taken out, I said, "Ollie, I don't think you should have taken me out." Oh, did he get hot! Two days later I was on my way to Lynchburg in the Piedmont League, Class B. In those days you didn't rub the manager wrong.

CHICAGO CUBS

RANDY JACKSON:

My father had played baseball at Princeton and always had aspirations for me, but while baseball came easy to me, I never took it seriously. Growing up in Little Rock, Arkansas, I didn't listen to baseball on the radio or have a favorite team or player. When I got out of high school, I went to the University of Arkansas, where after six months, I opted to go into the navy's officer training program. However, in February 1944, when I turned 18, I had to immediately drop out and enroll in the officer training program at Texas Christian University. Of the 1,400 students at TCU, about 800 of us were apprentice seamen making $50 a month. I was taking calculus and chemistry, and knew that I had to study because if I flunked out, I would be sent to where the fighting was. Then in June of 1945 the navy said all the midshipmen schools were full, so they sent me to the University of Texas.

I hadn't played sports in high school, but to pass the time, I played football for Dutch Meyer at TCU and Dana X. Bible at Texas, where Bobby Layne was the quarterback. I was a halfback and punter and became the only man in history to play in consecutive Cotton Bowls with two different schools in the same conference. TCU lost, but Texas won. I also played baseball for both colleges. At TCU, I batted .500 to lead the Southwest Conference in average. The next spring at Texas, I played third base and hit about .420 to lead the conference again. I played football for a third year and then played baseball again in the spring of 1947 and won my third consecutive batting title.

There were a few scouts around, but the one who was most interested was Jimmy Payton of the Cubs. He asked me if I'd like to play professional baseball. I truthfully replied that I'd never thought about it. (By this time I was 21 and out of the navy after two years and four months, during which time the Japanese did not invade Texas.) He said they could pay my way to Chicago for a tryout. My dad and I flew up to Chicago. The Cubs were on the road, but a sore-armed player who stayed home pitched to me at Wrigley Field. I was in awe of being in a major league park. I hit two or three into the seats and played the field. In August, the Cubs offered to sign me to a major league contract that included a bonus. But the bonus rule that was in effect stipulated they wouldn't have been able to send me to the minors for the seasoning we all knew I needed. So I signed a two-year major league contract for $6,000 each year, without a bonus, on the condition that I'd go to the minors but still be on the Cubs' 40-man roster. Then after two years both parties could decide if I should play in the majors.

JIM BROSNAN:

I was born in Cincinnati in 1929. My father worked for the Cincinnati Milling Machine Company. My mother had been a nurse before they married but she was pretty much stuck at home after giving birth to five children. My father had been a minor league umpire but had no influence on any of his three boys playing baseball. Without fear of contradiction, I'd say that he didn't have any interest in any of his children. I played baseball because that's what kids did. There were good recreational programs in Cincinnati and I played in organized ball from the time I was eight or nine. I wasn't a Reds fan, but I'd watch them play at Crosley Field. Rather than taking two trolleys, I'd walk the twelve miles and save the twenty cents fare to buy a hot dog and Coke. A few years later I was a member of the Knothole Club and saw an occasional free game.

I played hardball with Knothole kids, and when I was 16, I first played American Legion ball. I didn't display any unusual talent when I batted or played shortstop, but when I pitched I threw hard and was consistently effective. Tony Lucadello of the Chicago Cubs was the first scout to show an interest in me. After graduation, I wanted to go to Notre Dame and figured if I signed with

the Cubs, I could use the bonus money to go there. But the Cubs gave me just $2,500—a $2,000 bonus plus $125 a month for four months—and with $500 of that going to the government, I didn't have enough money left to pay for even one year at Notre Dame.

In the spring of 1947 I went to a special Cubs spring training camp in St. Augustine, Florida, for new signees, bonus players, and all those guys coming back from the army. There were 159 players on hand and everyone was charted for what the Cubs expected of them. Interestingly, many players were expected to merely fill up the extensive farm system rather than make it all the way to the majors. Because there were so many players in camp, we didn't get many opportunities to impress the Cubs brass.

I was assigned to Elizabethton, Tennessee, which was Class D. There was an incredible turnover rate there, with young signees and demoted players constantly filling roster spaces left by players who moved up, didn't make it, or, as in the case of some war veterans, just quit. At the end of the year there were only 5 guys left of the original group. I lived on $5 a day, so it helped that I didn't much socialize with other players. I wasn't so much shy as I was aloof. The only player I spent time with was Charley Morrison, an older pitcher who had gone into the army as a member of the Cubs organization, so was entitled to a job for a year. He and Bob Borkowski, who had been demoted from B ball, showed me the ropes and helped me grow up a bit. They told me not to pout so much after I got beat. I was a .500 pitcher for the first half of the year and then won 7 or 8 games in a row in the second half. I moved ahead of Morrison to become the number one pitcher on the team.

BROOKLYN DODGERS

SPIDER JORGENSEN:

I went to spring training with Montreal in Havana, Cuba. Just before the season started we played a 3-game exhibition series against the Dodgers in Brooklyn, with plans to open the season in Syracuse. The night before the season started they notified me that I would play third base for the Dodgers on Opening Day because Cookie Lavagetto and Arky Vaughan were both hurting. My contract had been transferred to Brooklyn and I was told to show up the next morning at the Dodgers' office at 10 A.M., prior to a one o'clock game. All my equipment had been shipped to Syracuse, so Ray Blades, the Dodgers' third base coach, lent me his shoes, and Jackie Robinson let me use his fielder's glove because he would be playing first base, since Eddie Stanky was the Dodgers' second baseman. It was scary coming to the big leagues in this way.

My first game was Opening Day against the Braves and was the game in which Jackie Robinson debuted in the majors. There was extra attention because of Robinson, but I didn't care about the significance of that game—I was just wanting to play well. As it turned out, neither of us got a hit, but we won anyway.

Right before the season began, Leo Durocher had been suspended for the entire year by Commissioner Happy Chandler for unspecified reasons. Supposedly, Leo had done something or several things wrong that Chandler considered a detriment to baseball, but he wouldn't say what. I knew Leo slightly because Montreal and the Dodgers had trained together in Daytona Beach in 1946. I was in awe of him because of the success he'd had managing Brooklyn since 1939, when he was a player-manager. He had won the pennant in 1941 and just missed in 1946. I realized that he was smarter than other managers and could think several innings ahead of them. I also was wary of him because he was very strict and had a fierce temper that he had directed at players and fans, as well as at umpires. In 1947 the Dodger players didn't really know why Leo was suspended, and we didn't talk too much about it because we were in the middle of a pennant race and trying to show we could win without him. If it was because the Catholics were mad at him for marrying actress Laraine Day in Mexico right after her divorce, I didn't know. I thought it was more likely because he was friendly with gamblers and other characters. He spent a lot of time at the racetrack. I know he was good friends with actor George Raft, who had a shady background of sorts. But I never found out the reason.

With Durocher gone so suddenly our coach Clyde Sukeforth opened the season as our temporary manager. He was a great guy. Then Burt Shotton, a Dodgers scout, took over and Clyde would sit next to him in the dugout and be his right-hand man. Shot was a soft-

John "Spider" Jorgensen had an excellent rookie campaign in 1947, batting .274 and playing solid third base for the National League champion Brooklyn Dodgers, but an arm injury would prevent him from ever playing regularly again.

NATIONAL BASEBALL LIBRARY, COOPERSTOWN, N.Y.

spoken man in his early sixties who had managed the Phillies back in the 1930s. He never wore a uniform, but wore a suit like Connie Mack. Shot knew a lot about baseball and held a daily meeting in which he'd go over the opposition. At the end, he'd usually tell a little story, and that would calm me down. He had a curfew, but he wasn't a strict manager and wouldn't badger players or talk behind their backs. I liked him very much. I assume he made all the decisions because Branch Rickey never came into the clubhouse. I'd see him only if I glanced up at the press box.

I got off to a good start and Shot kept me in the lineup. I was just trying to break into baseball, so I kept my mouth shut and only was loud when I struck out or grounded out on a pitch I should have hit. I was nervous and out of place, but Pee Wee Reese and a lot of other players helped me adjust. We all rallied behind Pee

Wee, our leader. He kept us focused on winning, which made us a close team. We knew he was going to make the right play or say the right thing. He was always helpful, to Jackie and the other players, too.

I'd say pitcher Rex Barney helped me the most. For instance, on the first day against Johnny Sain, he told me, ''All you're going to get is curveballs, curveballs— if he throws a fastball, don't swing because it will be a ball.'' He was exactly right. Throughout the whole season we talked about different pitchers and he'd tell me what they threw. Rex was a hard-throwing right-hander who could be wild, but if he was frustrated because of that in 1947, he didn't show it.

I knew a few guys on the team already. Jackie had been on Montreal in 1946. At Santa Barbara in 1941, my first year in pro ball, I'd played with Bruce Edwards, the Dodgers' strong-hitting catcher, Hal Gregg, who was a tall right-hander from California, and Vic Lombardi, who was a short left-hander from California. There were several of us who would go out to dinner together, including Bruce, my roommate Eddie Miksis, Pee Wee, Gene Hermanski, and once in a while Barney and Carl Furillo. We would have a few beers together, but no one really got drunk and we'd get back by quarter to one, in time for the curfew. Some of the single guys would go across the street from the St. George Hotel to a place called, I think, Vince and Paul's. But in Brooklyn, we married guys never went to bars. When we'd have a Wednesday afternoon game, some players and their wives might get together at someone's house that night for a charades party. There might be Pee Wee, Barney, pitcher Paul Minner, outfielder Dick Whitman, myself, and a few other guys. We had a lot of fun.

There was cardplaying in the clubhouse. Gin rummy was a popular game. Stanky and Hugh Casey, the veteran right-hander, played all the time. Pee Wee played occasionally. I know Durocher had liked to play. There'd be cardplaying on the trains—often poker for pennies and nickels, or dimes and quarters. I never won in the army, so I wasn't interested anymore.

I preferred going to the club car to listen to the reporters argue. I got along very well with the guys on the sports beat. The newspaper that was most associated with the Dodgers was the *Daily News,* which was friendly to Leo and fair to the players but really tore into Branch Rickey. I liked Dick Young, who covered us for

the *News.* Most guys did, I think. Or maybe I was one of the few. He was a good writer but we were all cautious around both him and his sports editor, Jimmy Powers, because they liked to dig up things. We worried that if there was something in the paper, we'd get called in and get our asses chewed out. So while we were on good terms with the writers, we kept our guard up on the trains and in the clubhouse.

One of the players the reporters loved was Kirby Higbe, who had been a successful pitcher with the Dodgers since before the war, and was their top winner in 1941. He wasn't as fast as Barney, but he threw hard. And he threw a knuckler. He was a friendly, colorful character, who was always willing to talk to the writers and give them some good quotes. He was a fun-loving guy from the South, who'd drink a lot and was always joking around or pulling off pranks to keep everyone loose. You'd have a good time around Kirby. He was traded to the Pirates early in the season, but I don't think it was because he was a disruptive force. I wouldn't describe him as disruptive.

Another good guy in the clubhouse was Hugh Casey, who was a good friend of Kirby's. I *loved* Hugh Casey. I had my locker next to his and he was always helpful. I was making just five grand and he'd take out a big roll of money and give me a $100 bill and ask if that was enough. Hugh owned a restaurant and my wife and I would go there on occasion, and we'd get treated well. He was a nice guy but he was also extremely tough and a good fighter. He wasn't in his best shape by this time, but in Havana during spring training, he and Ernest Hemingway got into a big fight. Hemingway used to challenge players for sport and Casey was goaded into fighting him one day. Casey got the best of him. On the mound, Casey was mean and a real good competitor. He was one of baseball's first great relievers, and had been since the early forties—he's the one who threw that famous strike-out pitch in the '41 World Series that got by catcher Mickey Owen. He had good control and threw an effective sinker—which is why he was often accused of throwing a spitter—and would get batters to hit into a lot of double plays. I think he would have been in trouble pitching for another team because Reese and Stanky scooped up a lot of grounders that other infielders wouldn't have reached.

In the spring, my wife and I lived in the St. George

(before we got an apartment at 2015 Foster Avenue). Pee Wee and the majority of the players lived there. Bobby Bragan, who was one of our catchers, was also there, and since I didn't have a car, I often rode with him to the ballpark. Other times I'd grab the subway.

After a game, we'd stick around and have a beer or two—later, Rickey banned beer from the clubhouse—or just mull around until we thought the crowd was gone and it was safe to head for the subways. Barney warned me, "Don't stop and sign autographs." One day, long after a game, I was walking the three or four blocks from Ebbets Field to the subway when a kid recognized me. So I stopped to sign one autograph, and the next thing I knew, there was a flock around me like a bunch of bees. I actually got pushed onto the hood of a car and they were poking pencils at me. I fought my way out of there and ran to the subway. I never stopped again because it was too dangerous.

But the Dodger fans were good. They'd just come out to see good baseball and to see us win. If the crowd was small you could hear a few loudmouths, but we were winning and Robinson was there, so we didn't have many small crowds. All Brooklyn loved the Dodgers. It was said that you could walk down any street during a game and hear Red Barber call every pitch because every radio was tuned in.

Red Barber had contributed a great deal to the popularity of the team ever since Branch Rickey brought him in to broadcast our games. All the fans became familiar with such Barber phrases as "Oh, doctor" and "Hold the Phone." They didn't mind that he was from Mississippi and had a Southern accent. Red mingled with the players before games, and I got to know and like him. He was a good reporter and broadcaster who was never critical of the players.

I suppose it was strange living and playing in Brooklyn because I had been born in 1919 and raised in Folsom, California—I was half-Danish and half-Irish and named John—attended Sacramento Junior College, and even played my first year of pro ball in the California League, before I entered the army. But it was even stranger that I reached the major leagues at all. My father, who worked for a company that tore up the land looking for gold, hated baseball and never encouraged me or watched me play high school or semipro ball. I knew I had talent, but I weighed only 90 pounds at the age of 16. I got up to only about 5′9″ and 155 pounds. I made the team at college as a walk-on. When the third baseman flunked out, I moved there. In my second year, Bill Svilich, a bird dog who worked at the haberdashery, recommended me to Tom Downey, the Dodgers' West Coast scout. I went to a tryout camp in San Mateo and was signed for $75 a month. That was in 1940. Seven years later I was a rookie on a great Dodgers team.

Of course, Robinson also was a rookie. Gil Hodges had played a bit before the war, but this was really his first year, too, and he was our third-string catcher. He was solidly built and very strong, but he was a quiet young man and a peacemaker in fights. Edwin "Duke" Snider also was a rookie. He had talent but would sulk a bit when things weren't going well for him. He didn't play too much because we had an outfield of Carl Furillo, Dixie Walker, and Pete Reiser, who all hit around .300.

Furillo had come up in 1946 and was a good player right away. He was a tough player and excellent hitter. He never said much off the field and was somewhat of a loner, but he was a nice guy and I liked him very much. Dixie was the brother of Harry Walker and had been playing since the early thirties. He was a former batting champion and an all-around good hitter. He was just a fair fielder at this point, but he was in his mid-thirties. He had been extremely popular with the Brooklyn fans and players, but the business with Jackie Robinson made his position a little cloudy.

Pete Reiser was a friendly guy and great player. Pete, Walker, and I were the only left-handed hitters in the lineup—though Gene Hermanski got a lot of playing time. Pete had tremendous speed and was the league's best center fielder. Balls would go into the outfield and I'd run out there expecting a single and a relay throw, but he'd catch the ball easily on the fly. Unfortunately, Pete was injury-prone. Parks didn't yet have warning tracks, so by this time he had crashed into walls several times. He had damaged his arm but it finally was healing when in the middle of the year, he ran smack into the concrete wall in Brooklyn. I thought he'd killed himself. Supposedly they gave him his last rites and he was paralyzed for days before coming around. Later on, they had to operate to get rid of a blood clot in his head. He came back—and even played in the World Series with a broken ankle—but was never the same.

Pete was fearless and went overboard sometimes, but if you were a Dodger, you put out all the time. We ran balls out hard, even obvious outs, trying to rush the opposition into making mistakes. Branch Rickey used to teach his young players that if you hit a single, treat it like a double. So we'd come around first base and if the outfielder hesitated, we'd keep going. That's how we were trained. Lots of times, they called us lucky, but that wasn't true.

It took a while for me to adjust to third base, but once I learned the hitters I became more relaxed. I was a wiry, mobile third baseman who could move from side to side and pick up grounders—that's why I was nicknamed "Spider." I was part of the best all-around infield in the league. Of course, I learned a lot playing next to Pee Wee. I thought he was the best shortstop in the league. He had a very strong and accurate arm and knew exactly where to play hitters. I kept my eye on him when I wasn't sure of a hitter and that gave me an edge.

Eddie Stanky, our second baseman, couldn't move in the field, couldn't hit, and couldn't run, yet he was a helluva ballplayer. He was a smart, tough competitor who could do a lot of things. He was a good second baseman because he knew all the batters and was always in the right place on grounders. He could bunt. He could steal because he could lull the pitcher to sleep and then take off. He always got the bat on the ball, and got so many walks because he kept fouling off pitches until he got ball four. He also would stand in there and be hit by pitches so he could get to first.

RALPH KINER (PIRATES):
Stanky wore an extra-baggy shirt so he would be grazed by more pitches and be awarded first base.

S. JORGENSEN:
On the bench he'd always get on the opposing pitchers, although I don't know if they heard him. On the field, Eddie shouted encouragement to our pitchers and razzed the batters. He wasn't as gentlemanly as Pee Wee, but loved to antagonize. Once the Cubs' Bill Nicholson was on second base and Eddie called for a pickoff. He knew he wouldn't get Swish, but he wanted to hit him in the face with the glove in the hope that Swish would get so mad that he'd leave the base to fight him and be tagged out. We laughed at a lot of the stuff he did.

Because Stanky played second, Robinson began his major league career as a first baseman. To me, Jackie was just another guy. I had played against blacks in California dating back to junior college and had played with Jackie at Montreal, so it wasn't a big deal for me. When Jackie was promoted to the Dodgers just before the season, Branch Rickey told him to be quiet, take a lot of abuse, and just play like hell. That's what he did. He had a lot of talent and led the team in homers, stole a lot of bases, hit to all fields, showed that he was a great bunter, and hustled every second he was on the field. He had a great season. He was better than anyone expected, including me. He proved to be an excellent curveball and two-strike hitter. And he ran the bases with abandon, stealing or catching outfielders napping. Dixie Walker, who was from Alabama, and a few other Dodgers protested that a black player would join the team, but when they saw how good Robinson played, there wasn't any trouble between them—although Walker was traded to Pittsburgh at the end of the year. Robinson was accepted because everybody wanted to win.

A few Southerners resented Robinson. Ben Chapman, the Phillies' manager, really got after him from the bench. He was from Alabama. The Cardinals got a little vicious. Pitchers would knock him down and Enos Slaughter and Ducky Medwick would step on his foot—or as high as his thigh—when they ran down to first. I wouldn't say we rallied behind Robinson just because of what he was going through, but we were a team and protective of all our players. So we warned the Cardinals that we would no longer put up with the frequent spikings. One Cardinal we got along with was catcher Joe Garagiola. He was a happy-go-lucky guy. Over the years I would read how Jackie and Joe got into a shouting match after Joe spiked him. But that never happened. Joe never spiked him.

Early in the season, the Cardinals were late getting out on the field. Only later were we told that their players almost didn't play us because of Robinson. Our players often weren't told what was going on. When we went to Philadelphia on the first road trip, the bus picked us up at the train depot and stopped at the Benjamin Franklin Hotel. After a few minutes we were told that we were going directly to the ballpark and not checking in. After the game, we checked into the Warwick Hotel, a much plusher place. The club might have told Pee Wee or a couple of others what was happening, but they didn't say much to the rest of us. (Only 40 years later would I learn that the Benjamin Franklin Hotel had turned us away because of Robinson.)

The people most concerned about Robinson were the black reporters. Wendell Smith, out of Detroit, followed Jackie all over the place and even roomed with him on the road. He was a good guy who I got to know pretty well.

Jackie was voted the National League's first Rookie of the Year. Although I wasn't a candidate, I thought I had a pretty good rookie season. I strove to hit .300 but wound up at .274 and had 67 RBIs. I hit only 5 homers, but nobody on our team had more than 12. The Dodgers didn't hit too many homers in Ebbets Field that year. Everyone had trouble homering to the opposite field. I'd say it was because the ball wasn't too lively that year, but the Giants set a home run record. We just didn't start hitting a lot of homers until 1949.

We relied on hustle, defense, timely hitting, and pitching. We had a good rotation with Ralph Branca, Joe Hatten, Vic Lombardi, and Harry Taylor, with guys like Barney and Clyde King in reserve. And Hugh Casey did a good job in the pen. Branca was a tall young right-hander from the New York area. He was one of the few other Dodgers who had attended college. He hadn't done a lot of pitching for the Dodgers before 1947. He became the ace of our staff and won 21 games. He threw hard, had a good curve, and was a tough competitor. After he threw a home run ball, he'd really stomp around that mound. When he pitched, I was confident he'd give us between seven and nine strong innings and we had a 90 percent chance of winning. Hatten was a hard-throwing left-hander who won 17 games. He was a reliable pitcher who had a good fastball and curve and gave us a lot of innings.

The pennant race was very exciting. We were ahead of the Cardinals by several games in September but were struggling. We won 91 games and clinched the pennant when the Cubs' Johnny Schmitz, a left-hander who always beat the Cardinals, beat them again. Bragan

and I were in the clubhouse getting updates on that game. Finally we heard that the Cubs had won and the team had a pretty good celebration. Brooklyn threw a ticker tape parade for us and all the players received watches.

DON NEWCOMBE:
When Jackie Robinson was promoted from Montreal to Brooklyn and broke the major league color barrier in 1947, Roy Campanella was promoted from Nashua to Montreal. With him there, I was left behind to pitch another year at Nashua, and Nashua brought up another black, from Cuba. Because of Mr. Rickey's stair-step procedure for getting blacks to the big leagues, I couldn't move up to Montreal with Roy already there.

Dan Bankhead, who was purchased from Memphis, Tennessee, was brought up by the Dodgers in August to become the first black pitcher in major league history. He was an excellent hitter and homered in his first time at-bat against Fritz Ostermueller of the Pirates—the first National League pitcher to do this. The Pirates hit him hard in his debut and after that he was in only a few more games. He was a pretty good pitcher who struck out a lot of batters, but I think he was brought in mostly as a companion for Jackie.

Before Bankhead's arrival in late August, Robinson was the only black player in the league. The American League's first black was former Newark Bears star Larry Doby, who joined the Indians in July. Then the St. Louis Browns brought up Hank Thompson and Willard Brown. All these men were talented, but it says something that only Jackie Robinson had a good year in 1947. Jackie alone in the National League received letters full of threats and insults, and suffered abuse from players, managers, and fans.

Along with everything else, Jackie had to cope with teammates who weren't happy he was now part of their team. It's a funny thing about people, especially if they're white and have position and also care about money—and most ballplayers are born capitalists—that if you can help them make some money, your color becomes insignificant. And that's the way it was in 1947. Dixie Walker even tried to generate a petition against Jackie playing with the Dodgers in Panama. When Jackie helped the Dodgers break their attendance record—almost every National League team set records because of Jackie—and make the 1947 World Series, Walker forgot all about his objections. Here was a cracker from the South who hated everything black, but he changed when Jackie helped him get into the World Series and make some extra money.

A classic photograph was taken of Pee Wee Reese standing near second with his arm around Jackie. Many people insisted that Reese was making a public gesture to show he had accepted Jackie, thus paving the way for other Dodgers to do the same. That's funny because Pee Wee said the gesture was something he hadn't given any thought to. He said he was tired and just put his arm around Jackie while they were laughing and talking. Jackie always was very jocular. Pee Wee didn't even remember what they were talking about, but someone took a picture of it and made a big deal of it. He said, "It was no big deal; I was just talking to my second baseman." Despite the early hostility Jackie received from Walker and some teammates—even Dodgers announcer Red Barber thought of quitting—it never was said that Pee Wee Reese was the protector of Jackie Robinson. Jackie didn't need any goddamn protector. He needed somebody to understand. Pee Wee understood, or tried to.

Jackie wanted to show everyone that he was the same as everyone else. "Why do I have to be treated differently," he asked, "just because my skin happens to be black?" He wanted to know why people called him "nigger" when they didn't call Pee Wee Reese "nigger." Only the color of his skin made him a "nigger" and he resented that to the core of his being. He hated that word. Yet he knew things were going to change. He knew that if he made a mistake in 1947 and that safety valve on his emotions shot off, Branch Rickey would call the whole thing off. Were it not for a beautiful woman named Rachel Robinson, his wife, he would have exploded. He had to keep everything inside of him because, like the rest of us, he felt obligated to Rickey. Jackie wasn't the type who could do that. I know it took a big toll on him and that he almost had a nervous breakdown after the season.

Branch Rickey's decision to break down the color barrier in baseball came from his heart, not because of financial interests. I always believed that and will go to my grave believing that. Mr. Rickey always said, "How can baseball be America's pastime when all Americans aren't given the opportunity to participate in the goddamn game?"—only he didn't say "goddamn" because he didn't curse. He would say that anyone in the world—Cubans, Elmer Valo from Czechoslovakia— could play major league baseball, except for black people. You could play as long as you had white skin. Silvio Garcia, Martin Dihigo, one of the great baseball players ever, couldn't play, not because he was Cuban, but because he was black. But those who had nowhere near the talent but were white could play. Branch Rickey wanted that to change. He was a businessman and saw wealth, not only of baseball talent but of fans who were not coming to see the Dodgers play. He envisioned a stadium that would seat 50,000 people and many would be blacks seeing black players playing with white players and baseball would be the true *all* American pastime that it was advertised to be.

NEW YORK GIANTS

BILL RIGNEY:

At the Giants' spring training in Phoenix, those of us who were unsure of our jobs were housed in one section of the motel while all the heavies were in another section. Having seen me in 1946, Mel Ott concluded, "You're the worst leadoff hitter I've ever seen." I didn't disagree. I never got bases on balls. I thought I'd have been a better second-place hitter because I could spray the ball to all fields and move runners along. But we didn't have anyone to bat leadoff. All we had were home run hitters because that's what the Giants' owner, Horace Stoneham, liked. So while they decided to keep me on the team and have me continue batting leadoff, they wanted to make a homer hitter out of me, too. Ernie Lombardi, who was a player-coach, changed me during spring training, turning me into a pull hitter by putting me right on top of home plate. Before that I just put my feet in the two holes where everybody else stood. Now when I batted in the Polo Grounds, I would hit down the short left-field line, rather than to center, where it was 460 feet.

I had a good spring and returned to New York. Before my wife and child joined me from California, I lived down at the King Edward Hotel on 44th, between

Broadway and Sixth Avenue. Several players lived there before their families joined them. When my family arrived, I rented a house in Westchester. That would be our pattern every year.

I fell in love with New York. There was Billy Rose's Diamond Horseshoe, the Copacabana, Birdland, the Stork Club, the Blue Ribbon, Toots Shor's and all the great restaurants and supper clubs, there were stores and Automats, there was music and movies and shows, there were subways and els and double-decker buses, there were newsstands everywhere you looked, and Central Park was a beautiful playground. Stoneham didn't really like night baseball, so in 1946 and 1947 we played only one night game with each club. So we were free at night. I guess I started to feel a bit like a celebrity because I'd be walking down Broadway at night and Giants fans would call to me. The New York fans knew who you were and who they were. They were proud of their teams. That made a huge impression on a young player like me. Until I came to New York, I didn't realize fans could care so much whether a team won or lost. New York was a baseball-crazy town. There were all those newspapers and great sportswriters: Jimmy Cannon of the *Post,* Arthur Daley of the *Times,* Red Smith of the *Herald Tribune,* Dick Young of the *Daily News.* And we had the best broadcasters: The Giants' Russ Hodges, the Dodgers' Red Barber, and the Yankees' Mel Allen.

Stoneham built a team around the home run rather than pitching and defense. He liked to watch guys who could hit the long ball. He got my roomie, first baseman Johnny Mize, and catcher Walker Cooper from the Cardinals. Cooper hit 6 homers in 3 games at one point. Outfielders Bobby Thomson, who had come up briefly in 1946, Willard Marshall, and Sid Gordon were all pull hitters with power. In 1947 we set a major league record with 221 home runs. Mize tied Pittsburgh's Ralph Kiner for the homer title with 51, Marshall was third with 36, Cooper was fourth with 35, and Thomson was fifth with 29. I hit 17 homers batting leadoff—all to left field. We were the only National League team with more than one player with 100 RBIs, and we had three, with Mize, Cooper, and Marshall. We'd win 10–9, not 1–0.

Mize's nickname was the "Big Cat," but he couldn't move at all around first base. However, he could hit. He had a great eye and a beautiful compact swing. He hit .337 in 1946, but injuries kept his homer total down to 22. Then in 1947 he hit those 51 homers and led the league with 137 runs and 138 RBIs. What a year! He was a cigar smoker. The first thing he'd do every morning on the road was light a cigar—oh, swell, John. He'd get up and walk to the window and lift the shade and look out and find a flag. He'd figure out from the direction that flag was blowing the direction of the wind at the ballpark. If the wind would be blowing out, Mize would lie back in bed and puff that cigar and say, "Roomie, I'm going to hit one or two today." And he would. If the wind was blowing in, he'd come back to the bed and put out his cigar and just lie there. I'd think, "Oh boy, our pitcher had better throw a shutout."

When we'd go out to dinner on the road, John had a little scotch whiskey while I drank my beers. Who cared? But John didn't want anyone to know it. I was kind of a prankster, and I played a terrible trick on him regarding his drinking. We had an off-day in August, and Ott wanted us to work out. It was extremely muggy and John put on a long-sleeved wool shirt and a rubber shirt over it. Afterward he came into the clubhouse and took off his two shirts, and so much water poured out of him that a puddle formed underneath him. I said, "That may be some of that scotch whiskey coming out of you." And Mize, who had no sense of humor, snapped, "Hey, you know better than to talk like that." He went upstairs to shower. Doc Bowman, our trainer, took out some lighter fluid and added it to the puddle. When John got out of the shower, I said, "John, some of the guys think that's whiskey pouring out of your pores." And Doc Bowman said, "There's only one way to find out." He lit a match and dropped it into the puddle and it went poof! You should have seen John's face when he saw the fire. He came over to me and said, "Jeez, I didn't know that stuff comes out of your pores." I told him before the season ended what we had done. He wasn't too happy about it.

Mize was an introverted, private individual, who was not a lot of fun. Otherwise, this was a pretty close team. I was outgoing and became very close friends with guys like Marshall and Gordon, and Buddy Kerr. Infielder Buddy Blattner and I were close. We had both come out of the PCL. Buddy was talkative—he'd become a broadcaster.

I also became close friends with Larry Jansen, a tall,

26-year-old rookie right-hander. Stoneham had a good relationship with the San Francisco Seals in the PCL and got players from them, including Jansen in 1947. Larry had an outstanding curve, a good fastball, great control, and a big heart. He had been a big winner in the Coast League but got off to a tough start. We were in Tucson playing Cleveland when Bob Feller hit a line drive that broke Larry's jaw, knocking teeth out. I was the shortstop and I remember him saying, "Rig, get it out, get it out." He felt the ball was still in his face. That set him back. After 6 games during the regular season, he was 3–3. He said, "Rig, this isn't good enough, I've got to change my style." I said, "You've got to change nothing. You're pitching good." He ended up winning 18 of 20, including 10 straight complete-game victories, and finished his rookie year with a 21–5 record. He became our ace.

With Stoneham's emphasis on hitting, our pitching was weak. All we had was Jansen and lefty Dave Koslo, who won 15 games by keeping batters off stride with a sidearm delivery and breaking balls. The Giants' organization did have high hopes for rookie Clint Hartung. He was a 6'5" pitcher and outfielder from Hondo, Texas, who was considered a "can't-miss" prospect after playing in the service. He went 9–7, which was pretty good for a rookie, but far too much was expected of him. He couldn't get over his wildness and would fail in several seasons with us, although he would win 9 games again in 1949. He was a nice guy and it's too bad it didn't work out better for him.

Mel Ott would have been a better manager if he'd had better pitchers. Another problem is that he hired his friends as his coaches. Ott was a great guy and everyone loved him and wanted to play well for him. Dodgers manager Leo Durocher was talking about Otty when he said, "Nice guys finish last."

Even in my first exhibition game against the Dodgers, I could tell there was a strong, strong rivalry between the Dodgers and Giants. I could taste it, smell it. There was never a rivalry to match it. On the field, the two teams detested each other. As the Giants got better, beginning in 1947, the rivalry became even more intense. There were now three good teams in New York. The rivalry wasn't based on jealousy. It was competitive, it was fun. Much had to do with our being in the same area. There was no such thing as a fan of two teams. You liked the Giants, Dodgers, or Yankees, and hated the other two teams. That the fans cared so much about their favorite teams fed the rivalries. I felt the Giants had an aura because they had a great tradition. There was also an aura around the Dodgers—the "Bums"—and they were always good because Rickey's tremendous farm system kept spewing out great players.

When Jackie Robinson joined the Dodgers in 1947, there was no better player in the league. He was the toughest out and there would be no better competitor during my entire career. He was carrying the cross for the black man and was he ever the right man to do that. He had a lot of talent and a strong personality. He could do so many things on the field, including hitting the long ball. There's a good reason I remember his first home run. It came in the Polo Grounds on April 18, but we won 10–6 and I hit 2 homers, one a grand slam, and drove in 6 runs. That was my biggest offensive output in my career.

There were a lot of people who didn't like baseball being integrated. Prejudice was prevalent, without a doubt—even in the Dodgers' ranks, with guys like Dixie Walker—"the People's Cherce"—and some of the other Southerners. Pee Wee Reese had a lot to do with solving the problem. He came from Kentucky but accepted Jackie for who he was, no matter what color he was. Reese was blossoming as a leader on the Dodgers and he was a great influence on the other players. Of course, Jackie's great ability and desire to win had to be admired by his teammates. All professional ballplayers had to admire him. We all kept an eye on him, watching his progress. It didn't matter if we rooted for him to make it, which many of us did, because he was going to make it in spite of everything. He was that dedicated. He was also mature, not a brash young man. People forget that he wasn't young but almost 30.

Robinson played first because Eddie Stanky was the Dodgers' second baseman. Stanky was a character. This was the era that we'd leave our gloves on the field when we came up to bat. And playing against that damn Stanky, a lot of times you'd come out to retrieve your glove and it would be full of dirt or be stuffed under second base.

Of the other shortstops in the league, I thought Reese was the best. He anchored the Dodgers' infield. I also was impressed with the Cardinals' Marty Marion, who had those long strides. Buddy Kerr, for us, wasn't much of a hitter but he was such a good shortstop, better than me. He had great hands and set a record for errorless games in 1947. Beginning in 1946, I played mostly at third because of Buddy. After 20 games at third in 1947, I was hitting .398, just behind Dixie Walker's .401. I was on such a roll. Then they asked me to play second because Blattner was having trouble turning the double play. The first time I played second, we turned 5 double plays, and they thought I was the greatest second baseman since Burgess Whitehead. But I was no second baseman. I wasn't comfortable there and never even tagged the bag. I had a great arm and was better suited for short or third. Later, Chub Feeney, our GM, said that they should have just gone out and gotten a second baseman and left me at third. If I'd just been stubborn and stayed at third, I could have played more.

I was one of the few infielders who wore glasses. Bob Dillinger, the third baseman of the Browns, wore them. Eddie Joost of the Athletics finally put them on. When I first found out I had to wear them I worried that would keep me out of the majors. I was called "Specs." I had another nickname which I got because I used to chatter while playing the infield and the guys in the center field bleachers could hear my voice. They knew it was me because Mize and Blattner never said boo, and they named me "Cricket."

I batted .267 over the year, an improvement of 31 points. But I think I hit about .100 against the Reds' Ewell Blackwell. He was the toughest pitcher I faced. Left-handers could hit him, but not right-handers. He was a lot of fun. Over the years he would hit me about 6 times. The ball would just bore into me. I knew if I ever kept my ass out of the lineup once, I'd never get back up there.

On the other hand, I must have hit .500 against his teammate Bucky Walters. Walters would tell me that the Reds' pitchers and catchers went over the Giants during the train rides to New York, and as they went through all the sluggers, Bucky would say, "Forget those guys. Tell me how to pitch to that four-eyed infielder!"

PHILADELPHIA PHILLIES

ANDY SEMINICK:

I was born in Pierce, West Virginia, in 1920, but from the age of three, was raised in Muse, Pennsylvania, along with my six older siblings. Although my parents met in America, they were from Russia and didn't know anything about sports. My father just knew hard work and was against me playing baseball. Fortunately, my brothers encouraged me. I had skills right away, and when I was 15, I began playing with adults on the town's semipro team against teams throughout western Pennsylvania. When I finished school, I went to work in the coal mines and toiled there three years to the day. Then, in the spring of 1940, Pittsburgh had a tryout at McKeesport and I went down there. They signed me to a minor league contract for $75 a month, good money then, and sent me to the PONY League. After about six weeks, they released me.

No player of the postwar era was any tougher than the Phillies' power-hitting catcher Andy Seminick, a product of the Pennsylvania coal mines.

NATIONAL BASEBALL LIBRARY, COOPERSTOWN, N.Y.

If I didn't make it as a ballplayer, I had to go back to the mines. So I continued to pursue a baseball career, going to Florida on my own for a tryout with the Knoxville, Tennessee, club of the Southern League. They signed me and sent me to Elizabethton, Tennessee, in the Appalachian League. I made the All-Star team as a second baseman, but I also caught a little bit. I could run at that time, and had a good arm, and was very strong from having worked in the mines and having done manual labor on a farm when I was young. I got married that year and worked as a heavy equipment operator in a defense plant in the off-season and made pretty good money, about $100 a week. The next year I got a $10-a-month raise. In 1943 at Knoxville, I batted .325 with 18 to 20 homers. I was playing first and the outfield when catcher Bob Finley was sold to Philadelphia. I took over the position and stayed there for the rest of my career.

After the season I got my draft notice to report to the army in a few weeks. That's when I got a call from Bill Veeck, who was the owner–general manager of the Milwaukee Brewers. He had bought me from Knoxville and then sold me to the Phillies. I was reluctant to go to Philadelphia, but he offered me $500 just to report. When I got there, the check was there, so I went downtown and bought me a new pair of spikes. Then I went to Shibe Park, which I thought was huge. Bill Cox was the owner, at least until the end of the year, when he had to sell the team because he'd bet on some games. Herb Pennock was the general manager, and Freddie Fitzsimmons was the manager, and he put me into the lineup. I was very nervous rubbing shoulders with big leaguers and struck out my first 5 times up. My first big league hit was a homer off Harry Feldman, a right-hander for the Giants. I then hurt my wrist stumbling after a pop-up. When we went on the road, it was hurting really bad, but I didn't want to say anything. After the season I learned I had broken a bone, and a cast was put on my wrist. I also had hurt my knee in the Southern League and it would pop out on me. So when I had my physical at Fort Oglethorpe in Georgia, they 4-F'd me. That's why I continued to play in the majors during the war.

When the war ended there were a lot of players at the camps and there was a lot more competition for jobs. We had our first spring training in the South in 1946, in Flamingo Park in Miami Beach. We stayed at the Broadway Hotel. Freddie Fitzsimmons had been fired in the latter part of 1945 and Ben Chapman came in. I became a regular for the first time, and my play improved. One guy who helped me was Schoolboy Rowe, the smartest pitcher I ever caught. He started back in 1933 and I learned from him.

The Phillies tied with the Pirates for seventh place in 1947, winning just 62 games. So it's hard to remember many bright spots. Rowe and Dutch Leonard, the knuckleballer, won half our games, and Harry Walker won the batting title. I had another fair season, batting over .250 with a team-high 13 homers and 50 RBIs in about 110 games. Still, I didn't feel I was playing top-notch major league baseball yet. I was a little shaky in the field, calling the game, catching the ball, mostly throwing the ball. I had a strong arm but was erratic. Chapman's coaches Benny Bengough and Cy Perkins, who were both former major league catchers, worked with me on all phases of the game. And Ben, a meticulous manager, rode me about things I wasn't doing right, maybe too much, but I responded to it. I respected everybody with authority. But one time I did stand up to Ben because he was criticizing me in front of everyone in the clubhouse. Outfielder Johnny Wyrostek was sitting next to me and he grabbed me and pulled me down. Fortunately, the coaches gave me encouragement and got on Chapman for getting on me. I still thanked Ben for giving me a chance to be a regular catcher. I worried about losing my job and being sent to the minors, but as the season went on, I gained confidence that I was going to catch the ball and throw guys out.

A few guys had trouble with Chapman. Willie Jones had an incident with him in spring training in Clearwater. "Puddin' Head"—he got his nickname when he was a little boy for eating pudding—had come up from Terre Haute, Indiana. He had an old pair of shoes and glove. Chapman bought him a glove and a pair of Spalding shoes for $22, big money then. After the workout, Jones was sitting in front of his locker. Chapman came by and asked how he liked his shoes and glove. I don't know what their problem was, but Puddin' Head looked at him and said, "Jam 'em up your ass and nothing good will hurt you." Imagine a rookie saying that to a manager! Chapman sent him back to Terre Haute immediately.

We didn't really have a conduct code, but you were expected to conduct yourself in a gentlemanly manner.

Of course, we weren't required to go to church, though a lot of guys went on their own. We had a dress code. We had to wear a jacket and tie and couldn't wear jeans.

Playing in Philadelphia was hard, especially for a young kid breaking in. If you didn't succeed right away, they got on you. Del Ennis was from Philadelphia, so they never gave him the chance to win them over. But as an outsider, I was able to turn them around. I had a lot of desire and their booing helped me push to succeed. Because I hustled all the time, they eventually started cheering for me, even when I wasn't going good. They liked competitors.

The Phillies had a rivalry with the Athletics. Philadelphia was known as an American League town. The Athletics had been successful over the years, but the Phillies had never been. Also, Shibe Park was owned by Connie Mack, so we were just tenants of the Athletics. Mr. Mack had moved the Athletics there in 1938 from Baker Bowl. He was a great, dapper guy, with high stiff collars, and a hat, and everything fit just so. He knew the Phillie players. If he saw me, he'd call to me and ask how I was.

The most significant event of the year was Jackie Robinson integrating baseball. Some of the clubs wanted to strike before he came in—St. Louis and Pittsburgh, I think. The Phillies had a meeting at which Skeeter Newsome got up and said, "Men, you can't strike. You can't do this." And we voted against striking. A few voted for a strike. Chapman was from the South and didn't want to play against Robinson. But he never told the pitchers or catchers to throw at him. We were on our own. When the Dodgers first came to Philadelphia, fans were hanging from the rafters to see him. He had a following all over the circuit. Sometimes we'd pass the Dodgers on the road and he had an entourage that would follow him all over. Players would get on him more than any other player in baseball. I don't think white players worried about losing jobs to black players if Robinson succeeded. Some were just concerned about the ending of segregation. Some players were real staunch rednecks. And some fans were hostile.

There was a fear of someone being hurt, shot. It was pretty rough in some of those towns. In Philadelphia, the park wasn't far from the black community and blacks filled the stands to see him. We thought of white players being shot by black fans and Robinson being shot by white fans. In Shibe Park we had to go through the crowd to get into our clubhouse and get to the field. For the visitors' clubhouse, they had to go under the stands and through a hallway. We had tight security.

DEL ENNIS:

We had clubhouse meetings about Robinson and decided not to call him names or rouse him in any way because he could then do much to hurt us. He was quite an athlete. He played first that year so players couldn't try to take him out sliding into second. In the Phillies clubhouse, we'd still say, "Try to get him!"

I had won over Ben Chapman in my rookie season. He also impressed me with his knowledge of baseball and how well he worked with young players. One day in Florida he bet $100 that I could beat the fastest player on the team, pitcher Dick Mauney. I was ahead by 10 yards but stumbled in the sand and lost. I thought Chapman would be mad at me for costing him the money, but he told me not to worry. But Chapman could be tough. I once scored the winning run from second base by barreling into the catcher and Chapman fined me $25 for not sliding. He taught me the game.

Jimmy Wasdell had been traded during the 1946 season, and then I started rooming with Schoolboy Rowe. He was 15 years older, a good guy, and a pretty good drinker. He was one of the team leaders. He'd sit on the corner of the bench and let us know what pitches were coming. He'd whistle on curveballs and on everything else, so he was a big help to me. He was one of several players who lived near me in Crescentville and we drove together to Florida to meet the club. He advised me to turn down the Phillies' offer of a two-year contract. He said I'd make more in two years even if I had a bad year in 1947. So I asked for $13,000 for one year. It turned out that in 1947 I hurt my back sliding and couldn't bend over for half a year. My RBIs went up slightly and were the most on the team by a large margin, but my average dropped to .275, with just 25 doubles and 12 home runs. His advice paid off.

Another roommate was Emil Verban. He played 155 games for us at second base and hit .285. He was a good guy, but he was chintzy. He always went shopping for suits and clothes for his wife, especially in New York. But he'd buy only wholesale.

PITTSBURGH PIRATES

RALPH KINER:

Nineteen forty-six hadn't been a great year for baseball. It was a catch-up year. A lot of the players from the war years who hadn't been in the service weren't that good. They were weeded out, along with veterans who no longer could play at a major league level. Then in 1947 baseball's greatest era began.

We still had a lot of wild-living guys on the Pirates. And during the season we acquired another one, veteran Kirby Higbe from Brooklyn. He was a great pitcher. Of all the knuckleballers, he threw the hardest fastball, which made him extra-tough. He also had a good curve. He wasn't as effective as he'd been with the Dodgers, and walked too many batters. But he was our workhorse and won 10 or 11 games. In the clubhouse, he was another disruptive force. He was one of the all-time characters who ever played. He certainly tried to live life to its fullest.

What saved me was Hank Greenberg coming over from the Tigers. Hank had led the American League in homers and RBIs for the Tigers in 1946, but he had salary problems and Detroit waived him out of the league. The Pirates purchased his contract in January for $75,000. The Pirates had to convince him to play one more year by making him the National League's first $100,000 player. Also, the Pirates placed a bullpen in front of the left-field fence at Forbes Field that significantly shortened the distance for a homer. The fenced-in bullpen area was dubbed Greenberg Gardens because Hank was supposed to benefit from it. But in his one year with the Pirates he hit only 25 homers. He hated his final year. All year he was bothered by an arm that had been operated on to remove bone chips. He also didn't like playing on such a bad team or being managed by Billy Herman, who he thought was too lenient.

I lived in Glimster Hall, a hotel near the ballpark, but on the road I roomed with Hank some of the time. That was quite a thrill because as a kid in the 1930s I was a big Detroit fan and he was one of my idols. Nobody helped me in any respect until Hank. He taught me to set goals and achieve them through hard work. I went from doing the regular routine work of an average ballplayer, which was just taking batting practice and playing, to spending hours and hours before and after games working on my hitting and everything else, even spending time sliding into sliding pits, learning to flip my legs to get into the air and land on my rear. I hated that. Hank improved my hitting by telling me to move on top of the plate. He gave me a lot of inside information about pitchers so I'd know what to look for. I'd say he gave me an accelerated course on how to play baseball.

I started off terribly with only 3 homers by the end of May. In one game I was struck out 4 times by the Cubs' Hank Borowy. I hadn't lost my confidence, but the Pirates would have sent me to the minors if Hank Greenberg didn't go directly to our owner, Frank McKinney, to plead my case. So I stayed on the Pirates and I had a great year. I hit .313, which would be a career high, scored 118 runs, and drove in 127 runs—the first of 5 consecutive years I would be over 100 in both categories—and led the league for the first time in slugging percentage. I jumped from 23 homers to 51 and won my second consecutive homer title, again tying Johnny Mize. After June 1, I hit 48 homers, which had to be some kind of record. In July I set the Pirates' single-season record with my 24th homer of the season. In August I equaled major league marks by hitting homers in 4 consecutive at-bats—3 coming in one game against the Cardinals—and 5 homers in 2 games, 6 homers in 3 games, and 7 homers in 4 games. Then in September I hit 8 homers in 4 games to set a new record. That may have been my greatest home run feat and was written up a lot. However, my biggest thrill came 5 or 6 games later when, in just my second year, I became only the second National Leaguer to hit 50 homers in a season. That homer put me in a special echelon.

Mize would hit his 50th two days later. There was a lot of press coverage of the home run race and Mize and I had pictures taken together. We became friends years later, but at the time I thought he was very gruff and not easy to get along with. We went back and forth until we each hit 51 and then both of us were shut out the last few days of the season. Mize even hit first in the lineup to get more at-bats and beat me. Herman offered to bat me first, but I didn't want to jinx myself.

During the year, Greenberg Gardens also started to be called Kiner's Korner. I became a big celebrity in Pittsburgh and attendance improved dramatically. It was a small town and everyone knew me, so I couldn't go anywhere. The only place people left me alone was New York. It was a big city and they knew how to treat so-called celebrities. I wasn't unprepared for my increased celebrity status. Bing Crosby had become a minority owner of the Pirates in 1946, and through him I met Bob Hope and a lot of Hollywood stars.

Baseball most changed in 1947 because of the integration of black players. At the time, major leaguers didn't think that the black—then called colored—players would have a strong impact in baseball. No one realized how good they were. I played against a lot of black players when I was in high school in southern California. They didn't impress me, but I didn't know anything.

I knew Jackie Robinson slightly from California because I had played softball against him. I knew of him when he went to UCLA, where he was an unbelievable football player, great basketball player, and fantastic track star. Baseball was his worst sport! Robinson wasn't by any means the best black baseball player, but he was the best athlete and best competitor to ever play baseball. He was the best baserunner who ever played. He had some problems with our ballclub because there were guys who harassed him. He took it that first year because of his agreement with Branch Rickey to turn the other cheek. But he wouldn't take it after he established himself. He was willing to fight.

Greenberg showed a lot of compassion for Robinson. He spoke to Jackie and told him to hang in there and not let the agitation get to him. He told Jackie that he got the same abusive treatment when he broke in as a Jewish ballplayer in the early thirties. I don't know if that helped Jackie at all, but Hank was definitely on his side. Even then Hank was still experiencing some degree of prejudice from other teams because he was Jewish.

We finished in a last-place tie with the Phillies, but there were a few guys in the lineup that supported Greenberg and me. Rookie Wally Westlake—I played left and he played right—hit 17 homers. And Billy Cox added 15. Cox had been a Pirates rookie in 1941. Then came the war, which he came out of with malaria. As a result he was very frail and weak-looking. He was being touted as one of the great shortstops of all time. But he and left-handed pitcher Preacher Roe were traded to the Dodgers after the season and he became the league's best-fielding third baseman and a great all-around player. Roe, who had a terrible record for us, would become one of the best pitchers in the league.

GENE WOODLING:

When I was in the navy I played a lot of baseball with Billy Herman. In 1947 he became manager of the Pirates and wanted me on his team. This was a bad ballclub although we had Greenberg and Kiner. Herman didn't last out the season and neither did I. I was only in 20 games or so.

I did play against Jackie Robinson. He was a fine player who could steal his way around the bases. There was some resentment at first and he did get mistreated somewhat, but it wasn't to the extremes that have been suggested. I didn't see any bad incidents. There was more talk than action. The Pirates didn't have any problems playing against a black player. In fact, I had played against him already in the International League.

FRANK THOMAS:

I was born in Pittsburgh in 1929. I had a brother and two sisters. My dad came from the Old Country and my mother was from Johnstown, Pennsylvania. Their marriage was prearranged, and she was 15 years younger and had a hard life with him. My dad was very strict and very mean. He lost his arm the year I was born, and his left arm became doubly strong and when he'd swing and hit you, you'd feel it. I can't remember much of my childhood because I blocked it out. But I do remember my Uncle Mike playing baseball with me and walking three miles to Schenley Park every Saturday to play ball all day long. My mother said I never went to bed without a bat or ball in my hand. I first used my dad's pick hammer for a bat. I got my first baseball from Josh Gibson. He gave me two. I was a Knothole kid and sat in the right-field bleachers at Forbes Field watching the Pirates or Homestead Grays.

Right after grammar school, when I was 12, I was sent to a seminary in Niagara Falls, Ontario, Canada, to study for the priesthood. We played intramural ball against some of the local high schools. They wouldn't let me pitch because I would strike out everyone and they wouldn't let me bat right-handed because I hit the ball too far. When I turned 17, I decided to go home and become a major league baseball player. My father didn't like my decision to quit the seminary. He didn't think baseball was a good job. (Years later, when I hit a grand-slam homer against the Giants, my dad came up to me in the runway and gave me a big kiss as if to say everything was okay.)

I left the seminary on January 27, 1947, and came back to Pittsburgh. That summer I played for a neighborhood sandlot team sponsored by a butcher shop. The butcher asked me if I wanted to play for a better team and got me on the Little Pirates, a club sponsored by the major league team. I played the outfield and went 4 for 4 the first night and kept hitting. Several scouts took an interest. Roy Hamey, the Pirates' general manager, made a small offer for me to turn pro. In his broken English, my dad said, "My boy worth more than that." I tried out with Cleveland and they offered me $3,100, and my dad wanted me to sign. But my dream was to play in my hometown, with my favorite team, and in Forbes Field. I went back to Hamey and said, "My mom and dad have a mortgage on their house of $3,200. If you can pay off the mortgage, I'll sign with you." That's what happened. I felt I owed my parents that much for sending me to the seminary. So I signed a contract with the Pirates on July 23, 1947, only six months after leaving the seminary and having played 41 games total of sandlot ball. It was like a miracle.

CINCINNATI REDS

EWELL BLACKWELL:

I was born in Fresno, California, in 1922, and was given my grandfather's middle name. I had an older and younger sister. When I was three, we moved to San Dimas, between Los Angeles and Riverside. We were a poor family who experienced the Depression at all times. My father was a contractor who originally came from Texas and had played a little semipro ball. I used to listen to ball games on the radio, mostly of the Los Angeles Angels and Hollywood Stars in the Pacific Coast League, but I wanted to be a major leaguer. I started out like many kids, playing in vacant lots. I always had a strong arm, but I began as a shortstop, not a pitcher. I wasn't yet 6'6". I was just 5'3" as a sophomore in high school before shooting up my junior year. I then started pitching—I already had a sidearm delivery—and

had a lot of success. But I still thought I was a better hitter. I *never* knew I had special talent.

After graduating from high school, I went to Laverne College, where I played baseball and basketball. On Sundays I pitched semipro ball. No money, but fun. I did well and was written up in the papers. I was a shy kid, but on the field I was a different person. I didn't pay attention to anybody watching the game, including scouts. Nine of them made offers, but my dad and I signed with Pat Patterson of the Reds in December 1941 because they agreed to take me to spring training in 1942. Dad figured that if I was sent to the minors nobody would hear of me again. I would have signed with Brooklyn, but they wouldn't take me to spring training.

I rode down with one of the head scouts, Bobby Wallace, to the Reds' spring training camp in Sanford, Florida. It was exciting going so far away from home for the first time. I was just 19 but had a lot of confidence and didn't feel out of place surrounded by veteran pitchers like Paul Derringer, Johnny Vander Meer, and Bucky Walters. When the season started, I pitched twice, giving up 3 hits, 3 walks, and 2 runs in 3 innings. I stayed with the team until the final cutdown day in May. I needed seasoning, so I was sent to Syracuse in the International League, which was still a high level for someone so young. I wasn't upset because originally I was supposed to be sent to Ogden, Utah, in Class D. And Bill McKechnie, the manager, said I'd be back. I had a good year and Cincinnati put me back on its roster in September. But I got pneumonia, so I didn't pitch for the Reds again until 1946, when I got out of the army.

In 1947 I went to spring training with the Reds in Tampa. Johnny Neun, a real nice guy, had replaced McKechnie as manager. I don't think I could have pitched any better than I did in 1947. I went 22–6. I led the league in strikeouts, complete games, and wins, pitched 6 shutouts, and had a 2.47 ERA. I won 16 games in a row, starting and finishing every one. I felt unbeatable. I went early to the park.

On June 18 against the Braves in Crosley Field, I was just trying to win. I won 6–0 and pitched a no-hitter in the process. I had particularly good stuff. I was young but was relaxed the whole game, even in the ninth inning. Grady Hatton, our third baseman, never even knew what was happening. On June 22, in my next start, also in Cincinnati, I had another no-hitter going into the

Called "the Whip" because of his unorthodox sidearm delivery, the much-feared Ewell Blackwell led the National League in strikeouts and victories in 1947 and came within 2 outs of pitching back-to-back no-hitters.

ninth against the Dodgers and had a chance to match Johnny Vander Meer's double-no-hit feat of 1938. I was pitching a better game than on June 18. I had better stuff. Stanky came up with one out in the ninth. I'd struck him out twice before. I threw a fastball that went in on him and sank. It hit the handle and broke his bat. The ball came right back at me and I mistakenly thought he hit it hard. I went down too early. When I came back up, the ball went through my legs. I didn't touch it. I'm glad it wasn't called an error because I wouldn't have wanted a no-hitter that way. I wasn't the type to get upset, but I was disappointed. I had almost equaled the impossible. The fans stood up and cheered me. The next batter, Gene Hermanski, hit a pop-up that would have been the final out. But it was only the second out. Jackie

Robinson then blooped one over the first baseman's head for the Dodgers' second and final hit. I won 4–0. Vander Meer was now on the Reds, but he didn't talk to me during the game. Nobody did. I talked to Johnny afterward in the clubhouse. He told me that he had hoped I would duplicate his record. I knew that because he was on the top step in the ninth inning, waiting to come out and congratulate me.

My sidearm style just came natural to me. There was nobody that I was copying. My high school coach had tried to make me come over the top, but I couldn't throw that way. Even when I had played shortstop, I almost always threw sidearm. I'd throw sidearm to right-handers and a little higher to left-handers, never underhanded. "The Whip" was an appropriate nickname. They held a fan contest in Cincinnati that year and they chose that one. I had a fluid motion and quick release. I had a high kick and tried to hide the ball.

Of every 10 pitches I threw, 9 were fastballs. They would sink, low and inside to right-handers and low and away to left-handers. I was clocked at 99.8 mph in either 1946 or 1947. Bob Feller had the identical time. I was always wild. I didn't walk too many batters but I would lead the league 6 times in hit batters. I always was aware of my control problems. I realized my sidearm delivery was intimidating and I took advantage of it any way I could. I was a mean pitcher. I know Ralph Kiner didn't like me. I could tell he was scared, and like most right-handers, he'd bail out because my fastball would break toward the batter. But he'd homer off me every once in a while.

RALPH KINER (PIRATES):

Ewell Blackwell was a scary pitcher because he was mean and would throw at you anytime. Your legs shook when you tried to dig in on him because of his sidearm delivery. Yet I hit more home runs off Blackwell than any right-handed batter. It was a real challenge to bat against him.

E. BLACKWELL:

I also did all right against the game's best left-handers. Neither Stan Musial nor Johnny Mize would homer off me. I never had trouble holding men on base. At Syracuse, I picked off stolen base champ Snuffy Stirnweiss 6 times.

I ran every day but the day I pitched. I pitched every fourth day. The next day I'd throw for about 15 minutes. I'd rest the day before I pitched. I didn't keep a book on batters, but would just sit with the catcher before the game and go over how we should pitch them. In this era, the competition was tough and every man in the lineup could hurt you. We were tough guys who played hurt and put our bodies on the line, not for money but because that's the way the game was supposed to be played. It was a hard-played game—a *sport,* not a business.

We finished in fifth place, despite having some decent pitchers. I was the only pitcher to win in double figures. Johnny Vander Meer still threw hard and Bucky Walters could still throw a good sinker despite having arm problems. Our trouble is that Grady Hatton, Eddie Miller, and Frank Baumholtz were the only guys to provide any offense.

I got real good press coverage in 1947, much more than in 1946. I was being singled out. I pitched in my second straight All-Star Game and started for the only time. I went against the Tigers' Hal Newhouser and we both pitched 3 scoreless innings. The American League eventually won 2–1. That was an exciting game.

FRANK BAUMHOLTZ:

I was 28 years old when I was a rookie in 1947. I had spent four years in college, a year in the minors, more than four years in the navy, and another year in the minors. But that had been the easy part. I was born in 1918 in Midvale, Ohio, which always seemed to have a population of exactly 348 people. That included the seven in my family. We were one of seven white immigrant families living in a row of company houses situated between two black settlements and across from the train depot, about a mile from the main section of town. We had oil lamps instead of electricity. My dad, who came from Germany, worked in a sewer-pipe plant and made $29 a month. Food was scarce, so we ate a lot of potatoes. We didn't notice the Depression because we never had anything.

I made my own hoops and boards for basketball. For baseball, I'd round up all the girls in the neighborhood—that's how I learned to play. One of the nearby black settlements had a team, and I eventually became its only white player. I dreamed of playing both professional baseball and basketball. I also wanted to work my way through college and study medicine. I was first-team All-Ohio in basketball in my senior year, and took my team to the state tournament in Columbus—the farthest I'd been away from home—so a lot of coaches saw me. I went to Ohio University and on the first day met the woman who would become my wife. The basketball coach arranged for me to have a place to stay, found me work to pay for my room and board, and saw to it my books were paid for. I was voted the most valuable player in the NIT tournament, in which we finished second. I also played baseball. As a freshman, I was a pitcher. I almost killed a coach with a wild pitch and for the next three years I was an outfielder. A Reds scout watched our baseball team. Scouts also saw me play semipro ball in Dayton during a summer I worked there. Frank Lane, the head of the Reds' farm system, signed me before graduation. I got a $1,000 bonus. In 1941 I played in Riverside, California, before the California State League folded, and finished the year with Ogden, Utah, in the Pioneer League. Soon after that I was in the navy until 1946.

I should have played in the majors in 1946, and might not have played for the second straight year if Bill McKechnie still managed the Reds in 1947. Fortunately, Johnny Neun was the new manager. He was a nice guy who had been in baseball all his life. He let me play. Not that the older players were unfriendly, but nobody on the Reds took me under their wing. I did stuff on my own, running, shagging fungoes, anything I possibly could. Nobody was going to stop me. I made myself a major league player by working at it. I had the skills before the war, but they weren't developed.

I had a very good rookie year. I was hitting about .300 until the last three weeks of the season and finished at .283. Batting leadoff, I had 643 official at-bats and walked 56 more times. Counting walks and hits, I got on 238 times. The Reds had some good players but didn't have a good team. We finished 8 games under .500. We finished last in runs scored and next to last in homers. Only first baseman Babe Young, shortstop Eddie Miller, third baseman Grady Hatton, and part-time outfielder Eddie Lukon hit more than 10. I had 32 doubles and 9 triples, but I wasn't a homer hitter. It was unusual that almost all our good hitters but Miller were left-handed. Young, Hatton, Lukon, and I were left-handed hitters and outfielder Augie Galan, who was our only .300 batter, was a switch-hitter.

Infielder Bobby Adams was my roommate and we became good friends. He was from California and was about 25. This was his second year in what would be a long major league career. Eddie Miller had been playing since the mid-thirties, including the war years. He made a statement at the end of the year to the effect that I wasn't a big league ballplayer. He told me those words were taken out of context and were just supposed to be off the cuff. We were friends, so I didn't hold it against him. But there was always something on his mind. He didn't talk to anybody unless they said something to him. He wouldn't show up at Crosley Field until just before game time and wouldn't take batting practice.

The star of the team was Ewell Blackwell, one of the best pitchers in baseball. Blackie liked to sidearm right-handers from third base. I played right field the day he pitched his no-hitter against the Braves, and got 4 hits. Then I played on the following Sunday when he almost got his second no-hitter against Brooklyn. Oddly, the excitement didn't really come until the seventh or eighth inning. In those days, no one would mention a no-hitter was being pitched out of fear that you'd jinx the pitcher. Which is crap, since the guy on the mound knows what he's doing.

I think we also had the best relief pitcher in Harry Gumbert, a tall right-hander who had first pitched in the majors with the Giants in the mid-thirties. He was once an effective starting pitcher but was only a reliever for us, coming in almost 50 times in 1947 (and over 60 times in 1948). Harry didn't have much speed but knew how to pitch and did an excellent job. He won 10 games for us in 1947, which was second most on our team to Blackwell (and he would equal that in 1948). He showed me how he doctored the ball to make it sink. I liked Harry because he was very, very pleasant. In the off-season, Harry was an insurance salesman where he lived in Texas. I bought my first policy from him.

Otherwise, our pitchers didn't have much success. Johnny Vander Meer was just an average pitcher by this time. He had been around for a long time. He was a fine, fine guy. He worked hard and threw hard and wasn't allergic to hitting somebody. Bucky Walters, who had been the Reds' ace from 1939 until Blackwell devel-

oped, still pitched pretty often, but he was losing his effectiveness. He was in his late thirties and had the respect of the younger players, but I don't think he was a leader. I don't think there was any leader on the Reds.

In the winter of 1946–47 I had played with the Cleveland Rebels of the Basketball Association of America and made All-Pro. I was the first major league player to play major league basketball at the same time. I talked to my wife about quitting basketball because I had to start playing baseball before the season ended and because by the end of the baseball season I was underweight from continuous activity. As luck would have it, near the end of the 1947 baseball season, Warren Giles offered me a turned-down check if I didn't play any more basketball. I turned the check over and it was for more than the $4,000 I made playing with the Rebels. Then, at the end of the year, he also raised my baseball salary to $10,000, which was a good raise in those days. As it turned out, the Cleveland Rebels were sold and moved to Providence, Rhode Island—I wouldn't have wanted to play there all winter with my family home in Cleveland. So I was happy with my decision to play only baseball.

HANK SAUER:
I was born in Pittsburgh in 1917. I was the fourth of five brothers. My younger brother Ed would play on the Cubs from 1943 to 1945, their World Series season. I played only sandlot ball until I was a semipro at 16 or 17, playing with adult men. I didn't realize I had special talents, but Paul Krichell, the Yankee scout who discovered Lou Gehrig and Tony Lazzeri—and later Vic Raschi and Whitey Ford—asked if I wanted to play professional baseball. I said I'd love to.

I got out of school and played with Butler for a couple of months in 1937 and 1938, when I led the league in hitting. In 1939 I went to Akron, Ohio, in the Mid-Atlantic League and hit over .300. The Yankees made me a pull hitter to take advantage of my power, and I think it hurt me because I originally had power to all fields. Frank Lane was intent on acquiring me for the Reds, and when the Yankees sent me to A ball in 1940, he drafted me and sent me to the Southern League. The next year I was with Cincinnati, getting 10 hits in 33 at-bats. In 1942 I went 5 for 20, with my first 2 major league homers. Then I went down to the International League, where I played until I entered the service.

I got out in September 1945 and rejoined the Reds, a seventh-place club. I had a pretty good finish for them. In 1946 I went to spring training with the big club. After the war, spring training camps were packed and there was tremendous competition. Bill McKechnie, the manager, left to look after his wife, who was ill. One of the coaches took over and never even took a look at me before sending me to Syracuse in Double A. That was discouraging.

In 1947 I had the Reds' first-base job won in spring training but tore up my knee sliding into third. That took a couple of steps off my speed for the rest of my career. I went back to Syracuse and led the league in homers and RBIs and was only a percentage point behind in the batting race. I was voted Minor League Player of the Year.

AMERICAN LEAGUE 1947

"WHEN I TORE LIGAMENTS IN AN EXHIBITION GAME AGAINST THE BOSTON BRAVES, THEY DIDN'T SEND ME TO A DOCTOR. THEY SIMPLY PUT ON ICE PACKS AND HAD ME WALK AROUND ON CRUTCHES FOR A COUPLE OF WEEKS. THEN THEY HAD ME PLAY AGAIN. IT WAS AMAZING."

JOHN BERARDINO

PHILADELPHIA ATHLETICS

EDDIE JOOST:

In February of 1947 I got a call from Connie Mack, the manager and owner of the Athletics. He said, "Son, I just want you to know that you are now a member of the Philadelphia Athletics. We just bought your contract. I have all the faith in the world in you. I don't even want us to discuss some of the bad things I've heard about you. Because I've heard some good things about you, too. I've heard you're a great player, and I want you to be our shortstop and leadoff hitter." So I was suddenly rescued from the blacklist and in the American League.

I met Mr. Mack in spring training and we sat down and talked about the contract I wanted. He was receptive but said, "Son, we aren't a rich ballclub." I said, "I understand that. But don't forget I have to make a living. I'm a 30-year-old married man with two kids." He said he couldn't give me what I wanted, but we agreed to a bonus system. Back then they didn't have performance clauses in contracts, so what we decided was between the two of us.

Connie Mack wore a suit when he managed. That was strange when I first saw it, but I became accustomed to it. He spent most of his time sitting on the bench but occasionally walked back and forth. He never came to the mound. Al Simmons told me that he was given credit for shrewdly moving the outfielders around by motioning with his scorecard from the bench when actually all he was doing was fanning himself.

In my first game with the Athletics, I learned of Mr. Mack's standing in the American League. Elmer Valo threw the ball from the outfield to try to cut down a runner at second. I caught it and thought I'd blocked the runner's foot off the base. Charlie Berry, the umpire, called him safe and I complained. He said, "You're new in this league. Don't ever show me up again or you'll never get a close call as long as I'm on this field." I said, "Do you mean that?" He said, "You heard me." I said, "You watch me, Mr. Berry. I'll go in the dugout and sit right next to Mr. Mack and tell him what you told me." He said, "You won't do that, will you?" I said, "You watch me." So I did it. After the game, Berry and the other umpires came through our dugout on the way to get showered and dressed. Mr.

Mack called him over and sat him down. He had me repeat what Berry had said on the field. Charlie's eyes got really big. Mr. Mack leaned forward and said, "Mr. Berry, I want to tell you something. If you do this to this boy—I'll have you know this right now—you'll no longer be an umpire in the American League because I'll see to it that you're disbarred." Berry stammered, "Mr. Mack, I don't recall exactly what I said, but if he thinks I said that, then I apologize. You know I wouldn't do that to you, Mr. Mack." So Mr. Mack said both he and I accepted Berry's apology. The next day, Berry comes up behind me at short and says, "I found out something about you—you've got a lot of guts." I said, "Charlie, this is my living out here and I'm going to squawk every once in a while." He said, "We won't have any more trouble. It'll just be bang-bang and walk away." Connie Mack had a lot of power in the league.

A mediocre player from 1936 to 1945 in the National League, 30-year-old shortstop Eddie Joost revived his career with the Philadelphia Athletics in 1947, anchoring the best-fielding infield in the league and becoming a standout leadoff batter.

COURTESY OF EDDIE JOOST

In 1947, when baseball was integrated by Jackie Robinson in the National League and Larry Doby in the American League, the white players didn't have all that much animosity toward them. But I'm sure there were a lot of players who said, "Why? They've got the Negro Leagues, let them play there." I don't think there was much fear of black players taking the white players' jobs because most of the white players didn't think there were a lot of good players in the Negro Leagues. I had seen Josh Gibson and a lot of the Negro League players. Man, some of them were great.

My best friends on the Athletics were Sam Chapman, Barney McCosky, Elmer Valo, and Pete Suder. On the road we'd go to shows, eat together, play cards, talk baseball. There were other groups of three to five players and perhaps their wives. Between two night games, there was a lot of time involved. We needed something to do before about four-thirty in the afternoon, so we'd go to a lot of shows and then have a light meal and go out to the ballpark.

Sam Chapman played for the Athletics from 1936 to 1951. Not many people gave him the credit he deserved. He was one of the best center fielders in the American League, including Joe DiMaggio. He'd usually hit over 20 homers and occasionally drive in more than 100 runs.

Barney McCosky was one of the best hitters you ever saw. When he was on Detroit he patterned himself after their great second baseman Charlie Gehringer, using the same stance and standing the same place in the box. He had a perfect swing, hit the ball solidly, and seldom struck out. He battled .300 every year, .312 lifetime. But if there was a man on base, look out—he couldn't drive in anybody in the Little League. He was terrible! That's why Detroit traded him to the Athletics in 1946 for George Kell (and why the Athletics would send him to Cincinnati in 1951). I used to go up to him and say, "Barney, how can you swing at such bad pitches with a man on second when the other times you hit line drives all over the field?" I liked Barney, but it was important to confront him.

Elmer Valo put out 100 percent every day, running, catching, throwing. He'd run into fences or go over fences and into the stands. He'd always disappear over the low railing in right field in Yankee Stadium. He was a good hitter, a complete player. He was a lot of fun off the field, an easygoing, nice, funny person. Everyone liked Elmer.

Pete Suder and I were the best double-play combination I ever saw. He was a good fielder, a good thrower, and did a good job at the plate. He was a complete player. Yet he got no credit, especially before I got there.

The Indians had the best-hitting infield in the league, but we had the best defensive unit with me, Suder, Hank Majeski, and Ferris Fain. Majeski was a great third baseman, as good as I ever saw defensively. He set a major league record for fielding percentage that year. He was a loner but a much respected, hardworking player. He either liked you or disliked you and would let you know it. He'd even walk away from you. If something went wrong on the field, he'd let you know about it.

Ferris Fain was his own worst enemy. He had a lifestyle of his own and would do exactly what he wanted to do. There were many things the players didn't like about him. No one drank as much. He wouldn't drink every day, but occasionally he'd overdrink and wouldn't be as attentive on the field. Majeski and a couple of the other players would challenge him now and then. But I don't think it was a real problem. Connie Mack would rely on his coaches for bed checks and discipline and they'd know what was going on off the field. For a time, Fain was successful on the field. He was a good first baseman, not a great hitter but a good hitter who could move it around the field. He told me that the reason his average was so high was that I was always on base and we'd employ the hit-and-run on every play. The infield would be moving and he'd pop the ball through the open spaces.

The 1947 season went by and I wasn't having the type of year I wanted. The reason was that I needed glasses. I had astigmatism, but I didn't want Mr. Mack to know it because only Bob Dillinger, the Browns' third baseman, wore glasses. But it got worse. When we played night games, I'd see two balls coming at me. I struck out 110 times. I finally got up the nerve to tell Mr. Mack that I'd probably have to wear glasses. He said, "So?" So I got my glasses. The first time I came up to the plate at Shibe Park, the pitcher looked 10 feet away. I couldn't believe my eyes had been that bad. It was too late to help my average—I batted just .206—

but I did other things better. I drove in 64 runs and walked 114 times. I also stabilized the infield, leading the league in putouts. I think I provided some of the leadership the Athletics were lacking on the field and off, and I was selected player rep. I had been a mediocre player in the National League, even a bad fielder. Now I was much improved. Mr. Mack just let me play, and it relaxed me.

ST. LOUIS BROWNS

JOHN BERARDINO:

I probably should have quit baseball in 1947, which was 10 years after I signed with Browns scout Jacques Fournier. Then I could have become a full-time actor five years before I did, resuming the career I began as a nine-year-old in Los Angeles. But then I wouldn't have had the distinction of playing for two of the worst teams of the postwar era, the St. Louis Browns and Pittsburgh Pirates. Twice!

When I was in my twenties, it was just exciting being in the big leagues, no matter what the Browns did. But I had turned 30, and the constant losing became demoralizing. I waited for the season to end. We did the best we could and went out and played the game, not knowing quite how or when we would lose. We scored a lot of runs but the other team scored more. The worst problem was that we never had good pitching, before or after the war. The Browns' scouts didn't have the ability to find pitchers, and the minor league system couldn't develop any.

What made it even harder for me was my bad back and other ailments. The Browns had a team doctor but he didn't travel with us, so I had to wait to get back to St. Louis to get therapy. There wasn't much therapy in those days. When I tore ligaments in an exhibition game against the Boston Braves, they didn't send me to a doctor. They simply put on ice packs and had me walk around on crutches for a couple of weeks. Then they had me play again. It was amazing.

There was competition with the Cardinals, with whom we shared Sportsman's Park. They had won the world title in 1946 and finished second in the National League in 1947, while we finished seventh in 1946 and last in 1947. They had Musial, Schoendienst, Moore,

Slaughter, and Marion, and we didn't have any stars. And our minor league system didn't compare to theirs. Of course, they always drew fans and we drew very poorly, attracting people who didn't mind seeing a losing team. We looked forward to playing the Cardinals in an exhibition series prior to the season in front of fans from both teams. We played our best and did well against them.

Our three best players were shortstop Vern Stephens, and my best friends on the team, left fielder Jeff Heath—who hit 27 homers that year—and Jack Kramer, our only pitcher with over 10 wins. The Browns had a habit of trading away or selling their best players to help pay their operating costs, and in November they sent Kramer and Stephens to the Red Sox for about 6 mediocre players and about $300,000. A few days later they sold Heath to the Red Sox. Kramer won 18 games and Heath hit 20 homers for the Sox in 1948 and Stephens's career took off. In St. Louis it was 360 feet down the line, but in Fenway Park, with the Green Monster, Vern could hit 30 homers and drive in way over 100 runs every year, which were terrific stats for a shortstop.

The Browns also kept switching managers, which kept us from having direction or solid leadership. Our team philosophy was to score runs and that was about it. One of our managers expressed his personal philosophy in spring training. He said, ''I don't want any boys on my team who squat to pee.'' Meaning: you hurt, you play. You know what that sounds like in the clubhouse. So there wasn't much respect.

Donald Barnes, the owner, and Bill DeWitt, the general manager, had no idea how to improve the team, so they just kept shuttling personnel back and forth. In the fall of 1947 they traded me to the Washington Senators for Gerry Priddy. I was going from an eighth-place team to a seventh-place team, which wasn't much of a thrill, so I announced I was retiring to become an actor. At that point, Happy Chandler, the commissioner, canceled the trade. So I was back with the Browns.

LES MOSS:

I knew I had a good shot to make the Browns in 1947. I had hit over .370 with them at the end of the '46 season and the team's top two catchers from the previous year

were gone. Muddy Ruel, who had replaced Zack Taylor as manager, also had been a catcher and thought I was a good prospect. I was young, big at 5'11" and 200 pounds, hit for average and power, and had a good arm. In fact, Muddy probably liked me too much. Once the season progressed I struggled terribly, but he wouldn't send me down to Toledo for more seasoning. A couple of times I tried to get him and DeWitt to demote me so I could play and straighten myself out. They wouldn't do it. Instead I sat on the bench for much of the season and I couldn't get out of my slump. I ended up hitting .157!

I shared playing time with Jake Early, my roommate. He was in his mid-thirties and in the twilight of his career, so the Browns put us together so he could help me. We didn't compete. I palled around with Jake most of the time, but there were other friendly guys on the Browns. John Berardino was a first-class guy. He had been around but he was too quiet to be a team leader.

After struggling at the plate in 1947, part-time catcher Les Moss would have several fine seasons with some awful St. Louis Browns teams of the late '40s and early '50s.

NATIONAL BASEBALL LIBRARY, COOPERSTOWN, N.Y.

Vern Stephens also might have been a leader, but he was too happy-go-lucky.

Despite my bad rookie season, it was a fun time for me and other players in the league. The baseball games were competitive and then we'd get on the train and play cards. We played poker, hearts, pinochle—double-deck pinochle was the game I played most. I also was a big reader. I read Westerns, war books, and history. I wasn't teased because there were other guys who read, too.

We had a good offensive ballclub. Stephens was the best player on the Browns during my years there. He had good power, hit for average, and was a decent short-stop. Bob Dillinger, our third baseman, didn't hit home runs, but he always batted .290 or .300 and led the league in stolen bases. Jeff Heath was a good player with a lot of power, and he ran pretty good for a big man. Back in 1941 with Cleveland, Heath had 20 hom-ers, 20 triples, and 20 doubles in one season. Walt Jud-nich, a first baseman–outfielder, was a pretty good ball-player who had some power, and Al Zarilla, another left-handed batter, could hit for a high average. So we could score some runs. But except for Jack Kramer, our pitching was short, no doubt about it.

We didn't think much about how blacks were play-ing in the majors for the first time. If anyone on our team didn't like it, they didn't show it. We got our own black player, Hank Thompson, a left-handed-hitting second baseman, about two weeks after the Indians brought up Larry Doby. We then brought up Willard Brown, an outfielder from Louisiana who was already in his early thirties. He hit one homer for us, against De-troit, and it was the first homer by a black in the Ameri-can League. This was his only season in the majors. I didn't get to know Thompson that well either because he also wasn't there that long. Like many Browns' play-ers, he had his best years after he went to a different team.

CLEVELAND INDIANS

GUS ZERNIAL:
I had been in the Philippines when we dropped the Big One. When I got out of the navy, I weighed 230 pounds, about 55 pounds more than in 1941, when I was 18 and living in Texas and Branch Rickey signed me for the Cardinals. I had better tools and in 1946 hit 42 homers, drove in about 130 runs, and batted .336 for Burlington, North Carolina. I was drafted by Cleveland although it was atypical for a major league team to draft someone from as low as C ball.

In 1947 I reported to Tucson for spring training with the Indians. I looked around at Cleveland's team and saw Lou Boudreau at shortstop, Joe Gordon—who had just come over from the Yankees—at second, Kenny Keltner at third, Jim Hegan catching, and Bob Feller on the mound. I followed baseball and these guys were my idols. I didn't want to be who they were but *where* they were, in the big leagues. I had no thoughts that I would fail to get there.

Bob Feller probably had his best year in 1946, when he won 26 games, threw his second no-hitter, and struck out a record 348 batters. He had a lot of years left at the top. He and Bob Lemon would throw batting practice and none of us could hit them. Feller was particularly difficult because he was so unorthodox. He had a high leg kick and threw everything up there before the ball. Then the ball moved all over.

BILLY JOHNSON (YANKEES):
The toughest pitcher in the American League was Bob Feller. What made him hard to hit was that he was so deceptive when he cranked up before releasing the ball. You'd expect his 100 mph fastball but he'd give you an outstanding curveball. I thought he was much tougher than Lemon.

EDDIE JOOST (ATHLETICS):
I faced Feller for the first time this season, my first time in the American League. The score was tied going into the ninth. I climbed up the steps of the dugout to lead off the inning. I heard Mr. Mack call me. He said, "How many times has he struck you out today?" "Three." He said, "I tell you what: I'm going to put in a pinch hitter for you because I don't want you to tie the record."

G. ZERNIAL:
Without being disrespectful to Lou Boudreau, the player-manager, I'd say he wasn't really the leader of

the players. It was hard to be the one leader on a team that had a Joe Gordon, Kenny Keltner, and Eddie Robinson in the same infield. Boudreau called the shots, but these players were leaders themselves. That spring, Boudreau was in a quandary because he had about 15 outfielders. He played me a lot and I really hit the baseball, but I was very green. Nobody taught anything at C ball, and I didn't know the fundamentals from an outfielder's standpoint. I didn't even know about hitting the cutoff man. I would learn all the fundamentals, but Boudreau correctly thought I wasn't ready. The Indians already had several outstanding outfielders, and in July, Bill Veeck, the owner, would bring up Larry Doby, the American League's first black. Boudreau tried to sneak me to the minors, to Baltimore, without putting me on the waiver list. The rule stated that if a team drafted a player from another organization and then he didn't make its roster, the other teams had to be given the chance to claim him before he could be sent to the minors. The Indians tried to get around this. I was at Baltimore for only one game when Joe Brown, who was aware of my status, claimed me for the Chicago White Sox. The Indians would win the pennant only a year later and it was a disappointment that I hadn't made the ballclub.

BOSTON RED SOX

AL KOZAR:

We had such a good year in Scranton in 1946 that about eight of us were invited to spring training with the Red Sox in Sarasota. I had never been to Florida and had never been to a major league spring training camp. It meant so much to me because I had struggled for so long to get there. I still remembered back to that day in 1939 when I left home. My mother, who didn't speak English, and I hugged in the kitchen. My dad, who was a tough guy who worked in the mills all his life, was on the porch and he said, "Alberto, don't you come back." My dad had been warned by men in the bars that good ballplayers had left that area of Pennsylvania and had returned in a month or so. He didn't want me to fail. That's one reason I never gave up. Also, I remembered

being a youngster and seeing people every day who were waiting for the bus to the steel mill. I didn't want to do that.

The Red Sox had a big charter plane and we stayed in the best hotels in Sarasota and on the road. I thought the Red Sox were a first-class organization. I was happy to be given a contract for $5,000, the major league minimum. When we went to West Palm Beach for a spring training game against the Philadelphia Athletics, I asked Eddie Joost for the whereabouts of Fritz Bernardi, who was a friend of mine from the service. Eddie told me he was holding out because he wanted $5,000 and Connie Mack was offering half that. I said that I was under the impression that if you got a big league contract, you were guaranteed $5,000. He told me I was reading the contract wrong. Apparently they could offer you a contract for any amount, even $1,000 for you to sign. You only got the $5,000 major league minimum if you made the club and were with them at the beginning of the season. That was the rule. They told me I was getting $5,000 only because I was with the Red Sox, a generous team. Bernardi got into trouble for speaking up.

I thought I was a good prospect. I got good wood on the ball most of the time. I hit it through the box and to the right of the mound. I could hit an occasional long ball. I didn't choke up as much as Frank Crosetti, but I choked up about 1½ to 2 inches and used a bat with no knob. My real value was that I was a very good defensive second baseman. But I knew Bobby Doerr was there at second and it was going to be tough for me to move him out. I figured that if I played hard and didn't make the team, at least I would move up from Scranton to Louisville and have a great shot in 1948.

I had a locker next to Ted Williams and we talked all the time. Of course, I didn't talk to him unless he approached me. I'd even eat with him. He ate one shrimp cocktail after another. We weren't great buddies but he was nice to a lot of rookies. He was genuinely friendly while Doerr and the other big leaguers wouldn't really talk to me. Ted always had a bat in his hand. He'd pick up his bat and ask, "Don't you think this is too heavy?" And I'd say really quietly, "Ted, don't ask me that. . . ." And he'd say really loudly, "What did you say?" and all the regulars would look up while he tried to get me to hold it. He would weigh his bats and they had to be right to the ounce. I didn't want the other players to snicker at me, so I never answered him. Then he'd ask some other rookie. Ted would help me with my hitting in spring training. He would say, "Okay, Bush, hit the way you're hitting. . . ." He liked the way I stepped into the ball and drove it to right center. I was on deck when he homered in Dallas and I touched his hand and he said, "I'm going to watch you do the same thing." My ball hit the top of the fence and dropped back in.

Ted Williams was the greatest hitter I ever saw. In 1946 he had hit over .340 and been voted the American League's Most Valuable Player. In 1947 he would hit over .340 again and win his second Triple Crown, yet the writers—many of whom feuded with Williams—would give the MVP award to Joe DiMaggio.

There were about five second basemen in Sarasota, including Doerr and me. Joe Cronin, the manager, had Johnny Pesky at short, Doerr at second, and Walt Dropo at first base. He had a lot of guys trying out at third, but he saw my arm and didn't try me there. Then he had me at second. He would bury me with balls from the fungo hitter and outfielders just to see what I could take. Cronin was a tough, sarcastic guy. And if you weren't a pull hitter from the right side, like Doerr, he didn't look at you too much. Doerr had a bad knee and wasn't playing much. I'd take over for him in the early innings. I was doing good. Then all of a sudden I'm not playing. A sportswriter from Cincinnati sat down on the bench and asked Cronin why. Cronin pointed down the bench and said, "You see that guy there? His name is Bobby Doerr. He's hurt but he's going to be all right. When the season starts, he's my second baseman. If I play this kid anymore, I may have to keep playing him. So he's not playing anymore." Those were the days when you didn't say nothing. So I didn't say nothing and I didn't play. Maybe I couldn't have produced like Doerr at Fenway Park, but I could have played second with anybody.

We went to Fort Worth and Dallas and I got hot again, but I was playing only because I was going to be gone. They dropped me off in Dallas. The Red Sox said they were going to send me to Louisville. I didn't mind. I was told that I'd be back and that they wanted me to be

happy. I still got $5,000 even after the Red Sox demoted me. I took a train to Louisville. I played only 3 or 4 games when they sent me down to New Orleans in Double A to make room for another second baseman the Red Sox were demoting. I finally got talkative and asked what was going on. I was unhappy to take another train to New Orleans. The first thing I heard from the owner was "Where the hell have you been? You weren't supposed to go to spring training with the Red Sox. They promised you to us last year." That's how things worked.

Maybe I was feeling sorry for myself or just angry. I started drinking beer—me and Sam Mele. Then Gus Niarhos and I used to put away the Schlitz. No more Orange Crush, which I'd been drinking since playing semipro ball. 1947 in New Orleans was the best year I ever had in baseball. I hit .339 and for a time was around .380. I was polished at this point and knew I had to go right to the majors. I was no secret anymore. The Detroit Tigers were offering a lot of money for me, but Joe Cronin didn't want to sell me. He didn't need the money. He needed another ballplayer. I learned later that he told a sportswriter, "I wouldn't trade him for any second baseman in the league except Bobby Doerr."

I went home, and in the winter some kid called me up and told me to pick up the *Pittsburgh Press*. I read that I had been traded to the Washington Senators. Boston hadn't even told me. Players were cattle. They told you nothing.

In my opinion, they traded me because it was a family affair. Cronin had an informal arrangement with Washington. Cronin used to play for Washington and he married one of Clark Griffith's nieces, one of the Robertsons. He figured that if Doerr's career ended and I proved myself with Washington, he could get me right back without a problem. Back then I wouldn't say anything.

I had mixed feelings about being traded. While I didn't feel loyalty toward the Red Sox, I would have liked to have played with them because they were a winning team. But at least I was going to the big leagues.

DETROIT TIGERS

GEORGE KELL:

After half a season in Detroit, I now considered myself a Tiger. I knew the players and I knew the manager, Steve O'Neill, who was very nice as long as you didn't cross him. I also had gotten to like the city. I rented a nice house about 10 miles from the ballpark from pitcher Steve Gromek, who played in Cleveland. I would pay him $750 total for the period between March 1 and the day the season ended. My wife would leave spring training early and drive to the house to set things up for when I arrived.

This year the Tigers started playing what we called twilight ball. We didn't have lights yet, so we'd start at 5:30 and often played in semidarkness. It wasn't always easy to see, but I hit .320 with 93 RBIs. This followed a 1946 season in which I had batted .322. I was playing much better after the war than during it when the veterans were away. I had proven that I could play major league baseball when it was at its peak, from 1947 on. You know what I thought about? My father. He was a barber who made $25 to $35 a week during the Depression. He was also a Sunday school superintendent, Sunday school teacher and church lay leader at the Swifton Methodist Church in Arkansas. And he was a good amateur and semipro baseball player who raised three sons, convinced that all of us would be major leaguers, if not stars. (Skeeter would play with the Philadelphia Athletics in 1952; Frank was killed in the army of occupation—or he might have been a big leaguer too.)

I thought back to a July 4, when I was 12, and my daddy was pitching for the Swifton semipro team. He had a big lead in the ninth inning and, also being the manager, told me to get my glove and go out to second base for one inning. This was a men's team and there were about 4,000 people watching. On the way home my mother threw a fit. She told my father, "How could you put him out there? He could have been killed!" She asked, "What do you think would have happened if one of those big, strong men had hit the ball at him?" My daddy said, "He would have caught it. That's what would have happened." My father believed I could play ball. I thought about that during my major league career, especially in those first few years.

I was a contact hitter, not a slugger, so I used a small bat of 34 inches and 31 ounces. I stood very close to the plate and up front so I would be alert for the fastball or be able to hit the curve before it broke too much. My glove was average size but I had it made with a larger-than-usual web because I needed that at third base. I always could hit, but fielding I had to work at. I took as much pride in fielding as hitting. I became a complete ballplayer. I knew when to take the extra base, I knew about the outfielder hitting the cutoff man, I knew when and how to bunt, I knew when to hit-and-run. Guys much older than me weren't as grounded in those fundamentals. I got that early training from my father.

The Tigers were lacking in offense. I was the only .300 hitter and the only player with over 80 RBIs. However, my best friend Hoot Evers had a good season, hitting about .295, and playing great defense in center field, and first baseman Roy Cullenbine hit about 25 homers in his final season. We also brought up Vic Wertz, who was an outfielder then. He already could hit for average but hadn't yet developed into a power hitter.

We finished second because of pitching. There were a lot of good starting pitchers in the league: Allie Reynolds and Spec Shea on the Yankees, Joe Dobson and Tex Hughson on the Red Sox, Bob Feller and Bob Lemon on the Indians, Phil Marchildon and Dick Fowler on the Athletics, Eddie Lopat on the White Sox, Early Wynn and Mickey Haefner on the Senators, and Jack Kramer on the Browns. But no team could match a rotation with Hal Newhouser, Virgil Trucks, Fred Hutchinson, and Dizzy Trout. Even our spot starters, Stubby Overmire, Al Benton and rookie Art Houtteman, were excellent.

Hal Newhouser was the greatest pitcher I ever played behind. They said he was good only during the war years, when he won back-to-back MVP awards, but that wasn't the case. He followed up his 29 wins in 1944 and 25 wins in 1945 with a league-leading 26 wins and an ERA under 2.00, in 1946, and 17 wins in 1947, and would keep winning after that. He was still effective and struck out a lot of batters. Newhouser had a terrible temper and nobody liked him. On the day he pitched he wanted everything to be serious and for us not to talk or joke around. Yet on days he wouldn't pitch, he'd be leading the parade.

Virgil Trucks and I were good friends, but he was a

mean pitcher. He threw so hard that he could hurt you. Ted Williams hit Trucks very good. Once he got a big hit off Trucks in Detroit. When Trucks got back to the bench, he said, ''Next time he comes up, I'm drilling him right between the eyes.'' O'Neill said, ''You're not going to hit Williams. Don't throw at him.'' But Trucks kept saying, ''I'm going to hit him.'' And he did, but in the back. Then O'Neill took him out of the game and they got into it.

I knew Fred Hutchinson mostly as a brilliant scholar who came from a family of intellectuals. His father and brother were doctors. I liked to think I was the biggest reader in baseball because I never made trips without a couple of books and read every night. Fred was the first other reader I ever knew in baseball—he also carried books with him. He studied all kinds of fields. He also studied baseball. He had a plan the night before on how he would pitch and usually it worked. He was just a tremendous competitor, who was a good hitter and fielder and could have played anywhere. In 1947 he won a career-high 18 games, but he always won between 13 and 17 games for us. He had been a fastball pitcher but hurt his arm and became one of the first hurlers who changed from being a thrower to a pitcher. He'd finesse batters to death. I remember him beating the Yankees in a day game in Detroit, 1–0, in about 90 minutes. He didn't throw the ball hard all day.

Unlike Newhouser, Fred was liked despite having a terrible temper. Fortunately, his tantrums lasted only a few minutes. Once, in Briggs Stadium, he had the Browns beat 2–0 with 2 outs in the ninth inning. Then they got 4 or 5 straight hits and he was taken out with the score 2–2. Then the Browns got another hit and he was the losing pitcher. When he walked down the runway, under a row of unguarded light bulbs, he just took his glove and whacked about 15 of them. I remember another day when he was taken out of a game that he should have won. He went into the trainer's room and locked the door, not letting anyone in, including the trainer. One day he walked home mad, 7 to 8 miles from the Stadium. But the next day he was fine. I could go to the mound to calm him down. Probably a lot of other players couldn't. I was the captain of the club, roomed with him, ate with him every night on the road. He might even grin at what I had to say. I knew better than to give him any advice or tell him to get the ball over the plate. We understood each other and respected each other.

Evers and Hutchinson were my best friends on Detroit. I roomed at times with Hoot and I roomed with Fred, and Fed and Hoot roomed together. There were several groups of players who would run together on the Tigers. I guess you could call them cliques, although no one felt like an intruder if they joined in. Hutchinson, Evers, and I would always be together. Johnny Lipon, the shortstop, was also part of our group. There was very little drinking among the group that I ran with. I didn't drink. We went to movies instead of bars. I didn't see evidence of other players hanging out at bars on our team. I know it went on, but not to the degree one would suspect.

The color barrier was broken that year. It wasn't a big deal for me to play with black players, even having come from the South. When I was in high school in Arkansas, I asked my father why black players couldn't play in the major leagues. I couldn't understand it. I never could understand why blacks let it go so long without demanding a reason for not being allowed in the major leagues. It was one of the great tragedies of baseball that blacks were excluded from playing major league baseball until 1947. I don't remember any particular incident of Tiger players getting out of line, but we had bench jockeys and I'm sure some of them got on Larry Doby and the other pioneer black players more than they did the average opponents. I'm sure they didn't escape anything. Especially from guys like Jimmy Dykes, who had managed Chicago and then coached with the Athletics in this period. When I first came up, he would sit in the corner of the White Sox dugout and yell vicious insults. I'm sure he later let blacks have it, too. But he probably wasn't doing it as a racial thing. He was nasty to everybody.

BILLY PIERCE:
I was born in Detroit in 1927 and raised in Highland Park, a mixed section of the city. I was an only child and grew up playing ball in the streets, the alleys, the school yards. From 14 to 16, I played in the Detroit Baseball Amateur Federation, on a team we called the Owls. My dad, who owned a drugstore for 30 years, was one of our sponsors. I was a first baseman, but then our pitcher deserted us because another team had snazzier uniforms. I

was wild, but I could throw harder than anyone else, so I became the pitcher. Then I pitched high school ball. We had tremendous coverage in the *Detroit Free Press* and the *Detroit News,* so this attracted scouts. In 1944 I went to New York for the *Esquire* amateur all-star game. I had never thought about being a major leaguer—I was taking Latin and physics in anticipation of becoming a doctor—but after going to the Polo Grounds and Ebbets Field, I got more of a feeling of what it would be like. The Tigers were my favorite team and I signed with their head scout, Wish Egan, when I was still 17. I finished classes on March 15, joined the Tigers, and then came back in June and got my diploma. In 1945 I went to spring training, which was held in Evansville, Indiana, since major league teams weren't allowed to go south beyond a certain line because of the war effort. For the first six weeks of the season, I sat on the Tigers' bench and didn't pitch. Then I was sent to Buffalo. I returned to the Tigers before September 1, so I was on Detroit for three-fifths of the year and we won the World Championship. I pitched only 10 innings all year and didn't pitch in the World Series—but I was eligible to pitch and received a ring at the age of 18! I didn't know it would be my only world title.

I went to spring training in 1946 in Lakeland, Florida. A lot of players returned from the service and there were lots of ballplayers in camp. Most of the old-timers who couldn't cut it anymore were soon gone and a wave of talented new players came up to take their place. A lot of new fellows came along with different backgrounds and new ideas. More college guys came into the league. The older ballplayers told me that the new breed was tamer. I figured I'd be sent down for experience and to make room for all the veterans. I hurt my back in June and didn't play anymore that year. I was in the Ford Hospital for a while. During the winter they would bake me in an oven three days a week. They decided the pain came from my being a boy doing a man's work. So I rested.

I rejoined Buffalo in 1947. Paul Richards was the player-manager. He had been a catcher on the Tigers during the war years, when he lived about five blocks from my dad's drugstore and would come there to get gum. I got to know him a little better when I worked out with the Tigers in 1944. Then in 1945 we were teammates on Detroit. Now I played under him in Buffalo.

He said Detroit wanted me to pitch only on occasion because of my back. He'd catch when I pitched and tried to slow me down by holding on to the ball.

CHICAGO WHITE SOX

GUS ZERNIAL:

Now that I was in the White Sox organization, I was sent to Hollywood in the Pacific Coast League. It was a step up because the league was full of former major league players as well as top prospects. The previous year, in the minors at Baltimore, my contract had been $500 a month—to a kid like myself who had been getting army pay, that was big money. When I reported to Hollywood, the general manager called me in and tore up my contract. He said, "We don't have anyone playing for us making $500 a month. You're making $800 a month." I had never seen that much money in a month in my life. It was fantastic.

I had a good year with Hollywood, hitting about .340. I didn't expect to hit the pitchers in this league for a lot of homers—I had only about 12—so I just concentrated on being a good hitter. I didn't pull the ball as much as I had done. In that period I met Hank Sauer, Peanuts Lowrey, Gene Mauch, Dick Williams, all guys who would remain close friends through the years. I picked up knowledge from these guys.

The PCL was comprised of independent teams, so I assumed I had become property of Hollywood when Chicago sent me there. Only after the 1947 season did I learn I still belonged to the White Sox. That's when I had to negotiate with the Sox general manager, Frank Lane.

BOB BUHL:

As a teenager in Saginaw, Michigan, I was cocky and wild, but I was no troublemaker. I sold cars part-time for my stepfather when I was in high school. But I had no intention of going into the car business. I wanted to be a ballplayer from the time I was in junior high. I used to listen to Tigers games all the time, but I only saw one game, on my 12th birthday. I asked one of the Tigers' players, Boots Poffenberger, to sign a baseball I got in the stands. I walked down to him, and he said, "Kid, can't you see I'm busy?" That really hurt me and I said right then and there: if I ever play in the big leagues I will never be like that man.

I played sandlot ball while in junior high and high school. If there were scouts looking at me, I didn't know it. In 1946, when I was 18, the White Sox had a tryout camp in Saginaw. I pitched one inning and they said that was enough for them to offer me a contract. My father had passed away, so my mother and I agreed to the contract. I wasn't allowed to sign because I was still in school, but I didn't know it at the time. The next season I was still a senior. I got out in midterm and reported to spring training. I graduated with my class in 1947 but I had already signed, and played a full season down in Madisonville, Kentucky. I wasn't being groomed for the majors. We didn't even have a pitching coach, and the instruction I got came from the player-manager, who was an old catcher. We were expected to pitch complete games even then and I pitched every third or fourth day. You didn't know what a sore arm was in those days. I had a pretty good year, going something like 18–10 and winning 2 games in the playoffs.

I got no bonus to sign, and $100 a month. And I had to pay room and board out of that. On the road, we got $2.50 meal money. No one could live on the money I was making. I knew the other players had to be making more than me. I just wanted to play ball, so I didn't feel bad about the money the first year, but I was upset when the White Sox sent me a contract for the next season for only $200 a month in Class C ball. I said, ''Wait a minute. I'm better than that.'' I sent it back unsigned. Then I read in the paper about a pitcher who had been signed by the Cleveland Indians while he was still in high school and he had been declared a free agent because of that. So I wrote Happy Chandler and convinced him to investigate my case because I had signed before I graduated. A couple of months later, I got a telegram back saying, ''You are declared a free agent. Every club can sign you except the Chicago White Sox.''

NEW YORK YANKEES

BILLY JOHNSON:

I was born in 1918 in a Catholic neighborhood in Montclair, New Jersey, and religion was very much part of my youth. My father worked on the trolley cars. The

An unsung hero of the Yankees of the late '40s, third baseman Billy Johnson drove in 95 runs and batted .285 for the 1947 American League champions.

Depression made it extremely tough, so I worked in a grocery store and did a few odd jobs to pick up a few pennies. I played organized baseball—mostly semipro ball—from an early age on. My parents wanted me to stop playing because I wasn't doing anything else that amounted to anything. I didn't think I had the talent to realize my dream to be a major leaguer, but in 1937 I was tapped on the shoulder by Yankee scout Paul Krichell, who said, ''Can I speak to your mom and daddy?'' After I graduated from Immaculate Conception High School I signed a contract, receiving a small bonus of $1,200. But it wasn't until 1943 that I was invited to spring training with the Yankees. That was in Albany Park, New Jersey. The players looked at the bulletin board every morning to find out what they were supposed to do each day, but I could never find my name there, so it wasn't planned for me to do anything. That was frustrating. Then one day I asked Frank Crosetti, the Yanks' shortstop, if he'd mind hitting me some grounders so I could get a little exercise. While he did that there was a little sprinkling of snow. I wasn't aware that the Yankee manager, Joe McCarthy, had come out and was watching me from the stands. After we finished, McCarthy called me over and told me, "Son, starting tomorrow, you're my third baseman." And I played there from then on. I remember putting on the Yankee uniform the first time. The pinstripes fit perfectly. The clubhouse boy got me the right size. I played 155 games, batted .280, and drove in 94 runs. We won the pennant and the World Series.

I spent 1944 and 1945 in the service. Then, like it was with so many other players, when I came back, it took a month or two to get adjusted and get back into form. Playing for McCarthy, Bill Dickey, and Johnny Neun, I batted .260 in less than 300 at-bats, while the Yankees finished behind the Red Sox and Tigers. The caliber of baseball was a little higher in 1946 than it had been in 1943. Then in 1947 baseball blossomed.

The Yankees were the team to beat, even in 1946 when we didn't win the pennant. Every team in the league wanted to beat the Yankees. Whenever we went anywhere fans would turn out to root against us. But we usually won because we had a great team.

Our star, of course, was Joe DiMaggio. He was a very quiet player but he was a leader, who did whatever it took to win. He didn't play for himself, but for the team. That's why he was voted Most Valuable Player in 1947, when he led us to the pennant. He made it look easy but he played hard. All the time. He was the greatest player I saw in my life, better than Ted Williams and Stan Musial. No one compared to Joe. He was an all-around player who could hit way over .300, hit for power, run, field, throw. He didn't make mistakes. He was seldom thrown out taking an extra base. He just knew when to go and when not to. And if you needed either a single or home run, he'd get it for you.

RALPH KINER (PIRATES):

Joe DiMaggio was motionless at the plate, as opposed to Ted Williams and Stan Musial, who moved their hips when they batted. To be motionless when you hit makes it very difficult, but Joe had exceptional hand speed and weight transfer.

GEORGE KELL (TIGERS):

Joe was as good a hitter as you'll ever see. He wasn't the pure hitter that Ted Williams was, but he was as

much of a perfectionist. He was the symbol of the great Yankee teams as far as I was concerned.

EDDIE JOOST (ATHLETICS):

No superlatives were too great for Joe DiMaggio. I had seen him with the San Francisco Seals in the early thirties when I was with the Missions. I used to play third and he'd hit the ball between my legs before I could get the glove down. In the majors, I'd still always stay down because he hit the ball so hard. I played him straight away. His power was to left-center, but he hit a lot of balls right up the middle. Everyone knew he could hit when he came to the majors, but what they didn't know is that he would be one of the greatest defensive center fielders ever in baseball. He had those long strides. He never showboated at all. He knew he could catch it and he'd go catch it.

B. JOHNSON:

Joe made you feel confident. If another player got too emotional about an umpire's call or something like that, Joe would simply gaze in his direction or mumble a few words and the other player knew it was time to relax. Joe was the only guy who would sit in the clubhouse long after a game ended. He'd stay a few hours for two reasons: he was tired because he had played hard; and he didn't want to sign a lot of autographs outside the ballpark. If Joe ever slumped, I didn't see it. Because he never bothered anyone or asked anyone questions about hitting. He just went off on his own and worked out of it.

Tommy Henrich was another Yankee who didn't care what it took to win. He'd been playing outfield for the Yankees since the late thirties and always put up good numbers, which is why he was called "Old Reliable." He was a leader on the Yankees in the years after the war. He was an intense player who would tell young players, "If you don't want to hustle with this club, there's no use in playing. Everybody has to go all out, everybody has to play together, or we won't win." In 1946 we were asked who we wanted to room with, and I bumped into Tommy and asked if he'd want to room together. He said it didn't matter to him. So Henrich became my roommate for my entire time with the Yankees. We'd pal around, going to eat and to shows. The Yankees were a very close team so Phil Rizzuto, who was from New York, Yogi Berra, who was just 21 or 22 then, and a lot of other guys would go out with us at times—however, I wouldn't go to all the fancy New York clubs. As on the field, Tommy didn't joke around too much. He was always all business.

Rizzuto became the Yankee shortstop before the war and then spent three years in the army. He was a good double-play man. He was very quick at touching second and getting out of the way of runners. He could cover a lot of ground, but his arm was kind of poor, so he compensated with a quick release and by playing shallow except against slow runners. A Cleveland batter once hit a ball that Rizzuto caught in the hole. Because he didn't have a strong arm, Phil tossed it to me at third and I tossed the guy out at first. Rizzuto was a good leadoff hitter because he could also bunt for a base hit. He sparked a lot of rallies. He was a pretty good ballplayer.

EDDIE JOOST (ATHLETICS):
Phil Rizzuto was a little guy—just 5′6″—who took quick steps and had quick reactions. He was accepted as a great-fielding shortstop, but he wasn't. He was a good shortstop. He was a showman, a Yankee-type player who was in the right place at the right time. There were a lot of shortstops in the league, including myself, who were as good or better overall. He was accepted as the best because he was with the Yankees and got the exposure.

B. JOHNSON:
Snuffy Stirnweiss and I had both been rookies in 1943, and he played shortstop then. In 1944, Snuffy became the Yankees' second baseman and had a couple of big years during the war. He did a good job for us in 1947. He could still run, although he no longer stole a lot of bases. He was also a good hitter and good fielder. Rizzuto and Stirnweiss were a good double-play combination (better than Rizzuto and Jerry Coleman would be, starting in 1949).

Johnny Lindell was a very nice guy. He was tall, about 6′4″, and weighed about 220. He was a pitcher when he came up with the Yankees in the early forties, but he was such a good hitter that he was converted into an outfielder. He was a pretty good ballplayer who hit the long ball on occasion and did a good job defen-

sively. He played a lot in 1947 and did a very good job. After that he would be an effective part-time player.

I enjoyed playing with Yogi Berra, who was just breaking in. He caught and played the outfield. It was obvious that he was going to be a great player. He wasn't even 5′8″, but he weighed over 180 and had a lot of power. He could pull the ball into Yankee Stadium's right-field stands, even on pitches out of the strike zone. There were two sides to Yogi: he was a fun guy and also serious. On the field, he really bore down and played well. He never joked, though he always tried to distract batters with light chatter. In the Yankee organization, you had to be all business on the field, so he was more inclined to joke around in the clubhouse, as were all the other players.

EDDIE JOOST (ATHLETICS):
Yogi Berra was a phenom. The way he looked, the way he did things—you'd never expect he would be a star. When he first came up in 1946 and 1947, he couldn't throw anyone out at second base. They worked with him and he became a real good catcher. As a hitter, he was impossible to explain. If you'd bounce the ball to the plate, throw it over his head, or throw it at him, he'd hit it solidly. He always got the bat on the ball and hit it hard.

B. JOHNSON:
Charlie Keller was an outstanding fellow. He was another left-handed hitter. He was called King Kong. He was a good hitter and decent outfielder. He had been a home run hitter before he went into the service and had hit 30 in 1946, but he had a bad back and became just a part-time player and pinch hitter.

The Yankees were a very strong team after the war and needed very little, so they were careful about making trades, making sure they got players who would fill gaps and really help the ballclub. Nick Etten, the Yankees' first baseman, hadn't done as well in 1946 as during the war, so the Yankees picked up George McQuinn to replace him. He had been with the Browns and Athletics. He was a quick, outstanding fielder who could jump or stretch or scoop up any bad throw. He batted over .300 and hit a homer every once in a while. This was near the end of his career.

We got Allie Reynolds from the Indians that year

and he became our ace pitcher, winning 19. He was great. He threw hard and inside and batters didn't like to get in against him. He was a fastballer, so our managers would like to use him in relief when it got hazy and dark at night. He made up for Spud Chandler's retirement.

Frank Shea went 14–5 in 1947. Spec did a fine job all year. His ball would move in or out, or even sail, and that's why he was so effective. He was about 26 or 27, but this was his rookie season.

Bucky Harris became the Yankee manager that year. He had managed for about 20 years and the 1947 Yankees were his first pennant winners since the mid-twenties, when he was player-manager for the Senators. He was very quiet and very lenient. I think he did a good job. The team had so much talent that a manager didn't have to be hard-boiled. The players would do what the manager wanted without being told.

There was a "Yankee Way." They did things the perfect way. For instance, you couldn't have long hair, you had to shave all the time, and when you went to a hotel you had to wear a jacket and tie rather than a sports shirt. It was all first class. The ballplayers didn't have trouble adjusting to the rules of the club or to life in New York. Nobody really got out of line or messed around more than they were supposed to. The players were married, so that kept everyone in place. After the season started, the players had their wives with them, so after a game was over they would either go directly home or go to a show with their wives and then go home. We didn't go to nightclubs. I didn't like that kind of thing anyway.

The first two months of the season, I stayed in Manhattan, at the Hotel Edison on 47th near Broadway. The rest of the season, my wife and I rented a home in New Jersey. Some players lived in hotels during the entire baseball season, and others owned or rented homes in New Jersey or New York. The New York sportswriters were kind to me. I became friends with a few of them, especially those who followed the Yankees on train trips, but I didn't pal around with any of them. I'd see my name in the paper, but I didn't consider myself a celebrity. However, I would be recognized all over the city. It was hard to go anywhere without being spotted. The Yankee fans were great. They appreciated us winning. They'd take us out to dinner and really look after us. If you didn't play well, the fans would get on you

and make you feel pretty bad. They'd boo some guys, but I never had any trouble with them—especially in 1947, when I batted .285, with 95 RBIs, and made the All-Star team.

It meant a lot to make the All-Star team. I didn't get to play in the game, but it was exciting to be on a team with so many great players. The Yankees were represented by such players as DiMaggio, Spec Shea, and Joe Page, who was the best reliever in the league. The game took place in Wrigley Field and the American League won 2–1. Shea was the winning pitcher, the first rookie to get a victory in an All-Star Game.

It meant just as much to win the pennant. And we did it easily. We won 97 games, 8 games more than Detroit. This is when the Yankee dynasty began.

LEW BURDETTE:

I was born in Nitro, West Virginia, in 1926. That was near Cabin Creek, and as a boy I'd play half-court driveway basketball with a gangly but talented younger kid named Jerry West. Growing up, I played sandlot baseball. We had American Legion, but they took my uniform away and gave it to someone else. The next year I started playing with one of the plant teams in Nitro, semipro industrial ball. In Nitro we picked up the Reds on the radio, so I was a fan of theirs and pitcher Bucky Walters. But pitching in the majors never even crossed my mind.

I entered the Air Force in 1944, when I was 18. After I got out, the Presbyterian minister, Reverend Montgomery, told me to go to the University of Richmond on the G.I. Bill because Richmond had a good baseball program. So my way was paid. I was making $65 a month from the army. I was planning on going into business administration, not baseball. I dropped out for one semester to work and save money to go back to school, but I got a telegram from Norfolk asking me to try out for the Yankee organization. I didn't want to do it, but my older brother Les wrote back and told them I would come. They sent me a ticket, so I decided to go down and see what it was like. This was the 1947 spring training for Norfolk of Class B, the Piedmont League. The Yankees painted a big picture of playing in the House That Ruth Built and offered me $175 a month. I said my daddy wouldn't let me sign for a penny less than $200, so they agreed. I should have said $300 or

$400. I also was offered a bonus of $500 if I was still in the organization after June 15. That's how I got into baseball.

I didn't start playing in the minors until I was 20, with my 21st birthday coming in November of that year.

I pitched a shutout my first game at Norfolk. Buddy Hassett was the manager and he was peeved because he had planned to demote me. I pitched just 2 or 3 games for them. As soon as I lost, I was on the train to Amsterdam, New York, in Class C.

WORLD SERIES

1947

YANKEES

VS

DODGERS

BILLY JOHNSON · YANKEES:

The Yankees played the Brooklyn Dodgers in the first of their postwar World Series. When the Yankees won the pennant in 1943, Bill Dickey asked me how I would feel playing in the World Series against the Cardinals. I told him, ''It will be just like playing in any other ballgame.'' Well, I found out differently once I got out on the field and there was all that excitement. And that's the way it was in 1947 when we faced the Dodgers. I think this was the first World Series that was on television, at least in New York.

For each game in Brooklyn, our team bused from Yankee Stadium to Ebbets Field. The people knew our route, so our police escort had to blow sirens in order to get us through the traffic. Then at Ebbets Field, the darn Dodger fans jumped up and down on top of our dugout and kept hollering. And they had a band playing in the stands. It was much more informal than at Yankee Stadium. It was exciting, but I didn't like that kind of thing.

We knew the Dodgers had outstanding, hustling players like Pee Wee Reese and Jackie Robinson. And Rex Barney was one of the fastest pitchers I ever hit against. But we weren't worried about them. We didn't worry about anyone. We went through their batting order and figured out how to pitch their batters and how to play them defensively. During the year, the plan was for the starting pitchers—other than Allie Reynolds, who usually went the distance—to go at least 7 innings and then have Joe Page come in from the bullpen. But it didn't work out that way in the Series.

In Game One, Spec Shea went just 5 innings and then left with a 5–1 lead—we broke through against Ralph Branca for 5 runs in the fifth inning—and Page came in early and went the final 4 innings in our 5–2 victory. Allie Reynolds didn't need any relief help from Page in Game Two because we won, 10–3. The Dodgers jumped on Bobo Newsom and Vic Raschi for 6 runs in the second inning of Game Three and held on for a 9–3 win. Page shut them out for the final 3 innings, but by that time it was too late.

Bill Bevens certainly didn't need any relief help in Game Four. That day he had a good fastball and curve, and great control. I didn't think he'd go very far but he no-hit the Dodgers for 8⅔ innings before Cookie Lavagetto hit that pinch double off the screen to beat us 3–2.

After the game, we went over to him and told him that was one of the things that happens in baseball. Rather than being very disappointed that he didn't pitch the first no-hitter in Series history and lost the game, he was jolly that he had pitched that good.

Shea had another excellent start in Game Five, four-hitting the Dodgers, and we won, 2–1. In Game Six, Harris brought in Page in the fifth inning to protect a 5–4 lead, but the Dodgers hit him hard and won the game, 8–6, to even the Series. We might have won that game, but in the sixth inning their left fielder Al Gionfriddo made that famous catch on DiMaggio's long drive, running it down in front of the fence over 400 feet away. There were two men on base. Joe ran around the bases and, when the ball was caught, kicked up the dirt in frustration, which I'd never seen him do before. That ball would have been way out of Ebbets Field.

There was a lot of tension in Game Seven. Shea started and Bevens pitched, but Harris came back with Joe Page to protect an early lead and he pitched 5 innings of shutout ball. We won, 5–2, to win the Series.

After he won Game Seven in relief, Page was in the training room. I went back there and said, "Joe, how about going into the clubhouse and congratulating some of the players who did well today?" And his response was "You mind your own business." All those guys had played good in the Series and had made money for Joe, but he didn't want to congratulate them. I was surprised. But he was that type of guy. If he wasn't in the limelight he didn't want to take part. DiMaggio palled around with Page, but I didn't get along with him too well.

I led the team with 8 runs and had 3 triples in the Series. I found out later that the 3 triples tied a record.

SPIDER JORGENSEN · DODGERS:
Being in the 1947 World Series was an incredible experience. But it was tough playing because I was beat after the regular season. We went into Yankee Stadium for the first game. I had never played there, but I wasn't too awed by it. The bad part was the shadows. Branch Rickey and Yankee president Larry McPhail were feuding, and we weren't allowed to work out at the Stadium before the Series. Shotten said, "To hell with them!" I think it cost us the Series. I know I would have liked a couple of days to get used to those shadows. When you

were at the plate, the sun set behind home plate and you looked into a mass of light out there with shadows between the mound and the plate. I couldn't see the ball very well and, being tense already, got only a few hits, though I did drive in 3 runs. I didn't have any trouble seeing at third base, but our outfielders did. Pete Reiser had a lot of trouble in center.

Our strategy against the Yankees was the same old thing: pitch them high and tight and low and away. It was the same in both parks. DiMaggio was the star of the Yankees and the scouts told us that he was a dead pull hitter. But I had seen him during his 61-game hit streak with the San Francisco Seals in the Pacific Coast League in 1933 and remembered him getting a lot of hits between third and short against right-handed pitchers. So without consulting anyone, I moved away from the line, where they had wanted me to play, and into the hole and caught a couple of ground balls.

In those days umpires sat in the stands to make sure players on opposing teams didn't fraternize, so I didn't get to know any of the Yankees. I didn't talk to Billy Johnson, who, I suppose, the press compared to me since we were the two third basemen. But I saw he was a tough player who hit in the clutch.

For me, the games in Ebbets Field were more exciting. Our fans were cheering and stomping and the three-piece Sym-Phony Band roamed through the stands playing. I think they wore hats or pins that said "Our Bums," which was our affectionate nickname. The Dodger fans didn't like the Yankees because they were considered a rich team. They got on them pretty good.

Spec Shea really impressed me in the first game. He gave up only a first-inning run before Joe Page relieved him in the sixth. Shea had good stuff and kept hitting the outside corner with his slider. Reynolds was also tough in Game Two. He had tremendous velocity and came in tight.

We won Game Three in Brooklyn, but in the fourth game of the Series, Bill Bevens no-hit us for 8⅔ innings. It was an exciting game, but was really irritating because we hit the ball all over and it was caught. He'd change up just enough to keep us off stride. I was so involved in that game that it didn't sink in that I was the one who scored our first run in the sixth inning. I walked and eventually scored on an infield out, I think, cutting their lead to 2–1. We thought the entire game that we could pull it out. I made the second out in the ninth inning. Furillo was on first after a walk. Bevens threw me an inside change. I shouldn't have swung, but I thought I could line it down the left-field line, and instead I fouled out to George McQuinn at first. Then Al Gionfriddo went in to run for Furillo and stole second, prompting Bucky Harris to have Bevens intentionally walk Pete Reiser. That was controversial because it put the winning run on base. Then Cookie Lavagetto, pinch-hitting for Eddie Stanky, got our only hit, doubling off the right-field fence to drive in the tying and winning runs. It was an incredible ending.

After we evened the Series in the fourth game I thought we would win it. But Spec Shea was sharp again in the next game and beat us, 2–1, on a DiMaggio homer against Rex Barney. We had to come back and win the sixth game in Yankee Stadium. They might have caught us if Al Gionfriddo hadn't made that great catch on DiMaggio's long fly to left against Joe Hatten. I didn't think he was going to get to it. The shadows were bad and he couldn't pick up the ball at first and came in on it, so I thought it was going to bounce

around out there and DiMaggio would wind up with a triple. Hatten thought it was an easy out, and as soon as it was hit he walked off the mound toward the dugout.

In the seventh game we took a 2–0 lead against Shea, but our pitching didn't do so well and we lost, 5–2. Joe Page shut us out the last few innings. Page wasn't as overpowering as I'd expected, but he threw the ball over and it tailed and gave some of us trouble. In Brooklyn, he hung a curve to me and I singled. Shea and Reynolds impressed me more.

We were disappointed we lost because we expected to win. And if it weren't for those shadows in Yankee Stadium I think we would have done it. Hugh Casey and a few other players went over to congratulate the Yankees. I didn't congratulate anybody.

The season really wore me out. After the World Series, I went to have a relaxing beer at the bar at the St. George. I was really looking forward to it, but I apparently needed a day to unwind because I took one gulp and it went to my stomach like a sack of rocks. I couldn't even taste it.

NATIONAL LEAGUE
1948

"BECAUSE OF OUR TREATMENT BY

THE CARDINALS WE DIDN'T WASTE

OUR TIME WHEN ANOTHER TEAM

INVITED US TO A TRYOUT. IF THEY

WANTED TO LOOK AT US, THEY

COULD WATCH US PLAY IN THE

NEGRO LEAGUES."

MINNIE MINOSO

BOSTON BRAVES

JOHNNY SAIN:

Bill Lee was gone, but I again asked Mort Cooper and Si Johnson what salary I should ask for after another 20-win season. They said $30,000. But management sent me a contract for $18,000 again, and they wouldn't budge. I decided that I could hold out to the 15th of March and still be in shape to pitch in the season. However, the Braves knew I was working out and waited me out. On March 15 in Bradenton, I signed their contract, but I told them I wasn't satisfied.

I won 11 games by the All-Star break. I told Billy Southworth that I was going to again ask for the $30,000 and that if they didn't give it to me right away, they couldn't stack enough goddamn money in front of me to get me to pitch for them again. He knew I meant what I said. I took a train to St. Louis to play in the All-Star Game. There was a knock on the door of my compartment. It was our publicity director, Billy Sullivan, telling me I was supposed to talk to Lou Perini the morning of the All-Star Game. I figured Mr. Perini was a businessman, like I was. I wasn't going to retract what I said. I said I'd gambled on my future: either I make money in baseball or I was in the wrong business. The next morning I went to Mr. Perini's room. He said, "John, without pulling too many bones out of the closet, what do you want?" I said, "$30,000." He said, "What about next year?" I said, "If you think I'm going to hold you up next year, make it a two-year contract." He agreed. Then as I was heading out the door he added, "John, I realize that winning 20 is a heck of a season, but for every win you go over 20, I'll give you an extra thousand." So I won 24 and another in the World Series. I had to ask him for the money the next spring and he said, "I didn't mean in the Series, too." But he gave me $5,000.

In late June the Braves had signed Johnny Antonelli to a $75,000 bonus. He was a left-handed 18-year-old high school pitcher. Braves management said I threw that up to them when I was negotiating. It wasn't true. I didn't care what he got. But I did know that if they could pay that money for a young kid, they needed to pay guys fairly who were doing the job.

The Dodgers, who were the defending champions,

and the Cardinals, who won in 1946, were the preseason favorites in the National League. On paper, both teams were stronger than us. The Dodgers added such players as Roy Campanella, Billy Cox, Gil Hodges, and Preacher Roe to go along with Robinson, Reese, Furillo, Branca, and Barney. And the Cardinals still had Stan Musial, Enos Slaughter, and all their other veterans. But we got terrific seasons from our entire team.

The Braves easily led the league in hitting, as 5 players batted over .300: outfielders Tommy Holmes, Jeff Heath, and Mike McCormick, second baseman Eddie Stanky, and shortstop Alvin Dark, the National League Rookie of the Year. Bob Elliott followed his MVP season with another great year, hitting over 20 homers and driving in 100 runs. Heath also hit 20 homers although his playing time was limited by injuries. In fact, he broke his ankle sliding into home in Brooklyn at the end of the season and knocked himself out of the World Series. Earl Torgeson did a good job at the plate and at first, and Phil Masi and Bill Salkeld were both good catchers. The 1948 Braves were a very close, proud team. Spahn and I were loners off the field but we got along with all the other guys. I got along especially well with Stanky, Torgeson, Sibby Sisti, and Nelson Potter. Stanky and Dark chummed together, as did Torgeson and Vern Bickford, and Tommy Holmes, Sisti, and Masi. Elliott was part of another group. Leadership and stabilization came from Elliott, Holmes, Heath, Torgeson, and the other first baseman, Frank McCormick.

Stanky came over from the Dodgers after they decided to move Robinson to second. He was from the old school, a tough competitor who knew the game, so we respected each other. He irritated a lot of people, but I thought he was great. A lot of people condemned him for what they perceived was his domination of Dark. But I thought he helped Dark think baseball. Stanky was a good player who did it with less. If he'd been fluid or powerful or fast, then he might have come across a bit differently and not bothered anyone. He was all business, a real pro. He broke his ankle in 1948, but came back and hobbled through the World Series.

HANK SAUER (REDS):

I didn't dislike Eddie Stanky, like a lot of his opponents did because of his hard-nosed brand of baseball. I thought he was a good competitor. A couple of times he went flying when I slid into him at second, and instead of getting mad, he gave me an approving look. That's the kind of guy he was.

J. SAIN:

The Braves had a good staff with me, Spahn, Vern Bickford, Bill Voiselle, and Nelson Potter and Bobby Hogue in the bullpen. Bickford was 27 or 28, but he was a rookie. He was an aggressive right-hander from Kentucky, who had success with a maneuvering, sinker-slider style.

Nelson Potter was purchased by the Braves in late May from the Philadelphia Athletics. He had started the season with the St. Louis Browns. He'd been a successful starting pitcher for them during the war years, but he did a great job for us coming out of the bullpen. His money pitch was a screwball, which was really difficult to hit.

Johnny Antonelli was a super young guy. But he mostly sat and watched us in 1948. When they gave him the bonus they had to keep him with the club. I resented that a little bit because we needed that extra body to help us. Not that he didn't have the strength to do it, but we couldn't afford to use him with so much at stake. It couldn't have been easy not playing after having received so much money while the underpaid veterans played, but if there was anyone who could handle it, it was John. He turned into a terrific pitcher.

I won 24 games and lost 15. That was the most wins in either league and we won the pennant, so I had a chance at MVP. But Stan Musial had his greatest year: he hit .376, which was more than 40 points higher than anyone else, and also led the league in hits, including a lot off me, runs, runs batted in, total bases, slugging percentage, doubles, and triples. He only missed by one tying Ralph Kiner and Johnny Mize for the homer title. I said that I'd vote for Musial for MVP. I also said there should be a reward for the year's best pitcher. Ironically, Cy Young saw me pitch in the 1948 World Series and he praised my pitching in the newspaper, comparing it to his own. So I always felt I got the first Cy Young Award, although pitchers wouldn't be recognized officially until 1956.

Down the stretch both the Dodgers and Cards faded, while we kept going strong. In September, Southworth started pitching me with two days' rest, and then did the same with Spahn. Spahn would pitch, I would pitch, and it would rain, so then we'd pitch again. That's how Southworth came up with that phrase, "Spahn and Sain and pray for rain," which the writers picked up on. Unfortunately, that diminishes the contributions of our other starters that year. Voiselle won 13 games, which was only 2 less than Spahn, and Bickford went 11–5. As it worked out, I pitched 9 complete games with two days' rest in twenty–nine days, winning 7 and losing 2 by the scores of 2–1 and 1–0. I thought I needed three days' rest to be at my best and felt myself becoming tired late in the games, but I went along with Southworth. I ended up leading the league with 39 starts, 28 complete games, 314⅔ innings, and 24 victories. Spahn actually had an off season, going 15–12 with just 16 complete games in 35 starts. In the next few seasons he'd usually lead the league in starts, complete games, and strikeouts.

When I was pitching all those games, we got off the train at Grand Central Terminal in New York. We were staying at the Commodore Hotel, which was next to the terminal. As I started down to pick up my bag, Billy picked it up and carried it all the way to the hotel. That was embarrassing, but it meant a lot to me.

In 1942 Braves manager Casey Stengel had told me that I wasn't a 9-inning pitcher. That always bothered me and I proved him wrong. From the time I got out of the service until the last day of the 1948 season, I had completed all of my 64 wins, 20 in 1946, 21 in 1947, and 23 in 1948, leading the league in complete games in both 1946 and 1948. Southworth gave me the option of not pitching against the Giants on the last day of the season and having five days off before the World Series or pitching for as long as I wanted and having two days off. Since I was pitching with two days' rest during that time and that would continue in the Series, I chose to pitch. So I pitched 5 innings and took myself out of the game with us ahead. Voiselle pitched 2 innings, and it was called on account of darkness. I got credit for my 24th win, the first of my 65 victories since the war that I didn't complete. Then I came back and pitched 2 complete games in the World Series.

JOHNNY ANTONELLI:

I was born in Rochester, New York, in 1930 and raised in the Italian section of the city. Of course, Catholicism

was important to everyone's lives there. My mother was born in Buffalo, but my father had immigrated from Italy in 1913. He went to work with my grandfather on the New York Central Railroad, and later became a contractor who built railroad sidings.

At Jefferson High, I played organized hardball for the first time. It came pretty easy to me. I was left-handed and could throw and hit. I started out playing first, but my coach, Charley O'Brien, noticed that when I threw the ball it had a little tail to it, so he tried me out as a pitcher. My coach was excellent and taught me how to wind up and all the basics, which I never had to deviate from. I also pitched in a very good American Legion program in the summer. I'd get attention in the press when I'd throw a no-hitter or strike out a lot of batters. Because the baseball season was so brief in the North-

One of baseball's most prized "bonus babies," Johnny Antonelli already had skills as an 18-year-old rookie in 1948, but he wouldn't get many opportunities to pitch until 1953, after the Boston Braves moved to Milwaukee.

east—we played only between 12 and 16 games—there wasn't much scouting done. I didn't know if they had been watching me because they weren't allowed to talk to me while I was in high school. In fact, several major league organizations were fined in 1948 for signing high school kids.

After I graduated, my father, coach, and a local semi-pro team set up an exhibition game so that scouts from almost every team could see me pitch at a higher caliber than high school. It was played at Red Wings Stadium, the ballpark for the Cardinals' Triple A affiliate. I pitched against a team of men in their twenties and thirties. I hadn't pitched in a few weeks, so they were going to limit me to 3 innings. But they would say, ''Can we watch him for two more,'' and ''Can we watch him for two more,'' and before you knew it, I pitched 9 innings, 2 more innings than I'd pitch in high school games. I didn't give up any hits and struck out about 17. If I pitched under those conditions later in my life, I probably wouldn't have achieved what I did. I was so young I wasn't really aware of what was going on and didn't feel pressure. The next day all the scouts came by the house with offers. I let my father make the decision. I signed with the Boston Braves for $52,000, less than was reported. That wasn't the highest offer, which came from the Red Sox. If I knew that the Yankees were going to be in so many World Series in future years, I would have signed with them, although I wasn't a Yankee fan. My father and I were fans of the Rochester Red Wings, and my father was surely influenced to sign with the Braves because Billy Southworth had once coached at Rochester. I'm sure he also took note that the Braves owner, Lou Perini, was a contractor like him and had an Italian name.

I think bonus signings began in 1947. I remember Curt Simmons signing and joining the Phillies. The intention of the bonus rule, which stipulated that players who signed for more than $5,000 had to stay in the majors for the next two years, was to prevent rich teams like the Yankees from signing all the young prospects and stockpiling them in the minors. Teams had to be selective because they didn't want a half-dozen 18-year-olds in the majors.

Outwardly no one on the Braves was unfriendly toward me because I'd gotten so much money at a time

the average salary was less than $10,000. I'm sure they figured that if I could help the team it would benefit them. I assume that the older players were bitter about salaries and security after retirement. We didn't have the television money or All-Star money to work with then, and we paid $2 a day for the pension plan. So money was scarce. In fact, the best thing that ever happened to Johnny Sain was my getting a bonus—because John went up and got a raise. Other players on the Braves who were looking for money pointed at me and got their raises. So I didn't have any problems. In fact, when Billy Southworth asked other pitchers to help me, Johnny Sain, Warren Spahn, Clyde Shoun, and Red Barrett were more than willing to help. Basically, most ballplayers were pretty nice people.

In high school I had always tried to throw the hardest fastball and best curve. I was now taught to change speeds. I learned variation. In high school, when I was striking out between 15 and 20 batters in 7 innings, I didn't need a good pickoff move. But I needed it in the majors, and Warren Spahn, who had an excellent move, worked with me. Clyde Shoun, who had a very bad move to first, tried to teach me his balk move. Southworth put a stop to that and sent me back to Spahn.

Unfortunately, Southworth didn't pitch me in games. Maybe he was afraid that the press might question him for using an untried rookie instead of seasoned pitchers, even if they were less talented. I should have been used in place of some of the other pitchers, even to do mop-up work, because I had the talent to get by. I couldn't sit for six weeks and then go out there with any timing or confidence.

Although not pitching was frustrating, it was still very exciting being in a pennant race. I had never seen more than about 12,000 fans at a ballpark. I arrived at a night game and there were 32,000 fans at Braves Field. I was very much taken by the spectacle. Johnny Sain was pitching that night and we won the ballgame.

Sain was a heck of a pitcher. And so was Spahn. But people forget about Vern Bickford. ''Spahn and Sain and pray for rain'' just sounded good, but in between there was Bickford.

I thought the leaders on the Braves were Bob Elliott, who all the other players looked up to, and, to a lesser degree, Earl Torgeson, who held court in the clubhouse every once in a while. But among the pitchers, Sain was the leader. We all liked him. Red Barrett kept everybody laughing—he was like a vaudeville comic. Bill Voiselle loved his country music and would do his singing and stomping, as big as he was—we enjoyed him. Nelson Potter was a soft-shoe specialist. A great guy. They were nice people, and it was fun being around them at the ballpark. I never had trouble getting along with anybody.

BOB BUHL:

Once Happy Chandler declared me a free agent, it was like starting over again. Every team came to the house except the Dodgers and White Sox. I had a good friend, a judge, who was good friends with John Quinn, the Boston Braves GM. He told me what kind of contract he could get for me from Quinn. The Braves weren't a very good club and some of their pitchers were old, so I figured I could make it to the majors quicker than I could in another organization. So I signed with the Braves. I received a new car and a Triple A contract at $800 a month. About an hour after I agreed to a contract with the Braves, a scout from Detroit came in and offered me a bonus of $50,000.

My contract was with the Milwaukee Brewers, the Braves' Triple A team, but the Braves assigned me to an independent Class A team in Saginaw, Michigan, my hometown. The Braves didn't have to call me up for three years without losing me. The Braves' system had a lot more coaching than the White Sox system, but not at Saginaw. However, if you produced they kept you moving along.

ST. LOUIS CARDINALS

JOHNNY KLIPPSTEIN:

In 1948 I went back to Columbus, the Cards' Triple A team. I had hopes of making the parent club if I had a good season. I saw that the Cardinals had three left-handed starters in Howie Pollet, Harry Brecheen, and Al Brazle, but only two right-handers who started, Murry Dickson—who was past thirty—and George Munger. But again I was demoted. I was sent to Lynchburg, bypassing Omaha. I was getting discouraged be-

cause I felt I was failing. Every time I would move up a step, it seemed like I would go a step back. I didn't think about quitting because I was still very young. But the Cardinals didn't have me in their plans and allowed the Dodgers to draft me.

MINNIE MINOSO:

I was born Saturnino Orestes Minoso in 1922 in the small town of Perfico, Matanzas, Cuba. I had two brothers and two sisters and was raised on a small ranch, where I cut sugarcane. I played baseball at the ranch from the time I was 11 or 12, managing the team and telling the older kids how to play. We would beat the city teams. I was a pitcher, played third, played center. I got the reputation for being the best player. I was ''something else.'' When I first started playing, I had no idea that I'd be able to play anywhere but Cuba. My ambition was just to play professional ball in Cuba. That was every boy's dream on the island. I didn't know anything about the major leagues. My mother never saw me play professional ball because she died in 1941, a year or two before I quit high school and went to Havana. I played semipro ball for two years there, but since I got only pocket money, I worked as a mechanic for a Buick dealer. I'd get $60 a week. Then I played on the Marianao team in the Cuban Winter League. My father saw me play in my prime only in Cuba in winter ball.

I became one of the stars in Cuba and was signed to a contract by the New York Cubans in the Negro National League. So I came to the United States in 1946. I played third base and made the Eastern All-Star team in 1947, when the Cubans won the World Series, and in 1948, my last season in the Negro Leagues.

When Jackie Robinson signed to play in the major leagues, many players in the Negro Leagues thought they had the opportunity also. I wanted to play in the major leagues to prove that I was one of the best ballplayers. I was invited to a tryout with the St. Louis Cardinals, along with a pitcher on the Cubans, José Santiago from Puerto Rico. We were so much better than anyone else there. Santiago struck out all 3 batters he faced, and they had to tell me to ease up on my throws because the first baseman wasn't able to handle anything so hard. But the Cardinals didn't really want to look at us. They sent us home. Because of our treatment by the Cardinals we didn't waste our time when another team invited us to a tryout. If they wanted to look at us, they could watch us play in the Negro Leagues.

CHICAGO CUBS

RANDY JACKSON:

Because I was on the Cubs' 40-man roster, I spent spring training with the parent club and went with them on the road to play exhibition games. I wouldn't even see the minor league team I was going to play for in 1948 until its regular season began.

The Cubs held spring training in California, out on Catalina Island, which the Wrigley family owned. Catalina had few people and was away from everything, so there was no trouble that the players could get into.

Most afternoons were free, but there wasn't anything to do. So we hung out at the hotel, played cards, and wandered around town, which took 15 minutes. There was no movie house or pool hall. Tourists would come over by boat and wander around, too, about a half boatload a day. The airport was only about 1½ blocks long and the planes needed good brakes to land, and when you took off you dropped down to almost sea level. We'd fly out of there to play exhibition games and it was scary at times, but nobody ever crashed.

Usually, we'd have one good 3-to-4-hour workout each day. Most of the rookies had some experience in the minors, so I was kind of the rookie-rookie-rookie. Maybe I was better educated, but that didn't matter to anyone. We were all in the same boat, trying to make a living playing baseball.

The manager was Charlie Grimm, who stayed in the organization a long time. He had no idea who I was. I didn't feel any pressure because I didn't know what they wanted of me. They didn't know what I could do. I'm sure the general consensus was that I'd be sent to the minors, but it was just a matter of what classification I'd be headed to. I played in some exhibition games and did pretty good, so I guess I was considered a prospect after that.

I was sent to Des Moines in the Western League, which was Class A. This was fortunate because Stan Hack was the manager. He had been a great third baseman for many years with the Cubs and helped me learn

that position. I had to learn the basics as far as keeping my balance when throwing and keeping my eye on the ball, and I had to familiarize myself with what to do in different situations. I never had anyone work with my hitting because I didn't have problems with that. I was mostly a pull hitter though I could hit to the other field occasionally, with power. I stood very close to the plate and hit mostly from the middle of the field to left.

It was all exciting and fun, being with 19 or 20 other guys and traveling by bus and playing baseball. It was a pretty good life. A few of my teammates made it to the majors and a few made it to Triple A, so there were genuine prospects. I don't think there was any real competitiveness between us because we all played. The rosters were so small that we had four infielders and one utility player. We played six months and then I went back to take a postgraduate course at Texas. But instead I just messed around. I played golf and had a few dates, and just had fun.

BEN WADE:

I was born in 1922 in Morehead City, on the eastern coast of North Carolina, about 70 miles from Wilmington. There were 14 in the family and I was the youngest. We never had any money, so I wasn't really aware of the Depression. My father worked for a fish buyer. He would go out Sunday afternoon and load the boat up with ice and take off and buy fish along the coast for five or six days each week. We ate a lot of fish. My father never played baseball, but I had two brothers who played professional ball. Jake, who was 10 years older than me, was in the majors from 1936 until 1946, pitching for every American League team but Cleveland and Philadelphia. Charley, who was 10 years older than Jake, got as far as Seattle in the Pacific Coast League.

I was a big kid—I would be 6'3" and weigh 195 in the majors—and I had a live right arm. I pitched high school baseball, but when the summer came I would visit Jake in Detroit, Boston, and St. Louis, and throw batting practice. In St. Louis in 1939 I got to work out with the Yankees, Red Sox, Cincinnati, and a few teams. I even pitched batting practice to Ted Williams. I worked out several times with Cincinnati and went to spring training with Indianapolis, their Triple A team. That's when Warren Giles signed me. I got a bonus of $2,500, which was a large amount of money, and was lucky enough to start right out at Indianapolis. I would have gone anywhere. I think I was ready. I had a good year. The next year I was sent to Syracuse, which also was Triple A. Hank Sauer and Ewell Blackwell were on that team with me. Blackwell had that sidearm delivery and even then I could see he was special.

After two years in Triple A, I went into the service from 1942 to 1945. I was stationed in California and France. I played baseball in California. I don't think the layoff affected my career at all. Many players came back from the service in 1946, when there was an overflow of ballplayers. I came up with a sore shoulder and was laid off for a year. Cincinnati left me on their Birmingham Barons roster and the Hollywood Stars of the Pacific Coast League drafted me. Then I was traded to the Los Angeles Angels, which was the Cubs' Coast League team. By this time my arm didn't hurt anymore.

In 1948 I went to spring training with the Cubs at Catalina Island, the worst place I trained in my life. It was cold, foggy, and damp. I liked Charlie Grimm and I impressed him enough to make the team. It was thrilling to make the majors, but I didn't play long enough to get a feel for it. I pitched only 5 innings. However, I got to know some of the guys. Some veterans like catcher Bob Scheffing, Phil Cavarretta, and Bill "Swish" Nicholson made rookies feel at home. Cavarretta, who joined the Cubs in the early thirties, was a fixture in Chicago and the player leader. At this time he was playing part-time at first base and in the outfield.

In those days young pitchers did the best they could and didn't worry about other pitchers they were competing with. Everyone got along. Bob Rush and I hung around together. He came from Michigan and was in his early twenties. He was another tall, rookie right-hander trying to make it with the Cubs. He would make the team and for many years be a good pitcher with a bad ballclub. I was also friends with Eddie Waitkus, who was young, single, and very congenial. He was a pretty good left-handed hitter—he hit doubles rather than homers—who had replaced Cavarretta at first base a couple of years back. He'd be traded to the Phillies after the season.

Teams could carry a couple of extra players until cutdown day. That's when I was demoted to Nashville. It didn't upset me that much because I knew I was an extra player. I would never pitch for the Cubs again.

RUBE WALKER:

I was born Albert Bluford Walker in Lenoir, North Carolina, in 1926. Growing up, I listened to Senators' games, but I was such a big baseball fan that I liked everybody. I had a strong arm and thought a little about pitching, but in high school I was a catcher. I was too slow to play another position.

In the forties there was much scouting of the high school teams in western North Carolina. Several teams scouted me, but only the Cubs really came after me. I was given a bonus when I signed in 1944, on the same day the Cubs also signed Smoky Burgess, who was from Forest City. I had never played against Smoky but I had heard about him. I didn't think that I should sign with another organization just because they signed another catcher. The Cubs had a good minor league system and they separated me and Smoky so we could both play.

I spent several years in the minors, starting out at Irvin, Tennessee, playing for Jim Poole, and ending up at Nashville, playing for Larry Gilbert. I was a left-handed pull hitter, and no one tried to change my swing. But Gilbert talked to me about being a receiver and expected me to do a little more in terms of running a game. One day he told me I was going to the Cubs. I was very happy. Larry sent me to Chicago with advice on how to conduct myself in the majors. I was told not to be a pop-off. And I was told to listen.

In Chicago, I moved into the Embassy apartment building off Lake Shore. Visiting players would stay at the Sheraton Plaza. I discovered that the Cubs players didn't really feel like celebrities. Maybe it was because the fans sat so close to us in Wrigley Field that we got to know them. When we walked out of the dugout, they were waiting for us. We recognized each other.

The Cubs had won the pennant in 1945, so I thought of them as a good team. But in 1948 the team struggled, finishing in a tie for seventh place with Cincinnati. Our biggest problem was that we had only a couple of good starting pitchers, left-hander Johnny Schmitz, who won 18 games and had a very low ERA, and young right-hander Russ Meyer, who won 10 games in his first full season. Rookies Bob Rush and Cliff Chambers, a southpaw, showed a lot of promise, but they didn't contribute much that year.

I thought we had a decent offensive ballclub. Our star was Andy Pafko. That year he played third base and batted over .300, hit over 25 homers, and drove in over 100 runs. He was an excellent player and a super guy. The fans loved all the Cubs players, but it was much stronger with Andy.

Bill Nicholson was our other big gun. He had been the Cubs' power hitter from the late thirties until Pafko came along. He still hit about 20 homers a year. I liked "Swish" because he was nice to young players. So was Eddie Waitkus. Eddie batted close to .300. So did our left fielder, Peanuts Lowrey, and Emil Verban, who was a part-time second baseman. Bob Scheffing, the starting catcher, did reach .300. Bob and our other veteran catcher, Clyde McCullough, who was from Tennessee, were great to me. We also had Hal Jeffcoat, a rookie from South Carolina, doing a good job as our center fielder, and the ageless Phil Cavarretta, who hit around .280. We talked baseball all the time, especially Scheffing, Cavarretta, and Nicholson. We talked about who we'd be facing the next game.

I batted a respectable .275, which I would never come close to equaling. Actually, besides hitting about 30 or 40 points higher than I would hit in the future, I had a year that would be pretty typical. I batted around 170 times, had 8 doubles and 5 homers, scored 17 runs and drove in 26. Other than the high average, the only thing that was different is that I pinch-hit a lot. As my average went down, managers used me less as a pinch hitter.

JIM BROSNAN:

I played half a year at Fayetteville, jumping from D ball to B ball. I couldn't have done that with a team like the Cardinals because they had more farm teams and it was a step-by-step process. As it was, five years was the time it was expected for a player with major league talent to reach the Cubs. My manager was Skeeter Scalzi. When I gave up a grand slam early in the season, he asked the infielders who gathered on the mound if any of them wanted to relieve me. That didn't help my confidence any. By the end of the year, in which we won the pennant, he had much more faith in me.

BROOKLYN DODGERS

SPIDER JORGENSEN:

Leo Durocher returned from his one-year suspension to manage the Dodgers. We trained in Santo Domingo in the Dominican Republic. Laraine Day came down with Leo, and all the players really liked her. She wrote a skit, full of all kinds of hijinks, for the players to perform. I don't think Jackie Robinson participated in it, but a lot of the guys did. It was all in good fun.

When Robinson came to spring training, Leo got after him in person and in the press to lose some of the weight he'd gained doing banquets in the off-season. Jackie weighed well over 200 pounds and looked like a balloon. The Dodgers intended him to play second base in his second season, and had made room by trading Eddie Stanky to the Braves. Stanky had been Durocher's favorite, so Leo made sure Robinson got down to his playing weight of about 185. The two of them got after each other pretty good and I think the resentment lasted. I could see it on the field after Durocher jumped the team in mid-season to manage the Giants. We were below .500 at the time. Burt Shotton returned as our manager. We played much better baseball under him, but still finished behind the Braves and Cardinals. That was disappointing.

It made sense for Robinson to move to second because when he had played there with me at Montreal, he had been much more relaxed than at first base. He had very good hands and rarely booted anything hit his way. Robinson would have an even better year at the plate—he led the team in RBIs—and would also make more contributions as a fielder and as vocal infield leader. Robinson was much more demonstrative. Rickey had turned him loose and he didn't take any flak from anyone. Now he was independent and let loose his anger.

ANDY SEMINICK (PHILLIES):

Robinson wouldn't take as much abuse as he had as a rookie. Now he'd talk back to umpires and talk back to players, just like other players would. He was a tough cookie.

DEL ENNIS (PHILLIES):

In 1948 everyone went after Robinson at second base on force plays. He had one rhythm and it was easy to time him. He took more knocks than Carter had liver pills. But he was agile and strong and avoided getting hurt. He'd also retaliate, using his spikes when he came down on runners and sliding with them up into those infielders who slid hard into him.

S. JORGENSEN:

When Robinson moved to second, Gil Hodges moved to first from behind the plate and got much more playing time. He did an excellent job fielding and showed improvement as a hitter, hitting some homers and driving in a few runs. I don't think he would have developed into a good hitter if he had remained a catcher. In fact, nobody thought he'd be much of a hitter at all because he chased curve balls outside the strike zone. That was the same problem Duke Snider was having, but I could tell he was going to learn to lay off the curve in the dirt that everyone was throwing him and become a very good hitter.

Hodges wouldn't have gotten much playing time behind the plate because we brought up Roy Campanella from St. Paul during the season. Bruce Edwards had hurt his arm during the off-season, so we needed help. Roy was a great, great catcher and hitter. He hit 2 homers in his first game, against the Giants. How he loved to play. Even on hot days he'd say, "If we had three games today, I'd catch them all." He'd done that in the Negro Leagues. I didn't see him as a leader yet, but the pitchers listened to him and he was solid.

We also improved ourselves by acquiring Preacher Roe from the Pirates in December. He fit into our rotation with Branca, Hatten, and Barney, who led our team with 15 wins, including a no-hitter against the Giants in the Polo Grounds. Roe was an excellent control pitcher and outstanding competitor. He threw a lot of change-ups and spitters to good hitters, and when he needed a strike he could reach back and throw a heater better than most.

In the Roe deal, in which we traded away Dixie Walker—probably in response to his early resistance to Robinson—Hal Gregg, and Vic Lombardi, we also picked up Billy Cox, who would become an important member of the Dodgers. He was expected to back up Reese at short, but third base became open. During the off-season I had returned to El Paso, where I now lived, and did a lot of dove and pheasant hunting, and I think the recoil of the rifle damaged my shoulder. But it could have been that I didn't do any throwing or playing in the off-season, as I had done in previous years. At spring training in Santo Domingo my shoulder was tight from the start and I couldn't work it out. I finally was sent down to St. Paul, which was a real disappointment. They gave me a couple of shots of Novocaine and the pain went away. I did a lot of pushups to strengthen my shoulder. But they didn't really know how to treat shoulder injuries then. I hit .300 for the Dodgers, but I batted only 90 times all year.

Tommy Brown seemed to have the inside track to play third. Tommy broke in with the Dodgers in 1944 at the age of 16 to become the youngest National League player in history, and then at 17 the next year became the youngest major leaguer to homer. He was 20 in 1948 and was being groomed to play third, but I think my injury came along too soon for him to step in. He still had trouble hitting major league pitching. So Durocher shifted Cox from short and he became the Dodgers' regular third baseman. He proved to be an outstanding ballplayer. He played great defense, ran well, and, despite being a small guy, hit for power. I didn't feel I was unfairly treated when I couldn't get my job back from Cox. In those days you always had guys to beat out to secure your job.

DON NEWCOMBE:

I knew I wasn't going to the majors, but at least after two years at Nashua I was assigned to Montreal. Campanella began the season at St. Paul, the Dodgers' other Triple A team, before being called up by the Dodgers and immediately establishing himself as the best all-around catcher in the National League. After failing with the Dodgers, Dan Bankhead was sent all the way down to Nashua. He became the team's first 20-game winner and at the end of the year moved up to St. Paul.

I also won 20 games at Montreal, including 3 in the playoffs, and, like Bankhead at Nashua, impressed the organization with my strikeout numbers. However, the Dodgers were probably still wary of my willingness to hit white batters. One white player charged out to the mound and jumped up into my face with his spikes. He was going "to grind this nigger's face," he threatened, for daring to throw at him. But I just sidestepped him and Chuck Connors, our first baseman, caught him and kicked the shit out of him. I could have broken his fucking arm, but Chuck had to protect me, because I couldn't fight him because I was black—which is what Jackie had to go through at Brooklyn. There was another Robinson in the stands that night watching me pitch: the great dancer Bill "Bojangles" Robinson—"the Mayor of Harlem." The next morning at breakfast he told me, "Don, I'm so happy you didn't lift your fist when he charged you on the mound."

ED ROEBUCK:

I was born in 1931 in East Millsboro, Pennsylvania, a mining town 50 miles south of Pittsburgh. I had five brothers and three sisters, all older than me. My father and brothers worked in the mines. Some of my brothers joined the service just to get out, but they reluctantly came back. I was very aware of the Depression. We leased a farm and managed to get by because of what we grew and raised. We had no money.

I played high school ball, American Legion ball, and semipro ball with a mining team that was comprised of the Roebuck brothers and brothers from another family. I didn't have any inspiration about playing pro ball until I was a sophomore in high school and threw a couple of no-hitters. Besides pitching, I played shortstop. Several teams were scouting me, but they weren't allowed to sign me until I graduated from high school. My high school coach and brothers encouraged me because they wanted me to avoid the mines. My father was reluctant. He was a Polish guy who based everything on hard work. He also thought that being in a family meant never going away.

I was a Pirates fan because they were close by. They were one of the teams that invited me to try out, but they weren't that committed to signing me. A Red Sox scout was practically living in my house. One day a black car pulled up in front of our door. It was a scout from the Dodgers, who wanted me to try out in Brooklyn, which I thought was across the world. They flew me to Brooklyn and I tried out in front of Branch Rickey. I did some hitting and running, but they saw I was slow. The Dodg-

ers were interested in signing athletes, so I didn't think I fit their needs. The Dodgers' system was based on pitching, speed, athleticism, and defense. After the tryout I didn't hear anything. Then in the winter of 1948 the Dodgers sent me a Triple A contract for what was pretty good money at the time, around $3,600 a year. Although I got a Triple A contract, I would play for Newport News in the Class B Piedmont League in 1949. I was just 17 and most of the players were around 30.

CHICO CARRASQUEL:

I was born in Caracas, Venezuela, in 1928. I had two brothers and seven sisters. We all played sports and my brothers, Domingo and Martine, eventually played minor league ball in the States. We didn't have any money for equipment, so we'd use whatever was available, often playing with sticks and bare hands. Latin boys didn't have time to go to school because we knew we had to play every day to become good enough to play professionally. I started playing professional baseball in Caracas in 1946, when I was 17. In my first game I hit a homer to win the game, and in time I became one of the star players. During my entire youth, my mother hadn't wanted me to waste time playing baseball, but when I brought home money, she said, "You can play baseball every day if you want to." My dream was to play in the major leagues. We listened on the radio and read in the papers about major league baseball. My uncle Alex Carrasquel had pitched for the Washington Senators from 1939 to 1945 (and would pitch for the White Sox in 1949), along with winter ball in Caracas. I knew a lot of the Negro League players because they played winter ball in Venezuela, Puerto Rico, the Dominican Republic, and Mexico. Roy Campanella, Don Newcombe, and Sam Jethroe were heroes in Venezuela. I was happy when Jackie Robinson broke the major league color barrier because it opened the doors for Latin players, as well as American blacks.

Fresco Thompson, the Dodgers scout, came to Venezuela in 1948 to see me play. But that year we had a revolution and baseball stopped for about a month. So he just called and asked if I wanted to come to the States. He signed me for $1,000 without seeing me play.

NEW YORK GIANTS

BILL RIGNEY:

I had played my butt off in 1947 and batted .267, with 17 homers, 24 doubles, and 84 runs and 59 RBIs in 130 games. I had a .420 on-base percentage. So I held out for $22,500. We didn't talk money among ourselves and salaries weren't common knowledge in those days, so I didn't know what most of the other guys got. But I know that after Mize's big year in '47, he got $51,000. Then he went out in 1948 and drove in 125 runs and again tied Ralph Kiner for the homer title, with 40. Walker Cooper had a contract that stipulated he must be the highest-paid player on the Giants. So they paid him a few hundred more than Mize.

After half the season had gone by, the Giants were under .500. Suddenly Stoneham fired Mel Ott and replaced him with Leo Durocher, who quit the Dodgers. It was a shock! We had hated Durocher on the Dodgers. He was our worst enemy. When he took over, in Pittsburgh, he laid it right out to us: "They made a change. I'm the new manager. Let's see who the hell can play here and who can't play and why the team's not playing better." It was that simple. I could tell right away who wasn't going to be around much longer. Walker Cooper didn't like him. He said, "You'd better watch your wallets, guys." But that was Coop. I liked that Leo was a gambler and spontaneous, would take any advantage to win the game, and would fight with umpires when he believed he was right. We all learned from him, especially that the little things were important. There were a lot of talented players on the team who were eager to put their talents to better use—so they accepted what Leo taught them.

Leo was a well-known disciplinarian, so we tried to guess who would get his first ass-chewing. Ken Trinkle came in to relieve a guy in St. Louis. He was a good sinkerball pitcher, but he hung a curve in the bottom of the ninth that Nippy Jones hit for a homer to beat us. We knew something was going to happen. Trinkle dressed right alongside of me. Leo walked back and forth and cursed Trinkle up and down. Trinkle was a tough guy who had gotten the Silver Star for saving a guy's life in the army, and he started to get up. I reached over and got him by the pants and pulled him back down. He started

to get up again, and I pulled him back down. Finally Leo got through chewing his ass. Trinkle was mad at me, but I asked, "What were you going to do, deck him? He was right—you hung a curve." Leo made his point: don't get beat on your second-best pitch. The next day Leo's anger was gone. He had personality conflicts with certain players, but if they could help win games he wouldn't hold them back.

As soon as Leo became manager, the whole picture changed. He wanted a club that could operate better and not just rely on home runs. He told me to go back to hitting the ball to right field because we had other players to hit the long ball. So I finished with just 10 homers. Mize got his 40 homers and Sid Gordon had 30, and Cooper, Bobby Thomson, Willard Marshall, and our rookie center fielder, Whitey Lockman, all hit between 14 and 18 homers. Whitey, a left-handed batter from North Carolina, was the type of player Durocher preferred to sluggers like Mize, Marshall, Cooper, and Gordon. Like Bobby Thomson, another favorite of Leo's, Whitey could run and execute the hit-and-run in addition to hitting home runs. Whitey was a great guy and he'd run around with me, Thomson, and Larry Jansen.

Jansen was again the ace of the Giants, pitching over 275 innings and winning 18 games. Dave Koslo and Clint Hartung won only a few games, but we got a boost from Sheldon Jones, a hard-throwing right-hander who won 16 games in his first full season. He was another workhorse, who started and relieved. We needed him to do both because we still had weak pitching.

PHILADELPHIA PHILLIES

ANDY SEMINICK:

We were playing much better ball than in 1947, when we had finished in a last-place tie, but Ben Chapman was fired halfway through the season. I don't know if it was because of the way he had treated Jackie Robinson, but there were some reporters who were after him. Eddie Sawyer got his first managerial assignment. He was only in his late thirties and was several years younger than Chapman. He wasn't as much of a disciplinarian as Chapman, but you couldn't fool him. There wasn't a lot of curfew breaking. We loved Sawyer because he let us play. Unfortunately, we didn't play well for him in 1948 and finished in sixth place, only a couple of games ahead of the Reds and Cubs.

However, our team improved dramatically with the addition of Richie Ashburn, who batted leadoff and hit over .300 as a rookie. He was very aggressive, competitive, and intense—although off the field he was a funny guy with dry humor. He was a left-handed hitter, but hit the ball to left, often shooting it to the right of the shortstop in the hole. He was more of a singles hitter than Pete Reiser. He was always on base and even set a rookie record by getting hits in 23 straight games—Alvin Dark also did it that year for the Braves. If Richie didn't like a pitch he'd foul it off—he would do that for several pitches in a row, until the pitcher would either walk him or give him something easier to hit. Richie could fly on the base paths and in center field and led the league in both stolen bases and putouts. One time he beat out a two-hopper to the mound against the Giants' lefty Thornton Lee. Those kinds of things sparked the ballclub. In Shibe Park, our pitcher would warm up in front of the dugout, and Richie would always walk up and eyeball him. He'd step in and try to hit the ball lightly back to the pitcher. But he'd often overswing and miss the ball or have it just graze the bat. I'd get mad because I wasn't wearing my mask. (One day—I'm not sure in what year—our coach Benny Bengough was warming up a pitcher and Ashburn swung too hard and hit the ball right into the stands and knocked a guy's eye out. The guy sued and collected, probably from the ballclub.)

Granny Hamner had come up to the Phillies in 1944, when he was just 17. But 1948 was his first season as a regular. He was a shortstop but played mostly at second this one year, while Eddie Miller played short and hit 14 or 15 homers for us. Granny was a .260–.270 hitter and a clutch player at bat and in the field. When he played short, he was the best at that time at making a relay throw to third or home. He'd take all the relays unless it was down the right-field line. He had such a good arm. He was a good guy, very confident in his talents. Granny—which was short for Granville—became a leader of the team and would be named captain.

The big gun in our offense was again Del Ennis—and that wouldn't change over the years. But the fans got on him pretty heavy. If he homered the first time up,

they got angry if he didn't homer the second time up. It was weird. The poor guy was in the outfield, where they could yell at him.

Del would hit third or fourth and I'd hit fifth, sixth, seventh. I used a big, heavy bat, 39 ounces at one time, but as the season went on, I went down. I was usually better at the beginning of the season than the end, but most players were like that. I'd get tired. I hit most left-handers well, except for Warren Spahn. Of the tough right-handers, I hit the Reds' Johnny Vander Meer pretty good. Ewell Blackwell wasn't as easy.

By this time I had become a good defensive catcher, and led the league's receivers in most fielding categories. I liked to watch the other catchers around the league. Walker Cooper of the Giants was outstanding. So were Clyde McCullough of the Cubs and Phil Masi of the Braves. They were all good at working with pitchers, knowing what they could and couldn't do. Roy Campanella came up to the Dodgers during the season and I could see he was a great catcher. He'd get your eye. He was kind of a roly-poly guy with that gear on, but he moved good for his size and he hit, threw, and received the ball so well. He did everything good. He was also a great guy, an ideal man to have on a ballclub. We got to know each other, both being catchers.

Only a few players stole 20 or 30 bases in those days, but most teams did quite a bit of running, so it was important for a catcher to have a good arm. In a close game, they'd let loose anybody who could run. Only if the score wasn't close was there an unwritten rule that you stayed put. On the Dodgers, Jackie Robinson and Pee Wee Reese always ran, and I didn't have much success throwing them out. Reese was the toughest. Pete Reiser, who was a super ballplayer, was still tough on the base paths, but by this time he was banged up and Duke Snider was being groomed to replace him. Even Duke was a good baserunner. We worked with the pitchers on keeping runners close, but even if they didn't, the catchers should have been able to throw some of those runners out. I was hard on myself.

Our best pitchers in 1948 were Dutch Leonard and Schoolboy Rowe, the two veterans. However, both Robin Roberts and Curt Simmons joined the rotation. Simmons, a left-hander, turned 19 during the year. He had pitched one game for the Phillies in 1947, but 1948 was his rookie season and he was our most used pitcher after Leonard. He had a good fastball and great curve. Roberts debuted in '48. There was something special about him. He had a lot of velocity and his control was fantastic. You put a glove here and there and he'd hit it, even as a rookie. He had a losing record but, after Leonard, had the team's best earned run average.

At some point, Roberts became our player rep. There were meetings, and if we had gripes, Roberts would take it up with the owners. Then there would be meetings of all the player reps. It had to do with the pension plan. The owners didn't want it, but I think the Phillies were for it 100 percent. For the pension plan, players and coaches had to put up $250 each to begin with. At least one of the coaches didn't want to put it up, so Bob Carpenter, our owner, put up the money for him. We were in favor of a players' union, only we didn't call it a union then. Roberts and guys like Ralph Kiner, Bob Feller, Allie Reynolds, and Marty Marion were the ones who were important in getting it started.

DEL ENNIS:

My back recovered and I had my first big season with the Phillies, with 40 doubles, 30 homers, and 95 RBIs. I was unhappy that Ben Chapman was fired, but I liked Eddie Sawyer because he could teach us all about the game. He was easy to play for. The Phillies' style under him was quite simple: Richie Ashburn would get on base leading off and we'd knock him in. We'd win a lot of one-run games.

The players dressed in coats and ties on the road. Ashburn always wore a hat. Actually, I got all the players Stetson hats from my father, so we all wore hats.

PITTSBURGH PIRATES

RALPH KINER:

Billy Meyer became the Pirates' manager in 1948 and was outstanding to play for. He got rid of all those disruptive players who were just there for a good time. There was a big change in personnel. Our team won 21 more games than in 1947 and finished 12 games over .500 at 83–71, finishing fourth. We even had a chance to win the pennant.

I had another solid year, hitting 40 homers and driving in 123 runs. I made my first All-Star team. In those days the American League won almost every year, and

Phillies outfielder Del Ennis had 30 homers and 95 RBIs in 1948 to take his place as one of the league's top power hitters, a position he'd maintain until 1958.

they won in 1947, 5–2. We got our runs on a Stan Musial homer. Johnny Mize and I tied again for the homer title. At one point I homered in 17 of 35 games. I homered on 8 successive Sundays, but in those days we always played 2 games on Sunday. I loved doubleheaders because it gave me a chance to hit 8 or 9 times. There was no mutual admiration society among home run hitters. There was no animosity, either. I didn't have hatred or compassion for Mize in the three successive years we competed for the homer titles. I wanted to win, but my nature was to just let the chips fall where they may.

I started out using 35-inch bats of between 33 and 35 ounces, which was what most hitters used at the time. Afterward I used a bat from 37 to 42 ounces, depending on the pitcher. I had a pretty upright stance, holding my hands high to compensate for the high fastball. Actually, the most important thing I learned about hitting was how to get out of the way of a pitched ball at my head. I was thrown at a lot because now that Hank

Greenberg had retired, Wally Westlake was the only guy besides me on the team who hit homers. My high school coach taught me how to turn my head away from the pitcher. Once I could do that, I had confidence. My head was safe and I didn't worry as much about the rest of my body.

FRANK THOMAS:

I spent my first year in the minors at Tallahassee in the Georgia-Florida League. My manager was Jack Rothrock, who had been an outfielder for the Cardinals' Gashouse Gang. He told me, "You can't get to the big leagues walking." So I left the dugout swinging. I led the league in RBIs and hit a few homers. My salary was $150 a month, but I made more than that hitting home runs. Every time I homered they would pass the hat around in the stands, which was a common practice in the minors at that time. I made $750 in salary and $900 in tips.

CINCINNATI REDS

EWELL BLACKWELL:

There was no money in these days. Even after my great 1947 season, I got only a small raise, up to $13,000. I asked for more, but it didn't do any good. They told me I had to have a couple of years like that to get a big raise. This disappointed me. But in those days there was no free agency, so you couldn't do anything about it.

I never feared that my sidearm delivery would hurt my arm, although various people warned me that I'd develop pain in my elbow. That didn't happen. I hurt my shoulder and it had nothing to do with my delivery. We were coming north after spring training and stopped to play an exhibition game in Columbia, South Carolina, on a cold, windy, rainy day. I was supposed to start Opening Day and they wanted me to go as far as I could. It was the wrong day to do it. Afterward my shoulder hurt, but they didn't know what was wrong with it. There was no disabled list in those days, so I stayed with the team. In fact, I pitched Opening Day. But I started only 20 games all season and completed only 4. I won only 7 games. It was a frustrating season.

What made the year tolerable was the tremendous camaraderie among the players. We always sat around and talked baseball—not the stock market. Bucky Walters, who was one of the team leaders, would talk a lot of baseball and tell us younger players stories of the past. We didn't play much cards, only on the train rides. I didn't drink and didn't see too much drinking around me. Many of us stayed out of public places. Guys didn't really go out together. On the road we ate in the hotel. In Cincinnati, I stayed in a hotel when I was single, and when I married, we rented a house outside the city. My wife went to almost all the games and sat with the wives of other players. Afterward we went home together.

Everybody got along. Outfielders Frank Baumholtz and Hank Sauer were good friends of mine, and we spent a lot of time together. Hank was wilder than me. I was glad Hank made our team because in my years in Cincinnati he was our first home run hitter. Grady Hatton, one of my roommates, was another good friend. He was a fiery guy. He wasn't very tall but he was strong. I also became close to outfielder Johnny Wyrostek, who came to the Reds from Philadelphia before the season. He was a good left-handed hitter. Ted Kluszewski, our rookie first baseman, was a big, strong Polack. He also was a kind, gentle guy.

Johnny Neun got fired in the middle of the 1948 season for the same reason Bill McKechnie was let go: we couldn't score any runs for him. Bucky Walters replaced Neun and stopped pitching. It wasn't hard to readjust to him as a manager. He was real good. But we couldn't score runs for him either.

FRANK BAUMHOLTZ:

There was an almost complete turnover in the Reds' lineup in 1948. Only third baseman Grady Hatton, catcher Ray Lamanno, and I were still starters from 1947. Our strength was our outfield. I played right and batted .296. Hank Sauer rejoined the Reds from the minors and provided us with a legitimate power hitter. Johnny Wyrostek played center field. He had decent power and hit 15 to 20 homers and drove in about 75 runs. He was a likable guy. I think he lived outside St. Louis and eventually became sheriff of his town.

Ted Kluszewski was up briefly in 1947, but didn't become our everyday first baseman until 1948. He was still a couple of years away from being a big home run hitter and had only about a dozen. He was still learning. He was a great big friendly guy. I liked him very much.

(I heard years later that he became somewhat of a loner, which is hard to believe.)

Sauer and I were roommates. He was always my best friend in baseball. Sauer, Kluszewski, pitcher Herm Wehmeier, myself, and three or four other guys were in a group that seemed to wind up together. I also got along well with Howie Fox, a big, strong, very nice right-hander who would start and relieve for the Reds into the early fifties. There were also friendships between the wives. My wife, Ewell Blackwell's wife, Bobby Adams's wife, Hank Sauer's wife, Ted Kluszewski's wife, and several other wives got to be close and sat together at ball games. As couples, we'd always have get-togethers at one of our houses.

The guys on this team were very compatible and the fans were good to me—everyone in southwestern Ohio knew me—so I liked playing for the Reds. I had a happy life.

HANK SAUER:

Warren Giles was the type of general manager who would say, "Sign this contract or stay home." I came up in 1948 after being the minors' Player of the Year and was offered essentially the same money. I was making $300 a month. The Reds were considered a cheap outfit. They got their players for nothing.

The Reds were a close-knit team. I was great friends with my roommate Frank Baumholtz and Ewell Blackwell, and our families were close. I had come up through the minors with Blackie. What a pitcher he was! Off the field he was the nicest guy in the world, but on the field he was a competitor. Everybody was intimidated by him. If you got a base hit off him, you got hit the next time up.

Blackwell was hurting in 1948, and Johnny Vander Meer became our top winner, with 17 victories. Other than Blackwell, Vander Meer and Bucky Walters were our only veteran players of star caliber, which is why we finished in a tie for last place with the Cubs. This was Johnny's last good season. Walters was also finishing his long career. When I came up to the Reds in 1941, he was the only player who treated me like one of the guys. No one else even talked to me. Bucky even bought me dinner. So I remembered that. He pitched only 7 times in 1948. About two-thirds of the way through the season, he replaced Johnny Neun as manager. But he didn't have any better luck.

We traveled only by train. Those trips took forever. The team had about three Pullmans. We drank beer, nothing else. We talked a lot of baseball, we played cards. We got to know each other.

I had a good year, playing the outfield for the first time in my career and a little at first. They wouldn't let Kluszewski hit against left-handers, so I'd take his position when southpaws pitched. I hit 35 homers and drove in 97 runs. I drove in one run in the 14th inning against the Cardinals and ended Ted Wilks's 12-game win streak and gave him his first loss in 77 games, dating back to 1945. That game was in April. I then went on to hit more homers than anyone ever had in Cincinnati.

AMERICAN LEAGUE 1948

"EVERY ONCE IN A WHILE, HE'D START TO SHAKE AND NOT BE ABLE TO CONCENTRATE. WE'D WALK TO THE MOUND, BUT WE COULDN'T SETTLE HIM DOWN. THE ATHLETICS FANS NEVER GOT ON HIM BECAUSE THEY KNEW SOMETHING MIGHT BE WRONG."

EDDIE JOOST

PHILADELPHIA ATHLETICS

EDDIE JOOST:

In 1948 I wore glasses all season and improved greatly. I hit .250, had 16 homers, scored 99 runs, walked 119 times, drove in 55 runs leading off, and again led the league's shortstops in putouts. The Athletics finished above .500 for the first time since 1933, fifteen years! We had a real chance to win the pennant. Barney McCosky, Elmer Valo, and Hank Majeski hit over .300, and Hank drove in 120 runs. Ferris Fain, Pete Suder, and I had good years. We had terrific defense and our pitching was solid: Dick Fowler won 15 games and Joe Coleman, Carl Scheib, who first pitched in the majors when he was 16, and Lou Brissie each won 14. We went into Cleveland in early September for a doubleheader and we lost two low-scoring games. It went down from there and we ended up in fourth place, 13 games behind the Indians. By this time it was apparent that Mr. Mack, who was 85, didn't manage with the same intensity that he once did.

One of our disappointments was pitcher Phil Marchildon. Like Fowler, he was a pitcher from Canada, and was friends with Fowler and McCosky. We called him "Fidgety Phil." He could never sit still or stop moving his hands. I was told he had been gassed during the war and that had changed him.

GEORGE KELL (TIGERS):

I was Marchildon's teammate in 1946. He had been an established pitcher before he went into the service. He had been confident and gung-ho on the mound. The way I heard it, and I never could get it confirmed, was that he had been a prisoner of war. All the guys told me that he became a different fellow. He could still pitch, but he had a funny look in his eye that hinted his thoughts were about the war and not baseball. He was extremely nervous.

E. JOOST:

Marchildon no longer had the composure of someone you'd think would pitch in the majors. But, my, he had good stuff. He could throw the ball as hard as anybody and had a good knuckle-curve, putting two knuckles on the ball instead of one. In 1947 he was one of the best pitchers in the league, winning 19 games. But after that he'd often get into what I called a "thinking trauma," and would wander behind the mound, fool around with the resin bag, and hit his palm with his glove for maybe thirty seconds. You'd know something was wrong. And sure enough, the next pitch was in the dirt or up in the screen—one day in Detroit, he threw one up in the stands. Every once in a while he'd start to shake and not be able to concentrate. We'd walk to the mound, but we couldn't settle him down. The Athletics fans never got on him because they knew something might be wrong. He had only 9 victories in 1948 and never won another game.

ST. LOUIS BROWNS

LES MOSS:

I expected the Browns to be even worse in 1948 because we had traded Vern Stephens, Jeff Heath, John Berardino, and Jack Kramer. But we moved from last to sixth place. That's because Bob Dillinger and Al Zarilla both hit over .320, Gerry Priddy, who we picked up from Washington, hit almost .300 and led the league's second basemen in every fielding category, and left-hander Cliff Fannin and rookie Ned Garver picked up some of the pitching slack. After Kramer left, Garver became our best pitcher. He was smart and all business on the mound, using sliders and change-ups to keep batters off stride.

I think I made my contribution to the team's improvement. I had a decent year at the plate, batting .257, with 14 homers. I was a dead pull, fastball hitter who held the bat all the way on the end. Every year I'd order about a dozen 36- or 38-ounce bats. I used a heavy bat because it lasted longer and kept me back a little in the box so I wouldn't commit too early. In those days I was one of the few players who worked with weights, having started in the service. Nothing heavy, just repetitions. I did it on my own and I think it paid off with all those homers.

Although we still won less than 60 games, the Browns' fans were great. We'd have the same ones out there every night. Of course, we had very small crowds. It wasn't easy to get people to come see a team that lost one game to the first-place Indians by the score of 26 to

3. We played 7 games in Cleveland and drew more than we did all year at home.

In St. Louis, the Browns and the Cardinals played in Sportsman's Park, and by the middle of July most of the grass was gone and it was like playing on a cement street. They couldn't keep it covered because there was a game almost every day. How Stan Musial would hit there. And Ted Williams would come in and hit about .550 every year. Williams was the best hitter in baseball. He'd hit 2 or 3 balls on the button every game. It was uncanny. When he came up, I put a sign down and hoped. The only type of pitcher who could give him any trouble was a junkball left-hander who could flop a curveball at him. Frank Biscan was the only guy on our staff who could give him trouble, and his last year was 1948. I'd try to get Williams to talk when he was at bat, but he was all business.

I always tried to talk to batters and do anything to attract their attention. I wasn't trying to be friendly. I was a tough catcher. I wasn't adverse to calling knockdown pitches. My hand would be on my thigh and I'd shoot out my thumb. I think every catcher did it that way. There was no sign to hit a batter because we didn't try to hurt anyone. The only guy pitchers wouldn't throw at was Philadelphia's Hank Majeski because he'd freeze if the ball was at his head. Majeski had been beaned and no one wanted to do it to him again. There weren't batting helmets in those days.

BOB TURLEY:

Browns chief scout Jacques Fournier had discovered me pitching in a municipal league in East St. Louis, Illinois, in 1948, and asked me and a couple of other guys to take the nickel bus ride across the river to try out at Sportsman's Park. They wanted me to sign right away, but I had to wait until the night I graduated from high school in June. They signed me for $1,200, covering June, July, and August of 1948, and gave me a $600 bonus and $200 more a month.

I played with Belleville in the Illinois State League and went 9–3. Then in 1949 I went to Aberdeen, South Dakota, in the Northern League. We played only about 100 or 110 games and I went about 25–3, struck out 200 batters, and hit over .300. I set a record no one could break: I finished every game I started and every game I relieved. At the end of the year I was called up to the

Browns. The manager, Zack Taylor, didn't seem to have any interest in me and I didn't get into a game, but it was thrilling to sit in the dugout at Sportsman's Park and be on a major league team. The Browns were a lousy club, and had been since their 1944 championship year, but I was awed by the players. As a kid, when I played everything from neighborhood pickup games to what was the equivalent of Little League, I never dreamed I'd make it to the majors.

Ned Garver was the player who impressed me most. He was a rookie but was by far the best pitcher on the team. He was friendly but not as open as some of the other players. He was a loner and didn't socialize with a lot of players, especially those who were 19 and single.

CLEVELAND INDIANS

JOHN BERARDINO:

I was going to retire to become a full-time actor rather than play with the Browns again. Then Cleveland owner Bill Veeck flew to my home in Los Angeles and offered to double my salary if I'd agree to a trade to the Indians. He wanted me to back up Joe Gordon at second and Lou Boudreau at short. That sounded good because the Indians were a legitimate pennant contender. I even got Veeck to agree to an attendance clause and that really paid off in 1948, when the Indians drew over 2.6 million fans to set an all-time record. More than 82,000 fans came to one doubleheader!

I was the rare player with an option to quit if I didn't like the deal offered me. Other players didn't have winter jobs that were so good they could afford to give up baseball, so the owners had the players strapped. But I was acting in the off-season in Los Angeles. Unfortunately, there wasn't much television at all, but I did theater at the Pasadena Playhouse and had minor roles in a few movies. It was hard to break into the movies because I was considered an athlete first. One of my first auditions was for *The Stratton Story,* starring James Stewart as Monty Stratton, the White Sox pitcher who lost his leg in a hunting accident. Sam Wood, the director, walked past a bunch of us actors who hoped to play ballplayers in the film. The son of a bitch had never heard of me and said I didn't look like a major league ballplayer!

The Indians were an entirely different team from the lowly Browns. We hit about .285 as a team. There were some excellent hitters: Boudreau hit over .350, my road roommate Joe Gordon and Ken Keltner—who were my best friends on the team—hit over 30 homers each, and we had Larry Doby, Eddie Robinson, and Dale Mitchell. Dale had over 200 hits and battled over .330.

AL KOZAR (SENATORS):

Other than Ted Williams, Dale Mitchell was my favorite left-handed hitter. I had to move in from second and stand near the pitcher when he batted because he'd lay his bat out and punch the ball by the mound. He was hard to throw out because he was fast and would already be running when he hit the ball.

J. BERARDINO:

We had a great pitching staff. That year, both Bob Lemon and rookie Gene Bearden won 20 games and Bob Feller won 19 and led the league in strikeouts.

EDDIE JOOST [ATHLETICS]:

Feller couldn't throw 100 miles per hour anymore, but he was still intimidating. Rudy York, who joined the Athletics in spring training, was a great student of pitchers and told me how to tell if Feller was going to throw his fastball or curve. Feller had a big windup, and when he dropped his right hand to swing it behind his back, his hand would be straight if he was about to throw a curve and cupped if he was going to throw the fastball. With this knowledge, I hit the hell out of Feller. He asked me why I was hitting him so good, but I wouldn't say anything. Then we played them in the final series of the year. I was licking my chops. I got up there and watched his hand. I was expecting a curveball when the hardest fastball I'd seen in my life goes whizzing by my head. I went down on the ground. He looks at me lying there and says, "We found out!" I said, "Who told you?" He said, "Never mind, but it's going to be tougher from now on."

J. BERARDINO:

We also had Steve Gromek, and Sam Zoldak came over from the Browns. Russ Christopher, who was in his last season, was an outstanding reliever. Our catcher was Jim Hegan, who was the best. He called a great game

Putting an acting career on hold, John Berardino joined owner Bill Veeck's Cleveland Indians for their pennant run in 1948.

and was the best defensive receiver in baseball. He had soft hands, which he needed for Feller and Lemon.

On this team we did a lot of singing in the shower, which we hadn't done on the Browns. Obviously that was because we were winning. We had a real nice bunch of players and the team was close and loose. We played cards in the clubhouse, there was partying, there was drinking.

Boudreau was a still a player, but he stayed clear of the partying because he also was the manager. It didn't bother me that Lou had both jobs because he had backup coaches. He always consulted Bill McKechnie, who had managed 25 years in the big leagues. McKechnie didn't get the credit, but he was always huddling and discussing strategy with Boudreau.

Bill Veeck had integrated the American League the previous July with Larry Doby. Larry didn't have much of a 1947 season in limited playing time, but he came on strong in 1948 and batted over .300. He was horribly

mistreated in Washington the first time he traveled there. I was standing beside him while the hotel management was making all kinds of overtures about him. They wouldn't let him stay, which was strange because among the hotel guests were African blacks in robes. He didn't protest, but I could tell he was embarrassed and incensed. The team should have checked out of the hotel. In other cities, except for St. Louis, he was treated better. I don't know about Cleveland because he stayed pretty much to himself and I lived in Euclid.

A year after Doby debuted, Veeck signed Satchel Paige to a major league contract and he became a 42-year-old rookie. His signing generated a lot of negative publicity and *The Sporting News* called it a publicity stunt that was bad for baseball. But Paige could still pitch and was vital to our stretch drive. He pitched great in relief and threw shutouts against the White Sox and Senators. Enormous crowds came to see him because he was a baseball legend. It was exciting to watch him. Everyone on the club welcomed him. He was a fun guy who liked to have a good time. Before the playoff game against the Red Sox, he got a bunch of us to shoot craps until the wee hours of the morning. The year before, I had gone on a barnstorming tour with Bob Feller's all-star team and we played against Satch's Negro League all-star team for a whole month. Feller and Paige were friendly competitors and would pitch against each other, about 3 innings each. They matched up pretty evenly. Satch was really something. He could put the goddamn ball anywhere he wanted.

DON NEWCOMBE (MINORS):

I was very satisfied that Satchel Paige made the majors. However, I felt sad that he didn't get the chance when he was 25 or 30. I would have loved to have seen him do to major league batters what he did to batters in the Negro Leagues.

J. BERARDINO:

This was my most exciting season in baseball. Both the Indians and Red Sox won 96 games, so we had a single-game playoff. Joe McCarthy, Boston's manager, decided to start Denny Galehouse, a veteran right-hander. I learned that Eddie Robinson, a left-handed hitter, wasn't going to start, so I went to Boudreau and suggested I play first base. But he told me he had made up his mind to play Allie Clark. I thought I deserved the shot. Clark had never played first base and I had. I had played first when Bob Lemon no-hit the Tigers in June. I was angry and told Lou so. And apparently he didn't like that.

Lemon was probably the best pitcher in the league, but Gene Bearden pitched and won the crucial playoff game in Boston, beating the Red Sox, 8–3. Boudreau hit 2 homers and went 4 for 4, and Keltner homered and drove in 3 runs. But Bearden was the star, throwing a 5-hitter against a great-hitting team with Ted Williams, who hit nearly .370 that year, Vern Stephens, Bobby Doerr, Johnny Pesky, Billy Goodman, and Dom Di-Maggio. Bearden didn't have overpowering stuff but he had a terrific knuckle curve that tied up batters. His arm gave out much sooner than he wished and he never was as good as he was as a rookie.

MINNIE MINOSO:
Bill Veeck sent a Cleveland scout to New York, and he signed José Santiago and myself at the Roosevelt Hotel. We thought we were too good to play in the minor leagues, but we agreed to go to Dayton. I was hitting .525 when Cleveland wanted to bring me up. But I asked to stay in Dayton to the end of the year rather than go up to Cleveland and warm the bench. Besides, I wanted to go back to Cuba at the end of the minor league season because I needed to play winter ball in order to make a living.

AL SMITH:
There were 6 boys and 6 girls in my family and I was the baby. I was born in Kirkwood, Missouri, in 1928. My oldest brother, Claude, was born in 1900. My father was a high school janitor, and after he died, when I was 7, my mother and siblings raised me. As a boy I sat in the bleachers and watched Terry Moore and the other Cardinals. I was big for my age and played sandlot ball with the men when I was just 12 or 13. Our team was all-black and we'd often play all-white teams.

I played baseball, softball, football; I boxed. I did everything. I was tough. I played halfback on my high school football team and was considered one of the best players in the state. Baseball was just a side thing. Recruiters from white colleges came to take a look at me, not realizing from my name, Alphonse, that I was black.

When they saw me they didn't want me. I wanted to be a football player, but in 1946 I signed to play baseball with the Cleveland Buckeyes of the Negro American League. I played with them until 1948. Meanwhile, a few Negro League players signed to play in the major leagues, including Buckeyes center fielder Sam Jethroe, who signed with the Braves. Larry Doby was already on the Cleveland Indians. And the day Satchel Paige signed with them, I also signed. Hank Greenberg was scouting pitcher Sam Jones and saw me. I was signed by Greenberg, who had just become Bill Veeck's farm director, and Laddie Placek. I think I was about the fifth black to sign with the Indians.

Satchel Paige went directly to the Indians, but I was 20 and was assigned to the Indians' Class A farm team in Wilkes-Barre, Pennsylvania, in the Eastern League. I would have gone to Double A, but they couldn't send a black to Oklahoma. I was aware of the troubles Jackie Robinson and Larry Doby were having in the major leagues because I was experiencing the same thing at Wilkes-Barre in 1948. I was the only black in the league, so it wasn't easy dealing with some of the fans, opposing players and managers, and even teammates. I'd ride the bus with the team, but when we got to the hotel I'd have to get a cab and go stay in a black hotel or black rooming house. I wasn't surprised by what I went through because I knew I had one strike against me. Fortunately, my manager, Bill Norman, was in my corner, so I didn't worry about anything, and Bill Veeck and Hank Greenberg would occasionally come down and they'd see how I was making out. The first black players felt they had something to prove. We were playing for the guys who never got the break we were getting. I wanted to prove we could, as Bill Norman used to say, ''cut the mustard.''

BOSTON RED SOX

FRANK MALZONE:
I was born in New York City in 1930, in the Clason Point section of the Bronx. My parents came from Italy. My dad worked for the water department, but it was tough to support a wife and five kids, especially for an immigrant. He never played baseball. However, my two brothers and I played in the streets, usually using a stick

or just hitting a rubber ball with our hands. Also, there were a couple of baseball diamonds in the neighborhood that the kids maintained themselves, cutting the grass and clearing the field.

When I was 15 and 16, a couple of semipro teams would invite me to play if they needed someone. We didn't get any money, but everyone would make $20 side bets, which was a lot of money. We played competitive baseball. I already was a third baseman. My high school team was very strong and played in tournaments. I also played in a couple of high school all-star games at the Polo Grounds and once hit a triple off the wall in left-center, which was a long way. I was written up in a couple of newspapers, including the *New York Herald Tribune*. The Giants talked to me, but told me to wait a year to see if I grew. I was strong but was considered small. My goal in life was to be an electrician.

Then I went to buy a pair of shoes at a sporting goods store over by Yankee Stadium. The owner was Si Phillips, a bird dog for the Boston Red Sox. He asked me if I was interested in playing professional baseball. That's the first time I had an inkling that I was good enough. Si thought I should sign right away so I'd be ready for spring training. So he brought an official Red Sox scout—I think it was Frank McGowan—over to my house to meet me and my father. I heard, "This is what we're going to pay you, sign your contract, here's a train ticket to Florida," and my dad was tickled pink.

I graduated from high school in January 1948. And in March, not long after my 18th birthday, I went to the Red Sox minor league spring training and then played for Milford, Delaware, in Class D for $150 a month. The Red Sox made no projections for me. I was supposed to be a professional ballplayer, not specifically a major leaguer. It would be seven years before I went to the Red Sox major league camp.

WASHINGTON SENATORS

AL KOZAR:

I went to the Senators' spring training camp at Tinker Field in Orlando. I was very happy to be in the majors finally and knew I had the team made. I was considered a hot prospect and was hit by sportswriters left and right. And I couldn't handle it. I was known as "Mum-

bles" because I was so shy. I didn't like Shirley Povich of *The Washington Post*. He was all over me, trying to get a story. He asked me, "You're going to show them how to play ball, aren't you?" I said, "No, I'm not. I'm just trying to make the team." He said, "Your trouble is that you don't have any confidence." I said, "I have confidence. But I'm just a minor leaguer." He kept knocking me down and trying to put me in a hole, hoping I'd say something brash. So I wouldn't tell him anything. I wasn't even in uniform yet, because it was raining, when Povich's story came out on me. It was Shirley Povich interviewing Shirley Povich, saying how he couldn't get nothing out of this rookie prospect. He said, "Washington expects a man in Kozar and gets a boy." I cut that out and put it in my scrapbook and wrote in ink, "This guy is full of shit." Povich stated that the best I'd do with Washington was hit .250. Being quiet ruined me. I felt Povich was my enemy and it hurt me. Arch McDonald, a big guy who was an announcer for the

Senators rookie Al Kozar was one of the most promising second basemen in baseball in 1948, but then fought losing battles to injuries and managers.

Senators, asked me to do him a favor and say good morning to Povich the next time I saw him. I said, "What for?" He told me that Shirley would bury me and run me out of the league if I didn't talk to him. I said, "Arch, I played a lot of years in the minors and I went through World War II. If I go down, it will be because I'm not doing my job."

Just like Povich predicted, I hit .250, right on the nose, and I could have killed myself for that. But I had the most hits on the team and tied Phil Rizzuto with the most games played in the American League. I even made *The Sporting News'* All-Rookie team. Later on, Shirley wrote me up in *The Sporting News* in halfway decent terms.

But it wasn't a good season for me or anyone else on the team. At first I was batting second and hitting the ball pretty good, but I was getting my fingers ripped open by double plays and my throws were sailing off. I was hit so hard by slides that two nails tore off. I finally got racked up at Yankee Stadium and had to wear aluminum caps taped on my fingers for two weeks. But they wanted me to play and my average and defense suffered. When I'd hit or field, my fingers would sting.

I played, but it didn't matter how I did. If an individual did anything good, it didn't matter because we still lost. Our team was so bad. We won only 56 games and finished seventh. Our first baseman Mickey Vernon, our only polished regular, had led the league with a .353 average just two years before, but he hit only .242 because he got nothing good to hit. Our third baseman Eddie Yost was a good kid but he had only a so-so year—he had trouble reaching the seats in Griffith Stadium. Early Wynn was our best pitcher and had tremendous talent, but on this team he won 8 and lost 19 and was traded to the Indians at the end of the season. Only Ray Scarborough did well, winning 15 games.

Most of the players laughed in the clubhouse after a loss, but the constant losing depressed me. I would have preferred being on a winning team in the minors. I couldn't understand why our rookie manager, Joe Kuhel, wouldn't get more upset. I'd played for minor league managers who tore up the place if we lost. He was quoted as saying, "I can't make chicken salad out of chicken shit." That summed it all up. Clyde Milan, an old-time coach who'd take the lineup out every day, saw me sulking in front of my locker and told me,

"You're a hell of a ballplayer, but you're down all the time. Just play for yourself and hope you get traded." It was now a job and the sportswriters were on us. And the Washington fans liked any visiting team more than us, because most of them were out-of-towners. They weren't against us; they just weren't for us. If we'd have won more, they would have supported us.

In addition to my troubles on the field, I couldn't handle being a celebrity. I wasn't good at banquets, giving speeches. Yost and I had to go to an annual luncheon at the Shoreham Hotel. I hated that and we didn't even get money. I had to make a speech and couldn't say nothing. I discovered it was easier for me to answer questions than make speeches. So from then on, Kuhel would ask me questions at banquets. But I still hated it. I remember posing for baseball cards, and once for a keychain, for small amounts of money. I didn't want to do that either. I couldn't stand when I had to appear on television in Washington, before or after games. I'd get red in the face and sweat. I often didn't show up at the station. I'd be outside sweating and couldn't do it. I felt so stupid. I wanted to be left alone and just play.

My troubles with Joe Kuhel began with my troubles with Bill McGowan, the veteran umpire. We were playing in Washington and the Browns' Pete Layden took off from second after a fly to center. I thought he'd left too early, so I tagged second and looked at McGowan. He said, "Safe." I said okay and returned the ball to the pitcher. I was never told off so bad in all my life. McGowan said that if I didn't like his call, he would send me back to the minors. He kept screaming at me, calling me rookie and cursing. I told him that I hadn't complained, yet he wouldn't let up on me. He looked up in the stands and said, "Do you think you're going to get those people on me? I'll rub your ass in your nose." I'd walk away and he'd follow me. Finally he quit. But the next inning he started on me again, cursing at me and spitting on me. Here comes Joe Kuhel. He said to me, "Christ, you never say anything. Why don't you leave this guy alone? He's been in the big leagues for 30 years." I said, "Joe, I'm not arguing." I didn't argue with anybody. After that game we went into Chicago and we're getting beaten again. During a pitching change, I was talking to the reliever Forrest Thompson, when all of a sudden I was pushed in the back. It was Bill McGowan again, cursing me and demanding the ball because I was holding up the game. Here comes Joe Kuhel. Kuhel says, ''If you say one more word to McGowan, I'm taking you out of the game.'' He wouldn't listen to me. McGowan kept it up. He was talking to himself and swearing. I saw that he was sick and figured he was having a nervous breakdown. Near the end of the season we played Cleveland in a seesaw battle. I went into the dugout at the end of an inning and wondered where everyone was. It turned out that McGowan, as the home plate umpire, had thrown out Kuhel, the coaches, and a rookie for jockeying him. I think he threw his ball-and-strike indicator at someone at some point. Later he threw out Eddie Stewart for protesting a play at the plate. After the game, everyone in our clubhouse had a pad and pencil and they were calling for ''Kozar!'' They wanted me to write him up in their report to the commissioner. I told Kuhel, ''You didn't want to listen to me before. You wouldn't believe me. I had no beef with that guy tonight.'' I wouldn't write down anything, despite Kuhel and the coaches coming down on me. They got McGowan suspended without my help.

DETROIT TIGERS

GEORGE KELL:

Most teams got into a few fights each year, and we had our share. The worst brawl took place in Boston. Tigers rookie George Vico, who was a 6'4" left-handed first baseman, got into it with veteran catcher Birdie Tebbetts, whom we had traded to Boston during the 1947 season. They were both thrown out of the game. In Fenway Park, all players would exit by going through the Red Sox dugout and through the one runway. Birdie waited in the tunnel for Vico and they resumed their fight. Both teams emptied in there and started brawling. It was just like a fire down there.

This was the first year in which I suffered injuries that sidelined me. Both times Yankees were the culprits. In the first case, Vic Raschi fractured my wrist with a pitch. The second time, we had a one-run lead in the eighth with Fred Hutchinson pitching. Joe DiMaggio was the batter, with the bases loaded. I moved in a little, thinking of my options if he hit the ball slowly, hard, or close to third. Joe hit an in-between hop and I went

NATIONAL BASEBALL LIBRARY, COOPERSTOWN, N.Y.

The best of the players who developed in the war years, Tigers third baseman George Kell actually hit better after the veterans returned, batting over .300 nine times in what would be a Hall of Fame career.

down to block it. I saw it hit something and fly up and I just turned my head. It hit me on the side of the jaw. I picked up the ball and stepped on third and intended to throw to first. But I just collapsed. They said I never lost consciousness, but I blanked out until I was lying on the trainer's table having ice packs applied to my face. Steve O'Neill told me later that they had to pry the ball out of my hand. DiMaggio had broken my jaw with his blue goose. I told Hutchinson, ''You're going to get people killed with the stuff you're throwing.''

I missed over 60 games during the year. But I still hit over .300 again. Hoot Evers was our hitting star, with an average of over .300 and over 100 RBIs, and Hal Newhouser led the league with 21 wins. But overall it was a bad year for the Tigers, as we slid into fifth place. Still, one of the things I really enjoyed was playing with our three hard-throwing young pitchers, Art Houtteman, Ted Gray, and Billy Pierce. They were all from Detroit and were inseparable friends. They called me ''Cap'n.'' I was a deadly fastball hitter, and they'd often challenge me to hit balls to certain areas of the field, and I'd do it for them. I was impressed by them as well. I thought Houtteman would be the best of the three. He had gone 7–2 in 1947 when he was just 20. Ted Gray was a left-hander. He was somewhat wild, but he might have been better than either Houtteman or Pierce if he had their desire. But he never would be more than a 10-game winner. (He had other interests—he went on to become a rich businessman.)

Pierce was the smartest of the three. Even at an early age, he realized that you don't throw certain batters certain pitches in certain situations. Unlike Houtteman, he realized that it was all right to walk a batter in a crucial situation if you had a better chance to get the next guy out. The Tigers should never have traded him.

BILLY PIERCE:

I had been optioned to the minors three times by 1948, so the Tigers were forced to keep me on their roster. I went 3–0 in the first 3 decisions of my career, but I started only 5 games and pitched only 55 innings all year. I wasn't surprised by how little I was used because Steve O'Neill had been my manager in 1945. That year I didn't pitch for six weeks until I debuted in Boston, when Red Sox had the bases loaded in about the third or fourth inning. O'Neill brought me in to face Boo Ferris, who was a right-handed pitcher but batted left-handed. It went to 3–2 on Ferris and I walked him. Then I pitched 4 shutout innings. We lost 4–3. I came back to the hotel that night and O'Neill told me, ''You did great. I'm really proud of you.'' Six weeks later I was demoted to Buffalo, having never pitched another inning. I wonder what would have happened if he hadn't been proud of me.

With so much free time, I was able to watch the veteran pitchers to see what made them successful. Hal Newhouser and Dizzy Trout had been the big guns for a while, going back to the war years. Newhouser was also a left-hander, so I was interested in how he went after batters. He had a good fastball and slider and a great curveball. He was still a terrific pitcher.

LES MOSS (BROWNS):

Hal Newhouser had won the MVP award twice during the war for winning about 25 games a season. I think he was just as strong after the war, and was still the toughest left-hander in the league. He could change speeds real good, had good control, and had a hard curve ball. I wasn't a great hitter to begin with, so I was pretty much overmatched against him. If he didn't strike me out, I'd hit the weakest ground balls and little pop-ups.

AL KOZAR (SENATORS):

Virgil Trucks and Dazzy Vance got me out by throwing the ball on my hands, but everyone called Hal Newhouser my ''cousin.'' Joe Kuhel would move me up in the order when he pitched. He'd try to throw a high fastball by me on the outside corner, but I'd just go the other way with it. He'd get so mad that his face turned beet-red. He later tried to pull the string on me, changing up. But I adapted.

B. PIERCE:

Trout was a fastball-slider pitcher. Virgil Trucks threw a hard fastball and hard slider. He worked hard, doing a lot of running. Watching him was instructional because he was an aggressive pitcher. When he got two strikes on a batter, he didn't try to finesse the corners but attacked him. He struck out a lot of batters. Newhouser, Trout, and Trucks were power pitchers, but Fred Hutchinson was different. He didn't have a fastball. He had a deceptively quick motion and threw a lot of change-ups. He could get a strike on you before you turned around.

They still had the veteran pitchers, but they also had Teddy Gray, Art Houtteman, and me breaking in. We were the youngest players on the team and all came from Detroit. So we hung out together.

Teddy was left-handed, like me. He also went to Highland Park High, but was about two and a half years ahead of me. He went into the navy and got out in 1946. He pitched 2 or 3 games for them that year, but 1948 was his rookie season. He didn't pitch much more than I did, but he did pretty well, winning 6 out of 8 decisions. Art was a right-hander with great potential. He'd done well in 1947, so he got a lot of work in 1948, starting and relieving. But he went just 2–16.

Although I left the Tigers at the end of the season, the three of us would stay in touch over the years because I continued to live in Detroit. Art, Ted, and I would get together with Leon Hart of the Detroit Lions and Marty Pavelich and Ted Lindsay of the Red Wings.

Our wives were all friends, too. Ted would win 10 games in each of the next two seasons but would develop arm problems and never became a big winner. However, Art would win 15 games in 1949 and 19 games in 1950. (Art would have two unhappy situations. He would fracture his skull in a car accident and miss the entire 1951 season. And he would lose his baby daughter in an automobile accident involving his wife and mother. It would be a very, very tough time for him. He would lose 20 games in 1952, and the next year be traded to Cleveland, where he would revive his career.)

The Tigers were a fairly loose team. Dick Wakefield was a real loose guy, Evers was more of a bear-down guy, Vic Wertz was kind of in between. George Kell was a good ballplayer and the infield leader. There weren't too many rah-rah types. I was very quiet in those days. I talked more as my career progressed.

In November, I went over to my fiancée's house. We turned on the radio and I learned from a disk jockey that I had been traded to the White Sox. I was traded for Aaron Robinson and 10 grand because the Tigers wanted a left-handed-hitting catcher who could take advantage of the short porch in right field. The Tigers wanted to give the Sox Ted Gray instead of me, but Chicago wouldn't go for it. The Tigers thought they were strong on the mound, but in 1949 Trout would have arm problems. It was a bad shock to be traded from Detroit.

CHICAGO WHITE SOX

GUS ZERNIAL:

I went to spring training in Pasadena with the White Sox. They had good players like shortstop Luke Appling, second baseman Cass Michaels, and outfielder Dave Philley. Ted Lyons was the manager. I did well and he told me I made the team. Then I stepped on a ball and tore my thigh all to pieces. So Lyons told me that the Sox weren't going to take me back to Chicago, but would leave me with the Hollywood Stars again with the intention of bringing me up when I healed. I didn't want to come up in mid-season, so I said, "If you send me to Hollywood, I want to stay all season." They honored my decision.

I hobbled into the clubhouse with Hollywood, and Jimmy Dykes, who had taken over as manager at the

end of 1947, was aghast: "What are you doing here? Can you play?" I said, "Jim, I can't run for the ball, but I can still hit." I opened the season with Hollywood. On opening night, I hit 2 homers. I went to bat officially 737 times in a 189-game season. I led the league with 237 hits, including 40 homers and 50 doubles, and drove in 159 runs. That was my biggest year in baseball. At that point I had no doubt that I could play in the majors.

Around then I got my nickname, "Ozark Ike," from former major league infielder Fred Haney, who would broadcast Hollywood Stars games until he would become their manager in 1949. He named me after a comic strip character. I liked it.

BILL WILSON:

I was born in 1928 in Central City, Nebraska. My dad was a mechanic, and during the Depression, his customers would pay him in trade with beef, pork, chickens. . . . He used to play semipro ball and had caught Grover Cleveland Alexander at St. Paul, Nebraska. So I loved baseball because of him. When I was 12, my family moved to Long Beach, California, and I played sports all year round. In my senior year of high school, I was an end on the football team and played shortstop and outfield on the baseball team, where I developed into a power hitter. I received scholarship offers from USC and Notre Dame to play football, but my first choice was baseball, specifically the Pacific Coast League. I used to love to see the Los Angeles Angels and Hollywood Stars. I wanted to be a major leaguer, too, but I read an article that said only one kid in several thousand made it. So I signed with Sacramento in the Coast League for about the same money a major league team would have offered. We agreed that if Sacramento later sold me to a major league club I would get 10 percent of the purchase price.

After a year with Wenatchee, Washington, in Class B, I played with Sacramento in 1948. I was a young, fast center fielder playing between a right fielder who was 38 and a left fielder who was 36, and all I could hear all year was "It's all yours!" Both the White Sox and Red Sox were interested in purchasing my contract after watching me for about a week. I'd go to a movie and see their scouts sitting behind me because they were following me around. They thought I was a good prospect because I had youth, speed, power, and size—I was 6'3" and 190 pounds. Finally Frank Lane came out to the coast and bought my contract for $100,000, of which I got $10,000.

Lane didn't promise me anything about playing with the White Sox, but he gave me a $5,000 major league contract. He was okay at that point, but later on, when we negotiated contracts each year, he was like any other general manager, who remembered only what you did bad.

NEW YORK YANKEES

BILLY JOHNSON:

We won 94 games but finished third behind Cleveland and Boston, who tied for first. Bucky Harris got fired after the season because we didn't win, but it wasn't his fault. Other than DiMaggio—who led the league with about 40 homers and over 150 RBIs—Henrich, and a few other hitters, and pitchers Allie Reynolds, Vic Raschi, and Eddie Lopat, most of the players had off-years. Too many guys played lousy.

I hit .294, which was a career high, and had 12 homers. I was a curveball hitter who stood even with the plate. When I first came up in 1943, I hit everything to left, but Joe McCarthy told me that if I wanted to stay in the majors I would have to hit to all fields. So I learned to hit to right. I got my share of doubles and triples, but I would have hit a lot more homers if I didn't play in Yankee Stadium, where the left-field fence was so deep. I had power, which was why my teammates nicknamed me "Bull," but I hit many balls against the wall that would have been homers in other parks. It's amazing DiMaggio won homer titles playing half his games there.

We had a pitching staff as good as any in the league, including those in Cleveland and Detroit. Lopat, Raschi, who came into his own in 1948, and Reynolds could be counted on to win between 16 and 20 games each year. Tommy Byrne also was very effective. Like Reynolds and Raschi, he was a power pitcher, but he came from the left side and was very wild, so left-handed batters had a hard time not bailing out.

We had just acquired Lopat from the White Sox. He

was a finesse pitcher. He would wind up real hard and then throw the ball 6 miles an hour over the plate. He had a very good change-up and got by with a lot of junk.

EDDIE JOOST (ATHLETICS):

What a rotation the Yankees had! Holy mackerel! Eddie Lopat had great motion and control. He also cheated like hell. He'd throw spitters. He'd throw everything up there but the glove. Vic Raschi had a good fastball and he'd pound the ball on the inside, knocking you down. He was the first pitcher I saw who had a quick slider that would move away from right-handed hitters. And he threw a heavy ball and when you hit it you'd feel it clear up to your shoulder. Raschi was a good pitcher. Reynolds was one of the best. He had a great fastball and great curveball and he'd give you nine innings without losing anything. He would knock you down. One Opening Day in Yankee Stadium, Reynolds was on the mound warming up. I'm standing near home plate chatting with Berra. All of a sudden Berra yells, "Look out!" Down I went as the pitch whizzed by me. I looked out at Reynolds for an explanation. He said, "You don't belong there. The game hasn't started." Berra said, "He's tough. He meant it."

B. JOHNSON:

Byrne, Lopat, and Reynolds were serious about batting practice. In fact, they had competition to see who was the best hitter. I don't think there was any doubt it was Byrne. He hit about .325 that year and was used as a pinch hitter. He could hit the long ball.

Just as our pitchers kept track of all the hitters in the league, many of the Yankee batters kept a record of opposing pitchers so we knew what they'd throw if they got ahead or if they were in the hole. I also learned where batters hit the ball so I'd know where to play them in different situations.

I got to know almost everyone in the American League just chatting with them prior to games or when they were on third base. George Kell became one of my best friends in baseball. We talked on the field prior to Yankees-Tigers games and whenever one of us reached third. We used the same size bats and during the season we would trade bats and use them.

GENE WOODLING:

I played just a little with the Pirates in 1947. Then I went to Newark. That was the Yankees Triple-A team, but I didn't belong to the Yankee organization. At the end of the year the manager, Bill Skiff, told the Yankees they'd better sign me. They didn't and let me go to the San Francisco Seals in the Coast League. I played for Lefty O'Doul, who taught me more than anyone else ever did. He saw that I was a major league hitter but realized he had to change my style so major league teams would be interested in me. When I first started I had a straight-up stance, but since teams didn't like that I hit in the high .300s, I switched to a crouch and moved on top of the plate so I could hit 100 points lower. Still, I led the Coast League in batting in 1948 and was Minor League Player of the Year. Then the Yankees paid a bundle of money plus players for my contract. They could have had me for nothing a year earlier.

WORLD SERIES

1948

INDIANS

VS

BRAVES

JOHN BERARDINO · INDIANS:

I didn't get to play in the World Series against the Boston Braves. It was Lou Boudreau's decision. We didn't get along after I questioned him for not starting me at first base over Allie Clark in the playoff game. Naturally, I was annoyed because there were occasions I thought Boudreau could have played me. But I could still root for the team. It was a very well played Series with great pitching on both teams. Feller was beaten 1–0 in a tremendous pitching duel with Johnny Sain in the opener, but then Lemon beat Spahn, Bearden pitched a shutout, and Gromek outpitched Sain. We lost Game Five, but took the Series in Game Six, 4–3, behind Lemon and Bearden.

JOHNNY SAIN · BRAVES:

When the Indians played the Red Sox in the one-game playoff to determine the American League champion, I went over to Fenway Park to familiarize myself with the players on both teams. I stayed about 6 innings. It would have been nice to have had an all-Boston Series, but I felt I'd have better success against Cleveland because I'd pitched against them more in spring training. I also liked Municipal Stadium more than Fenway Park. So I wasn't upset that Cleveland won.

Cleveland outsmarted the Braves' front office people by talking them into saving money by not having an off-day. They didn't realize that Cleveland was deeper in pitching. Cleveland also had field glasses in the scoreboard and a buzzer on the bench so that they could call our pitches. That didn't hurt me because I always used the switch. I'd do things like drop the resin bag as a sign to the catcher for what I'd pitch. I might stand on the mound, and if I showed the face of my glove I'd throw the opposite of what was called for.

The Braves hadn't played in a World Series in 34 years, and it had been 28 years for Cleveland. The Indians were an outstanding team and we were supposedly the underdog. It was important not to fall behind. I hooked up against Bob Feller in the opening game in Boston. I gave up 4 hits but no walks, while Feller gave up only 2 hits but walked 3. His second walk came to our catcher, Bill Salkeld, leading off the eighth. Phil Masi pinch-ran and moved to second on a sacrifice bunt. Then Feller and Boudreau, the shortstop, worked a timed pickoff play at second to perfection. I was afraid Masi would be called out, but umpire Bill Stewart said he got back to second ahead of the tag. Feller then intentionally walked Eddie Stanky to get to me—later, he told me that he would rather have pitched to Stanky. However, I lined to Walt Judnich in right for our second out. Then Tommy Holmes hit a dying quail to left that scored Masi for a 1–0 lead. In the last of the ninth, Ken Keltner hit a slow grounder toward third that Elliott threw 10 feet over the first baseman's head. Keltner went to second. Now I was in the same position Feller had been in in the eighth. The batter was Judnich, who was a powerful left-handed hitter. There was a chance he would homer over the right-field fence, just 315 feet away, and the next day we would have to read about Elliott's error instead of the umpire's safe call on Masi. But I struck out Judnich looking with a sidearm curve that broke 2 feet. After the Dodgers' Pete Reiser beat me on that pitch on Opening Day, Southworth told me not to use it anymore against left-handed hitters. But I used it against Judnich. That gave us a 1–0 victory in 1 hour and 42 minutes.

I was happy I did so well because this was the first time I experienced much media coverage. The radio announcers were Mel Allen, the Yankees' broadcaster, and Jim Britt, the broadcaster for the Braves. Joe DiMaggio advertised Blue Blades. Tris Speaker was writing about the Series in the newspaper and he compared me to Christy Mathewson, saying we both used fastballs to set up our other pitches. I was extremely flattered.

Bob Lemon beat us 4–1 in the second game, besting Spahn. Then, in Cleveland, Gene Bearden shut us out on 5 hits, 2–0, although Vern Bickford, Bill Voiselle, and Red Barrett gave up only 5 hits themselves.

I pitched again in Game Four in front of almost 82,000 Cleveland fans, a World Series attendance record. I gave up a run in the first inning when Dale Mitchell, who was an excellent hitter, singled leading

off and Boudreau knocked him in with a double down the right-field line that he tried to stretch into a triple. In the third, Larry Doby tagged me for a solo homer off a straight change. He told me later that he wasn't told which pitch was coming. I shut them out the rest of the way on just 1 more hit, for a total of 5 hits. We got 7 hits off Steve Gromek, but Marv Rickert's solo homer in the seventh was our only run. Gromek was a short-armed-type pitcher who you'd run up to hit against and he'd get you out. We lost 2–1, falling behind 3–1 in the Series. I think if we'd beaten Gromek we would have won the Series. Then Southworth could have held Spahn to start in the sixth game, instead of having him relieve in the fifth and sixth games because we couldn't lose another game.

We busted loose against Feller in the fifth game, 11–5, with Bob Elliott smashing two homers off him. Spahn was the winning pitcher in relief of Nelson Potter. But, with Voiselle and Spahn pitching, we fell short against Lemon and Bearden in the sixth game, 4–3, and lost the Series 4 games to 2. I was ready to pitch the seventh game with two days' rest.

We weren't that upset to have lost. Winning is great, but it was such a thrill to have played in a World Series. As much as anything, I enjoyed my mother and dad being there. My parents were the greatest people in the world and followed my career the best they could down in Arkansas. My mother listened to whatever games she could find on the radio just so she could pick up the scores of Braves' games. I offered them enough money to travel to the Series but let them know they could just keep it and not come because the money was that important to them. I had an uncle who played baseball in the Cotton States League, and he drove them to Boston to watch me pitch the first game of the Series and then drove them to Cleveland and saw me pitch the fourth game. Their presence made it so much more gratifying.

NATIONAL LEAGUE

1949

"WILLIE ALWAYS BROUGHT BINOCULARS ON ROAD TRIPS SO WE COULD SCOUT FOR WOMEN. WE WERE SURVEYING THE WINDOWS IN THE HOTEL WHEN EDDIE WAS SHOT. WHEN WE WENT DOWN TO THE LOBBY AND FOUND OUT WHAT HAD HAPPENED WE COULDN'T UNDERSTAND HOW WE MISSED IT."

DEL ENNIS

BOSTON BRAVES

JOHNNY SAIN:

My arm had felt fine in the World Series despite my pitching with just two days' rest late in the season. However, in the spring my shoulder hurt and I couldn't put anything extra on the ball. I didn't tell anybody because I didn't want them holding me back. I was either going to throw my arm back to where it was or throw it out for good. I struggled through the year, winning just 10 of 27 decisions. And my strikeout dropped dramatically. The sportswriters thought I was experimenting with different motions, but I was just trying to maneuver my arm so it wouldn't hurt. Even Grantland Rice wrote an article about how I was lying down on Southworth and not giving my all.

I pitched over 240 innings despite the pain, but with my wins down, the other pitchers had to pick up for me. Spahn pitched over 300 innings and won 21 games, to lead the league, and Vern Bickford won 16 games, but no one else won more than 7. Also, our offense wasn't nearly as productive as it had been. Where we had five .300 hitters in our title year, we had none this year and Elliott's 76 RBIs was enough to lead the team. We fell to fourth place behind the Dodgers, Cardinals, and improving Phillies, and were 4 games under .500.

We couldn't match the Dodgers, who got even stronger by adding pitcher Don Newcombe and moving Duke Snider into the starting lineup. The Dodgers had mostly right-handed hitters, so teams would throw right-handers against them, which made it easier for Snider, their one left-handed power hitter. Snider hit me the best on that team. Gene Hermanski, another lefty, didn't play often, but he played too much against me because I couldn't get that son of a gun out.

One reason our team faltered so badly is that some of the guys didn't like Billy Southworth's heavy drinking. Guys like Eddie Stanky and Alvin Dark wanted out of Boston because of Billy. In August, Lou Perini convinced him to take a leave of absence because of all the discontent in the clubhouse. Our coach Johnny Cooney took over, and we played a bit better. Southworth's drinking usually didn't bother me, but once in 1949 when he was loaded, I heard him say, "We didn't have a good ballclub in 1948. They didn't win the pennant. *I* won it.'' That just chilled me.

JOHNNY ANTONELLI:

Del Crandall was also 19 when he arrived in 1949 to catch for the Braves. When he told me that the team hadn't gotten him a room, I invited him to come stay with me. I lived close to the ballpark in a rooming house run by a nice lady, and I had a large room with two double beds. Del became my best friend on the team. We were called the "Milk Shake Twins" because we drank milk shakes and the other players drank what they wanted. I believed that an athlete shouldn't ever smoke or drink. That was the rule I lived by. However, it didn't bother me that my teammates smoked, drank, and chewed tobacco. Those men Del and I played with seemed older. *Much* older. We didn't try to fit in with them, but let them travel in their own circles. We went to movies and to soda fountains.

Del was a leader as a rookie. He'd wake up the senior citizens by firing the ball around the infield. He liked to hear chatter around the diamond when he was catching, and one day he gunned the ball down to third, saying, "Come on, Elliott, wake up!" Elliott was a seasoned player and warned, "Don't do that again, kid!" But he would—that's the way Del would be his entire career.

Del and I established the record for being the youngest battery in a game against the Cubs in Boston. Dutch Leonard pitched against us. He was 42, older than our combined age of 38. I beat him 2–0. The next time Billy Southworth let me touch the ball, even in relief, was six weeks later. What kind of judgment was that on the part of a seasoned manager? Southworth was protecting his job.

CHICAGO CUBS

RUBE WALKER:

I didn't speak to P. K. Wrigley when I signed with the Cubs the previous year. But I saw him on Catalina, where we trained for a week to ten days during spring training. He was very nice. I also liked Charlie Grimm. Despite our poor record, he was an excellent manager.

He was in his fifties and liked to teach us young players. We were taught "Cubs baseball." I suppose it wasn't any different from what was taught by other organizations, but Charlie might have phrased things differently.

I roomed with Bob Scheffing, who took me under his wing in spring training. He took it on himself to tutor me about how to work a pitcher. He told me to find out his best pitch and how to determine whether it was working that day. I'd sit with the pitchers on the bench. I learned the most working with our ace, Johnny Schmitz. He was an excellent pitcher.

Schmitz led our team in victories again, although his total dropped from 18 to 11. Bob Rush won 10 games in his second year and did a good job despite losing 18. 10–18 on the Cubs was a good record. Because Eddie Waitkus and Swish Nicholson had been traded, our only offense came from Andy Pafko, who also played an excellent center field, and our new left fielder, Hank Sauer, who led our team in batting, homers, and RBIs.

After a game, Scheffing—who liked good food— would want to go to a good restaurant. So in Chicago, several of us might go to the Columbia Restaurant, which was a steak house. Scheffing liked his steaks, but most of us ate hamburgers. Everybody on this team was very friendly and hung out together. I was lucky that Bob and the majority of players were married, so there wasn't much partygoing. The Cubs were strict. They would do bed checks and they'd sit in the lobby and make sure no one snuck in after curfew. I was never fined for breaking curfew. In fact, I'd want to get up early and go to church when it was possible. The Catholics in particular went to church. They had to find out what time mass was in cities we'd visit.

The leaders on the team were Scheffing and Phil Cavarretta. The Cubs had sent Waitkus to Philadelphia, so Phil now shared first base with Herm Reich—Reich played one year in the majors, did a good job, and, for some reason, that was it. Phil spent time with the kids: me, Rush, and outfielder Hal Jeffcoat. We young guys kept quiet at clubhouse meetings and didn't complain about being on a last-place club. We understood there was rebuilding going on. But I know some of the veteran Cubs got depressed because of the continuous losing and the realization that we couldn't be contenders for years, even after picking up a good power hitter like

Sauer. But guys like Pafko never showed anger. Cavarretta or Scheffing might say something to me every once in a while, but they were never critical of the team.

But I guess Wrigley wasn't happy with how the team was performing because about a third of the way through the season, he fired Grimm and replaced him with Frankie Frisch, the old "Fordham Flash." I loved being around Frisch because I was interested in baseball history and the Gashouse Gang, and he loved to talk about such things. But Frisch wasn't a popular choice among the players.

FRANK BAUMHOLTZ:

Unfortunately, when I came to the Cubs and played for Frankie Frisch, I ran into the same situation I had at Cincinnati. Frisch was a very strange person. He always spoke of his past and how "the Old Flash did this" and "the Old Flash did that." I made some kind of remark about "the Old Flash" and I think he might have overheard me. Because he didn't like me and didn't play me.

HANK SAUER:

When Frank Baumholtz and I came to Chicago after being traded for Harry Walker and Peanuts Lowrey, Frisch told me, "Hank, we brought you here for just one reason: to hit homers and drive in runs." And I did exactly what he wanted. In my first month there I hit 11 homers. I hit 27 homers and drove in 83 runs from mid-June on, giving me 31 homers and 99 RBIs for the season, and my average went up from .260 to .275.

Frisch ddn't get along with a lot of players, but we got along well because I gave him what he wanted. We had a last-place ballclub and he said, "I've got one ballplayer on this team and the rest are minor leaguers." I didn't approve of that, since we had Andy Pafko, Phil Cavarretta, Hal Jeffcoat, Frank Baumholtz, Johnny Schmitz, Bob Rush, and some other very good players. But I was the only guy who would argue with Frisch, and he liked that. He didn't like guys who shied away from him. Of course, I was already 32 and had the nerve to stand up to him. He was tough on young kids, and they couldn't handle when he cut them up. But as far as I was concerned, he was a hell of a guy.

Cavarretta was the only leader among the players. He was a veteran, so he had no problem with Frisch and paid no attention to his insults of the entire team. I don't

Acquired during the season from the Reds, Hank Sauer became instantly popular with Chicago Cubs fans by having his second of five consecutive 30-homer seasons.

know how Andy Pafko felt. Andy had been with the Cubs since 1943 and had become a star when he led the team to the title in 1945. He was too quiet to be a leader, but he was extremely popular with his teammates and adored by the fans. He was a nice, handsome guy, one of the Polacks of Chicago. I wasn't a leader type and I didn't want to get into that role. I didn't want to be accused of popping off because I considered myself a star.

RANDY JACKSON:

After the Cubs left spring training to go back to Chicago, I was left with the Los Angeles Angels. I played about 20 games with the Angels and was hitting just below .320, but for some reason I was sent to Double A, to play with Oklahoma City in the Texas League. They were owned by the Cleveland Indians. Back then several organizations had players playing for teams owned by other organizations. It didn't bother me because it was nice to play near Texas. Oklahoma City was a fun town. We had a powerhouse, with three guys who knocked in over 100 runs. So I enjoyed another year of just playing baseball. At the end of my two-year contract with the Cubs, I was confident that I had major league talent. I had made the All-Star team in both leagues, so I didn't think Chicago would get rid of me.

BROOKLYN DODGERS

SPIDER JORGENSEN:

I returned to the Dodgers in 1949 and spent the whole year with them. I played part-time, giving Cox an occasional rest at third. I hit .269 in 134 at-bats.

I think this was the year that the Dodgers really came into their own. Pee Wee Reese was named our captain and had a great season. He scored over 130 runs. Gil Hodges became a star, hitting over 20 homers and driving in well over 100 runs. Duke Snider became our regular center fielder. He batted over .290, with over 20 homers and 90 RBIs, and showed he could cover as much ground as Pete Reiser had. With Snider in center, Furillo moved over to right field, which was a much better position for him because of his tremendous throwing arm. He also hit around .320. We had traded Reiser to the Braves in December, and when we learned one day that he was lying on the training table with a hurt leg, Bruce Edwards and I went over and jokingly administered the last rites to him.

We had three great black players that year. Robinson led the league by hitting about .340, drove in about 125 runs, and was voted the league's Most Valuable Player. Roy Campanella hit over 20 homers and did a great job behind the plate. And Don Newcombe came onto a team with great pitching and immediately became our ace. I think the three were different types. Robinson was the most outgoing and outspoken. He was a public figure. (I know he testified against Paul Robeson that year—but I didn't know what that was about.) Campanella was more conservative and stayed to himself. He wasn't as intense. Newcombe was still a rookie and not that secure yet, but he became more outspoken as the year progressed. He apparently did some drinking,

but I was unaware of that. All I could see was talent. He led our team in wins and was the Rookie of the Year. He was 6′4″ and weighed about 240 pounds and was a big monster out there. He could muscle up and throw the ball right by batters. His ball always sank. He didn't have much of a curve, but his nickel slider was effective because it would break at about the same time as his sinker but break into the hitter instead of away.

Branch Rickey had assembled a talented team and a racially-mixed group of men that jelled on and off the field. The fans loved this team and other teams admired how we played and conducted ourselves. I think this is when the Dodgers' aura really came into bloom.

RALPH KINER (PIRATES):

The Dodgers definitely had an aura. Of course, they had an unbelievable ballclub that with the exception of left field pretty much had the same guys going out there every day through the years. It was a thrill coming to Ebbets Field, which was such a wonderful place to play. It was an intimate park and the fans were great. It was a fantastic place to hit, but they had such a tough pitching staff. They were all about the same. They all had great curveballs, great change-ups, and good fastballs. Newcombe had a great fastball, his best pitch. He was tough. I think Rex Barney threw harder than any pitcher in baseball. He really brought that ball up there in a hurry, at over 100 mph. But it was straight down the middle of the plate and hittable, unlike Robin Roberts's fastball. I could hit Barney. So could a lot of other guys, because his record was mediocre. He won 15 games in 1948, but that was the only time he won in double figures. New York sportswriter Bob Cook would write: "If high and outside were a strike, he'd be in the Hall of Fame." He went to a psychiatrist to try to cure himself of his wildness. But it didn't work.

Roy Campanella did a tremendous job of handling that staff. He was black, but Newcombe wasn't the only guy who listened to him. They all did. Roy was a tricky catcher. He would pound the mitt low and outside and batters would hear that and think that's where the pitch was going. But the ball might come in high and inside. Also, he distracted you with his constant chatter.

Carl Furillo was the Dodgers' secret weapon. He was a great hitter and he had an amazing arm. You didn't run on the "Reading Rifle." At Ebbets Field, where the right-field fence was so close, the batter had to think of him as another infielder and run out line drives to short right because he could throw you out at first.

S. JORGENSEN:

This was a tough season. We were in a tension-packed pennant race with the Cardinals. We couldn't pull away from them. Musial, Slaughter, Howie Pollet, and many others were having excellent seasons. They were up by a game with 4 games remaining. Then they started losing. Meanwhile we won a doubleheader in the rain from the Braves. Newcombe beat Johnny Sain in the second game, a rain-shortened shutout. So going into the last day, *we* were one game up. I was very confident that we were going to win our final game against the Phillies because we had Newcombe going against Russ Meyer. With a right-hander pitching for them, I was really looking forward to hitting. I drove in the first run of the game and we went on to take a 5–0 lead. Later, when a left-hander came in for them, I was lifted for a pinch hitter and Eddie Miksis finished the game at third. Unfortunately, the Phillies tied the game in the middle innings against Newcombe, who was tired from pitching so soon after beating Boston, and Rex Barney. But then Shotton brought in Jack Banta, a sidearmer who pitched very well for us during the year, and he shut the Phillies down for four innings. We had to win because the Cardinals won that day, and we finally did in the 10th inning, 9–7, on singles by Snider and Luis Olmo. That was the most exciting game I ever played in.

DON NEWCOMBE:

My turn had come to join the Dodgers. But after a great spring, they returned me to Montreal. I was very frustrated but stuck it out until I was recalled by the Dodgers in late May. In my debut I shut out Cincinnati. I was reunited with Roy and got to play with Jackie Robinson for the first time. The three of us became the first blacks to make the All-Star team, which was a thrill—it felt good to be around all those stars—but how could they have left Jackie off the team in 1947 and 1948? Of course, they couldn't have had that All-Star Game in Brooklyn and not have had the three of us. Although I missed a month of the season, I went 17–8 and led the league with 5 shutouts—3 came in succession against St. Louis, Pittsburgh, and New York, and I set a Dodger record with 31 scoreless innings in succession. It was gratifying being successful, but it was not surprising to me because although I just turned 23 in June, I felt I could have pitched in the majors three years earlier.

I had the talent and desire. And I was cocky. I knew I was good, as good or better than the white guys who were trying to keep me from being there. They knew it, too. White pitchers around the league couldn't do a damn thing about my quick rise to the top. There hadn't been a successful black pitcher in the National League and many were hoping I'd fail. The same applied to the Dodgers' pitchers. But as it had been with Jackie, they welcomed me once they realized I would help them win the pennant and receive World Series money.

Unlike what was often reported, the Dodgers weren't always unified. There was a lot of infighting that went on, much hate and animosity—especially once we black players got there. We were going to take away someone's job. Jackie's arrival had meant that Eddie Stanky, the second baseman, got traded from the team he loved. Roy's arrival made Bruce Edwards into a backup catcher and a first baseman out of Gil Hodges—and he became the best in baseball.

I didn't socialize with the white players on the Dodgers. The wives didn't sit together in Ebbets Field, and their husbands didn't socialize in the early stages of integration when we were tearing down that barrier. Jackie finally got to the point where he would play cards with them. Roy was always very sociable. He came from a mixed family, with a white father and black mother, so he was raised in an integrated life and knew how to act and react. A lot of times people didn't like how Roy did it so easily, but that was his way. He was half-Italian but was still black as far as his teammates and opposing players were concerned. He was "a nigger," as were Jackie and myself—and Dan Bankhead in those years he was on the Dodgers. We had to bond together because we were all we had. We didn't know when that would change and if we'd be around when it did.

We were extremely angry. Jackie always used to say, "I'm *bitter* right now but I'm going to hang around long enough to change one letter in that word, the *i* to an *e*." And he did make it significantly *better* for blacks in baseball. He, Roy, Larry Doby, and myself were re-

On his way to establishing himself as the major league's first great black pitcher, Brooklyn's hard-throwing, 6′4″ Don Newcombe won 17 games in his 1949 Rookie of the Year campaign and became the ace of the Dodgers' impressive staff.

sponsible for the progress. We were not truly cognizant of our role in history, but we did know that we were writing a chapter.

Now that I played with Jackie, I got to see what he had to go through. He was fully aware of his responsibility, and though he accepted it, it was a great burden. There were now other blacks in baseball—and we suffered much abuse ourselves—but he was still the man who integrated baseball, and he lived under more pressure than any human being I met in my life (and that includes Martin Luther King, Jr.). Yet he never drank or smoked. Maybe he should have had a drink every once in a while because it might have relieved some of the tension. It also might have taken away some of that ingrained hatred he felt because of how people were treating him simply because he happened to be black and wanted to play baseball in this country. That's all any of us wanted to do—play baseball.

If anyone else could have integrated baseball, it would have been Larry Doby or Roy Campanella. They made tremendous contributions as it was. I think Larry would have had a hard time controlling his temper. He had a violent, fly-off-the-handle attitude when he got mad. Unlike with Jackie that first year, if you fooled with Larry, you might get knocked on your ass. He was young then.

Campanella was a quiet man with a natural safety valve on his emotions. Unlike Jackie, he could keep things inside. He had the right temperament, but I don't know how much he could have taken physically. Even in the majors, he used to get hit in the head a lot. I never saw Jackie get hit in the head—the ribs, the arm, but never in the head. (The same with Willie Mays, after he joined the Giants in 1951.) Roy didn't have those kinds of reflexes. I saw him get hit in the head by Bill Werle on a curveball. They would have killed Roy. They would have actually set him up and killed him with a baseball.

Jackie Robinson probably had the least talent of the players I'm talking about. But he had other attributes that made him the right man to integrate baseball. He was a leader—he was the leader of the Dodgers and the player who drove them to so many pennants. And he was someone who refused to lose. He didn't like to lose at anything—marbles, table tennis, golf, or betting on racehorses, which was one of his hobbies. And he wouldn't accept any of us feeling any different.

Brooklyn Dodger fans were the best there will ever be in baseball. They truly wanted Jackie, Roy, and me to do well. They were proud of us and glad we were part of the team they loved. They were for the Dodgers, win or lose. They even cheered opposing players, like Stan Musial. When we went to St. Louis, Jackie Robinson never got the kind of idolatry that was shown Musial in Brooklyn. Roy Campanella never got that in Cincinnati. Only the Dodgers fans were so generous.

JOHNNY KLIPPSTEIN:
Branch Rickey drafted me out of the Cardinals' organization because he was impressed by my 90 mph fastball, which moved into batters. He thought I had potential. I was happy because I was getting a new start. I went to the Dodgers' training camp in Vero Beach. That's where Chuck Connors would always recite

"Casey at the Bat" for Mr. Rickey. He could do that better than anyone and would do it every spring in a large hall for all the minor leaguers.

The Dodgers intended to assign me to Greenville in the Sally League, Class A. Fresco Thompson called me in and said I was going to get $300 a month. I said, "Wait a minute, I got $350 a month last year playing in Class B. I'm not being ornery, but you'd better take an extra pitcher to Greenville, because that's closer to my home than Florida, and home's where I'm going if I don't get more money." The next morning I looked on the bulletin board and discovered I had been moved up to Mobile in Double A. I would get $425 a month there if I made the team. Mobile had one exhibition game left against the Cincinnati Reds and that was the first time I pitched against major leaguers. I pitched 5 scoreless innings and made Mobile. But I was considered a wise guy. I really wasn't but I was sticking up for my rights. By the middle of the season I had won 8 games. A couple of players, who were probably putting me on, told me that I should go see Edgar Allen, the president of the Mobile club, to ask for a bonus if I won 15 games. They told me other players got bonuses. So I went to see Allen about the bonus and he wanted to throw me out with help from policemen. He called up Branch Rickey and I could soon hear Rickey screaming on the phone. Rickey had me suspended for three days without pay, and I was informed that if I didn't want to continue playing with Mobile at my current salary, I could go home. I sat for three days, then finished out the season. I won 15 games. The Dodgers intended to promote me to Montreal, but instead I got drafted by the Chicago Cubs, who wanted me for their parent club. My dad died three days after he knew I was coming to the big leagues.

CHICO CARRASQUEL:

I flew to Miami and on to the Dodgers' camp in Vero Beach. I had never been out of Venezuela before. I didn't know any English and nobody spoke Spanish, so I was there 20 days and couldn't talk to anybody. I used to go to the restaurant and point with my finger. I figured my glove would speak for me.

I was assigned to Fort Worth in Double A. I received about $600 a month. I expected $300 every fifteen days. However, my first check was for $210, so I went to the office and asked about the missing money. I was told,

"Uncle Sam." I said, "Uncle Sam? I don't have any uncle in the States." They explained to me about taxes. Bobby Bragan was my manager and he spoke a little Spanish. It was a friendly team with outfielders Dick Williams and Cal Abrams, and pitchers Billy Loes and Carl Erskine. I roomed with Abrams, who spoke some Spanish and was my interpreter. He invited me to restaurants, movies, swimming. At that time many restaurants in Texas would have signs that said: "We serve no Mexicans, no Negroes, no Dogs." Still, I had a good time. I hit about .315 and was good defensively. We won the pennant.

I returned to Caracas after the season. When I arrived at the airport, a sportswriter told me that I had just been traded to the White Sox. That's how I learned. I was glad because I thought it would take me several years to make the Dodgers because Pee Wee Reese was the shortstop. I'm sure I was traded because the Dodgers had Reese and not because I didn't know English.

NEW YORK GIANTS

BILL RIGNEY:

Durocher continued to shape the Giants into the type of team he liked, getting rid of the sluggers and bringing in versatile players. In June, Walker Cooper was traded to the Reds, allowing Wes Westrum to become our starting catcher. Wes would never be much of a hitter—although he would hit over 20 homers in both 1950 and 1951—but he was an excellent receiver.

In July we brought up both Hank Thompson and Monte Irvin from Jersey City. They were the first blacks on the Giants. Thompson also had been the first black on the St. Louis Browns in 1947. He had done some time—it had something to do with someone being killed in Texas. He played second base for us and did pretty good, hitting 9 or 10 homers in half a season. Every once in a while Thompson would get out of line and Monte would get on his case. Monte was a super guy. He was a strong, very talented right-handed-hitting outfielder-infielder from Alabama. He had been a superstar in the Negro Leagues—one year he batted over .400—and had played in the Polo Grounds with the Newark Eagles before signing with the Giants. He was already 30, but it was fortunate that he could have a few good major league seasons.

In August, Johnny Mize, whose homers were way down, was sold to the Yankees for their pennant drive. And after the season, the Giants sent Sid Gordon, Willard Marshall, and Buddy Kerr to the Braves for second baseman Eddie Stanky and shortstop Alvin Dark.

Leo had a very busy season. He had run-ins with heckling fans and umpires and was suspended for a little while. I don't think he was as tough on umpires as he was supposed to have been. He made a little more out of it because he tried to live up to his reputation. He wanted a fair shake. Leo also had a lot of run-ins with the Dodgers—our rivalry was becoming much stronger now that Leo was our manager. He'd really razz Jackie Robinson and Don Newcombe. Leo was never calm and couldn't sit still on the bench, but he knew what was going on all the time. He thought better when moving around. He chatted all the time. Someone would say something and he'd echo it. A player would yell to our pitcher, "Come on, pop him up!" and Leo would say, "Yeah, pop him up!" When we were on the bench, we would kiddingly yell something just to hear him repeat it. On our club, he had a third of the guys afraid of him, a third who weren't sure, and a third of us who knew him. That's the way he liked it.

After you had a good year, the Giants tried to sign you before you went home and thought about what salary you really deserved. I'd hit .278, with 19 doubles, 6 triples, and 6 homers, and had played all over the infield, including 80 games at shortstop. I wanted a certain amount of money for the 1950 season. Leo was there when I negotiated with Stoneham. Horace said, "Schoendienst doesn't make that much with the Cardinals." My response was "At this time, I'm the only guy on the Giants who plays the game the way Leo wants it to be played. I'm the only one." And Leo said, "He's right." So Horace gave me what I wanted.

ART FOWLER:

I was born in 1922 in Converse, South Carolina, where everyone in town worked in the textile business. I was the youngest of ten children in a poor Baptist family and didn't even have a pair of shoes. Jesse, the oldest of my five brothers, was 24 years older than me and pitched with the St. Louis Cardinals in 1924. They wouldn't give him the raise he wanted and he quit after only one year in the majors. I was the only other boy in the family

to play baseball. I dropped out of school after seven grades and learned more playing ball than I did in school.

I was working in a cotton mill and pitching in semi-pro ball when Pat Murray, a scout for the Giants, asked if I was interested in playing pro ball. I had never been away from home, but my family supported my decision to sign a contract. So in 1944 I went to Bristol, Tennessee, my first professional team. That was the Appalachian League, and I got $37.50 a week and that was good money. I got my first pair of shoes. And for $20 every two weeks, I got a room and two meals a day at a boardinghouse. I was homesick, but my manager, Hal Gruber, took care of me. I won 13 games and also played 30 games in the outfield.

The next year I went to Danville, Virginia in the Carolina League, and went 23–6, completing 27 of 28 starts. I could really throw the ball. By 1947 I was in A ball with Jacksonville. I was 11–5 and then lost the next 9 in a row and ended up 11–14. That didn't bother me. The next year I went back and won 19. I threw a fastball and picked up the slider. I was hoping to move up to Minneapolis, the Giants' Triple A team, but the organization sent me to the independent Atlanta Crackers in Double A, for Davey Williams. He played a little for the Giants in 1949, and eventually became their starting second baseman. I bided my time.

PHILADELPHIA PHILLIES

ANDY SEMINICK:

The Phillies finally turned the corner and became a winning team. The veterans produced—Ennis hit 25 homers and drove in over 100 runs, I hit 24 homers and had 68 RBIs in just 334 at-bats, left-hander Ken Heintzelman won 17 games—and young players like Hamner, Ashburn, Willie Jones, Roberts, Simmons, and Russ Meyer had impact. Meyer got 17 wins after coming over from the Cubs. Roberts had 15 victories and proved he would be a big winner for us. Jones had been up twice before, but this was his rookie season and he showed he was a good hitter who had power and was a sure-handed third baseman with a good enough arm. He played shallower than any third baseman in the league.

I had my biggest game against the Reds. I hit 3 homers, 2 in the eighth inning, when Ennis, Jones, and Schoolboy Rowe also homered, tying the record of the 1939 Giants. We could have had 6 homers that inning. Hamner hit a ball that ricocheted off the fence—if he hadn't coasted into third, he could have had an inside-the-park homer. That was my personal highlight except for winning the 1950 pennant on the last day.

This was a very close team. We'd get together at home or on the road. On the 28-hour train trips from Boston to St. Louis, you had better get along. We'd go out to eat together and have a beer or two. There was also beer in the clubhouse, and eventually beer companies sponsored our games—Ballantine, then Schmidt's, a local beer. One of the sponsors would throw an annual party-picnic for us. Most guys drank. Ashburn was a milkshake drinker at the beginning, but then would drink an occasional beer. Hamner would have his beer, but I don't think he had any real problem.

On the field I wouldn't fool around, but off the field I was a lively guy who liked to have fun. I'd have a couple of beers, I'd sing, I'd play cards. A lot of the guys would play pinochle, others poker and hearts. Hamner liked to play pool, but not too many other guys did. There wasn't much golf playing either. Ashburn played tennis and golf and was big on squash. Most of the players were married, but everyone would be together. Hamner was married when he was young, Del Ennis, Puddin' Head Jones. . . .

Eddie Waitkus, who we got from the Cubs to play first base, was a single guy and sometimes he'd go his own way. Sometimes he'd bring his girlfriend along. When Eddie was shot we were staying at the Edgewater Beach Hotel in Chicago and I was rooming with Eddie Miller. At about two A.M. the phone rang and a friend of ours was calling from Philadelphia, wanting to know about Eddie Waitkus. It had just come over the radio that he'd been shot. I literally fell out of bed. Eddie and I got dressed and went down to the lobby, and sure enough, some gal named Ruth Ann Sternhagen had shot him. This gal had run a thorough check on Eddie, learning where he lived, who his neighbors were, street numbers, where he came from, and everything else about him. After the game that day, she checked into the Edgewater and he came in late and she called his room. She introduced herself as a friend of his neighbors. She knew their names and said she had a message or present

from them. He went into her room and sat in a chair to the side of the bed and she was standing by the front door and closet door. She said she had a present for him and reached into the closet and took out a .22 rifle and shot him. He was severely wounded. Eddie Sawyer called a meeting the next day and told us what happened so none of us would talk out of turn. He told us not to go to the hospital because we weren't allowed to see Waitkus anyway, and we left town the next day. Fortunately, the media didn't really bother us much about Waitkus. Our trainer spent the winter with him in Clearwater to get him ready for the 1950 season. We certainly felt terrible about what happened, but it didn't affect our play for the rest of the year. Maybe the single guys in baseball were more careful after that.

DEL ENNIS:
When Eddie Waitkus was shot, I was in my hotel room with Willie Jones. Willie always brought binoculars on road trips so we could scout for women. We were surveying the windows in the hotel when Eddie was shot. When we went down to the lobby and found out what had happened we couldn't understand how we missed it. Eddie didn't even know the woman. She was a fan obsessed with him. If she couldn't have him, nobody could. Oddly, Eddie was on another date at the time. He left his date in the lobby while he went upstairs for a few minutes. He received a phone message from this woman who said that she had just seen Eddie's father in Boston and that he was sick. So he went to her room to get more information, and as soon as he walked past her into her room, she shot him. It was a strange thing to happen.

Willie Jones would be my roommate for about six years on the Phillies. He was a real good guy. He'd complain every day that he had sore feet and would go onto the field with a tippytoe act. It got to be a habit with him. He was a terrific third baseman and a good hitter. But when I'd homer he'd try to do the same and couldn't do it. Willie loved women. I got to be the best bed-musser in the league. Anytime there was a bed check I'd muss up his bed.

We called the girls who hung around baseball players "Queens." They came in all shapes, sizes, and ages. They were at train depots, at the ballparks, and in hotel lobbies, challenging players to take them on. They weren't considered a problem by the players—more truthful is that they thought having women around was one of the side benefits they got from being ballplayers. Players saw a lot of women. The guys who went out with them had to have good constitutions because they had to be in shape the next day at the ballpark.

The road trips gave players the chance to get to know each other. We talked baseball and played cards—hearts was a popular game. Other players would drink beer, but not to excess. We slept to excess. I didn't drink. Richie Ashburn never drank. He didn't swear either. But he fit in, like me. He wasn't so innocent. Forget the story that went around: He didn't sleep with his *bat* on road trips.

On the road we'd find our spots to have dinner. I'd go to first-class restaurants and usually eat steak or roast beef. A lot of us would go out together, but it wouldn't be everybody because certain guys were too cheap. In Philadelphia I'd eat at home. Other players would go to familiar spots downtown. It wasn't hard being married. I didn't want to go anywhere at night. The single players stayed out late. They didn't hurt the Phillies because we used to get on them as a team to make them behave themselves. If word got around that they were stepping over the line, we would get on them without management being brought in. Nobody got into trouble.

I led the Phillies in batting average, homers, and RBIs. I had 110 RBIs, the first time I had more than 100. That would be my goal every year because I had it put in my contract that I'd get paid an extra $5,000 for 105 RBIs, $10,000 for 110 RBIs, $15,000 for 115 RBIs, and $20,000 for 120 or more RBIs. Three times I would collect the biggest bonus.

I also did well in the field. We had a good defensive outfield in 1949. I led the league in assists playing left, Ashburn led in putouts playing center, and Bill Nicholson did a good job playing part-time in right. Swish was a pretty good player with homer power, and he was a professional all the way. He was already 35 when he came over from the Cubs that year, but he was good to have around and stayed with us for about five years as a backup outfielder and left-handed pinch hitter.

ELROY FACE:

I was born in 1928 in Stephentown, New York, a small town east of Albany. I had two brothers. My father was a carpenter by trade but at times worked in the woods cutting logs and in a factory. My mother was a homemaker but worked briefly gathering eggs at a chicken farm. I wasn't a baseball fan and couldn't have named 10 players in the big leagues—but I was the first in my family to play ball. We didn't have Little League, so I just played pickup ball. One older, bigger kid was the manager and didn't let me play much because I was small. I was still small in high school, but I played two years of varsity basketball, football, and baseball, pitching and playing short and second. I realized I had special talent when I was 8–1 and pitched a shutout to give us our first league title.

I quit high school when I was 18 and spent a year and a half in the army. I got a high school equivalency diploma when I was stationed in Guam, but when I came home they wouldn't recognize it. I had been a mechanic in the army, so I got a job in an Oldsmobile garage. On weekends I played sandlot ball with the New Lebanon town team. I pitched and played infield, batting fourth. I struck out 18 in one game and 19 in another, and Fred Matthews, a Phillies bird dog who was vacationing in the Berkshires, saw this written up in the paper. On Memorial Day he stopped by to watch me pitch in a game before heading home. Ironically, I was beaten that game by the same guy who gave me my only loss in high school a couple of years before. Matthews signed us both, but I would be the only one from our town to make the big leagues. Matthews told me I had two strikes against me: I was just 5'8" and I would already be 21 going into spring training. But he said he'd give me a chance. I signed with Carbondale in the Mid-Atlantic League, Class D, and went to spring training as a pitcher and infielder, but all I did was pitch. Then Bradford of the PONY bought my contract from Carbondale. So I pitched for Bradford in 1949. I went 14–2 and we won the pennant. At the time I gave no thought to becoming a reliever. That wasn't any pitcher's goal in those days.

PITTSBURGH PIRATES

RALPH KINER:

The Pirates trained in San Bernardino, California, then went to New Orleans where our minor league team was. Then we'd work our way north back to Pittsburgh, or maybe to St. Louis to open the season. We'd go by train, stopping every day to play a game. We'd play ball, check into hotels, ride the trains, until we reached our destination. Baseball was fun to play, but the travel made it a hard life. At least during the season we could stay in one city for a few days before getting back on the train.

We dropped to 71–83 and fell to sixth place, but we still had a pretty good ballclub. Wally Westlake hit over 20 homers and drove in over 100 runs, and we got good starting pitching from Murry Dickson, Bill Werle, and Cliff Chambers. Johnny Mize was going downhill, so I didn't have any real competition in the homer race. I hit 54 homers to finish with 18 more than Musial, the second-place finisher. I became the first National Leaguer to hit over 50 homers twice, which still didn't mean as much to me as hitting 50 the first time. I hit 16 of those homers in September, and again had homers in 4 successive at-bats.

I always had close friends on the ballclub. There was no open hostility toward me because I was the lone All-Star. Every club has its cliques and you have both detractors and people who join you. But I think most of the guys liked me because with my success I elevated their positions and salaries. The other thing that made a big difference is that I was the player representative and was fighting for their rights in the pension plan. In 1947, when the pension plan went into effect, I became player representative of the Pirates. By 1949 I was the National League representative.

I liked the ballplayers of this era. They had an *esprit de corps* that was outstanding. When you were a teammate, you really were a teammate because there wasn't much movement between ballclubs in those days. We bonded together because baseball was very competitive and we all hated the enemy. We now had a good group of guys. Westlake, who was one of my roommates, and I were usually together. Catcher Clyde McCullough was a fun guy, and I got along well with Chambers. I spent a lot of time with Rip Sewell, who was best known for his "eephus" pitch that went high in the air before crossing the plate. Rip had been with the Pirates since 1938 and this was his last season. He was still a good pitcher and tough competitor, and off the field he was a very nice guy who really enjoyed life. He had gone to the University of Alabama and was very smart, literate, and opinionated.

We played mostly day ball, so while on the road four or five of us would go out to a good place for dinner or to a nightclub. We weren't cliquish, so anyone could come along. Even the reporters, who rode the rails with us and were part of our social lives. We were steak eaters. I can't remember anyone going for French cuisine or more exotic fare. There was a lot of social drinking, but I can't say there was too much drinking. It depended on the individual. Some guys drank a lot and some guys didn't drink at all. We'd usually be in by midnight for a day game the next day.

When we came to New York we had a regular routine. We'd go to places that were popular with players. We'd always go to Toots Shor's. We'd start out there and have dinner and hang out. Sewell and I always went to Bertolotti's, a supper club in the Village. Whenever the Cardinals were in town playing the Dodgers or Giants, we'd always run into Stan Musial and Red Schoendienst there. I always went to see Eddie Condon play guitar down at Condon's on West Third Street in the Village, and uptown we went to see George Shearing play the piano at Amber's. New York was loaded with good entertainment in those days. Ever since 1947 I had been going to the "in" places in the city, like the Stork Club, El Morocco, Copacabana, and Latin Quarter. We were like the old-time ballplayers who always went out on the town. I liked going to all the top spots, so I really enjoyed New York. I envied the players on the New York teams and could never understand those who thought there was too much pressure to play there. We had so much fun that it's a wonder we ever won a ballgame there. . . . Actually we didn't win many.

In Cincinnati we went across the river to Kentucky to the Beverly Hills Club and the Lookout House. There was open gambling with great floor shows. The Lookout House was closed down, then reopened illegally, and finally closed down for good. There was always pressure put on players to disassociate themselves from gamblers. I don't think it meant much. I never saw gamblers hanging around players. Among the players, we didn't know who was gambling and who wasn't. At least, my group didn't.

Pittsburgh had a couple of good nightclubs. There was Lenny Littman's, which is where I first saw Sammy Davis, Jr., performing with his dad and uncle. And there was the Carrousel, which was run by a fellow named

Jackie Heller. Otherwise, I didn't go out much because the fans wouldn't leave me alone.

I had a tremendous following in Pittsburgh, but there were some fans who didn't like me. In Pittsburgh they would boo you for anything. A few years back, they booed Bob Elliott for making an error during infield practice. It was a tough town.

I was well known for my home run exploits and was treated like a celebrity when I returned to California in the off-season. One year I escorted Elizabeth Taylor, who was then a young starlet, to a movie premiere at Grauman's Chinese Theater. Later, we came out and stood there while the valet went to my car. We waited and waited. Finally the valet informed me that my chauffeur must have fallen asleep. I told him I didn't have a chauffeur. Whereupon I was directed to an enormous parking lot and told my car was in there somewhere. So for a long time Elizabeth Taylor and I ran around this parking lot looking for my car. It was some date. But she was great—she was a real sport about it.

FRANK THOMAS:

After my good year at Tallahassee, I was promoted to Davenport, Iowa, in Class B. Then I was sent to Waco, Texas, in the Big State League. They had a hard-throwing pitcher by the name of Bill Pierro—"Wild Bill." He would pitch for the Pirates in 1950 and walk 28 batters in 29 innings. He was always popping off about how fast he could throw. I told him I could catch his fastball bare-handed. He didn't believe me. He didn't even want to warm up. After I caught a couple of them, he said he needed to warm up. So he warmed up. Then I caught 5 in a row. As a kid, I played shortstop without a glove in fast-pitch softball games. My hands toughened up and I had a good pair of hands, so I could catch hardballs bare-handed. I would do it over my career to lower players' egos.

I was hitting .352 when the manager held a meeting in which he discussed players having the desire to move up to the majors one class at a time. During the meeting the phone rang, and it was the Pirates, who told him they were sending me back down to Tallahassee. I decided that if this was the way baseball was, it wasn't what I wanted to do. At the time I was dating the woman I'd marry and she talked me into staying. I flew back to Tallahassee, the first time I ever was in a plane, and went

through a hurricane. I hadn't eaten anything and got really sick. At Tallahassee, my return meant they started drawing fans.

CINCINNATI REDS

EWELL BLACKWELL:

One of my kidneys didn't work from birth. It had hurt during the off-season, so I had surgery to remove it in January. Consequently, I didn't get to pitch much in 1949. I went just 5–5 and started only 4 games. Bucky Walters used me in relief the rest of the time. That was frustrating because I wanted the chance to go 9 innings because we used our complete games in contract negotiations.

The Reds made a mistake early in the season trading Frank Baumholtz and Hank Sauer to the Cubs. Frankie

Ailing Reds' right-hander Ewell Blackwell struggled for the second consecutive season, but he would return to dominant form in 1950.

was a good left-handed average hitter and Sauer was our only genuine power hitter. We had no one to take Hank's place, so we picked up catcher Walker Cooper during the summer. He hit the long ball on occasion and even had 3 homers and 10 runs batted in one game, but he couldn't make up for all the power we lost when Sauer left. Consequently, we lost more than we did the year before and finished just a game ahead of the last-place Cubs. Bucky Walters was fired just before the end of the season and was replaced by coach Luke Sewell, the long-time catcher.

FRANK BAUMHOLTZ:

The last thing I expected was to end up on the Chicago Cubs in 1949. It came about because in 1948 Bucky Walters replaced Johnny Neun as manager of the Reds with one-third of the season remaining. When he was just a pitcher, Bucky had been the person who did the most for me. When my wife's father had died and when she had been hospitalized with a serious illness, Bucky befriended me and made sure I was never alone and that my spirits were up. Then he became manager and turned into a Mr. Hyde. After hitting .283 in 1947 and .296 in 1948, I was in and out of the Reds' lineup and then wasn't playing at all. He was no manager. A perfect gentleman and helluva ballplayer, but you don't change just because you change jobs. That was the end of our friendship. Apparently, he didn't like Hank Sauer either—although Sauer had a big year in 1948—because Warren Giles traded both of us to the Cubs for Peanuts Lowrey and Harry Walker, who both had their good days behind them. (Years later, Giles would tell me that this deal was the worst mistake he ever made in baseball. That made me feel good.)

HANK SAUER:

I didn't know I'd be traded to Chicago because I felt secure after setting a Reds home run record my first year with the team. But apparently, they weren't satisfied. When I came to spring training, Walters told me that he wanted me to learn how to hit to right field. I said, "You wanted me to provide power and I hit 35 homers. What the hell is wrong with that?" So I started hitting the ball to right and my thumbs swelled up like boxing gloves. At that point Walters told me I could return to pulling the ball.

I started the season hitting very poorly. I had just a handful of homers by June at the trading deadline. So Frank Baumholtz and I were traded to Chicago. I didn't know about it until Blackwell called me up and asked me how I wanted him to pitch me now that we were going to be on different teams. I said, "I don't know. Where are you going?" (When I did face Blackie soon after as a Cub, there were men on second and third, and he approached me and said, "Boy, I wish I had my fastball now." That's when he was hurting.)

I didn't want to leave because I had a lot of friends in Cincinnati. Walters told me he traded me because "I couldn't make an all-around hitter out of you." Warren Giles had already traded me to the Cubs when he wrote me saying, "I hope that the background in Chicago doesn't bother you as much as it bothers all the rest of the ballplayers." He wanted to make me think about those fans in the stands who were in the batter's line of vision. He didn't want me to hit once I left the Reds. But I would fool him. I would always hit particularly well against the Reds. (One year I would open up the season by hitting a grand slam to beat the Reds in the snow in Cincinnati. That gave me a lot of satisfaction!)

AMERICAN LEAGUE 1949

"THE FIRST BIG LEAGUE GAME I EVER PLAYED IN WAS AGAINST THE TIGERS, MY FAVORITE TEAM AS A KID. ONE OF THE PLAYERS I IDOLIZED AS A KID WAS HAL NEWHOUSER. WHO WAS PITCHING THAT DAY? HAL NEWHOUSER. I CAME UP TO FACE HIM. HOW DO YOU EXPLAIN A DREAM?"

GUS ZERNIAL

PHILADELPHIA ATHLETICS

EDDIE JOOST:
I had my best season. I hit .263, with 23 homers, 25 doubles, 149 walks, 128 runs and 81 RBIs batting leadoff. I drove in a lot of runs with two outs, and that to me was an accomplishment. I loved to hit with men in scoring position. It got to the point where they'd walk me intentionally and, Jesus, my ego went up and I'd go up the first-base line laughing and clapping my hands. I made the All-Star team for the first time. That was the biggest thrill of my life because there were some good shortstops in the league: Boudreau at Cleveland, Rizzuto in New York, Appling at Chicago, and Vern Stephens at Boston, who wasn't a good defensive player but hit 39 homers and led the league with 159 RBIs.

I missed several games because I got banged up in New York. Casey Stengel was the Yankees' new manager, and he and I were on each other all game. We still had animosity from when he managed me in Boston— I'm sure he remembered the time he was babbling during a clubhouse meeting and Eddie Miller and I turned our chairs toward the locker and read *The Sporting News.* I got a couple of hits and we were ahead in the eighth inning when Johnny Lindell walked for the Yankees. The next guy hit a double-play grounder to Pete Suder. I took the relay, tagged second, and threw to Fain. I was way off the bag watching the play at first and suddenly I'm flying through the air. Lindell, who was a big guy, slid into my planted leg ten feet from the bag. I started cussing him and Stengel. Luckily, it was just a bruise.

We finished in fifth place, but we won 81 games and had some bright spots. For a change we had solid pitching. Alex Kellner, a big, strong right-hander, became the Athletics' first 20-game winner since 1933. Although he had only a few wins, Bobby Shantz, a gutty 5' 6" southpaw, showed a great promise as a rookie—in his debut, he came in in the third and threw no-hit balls the rest of the way. Dick Fowler won 15 games, and Lou Brissie won 16 games, giving him 30 over two seasons. Brissie was an amazing case. He was a tall left-hander from South Carolina whose leg was shattered during the war. It didn't look like he'd ever play in the majors. Some surgeon put in a steel plate, and he had therapy and regained use of the leg. He made the team in 1947 and did a good job for us in 1948 and '49 with nothing but a high fastball and a curveball that would hang.

Another small guy with great heart, Nellie Fox first made the team in 1947, when he was 19, but it wasn't until 1949 that he got any significant playing time at second base. For some unknown reason, Mack wasn't impressed with him. Nellie used to stuff almost half a pack of chewing tobacco in his cheek. I'd warn him that it might hurt him, but he laughed it off. Years later, he would even endorse Red Man chewing tobacco. I used to smoke but not chew tobacco. I tried it once: I swallowed it, threw up, and that was it. The tobacco would sear the inside of your mouth, but unbeknownst to anyone at the time, the juice from the nicotine got under your tongue and went right into your bloodstream. (Of course, Nellie got cancer in the 1970s.)

In my years with Athletics, Mr. Mack had only one meeting. After we had made a terrible play that cost us a game, the players walked into the narrow clubhouse in Shibe Park. Mr. Mack's office was on the far end. We were sitting there, disconsolate, cursing because we'd blown the game. All of a sudden Yitz Crompton, the clubhouse man, called out, ''Hold it right where you are. Mr. Mack is going to hold a meeting.'' We all were surprised. Mr. Mack, in his straw hat, came in and they closed the door. He walked down the middle of the clubhouse in between all the players and just kept looking for something. He finally said to Hank Majeski, ''You, sir, are a great player and I admire what you do.'' He turned to me and said, ''You, sir, are a great player and I admire what you do.'' Then, looking around, he raised his voice and said, ''But there are some people on this team that don't do very good.'' And he left.

ST. LOUIS BROWNS

LES MOSS:

The Browns won just 53 games in 1949 and dropped to seventh place, just 3 games out of the cellar. I was pretty even-tempered, so I just chewed my tobacco, had a little snuff, and played the game, without worrying about our losses. And I had a pretty good year, batting .291 with 10 homers and about 40 RBIs in about 275 at-bats. The

reason I didn't play more is that I split time with Sherm Lollar. He was a great guy and good player who we acquired from the Yankees. Our other major addition was Roy Sievers, a modest young outfielder from St. Louis. He was one of the best-looking young hitters, with a good swing, good balance, and good power. He hit over .300 and drove in 90 runs, and was voted the American League's first Rookie of the Year. Sievers, first baseman Jack Graham, center fielder Stan Spence, right fielder Dick Kokos, and whoever caught—Lollar or me—gave us five guys in the lineup who could hit the long ball. Bob Dillinger and Gerry Priddy were our two best average hitters. Our offense wasn't bad, but except for Ned Garver, we still didn't have any pitching.

RYNE DUREN:

They wouldn't let me pitch in high school in Cazenovia, Wisconsin, because I threw so hard and wild that I hit a kid and broke a couple of his ribs. So I played second and threw underhanded to first. I only started pitching again after high school when I played in a town-team league. We'd drink and fight in the bars on Saturday night and on Sunday we'd continue to brawl on the ballfield. I could throw so hard that I'd strike out 21 to 23 batters a game and went through 33 consecutive no-hit innings. One day Ernie Rudolph, a bird dog from Black River Falls, drove across the bridge in Cazenovia and saw the ball diamond. So he stopped to watch us play and sat down next to my sister, who was keeping score. He watched as I struck out about 12 in a row, and maybe 18 or 19 for the game, and he asked her if I always struck out that many. She said, ''Usually more.'' He couldn't believe what he was seeing. He called the higher-up scout for the St. Louis Browns and I signed a professional contract. The first time I saw a professional game I pitched in it.

I already was an alcoholic. I had been drinking from the time I was about 13. My dad, who became a postmaster after being shot up pretty bad in the war, used to tell me that his hero, an ex-army buddy named Big George, could outdrink everybody and never be whipped. I had a macho concept about drinking, believing that the more you could drink, the better man you were. I also believed that saying: ''Never trust a man who won't have a drink with you.'' I was proud that I could drink. Nobody ever told me that I was an alcoholic. I didn't realize it myself until I was pitching in the majors.

It was obvious from the start that I had talent, but my wildness alerted the Browns less to my alcoholism than to my poor eyesight. So in 1949, when I was 20, they sent me to an eye doctor. He reported back that I had 20/70 20/200 vision and bad depth perception, and recommended that I give up baseball because they couldn't correct anything. I wasn't going to quit. Instead I began a long climb to the majors.

CLEVELAND INDIANS

JOHN BERARDINO:

I didn't want to be traded after Lou Boudreau benched me in the playoff and World Series in 1948. Anyway, in those days, you didn't suggest or demand to be traded. They were more likely to send you home than trade you.

Unfortunately, 1949 wasn't as much fun as 1948. I got into only 50 games and for the second straight year batted less than .200, which not playing can do to a batter. I think our team tried to live off the fact that we were world champions. Consequently, we slipped to third, behind the Yankees and Red Sox. But there were two positive developments. Larry Doby emerged as a power hitter, and Early Wynn, who we acquired from the Senators, and rookie Mike Garcia joined Bob Lemon and Bob Feller to form the most formidable starting foursome in baseball, perhaps in baseball history.

MINNIE MINOSO:

I went to the Indians' camp in Tucson, Arizona. During their spring trainings, the black players—me, Larry Doby, Luke Easter—couldn't stay at the same hotel with the white players. We would often stay with black families. I knew Larry Doby because he had played for the Newark Eagles in the Negro Leagues until he signed with the Indians in 1947. He had been my enemy and we'd slide hard into each other—he played second and I played third then—and cuss at each other. Now he was my teammate and my friend. He was an impressive, aggressive, tough ballplayer. Luke Easter was another

Speedy, muscular former Negro Leagues star Orestes "Minnie" Minoso wouldn't get much chance to play after signing with the Cleveland Indians, but he would become an All-Star after being traded to the Chicago White Sox in 1951.

friend. He had been a star in the Negro Leagues with the Homestead Grays. He was such a nice man. I didn't speak good English, so he'd take me to restaurants and other places and translate for me.

When you don't know anybody and have trouble talking to anybody, it's a little bit difficult. At least nobody had to teach me how to play baseball. I always watched the game closely and tried to pick up what was necessary to be a good ballplayer.

I batted only 16 times with the Indians during the season, with one home run. The rest of the year I spent in San Diego in the Pacific Coast League, much of the time with Luke Easter, who became a big star there. I was happy to have even a brief stay with the Indians. When you come from nowhere—cutting sugarcane in Cuba—and get somewhere, you have to be happy.

WASHINGTON SENATORS

AL KOZAR:

We opened the season against the Yankees. I didn't pay attention to the umpire, as usual. The first pitch Allie Reynolds threw was a waist-high pitch. A perfect pitch. And I heard, "Ball one!" It was Bill McGowan, the umpire who had told me off twice in 1948 and who Joe Kuhel wanted me to write a negative report about. Yogi grumbled, "Oh, come on!" I fouled one off. Then Allie threw a low strike, but again I heard, "Ball two!" Right down the pipe. And Yogi said, "Goddamn, Bill, let's cut out that shit!" McGowan said, "Berra, do you want me to shove the ball down your throat?" Then he called time and walked by Berra and he was face-to-face with me. He said, "Kid, you were the only Washington Senator not to write me up last year. I gave you two, I'm not giving you any more. We're even! Take that goddamn bat off your shoulder and swing!" And he turned around to Yogi Berra and said, "You shut up!" How about that? I could tell that McGowan had gotten better during the off-season.

Kuhel decided to platoon me with Sherry Robertson. He did this because I didn't sign those statements against McGowan and because Robertson was a nephew of Clark Griffith. Robertson was okay at the plate but he was no fielder. Soon I wasn't even playing against right-handers, so I quit playing hard. I never was a bench warmer. Once, on a train, Kuhel said, "You don't want to play, do you?"

Kuhel wasn't one to give players encouragement, especially me. He didn't like much that I did, even when I made good plays in the field. In the minors I had a reputation for being a really good fielder. But not with Washington, although I was still a good second baseman when my hands didn't hurt. I wasn't as flamboyant or acrobatic as the Indians' Joe Gordon, but I made the same plays. I loved to get in front of everything. I got hit in the mouth and ripped off uniform buttons picking up and throwing balls. I hustled and would get balls that caromed off the first baseman's legs. I got a lot of errors because I went after everything and made daring throws home trying to save runs. (It seems strange in hindsight, but we used to leave our gloves out on the field when we went in the dugout. Only the pitcher, first baseman, and catcher took their gloves into the dugout. I'd throw my glove out a little ways, and if it was too close to the infield, the other team's outfielder would kick it out a little farther. I would put water in mine and it would stay right up and the outfielders or umpires would kick it over. That's the way we did it. Sometimes my glove would stand up the whole inning. The ball hit the gloves many times, but no one said anything. They changed the rules soon after, but I'd often forget and leave my glove out there, and the shortstop would bring mine in and throw it, which made me mad because that would make it like a pancake again.)

Joe Kuhel didn't appreciate my fielding, but some of my teammates did. At the end of the season we held a team meeting before a game with the Red Sox. Boston and New York were battling for the pennant and it was a vital game for the Red Sox to win. Kuhel asked our starter, Ray Scarborough, how he intended to pitch the Sox players, beginning with Dominic DiMaggio, who recently had a 34-game hit streak. Ray said we should play him straight away and he asked me and Sam Dente, our shortstop, if we went along with that. But Kuhel interrupted, saying that Sherry Robertson was going to play second, not me. Ray said, "When I pitch, I want a second baseman out there." Ray was good friends with Sherry, but it didn't matter. Ray continued, "Pesky's up second, I'm going to jam him. Al, you're playing second." Kuhel said, "Al, you're playing second."

As it turned out, Ray kept jamming the left-handed Pesky, and Pesky kept hitting balls to me near first baseman Mickey Vernon. Pesky batted .300, got 200 hits, and scored 100 runs every year, so it was important to keep him off base. Ray also stopped Ted Williams. That wasn't easy because that year Ted was the league's MVP and homer champion, and tied Sox shortstop Vern Stephens for the RBI title. They each drove in 159 runs! Ray was right-handed but loved to pitch against Williams because he could jam him. I was lucky all day. Chuck Stobbs was pitching for the Red Sox, and I could hit left-handers. I got 3 singles, and the hardest ball I hit was a liner to Pesky at third that almost tore his head off. I went 3 for 4. In the last inning, with the score tied, I singled and moved around to third after a couple of plays at home. When I got to second, Bobby Doerr told me, "What a day—you are knocking us out of $5,000 per man." Mel Parnell came in to pitch for the Red Sox.

He was a great pitcher and led the league with 25 wins and in earned run average. It was raining, so it was hard to see. After a couple of pitches, the ball hit the plate and skidded off catcher Birdie Tebbetts. I thought it went through his legs, but our third-base coach couldn't see it. Tebbetts wasn't moving, as if he had it in his mitt. It was like 15 seconds before I charged in. If he had it, it would have been quite embarrassing. But I scored and we won 2–1. Parnell said, "Nice going, Mumbles. You son of a bitch, you just knocked us out of the pennant." They could have still won it after beating us the next day, but they lost the final two games of the season to the Yankees. Getting the winning run that game and preventing my former team from clinching the pennant was my biggest thrill in the majors. Kuhel didn't say anything afterward. I didn't want to have pictures taken with Ray, but I did. Other than being honored with an Al Kozar Day in Cleveland by everyone from McKees Rocks, Pennsylvania, this game brought me my only pleasure in Washington.

DETROIT TIGERS

GEORGE KELL:
This was the train era. Everybody would have a private compartment. It was like a sitting room in the day and then you'd step out in the hall and pull your bed down and make a bedroom at night. I remember the trip from Boston to St. Louis after a Sunday doubleheader. We got on the train at about 7 P.M., and traveled all night and then all day and all night on Monday, and finally got off the train Tuesday morning at about 7 A.M. Then we'd play ball that night. We had a lot of idle time, so I read and played hearts, which most of the Tigers played. I never played any poker. I became roommates and good friends with Charlie Keller, the former Yankee, and he taught me bridge. On every train trip for two years, we'd have supper, and then play bridge all night with coaches Ted Lyons and Rick Ferrell. The four of us also would play in spring training. It was unusual for players and coaches to play cards together, but both Keller and I had played ball against Lyons and Ferrell, so we didn't have the standard player-coach relationship.

I read a lot about Jackie Robinson, but I never saw him until the 1949 All-Star Game at Ebbets Field. That was the first All-Star Game in which blacks played, and Robinson, Roy Campanella, Don Newcombe, and Larry Doby were there. I went to the National League clubhouse specifically to meet Robinson. He was a symbol of greatness to me and someone who had broken down a terrible barrier. I told him I had great admiration for him and had read all about him. He thanked me for coming over. That was a thrill. We didn't know it yet, but that year we would end up leading our leagues with almost identical batting averages: I would hit .343 and he would hit .342.

I really didn't think of winning the batting title until the last couple of days. Ted Williams and I were neck and neck, but he always was a couple of points ahead and you didn't figure on beating him. When I came to the park to play Cleveland on the final day of the season, a Sunday, I got a call in the clubhouse from my wife, who had gone back to Arkansas to put the kids in school. She wished me good luck. Hoot Evers then told me that I was going to win the title if I got 2 hits. I said, "Yeah, but Bob Lemon's pitching." He said, "I don't care who's pitching. Two hits and I guarantee you'll win it." Well, I singled and doubled my first two times up. In the sixth inning or so, they were ahead and brought in Bob Feller. He walked me. Then he struck me out in the seventh inning. In the ninth inning, I was due up fourth.

Communication was such that I didn't know what Williams was doing in his final game, so I didn't know if I was first or second in the race. Dick Wakefield pinch-hit and got a leadoff single. That meant I was going to bat unless there was a double play. The second batter flied out. That brought up Eddie Lake. I was in the on-deck circle. I looked into our dugout, and Joe Ginsberg was swinging a few bats as if he was going to pinch-hit for me. But he didn't get a chance because Lake grounded to Ray Boone at short, who touched second and threw to first for the game-ending double play. I didn't want to bat again because I thought 2 for 3 might be good enough to win the title. I got back to the dugout and Steve O'Neill said, "I was going to pinch-hit for you." I said, "Without asking me?" He said, "They called down and said you had the batting title won, and I was not going to let you lose it on the last day of the season on your last time at bat." So I don't know what would have happened if there hadn't been a double play. Williams went 0 for 2 in New York and also ended up with an official .343 average. But I won the title by 2/1000th of a point!

CHICAGO WHITE SOX

GUS ZERNIAL:

I was confident that I would make Chicago's Opening Day roster because my thigh injury had healed. I was getting a lot of publicity from the Chicago press because of my big year in Hollywood. Jack Onslow had been made manager—I had never heard of him before—and he made no bones about it that I would be his left fielder.

The first big league game I ever played in was against the Tigers, my favorite team as a kid. One of the players I idolized as a kid was Hal Newhouser. Who was pitching that day? Hal Newhouser. I came up to face him. How do you explain a dream? There were 54,000 fans in the stands and I was from a town that didn't have that many people in it. I'm looking all over and feeling just like a kid again, thinking that this was a fantastic experience. Newhouser just beat the tar out of us, but I got 2 hits off him—and this day was one of the highlights of my life.

Chicago could use my power. We had some pretty good hitters, but I was the only guy who could hit the long ball. I hadn't gotten my home run stroke down and had hit only 5 by late May, but I was hitting well over .300. Then, against Cleveland with the game on the line with two outs in the ninth, Thurman Tucker hit a ball down the left-field line and I dove for it. I caught it but hit the ground and rolled over, ripping apart my right shoulder. Other than whirlpool baths, there was no therapy in those days: they wired me back together and said good luck. I whirlpooled it, stretched it. But when the season ended I couldn't even throw a ball. I worried that my career was over.

BILLY PIERCE:

When I came to spring training in Pasadena, I didn't know if I'd make the White Sox. There were nine other left-handed pitchers in camp. But I made it because I could throw extremely hard. I assume that's why Frank

Discarded by the Tigers, shrewd and talented southpaw Billy Pierce would win 185 games from 1949 to 1961 with the Chicago White Sox.

Lane traded for me. He counted on me harnessing my control.

Leaving Detroit was hard enough, but other than Philadelphia, Chicago was the place I least wanted to go. The White Sox had a last-place team in 1948 that had no offense and no pitcher that won in double figures. Furthermore, Comiskey Park was dim, and the nearby stockyards were going full blast and the aroma was terrible. I couldn't imagine ever enjoying pitching there. It turned out that the trade was the greatest break in my life. The White Sox had lost 101 games and finished last in 1948, so the organization was changing everything around and I got the opportunity to pitch, which was what I needed at that point. So did Bob Kuzava and Randy Gumpert. The three of us joined Bill Wight in the rotation. I started 26 times and pitched about 170 innings. My record was just 7–15, but I had a decent earned run average.

Jack Onslow replaced Ted Lyons as Chicago's manager in 1949. He had been a minor league manager. He was about 60 and it was tough on him because we had young players who were prone to making mistakes and some veterans who would have listened more to someone with major league experience.

A lot of the young players looked up to Luke Appling, who had been around 30 years and was still a good-fielding shortstop and .300 hitter.

EDDIE JOOST (ATHLETICS):

We'd challenge Luke Appling. He was a great right-handed hitter but couldn't pull a ball if you held it by a string. I said, "Lucius, I'll play you behind second base because I know you'll hit it down the middle or to right-center or right. If you hit the ball through shortstop I'll buy you a dinner the next time you're in Philadelphia." That would foul him up so badly because he just couldn't pull the ball. So one day he says to me, "Bets are off."

B. PIERCE:

Luke became a very good friend of mine. He said, "Kid, you've got to learn to drink scotch. It's good for you and will give you strength." So I drank a little. It was the ugliest-tasting stuff I had in my life. I thought it was medicine. That's why I didn't drink. It had nothing to do with religion. I had no problem adjusting. If another player wanted to drink, fine. I could go along and have a Coke. I never had problems with other ballplayers, where if I didn't drink I wasn't part of the group. They understood that I'd rather be at the movies.

BOB CAIN:

After high school graduation in 1942, I left Salina, Kansas, a small town where my father had a line of taxicabs, and went to Coffeyville to play Ban Johnson League amateur ball. I pitched and played in the field. I had known I had special talent since pitching my American Legion team to a state title and getting offers from scouts. Then I got new offers from eight clubs and accepted a contract for a couple of hundred dollars a month from the New York Giants. They were my favorite team because they always had left-handed pitchers.

Although I had signed a Triple-A contract, I pitched and played first base and the outfield in Bristol, Tennessee, in the Appalachian League, which was Class D. Then I went in the service. Afterward, I was assigned to Manchester, New Hampshire, where I played against Nashua's Don Newcombe and Roy Campanella—that was the first time I played in an integrated game. I then played with Jersey City in the International League and ran up against Montreal and Jackie Robinson. I'd never forget how he ran the bases. He always caught players napping and took the extra base. Then I played with Minneapolis in the American Association, until they sold me to the Memphis Chicks in the Southern League. Memphis was affiliated to the White Sox.

After our season ended in 1949, I went up to the White Sox. It was exciting to come to the majors. I had never even been to a major league ballpark. I made only 6 appearances for Jack Onslow, all in relief, and though I pitched well I got no decisions. In my first appearance, I relieved against Boston. We were far behind. The batter was Ted Williams. I struck him out on a called third strike! He was surprised that a rookie would throw a 3–2 curveball. That was the last time I struck him out. He could remember what a pitcher threw him and he didn't forget that I would go with my curve in such a situation. He was the best hitter I saw. He'd stand up there with his hands eagerly sliding back and forth on the bat as you wound up. Williams was fearless at the plate and wouldn't bail out against the toughest left-handers. He'd have stood up there if a cannon were on the mound.

NEW YORK YANKEES

BILLY JOHNSON:

Casey Stengel became the Yankees' manager in 1949. He was hard and strict, but he got along with most of the players, including Joe DiMaggio. Stengel believed in platooning players, so everyone on the bench got a lot of playing time. Only Rizzuto at short, and DiMaggio in center—when he wasn't injured that year—were sure to be in the lineup every day. He believed a right-handed hitter like me couldn't hit a right-handed pitcher as well as a left-handed batter could. To prove it, one day we needed a pinch hitter, and instead of choosing a right-handed .300 hitter, he picked pitcher Tommy Byrne, who batted left-handed. Byrne was a good hitter, but he made an out. The writers, who loved Casey because he gave them great quotes, questioned Casey on his move the next day and he responded, "If Byrne got a hit, you'd say I was the smartest manager in the world. But he didn't get a hit, so now you're saying I'm the dumbest."

EDDIE JOOST (ATHLETICS):

Casey Stengel was never a good manager until he got to the Yankees, where he came to be regarded as one of the greatest managers in history. He got accolades he didn't deserve because the press loved him—he'd tell stories and go on and on and on in his Stengelese, talking for hours and never saying a thing. I told him I could manage his team just by sitting in the office. In fact, he never made the decisions. His coaches Frank Crosetti and Jim Turner ran the Yankees. Turner was a great student of pitching and was out in the bullpen, and Crosetti was at third base giving the signs. Stengel was in the dugout not having any idea what was going on. When he would make a decision, it was usually wrong. But he had two ballclubs on the Yankees. He could play either one and win. Hank Bauer would come up to me and ask who we were pitching the next day. He'd want to know if he was going to play. I'd tease him and not tell him. There were several guys who hated being on the Yankees because they either sat on the bench or were platooned when they knew they had the talent to play every day on another team. Stengel would laugh if we'd change pitchers because he had several guys on the bench with bats in their hands.

The Yankees would come to Philadelphia and we'd beat their pants off. I had some of my greatest games against them. Stengel didn't like that. During games I used to talk to Berra and Rizzuto, but one game I got a double and found that Rizzuto wouldn't speak to me at second. Then, when I came up again, Berra said, "Don't talk to me. Stengel told us not to talk to you guys because you're always beating us. Why don't you beat Cleveland instead?"

B. JOHNSON:

I never argued with Casey about platooning. I was a team player, so it was fine with me if Casey played

Bobby Brown at third. He was an excellent left-handed batter who could hit to all fields. Sometimes Casey would have us both in there, playing me at first and moving Tommy Henrich, a left-handed hitter, back to the outfield or resting him against a left-hander.

AL KOZAR (SENATORS):

Tommy Henrich would go to the middle or to left field his first three times up in a game. Then, in his last time up, I was told to play him straight away and back toward right field, even at Yankee Stadium. He'd always homer to right.

B. JOHNSON:

Bobby Brown and I were very good friends and I didn't have problems with anybody about his playing. Bobby was very intelligent. He was a medical student. He roomed with Yogi Berra. That was an unusual pair, but they worked out fine. Yogi was smart in his own way.

Another thing Stengel—or the Yankee executives—liked to do was acquire a veteran to help down the stretch. In 1949 we purchased Johnny Mize, the former home run champion with the Cardinals and Giants. He had a bunch of key hits for us in September. He did so well that the Yankees would make it a practice to pick up veterans for stretch drives in future years.

I used to watch Stengel get on umpires every once in a while. It was funny. He'd go argue and have his say, but after the argument was over, the umpire would say, "What was he talking about?" He couldn't understand Casey—it was all mumble and grumble.

Stengel might have been a good manager, but anybody could have managed the Yankees at this time. We had the caliber of players that could win. We had a terrific race with the Red Sox, who had such great players as Ted Williams, Bobby Doerr, Vern Stephens, Dom DiMaggio, Johnny Pesky, Mel Parnell, and Ellis Kinder. They were managed by Joe McCarthy, who brought me to the majors in 1943 when he managed the Yankees. They were strong competition, but we edged them in the final week, winning the pennant by one game. We refused to lose to the Red Sox.

GENE WOODLING:

In 1949 I joined the Yankees. In 1948 Casey Stengel had managed Oakland in the Coast League, and I murdered that team, so I imagine he had some influence on the Yankees' getting me.

This was the year the Yankees officially began their dynasty, but everybody was already trying to beat them. Let's face it: we had a great ballclub. We had outstanding pitching and hitting, and our defense was never given proper credit. And we all could run, so we didn't hit into ground-ball double plays. Casey said he didn't want guys who took one swing and made two outs. We hit into far fewer double plays than anyone else. That's what wins ballgames.

We also led the league in being "RAs." We had some of the best Red Asses who ever played baseball. If you fooled with Chief Reynolds, Vic Raschi, Hank Bauer, or me, you were in trouble. Raschi may have been the nicest person in the world off the field, but you didn't mess with him on the field. We were serious. And we got on each other. Casey sat over there and watched us do his job. We never went out to hurt anyone, but if someone took advantage of one of our guys, they were going to be in trouble. We played tough baseball.

You think we were determined? You bothered DiMaggio and you were really going to be in trouble. You know where he did his grumbling? In the outfield. He'd grumble if the pitchers didn't get the ball over and were fooling around. He had no patience for that. He came to play and was a bear-down no-nonsense player all the way. Not just on the field, but in his whole life. He had a lot of pride in himself. He always looked like the part he played—he was all class in everything he did. He was the type who wouldn't do anything that he couldn't do right. I doubt if he ever told a joke, and he didn't laugh too often. But he was a great guy. He'd do anything for any of us. His personality reflected the personality of the Yankees. He was a leader.

DiMaggio never talked about Ted Williams. DiMaggio didn't talk. He didn't say anything all year. He wasn't cold or aloof—he was just a quiet, bashful individual. He didn't have to say anything. We just watched him and tried to play as hard as he did. It was a thrill to play alongside of him because he had been a hero when I was a boy. Bauer and I just stayed in our little circles in right and left fields, and when the ball was hit anywhere else we'd say, "Go ahead, Joe." After the game, Bauer and I would go home, while Joe had to wait three hours to avoid fans and sportswriters. I expected him to be

great, but still his talent surprised me. He was out the first 69 games of the season with a painful heel, then came to Fenway Park and had 4 homers and 9 RBIs to lead a 3-game sweep against the Red Sox. I have no qualms with DiMaggio being voted the best ballplayer who ever lived. Of course, no player was perfect, not even DiMaggio. I remember him forgetting there were only two outs and letting the winning run cross the plate. But let me tell you—that didn't happen too often. More likely it was Joe driving in the winning run for us with two outs in the ninth.

Yogi Berra wasn't the best catcher, but he was a terrific hitter. He didn't have that "RA" desire a lot of us did, but he got the job done. Yogi wouldn't hurt a fly. For the public, Berra built an image of being a dumb, funny guy. He did make those absurd nonsensical statements he was famous for—I'd say, "Jesus, Yogi, what

A marvelous left fielder and dangerous left-handed batter, Gene Woodling would be one of the Yankees' steadiest players as they went on to win 5 straight world titles from 1949 to 1953.

are you talking about?''—but he was a serious player. He wasn't dumb. He didn't read comics. Bobby Brown came up with that: he said he was reading medical books and Yogi was over there reading comic books. Yogi got good mileage out of the publicity.

I think there was the right degree of levity and seriousness on this team. I was serious for three hours a day. You just didn't fuss with me when I went to the ballpark. I didn't care who the manager or owner was; I didn't care about the uniform. I played the best that my body let me. Then I relaxed. I could be a fun guy. I didn't agree with that false crap about eating, sleeping, and dying baseball 24 hours a day. I didn't do that. I didn't owe anybody anything when I walked out of that clubhouse at the end of the day. I even used to say, ''Stick baseball up your butt.''

Casey got to see that side of me and, I think, know me better at our World Series victory party. I had complained all year to Casey about being platooned with Hank Bauer and batting less than 300 times. Stengel talked to my wife, Betty, and casually brought up my fussing about playing time, expecting her to know what he was talking about. She said, ''Casey, I'm glad you told me because Gene never brought one word home.'' From that moment on, he had new respect for me. You see, I never took baseball home with me. It didn't belong in my home. It's not right to burden your wife and children about not getting any base hits or enough playing time.

We got into the World Series by getting past the Red Sox. Boston came into New York for 2 games to conclude the season. They had to win one game to eliminate us; we had to win both games. Johnny Lindell got the biggest hit of *my* entire career in the Saturday game. That was Joe DiMaggio Day and they had a celebration for him before the game. There were 65,000 fans in Yankee Stadium. Joe had been terribly sick but insisted on playing. For one of the few times all season, Allie Reynolds wasn't sharp and the Red Sox took a 4–0 lead before we started to come back. We knocked out their ace, Mel Parnell. Then we tied the game when Billy Johnson grounded into a double play with the bases loaded. Meanwhile, Joe Page was masterful, holding Boston scoreless inning after inning. In the eighth inning, with two outs, after two left-handed pinch hitters made outs, Stengel decided to leave in Johnny Lindell against right-hander Joe Dobson. Dobson threw him a high fastball and Lindell hit it over the fence. We won 5–4. Lindell gave us a chance to play for the pennant the next day. That game Raschi went against Ellis Kinder. We scored a run in the first inning when Rizzuto tripled and Henrich grounded out to second. And Raschi made it hold up—he was some pitcher. In the eighth, with Kinder gone, we scored 4 more runs on a Henrich homer off Parnell and a bloop bases-clearing double by Jerry Coleman. Boston rallied for 3 runs in the top of the ninth, but we held on to win 5–3 for the pennant. So I have Johnny Lindell to thank for getting me into my first World Series—a poor boy's dream.

WORLD SERIES

1949

YANKEES VS DODGERS

BILLY JOHNSON · YANKEES:

Both the Yankees and Dodgers won 97 games and clinched pennants on the last day of the season. The Dodgers were a much better team in 1949 than in 1947. They now had Roy Campanella, Duke Snider, and Billy Cox in their lineup and they had added pitchers Don Newcombe and Preacher Roe. They were better with Jackie Robinson at second and Hodges at first. But we also had improved and beat them in just 5 games. The key to the Series was our pitching. Roe shut us out in Game Two, but that was it for them. Tommy Henrich's 9th inning homer beat Newcombe in the first game, and Raschi, Reynolds, Lopat, Byrne, and Page did all our pitching and were all great. That was a very exciting Series. Bobby Brown, my platoon mate, did real good job batting .500, with 5 RBIs.

GENE WOODLING · YANKEES:

Going into the World Series, I was nervous. Any guy who said that he wasn't would be lying. Even DiMaggio and Berra were nervous. I had a nervous edge my entire career and I think it was a good thing. It made me a better player and competitor.

Stengel prepared us for the 1949 World Series quite simply. He said, "Go get 'em!" I'd have to say that Jackie Robinson and Pee Wee Reese were the keys to the Dodgers. Reese had a good Series, but our pitchers pretty much stopped Robinson from getting on base. Pee Wee was a good leader. I knew him because we spent time together in the navy. He was good people and a helluva ballplayer.

Pitching dominated the first three games. Chief and Don Newcombe hooked up in a scoreless tie for 8 innings and then Tommy Henrich won it for us, 1–0, on a leadoff homer in the ninth, the first time a Series game had been won like that. The Dodgers won the second game, 1–0, behind Preacher Roe, who bested Raschi. We went to Brooklyn for Game Three, with Tommy Byrne going against Ralph Branca, and that game was tied 1–1 until the ninth inning. Joe Page pitched great relief for us from the fourth inning on. Then, in the ninth, Johnny Mize had a big pinch single and we scored 3 runs. The Dodgers came back with 2 homers off Joe Page, but we won 4–3. We had an easier time in the final two games, jumping off to big leads. We won all three games in Brooklyn. So we had won the first of 5 World Series in a row.

SPIDER JORGENSEN, DODGERS:

I was much looser than I'd been in the 1947 Series. I thought we were going to bowl over the Yankees. But we didn't hit. Snider had a bad Series and didn't drive in any runs. The first game was a killer. I guess that's when Newcombe started to be called a choker. He wasn't that. He'd won big games all year, including the one that put us up in the pennant race. He was a good pitcher and we had faith in him. Rather than being disappointed that the Yankees won the Series, I was dumbfounded that they had won it so easily. I couldn't believe it, because our team was very good. Maybe we lost because after the pennant race we felt that the Series was an anticlimax.

Later, I heard Branch Rickey was criticized for being so cheap that he made us give back our 1947 World Series rings to get rings from 1949. But I don't recall being offered rings after either Series. Only the winners, the Yankees, got rings.

NATIONAL LEAGUE 1950

"EDDIE STANKY, THE GIANTS' SECOND BASEMAN, GOT IN LINE WITH ME AT THE PLATE AND MAGLIE ON THE MOUND, AND JUMPED UP AND DOWN, DOING WHAT WE CALLED THE 'HOP-STRADDLE' TO DISTRACT ME. AFTER I COMPLAINED TO THE UMPIRE, MAGLIE DRILLED ME IN THE DAMN RIBS."

ANDY SEMINICK

BOSTON BRAVES

JOHNNY SAIN:

In 1950 I learned how to pitch with discomfort. I decided to throw like I threw in the outfield before games because that didn't hurt. I loosened my grip and made my throws more fluid. I'd stay loose all through my windup until I used power when I released the ball. I adjusted my whole body according to the position of my hand upon release. I came back and won 20 games with the same arm. But I did struggle and even needed relief help on my 20th win, which was unheard of. And though I increased my innings pitched to 278, I was still behind Vern Bickford, who led the league with over 300 innings, and Warren Spahn, who threw over 290 innings. The three of us combined for 60 wins, with Spahn winning 21 games and Bickford 19. We also got some good offensive production from Bob Elliott, Earl Torgeson, and Tommy Holmes, and several newcomers: rookie outfielder Sam Jethroe, and former Giants Walker Cooper, Sid Gordon, and Willard Marshall—we got Gordon and Marshall for Alvin Dark and Eddie Stanky prior to the season. With so many players having good years, our record improved, but we still finished fourth behind the Phillies, Dodgers, and Giants.

JOHNNY ANTONELLI:

Sam Jethroe joined the Braves in 1950, having played several years in the Negro Leagues. He was the Braves' first black player. What we had heard about his speed was true. As a rookie, he led the National League in stolen bases and scored 100 runs. He had bad eyesight and wasn't a good outfielder but he was a good offensive player and was voted National League Rookie of the Year. Some pitchers probably threw at him, but I don't remember him having trouble with our players or fans because he was the only black player in Boston. No one gave Sam a hard time unless he dropped the ball or got hit right in the head by a line drive, as happened in Philadelphia. We'd kid him about stuff like that, but there was nothing racial about it. We liked Sam. He was a nice guy.

Again, Billy Southworth didn't pitch me very much. In fact, I pitched almost 40 innings less than in 1949 and got fewer starts. They kept saying, "He's never had any minor league experience.'' I didn't think I needed it—I just needed to pitch in games rather than on the sidelines. But I got the equivalent of minor league ball after I was drafted into the service and played ball there in 1951 and 1952.

BOB BUHL:

In the minors, I used to strike out as many as I walked, and sometimes I walked more. I just threw fastballs and tried to throw a curve. I was cocky on the mound and tried to make batters look foolish and laugh at them, and if they got a hit, they'd laugh at me. It was fun. In 1949 I had played at Hartford in the Eastern League. It was like a baseball school and I started learning about fundamentals.

In 1950 I had a good spring training with the Triple A Milwaukee Brewers in Austin, Texas. But when the season started, I wasn't used. I got disgusted and told the manager, Bob Coleman, to send me someplace where I'd get to pitch. Meanwhile, I went home, just across the lake. The next day the Brewers sold my contract to Dallas, an independent team in the Double A Texas League. I flew into Houston in a two-engine plane and met the Dallas club at the Shamrock Hotel. The manager, Charlie Grimm, got me a room and I started playing for Dallas. Grimm had been the Cubs manager until the year before. He was a peach to play for. I roomed with three younger fellows in a house and we spent a lot of time playing pool and riding buses. I stayed with Dallas all season and had something like a 10–14 record. I could feel myself developing, but still all I had was a fastball and mediocre curve. I still didn't know anything about pitching.

The Braves bought my contract back in August and wanted me to report for the last 30 days of the season. I told Grimm I'd prefer staying with Dallas through the playoffs and reporting to the Braves in the spring and starting the new season fresh. He called John Quinn and I was given permission to stay with Dallas in the playoffs. We lost. After that I went home. Now I had a major league contract for $5,000 and was looking forward to spring training. Come December I get a notice: ''Uncle Sam Wants You.'' When I had tried to join the Marines when I was 17, they had turned me down. They sent me to the navy. They turned me down, too, and told me to go to the army. I said, if I wanted the army I'd have gone there first. So now, at 21, I'm ready to make my move in life, and I get drafted by the army for two years. The upsetting part was that if I'd have played with the Braves in September I'd have gotten two more years in the pension program.

CHICAGO CUBS

HANK SAUER:

In 1950 Andy Pafko and I were the best one-two punch in the league. He had 36 homers and 92 RBIs and I had 32 homers and 103 RBIs. We finished second and third in homers, behind Ralph Kiner. Also, our shortstop, Roy Smalley, and third baseman, Bill Serena, each hit about 20 homers, so we were getting pretty good offensive production. We also got good pitching from Bob Rush, Johnny Schmitz, Paul Minner, and Frank Hiller, and moved out of the cellar, ahead of the Pirates and only 2 games behind the sixth-place Reds.

When I first came to the Cubs, it was hard to hit in Wrigley Field. People were sitting in center field, so the white ball came out of the white shirts. We used to pray for sidearmers, and those guys were tough to hit. At least their pitches would come out of the vines so we could see the ball. I had success because when I batted I never looked beyond the pitcher. I'd just watch his arm and the ball come out of his hand. If you looked beyond his hand, you had problems. It was the same at Ebbets Field in Brooklyn. Eventually they blocked off that area of Wrigley and it became easier to hit. But there were other obstacles. The winds were strong and would change. It could blow straight in and be extremely cold. Once when the wind was blowing in, the Pirates' Murry Dickson told me he was going to throw every pitch down the middle and let me hit it as hard as I wanted. I hit three shots that went out of the ballpark and blew back in and were caught. The last time up, I hit the best shot of my life and it barely hit the fence. Guys like Stan Musial questioned how I could hit so many homers there.

Still, I loved playing in Wrigley Field. The fans were great. They knew baseball better than anybody—the only ones who came close were the fans of New York and Brooklyn. I became so popular there that I got to be known as ''the Mayor of Wrigley Field.'' There were those who suggested I run for mayor of Chicago. Fans would throw tobacco to me. What I couldn't put in my pocket I'd store in the vines. I supplied the whole club with tobacco. Even Yosh Kawano, the clubhouse man, who I roomed with that year, got tobacco. He was a chewer. As soon as I put on the uniform I had to have a chaw of tobacco. But I never chewed out of uniform and what I had left over I'd give to him.

The Chicago fans were the nicest in baseball. They would boo opposing players, but if they did something good, they cheered them. If an opposing player homered, they'd clap for him—they wouldn't throw the ball back on the field. If you gave 100 percent, the Chicago fans never got on you. But if you loafed once or twice you would really be hassled. Roy Smalley was the only Cub they really booed. He loafed a couple of times going to first, and after that he couldn't go out on the field without being booed. And he was one of the nicest guys. After the 1953 season the Cubs would have to get rid of him. Seeing what happened to Roy, I never would loaf in that town, especially since I played in the outfield where fans could throw things at me. So I never had problems.

The only time I ever had anything thrown at me was during an exhibition game between the Cubs and White Sox at Comiskey Park. I was in the outfield and a Sox fan threw one of those heavy circular iron grates and just missed me. That would have done some damage. I moved in so far that nobody could reach me with anything. I thought that if someone hit the ball over my head I wasn't going after it. They were tough on the South Side.

There was definitely a rivalry between the Cubs and White Sox, which was very apparent when we'd open up the year with a 3-game exhibition series. It was hotly contested. The media didn't favor one team over the other. The media was never a problem in Chicago. I got nothing but good things from them. No one gave players trouble except for Warren Brown. The rest of the reporters were great guys. There weren't any hatchet guys. And there weren't any reporters following us around to see if we missed curfews.

On the other hand, Frankie Frisch tried to catch me missing curfew in Boston. We had just lost a one-run game, and I decided to have fun that night. I went out with a few of the guys and had a couple of beers—not too many because I wasn't much of a drinker—had something to eat, and found me a little girl I was running around with at that time there. I came back to the hotel at about one-thirty. I saw Frisch and his coaches sitting in the lobby. They were looking the other way, so I raced past them and up to my room, where Ron Northey tells me, "Goddamn, Hank, they did a bed check and caught you out." The next day Frisch calls me to his suite and says, "My big guy had to go out and have a good time. I'm going to fine you $200 and the others $100." $200 was a lot considering my low salary—I was still working in the off-season to make ends meet. At the end of the season, he said, "Hank, if you hit a home run today, I'll give you your money back." I said, "What about the other guys?" He agreed to give them back their money if I homered. I told them that they had better pull for me so they could get their $100 back. I hit a homer and you've never seen guys so happy.

FRANK BAUMHOLTZ:

Frisch's attitude toward me hadn't changed and he sent me to the minors although I was better than a lot of players on the team. He told me, "There's room for only two Germans on this ballclub and you're not one of them"—he didn't realize that Sauer was Hungarian, not German. Before the season, Frisch dumped me with the Los Angeles Angels in the Coast League. I hit .400 until the last two weeks and ended up at .379. Still, I didn't even get to play with the Cubs in September.

JOHNNY KLIPPSTEIN:

I was 22 when I went to spring training with the Cubs on Catalina Island. New players were invited a week early, and that sounded like fun, but then they had to climb through the mountains on the goat paths. I'd heard about that, so I didn't come until a day before camp. The guys who came early were covered by bumps and bruises and sores.

I dated one of the three or four girls on the island, and one night I got in five minutes before the midnight curfew and Frankie Frisch and his coach Spud Davis were out front making comments about my trying to make the club yet staying out late. I said, "Mr. Frisch, your curfew is midnight and I got back in time. If you had made it an eleven-thirty curfew, I would have made that, too.

I'll see you in the morning." Frisch liked that and we got along from then on. If you wouldn't stand up to him, he would get all over you.

Frisch really used to pick on Carmen Mauro, a left-handed-hitting outfielder. Every day he'd agitate poor Carmen about everything from swinging on the wrong count to wearing old shoes. Frisch wasn't a good manager for this ballclub. He was at the end of his career and just lollygagging around. There were times at Wrigley Field when we'd be in the seventh or eighth inning and he'd say, "I can't stand to watch minor league baseball—somebody give me a bucket, I think I'm going to puke." Then he'd take off for the clubhouse. We weren't a good team, but we weren't that bad at times. I don't know if Wrigley knew about his actions.

I was happy to finally make the majors but I had a tough rookie year. I went only 2–9, and won only 1 of 11 starts. I actually had a better year at the plate, where I went 11 for 33 and hit my first homer. Frisch was such a maniac that he sent me up to pinch-hit against Ewell Blackwell. I grounded out to second and was just glad to get out of there.

Phil Cavarretta was the team leader. He had played

Although he had a difficult rookie season with the Cubs, right-hander Johnny Klippstein would go on to pitch in the majors for 8 teams over 18 seasons.

first base and outfield for the club since the mid-thirties and was a fixture on the team. He was as gung-ho about winning as a player could be. He'd want to win at all costs and he didn't care if we were behind 10–0. It's not surprising that when Wrigley got around to firing Frisch in 1951, he made Phil the player-manager.

The Cubs had two offensive stars, Andy Pafko and Hank Sauer. Pafko was a great hitter and outfielder. Hank was a free-swinging home run hitter, and he'd get so mad when he took a third strike. He would come back to the dugout moaning and complaining about the umpire, but he was really mad at himself for not swinging. At times he was accused of being a bad fielder, but while he didn't cover a lot of ground, he caught anything he got his hands on. When he'd go to left field in Wrigley Field, fans would throw him Beechnut and Red Man tobacco.

Both Andy and Hank were likable guys. So were Cavarretta and Rube Walker. Rube had a good sense of humor, and we had a lot of good times together. My best friends were Roy Smalley and pitchers Warren Hacker, Bob Rush, and Dutch Leonard. Roy hit over 20 homers and drove in 85 runs that year, but he had a low average, led the league in strikeouts, and had some trouble at short, and as a result would get booed at Wrigley every time he ran onto the field. He claimed it never bothered him, but I lockered next to him over the years and saw that it did.

Bob Rush lost 20 games in 1950, but he led the team with 13 wins and was our best, most consistent pitcher. The Cubs' one-time ace Johnny Schmitz was finishing his long stay with the team. Warren Hacker and Paul Minner, who came over from the Dodgers, were beginning their stays. Dutch Leonard had already pitched about 15 years when he came to the Cubs in 1949 from the Phillies. In 1950 he became a reliever, so we spent a lot of time warming up together. He was a knuckleball pitcher, so he couldn't really help me too much with my pitching. Dutch and I roomed together when I first came to the Cubs. When I hung my pants over a chair, he'd say, "In the big leagues, we hang them up." He set me straight. He was a great guy. In 1952 I'd marry his niece.

When I was a single guy, I lived in an apartment on the North Side of Chicago, near Wrigley Field. Most of the girls I dated lived in the neighborhood, so I never went downtown. One day after a game I was in a bar having a couple of beers with Ron Northey, a likable, funny, straight-talking outfielder and pinch-hit specialist we picked up from Cincinnati during the season. Ron went over to a young lady and told her I was quite a ladies' man and had been talking about her for an hour. Of course, I hadn't said anything. Ron invited me to their table and said, ''John, this lady is really attracted to you.'' She said that she'd like to have a date with me, but already had a date that night. Ron convinced her to break the date. So I had a date with her. She had a Cadillac and drove us to dinner at a country club. I couldn't even pick up the tab. The next day, Ron said, ''That should have been me.''

In those days players kept their relationships with women fairly private. On every club there were two or three guys who were known for going out looking for women at night, but very few flaunted it. There were a lot of girls hanging around, but guys definitely thought about what happened to Eddie Waitkus and most were more careful. Some guys didn't care. There was a place we used to go to have a few beers. One time Russ Meyer, who pitched for the Cubs before being dealt to the Phillies, was in there talking to a girl. He was kind of a crazy guy who had the nickname ''the Mad Monk.'' He got fresh with her and she leaned over and bit almost half his nose off. Of course, he got kidded about that for years.

The men who played baseball in the late forties were tough mentally and physically. They worked hard and were very serious about what they were doing, and were in love with it, too. They might have played for free. Most weren't well educated, but they were knowledgeable and well versed about all aspects of life. I think few had come from above middle-class homes. They had never had it too easy and had grown up with the work ethic. I think about half the players were religious. The Catholics were the ones who went to church on Sundays, while services were too late for everyone else. By and large, the players were private. They kept their most serious problems to themselves or just shared them with their closest friends on their teams. They rarely talked politics or religion; they mostly talked baseball.

The players on most teams, including the Cubs, were unified. After a game, we'd sit around the clubhouse and have two or three beers and talk about the past game and what we hoped to do in the next game. If you were sitting in a hotel lobby and a few guys would be on their way out, they'd invite you along. For relaxation a lot of us played golf during spring training. During the year we'd go to movies, eat together, hang out together. In every town we'd try to find a pretty nice restaurant. In New York we'd often go to Mama Leone's; once in a while we'd go to Toots Shor's.

Guys would go out to have a good time but always be back before curfew. Very few were heavy drinkers and very few were carousers or partygoers. I liked to drink beer but I'd stop if it affected me. Lots of players drank—but everyone drank back then, not just ballplayers. I also smoked cigarettes but would quit when it got too heavy. I smoked in September when it was tense. Most players smoked. There was also a lot of tobacco chewing. I chewed tobacco until it got the best of me and I felt a little queasy. It was kind of a superstition that you would hit better when you chewed tobacco. All ballplayers were superstitious. Very few stepped on chalk lines. When I went to third, I'd give the base a kick.

We didn't feel like celebrities, but it made us feel special to have fan clubs. Almost everyone had one in those days. And girls would come to the park wearing jackets with their favorite players' names on them. That was nice. There was a girl who formed a fan club for me in 1950, and would keep it going for the full time I was in Chicago.

RANDY JACKSON:

Somebody got the brilliant idea for everyone to come out a week early to Catalina. And you couldn't touch a baseball during that time. They had a lot of wild goats on the island and they thought that if we came early and walked the goat paths we'd get our legs into real good shape. What were we going to say? For a week we walked up and down the mountains. Of 30 guys, 28 came down with shin splints, including me. I'd never had them before.

The Cubs offered me a contract that gave me just a $500 raise. It wasn't fair after my making two minor league All-Star teams, but it didn't bother me. I made the team and played 18 games before I went to the minors. Then I came back and joined the Cubs in Boston.

That first night I homered off Vern Bickford, who was trying to win his 20th game. He never got it. I finished the season with 3 homers in a little over 100 at-bats, and batted .225.

Frankie Frisch was my first manager. I think this is true of a lot of great ballplayers: Frisch assumed that everybody should know what to do and that everybody was as good as he'd been. He didn't think anybody should make mistakes, but it doesn't work that way. Another former great, Rogers Hornsby, was our batting practice coach, but we never talked about hitting. I never saw him help anybody.

The star of the team was Hank Sauer. He was a terrific hitter and a peach of a guy, just an old country guy. Everyone looked up to Phil Cavarretta, who was the team captain. He was a first baseman and he took the lineup out each day and I guess that made him a leader. He didn't really help ballplayers. Nobody really did.

JIM BROSNAN:

I went to spring training in Fullerton, California, with the Los Angeles Angels in the Coast League. I had no chance to make it there because it was a super team of veteran ballplayers, some who had been in the league about a dozen years. So I was sent to Springfield, Illinois. Then I was sent to Nashville in Double A, playing for Don Osborn. The only time he spoke to me was when he reamed out my ass for throwing my glove high in the air after an error cost me a game. I was a poor loser. I did badly at Nashville and was sent to Des Moines in A ball. I pitched for Charlie Root, a no-nonsense type, and made a mistake with him. I went all the way in a game and got beat 2–1 when the right fielder jumped up and the ball bounced off his glove and went over the fence. Having learned the hard way not to get angry at my fielders, I didn't overreact and throw my glove in the air again. I didn't say anything. I walked into the clubhouse and sat down and started reading *Time* magazine. Root saw me and blew his stack. He said that I displayed the worst attitude he'd ever seen from a ballplayer in his life. That night he wrote his regular managerial report and sent it to Cubs general manager Wid Mathews at Wrigley Field. It said: "Get rid of him. I don't want him playing on my club." The next day I was on my way to Decatur in B ball.

Third baseman Ransom "Randy" Jackson was another rookie who had a shaky start in 1950, but until the mid-'50s would contribute a steady glove and the strong bat to complement Hank Sauer in the otherwise weak Cubs lineup.

I certainly wasn't encouraged. And I didn't pitch well at Decatur, for that matter. But this was a club with the dregs of the system. We didn't even have young prospects. They were all guys like me who couldn't make it any higher or had some problems of one sort or another. It was like being with a bunch of cutups at college. In August I got my draft notice. I thought, "Hell, I'm going into the army anyway. I don't give a fuck about this organization. We were gonna have fun every night." And that is what we did. I was actually sociable for a change. I never drank so much beer in my life.

It was at Decatur that I began to write. As a kid I spent as much time in libraries as I did playing ball. If I had any adult ambitions, it was to have a book with my name on it on the library shelf. I always was interested in writing but never pursued it seriously until I started keeping a diary. I'd write about 250 words a day, injecting personal thoughts and some dialogue. This was the genesis of my later journalistic books. I intended to continue the diary in the army, but found I didn't have time once basic training began.

BROOKLYN DODGERS

DON NEWCOMBE:

I had another big year, pitching almost 270 innings and tying Preacher Roe for the most wins on the staff with 19, 4 of them shutouts. One Sunday, I started both ends of a doubleheader. Again we had a strong offense. Jackie, Duke Snider, and Carl Furillo batted over .300, and Roy, Snider, and Gil Hodges each hit over 30 homers. In August, Hodges hit 4 homers and a single in a game against the Braves. Nobody could hit like the Dodgers. Not the Phillies. But the Phillies edged us in the pennant race because only Roe, Erv Palica, and I won over 10 games. We won only 89 games.

ANDY SEMINICK (PHILLIES):

I suppose some of the Brooklyn press and fans got on Don Newcombe pretty badly because he was the losing pitcher in the final game of the season, when the Phillies clinched the pennant. It's true that he gave up the three-run homer to Dick Sisler that gave us the victory, but that came in the tenth inning, don't forget. He did more than the Dodgers could have expected of him in the first nine innings. The only run we got came after a pop fly that fell between Snider and Robinson in center. It should have been caught. Then the Dodgers should have won the game in the ninth, but their third-base coach Milt Stock waved Cal Abrams home with none out on a short single and he got nailed. They could have had a big rally, but they didn't score and Newcombe, who probably assumed that he had a win in his pocket, had to try to gear himself up again and pitch some more. That's when we got to him. I wouldn't have blamed Newcombe. Maybe I'd have blamed Stock—I know the Dodgers fired him after the year—or his team for not giving him any runs. Newcombe did his job.

D. NEWCOMBE

Dan Bankhead returned from the minors and won 9 games, but he was hit pretty hard. Dan and I were room-mates for a while. He was a good pitcher, but didn't have that much desire to play in the majors. At the time you couldn't play major league ball and winter league ball, and Dan preferred playing in the wintertime because he had fallen in love with a woman in Mexico. He'd pitch briefly for the Dodgers in 1951 and then his major league career was over.

SPIDER JORGENSEN:

I was always insecure about my job. My expression was "running scared." I never knew from year to year if I'd be traded to another team or be sent to the minors. I didn't ask Branch Rickey what my status was. We didn't speak. I wouldn't negotiate my contracts with him directly. I'd either do it through the mail or with Branch Jr., who would come into the clubhouse every once in a while.

I hated to leave Brooklyn because I had made a lot of friends there. But I could see the writing on the wall. Bobby Cox was now the everyday third baseman. The Dodgers could have used me if I were a utility player, but I could only play third and Bobby Morgan, who had a couple of good years in Montreal, could play second, short, and third. So I wasn't really surprised when the Dodgers traded me, although it did surprise me that I was dealt to the Giants. At least I didn't hate the Giants—our games with them had been intense, but nowhere near as dirty as our games with the Cardinals.

NEW YORK GIANTS

SPIDER JORGENSEN:

Leaving the Dodgers was the biggest disappointment of my career. But I wasn't upset going to the Giants because Leo Durocher, my former manager on Brooklyn, was managing over there; Herman Franks, who had been a teammate at Montreal, was a coach and Leo's gin rummy opponent; and ex-Dodger Eddie Stanky was the second baseman. I discovered that the Giants weren't as close as the Dodgers. When the game was over, everyone disappeared. We didn't have the parties or get-togethers that we had on Brooklyn. I did become good friends with my roommate, Bill Rigney.

At first it was a little hard to play against the Dodg-

Joining the Giants in 1950, ex-Dodger Spider Jorgensen became one of the few players of the era to play for both National League New York teams.

ers, but I got used to it. They were still good guys, but I wanted to beat them bad. There was a strong rivalry between the two teams, so we didn't want to lose to them. Leo really wanted to beat his former team. He wasn't friendly to those guys. In fact, he got into razzing battles with Jackie Robinson and Don Newcombe at Ebbets Field.

I liked Leo. I think he was well liked by the players, if not as popular as his wife, Laraine Day—she had a daily radio show and the players were happy to be her guests. I thought Leo was a great manager who was always a few innings ahead of everybody. He used to coach third base, which was a common practice of managers back then. He wanted to be in the game and to pester the umpires a little more than he could do from the dugout. Leo was a superstitious man, and when he'd go out to the coaching box each inning, he'd always jump over a water bucket in the dugout. One day the Pirates were having a hell of an inning against us. He

was in the dugout and he looked down and saw that the water bucket was gone. He went crazy looking for it. But earlier Eddie Stanky had kicked it over and it hadn't been replaced. Leo raised all kinds of hell. Our trainer, Doc Bowman, found a bucket and filled it with ice and water and put it in front of Leo. That calmed him down, and when the inning was over, he jumped over the bucket and ran to the coach's box.

For Leo I became a utility player because Hank Thompson was the regular third baseman. He had a good year with about 20 homers and a lot of runs batted in. In one game at the Polo Grounds he hit 2 inside-the-park homers. He was also a very good fielder.

Alvin Dark played every game at short. He was a good ballplayer. He played hard and was a good guy. He didn't cover as much ground as Reese and his arm wasn't as good, but he was a better hitter. He could do a lot of things with the bat. Dark and Stanky were roommates and would stick together. They'd stay in their room.

Since I was a utility player, I had a lot of spare time. One thing I did was warm up Sal Maglie all the time. He gave the right-handed Dodgers fits—he started a long winning streak in Ebbets Field. Sal was a tough guy on the mound and threw inside. We'd always say that "the Barber," which Leo nicknamed him, was giving a batter a close shave. But off the field he was a really nice guy, who I liked a lot.

I didn't finish the season with the Giants. Instead I wound up in Minneapolis, playing right field. Kirby Higbe was my roommate there. He'd become serious when he went to the Giants organization. He'd seen Billy Graham and had become religious. There was no more swearing or drinking. But he changed back because he needed to drink to celebrate.

BILL RIGNEY:
When we got Alvin Dark and Eddie Stanky from the Braves in December, I knew my days as a regular were numbered. I realized I couldn't play second base as good as Stanky, and knew I couldn't hit and play shortstop as good as Alvin. Of course, I was upset. I had just had a good year and was a solid player, but all of a sudden I got caught without a position. I dropped from 389 to 83 at-bats in one season. I thought of asking to be moved because I knew I could still play, but being a

Giant was part of my life. I wanted to end up a Giant. Only in 1950 did I think about what I'd do after my career ended. I paid special attention to how the game was played because I had nothing else to do.

Stanky had been with Durocher in Brooklyn before being traded to Boston, and Dark had been Rookie of the Year in 1948 with the Braves. They both had a falling out with Billy Southworth, the Braves' manager. They fit in because Durocher was putting together a team of players who could both hit and run. I had no trouble seeing Stanky, an ex-Dodger, as a Giant. I accepted his ability and knew he was a plus. He wasn't a lot of fun on the field because he was all business, but off the field I enjoyed him. He was a "neat" guy.

Alvin Dark was an ugly-looking shortstop but got the job done. He wasn't as slick as the other two New York shortstops, Reese and Rizzuto, but he was better offensively. He could really hit. He was a tough out, a perfect number two hitter behind Stanky. Religion was always a gray area with Al. But he certainly knew the game.

Sal Maglie rejoined the team. After the Mexican League had disbanded, he played in Latin America until Happy Chandler lifted the ban on all the players who defected to the Mexican League. Sal was already 33, but he could throw hard. He was very tough against the Dodgers' right-handed hitters because he pitched tight. Sal came in and won 18 out of 22 decisions, including 11 in a row. He threw 45 consecutive scoreless innings at the end of the year and lost his streak only because Gus Bell of the Pirates hit a 257-foot homer. Sal was a great guy despite being mean on the mound and was a tremendous addition to our team. He and Larry Jansen, who won 19 games, gave us the strong one-two pitching punch Leo wanted.

HANK SAUER (CUBS):

We had dreaded going to New York because of the Dodgers' pitching, but now we didn't look forward to going to the Polo Grounds either because they had Maglie and Jansen. Maglie had as tough a curve as Johnny Sain's. It would explode. Jansen beat you with control.

B. RIGNEY:

Sheldon Jones and Dave Koslo, who each won 13 games, were also effective. Then in mid-season Chub Feeney shrewdly got Jim Hearn on waivers from the Cardinals. He quickly won 11 games for us and had a very low earned run average. He would be a great number three pitcher, a dependable winner for years for the Giants. We still had a lot of good hitters—Thomson, Lockman, young outfielder Don Mueller, Irvin, Stanky, Dark, and others—but we finally had the pitching we needed to challenge the Dodgers.

PHILADELPHIA PHILLIES

ANDY SEMINICK:

The Phillies already had a winning attitude going into the 1950 season. We played in Brooklyn on Opening Day and scored a few runs one inning. When Jackie Robinson came up to hit, he said to me, "You guys look like you want to win a pennant." I said, "You're damn right we do." Roberts beat Newcombe that game, which gave us confidence. We realized we had a shot at the pennant early in the season when we were beating all the other teams and it was apparent that our young players—the "Whiz Kids"—had matured.

We had a lot of fun. Players had appeared on radio and some television, beginning in the late forties, but now we were wanted by a lot of talk shows—mostly local shows, but I also went on "Don McNeil's Breakfast Club" when Philadelphia went into Chicago. At some point, Dick Sisler, Ashburn, Hamner, Willie Jones, and I went on a show hosted by Ed McMahon, and we sang a song about the Phillies: "The Fightin' Phillies" or something. We would always harmonize in the showers. Mostly country and western songs. "Blood on the Saddle" or something. I think I was the lead singer.

Roberts won 20 games for the first time and Simmons won 17 before entering the army to fight in Korea. And Jim Konstanty was tremendous in relief, winning 16 games—they didn't keep track of saves then, but I know he had a lot. I had a career-high .288 average, and tied my career highs of 1949 with 68 RBIs and 24 home runs, which was third best in our lineup, 1 less than Willie Jones and 7 less than Ennis. Del led the team in batting average, homers, and RBIs. We also got good years from Ashburn, who batted over .300, Hamner, Sisler, who played left, second baseman Mike Goliat, and Eddie Waitkus, who came back from the shooting.

Eddie had 5 hits in 3 different games. He hadn't changed, at least not in the clubhouse or on the field. He didn't talk about the incident and we didn't ask. We did see his scar. It was a small scar where the bullet went in, but his back was ugly because they cut into him. Some of the bullet got lodged in his back permanently.

By this time I had assumed much of the leadership on the team. I took charge and moved our fielders around and the pitchers listened to me. If I called a pitch and Roberts didn't like it, he shook me off. If I knew it was the right pitch to throw, I'd go to the mound and explain why I wanted that pitch in the situation. Say Roberts would want to throw a change-up when the batter was hoping to pull the ball. I'd tell him to throw a fastball instead because it was harder to pull. Sometimes he'd have a lead and would get behind in the count and want to throw a freak pitch. I'd tell him why he couldn't do that. I'd also tell the pitchers if they were working too fast or too slow. We never had any problems. I called more than 90 percent of the game.

With Roberts, I'd call 8 fastballs out of every 10 pitches. He had a little curveball, which was more like a slider and hit the corners. His ball was so quick that even if he made a mistake in a batter's wheelhouse, he got him out. Almost all of the homers he gave up came when we were way ahead. He'd get careless. Maybe he was trying to save himself and didn't exert himself. Simmons had better stuff than Roberts. He came up with a change-up, which made his curve and fastball even more effective. His ball would move so much. But he couldn't hit the corners like Roberts could. With Simmons, I'd have him pitch up and down. With Roberts, it was from side to side.

Both Roberts and Simmons always rose to the occasion. With a man on third with less than two outs, they'd get the batter to pop up or strike out. Both were calm and confident. Sometimes I'd go out to the mound and remind Roberts that there was a runner on base. And he'd say, "Don't worry, he's not going to score." That was Roberts. They were both tough competitors—and bosom friends.

When we'd go into a town for a 3-game series, we were confident we'd win at least 2 games. We'd have Simmons and Roberts and maybe Russ Meyer, who had a full repertoire of pitches. Roberts pitched over 300 innings for the first time and led the league in starts and shutouts. It was a typical season. They were all work-horse pitchers who liked throwing complete games, but they didn't get upset to be taken out by Eddie Sawyer, our manager.

Sawyer couldn't make a mistake if he brought in Konstanty. He was one of the few relief specialists in those days and he was outstanding. He didn't throw hard, but he had good control and was deceptive. He'd throw a hitter's timing off with a palm ball and slider. He set a record with 74 appearances in 1950. He thrived on pitching. If he didn't get into a game, he threw in the bullpen anyway. If he felt like he wasn't right, he'd call a friend in Oneonta, New York, where he lived. His name was Andy Skinner and he was an undertaker. He would come down and watch Konstanty pitch and work out, whether we were in Philly, New York, or Boston. Then he'd talk to Konstanty and get him back on track. I'd talk to Konstanty, but Skinner was almost like a god to him and he'd respond much more to him. It was psychological. Konstanty was a good guy and everyone liked him, but he didn't mix too much with the other players. He looked more like a professor than a baseball player. He was unusual. (He didn't drink yet would eventually die of liver cancer.)

One day in August, I was facing Sal Maglie. I had good luck hitting the Giants, so Eddie Stanky, the Giants' second baseman, got in line with me at the plate and Maglie on the mound, and jumped up and down, doing what we called the "hop-straddle" to distract me. After I complained to the umpire, Maglie drilled me in the damn ribs. I liked and respected Maglie, but I didn't like him hitting me. That night I didn't sleep much, thinking how I had to get back at the Giants some way. When I got up the first time the next day against veteran pitcher Jack Kramer (who I remember best for being a sharp dresser), Stanky didn't move because he had been warned that he couldn't jump up and down to distract batters. I got on base. A ball was hit to left and I didn't stop at second but ran to third, where I slid hard into Hank Thompson. He turned some flips. I got up and scored. They had to take Thompson off the field. The next time I came up, Stanky started jumping up and down because he was upset about Thompson. Durocher had given him the go-ahead. So I let the bat loose and it landed near the mound. When I retrieved it, I warned Kramer, "The next time I ain't going to miss you."

Meanwhile, Stanky was thrown out of the game and Bill Rigney replaced him. Again I got on base. Then a ball was hit to short and I lightly bumped Rigney on the play at second. We started going at it right there. I grabbed him, pulled him down, and started punching him. By that time the whole crew was out there from both teams. Three or four of us were thrown out. I was called on the carpet in Ford Frick's office in New York. I was fined, which upset me. That was the best fight we had.

The Phillies broke out to a big lead in the pennant race and then had to hold on against Brooklyn. Our pitchers disappeared. Simmons was drafted, Bob Miller hurt his back; Bubba Church was hit in the face by a line drive by Ted Kluszewski. Church had been pitching well for us as a rookie. In the last week of the season, at the height of the pennant race, we were playing the Giants again and Monte Irvin ran into me and broke my leg by the ankle. I didn't know how bad it was until the end of the season. I was all taped up but caught the next day. Then we went to Brooklyn for a 3-game series. My leg was killing me. They'd shoot it up with Novocaine and wrap it up with tape and it would be just like a stump. It was difficult for me to stand up, catch, run, do anything.

In the classic game in which we beat the Dodgers to clinch the Phillies' first pennant in 35 years, Robin Roberts was pitching and I was catching. Roberts was going for his 20th victory for the seventh time and was pitching for the third time in five days. Don Newcombe also was going for his 20th victory. This was the last day of the season and the Dodgers were one game out and would either tie us if they won or be eliminated if they lost. At one point, I caught a pop foul and fell over the fence—Ebbets Field had low fences—onto a woman's lap. We got a run off Newcombe in the sixth. In the bottom of the sixth, Reese hit a fly ball that landed on top of the fence and stayed there. At Ebbets Field there was a thick concrete wall with the fence embedded in the middle. I yelled for Del Ennis to throw his glove at the ball and knock it off so it would just be a triple or something. Of course, he was too far away to hear me. Pee Wee circled the bases for a home run and the game was tied, 1–1. In the bottom of the ninth Cal Abrams got on second for them, with no one out. I had been taken out for a pinch runner in the top of the ninth, so Stan Lopata was catching now. For some reason, Ashburn in center

started creeping in. Duke Snider hit a screaming line drive right over second base and Ashburn got it on the first or second hop and threw it home. Abrams was the winning run coming home. The throw was up the line about 10 feet and Abrams was out by another 10 feet. It wasn't close. It was a bad decision by the Dodgers' third-base coach, Milt Stock, to wave Abrams home with no one out. The Dodgers still had a chance to win the game when they got the bases loaded with one out. But Furillo fouled out to Eddie Waitkus and Hodges hit a high fly to Ennis. After the inning was over, Ennis told me that the ball got lost in the sun and hit him at the base of his glove and rolled up his arm. Then, in the tenth inning, Dick Sisler hit a 3-run homer off Newcombe and we won the pennant, 4–1! That was the highlight of my career. We swarmed onto the field. We didn't realize how great the tension had been until the game was over. We were drained.

I was happy for Dick Sisler, a super guy. Dick and I were roommates for quite a few years. His father was Hall of Famer George Sisler. The pennant-winning homer was his own claim to lasting fame. He loved his father very much, and his father loved him and his other brothers, George and Dave, who played in the big leagues for a while. Dick studied hitting and talked to his father a lot. He was a pretty good hitter and, fortunately, had occasional power.

I remember the celebration. We came in from New York on a train and got to the North Philadelphia station, where many of us usually got off. But the crowd there was so big that we decided to go to the next stop. But we got down there and it was the same thing. Somehow I got home. I got my wife and we went to the Warwick Hotel. Sunday in Philadelphia is pretty much dead, but they had a pretty good party for us and there was a parade.

DEL ENNIS:

I got along with everybody on the Phillies in 1950. We all worked together like buddies, like a big family. Players would help each other, correcting each other's mistakes on the field. Sawyer played basically the same players every day, though Andy Seminick was occasionally spelled by Stan Lopata. Even Eddie Waitkus, who was all scarred up his back and had slowed down a bit, played 154 games and had a good year. We just jelled. When one of us would go after somebody on another club, there would be eight more of us going after him. We all would fight. When somebody spiked one of us we'd say, "We gotta get that guy." So nine of us would get him. We were a tough bunch.

I was a tough guy, ever since I was a kid. My father was a boxer and I couldn't come home unless I could handle myself. Seminick was as tough as they came. He was built like an ox. He played on a broken ankle. Now that Schoolboy Rowe's career was over, Seminick and Granny Hamner assumed leadership of the team. Hamner was the captain. He liked to drink and play cards. He was a take-charge guy. I wasn't a leader. I just minded my business.

We had a good offense. Only the Dodgers had a better batting average. We also had good defense with Seminick behind the plate, Waitkus at first, Jones at third, and Ashburn and me in the outfield. In 1950 I moved to right field. I was known best for my arm. I'd dare runners to go to third. In one game I would throw two guys out at home plate. A couple of times I threw out batters at first base on sharply hit balls. I covered a lot of territory and was fast enough to play center if Ashburn hadn't been out there. I was a good athlete, with speed and agility in addition to strength. I had my share of good catches. I remember one line drive I caught off Jackie Robinson. When he went past first base, he continued into right field and said, "How did you catch that ball?" I said, "Bare-handed. Like picking cherries." Once a batter hit the ball down the foul line. I saw it at first but lost it while I was running. I kept running and suddenly the ball went right into my glove. I still don't know where it came from.

I used a heavy bat: 40, 42 ounces. I had a dozen 36-ounce bats that I'd dip up to the trademark in linseed oil all winter. The oil would seep through the wood and the bat would become as hard as a golf club. You could really bang that ball and not dent anything. In 1950 I used only one bat. Andy Seminick and I both used it. It never broke because it was so hard. Other batters would have their own gimmicks. Batters wouldn't let other players use their bats because they didn't want to be detected.

We wouldn't have won the pennant without great pitching. Back in 1948, I could tell Roberts and Simmons were better than typical pitchers. Roberts was the best pitcher I ever saw. If you had to win one game,

you'd put him on the mound. He wouldn't beat himself. He would just throw hard and throw strikes. He'd go right after the hitter: *voom-voom-voom*. If he lost he would sulk. He also hated to be taken out of a game. He usually stayed in because he was as good a hitter as anyone coming off the bench. He was a tough competitor.

Brooklyn was a better team than Philadelphia, but Roberts could beat them. Every time we played them, Roberts would pitch against that right-handed lineup and come out on top. I didn't realize we had a real shot at the 1950 pennant until the last week of the season. Then we couldn't win a game until Roberts beat Brooklyn to give us the pennant. We knew we were going to win that game because Roberts was out there pitching his heart out. We ended their rally in the ninth when Hodges hit a fly to right that I lost in the sun. It hit me right in the chest, left its imprint, and fell right in my glove. I listened to the tape of the radio broadcast later. The announcer said, "There's a fly ball to right. That's the end of the inning." That's all he said.

Winning the pennant was a thrill. There was a parade in Philadelphia and everyone was in the streets cheering for the Whiz Kids.

My only real regret in baseball was not winning the Most Valuable Player award in 1950. I played 153 games, batted a career-high .311, had 31 homers, 34 doubles, 8 triples, scored 92 runs, and led the league with 126 RBIs. In one game against Chicago, I drove in 7 runs in the seventh and eighth innings with a bases-loaded double and a grand slam. Jim Konstanty did a heck of a job for us in relief, but I felt they shouldn't have taken a pitcher over an everyday player.

Konstanty was a weird guy. He was a nickel pincher: he'd steal newspapers on the way down to see his mother in the lobby. When he was going bad, he'd call his undertaker friend. He'd ask if his palm ball stopped. He'd throw a palm ball that he expected to stop in mid-flight and drop. That ball never stopped, but he thought it did and that this was the reason he was so good.

ELROY FACE:

I returned to Bradford for a second year. I went 18–5, to give me a two-year PONY League record of 32–7. I got a Class B contract from the Phillies, but in order to protect me from the draft they would have had to give me a Class A contract. Mr. Rickey drafted me to the Dodgers organization in the winter of 1950, just before he moved over to Pittsburgh as general manager. I was the number one draft choice.

HAL WOODESHICK:

My mother was born in England. My father was born in America but was of German descent. And in 1932 I was born in Wilkes-Barre, Pennsylvania. We lived there until I was 10, and then moved to Pittsburgh. My father, who was a coal miner, would take my younger brother and me out to play ball. I played hardball from the time I was 12, always in pickup games. Then I played in high school as a junior and senior, after being cut from the team as a sophomore. I was a pitcher from the beginning, a left-hander. In 1950 I realized I had special talent when I pitched a perfect game against New Brighton, which had Tito Francona. The scouts saw me and the Phillies had me work out for them at Forbes Field. They signed me to a minor league contract for $125 a month. A few days later they put me on a Greyhound and I went to Carbondale, Pennsylvania, in Class D. I was there only a month before I was released.

PITTSBURGH PIRATES

RALPH KINER:

In January the Pirates gave high school pitcher Paul Pettit about a $100,000 signing bonus. He was a left-handed kid from Los Angeles who had thrown 5 or 6 no-hitters. We were curious about his talents when he came to spring training. He'd even signed a movie deal. When he finally took the mound everybody watched and waited. Nothing happened. He didn't have anything on the ball. He had hurt his arm. He would win one major league game in 1953 and pitch a total of 12 games. He was considered the biggest bonus bust.

In July there was an unbelievable All-Star Game at Comiskey Park. It was over 100 degrees in Chicago, yet the pitching was strong and there were many great fielding plays. In the first inning, Ted Williams broke his elbow catching my line drive against the fence and would be out until mid-September. We hadn't scored since the second inning, when I homered off Art Houtteman in the ninth inning to tie the game at 3–3.

Red Schoendienst finally won the game with a fourteenth-inning homer off Ted Gray. My old nemesis, Ewell Blackwell, was the winner. I thought it interesting that I played the whole game.

I was voted the Player of the Year by *The Sporting News.* I led the league with 47 homers, beating the Cubs' Andy Pafko by 11. I also drove in 118 runs, which was second to Del Ennis, and was second in walks to Eddie Stanky, and third in the league in runs scored. In one game against the Dodgers, I hit for the cycle, had 2 homers, and drove in 8 runs. Wally Westlake was the only other guy in the lineup who did any damage. He hit over 20 homers and drove in close to 100 runs, and nobody else had more than 8 homers and around 50 RBIs. First baseman Johnny Hopp was hitting about .340 when we sold him to the Yankees in September, but he didn't drive in many runs. Murry Dickson, Cliff Chambers, and Bill Werle didn't have much to work with and we dropped into the cellar, where we'd stay for three more years.

Having already played for the St. Louis Browns, John Berardino had the experience necessary to survive playing with the dismal Pittsburgh Pirates in 1950 and 1952.

JOHN BERARDINO:

At the end of the Pacific Coast season, a Pittsburgh scout offered me a bonus to sign with the Pirates for the rest of the season. They were already in the cellar, so probably they were just thinking of plugging up holes for the next season. I got into about 40 games, mostly at second base when Danny Murtaugh was out a while with some ailment. Danny was a scrappy player and a pretty good hitter. I had no idea that he'd eventually be a Pirates manager.

When you get on a losing team, there's no joy. It's like reporting each day to a penitentiary. The Pirates were like the Browns team I had been on. We scored runs, but our pitching was so weak that other teams always scored more. We had Ralph Kiner and Wally Westlake, and our other outfielder, Gus Bell, was developing into a good player. Our best pitchers were Murry Dickson and Cliff Chambers. Vernon Law was a rookie in 1950: I could see he was talented. ''Deacon'' was a Mormon, but his religion wasn't disruptive.

The only thing the Pirate fans had to root about was Ralph Kiner crushing homers. He was a very good hitter, who didn't only hit home runs. He also came from Los Angeles and was easy to get along with. Despite his star status, he wasn't a leader type—when you're losing there are no leaders. But he'd drive in 5 or 6 runs some games.

The Pirates would make changes in their infield in 1951, but I wasn't in their plans.

FRANK THOMAS:

I went to spring training with Pittsburgh in San Bernardino, California. It was exciting. I picked up one of Ralph Kiner's bats and he said, ''That's my bat and rookies don't touch it.'' He wasn't unfriendly—it's just the way they were at that time.

I was sent to New Orleans in Double A, but I knew I wasn't going to stay. They sent me to Charleston, South Carolina. At the time, everything I hit was to right, right-center, or dead center. I was changed into a pull hitter by my manager, Rip Sewell, the former Pirates pitcher. He brought me closer to the plate. I was so strong that I could still hit homers off inside pitches.

CINCINNATI REDS

EWELL BLACKWELL:

My shoulder still hurt but I had to grin and bear it. I came back and won 17 games, including 2 one-hitters. I completed 18 of 32 starts, my ERA was 2.97, and I struck out 188 batters. I was the National League's last pitcher in the All-Star Game, throwing 3 scoreless innings and getting the victory when Red Schoendienst homered in the top of the fourteenth.

Other than Johnny Wyrostek and Ted Kluszewski, who finally showed the power that was expected of him, with 25 homers and over 100 RBIs, our offense was still weak, so it was the pitching that moved us up a notch to sixth place. Ken Raffensberger, Howie Fox, and Herm Wehmeier also won in double figures. Ken was a lefty who came to the Reds during the 1947 season. He threw curves and change-ups, much like Whitey Ford would. Beginning in 1948, when I hurt my shoulder, he became a workhorse for the Reds and our ace left-hander. He won 18 games in 1949 for our seventh-place team, and in 1950 we combined for 31 wins and pitched 500 innings between us. Most of the good teams had strong righty-lefty combinations—Roberts and Simmons on the Phillies, Newcombe and Roe on the Dodgers, Sain and Spahn on the Braves—and I thought we were right up there.

Ken didn't like to pitch to all those right-handed batters on Brooklyn, but being right-handed, I was really tough on them. Some of those right-handers wouldn't play against me. Campanella, Hodges, Cox, and Furillo usually weren't in the lineup. I also loved to pitch against the Giants in the Polo Grounds. There were small porches down each line, but the Giants couldn't pull the ball against me. The Pirates, Phillies, and any other team with right-handers were easy for me. The only right-handers who did well against me were guys who tried to punch the ball against me. The Braves' Del Crandall hit me the best of the right-handed hitters. I didn't protect the batters on my own team who were brushed back—pitchers didn't have that responsibility in those days. I protected myself as a pitcher and didn't need a reason to come inside. I owned three-quarters of the plate. But I didn't try to hit anyone. I brushed them back. Who I brushed back depended on the circumstances. One day Richie Ashburn bunted on me. I threw him out and warned him never to bunt on me again. He tried once again but fouled it off. On the next pitch I hit him on his knee. I tried to brush him back, but he didn't get out of the way. The only time I hit anyone and got scared was in the minors. I got two strikes on Joe Abreau, a little outfielder on Newark. Then a fastball got away from me and hit him on the back of the head and knocked him unconscious. I nearly killed him. I went to the hospital with him.

I was all business on the mound. I didn't joke around. I never felt pressure, but I did display a temper. Mostly it was directed at umpires. I tried not to get too pumped up. Only in certain situations would I go for strikeouts: for instance, if there was a man on third with less than two outs. In other situations, I was content to let them hit the ball. Often they couldn't, which is why I got a lot of strikeouts.

AMERICAN LEAGUE
1950

A leadoff hitter with both power and patience, the Athletics' Eddie Joost missed more than 20 games in 1950 yet still hit 18 homers and walked 101 times.

"I ALWAYS SET GOALS. I'D WANT TO HAVE A CERTAIN AMOUNT OF HITS EVERY GAME, EVERY SERIES, EVERY WEEK, EVERY MONTH, AND I WAS DETERMINED TO REACH MY GOALS. IF I DIDN'T GET A HIT FOR A COUPLE OF GAMES, I WAS READY TO UNCOIL."

GEORGE KELL

PHILADELPHIA ATHLETICS

EDDIE JOOST:

This was the 50th and last year that Connie Mack managed the Athletics. He was the figurehead of the team and was much respected by the players, and he had an aura because of all he had accomplished. However, by this time, he was 88 and the coaches and players were collectively running the ballclub. The pitchers would take over at meetings and tell how they'd pitch, and the infielders and outfielders worked out their defenses. If the pitcher didn't want to call his game, the catcher would take over. Everything was done as a team. There were players with personalities that conflicted, but on the field we were unified.

Like most of the Athletics, I had a worse year than in 1949. I had over 100 walks and hit 18 homers, but my average dropped into the low .230s. Only Sam Chapman and Ferris Fain had good offensive years. Our pitching was dismal. After winning 20 games in '49, Alex Kellner lost 20 games. And our most used pitcher, Lou Brissie, went 7–19. One day in Boston—I think it was in 1950 and not late in '49—a line drive hit Lou on the leg, on the shin guard he wore. We all grimaced. He fell down and it was a sad moment. When he got up, his leg was bruised and he was ineffective for us after that. We would trade him to the Indians in 1951, and he would have a couple of fair seasons as a reliever. Lou would have been a very good pitcher if it hadn't been for his leg.

The Phillies won the National League pennant, while the Athletics lost 102 games and finished in last place in the American League. Their success certainly didn't do anything to bolster our attendance, but there really wasn't much of a rivalry between the Athletics and Phillies. Both teams had tough fans. I'm sure some of their fans would come out every once in a while and root like crazy against us—but it may have been our fans who were booing. Fortunately, I got along with the fans in Philadelphia and wasn't booed.

ST. LOUIS BROWNS

LES MOSS:

Bill DeWitt, our general manager, was a hard negotiator, so none of our players had high salaries. Almost everyone on the Browns—and on other teams as well—worked during the off-season. I was a metal finisher for several years in Toledo. I also drove a truck for my father-in-law for a couple of winters.

But each year I'd come back with high expectations that the Browns would do better. We went out and did the best we could, yet our record never improved. I never noticed anyone on the Browns getting depressed, except after a doubleheader in June of 1950 in which the Red Sox beat us 20–4 and 29–4. But I remember how lousy it felt when we finished the season playing the White Sox to see if we could tie them for sixth place rather than end up in seventh place again. We looked up at the scoreboard and every other team was done and we were still playing for sixth place. That was disgusting. And we lost.

Despite our poor records, we got fair coverage from the sportswriters. They were kind to us and didn't try to compare us to the Cardinals. Reporters like Bob Burnes and Ray Gillespie were friendly to the players. There were always 1 or 2 of them with us at all times. They hung around us in the trains.

I continued to split time with Sherm Lollar, and we both had a good year, hitting over 20 homers and driving in nearly 100 runs between us. Dick Kokos had another good year, and we added first baseman Don Lenhardt, a tall right-handed hitter who led the team with over 20 homers and about 80 RBIs. But our offense suffered because we had traded Bob Dillinger and Gerry Priddy, and Roy Sievers broke his collarbone. Ned Garver continued to improve and we added one guy who could help him, Stubby Overmire, who came from the Tigers. He and Dick Starr threw knuckleballs. No one liked catching knuckleballs, but, luckily, I didn't think Stubby's was that difficult to catch. The other pitchers were mostly veterans who were stuck in the bullpen at a time relief pitchers weren't specialists. The Yankees' Joe Page was the first specialist I remember.

CLEVELAND INDIANS

JOHN BERARDINO:

Because of Cleveland's disappointing 1949 season, some major changes were made. Ken Keltner was sent to Boston and rookie Al Rosen became the starting third baseman and would lead the league in homers and drive in well over 100 runs. Lou Boudreau cut his own playing time and Ray Boone became the primary shortstop and batted .300. And big Luke Easter, who had been a big star with San Diego in the Pacific Coast League, became the starting first baseman and hit close to 30 homers and drove in over 100 runs. One homer went over 470 feet, the longest ball ever hit at Municipal Stadium. His addition meant we would return Mickey Vernon to the Senators after just one year. I didn't stick around to see the new revamped offense. I hurt my leg playing an exhibition game at USC before the season and it gave me a lot of trouble. I also got a strange case of pleurisy. The cold weather made it worse, so the Indians sent me to San Diego. I was there for about a month, and then they shifted me to Sacramento. Then Cleveland released me.

BOSTON RED SOX

FRED HATFIELD:

I was born in 1925 in Lanett, Alabama, a small cotton-mill town where only half the houses had radios and there was no newspaper. I was supposed to be a direct descendant of the West Virginia–Logan County Hatfields, but I never knew a Hatfield because my dad disappeared mysteriously six months before I was born. From the time I could walk, I had some ball in my hand all the time. Although I grew up in Lanett, I went to high school in North Carolina, which was a hotbed for semi-pro and American Legion ball. The town's Rotary Club businessmen helped foot the bill and I even lived with my high school coach my last year. They drew up papers that stated that the guy who owned the Ford business was my guardian, but I never saw him. The Boston Red Sox approached me when I was 17. I signed with them in 1941 while in high school, after my eligibility in American Legion ball was over. They told me I would get a $1,200 bonus if they retained me for 30 days after a month's tryout the following March but would get nothing if they let me go. They promised my coach an overcoat and hat, but he told me he never got them. I did get my money and was assigned to Canton, Ohio. Canton was in the low minors but it was the majors to me. In those days we figured on playing four, five, seven years in the minors and would just dream and wait for the opportunity to get to the majors. Counting two years in the paratroopers, it would take me seven years to reach the majors.

When I made it to the Birmingham Barons, which was the high minors, the Red Sox planned for me to be their next shortstop in Boston. I had range problems and our third baseman, George Strickland, had trouble coming in on a tapped ball. My arm was strong but not as accurate as George's. So we switched and it worked out for both of us. The Red Sox minor league system didn't teach fundamentals as well as the Dodgers, Yankees, Cardinals, or Pirates, but I learned through experience to play the position.

I was playing for Birmingham in 1950 when I was called up to the majors. It took me only 15 minutes to pack and I arrived in Boston the next day. I got to the park before the ushers. I wanted everyone to know I was

there. I reported to the clubhouse and somebody called me to go up and sign a contract.

Twenty-five thousand fans came early to Fenway Park just to watch Ted Williams, Bobby Doerr, Junior Stephens, and the other Red Sox take batting practice. There were big stars on this team. I didn't start any conversations, but I wasn't intimidated. I was 27 and pretty mature.

I debuted as a pinch runner. In my first at-bat, I faced Bob Lemon, who led the league with 22 wins in 1950. It was in Cleveland with about 60,000 people in the stands. My legs were shaking. I told Jim Hegan, the catcher, "How about holding my legs still while I hit." I struck out, but Lemon struck out more than 10 others that day, so I didn't feel too bad. I usually swung—I didn't take too many. I don't remember my first hit or first homer. But I do remember a fielding play. In extra innings in Washington, I picked up a slow-tapped ball down third when they had the winning run on third and made an underhand throw on the dead run and we went on to win the ballgame. Nobody could believe I made the play, but I thought it was routine.

I wasn't with the team that long in 1950, so I didn't get to know most of the other veterans. However, I already knew Walt Dropo because we played together on Scranton in 1947. He was a shy, powerful first baseman who came out of the University of Connecticut, I think. He was one of the biggest guys around. Lefty Gomez would say, "Pull a bale of hay and a dozen apples so he can have something to eat." For a big guy, he was shy. He had a tremendous rookie season in 1950.

My only problem in adjusting to the city of Boston was not being able to get grits for breakfast. Visiting players stayed right downtown at the Kenmore Hotel and walked to the ballpark. I stayed there until I was able to rent a house. I was married with a small child, so my life was different from that of the single Red Sox players. I'd always go home after leaving the ballpark, or my family met me and we stopped for something to eat. Each day I'd report to the ballpark a half hour or hour before we were supposed to. I always ate two hours before a game to help digestion.

Now that I was in the majors, I had to contribute to the pension fund out of my paycheck. I was a little leery of investing my money when I was making very little. I had the secure feeling that somebody I was working for would take care of us—so I just played ball and let other people handle it. Each team had a player rep. You picked a popular guy who knew everyone and was willing to take the job.

Dominic DiMaggio, who was a great hitter and fielder but had the misfortune of being overshadowed by his brother Joe, was player rep on the Red Sox. They called him "the Little Professor," and he could get things done. Once we were driving through Cleveland and stopped temporarily at the hotel we usually stayed at when we played the Indians, and went into the dining room or bar to have a drink and something to eat. The management wouldn't let us in there because we weren't wearing ties. So Dom said we wouldn't be staying or eating there anymore. And he complained to the team. So when we came to Cleveland from then on, we got meal money so we wouldn't have to eat there. That also happened in Washington at one of the hotels. With the Red Sox, we usually just ate and then signed for it.

There was so much media attention and so many writers that there were a lot of players on Boston who played for themselves. But Bobby Doerr, the All-Star second basemaan, and catcher Birdie Tebbetts were nice enough to take me under their wings and tell me how to adapt to being a major league backup player, playing behind third baseman Johnny Pesky. We all had lower berths in the train and they said, "Sit down, kid, let's have a little talk." They told me to play hard and be ready, because I'd get a chance to play. They told me to work out just like I was going to play, stretching my legs and arms before a game. Then, in case I'd pinch-hit, I was instructed to loosen my back by swinging a heavy bat. If I got into a slump, I'd try to work it out myself, and if I got hurt, I wouldn't tell anybody. I wanted to play and anxiously checked the lineup every day, knowing that I'd play only if someone got hurt or sick. But I didn't root for that. Birdie said that as a bench warmer I should always pull for the guy on the field because someday I'd get a chance to play and there wouldn't be any pressure on me. If I put pressure on him, then I put pressure on myself. Tebbetts used a lot of psychology.

Tebbetts and Doerr told me what went on in the big leagues and with the Red Sox. Everybody didn't like rookies. The regulars always hit more than rookies during batting practice. Some days on the road, I might get

A homer hitter in the minors, Fred Hatfield was converted into a scrappy singles hitter when he joined the power-laden Boston Red Sox in 1950.

two swings and the starters did all the rest of the hitting. On a 10-day trip, I might swing the bat only nine times. Nobody ever told Ted Williams to get out of there. Of course, they were happy to see Williams back in uniform in September after he fractured his elbow in the All-Star Game. He hit 28 homers and drove in almost 100 runs although he played in less than 90 games. In the little time I saw him, he was fantastic.

The Red Sox had an amazing offense in 1950. The team batting average was over .300 and we also walked more than anybody! Billy Goodman led the league with a .355 average, and he couldn't even find a set position. He played in the outfield and all over the infield. Everyone in the starting lineup hit over .290, and guys like Walt Dropo, Al Zarilla, and Dom DiMaggio hit over .320. Both Dropo and Vern Stephens benefitted from being pull hitters in Fenway Park and hit over 30 homers and tied for the league RBI crown with 144 each.

These guys were amazing. Yet the Red Sox lost the pennant to the Yankees by 4 games and finished 3 games behind the second-place Tigers.

Mel Parnell was a great left-hander and Ellis Kinder was a top relief pitcher, but overall we couldn't match the Yankees' staff. You had to face Vic Raschi, Allie Reynolds, Ed Lopat, Whitey Ford, who was a rookie in 1950, and Tommy Burns, a reliever you didn't want to bat against. And with Joe DiMaggio, Yogi Berra, and Hank Bauer, they had three .300 hitters with power. Heck, that year Phil Rizzuto hit way over .300 and was voted the league's Most Valuable Player. He was a much better-fielding shortstop than Stephens. In fact, their whole team was better defensively—even if Dominic may have been even better than Joe in center. They never beat themselves. We believed we could beat them, but when we walked into Yankee Stadium, we felt we were playing with a stacked deck. But to be honest, in my first couple of years, I was so busy taking care of myself and making the club that I didn't worry about who won the pennant.

JOE DE MAESTRI:

When I played sandlot, high school, American Legion, and semipro ball as a teenager in the San Francisco area, I was scouted by the Red Sox, Yankees, and Indians. After I graduated in 1946, I picked the Red Sox because their scout, Charlie Walgreen, was a family friend and because two friends from my high school team also signed with them. One friend signed for $12,000, another signed for $12,000, and I got just $600, which was peanuts. Ironically, I was the only one who would make it. I would have signed that contract even if they told me I would never be a major leaguer because at that time I really didn't set my sights on the majors.

As I moved up the ladder, I saw that the Red Sox had a wonderful minor league system with a good record for getting their teams into the playoffs. They also prepared you for the majors by teaching fundamentals—but to be honest, most of what I learned was through experience. In 1950 I was promoted to Birmingham, Double A. We had a great ballclub with guys like Dick Littlefield, Leo Kiely, and Norm Zauchin. Talent-wise, I really think I started developing in Birmingham because I did well against some tough competition, including major league teams in exhibition games.

After three years, an organization had to protect a minor league player by placing him on its 40-man roster. There were seven other guys on Birmingham who would be on the Red Sox in 1951, so I was left unprotected without ever having been invited to Boston's spring training camp. I was drafted by the Chicago White Sox, who were looking for infielders. I think it was a good break for me because I might have stayed forever in the Red Sox system.

WASHINGTON SENATORS

AL KOZAR:

Bucky Harris, who had managed the Yankees to the pennant in 1947, replaced Joe Kuhel as the Senators' manager in 1950. Harris knew his baseball, so I knew I'd be the regular second baseman again. Sherry Robertson never even took a grounder now that Harris was there. The Opening Day starting lineup was Gil Coan, left field; Sam Dente, shortstop; Irv Noren, right field; Eddie Robinson, first base; Eddie Stewart, center field; Eddie Yost, third base; me, second base; Al Evans, catcher; Ray Scarborough, pitcher.

Unfortunately, I got too cute and tried to hit homers. I figured if I couldn't hit .300, I had to hit the long ball. But I couldn't pull the ball. I hit everything to right and the ball wouldn't reach the fence. Lou Boudreau used the same shift on me that he used on Ted Williams, and I was a right-handed hitter!

At the time, there were a lot of screwballs in baseball. Guys who couldn't handle pressure. Guys who were violent and got into fights. Fortunately, they were on other teams. I liked my teammates on Washington. Eddie Yost and I went to church together on Sunday, and sometimes on Thursday or Friday just for an hour to meditate. Clyde Vollmer and I got along. He was an outfielder with pretty good power. He hit homers in every ballpark in 1949 and 1950 and was doing great and all of a sudden he was traded to Boston, where he spent a couple of years before the Sox returned him to Washington—I think it was that family connection that brought me from the Red Sox. Clyde was thrilled to get out of Washington. I lent him my suitcase and it took a month to get it back. I drank a lot of beer with Mickey Harris, who came over from the Red Sox in 1949. Then we might go eat a big steak at one in the morning, and I'd have a glass of milk. There wasn't much socializing with players on opposing teams. You'd have to do it fast after a night game. But I did drink a few beers with Vern Stephens of the Red Sox and Joe Gordon of the Indians. Gordon and I became good friends. Anytime he came to town, he'd borrow a tie from me. Once I lent him my car.

On some days off, the Senator organization would ask players to go out to Beverly Beach on the Chesapeake. The Robertson family wanted me because I was a single guy and they'd have single women there from the front office. Everyone would bring beer. They also asked Eddie Yost, but he didn't drink much. We'd have a barbecue and swim and talk. There would be a boat for us and we'd fish. That was fun. There also would be gatherings in New York at the Copacabana and the Travelers Bar across from the New Yorker Hotel. They would be sponsored by our owner, Clark Griffith, who was getting along in years and talked to me with a handkerchief over his mouth. Again, they wanted me there because I was single. I wouldn't show up and they'd holler. That wasn't my crowd.

Ted Williams said that the postwar period had the toughest, best baseball that he ever saw. I have to agree. There were only 16 teams, so every team was strong. Yet great teams like the Yankees would beat you almost every time out. The game was tough psychologically, especially when you played for the Senators. If you made an error on the Yankees, another player would pick up for you. If you made an error on the Senators, it would cost us the game because the team never came back. It was too hard to play that way.

Baseball was also tough physically. You'd injure your body, there'd be wear and tear. The fields were bad and you'd slide through rocks. Wally Moses hit a ball that split my mouth wide open. I got 9 stitches. In Washington, I hit an inside-the-park homer and collided with the catcher and had a rupture and got bursitis and was out for a month. I ripped up my fingers on plays at second. I'd get hit in the back with a fastball when the guy in front of me homered. Joe Tipton, a feisty catcher on the Athletics, always called for his pitcher to hit you. I never cried. I was no homer hitter and was happy to get on base.

My body was so banged up that I didn't produce for

the Senators in 1950. Then, in May, my unhappy time in Washington came to an end when Eddie Robinson, Ray Scarborough, and I were traded to the Chicago White Sox. I felt fortunate because I knew the Senators would be at or near the bottom of the standings for the next few years.

DETROIT TIGERS

GEORGE KELL:

Although Walter Briggs didn't like night baseball, he had reluctantly installed lights in 1948, and we played 7 night games that year. In 1949 we had played 14 night games, and in 1950 we played 21 night games, before the floodgates opened and we started playing every weekday night, as did most of the other teams. You couldn't get a ticket to a night game in 1949 and 1950 because they were so much in demand. The players couldn't even get tickets. Then we were allowed to buy 10 tickets apiece for family and friends. I had a lot of friends in Detroit, so I'd have to scurry around the clubhouse asking players if I could buy their tickets. Our capacity was almost 53,000, and we drew over 1,950,000 in 1950, a new Tigers record.

Red Rolfe replaced Steve O'Neill as manager. Red was an excellent manager, but he didn't get along with players because he was all business. He would criticize you on the spot if you made a mistake rather than waiting until he had you alone in the clubhouse. Hoot Evers really didn't like him.

Rolfe had the idea that veterans should room with kids to help them break in. I was established as one of the leaders on Detroit, so when we'd bring up youngsters, I'd room with them and help them out. I think young players could learn a lot from me. I was a contact hitter who usually struck out less than 20 times a season. I never hit more than 12 homers in my career, but I got a lot of doubles. I hit a lot of balls down the lines and always rounded way past first base at full speed to see if I could make it into second. I hustled all the time. Once I spoke to Stan Musial before a season, and he told me confidently that he would hit between .315 and .340 during the year. I questioned how he could predict such lofty stats and he said that he'd been around long enough to know exactly what he could do. After I'd been in the league a few years, I could predict that I'd hit well over .300 each year. I knew my talent. Not that I was ever complacent. I always set goals. I'd want to have a certain amount of hits every game, every series, every week, every month, and I was determined to reach my goals. If I didn't get a hit for a couple of games, I was ready to uncoil. Young players certainly picked up on my intensity.

I had my best year. I batted .340, which was second in the league. I had career-highs with 157 games, 101 RBIs, and 114 runs, and led the league with 641 at-bats, 218 hits, and 56 doubles, which were also career highs. (No one has equaled those 56 doubles since.) I wasn't the only player in the lineup who did well. Both Evers and Vic Wertz, who came into his own by hitting .300 with 133 RBIs in 1949, again batted over .300 with over 120 RBIs, and we also got big years from second baseman Gerry Priddy, who we just got from the Browns, shortstop Johnny Lipon, and Johnny Groth.

Groth was an interesting case. He became the Tigers' center fielder in 1949—and was part of our "Million Dollar Outfield" with Vic Wertz in right and Hoot Evers in left. He showed in those first two years that he had the talent to become a star. But he didn't seem to want that. He underestimated himself and after hitting .290 and .300, underachieved during the rest of his time with the Tigers and for the rest of his career. I think he was afraid to be in the spotlight.

We had excellent infield defense and our usual fine pitching. Art Houtteman had 19 wins and Hal Newhouser won 15 at the age of 39. I thought we were going to win the pennant. We were ahead in the race, but Virgil Trucks hurt his arm and was lost for the season and the Yankees brought up Whitey Ford, who won 9 out of 10 games. The Yankees slipped by us and repeated as American League champions by 3 games. That was discouraging.

I didn't consider the Yankees to be a great team until then. This is when I realized that few teams in the league had a real chance to beat them. They were just loaded with players, and if they needed somebody late in the season, they'd either bring him up from their tremendous farm system or purchase him. It was definitely frustrating competing with the Yankees because they had the advantage.

CHICAGO WHITE SOX

BILL WILSON:

I went to spring training with the White Sox in Pasadena, at Brookside Park by the Rose Bowl. Most of the players stayed at a hotel, but I stayed at home in Long Beach and drove over there each day. We already knew the fundamentals, and the purpose of the camp was to see which players could stick with the major league team. The manager, Jack Onslow, was a short, fat, grumpy-looking man. I tried to stay out of his way.

The player who caught my attention was Luke Appling, who was about to play his last season. He was a real character, a funny guy who could get away with anything because he knew he was a fixture. He was probably the leader of the team. Nellie Fox had just come over from the Athletics and wasn't yet a leader. Cass Michaels had played 154 games at second base in 1949, but Fox would take over when Michaels got hurt and Cass would be traded. Both Fox and Michaels were real nice guys. Jim Busby, another rookie, was also friendly. I became lifelong friends with Gus Zernial.

The White Sox sent me down to Memphis in the Southern Association. I had never been in the South but enjoyed it very much. The manager was an ex-catcher, Al Todd. I had a good year, with 36 home runs, which was a league record for right-handed hitters, 125 RBIs, a .311 average. I stole about 28 bases. We had a good team and won the pennant. At the end of the year the Sox brought me up for a bit. Then I went into the army for two years.

GUS ZERNIAL:

During the off-season, Frank Lane had assigned two scouts to make sure I strengthened my shoulder by working all winter under a trainer at the Hollywood Athletic Club, Jerry Hatfield. I was concerned because in February I still couldn't throw a ball. My arm had no elasticity. But I went to spring training in 1950 and kept working at it until I was ready to play.

The White Sox trained in Pasadena. I had been living in Hollywood since I played there, and had met a lot of movie people, mostly men who liked baseball but also a lot of the starlets. Some agents requested that a few of us players pose with a rising young starlet. She was a lovely, well-proportioned young lady. We were introduced to Marilyn Monroe. I thought, ''Man, could a girl be any prettier?'' So I was willing to pose with her. And they took pictures of us all over the Pasadena ballpark. I was probably in more pictures than any of the players. Soon there was about a 12-page layout of Marilyn in *Esquire* that included some of the photos of us walking and posing together. My wife didn't appreciate the layout very much, although there was nothing to it. Hank Majeski and Eddie Robinson were in there, too. I had no designs on Marilyn, and as the season progressed, there was no contact between us. I was playing ball and she was making movies. The White Sox went into New York to play the Yankees. At the same time, Marilyn was coming to New York, so there was a lot of publicity. Joe DiMaggio had never met Marilyn, but when he saw the magazine he made a comment like, ''Why does a rookie like Zernial get to take a layout with someone like her?'' He had never met Marilyn, but that comment set off a chain of events and finally he was introduced to her. So the magazine layout led to their meeting, although a story developed that I introduced them. He never asked me ''Who's the blonde?,'' which became a famous quote. He never called me to ask about her. Joe and I knew each other, but we never discussed any of this. He was a private man, particularly in regard to Marilyn.

I played the whole season, batting .280 and hitting 29 homers and driving in 93 runs. On that ballclub, driving in 93 runs was like driving in 130 on another club because we didn't score many runs. Eddie Robinson and Dave Philley were the only other guys on the team with more than 60 RBIs.

On the last day of the season we played the St. Louis Browns in a doubleheader. We lost both games, but I hit 4 homers, 3 in the first game. It was an American League record, but was no big deal because other players have equaled and, in the National League, surpassed that. However, I don't think anyone else ever hit 4 home runs in a single day in Comiskey Park, which was a tough stadium because of the winds blowing in. Also, I broke the single-season White Sox homer record that day, passing Zeke Bonura's 27. So that was one of the highlights of my career.

My best friend on the White Sox was Gordon Goldsberry, a part-time first baseman. He was a good young left-handed hitter, but he would never develop. In the first game of that season-ending doubleheader, Gordy was up in the last inning, hoping to get on base so I'd have a chance to hit 4 homers that game. He had a 3–0 count and took 3 straight pitches and struck out.

I also spent a lot of time with Luke Appling, who had spent his entire 20-year career with Chicago. I learned a lot from him. Another friend was Phil Masi, the veteran catcher. His career also was winding down—he started out with the Boston Braves in 1939. Dave Philley was a good friend. He had come up with the Sox before the war and was already 30, but he'd play another dozen years. He was with me during all my early years in baseball. He was a hard-nosed all-around player, a switch-hitting outfielder with some power and good speed. He came from Paris, Texas. Eddie Robinson also was born there. Since I was from Beaumont, the three of us had a lot in common.

The Sox got Nellie Fox from the Athletics before the season. We didn't chum together, but he was a great guy. If there was anybody who was a self-made ballplayer, it was Nellie. He didn't have the athletic ability of a Bobby Doerr, but he was as reliable as any second baseman in the league. And it got so that I would rather see Nellie at the plate in a clutch situation than anybody on our ballclub.

The White Sox weren't a drinking team. Floyd Baker and Cass Michaels didn't drink; Appling drank just a little. We'd play cards rather than drink. We weren't a close team because Frank Lane was too much in control. He fired Jack Onslow and replaced him with Red Corriden, and was always making out the lineup. He wasn't a ballplayer's general manager. He kept turmoil among the players, which is what I think he wanted. I don't think there was much leadership on the team. Appling wasn't a leader. I never wanted that role—I just tried to do my job. I wasn't a rah-rah type of guy. If I led, it was only by example.

BILLY PIERCE:
Again we had spring training in Pasadena. We had a nice facility by the Rose Bowl, but the smog got so bad that we couldn't breathe. It really made it hard. So that was our last spring there.

In my second year with the White Sox, I pitched more innings than anyone on the staff and led the team with 12 wins. So it was apparent I was progressing. Frank Lane gambled a lot for a few years and in my case it worked out. I came for a player the Sox weren't going to use in 1949 and I stayed 13 years. Nellie Fox came from the Athletics for Joe Tipton, another catcher the Sox weren't going to use in 1950, and Nellie stayed for 14 years. During our years together, Nellie and I were roommates and best friends. He was a left-handed batter and at the time used a thin-handled bat and tried to pull everything to right, though he was a small guy. So he struggled at the plate his first year with the Sox, hitting below .250. He also needed work at second base, though he and Chico Carrasquel were more than an adequate duo out there.

Lane got Chico from the Dodgers' organization and he replaced Luke Appling at shortstop. He was another Lane acquisition who cost the team very little and stayed for years. He got the nickname "the Caracas Cat" because he could get the ball all over the infield. He was great. When he had been at Fort Worth, the only things he ate were apple pie and eggs because that was all he could say. But by the time he came to the White Sox, he could speak just enough English to be able to communicate with us—as long as it was simple. Chico wasn't alone in speaking Spanish because we had pitcher Luis Aloma. They'd converse with each other.

CHICO CARRASQUEL:

I thought I'd have a better chance with another team than the Dodgers. But when I checked the paper I discovered Luke Appling was the White Sox shortstop. He'd been the shortstop since 1930! And in 1949 he hit over .300! So I figured I might not have a chance to play in the big leagues but would do my best wherever the White Sox sent me.

I reported to the White Sox spring training camp in Pasadena. Jack Onslow helped me feel that I was wanted by encouraging me and giving me good advice. I was 6'1", tall for a shortstop, but they didn't try to move me because I was quick and had a lot of range. I played a deep shortstop. After we had played some exhibition games, the sportswriters asked Onslow about the Opening Day lineup and he told them that he had a kid from South America who would be his starting shortstop.

Appling was thinking of retiring after the year. He

was a nice gentleman who tried to help me play shortstop. Every day he would talk to me, some in English and some in Spanish. I listened to him because I knew he was one of the greatest players.

I was scared when we played our first game in Chicago because I was replacing the team's most popular player. They loved Appling. When my name was announced I heard so many boos. I didn't blame them. After a couple of games the fans welcomed me. I had a good year, batting .282 and playing good defense. I missed only a few games because I hurt my knee in St. Louis. I finished third in the Rookie of the Year vote to Walt Dropo of the Red Sox and Whitey Ford of the Yankees.

Frank Lane bought Luis Aloma, a right-hander from Cuba. It was said he wanted Aloma just so I would have someone to speak Spanish to, but I don't think so. Luis was a real good relief pitcher. He went 7–2 that year. His record in the big leagues, from 1950 to 1953, would be 18–3! We became roommates and real good friends. I had problems adjusting because of food and language. The manager would have an hour-long club meeting and I'd have no idea what he was talking about. Luis helped me with my English.

Nellie Fox was a real good infield partner. He was a nice guy and a fiery leader on the field. Nellie couldn't speak Spanish and I couldn't talk English, but we let each other know how we wanted the ball on double plays. At that time the best double-play combinations were Johnny Lipon and Gerry Priddy at Detroit, Phil Rizzuto and Jerry Coleman at New York, and Eddie Joost and Pete Suder on the Athletics, but we weren't far behind in our first year playing together.

I continued to play winter ball in Caracas. I was considered a hero and was greeted by a lot of fans when I arrived home. A lot of señoritas were waiting for me. In Venezuela I was called Alfonso, but in America I was called Chico. I liked Chico because in Spanish it means "friend."

BOB CAIN:

When I went to spring training, I wasn't sure I was going to make the ballclub. Chicago already had several other left-handers, including Billy Pierce, Bill Wight, Mickey Haefner, and Jack Bruner, an expensive bonus player who didn't last very long. I made the club because I happened to have a pretty good spring training. I was surprised.

Jack Onslow had been a Dodgers coach. He was a pleasant manager to play for and we called him by his nickname, "Happy Jack." He knew baseball pretty well. We'd have regular clubhouse meetings to go over the batters; then, before the game started, the pitcher and catcher would talk.

We had a terrible start, losing 22 of our first 30 games. Onslow was fired and replaced by Red Corriden, another former coach at Brooklyn. He was a very easygoing manager. His style was to explain situations, but he never bothered going into baseball fundamentals. I guess he assumed we should have gotten that training in the minors.

My first major league start came in New York on May 4. I went against Ed Lopat. I got over my jitters quickly. We scored 4 runs in the first inning and got 8 runs off Lopat in 5 innings. We won 15–0 on 23 hits off Lopat and Don Johnson. That was one of the worst beatings the Yankees ever had, especially in their home park. Jim Busby, Dave Philley, Luke Appling, Cass Michaels, Gus Zernial, Hank Majeski, Eddie Malone, and Chico Carrasquel were in the lineup for the White Sox. They all hit the ball hard—the balls the Yankees hit hard went right at somebody. In 1950 I had a lot of success against the Yankees. They beat me a couple of times, but I got 4 of my 9 victories against them. That's what kept me in the league.

Joe DiMaggio didn't get a hit off me that first game. But he usually hit me pretty good. There was no way to pitch to him. He was far from being over the hill. He was dangerous—I remember him beating me in Chicago with a single that year.

I liked pitching in Comiskey Park. It was about 345 feet down the lines and there was always a strong wind. If you could get batters to hit to center field, you were in good shape because the wind would hold it up. Our center fielder was Jim Busby and he could really go get 'em. We could draw fans to Comiskey Park, but the Cubs had the better of the deal simply because Wrigley Field was in a better location. After a home game we didn't hang around the ballpark or go anywhere in the area. We stayed at the Piccadilly downtown. They gave players a discount on rooms, and they'd always have rooms ready for us when we came back into town.

Anticipating Luis Aparicio, Chico Carrasquel came out of Venezuela to become a fancy-fielding shortstop for the Chicago White Sox.

This was a fairly close team. We traveled by train and played cards. Luke Appling was a big card player. Our favorite game was hearts, which we played from one town to the next. I didn't go to movies. If I had a day off, I'd play golf. In every town there were one or two restaurants ballplayers frequented. Even in Cleveland, players went out to Cavoli's, a very nice Italian restaurant on Clifton. Joe Cavoli catered to the ballplayers. There was a downtown bar-restaurant that the managers and coaches would go to, so players stayed away from there. There was no pressure from older players to make young players drink. Some guys drank and others didn't. I don't think it caused problems. Management didn't try to discourage it. In fact, when I was coming up through the minors, I was encouraged to drink ale to put on weight because I was 6' tall but weighed only 150 pounds.

Luke Appling was the leader of the team. He was a nice man who would help me and the other young players learn the ropes. When Chico Carrasquel joined the team to take his place at short, Luke helped him like a baby. They'd work extra time and during games he'd help position him. So even as a rookie, Chico was a tremendous shortstop. Appling was 41 years old, but he had hit over .300 the past 6 years and about 15 times in his career. He didn't play much in his final season but he could still give pitchers fits. He had amazing instincts and could always place the ball through positions vacated by infielders when they moved. He was so impressive. I never saw a batter who could hit so many foul balls—up to a dozen. I think he enjoyed doing it. In Chicago, they'd get after players for giving balls to fans, so Luke said, "I'll cost them a few dollars in today's game."

Probably my best friend on the team was Lou Kretlow, who came over from the Browns during the season. He was a tall right-hander from Apache, Oklahoma, who could throw at about 95 mph through a brick wall, but he had no idea where it was going. We'd often play golf together. Lou could really hit the ball.

We had some pretty good players, which is why we were able to come back from our horrible first month and at least finish ahead of the Browns and Athletics. Gus Zernial was our best power hitter. He could hit home runs, especially if the pitch was down around the knees. Pitchers had to keep the ball up on him to keep him from getting full leverage. Eddie Robinson was our best average hitter and also had a lot of power. I saw him hit a ball into the right-field lights in Detroit. What a wallop! And he hit one on the roof at Comiskey Park. Dave Philley was the only other player who had long-ball power, although not on the level of Zernial and Robinson. Philley was a no-nonsense player. After games were over, he stayed to himself.

Chico Carrasquel, Hank Majeski, and Phil Masi were all good hitters. But Nellie Fox impressed me the most. He was a great ballplayer and very clean-cut young man. Even as a youngster, he was one of the best contact hitters in the league. He would soon develop into one of the best defensive second basemen.

Watching Billy Pierce and Bill Wight helped me. Pierce was a very good pitcher. He could throw hard. Wight didn't throw hard at all. He had one of the best pickoff moves to first. There was a picture taken of the three of us left-handers after we beat the Yankees three games in a row in Chicago.

I was a little wild, but I threw hard and had a pretty good curveball. I threw overhand or three-quarters.

Only on occasion would I throw sidearm to a left-handed batter. For some reason—maybe I didn't concentrate enough or got lazy—I had less luck with left-handed batters than right-handers. My philosophy was not to throw in the same place two pitches in a row. I'd move the ball around to keep batters off balance and guessing.

Ballplayers would talk to umpires after games. I would stand out by the hotel after a game talking to an umpire for an hour at a time. We might talk about a certain play, but not controversial calls. Among the good American League umpires were Bill McGowan, Ed Hurley, John Stevens, Art Passarella, and Joe Paparella. Hurley and Passarella had low boiling points. You had to watch them.

McGowan called them pretty close. If the pitcher seemed to be on, he'd go along with him, but if he was a little wild, McGowan wouldn't give him the benefit of the doubt. When he had his mind made up, he was too stubborn to change. McGowan said that I was a little cocky because I was questioning some of his calls. I saw him and another umpire after a game in 1950 or '51, and he politely warned me that if my attitude toward umpires didn't change, the umpires would screw me. I took heed. After that I stopped questioning calls and, in turn, felt the umpires were giving me calls.

AL KOZAR:
In May, Eddie Robinson, Ray Scarborough, and I were traded from Washington to the Chicago White Sox for Cass Michaels, Bob Kuzava, and John Ostrowski. Clark Griffith gave Eddie and Ray $500 because they were married—I didn't get anything. We joined the White Sox in Yankee Stadium and Dizzy Dean interviewed me. I usually didn't like interviews, but we had a lot of fun and it was a good interview. He said nice things about me. I wasn't used to that from the media.

I had started getting a sore back with Washington, probably because I was muscle-bound. Soon after I got to Chicago, I faced Tommy Byrne of the Yankees. I hit a homer but could barely get out of the box because I had pain down my left side and back. It was embarrassing running around the bases. This was my last homer. I got around second and Phil Rizzuto says, "*Now* what is the matter with you?" Then I went to get my glove and fell down on my knees and couldn't get up. I was out for

COURTESY OF AL KOZAR

Al Kozar's abbreviated major league career concluded with a brief stint on the White Sox, which would be followed by years in their minor league system.

a month. Nellie Fox went out to play second in my place. I gave him his job.

That evening I went out with Scarborough and Hank Bauer and Gene Woodling of the Yankees. I was sitting there drinking a beer and I had tears in my eyes. I was miserable. I had to walk with my arms spread. No one cared. When we got to Philadelphia, they made me put on a uniform for batting practice. But I couldn't do anything because the trainer had taped me up real good.

On my birthday, July 5, they sent me by train to the Oakland Oaks in the Pacific Coast League on 24-hour recall. I was never recalled. This began my worst years in baseball. I didn't want to go to the minors, but I had to play somewhere to work my back into shape. And I was happy to play with the Oaks because they were a

good, winning team. Charlie Dressen, the former third baseman and Dodgers coach, was the Oaks' manager, and he put me on third, and player-coach Cookie Lavagetto taught me how to throw overhand again. However, I moved back to second when we went up to Seattle for 4 games. Paul Richards was the manager there, and his team was in fifth place. I had a big series and even thwarted a double steal that I figured out Richards would be calling. After that we were 11 games in front and Dressen was raving about me being a big league second baseman. I thought I would go back to third, but instead Dressen tells me Chicago called up my contract and then sent it back down to Paul Richards at Seattle, which did more business with the White Sox than the Oaks did. Richards was part of the White Sox organization. Richards wanted me to help his team get into fourth place. I told Charlie, "The winner of this league gets $1,300 per man. I want my $1,300." I never said things like that before. I loved the game, but I was playing for money, not buttons. I felt gypped. He said, "Ask Richards for money. You're not with us anymore."

So I reluctantly went over to Seattle. Paul Richards, the Big Texan—you don't tell him nothing. But he did offer me $600 out of his pocket as compensation. I said I wanted $1,300 or I'd jump the club. And I did. I got off the train and went to Hollywood and stayed with an ex-army buddy and didn't play for the rest of the year. I was hoping for a fresh start with the parent club in the spring. How did I know that the next year Richards was going to be promoted to manage the White Sox? Did I get into the wrong person's doghouse!

NEW YORK YANKEES

BILLY JOHNSON:

This year we had a pennant race with both the Red Sox and Tigers. Again we prevailed, winning 98 games. We got great pitching all year from Raschi, Reynolds, Lopat, and Byrne, who all won over 15 games, but one of the keys to our victory was Whitey Ford being called up from the minors. He was very effective, winning 9 out of 10 decisions for us. He was left-handed, and not only had a good fastball, curve, and change-up, but also was very confident and intelligent on the mound. He knew what he was doing. He was very crafty. Even as a rookie, he impressed me with his ability to pick runners off first.

We had a tremendous offense that season. DiMaggio and Berra each drove in over 120 runs, and DiMaggio, Berra, Hank Bauer, and Rizzuto all hit over .300. Phil hit about .325 and was voted the league's Most Valuable Player. He was always on base and scoring runs.

AL KOZAR (WHITE SOX):

Phil Rizzuto got a lot of hits on bunts. He was considered the best bunter in baseball. He told me how to do it. He told me to bunt down the baseline, not between third and the pitcher. This meant a longer throw for the third baseman. If it went foul, you got another at-bat. It made sense.

B. JOHNSON:

Stengel could have played the same guys every day and won the pennant. But he continued to platoon, and Rizzuto, Jerry Coleman, and DiMaggio were our only everyday players. Bobby Brown and I shared third again and we both had pretty good seasons. Stengel also did a lot of shifting around in the outfield so that Gene Woodling, a pretty good left-handed hitter, Bauer, a hard-nosed, good-hitting right-handed hitter, and Cliff Mapes, a left-handed hitter with an excellent throwing arm, all got a lot of playing time. At first base, Tommy Henrich and left-handed rookie Joe Collins, who was a good fielder and occasional power hitter, shared time with Johnny Mize. Mize had a great year, hitting about 25 homers and driving in over 70 runs playing part-time and pinch-hitting.

We had a powerful team that was good enough to win in a tough American League. In the World Series, Philadelphia wasn't much of a challenge.

GENE WOODLING:

I liked Stengel, but I did a lot of fussing with him. Our arguments over platooning were well known. I was serious. Bauer and I called him names occasionally. Stengel responded by saying, ''Those two squareheads—if you can't get them mad, they can't play.'' The reporters said we disliked each other. But he made me money, so how could I hate him? Years later, Stengel cleared it all up. ''How could I hate Woodling?'' he asked. ''All he was fussing about is wanting to play.''

Beginning in 1950, Stengel didn't really platoon Bauer and me as much as reported. I was usually in left and Bauer in right, especially in important games. Bauer asked him, ''How come when we have a 5-game lead, you platoon Woodling and me, but when we're tied, you play us both?'' That's what he did. We couldn't really object when he did platoon us because we were winning.

VIC POWER:

I was born in 1931 in Arecibo, Puerto Rico. My father worked in a factory, but when I was 13 he cut his finger in a work accident and died from tetanus. My mother somehow raised three boys and three girls by sewing dresses. I had a lot of artistic talent, but I decided to become a lawyer so I could get the $10,000 compensation the factory should have paid my mother after my father's death. I played a lot of baseball, but at the time nobody in Puerto Rico thought about playing in the major leagues. In fact, while I had heard of the Yankees and even once wore a Yankee uniform my parents bought in a drugstore, I didn't know who they were or what the major leagues was.

In 1947, when I was 16, I became the first baseman for Caguas in the winter leagues. I was a good hitter and could catch anything with one hand, so I became a star player in Puerto Rico. In 1948 I received $2,000 for the 4-month season and bought a house in San Juan for my mother and brothers and sisters, who I would support until all the kids graduated high school and were married.

In 1949 I attracted the attention of Quincy Trouppe, who caught and managed in the Negro Leagues. He signed me to play in the summer in Drummondville, Canada, in the independent Provincial League, for $800 a month. It was the first time I had been away from home—I got so sick flying there—and I didn't speak French or English. But the people were friendly and Quincy treated me like his son, cooking and looking after me. It was a tough league because they had former major leaguers who weren't yet allowed back in because they had jumped to the Mexican League in 1946. Sal Maglie and Danny Gardella were there. I played right field and hit .329, two points from the batting title. Back in Puerto Rico, I was called Victor Pellot because I used my father's last name, but in Canada I went by my mother's name, Power. That was because when they mispronounced Pellot, with an *l* rather than a *y* sound, it sounded like a French sexual term.

In my second year at Drummondville, my salary increased to $1,000 a month and I moved to first base. I had an even better year, leading the league with a .334 average and driving in 105 runs in 105 games. I played in the Provincial League All-Star Game and did well at the plate but made an error. The Yankees had sent their scout Tom Greenwade to watch me. He was the scout who signed Mickey Mantle. He reported that I was a good hitter, average runner, and poor fielder. The Yankees purchased my contract for $7,500. I didn't care about the Yankees, so I threatened not to sign unless the Drummondville general manager gave me a share of that money. He got nervous and handed me a stack of Canadian paper money. I thought it was a lot of money, but it turned out to be only about $500. I found out later that Drummondville didn't own my rights and that I should have gotten the entire $7,500 from the Yankees.

WORLD SERIES

1950

YANKEES
VS
PHILLIES

GENE WOODLING · YANKEES:

We swept the Phillies in the World Series, so a lot of people assume they were overmatched. But that Series was tight. It's fortunate Vic Raschi pitched a 2-hitter in the first game because we got only 5 hits off Jim Konstanty. We squeaked by, 1–0, scoring our only run on a sacrifice fly by Jerry Coleman in the fourth inning. Game Two, in which Reynolds outpitched Robin Roberts, was just as tight. We won, 2–1, when DiMaggio hit a tenth-inning homer. Then we edged them, 3–2, in Game Three, tying the game in the bottom of the eighth when Granny Hamner made an error, and winning it in the bottom of the ninth when Coleman drove me in. The easiest game was the fourth game, in which we took a 5-run lead with Whitey Ford on the mound. Then I decided to let them know I was on the Yankees by dropping a fly ball in the ninth. As a result, the Phillies scored 2 runs. They had the tying run at the plate, but Reynolds struck out Stan Lopata to end the game. We didn't beat the devil out of them.

I got so much negative publicity from dropping that ball, though the reporters knew I didn't see it. I thanked the writers the next year for making me a lot of money. Everyone felt sorry for Gene Woodling after the press wrote how I cost poor Whitey Ford a World Series shutout. So I got a ton of speaking engagements all over.

ANDY SEMINICK · PHILLIES:

The World Series was a good experience although we lost. We were in every game until the last out. Hamner hit well, but the rest of us didn't. Of course, their pitching had a lot to do with that. I think we were somewhat awed by the Yankees. DiMaggio, Reynolds, Berra, Woodling, Bauer, Bobby Brown—they were all experienced. You knew by the way they carried themselves that they were a class act. They looked like champions. We carried ourselves pretty good too, but this was our first shot.

It was interesting watching Yogi Berra. It would have been hard to copy him: he approached things differently. But he caught the ball and threw it well, and hit the ball well. His style of hitting amazed me. He hit bad pitches. Finally we decided to just throw him strikes and see what happened. He didn't have that good a Series at the plate, but he homered in the fourth game against Konstanty, when they pulled away from us.

DEL ENNIS · PHILLIES:

We would have done better in the Series if we had won the pennant earlier. The World Series was anticlimactic. The Yankees didn't awe me. They had good pitching, that's all. But the reason we couldn't hit against them is that we were worn out. I couldn't get started and neither could anyone else. Another big problem was that Curt Simmons wasn't allowed to pitch although he was on army furlough. Since Roberts had pitched in our pennant-winning game, Sawyer had to start our top reliever, Jim Konstanty, in Game One. We never could get adjusted. It was a shame because the Phillies had never won a world championship.

NATIONAL LEAGUE

1951

"IN NEW YORK THERE WAS A STEAK PLACE NEAR YANKEE STADIUM WITH SAWDUST ON THE FLOOR AND YOU JUST PICKED YOUR HUNK OF MEAT AND TOLD THEM HOW THICK YOU WANTED IT SLICED. THEY HAD A PITCHER OF BEER FOR YOU AND YOU'D GET YOUR STEAK AND FRENCH FRIES—THAT WAS REALLY LIVING."

RANDY JACKSON

BOSTON BRAVES

JOHNNY SAIN:
In 1951 I still felt pain in my shoulder. I was ineffective, winning just 6 and losing 13 through August. Only Spahn and rookie left-hander Chet Nichols were pitching well. The team was floundering in the middle of the pack, so I thought I was on my way out of Boston. Tommy Holmes, who had replaced Billy Southworth as manager, called me on an off-day and told me to come over to the ballpark. He then told me I had been traded. I'm an emotional guy and I was choked up a little. The Braves, possibly to cut down on their payroll in response to plummeting gate receipts, had sent me to the New York Yankees for pitching prospect Lew Burdette. It was a deal that turned out to be good for both of us.

LEW BURDETTE:
I was glad to be traded to the Braves because I got a chance to pitch. Fortunately, they were rebuilding and I got to go straight to the parent club. My one-time hero Bucky Walters was the pitching coach for Boston, and he said there was one job opening. I said, "What is it—water boy? I'll take anything I can get." He wanted me to be a short man in the bullpen because Tommy Holmes already had Warren Spahn, Max Surkont, Vern Bickford, Chet Nichols, and Jim Wilson to start. Unlike what is usually said about this era, it wasn't only old guys who were used in relief. I had been a reliever and starter in Triple A, so I knew how to do the job.

ST. LOUIS CARDINALS

BILLY JOHNSON:
When I was notified in mid-May that the Yankees had dealt me to St. Louis, I was disappointed. I felt that I was going to a lower classification. But once I got to the Cardinals I was treated just as well as I had been on the Yankees. Also, I had played against the Browns, so I was ready for the hot weather and the hard infield.

RALPH KINER (PIRATES):
All the fields were chopped up in those days, especially those in towns that also had football teams. But the

worst field was Sportsman's Park in St. Louis. It was always in bad shape because both the Cardinals and Browns played there.

B. JOHNSON:

We moved close to St. Louis. When I arrived, everyone already had roommates, so I said it would be fine if I roomed by myself. I didn't pal around with anyone in particular, just whoever was around. The Cardinals were a very close team and we had good times. On the road we'd go to movies or an occasional party—they were never parties thrown by the club. We got to know each other best on train trips. But I didn't like those trips because the air conditioner often broke down and we'd have to spend hours and hours in the summer in heated trains. There really wasn't as much cardplaying as you'd expect. I didn't play at all. Peanuts Lowrey, our center fielder, was a great cardplayer. He was a magician who could do anything he wanted with cards. The other guys tried to stay away from him.

After being platooned by Casey Stengel in New York in 1949 and 1950, Billy Johnson again became an everyday third baseman for the St. Louis Cardinals and responded with a career-high 14 home runs.

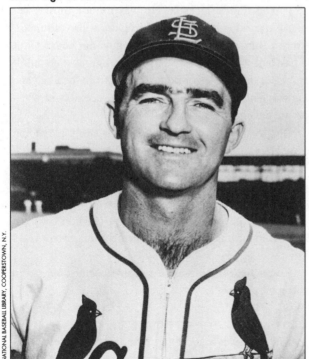

NATIONAL BASEBALL LIBRARY, COOPERSTOWN, N.Y.

Marty Marion was the manager. He had been the Cardinals' shortstop since before the war, but wasn't playing this year. I thought he did a good job his first year as manager. He was the type who would change the batting order around and move players in and out of the lineup to win. I thought he got along with all the players.

Other than Marion, who'd become our player-manager in 1952, there weren't many leaders on the team. Stan Musial was a bit of a leader, but I didn't notice any of the other players taking up that role. Stan was a good guy of exceptional character. He also was a tremendous hitter who led the league with a .355 average, hit over 30 homers, and drove in over 100 runs, by far the best on the team. He and Red Schoendienst were roommates and close friends. Red was a good hitter and fine second baseman. I liked that he played hard all the time.

Right fielder Enos Slaughter was one of those old-style hard-nosed players. He didn't care who he hurt on the ballfield. He was a good presence on the club, an outspoken player who was always hollering. He was a terrific bench jockey, but I didn't see him hassle Jackie Robinson or other black players.

Gerry Staley was considered the ace of the Cardinals' staff. He came close to winning 20 games each year. He was a pretty good pitcher who was very businesslike on the mound. His best pitch was a sinkerball. I think Max Lanier was our best pitcher. He was a left-hander who had been on the Cardinals since the late thirties, but he still had good stuff and won a few games for us in 1951. In 1952 he would go to the Giants. Harry Brecheen also had been with the Cardinals for a long time. He was still a quality left-hander. In 1952 "the Cat" would go crosstown to the Browns. Al Brazle was the top relief pitcher on the Cardinals. I remembered him from the 1943 World Series because I tripled off him. Now that we were teammates, he never said anything about it.

The Cardinals finished third, well behind the Giants and Dodgers. I had a good year, leading the league's third basemen in fielding and hitting a career-high 14 homers. I didn't have trouble adjusting to National League pitching. The toughest guy I faced was the Dodgers' Preacher Roe. He was a left-hander with a tough sinker. But he didn't give me any more trouble than Bob Feller.

CHICAGO CUBS

FRANK BAUMHOLTZ:

In 1951 Frankie Frisch couldn't keep me off the team or out of the lineup. For much of the year he had me batting third, the only time in my career I wasn't a leadoff hitter. I hit .284, with 28 doubles and 10 triples and a career-high 50 RBIs. That was a lot better year than he had—he was fired.

Hank Sauer was the Cubs' star and most popular player. Every year he'd hit over 30 homers, and nobody could bring runners around like Hank. On the road, Hank and I were roommates and would go to a lot of movies together: whodunits, shoot-'em-ups, war movies, intrigue. We would play pinochle and hearts on train trips. When we'd have a day game and not have another game until the next night, we might start up a five-and-dime poker game.

There were all-night poker games, but I can't remember there being any wild parties. When Phil Cavarretta was the team captain, he was a good friend who ran around with Sauer, Bill Serena, Bob Ramazzotti, and me, and we'd play poker together. After Phil became manager halfway through the 1951 season, he couldn't play poker with us anymore and seemed a bit disappointed. One time he came to me and asked if we had been playing poker in the hotel the night before. I said, "Phil, why do you ask when you know we were? We were waiting for you to come up and join us." He said with a touch of embarrassment, "Some older people were saying they heard a lot of noise coming out of the room. Can you see if you can get the guys to call it a night a little earlier?" I smiled and said I would.

There were strict rules about when we'd have to be in after both day games and night games. Different managers would have bed checks. Cavarretta would send Yosh Kawano around to check rooms—Phil knew what was going on because he was a player. He knew that after a game at, say, Crosley Field or Wrigley Field, there were a lot of women standing outside the ballpark hoping to meet players; and that in New York at the Commodore Hotel, there were women on the mezzanine. To tell the truth, I don't think Phil was that interested in what the players were doing as long as they didn't stay out past curfew, or do anything that would get them into trouble

or hurt their play on the ballfield. Neither did I.

Hank and I used to eat a lot at a place called the Cottage, which was about 1½ miles from Wrigley Field. When I went out, I drank scotch and water, and had an occasional martini, until I drank too many one day after I tore both my groins. A lot of guys drank. Not that there were drunkards. It's just that players had so much time on their hands. I had beer after a game only on a really hot day. We had beer in the clubhouse but had to buy it ourselves. We gave Yosh money and he took care of that. He kept a record of what everybody bought. The only thing we got free were sandwiches between games of doubleheaders.

We had a good group of players. Chuck Connors had a stint at first for the Cubs. I first met him when I was playing basketball with the Cleveland Rebels and he played with the Boston Celtics in the NBL. He had been with the Brooklyn organization, but this was really the only time he got playing time in the majors. My wife and I went out a few times with him and his wife. I was the only guy who called him Kevin, his real first name. He was a very nice guy and extremely talented as an actor. He could recite everything from Shakespeare to "Casey at the Bat"—and he could be so funny. I told him, "You oughtta be in movies."

I liked Randy Jackson. He was a good third baseman—a good golfer, too. He had a dry sense of humor. Smoky Burgess was a pudgy little guy, but he could hit a baseball. He was a nice guy and religious—he didn't smoke or drink. We got Eddie Miksis from the Dodgers. He was a nice guy and played a good second base when he got the chance.

Bob Rush was very likable. He was a big, easygoing guy. He was our best pitcher and threw a ball that felt like a rock when you hit it. Johnny Klippstein was a super guy. Frisch said, "I'm going to pitch him every day if it kills him"—he thought his stuff was that good. Johnny did have excellent stuff, but he didn't get the proper opportunity then. He became much better years later.

I didn't get to know Hal Jeffcoat because he ran in different circles.

JOHNNY KLIPPSTEIN:

Hal Jeffcoat was a good guy who talked and told jokes all the time. Jeff would laugh louder at his jokes than anyone else—because they usually weren't funny.

Frank Baumholtz was a fine guy, good hitter, and helluva competitor. He was a good outfielder, with a good arm, but if he had a shortcoming it was that he tried to throw out too many runners at home on singles and the batters would end up at second base. He wouldn't have done this on other teams, but he knew that the Cubs' pitchers couldn't afford to fall behind.

Turk Lown and first baseman Dee Fondy were brought up by the Cubs and we became good friends. Turk and I roomed together quite a bit. He was a right-hander out of Brooklyn and, like me, struggled with his control. But, also like me, he stayed in there and would have a long career. Turk was fun to hang out with because he knew someone in every town who was good for a free meal. We'd come into any town, and Turk would remember someplace we could go. I'd kid him for being the world's biggest freeloader.

Fondy was a tall, strong left-handed batter from Texas. It was obvious that he would become our regular first baseman, but he didn't play much as a rookie because of Chuck Connors. Connors was a funny guy. He'd walk down a crowded street with his son on his shoulder and recite poetry very loudly: "Today, I killed a man. . . . But I'm not sorry." And everyone would turn around. Or we'd walk down a crowded street in New York and he'd ask excitedly, "Don't you see him? Where's he at?" And everyone would start looking for someone who wasn't there. This was his way of having a good time. He had acting ability.

Once Andy Pafko was traded, Hank Sauer was the only star on the Cubs until Ransom Jackson started to hit a few home runs. Randy was a likable guy and a good competitor, but he was so quiet it was almost scary. He had a very dry sense of humor and when he did say something it was funny. He'd crack you up with one-liners. I'd wonder why someone so quick and witty didn't talk more.

RANDY JACKSON:

Nineteen fifty-one was my first full year in the majors, and I hit 16 homers and drove in 70-some runs. Unfortunately, I had played enough games in 1950 to disqualify me as a Rookie-of-the-Year candidate. In 1950 I hadn't really felt like a member of the team, but when you play a whole season, it's different. You make friends and go on trips together and are with everyone the whole time.

On the whole, the players were friendly. Some guys ran around together, but it was never cliquish. On the road, you might do something only with your room-mate, but often you'd run into teammates at the place you ate. In some towns without good restaurants, we ate in hotels and signed checks, which made it easy. Sometimes we had already snacked at the ballpark—the clubhouse guys always supplied us with sandwiches or fruit, candy or cookies. When they gave us meal money, most of the time we went to a non-fancy place that would have a good steak or seafood. Bookbinder's in Philadelphia was a popular hangout. In New York there was a steak place near Yankee Stadium with sawdust on the floor and you just picked your hunk of meat and told them how thick you wanted it sliced. They had a pitcher of beer for you and you'd get your steak and french fries—that was really living. Nothing fancy. I'm sure some players snacked during games, because you didn't want to play on an empty stomach.

At home, you took care of your own accommodations. Before I was married, I had an apartment about 10 blocks from Wrigley Field. The clubhouse guy, Yosh Kawano, a nice guy who was my age, and another player lived with me to cut expenses. The only guy I ever wanted to get away from as a road roommate was utility infielder Bob Ramazzotti. He was a wonderful guy but smoked Italian cigars that just curled your hair. I didn't smoke, so I told him he'd have to get someone else.

Ballplayers couldn't help but consider themselves celebrities to a certain extent. We were recognized when we went out and fans were always asking for autographs. But we didn't feel like movie stars, even though they came out to see us play and introduced themselves to us. The Wrigley Field fans were great. They were used to bad teams but still they'd come root for us. The bleacher bums would sit in the sun with their shirts off. They wouldn't cause much trouble. They weren't very vocal. They just enjoyed a nice afternoon in the sun watching a baseball game.

The Cubs' infield consisted of me at third, Roy Smalley at short, Eddie Miksis at second, and Chuck Connors or Dee Fondy at first. When I was on the L.A. Angels in 1949, Chuck was playing for Montreal in the Dodgers' organization. The Cubs' general manager called me up and asked what I thought of him. I told him that he could hit and field, so they bought him. He came out to Catalina in 1951 and he was funny. As long as there were two people near him, he'd recite "Casey at the Bat." He did a great job, and he'd do it for anybody. When the season began, the Cubs sent Fondy back to the Pacific Coast League and kept Connors. Fondy burned up the PCL and Connors couldn't hit major league pitching, so they swapped them in the middle of the year. Connors did great in the PCL and Fondy had a bad first year with the Cubs. Of course, once Connors got out in the California climate and met some Hollywood types, it worked out great for him in show business. He didn't have to play baseball anymore because he became a successful actor.

Having gained more experience in the majors, I realized that ballplayers had to accept certain facts: you had no control over what they paid you, if they played you, if they traded you, or where they sent you. I never thought about one organization being much better than the others. Being on the Cubs didn't seem any better or worse than being anywhere else. Nobody wanted to be traded to the Boston Braves because there would be more people in church than at the ballpark. We didn't like playing in a town like that. St. Louis had a bad ballpark, Sportsman's Park, and it was like playing on concrete. And St. Louis and Cincinnati were really hot all the time. The Dodgers were considered a good organization—and I'd seen evidence of that in the minors. The Giants were considered a good organization, but they had the worst ballpark. In the Polo Grounds, you could hold back your bat and hit one into the seats to the opposite field because it was so short, but it went about a mile and a half in center field. I didn't really think of playing with other teams despite being on a losing team. I believed that you do what you can for whatever team you are with.

HANK SAUER:

Our general manager, Wid Matthews, came over from the Dodgers' organization. When he thought he'd make a few deals he looked to the Dodgers. It was either Pafko or me going to Brooklyn. I was told that they wanted me. I would have loved to have gone there just because of that tremendous pitching staff they had. I

would have liked to play in a World Series. When Pafko was traded there was an uproar because he was so popular in Chicago. I'm sure that if I had been the one in that trade they would have been unhappy, too. When we lost Pafko we lost a big part of our ballclub. I hit fourth, and after the trade there was no fifth-place batter who could keep hurlers from pitching around me. Pafko and I were good to start with. And with me in left, Pafko in right, and Frankie Baumholtz in center, we had a good outfield offensively and defensively. Our problem was our middle infielders, and they tried to improve that in the Pafko deal. But it didn't work out because Eddie Miksis couldn't replace Pafko, who was a star. We gave up too much. I didn't like losing Johnny Schmitz either, because he had been our best pitcher and was our left-handed complement to Bob Rush—Joe Hatten wouldn't do much for us. And I also was sorry to lose Rube Walker. He was our "fleet-footed" catcher. He also was a great guy.

I was glad that Baumholtz was brought back from the minors because he shouldn't have been there in the first place. He was a good center fielder and excellent hitter. In fact, he was a tremendous athlete. As in Cincinnati, we roomed together, and our families were close. He was one of the nicest men who ever lived, an outstanding person. We had a lot of fun together.

Frank and I palled around a lot with infielder Bill Serena. He was a happy-go-lucky guy. A bunch of us would go to a bar and drink a few beers, and every time it came time to pick up the tab, Bill would disappear. One day he slipped into the bathroom. We saw that Bill had left behind a $20 bill, and we used it to order a round of beers, letting the bartender keep the change.

When we went out, we didn't feel like celebrities. We felt we were somebody but nothing outstanding. I didn't forget that back in 1937, when I became a pro, ballplayers were considered bums. Most of the guys lived modestly on the North Side—I lived in the Sheldrake Apartments—and you'd usually have a companion or two going to and from the park each day.

The Cubs were a close club, with no dissension. The only problem was that the young players didn't like Frankie Frisch. They spoke up about their troubles and Frisch was fired halfway through the season, when we were in Philadelphia. He blamed the young kids for getting him fired.

RUBE WALKER:

The Brooklyn Dodgers were the team I liked to play most. I knew that Reese and Robinson would run against me, and that revved me up. I had a strong arm and liked the challenge. We didn't do that well against the Dodgers, but no one else did either. Of the teams in the National League, they were the only one that had an aura. I admired them, so it was a happy day in June when the Cubs sent me, Pafko, Johnny Schmitz, and infielder Wayne Terwilliger to the Dodgers for catcher Bruce Edwards, pitcher Joe Hatten, infielder Eddie Miksis, and outfielder Gene Hermanski.

BROOKLYN DODGERS

RUBE WALKER:

I was shocked to be traded to Brooklyn. I looked up the next day and I was in a Brooklyn uniform. It was strange putting it on. I was number 10.

Branch Rickey had moved on to Pittsburgh and Walter O'Malley was now the majority owner of the Dodgers. Before the season, he had fired Rickey's manager, Burt Shotton, and replaced him with Charlie Dressen, an upbeat guy who had been Leo Durocher's coach before managing out in the Pacific Coast League.

When I came to Brooklyn, Dressen and Buzzy Bavasi, the GM, told me I was there to back up Roy Campanella and be a left-handed pinch hitter. I put on the gear in about a third of our games. I didn't regret not being a starter and backing up Campanella. I felt I contributed. Damn right! I admired Campanella a great deal and we were good friends. He is remembered for his happy demeanor, but he was a serious player. And a tough, long out. I always think of him swinging that bat. He swung hard and was more of a pull hitter than Snider. He batted .325, led the team in RBIs, and hit 33 homers, which was behind only Gil Hodges. As a receiver, he was excellent. I watched the way all catchers called a game and he was the best in the league. He had a good arm and a great, quick, short throw to second base.

In those days, catchers on opposing teams talked more before games, on the field. Campy and I had talked a lot when I was on Chicago. I'm sure we learned from each other. Like Campanella, I tried to talk to batters to distract them. Anything you could do to distract them, you did. We'd also scuff the ball anytime we could. When we picked up a ball we'd grind it into the dirt. We tried to hide it, but the umpires were aware of it. We got along with umpires, so they left us pretty much alone. Roy and I called similar games because we had the same staff. If we had a fastball pitcher, we damn sure couldn't make him a breaking ball pitcher, could we?

Don Newcombe was our ace and the man Dressen went to down the stretch. He was a fastball pitcher who could spot it as good as anybody. He had great control and pitched inside. He got better when he came up with a hell of a change-up. So here was a guy who throws as hard as a son of a bitch and suddenly he could take something off. He got to where he'd use his curve and change-up 33 percent of the time. It's likely that Carl Erskine helped him. Erskine had one heck of an overhand curve and a super change-up that looked like it backed up. He was the only Dodger who didn't like to pitch tight. He didn't want to hurt anybody. He was just coming into his own and felt that he'd have come along sooner if Burt Shotton hadn't pitched him in pain when he was just 20 or 21.

Clem Labine, who was very cocky for a rookie, occasionally threw a fastball up and in, but mostly he threw sinkers and curveballs. Both pitches were excellent. His fastball was a hard sinker. After being brought up in late August he won 4 straight, including 2 shutouts and two 1-run games. But Dressen seemed to forget about him down the stretch. Clem thought he was mad at him. Ralph Branca could throw all kind of pitches. He had great stuff, but he had hurt his shoulder and it affected him. Preacher Roe was amazing. He was a skinny left-hander who looked old and weak, but he had strong hands and was a tough pitcher. He had great control and could throw a ball in a cup. Preach went 22–3 in 1951. You couldn't get much better than that. The pitchers would talk among themselves. Some guys were quiet in the clubhouse, like Erskine, Labine, and Preacher, but on the mound they were extremely competitive and would do whatever it took to win.

This was a great team and just being on the Dodgers made certain players more competitive. It rubbed off. Watching Newcombe, for instance, made other pitchers more competitive. Certain guys didn't believe they'd lose. My attitude changed when I was a Dodger and I became more competitive and played better.

The Dodgers' winning attitude is what I remember most. The Dodgers were a proud but humble team. We expected to win, but didn't gloat when we did. Winning is all that was talked about from the first day of spring training. If someone got down, Gil, Pee Wee, Campy, or Robinson would sit and talk to them. Reese was the on-field leader. Hodges, Snider, and Robinson were all leaders. We all thought Pee Wee could have been a great manager, but he didn't want to manage. We all felt Gil would be a manager. He'd get mad every once in a while, but I'd say he didn't really have a temper. He was very quiet. Gil was a great guy and we were very close although we didn't socialize very much. What a hitter he had become since the mid-forties. He was a dead pull-hitter. He hit 40 homers and drove in 100 runs—

The acquisition of strong-throwing, left-handed hitter Albert "Rube" Walker gave the Dodgers a dependable catcher to spell Roy Campanella for their remaining years in Brooklyn.

NATIONAL BASEBALL LIBRARY, COOPERSTOWN, N.Y.

he'd have 100 RBIs seven straight years. He and Snider were the best righty-lefty power duo in the league.

Snider was a good guy. He was also our most consistent power hitter. We had mostly right-handed hitters, so, being left-handed, he had the advantage in that other teams would throw right-handers against us. In Ebbets Field, Snider could hit any right-hander out of the park.

Jackie Robinson was a unique player, a tough competitor who got the attention of other players. When he was on base, he distracted pitchers. He was the most daring baserunner in the game. He could hit to all fields. He could hit with power. He was hitting fourth when I got there, although sometimes Hodges batted fourth. By this time, Robinson wasn't having many racial problems. Once in a while, he'd get harassed by someone on the opposing bench but he'd handle it so damn well. He had a lot of inner strength and wasn't afraid to speak his mind. He had friends other ballplayers didn't have— politicians, Edward R. Murrow. He was a fine guy. I know he was unhappy that Branch Rickey had left and he didn't care much for Walter O'Malley, but he still hit .338 in 1951 and drove in about 90 runs. He also was an excellent second baseman.

HANK SAUER (CUBS):

Jackie Robinson was something. On many occasions I slid into second trying to break up a double play and get him. I always missed him until one day when I almost cut the shoe off his foot. He still said, "That's the way to play the game." He was a great player. Willie Mays, who was a rookie in 1951, had more power than Robinson, but he couldn't run with this guy. Robinson could steal a base any time he wanted. When Bob Rush pitched, I said, "Why don't we just put Robinson on third base and get it over with." Because with Rush pitching, he'd steal second and third on two pitches. With his first step he was going full blast. Nobody in baseball history ever took the abuse he took. I saw it first when he played in the minors at Montreal. When he played in Chicago, they gave him a standing ovation.

R. WALKER:

Jackie and Pee Wee hit to all fields. So did Carl Furillo, who was a great hitter. And a great fielder. His arm—

goodness gracious! He threw strikes from the right-field fence. At Ebbets Field, the right-field wall was thirty feet high with a twenty-eight-foot screen on top, and there was a scoreboard on the wall in right-center with a Bulova clock on top of that. It wasn't easy to play right because the ball would carom off all those things in different ways and give a right fielder lots of trouble. Skoonj, as we called him, studied the wall and mastered it. No one played the caroms as well as he did.

The Dodgers were known for their unity. We were all good friends, and after a road game two or three players would go out for dinner and by the time they got to the place there would be fifteen of us. Some of the Dodgers played golf. I did; so did Hodges, who was a lot of fun to play with. Pee Wee could really play. Some Dodgers played pool, bowled. There were several card games going on all the time. Reese, Hodges, Snider, and Jackie played cards, mostly bridge. Clyde King, Billy Cox, and Carl Erskine liked bridge, too. There'd always be games for money on the train. Guys would sing. Branca was a good singer and would sing pop songs. A few of us from the South would play country and western music. The Dodgers would throw parties for the players in downtown Brooklyn—we didn't go to Manhattan for functions—or we'd organize one ourselves on an off-day. However, there wasn't much socializing in Brooklyn. We were very close and were concerned about each other but didn't really show it. I got married that year and lived in Bay Ridge and saw a few guys who lived out there—Duke, Pee Wee, Eskine—but when players went out it was usually just with their families or another couple.

The fans were a bit wilder in Brooklyn than Chicago. At every game, there were single people, fathers and sons—or daughters—entire families, groups of kids, people of all ages, and in Ebbets Field you were so close to them that you got to know them. They got to be like our family. Snider and the others would call them by their first names. When you were going to the bullpen, you'd holler to them all the way down. It was fun signing autographs. Some kids wanting autographs put postcards under players' windshield wipers and we'd mail the signed cards back to them. We couldn't do it every day, but after a game some of us would park at a service station in back of right field. And there'd be a hell of a

crowd there every time we went out. Reese, Jackie, and the others would sign autographs. I think everyone in Brooklyn identified with the Dodgers—we symbolized the "city."

Of course, the Giants were the Dodgers' chief rivals, and in 1951 we were in a two-team pennant race. We didn't really hate the Giants. We just wanted to beat them badly and we didn't care how. There were several knockdown contests. They had Maglie, Jansen, and Hearn coming in to our batters, so we had to match them. Newcombe was always knocking them on their backs. The catchers didn't have to call knockdown pitches. The pitcher would just throw one whenever he wanted to. We'd knock anybody down—"the ball got away." As I said, only Erskine didn't pitch tight.

The Dodgers got off to a great start before I arrived—Cal Abrams hit in the high .400s for two months—and we were up by 13½ games in August. But then the Giants got red hot. As our big lead over them shrank, we didn't panic because we knew better than to assume that we'd already won the pennant. But yes, we were surprised that the Giants came back from so far behind so late in the season. They had an excellent ballclub, but we felt we were better. They finally tied us with two games to go. Then we both won. Newcombe shut out the Phillies and Sal Maglie shut out the Braves. Newcombe got a lot of dumb criticism for not being a big-game pitcher, but he was super in the clutch. He won that game against Philadelphia, and came back the next day when we needed him. We played again in Philadelphia on the last day of the season, and found out in about the sixth inning that the Giants had won their final game. That meant we had to win. It was a high-scoring game and Dressen ran through a lot of pitchers—Roe, Branca, King, Labine—before Erskine held the Phillies in check for a couple of innings. We caught them by scoring 3 runs in the top of the eighth. I got a pinch double off Karl Drews that scored 2 runners, and then Furillo singled off Robin Roberts to bring home the pinch runner. That's when Dressen brought in Newcombe, and he held the Phillies scoreless until the thirteenth inning, while Roberts stopped us cold. Pafko bailed Newk out with a catch down the line off Seminick in the eleventh inning, and Robinson made a game-saving diving catch off Waitkus with the bases loaded in the twelfth inning. He almost knocked himself out. Newcombe tired with 2 outs in the thirteenth and Bud Podbelian finished the game, doing a great job. We won when Robinson homered in the fourteenth inning against Roberts. What a way to tie the Giants for the pennant!

We were confident going into the best-of-three playoffs. Our team had been together for so long that there was no reason for a pep talk. The Giants won the first game 3–1, beating Ralph Branca. Campanella pulled a muscle, so I caught the last 2 games of the playoffs. The second playoff game was one of the highlights of my career. Dressen gave Labine a rare start. Clem shut out the Giants 10–0 and I homered and had a couple of hits.

Going into the last game, in the Polo Grounds, I thought only of winning. Maglie was knocked out and going into the bottom of the ninth with Newcombe ahead by 3 runs, 4–1, we couldn't help but be confident. Our best reliever, Clyde King, had a sore arm, so we didn't question Dressen bringing in Branca when Newcombe tired. He'd had a good year and had picked up a few saves. We figured he could get out of the jam. But with two on, Bobby Thomson hit a fastball off Branca to beat us, 5–4. He didn't hit it that far, but I knew it was a homer as soon as he hit it. I knew it was a long walk to that goddamn clubhouse in center field. I watched the homer but not the Giants' celebration near home plate. God, that was the toughest moment in my career—and for the other Dodgers as well. For a few seconds, our players were too stunned to leave their positions. They couldn't believe it was over. It's kind of hard to explain my feelings for Branca at that moment. He cried afterward in the clubhouse. That was tough. Of course, none of the Dodgers blamed him—we supported him. He wore number 13, and that sure came into play that game. He and I had planned to go out to dinner that night with my wife and his fiancée, and we still went. We didn't talk about the game at all. But we were sure thinking about it. "Heartbreak" is the right word to describe how we felt. It hurt.

DON NEWCOMBE:

I started 36 times and pitched over 270 innings in 1951, and I led the league in strikeouts and won 20 games for the first time. Jackie also had a great year, batting close to .340, and Roy was voted the league's MVP. We had

as good a Dodger team as there had been, but the Giants rallied in August and September and beat us in the playoffs. Our rivalry with the Giants was the real thing and it got out of hand sometimes. But it wasn't racial. Sal Maglie would throw at Carl Furillo and Gil Hodges the same as he would throw at Jackie Robinson. And I'd throw at Willie Mays the same as I'd throw at Alvin Dark and Don Mueller. We were out there trying to win championships. I won a lot of big games for us during the year and would like to have won that third playoff game. Maybe it just happened to be the Giants' time to win.

After I became reasonably successful with the Dodgers, I went to see Hermie Kaufman, who was coaching at the high school where I grew up, near Maplewood, New Jersey. Back then he coached at my junior high, and when I tried out, he told me I'd never make it as a pitcher. Now he asked me to come back and talk to the kids. I used Hermie as the butt of my jokes to the kids, because I made it despite him. He laughed now, but I didn't think it was too funny when I was 14 and my coach told me I'd never make it. In fact, he didn't pitch me much on his team because he said I didn't have the talent and wasn't smart enough.

As a kid, there was one man who encouraged me. His name was Johnny Grier and he was my next-door neighbor and probably one of the best amateur athletes in New Jersey ever. He was about 12 years older than me. My mother, Sadie, and my father, Roland—who was a chauffeur for a real estate man for 30 years—liked that he took me under his wing and taught me a lot of things about life. He got me dates and taught me about women, about driving cars, how to paint houses—I worked with him part-time when I was going to school. I owe a major part of my life to him, especially my young life. I could have wound up in jail. I didn't carry weapons, but we had our own gang, and if guys from the other side of town came into our neighborhood we'd kick their asses. We didn't want anyone coming over to our side of the highway and messing with our girls. Johnny kept me out of a lot of trouble. I didn't give him the due he should have gotten when I was successful with the Dodgers. I'd mention him in interviews, but I never brought him out front to tell what could happen to ghetto kids without a big brother to help them get on the right track. Johnny made sure I got the chance to work and play baseball. Around Elizabeth, we'd work out and people would watch us. We'd pitch to each other with a ball of thick black tape. Johnny taught me the big wind-mill windup and high kick I would use my entire career. He said, "Get momentum behind your body." That's exactly what I was doing now that I was winning in the major leagues.

I felt that I was peaking as a pitcher and that the Dodgers would rebound from that tough playoff loss and become a pennant winner in 1952. It wasn't a good time for me to be drafted into the army. I would lose two years from my career, which was just getting started after I'd already lost two or three years in the minors waiting on the Dodgers. Naturally, I was bitter.

NEW YORK GIANTS

SPIDER JORGENSEN:

I returned to the Giants from Minneapolis, and Durocher used me as a pinch hitter and spare right fielder. I played only once at third base. This year the team became closer and that contributed to its improvement into a pennant-winning team. I think a key to our success was the development of Jim Hearn. Our pitching coach, Frank Shellenback, dropped Hearn down from overhand to a three-quarters delivery, and all of a sudden he was throwing strikes and his ball was moving. That gave us a third big-winning starting pitcher, behind Sal Maglie and Larry Jansen.

Another major reason for our success was Monte Irvin. He played every day for the first time in the major leagues and became a star. Every time you looked up, he was driving in a big run. I was happy for him because he was a good guy. He was an excellent hitter and steady outfielder, a real plugger.

Bobby Thomson struggled a bit at the beginning of the year, and it's not surprising that the whole team did poorly. He and Whitey Lockman were pretty close and I think Whitey got him to close his stance and stand straighter. Then he started to hit the hell out of the ball. And the Giants started to win.

Willie Mays came up in May and was immediately starting in center field for us. He was accepted on the team right away. We knew he had talent. He was a young rookie just breaking in so he made a few mis-

takes now and then. He started out in a slump, but he worked hard and had a fast bat and good swing, so I didn't worry about him. Once he started hitting, he didn't stop.

I hit about .250 when I played in the field, but I struggled as a pinch hitter for the second straight year and my overall average was only .235. Then the Giants got utility player Hank Schenz from Pittsburgh, and at the All-Star break they sold me to the Oakland Oaks in the Pacific Coast League. (Oddly, the next year Schenz was also sold to Oakland.)

My major league career, which began in 1947 and included two World Series, was satisfying. But I was disappointed that I didn't put in a full five years and qualify for the pension. I wanted that.

BILL RIGNEY:

The 1951 season couldn't be scripted. We lose Opening Day, win the next game, and then lose the next 11. So we start 1–12. The fans didn't turn on us and we continued to believe in ourselves. Leo was trying to shake up the lineup and for a time benched Eddie Stanky, who was kind of a sparkplug for him. Finally, when we were trailing the Dodgers by 13½ games in August, and Charlie Dressen said, "The Giants is dead," we won 16 straight—our rookie Al Corwin won 5 in a row—and closed the gap on the Dodgers. Still, there was never a lot of positives in the press. They'd write, "They're playing good now but it's too late." Only we thought we had a chance to win it. And Leo would never let us give up: "Hey, it's not over, come on, come on, just keep coming!" We'd win one more and win one more. Every time we lost and the Dodgers won, we'd sag a little but then we'd come back and start a new streak. Larry Jansen was our lone pessimist. He'd say, "If the Dodgers play just .500 ball the rest of the way, we have to play .800 ball. Come on, face reality!"

We were a very smart team, a club that was a marvelous fit of talent and guys who cared about the game, wanted to play it correctly, and wanted to stay in the game after retiring. (Dark, Stanky, Westrum, Lockman, Herman Franks, and I would become major league managers and Maglie and Jansen would become pitching coaches.) Other than Leo, Dark and Stanky were the leaders on the team. They knew the game. If I wasn't considered a leader, I was at least a prospective leader because already they were saying I'd manage someday.

Every night on the road, after the game, Stanky, Dark, Lockman, Jansen, Westrum, maybe Maglie, and I would come back to the hotel and gather in my room. I used to keep a book on opposing pitchers, watching their fingers on the ball so that I could tell what pitch was coming. We'd have a couple of beers and I'd go over the next day's opposing pitcher with my teammates. If you told Monte Irvin or Willie Mays how they could tell what pitch was coming, then you'd have to buy a plane ticket to find the ball after they hit it. I think we lost only one game in our last western trip. Pittsburgh, Cincinnati, and Chicago were out of it, so they got a little careless and their catchers wouldn't bother to disguise their pitch calling. Our baserunners would relay signs to the hitters. If you crossed over with your left foot when taking a lead, it was a breaking ball; if you started out with your right foot, it was a fastball.

Most of our players were family-oriented. That makes for a good team. We were low-key but dedicated. Leo didn't really have to be a disciplinarian with us. Nobody was ever late getting to the ballpark and everybody was getting their rest. Leo never had bed checks. There were always a couple of guys who took advantage, but not the guys on the field every day.

We were in Cincinnati with one game to go on the last road trip. I had played that night—someone needed a rest against a tough left-hander. After our nightly meeting I went out to get the papers. At this late hour I spotted Monte Kennedy, one of our little-used pitchers, going out. He fibbed that he was going out to pick up a paper, but I said he could have mine. "Rig, this is the best-looking thing you've ever seen. You can't believe the boobs. . . ." I said, "Hey, we're hanging by our nails." He said, "Christ, Leo's not going to use me tomorrow." He wouldn't pass it up. The next day we went into the ninth inning ahead by a run. Kluszewski was the batter, with two men on. And Leo brought in Monte because he was a left-hander. I was the only one who knew about the previous night, so I was more nervous than anyone. He threw one pitch and Kluszewski hit it against the right-field screen for a double. We lost. I was so pissed. I came into the clubhouse but I couldn't find the son of a bitch. I wanted to kill him, but he locked himself in the john. Monte wouldn't look at me all the way back in the train. I'm sure his being out that night didn't cause what happened, but it bothered me that winning meant so much more to me than it did to him.

Leo managed his butt off because there was no room for mistakes. Give him credit. He took Thomson out of center field and put him back on third, where he'd played in the minors. And Whitey Lockman was moved from left and became a good first baseman—he must have saved Thomson 20 throwing errors. Both Hank Thompson and I were usually on the bench because Thomson was at third.

My teammates knew I could play and that I knew what to do at the right time. They said that they could depend on me. I could bunt a man over or score a man from third with less than two outs. I got to be the hitter Leo saved to pinch-hit late in the game. I knew he counted on me because I won the 10th and 16th games in our winning streak. I always knew I'd hit for Westrum or the pitcher.

One of our scouts told me, "Don't let the guys give up, because we're going to bring up a young player from Minneapolis and he might be just the difference for this club." Willie Mays was 20 when he joined the Giants in late May of 1951. He was unbelievable! We had first heard of Willie during spring training when Leo left us for a day and went to our minor league camp in Melbourne just to watch him play. You couldn't believe the things he said the next day about this black center fielder. He was hitting .477 at Minneapolis when he joined the team in Philadelphia, just as we were finishing batting practice. He was going to play, so Leo let him take the last five minutes of batting practice. He popped it up, hit a weak grounder, fouled one back . . . then all of a sudden he hit a rocket that landed in the middle of the upper deck in left field. Then he hit another rocket that went over the roof. Then he hit one that hit the right-field scoreboard. Everything stopped. The Phillies stopped warming up and Ashburn and Hamner and Puddin' Head Jones and all the others stopped to watch him hit. He got everyone's attention. He was amazing.

DON NEWCOMBE (DODGERS):
Athletically, Willie could do anything he wanted. I first saw him in 1949 when I was in Birmingham, Alabama, playing on a black all-star team with Jackie, Roy, and

Larry. We saw this young center fielder who threw Larry Doby out by a mile. Larry said, "Who the fuck is that?" Roy called Brooklyn and told Al Campanis, who had just become a scout, about him. The Dodgers sent a scout down and he said that Willie couldn't hit a curveball, so they passed on him. The next year he was on the Giants and the rest is history.

B. RIGNEY:

Willie started out going 0 for 12. He was anxious at the plate. He was in tears because he wasn't helping us and asked Leo to return him to Minneapolis, where he'd been a star. Leo said, "You're our center fielder, even if you never get a hit." It was a marvelous thing to say to a young black kid from the South who suddenly found himself in center field in the historical Polo Grounds. Then on May 28 he got his first hit, a homer against Warren Spahn. And after that he had no problem. He just got better and better. He made some incredible defensive plays and hit 20 homers. He would be voted Rookie of the Year. He was a little shy socially, but the exuberance and joy of playing just poured out of him. You could see the way he ran the bases, the way he caught the ball, the way his hat flew off—he gave a lift to everybody. Everybody took shots at Mays. Newcombe and some of the others would throw it behind his ear. He'd get up and screw his foot right back in there and hit a double down the left-field line. He had no fear at all—zero. Durocher was the right manager for Mays. Willie started to copy Leo's style, even dressing like him. He was a father figure to Willie. The other players didn't resent it at all.

We got great defense and a lot of timely hits from Mays, Wes Westrum, Don Mueller, and everyone else. We called Mueller "Mandrake" because he was a great bad-ball hitter. He hit singles, yet set a National League record with 5 homers in 2 games against the Dodgers in early September. What a hitter he was. But the best clutch player on the 1951 Giants was undoubtedly Monte Irvin. He drove in 122 runs, many in key spots. We'd get two men on and two outs and he'd single to center field. He was marvelous. Thomson was the only other Giant to have more than 100 RBIs, and only Bobby had more homers, 32 to 24. Monte also led our team in average, hitting .312.

On the mound we still had Jansen and Maglie and both won 23 games, tying for the league lead. And Jim Hearn won 17. All three were very tough against the Dodgers. Dave Koslo and Sheldon Jones were also reliable starters, and George Spencer was a good man in the bullpen.

We came into Boston for the final 3-game series, and the Dodgers were in Philadelphia. Maglie beat Boston, 3–0, on Saturday to tie us with the Dodgers. On Sunday, Jansen beat Boston, 3–2. We were up 3–1 and Stanky booted a double-play ball, a rare occurrence, and the score was 3–2, with two men on and two out. Willard Marshall, a former Giant, was the hitter. Leo left the bench and I knew he wanted to replace Jansen with Spencer. Larry was a quiet, unassuming guy, but he walked right off the mound and met Leo. I thought, "Uh, oh." But when Larry said what was on his mind, Leo returned to the bench and sat down. Marshall, my pal and former roommate, was the batter and I'm thinking, "Willard, you wouldn't be the one. Not you." Larry made one pitch and Marshall hit a line-drive spear . . . right to Monte Irvin. The game was over and we'd won, assuring us of at least a tie for the pennant.

Now we were on the train going back to New York. Our wives were with us. Every time the train stopped, someone would jump off and find out the score of the Dodgers' game with the Phillies. That game went 14 innings before Jackie Robinson won it with a dramatic homer, forcing a playoff. Meanwhile, I had a beer or two and asked Larry what he said to Leo. He said, "Rig, I never did what I did in my life. When Leo walked out, I just said, 'Leo, I want to tell you something. I have never come so far in my life as I have right now. I'll get this last out, so get your ass out of here!' "

We won the first game of the playoffs, 3–1, when Jim Hearn outpitched Ralph Branca and Thomson and Irvin homered for us. But then they clobbered us 10–0 behind Clem Labine. Sheldon Jones was our losing pitcher. So the whole season went down to Game Three, with Sal Maglie going against Don Newcombe, the toughest opposing pitcher in the league. We were behind, 1–0, in the fifth inning of the third playoff game, when Eddie Stanky says about Newcombe, "The big guy's losing it. Just stay close and we'll get his ass." We tie it in the seventh, but they get 3 more in the eighth and it's 4–1. Maglie's gone, Jansen's in for us, and Newcombe still looks strong. In the eighth, Hank

Thompson got into the on-deck circle intending to pinch-hit for Jansen. Meanwhile, I go up to pinch-hit for Westrum. I wanted to take a pitch. Newcombe blazed it by me. The ball looked as big as a pea. I backed out of the box and gazed at Stanky with a look that said, "Yeah, he's really lost a lot." He struck me out, he got out Thompson, and got out Stanky. But that was it. Alvin led off the ninth with a single. Then, for the only time I can think of, Charlie Dressen stumbled as a manager. He had Hodges hold Dark on at first—despite the 3-run lead and the fact that the batter, Don Mueller, was a left-handed hitter. Mueller hit a line drive that nicked Hodges's glove and went through for a single. If Hodges had been playing behind Dark, it would have been a 3–6–3 double play. Lockman followed with a double to left to score Dark and send Mueller sliding into third. Don broke a bone in his leg and I helped carry him into the clubhouse as Ralph Branca came in for Newcombe to face Bobby Thomson. People forget he had already homered off a Branca fastball in the first game. I was in the clubhouse looking out the window at the field when Thomson hit the pennant-winning 3-run homer off Branca. "The Shot Heard Around the World!" "The Miracle of Coogan's Bluff!"

Jim McCulley, the Giants' writer for the *Daily News,* was in the clubhouse after the game. He was a good friend and asked me, "How do I write this story? You guys came back from the dead." And Arch Murray was there, too. He wrote for the *Post* and couldn't believe it either, even when we were closing the gap on the Dodgers. After the game, Jackie Robinson and a few other Dodgers congratulated us. As Robinson said, "The Dodgers didn't lose the pennant, the Giants won it." We had gone 39–8 down the stretch.

There really wasn't a celebration because we didn't have time. Jim Hearn, his wife, Marianne, and my wife and I went down to Toots Shor's for a late dinner. When the guy brought back our car, I was about to hand him $10 when Marianne stopped me and said, "I'm not going to let you spend all the money yet." She gave him $2 out of her purse.

I think we were better than the Dodgers in 1951. I really do. You look at their team with Pafko, Furillo, Snider, Gil, Jackie, Pee Wee, Cox, Campy, Newk, Preacher, Erskine, Labine. . . . And then you look at our team: Maglie and Jansen won 46 games, Lockman had a

great year, Stanky and Dark were solid players, Bobby Thomson played his ass off at third, Monte coming out of the blue with big RBIs, Willie, Mueller—the purest hitter we had on the Giants. They were just two marvelous teams. There was such quality and I was proud to be part of it.

ED BOUCHEE:

As far as we could determine, the name Bouchee came from my great-great-grandfather, who came from Quebec. I was born in Livingston, Montana, in 1933. My father was a boilermaker for the Northern Pacific Railroad, and when I was ten he was transferred to Spokane, Washington. As a kid I was more interested in fishing and hunting than playing ball. However, I could hit as soon as I picked up a bat. I was a good left-handed hitter. In junior high I played fast-pitch softball. Then I played hardball in the Park League before entering high school. My desire to become a professional ballplayer came from hanging around the ballpark where the Spokane Indians played. They were an independent team in the Western International League. I shagged flies and talked to the some of the Indians, who were very friendly.

In high school I played baseball and was an All-City basketball player and All-State football player. Jack Spring, who was a future major league pitcher, was a buddy of mine, and we played baseball together in high school and American Legion. In the summer after we graduated, he and I played amateur ball in Troy, Montana, on a team with 11 guys. We won a tournament in Watertown, South Dakota. Then we bused to Battle Creek, Michigan, where we played the Eastern champs from Kalamazoo, Michigan. Their star was Ron Jackson, the tall first baseman who would later play with the White Sox. We got beat 3 games to 2 for the national title, but I hit 3 or 4 home runs in that series. A lot of scouts were on hand. The New York Giants offered both me and Spring $10,000 if we'd sign on the spot. We didn't sign with New York because we wanted a college education, or so we thought. Perhaps we would have signed to play professional baseball if we could have gone to college and still played other sports. But you weren't allowed to do that. I think that's what kept a lot of guys from signing. So I entered Washington State University, thinking I'd major in history, and as a freshman I played junior varsity basketball and varsity baseball and football. I was still getting attention from scouts, but fortunately in those days they didn't like to pester college kids too much.

PHILADELPHIA PHILLIES

ANDY SEMINICK:

In the off-season my friends and I would always go bird-hunting down in western Tennessee and stop off in Nashville. I was once a guest on the Grand Ole Opry because my wife's sister was married to a country and western singer. I met Roy Acuff and all those guys and answered a few questions.

I had to work during the off-season because my salary was so low. I had a lot of jobs. I was a pretty good meatcutter, an undertaker, a construction worker using heavy equipment, and a factory worker in Tennessee and Detroit. In Philadelphia, I worked in an Acme store, in the meat department. My sister and her husband had a meat market in Detroit and that's where I learned, while in the minors.

After the 1950 season I got $28,000. I always felt that when I signed I was satisfied. It would get out what the other players got and it would give you incentive. I sent back contracts unsigned. One year I held out almost all spring. With the Phillies, you didn't go to the front office unless you were asked, which maybe happened when they were giving you your release.

We dropped from first to fifth place and had a losing record. Ashburn batted in the .340s and Granny Hamner and Willie Jones had solid seasons, but the rest of us in the lineup had off seasons. Robin Roberts won 21 games and Bubba Church won 15, but Simmons was in the service and none of the other pitchers did particularly well. Konstanty was nowhere near the reliever he had been in 1950.

This time when we played the Dodgers at the end of the year, we weren't in the race. Brooklyn clinched a tie with the Giants for the pennant on the regular season's last day by beating us, 9–8, on Jackie Robinson's homer off Roberts in the 14th inning. I walked 5 times that game. The record was 6 times. The umpire, Larry Goetz, said, "I'll get you to swing that bat." I said, "Larry, you can't do that." It wasn't any surprise that

Robinson hit the homer. He rose to the occasion many times. He had already saved the game on a great play against Waitkus.

That year I was hit on the head by Max Lanier, the Cardinals' left-hander. Pitchers used to throw inside in those days, before batters wore helmets. That day we had some helmet liners come in and I was looking at them. I tried one on and figured they wouldn't help me much. After I got hit, I was in bad shape. My heartbeat went down to 38 and I could hardly raise my arm. I stayed in the hospital for a day. I tried to come back too quick, on the third day. That's when I got to feeling real bad. They rushed me to the hospital again. But I was okay. I didn't think it affected my hitting, but it must have, because I never could get in the groove again that year. I came up with yellow jaundice, and other things happened to me.

It was strange what happened to Mike Goliat. In 1950 he had been a good second baseman, allowing Hamner to move back to shortstop. Mike could hit 4 line drives off Don Newcombe every time he faced him. If you hit a couple of balls hard against Newcombe it was pretty good. In 1951 Mike was very fat when he came to spring training and that probably was his downfall. But he hit good in spring training. Then all of a sudden he just went downhill. I remember him being benched and saying, "Well, if they don't want me here, I can go someplace else." Then he was gone. It was the strangest thing. He never did come back. I realized nobody's job was secure.

In December I was on a hunting trip in west Tennessee when I was called and told I'd been traded to Cincinnati. That upset me very much. I had no indication that would happen. It may have been a good thing to happen, however, because it fired me up again. I wanted to prove the Phillies wrong for trading me.

DEL ENNIS:

I was a starter in the All-Star Game, but I missed a few games and this would be the only time in seven years I didn't have 100 RBIs. As the Phillies' top RBI man, I expected to be pitched inside. Ewell Blackwell was the toughest pitcher I faced, followed by Don Newcombe and Sal Maglie. Blackwell's sidearm delivery was murder on right-handers. He'd start the curveball at you and it would curve over the plate. But I hit him pretty good after a while. He was a mean pitcher. There were pitchers who angered me. I never liked Rex Barney of the Dodgers—who was out of the league by 1951—or Sal Maglie of the Giants. They threw right at you. They would tell you when you came to the plate, ''I'm gonna put this right in your ear.'' And they meant it. I never charged the mound after being knocked down. It just made me eager to hit. I'd wake up and hit the ball hard after getting up off the ground. I was hit many times. I got hit hard in the head once. I was hit twice in one game on one spot on my elbow. I couldn't bend my arm after the first time! That made me mad. Our pitchers would protect us by knocking down opposing players.

Ballplayers in the late '40s and early '50s were hard-nosed. Pitchers would throw at batters all the time. Since we didn't have helmets, we had to be tough. I never wore a helmet in my life. Baseball would become softer when they brought in helmet liners and then helmets. I'd rather they changed other rules, like charging an out in your batting record for hitting an RBI fly. They wouldn't have the sacrifice fly rule until 1954. (That would have raised my average 20 points a year.)

PITTSBURGH PIRATES

RALPH KINER:

We had another bad club in 1951, finishing just 2 games ahead of last-place Chicago. We won only 64 games, so it was amazing that Murry Dickson won 20. No one else won more than 8 games. Like all knuckleballers, Murry was always filing his nails.

FRANK BAUMHOLTZ (CUBS):

On Pittsburgh there were several pitchers who looked like they couldn't get anyone out with their stuff, but their balls moved. Dickson was the toughest. His ball moved all the time and occasionally he'd sneak a fastball in on your fists. He was no fun to bat against.

R. KINER:

I batted over .300 for the third time, drove in 109 runs although they wouldn't pitch to me with men on base, and led the league in walks, slugging percentage, and home runs, with 42. Our outfield did pretty good be-cause our right fielder, Gus Bell, drove in around 90 runs and our center fielder, George Metkovich, batted over .290 in his first year with Pittsburgh. George was a good guy with a great sense of humor. He also was from California and we became very close. We called him ''Catfish,'' ''the Cat,'' ''Poor George,'' everything. One time he was struck out by Max Surkont of the Braves. I asked him, ''What did he throw you?'' ''He threw me the radio ball.'' ''The radio ball?'' ''Yeah. You can hear it but you can't see it.'' Once Catfish was lazing by a swimming pool when a woman who walked by expressed horror at his feet. He said, ''Lady, if you'd fouled as many pitches off your feet as I have, your feet would look like these, too!'' I was glad George and rookie pitcher Bob Friend were now on the team, because Branch Rickey, the Pirates' new vice president and general manager under John Galbraith, traded away a couple of my other good friends. Cliff Chambers no-hit the Braves in May, yet he and Wally Westlake were traded to the Cardinals a month later. Rickey was trying to cut costs, and since I had signed a two-year contract with John Galbraith for a league-high $90,000 a year, I didn't feel that secure in Pittsburgh despite my great numbers.

The National League won the All-Star Game, 8–3. It was played in Detroit, and Tigers stars George Kell and Vic Wertz homered for the American League, and Musial, Hodges, Bob Elliott, and I homered for the National League. The National League had never won consecutive All-Star Games before.

FRANK THOMAS:

I went to spring training with the Pirates for the second time. Again I was assigned to New Orleans. I got so mad I went home. The Pirates kept calling me, but it was my wife who convinced me to go back. So I went back, and for the second time they sent me down to Charleston. Then Branch Rickey called Rip Sewell to ask if he had anybody who could help the Pirates. Sewell recommended me.

When I got to the big leagues for the first time, Ralph Kiner told me, ''Watch the way they pitch me, because you're a home run hitter and that's the way they're going to pitch you, too.'' That was good advice. But I didn't model myself on him or anyone else.

Twenty-two-year-old rookie Frank Thomas was seldom in Pittsburgh's lineup in 1951, but in two years he would smash 30 homers and drive in 102 RBIs, prompting the Pirates to trade their longtime slugger Ralph Kiner.

I played in 39 games with the Pirates, batting .264, with 9 doubles and 2 homers. I got my first hit off Paul Minner, a tall left-handed starter with the Cubs. I would get 10 straight hits off him. I couldn't make an out against him. Outfielders would run into each other and the ball would drop, infielders would stumble going after the ball. Finally he hit me in the leg and he laughed all the time I went down to first, saying, "That's one time I got to hit you instead of you hitting me."

DICK GROAT:

I was born in 1930 in a hospital in Wilkinsburg, Pennsylvania. But our home was actually in Swissvale, a small industrial town outside of Pittsburgh. My father, who was of German-Dutch descent, was in the real es-

tate and insurance business in Braddock, another suburb. I was the baby in the family, following two brothers and two sisters. I started playing basketball when I was five or six, and probably played ten times as much basketball as baseball from the time I was an eighth grader. I didn't play organized baseball until I was a sophomore in high school. I was fortunate enough to be one of two players picked to represent Pittsburgh both as a junior and a senior in high school in Hearst All-Star Games in New York. That's how I knew I had special talent. Scouts saw me both years, but I turned them down when they offered me contracts after I graduated. As much as my father wanted me to play major league baseball, he wanted all his kids to get college diplomas before doing anything else.

I had the opportunity to get my college education through basketball because Duke gave me a scholarship to play. At this time I dreamed of being an All-American basketball player and then playing in the NBA, and also playing major league baseball with the Pittsburgh Pirates. At Duke I played 2 years of baseball and 2½ years of basketball. I was an All-American in both sports each year. Basketball was my first love, and I was a much better player. I set NCAA records for most points and free throws and then averaged even more points the next year. I led the nation in assists both years. I was voted College Player of the Year.

In order to get my senior year of athletic eligibility, I spent six weeks in the Marine Corps at Parris Island during the summer of 1951. When I got out, I played some semipro baseball for a team in South Boston, Virginia. During the playoffs, Rex Bowen, a longtime scout for Branch Rickey, told me that if I went home before going back to Duke, Mr. Rickey wanted me to work out with the Pirates. You can't imagine how excited I was to spend two weeks working out with my favorite team. In the morning, Mr. Rickey watched me and some other prospects and in the evening I worked out with the Pirates before their games. One night, when the Pirates played the Reds, I sat in Mr. Rickey's box, with my parents sitting behind me. He said, "Young man, if you'll sign a contract tonight, I'll start you at shortstop tomorrow night against the Reds." My exact words were "Mr. Rickey, that isn't even fair." Then I said, "I'm going back to Duke. I owe them my senior year of athletics. But if you make the same offer after I graduate, I promise I'll sign with the Pittsburgh Pirates.'' He never once mentioned anything again until I finished with my college eligibility.

CINCINNATI REDS

EWELL BLACKWELL:

I had another good year in 1951, tying Ken Raffensberger for the team lead with 16 wins. We were the only pitchers on the Reds to win in double figures. All the starters lost in double figures because we were last in the league in runs scored, homers, batting average, and almost every other offensive category. We were lucky to finish sixth again. One bright spot was our 20-year-old rookie shortstop, Roy McMillan. He couldn't hit at all and wasn't very fast, but he was already a tremendous shortstop.

I was the National League's final pitcher in the All-Star Game for the second straight year, finishing up for Robin Roberts, Sal Maglie, and Don Newcombe. I pitched a scoreless inning in an 8–3 victory. I established a record by pitching in 6 consecutive All-Star Games, which only Early Wynn would match. Another highlight was hitting my first and only major league home run. I hit it over the center-field fence in Brooklyn against Preacher Roe. Old Preacher was running around the bases with me, cursing me out. I was a good-hitting pitcher. That year I hit .293.

AMERICAN LEAGUE
1951

"I WAS WONDERING HOW I WAS SUPPOSED TO PITCH TO A MIDGET. I DIDN'T KNOW WHETHER TO THROW THE BALL UNDERHANDED OR OVERHANDED TO GAEDEL. I JUST WANTED TO BE CAREFUL NOT TO HIT HIM. DIZZY TROUT TOLD ME LATER THAT IF HE'D BEEN THE PITCHER, HE'D HAVE THROWN THE BALL RIGHT BETWEEN HIS EYES."

BOB CAIN

PHILADELPHIA ATHLETICS

EDDIE JOOST:

Jimmy Dykes became the Athletics' manager after Connie Mack retired. He was knowledgeable and was respected by all the players. I thought he was a great guy and one of the team. Hearts was the game we played on one end of the train to the other and Dykes played, too. He never was without a cigar in his mouth. I'd warn him, but he loved those cigars. He was so well liked that in every clubhouse on the road the clubhouse man had six to eight boxes of cigars waiting for him. And he smoked them all. (In 1976, he would die of cancer.)

The Athletics acquired Dave Philley and Gus Zernial from the White Sox during the season in a big three-team deal. They were inseparable. Philley was a switch-hitting, good-fielding veteran outfielder who played hard every day. He'd challenge everyone. He'd knock you down or fight you, opponents or teammates. We didn't socialize together, but we got along.

GUS ZERNIAL:

Philley and I reported to the Athletics at the beginning of May. I moved to Germantown. Although I was disappointed to leave the White Sox, I was looking forward to playing for Jimmy Dykes, who had been my manager when I had a big year for the Hollywood Stars. Also, Philadelphia was a good, experienced team. Philley and I joined Elmer Valo and Wally Moses to make up a good outfield. Defensively, our infield was the best in the majors, better than the Indians or Yankees. Offensively, third baseman Hank Majeski was no better than a steady hitter who'd plod along without doing anything exciting, and second baseman Pete Suder wasn't much at the plate, but Ferris Fain was a .300 hitter and Eddie Joost could get on base and had a lot of power for a shortstop.

Even in 1951 I could tell Connie Mack was in trouble. The Phillies had deservedly stolen the town in 1950 with the Whiz Kids, a young, aggressive, winning ballclub. Meanwhile, the Athletics went downhill. Connie didn't have any money. Everybody was propping him up. His sons, Earle and Roy Mack, took over the club

NATIONAL BASEBALL LIBRARY, COOPERSTOWN, N.Y.

In his first year with the Philadelphia Athletics, Gus Zernial won the American League home run and RBI title.

and didn't have administrative skills. Earle was on one side of the stadium and Roy was on the other side, and they had differences. It split everything.

The first 6 homers I hit in 1951 were hit in 3 consecutive games, 2 each game, tying Tony Lazzeri's record. A photographer from a Philadelphia paper came out to get pictures. I came up with the idea of taping 6 balls to a bat I held—that's the photo that ended up on my 1952 baseball card. The day of the photo shoot, I hit another homer against the Browns for my 7th in 4 games, another record.

I came on strong to lead the league with 33 homers and 129 RBIs. Ferris Fain led the league with a .344 average and Bobby Shantz had a great year, winning 18 games. Valo hit .300 and Joost got his 18 or 19 homers, 75 RBIs, and 100 runs. So although we finished in sixth place, I thought we had enough talent to be a pennant contender in 1952.

ST. LOUIS BROWNS

LES MOSS:

In 1951 Ned Garver proved how good he was by winning 20 games for a team that won just 52 games. Duane Pillette was second on the staff with 6 victories. This may have been the worst Browns team of all. We could never improve because they kept trading our best players. Bob Dillinger, Ellis Kinder, Al Zarilla, Jeff Heath, Hank Thompson, and Jack Kramer had passed through St. Louis. Then, in May of 1951, I was sent to the Red Sox for catcher Matt Batts, a couple of other players, and a large sum of money. I suppose they wanted to give Sherm Lollar the chance to catch every day, but at the end of the season they traded him, too.

JOHN BERARDINO:

I re-signed with the Browns, returning to my original team after 3 years with the Indians and Pirates. Bill Veeck, who had owned the Indians when I went there, now owned the Browns. He liked to pull publicity stunts with the Browns because it was hard to get the fans interested in such a bad team. Because I was an actor, he decided to insure my face for $1 million.

I was at the Eddie Gaedel game, Veeck's most famous publicity stunt. Veeck had announced a big surprise, so we drew more people to that game than we had in two months. We were really surprised when a midget popped out of the cake and came to the plate with a tiny bat. It was a three-ring circus, a comedy. I don't know if it was good for baseball, but we were such a bad, losing team that Veeck needed something to draw people to the park. Veeck was good with promotions, but that event was hard to top.

I played less than 40 games during the year. It wasn't a whole lot of fun sitting on the bench for a last-place team, so I tried to do things that would relieve my boredom and the team's tension. I'd pull pranks, like giving hotfoots, and I'd also razz umpires. I once got thrown out of a game for not saying a word. During a home game against the Yankees, I was getting on home-plate umpire Art Passarella, and the Yankees told him to shut me up. So he came over and warned me that if I didn't keep my mouth shut, I'd be out of the game. So I borrowed some tape from the trainer and taped my mouth shut. Now the Yankees were hollering and pointing to me. Passarella ran over and said, "You're out of the game!" I tore the tape off and said, "What for?" He looked around at the nearly empty stands and said, "For inciting a riot!"

Art was a good guy and one of the better umpires. Players weren't really allowed to consort with umpires, but Art and I wanted to get together because we grew up in the same neighborhood. So a lot of times we'd have to sneak off to have a beer together.

BOB TURLEY:

I had pitched well in 1950 in Wichita, Kansas, and in 1951 at San Antonio, where I went 21–7 and was voted the league's best pitcher. I felt that the Browns weren't even noticing what I was doing in the minor leagues because there was no personal contact. But at the end of the year I came up to the Browns again. I was there when outfielder Bob Nieman set a record by homering in his first 2 major league at-bats against Boston's Mickey McDermott. I pitched my first major league game in St. Louis. I started against the White Sox. Almost everybody in the stands was my family. I lasted into the eighth inning and struck out 5 batters, including Eddie Robinson. I got the loss but it was still a real thrill.

CLEVELAND INDIANS

JIM FRIDLEY:

It was strange that I made it into professional baseball at all because Philippi, West Virginia, wasn't a place scouts usually went looking for prospects. But the Indians' Bill Bradley and scouts from the Dodgers and other teams saw me play with the Philippi Red Sox, a semipro team. I pitched, but they were more interested that I was 6'2" and 215 pounds and could hit the ball 10 miles. Bingo Levicki took me to Cleveland for a tryout with other prospects in League Park. I went about 8 for 10 in intrasquad games and they offered me a small bonus and offered me a minor league contract. I was a raw kid and had to learn the fundamentals in the minors. It was difficult. There was a lot of competition, the pitchers threw harder than I expected, there was a whole lot of pressure, and I felt out of

place a lot. I was even teased about being a big, ol' country boy and wearing white knee socks, although, having spent three years on a football scholarship at the University of West Virginia, I was one of the few guys to have been to college.

I went up through the ranks—Burlington, Spartanburg, Dayton. After I batted .321 at Dayton in the Central League, the Indians invited me to my first major league camp in 1951. There was a high level of play with a lot of veterans. The Indians' farm system didn't have much coaching and there was no real hitting coach at the major league level, but I got instruction every day. People fooled with my batting stance, trying to get me to hit the ball more to right. They changed the size of my bat, they changed how I moved my legs. I had too many guys instructing me. They messed up my swing. Hank Greenberg, who had become the Indians' GM, tried to get me to pull the ball more in both the minors and majors. He thought I was so big I should pull everything out of the park. Greenberg did teach me something valuable, though. He said that if a guy gets you out with a particular pitch, watch for it the next time. I wasn't a smart player to begin with and I wasn't given enough time to learn.

The Indians would have three 20-game winners and almost win the pennant, but after spring training the Indians returned me to the minors. I went to Dallas in the Texas League, where I hit .299 with power. I knew I was a major league prospect and hoped I'd get a chance to prove that at the Indians' spring training camp in 1952.

MINNIE MINOSO:

I spent most of 1949 and all of 1950 with the San Diego Padres in the Pacific Coast League, so I was glad to make the Indians in 1951. I had a good year at San Diego, so I knew I was ready to be a good major league player. Al Lopez had replaced Lou Boudreau as the Indians' manager. He didn't play me much, but in 8 games I batted .429. I had some close friends on the team—including Larry Doby, Luke Easter, and Harry Simpson, who had been my teammate and a star player with 150 RBIs at San Diego—so I was disappointed and upset when Cleveland traded me to the Chicago White Sox in a 3-team, 7-player deal on April 30.

HAL WOODESHICK:

After being released in 1950 by Carbondale, a Phillies' Class D team, I went home to Wilkes-Barre and pitched semipro ball with National Electric. I did well and Cleveland signed me. In 1951 I went to spring training with Cleveland's farm teams in Daytona Beach. Then I was assigned to Batavia, and from there I went to Duluth in the Northern League. That was C ball. I was supposed to get a bonus if I stayed on the team for 60 days, but they cut me after 30 days. So I went home again.

BOSTON RED SOX

FRED HATFIELD:

In my last two years in the minors I batted third and hit 27 or 28 homers, and drove in over 100 runs. But after I came to the Red Sox in 1950, they put me eighth in the lineup in my infrequent appearances and that made a big difference in my production. They took the home run stroke away from me. Joe Cronin said, "Hatfield, you're going to hit .250 and you'll make $20,000 in this game. So you go ahead and do that and let the big guys hit you in." I played for him, so I did it. I continued to be a pull hitter, but I choked up on the bat and leveled off my swing to become a line-drive hitter.

Because I didn't play regularly, I was a professional bench jockey. I learned that in the Red Sox system, where you hated everyone in a different uniform. Our manager, Steve O'Neill, liked bench jockeys, so I figured that's the only way I could make that ballclub with infielders like Pesky, Goodman, Doerr, Stephens, and newly acquired Lou Boudreau. I touched up everyone, including opposing pitchers when they'd get knocked out of a game and have to come through our dugout in Boston on the way to the shower. I'd say, "Hey, you got time to catch that three o'clock movie!" when they passed by. Some Yankee pitchers told me, "Hatfield, I'll be glad when you start playing, so you'll shut up." One day we were playing Detroit and Fred Hutchinson was knocked out of the game. O'Neill warned me, "Freddie, Freddie, don't say nothing when Hutchinson walks through here." Everyone in baseball knew Hutch's temper. He broke the lights in the runway

that were covered by steel frames, using his fist to clear them out. Then he went upstairs and tore up the water cooler and some other things. I imagine he would have preferred banging on me if I'd said something.

I think I earned the reputation for making big plays. The tougher the situation, the better I was. With the bat or glove, I didn't choke. I also got the reputation for being a tough baserunner. I got the nickname "Scrap Iron" because, instead of sliding, I'd knock infielders to the ground with cross-body football blocks, throwing myself against their legs to break up double plays. I never cut anybody, but Phil Rizzuto was the only middle infielder I never knocked to the ground. He got rid of the ball so quick. But I took out Jerry Coleman and Nellie Fox. Indians second baseman Bobby Avila was scared to death of me when I'd get on first. He'd catch the ball and run onto the grass to avoid my blocks. I never had a run-in with Billy Martin. The occasion never came up. We both knew we'd knock each other down.

Nobody would get mad at me for knocking them down. It was as much part of the game as knockdown pitches. I accepted that. My former roommate Jim McDonald was traded by the Sox to the Browns in 1951. He knocked me down in the day and had dinner with me at night, at which he said, "You son of a bitch, don't drag-bunt on me or I'll knock you down again!"

You usually picked your own roommate unless you were part of what they called "the Dalton Gang." They'd separate the wild guys and drinkers. On Boston, Ellis Kinder was known as a heavy after-game drinker. He loved the night life. I always went out after the game and had my beer. I was pretty much a loner or with my roommate. I had my own life and knew what I could and couldn't do. McDonald had been my best roommate. We went to movies and did everything together. Johnny Pesky and I were roommates for a time. We talked a lot of baseball—most of the players would talk baseball during card games on trains. Johnny and I would eat breakfast together, but I might go to some Western movie by myself in the afternoon, and we went our own ways at night. He knew a lot of people in every town. In fact, most of the veterans knew people in every town. Your first night in, you didn't have time to see them, but you'd see them the second night. The third night you'd leave. That was the routine. Wives hardly traveled with players because the teams wouldn't pay for their rooms or transportation. They stayed home during road trips unless we went to a town that was close by, maybe New York or Philadelphia. My wife never made a big league trip.

I always liked the cities that had a lot going on near the hotel, like New York, where restaurants and movies were close by. And Detroit was a sports-minded town where you were known in every bar and restaurant near the ballpark. Every now and then you got free drinks. I wouldn't stay in the same place and drink all night because I didn't want people to think I was a boozer.

In Chicago, Detroit, or New York, you'd always run into a celebrity of some kind. There were guys on each club who had friends in the entertainment world, movie world, boxing world, so we had the opportunity to meet all those people. Celebrities went out to the ballpark because there was more day ball in those days and games didn't interfere with their night life.

Ted Williams was a loner. If you ever accidentally went somewhere he was, like a restaurant, and if you went to the rest room and came back, he'd be gone. He was by himself everywhere. I never saw him with anyone. I didn't know if he had a social life.

JOHN BERARDINO (BROWNS):
Ted Williams and I were both rookies in 1939. I called him up once then and said I was with a couple of pretty girls and asked if he wanted a date. He said, "No, not really." I added, "We're going to go have hamburgers and milkshakes." He said, "Oh, I'll go for that."

F. HATFIELD:
Ted talked to me during ballgames. What made me feel funny was when I was waiting to hit and he came back from the batter's box raving, "That guy's got great stuff." That makes you feel confident. I think everybody had a lot of respect for Ted Williams. The only criticism I ever heard was from a couple of players who thought he should have swung more with runners in scoring position instead of taking bases on balls. Nobody ever said anything to him about it. They were just slight backroom remarks about him not driving in runs on close pitches. And the media didn't attack him for anything other than making gestures at them and spitting when he was jeered by the Fenway crowd for making errors. Ted was no gazelle—in fact, he was a one-gait fielder—but he could play left in Fenway as well as anyone. He didn't need a great arm. Of course, you talked only about hitting with Williams. You didn't talk about great fielding plays like you would with Willie Mays. Williams caught the ball and threw to the right base. That was enough.

It was a joke when I saw him and Stan Musial standing together in spring training. I'd say, "Hey, how does it feel to know you're going to hit .340 before the season starts?" They just laughed. I'd say, "Yeah, you guys laugh all the way to the bank." It was understood he'd hit .340. He was the only player I remember who had everyone watch him take batting practice. I saw that eye-hand coordination, bat quickness, and a little strength were the secret to hitting. When Ted pulled the trigger, the bat exploded.

RALPH KINER (PIRATES):
Fingers take a great deal of abuse in baseball so Ted Williams did finger push-ups to strengthen them and take out some of the pain.

F. HATFIELD:
Even at Fenway, Williams might hit for an hour before a game, 3 to 4 times a week. He'd pay someone to pitch batting practice. At home, he'd go out to the park early, religiously. He was dedicated to *hitting*. During a game he'd sit and grind that sawdust out of the bat, waiting in the on-deck circle. He may have been the only hitter who a pitcher would never have to wait for. When the ball was hit while he was in the on-deck circle, by the time the ball got back to the pitcher, Ted was standing in the batter's box ready to hit. He had a chain of thought and it never got interrupted. He loved to swing that bat.

After a homer or after striking out, he had the same expression. I never saw him lose his temper, cuss, throw the bat, or break the bat. I saw him take 3 straight strikes one day, never taking the bat off his shoulder. And the next time up, he hit one in the upper deck, sitting on that pitch that got him out earlier. He hit 30 homers that year without much effort.

LES MOSS:

I was happy to be traded from the Browns to the Red Sox in mid-May. I hit a grand slam when I first went there, and that was as good a hitting memory as I had in the major leagues.

I felt like I was with a field of stars. There was Williams, Dom DiMaggio, Doerr, Goodman, Stephens, Dropo, Pesky. Our ace pitcher was Mel Parnell. He was a good pitcher who threw sinkers and sliders. He had good command and kept everything down. I liked catching him and thought we worked well together.

I thought we'd win that thing. We were 3 games out with 8 games left, but lost the last 8 games and wound up 11 out. We couldn't believe it. Everybody outscored us. Allie Reynolds even threw a no-hitter against us in Yankee Stadium. The Red Sox weren't an emotional team, so there wasn't any sad reaction to what happened. I guess they were used to losing to the Yankees.

Boston wasn't a close team. The only time you'd see any of the other players was on the train or at the ballpark. When the game ended, everyone would go home, and that was it. Some of those guys stayed in their hotel rooms because if they went out they'd be recognized.

Ted Williams was great to have on a ballclub. I really enjoyed him. He didn't act like a star. He'd work with anybody on hitting. He gave me little tips. I had a heck of a time getting started, so I'd listen to him, trying different ways to hold the bat. They were all pretty good suggestions.

However, I couldn't hit all season. As a result I was traded back to the Browns. It was just part of the game.

DETROIT TIGERS

GEORGE KELL:

When I first came to the majors, during the war, they didn't give players meal money. We ate in our hotel and signed a tab. We'd stay in the Warwick Hotel in Philadelphia, and it had the best food in the world. It was expensive. In Chicago we'd stay at the Del Prado, a nice hotel on the South Side. Every team would stay there. They had an enormous dining room with white tablecloths and black waiters who took great pride in their work and were extremely efficient. Every once in a while we'd go downtown and eat. Once I got estab-

lished and was making the All-Star team every year, I became one of the highest-paid ballplayers. I was making $45,000 and Freddie Hutchinson and Hoot Evers were probably making over $30,000, so we treated ourselves to good food. We'd meet every night in the lobby at seven and go to one of our favorite spots. Sometimes we'd ask a young player along and pick up his tab. In Philadelphia we'd go to Bookbinder's for seafood. In Chicago we'd go downtown to George Diamond's, which had great steaks. In New York we'd often go for steaks at Gallaghers, or if we wanted Italian food, we'd go to Mama Leone's, early on, before it became a tourist spot. We didn't go to nightclubs, but more and more we went to Broadway shows.

I had a pretty good year, batting .319, but Vic Wertz was about the only other guy in the lineup to do well. And this time our pitching didn't pick us up. The only guys to have decent years were Virgil Trucks, Fred Hutchinson, and Bob Cain. Cain was a lot like Hutchinson. He didn't throw that hard but instead threw a lot of curves and hit spots. Being left-handed helped him a lot, especially in our stadium. He was a tough, tough competitor, who was particularly strong against Bob Feller.

BOB CAIN:

We didn't know anything specific would happen when we played the Browns on August 19. We knew only that it was the 50th anniversary of the Browns and Bill Veeck had promised the fans a surprise. There were 18,000 fans, an enormous crowd for the Browns. I was scheduled to pitch the second game of a doubleheader. We batted in the first inning and wondered why Frank Saucier was out in center for the Browns because he'd had an operation on his arm and couldn't throw 50 feet. We were retired in the first and then I went out to the mound and warmed up with Bob Swift. Meanwhile a big four-wheeler rolls onto the field carrying a big papier-mâché cake. Out jumps 3'7" Eddie Gaedel, wearing a uniform. We still didn't think anything about it. He trotted over to the Brownie dugout. I could see umpire Ed Hurley's neck turning red. He was surprised, too. Hurley walked over to the Brownie dugout and out comes Browns' manager Zack Taylor with a signed contract in his back pocket. Veeck had mailed a copy of Gaedel's contract to the league office the night before, knowing full well that there was no way it would arrive in time for Gaedel to be disqualified before the game. Hurley looked over the contract, showed it to Red Rolfe, our manager, and then came back to home plate and yelled out, "Play ball!" At this point Eddie walked to the plate carrying a miniature wooden bat and the announcer told us: "Eddie Gaedel batting for Frank Saucier." Meanwhile, Swift and I talked on the mound. I was wondering how I was supposed to pitch to a midget. I didn't know whether to throw the ball underhanded or overhanded to Gaedel. I just wanted to be careful not to hit him. Dizzy Trout told me later that if he'd been the pitcher, he'd have thrown the ball right between his eyes. Swift went behind home plate and lay down on his stomach to give me a real low target. Hurley got after him and made him get up on his knees. All 4 pitches were across the plate at head level, strikes on the typical ballplayer. The crowd was howling with laughter. There was a lot of yelling back and forth between the two dugouts. I laughed a little bit but was a little angry. I'd have given my right arm just to have gotten one strike on him. Swift kept trying to encourage me to get the ball lower. Veeck had told Gaedel that he would shoot him if he swung at a pitch, but it looked like he was itching to swing if I'd gotten the ball any lower. But I walked him, and all the way down the first-base line he tipped his hat to the crowd—the crowd ate it up. Then he stood on first until outfielder Jim Delsing came in to pinch-run. Gaedel patted Delsing on the butt and ran across the diamond toward the Browns' dugout, tipping his hat the entire time. We had no idea that this was going to be part of baseball lore.

I'm glad Eddie led off the game rather than coming up with the bases loaded. That really would have been a farce. As it was, he got me into trouble in the first inning. I had to get out of a bases-loaded jam. We won 6–2, so it didn't hurt anything. After the game was over, we didn't even think about the midget episode. It just grew in fame. The main reason for that is that St. Louis sportswriter Bob Broeg knew about the publicity stunt, so he had a photographer stand between home and first to take a picture of Gaedel. He didn't know how he could get away with this, but nobody made them move the camera. All the other photographers had left the ballpark after the first game. So if it hadn't been for him there wouldn't have been that famous picture of Eddie with the small bat, Hurley, and Swift. (In 1961, when

we found out that Eddie had been murdered in Chicago, my wife and I drove up to go to the funeral. We were the only ones from baseball there. However, Bill Veeck sent flowers and would have been there if he hadn't been sick at the time. When we got out of the car, Mrs. Gaedel, who was not a midget, ran over and hugged and kissed me. It meant something to her to see us there. And it meant something to us to be there. I remember how small the coffin was. We kept in touch with Eddie's wife for a few years before losing track.)

I had come to Detroit from Chicago early in the season in a trade for pitcher Saul Rogovin. I hated to leave because I liked Comiskey Park better than Briggs Stadium. But I learned how to pitch around the short right-field fence and got to like the Detroit park. I also discovered that the Tigers had the best fans in the country. You wouldn't hear the boos if you got beat or made an error as you would in Chicago.

Red Rolfe was a stern manager and we had to stick to his rules. But I thought he was a good man to play for. I liked that he fought for his players against the umpires. I also liked that he wouldn't banish you after one shaky outing. I started one game on a hot day in Washington when I had one of those summer colds. The first 5 hitters got on base. There wasn't one ball hit out of the infield. One guy bunted it to me. I put my glove down and the ball hit something and bounced over it. Rolfe took me out of the game. Then we went into New York. I still had that cold. Hal White was pitching and we were ahead 2–0. Rolfe brought me in with the bases loaded, and 2 balls and no strikes on Johnny Hopp, a .300 career hitter. I thought my first pitch was a strike, but the umpire called it a ball. Then I threw a ball inside that he called a strike. I struck out Hopp. Then I struck out Billy Martin and Gene Woodling. I finished the game, giving up only one hit. Rolfe said, "Cain's one of the best left-handers in the American League." He probably forgot my previous outing. My luck had just reversed itself.

The Tigers were a fairly close team. The only loner I can think of was second baseman Gerry Priddy. My roommate was catcher Joe Ginsberg, a Jewish player from New York. He was full of fun and loved baseball, and never talked about any prejudice he'd experienced. George Kell, Hoot Evers, and Johnny Groth were pretty close. Pat Mullin and Steve Souchock, two good-hitting backup outfielders, and reserve first baseman Don Kolloway were all fun guys you could kid around with. We played a lot of hearts on train trips. Kell, Evers, shortstop Johnny Lipon, Vic Wertz, Ginsberg, first baseman Dick Kryhoski, Mullin, Souchock, Kolloway, and I played marathon games.

Kell was one of the leaders on the Tigers. He was our best all-around player and our biggest star, yet he was one of the few who liked to help younger ballplayers. He was full of tips. Before I played with him, I dreaded seeing him come to the plate with runners on base because he was such a good hitter. Bob Swift, who had been a part-time catcher on the Tigers since 1944, was another leader. I knew him and his father back in Salina, Kansas.

The Tigers were known to have TNT, supplied by Virgil Trucks, Hal Newhouser, and Dizzy Trout. Newhouser had slowed down a bit, but Trucks and Trout threw real hard. Trucks was a fun-loving guy. He'd often go with me and Ginsberg to play golf on our off-days. But Virgil had his problems. He drank quite a bit off and on, and I think that hurt his pitching.

Trout was one of the meanest pitchers. If you got a hit off him, you'd go down. But I thought he was a good guy, and when we went to Boston we'd go to the racetrack together. Hutchinson also would throw at a hitter. If a guy homered or got a key hit, Hutchinson would bury him the next time up. You didn't want to be too close to him when he lost because he could break things pretty good. Outside of that, he was a real gentleman. In fact, of the pitchers, my best friends were Fred, Dizzy, Marlin Stuart, and Gene Bearden, who had won that 1948 playoff game for Cleveland. There weren't any good losers on our staff. I took losses pretty bad, although I didn't break things like Hutchinson or Trout would.

Early in the year, we didn't assume the Yankees would win. We felt that we were starting out even. But it was soon apparent that the Yankees were so much better than the other American League teams. Casey Stengel didn't impress me. I think anybody could have managed the Yankees. The moves he made always seemed to be the right moves, but with the bench he had, he couldn't go wrong. They could have brought in the Yankees' Newark team and they could have finished second.

Our main concern when facing the Yankees was not to get in trouble with walks—too many batters could hit the ball out of the park. In Yankee Stadium we'd try to keep the ball away from hitters so they'd hit to center field, which was a wide-open space. Joe DiMaggio, who was in his last season, knew pitchers and was a choosy hitter, though not as selective as Ted Williams. Unlike with Williams, you could get him to chase a ball just off the plate. I had a lot more trouble pitching to Yogi Berra, although he was left-handed. I finally discovered that the best place to pitch him was belt-high, right over the plate. He'd hit that to center field. He'd homer on any other pitch, including balls that were sinking into the dirt. I think he was underrated in that he was a darn good receiver.

Although he would be remembered most as the pitcher who walked midget Eddie Gaedel, Bob "Sugar" Cain had a strong season in 1951, finishing second in victories on the Detroit Tigers' staff.

Boston had a lineup that was as strong as New York's, but they were one of the teams I liked to face. I had success against them. However, I didn't pitch much against them in Fenway Park, where left-handers had trouble because of the Green Monster. Yet it seemed that any time we played the darned Yankees or darned Indians it was my turn to pitch.

Cleveland also had an excellent team and finished second almost every year, ahead of Boston. I respected Al Lopez much more than Casey Stengel and think he did much more with less talent. Which isn't to say that they didn't have good hitters. Al Rosen was a very good hitter. (After I was traded to the Browns, he would hit a ball off me over the left-field bleachers in St. Louis that I swear is still in orbit. It was a country mile out there.) I tried to pitch Rosen inside. He had an injured thumb at one time and would curse me out for pitching him in.

Larry Doby was a good hitter. He was a free swinger and would hurt me a lot of the time. But Luke Easter gave me more trouble than any of his teammates. He had an awful lot of power. You could pitch to him down and in or up and in. But if you threw the ball to where he could stretch his arms, he could kill you. He'd hit balls over 450 feet. It's amazing that he played only softball until 1946.

Of course, Cleveland's strength was its pitching. Bob Feller pitched his third no-hitter against me in Cleveland. He beat me 2–1. A couple of weeks later, Bob Lemon pitched a near-perfect game against me. Our only baserunner was Vic Wertz, who homered in the ninth inning. I lost that game 2–1. Lemon had the most natural stuff of any pitcher. He couldn't throw the ball straight. Every pitch moved. Batters found him harder to time than Feller.

The Indians pitcher I was fond of was Early Wynn. At the tail end of 1950, when I had played for Chicago, we were in Cleveland and Wynn knocked me out of the game with a line drive that hit me about 18 inches above the kneecap. I didn't suit up the next night, but sat up in the stands with our trainer, Packy Schwartz, his wife, and their friend Judy, a young woman who ran the flower shop at the Statler Hotel. Judy and I started writing. Now, almost a year later we were married at the Statler Hotel—so Early Wynn was responsible for my getting married.

I was a lot better off once I had married. I had a place to go when I was home. I had more responsibility, yet I had someone to give me support. I would talk about bad games with my wife. She was a baseball fan and helped me go through it all. Win or lose, she was still with me.

In 1951 I finished with an overall 12–12 record. However, I was 11–10 on Detroit to make me the Tigers' biggest winner after Virgil Trucks, who won 13 games. I enjoyed my year and was disappointed that the Tigers didn't want to give me more than a token raise. So I refused to sign the contract Walter Briggs offered, leading to my departure.

CHICAGO WHITE SOX

GUS ZERNIAL:

I thought that with myself, Golden Goldsberry, Nellie Fox, Chico Carrasquel, Billy Pierce, and Jim Busby, the White Sox had a young nucleus that could develop into a contending team. However, Frank Lane liked to trade anyone who shared his limelight. I had played only one full year in Chicago and I broke the club home run record. So in late April he made me part of a 7-player deal. The White Sox wanted Minnie Minoso, who had speed. Dave Philley and I had to go to the Athletics. And Lou Brissie, who was still a pretty good pitcher, went from the Athletics to the Indians. We were the 4 key players. I was disappointed to be traded coming off my first full year, when I had finally established myself. During the year, Philley and I would always beat the Sox and we'd kid Lane that he made a mistake.

MINNIE MINOSO:

I worried about adjusting to another team and city, but I felt right at home in Chicago. Paul Richards, who was the new manager, had seen me at San Diego and wanted me. He told his players about me, and I was welcomed. I was the first black player on either Chicago team, but to be honest, I didn't know if there was publicity surrounding me because of that. All I knew is that I had to do my job if the White Sox were to keep me.

In my first game with the White Sox, we played against the Yankees in Chicago. I hit a homer in my first at-bat on the first pitch by Vic Raschi, a good man and good pitcher. It went into the bullpen in center field. But I also made an error at third base and we lost, 4–2.

Mickey Mantle hit his first major league home run in that game. The fans were so nice to me from the start. They saw that I was a good hitter and that I played hard at third base and in left field and hustled all the time. They cheered me. They *never* booed me. I had a good season. I hit .325, to finish second in batting to Ferris Fain; I scored 112 runs, which was just one behind Dominic DiMaggio; and I led the league with 14 triples and 31 stolen bases, which would be my career best. I was chosen Rookie of the Year by *The Sporting News,* but the sportswriters—most were from New York—picked the Yankees' Gil McDougald.

I liked the discipline of major league baseball and playing for Paul Richards. No matter how tough you were on the streets, when you played in the major leagues you had to follow the rules, you had to listen to your manager, you had to respect the umpire. It was like a university. Richards was a 100 percent better manager than Al Lopez, my manager on the Indians. 101 percent! He was the best manager I would ever have in baseball. He didn't talk too much, just what you needed to know. He was a great teacher and I learned so much. I tried to play hard for him because he had faith in me.

BILLY PIERCE:

When we acquired Minnie Minoso by trading two good players, Gus Zernial and Dave Philley, it was another gamble on Frank Lane's part that brought the White Sox a player who would stick around for many years. Gus looked good for us and supplied a lot of power, but he had once broken his collarbone and maybe the White Sox worried that would happen again. I do know that Paul Richards wanted Minoso's speed. It turned out that Minoso had a pretty good bat to go along with it. Minnie was the first black player in Chicago, but in those days I don't even think that fact registered. We just got a prospect named Minoso with great speed, and when he hit that Opening Day home run against Vic Raschi we saw that he was an all-around player. He was a great player and perfect third-place hitter to bat behind Nellie Fox. That was a good setup. Both batted over .300. So we started the "Go-Go" Sox and emphasized the running game.

We started to improve and were in first place at the All-Star break. Everything went right the first half of the year, but we were a young team and in the second half nothing went right. Paul Richards, my former Tigers' teammate and manager at Buffalo, helped solidify our team. Richards was the greatest teaching manager in baseball. He worked hard with all the position players and pitchers. Chico Carrasquel was falling away from the ball and Richards forced him to stick in there. Richards and Doc Cramer worked with Nellie Fox. They were the ones who gave him a bottleneck bat. The bat gave him more control, allowing him to spray the ball to all fields and helping him become one of the best bunters in the league. He upped his average over 60 points.

FRED HATFIELD (RED SOX):

Fox was the best bunter down the third-base line I ever saw. He could control the ball a little better than Rizzuto. If I played Rizzuto in, he'd hit it by me, but if you played Fox even with the bag or deep, he'd lay it down safely and deaden it, making it come back a little like a golfer. He could get backspin on the ball.

B. PIERCE:

Richards also brought in Joe Gordon, who had retired, to help Nellie with the double play. He accepted all this instruction and became a tremendous ballplayer, a guy who got the most out of his talent.

Richards also helped me. In 1950 I had walked 137 and was lucky Tommy Byrne was also in the American League or I might have had the most. But in 1951 I pitched about 20 more innings and walked 60 fewer batters. This resulted in my earned run average going down to about 3.00 and my win total going up to 15, again tops on the team. I learned to control my fastball better and, at Richards's request, learned a third pitch to go with my fastball and curve—a slider. Developing the slider helped me tremendously because it gave me a third out pitch. I threw it almost as hard as my fastball, but I could throw it for strikes better than the fastball or good curve, which meant it was very useful when I was behind in the count. This eventually helped me become a control pitcher. Richards made me work on it, and it took me about two years before it was consistent.

BOB CAIN:

I was with the White Sox in spring training and early in the season. That gave me the chance to play for Paul Richards. He played fundamental baseball. He had us running and employing the hit-and-run more often. He expected the infielders to make the plays. He expected his pitchers to get the ball over the plate and let the batters make contact. He was very stern in his actions and what he said he meant. Richards was the most hard-headed manager I would have in regard to knocking down batters, either ones who homered off us or who batted behind batters who homered. I did what he said, but I didn't agree with him. Throwing at a batter who'd homered earlier could only wake him up. It was too late to stop the first homer. And I didn't know why I should take it out on another player. Richards was also one of the roughest managers on umpires. He knew the rules as much as they did.

I liked Minnie Minoso, who came over from the Indians. He was a very good all-around ballplayer. He stood close to the plate and liked the ball out over the plate, belt-high and up. The way to pitch him was down. But even that didn't work because he'd slash the ball all over the park. Minoso played left, and Al Zarilla was acquired from the Red Sox to play right, with both new players flanking Jim Busby. I liked Al, too. He reminded me of Catfish Metkovich, who had been on the Sox when I joined the team in 1949. They were both colorful guys and cutups. They were always playing tricks, like moving things from one player's locker to another player's locker. That sure could stir things up.

I could see that the White Sox were improving under Richards, but he pitched me so infrequently that I didn't know if I'd be around very long. Then, in May, I was traded to Detroit for Saul Rogovin.

JOE DE MAESTRI:
I went to my first major league spring training and had a pretty good camp. The hardest night of a young player's life is the night before the team breaks camp and the final cuts are made. I'll never forget that night in 1951. A few players were going out to dinner when our coach, Lum Harris, came over to me and said, "Joe, don't worry. You're going to be on that train tomorrow." And my dinner tasted a lot better.

It's funny. My father had come from Italy when he was 3 and along with his two brothers—one who would always insist on spelling De Maestri with no space or capital M—grew up in an American orphanage, without having known his parents. Now his son was a major league baseball player.

I had just gotten married in January, and my wife and I moved into a big hotel on Lake Michigan. There were about four or five other players who lived there, and since I didn't have a car, I relied on them to drive me to the park. Our families socialized, and when the players were on the road, the wives had picnics and stayed together pretty much. When we played at Comiskey Park they would sit together in a designated section.

My first game was against the St. Louis Browns and they had a left-hander pitching against us and I got a base hit. I better remember another game against the Browns. We were playing in St. Louis and I hit a home run off their ace, Ned Garver. But Garver came back and hit a home run and won his own ballgame. I guess that's the only way he could have won 20 games on that team.

Paul Richards was a real quiet guy, a real thinker, who was three innings ahead of everybody else. He was a former catcher, and I think he was the best teacher of pitchers and catchers the game has known. Paul was a leader and a disciplinarian and what he said went and that was it. He was the toughest guy I've ever played for. If you made a stupid mistake, he would pull you to the side and chew you out, and you'd correct it real quick. I liked that you always knew where you stood with him.

I really wasn't worried about my hitting because I was told they wanted me for defense. I was able to do the job. The only times I even remember pinch-hitting was when we ran out of people, and I never pinch-hit with a runner on base. I didn't have a playing schedule. I just went out every day and ran, fielded ground balls, took batting practice, and made sure I was in shape and ready to play. I was never discouraged about it. I didn't sit alone on the bench and pout. I was a very outgoing guy who always tried to keep everyone's spirits up.

I batted only about 75 times. I didn't mind because I was just amazed to be in the big leagues. I played behind Chico Carrasquel. He was a big guy and not very fast, but he had good hands and a great arm and was a pretty good hitter. I would work out with Chico, playing second base. Nellie Fox and I didn't really work out much together, with me at short. Nellie almost didn't make the ballclub. A coach took him down to Pasadena and worked with him every night on hitting. He got that old-model bottle bat and made himself a .300 hitter. He'd just stand there and blump, blump, blump. Nellie wasn't a power hitter but he could do everything else with that bat.

Gus Zernial was like my big older brother, and I was upset when he was traded so soon after I joined the team. Richards was converting to a younger team, but there were still older guys around, even after Zernial left. Guys like Eddie Robinson, Hank Majeski, Bob Dillinger, and Phil Masi offered the younger guys a whole lot of experience. I hung out pretty much with Robinson and Majeski, who both treated me real well. They would say, "Hey, you're coming with us." We might have a beer or something after a game, but we didn't really go out drinking. It was dinner, a show. Like all teams, the White Sox played a lot of cards. We played pinochle and hearts. A few guys played gin.

Bob Dillinger came over from Pittsburgh to play third base. He was a tough guy, a loner who didn't mix with the rest of the guys. He was always a .300 singles hitter and he still had good speed although he was at the tail end of his career. He hit line drives in his sleep. He was what you would call a cheater. He was the first guy I ever saw who doctored his bats. Dillinger was a master. He would take a bat and file it down so that it looked round but was actually flat. Or he'd use an ice pick and work on the wood between the grooves and make it really rough so it would catch the ball. He just wanted good contact. Everybody finally caught on about Bob, and on a couple of occasions the catcher called time and had the umpire look at the bat. The umpire would throw out the bat, and Bob would just get out another of his fixed bats. He'd replace the flattened one for the grooved one or vice versa.

Minnie Minoso wasn't that young but he was just beginning his major league career. He was more of a Richards-type player than Zernial. He was a slash hitter with good speed and was an excellent outfielder. The fans took to him immediately. But I'd say that in 1951 at least, Billy Pierce, Nellie Fox, and Chico Carrasquel were the most popular players on the team.

It was an easygoing club. We didn't feel pressure because nobody expected us to wind up in the first division or to beat anybody. But we had a good team. Fox,

Dillinger, and Minoso all hit over .300; Eddie Robinson hit almost 30 homers and drove in over 100 runs; we had good defense up the middle with catchers Phil Masi and Gus Niarhos, Carrasquel, Fox, and center fielder Jim Busby; Billy Pierce won 15 games; and good old Saul Rogovin led the American League in earned run average. At one point we won 14 straight games on an eastern swing that included Cleveland, New York, and Boston. When we were in first in July, everybody was shocked and excited. The fans filled the stands, giving us a great deal of support. We dropped to fourth place, but that was the first time in 20 years the Sox made the first division. And we won 21 more games than the 1950 team. It was great finishing fourth because we even got a small World Series share. That was a nice ending to my 1-year White Sox career. That winter I was included in an 8-player deal with the St. Louis Browns in which Sherm Lollar came to the White Sox.

AL KOZAR:

I got a call from Frank Lane, asking if I wanted to play in the big leagues again. I complained about being sent to the minors because of my bad back. He said I'd get my same contract, for $9,000, and told me to report to Pasadena. I reported, roomed with Joe De Maestri, a nice, younger guy, and got very sick from the water, as did all the players. And there's Paul Richards managing with Nellie Fox playing second. Richards remembered I had jumped his Seattle club the previous year and looked at me like a rattlesnake. Everyone was scared of him, acting like he walked on water. He didn't mean anything to me, but his word was law. He'd get a dozen new baseballs, and send me to second and Nellie to short. He'd throw balls to Nellie, who'd throw them to me so Nellie could watch how I turned the double play and learn from that. I had a system where I wouldn't do things the same at second each time so sliders wouldn't know what to expect. Then, when Nellie and I switched positions, I had to show him again. We did this for a week. Then the exhibition games started and Richards wouldn't play me. I was the only guy on the bench. I played only on the B squad. I hit 2 homers against Toothpick Jones, and right after that game, Richards told me I was going to Memphis in the Southern Association. I knew I was doomed for the rest of my life. Richards had chosen Fox over me. He turned out to be right—the son of a gun.

I went down to Memphis and played with Luke Appling, who was the player-manager. His reflexes were gone and he'd moved to first base. We got so tired of hearing him whining like a baby that he lost his job to Chico Carrasquel. He'd whine all the time, including at the back of the bus. One day we stopped off for lunch and all the players filed into a steak house. Another player pulled me aside and said we shouldn't go in there because he couldn't tolerate Appling's whining anymore. We went to a nearby place and bought our steak and beer—not knowing this was the rare day management picked up the tab in the steak house. I should have been playing in the majors, but here I was stranded with Luke Appling. But in those days, you couldn't get out of an organization unless they traded or released you. I felt Richards was punishing me.

CHICO CARRASQUEL:

I loved Paul Richards because he was 100 percent baseball. He tried to explain what you had to do in every situation on the field, and I wanted to learn. He helped me a great deal. I played 53 straight games without making an error, handling 297 chances. Playing for Richards, I had another good year at the plate, batting .264, with 22 doubles and 58 RBIs. I even beat out Phil Rizzuto as the All-Star shortstop, and was the first Latin to play in an All-Star Game. I got to Detroit and my teammates were Ted Williams and Joe DiMaggio. What a thrill! That was the highlight of my career.

It was exciting playing against the Yankees and seeing players like Rizzuto, DiMaggio, and Yogi Berra, who I had heard so much about. I played my best against them. At the beginning of every season, we said we were going to beat the Yankees and we tried. So I'd play hard, hoping to beat them. But they'd win.

NEW YORK YANKEES

BILLY JOHNSON:

Nineteen fifty-one was Joe DiMaggio's final year and Mickey Mantle's rookie year. Mickey was a very powerful switch-hitter, an excellent runner with a lot of speed, and he played right field pretty good. I saw he had the ability to be a great player, but I couldn't tell if he would succeed.

I wouldn't get the chance to see Mantle develop or be around for DiMaggio's final game because in May I was traded to the Cardinals. They had to make room for rookie Gil McDougald, who would bat .300 and play all over the infield. It had been a thrill to have played on 4 World Series winners with the Yankees and an honor to have put on the pinstripes and played with such players as Henrich, DiMaggio, Berra, and Rizzuto. I had accomplished a lot.

GENE WOODLING:

If you played for Casey, you hit everywhere in the batting order. Only Joe DiMaggio, our cleanup hitter, stayed in the same spot in the order every day. I hit first, second, sixth, seventh, all over. I stood right on top of the plate, bent over. I was one of the toughest to strike out. Every pitcher in the league said they'd get me off the plate. They couldn't do it. If you're going to run scared when you go up to bat, go on home.

The reason I could stand pressure is that I had been a competitive swimmer from the time I was five. My brother was a champion swimmer, and we Woodlings weren't allowed to lose, not ever. Baseball was a joke compared to swimming. You just showed up and played. I was a winner. They had nicknamed Tommy Henrich "Old Reliable," and since I came from near him in Ohio, Yankee broadcaster Mel Allen nicknamed me "Old Faithful." I liked to think that nickname applied to my playing, too. I had the good fortune to be able to win ballgames with late-inning hits. That was where I excelled and how I made my money. Opposing managers would go to the mound and scare pitchers into throwing me fastballs down the middle so they wouldn't fall behind in the count. I was known to take the first pitch all the time, but in late innings I would surprise them—I wasn't going to let the pitcher get ahead with an automatic strike. Ted Williams once signed a picture to me with the inscription "The toughest guy to get out in the American League in the years I played against him."

Joe DiMaggio used perfect timing on when to retire. He still could have played more—I'd like to have played like he did in his last year—but he knew his skills had diminished to a point where fans could tell the difference. The fickle fans outside New York were even booing him some. I'm sure he didn't like that.

LES MOSS (BROWNS):
Early in DiMaggio's career, pitchers would try to change patterns on him. In his last couple of years, you could pitch him hard because his reflexes had slowed down. That's when he started hitting to right field more. He could still get around on the curveball, although he said he had trouble with the slider.

G. WOODLING:
We were in Arizona training that spring. My friend Ralph Houk, who was a backup catcher, and I always found places for our families. Houk came out a little earlier and when I got there he said, ''This kid Mickey Mantle is something else.'' I had never heard of him. He was hitting in the light air of Arizona and the ball was going for miles. Nobody else would come along with ability like that. He was awesome right from the beginning, yet he was not a great *hitter*. If he would have worked at it like DiMaggio or Williams, he would have broken so many more records. But he had a different attitude. Hank Bauer and I used to talk to him to keep in line. But he was just a good kid out of Oklahoma who everyone took advantage of. New York was a great place to play ball, but it was the wrong place for him to grow up. He hung around with the wrong people. Mickey played right field and struggled his rookie year and even was demoted for a time. He had trouble hitting the slider. Then he stepped in a drain on the field and was injured and didn't play much in the World Series.

LES MOSS (BROWNS):
Mantle and I were friendly because we were both Okies. When Mickey came up, we tried to pitch him up when he batted left-handed. As time went by, he improved and wouldn't chase that pitch. But we still pitched up on him pretty much. He was outstanding as a right-handed hitter. We pitched him like we did DiMaggio.

G. WOODLING:
Even with Whitey Ford in the service, we had excellent pitching with Reynolds, Raschi, Lopat, Tom Morgan, Bob Kuzava. . . . Reynolds pitched 2 no-hitters in 1951. On July 12, I hit a homer off Bob Feller, the league's top winner, to give him a 1–0 victory. I also homered when Chief no-hit the Red Sox on September 28, but we won that game easily, 8–0. Ted Williams was the last batter, and Chief busted him in tight and he hit a foul pop to Berra. And Berra dropped it! DiMaggio was baseball's best all-around player, but Williams was the best hitter and Chief didn't want to give him a pitch he expected. Chief stayed composed and for the first time, he would tell me later, gave Williams the same pitch twice in a row. Again Ted hit a foul pop and this time Berra hung on to it. In the second game of the doubleheader, Vic Raschi beat the Sox 11–3 and we clinched the pennant.

VIC POWER:
During the winter, the Yankees told me they were going to send me to Kansas City, to play for the Blues. So when I was home in San Juan, I read in the encyclopedia about Kansas City. I thought it was still the Wild West and that everybody wore guns and holsters and rode through the streets on horses. But three weeks later the Yankees sent me a letter saying I was going to Syracuse in the International League. My contract called for $1,200 a month. I stayed there all of 1951 and batted .294. The Yankees didn't add me to their roster in September, but I went to New York for a physical and was invited to Yankee Stadium to watch them play Boston. Ford Frick, the new Commissioner, was there, too. I sat behind Yogi Berra, the American League's Most Valuable Player, when Allie Reynolds pitched his second no-hitter. In the second game, I saw Joe DiMaggio hit a 3-run homer. I was happy to see him before he retired.

LEW BURDETTE:
I was glad that the Yankees traded me to the Braves but felt fortunate that I had come up in the Yankees' system. The Yankee, Dodger, and Cardinal organizations were the best. They all had over 20 farm clubs and taught fundamentals. When you reached the majors in the Yankee organization, a mental error was inexcusable.

I spent several years in the Yankee system. I was

doing well in the minors, but I could win 8 in a row for the Kansas City Blues and the Yankees still wouldn't have a place for me because they had Raschi, Reynolds, Lopat, Byrne, and Ford as starters and Joe Page in the bullpen. There was no place for me. Everyone in the Yankee organization went through the same thing. Joe Collins played in Triple A for something like 10 years and he was good enough to play first base for other major league teams. I had pitched only 1⅓ innings in 2 appearances in 1950. In those days, there was no union, so you couldn't question anything. If you wanted to play ball, then you kept your mouth shut. Your manager couldn't complain on your behalf because someone would take his job. There was an awful lot of people looking for jobs. I didn't think of quitting. I wasn't frustrated.

I got my break at the end of August when the Yankees traded me and $50,000 for Johnny Sain.

JOHNNY SAIN:
I was surprised that I was going to New York for their pennant drive, but Casey wanted me again. I had pitched for him as a rookie with the Braves in 1942. I thought Casey was great. He always had a friendly expression when he looked at me. For the most part, everyone liked Casey and responded to him. However, since he used the platoon system, there were always a few who grumbled about their playing time.

The Yankees brought in veterans better associated with other teams: former Cardinal and Giant Johnny Mize, one-time Cardinal outfielder–first baseman Johnny Hopp from the Braves, me (and in 1954 they'd deal for the Cards' Enos Slaughter). But they always had a nucleus. They had a club that could win even if the superstars weren't hitting. That was the key to their consistent success. The superstars were just icing. Without Gene Woodling, Hank Bauer, Joe Collins, Gil McDougald, and some others, the superstars wouldn't have had the opportunities to be superstars. I knew I wasn't going to be the Yankees' star pitcher at this point in my career, but felt I could fit into that other category. If I didn't do what I did, what the superstars did wouldn't have been so important.

The Yankees were a classy organization steeped in tradition. They even had the greatest clubhouse man,

Pete Sheehy. All anybody had to do was mention something, and Pete would take care of it. When I put on the Yankee uniform for the first time, I couldn't help thinking about Ruth, Gehrig, and Bill Dickey and all the greats. I received the highest salary of my career, $32,000, but the Yankees were notoriously stingy. They weren't giving players anything. They would factor World Series money into salaries. Gene Woodling, who was a super person, and I were real close. I used to kid him and say, "Why don't you climb the golden stairs?" I encouraged him and he improved his contract negotiations.

It was unreal playing for the Yankees, especially that year, with Joe DiMaggio going out and Mickey Mantle coming in. It was sad watching Joe play his last season. But he was still such a good player. All eyes were always on him, whether he was taking batting practice or shagging flies—just like it was with Ted Williams. Joe was a leader on the Yankees without having to say anything. He was all class.

There was no doubt that Mantle was going to be a great player. It wasn't just his power from both sides of the plate. It was also his speed. No one was faster running to first. Mantle would be running at what everyone thought was top speed and then he'd turn it up another notch. I saw him run to first and try to speed up and have his knee buckle, causing him to roll over the base. That was scary. He was injured running in right center down a slope and his knee buckled. He'd pull muscles in his legs and shoulders. He applied so much strain to his muscles instantly that he was prone to pulling them. Mickey and I became close. He grew up in Oklahoma and I grew up about 100 miles from him in Arkansas, and we spoke the same language. We were standing in the outfield one day talking. At the time he had been doing a few off-field things that were worrying a few people. I said, "Mickey, you remind me of a beautiful gold watch with the movements of a dollar watch." He understood what I said. I didn't know that he even heard me, but the next year I was standing in about the same place and he walked up to me and asked, "John, do you think the movements are getting any better?"

It was a close team on which everyone respected one another as players and individuals. Like on any other team, there was a partying element and a quieter element. There were no rah-rah leaders on the Yankees but there were many leaders: DiMaggio, Berra, Rizzuto, Bauer. . . . They were an unusual group, a loose team. I felt fortunate just to rub elbows with these guys.

The Yankees were a seasoned team who had already won pennants in 1949 and 1950. From the first day of the season, they had set out to win the pennant. In September we didn't know we'd win, but we expected it. If we were a couple runs down late in the game, we'd say, "Okay, this is our part of the game, let's win it." We finally clinched the pennant in mid-September when Rizzuto beat the Indians with a suicide bunt.

Feller, Wynn, and Garcia had 20 victories and Lemon won 17 for the Indians, but our pitchers weren't outclassed. I was close to all the pitchers. I dressed next to Allie Reynolds. He went 17–8 in 1951. I used to kid him that I wanted 10 of his fastballs per game. I would have probably thrown them as the first 10 pitches and

In the second phase of his career, former Braves standout Johnny Sain would be both an effective starter and reliever while helping the New York Yankees win pennants in 1951, 1952, and 1953.

let batters look for more of them the rest of the game. Reynolds could really throw the ball. He had a great curve and super fastball. He loved pitching in pressure situations and was dominant in the World Series every year. He was also a good guy. One day I was a little upset and withdrawn, and Reynolds walked up to me and grinned. Reynolds was part Creek Indian and he said, "My daddy always told me you could fence more out than you can fence in."

Eddie Lopat went 21–9 in 1951. He was called a junk pitcher. I told him he could throw those maneuvering-type pitches to set up the fastball and then just sneak it right by them because they were expecting something slow. I was a junkball pitcher, but I couldn't sneak by my fastball because my motion was such that they'd expect something hard.

Vic Raschi won 21 games in 1951 for the third straight year. He was a fantastic person. He was an Italian, but much bigger than Phil Rizzuto and Billy Martin. On days he pitched, he was quiet and so serious about everything. When he took the mound, he was all business. He was more of a location pitcher than Reynolds. He worked on the theory that if someone hit a pitch in one area he didn't pitch him in that area anymore. I paid more attention to what the pitch was doing than to where it was when it was hit.

A lot of the credit for the success of the Yankee pitchers had to go to Jim Turner. He was the first pitching coach I ran into who had been a pitcher, having finished his pitching career with the Yankees during the war. He had a system for record keeping that I would use when I became the Yankees' pitching coach in 1961 for Ralph Houk. At this time Houk was a seldom used catcher. We got along really well. We sat together in the bullpen and did a lot of talking about pitching. That's when I realized that he would make a good manager and he realized I would make a good pitching coach.

To show how important our pitching was that year: Yogi Berra led the Yankees with just 27 homers and 88 RBIs, and was the only player on the team with more than 15 homers and 71 RBIs. Berra carried the offense. As a batter, Berra had the pitcher in the hole when he had a count of no balls and 2 strikes. He'd swing if he had 2 strikes on him, and if he could reach it, he'd hit it, often into the stands. In addition, Yogi called a good game and led the league's catchers in every fielding category. He was a good receiver and surprisingly quick and agile. No one could take advantage of his arm. He threw out two runners in a row at third base on bunts in the World Series. There was no way in the world I could have fielded those bunts, but he pounced on both, killing a rally.

I joined the Yankees for the September pennant drive in 1951. I won 2 games that month and for that was voted a full World Series share. Maybe those 2 victories made the difference, even though we pulled away to win by 5 games over Cleveland. I always felt I did more to help the Yankees get into World Series than I did pitching in them.

WORLD SERIES

1951

YANKEES VS GIANTS

GENE WOODLING · YANKEES:
The Giants weren't as strong a team as the Dodgers. That's not knocking the Giants. We were glad to play them because the Polo Grounds held 55,000 and Ebbets Field only 32,000. We got our cuts based on attendance. The Yankees won the Series in 6 games. I hit under .200 in that Series—the only one of my 5 World Series in which I was below .300—but my 3 hits were a double, triple, and homer, and I walked 5 times and scored 6 runs in 6 games.

JOHNNY SAIN · YANKEES:
The main thing I remember about the 1951 World Series against the New York Giants is that I was scheduled to pitch the fourth game. But it rained, and that gave Reynolds an extra day off and he started. At the time I thought it was best for the team for him to start and me to relieve. But I didn't need to relieve: Reynolds went the distance on an 8-hitter, beating Maglie, 6–2. The highlight was Joe DiMaggio's final major league home run! That evened the Series at 2 wins apiece. We won the fifth game 13–1 on Lopat's 5-hitter. And we won the final game 4–3. I relieved Raschi in the seventh inning and ran into trouble in the ninth. Then left-hander Bob Kuzava came in to get out of a bases-loaded jam and give us the title. It was his only appearance in the Series. That was Joe DiMaggio's last game. He doubled in his last at-bat in the eighth inning and after being forced out at third received a tremendous ovation from the crowd.

BILL RIGNEY · GIANTS:
It was a kick in the World Series against the Yankees. They were such a proud team and it was thrilling to play in Yankee Stadium. Once I had worked out there. I had hurt my arm and the Giants were out of town. I went into the clubhouse and started to put on my Giants uniform. But Joe DiMaggio came over and said, ''There's never been a uniform put on in this clubhouse other than the one with stripes.'' He called over a clubhouse man and I had to wear a Yankee uniform to work out.

This was the first World Series that was broadcast coast-to-coast. Dave Koslo went the distance to beat Allie Reynolds in the first game, 5–1. Alvin Dark hit a 3-run homer and Monte Irvin got 4 hits and stole home. Don Mueller, our right fielder, had broken his leg in the playoffs, so I went to Herman Franks and asked to play right field in Yankee Stadium in Game Two against Eddie Lopat, the left-hander. Herman said he liked that idea. I urged him to go to Durocher that night. But he wouldn't do it because I had never played the outfield. I said, "Who cares? Tell Leo I played it in high school. He'll never know." I just wanted to play. Leo put Henry Thompson out there. He was nervous but he didn't hurt us. We were behind 3–1 in the eighth. There were men on first and third with one out and Westrum due up. And Leo's shouting to Herman, "Where's Rigney? Where's Rigney?" Leo used to talk to pinch hitters so if they got a hit, fans would yell, "Thataway, Leo!" So I'm up at the plate and Leo's yelling that he wants to talk to me. I ignored him. Yogi told me that he was walking toward me from the third-base line. Finally I acknowledged him. He just wanted to tell me not to hit into the double play. I told him to give me one swing on my own and let me pull it, and if that didn't work I'd then hit to right like he wanted. But he wouldn't let me. Anyway, Lopat started throwing his slop. I finally jumped on a pitch I could handle. I shouldn't have been so eager. The next day Lopat told me, "You just didn't wait on that pitch long enough." If I'd waited a split second longer it would have gone into the right-field seats for a 3-run homer and we would have won 4–3. But I didn't get all of it and Hank Bauer caught it against the right-field wall. So instead of being up 2–0 in the Series, we were even. We would have been up 3–0 because Hearn out-pitched Raschi and Lockman hit a 3-run homer as we won Game Three, 6–2.

Casey Stengel was furious about being behind by even one game, especially since we'd scored 5 runs in the fifth inning of Game Three after Stanky had kicked the ball out of Rizzuto's glove. Jerry Coleman told me they held a meeting in which Stengel said, "Are you going to let those . . . those . . . those . . ." Stengel couldn't find the right words to describe the Giants. He happened to look at a garbage can and, inspired, he said, "Are you going to let those garbage collectors steal your money?" He was so mad at us. We were up 2 games to 1 and had Maglie scheduled against Johnny Sain. Then it rained. That gave Allie Reynolds another day's rest and he pitched in the fourth game, going the distance in a 6–2 win. Joe DiMaggio hit a 2-run homer. Then they killed us in the fifth game, 13–1. McDougald hit a grand slammer and Rizzuto hit a 2-run homer and Lopat pitched a 5-hitter. That put the Yankees ahead 3 games to 2. In the sixth game, in Yankee Stadium, Koslo went against Raschi. It was 1–1 until Bauer cleared the bases with a triple in the sixth inning. We rallied for 2 runs in the ninth inning and had a man on third with 2 out. Pinch hitter Sal Yvars hit a liner to right against Bob Kuzava, but Bauer made one of his sliding catches to end the Series. Irvin and Dark were the only guys who hit well for us, and neither Maglie nor Jansen got a victory. So the Yankees won. The loss wasn't so bad because the Series was anticlimactic after the pennant victory. Somebody said we had needed a week's rest. I said that we needed a month's rest. All of us were strung out. We had come from so far behind to catch the Dodgers.

NATIONAL LEAGUE
1952

BOSTON BRAVES

LEW BURDETTE:

I met Warren Spahn in September of 1951, after my trade from the Yankees. In 1952 we became roommates, and that would last my entire career with the Braves. He would be my best friend in baseball. We got along terrifically. We were very lucky because we had everything in common, including our senses of humor and our love of outdoor activities. My main hobby was fishing and Warren had his cattle. He also fished once in a while because he had lakes on his property in Oklahoma. We had fun talking baseball 99 percent of the time. But with his being a lefty and me being right-handed, we could tell each other only whether a particular guy was an egotistical hitter and whether he swung at bad pitches when he was behind in the count. Also, he was a starter and Tommy Holmes and his replacement, Charlie Grimm, used me almost always in relief. Both

No longer stuck in the Yankees' system, Lew Burdette chalked up his first starts and victories in what would be a long, productive career with the Braves.

of us pitched well that year, but we had losing records because other than Sid Gordon, Eddie Mathews—who was a rookie—and a couple of other guys, no one was giving the pitchers any help.

BOB BUHL:

I spent two years as a paratrooper when I should have been in the major leagues. I played ball while in the service, for the company team and on weekends for an independent man. I was pitching twice a week. On the base, I just played for Lieutenant Brown, a heck of a nice guy. He was a colored man but let me use his name when I played off-base. So I played for a Mr. Brooks, and we traveled around Tennessee playing every Sunday. He was in the cattle business and all he wanted to do was manage a baseball team. He used to bet a lot of money on those games, so he paid me more money than I was making in the army. I was sort of a ringer. While I was in the army, Charlie Grimm was appointed the Braves manager. So I was happy there'd be someone I knew when I rejoined the Braves. I didn't know any players. Every once in a while someone would send me a Boston paper saying, "Grimm counting on the rookie Buhl once he gets out of the army."

JIM GRANT:

For just a moment in 1952, I thought I was a member of the Boston Braves. I was born in 1935, in Lacoochee, Florida, a segregated town of 500 people where everyone either worked in the lumber mill or picked oranges and beans. My dad, uncle, and even my mom from time to time worked at the lumber mill. My mom also worked at the Pasco Packing Company in Dade City, about seven miles away, canning orange, tangerine, and grapefruit slices. I was one of nine children, and when I was old enough I worked, too, delivering the black *Pittsburgh Courier* and doing an assortment of jobs at the lumber mill.

Transition was slow in terms of civil rights. At ballgames we blacks had to sit down on the side, and I didn't want to do that. I had problems at the mill because I spoke out. I had problems in the stores. I had problems with white insurance agents who always called my mother by her first name. I was thrown in jail once because I didn't say "Yes, sir," to a policeman.

My mother and sisters, who were older, were protective of me, but they never discouraged me.

I thought that everywhere in the world was segregated. But I thought of leaving Lacoochee to get an education—my mom never got past elementary school, but she was a real bright lady, and she and my sisters instilled in me that an education was very important to better myself. I always thought about doing better educationally and financially and then coming back home to share whatever I had . . . which is what eventually happened.

My life was rich with black history and culture. I was inspired by all blacks of accomplishment. I knew all about Jesse Owens, Mary McLeod Bethune, Duke Ellington, Paul Robeson, Marian Anderson. We remembered Joe Louis's saying, "I'm going to win because God is on our side." We knew about Jackie Robinson and when we heard on the radio that he signed with the Dodgers, everybody spilled out onto the streets and there was a celebration.

I was about 7 or 8 when I started hanging around the local sandlot lumber mill team watching an uncle play baseball. They were the Lacoochee 9 Devils and I became their bat boy. When I was around 13 they put me in a ballgame and I was able to compete. By the time I was 14 I was probably one of the best players in the state. I didn't pitch that much, even at Moore Academy High School in Dade City. The only times I always pitched were in tournament games. All of the guys could throw the ball hard, but I was one of the few who could throw hard and throw strikes.

I avoided major league spring training games in Florida because I didn't want to sit in the sections designated for black fans. But I would see the black teams that barnstormed through Florida and played against local all-star teams. When I was 14 or 15, I played center field and third base on a couple of those local clubs. To leave small Lacoochee and go all the way to Tampa, a "big" city, was exciting, and it was fantastic to be able to talk to my heroes, Satchel Paige, Larry Doby, Jackie Robinson.

The Lacoochee 9 Devils had a good reputation and on Saturdays would play the prisoners at the state penitentiary in Raiford. The prison itself was fully integrated, but our games were only between blacks. They would feed us for coming to play. I'd hear the prisoners ask if they brought ''that Grant fellow,'' and when they heard I was there, they'd say, ''Uh, oh!'' At the time I was 5'11", about 145 pounds, not particularly big, kind of wiry. In 1952 a scout from the Boston Braves, who was a friend of the warden, came to see me play. Afterward he wanted to sign me. Everybody crowded around because they were so happy for me. I filled out his contract and put down my age. He said, ''Oh my God, you're 16!'' He tore up the contract. So I didn't become a Brave. That's when I learned you had to be 18 to sign a contract. And I knew my mother wouldn't sign for me even then because she had other things in mind for my future.

ST. LOUIS CARDINALS

BILLY JOHNSON:

Eddie Stanky became the Cardinals' manager. Players didn't get along with him. He wasn't too good a manager. If he gave a bunt signal to a batter, he might turn to a player on the bench and ask him what the signal meant. He'd try to keep you in the game but it didn't make any sense for us to know about signals sent to someone else. What good would that do? Stanky was mean when it came to arguing with umpires. ''The Brat'' was the right nickname for him. He was just like a little kid and would kick dirt all over the umpire's suit. That kind of stuff embarrassed the players.

Despite Stanky, there was no dissension on the team and we maintained a winning attitude. Again we finished third, but this time we won more games and ended up only 8 games behind the Dodgers and 4 behind the Giants. Musial led the league in hitting again for the third straight year, and in several other categories, and he and Slaughter drove in a lot of runs. Musial was a great hitter and a pretty good left fielder, but he couldn't run like Joe DiMaggio.

DICK GROAT (PIRATES):

When I first came up in 1952, Stan Musial could fly. I remember going over to second base and making a hell of a play on a ground ball he hit through the middle. I stood up and got ready to throw and saw that he was *already past first base. ''Whoa! Wait a minute!'' At that time, he went to first base in a class with Mantle, before Mickey hurt his knee. He was that quick.*

RALPH KINER (PIRATES):

Almost all the dents on Stan Musial's bat were by the label. Bad hitters had dents all over.

B. JOHNSON:

We got good pitching from rookie left-hander Wilmer Mizell. ''Vinegar Bend'' was a tall good ol' country boy. He was so quiet that you would never know he would go on to become a politician. He just did his job and that was it.

TOM CHENEY:

I was born in 1934 in Morgan, Georgia, and raised on a farm during the Depression. We were very poor. My mother skimmed cream and they would pick it up every 2 weeks and she'd get $1. But we didn't want for anything. We grew our own vegetables and had hogs for meat and cornbread and biscuits at every meal, and we lived in a house from which you'd never lose sight of the moon. I hunted and fished. We used to get a mule and wagon and go visit neighbors. We went to Sunday school and church. Thursday afternoons my father gave me the choice of working on the farm or playing American Legion ball. It was an easy choice. My father always made sure I got to the game. In high school and in American Legion ball, I pitched and played shortstop. I didn't think at all of becoming a professional ballplayer because I was just 5'7" and weighed only 135 when I completed eleventh grade, which was the final grade at Morgan High.

I thought some about becoming a veterinarian, and I went to Abraham Baldwin Junior College, down in Tiffany, Georgia. There were only 250 students then—it was strictly a farm school. Of course, I played ball there, pitching and playing the outfield. Once I pitched the first game of a doubleheader and caught the second game. I had shot up to 6 feet and weighed 150 pounds. At Baldwin we won the state championship of junior colleges. I think I was 8–1.

After my first year at Baldwin, I traveled to Atlanta to work out with the Boston Braves' farm team in the

Southern League. Dixie Walker was the manager. They offered me a Class C contract. But the Cardinals were my favorite team because they had a Class D Georgia-Florida League team closer to Morgan, in Albany. So 4 or 5 of us went over to try out. I wanted to try out at short, but after they saw me pitch, they said there was no need to play the infield. I was signed to a contract by Mercer Harris, who was a Cardinal scout in Georgia, Florida, and maybe Alabama. My dad loved baseball but didn't want me to sign. It meant I had to drop out of college after 1½ years. I got $1,500, which was like $1 million to me. At Baldwin, my dad had given me $5 a week. Material things never meant much to me, though—I just wanted to make enough to buy a couple of thousand acres in Georgia for hunting and farming and to set my mother and father up for life.

I signed in September 1952 and joined Albany. We stayed in private homes and I believe we got $2.50 a day for 3 meals—I'd get a good balanced meal at my boardinghouse for $1.25. I had 7 or 8 games left in the season with Albany. I showed I had a good fastball and curve and got my share of strikeouts.

We weren't a very good team that year or in 1953. My manager was Russ McGovern. He wasn't a bad guy, but he once called me a gutless S.O.B. on the mound. I told him that if he ever called me that again, one of us would get killed, and I meant it. I was raised in the South and that was one thing you didn't call a guy and mean it.

CHICAGO CUBS

RANDY JACKSON:

The Cubs sent me a contract offering something like $7,500 or $8,000. I'd seen in the paper how other teams were trying to get me, so I sent the contract back, saying, "I really thought I'd done better than that. I led the team in stolen bases and led the league's third basemen in putouts and assists and I understand some other teams are looking at me. I really think I deserve more than a $1,000 raise." And I got a letter back from Wid Matthews saying, "Let me tell you something. There has been only one team asking for you and all they offered was an old ball, a caved-in catcher's mask, and a broken bat. Get your so-and-so down to spring training and don't let me hear one more word from you." I signed that contract so fast and put it back in the mail. At that time we thought of ourselves as employees and didn't figure we had many rights. We didn't argue with general managers. So he conned me with a few choice words into signing that contract.

HANK SAUER:

Back in 1948 my brother Ed was out in southern California playing in the Coast League, and he invited me to come live with him. So I went out intending to stay one year and never left. During my first 5 years in the big leagues I had to take part-time jobs in the off-season to make ends meet. In Hollywood I worked as a carpenter at the studios. I wasn't much of a carpenter—I was more of a helper. I also was an extra in movies and television shows with Bob Hope, Ronald Reagan, Dan Dailey, and others.

During the winter I played golf in California. I never took a lesson but immediately was a scratch golfer. At the peak of my baseball career I could have turned pro. Gus Zernial of the Athletics, who was a gentleman and a real close friend, also lived in Los Angeles, so every year we worked out together before spring training. He had trouble losing weight, so we'd play golf, take batting practice, and have daily handball games. Afterward I'd drink beer and he'd get mad because he couldn't drink it without gaining back the weight he'd lost.

I picked up very little money each year through endorsements. I got just $1,500 a year for my signature on a Wilson glove. I got about $100 from the baseball card companies, Topps and Bowman. I also had a bat contract with Hillerich and Bradsby, but I didn't get any money. For their use of my signature year after year, I got one set of golf clubs.

I always used a 36-inch, 40-ounce bat, which was very heavy. Ted Williams saw my bat in spring training and was surprised by its size. He had a scale and weighed it. Then he believed me. I stood close to the plate. I was known for my swing. I wasn't against swinging at the first pitch because I didn't like a pitcher getting ahead of me in the count. I always swung at close pitches. If a pitcher wanted to get me out, the best way was to throw the ball high and tight and then low and away. If the pitcher got the corner he was successful, but if he missed I would hurt him. I preferred hitting against a fastball pitcher. But through my entire career, I didn't believe anybody should get me out.

I didn't break bats when I failed in a clutch situation. But when I first started, I threw them. My manager at Syracuse made me realize that my biggest enemy was myself. He instructed me that when I lost my temper I was supposed to walk down the third-base line to the coach's box and let him settle me down. So the first time it happened, I did it. It was embarrassing. After 2 times walking down the base line, I got over my habit. I changed from a vicious person to a calm player.

I was known as a nice guy, off the field and on. For instance, I never beefed with umpires. But if you gave me problems, I would give problems back. I was terrible like that—before I learned to control my temper, I'd fight at the drop of a hat. From an early age on, I was willing to mix it up. Once in Birmingham a catcher named Felner blocked me off home plate and tore up my knee. It took me six weeks to come back. We played the same ballclub and Felner was catching. That day my general manager, Paul Florence, told me he'd give me $100 if I got into a fight that day. I was making only $200 a month, so $100 was a pretty good piece of change. I reached second and wanted someone to hit a ball through the infield because I wanted to go after Felner. I rounded third, a dead duck on a play at home, and just jumped right on top of Felner as he tried to apply the tag. I knocked him down and we started swinging. Florence gave me the money the next day. I suggested that I do it again that day, but Florence said, ''No, no, no, that's enough!''

I seemed to intimidate a lot of pitchers. For some reason I had a vicious look. I didn't know that until some pitcher came up and said, ''I don't mind your hitting a home run off me but, jeez, don't look at me as if you wanted to kill me.''

In 1952 I had my best season, leading the National League with 37 homers and 121 RBIs. We won a game against Curt Simmons and the Phillies, 3–0, when I hit 3 homers. It was a big honor getting the National League's Most Valuable Player award, no doubt about it. An hour after I was called about winning the award, my son was born. It was quite a day!

The greatest thrill I had in baseball was hitting a homer off Bob Lemon to win the 1952 All-Star Game. Stan Musial was on base. It came in the bottom of the fourth inning in a game that was called after 5 innings. My Cubs teammate Bob Rush was the winning pitcher.

The year was made more enjoyable because Chicago moved up to fifth place and had a .500 record. It was the best year the team had in my 7 years in Chicago. We were actually at the top of the standings at the All-Star break, but then we lost 10 or 12 in a row and it just fell apart. I got some good support in the lineup from Frank Baumholtz, who hit .325, first baseman Dee Fondy, who batted .300, Bill Serena, who hit 15 homers, and guys like Randy Jackson and catcher Toby Atwell.

But the big difference was our pitching. For a change, we had several pitchers who did well. Rush won 17 games, which was the most by a pitcher during my years on the Cubs, Warren Hacker won 15, Paul Minner 14, and Johnny Klippstein gave a good effort. Also, Dutch Leonard was excellent in relief. In other years our pitching was mediocre at best, with only Rush holding his own against tough teams. Bob threw hard and had a good curve and change-up and was a terrific competitor. He would have been a 20-game winner on a better team, but we couldn't afford to trade him and give him the opportunity.

JOHNNY KLIPPSTEIN:

For the first time I started more often than I relieved. Cavarretta pitched me 41 times, 25 times as a starter, and I threw over 200 innings, second only to Rush. I had only 9 victories, but I had many good outings and was pretty satisfied considering this was only my third year and I was still only 24. It also was hard to pitch at Wrigley Field because the wind direction changed so often.

If you were in the 4-man rotation, you wouldn't do anything the day after you pitched. The second day you'd run and sweat and throw a little bit to loosen up. The day before you pitched again, you'd throw for 5 minutes. I'd get rubdowns from Andy Latshaw, the Cubs trainer. He was famous for his Coca-Cola rubs. When guys would come in too often, instead of rubbing them with liniment, he'd secretly rub them with Coca-Cola, which was pretty much the same color.

I was all business on the mound. My wife would say that when she was at games I wouldn't even acknowledge she was there. The minute I walked into the ballpark I was in another world, thinking what I'd do that day. I kept a book on hitters those years. After that it was a memory thing.

In most instances the mound is what determined whether a park was good to pitch in. The best pitching park in either league was the Polo Grounds. They had a clay-like dirt that gave you excellent footing. There was also a mile behind home plate for catchers to run down foul pop-ups. Cincinnati had the worst mound. It was like pitching off a flat table. It was very difficult to throw a curveball there. Philadelphia was a great park to pitch in because it had a good mound. St. Louis was a good park to pitch in although it was a little short in right and you had to be aware of Musial and other left-handed power hitters. Ebbets Field was short all the way around, particularly the right-field screen, which was only 297 feet away. There was a lot of room in Forbes Field. It was only 365 feet in left after they constructed ''Greenberg Gardens,'' but it was still a long way to center. Every park was different and every lineup was different.

Pitching against the Dodgers in Ebbets Field was tough, perhaps the biggest challenge a pitcher could have in those days. If you went through their lineup 4 times, you earned your money. You had to score a lot of runs to beat them because they weren't going to be shut out very often. When they took the field, they expected to win. They were somewhat on the cocky side, but maybe deservedly so. They were aggressive and confident and had staying power. The Dodgers had a camaraderie that few teams had. It extended to their fans. The Ebbets Field fans were my favorites because they were good to the opposition. If they got on you, it was in a good-natured way, and if you did something good, they'd applaud you.

FRANK BAUMHOLTZ:

I was the batter who faced Stan Musial the only time he pitched. It was the last day of the 1952 season in St. Louis. The weekend before, the Cards were in Chicago for a doubleheader, and when they left town he led the league in hitting, only $\frac{1}{10}$ of a percentage point ahead of me. We had three off-days during which Musial did well against Cincinnati to increase his lead over me. On the last day I didn't have a chance to read the morning paper, so I didn't know why there were so many people

One of the most consistent hitters of the period, Frank Baumholtz batted .325 for the Cubs in 1952, finishing second in the National League to Stan Musial.

NATIONAL BASEBALL LIBRARY, COOPERSTOWN, N.Y.

in the stands. It turned out that the day before, Eddie Stanky announced that Musial would pitch to me when I led off the game. Stanky called time before the game even started. He motioned Musial in from center field and sent the day's pitcher, Harvey Haddix, out to center. So Musial warmed up. I didn't know what was going on. Cavarretta told me, ''They're trying to make a fool of you, Frank.'' I said, ''I don't think so. I think it's just a gimmick to get a lot of people in the stands to watch two also-rans on the last day of the season.'' I told Phil that if Musial pitched to me, I was going to turn around and bat right-handed. Jocko Conlan ordered me to hurry into the batter's box because he was eager to get back to California. I'd never batted right-handed before. Musial threw one pitch and I connected and I swear it was the hardest ball I hit in my life. Third baseman Solly Hemus was crouched over and he couldn't even get his glove down fast enough. The ball hit him on the inside of his right shin and went into the left-field corner. I pulled easily into second base with a double—only they flashed ERROR on the scoreboard. Musial and Haddix then switched positions. At the end of the inning, Stan called the press box and said, "If I ever saw a base hit in my life, that was a base hit." But they wouldn't change it. I got only 1 official hit that game, off Haddix, to finish at .325, and Musial got 3 hits, so he would have won the batting title anyway with his .336. Six months later, that event with Musial changing positions and me becoming a switch-hitter appeared in *Ripley's Believe It or Not*.

BROOKLYN DODGERS

RUBE WALKER:

We had lost the 1951 pennant race in an upsetting way, but in 1952 we were ready to go. We arrived in spring training with a new determination to win. And that feeling carried us through the whole season. This time we held off the Giants by 4 games.

We won the pennant although our best pitcher, Don Newcombe, was in the army. Carl Erskine went 14–6 and no-hit the Cubs, and Preacher Roe had another phenomenal season, going 11–2—he was 33–5 in 1950 and 1951. And three new pitchers helped fill the void. Ben Wade came from nowhere to win 11 games. Billy Loes won 13 games. He was a local schoolboy sensation with great stuff. He came to the big leagues, and, my goodness, he had all the pitches. In fact, I think he went a little too often to his curve, slider, and change, because his fastball was so good.

Probably our key addition was Joe Black, a big right-handed reliever who, like his name, was black. Dressen used him all the time and he won 15 games and saved about the same number. He had a good fastball and a good slider, and he came up with a change.

RALPH KINER (PIRATES):

In his rookie year, which was by far his best year, Joe Black was extremely tough. He had a great fastball and

a very, very sharp . . . whatever-it-was. It may have been a slider, though I think it was a spitball.

Of the starters, I hit Carl Erskine better than some of the others, but I think he was actually the toughest of the group.

R. WALKER:

We got good years from everybody in the lineup, as well as substitute outfielder George Shuba, who gave us another left-handed hitter with pop. Hodges led our team with over 30 homers and 100 RBIs, but Robinson, Furillo, Pafko, Campy, and, of course, Snider provided a great deal of power. And we had our usual outstanding defense.

BEN WADE:

I was drafted out of the Cubs' organization by the Dodgers' Hollywood Stars team in the PCL, and I had played with them in 1950 and 1951. When I was with Hollywood, Brooklyn broke its working agreement with them, but it was allowed to take one player after the 1951 season, and I was the one they took. I had gone 18–6 and was the best pitcher on the club. I went to spring training with the Dodgers in 1952 and felt all along that I would make the ballclub. Chuck Dressen had managed Oakland in the Pacific Coast League and knew I could pitch.

My biggest thrill was the day I walked into Ebbets Field and saw that I had a locker next to Jackie Robinson. We became good friends. Robbie was the leader of the Dodgers and everyone looked up to him. He was no longer in his prime, but he was still the best ballplayer on the club. There were a lot of great players on the Dodgers, but he was the one who got it started. He was an inspirational player, a gung-ho guy, the best competitor I ever saw. I didn't see anger in him, except when he was playing and opponents tried to upset him. That made him a much better player.

His locker was where all the action was. He was friendly toward the media, and all the reporters came up to him before and after games. It was interesting to sit there and listen to him and then get up the next morning and not find one thing in the paper that you heard him say. But I wasn't displeased with the media. I thought all the New York sportswriters were great. They knew how to write. If they wrote something a player didn't like, the player would tell them. After that, it was all over. The media was always welcome in our clubhouse.

Don Newcombe was in the service in 1952 and Ralph Branca didn't pitch as much because he had back and shoulder problems, so Billy Loes and I moved into the rotation with Carl Erskine and Preacher Roe. We had 45 starts between us. Loes was pretty much a loner, but he was popular with his teammates. He was only 22, but he was a real, real good pitcher.

All the starting pitchers had the same routine. If you pitched on Monday, you rested on Tuesday and didn't do anything but run, you threw batting practice on Wednesday, you rested and ran on Thursday, and you pitched again on Friday. You pitched a day, then rested the next. All we did was run and pitch. We did a lot of running. It was the same with every team. Every team had 4 starters. Pitchers generally didn't get sore arms in

Twenty-nine-year-old Ben Wade finally got a real chance to pitch in the majors in 1952 and won 11 games for the National League champion Brooklyn Dodgers, helping fill the void left when Don Newcombe entered the service.

those days. If your arm hurt, you didn't say anything. I don't remember a Dodgers pitcher getting a sore arm. We didn't do any exercises.

We didn't have a pitching coach on the Dodgers. Cookie Lavagetto, Billy Herman, and Jake Pitler were our coaches. There weren't pitching coaches in those days. There wasn't an official hitting coach either.

I started 24 of the 37 games in which I pitched and went 11–9, with a 3.60 ERA. I struck out 118 batters in 180 innings, including 6 batters in a row against Pittsburgh in one game. If that had been against the Giants, in a game that meant something, it would have been much more special. It didn't mean that much. My personal highlight was hitting 2 homers in a game against Warren Spahn.

Pitchers would always go over the lineup of the other club with Roy Campanella or Rube Walker, depending on who was catching. I had known Rube in Nashville and we were both ex-Cubs, so we got along great. The catcher called the game, but we could shake him off. Sometimes he'd come back and signal for the same pitch until you threw it. I threw fastballs mostly, but then I came up with a half-decent breaking ball, though I wound up throwing the slider more. Out of 10 pitches, about 7 would be fastballs. In time, I'd throw more sliders. My fastball was my best pitch, so it was my out pitch.

Roy Campanella was much more competitive than he looked. He seemed happy-go-lucky, but he was tough. In New York everyone always argued about who the better catcher was, Campanella or Berra. They were both great.

New York also had 3 great shortstops. Phil Rizzuto and Alvin Dark might have been even better than Reese. Dark was about as good a competitor and athlete as there was.

The biggest arguments were about center field. Duke Snider wasn't as good a fielder as Mickey Mantle or Willie Mays, but he was a good fielder. He wasn't as exciting as the other two and didn't get the same publicity, but his average, homers, and RBIs during the fifties matched them. He was a great hitter, especially in Ebbets Field.

The Dodgers had so many stars that Carl Furillo was pretty much taken for granted. If he didn't have that great arm, not many people would have known he was as good as he was. He played right field in Brooklyn like no one else could play it, and he was a terrific hitter.

People may find this surprising, but if we were in a jam and needed a base hit, I wanted to see Billy Cox at the plate. Not only was he a peerless third baseman, but he was also the best clutch hitter on the ballclub. He was a quiet guy who never said a word. He was the best fielder I ever saw. He was quick and had great hands and a great arm. No one could ever be better than Cox.

Charlie Dressen was by far the best manager I had in the majors. He knew how to utilize his players, including his pitchers. The rivalry that existed between the Giants and Dodgers was mostly a rivalry between managers, Durocher and Dressen, Durocher's former coach. Every club was tough, but when you have two talented clubs from the same city, it has to be a big rivalry. We never saw Giants players except when we played them.

I didn't mind pitching in Ebbets Field because the Dodgers were playing with me. The fans were great. They gave you hell when you lost but cheered you when you won. They were fair.

ELROY FACE:

I had been drafted by Branch Rickey out of the Phillies' organization in 1950, but soon after that he sold his percentage of the Dodgers to Walter O'Malley and moved to Pittsburgh. I reported to Vero Beach in 1951 but didn't get to pitch to major leaguers. I was assigned to Pueblo, Colorado, where I started 33 games, completed 25, and was 23–9 with a sixth-place club. In 1952, I played in Fort Worth, where Bobby Bragan was my manager. I didn't work with a pitching coach even once. What I learned was self-taught. I still didn't think about becoming a major leaguer because I realized it was difficult to break into the Dodgers' staff. So it was my biggest break to be drafted by Mr. Rickey for a second time and go to the Pirates' organization.

NEW YORK GIANTS

BILL RIGNEY:

It was upsetting that we didn't win the pennant again and finished in second place, 4 games behind the Dodgers. But we had reasons. Willie Mays began a 2-year

stint in the army and Monte Irvin broke his leg in Denver. Henry Thompson moved into center field, and we picked up Bob Elliott to replace Irvin in left. Bob did as good as he could, but he was no Irvin. Bobby Thomson hit 24 homers and drove in over 100 runs, but no one else was close to him in either category. So our offense sputtered. Maglie went 18–8 and Hearn went 14–7, but our pitching also declined a bit. Jansen pitched only .500 ball.

However, Hoyt Wilhelm, the great knuckleballer, was about to rise out of the ashes of Minneapolis. He'd been in the minors for ten years. Leo didn't like pitching Wilhelm because he didn't like that there was always the potential of his knuckler going to the backstop because it was as hard to catch as it was to hit. He finally kept him on the club in 1952 and Hoyt was amazing. He could pitch every day without tiring or losing his effectiveness. Hoyt pitched 71 games and almost 160 innings in relief, going 15–3, with the best ERA in the league. He even homered in his first at-bat. That was funny because he was a horrible hitter and would never homer again. But as a pitcher he would go on forever, right into the Hall of Fame. He was already 29, but would pitch another twenty years, setting all kinds of records.

This was the final season when I played a fair amount. I was mostly used as a pinch hitter, but I played all over the infield and batted 90 times. I hit .300 for the only time in my major league career.

HAL WOODESHICK:

After returning home after just 30 days in the Cleveland system, in 1951, I was told by my dad that I just got a call from the general manager of the team in Oil City, Pennsylvania, in the Mid-Atlantic League. So my dad drove me to Oil City and they signed me that afternoon. I pitched that night and got knocked out in the first or second inning and was released that night. So my dad drove me back home.

In the winter of 1951, I went to work at a mill and saved some money. I saw an announcement in *The Sporting News* about a tryout being held by the New York Giants in Melbourne, Florida. So my buddy and I drove to Florida, knowing that we would get reimbursed if we signed a contract. We got down to the camp and there were about 400 guys there. They put numbers on our backs and we waited our turn to play. When my turn to pitch came, I struck out all 9 guys I faced. They called me into the office and said, "We can't sign you." I said, "Why not?" "You've been released three times," they said. "There's something wrong with you." I said, "Gimme a break." So they did and signed me for $125 a month. I was sent to their Class D team in Kingsport, Tennessee. I won 13 games and made the All-Star team. I was expected to move up the next year, but in January I was drafted into the army.

PHILADELPHIA PHILLIES

DEL ENNIS:

Bob Carpenter, the Phillies' owner, wouldn't allow his players to accept endorsements for the first few years. Otherwise, I could have made a lot of money on the side, especially because I was so well known in Philadelphia. We also couldn't go to banquets during the season because he didn't want us to leave the club. However, in the off-season we'd go to local banquets for about $100 a time. One year I went to 87 of them. I felt I was always at a banquet. Later on I got some endorsements because Carpenter got more lenient.

Carpenter was like a father to me from the time I joined the Phillies. He took care of his players throughout the organization. He acted as the general manager, so he'd handle contract negotiations, and I felt I was treated fairly. I think all the players liked Carpenter. The players would get together about once a month and have barbecues and parties by somebody's swimming pool, and one of the best times we had was at Carpenter's house.

The Phillies had a bad first half of the season, so Carpenter fired Eddie Sawyer and replaced him with Steve O'Neill. Steve was a much older guy. He was in his early 60s and had been managing since the mid-thirties, but only in the American League. He had recently been the manager of the Red Sox. Once O'Neill took over, we probably played the best ball in the league. We finished 20 games over .500. I rebounded to have a good year, with 107 RBIs. Robin Roberts was great, winning 28 games, which was the most in the league since Dizzy Dean won the same number in 1935. He was the only pitcher in the league with 20 wins. He won one game, 7–6, when I homered in the seventeenth inning. Roberts

went the entire distance. So did I, though I broke my wrist early in the game and had to put it in a pressure cast to keep playing.

PITTSBURGH PIRATES

DICK GROAT:

I signed a contract with the Pirates the night I graduated from high school. I joined the team the next day. George Strickland was the regular shortstop, but our manager, Billy Meyer, could afford to play me because we were such a terrible team. We lost 112 games and 21 out of 22 games to the Dodgers. Meyer, who came over from the Yankees' organization in 1948, was one of the finest people I have ever been associated with. We set an all-time record for losses that year, but he was so patient and understanding.

Ralph Kiner was the only player we had who could hurt anybody. I don't know how he hit so many home runs, because all they did was pitch around him. He had been my idol when I was in high school, so you can imagine my anxiety when I learned he was going to be my roommate. On the morning I found out, he had gone out to breakfast and I checked in for us at the Knickerbocker Hotel in Chicago. I got to the room and had Ralph Kiner's bag and mine delivered upstairs. I wanted to lie down because I had a hard time sleeping on the train. But I didn't make a move. I just waited until he came to the room and told me which bed he wanted. Then I collapsed into the other one.

Ralph was the only star and high-salaried player on the team, and when he went out, he was treated royally. It was a thrill for the young players to go out with him. One night in Cincinnati he went out to dinner with four of us rookies. We were all making the minimum salary of $5,000 a year. Before dinner we had a few drinks, and Ralph let us take pride in buying him a drink. Then we ate dinner and Ralph picked up the big tab for all of us. That was his pattern. He was a first-class gentleman in every way. He was the nicest guy in the world to be around.

Ralph gave me advice about being a ballplayer and about hitting. George Metkovich also helped me with my hitting. George Sisler was the chief of scouts and the batting instructor and he taught me so much. I also went out to Paul Waner's batting cage and worked overtime. I took more extra hitting than you can imagine. At the time, I would consistently hit to right field. I had an inside-out swing that made it easier to hit the breaking ball because I could wait a little longer and hit it to right. Now I changed the position of my arms, which had been too close to my body, and lifted them so I pretty much had a Ralph Kiner stance without his power. I was not a very confident person, or I wouldn't have worried as much as I did all through my baseball career. I had a lot of pride and was a perfectionist. I told myself that the day I couldn't hit .260 in the majors I would quit. And if I hit below what I thought I deserved, I wouldn't think to ask for a raise. In my rookie year, I played 95 games and ended up leading the team with a .284 average.

George Strickland was traded in mid-season, but before that, he taught me a lot about how to play the position. I tried to model myself after Pee Wee Reese of the Dodgers and Alvin Dark of the Giants. There was a fraternity among shortstops in those days, and Alvin taught me a lot about fielding and hitting. I was just a kid and was getting killed at second base on double plays. As a rookie, I was afraid to use the phantom play at second and made sure I always touched the bag, even if it meant having the runner slide into me. In college I got knocked down once in a while, but in the majors I was getting beaten up all the time. I had marks all up and down my legs and I worried that my career was in danger because I couldn't take too much more of it.

Then, after a game at Forbes Field, Alvin took the time to show me how to make the pivot and get out of the way. He explained that on every double-play grounder, the one thing the runner on first is supposed to do is break up the double play, meaning whoever covered second was his target. He confirmed that in the majors you needed to touch the bag *before* you actually had the ball so you could throw the ball and move away before getting slammed. His advice helped me tremendously. The umpires went along with the play. In the majors, if the ball beats the runner to the base, the runner is out. (A few years later, I would have a very badly jammed thumb and be scared to death of somebody sliding in. I went three weeks without ever tagging the runner at second, yet never had anyone called safe. Nobody even argued.)

Oddly, the guy I would consider the most notorious

NATIONAL BASEBALL LIBRARY, COOPERSTOWN, N.Y.

Already known to basketball fans for having broken the NCAA scoring record while at Duke, Dick Groat began an excellent baseball career in 1952 as a shortstop on the 42–112 Pittsburgh Pirates, whom he would lead to a world title in 1960.

slider in the league was Daryl Spencer, who broke in the same year I did, for the Giants, and would eventually replace Dark as their shortstop. He'd cut you. He would spike more middle infielders than anybody. He was a big guy for a shortstop.

If I eventually became the best hit-and-run man in baseball, it also was because of Dark. We both had reputations for hitting the ball to right with a guy running from first, so opposing teams were ready. Alvin explained to me that I couldn't hit-and-run on the normal counts but had to cross teams up by doing it on odd counts. Teams knew what I was going to do, but I was still effective because they couldn't predict the count when I'd do it.

I got along with all the Pirate veterans—Kiner, Metkovich, Murry Dickson, Howie Pollet, Clyde McCullough. Joe Garagiola was someone I liked very much.

He wasn't as bad a hitter as he'd later make himself out to be once he became a television personality. He hit about .275 that year, second on the team to me.

Of course, I spent more time with the young players. There were a lot on the Pirates that year. I probably became closest to Bob Friend. He was a 21-year-old right-handed pitcher from Indiana. He had come up in 1951 and immediately became part of the rotation. He was very intense, and we'd call him ''Nervous-Nervous.'' Bobby would take the ball every fourth day and never missed a turn. He had tough years in the beginning when the Pirates kept losing, as we all did. He went 7–17 in 1952. He took his losses hard, but he didn't have much chance of winning. He was still learning how to pitch, and we were a bad ballclub behind him. Friend, Dickson, and Pollet were good enough to keep us in games, but if we had the tying run on third with nobody out, we couldn't bring him in. It was frustrating for everybody. Ronny Kline went 0–7, so you know how he must have felt. Another pitching prospect, Ron Necciai, who had a tremendous fastball, went 1–6 and never pitched in the majors again.

HAL WOODESHICK (MINOR LEAGUES):

I was on the Giants' Kingsport, Tennessee, team in Class D, and we'd play Bristol, a Pirates' farm team. Ron Necciai pitched for them. He could throw hard. He had a no-hitter in which he struck out 27 batters! I pitched against him and he struck out 24 or 25. That year he jumped from D ball to B ball to the big leagues. He pitched some for the Pirates but failed. The reason he didn't make it was ulcers. Years later, after I had seen all the great major league pitchers, I'd say Necciai was the fastest guy I ever saw. Faster than Herb Score, Sandy Koufax, or Sudden Sam McDowell!

D. GROAT:

After the season ended, I returned to Duke to get the 10 credits I needed for a degree in social studies, political science, and education. Then the Fort Wayne Pistons called and offered me twice the money that I had made as a rookie in the majors. Soon a plane was shuttling me back and forth between my Durham campus and wherever the Pistons played. The Pistons were a pretty good NBA team, with guys like Larry Faust, Freddie Schaus, Don Meineke, Jack Kiley, and Dike Eddleman. We had

a winning record and finished third in the Western Division. I played with them half a season. I loved pro basketball, but I didn't get to play as much I would have liked. I only had one chance to start, against the Knicks, and scored 20 points at the half. Some games I never played a minute. I was in about half the games and averaged over 11 points a game. Bob Cousy was my basketball idol, and I got to play against him twice. He outplayed me the first time, but I got the better of him the other time. I could play. But I would never play in the NBA again.

After I graduated, I had to go into the service immediately, putting my two-sports career on hold. I was gone for two years.

RALPH KINER:

I always lived in the ballpark area. I had married in 1951 and we first lived in a co-op situation, and then moved into an apartment right across the street from Forbes Field. Being a player rep didn't take up too much of my free, family time. The time we devoted was very unorganized and generally consisted of meeting a day or two before meeting with the owners. There was a yearly meeting during the All-Star break and the winter meetings. I didn't think my career was placed in jeopardy because of my involvement with the pension plan. One reason the players wanted guys like me and Allie Reynolds, the American League rep, is that the owners really couldn't put much pressure on us.

I enjoyed rooming with Dick Groat on the road. Dick was a young kid who was scared to death. But he played well. His first game was in the Polo Grounds and he got 2 hits against the Giants. He was a nice, classy, intelligent kid and he listened most of the time, which is why he became good. He worked very hard. I never saw him play basketball. He supposedly invented the jump shot.

Groat was a good addition to our club, but Branch Rickey tried to bring in too many young guys and the results were terrible. We started losing over 100 games a year. I couldn't tell Rickey to get better players because he was too pompous to allow us to talk to him about such matters. I was around him a lot, but it was a one-way deal with him—he was always the speaker. There was no conversation.

The one change Rickey made that met with approval was that the Pirates became the first team to wear batting helmets, in 1952. Unfortunately, he insisted that we wear them all the time, including on the bases and in the field. In the field, it was pretty discouraging.

I don't think there was added pressure every year to continue my home-run title streak. Either that or players lived with pressure better in those days. In 1952 I won my seventh consecutive homer title, tying Hank Sauer with 37 homers. Our last series was in Cincinnati and we were scheduled to play 2 games. I was 1 homer behind Sauer. Rather than taking the train with the rest of the team, I flew to Cincinnati. I paid my own way so I could get a good night's sleep. Before the first game, I got Dick Groat to pitch batting practice to me for about an hour and a half, which he was very happy to do. And I hit a home run that game. On Sunday I didn't hit a homer. We were on the train going back to Pittsburgh and I couldn't get any news about Hank's final game. I didn't know if he had homered and won the title. It was important to me because 7 straight homer titles would break Babe Ruth's record. The train stopped in Indianapolis and I got out and found the stationmaster. Through Western Union, I discovered that Sauer hadn't hit a homer, and we ended up tied. I had broken Ruth's record. So when I got back on the train I ordered champagne for all the players.

I went to Rickey for a raise and he told me that I wouldn't get one because the Pirates could finish last without me. I argued that we drew a million people and many came out to see me. I said, "I don't want to take a 25 percent cut because you didn't put together a decent ballclub that would put us in a pennant race." But he was impossible. I knew he wanted to trade me and get rid of my salary. So I got him to agree to tell any team I was traded to that I was to get an extra $5,000.

FRANK THOMAS:

I went to spring training with Pittsburgh for the third time—and they sent me to New Orleans again. I guess that was good luck in disguise because I had one heck of a year. I hit 35 homers and led the Southern Association in a lot of offensive categories. Pittsburgh brought me up for just a little time. I played only 6 games, but felt that I finally had made the team.

JOHN BERARDINO:

When the Indians dealt me to the Pirates in August, with George Strickland going to Cleveland, it meant that I had the distinction of having played with the Browns twice, Indians twice, and Pirates twice, in the same order each time.

I had left the Pirates in 1950 when they were a last-place club, and if anything, they had gotten worse in my absence. They were still a last-place club, but had a record of 42–112. So it wasn't a happy experience coming back, although I did get to play again with Ralph Kiner, who was still hitting those long homers into Greenberg Gardens. Catcher Joe Garagiola was also a pretty good player and we had a lot of laughs together. On this team, you had to laugh or you would have gone crazy.

I had only one meeting with Branch Rickey. At the end of the season, he told me he wanted me back for the next year. I said I thought I should get a bonus. He said no. That's when I decided to retire.

I wish I could have tried my career over again. I think I could have done better. In those days we didn't train enough during the off-season. You might run, but that was all. Who knows? Maybe I could have stopped myself from being injured.

CINCINNATI REDS

EWELL BLACKWELL:

I could see improvements in the Reds in 1952. Roy McMillan became the regular shortstop, Ted Kluszewski and Ken Raffensberger had much better seasons, left fielder Joe Adcock showed he could become a big hitter—he was tall, muscular, and very strong—and Andy Seminick, who we acquired from the Phillies, was an excellent receiver and solid hitter. He was a tough player, but he was a fun guy off the field. He was bald, so we'd kid him that he had to glue his hat on his head.

I didn't get along with Rogers Hornsby, who replaced Luke Sewell as manager during the season. He was too temperamental. I wouldn't let him get after me. I was having arm problems and didn't pitch while he was manager. I wanted to be traded, and they accommodated me by sending me to the New York Yankees.

My years in Cincinnati had been wonderful. It was a great, friendly town. I even liked pitching in Crosley Field, although it was the smallest park in the league.

ANDY SEMINICK:

I went over to the Reds and had a fairly good year, hitting 14 homers and driving in 50 runs in about 340 at-bats. Cincinnati was a good town to play in, a big country town. There were a lot of restaurants the players went to, like Sam Framo's, where shrimp was the specialty. There wasn't much difference in the way fans in Philadelphia and Cincinnati treated players. They didn't get on anybody like the Phillies fans got on Del Ennis, but they'd razz Herm Wehmeier pretty good because of his wildness.

Luke Sewell was an ex-catcher, so we got along pretty well. But the team did poorly and he was replaced by Rogers Hornsby, who proved to be a bad, unpopular manager. He wasn't great with his moves on the field or with the players off the field. The Browns had fired him.

After 9 years with the Phillies, Andy Seminick would spend 3 years with the Cincinnati Reds before returning to Philadelphia.

Grady Hatton had been with the Reds since the war ended and was a team leader. He was only about 5'9", but he had power and was a hard-nosed, dependable player. He had switched from third to second to make room for Bobby Adams, and it affected his hitting.

Ted Kluszewski was another leader. He was a big, quiet, easygoing guy who could hit like hell. He hit .320 with good power. He was still young, and I expected him to really hit a lot of homers. He didn't get much credit for it, but he was a good first baseman, with good hands.

Joe Adcock was a great guy and more of an extrovert than Kluszewski. We roomed together a lot. He was another player I expected to hit a lot of homers after he gained a little more experience. Unfortunately, the Reds would trade him to the Braves at the end of the year. They should have waited just another year.

One guy the Reds held on to was Roy McMillan. He was a super shortstop, as good as I'd seen. He had great range, great hands, and a great arm. In his first full season, he already led the league's shortstops in assists. And his hitting was improving. He was also a great person. I loved Roy McMillan.

We had a good crew at Cincinnati, but we lacked pitching. Our best pitcher that year was veteran Ken Raffensberger, who threw about 250 innings and won 17 games. He had excellent control and really bore down with men in scoring position. He had one of the best earned run averages in the league. Another left-hander, Harry Perkowski, won 12 games, but Wehmeier and the other starters only had a few wins each.

We had Ewell Blackwell, but this was late in his career and he would be traded near the end of the season. You had to be on your toes to catch him. Blackwell would throw a fastball down the middle, but it would move so much that often it would go out of the strike zone. Or he'd throw a curve that started right toward a right-handed hitter and then would veer across the plate. Batters were nervous facing him. It was kind of funny when my old teammate Willie Jones batted against him. Willie's front leg would be going out more and more with each pitch. He'd always bail out. Most guys bailed out against Ewell. He threw inside and knocked you down. When I was a Phillie, he was the toughest pitcher I faced as a hitter.

Blackwell wasn't alone in the league in knocking

down batters. Lew Burdette was tough. So was Sal Maglie, Mort Cooper, Max Lanier, a lot of guys. There weren't mean pitchers. They all just pitched inside and sometimes would come too far in and knock a batter down. There weren't many pitchers who wanted to hit anyone. If you wanted to hit a batter, all you had to do was pitch at his armpit and it was difficult to get away.

The most successful pitchers threw inside for balls to push the batter off the plate and straighten them up a little bit. Batters expected a pitcher to throw inside. You didn't charge the mound after he did it. If you wanted to get back at him, you could bunt and run at him when he covered first.

AMERICAN LEAGUE 1952

"THEY'D HAVE HIM PAGED AND HE'D COME SLIDING THROUGH THE HOTEL LOBBY. I COULDN'T GO ANYWHERE WITH HIM BECAUSE HE'D STOP A TOTAL STRANGER ON THE STREET AND TELL HIM, 'HEY, YOU HAVE TO MEET MY ROOMMATE FREDDIE HATFIELD. HERE'S A PICTURE OF ME—JIMMY PIERSALL.'"

FRED HATFIELD

PHILADELPHIA ATHLETICS

EDDIE JOOST:
Philadelphia had its last good year, finishing fourth. This was my final year as a full-time player, and I had 20 homers, 26 doubles, and 75 RBIs, good numbers for a leadoff hitter. I knew what a leadoff batter was supposed to do: get on base. And I worked at it. I walked more than 100 times for the sixth straight season. I helped the guys behind me drive in runs. Until he became the batting champion in 1951 and 1952 and his production went down, Ferris Fain would drive in 70 or 80 runs a year. Hank Majeski drove in 120 runs in 1948, Sam Chapman drove in 108 runs in 1949, and Gus Zernial drove in more than 120 runs after coming over to us in 1951 and another 100 runs in 1952.

But the star of our team in 1952 was Bobby Shantz, our 5'6" lefty. Nobody was better than him that year. He missed most of September with a wrist injury, but still won 24 games, had an ERA of less than 2.50, and completed almost every game he started. He had unbelievable stuff: a good, moving fastball and a great curveball that was always around the plate. Later, it was said that Jimmy Dykes overused him, but I don't agree. His arm wasn't hurting and was strong every time he pitched. We watched him warming up to make sure his arm wasn't tired.

JIM FRIDLEY (INDIANS):
The first time I saw Bobby Shantz, I assumed he was the Athletics' batboy. He turned out to be the best left-hander I faced in the major leagues. He had a really good curve and could throw faster than you'd expect. The little guy could get you.

E. JOOST:
Shantz would come to spring training the next year and it wouldn't be there. He would make only 16 starts all season.

GUS ZERNIAL:
Shantz was one of the greatest pitchers I ever played behind. He deservedly was voted the American League's MVP. He didn't have much help in the pitching depart-

ment. He also didn't get much offensive support. I hit 29 homers and had 100 RBIs; Fain led the league again, with a .327 average; and Eddie Joost had a solid season, but that was about it.

Fain hit for a high average, but he didn't drive in many runs. So when I came up, there were always 2 guys on base—2 of our first 3 hitters, Eddie Joost, Ferris Fain, and Dave Philley. That's why I thought that I should have driven in a lot more than 129 runs in 1951 and 100 runs in 1952.

We called Ferris Fain "Burrhead" because of his haircut. He didn't mind that, but too often he thought people made fun of him. He wanted to fight someone all the time. He was fiery in the clubhouse and on the field, and if there was a fight, he was in the middle of it.

JIM FRIDLEY (INDIANS):

Ferris Fain was friends with Joe Tipton, who the Athletics traded to the Indians during the 1952 season. Once, after a game between the two teams, they were socializing. I came over to talk to Tipton, and the next thing you know, Fain wanted to fight me. I was willing, but Tipton held him back. That guy had a short fuse.

G. ZERNIAL:

Fortunately, on our ballclub there were players Fain couldn't challenge: I never had problems with him; Billy Hitchcock was able to take care of himself; Elmer Valo, "the Bull," didn't know how to fight but he kept Fain in line; Hank Majeski was a quiet guy but wouldn't back down to anybody. I liked Fain very much but more as a man's ballplayer than as a friend. It was well known that he had a drinking problem, but I don't think his drinking hurt us or was the reason the Athletics traded him to Chicago after the season for Eddie Robinson. The Athletics preferred Robinson because he could drive in more runs. And the White Sox badly wanted Fain because he was a batting champion and a tremendous fielder. He was the best first baseman at cutting off runners—he'd take a relay and throw out a runner, or on a bunt, he'd throw out the runner at second or third.

ST. LOUIS BROWNS

LES MOSS:

When I came back to the Browns, the team was only slightly better than when I left it. Sherm Lollar was gone, and the starting catcher was Clint Courtney. He would be my roommate for two or three years. He was the first catcher to wear glasses, but no one teased him because he was a tough guy. "Scrap Iron" would fight all the time, though I don't know how many he won. I spent two weeks with him on his place in Coushatta, Louisiana. They kidded about him being a dumb hick, but if you saw his farm you'd see who was dumb. He had cattle and he had hay. He said, "Les, there's 50,000 bales of hay in that barn and I'm going to sell every one for $1 a bale. They'll all be gone this spring."

Bill Veeck had become the owner and general manager of the Browns the previous June, when I was on the Red Sox. He was in a class by himself. If you had a good day, you might find two dozen shirts of the kind he wore in your locker. He would keep me supplied with shirts for three years. He once gave Courtney a pig to put on his farm. Anything for a laugh. Every now and then he'd throw a team party and would start squirting the champagne, and by the time we left, the place would be a mess. Veeck wasn't a tough negotiator, but he wasn't overly generous. He was fair. He paid the same salaries as everyone else. I never turned down a contract with him, as I had with Bill DeWitt.

Probably the most pleasure I got returning to the Browns was playing with Satchel Paige, who was signed by the team in 1951, after his time with Cleveland. He was something else. One time a cop wanted to arrest him in the St. Louis train depot. He knew Paige's face and thought he saw it on a wanted poster instead of the sports pages, and Satch was just leading him on. I had to come up and explain to the cop who he was. The guy was really embarrassed. One time Satch brought a five-pound catfish into the clubhouse and said he caught it. He would never crack a smile, so he could make you believe anything he wanted. But there wasn't a hook mark anywhere, and we knew somebody on the river gave the fish to him. He was a lot of fun and very popular on the team. I talked to him all the time, but he was a loner. Bill Veeck bought Satchel a chair and set it out in the bullpen. He was proud of the chair and wandered down to the pen in the third or fourth inning, sat in it for a while, and then returned to the dugout.

Satch was all business on days he pitched, not showing any emotion on the mound and being very quiet in the dugout. He was about 46 or 47 and no longer had much of a curve, but he could still throw his fastball in the high 80s and put it right where he wanted. He was easy to work with because he'd throw 8 or 9 fastballs out of every 10 pitches and just 1 or 2 little curves or sliders. He didn't throw junk.

JOHNNY SAIN (YANKEES):
One of my favorite pitchers was Satchel Paige. He was one of the few power pitchers who could also be a finesse pitcher. I pinch-hit for a pitcher against the Browns, and the St. Louis hurler got 3 straight balls on me. Then he was relieved by Paige. On the first pitch he spun a little curve over for strike one. I was taking. Then he threw a little-better breaking ball. I didn't swing. Strike two. Now, here's a guy who can do anything he wants to, so I didn't know what to expect. His third pitch was a great curveball that came in at throat level and dropped across the plate. I swung and missed. Strike three. That was one of only 20 times I struck out in my career in 774 at-bats, and the only one I didn't mind. I was a breaking-ball pitcher, yet he struck me out with breaking balls. Three different breaking balls. That meant a lot to me.

JOE DE MAESTRI:
During the winter I was included in an 8-player deal with the St. Louis Browns that sent Sherm Lollar to the White Sox. I was disappointed, but I looked forward to playing for Bill Veeck because I knew how much the players had liked and respected him when he owned Cleveland. He was such a class guy and made everyone on the Browns feel like he was an important member of the team. However, during the year he sat in his box and didn't visit the clubhouse much or travel with the team.

Unfortunately, Rogers Hornsby was our manager. He was the worst manager and worst person I ever played for. Everyone hated him.

RALPH KINER (PIRATES):
I heard that one of the reasons Rogers Hornsby was despised by the Browns was that he would climb on the bus and order the driver to leave before some of the players got there.

J. DE MAESTRI:
The only time that I saw Satchel Paige upset was when Hornsby got after him in spring training in Burbank. Hornsby didn't like Satch, and I think it was simply because he was black. One day Hornsby was holding a meeting before workouts and Satch got there late. Satch had to walk from the clubhouse, which was on the other side of the field, and he was unable to sneak to his seat. Hornsby sees him and says, "You're fined $200." Satch says, "No I'm not." Hornsby repeats, "You're fined $200." Satch repeats, "No I'm not." Hornsby says, "You can go change. You're fined $200." This prompts Satch to say, "Well, I'm going to call Mr. Veeck." Of course, there was no $200 fine.

Hornsby came from the old school. He had two pets on the team, my friends Clint Courtney and Jim Rivera, who came over with me from the White Sox in November, after having led the Pacific Coast League in batting at Seattle. Hornsby even stated in the newspaper that they were the only two guys he'd ever pay to see play ball.

Rivera was a left-handed batter who could run and was as strong as a bull. He always slid in headfirst and was covered with bruises on his face and head at the end of the year. Hornsby loved that brand of baseball. He liked that Courtney got into a lot of fights. "Scrap Iron" was always in fights with players on the Yankees, whose chain he'd been in. He had some terrible fights with Billy Martin over the years. (They'd start a brawl in 1953, after Courtney slid into Martin's pal Phil Rizzuto with his spikes high.) We liked Courtney off the field, but to be honest, not too many guys from our side went out to help him when he starting punching somebody. We felt that he started it, so he could finish it.

I thought I'd have a better chance to play regularly than in Chicago. But after a year as the Cardinals' manager, Marty Marion had moved to the Browns to play short and I didn't play much. Marty was a different kind of shortstop. He was about 6'3", with long, long arms, and he played the position like a spider, drifting from side to side. We got along fine, but I couldn't learn much from watching him play and he didn't really take the time to teach me anything.

The best thing that happened was Bill Veeck coming down in the elevator one day and saying, "Well, I just fired Hornsby. Marty is your new manager." We celebrated as if we had just won the World Series. Everybody was really sick of Hornsby.

However, the team didn't really relax under Marion. When Marty took over as manager, he split away from the team as a player and as a friend. He really started laying down the law on everybody. I know he and second baseman Bobby Young were very close friends, but after Marty became manager, they weren't friendly. It was odd.

When Marty took over in Boston, he held a meeting before the next game started, and said, "Anybody that goes 4 for 4 tonight doesn't have to go to Dayton for tomorrow's exhibition game. He can just go right home to St. Louis." Wouldn't you know it? I had 2 singles, a double, and a triple—4 for 4, and we won the ball game. But I was stuck playing in Dayton the next night. That showed how much I could trust Marty's word. At least when Marty became player-manager, I got more playing time. It was like going back to school.

I vaguely remember rooming on the road with Bobby Young and outfielder Jimmy Delsing. When we had an off-day we'd usually go to movies, maybe seeing two or three a day just to kill the time. But in general, the players didn't hang around together as much as on other teams I played on. If the guys were depressed, it was just because we had trouble with our managers and had a hard time winning. We did finish about 15 games ahead of the last-place Tigers, but we ended up about 25 games under .500. I'm sure that some guys were discouraged by all our losses. And there were days that I got discouraged. But I think most of us enjoyed that year. Nobody was making money, and all we thought about was going out and doing the best we could.

That summer it was scorching and some days it was too hot to play ball. At night my wife and I had to soak the sheets in cold water, or it would have been impossible to sleep. We lived way out in Ferguson. We rented Sherm Lollar's house, which he didn't need during the summer since he had been traded to the White Sox. St. Louis wasn't as exciting as Chicago and we wouldn't go into the city, except to see an occasional show.

There was no rivalry with the Cardinals because we couldn't compare to them. We were a bad team and they were a pennant contender. There was no jealousy. We didn't pay any attention to them, and I'm sure they didn't pay any attention to us. They got more media coverage, but they didn't get so much either. If you had a good day, you got a write-up on it. If you didn't, they ignored you.

Satchel Paige was a classic. I never did find out how old that man was, but I used to try. Everybody tried. Satch and Clint Courtney were great friends. They would give each other a bad time. They argued all the time, but they were friendly arguments. One time Satch told Clint he should throw out more baserunners. He said he could throw out a runner at second base from his haunches. So before a game Satch put on all the catching gear and demonstrated while one of us ran to second base on a pitch. Satch took the pitch and threw the guy out without moving at all. Oh, he had a great arm! He never let the trainer touch his arm. He would put it under scalding-hot water every day. You could actually see it get red, and that's pretty hard considering he was a black man. Then he'd towel himself off and that would be it.

DON NEWCOMBE (DODGERS):
I played against Satchel Paige and talked to him many times about why he didn't get sore arms. I was concerned because my arm was long and skinny like Satchel's. He told me that all you do is rub in some snake-oil liniment and pour hot water over the arm. He gave me a bottle of his snake oil in 1949 or 1950 in Miami.

J. DE MAESTRI:
Satchel went his own way because he lived in a different area and had his girlfriends pick him up after games. During games, he'd be rocking in his chair. It had a little sun visor on it and he'd sit there basking in the sun. A couple of gals would sneak him some libation in perfume bottles. When he thought no one was watching, Satch would tilt back his head a little and take a swig.

Sometimes Satch seemed to be in a different world from the rest of us. I think that was an accurate way to describe him. But I'm sure he was still serious about his pitching. He was the only guy I ever saw who needed only 3 or 4 warm-up pitches. And he never threw them hard; he just moved his arm a little bit. It worked because he was one of our best pitchers that year, starting and relieving. In fact, his 12 wins tied him for the team lead with Bob Cain.

BOB CAIN:

On Valentine's Day in 1952, I got a call from Bill Veeck, who said he had just traded 3 Browns to the Tigers for Gene Bearden, Dick Kryhoski, and me. He asked me why I hadn't signed my contract with Detroit. I told him about the low Tigers' offer and then he asked what I thought I should be getting. I told him, and he said, "Come to St. Louis and sign your contract for that amount." So getting traded from a team that had finished fifth to one that had finished eighth was not upsetting. It was especially gratifying when we beat the Tigers out for seventh place in 1952.

Bill Veeck was one of the nicest, most honest men in baseball, a great guy to play for. For instance, one day we beat Cleveland, and the next day every player—whether he had been in that game or not—looked into his locker and found a miniature hat containing a $25 gift certificate from a downtown department store. At other times he might give you a dozen sports shirts with his picture on the labels. Veeck promised me a new suit if I could beat the Yankees one game. We were leading by a couple of runs late in the game, and I figured I had the suit won. Then Gene Woodling homered to right to beat me.

Rogers Hornsby would always sit in the lobby reading or pretending to read the paper. We couldn't figure out why Bill Veeck would have him as a manager. He was no manager. He was pretty unapproachable. He didn't care that he was disliked. He had his favorites, like Clint Courtney. Hornsby did a lot of betting on the horses, and when we'd go into Washington he'd send Courtney out to the track with his bets—during the game!

Courtney liked to block the plate on close plays and to throw hard. I'd always get on him because if I didn't have my real good control, he'd just blister the ball back to me. The area around the bone on my glove hand would puff up. One game, with a runner on base, he got

A year after pitching against the St. Louis Browns in the historic Eddie Gaedel game, former Tiger Bob Cain tied Satchel Paige for the most wins on the Browns.

provoked by me and fired the ball back to the mound. I stepped aside and the ball went into center field, allowing the runner to advance. The manager got us together and we gave our explanations. After that, Courtney would throw the ball back a little softer. I wasn't going to put up with that, even if we were friends.

Hornsby also took good care of Jim Rivera. He may have been instrumental in getting Rivera out of an Atlanta prison and into baseball. Rivera was almost 30 when he was a rookie center fielder with St. Louis in 1952. He was a good, hustling ballplayer, but he always got himself into trouble. Away from the ballpark, players pretty much stayed away from him. One reason is that we knew he had been charged with rape in the army, although he claimed it was a phony charge and would be cleared at the end of the year. Rivera didn't associate with the best people in St. Louis, and Hornsby asked a few of us to take him home a few times and away from gambler types. He was on his last legs in St. Louis. Rivera had quite a temper and one time beat up his wife pretty badly. Either she wanted to leave him or he wanted to leave her. This took place in our hotel, and they called for my wife. She went to see Rivera's wife and she was beaten to a pulp. My wife called Bill Veeck, and Bill told her to take Rivera's wife to the hospital and to a certain doctor, and to keep what happened quiet. At the end of July, Veeck traded Rivera to the Chicago White Sox. I think he calmed down over there.

By that time Hornsby had been fired and replaced by Marty Marion. Ned Garver, who was the Browns' best pitcher, and some of the other players had gone to Veeck with complaints against Hornsby, which led to his firing. Veeck sent in many cases of beer to celebrate the firing.

I'd like people to remember how I pitched against Bob Feller. It was a good rivalry from my point of view because I lived in Cleveland and knew Feller pretty well. Being able to pitch against someone I knew would be a Hall of Famer gave me inspiration. He was a real competitor who fought for everything that he got. He had that great fastball, but he also had as good a curveball as anyone in the league—although the reporters didn't write about it nearly as much. On April 23 I got halfway even with Feller for having thrown a no-hitter against me in 1951. It was 40 degrees in St. Louis, and batters were at a decided disadvantage. I pitched my best game, giving up only a fifth-inning single to Luke Easter. There were no hard-hit balls. Feller gave up only a first-inning triple to Bobby Young, the leadoff hitter. Young was a left-handed batter, and the ball curved over the head of Jim Fridley in left. If he'd had more experience, Fridley might have caught it. Young then came home when Al Rosen mishandled Marty Marion's grounder and had to throw to first for the sure out. That was the only run of the game. This was the first time in the American League that both pitchers threw one-hitters. This was the only one of Feller's 12 one-hitters that he lost. I even had more strikeouts than him that game. I struck out the first 3 batters, 1 in the middle of the game, and the last 3 batters, the last being Harry Simpson.

It was strange pitching in Sportsman's Park. If it weren't for the ushers, players' wives, and pigeons, it might have been completely empty during our games. I also wasn't crazy about the short fence in right. Still, I had my best year in the majors, going 12–10. Tommy Byrne, the former Yankee, and I formed a good left-handed duo. He could throw hard. Whew! But he was wilder than a March hare. He come around from the side and there weren't too many hitters who dug in on him. Byrne was also one of the best-hitting pitchers. I saw that he had a few good years left and thought the Browns made a mistake by trading him after the season.

CLEVELAND INDIANS

JOHN BERARDINO:
Before finishing both the season and my career with the Pirates, I had returned to the Indians after almost two years. The Indians were still pennant contenders, since Wynn, Garcia, and Lemon were each winning 20 games a season. But Al Lopez had replaced Lou Boudreau as the manager and third baseman Al Rosen had emerged as the leader of the team. Rosen led a very strong offense. He, second baseman Bobby Avila, and left fielder Dale Mitchell hit over .300. And with Rosen, Larry Doby, and Luke Easter, the Indians had 3 men at the heart of the order who could hit 30 homers and drive in over 100 runs. Rosen led the league in RBIs, and Doby led the league in homers. Easter was a dangerous hitter who hit some mammoth homers and knocked in a whole lot of runs—which is why he got knocked down a lot. He was a good-natured guy, full of laughs all the time.

EDDIE JOOST (ATHLETICS):
Luke Easter, the Indians' first baseman, was a great homer hitter, but he couldn't get out of his own way running. When he ran to second he wouldn't slide. He would wave his hands, and shortstops would have to throw around him. Once when I had reached first I told him that the next time he ran toward second waving his hands, I would throw the ball directly at his mouth. He said, "I hear you, boy." Three innings later he runs toward second. You've never seen such a hook slide, halfway between first and second.

J. BERARDINO:
My second stay with the Indians was brief and didn't include much playing time. It ended in August when I was traded to Pittsburgh.

JIM FRIDLEY:
I was invited to my second Indians training camp and I had a terrific spring in the Grapefruit League, batting .346 and hitting 7 or 8 homers. But I still didn't know if I'd made the Indians because the competition was so strong—the Indians had a really good team. But I beat out Dale Mitchell and was named the Opening Day left fielder against the White Sox in Chicago. That was a memorable day because my first hit was a homer that won the game, 1–0. It came in the middle innings on a high fastball by Joe Dobson and gave Bob Lemon the victory. That night Lemon took me to the fights and I saw Sugar Ray Robinson defeat Rocky Graziano.

I had one game that equaled that. I had the best day of my career on April 29 when I went 6 for 6 in Philadelphia. I later learned that was a rookie record for a 9-inning ballgame. I shared the spotlight with Al Rosen, who hit 3 homers in that game.

The Indians were a unified team, not cliquish. We ate together: steaks, spaghetti. I'd go to bed late and sleep late. But I rarely went to the movies or nightclubs, though I did see Don Cherry perform and saw Louis Armstrong in Boston. Luke Easter and Larry Doby both knew Louis Armstrong, so they introduced me to him and I got his autograph. That was a big thrill.

Easter was a big, strong happy guy, the kind of guy you wanted on a ballclub. I liked him very much. Doby was a lot quieter than Easter. He was shy and a good man. He could have been a better ballplayer, but when he got into a batting slump it would always show in the field.

Al Rosen was the team's best hitter and the leader of the team, someone the players looked up to. He was a great competitor and an emotional player. He was probably too emotional at times. He had a bad temper and got into it with some of his own players, like Easter and Doby. If Rosen would throw the ball in the dirt, he'd get mad when Easter wouldn't dig it up and Al would be charged with an error. He'd yell at Easter because he felt he had to throw strikes for him to catch it. Easter didn't take kindly to that.

Rosen did some nice things for me. If there was an autograph session at a store or some other place, Rosen didn't care about it, so he'd arrange for me to go instead so I could pick up an extra $50 or so. People thought I looked like Rosen, so when I'd leave the ballpark or walk down the street, fans would wave to me or congratulate me. And I'd say thanks.

I remember Rosen's helping me prepare to face the Yankees for the first time. He told me to watch out for Allie Reynolds, who he said was a great pitcher. I'd already batted against the White Sox and thought Billy Pierce was really fast and wondered if I needed any preparation. I was scared about what Rosen said and thought Reynolds would overmatch me with his fastballs. So I came up to the plate and dug in. I was surprised when Reynolds threw me 2 quick curves for strikes. So I said to myself, "This guy's a shitballer," which is what we called guys who threw curveballs and junk. So I spread out and relaxed and waited for another slow curve. Whereupon Reynolds threw a fastball right by my jaw. I could feel the wind. It knocked me down. Yogi Berra was the catcher and he told me, "You gotta quit guessing."

There were a lot of guys on the team I got along with. Early Wynn was my roommate and we got along well. I liked Bobby Avila, one of the class players on the team. I liked Easter and Doby. Harry Simpson was like me, quiet and just glad to be there. Much was anticipated of him because he'd torn the cover off the ball at San Diego, but he didn't live up to his potential. I think someone fooled with his batting stance, too. Dale Mitchell was an A-1 guy. Our competition for left field didn't bother either of us. We were friends. Mitchell thought his own talents had diminished and he might have slowed down. Ray Boone was an ideal, cheerful teammate. Ray would become a fine third baseman, but he wasn't mobile enough to play short and couldn't turn the double play, which was one of the reasons we didn't win the pennant.

My best friend was Bob Chakales, a pitcher. He couldn't break into the Indians' rotation and became rusty, wild, and frustrated. It got to a point where his mother questioned Hank Greenberg about why he didn't trade him. Greenberg told her no one wanted him, and he wasted his prime years with the Indians. Bob wanted to quit.

I think the best staff in baseball was the Yankees' Reynolds, Raschi, Ford, and Lopat, but Lemon, Wynn, and Garcia could compete. A major mistake Al Lopez made was to juggle his pitching rotation to make sure Lemon, Wynn, and Garcia would face the Yankees. By doing this he messed up the rotation so that we'd lose to Philadelphia and Washington because everything was out of whack.

Bob Feller had passed his prime by this point and was relying more on his breaking pitches. He told me, "I wish you could have seen me when I used to get 2 strikes on a batter and he'd just turn and want to go back to the dugout."

If I had to pick one pitcher from our staff for one game, I would have picked Lemon. And Al Lopez would have agreed. He had a hard slider and a fastball and was extremely confident and imposing. Plus he was a great hitter, even better than Wynn. He hit 7 homers one year.

Mike Garcia threw a heavy sinker that broke bats. He was sneaky-fast. It didn't look that hard from the dugout, but right when it would cross the plate it would pick up speed. Although Lemon and Wynn had mean reputations, Garcia could match them when he had that ball in his hand, although he was a nice guy.

Wynn was more of a finesse pitcher than Lemon, changing speeds and throwing an occasional knuckler. He threw inside. He and Virgil Trucks were the two pitchers I saw who thought everything they threw was a strike. They'd bitch at umpires.

Not all umpires responded well to complaints. Bill McGowan would turn against the pitcher if he bitched or showed him up. He'd call the next pitch a ball even if it was right down the middle of the plate. McGowan would occasionally tell batters he was calling them close, so we should swing if it was near the strike zone—the strike zone was bigger in those days. He didn't like calling a game pitched by Cubans because they were too deliberate and took too long. He had bad legs and feet, so he hated pitchers he thought "were fooling around on the mound." McGowan didn't like Cubans or black players. I remember McGowan kicking out Luke Easter for no real reason, after Easter disputed a low pitch he called a strike. Then I came up and said I thought that Easter had a point, and McGowan got furious and called me a "busher," and told me off. I didn't

Once the only boy who could throw a rock over a river in Philippi, West Virginia, "Big Jim" Fridley made it to the majors at the age of 27 for a season with the Cleveland Indians.

argue with him, and for some reason McGowan always liked me after that.

The only umpire I had disputes with was Ed Hurley. One time the bases were loaded and I had a 3–2 count and he called a third strike on a pitch that was an inch off the ground. I got furious, and Al Lopez came out and argued and was kicked out of the game.

Lopez didn't always take my side. If you did something wrong with him, he made you pay. I remember being on first and Early Wynn was on second. There was a base hit and I slid into third, thinking Wynn had scored. But Wynn was standing there. Lopez didn't say a word; he didn't have to. I knew what to expect from him. He sat me down and I got splinters in my rear end because I was there for so long. Dale Mitchell got his left-field position back then. What eventually happened was that Mitchell also made a base-running blunder, and Lopez benched him and put me back in left.

The only really bad thing Lopez did to me was put me in the outfield one game although he knew my arm was hurting. I couldn't even throw. Luckily Bob Lemon was pitching and there were no balls pulled to left. I had hurt my arm playing pickup basketball in Dayton and then hurt it again playing basketball against players from the Cleveland Browns. I was hit and knocked over by Marion Motley, the big fullback, and my arm felt dead. I developed calcium deposits. The Indians paid for my operation, but Hank Greenberg was really mad at me. He suggested I choose between baseball and basketball. Once I recovered from the arm injury, I could throw as well as I ever could and could play the outfield. But by that time I had the reputation for having a bad arm. I think that eventually got me demoted and traded to Baltimore. But I also might have been traded for the way I hurt my arm, which didn't suit Greenberg.

AL SMITH:

After a year and a half at Wilkes-Barre, a year at San Diego in the Pacific Coast League, and two years in the army at Fort Leavenworth, Missouri, I attended my first spring training with the Indians. I was glad to see Harry Simpson. In 1949, when I was no longer the only black in the Eastern League, Harry played with me on Wilkes-Barre and led the league in homers and RBIs. In 1951 he had become a starting outfielder with the Indians.

I was hopeful about making the Indians, but Al Lopez wouldn't play me. I assume he knew who I was, but we didn't talk. He didn't give any encouragement to young players or talk about the Indians' tradition or way of doing things. He was a quiet guy whose attitude was that you had to show him what you could do. But he didn't give me a fair shot to show him anything.

So I was sent to Indianapolis in the American Association. I was moved from shortstop to third base and had a helluva year. I thought I should have been brought up. But after the minor league season I went home.

BOSTON RED SOX

FRED HATFIELD:

During the off-season, my wife and I lived in Birmingham, where I had my best minor league seasons. From 1946 through 1950 I was attending Birmingham South-

ern each winter to earn credits for a physical education degree because I wanted to coach after my baseball career was over. (I'd finally get my degree in 1957.) After the 1951 season I worked as a salesman at a clothing store and officiated basketball in the Southeastern Conference. The Barons drew over 400,000 fans in 1949–1950, when I had big years, so the clothing store used my name for promotion. They would have given me the store if I quit baseball.

After the winter I reported to spring training. I looked around at the competition and saw that I could be the team's starting third baseman. Vern Stephens had played there a lot in 1951, but he was really a shortstop. Anyway, they were cutting back on his playing time. I played hard and realized I was going to get a lot of playing time from our new manager, Lou Boudreau.

Jimmy Piersall was brought up to play shortstop because both Stephens and Johnny Pesky had slowed down. He was a local favorite from nearby Waterbury, Connecticut. Unfortunately, they put him in a room with me. They'd have him paged and he'd come sliding through the hotel lobby. I couldn't go anywhere with him because he'd stop a total stranger on the street and tell him, "Hey, you have to meet my roommate Freddie Hatfield. Here's a picture of me—I'm Jimmy Piersall." I liked him but I said, "I'm not going to room with a crazy man. I'll pay the difference." We stayed at the Del Padre Hotel on Chicago's South Side and I shot pool with him, just so I could get his money. He was very emotional and would explode really easily. In those days, we didn't think about psychiatrists; we just thought he was nuts. I'd stay away from him after a ballgame. I don't think many guys would go out with him.

Jimmy believed in himself. He wasn't even intimidated by Ted Williams. Of course, Ted and Jimmy didn't play much together that year because Ted went back into the service. He left in April, which made us feel gloomy about our pennant chances.

JOHNNY SAIN (YANKEES):

During the war, Ted Williams and I received our commissions in the naval aviator program in Chapel Hill, North Carolina, qualifying us for active duty. At that time we were given a choice of going into the navy or the Marines, which was run by the Navy Department. They had us move to one line or the other. That's when I chose the navy and Ted chose the Marines. After World War II was over, the navy had so many reserve pilots I was able to get completely out of the reserves. But Ted had to go to Korea in 1952.

RALPH KINER (PIRATES):

I'm not positive about this, but I believe Williams got trapped. He was asked to join the Marines as a promotional gimmick and later on he had to fly combat missions in the Korean War. At one time he had to crash his plane, so that decision almost cost him his life, much less his baseball career.

F. HATFIELD:

There weren't any black players on the Red Sox. But I doubt it was because the Boston management was deliberately avoiding signing them. I think they just didn't find a black player who would help the team. I don't know if I resented it or not, but I thought the praise for black players was blown out of proportion. They all weren't that great. There were a lot of white players who were just as good as they were. I had seen that Willie Mays was a great athlete, so I didn't have to read the paper to see how great an athlete he was. As far as Satchel Paige goes, there's no way of knowing. All he did was throw hard and throw a slider. I don't know if he could pitch in the big leagues or not. I resented a lot of the publicity they got just because they were black. I thought it was overplayed. If you knocked down white guys, nothing was said. A black guy gets knocked down and it was racial prejudice. He's not a baseball player, he's a black guy. I thought it was a compliment to get knocked down. At least they had respect for you. Luke Easter wasn't thrown at because he was black—he was thrown at because he was a good hitter and was hurting you. When the blacks and Latins came along, they thought you were picking on them when all you were doing was seeing if they could be intimidated and what they were made of.

The Boston front office had always been fair to me. I hadn't had any hassles with them. When I came up at the end of the 1950 season and lost out on minor league playoff money, Joe Cronin took that into consideration and gave me $6,000 instead of the $5,000 major league minimum. So I liked him for that. And I liked that he gave me the potential to make an extra $2,000 if I

played regularly for the Red Sox. But just when I was hitting .320 and playing every day, Cronin traded me in one of the first big trades, a 9-player deal with the Tigers. Walt Dropo, Johnny Pesky, Don Lenhardt, Bill Wight, and I were traded for George Kell, Hoot Evers, Dizzy Trout, and Johnny Lipon. I went from a first-place club to a last-place club. So I was really disappointed and would always play my best against the Red Sox. At least they gave us the courtesy of calling us into the office to tell us of the trade. Cronin was under the impression that Kell would help Boston, and me being a third baseman, too, I was thrown into the deal.

GEORGE KELL:

Detroit had been my second home, but I looked forward to playing in Boston. I believed I could hit the wall in Fenway Park any time I wanted to. I couldn't, but I had another .300 year. Johnny Lipon, who had come over with me in the trade, played beside me at short, with Billy Goodman at second and Dick Gernert at first. I was glad Hoot Evers was still with me. He had a good year playing left field. The Red Sox had wanted him because Ted Williams was in Korea. Williams's absence really hurt the team, and we ended up in sixth place despite having several good players.

Lou Boudreau was a good manager for us veterans. He got along with guys who could execute real well and play like he could. However, he'd get exasperated with the younger ballplayers. I remember one game in Chicago when Jimmy Piersall got his goat. Boudreau loved to win in Chicago because that was his hometown. We'd won the first game of a doubleheader and he wanted that second game so bad. It came down to the ninth inning and we were ahead by one run. He inserted Piersall in right because he was truly an outstanding defensive player. The White Sox loaded the bases with 2 out in the ninth, and the last guy lifted a high fly to right. It should have been a routine play, but Piersall ran back about 10 steps, stopped, and sped in and caught it right above his knees and kept running right into the dugout. Boudreau called Jimmy into his office and let him have it. Piersall said, "Hell, I had it all the way, Skip."

Jimmy was a showman. He'd do things nobody else would and then laugh about it. A lot of players used to rag him and encourage him to do wild things, and when he had his breakdown everybody felt bad. I couldn't really see his breakdown coming. I witnessed it. He ran to the screen when fans were riding him. He grabbed the screen and had to be pulled away. It was really sad.

HERSHELL FREEMAN:

In 1948 I had been pitching for the University of Alabama when I got the urge to play pro ball. It turned out that a Red Sox scout named George Digby had been following me since I'd played semipro ball for the Goodyear Tire Company in my hometown of Gadsden, Alabama. He signed me to a minor league contract for $250 a month and a $500 signing bonus, and I began my career in Natchez, Mississippi, in the Cotton States League, which was Class C. As I moved up in the system, people would ask me if I was Jewish because of my name. Actually, my mother was Irish and my dad's great-great-grandmother was a full-blooded Cherokee.

In the minors I learned two essential things: to control my temper and to be a relief pitcher. When I entered professional baseball I'd hit my best friend if I got mad. I knew that I had to control my temper by my second year or I'd be labeled a troublemaker and not get anywhere in baseball. So I did, and everyone began to think of me as easygoing, which was a good thing to be for someone my size. I didn't really pitch in relief until I played for Red Marion at Birmingham in 1950 and was in about 80 games, counting playoffs. I had the live arm, and when I proved I could relieve, that sent my career into high gear. In 1952 I went to spring training with Boston.

I first met Ted Williams in spring training. He played only a couple of weeks before going into the service at the end of April. A day was held for him then, and in his last at-bat he hit a homer against Dizzy Trout to beat the Tigers. I was in awe of him, but I was never scared of him. We would fish together. I think he was the most misunderstood baseball player by the sportswriters. He wasn't self-centered at all but a tremendous team player. He would take up for us bush rookies. Here I am sitting in the clubhouse with 32 sportswriters breathing down my neck, and Ted comes over and says, "Hey, why don't you guys come over here and pick on me and let the kid alone." I admired him for this.

I knew Walt Dropo from when we played at Birmingham. He was just a big, strong, good-natured soul. In the minors, Dropo hit homers that may still be in orbit. We had a clothier in Birmingham that gave new suits for home runs and outstanding pitching performances. At one time Walt Dropo was the best-dressed man in the country. He hit 25 to 30 homers, so right there he got 25 to 30 suits.

Outfielder Faye Throneberry was a good ol' country boy from the hills of Tennessee. He was the older brother of Marv Throneberry, who would move up in the Yankees' chain as a top prospect. Both brothers loved to play baseball but didn't have too many skills. Faye could hit the ball, but he wasn't the greatest outfielder in the world. He was one of the nicest guys you ever wanted to be around. He wasn't funny, but we'd laugh at what he said. To him it might be a serious remark, but everyone would crack up. Like, "It was just a fly ball that I missed."

Billy Goodman was another good ol' country boy, from North Carolina. He was a good all-around player who played almost every position, but he just loved to hit. He was an outstanding left-handed singles and doubles hitter. You could count on him to hit .300.

Jimmy Piersall was a fellow rookie. We had become very close at Birmingham, where he hit way over .300. Our wives also became good friends. Jimmy and I ran around together on the road. Jimmy was always, as we'd say back then, "up-and-going." I could calm him down just by talking to him. And Mary, his wife, was a very strong influence. But the pressure got to Jimmy later. At spring training, the Red Sox started experimenting with him at shortstop although he was a natural outfielder. I think that with all the other troubles in his life, he wasn't able to handle the extra pressure of playing a new position. He tried so darn hard to be a shortstop that something had to snap, and later in the season it did and he had a nervous breakdown. When that happened I was pitching for Louisville. I was sorry that I wasn't around to see if there was anything I could do. I was somewhat surprised by Piersall's breakdown, but on the other hand I wasn't once I thought about it—he was so hyper. We'd all sit down to eat steaks, and Jimmy could finish two before we ate one because he was always going at a faster pace. You figured something had to give. I was surprised at how serious it was. I thought he might have a nervous breakdown and be back after two to three months in the asylum, but it almost killed him.

Jimmy blamed his father for his condition. I had met his father and I didn't think he expected any more of Jimmy than my parents did of me. However, he was the type who'd say, "You did so-and-so wrong. Don't do it again." The trouble is that every ballplayer will make the same mistake over and over until it dawns on him how to correct it. If you make a mistake and someone insists that you don't do it again, that adds extra pressure and you'll make the same mistake trying not to. My dad never told me that I did bad. He said, "Son, you can do better," but he never made it a point that it was life and death.

At the end of 1952 the Red Sox called me up from Louisville, where I had pitched before 2,000 to 4,000 fans each game. I joined the team in Cleveland, and when I came in to relieve the first day, there were 80,000 people in the stands. It was a good way to grow

up in a hurry. I was scared debuting in front of so many people against Al Rosen and that great Indians lineup. But I said, "What the heck—they either hit me or they don't." I figured I'd control my fear instead of letting it control me, which was pretty much my pitching philosophy. I thought I was ready for the big leagues. I knew what I was capable of doing and felt I was as good as anyone. Soon I got the first of the 3 major league starts I would have in my career, all with Boston. It was against Washington, and I came away with a victory. I thought I'd died and gone to heaven.

WASHINGTON SENATORS

PEDRO RAMOS:
I was born in Pinar del Rio, Cuba, in 1935. My father was the foreman in a tobacco field and later opened a handmade cigar factory. In high school I played baseball and was on the track team. When I was 17, in 1952, Billy Herman, who was in the Dodgers' organization, wanted to sign me, but I signed with Joe Cambria. He worked for the Washington Senators in Havana and had signed other Cuban pitchers. Cambria came to my hometown and offered me big money: $150 a month. I took it because all I wanted to do was play baseball. (If I had a chance to do it over again, I would have gotten a better education.)

DETROIT TIGERS

GEORGE KELL:
The Tigers had finished fifth in 1951 and were heading for a last-place finish in 1952, so the organization—Walter Briggs had died in January and was succeeded by his son as president—decided to make some major changes. I would have liked to have played for Fred Hutchinson once he replaced Red Rolfe as the Tigers' manager at mid-season. But by that time my wonderful period in Detroit had ended. On June 3 I was traded along with Hoot Evers, Johnny Lipon, and Dizzy Trout to the Red Sox for third baseman Fred Hatfield, Walt Dropo, and 3 other players.

Having played with the Tigers since 1946, I would find it strange to play against them. I particularly re-

Hershell Freeman began his major league career with the Boston Red Sox in 1952 but wouldn't have much success until he became a relief pitcher for the Cincinnati Reds in 1955.

member when I faced Art Houtteman for the first time. I knew him so well, having watched him since he was a rookie. I knew that he was stubborn enough to test his fastball against me although I was a good fastball hitter. So on the first pitch, I guessed correctly that he'd challenge me with his best fastball down the middle. I jumped all over it and drilled it for a double off the wall. As I glided into second, Art looked at me and said, "You really can hit a fastball, Cap'n."

FRED HATFIELD:

It wasn't easy to follow a legend at third base, but I was happy to finally get a chance to play regularly at Detroit. I hit only in the .230s, but I did lead the league's third basemen in assists and fielding percentage. Coming to the last-place Tigers from Boston, I noticed the difference in attitude. After the game was over, I looked around and the only people in the Tigers' clubhouse were those of us who had just been traded from Boston. We hadn't even completed our showers and the rest of the players were on the bus, hollering, "Let's go to town!" They had developed a defeatist attitude. When you start winning it's catching, and the same goes for losing. It's easy to lose: just go through the motions. The Tigers had pride, but it was evident much more when they played at home. The Tigers were even worse than the St. Louis Browns that year, but the Detroit fans still loved us.

There wasn't much for them to cheer about except for Virgil Trucks and Walt Dropo. Trucks won only 5 games all year, yet he no-hit Washington before I came to Detroit, and then in August no-hit the Yankees, also by the score of 1–0. Early in the Yankee game, Phil Rizzuto beat out a grounder to Pesky at short that was scored an error, then a hit, and finally an error when Pesky told the scorer it was his fault that the ball got stuck in his glove. Our other highlight came in July when Dropo tied Pinky Higgins's major league record by getting 12 straight hits, 5 against New York and 7 against Washington in a doubleheader. It was uncanny. Walt was the only power hitter the Tigers had after trading Vic Wertz to the Browns in mid-season. He hit 22 or 23 homers.

When Walt and I got to Detroit, Red Rolfe was the manager, although he would last only about another month. He liked me because I would put my body on the line for the club. He saw that I never got out of the way of a right-hander's curveball unless it was at my head. I just turned in to the catcher to make it look like I was trying to avoid the ball, and let it hit my leg or back. I think Rolfe would have let me play for him forever because it was obvious I'd do anything to get on base. Rolfe liked that no pitcher intimidated me, and that if one knocked me down, I'd try to step on him if he covered first when I grounded out. I would have cut him. As we said, "Payback is hell." Everybody had a little elephant in him. You pay him back, even if it takes a year. I didn't have feuds with any individual—unless if there was a pitcher who had the reputation of throwing at you, you usually hated his whole club.

COOT VEAL:

My name was Inman, but the coach at Lanier High School—the only white high school in Macon, Georgia—nicknamed me "Kook" after a third baseman on a black team that barnstormed through the area. When I went to Auburn, everyone thought "Kook" was "Coot" and started calling me that. I was scouted through high school and college by Bill Pierre, who worked for the Tigers. He was an older fellow, a real nice, well-dressed father figure. He finally got tired of following me and said, "Coot, when you're ready to sign, call me." After my sophomore year, I called him. It was my aspiration to go to Detroit because he had taken such a personal interest in me.

My father went with me to Detroit for my tryout. He was a railroad employee who used to hit grounders to me from the time I was four, when I started dreaming of being a major leaguer. Jim Campbell, the Tigers' GM, signed me for $18,000. I would have gotten more, but Harvey Kuenn, another shortstop, had signed earlier in the week, for $45,000 to $50,000. They kept that quiet until after I signed. I also was supposed to try out with the Indians, but I couldn't because I was getting married. A week later I learned that they had signed Billy Moran for about $40,000. So I got caught right in the middle—which would be the story of my baseball career.

I signed on a Friday because I had to get back to get married the next day, June 21, 1952. I took a week off and then reported to Durham in the Carolina League. That was B ball. Two weeks later I went to Williamsport in Triple A. A week later I went to Jamestown in the PONY League, Class D. I had a good month there and wound up the season back at Williamsport. There were about 18 players per team, of which half were major league prospects. I felt I was one of them, but I got no special attention.

I had never been away from Georgia, but I had my wife with me, which made it easier. Starting a marriage and a baseball career was compatible with her. We started dating my first year in high school, so she always knew that baseball was my life. She enjoyed it, so everything worked out fine.

CHICAGO WHITE SOX

BILLY PIERCE:

I again won 15 games in 1952. My earned run average dropped into the 2.50s and my losses and walks went down, while my strikeouts went up. It was very satisfying because the team moved up to third place, behind only the Yankees and Indians. We also got good starting pitching from Saul Rogovin, Joe Dobson, Marv Grissom, and Chuck Stobbs, and relief pitching from Harry Dorish, Luis Aloma, and Sandy Consuegra, who went 6–0. But I was the guy who Richards would send against the Yankee and Indian aces. I held my own against Reynolds and Raschi, and Lemon, Garcia, and Wynn, but they hurt my batting average!

Sherm Lollar was the best addition the White Sox made that year. He was a hard-hitting, fine defensive catcher and we were lucky that he was available. He had come out of the Yankees' system but couldn't displace Yogi Berra, and then had played with the Browns, who also didn't realize how good he was. He became part of our nucleus. Sherm was a quiet guy, but he was the catcher and became somewhat of a leader. We were a battery for many years and worked well together. We'd do most of our talking before a series started and prior to the game I pitched. So during the game, I'd shake off only about 20 percent of his calls. I'd brush my chest, adding or subtracting from the fingers he put down by the number of brushes. No one knew I was shaking him off because I didn't shake my head.

Jim Rivera came over from the Browns about two-thirds of the way through the season and became our starting right fielder for 6 or 7 years. That year he stayed around Nellie and me almost all the time. We'd all go out to eat, and Jim and I would go to the movies. He was the ultimate hustler and always seemed to put his body on the line—that's why we called him "Jungle Jim." He was a good outfielder and ran the bases exceedingly well. Minoso beat him out for the stolen base title by just one base, so they were a good tandem. Jim had a little hitch in his swing but was a good left-handed hitter with extra-base power. He was funny, and if there was a rainout, he'd do something to pass the time, like a mime routine in which he played pool. Soon he'd have us in stitches.

CHICO CARRASQUEL:

When we Latin players came to the States, we knew that we had to do something extra. In those days, if a Latin player wasn't a regular, he'd be sent to the minors. I played regularly my first year and throughout my career, but I knew I couldn't let down. I didn't feel any prejudice in the White Sox organization toward Latin players because they had as many as any major league team. Most of us were married. I got married in Caracas. No more señoritas! I had an apartment in the Piccadilly Hotel on the South Side. Most of the players lived there, including Nellie Fox, Jim Busby, and Latin players like Luis Aloma, Mike Fornieles, Sandy Consuegra, and Willie Miranda. The wives were friends and would sit in the stands together. The Latin players would hang out together and come to the ballpark together. Latin players throughout the league were friends, and before and after games, we would go out to eat. I liked the Indians' Bobby Avila, who was from Vera Cruz, Mexico. We ate together and went to movies. If we were seen drinking beer, we were thought to be drunks because we were Latins, so we didn't go drinking much. We also made sure not to miss curfews. A White Sox coach would check every night at around midnight prior to a night game and 10:30 prior to a day game. If you weren't there, you'd be fined. Latin players couldn't afford to get reputations for breaking team rules.

Minnie Minoso was one of the best Latin players in the big leagues. He could run and hit and had good power. When he came to Chicago from Cleveland in 1951, we became best friends. I came from Venezuela, where no one cared about black or white, while Minnie came from Cuba, where there was a race problem. We'd go places together. Sometimes he couldn't get into a restaurant because he was black, so I'd go in and get the food. We both loved dancing—I was a real good dancer—so we'd go dancing. In New York we'd go to the Palladium. In Chicago there was a club for Latins called Tito Hacienda. We went a lot on Sunday nights after doubleheaders, because Monday was an off-day. Minnie, Luis Aloma, Willie Miranda, and I would all go together.

MINNIE MINOSO:

Chico Carrasquel became my good friend from the time I joined the White Sox in 1951. We had the same tastes in things and were together all the time. We played dominoes on the train, ate together, went out dancing together. When I was growing up in Cuba, everybody wanted to be a professional ballplayer or professional dancer. I became a professional ballplayer and dancing was my favorite hobby. I was also a fancy dresser. I didn't compete with the other players, I just dressed the way that felt right. In some years they would take polls and I would be considered one of baseball's ten best dressers.

In those first few years in the majors, some teams would call me names. Jimmy Dykes, the manager of Philadelphia, used to call me every name in the book—"you black nigger so-and-so." One or two of his play-ers would go along with him. After the game he'd come to the hotel and say, "Hello, Mr. Minoso." I was won-dering how he could now be so polite. I went along with the program and said, "How do you do, sir?" I think all he was trying to do at the ballpark was to get my atten-tion away from the game.

No one on the New York Yankees ever called me a name, so I admired and respected everyone. Even Casey Stengel, who was a comedian, was a great sportsman. I was prepared for the racial insults from opposing play-ers and fans in towns we visited. They went through one ear and out the other. I learned from my parents. The only way I'd answer is with a smile. They'd say "You black . . ." and I'd flash an insincere grin. Sometimes I'd insult them back in Spanish, warning them, "I can tell you worse things than you said to me, and I can tell you twice without you knowing what I said!"

JIM LANDIS:

I was an infielder at my high school in Richmond, Cali-fornia. I played strictly for the enjoyment and didn't re-ally realize my talents or even that I could run that fast until others pointed it out to me. I was never approached by a scout until I went to Contra Costa Junior College. My coach was a bird dog for big league clubs and said a couple of things about me, and not more than a month later I was offered a contract by Bob Maddox of the White Sox. He came to my house only twice. I was eager to play professional baseball, even if I'd never get past the minors, so I signed.

In 1952, when I was 18, I played third base at Wis-consin Rapids in D ball. It was like a rookie league and was the correct place for me because I was very green. I had never been away from home and got homesick. I'd sit at the end of the bed and ask what I was doing there. This was a bus league, and our driver was about 65 and his eyes weren't very good and he was so short he could barely see over the steering wheel. He was driving us all over the place and at times that was quite scary.

They always had contests in the minors. We had a running contest with a $50 bond as a prize. I ran around the bases in just over 13 seconds. That speed shocked me. Dario Lodigiani, a scout who had played for the Phillies and White Sox, told me that in all his scouting he had never seen anyone run faster from first to third.

NEW YORK YANKEES

GENE WOODLING:

Johnny Sain was an intelligent guy. We'd sit together on trains and he educated me on getting better sala-ries—because he was tough in salary negotiations. I be-came a good negotiator. I think I was paid fairly well, although you always think you're worth more. I dealt with George Weiss on salaries. The other guys dealt with Roy Hamey, his assistant. I said, "I'm not going to sign with a caddie." Dan Topping and Del Webb were tremendous owners. They didn't interfere. We saw them in spring training and at the World Series and that was all.

Hank Bauer and Gil McDougald roomed together, and Ralph Houk and I would pal around with them. We were like family. We had our fun, our drinks, but nothing more. We picked our places because if we went to a place where people knew us, someone would spread the word that we were drunk after just one drink. When I first came to the Yankees, we ate in the hotels and signed checks. Later we got meal money and went out to good places. Our group ate steak or roast beef every night.

Our life on the road was playing ball, playing cards, going to movies, eating meals, having a few drinks, and sleeping. We went to so many movies we should have been critics. We didn't bowl or play golf. Religion didn't play a big part in baseball. But players were church-minded. There were many Catholics. I'd go to Catholic churches for Sunday services because they had early mass. I couldn't go to my church at eleven because I had to be at the ballpark. I was a Christian, but I didn't believe religion had a place at the ballpark. The good Lord wasn't going to do any more for a religious batter than anyone else.

The Yankees were a card-playing team. Hearts was our game on trains. Guys like Eddie Lopat, Allie Reynolds, Vic Raschi, Hank Bauer, and I would play red-ass games. It was blood for a nickel. We would cuss at each other, and you would think we were going to kill each other. But we were best of friends. We were very protective of each other. Pros should never, never talk about another ballplayer. If a Jim Bouton type had written a book about his teammates in my day, he would have been in serious trouble. You just don't do those things. I was out in the business world and those guys did ten times worse than ballplayers.

The press didn't try to break into our card games. They weren't that dumb. We did some nice things to reporters on trains. They used to put their shoes out at night while they slept. The train would pull into a city in the morning and they'd discover that their shoes were missing. Somehow they'd fallen off the train during the night . . . along with their typewriters. In the clubhouses, they could find themselves in the whirlpool if they blinked their eyes. Some of this was done in fun, but I have to say I wasn't on good terms with the press. I didn't like when they wrote that I didn't want to play in New York or that I wasn't trying to get base hits or I didn't make an effort to catch a ball that I couldn't see because of the sun. It's not that I disliked particular reporters, but I didn't associate with them. Some players

on the team got a lot of publicity. I didn't get much because I wasn't friendly with writers. I thought they would hurt me in the long run.

I didn't consider myself a celebrity—of course, there was a difference between me and a DiMaggio or Mantle—and publicity or fame wasn't important to me. I just liked getting a sizeable paycheck and realizing I didn't have to work for a living. There was also a sense of pride that came with the winning that I enjoyed in New York. I enjoyed winning pennants, and we won our fourth in a row in 1952, beating out Cleveland by 2 games. That was the first year I batted over .300, and was only a couple of points behind Mantle for best average on the team. I also led the American League outfielders in fielding percentage.

JOHNNY SAIN:
I had a doctor friend in Dallas. He was the first person I mentioned my bad shoulder to. He gave me X rays and discovered fibrous tissue had formed in the muscle. He recommended radiation. I would have done anything to get rid of the pain. I took a series of three radiation treatments over three weeks. And I was healed! I told the Yankee club doctor about it in the spring, and he got mad at me for going outside the organization and trying some radical procedure. I told him it helped me and recommended that he use it. (Lopat, Ford, and other Yankees through the years—including Ralph Terry, Bill Stafford, and Ford in 1961—took the treatments and were back in the rotations within 10 days. Ford would later say that such treatments helped the Yankees win 4 or 5 pennants.)

Casey saw the change in me when I came to spring training, and knew he could use me effectively during the year. In 1952 my career was revived. Ford was still in the service, and early in the season Ed Lopat and Vic Raschi were having physical problems, so for a while Allie and I did the brunt of the starting and carried the club. When Lopat and Raschi came back, I went to the bullpen.

I finally developed a good pickoff move. I needed it more now that I was a relief pitcher because I'd come in when I couldn't afford to let runners get into scoring position. I also developed an unorthodox move to second in which I'd turn toward the runner—at the very least, I made him lean back toward second, so that he'd have trouble scoring on a base hit. I learned both moves in my backyard on a concrete-block contraption that I invented.

I always pitched better helping the Yankees reach the World Series than in the World Series. Overall, I was 8–5 in my 16 starts that year, with 8 complete games. I was 3–1 in 19 relief appearances, with 7 saves. My 11 wins was the third most on the team, behind Reynolds' 20 wins and Raschi's 16 wins. My ERA for the year was 3.46, my best since 1948. Moreover, I pitched the 1952 pennant clincher in Philadelphia.

EWELL BLACKWELL:
It was a thrill going to the Yankees and finally being with a pennant winner. The Yankees got me to pitch and not to work with younger pitchers and teach them my sidearm delivery. I never taught any other pitcher how to pitch in my life. I came to the Yankees at the end of the season, so I was in only 5 games. In that time I saw no difference between the American and National leagues. I won one game down the stretch, which I guess was important because the Yankees wound up just 2 games ahead of the Indians.

I got along really well with Casey Stengel. The Yankees were a close, united team because he made it that way. He was in control of the team. There were little dissensions, but everyone went along with him and I didn't notice anybody grumbling.

We had so much talent. Yogi Berra led the team in homers and RBIs, but three of the guys who I thought made the team go were Mickey Mantle, Phil Rizzuto, and Billy Martin. Mantle was an awesome talent. If he'd had good legs he would have been the greatest player ever. Rizzuto was a little pepper pot. He was one of the many leaders on the team. Billy was a favorite of Stengel's because he'd played for him with the Oakland Oaks in 1948. He became a starter in 1952. Billy was a good, aggressive second baseman and a real nice kid. Everybody had the wrong idea about him. He was a fiery guy who'd fight you at the drop of a hat if you did something wrong to him—but he only fought players on the other team.

VIC POWER:
After the good year I had in Syracuse in 1951, I should have been brought up by the Yankees. But instead they sent me to the Kansas City Blues in the American Association. I had a great year in 1952. I batted .331 with 40 doubles, 17 triples, 16 home runs, and 109 RBIs. Still the Yankees didn't bring me up in September.

WORLD SERIES

1952

YANKEES vs DODGERS

EWELL BLACKWELL · YANKEES:
I started the fifth game of the Series and Carl Erskine went for the Dodgers. I struck out 4 and gave up only 4 hits in 5 innings, but I gave up 4 runs, 2 on Duke Snider's homer. We eventually lost that game in extra innings. But having never been in the World Series during my career, it was a great experience.

JOHNNY SAIN · YANKEES:
I pitched only in the fifth game. I relieved Blackwell after 5 innings with us leading 5–4. Unfortunately, after we scored all 5 runs in the fifth inning—3 on Johnny Mize's third homer in 3 games—Carl Erskine retired the next 19 batters. I gave up a run in the seventh inning that tied the game and the losing run in the eleventh inning on a single by my old nemesis, Duke Snider. Duke had a great series with 8 RBIs, but we had several stars—Mantle, Berra, Woodling, Martin, McDougald, and Mize. And we had better pitching.

In the seventh game, Ed Lopat started against Joe Black, but Stengel brought in Reynolds in the fourth inning with us ahead 1–0. The Yankees scored 1 run in the top of the fourth and the Dodgers tied the game in the bottom of the fourth. The Yankees scored in the top of the fifth, and the Dodgers tied it with a run in the bottom of the fifth. Mantle homered off Black in the sixth to put us ahead, 3–2, and we scored another run in the seventh, to go up 4–2. Raschi came in to get 1 out in the seventh inning, but Stengel went to his bullpen once more when the Dodgers loaded the bases. I was warming up with Bob Kuzava, who had a good, hard, live fastball. Stengel went with Kuzava and he got out of the jam, getting both Snider and Robinson to pop up on 3–2 counts. On Robinson's pop near the mound, both Kuzava and Joe Collins froze, and Billy Martin saved the game by racing in to catch the ball on his shoe tops. Stengel stayed with Kuzava, although he was a left-hander facing the Dodgers' predominantly right-handed lineup. He just poured in fastballs and retired the next 6 batters to give us the championship. He did a marvelous job. It was the second consecutive year that Kuzava saved the final game with a gutsy performance. Oddly, Kuzava didn't pitch in either Series until the final game!

BEN WADE · DODGERS:

We should have won the Series because we had the better ballclub. That was the best Dodger team because, in addition to Furillo in right and Snider in center, we had Andy Pafko in left. But Furillo and Pafko slumped in the Series, as did Campanella, Robinson, and Hodges, who went 0 for 21. Reese, Cox, and especially Snider provided all our offense. We were up 3 games to 2 and we were heading back to Brooklyn to finish the Series. It was our own fault that we lost. We lost the sixth game, 3–2, when Loes hit the ball with his knee and it dropped to the ground, allowing the go-ahead run to score. He couldn't see Raschi's grounder because of the sun shining through the back of the stands. Loes was telling the truth when he said he lost a grounder in the sun. We then lost the seventh game, 4–2. Mantle homered in both games. Joe Black was a phenomenal relief pitcher in his rookie season, winning 15 games. Then Dressen started him in 3 games in the Series. He bested Allie Reynolds, 4–2, in the opener to become the first black pitcher to win a Se-ries game. But he lost to Reynolds, 2–0, in Game Four, and lost the seventh game.

RUBE WALKER · DODGERS:

The World Series was a combination of great pitching and home runs. There really weren't a lot of runs scored, but most came on homers. Snider hit 4 for us and old Johnny Mize hit 3 and Berra and Mantle each had a couple for them. In both the first and sixth games in Brooklyn 4 homers were hit. Raschi 3-hit us to win Game Two, 7–1, and Reynolds outpitched Black to win Game Four, 2–0, with a 4-hitter. Our 3 wins also came on complete games—Black pitched a 6-hitter in Game One, Roe pitched a 6-hitter in Game Three, and Erskine pitched a 5-hitter in Game Five. I thought we'd win the Series then, but they got good pitching from Raschi, Reynolds, Lopat, and Kuzava and home runs by Mantle, Berra, and Woodling and edged us in the final 2 games. It was disappointing, but not humbling. It was such a close Series that neither team deserved to lose. We were both great teams.

NATIONAL LEAGUE 1953

"I DON'T KNOW IF THERE WAS A SINGLE LEADER ON THE BRAVES, BUT EVERYONE RESPECTED WALKER COOPER, THE VETERAN CATCHER. HE HAD PLAYED THE LONGEST. IF A PLAYER HAD A PROBLEM, THEY COULD GO TO CHARLIE GRIMM. IF A PLAYER WANTED A PROBLEM, HE COULD GO TO COOPER."

BOB BUHL

MILWAUKEE BRAVES

JOHNNY ANTONELLI:
I had left the Boston Braves after the 1950 season to join the army. During the following two years, I was stationed in New Jersey, Florida, and Virginia, and pitched during that time, winning 42 games and losing 0. I got married in 1951 to a Boston girl, and when I got out of the army, we bought a house in Lexington, Massachusetts. But we didn't live there long because in March the Braves were given permission to move to Milwaukee. The Braves had been in Boston for 77 years, and the move caught the players by surprise.

RALPH KINER (PIRATES):
I know Warren Spahn didn't expect the Braves to move to Milwaukee, and he couldn't have been too happy about it. He had bought a diner next to Braves Field.

J. ANTONELLI:
The Braves were the first franchise to move to a different city since 1903. So we got the royal treatment from the fans and local businessmen of Milwaukee. We were all given Plymouths to drive, free gasoline, bread, and milk, all kinds of things. The people were very gracious. My wife and I rented an apartment in Milwaukee. Some players with families sublet houses, while some bachelors and some married players whose families weren't with them moved into hotels.

The Milwaukee Braves of 1953 were a much different team from the Boston Braves I'd played with in 1950. Warren Spahn, Del Crandall, Max Surkont, and Sid Gordon were among the few holdovers. We also had another manager, Charlie Grimm. He had replaced Billy Southworth's successor, Tommy Holmes, during the 1952 season. I got along well with Charlie, who was one of the nicest men I ever met in baseball. The Braves were fun to be on because Charlie set the tone. He lived in St. Louis and would throw a party for the team when we traveled there. All the players and his friends would gather in the party room and he'd take out his banjo.

Grimm made me a starter, along with Spahn, Surkont, and Bob Buhl, who was a rookie. Later, Lew Burdette moved from the bullpen into the rotation. I was 23 now. Although I was considered a fastball pitcher, there were times I threw more change-ups in a game than fastballs. I had good control and wasn't afraid to go with a curve or change on a 3–2 count. I threw inside and outside. I was glad to finally have the opportunity to prove to everyone, including myself, that it was not a mistake for the Braves to have given me all that money in 1948. It also felt nice to know that if I lost a game, I'd still be scheduled to pitch on my next turn. The Braves won over 90 games and finished second, and I felt that I was part of the team and important to its success. I was 9–3 at the All-Star break. Unfortunately, I then spent a few days in the hospital with pneumonia and then tried to pitch too soon. I never got my strength back and lost 9 of my last 12 decisions, finishing at 12–12.

We had a very good team. Eddie Mathews, who was an incredible athlete, was our third baseman. He hit over .300, drove in over 130 runs, and hit 47 homers to break Ralph Kiner's 7-year hold on the title. He was our star. Joe Adcock was at first; we had a good double-play combination in Jack Dittmer and shortstop Johnny Logan; Andy Pafko was in right, rookie Billy Bruton was in center, and Sid Gordon was in left. Del Crandall also returned from the service in 1953 and reestablished himself as a team leader. Now he was older, and Grimm made him the regular catcher. He called a good game and had a strong arm. We also had an excellent pitching staff top to bottom, led by Spahn. He led the league in wins and earned run average. Burdette, who had joined the team while I was in the service, won 15 games. Spahn and Burdette were best friends and two of the jokers on the team.

JOHNNY KLIPPSTEIN (CUBS):

I admired Warren Spahn as a pitcher, but he would walk by without saying hello and seemed arrogant. However, as the years went by, I learned that he was a really nice guy.

J. ANTONELLI:

The Braves looked like they were going to be the team to beat for the next 10 years, so I was upset to be traded in February to the New York Giants in a 6-player deal that brought Bobby Thomson to Milwaukee. The Braves felt they could deal me because they were high on left-hander Chet Nichols, who was returning in 1954 after two years in the service. The Braves also had a

couple of other promising left-handers in the farm system. Someone had to go, and they picked me.

BOB BUHL:

After two years in the service, I went to Bradenton, Florida, for my first spring training with the Braves. I was anxious because I knew I had to pitch well to make the team. They had quite a few pitchers, but except for Lew Burdette and Johnny Antonelli, they were from the older school. Of course, Spahn was secure in the rotation, but I couldn't say the same for Vern Bickford, Max Surkont, or Jim Wilson.

I don't know if there was a single leader on the Braves, but everyone respected Walker Cooper, the veteran catcher. He had played the longest. If a player had a problem, he could go to Charlie Grimm. If he wanted a

In the Braves' first year in Milwaukee, intimidating rookie pitcher Bob Buhl won 13 games and became part of a formidable pitching trio with Warren Spahn and Lew Burdette that would last until the early '60s.

problem, he could go to Cooper. One day Coop asked me if I was doing anything that night. I told him I'd go out with him if he promised to have me in by curfew. He had a car, so after the workout we went to the Sandbar on Anna Maria Island. We drank beer and played shuffleboard. At ten, I reminded Cooper I had to be in at midnight. But midnight passed. I said I wanted to make the team, and he said, "Don't worry, you've got it made." Finally it was 2 A.M., and it was the last call. He asked the bartender for two fishing poles that were in the corner. We got the car and went back. So we walked in holding fishing poles. For all the good that did us, we should have turned around and pretended we were just then leaving the hotel to go fishing first thing in the morning. The bellboy saw us and he was a squealer. That was the end of me going out with Cooper.

The pitchers and catchers arrived a few days before the other players. I had checked into the Dixie Grand Hotel. I was looking out the window and here comes a blue Mercury convertible. In the backseat was a guitar. I said, "Who in the hell is coming in with that?" Soon I heard a knock on the door. I opened it and the guy introduced himself, "I'm Ed Mathews." I said, "I'm Bob Buhl. Is that your guitar?" He said, "Yes." I said, "Do you play it?" He said, "No." I said, "Okay." He couldn't play and couldn't sing—we got along immediately. So we became roommates and that would last 9½ years, all the years I spent in Milwaukee. Ed was a muscular, left-handed-hitting third baseman. He had already played one year and hit 25 homers, and was about to become a star. During the spring I would tell him how I'd pitch to get him out, and he'd tell me what he would be looking for if he were batting against me. We talked about hitters and pitchers all the time.

I first met Warren Spahn when we were going north and stopped in Mobile, Alabama, for an exhibition game against the Dodgers. Eddie and I were waiting for the train and went to a little tavern and had some beers. And there was Spahn, Burdette, and Bickford sitting with us. Spahn said to me, "You don't think you're going to make this club, do you?" I said, "Yes, I do." He said, "Whose spot are you going to take?" And I said, "I don't care whose spot I'm going to take, but it will be somebody's." Bickford, who was a nice guy, was a bit older, but he wasn't worried about me. Everybody respected Warren. He was a good guy. Anyway,

he was smaller than me—I wasn't afraid of him.

I became friends with Spahn and Burdette at the same time during spring training and in the clubhouse. Lew was a real character. Players would play practical jokes on each other and Burdette was always getting blamed because he was always up to something. In spring training, Spahn, Burdette, Mathews, and myself started hanging out together. We got along pretty good. Mathews was the youngest. Spahn grew up old. We used to play jokes on one another and compete with each other.

When we got off the train in Milwaukee, there were many fans to greet us. And they had a parade for us, just like we'd won the World Series. We were treated so well in Milwaukee that first year. It was unbelievable. We got our milk free, our dry cleaning free, we had cars provided us. Players would stay at the Hotel Wisconsin and we'd go to the lounge and the dining room to eat and all the drinks were picked up by the Schlitz Brewery. The Braves were bad when they left Boston, and we were expected to be at the bottom again. But everybody had a good year, even the older fellows, and we drew a lot of people to the park.

I wasn't guaranteed to be a starter because we had enough starters. Max Surkont was doing a good job—he even struck out a record 8 batters in a row against Cincinnati. But Bickford was erratic and he came up with a stiff neck and couldn't pitch. It was about 20 degrees in Milwaukee, so I got to pitch my first game in the majors against the Giants, with Leo Durocher managing them. I started. I knew that it would sting batters' hands if I threw inside fastballs. If the guy was muscular I'd pitch him up and in. I believe I broke 8 bats that night and I got my first victory, 8–1. At one point I had 2 outs and Durocher had a guy try to steal home on me. He wanted to see if I was a rookie who would balk or if I knew what I was doing. I threw a hard pitch that knocked the hitter down and the runner was out. Leo never tried that with me again. He realized I knew the game a little bit and was old for my age. Everybody was happy for me after the game. I would get 18 starts in my rookie season, as Antonelli and I replaced Bickford and Wilson in the rotation. I pitched about 150 innings and had an ERA of 2.97, and had a record of 13–8. Only Spahn and Burdette won more on the staff.

I was liked on my team, but opposing teams didn't

care too much for me because I was mean on the mound. I'd brush guys back; I didn't care who they were. And I was wild to begin with, so that helped me out. Right-handed batters didn't like to face me too much. The fellows I didn't have trouble with I didn't have to bother with. I always figured they were looking for the brushback, so I'd keep them waiting. I wouldn't let them dig in. They were thrown off stride because I had a herky-jerky motion and was quick. I was a short-armed pitcher, and instead of moving way back and way forward, I'd let loose tighter to my body.

I was a fast worker. Neither managers nor catchers could slow me down. I was all business on the mound and hated to lose, but I never took a loss home. If I was mad I'd get away from everybody because I didn't want to talk about it. After a little while it was gone. Fortunately, I didn't have to wait for my next start to pitch, but could relieve for a couple of innings to keep sharp.

Bucky Walters was our pitching coach, and I learned the most from him my first year. He told me I was going to need another pitch, so I worked on the slider, which came to me quicker than the change-up. It was a new pitch then. It looked like a fastball but would break real quick down and away from a right-handed hitter. Every now and then I'd show it to a hitter just to show I had another pitch. But I wasn't using it enough to master it. Walker Cooper told me to throw whatever I wanted and didn't bother with signs. I started mixing in the slider and he would freeze. After about 3 sliders sent him to the backstop, he came out and said, "Kid, I think we're going to need a sign for that." From then on, we used signs.

It was fun pitching for a team that had a lot of power. No one came close to Mathews's 47 homers, but a few other guys had their share of homers: Joe Adcock, who had been acquired from Cincinnati before the season, Sid Gordon, Del Crandall, Andy Pafko—a real nice, quiet veteran who just did his job and went along with everyone else—and even shortstop Johnny Logan. Billy Bruton, who was a very fine gentleman, speedy center fielder, stolen base champion, and good team player, hit only 1 homer all year, but it was the first major league homer ever hit in Milwaukee's County Stadium—it came in the tenth inning and won our first home game, against St. Louis. Jim Pendleton had only a handful of homers, but 3 came in 1 game against Pittsburgh to tie a

rookie record. We won that game 19–4 and tied a major league record with 8 homers. Then we hit 4 more in the nightcap to set a record with 12 homers in a double-header. Eddie hit 4 homers that day.

Back in April, Adcock, who was a big, good-natured, down-home boy from Louisiana, homered into the center-field bleachers in the Polo Grounds against Hoyt Wilhelm. That was about 475 feet. Nobody expected the ball to go that far because it didn't look like he hit it that good. In fact, he ran hard to second base and then slowed up when he realized it was in the stands. We didn't know that had never been done before in the majors. Only Luke Easter had done it in a Negro Leagues game.

The Braves had a working agreement with Caguas in the Puerto Rican Winter League, and after the major league season they sent a few of us down there for experience. Guys like Vic Power, an incredible first baseman who was a Yankee prospect, and White Sox outfielder Jim Rivera were on that team, as well as players from the Braves and other teams. I saw that the Braves had one prospect who could really hit. He was a slim but muscular black player from Mobile, Alabama. Henry Aaron had been sent to Caguas to play second base. Apparently, he'd been a shortstop in the Negro Leagues before the Braves signed him in 1952. I got a phone call from John Quinn, and he asked me how Henry was doing. I said, "He's doing real fine with the bat, but if you don't get him off second base he's going to get himself killed." I suggested putting him in the outfield. Quinn asked what I thought he'd hit his first year in the majors. I told him if Aaron played right field, he'd hit .280 the first year and, after that, .300. I said that if given the chance he'd take Andy Pafko's right-field job away. Well, they moved him to right and Henry thanked me for doing that. We got to be pretty good friends. He had his little baby down there and we all lived on the same street, so the families got to know each other.

LEW BURDETTE:
Midwestern people are warm people and Milwaukee people are even more so. The Milwaukee fans were the greatest people I ever met. They enjoyed having us around. We made an awful lot of friends in Milwaukee, in West Allis, where we lived, and several other parts of town. While Fred Miller of Miller Brewery was alive, I

worked for him in the off-season in sports promotions. Billy Bruton did also. Johnny Logan worked for Blatz Beer. We had nothing to do with selling beer. We went to churches, schools, fraternal organizations, breakfast-luncheons-dinners five or six days a week. We didn't feel like celebrities, but we were treated nice. If we wanted beer, we could go to the city sales office and load up our trunks. The breweries, who sponsored baseball, always supplied beer.

It was a great year when the Braves turned a corner and became a winning team. In his second season, Eddie Mathews became the homer champion, Joe Adcock emerged as a power-hitting first baseman, Del Crandall got out of the army to give us a first-rate catcher, and we had a strong pitching rotation. Johnny Antonelli and Bob Buhl moved into the rotation early in the year, and when Antonelli and Vern Bickford broke their fingers, I got my shot. I finished the season at 15–5, second to Spahn's 23–7.

I was a sinker-slider pitcher from the beginning. My fastball was a sinker because I threw sidearm and three-quarters, and the ball sank. My slider went the other way. One went down and away and the other went down and in. When I came up, I came in. I pitched inside all the time. I became notorious for brushing back and hitting batters. Any kind of reputation if it's mean is not bad to have in baseball. Spahn would come inside once in a while and brush batters back, but not very often. I don't know if it was intentional when he knocked guys down.

Spahn and I were competitive, but we didn't compete with Buhl in the same sense because he wasn't a roommate. Spahn and I would say, "Anything you can do, I can do better." We played for steak dinners in the outfield before games. Spahn was a good hitter because he'd been a first baseman. In his career, he'd set the National League record for homers by a pitcher. I became a good hitter.

Spahn, Buhl, Mathews, and I would go out to eat a lot. That's how Spahn, Buhl, and I learned how to pitch against a power-hitting left-hander. Mathews told us what bothered him most was a flat slider in on his fists, and that worked with all power-hitting left-handers. Most were extended-arm hitters who liked the ball down and away or over the plate. If they got out in front and hit the side of the ball that was on their fists, they'd

hit a hard foul into the lights. The crowd would go ooh-aah. But the ump would say, "Strike one!" I used to pitch that way to the Reds' Ted Kluszewski, who was the other top left-handed power hitter in the league. I'd throw him 2 sliders inside upstairs and let him ooh-aah the fans to death, and then go dunk him one outside.

ST. LOUIS CARDINALS

BILLY JOHNSON:

Under Eddie Stanky, I had batted 200 fewer times in 1952 than in 1951, under Marty Marion. Then in 1953 Stanky gave the third-base job to Ray Jablonski, a powerful right-handed rookie who would drive in over 100 runs. So at the age of 35, my major league career ended. I had no regrets. I lasted as long as I did because I had a winning attitude and worked and played hard.

DICK SCHOFIELD:

I was born in Springfield, Illinois, in 1935, and that's where I always lived. I was an only child. Before I was born, my dad, John Schofield, played professional ball for 11 years, reaching Double A. He was about my height, 5'8" or 5'9", and also played shortstop. His nickname was "Ducky," which became mine after I introduced him to the Cardinals years later. We'd go out and he'd hit 9 million ground balls to me. I played shortstop and batted third or fourth on the high school team because for a little guy I had power. One night after a game, a couple of Dodgers' scouts asked me if I was intending to sign after what they thought was my senior year. I informed them I was just a freshman. I thought I was kind of hot stuff. There were several reasons scouts were interested in me. I always hit the ball hard. I had a super arm. And I didn't make many mistakes—my father had taught me how to play.

I also did extremely well in American Legion ball—in 1952 we were the state champions—so by the time I was a senior I could have signed with 14 of the 16 teams. I had worked out with the White Sox when I was a junior and they offered me a lot of money, but they didn't want to make me a bonus player and have me sit on their bench for 2 years. They wanted to give me the money in some strange way and send me to the minors. The Yankees and Tigers wanted me to fly out to work out with them, but I didn't want to spend the summer trying out with all the teams. I was a Red Sox fan—a Ted Williams fan—and wanted to sign with them, but they had just signed Don Buddin, Marty Keough, Haywood Sullivan, and some others for a whole lot of money and were being called the "Gold Sox." So I ended up signing with the Cardinals, who I had always rooted against. Joe Monahan and Walter Shannon signed me for a $40,000 bonus. I had a full scholarship to Northwestern to play baseball and basketball, but that was too much money to refuse. Unfortunately, I was so naïve about the bonus rule that I still didn't understand that I was required to stay in the big leagues for the next 2 years. Which meant I'd sit on the bench when I wanted to play. I was the Cardinals' first bonus player.

I had no clue as to what would happen once I joined the Cardinals after I graduated in June. I was scared to death. The team was playing Brooklyn and I checked into the Commodore Hotel in Manhattan. Then I rode to the ballpark with Stan Musial and Red Schoendienst! They asked me to come along. Imagine that! For some reason, Musial called me "Lefty" all the way to the ballpark—he had no idea what my name was. I didn't say I wasn't right-handed, I didn't say nothing. I didn't really say anything much for a couple of years.

There were a lot of players who didn't know my name and could have cared less about me. Vern Benson, who played the outfield and infield, probably didn't like me too much because my taking a roster spot meant he was going back to the minor leagues when I should have been the one sent out. But I was treated so well. Musial, Schoendienst, Solly Hemus, Peanuts Lowrey, Rip Repulski, Ray Jablonski, Harvey Haddix, Joe Presko, Tom Poholsky, and Hal Rice really treated me nice. I felt accepted.

I lived alone, first at the Melbourne Hotel and then at the George Washington Hotel. Some of the other players stayed there, but we didn't necessarily socialize. I lived close to Springfield, so some of my high school buddies would come to stay with me in St. Louis. I didn't hang out with a lot of Cardinals. I was younger, so I'd wait for an invitation. Andy Anderson, the team's bullpen catcher, was my road roommate. He was 36 and I was 18. He was like my dad and took good care of me. He made it easier for me.

Harvey Haddix was a real good friend. He was 10 years older, but he was single, too, and I'd hang out some with him. In St. Louis, we'd go to a little place called the Martinique Bar. On the road, we went to movies. We'd have fun together.

I wasn't a drinker, but there was a lot of drinking in those days. You could look in some drinking spots and you'd find half the team in there. We had guys who could drink beer, like Steve Bilko, Rip Repulski, and Ray Jablonski. I think when guys would have a few beers together, they'd hang together a little bit more. The Cards were really a partying team.

We called Bilko "Humpty Bumpty." He was a big, strong, beer-guzzling guy who looked mean but was a very easygoing, nice man. He struck out a lot but wasn't a bad player. He hit the ball a long, long way. He had been on the Cards since 1949, and 1953 was his first year as a regular. He hit over 20 homers and had about 85 RBIs, and though he was far from graceful, he led the National League first basemen in several fielding stats. But at the beginning of the next year the Cards would trade him to the Cubs, and he never would be a starter in the majors again. However, he did become a superstar in the Pacific Coast League.

Musial and Schoendienst were roommates, so they were together pretty much. But it wasn't a cliquish team. One reason we'd go to places in groups was to save meal money by splitting the cab fare. We had a pretty good bunch of guys, no different than on other teams. We had drinkers, we had partygoers, and we had poker players, especially on train trips—I didn't gamble. We had funny guys, like Hal Rice, before he was dealt to Pittsburgh. We also had religious guys like Vinegar Bend Mizell. He was a tall left-hander who was born in Mississippi, a big ol' country boy. He had come up in 1952, when he'd been 21, and was already one of the Cardinals' best pitchers. He'd win 13 or 14 games a year and strike out a lot of batters. He was as nice a guy as there was. Apparently, he'd been somewhat wild in his younger days, but had calmed down and was married and quiet. You'd never suspect he'd become a politician.

Eddie Stanky was in his second year as the Cardinals' player-manager. I had met him when I worked out with the Cardinals prior to signing. He was an infielder, so he spent a lot of time breaking me in at shortstop. He knew baseball better than anybody I ever met. Every once in a while he'd tell me to sit beside him in the dugout. Or he'd walk by and give me a pop quiz about the game we were playing. I'd be in trouble if I didn't know the count or how many outs there were. He might ask me, "How many times has that pitcher looked at second base?" "I don't know." "You oughtta know. What if I put you in and you have to steal third base?" So he scared me into paying attention to everything.

Stanky wanted his players to be enthusiastic, as if every game was their first or last game. He was great to me and other young guys, but he had trouble with the veterans. He was from the old school and wanted everyone to play like him or think like him all the time. He didn't handle players correctly and would get guys pretty upset. For instance, he was a real stickler on weight. I was 18 years old and he expected me to weigh a certain amount. He used to really harass our second-string catcher, Sal Yvars, about his weight. Yvars had to work out all the time, so he was tired before the game started. Yvars could hit, but I think Stanky was right about him—his weight hurt him defensively. Stanky would get on little things and wouldn't stop. Older guys felt that they should be allowed to take care of themselves, and there was a lot of grumbling. Stanky and Al Brazle didn't get along, but I'm not sure why. I remember once Schoendienst bunted with a man on second. So Stanky said, "If you want to bunt, everybody be at the park tomorrow morning at ten, so we can bunt." So we all had to come early to the park and bunt for an hour or so. I don't know why he did things like that. A lot of players resented such Mickey Mouse games.

Eddie loved Harvey Haddix, and I think he helped him. Haddix responded by winning 20 games, including 6 shutouts, in just his second full season. He was a real workhorse for Stanky. I don't know if Stanky favored short players, but we had a bunch of guys between 5'8" and 5'10"—Peanuts Lowrey—who tied a record with 22 pinch hits for Stanky—Solly Hemus, Harvey Haddix, Joe Presko, me—and he seemed to like all of us.

Stanky was a strict family man who believed a player's life should be his wife, his kids, and baseball. But everybody had different lifestyles. Some guys drank and some guys went out at night, and Stanky made it known that he didn't like that even if you were single. It was unrealistic of him, and he made trouble for himself. If he could have just accepted managing the

Eighteen-year-old bonus player Dick "Ducky" Schofield would be frustrated by a lack of playing time with the St. Louis Cardinals before being traded to the Pittsburgh Pirates in 1958.

game and not trying to manage the players' personal lives, he would have had it easier. He just got players' minds messed up and got them grumbling. In his defense, I think he was sincere about trying to help his players, and that if they had gotten into trouble he would have stuck up for them. With Stanky as manager, not too many people did anything other than what he wanted. He had his rules. We gave him a bullwhip as a joke, teasing him about how much he'd make us run. That was a mistake, because he made us run even more.

Other than Enos Slaughter, the Cardinals weren't a fighting team. Stanky razzed everybody pretty good but never got into fights. I remember playing against the Dodgers, and Stanky and a lot of our players would holler a lot of racist stuff at Jackie Robinson. However, nobody got on the other blacks on the Dodgers any more than they would white opponents. I think Robinson tried to stick it in our face a little bit, so some of the players were hostile toward him. He had guts and was a good player, but he wasn't the easiest guy to get along with. Our coach Dixie Walker, who had been a teammate of Stanky's on Brooklyn, had been unhappy when Robinson joined them on the Dodgers in 1947.

Del Rice was our catcher, so he pretty much had a say in how things went on our team. But Stan Musial was our leader. He was an enthusiastic player who really wanted to win. Losing would frustrate him, but he tried not to show it. Stanky left Musial pretty much alone. You couldn't tell him how to play—he'd won 6 batting titles by then and 3 in a row. You just penciled him in third on the lineup card and left it at that. Stan was a loose individual. In spring training he'd always take coat hangers and use them like drumsticks, beating them on any surface. He'd say, "This is going to be another tough year. I don't know whether I'm going to hit .330 or .350." He was serious. He was a fantastic hitter, who was focused every time he went up to the plate. In 1953 he hit .337, with 200 hits, over 50 doubles, 30 homers, and way over 100 runs and 100 runs batted in. And every year in my Cardinal career, he would have similar statistics.

BILL RIGNEY (GIANTS):

During my career, which lasted from 1946 to 1953, Stan Musial was the best hitter of the period. The numbers were that good. There was no way to play him in the field. And in those days he could fly to first base. I'd watch him play doubleheaders in St. Louis in 100-degree heat. I'd look like I'd been in a mud bath, covered with dirt and sweat, and he'd have maybe three beads of sweat on his entire body and his uniform would be nice and white. He'd go about 5 for 9. He played easy, just like Ted Williams and Joe DiMaggio.

D. SCHOFIELD:

Red Schoendienst was pretty much captain of the infield. He was a very good hitter and a super second baseman. He didn't look smooth in the field, but he was as good as anyone. In 1953 he had an outstanding season, batting .342, 5 points higher than Musial. This was Stanky's last year as a player, but he played second only a few times.

Shortstop Solly Hemus was a good guy who was helpful to me—not only playing the infield but dressing. He was the one who got a lot of the players to start wearing loud clothes, particularly sports jackets. I hadn't any money as a kid, so now I had my first opportunity to buy clothes, and I liked it. I got a reputation for my outfits. Solly, Stan, and I all wore unusual, bright jackets.

Stanky and Hemus helped me learn to play shortstop in the majors, especially turning the double play. In high school there weren't players who tried to kill you with a slide into second base. In the big leagues in those days, there were some guys who really came after shortstops.

There was a stretch when Stanky played me in about 10 straight games. I hit 2 home runs in a week. That made me think I would play a lot if the team had a bad year. But we had a good team, tying the Phillies for third, with an 83–71 record. So it didn't make sense for me to be playing, especially since the Cards had Hemus. I got to bat only 39 times.

CHICAGO CUBS

RALPH KINER:

I was traded from the Pirates to the Cubs in a 10-player deal in early June. I came over with Catfish Metkovich, Joe Garagiola, and Howie Pollet. Rickey arranged for the Cubs to pay me the $5,000 I had insisted on if traded, but National League President Warren Giles ruled that the payment was illegal. I got nothing to make up for Rickey's salary cut, which was disappointing. I had a slow start with the Pirates but did somewhat better hitting home runs after I arrived in Chicago. Still, I was never really close in the homer race. Eddie Mathews led the league with 47 homers, and Duke Snider, Roy Campanella, and Ted Kluszewski all hit over 40 homers. I ended up fifth, with 35 homers. I wasn't that disappointed that my 7-year skein was over, because it wasn't as if I lost the race in September.

I did play in my sixth consecutive and last All-Star Game. It took place in Cincinnati, and the National League won for the fourth consecutive time. We got 5-hit pitching from Roberts, Spahn, Curt Simmons, and Murry Dickson and won 5–1. All-Star Games were always an honor to play in, but a pain in the ass to get to. There were times when you had to take an all-night train trip, play the game, and then take another all-night train trip to get back to your team. It wasn't easy. We took the games seriously, and I was happy to be part of the teams that turned the damned series around for the National League.

I was disappointed that I was traded to the Cubs. I liked being a Pirate, and the Cubs were only a slightly better team. We finished in seventh place, with only Pittsburgh behind us. The Cubs didn't have much of anything and were going through the doldrums. It was a messed-up operation. But I liked playing with Hank Sauer and Frank Baumholtz, who were great guys. And Chicago was a great town for me because we played only day games at Wrigley Field, and at night we had our pick of restaurants and entertainment. We often went to the Cape Cod Room.

I continued to be the National League player rep. There was much going on in player-owner relations and with the pension plan. In 1952 Emanuel Celler's congressional committee had ruled that antitrust legislation of baseball was unnecessary, and in 1953 both the U.S. Court of Appeals and U.S. Supreme Court ruled that baseball was not subject to antitrust laws, thereby keeping the reserve clause intact. As far as the pension plan went, we had to either renew or renegotiate it. That's when Allie Reynolds and I became heavily involved. The December meetings took place in Atlanta, Georgia. We had to deal with the owners' executive committee. Walter O'Malley was in charge, and he was tough to deal with. We brought in our attorney, J. Norman Lewis, and the owners refused to meet with him although they had their own attorney sitting there. So we walked out. We were helped by the big-city newspapers, which criticized the owners for not allowing us legal representation. So the owners appointed a committee of Cleveland GM Hank Greenberg, Pittsburgh owner John Galbraith, and an attorney, to meet with Allie, me, and Lewis. That's how we worked out a deal in which the players got 60 percent of the television rights. That was my idea. I was living in California, where there was a lot of talk about pay television, and it was my opinion that if we ever went to pay TV, 60 percent of the money was better than getting a flat fee. We asked for 66.6 percent, which was based on the radio split the ballplayers got for the World Series, but settled for 60 percent.

Hank Greenberg had gone from being a player to the owners' side, but he was fair and a major reason we

were able to work out a plan. He had refused to be part of the negotiating committee unless the owners gave him full authority to say yes or no. When he took back the deal to the owners, they didn't want to give us the television percentage. So Hank and Galbraith had to fight the owners, and they did so successfully. We had three things going for us: the support of influential newspapers; the realization by many owners that the players deserved a pension plan; and Hank's acknowledgment that our terms were reasonable. Throughout the negotiations, we worried that it would all fall through because we really had no leverage other than threatening a strike during the World Series. And I doubted if that was possible because we didn't have the full backing of the players. We were really out on a limb and had to bluff our way through the early part of negotiations. That's why we felt such elation when the plan was approved. It was a tremendous step to secure a very strong pension plan. (Later on, they changed it and accepted flat fees instead of percentages. The owners shrewdly packaged the World Series with the Game of the Week, when the World Series was the money-maker and the CBS Game of the Week had been a loser since debuting in 1946. They watered down the amount of the principal.)

HANK SAUER:
When Ralph Kiner joined us in 1953, I shifted from left field to right field. I told Phil Cavarretta that he should let me stay in left and have Kiner play right instead of hurting two positions. I said, "My arm's not good enough to play right." He said, "Yeah, but it's still better than Kiner's." Ralph wasn't that bad an outfielder, but his legs were all taped up and he couldn't move that good. So we'd stand near the lines and Baumholtz would try to get everything in between. They said, "You have a good center fielder, but you're going to kill him before the season is over." They joked that Frankie started the season weighing 187 and wound up at 165 pounds, after Kiner and I got through with him.

We also got Joe Garagiola from the Pirates in the Kiner deal. He and Clyde McCullough, who had returned to the Cubs after 4 years in Pittsburgh, split the catching. Joe was a pretty good receiver and a good, .270-type hitter. He talked a lot, but I wouldn't say he was a leader. He was the club's comedian and a fun guy.

At the end of the season the Cubs got their first black players, Gene Baker and Ernie Banks. Baker came from the minors, but Banks came straight out of the army. He'd played in the Negro Leagues but not the minors. Gene had played short in the PCL, but that was Banks' position, so he moved to second base. He was a quiet guy and a good player. Ernie was so quiet that he wouldn't talk to anyone. I didn't know what his experiences were playing with and against white players, but he probably did that in the service. I saw right away that he was one of the nicest people in the game. And I could see that he could play.

RANDY JACKSON:

The media treated Ernie and Gene well when they joined the Cubs. They were both great people. I'm not a prejudiced person, and if a person does his job, he's fine with me. They did their jobs.

There was no team policy in regard to talking to the media. You had to use your own judgment. Reporters traveled with you, in style. We knew each other, but I wouldn't say we were friends. We didn't go to the movies together. I usually didn't care what the media said. But one time an out-of-town reporter who had interviewed me in Cincinnati wrote that I didn't care how the team did and that the only thing I was interested in was how I did. I hadn't said anything like that because I would much rather have played for a winning team than a losing team, whether I did good or not. I got a note from the front office to come up there and explain myself. I said there was no way I'd say something like that. And I wrote the guy asking for an apology.

There was only one other time I got annoyed with the media. That's when I was called "phlegmatic." Try that one on for size. Like I didn't care. I never got into arguments and I wasn't fiery, but I didn't figure that remark was necessary or valid. If you can catch ground balls and throw them out, and get the hits, what difference does it make?

In some cases, the sportswriters were little gods, who knew they could make or break players. I saw them almost run one of my managers out of Chicago. But on the whole, they were pretty nice guys and their stories were fair. You just didn't have to believe everything they wrote.

FRANK BAUMHOLTZ:

Ralph Kiner was super-nice and a super competitor. Unbeknownst to most people, he had two painful legs that never had a chance to heal, and had trouble running. Dee Fondy was doing a good job for us at first base, so the only place he could play was left field. Hank Sauer had been a terrific left fielder, but he moved over to right field. It wasn't fair that he had to shift to a new position. So in 1953 I played center field between 1952's co-homer champions, neither of whom was comfortable in the field. I'd have to catch all the balls hit to them.

We played one Sunday doubleheader in Chicago against Pittsburgh. It was so hot and humid that the insects were coming out of the ground and eating through our socks, sucking the blood from our feet. We sprayed our feet, but it didn't matter. Both games were high-scoring affairs, with each team getting about 20 hits and 13 or 14 runs. I got 7 hits off two left-handers. As the day wore on, all the players were worn to a frazzle, particularly Sauer and Kiner, who could move no more than one step from where they positioned themselves. Pirate batters kept hitting the ball into left center and right center, and I kept hearing Sauer and Kiner yell, "Go get it, Frank!" So I was running all over the field after balls. In the seventh inning of the second game, Cavarretta told me to shower and go home. The next day at the park, Phil said, "I suppose you're wondering why I took you out." "Yeah," I responded. "Jesus Christ, Phil, I was having the greatest day I ever had in baseball. Everything they threw up I was hitting the shit out of." He said, "The reason I took you out is that I thought you were loafing." I laughed. "Damn you, Phil."

On the Cubs, everyone liked Cavarretta and had good feelings about our owner, P. K. Wrigley. But players might have had problems with individual people in management, such as our general manager, Wid Matthews. After I finished second to Stan Musial in the 1952 batting race, Matthews sent me a contract with only a $500 raise. That would have given me $11,500. I made more money in the winter by selling clothes for the May Company. Two months later I sent the contract back unsigned. So Matthews called, and I told him that I'd rather quit and work full-time with the May Company than sign that contract. I said I'd make more money as it was and would make even more money when I became a buyer. So he sent me another contract. It contained a $1,000 raise. Having gone through what I had with Frankie Frisch in Chicago and now having this happen, I told my wife that I would quit. Two days before spring training was going to start, Matthews called me from Jackson, Mississippi. I told him I had reached the point where I'd had enough. He said, "Well, what do you want?" I said, "if my season didn't warrant at least a $5,000 raise, forget it." So he told me, "Pack your gear, because you got it." If the son of a bitch hadn't said that, I really would have quit.

So I got $16,000 in 1953. That was a good salary in those days. The word then was that the Cubs had one of the highest average salaries. As Ralph Kiner told us, Branch Rickey didn't pay anybody what they were worth on the Pirates, as had been the case when he was the Dodgers' owner. If you asked him for a raise, he made you cry. It wasn't that bad on the Cubs, but Matthews had it in for me because I wanted that raise. In 1953 I hit .306 and after the season got only a very small raise out of him. He tried to sell me to the White Sox but had to take me back because he hadn't put me on waivers. At the next spring training in Mesa, he walked out to me in center field and had the gall to ask, "Frank, are you mad at me?"

JOHNNY KLIPPSTEIN:

It wasn't easy to pitch for a losing team. In 1953 all 4 starters lost in double figures, with Warren Hacker losing 19, to lead the league. Hacker and Paul Minner led our staff with just 12 wins each, and Bob Rush slipped to 9 wins. I had the best percentage by winning 10 and losing 11. But I didn't pitch any better than I had the previous year.

I enjoyed pitching when Garagiola was my catcher. He was a funny guy. One day I was facing Dusty Rhodes in a touchy situation in the Polo Grounds. Dusty had the reputation for drinking a little Black Label. When Dusty came up to pinch-hit, Joe came to the mound and asked what I was going to throw him. I said I wasn't going to throw him any fastballs and would try to keep the ball away from him because of the short right-field fence. Joe said, "Thank God you said that. I thought you were going to throw inside and knock the

cork off the bottle in his back pocket and there'd be whiskey all over the place." I cracked up and had to turn around because I didn't want Cavarretta to see me laughing on the mound. That was Joe's way of relaxing me a little bit. We got him out.

JIM BROSNAN:

I won 30 games playing army ball at Fort Meade for two years. I had also hitched rides on the Chesapeake Ferry up to Millington, Maryland, to pitch for a semipro team. It was like being back in American Legion ball because I won all my games. The next year I played in a faster semipro league, in which I lost a few times.

When I came out of the army in 1953, I went to spring training with Springfield and made the club. That's where I got my nickname. As a boy I had gone to a school that was run by the Catholic Church and was intended to direct kids to the seminary. So religion had been part of my background. At first Ron Northey—who was trying to make it back to the majors—called me "Reverend." When I told him I didn't like that, he changed it to "Professor." I said, "That's insulting a lot of bright men in academia." But the nickname stuck.

It was one of the faults of the organization that we were never taught Chicago Cubs' loyalty or tradition. We were never taught anything. I played with Bruce Edwards and a couple of other guys who had come over from the Dodgers organization, and they talked about how at the Dodgers' spring training camp, everybody learned fundamentals over and over and over again. It would have been wise of the Cubs to have made fundamentals part of what we learned coming up through the system. As a pitcher at Springfield, I was lost when I had trouble. Nobody would help me. I tried to change myself, altering my delivery and becoming a sinkerball pitcher. I finished the season at 4–17. We had a terrible, terrible club, but my record spoke for itself.

I thought my career was over. I had taken an aptitude test that I was entitled to as an ex-serviceman. The results indicated I should go into accounting or writing. My wife said, "Well, you're no writer and you wouldn't make any money if you were." So I enrolled in Benjamin Franklin University, a specialized accounting school, in Washington, D.C. My wife worked, so we were getting by. And out of the blue comes a letter from Jack Sheehan, who had run the Cubs' farm system since I'd been in the organization. He wrote: "Despite your record, we are promoting you to the Cubs. We are looking forward to seeing you in spring training."

I didn't have a great arm, but they knew I had a major league arm. And they didn't have many of those at their minor or major league levels. If I had played in any other organization, I probably wouldn't have made it. Tommy Lasorda would win 18 or 19 games a year at Montreal, yet the Dodgers wouldn't bring him up, while I went 4–17 at Springfield and went to the big leagues. Tommy told me that he wished he could be traded to the Cubs because they had the worst pitching in baseball. And they probably did.

BROOKLYN DODGERS

RUBE WALKER:

There's no doubt we were the class of the league in 1953. We won 105 games, including 60 in Ebbets Field, and won the pennant by 13 games over Milwaukee. Our starters all had outstanding percentages: Carl Erskine went 20–6, Russ Meyer—who everyone seemed to forget about—won 15 games and lost only 5, Billy Loes won 14, and Preacher Roe went 11–3. In 3 years, Preacher had gone 44–8—no one in baseball could compare to that. We also brought up Johnny Podres, a 21-year-old from New York. He was a fine guy and excellent pitcher with pinpoint control, and a good fastball and curve. Dressen taught him how to throw a wicked change-up. He won 9 of 13 decisions as a rookie, pitching both in relief and as a starter, and he impressed us tremendously. Roe was already 38, so it was reassuring to get a young left-hander with Podres' potential.

Nobody liked to pitch against us because Furillo, Snider, Robinson, Campanella, and Hodges all hit over .300. Billy Cox hit over .290. Furillo had a cataract removed and led the league with a .344 average, but his season ended in early September when he had his finger stepped on while beating up on Leo Durocher, whom he hated—Carl actually charged into the Giants' dugout after Ruben Gomez plunked him in the ribs. He missed getting 100 RBIs. But Snider, who hit 42 homers, Hodges, and Campanella each drove in over 120 runs

for us. I got to back up the league's Most Valuable Player. Campy batted .312 and set the major league records for catchers with 41 homers and a league-leading 142 RBIs. What a great player he was! So I didn't mind playing a little less than usual.

It wasn't easy to break into the Dodgers' lineup, but Junior Gilliam came up from the minors and immediately became our second baseman, moving Robinson to left field. He was a nice, quiet young black man from Tennessee who fit right in. Jackie and Campy looked after him. Junior had a world of talent. He was a switch-hitter who had a lot of speed and led the league in triples, scored 125 runs, and stole over 20 bases. For a youngster, he was very patient at the plate and had a good eye. He walked 100 times and rarely struck out. He was voted Rookie of the Year, following in the footsteps of Jackie, Don Newcombe, and Joe Black.

BEN WADE:

All the Dodgers hated to lose. World Series losses, like the one we suffered in 1952, would get to us. However, we were a mature ballclub who knew that we had a chance to get beat, and if that happened it wasn't the end of the world. I never saw as much confidence on a team as with Brooklyn.

Also, it had the most togetherness. I was living in Bay Ridge and had two small kids, so I didn't socialize with other Dodgers when we played at home. However, on the road everybody was friendly. You went to movies and restaurants together. I played bridge with coaches Jake Pitler and Billy Herman, and Reese and Gilliam. We had a lot of good poker players, too, Robinson especially. He loved to play. Reese and Hodges were very close and spent a lot of time together. Snider and Erskine were together. Campanella and Newcombe—who was still in the service—were very close. Robinson had to be a loner because he came up that way. The closest he got to anybody was with Gilliam.

In 1953 I relieved in all my 32 appearances. As long as I got to work, it didn't make any difference to me if I started or relieved. I went 7–5 and completed every inning in which I pitched. I was never relieved during an inning. I guess that's a record you can only tie, not beat.

NEW YORK GIANTS

BILL RIGNEY:

In 1953 Bobby Thomson, Monte Irvin, Alvin Dark, and Hank Thompson each hit over 20 homers and Don Mueller, Irvin, Dark, and Thompson hit over .300, with Whitey Lockman and Davey Williams in the .290s. But Willie Mays was still in the service and our offense wasn't as formidable as it had been in past years. Also, our pitching wasn't very good. Ruben Gomez, a right-hander from Puerto Rico, led our top staff with just 13 victories. Jansen won just 11 and Hearn and Maglie won less than that. So it was a bad year for the Giants, who finished 14 games under .500 and dropped to fifth place.

I left the club to go off and be a player-manager for Minneapolis. Leo asked me to stay with the Giants and coach, but I said, "I've got to tell you: I can't because I

want your job." He replied, "Go off and manage, and someday you'll get it."

The best baseball ever in the major leagues was played in the late '40s and early '50s. The best baseball was found in New York, where there were three great teams: the Yankees, the Dodgers, and the Giants. We played at the same time, in the same place, and at the same level of excellence. Every day was a thrill, and a new story that became part of baseball lore and history. There would never be anything like it.

PHILADELPHIA PHILLIES

DEL ENNIS:

Under Steve O'Neill, we continued to play well. Our record wasn't quite as good as in 1952, but we tied for third with the Cardinals. Robin Roberts tied Warren Spahn for the league lead with 23 wins. Curt Simmons and Jim Konstanty also won a lot of games.

RALPH KINER (CUBS):

Curt Simmons had a herky-jerky motion that made him tough, particularly on left-handers. Robin Roberts didn't throw the fastest fastball in the National League, but he threw the best. It had the most movement.

HANK SAUER (CUBS):

I always hit good against Simmons. I had hit 3 homers in a game against him in 1952 and would do it again another year. That would be the first time a batter did that to a major league pitcher. It was just one of those things. Because of his motion, I didn't watch his body, his head, or his eyes. I knew he was coming three-quarters, and would concentrate on the moment his hand released the ball. Robin Roberts was tougher. When he got men on base he was the toughest pitcher to hit. His ball would go toward the middle of the plate and then sail. If it didn't sail, he was in trouble.

D. ENNIS:

I had one of my big RBI seasons, with 125, and hit 29 homers. Ashburn hit .330, and three of our infielders hit some homers—Jones, Hamner, and Earl Torgeson. Earl played first base for us from 1953 until part of the way through 1955. We called him Clark Kent because when

Bill Rigney's playing career ended in 1953, after 8 seasons with the New York Giants, but he would return as the team manager in 1956.

he took off his glasses, watch out. Earl got hit his first time up in a game in St. Louis. Off came his glasses. He laid them right on home plate. We all said, ''Uh, oh!'' He turns to the catcher, Sal Yvars, pops up his mask, and hits him in the chops. That started a free-for-all. Torgeson was a tough guy who could get rambunctious. He'd put his fist through a TV screen.

Our catcher, Smoky Burgess, was very different. We got Smoky the year before in the deal for Andy Seminick and Dick Sisler. He was very quiet, very religious, and very sincere. We were friends. Smoky's backup catcher, Stan Lopata, was even more religious. His sisters were nuns. He would go into the closet every night and read the rosaries. Not surprisingly, he was hard to get to know.

PITTSBURGH PIRATES

RALPH KINER:

When I was winning the 7 consecutive home run titles, I never thought about my place in baseball history or the Hall of Fame. I did have a goal of some year hitting 60 homers. It was always written about, and I lied when I told reporters that it didn't matter to me if I ever equaled Babe Ruth's record. I would have loved to hit 60 homers. But I never got close enough to do it. What made it too difficult is that many pitchers wouldn't throw strikes to me. Some games I'd be walked almost every time up.

In 1953, even before my trade to the Cubs, it was obvious that my home run title streak was ending. I knew I didn't have a chance to keep it going after I hit only 7 homers in 41 games for the Pirates. Frank Thomas was succeeding me as the Pirates' slugger. He was playing his first full year and proving to be a great ballplayer. I thought he copied my batting stance a bit.

I was disappointed to leave the Pirates in June. But obviously, it had been upsetting playing for those bad Pirate teams. I was saved because I had a good attitude because of Hank Greenberg, we had some good guys who tried, and I was motivated by being in home run races each year. It was very tough, and after my career was over I looked back and couldn't understand how I stood it. I would do well and nothing would come out of it. I just tried to be the best I could and be well prepared.

Having won the National League homer title in his first 7 years, Ralph Kiner's production dropped off early in 1953, resulting in the high-salaried star's quick trade to the Cubs.

I worked extremely hard and despite our defeats enjoyed every minute of it. It wasn't a task. I had been fortunate to live in Pittsburgh and play in a good-hitting park, but it would have been even better if we'd had good teams. I really missed not playing on a pennant winner.

FRANK THOMAS:

I talked to Branch Rickey about a contract for 1953. I was getting $6,000 and wanted another $1,000 for my good year at New Orleans. He wouldn't do it. I said, ''You're kidding. Don't I get a raise for what I've done?'' His response was ''I can't pay major league salaries to minor league ballplayers.''

Our manager, Fred Haney, put his arm around me and told me he'd give me a chance to show if I could play every day in the major leagues. It was like someone taking a blanket off me and letting me loose. I realized I was good. I had raw talent and could hit the ball a long way. I also got the bat on the ball. In the majors, I would never strike out 100 times in a season.

I hit 30 homers and drove in 102 runs in just 128 games. I went to Rickey at the end of the year, and the first words out of my mouth were "I'm a major leaguer now and I want to be paid accordingly." "What do you want?" "$15,000." "You go along with my offer of $12,500, and if you have another good year, I'll take good care of you." I didn't know any better, so I believed him.

ELROY FACE:

Branch Rickey had moved to Pittsburgh after drafting me to the Dodgers. Then, two years later, he drafted me again, out of the Dodgers' system. I went right to the Pirates as a 25-year-old rookie. I didn't deal much with Rickey. Contracts were handled by his son, Branch Jr., and that was probably just as well. If you demanded a raise from Rickey, he would scare you into thinking he would demote you rather than pay the salary increase. I know he did that to Bob Friend one time when Bob went in to see him, and Bob got so frightened that he took Rickey's lower offer in about half a second.

Fred Haney used me a lot—I was in over 40 games, mostly as a starter. That's what I wanted to be. In those days, only a few teams had relief specialists. Most relievers were mop-up men.

It was exciting to be in the majors, even with a last-place club that lost 104 games. There wasn't much leadership on the team. Maybe some of the older players, like Johnny Lindell or Joe Garagiola. Joe was our catcher until he was traded to the Cubs along with Ralph Kiner and George Metkovich. We got catcher Toby Atwell in that deal, and he became my roommate. Other than our left fielder, Frank Thomas, we didn't have any power and not much of a lineup. We had the O'Brien twins, Johnny and Eddie, playing at second and short, Danny O'Connell at third, Preston Ward at first, Cal Abrams and Carlos Bernier in the outfield, Atwell and Mike Sandlock behind the plate. The only guy who had been a 20-game winner was Murry Dickson, a knuckleballer. He did it in 1951, but then he lost 21 games the next year and 19 games in 1953. He was still our ace. We also had Paul LaPalme and Lindell, an ex-Yankee outfielder who came back to the majors in 1953 after

winning over 20 games using a hard knuckler in the Coast League, but they both had bad records. Bob Friend, our fourth starter, was a struggling young pitcher then, and Vern Law and Ron Kline had been sent back to the minors for more seasoning. That's what the Pirates had in mind for me after I went 6–8 with an ERA over 6.50 in my rookie season.

CINCINNATI REDS

ANDY SEMINICK:

We couldn't compare to the Dodgers, who scored 200 more runs than any other team, but the Reds' lineup made vast improvements in one year. I had one of my best seasons, hitting 19 homers and driving in 64 runs. As I predicted, Ted Kluszewski emerged as an All-Star player, hitting over .300 and breaking Hank Sauer's club record for homers with 40. He also was one of 3 Reds to drive in 100 runs. Center fielder Gus Bell, who came over from the Pirates, batted .300, hit 30 homers, and scored and drove in over 100 runs. And left fielder Jim Greengrass hit 20 homers and drove in 100 runs. Jim was a great guy who became very popular with the fans. He was a cutup who liked to have fun. Rogers Hornsby had brought him up for a brief time in 1952 because he saw the way he hustled. He had some good potential.

Joe Adcock had been traded to the Braves to make room for Greengrass in left. Rocky Bridges, who had been in the Dodgers' organization, became my new roommate and our second baseman. He was a tobacco chewer from Texas. He became part of one of the best defensive infields in the league. Rocky, Kluszewski, Roy McMillan, and Bobby Adams led their positions in various fielding categories.

Our problem was that our pitching became even worse with Ewell Blackwell's departure and Ken Raffensberger's sudden decline. Harry Perkowski led our team with just 12 wins. Because we couldn't win, it cost Hornsby his job with just over a week left in the season. Nobody was upset that we'd have a new manager in 1954.

AMERICAN LEAGUE 1953

"I DIDN'T FEEL IT WAS UNFAIR HOW

GOOD THE YANKEES WERE. I

THOUGHT THAT WAS THE WAY IT

WAS SUPPOSED TO BE. I LOOKED

FORWARD TO THAT EXTRA CHECK

EVERY FALL."

GENE WOODLING

PHILADELPHIA ATHLETICS

JOE DE MAESTRI:

Right after the 1952 season ended, the Browns traded me back to the White Sox for another young shortstop, Willie Miranda. I was beginning to think I'd be traded every year! Then, before spring training, I flew down to Florida because Paul Richards wanted me to attend a minicamp before the other guys got there. I was there two or three days when I was traded again! Eddie Robinson and I went to the Athletics for Ferris Fain. A couple of other players were involved. That's how my 7-year career as the A's starting shortstop began.

I loved being on the 1953 Athletics. My teammates were so friendly and really interesting guys. I was closest to Gus Zernial and Eddie Robinson. We'd all played together on the 1951 White Sox before Gus was traded. Gus and I were happy to be teammates again, and we roomed together. His average was only about .260, but he hit the ball long and hard. There were times he'd put on real exhibitions, hitting balls on the roof of Shibe Park. It was incredible. I remember him and Don Lenhardt of the Browns hitting homers in one series as if they were trying to see who could hit them the farthest.

I enjoyed playing in Shibe Park. It opened in 1909 and was like the old stadiums in Cleveland and Baltimore that were built like big bowls and had fences way out there. It was over 460 feet to dead center. The only way a singles hitter like myself could hit a homer was to hit the ball right down the line, where it was just over 330 feet. Still, it was a pretty good hitter's park.

Jimmy Dykes was like a father to me and everybody else. He was a good guy. His coaches, Bing Miller and Chief Bender, also looked after us. The Athletics had a lot of talented players, but we still had a tough year. Maybe it was because there wasn't much leadership in any direction. If I had to pick a player who was a leader, I'd say Eddie Joost. Some other guys had experience, too, but they were not as outspoken. Joost was a great leadoff man. The guy would stand there and not even blink an eye on a 3–2 count. He'd take ball four, drop the bat, and walk to first. And he had power, so pitchers had to be more careful than they'd be with the typical leadoff man. Eddie was an excellent shortstop with a great arm. He taught me how to get rid of the ball quickly. I learned a lot from him. In fact, he was the first guy to actually take time to help me in the field. Eddie got hurt in May. After that, I played regularly.

My second-base partner was Pete Suder, who was as good a fielder as there was in those days. He was always in the right spot. Pete was a very quiet, laid-back player who made everything look so easy, including difficult double plays.

Another player I admired was Elmer Valo, a team player who was a lot of fun to be around and who shared his experiences with younger players. He had a slight accent because he was born in Czechoslovakia—you'd forget where he was from but then hear him pronounce a word or two in a strange way. He was a good, good hitter, but he was like a bull in the outfield, a big-chested guy whose movements were far from loose. When he went after a ball, his hands were all over the place and he always looked awkward. But he'd catch the ball even if it meant diving on his stomach.

After being shuttled around the league for several years, Joe De Maestri found a home at shortstop with the Philadelphia Athletics, replacing Eddie Joost.

Elmer, Gus, Suder, Dave Philley, Alex Kellner, and I would all go fishing on our off-days. Alex would take us bass fishing at some nearby lake. I always loved fishing and Dave and Alex were big fishermen. Both Alex and his brother Walt, who pitched briefly for us, did a lot of fishing and big-game hunting. God! The stories you would get all year about all the great places they went to. So they talked Gus and me into going with them to Mexico. It was a hell of a trip!

EDDIE JOOST:

Joe De Maestri became the Athletics' shortstop. I gave him the job because he'd been sitting around too long. I told him I could play if he failed, but he did an adequate job and I couldn't have done much alone to improve the team. By 1953 the Athletics had fallen off to being a seventh-place team, just a little better than the St. Louis Browns. Our downfall was pitching. Over the years we had some talented pitchers like Phil Marchildon, Dick Fowler, Lou Brissie, Carl Scheib, Joe Coleman, Alex Kellner, Bob Hooper, and Bobby Shantz. They would have one or two great years for us, but then they got hurt or became ineffective overnight. It was eerie. Our two best pitchers in 1952 had been Shantz, who won 24 games, and rookie Harry Byrd, who went 15–15. This year, Shantz won only 5 games because of his bad arm, and Byrd lost 20 games and was traded to the Yankees after the season—which I had something to do with.

One of our rookie pitchers in 1953 was Bob Trice. He was the Athletics' first black player. I'm not sure why it took so long. But I know players and management didn't get together and decide to keep black players off the team. Connie Mack never mentioned the subject of integration.

Like the Griffiths in Washington, the Macks—and I'm including his sons Roy and Earle from his first marriage and Connie Mack, Jr., from his second marriage—owned the Shibe Park concessions, which was the prime source of income in those days. The Athletics disintegrated because several families were living off the franchise and they put nothing back into the team. They didn't have sidelines that would comprise other incomes, so they got everything from the team. When things got bad, they just borrowed money. In 1952 and 1953 there were serious financial difficulties.

Both Jimmy Dykes and Arthur Ehlers, our general manager, wanted to get out of Philadelphia because the team was broke. Mr. Mack told Dykes that the team was having such financial problems that he'd have to take a salary cut if he wanted to manage the A's in 1954. Ehlers was offered the general manager job when St. Louis moved to Baltimore, and he asked Dykes to become the first Orioles manager. Dykes confided in me: "I'm not going to manage here next year and I think they're going to offer the job to you. I think you should take the opportunity."

GUS ZERNIAL:

I was pretty optimistic about the Athletics becoming a contender. But then things started happening. Hank Majeski was traded to the Indians during the 1952 season; our best average hitter, Ferris Fain, was traded to the White Sox after the season; Bobby Shantz hurt his arm; managerial changes were talked about; there were front office problems. It got so bad that supposedly Connie Mack sold Allie Clark to Chicago in order to meet his payroll.

I hoped Alex Kellner would take up some of the slack once Shantz got hurt. When I was on the White Sox, he had been the toughest A's pitcher I faced. He won 20 games as a rookie in 1949 but was always around a .500 pitcher after that, including 1953. He tied Harry Byrd for most wins on the team, but that was only 11 wins. Alex and I became good friends, and in the off-season, Joe De Maestri, myself, Alex, and his brother Walter had a great time fishing in Mexico.

In my spare time during the season, I went to movies. I didn't play cards and I wasn't a nightclubber, though every once in a while I'd go in. I didn't stay there that long because I didn't like drinking that much and I liked to get to the ballpark early the next day. I enjoyed sitting down with people and just chatting. I would talk to players on trains or people I'd run into in hotel lobbies. I was always an extrovert, outspoken but not braggadocio. I had opinions about baseball, politics, everything. But I didn't say anything critical of our ballclub because I didn't want to get into trouble. I was critical of some reporters, however, because they didn't tell it like I had said it.

I finished the season with 108 RBIs. I thought that

was a greater achievement than driving in 129 runs in 1951. That's because I had Eddie Robinson hitting in front of me. He always made contact and hit 22 homers and drove in 102 runs, so he didn't leave me nearly as many men to pick up as Ferris Fain had in the previous two years.

In late September we were way out of the race, so I was thinking about my individual stats. I was leading the homer derby, 41 homers to Al Rosen's 40. For the last series of the year we were playing in Washington and the Indians were playing at home against Chicago. I was at a disadvantage because it was much harder to homer to left in Griffith Stadium than in Municipal Stadium. It was about 70 feet farther down the line. I was thinking that if I could just hit one more homer I would at very least tie for the title. I did homer on the second night, which made me feel more secure, but Rosen hit one later that night. I was still ahead 42–41, but on the final day Rosen came up with 2 homers and won the title 43–42. The second went to the opposite field and curved around the right-field foul pole. Eddie Stewart, a friend of mine with whom I used to work out, was playing right field for the Sox, and he later told me, "You know, Gus, the second one Rosen hit was foul." Of course, I would have liked to have won the title that year.

ST. LOUIS BROWNS

LES MOSS:

It wasn't strange that I played for Marty Marion after playing with him. I thought he was a good manager to play for. I was sorry that he stopped playing short almost entirely. If someone tried to steal second, Marion was the easiest guy I ever threw to, the one with the best tag. I'd throw it anywhere, and boom.

We had another terrible season in our last year in St. Louis, finishing in last place once more. We had one 14-game losing streak that ended when we ended the Yankees' 18-game win streak. We had one other high spot and that was provided by an unlikely player: Bobo Holloman, a tall, hard-throwing rookie right-hander from Georgia. Bobo wasn't really as bad as his reputation, but he didn't have command of his pitches. On May 6, with me catching, Bobo got his first major league start and threw a no-hitter against Philadelphia, beating them 6–0. It was said that Bobo was lucky because the A's kept hitting line drives to our fielders, but all I remember was Billy Hunter making two outstanding plays at short. It was a legitimate no-hitter. After the game, Bobo, Billy, and I posed for pictures together and the press made a big thing of the game because Bobo was the only pitcher in the 20th century to throw a no-hitter in his first major league start and the only Browns pitcher to have thrown a no-hitter since another Bobo did it in 1934—Bobo Newsom.

Another vivid memory I have of 1953 is hitting pitcher Bob Miller in the head with a line drive in Detroit. That ball had enough on it to still go into center field. It's a good thing he was leaning backward and didn't get the full blow. That was scary.

BOB TURLEY:

I had entered the army for a two-year stretch in October 1951. I pitched a lot in the service, keeping sharp and in condition. I heard very little from the Browns during this time. I was so darn broke that I asked Bill Veeck for $500, but he turned me down. Probably he was broke, too.

I saved my leave time in 1953, so when I got out there were still about 45 days left in the baseball season. I had a major league contract when I went into the service, so when I got out I automatically rejoined the Browns. I signed a new minimum-salary contract that was given to me by one of the men who worked for Veeck. They were trying to put one over on me. When I examined it later, I discovered it was for two years. I said, ''No way!'' I went back in and forced them to tear it up. If they hadn't, I would have received the minimum salary, $6,000, for two years without the chance of a raise. It would have cost me $3,000, because I got $9,000 for the 1954 season.

I had married in 1952, and my wife and I stayed with my parents. On the road, my roommate was Harry Brecheen. After spending his entire career on the Cardinals, he came to the Browns that year to both pitch and be a pitching coach. He was about 15 or 16 years older than me. When I was 11, a team I was on played a 3-inning game at Sportsman's Park before the Cardinals' game. Our manager gave each of us baseballs for autographing and I asked Harry to sign my ball. He was pitching that day and said he didn't have time. When we roomed together, you bet your life I reminded him of that day 11 years before. I liked Harry. He was a funny guy from Oklahoma, with a dry sense of humor and a lot of common sense. He taught me pitching fundamentals, which was important because in those days there weren't pitching coaches to help us develop.

I had two catchers on the Browns. Les Moss was a great guy, a joker. He was a good receiver for young pitchers because he could make us feel good and motivate us. He'd have me throw 8 of 10 fastballs. I preferred him catching me to Clint Courtney, but Courtney was a better hitter. ''Scrappy'' was a free spirit with a bad temper.

It wasn't depressing playing in front of empty stands in St. Louis. I was a rookie pitcher and wasn't looking into the stands. I just wanted to play baseball and improve. I pitched 10 games, losing 6 but winning the first 2 games of my career. I had a good earned run average and struck out 61 batters in 60⅓ innings. I also walked 45. Confidence was no problem—I always had a ton of that—but wildness was. As I had gone up the ladder to the major leagues, I never knew I was wild. All I was doing was winning almost every game I pitched, and I thought that was important. There were about 500 guys in the system, and they'd get rid of guys as often as they signed them—coaching them wasn't a priority. When I got to the majors they told me I was wild.

One guy who had great control was Satchel Paige. He pitched pretty well for us and made the All-Star team. I got to know Paige real well. He was a character, a loosy-goosy type of guy. But he had a lot of pride. We went to play an exhibition game in Charleston, West Virginia, and it was heavily promoted because he was going to pitch. But when he discovered that he wouldn't be allowed to stay in the hotel with the white players, he took off.

I was a movie fan and would go to a matinee every day before night games. I wasn't on the team so long that I'd have any one person to hang out with. There was a lot of drinkers on the team, but I wasn't a drinking person, so I didn't go with those guys. For a last-place team, the Browns had a lot of fun. There was always a lot of laughing in our clubhouse. One day I asked Marty

Marion how the players could be so cheerful after losing a tough game. He said in a comical way, "Bob, when you come to the point in your career when you get through a game without getting hurt, you'll be happy, too."

BOB CAIN:

The Browns players usually went their separate ways, but in the clubhouse they were a close team. Players cared more for each other in those days, and everyone on the team helped each other whenever they could. As teammates, they were real nice guys, and they were all approachable by fans. I made a lot of good friends: Billy Hunter, Dick Kryhoski, Vic Wertz, Bobby Young, Jim Dyck, Clint Courtney, Roy Sievers, Les Moss, Duane Pillette, Donny Lenhardt, Harry Brecheen, Don Larsen, Dick Kokos, Virgil Trucks, Satchel Paige.

Billy Hunter was a very good shortstop and a popular cutup who kept everyone loose. If you were shagging flies, you could count on Billy to cut in front of you and run off with the ball. Bobby Young was the one who got the only hit off Bob Feller in that 1952 game in which I beat Feller with a 1-hitter of my own. Now in 1953 Young got the only hit off Billy Pierce in a 1–0 loss. He was a pretty good left-handed hitter and not a bad second baseman. He was also a fun guy to talk to. Les Moss was a fun guy. He was always reading or playing cards. Don Larsen was nicknamed "Footsy." He was a very easygoing, nice guy. Nothing seemed to faze him on the mound, which was fortunate because on the Browns you didn't win many games.

Satchel Paige said, "Don't be in a hurry to get yourself into trouble." He was quite a guy, one of the greatest men in baseball. He became strictly a relief pitcher in St. Louis, and Veeck said he wouldn't have to be at the ballpark until about the fifth inning. One day he arrived in mid-game as usual, got dressed, and headed for the bullpen and his contour chair. After the game, the entire team filed into the shower only to discover that Paige had been fishing before coming to the ballpark. The whole shower was filled with fish. On trains, he wouldn't come and sit with you unless you asked him. I don't know if he was still a little leery, though he never said anything. When we'd invite him to play cards, he'd say, "You don't want old black Satch in your game be-cause I'll take all your money." He was a comical guy, and we got along really well. In spring training we were at the Mission Inn while on a road trip from our camp in San Bernardino. My wife went to check if we had any mail. Satch was in the lobby with a whole stack of letters. My wife joked, "I'll trade my one letter for some of yours." He said, "Just a minute, Mrs. Judy," and he shuffles through his letters, saying, "I don't like her . . . I don't like her . . . oh, this is the one that's got all the money—you can have all the rest of them."

I saw Bobo Holloman's no-hitter. Veeck intended to ship him out the next day, but he needed a starter against the Athletics. After the no-hitter, the fans wouldn't let him demote Holloman. He wasn't a good pitcher, but that day he got away with everything. When he didn't win any more starts, the fans weren't so taken with him, and Veeck demoted him and he never pitched in the majors again. I wasn't friends with Bobo. I heard he was pretty much of a skirt-chaser.

Women were all over the place. They were available to players in every town. You just had to watch what you were doing. It could have been a problem if you wanted it to be. Everybody knew which players went after women and which ones stayed away. You could disassociate yourself from the skirt-chasers.

I had a lot of trouble with Marty Marion. Before he became manager, everybody on the team really liked him. But overnight he changed. And it's tough when that's the guy who controls your life. He thought everyone should be a perfectionist like him. Early in 1953 he brought me in to relieve against Cleveland. I got Larry Doby to hit a perfect double-play ball to Dick Kryhoski at first. But Dick let the ball go through him for an error. Then Marty came to the mound and took me out. I went right into the clubhouse, despite his rule that pitchers who were taken out of a game had to sit on the bench. I took a shower and left the stadium. After that we didn't see eye to eye. I had my worst year in baseball pitching for him. I went 4–10, with an ERA over 6.00.

We finished in last place. That was the Browns' last year in St. Louis. The souvenir I kept was a tiny St. Louis Browns uniform that Bill Veeck gave to all the wives who had babies. It came with socks, a hat, and a miniature bat. We got the last uniform ever issued of any size by the Browns.

CLEVELAND INDIANS

AL SMITH:

I was disappointed that the Indians sent me back to Indianapolis in 1953. I showed I belonged with my bat: I batted over .330 and had 18 homers and 75 RBIs by July 4. Then they brought me up because one of their outfielders had been hurt. It was a thrill to finally be a major league ballplayer, to have reached the top. I played my first games in Chicago in a doubleheader, facing Billy Pierce and Harry Dorish, and went 3 for 6. I played outfield for the first time.

I felt pressure to succeed. If you didn't hit, you wouldn't be out there, and we blacks knew that if we

Previously a star in both the Negro Leagues and the minor leagues, Al Smith became a productive outfielder for the Cleveland Indians in 1953 and would be a pivotal player on their pennant team the following year.

didn't become starters, we would be demoted to the minors. Teams didn't have blacks sitting on the bench for very long. That was one reason we played even if we were hurt and didn't inform our managers or trainers. We didn't say anything because once we were on the bench we might have lost our jobs. I didn't play regularly until late in the season and batted only 150 times. One of my highlights was getting the only hit in a game against Boston.

Once you reach the majors, you can't just throw your glove out on the field. I had to work and study. The guy who helped me most as a fielder was Larry Doby, who played center field. I was in left, and he helped me learn where to play all the hitters. He'd tell me that when he moved 3 or 4 steps toward right field, I should move 3 or 4 steps to my left. He'd tell me that since Early Wynn was a high-ball pitcher, there would be a lot of fly balls hit off him, and that since Garcia and Lemon were sinkerball pitchers, batters would hit more line drives off them. Bob Feller wasn't throwing as fast as he once had, so with a pull hitter I wouldn't shade him to center but would guard the line. Larry also told me about the wind. After playing a while in Municipal Stadium I got used to the wind coming off the lake. Right field was the hardest because the wind would come in through an opening in left and swing around, often carrying the ball hit to right, or holding it up.

I also would adjust according to my shortstops. They would give a sign on their leg or something. Also the coaches, Red Kress and Tony Cuccinello, would move us in the outfield. After a while I knew where to play everyone except batters I'd never seen before.

I lived by myself in the southeast end of Cleveland, and palled around with the single guys. On the road I roomed some with Dave Hoskins, a right-handed pitcher from Mississippi who went 9–3 in 1953, but mostly I roomed with Doby. Some players thought Larry was quiet and a loner, but I didn't see him that way. Not only did he help me in the field, but we talked a lot when we were alone. He was a helluva nice guy. He wasn't angry, just stubborn about how he played the game, and a tough competitor.

The train trips were something. The Cleveland to Boston trip was long and boring. We had a baggage car, a diner, two sleepers for the players, and one sleeper for the sportswriters. In Cleveland we brought our own luggage to the station, but in hotels we'd just carry our bags down to the lobby. Like most teams, the Indians played cards. We played poker and bid whist. Early Wynn liked to play. Luke Easter loved to play cards. I loved Luke. He was a big, jolly fellow who kept me laughing all the time.

There were always sportswriters milling about in the trains and clubhouses. Back in those days, the reporters knew baseball. They were older guys like Red Smith and Hal Lebovitz of the *Cleveland News,* and some of the other Indians' reporters. I got along with them all. They were part of our lives. So was the Indians' announcer Jimmy Dudley. We all knew him.

The person who was the hardest to get to know was Al Lopez, the manager. He didn't talk too much. He'd just watch you, and if you did well, then he gained confidence in you. He was a difficult person to get along with. If he got riled, he revealed a temper that would shake you up. He could spit out some ''words'' to his players and he had some terrible arguments with umpires. However, I thought he was a pretty good manager. He'd tell you to take certain pitches, but when he found out you had a reason for swinging when you did—not wanting to fall behind in the count, for instance—he'd let you do what you wanted to do. After a while he left me pretty much alone.

The Indians won 92 games, but for the third straight year under Lopez finished second to the Yankees, 7 games back. Luke Easter broke his foot and didn't play much, so Al Rosen and Larry Doby carried the offense. Rosen was the star, hitting over .330 and leading the league in homers, and had 145 RBIs. He was the American League's Most Valuable Player and would have won the Triple Crown if Mickey Vernon hadn't batted one point higher than him. Doby also had a good year, with about 30 homers and over 100 RBIs. The pitching was tremendous. Bob Lemon won 21 games, Mike Garcia and Early Wynn had only a couple less. Bob Feller won 10 games, pitching a lot less. We called Feller ''Inky'' because he'd carry around and read about 20 newspapers that his wife packed for him in a bag. The Yankees stayed ahead of us because they also had great pitching, with Whitey Ford, Vic Raschi, Ed Lopat, Johnny Sain, and Allie Reynolds, who was the toughest pitcher I faced. But the Indians and Yankees didn't have all the good pitchers in the league. That's

why it was hard for me to come into the league and just start hitting. In my first year I batted .240. However, I'd shown enough improvement where I knew that if I played every day for a full season I could do much better.

BILLY MORAN:

From the time I was 11 or 12 I played organized hardball in the East Point area of Atlanta, where we had moved from Montgomery, Alabama. My father had played semipro ball with a cotton mill team and he worked out with me every day, developing my skills. By my mid-teens I was playing five or six nights a week during the summer in different leagues for different ages. I was a hard-hitting shortstop. I also played on my high school baseball team and got a lot of local press. I was seen by baseball scouts, particularly when my Atlantic Steel team in the City League won the regional tournament and competed for the national title, where I was lucky enough to hit a homer or two. Several teams approached me, and I had tryouts in Chicago, Cincinnati, and Cleveland. In 1952, when I was 18, I signed with Joe Sewell, the Indians' Atlanta scout. I signed because of the money. It was for $40,000, and that seemed like a lot to me because I didn't think even Early Wynn was making that much on the Indians. There were several shortstops in my area who signed then: Coot Veal, Bob Lillis. . . . I didn't know everything about the bonus rule, but I wouldn't have to stay on the major league roster and be stuck on the bench.

Meanwhile I was going to work for my degree in industrial management at Georgia Tech. I had an agreement with Cleveland that I could go to school and report late to spring training every year. That was rare in baseball, so eventually they talked me out of that. It would take me 11 years to get my degree.

The Indians had a good system with a lot of minor leaguers. When I went to spring training with the Cleveland farm clubs in Daytona in 1953, I was number 469. They had different-color socks to distinguish the players: brown socks were for Class D, red socks for Class C, and green socks for Class A, which was Reading, Pennsylvania. Indianapolis, the Triple A team, had the striped socks that the Indians wore the year before. All I wanted that first year was to get those green stockings. But I spent my first year in D ball with Green Bay. I think some of the players resented me at the beginning because I was a bonus player. But that didn't last. I was fairly confident and had a good year, hitting about .275. So I was on my way.

BOSTON RED SOX

GEORGE KELL:

The Red Sox were known for hitting—we won one game against Detroit 23–3 at Fenway Park, in which we got 14 hits and 17 runs in one inning; rookie outfielder Gene Stephens set a major league record with 3 hits that inning. However, it shouldn't be forgotten that we had some very good pitchers. Mel Parnell was the Red Sox ace. He was a fine pitcher, a left-hander who had suc-

In his one full season with the Red Sox, George Kell batted .300 for his eighth consecutive year.

NATIONAL BASEBALL LIBRARY, COOPERSTOWN, N.Y.

cess in Fenway Park. He was in the same class as Hal Newhouser but didn't throw as hard. He'd throw a hard slider down and in. One Opening Day in Boston it was about 32 degrees and we were going to play Washington. I was sitting in the clubhouse complaining about the weather when he said, ''I like it! I'll hit the first couple of right-handers right on the fists with my slider and they won't swing the rest of the day.'' He was right. They were just frozen. He knew when he went out there he had the advantage. He was one of the more intelligent pitchers.

Ellis Kinder had been a so-so pitcher with the St. Louis Browns in 1946 and 1947. Then he went to Boston and became outstanding. In 1949, as a starter, his record was 23–6. By 1951 he was one of baseball's top relief pitchers. I was on Detroit then, and he came in with the game on the line and got 3 outs so fast you couldn't believe it. Later, Charlie Keller reminded me that Kinder didn't pitch that way before. He had been lackadasical and now he was like a bulldog. He wanted to pitch more than anybody, particularly in tough situations. Boudreau couldn't keep him out of there. It didn't always work out. Kinder pitched against the Yankees in a tight game at Yankee Stadium with one out and men on first and third in the ninth. Boudreau came out to the mound and asked Kinder if he preferred pitching to Mickey Mantle or walking him and pitching to Yogi Berra. Kinder chose to pitch to Mantle because he thought he had a chance to strike him out, while he had no chance of striking out Berra. Then Mantle hit the ball into the monuments in deep center to beat us.

Frank Sullivan, a very tall rookie right-hander, pitched briefly in 1953. Sullivan had been to Korea but was just 23. They brought him into a tough situation and I walked to the mound to say something to him. I thought I'd calm the kid down. He said, ''Hey, I've been out there with machine guns firing all around me. They might get some hits, but they aren't going to kill me, are they?''

Billy Goodman and I hit over .300 and we got good years from Dick Gernert, Sammy White, and Jimmy Piersall, but with Ted Williams out until August, the pitchers had to carry us a lot of the time. Parnell, Kinder, Mickey McDermott, and Hal Brown did great jobs for us all season, and then Williams came back and was as good as he'd ever been and we finished in fourth place, 15 games behind the Yankees but 15 games over .500.

HERSHELL FREEMAN:

I got married in 1950 at Birmingham and my first child was born when I was at Louisville. It was probably the best thing that happened to me in terms of my career. I lived out of a suitcase for two or three weeks at a time, and it gave me a home and family to come back to. My look toward baseball was much more pleasant after I got married. Mike "Pinky" Higgins, who managed me at Louisville in 1951 and '52, taught me to leave the game at the ballpark. I tried never to take a bad ballgame home with me because it wasn't fair to my wife and kids. Because it wasn't their fault, it was mine for making the bad pitches.

We lived quite far from Fenway Park, out in West Newton, so on homestands I saw the other players only at the ballpark. Most of my good friends that year were pitchers. I got along well with Willard Nixon, a pretty good right-hander from Georgia who I had known since semipro ball. Mel Parnell was a good friend. He had been Boston's best pitcher since the late forties and, like Nixon, would spend his entire career with Boston. Parnell didn't have an overwhelming fastball, but he had great control and made batters hit his pitch. Left-handers weren't supposed to win in Fenway Park, but Parnell did. He would win 21 games in 1953, which was his last good year.

I spent the most time with Ellis Kinder, a tall right-hander who was the best reliever in baseball. He was one of the few guys who was paid to be a relief specialist. I knew I wasn't going to pitch very much because Kinder was a workhorse—he pitched in almost 70 games that year. So instead of learning only through experience, I learned a lot from him, as we relievers had to stick together. He told me how to prepare myself every day. He said that when the other guys were out doing 15 to 20 wind sprints, I shouldn't run as much if there was the possibility I'd pitch that day. He taught me how to take care of my arm, getting heat or some kind of oil on my arm or shoulder if it was cool weather.

The Red Sox had individual personalities, so on the road only a couple of guys would go out together and eat or see a movie. Kinder and I would do that. Occasionally a few other guys would join us. I don't think the lack of unity hurt the Red Sox. The Yankees were a club of individuals, and they won. You could win as individuals or as guys who hung out together.

The Red Sox drank, but not as much as people thought. I never had that problem. My dad was a real bad drinker, and it turned me against it. I was always the designated driver. But I never felt out of place or was teased about it—the guys would order a beer or highball and say, "Bring Hersh a ginger ale."

There was no number one leader on the Red Sox while Ted was off in Korea, but Billy Goodman and Vern Stephens provided leadership. Dominic DiMaggio was a quiet leader before he called it quits at the beginning of the season. He wasn't an outgoing person. From what I saw, he felt he was overshadowed by his brother Joe even though Joe no longer played.

George Kell was very easygoing and not very outspoken, but everyone looked up to him. After all, he was one of the all-time great third basemen and a real good hitter. Johnny Lipon played backup shortstop for us at the end of 1952 and about half of 1953. He was a very level-headed guy with leadership traits. He was a student of baseball, and I sensed he was destined to be a manager.

All the pitchers respected Sammy White, who was one of the best receivers I ever saw. I think he was almost on the same level with Jim Hegan and Roy Campanella. He let the pitcher work his own game, but if he wanted something he got his point across. Also, he was a big guy for a catcher—he was my height, 6'3"—and could hit the long ball, particularly in Fenway Park.

Lou Boudreau had become the manager in 1952. He had a great baseball mind, but I didn't think he could handle ballplayers, particularly a team with a lot of stars. He would have handled situations better if he had tried to deal with the players as individuals. He'd say what he expected the team to do without pointing out what each player's role was. If you didn't understand what he wanted from you as an individual, you couldn't just walk into his office. He was hard to talk to. I felt he would rather be doing something else. He managed the club, but he let his coaches work with the players. He didn't really work with pitchers but left that to his pitching coach, George Susce. I'm sure he felt the media pressure managing in Boston.

The biggest problem we had with the media was that

there were so many reporters. We'd go on a road trip and there might be three Pullman cars for the players and four for the writers. We'd have writers from all the small towns around Boston as well as the Boston writers. The sportswriter who criticized us most was Colonel Egan of the *Record*. He used to write personal things about the Red Sox, including me, and I don't recall ever seeing the man.

I think the Red Sox fit exceptionally well into the community. I think a lot of that had to do with Ted Williams and the Jimmy Fund. All of us were involved to some degree. I think the fans appreciated that. The Fenway fans were diehard Boston fans. Most of them were very knowledgeable. They were anti–New York Yankees. When the Yankees used to come to town, everyone would come to the park just to ride them. Of course, they didn't mind getting on our case, too. The fans even got on Ted pretty good when he came back from Korea in August. But he usually didn't mind it, though there were some incidents. What upset Williams the most was some player who was, as Ted would say, ''doggin' it.'' He wanted everyone to give 100 percent win or lose. He didn't mind letting you know it. He always made the full effort.

Thank God batting practice was the only time I faced him. When he took BP, he'd instruct our pitchers, ''Don't expose the ball until the last second.'' He had such quick hands, and such great eyes that he could almost tell you by watching the ball spin whether you'd held it across the seams, with the seams. . . . He had the best hand-eye coordination of anybody I've ever seen. He wasn't only a great hitter, he was a great outfielder. He could play the Green Monster as well as anyone who ever walked on that field. After coming back from Korea, he was unreal. He batted only about 90 times, but after being away a year and a half, he hit 13 homers and batted .407!

Jimmy Piersall also returned and did a great job. The Red Sox didn't find him disruptive.

BOB CAIN (BROWNS):

Jimmy Piersall was the most eccentric ballplayer during my career. Several times during batting practice, he'd walk on top of the Green Monster as if it were a tightrope. He was a little nutty.

H. FREEMAN:

One game, Jimmy went 6 for 6. And he was a tremendous right fielder that year. I would have been willing to pitch with only 2 outfielders if they were Willie Mays and Jimmy Piersall. He was the type to do anything in the world to win or help the ballclub. Oh, Lord, did he love to play. He would have played from morning to sundown—and if there were lights, until the next morning.

I got into only 18 games during the season and won only 1 game. The team also struggled, finishing in fourth place, far behind the Yankees. We were capable of beating anyone, but we couldn't beat the Yankees. DiMaggio was gone, but now Mickey Mantle was there. He was a helluva player. He hit a 565-foot homer against Chuck Stobbs that year in Griffith Stadium. It was the longest homer ever hit in the majors. Against Mantle, I'd throw it and let him do whatever the hell he wanted to, and I'd worry about the next hitter. Mickey was so damn strong, and even if he mishit the ball he could beat out routine grounders with his speed. And even if you shut out Mantle one game, Berra, Bauer, and the other guys would beat your brains out. I was no Yankee lover.

WASHINGTON SENATORS

PEDRO RAMOS:

I didn't speak any English when I signed with the Senators. I thought they were going to send me to Roswell, New Mexico, in the Longhorn League. After flying from Havana to Key West, Florida, and riding on a bus from Miami for three days, I was told I was in Morristown, Tennessee. We played in the Mountain States League. Most of our players were Spanish, from Costa Rica, Nicaragua, Panama, Cuba. We had only about 4 to 5 Americans. Nap Reyes, a Cuban who once played for the New York Giants, was the manager, and he didn't have to flash signs to the Latin players because he could get away with just calling out instructions in Spanish. On that team, I was the only one who made it to the majors.

At the beginning I was a little homesick. I used to walk to a little place called Rainbow Cafe in Morristown. I wanted to eat something that I liked, but I couldn't read the menu. So I pointed to something and hoped. It just happened it was pork chops with a little pineapple and fried potatoes. I ate that every day for two months. Later on, we'd go to the Bean House and eat beans every day.

DETROIT TIGERS

FRED HATFIELD:

Fred Hutchinson had replaced Red Rolfe as manager at the midpoint of the 1952 season, but it wasn't until 1953 that he really had the chance to turn around the club. We still didn't have a great year, but at least we moved up from last to sixth. I liked Hutchinson. He was the first

In his first full season with the Detroit Tigers, Fred Hatfield was a much-used utility player, even playing second base for the first time.

one to praise you when you did well and the first one to jump on you if you did something wrong. Hutchinson had just quit playing himself, so he knew how to get along with players. Plus he put a little fear in us. He was the type who could back up his temper. Nobody who knew him would have wanted to be in a dark alley with him.

With the exception of Ted Gray, Detroit's starting pitchers of the past few years, including Newhouser, Trout, Trucks, Houtteman, and Hutchinson himself, were all gone, so Hutchinson created a new rotation. He acquired the Browns' former ace, Ned Garver, and the longtime Indians pitcher Steve Gromek, who lived in Detroit. They were the right-handers. Our left-handers were Gray and 21-year-old Billy Hoeft. Gromek came over in a deal for Houtteman, which also brought us Ray Boone. Ray batted over .300, with over 20 homers and 90 RBIs, and once we got him to play third, I became a utility man. I played some third and some at second, where Hutchinson had inserted Johnny Pesky. I didn't play at all at shortstop because that position was filled every game by Harvey Kuenn, the league's Rookie of the Year. Harvey was one of the best natural young hitters I ever saw. He was a competitor, a tough out. He batted over .300 and led the league in hits.

I didn't complain that I was back on the bench. Pesky, Kuenn, and Boone were all doing good jobs. So I just waited until I was called on and did a pretty good job myself, in the field and at the plate, where I upped my average about 20 points.

COOT VEAL:

I was a tall shortstop, like my idol Marty Marion. Nobody in the Tigers' organization had problems with my fielding. But I got hitting instructions in the minors. I was a contact hitter who sprayed the ball around, hitting behind runners and stuff like that. I had always been a good hitter, but my first year in spring training, 1953, I was given three or four hitting instructors, including Joe Gordon, who taught me three or four different ways to hit: one to chop down, one to swing level, one to swing up, one to hit inside out. It was confusing. I was a front-foot hitter, but they were teaching me to swing off my back foot. Meanwhile, Harvey Kuenn was hitting line drives off his front foot. He was the best front-foot hitter I ever saw. They didn't try to change him, and he went on to be a batting champion. But they tried to change me, and I think that hurt me.

CHICAGO WHITE SOX

BILLY PIERCE:

The White Sox always had good defense to go along with the pitching. We didn't feel that we were doing it all ourselves with guys like Fox, Carrasquel, Rivera, Minoso, and Lollar supporting us. In 1953 we also added third baseman Bob Elliott and Ferris Fain, the best-fielding first baseman in the league. Elliott still did an adequate job at third, but had slowed down and didn't have the power he displayed with the Pirates and Braves in the forties. This would be his last season in the majors.

Fain was still an outstanding fielder, but we were also counting on his hitting. He had led the league in batting the previous two years with the Athletics, but Paul Richards placed him further back in the lineup and he tried to hit the long ball. And that hurt him because he was more of a singles and doubles hitter. I didn't socialize with Ferris, but we were friends in the clubhouse. There was no time that I could see on the field that Fain or any other player had been drinking the night before. Guys who drank would sleep it off and be in good shape for the ball game the next day. Baseball was their livelihood.

The White Sox finished third again, but we won 89 games, which was quite a lot considering Virgil Trucks and I were the only productive starters. Many of our wins could be attributed to Richards. He was always ahead of the game, knowing innings in advance who he'd pinch-hit for and who'd pinch-run. We were next to last in homers and sixth in average, yet we finished third in runs, behind first-place New York and second-place Cleveland. Once I was pitching against the Yankees and they had two right-handed batters coming up in the eighth inning, so Richards moved me to first base and had Harry Dorish pitch to the two batters before I finished up. I got one putout at first, so I made the baseball record books as a fielder. Richards had to come up with those kinds of things for us to win.

The White Sox didn't go into a game thinking our offense would give us 10 runs to work with. We had some good hitters—and Minoso could drive in 100 runs for us—but we often eked out runs. Once I lost a game 1–0 and then left the next game with the score tied 0–0. When we scored a run in the first inning of my next start, Nellie said, "There: you got your run—now hold it." That made me laugh. It turned out we did win, 1–0. We won a lot of close, low-scoring games.

In 1953 I won a bunch myself. I pitched 7 shutouts and had a stretch of 51 innings in which I didn't give up an earned run. Everything went well. This was the year I really came into my own, winning 18 games and leading the league with 186 strikeouts. My ERA for over 270 innings was 2.72. For the first time I was given recognition as one of the better pitchers in the league. I was selected to be the American League's starting pitcher in the All-Star Game. That was extremely exciting, particularly because it was my first appearance. The game was in Cincinnati and I started against Robin Roberts. We both pitched 3 scoreless innings. It was very tense. The National League went on to win 5–1. Minnie Minoso drove in our only run. I got to play with the players I usually challenged. Ted Williams and Mickey Mantle were now my teammates. Now, instead of my pitching against Yogi Berra, he was my catcher, and an excellent one at that. I loved mingling with those guys. We really didn't get to meet them during the season. Despite the team's loss, it was a childhood dream come true.

Oddly, Virgil Trucks won even more games than me. He had his only 20-win season. But he had won 5 of those games with the Browns before being traded to us, and then picked up 15 more wins in not that many starts. He finished second to me in the league in strikeouts. That year we were a hard-throwing one-two punch.

GEORGE KELL (RED SOX):

Trucks and I had been teammates in Detroit, but eventually he went to Chicago and I went to Boston. I got a triple off him with the bases loaded. The next time I came up, the bases were empty. Paul Richards came to the mound and took him out of the game. Later I asked Paul why he took out Trucks in that situation. He replied, "He's sitting on the bench saying, 'I'm going to get that Kell. Next time up I'll break his arm.' So I decided to take him out. I knew he'd throw at you." And Trucks liked me.

B. PIERCE:

Virgil hadn't liked his brief stay with the Browns. They were a last-place team and St. Louis was a hot place to play, where balls would shoot through the hard infield or take crazy hops to elude fielders. Still, I didn't mind pitching there because we had a first-division club and they had a second-division club, so our chances of winning were better. I got my 18th win of the season when I beat the Browns in that franchise's last game, 2–1. As time went by, I felt more nostalgic about pitching the last American League game in St. Louis, but at the time it didn't really sink in.

MINNIE MINOSO:

I stood close to the plate, but that's not the reason I was hit by the pitch so often. At the beginning, the pitchers tried to push me off the plate or to hit me. That was before there was any protection. They wanted to see if I was scared. If they had made me scared, I knew I'd never succeed in major league baseball. But I wasn't scared and didn't move away from the plate. That's why I would set records for being hit by the pitch. I remembered when I played with Luke Easter in Cleveland and at San Diego. They'd throw at us both, but neither of us got frightened and neither of us tried to fight. We just got back up and tried to pay the pitcher back with our bats. If we got hit, we were happy to get on base— sometimes I would then steal second so they would realize that when they walked me or hit me, it was like giving up a double.

The one pitcher who I knew threw at me on purpose and hit me was Hal Newhouser. Sometime in the early '50s, I hit a home run off him and the next time up he hit me. He broke the sunglasses in my pocket. Then he said a few bad words to me as I ran to first. He disappointed me because he used to be my idol.

By this time I think Sherm Lollar was the leader of the team, not Nellie Fox. Lollar was a quiet, very gentle, nice man. And he was always helpful to me. Another player who helped me was Ferris Fain, who came from the Athletics. He seemed tough, but he was a good man.

BILL WILSON:

When I was in the army in 1951 and 1952, I was lucky to be stationed at Ford Ord in Monterey, so I could play a lot of baseball. Hollis Thurston, a White Sox scout,

followed our team around. I pitched a few games and Frank Lane wired me to knock it off and go back to the outfield. Going into the army hurt my career. When I got out in 1953, it was like starting all over. My timing was off and I was no longer used to facing good pitching. So I went down to Cuba to play winter ball. I pulled a muscle in my leg and it blew up like one of those toy bazookas you blow up at parties. The Sox flew me back to Chicago and they had to cut out the muscle. I went home and ran to get in shape.

I reported to the Sox on the date that was scheduled and Paul Richards wanted to know where I had been for the last week. I told him I was on time, but he insisted I was late and got pissed off. He acted as if it were my fault and never got over it. The White Sox weren't too loose with Richards as manager. He wasn't a very happy fellow. I didn't get along with him and sat far away from him in the dugout. I might have been less shy with another manager.

Sherm Lollar had become the White Sox catcher in my absence. He was a nice guy and was the one who took the time to teach me the ropes. Normally, the White Sox weren't a team that sat around talking baseball after a game. Everyone would go his own way or go off with his roommate. I roomed with Vern Stephens before he was traded to the Browns in mid-season. He was a nice, happy-go-lucky guy. The rest of the time I hung out with Jim Rivera, Billy Pierce, and Nellie Fox. We'd get on a train or plane and immediately start playing hearts. Then we'd go out to eat. In different cities we had different places. In Detroit we'd go to a steak house; in Washington we'd go to a ribs place. In Chicago I'd stay at the Blackmore Hotel on the South Side and we'd eat around there. If we had a night game on the road, we'd go to a movie in the afternoon. We made our curfews, and followed team guidelines by wearing suits and sport coats and ties in the hotel when we'd eat breakfast or lunch. We were anything but a wild group.

The White Sox weren't really a drinking team. Nellie, Billy, and I would go out to dinner, and maybe Nellie and I would have a drink or two. That was it. Of course, Ferris Fain drank more than his share. With Ferris you might not see him for a couple of days. He was a wild one. He'd run around with Virgil Trucks. I had heard Jim Rivera was a wild guy, but I never saw him do anything wild. He was one of the funniest guys on the team. He was always cracking jokes and having fun, but not in front of Richards. Minnie Minoso was a terrific player and a real nice guy. I played with him in Cuba, where he was like a god. I also remember pitcher Saul Rogovin because all he would do in spring training was sleep—all the time.

I was a fastball pull hitter who stood deep in the box. The White Sox wanted to change my batting style. I held the bat low and they wanted me to hold it high. It felt too uncomfortable, but I had to try it. Then, when I tried to go back to my old way, it wasn't there anymore. Something was missing and I really struggled at the plate. It didn't help that I was rarely in the lineup.

I wanted to play, but Richards wasn't giving me a chance. He had his team and that was it. His coaches wouldn't say anything to him. At that time you were just like a damn slave. They told you what to do and where to go and you had no choice. Richards knew baseball, but a lot of guys didn't like playing for him. They'd grumble, but there was nothing anybody could do. There were no outspoken guys who were in the position to stand up to management.

I got depressed when I wasn't playing, so I asked to be sent down rather than sit on the bench. They sent me back to Memphis, where Luke Appling was the manager. I missed the first 47 games, but still tied for the homer title with 34, drove in 101 runs, and again hit .311. As a publicity stunt, a Memphis laundry offered me $200 for every homer I hit at home, so I picked up an extra $2,800. I could use the money because Frank Lane didn't want to give me anything. The White Sox were known for being a stingy organization.

AL KOZAR:
I was stuck playing for Luke Appling at Memphis for two years because Richards refused to bring me up. The Athletics tried to trade for me, and a deal was made. But the White Sox asked for a second player. The Athletics agreed to that. Then the Sox asked for money. The deal fell through. It was so frustrating. Then Appling was so afraid to lose me that he sent out the word that I didn't want to play in the majors. Here he was crying that he wasn't a major league manager and he was preventing me from moving back up. I blew my top.

JIM LANDIS:
In my second year I went to the Sox minor league camp in Texas. They wanted to take advantage of my speed by converting me to an outfielder. They taught me to use a crossover step in the field—I also used it to steal bases. John Mostil, who had been a great outfielder for the White Sox in the 1920s, took me under his wing and worked my tail off. Every day he kept me out there for a long time. They had me doing drills I still don't understand. To work on my reflexes, Don Gutteridge would hit hard BB's at me from 120 feet away for half an hour—in the air and on the ground. Even Paul Richards, who was at the camp, had to say, "That's enough for today." I think we were taught the White Sox way of doing things, although no one said that was what they were trying to do. They taught defense, speed, and pitching. That year I played in Class A in Colorado. I felt I was progressing at a good rate. Then I was drafted for two years.

NEW YORK YANKEES

GENE WOODLING:
I was a good outfielder, but I didn't get a lot of publicity for it. I went along and did a good journeyman's job and at the end of the year they gave the other guys credit. I didn't care. I got paid. I played left field, which was the sun field at Yankee Stadium. And in those days we played almost every game in the daytime. I never talked about the difficulties then because there was no sense in making excuses—I had to do it, and I did. There wasn't just the sun, but on hot, humid days it would become hazy from all the cigarette and cigar smoke. And by the time of the World Series, when the sun was closer to the earth, it was almost impossible to see the ball. I tell you I prayed a lot out there. I was hoping a lot of flies would go the other way. I felt sorry for guys before and after me (like the Yankees' Norm Siebern, who missed a few flies in the '58 World Series). I knew how difficult left field at Yankee Stadium was. I tried to figure out all the angles, but don't let anybody kid you—I got hit all over and was covered with black-and-blue marks. You stand in the outfield: you see it and then you don't and think, "Oh, my God!" Gus Zernial hit a ball once that almost killed me.

Ralph Houk and I both lived in New Jersey. We'd get to the park early and he'd do his backup catching chores and I'd go to the outfield and shag flies. The more I saw, the better chance I had to catch them. We won a lot of games at Yankee Stadium, including in the World Series, because the opposing left fielders had trouble seeing the ball. They'd come into town once a month, so they didn't have time to adjust. I almost felt sorry for them.

I didn't feel it was unfair how good the Yankees were. I thought that was the way it was supposed to be. I looked forward to that extra check every fall. "It's hard to repeat." That's what Casey told us after we won in 1949. He said, "That was the easy one. Everybody is going to be after you now." After we won in 1950, he said, "That was still the easy one. . . ." Pretty soon we shut him up.

We won the pennant again in 1953, beating the Indians by 7 games. We got great pitching from Whitey Ford, Eddie Lopat, Vic Raschi, Allie Reynolds, and Johnny Sain, and a lot of guys contributed with their gloves and bats. Berra and Mantle—who was no cripple—hit homers and drove in runs, but Bauer and I were the only .300 hitters.

At the time we didn't really realize what we accomplished by winning 5 pennants and World Series in a row. Later we realized that was a record that may never be broken.

JOHNNY SAIN:

I made the All-Star team with the Yankees in 1953. Stengel picked me. I had 8 wins and 2 losses with 2 saves at the time. I ended up 14–7 overall, with 9 saves, and an ERA of just 3.00. I was 10–6 as a starter, but I would never start again. So for my career, I ended up completing 57.1 percent of the games I started. That was third best of pitchers in my era, behind Bob Feller's 57.7 percent and Warren Spahn's 57.5 percent.

Whitey Ford returned to the Yankees in 1953, so I got to pitch with him for the first time. He went 18–6. He was a steady, consistent pitcher. His pitches were more alive than Lopat's: there was an active spin on the ball. His breaking ball was very sharp. He had 3 speeds on his curveball. (What would really make him a great pitcher—in 1961, when I was the Yankees' pitching coach—was when he started sinking the ball and throwing more of a controlled breaking ball.)

EWELL BLACKWELL:

I started only 4 games during the season, making 8 appearances overall. I got the last 2 wins of my career. Some people remember when I pitched against the White Sox and Paul Richards sent up pitcher Tommy Byrne, who was left-handed, to pinch-hit for Vern Stephens with the bases loaded. Byrne hit a grand slam. I didn't think it unusual because Stephens was right-handed and past his good years, and Byrne was an excellent hitter.

VIC POWER:

After my great season at Kansas City in 1952, I hoped that the Yankees would finally bring me up. But they decided to keep me in Kansas City for another year. I should have been brought up in 1951, but I lost two prime years in my major league career because the Yankees were reluctant to make me their first black player. In the winter, Jackie Robinson went on television in New York and criticized the Yankees for not bringing up a black player. They brought up my white teammates, including Bob Cerv and Andy Carey, but not me. I think they were waiting for my skin to turn white. Blacks and Puerto Ricans picketed Yankee Stadium so they would bring me up, and the Yankees got mad at me. They kept making excuses. They'd say I didn't prove I could hit major league pitching. But they wouldn't even invite me to spring training so I could face big league pitchers. Meanwhile they were saying how they wanted a "decent" black to be their first. That's why everyone started asking, "What's wrong with Vic Power?"

Maybe the Yankees didn't want a black player who would openly date light-skinned women, or who would respond with his fists when white pitchers threw beanballs at him. I was the only black on Kansas City, and every time one of my teammates would homer, the pitcher would throw at my head. There weren't helmets in those days, so I had to rely on my reflexes and my fists. I had to protect myself. I had a temper and got into some brutal fights. Being Puerto Rican, I would fight anybody, but I wasn't a troublemaker. We'd play games in Arkansas, Louisiana, and Mississippi, and the people would call me names, but I wouldn't respond. They'd yell, "You're black!" I knew that, so I didn't get mad.

In 1953 I had another great year. I led the league with a .349 average, had 217 hits, 115 runs, 93 RBIs. Now everyone knew about me. I figured the Yankees couldn't ignore me any longer. Elston Howard was my roommate on the Blues. He wasn't my competition to be the Yankees' first black. He wasn't a star. He was a conservative player, and his numbers weren't too good. The Yankees couldn't justify picking him as their first black as long as I was in their organization.

In December I was in New Orleans trying to ship my car to Puerto Rico when I looked down at a newspaper on the floor and discovered that I had been traded to the Philadelphia Athletics. That's how I found out I was no longer a Yankee. (In 1955, the Yankees would bring up Elston Howard as their first black player.)

I didn't care too much because I just wanted to play in the majors. I would have been a big attraction in New York because of all the blacks and Puerto Ricans, but the Yankees didn't want me. Or maybe they didn't want blacks and Puerto Ricans coming to Yankee Stadium. (In the mid-'50s, the Puerto Rican fans would hold a day for me in Yankee Stadium. They had a trophy to give me before the game, but the Yankee organization wouldn't let them give it to me at home plate, so they held the ceremony in the stands. That game I hit 2 homers, one against each pole.) I would always hit my best against the Yankees.

WORLD SERIES

1953

YANKEES
VS
DODGERS

GENE WOODLING · YANKEES:

What can you say about playing in the World Series? The fifth one was just as big a thrill as the first one. As always, the atmosphere in New York during a Yankees-Dodgers series was incredible. The team would meet at Yankee Stadium and then take bus rides to Ebbets Field, and the streets were loaded with people on the entire route. You wouldn't believe how many people. You talk about excitement. Then you'd go into Ebbets Field with the small field and the colorful billboards, and their little band would be playing in the stands and the crowd would be going crazy. The Ebbets Field fans were wilder than Yankee Stadium fans. The Yankee fans were very good, too. They were well-educated fans, the best I played for. They didn't boo anybody. They even applauded and were warm to the Dodger players.

There was nobody on the Dodgers to knock. We respected all those guys. They had one heck of a ballclub. Campanella, Hodges, Robinson, Reese, Cox—God, was he a great third baseman!—Snider, Furillo, and that great pitching staff. Newcombe was in the army, but they still had Preacher Roe, Carl Erskine, Joe Black, Billy Loes, Russ Meyer, Clem Labine, and Johnny Podres. These guys could pitch. We accomplished something beating them. I'd have to say the Yankees were better simply because we won. I'd often say, "We beat these guys three times in the World Series? It's unbelievable." I played three World Series against the Dodgers, and if you looked at their lineup and pitching, it tells you how good we were to have beaten them.

I had a pretty good Series, batting .300 and homering in the fifth game. I was glad that game was in Ebbets Field. It wasn't as big as my living room. I got a leadoff homer to dead center off Podres, and that was the first leadoff homer in Series history. If I'd hit it at Yankee Stadium, Duke Snider would have been running in to catch it. Anything you hit in the air had a chance to be a homer in that bandbox.

JOHNNY SAIN · YANKEES:

The Yankees had the utmost respect for the Dodgers. We knew they were a tough team. It didn't matter who was better because in a short series anything could happen. The Yankees entered the Series with a tremendous amount of confidence, but no team is really relaxed in a World Series because of the unknown.

I was the winning pitcher in the opening game against the Dodgers before over 69,000 fans at Yankee Stadium. Allie Reynolds started against Carl Erskine, and we jumped off to a 4–0 lead in the first inning when Billy Martin hit a bases-loaded triple. But the Dodgers pulled to within 5–4 in the fifth on three homers. I replaced Reynolds in the sixth and yielded the tying run. But I held them in check the rest of the way. Joe Collins put us ahead 6–5 with a homer in the seventh, and we scored three more times in the eighth inning, for a 9–5 victory.

RUBE WALKER · DODGERS:

After the previous year's defeat, we were looking forward to playing the Yankees. We had such a good year that we figured we had the upper hand. But we lost Game One despite homers by Gilliam, Hodges, and Shuba, and Game Two despite a 5-hitter by Roe, when Mantle hit a 2-run homer in the eighth inning for a 4–2 Yankee win. Mantle was so strong. He hit balls out of sight even in Yankee Stadium. That put us behind 2 games to 0. We won the next game when Erskine outdueled Raschi, 3–2, with a 6-hitter. He set a World Series record with 14 strikeouts, including Mantle 4 times. That was exciting. We also won Game Four, 7–3, when Loes and Labine pitched a good game and Snider drove in 4 runs. However, we lost the pivotal fifth game in Brooklyn, 11–7, when the Yankees slugged 4 homers, including a grand slam by Mantle. What a player he was. Then, in Game Six, they edged us in the bottom of the ninth, 4–3, on Billy Martin's single. Martin was a pest all Series, with 12 hits. We hit .300 for the Series but still lost in 6 games.

BEN WADE · DODGERS:

We were getting ready to start the Series and a sportswriter—maybe Dick Young—was walking around asking each Dodger why he expected to win this year after our loss in 1952. I was sitting close to Billy Loes when he was asked why the Dodgers would win. Billy said, "I didn't say we'd win." And the writer asked, "You don't think the Dodgers will win?" He answered, "No. I think the Yankees are going to beat us 4 games to 2." A lot of us heard him say it. We all took it as a joke, but the press made a big thing out of it. As it turned out, Billy was a good prophet.

I hadn't pitched in the 1952 World Series, but I relieved in the first game in 1953. I came in in the bottom of the seventh inning when we were 1 run down and Mickey Mantle was the batter with the bases loaded and 2 men out. Mantle took a third strike. The next inning, they scored 3 runs off me, but nobody hit the ball hard. I almost got out of it, but Johnny Sain got a big hit off me. I just told myself there was nothing I could do. The Yankees were a great team and they got runs off everybody: they won that game 9–5 and won the other game I pitched in 11–7. The result was bad, but I'm very glad I pitched. It was the World Series.

NATIONAL LEAGUE 1954

"WILLIE LIKED TO EXTEND HIS ARMS LIKE DUKE SNIDER, MICKEY MANTLE, AND OTHER POWER HITTERS, SO IF YOU CROWDED HIM WITH ONE PITCH AND THEN THREW A PITCH LOW AND AWAY YOU COULD GIVE HIM TROUBLE. OF COURSE, YOU COULD PITCH GOD THAT WAY, AND IT WOULD GIVE HIM TROUBLE."

DON NEWCOMBE

MILWAUKEE BRAVES

BOB BUHL:

I had gone to Puerto Rico in the winter to work on my slider and change-up with Mickey Owen, who was the manager of Caguas and one of its catchers. I was eager to try them out in the majors in 1954, but when I came back to the States I discovered I was worn out. I just couldn't get back into the swing. I won 2 and lost 7. This was my bad year in baseball. I couldn't get anybody out, so Charlie Grimm had to take me out of the rotation, which was already shorthanded because we had traded Antonelli, Surkont, and Bickford in the off-season. So now our rotation had Spahn, Burdette, Chet Nichols, who was returning from the service, and rookie Gene Conley. Grimm then reinserted Jim Wilson, who threw the majors' only no-hitter that season against the Phillies. They all did well. So did Dave Jolly and Ernie Johnson in the bullpen. That year I was the weak link.

Nichols was a good pitcher with a real good curveball. He would have a couple of good seasons and then all of a sudden not have it anymore. He chummed around with Spahn, Burdette, Mathews, and myself. Conley gave the team a big lift, winning 14 games. He was called "Stretch" because he was 6'8" and also played in the NBA. He also was called "The Hatchet Man" because he had big sharp elbows that would come down on you. I know, because on rainy days in spring training, we'd play basketball at a gym down in Bradenton. Gene ran with us every now and then, but he was pretty much on his own or with Ernie Johnson. He wasn't a wild guy. He was a funny guy.

We had acquired Bobby Thomson from the Giants to play left, but he broke his ankle in an exhibition game and Hank Aaron was given that position. It's odd: Thomson had the misfortune of losing jobs to Mays on the Giants and then to Aaron on the Braves. Hank hit his first homer early in the season in St. Louis off Vic Raschi, the ex-Yankee. He would hit only 12 more homers as a rookie, but as I predicted, he batted .280, and we got enough homers already from Mathews, Adcock, and Del Crandall. Adcock had the greatest slugging game in baseball history against the Dodgers in Ebbets Field on the last day of July. He had 4 homers and a double for a record 18 total bases. It's funny, but we tended not to get excited about such things and I can't even remember that game.

Walker Cooper was gone, and now we looked up to Crandall, along with Spahn and Johnson. They were the ones who would be our player reps over the years. Del had a good head on his shoulders. We called him "Jack Armstrong, the All-American Boy." He would never do anything wrong. For instance, he didn't drink. Yet he wasn't resentful of those who did, which was fortunate, because we were a drinking team. After the first year, when we'd get free Schlitz at our hotel, Miller's delivered a case of free beer to our houses every week. We'd also go out drinking.

If someone wasn't doing his job, we had clubhouse meetings without the managers or coaches: no fights, just expressing opinions. For instance, if someone looked like he was too tired to play or loafed, we'd get on him. I think there was a lot of respect between the players because we were winning. I was never accused of loafing because I always threw the ball as hard as I could and went as far as I could. Pitchers weren't blamed too much. Errors were never brought up. Hustle was the main thing. If a ball should have been caught, a player was told just that. If a guy dropped a ball he made an honest effort to catch, there was nothing to be said. We played smart baseball, patterning ourselves on the Dodgers. We knew how to advance runners, how to get a run home. We hustled and got one run ahead. When we were out on the field it was serious, except if you made a damn fool of yourself. We laughed at Del Crandall one day when Sad Sam Jones threw him three curveballs and he fell down on each one and struck out. On things like that, you couldn't help but laugh.

The Braves were very professional. We didn't throw or break bats, give umpires a hard time, or show up the other team. In those days, if you struck out the final batter, the catcher would flip you the ball and pat you on the back. The other players would pat you on the back as they ran past. There wouldn't be any handshaking until you got down to the dugout and clubhouse. Then everybody would come around. There would never be too much excitement because we figured all of us were just doing what we expected of each other.

LEW BURDETTE:

The Braves weren't very emotional. But we cheered for each other and jumped up and down and ran out of the dugout at certain times. Everybody pulled for each other. We were all happy for Adcock when he had his big day against the Dodgers. His double just missed being his fifth homer of the game. It hit that tiny red fence and rolled around the top of the wall in dead center field in Brooklyn. I told Joe when we went into the clubhouse that he'd better screw that helmet on tight the next day for his protection. And damned if Clem Labine didn't drill him the next day and split his helmet. He was okay but they had to carry him off on a stretcher, I knew it was going to happen. Gene Conley later knocked down Jackie Robinson, and Robinson and Eddie Mathews went at it. Adcock hit the Dodgers even more after being beaned—I think he set a record for homers against them that year.

We were united in that we all played for the great fans of Milwaukee, who set a National League attendance record, with over 2 million coming to County Stadium in 1954. We were very close. We'd fight for each other. If a batter charged me, it would get mighty crowded on the mound. We'd do anything for each other. I think Spahn was the leader of the team. He was the player rep most of the time; Crandall was later on. I always pretended I was too dumb to take that job. It didn't pay much extra and there was a lot of work involved, especially after the Players Association was formed that year. We thought about deferring a certain portion of our salary but they turned us down because we were independent contractors. I don't know why they wouldn't let us defer 10 to 15 percent of our salary and have it be tax-free, so we could collect it when we retired. But Washington wouldn't let us do it.

Henry Aaron almost didn't make the team. They were going to send him to Jacksonville after spring training because we just got Bobby Thomson in a trade with the Giants for Johnny Antonelli. That would have been a shame because it was obvious that he had a good stroke. Then Bobby broke his ankle. Later, I went in to take a shower. John Quinn came in and I overheard him saying they were going to keep Aaron. I got dressed and went out on the bench. I congratulated Hank. He said, "What are you talking about?" I said, "You just made the ballclub. I heard it inside.'' He was happy. He sure turned into a good product, didn't he?

ST. LOUIS CARDINALS

DICK SCHOFIELD:

None of the Cardinals seemed to mind that I was a bonus baby and taking up roster space. Enos Slaughter was a grouch, but that's the way he always was to everyone. He was from the old school, the type who sharpened his spikes before a game. I remember using his bat once in spring training in 1954. It was an old, beat-up bat that he used a long time. And I took one swing and it just split. I just laid it down real nice and walked away. Later he came up to the batting cage, hollering and screaming, trying to find out who broke it. I didn't say anything. I didn't have much to do with Slaughter, but he treated me okay. He was tough for anyone to get along with. He was married a few times and had personal problems.

Slaughter supposedly cried when he heard he had been traded to the Yankees, for Bill Virdon and a couple of other players, right before the season started. Stanky had to make room in the outfield for Wally Moon, who was a left-handed-hitting rookie outfielder from Arkansas. I lived next to him in spring training and we got to be pretty good friends. Wally had a little trouble in the outfield in Wrigley Field, but he was a super offensive player who hit for average and had extra-base power. He hit a homer in his first at-bat against Chicago and went on to bat over .300 and be voted Rookie of the Year.

Joe Cunningham was another good left-handed-hitting rookie. Steve Bilko had been traded, and Cunningham took over at first base after Tom Alston got a chance. Joe was more of an average hitter than a power hitter, but he hit 3 homers in his first 2 games in the majors in early July. We became friends. Once, when we were in New York playing the Giants, he invited me to his house in Paterson, New Jersey, and his mom fixed us dinner. He was a good hitter and developed into an excellent first baseman.

Tom Alston was another rookie, a 6′5″ first baseman from North Carolina. He was the first black to play with the Cardinals. He played a fair amount with us in 1954, prior to Cunningham's arrival, but spent most of the next three years at Omaha.

Brooks Lawrence came up in 1954 and went 15–6. Only Harvey Haddix won more games for us, with 18. Lawrence had pitched in the Negro Leagues and was already in his late 20s. He was the Cardinals' first black pitcher, but to be honest, I didn't think much about it, just as I hadn't thought about Tom Alston's place in baseball history. By that time there were black players throughout the league and several would come to spring training with the Cards. I assume Brooks was a loner because in those days not too many white players ran with black players.

Other than Haddix and Lawrence, our starting pitchers weren't very effective. We had acquired Vic Raschi from the Yankees prior to the season. His win totals had gone down for the Yankees and he was 35, so the Cardinals were able to purchase him. Everybody thought he was going to win 20 games and be our ace. He started out pretty good, but his arm went bad and he won only 8 games. I didn't get to know him well, but he was a nice guy and very professional.

Red Schoendienst batted over .300, and the Cards also got good offensive years from Moon, Cunningham, Rip Repulski, Ray Jablonski—who had over 100 RBIs for the second straight year—catcher Bill Sarni, and a few others. But, as usual, the biggest producer was Stan Musial, who batted .330, drove in about 125 runs, and hit 35 homers. He was a more dangerous power hitter in Busch Stadium—which is what Sportsman's Park was renamed after Bill Veeck sold it in 1953 to the Cards' new president Augie Busch, the president of the Anheuser-Busch Brewery. He'd go out and get the ball and flip it up on the roof. In a bigger ballpark, he might have hit half as many homers, but he'd have hit for an even higher average. He didn't have many slumps. When he had a bad day, you could sense he was unhappy, but he'd never vent his frustration. He cared a lot. For all his greatness as a player, he was a super-nice man. He never treated anybody badly.

I saw him do a lot of amazing things, so nothing he did really shocked me. But I was certainly impressed when he hit 5 homers in a doubleheader to set the major league record. It took place in early May against the

Giants in St. Louis. He went 6 for 8 in the two games, with 9 RBIs. He hit 3 homers in the first game, 2 against Johnny Antonelli and the other against Jim Hearn.

JOHNNY ANTONELLI (GIANTS):

Stan was such a nice guy that I was probably happy for him when he homered off me. He didn't have an enemy in the world. I remembered that he had played in my hometown of Rochester with the Red Wings on his way to the Cardinals, and in my youth that had been one of our city's claims to fame.

D. SCHOFIELD:

In the second game he hit 2 homers off Hoyt Wilhelm, both long drives that landed on Grand Avenue.

Eddie Stanky had Alex Grammas and Solly Hemus splitting time at short, so in my second year I played in the field only 11 times and batted only 7 times. Stanky used me primarily as a pinch runner. I think it hurt me spending so much time not playing, but I still believed I was correct in taking all that bonus money. I felt I would get my chance.

At various times in the off-season, I worked for the Illinois State Youth Commission and attended junior college, but that winter I decided I needed some playing time, so I went to Cuba for winter ball and played with other young Cardinals like Ken Boyer, Don Blasingame, and Bill Virdon.

BEN WADE:

I didn't mind going to the Cardinals from the Dodgers. They had a good system and such players as Stan Musial, Red Schoendienst, Ray Jablonski, and Harvey Haddix. I also was still in the National League, so I could go back to Brooklyn—although I didn't particularly like pitching against the Dodgers.

The Cardinals' fans didn't remind me of the fans in Brooklyn. I can't say the fans were particularly warm because we had a sixth-place team and we didn't draw well.

I pitched 13 times for the Cardinals, all in relief. I didn't have a particularly good year and knew there was a good chance I wouldn't be back in 1955.

When I joined the Cardinals' pitching staff, I was immediately one of them. Harvey Haddix and Brooks

Lawrence were the most effective pitchers that year. The Cards also had Vic Raschi and Gerry Staley. I roomed with Gordon Jones, a rookie right-hander.

Eddie Stanky knew more baseball and was the best baseball man I ever played for, but he was the worst big league manager I played for.

HANK SAUER (CUBS):

One year, when Eddie Stanky managed the Cardinals, I was hit 8 or 9 times. Hit, not just knocked down. Any time there was a guy on second and first base was open, Stanky would want to put me on. Only they wouldn't walk me, they'd hit me. Maybe Stanky felt he could get me out of the lineup that way. The Cubs played the Cards on the last day of the season. Neither team was going anywhere, so the game was unimportant. I came up with a man on second, and first base was open. Tom Poholsky hit me right in the kidney. I staggered out toward the mound. I wasn't going to fight him because I could hardly breathe. But I said, "You have three more shots at me. If you hit me again I'm going to kill you." He walked me the next 3 times up. When Stanky walked by, I said, "Eddie, I ought to pick you up and throw you to the wolves in the stands." He just kept walking.

B. WADE:

Stanky just didn't know how to treat players. I don't think the Cardinals were a close team, and Stanky was the main reason. He had been a little player who had a little-man complex that he hadn't gotten over now that he was only managing. Stanky was about 5'8" and he seemed to get close only to small players, like Solly Hemus and Sal Yvars.

Musial wasn't bothered by Stanky. He just went along and played. He was a great ballplayer. Musial was a better hitter than Mays or Mantle, but they were better all-around ballplayers. Stan and Schoendienst were the leaders on the team. Both were quiet and friendly. They were good friends and stayed together a lot. I wasn't on the Cards long enough to make any real good friends.

TOM CHENEY:

The first time I went away to a minor league spring training was in 1954. I flew from Georgia to El Centro, California, about 9 miles from the Mexican border. I was 19 and this was the first time I'd been out of Georgia. There were about 25 young guys who stayed in a hotel without air conditioning, and we pulled our beds into the hallway at night, hoping we'd get a little breeze. At least there was a pool. We had one workout a day and then there was nothing to do. We walked around town, maybe saw a movie. Or we'd go over to Mexicali, where you could eat cheap and get a good haircut for a quarter. We ate Mexican food. I learned to eat tacos, the only thing I liked. The toughest part is that we didn't have other teams to play and had to play among ourselves. I don't think they ever had spring training down there again.

We had one or two guys who'd been up to A ball, but everyone was young. I wasn't being told to do anything pitching-wise. In fact, I wouldn't talk to a pitching coach until I went to spring training with the Cardinals in 1956. I learned from the catcher John McNamara, who was 4 to 5 years older than the rest of us. He'd been up to A ball, and passed on his experience to me. He gave me an idea of how to work a hitter. There was no pitch that I couldn't learn to throw.

After that I was assigned to Fresno in the California State League, which was Class C. I got a ''big'' raise from $175 to $250 a month. Still, that was the most money I ever had. I went 12–11 at Fresno, with quite a few strikeouts. I think the Cards considered me a good prospect by this time, but I didn't expect to be in the majors for a while. In the St. Louis system, they didn't figure you'd reach Triple A or the big leagues for 5 to 7 years.

CHICAGO CUBS

RALPH KINER:

I wasn't sensitive to criticism about my fielding because I knew I did a decent job. I started out as a center fielder. What people saw toward the end of my career was me playing with a bad back and, with the Cubs, two severely pulled groin muscles. Guys in later years wouldn't play in my condition, but I played 158 games in 1953 and 147 games in 1954 and had a terrible time.

Everyone kidded Hank Sauer and me about letting Frank Baumholtz catch everything. I went along with it,

saying we made Baumholtz a star. It didn't make any difference to me. Sauer was very sensitive to the criticism. He was a good outfielder, but his natural position was left field and he moved to right to make room for me. Stan Hack, our new manager, kept him there.

Hank had a great year at the plate in 1954. I still managed to bat .285, but my 22 homers and 73 RBIs were career lows at that point. If I hadn't been hurting then, we could have been a very strong combination. Hank was a good hitter. He had good bat speed, so he was able to leave his bat out front while the pitcher wound up, and then in one motion bring it back and forward again.

Of course, Ernie Banks was a good hitter, even at the beginning. I liked watching him. He would lightly rap his fingers on the bat—he looked like he was playing the flute. I didn't play with him long because in November I was dealt to the Indians for Sad Sam Jones, another player, and $60,000. Finally I was going to a contender.

JOHNNY KLIPPSTEIN:

Ralph Kiner was a nice guy. I would have liked to spend more time with him, but it's funny that when guys are in a different salary bracket you can't afford to go to some of the places they go. Sometimes that separates players. However, I did attend Ralph's birthday party at spring training. We had our wives in spring training and he was kind enough to invite several of us to the Camelback Inn in Phoenix for dinner and pick up the tab.

I got married in 1952 and would have three children in four years. By this time I was secure in the big leagues and didn't have nearly the stress I experienced in the minors. When I had a bad outing I was eager to get the ball again rather than moping at home. It helped that my wife was a tremendous baseball fan. When she was young she'd watch her uncle Dutch Leonard pitch in Washington, D.C. I met her when she came to see Dutch pitch at Wrigley Field. She understood the game and she was definitely helpful. Playing in Chicago was great because we played day ball and could have a fairly normal family life. In those days, home stands could last two or three weeks, which was great. However, road trips were also that long and it was difficult being away from wives and children. I believe the Cubs had a harder time adjusting to road games than other teams because we had to adjust to night ball and change our hours around.

Stan Hack was probably too nice to be a manager. We lost 10 or 11 in a row and his attitude was "Boys, let's have another beer and get 'em tomorrow." We lost 13 games in a row to the Phillies in Philadelphia and were scheduled to play them in a Sunday doubleheader. On Saturday night, they threw a party for us at Bookbinder's. We ate and drank, and drank and ate. Then we went out the next day . . . and increased our streak to 15 losses in a row. That was the last party we ever had.

Speaking of drinking: Steve Bilko came over from the Cards during the 1954 season. I roomed with him for a while, and no matter when he would come into the room, he would be carrying a six-pack. He was a great guy. He was very serious when he was playing, but away from the park he was completely different. We first played together in the Cardinals' system. I couldn't believe how hard he hit some balls. They were 6 feet off the ground and would go 350 feet. He was a strong man.

Ernie Banks didn't look that strong, but he had powerful wrists and a quick bat and Wrigley Field was ideal for him. I had never played with black players before Ernie and Gene Baker joined the Cubs late in 1953. Ernie was pretty quiet, but he was very confident. One day a knuckleballer came in to pitch against us. Nobody liked to hit against a knuckleball. Nobody. Someone told Ernie, "Watch this guy because he throws a good knuckleball." He said, "I love to hit the knuckleball." He was the only guy I heard say that in my life.

In the 5 years I spent with the Cubs, they wanted me to throw the fastball. We played all day games and it would get shadowy in the sixth or seventh inning and they figured it would be hard for batters to pick up fastballs. The result is that I never got confidence in my curveball because I wasn't throwing it when I needed a strike. At 3 and 1, there was no way I'd throw a curveball. My curve wasn't bad and I wish I could have thrown it more because I could have been a better pitcher. Dutch Leonard, who became our pitching coach, was inclined to have me throw many more breaking balls. But during the game, the manager would have the upper hand, and whether it was Frisch, Cavarretta, or Hack, he would instruct my catcher—Mickey Owen, Harry Chiti, Rube Walker, Clyde McCullough, or Joe Garagiola—to call for fastballs.

I had a frustrating season in 1954, finishing at 4–11, and when the season ended, I was sent to the Cincinnati Reds in a 5-player deal. The first time you are traded is the toughest because you feel a team has given up on you. After that, you realize there are clubs that need different things—a fifth starter, a relief pitcher—so you feel it isn't that a team doesn't want you but that it needs to get someone in return who better fits the team. We didn't have a good ballclub during my years in Chicago, but at least we were last only once, and once had finished fifth. I had really enjoyed Chicago and playing day ball in front of the great, knowledgeable Cubs fans. So I looked at my time there as a good learning experience.

HANK SAUER:
The fans loved Ernie Banks right off the bat. He was a beautiful person and added enthusiasm to the team. Once he got used to the other players and came out of his shell, he lightened things up a bit. He was a super player, a good shortstop, and tremendous hitter with powerful wrists. He was one of the reasons I felt the Cubs were finally about to make a move. But we didn't go anywhere despite his contributions. Or Ralph Kiner's, or Randy Jackson's. Or mine. We all hit pretty good—I had 41 homers and 103 RBIs, Ralph hit over 20 homers, Ernie and Randy hit 19 each, and even Gene Baker hit over a dozen—but we still finished in seventh place, 8 games out of sixth. It could get very depressing on the Cubs.

RANDY JACKSON:
I proved my consistency by hitting 19 homers for the second straight year and driving in almost 70 runs again although injuries kept me out about a month. In April, with the wind blowing out at Wrigley, I hit my longest homer onto the third floor of a building on Waveland Avenue, in a 23–13 rout of St. Louis. I couldn't believe I hit it that far.

Making the All-Star team was the highlight of my career in Chicago, although I had winning hits, winning homers, grand slams. Not a whole lot of folks make the All-Star Game, and I was excited and in awe in the National League clubhouse. As soon as you walked into the dressing room, you signed several dozen baseballs. All the players got one autographed ball—a thrill. It's something to be there with all the great players from the various teams. Of course, some of them had to have respect for me because I wouldn't have been there if I hadn't been having a good season. It was an exciting game, the highest-scoring All-Star Game in history. The American League won 11–9 on a pinch-homer by Larry Doby and a 2-RBI single by Nellie Fox in the eighth inning.

I thought that when Ernie Banks joined the team, it was definitely a positive move, but we had problems that couldn't be solved by one player, no matter how good he was. We never had any great pitchers, guys who'd win 15 to 20 games, or good offensive catchers. There were always three or four weak spots in the Cubs' lineup. To be a contender, you could have only one or two. I wanted to be on a winner, but I never got depressed. I'd play my year out and we'd finish from fifth to eighth, and then I'd go home and watch the World Series.

Home was no longer Arkansas. My parents and sister had moved to Oklahoma, and I went back there in the winter. For several years my father and I had a laundry and dry cleaning business in Lawton, which was south of Oklahoma City. I never played in the winter leagues, nor was I told to. At the end of the year we just shook hands and said, "See you next year."

FRANK BAUMHOLTZ:
I liked playing for Phil Cavarretta because he knew baseball and was good to his players. He was a good manager, but he had trouble controlling his Sicilian temper. He also may have been too straightforward. Stan Hack replaced Cavarretta in 1954 because Wrigley got angry when Cavarretta told reporters during spring training that the Cubs were a second-division team. We finished seventh again under Hack. Stan was a nice guy who was known for his smile, but he didn't know baseball as well as Phil.

I had another good year, hitting .297, which was the best average of the regulars. A lot of guys asked me to help with their hitting. I did it only if they promised not to listen to anyone else because a batter would get messed up by too many instructors. I'd pitch batting practice to them hours on end. I could have hit a lot of homers, as I showed in batting practice, but that wasn't my role. Instead of pulling the ball all the time, I hit the ball to the biggest part of the field. I hit a lot of balls between outfielders, and since I could run fairly well, I got a lot of doubles and triples. I did this by trying to knock the pitcher off the mound every time I swung the bat. That's what I taught players who asked my advice. I hit a lot of pitchers. Before I joined Dutch Leonard on the Cubs in 1951, he'd yell when he pitched to me because he knew I'd try to hit his knuckler through his stomach.

I would order a dozen bats a year. Then I would spend time honing them with a big soup bone. I looked at the grains to see which would splinter, and those were the bats I'd use in batting practice. I'd use only two or three bats during the season. I used my own modification of a Babe Ruth–Ducky Medwick bat. It was 35″ to 36″ long and 33 to 34 ounces. I put two pieces of tape over the handle and choked up.

The team supplied the bats, caps, socks, and those heavy, baggy uniforms. We had to buy our own gloves, spikes, white socks, and sliding pants. I played with the same glove and the same spikes for years. My glove probably cost $15.

In general I played a medium center field, but I studied all the hitters to know whether to shade them or play straight away. Willie Mays had a lot of power to both right-center and left-center, so I played him straight away. I also played rookie Hank Aaron straight away, realizing that he hit the ball to all fields in those days, instead of trying to homer to left. I'd shade Musial to right because that's where his power was, but I knew he could hit the ball to left-center as well as anybody. Most of the time, Musial was a line-drive hitter, but when he hit the ball hard and high into right you could forget about it because it was a home run. He was a great, great hitter and one of the finest gentlemen I ever met—the top of the heap.

JIM BROSNAN:
Thinking my baseball career was over, I hadn't kept myself in good condition. When I got to spring training in Mesa, Arizona, I weighed 220 pounds. I was 6′4″, but that was still more than 20 pounds over my playing weight. I was fat and sick. For four or five days, all I did was run back and forth. I finally got back into shape. And the manager, Phil Cavarretta, told me I made the club. After we broke camp, we were on our way from

Jim Brosnan, one of the first intellects in baseball since Moe Berg, would eventually become a very good major-league pitcher but would be remembered more for his revealing chronologies *The Long Season* and *Pennant Race*, two critically acclaimed books that forever changed baseball literature.

Mesa to New Orleans, playing daily exhibition games along the way against the new Baltimore Orioles, formerly the St. Louis Browns. That's when Cavarretta made the mistake of being candid about our club to a sportswriter. P. K. Wrigley got so mad he fired him that night. (Wrigley apologized to Cavarretta for years every time he saw him, saying, "I should not have done that to you, Phil, but what you said upset me so much.")

We spent an eventful night in Shreveport on that trip. After a game, six of us from the two teams decided to go drinking in Bossier City, where we could have more fun because it wasn't a puritanical Baptist town. We found a wild club where there was liquor and women. One of our guys was Don Elston, but I forget the other, and the Orioles were Don Larsen, Bobby Young, and Howie Fox (who was killed outside his Texas bar the following October). Young was a very bright guy and we spent a few hours talking, drinking, and looking around. Larsen

drank, which is what he always did. The reason Larsen didn't care if he won or lost was that afterward he'd go out and have four or five drinks. Twice he took his bottle and disappeared with a woman. So I assumed he went at it twice, which may have contributed to why he had *nothing* left the next day. About four o'clock we returned to the Captain Shreve Hotel and there was Orioles manager Jimmy Dykes waiting for his tardy players. A few hours later, Dykes made Larsen pitch 7 innings in the sun. It was so hot that Larsen's uniform was soaked after only warming up before the game. It was torture for him pitching and he just kept getting slower and slower. But he never said a word.

Stan Hack was a very nice guy, but he didn't respect me much as a pitcher my rookie year. He said, "Everytime Brosnan sticks his head out of the dugout, somebody hits a line drive." (I ran into Hack again in 1958, when I was traded to the Cardinals, and we became much closer. He told me that in 1954 he didn't think I'd make it.)

If there was a leader on the Cubs, it was Hank Sauer, the team's one star. Whatever he wanted he could get. He was a smart guy who had a willingness to learn and then impart what he learned. He would always talk to players about certain types of pitches and patterns, and what to expect from certain pitchers in particular situations. He was a good teacher because he could be serious but also had a good sense of humor. Being accepted by Sauer was very important because it made me feel I was becoming part of the club.

But I didn't really socialize with anyone on the Cubs. My best friends were the trainer, Al "Doc" Scheuneman, and the clubhouse man Yosh Kawano. They took care of me. I was by nature a loner, so that was how I was perceived. Some players thought I was standoffish. It didn't bother me at all. I lived in Chicago, so I went home every night to my wife and two small kids. I didn't feel I was being left out.

As far as I knew, the Cubs weren't a drinking team. There was no beer in the clubhouse at that time. I was on a fitness kick that year and had sworn off both tobacco and alcohol, except for a glass of wine at dinner—which is a terrible thing for me to admit, since it was well known that I had two martinis before dinner every night during the off-season.

The only reason I made the Opening Day roster was

because Bubba Church was disabled. I was told that when Church returned I was ticketed for Des Moines. That's what happened, but Church got his nose broken by a line drive and I was back on the team. I pitched in 18 games, all in relief, and was lucky enough to win my only decision, but my ERA was 9.45, which was high even on the Cubs.

Howie Pollet, a soft-spoken lefty who had been pitching in the majors since 1941, offered me help. He said, "I don't know whether you've got the brain or the heart, but you've got the arm. However, you've got to have another pitch." He taught me the slider, which was unusual because he was a big overhand curveball pitcher. The slider Pollet taught me was actually a nickel curveball. If you threw it hard enough and with control, it was very effective. I learned that slider pitchers who just throw that pitch for strikes got killed because it's thrown harder than a hanging curve and can be hit farther. To fool overeager batters, it has to break out of the strike zone. Pollet said, "If you can control it, nobody will hit it well." His interest was fortunate because that was the pitch that would make me a successful major league pitcher. I had an average fastball—a little over 85 mph—but I became a finesse pitcher, relying on sliders and changes.

I had always been an indifferent learner. If a pitch didn't work right away, I'd abandon it and try something else, so I never mastered anything. Fortunately, the slider worked right away. After just 2 games I could throw it where I wanted, which was low and away to right-handed batters and—though this wasn't recommended by any pitching coaches—up and in to left-handed batters. I'd break the ball right in on the hands of left-handed batters and I'd get them out.

BROOKLYN DODGERS

BEN WADE:

Before I was picked up by the Cardinals from the Dodgers, I had just moved to downtown Brooklyn after two years in Bay Ridge. I lived about 8 to 10 miles from Ebbets Field and 3 or 4 blocks from Gil Hodges, with whom I'd go to the ballpark. I had a feeling I wasn't going to be on the Dodgers much longer. The Dodgers had always treated me well and paid me fairly, but I

knew I wasn't a player they were building their team around. Charlie Dressen had liked my pitching, but he had been replaced by Walter Alston because he insisted on getting more than a one-year contract and Walter O'Malley wouldn't give it to him. There were other pitchers Alston was more interested in, veterans and prospects. Campy had gotten hurt and Newcombe had come back from the service, so this was the year the Dodgers started to make changes. I pitched in over 20 games by early August, which is when the Cardinals claimed me on waivers.

RUBE WALKER:

The Dodgers won 92 games in 1954, but since we finished 5 games behind the Giants in the pennant race, we considered it an unsuccessful season. Roy missed a lot of games with a bad hand but most of our players had good years—Hodges hit 42 homers and Snider hit 40 and they each drove in exactly 130 runs—and we were given a lift by a young left-hander named Karl Spooner. Darned if he didn't come up from Fort Worth at the end of the year and pitch 2 consecutive shutouts, striking out a record 27 batters. I'd never seen anything like it.

JIM LANDIS (MINOR LEAGUES):

The pitcher who impressed me most in my career was Karl Spooner, even more than Herb Score. I saw him in A ball and nobody could hit him. I thought that maybe he was striking out 14 batters a game because the lights were dim in minor league ballparks. Then the Dodgers brought him up and he struck out 15 and 12 batters in his first 2 games, both shutouts. I said that he was as tough as I thought. He was the hardest pitcher I ever faced. He was unbelievable. But he got hurt before the next season.

DON NEWCOMBE:

When I returned from the service, I joined a rotation that was completely different. Preacher Roe and Ralph Branca were both gone, and now Carl Erskine was the top veteran and Johnny Podres, Billy Loes, and Russ Meyer filled the other slots. I was rusty after having been away two years. I won only 9 games, the lowest of the starters—but my innings pitched was also the lowest.

Jackie Robinson was still hitting .300, but was no

longer playing every day. Now Walt Alston more often played him in the outfield or at third than at second. Second now belonged to Jim Gilliam, who had been 1953's Rookie of the Year. When Gilliam came up, Jackie felt it his responsibility to talk to him. The first thing Gilliam did was sit down and talk to the godfather. Jackie told Junior what he was supposed to do as a human being, a person, a player. And not to do Uncle Tom "yes, sir!"/"no, sir!" shit. Instead it was "Act like a champion, carry yourself like a professional." Jackie nursed Gilliam along so that he overcame his shortcomings and became a star player himself.

I didn't socialize with Jackie because he lived on Long Island and I lived in New Jersey. At one time I almost bought a house on Roy's street in St. Albans, Queens. I changed my mind and was glad I did. Even though I had a 100-mile round trip every day, I was happy to do it because it gave me the chance to get away from the rat race.

ED ROEBUCK:

I was in the Dodgers' minor league system from 1949 to 1954, moving up to Elmira and Montreal, where I led the league in complete games in 1954 yet was converted into a relief pitcher. I never thought of making the Dodgers, even when I was pitching well in Triple A, because the Dodgers were just loaded with good pitchers. I was at Montreal for three years, winning 12, 15, and a league-leading 18 games. I just played to play. It was exciting being a professional ballplayer at any level.

Each year I went to Dodgertown with everyone in the entire system. It was a big family. Everyone liked each other. Gil Hodges and Roy Campanella were among those who came over to me and made me feel like part of the team. At spring training and in the minors, I wasn't really instructed on how to do anything. I learned from experience. But it was a good system. There was strong competition because the parent club rarely changed personnel and so many of us were stranded in the minors.

For instance, Roberto Clemente, a young Puerto Rican, played with me on Montreal. He was a kid with a lot of raw talent. The Dodgers wanted to hide him so he wouldn't get drafted by another team. He was a right-handed hitter, so they played him only against left-handers and sat him against right-handers. He could

have hit anybody. He was on an emotional roller coaster and almost quit. It was probably fortunate for him that Pittsburgh drafted him out of our system, so he could reach the majors quicker.

By the early '50s there were a lot of blacks in the minors. No one told the black players and us white players in the Dodgers' system how to coexist. We just did it. We were very cognizant of the quota system, which meant that only a certain number of blacks could make it to the majors, and that no team would have more than a few blacks, and that some teams didn't have blacks at all yet. So it was tough for the black players. Junior Gilliam, who was called up to the Dodgers in 1953, was the exception who made it to the parent team. He was someone who couldn't be denied. Once he made the team, he showed that he belonged.

STAN WILLIAMS:

I was born in Enfield, New Hampshire, in 1936, but my family left there about 18 months later and I grew up in Denver, Colorado. When I eventually made the majors in 1958, I was the only player from either state. My father was a carpenter and my mother was a housewife and they raised a daughter and four sons: one would become a ballplayer, one a mechanic, one a cop, and one a robber—not really, but he was a tough guy.

I was an easygoing small-town kid, very green, a big rube, didn't know much about life. My main hobby was fishing, and the opening of trout season was the big day of the year. I was 6'2½" and weighed 188 pounds when I entered East Denver High and started pitching. I had always played baseball—unorganized ball in a field right across from my house—but I got serious for the first time. In Colorado the baseball season consisted of only 8 high school ball games, followed by just 15 American Legion games. My team was called Duffy's Delicious Drinks, and I would just go out and throw the ball hard and strike out between 15 and 24 batters every time. Two years in a row we won the state tournament in American Legion and won the regionals, but lost in the sectionals. We would come to the regional tournament with a 14–1 record and play teams with records like 48–2. Especially the California teams played a lot of baseball compared to us. I played to have a good time, not to impress anyone. I got recognition from the results.

At the time I was a fan of the Denver Bears in the Western League because they were the only team we had before we had television. My sister and I took streetcars to see them play and they looked like the greatest players in the world. I was invited to throw batting practice when I was 15, and a couple of hitters told me I threw harder than anybody in the league. Not too many guys would hit against me because I was a little wild.

There was a major league rule that scouts couldn't talk to you unless you were 18 or had graduated from high school. However, there was a scout who talked to my American Legion coach after my junior year and told him I could expect a bonus in the vicinity of $50,000 from their organization once I graduated. But the year I graduated they came up with this bonus rule where the most you could get was $4,000 unless you went directly to the big leagues and stayed on the 25-man roster for two years, à la Sandy Koufax. But there was no way I was ready to go to the big leagues. Class D was more like it.

I received offers from 14 of the 16 major league teams, but I chose the Dodgers. My goal became to be a Dodger and beat the Yankees in the World Series. I hated the Yankees. I signed in June, after graduation. I was 17. I got the maximum $4,000, including my first year's salary, which was $700 a month for the rest of the year. I could have made it all salary, but I was told that if I had a high salary there was a better chance I'd be cut. So I took a $700 salary and made the remainder my bonus. When I signed to play baseball, I couldn't tell you the names of all the major league teams.

I started in Class D, Sooner State League, Shawnee, Oklahoma. When I joined the team in the middle of June, they had a 22½-game lead. Jack Banta, an old Brooklyn pitcher, was the manager. The Dodgers sent me there to pitch and Banta wanted to stick with the pitchers who had gotten the team so far. He didn't want a big wild kid on the mound because he had better-qualified people. In my first game, I lost 7–1, giving up 5 walks in a row and then a grand slam. After that he didn't want to pitch me and got in trouble with the organization. He got fired the following year, and supposedly his objection to me was one of the reasons. I would be the only player on that team to move up to a higher level the next year, and two years later, Don Le-

John (who'd play briefly for the Dodgers in 1965) and I were the only two players still playing pro baseball. I was surprised when I was told I was going to move up to Class B in 1955, after having had a losing year and walking a lot of batters in Class D. But I did have 77 strikeouts in about 64 innings.

NEW YORK GIANTS

JOHNNY ANTONELLI:

In February, Don Liddle, Billy Klaus, Ebba St. Claire, and I were traded from the Braves to the Giants for Bobby Thomson and Sam Calderone. It turned out to be the best thing that ever happened to me. I became the

With 21 victories and a league-leading 2.30 ERA, Johnny Antonelli was just as important as batting king Willie Mays in the Giants' world championship season.

lone left-hander in the rotation and pitched every fourth or fifth day.

My style didn't change when I moved to the Polo Grounds. All I did was work on change-of-speed pitches. I referred to one of those pitches as "a little snap screwball." I just turned the ball over a little bit. With the backing of the Giants' pitching coach, Freddie Fitzsimmons, a semiretired onetime minor leaguer taught me this pitch in spring training. It was meant to keep batters off stride. The pitch worked during the spring and I kept using it. It was the pitch that made me successful.

The Polo Grounds was a friendly ballpark for me. I was able to keep batters from pulling the ball down the lines. I made them hit the ball straight away and I had Willie Mays to track it down. I won 12 straight at home before losing in September.

Leo Durocher pitched me a lot against the Cardinals, Reds, Phillies, and Pirates. They had left-handed swingers, so he might hold me back a day to pitch against them. He'd hold back Sal Maglie for the Dodgers. Sal beat the Dodgers 10 straight times at Ebbets Field before losing—then he clinched the pennant by beating them there in mid-September. Being a left-hander, I didn't relish facing all those right-handed Dodgers. Even Warren Spahn didn't pitch too often against them. I did all right against them, however.

The press built up the rivalry between the Giants and Dodgers and we had to live up to it. The fans made a big thing out of it. In Ebbets Field, the fans would get on us from the time we walked into the ballpark until the game ended. And their band played music to accompany our every move, whether Leo went to the mound or I went to get a drink of water. I know there had been past incidents involving players like Maglie, Jansen, Robinson, Furillo, and Newcombe, but I didn't see much of that. Our games still had knockdown pitches and hard sliding and occasional arguments involving players, managers, and umpires, but I thought it was all good, clean fun.

I had nothing but deep respect for Durocher. He was an agitator and would get on opposing players before the game even started. He'd get some guys really upset. He had Newcombe's number. I think his greatest ability was to get the most out of his players. He understood how to deal with individuals as well as any manager in baseball. For instance, he knew that you didn't jump on Mays if he made a mistake—he knew that if he took care of Willie, Willie would jump fences for him. With Dusty Rhodes, he'd kick him in the pants every once in a while and that would wake him up. He handled me well. He realized that I wasn't the type of guy who liked to be bashed, but a good kick in the pants every once in a while wasn't such a bad idea. I had my greatest success with him.

Nineteen fifty-four was a pleasant surprise. Nobody thought the Giants would win the pennant. They had finished 14 games under .500 in 1953, in fifth place behind the Dodgers, Braves, Phillies, and Cardinals. Other than Willie Mays, we weren't the most overpowering team, position by position. We weren't a team that could put together a big winning streak. We'd win 5 and lose 2, win 6 and lose 4. We had Mays, Hank Thompson, Monte Irvin, Whitey Lockman, Dusty Rhodes, and even Alvin Dark to hit home runs, but we didn't score a lot of runs.

Our strength was our pitching staff. It was excellent. I went 21–7 and led the league with a 2.30 ERA. I had 6 shutouts and gave up 1 run 6 times and 2 runs 6 times. Ruben Gomez was 17–9, Sal Maglie went 14–6, Jim Hearn, Don Liddle and Marv Grissom were effective spot starters, and Grissom and Hoyt Wilhelm were tremendous in relief. Liddle was a rookie left-hander when I first played with him in 1953 in Milwaukee. He was a very quiet, nice guy and didn't look very big on the mound, but he was a tough competitor who had good control of his curve and could effectively change speeds. He did a good job relieving and spot starting both with the Braves in 1953 and with the Giants in 1954 and 1955, going 9–4 and 10–4.

We were able to win a lot of the low-scoring games because we threw 19 shutouts and had an outstanding team ERA of just above 3.00, both league bests. In April Grissom, Maglie, and I threw consecutive shutouts against the Phillies. We kept the team in the game and then somebody like Dusty Rhodes or Bobby Hofman would do something sensational to win it at the end. Once they both hit pinch homers in the same inning. Rhodes and Hofman were the best lefty-righty pinch-hit combination in many years. Dusty, being very confident, would say, "Hold them there, boys, and I'll get them in the ninth." Rhodes was a funny guy from Alabama who kept the bench relaxed. He backed up his boasts all year. He was amazing, batting way over .300 and hitting 15 homers and driving in 50 runs in something like 150 at-bats. He won a few games against the Dodgers with late-inning pinch hits. He started one doubleheader and tied a record with 6 extra-base hits. We also got timely hitting from regulars Don Mueller, Whitey Lockman, Alvin Dark, Monte Irvin, and Hank Thompson, who hit about 25 homers and played very good defensive at third. Davey Williams at second and Wes Westrum behind the plate did good jobs as well. Ray Katt was an excellent backup catcher, who I had very good luck pitching to.

Of course, we also had Willie Mays. To play with Willie Mays and watch him every day was a treat. I loved how he ran the bases or ran down long flies or got a base hit or home run we needed. He was just a great, great ballplayer. In 1954 he came back from two years in the service and really came into his own, playing in his first All-Star Game and being selected the National League's Most Valuable Player. He hit over 40 homers, drove in over 100 runs, and played with such enthusiasm. He and Don Mueller fought down to the wire with Duke Snider for the batting title, which made the season even more exciting. We were pulling for both guys. Don Mueller was what we called a banjo hitter. He had only 4 home runs but led the league with 212 hits. Going into the last game of the season, Mueller led Snider and Mays by percentage points. Then Mays got a single, double, and triple to win the title with .345, and Mueller slipped to second at .342. It was comforting to pitch with those guys in the lineup.

DON NEWCOMBE (DODGERS):
You didn't let Willie Mays hit the first pitch. Of course, he could hit the second pitch, too. Willie liked to extend his arms like Duke Snider, Mickey Mantle, and other power hitters, so if you crowded him with one pitch and then threw a pitch low and away you could give him trouble. Of course, you could pitch God that way, and it would give Him trouble.

J. ANTONELLI:
We were good but we were also lucky. We also had a lot of heady baseball minds like Whitey Lockman, Wes Westrum, Don Mueller, Joe Amalfitano, and Marv

Grissom. In the clubhouse and the club car on the train we'd talk a lot of baseball. There was a lot of joking around and a lot of fun.

I won my 20th game in St. Louis at the end of August, becoming the first Giants' left-hander to do this since Carl Hubbell and Cliff Melton in 1937. I should have won 24 or 25 games that year, but won only once more. I shut out the Cards 1–0, and I think Joe Garagiola caught that game. We picked him up from Chicago and he finished his career with us before going off to be a broadcaster.

I went out and tried to do my best. If I had a shutout going when I got to the ninth inning, I might try a little harder. I think I was a bear-down pitcher in the late innings. Once I got by the first or second inning, I'd usually get into a groove and be tough to beat. It was the same with a lot of the better pitchers.

PHILADELPHIA PHILLIES

DEL ENNIS:
I used to play a lot of tricks. Our coach Benny Bengough was a good sport, so he was often a victim. I'd do things like write on his bald head. If he'd pick me up for a banquet, I might invite Benny into the house, and while my wife engaged him in conversation I'd sneak outside, remove his hubcaps, and put some stones in there. Then when his car rattled on the way to the banquet, I'd tell him to take his car to a mechanic.

I'd nail shoes to the floor or hats to the ceiling and stuff like that. I would get the manager and coaches. Once we were ahead 9–1 against Pittsburgh, so Steve O'Neill rested me at the end of the game. I went back to the clubhouse and drove sixpenny spikes through their shoes into a corrugated wood floor. I figured they'd be in a good mood because of the easy victory. Then they walked in. They had lost the game! Here I was the only guy in the clubhouse with their shoes nailed to the floor. They weren't too happy with me.

We played over .500 ball for O'Neill for half a season, but Carpenter replaced him for the rest of the year with Terry Moore, the former Cards outfielder. We ended up 4 games under .500, despite Robin Roberts winning 23 games again. He pitched a 1-hitter against the Reds, no-hitting them after Bobby Adams got a leadoff hit. I felt loyal to the Phillies and had enough pride to play at the same level despite our drop in the standings. I had a good year, with 25 homers and 119 RBIs.

But the Phillies' fans didn't appreciate my effort. They booed me as much as ever. It's true that I did get some positive fan mail. Also, I had a fan club in Audubon, New Jersey. I gave them permission to form it and used to go over there and visit them all the time. They were helpful, but they were always on my back to do something. It got to be a real pain in the neck.

PITTSBURGH PIRATES

FRANK THOMAS:

I walked to the ballpark, past a lot of bars. I didn't drink, so I didn't go in. But guys I grew up with would come out and say, "Are you too good for us now?" I'd go in and have a 7UP or a glass of milk. Then if I made an error at the park, someone would point out that I was in a bar before the game. So you're damned if you do and damned if you don't. There were advantages and disadvantages to playing in Pittsburgh. Overall, people were kind to me, but hometown fans expect the impossible and there was a segment of the fans who didn't like me. I considered myself an entertainer and I did my best every day, so it didn't matter what any fan said. There were fans in the bleachers who were called the Bleacher Buc(k)s because they got in for a buck. If you did good or bad, they'd let you know it. That's the way it should be. They paid their way in and could do what they wanted as far as I was concerned.

When growing up in Pittsburgh, I never understood why the Pirates never played the Homestead Grays. I didn't know why there was no integrated baseball. I didn't even know there was friction between the races until I played professional ball and went to spring training in the South. In the minors, there were no blacks on my minor league teams, so I didn't play on the same team with a black until 1954, when the Pirates brought up their first black, Curt Roberts. He was a 5'8" second baseman from Texas who had played in the Negro Leagues and then a few years in the minors. He was a pretty good defensive player but didn't have much tal-

ent overall. He was a regular as a rookie, but after that he couldn't compete with Bill Mazeroski.

I roomed with two Jewish players on the Pirates: Cal Abrams and Sid Gordon. They were both really nice guys. They never spoke of being abused by fans or any discrimination, and I didn't witness it. Cal had a pretty good year for us in 1953, but he got off to a slow start in 1954 and was traded to the Orioles. Sid had a pretty good year for us in 1954, but he would get off to a slow start in 1955 and be traded to the Giants. It didn't matter at all that I was Catholic and they were Jewish.

I would go to church every Sunday and during the week, if possible. On Sunday, I'd call other Catholic players and say, "Wake up, we're going to church." Religion never got in the way. When I just got out of the seminary, I grabbed a player and said, "Don't you swear around me!" But I stepped back and realized I couldn't force them to change. I could only lead by example. It got to the point where if I came around, they wouldn't swear. I lived my life and let the other players live as they pleased. You hoped a little would rub off because there were a lot of temptations in the life of a ballplayer. He had to be strong because he was on his own. For instance, there was a lot of drinking, yet the managers didn't say anything about it because it didn't show up on the field. Most managers felt that whatever you did outside the lines was your business. If you wanted to stay out late for whatever reason, all you had to do was let the manager know, so that if you got into trouble the team would be there to protect you.

I loved being a ballplayer, but it wasn't as glamorous as it was made out to be. Being away from home and the family was difficult, and so was not eating at regular hours. Like me, the guys I played with weren't fairly compensated for their talents or contributions, yet they took pride in what they were doing and enjoyed playing. They even played when they were hurt because they were afraid to lose their jobs, as Wally Pipp did when he let Lou Gehrig take his place for one game. They didn't carry an attaché case and *The Wall Street Journal*. They were friendly men who recognized that it was important to be nice to kids. On the road, some guys would go to the movies, but I would answer my fan mail. I felt if a kid wrote me, I was obligated to answer him. I signed autographs. I visited kids in hospitals. They'd give me these big smiles despite their difficulties. It gave you a different perspective on life. I had my health. Afterward, I could go 0 for 41 or, as I once did, strike out 36 of 69 times, and it made no difference.

In 1954 I played 153 games in the outfield and batted .298, with 23 homers and 94 RBIs. I looked forward to getting my new contract from Branch Rickey because when he didn't give me the $15,000 I wanted after 1953, he promised to make it up to me if I had another good year. I expected a substantial raise.

ELROY FACE:

All I had was a fastball and curve, so after my rookie year, Mr. Rickey sent me to New Orleans in the Southern Association, Double A ball, to work on an off-speed pitch. So I wasn't around when the Pirates became the first team to charter planes. I was in New Orleans developing a forkball, the pitch I would be known for. In the spring, former Yankee reliever Joe Page had been in Pittsburgh's camp trying to make a comeback, and I had watched him throw his forkball. "Forkball" wasn't really part of the baseball vocabulary then, but Page threw one and Rube Marquard had thrown one back in the twenties. That's the pitch I decided to work on while on the sidelines. About halfway through the season I started using it in ballgames. It was effective immediately.

To throw a forkball, you hold the ball between your first and second fingers and let it slide through. I had long fingers and just wrapped them around the ball. You wouldn't get the rotation you got on a fastball. On the fastball, you had your fingers behind the ball, giving it force. Page would move the ball so that one of his fingers would catch on one of the seams and he'd get a little pull on the seam to break it in or break it out. I'd throw it with the same delivery as my fastball. I'd throw it three-quarters speed so batters couldn't tell it apart from the fastball. Usually it would sink, but sometimes it moved in and out and sometimes it would shoot upward. I didn't vary it on purpose. I threw it the same way every time, aiming it for the middle of the plate, and let it take care of itself.

CINCINNATI REDS

ANDY SEMINICK:

Our new manager was Birdie Tebbetts. He was a younger guy, having been catching just a couple of years before, so he could relate to the players much better than Rogers Hornsby, our manager in 1953. Birdie was a super person, an outstanding, knowledgeable baseball man, and a good manager. Everyone liked him very much. We moved up to fifth place under him. The Reds hadn't won over 70 games since 1947.

Our big gun was again Ted Kluszewski. He was phenomenal. He hit around .325 and led the league with 49 homers and 141 RBIs. Gus Bell drove in over 100 runs again, and Jim Greengrass came close to that and hit more than 25 homers. By this time the Reds were putting together a lineup that would last for a few years. Johnny Temple, a fine hitter and rugged player, moved into second base, and Wally Post, who had been around since the late forties, became the starting right fielder. He was a fun guy who could hit the ball a ton and was a good fielder with a strong, accurate arm. My backup was Ed Bailey, another guy who liked to have fun. He didn't hit much for average that year but hit a lot of homers for the limited time he played. I worked with him some and he was a good learner. I could see that he would soon be the Reds' regular receiver. (Surprisingly, when the Reds traded me back to the Phillies early in 1955, it was for another catcher, Smoky Burgess, and Bailey's advance to regular status would be delayed until 1956.)

The Reds' pitching still lagged far behind the offense, but it improved some. Joe Nuxhall went 12–5 and proved he could be an effective starter. Joe had pitched in 1 game in 1944 when he was 15—he was the youngest player ever in the majors—but didn't make it back to the Reds until 1952. He showed promise in 1952 and '53, but really came into his own in 1954. He was left-handed, so his ball moved, and he pitched inside.

Art Fowler tied Nuxhall and Corky Valentine for most wins on the team. He had a good arm, a good fastball, a good breaking ball, and excellent control. He knew how to pitch and worked hard. He was a very, very poor fielder but worked until he got to be one of the best-fielding pitchers. He was a good guy to have on a team. He liked to have a good time, and he did. Maybe that was one of his faults. He was a knowledgeable pitcher for a rookie, but he was older than most. I used to get on him for shaking me off. He just came up from the minors and shook me off and I went to the mound and said, ''No, you don't do that.'' He listened.

ART FOWLER:

I thought it would take me a total of 5 years to get to the majors but I pitched all those extra years with the Atlanta Crackers and Milwaukee Brewers, in the Braves system, and it took me from 1944 to 1954. I didn't think I'd make it. I never complained, but why did it take me 10 years to get to the big leagues when I was always a winner in the minors?

In 1953, I went 18–10 at Atlanta, and led the Southern Association in ERA, games pitched, innings pitched, and shutouts, with 6. So finally, in 1954, Cincinnati took me on a 30-day look-see basis. I was a 31-

After 10 years in the minors, Art Fowler reached the majors in 1954 and tied for the most victories on the Cincinnati Reds' staff.

year-old rookie. I'm there two to three weeks without doing anything, when they ran out of pitchers and Birdie Tebbetts told me I'd be starting. I gave up just 2 runs to the Cubs—Hank Sauer and Dee Fondy homered off me—and I won 3–2. That was my biggest thrill as a player. I didn't pitch anymore until the day before my 30-day trial was up. Then I beat the Phillies' Murry Dickson, 1–0. Gabe Paul told me he bought my contract. My rookie salary was $6,000 and I got $6-a-day meal money, which I thought was super. In those days, we didn't care about money, we just played ball.

It was a super feeling pitching back then. I got to go against some of the best players who ever played major league baseball. I'm not saying I was that good, because it was tough enough just to be a big league player, much less be a great player. I felt fortunate and lucky to be there, making a living playing major league baseball.

It was also great starting out with the Reds. Cincinnati was a super place to play ball. I lived right downtown, right in the square. Usually I was by myself, but sometimes I roomed with Corky Valentine, who had been in Atlanta. The fans were behind me and the players couldn't have been nicer. Joe Nuxhall was probably my best friend. There were no problems between players. Nobody griped because of what the other guys were making. We could have guessed, but it wouldn't have made any difference.

Birdie was the best manager I ever played for. He was like my father. No one had ever given me a chance to play and he gave me the chance. Birdie told his players, ''All you have to do is hustle 90 feet and give me 100 percent and we'll have no problems.'' So we never had problems. He had been a catcher with Boston and worked well with pitchers. Tom Ferrick was Tebbetts' pitching coach. He was a big right-hander whose major league career had ended just a couple of years before. He'd been a relief pitcher for five or six teams. He was a good guy. His philosophy was ''Throw strikes, buddy.'' When I got beat I'd say, ''Tom, I threw too many strikes.''

I won my first 4 games and ended up with a 12–10 record. I pitched more than 220 innings and led the team in earned run average and tied Nuxhall and Valentine for most wins on the team. I led the National League pitchers in fielding—I didn't make any errors. I wanted to be the first player to sign for next year because I was having a good year. Gabe Paul called me in before the season ended. I don't know anybody who liked Gabe Paul. He was a selfish individual. He didn't want to pay me nothing. I didn't know about salaries and what other players got, but I wanted $11,000 to $12,000. I said, "All you want to give me is $9,000? That's ridiculous." But I had to sign. For the first time since I became a professional ballplayer, when I went back home to South Carolina, I didn't take an off-season job.

AMERICAN LEAGUE 1954

"WYNN WAS THE TOUGHEST PITCHER FOR ME. HE WAS TOO SMART. HE'D FIND A BATTER'S WEAKNESS. HE'D JAM ME, HIGH AND INSIDE. I READ WHERE HE SAID HE'D KNOCK DOWN HIS GRANDMOTHER IF SHE GOT A HIT OFF HIM, AND I'M THINKING, 'I'M NOT IN HIS FAMILY—HE MIGHT KILL ME.' "

VIC POWER

PHILADELPHIA ATHLETICS

EDDIE JOOST:

As Jimmy Dykes had assumed, I was offered the job of manager of the Athletics. I did all right on salary because I would still be playing and getting money for that also. When I became manager I wanted to disassociate myself from contractual arguments, but I saw the contracts of Bobby Shantz and Pete Suder on Earle Mack's desk and said, "You're kidding me. That's all they're making?" He said, "That's what we've been paying them. They never asked for more." I said, "Well, they're going to ask for more now." I picked up the phone and called Pete Suder at his home in Aliquippa, Pennsylvania. I told him I got him a $5,000 raise and that for the first time he'd be able to bring his family to spring training at the team's expense. I heard Pete's wife in the background excitedly asking, "Eddie, do you mean that?" Then I told the Macks to give Shantz a $5,000 raise. "But, Eddie, Shantz has a bad arm." "Yeah, he has a bad arm. He made a lot of money for you two years ago and now you're going to tell him he's not worth it?"

Shantz tried a comeback with me. I told him that his arm wasn't where it should be and that he had to continue to work on a rehabilitation program with a therapist. I told him that he was still a member of the team and that he should tell me when he was finally ready. He began to pitch under the stands in Philadelphia. Then he told me he was ready. He threw for me and it was obvious his arm was hurting. I told him he would probably never be an effective starter again but that if he kept working he could be one of baseball's premier relievers. I held him out all year.

I needed players and the Yankees were the team that had them. We tried to get a couple of front-line players from them for Harry Byrd. We had a meeting with Casey Stengel and Dan Topping in Atlanta. They accepted the deal. But then they said that they had to call New York to get confirmation from George Weiss, the general manager. I knew it wouldn't work because Weiss wouldn't accept the deal because he hadn't been there. Sure enough, Weiss screamed at Topping and the deal fell through. Stengel had no say about players. He was just the manager up front.

When word got around that I was trying to make a deal with the Yankees, Joe Cronin, the GM of the Red Sox, approached me at the Commodore Hotel in New York and was upset with me. He said I was helping the Yankees become even stronger than the other teams. Some were willing to buy Byrd for $200,000 to $300,000, but I couldn't put that money out on the field.

Earle Mack resumed talking about a big trade with the Yankees. Eventually, we sent them Harry Byrd, Eddie Robinson, and 3 other players and we got 6 players Weiss wanted to unload, including Jim Finigan, Vic Power, and Bill Renna. I hated that deal. I didn't want us to get a reputation for being a dumping ground for the Yankees.

Jim Finigan was the first guy the Yankees mentioned when we talked about a trade. I couldn't understand why they were so eager to get rid of a guy who had done so well in the minors and wasn't a troublemaker. So in spring training I watched him closely. He could hit all right and had a fair throwing arm, but I discovered that he couldn't run. He'd get going at top speed and stumble, often falling down. If he went an extra step while playing third, he'd stumble and fall down. He wasn't a good third baseman, but he had one good year for us, hitting over .300 as a rookie. He was a very nice person.

Vic Power had tremendous ability but didn't show it in 1954. He didn't want to play with us—he wanted to play with the Yankees—but I kept telling him that the Yankees didn't want him. His demise was wine, women, and song. That was his forte. That's why the Yankees wanted to get rid of him—not because he was black. That's why I didn't want him, either. I wouldn't have had a problem, but he wouldn't pay attention. Then he'd come in and say, "I don't want to play center field, boss. I'm tired of playing center field—I want to play first base." Then he'd go out and dog it. He'd miss balls. The Yankees knew he was a hot dog.

Bill Renna was a big, husky kid from the University of Santa Clara. The Yankees had soured on him and he was mad: "Eddie, I sure got a raw deal in New York. They wouldn't give me a chance." I told him to forget what happened over there and to do it here. But he was

more of a football player than a baseball player. He could run well and was a pretty good outfielder, but he couldn't hit major league pitching. The Yankees knew that.

We also got Don Bollweg from the Yankees. He had bad legs, so they didn't want him. He was a good-looking first baseman . . . during infield practice. In the game, he didn't do nothing.

The players we got from the Yankees blended in with some players we already had. Lou Limmer was the first baseman. He is a bad memory. He was the nicest guy in the world, but he couldn't hit, he couldn't field, he couldn't run, and he couldn't throw. I don't know how he did it, but he must have had a good year someplace because we brought him up. Spook Jacobs was pushed down my throat all spring training. Supposedly he was the greatest second baseman since Nellie Fox and the greatest leadoff hitter of all time. I saw him in spring training and realized this wasn't the guy I'd heard about. This guy couldn't do anything. I told him, "You're doing this wrong, that wrong, this wrong." He was a hyper guy and he'd be up in arms as soon as I'd talk to him. I still preferred Suder at second.

Marion Fricano was a real nice guy but didn't have major league pitching ability. He wasn't overpowering but was aggressive and would knock you down with a fastball. Fricano wasn't a head hunter—Cass Michaels just lost the ball that hit him on the temple and nearly killed him. It wasn't intentional.

The 1954 team I managed was a mixed lot. We didn't have any players who were leaders. Gus Zernial wasn't a leader. He could hit homers but he was a terrible outfielder. He did a couple of things early in the season and I started taking him out of games early. He said, "Eddie, we've got to sit down and talk. There's something between us that I don't believe is right." I said, "I'm not trying to make it difficult but I'm the manager and if I think you're not capable of doing things, I'll tell you. If you blow up, that's up to you. I'm telling you that you should be a better fielder. You hit home runs but that's only one part of the game." So he said he'd work on his fielding and throwing. And he did. He tried. Then one day we were playing a doubleheader against Boston on a hot afternoon in Philadelphia. In about the fifth inning we were behind 7 or 8 runs, so Wally Moses said, "Why don't you take him out and save him for the second game." I said, "Wally, we're both going to be here for 9 innings, so let him stay and suffer with the two of us. If he can't stand it, tough luck." The very next inning, the ball's hit on the line to his left. Gus goes over to catch it, stumbles, and breaks his shoulder. Wally's looking at me, saying, "I told you to take him out." I said, "No, no, no!" It came back to haunt me, but fortunately it didn't end his career.

When I became player-manager of the Athletics in 1954 I didn't even try to disassociate myself from the players. I'd mingle with them, talk to them, do the best I could to keep them relaxed. Not that I was a great manager, but it was just the case that we had a bad ballclub. Everyone knew it.

Our staff was comprised of minor league pitchers. I had wanted Bing Miller to come back as pitching coach, but he retired. I contacted Bucky Walters, who had just retired, but he was through with baseball. He suggested Rollie Hemsley, who had been in the minors. I suggested Hemsley to the Macks and they lit up like Christmas trees. So he came to spring training and I talked with my new coaches, Wally Moses, Augie Galan, and Hemsley. Augie was knowledgeable and a good guy, and helpful. I told Rollie I was turning the pitching staff over to him and that I wanted daily reports. But Rollie had no intention of helping the pitchers. Instead he was going behind my back to tell the Macks what a bad job of managing I was doing, especially with the pitchers. I confronted him because he was intentionally undermining me. That's the kind of guy he was.

Connie Mack, Jr., assured me that the team wasn't leaving Philadelphia and that I'd stay on as manager in 1955. He wanted me in on an upcoming meeting three days later. We took the elevator up to the tower where Connie Mack's office was. Mr. Mack was there with his sons. And so was Jack Kelly, the old-time bricklayer and prominent Philadelphian. He made an offer for the ballclub to keep it in Philadelphia. He was going to pay $1.5 million and pay off all the debts. All he asked was that we involve his son in the daily operation of the ballclub so that eventually he would become the president and general manager. Earle and Roy Mack objected because they wanted to keep the team in the Mack family. They didn't understand that they had no choice because they were broke. So this deal went down the tubes.

I got along well with the Philadelphia newspapers, but at this time they wouldn't support the team staying in town. They said they didn't need us because the city had the Phillies. We had five sportswriters traveling with us all the time and I asked them, "Who are you going to write about if we go? You should find a way to get the Kelly offer back on the table so that we stay here." But it was too late. The Macks sold the ballclub to Arnold Johnson, an entrepreneur from Chicago, and he would take the team to Kansas City in 1955. And three or four of the Philadelphia reporters lost their jobs.

After the season, I called Arnold Johnson to get my status for the 1955 season. He told me not to worry about my job. He said he wanted to get together with me in New York. A week goes by and he calls to tell me he had hired Lou Boudreau to replace me. He said he wanted a name for when the team moved to Kansas City. I wasn't too upset.

GUS ZERNIAL:

In 1954 Eddie Joost was appointed player-manager. He and I had some problems. Eddie was a frustrated manager with a can't-win club and I got very irritated with him because I became the victim of what he was trying to do to improve the club. He was trying to find a lineup and would occasionally platoon me, which I resented because I had earned my spurs. If he'd found a way to win by platooning me, that would have been fine, but he didn't. We lost 103 games.

The differences Eddie and I had were personal. I don't know if Eddie realized the reason we had our biggest problems. Outfielder Wally Moses and I were good friends. I didn't have a car, so Wally would give me rides all the time. But when Eddie made Wally a coach, Wally stopped associating with me. Maybe Eddie had a rule that his coaches couldn't be friends with players, but I never forgave him for that. I was equally mad at Wally. I told him, "If your becoming a coach interferes with our friendship, forget it." And I meant it. Baseball is baseball, but a friendship is something different. I don't think Eddie himself distanced himself from players . . . no, I think he *did* do that. I would dispute that.

Dave Philley said he'd never play for Joost, and he was traded before the 1954 season started. Philley didn't like Eddie, but he didn't like a lot of guys. I did like Eddie and we would stay friends through the years.

However, I just think he got caught up in circumstances that were very difficult, caused by the lack of money and direction in the front office, and the rift between the Mack brothers. Jimmy Dykes had left to manage in Baltimore, and Eddie took on a hopeless role in which he was an inevitable loser. I recognized more in later years than I did at the time that Eddie was given an impossible task.

Eddie and I had had our problems, but I was back in the lineup and was having a solid season when I broke my shoulder. We were getting beat by Boston 18–0. I obviously wasn't having a productive day and I was tired of chasing down doubles and triples. A ball would go to my right, a ball would go to my left, and probably a ball went right through my legs. The fans were getting all over me. I'll never forget telling myself, "I don't care what comes my way next, I'll catch it." Billy Consolo was the first batter and he lined one to left-center. I raced for that cotton picker and stepped in a hole where the water came out for the sprinkler system in the stadium. They had left the rubber top off. So I tumbled and broke my shoulder. The fans were booing me. I said, "Thank God I don't have to come out here anymore." I lay on the field for quite a while, long enough for the public address announcer to tell the crowd I'd broken my left shoulder—everyone knew I'd already broken my right shoulder a few years before. Then they wheeled me off through a runway. The fans used a lot of foul language, and such sentiments as, "You should have broken your neck!" The fans were raw and bitter—we were having a terrible season, we were playing a horrendous game, and it was pretty well known that we were leaving the city.

I averaged 30 homers and 100 RBIs in my 4 years in Philadelphia. It was depressing from the standpoint that individually I accomplished a lot but we were a losing ballclub. I couldn't figure out how to generate enthusiasm. I hadn't had the experience of winning, so I couldn't teach my teammates how to do it. I thought we had a very lethargic ballclub beginning in 1953, when we hit the skids. By 1954 we were a disaster.

JOE DE MAESTRI:
I came along at the end of the Connie Mack era. Mack came to a couple of games, but he didn't visit the dugout or anything, so those were the only times I ever saw

him. He was 91 years old. Roy Mack and Earle Mack were in charge. The players were aware that there were financial problems. After the 1953 season, I negotiated my contract with Roy, whom I liked very much. I was making $6,000 and said, "I can't come back unless I get $7,000." Roy was trying to be fair and reluctantly gave it to me. It's funny today to think of holding out for a $1,000 raise from $6,000 to $7,000, but that's the way it was in those days.

Eddie Joost had become the manager of the Athletics, so he rarely played in the field. I was the regular shortstop from the beginning of the season. I batted just .230 but had a career-high 40 RBIs and had a good year in the field.

The Athletics had such bad pitching that Arnold Portocarrero, a rookie, led the team with 9 victories. He lost 18 games. How can I classify Portocarrero? He was a big kid, but he wasn't strong. He had very thin arms and legs for a big man. He had fluid motion, but his ball was too straight, with no movement on it. At times he showed signs of brilliance, but he just couldn't keep it up game after game.

Marion Fricano was another starting pitcher who wasn't very good. He had an okay fastball, but he couldn't overpower batters, so he relied mostly on breaking stuff—only he couldn't get many guys out with it. Fricano and Cass Michaels had been teammates on the Athletics in 1953. In 1954 Cass went back to the White Sox, who he played for in the '40s. One night Fricano started against Chicago in Philadelphia. Cass batted sixth for the Sox. The first 5 guys came to the plate and it was just boom, boom, boom, boom, boom and the score was 5 to 0 with no outs in the top of the first. Then Cass came up to bat. I was playing short and I looked at Marion. He had turned away from the plate and was looking out toward the outfield and rubbing the ball. I just knew that the next guy up was going to get hit or thrown at. Well, Cass had the craziest stance. He stood real wide over the plate with his left shoulder facing the pitcher and his jaw on his chest. It was the perfect stance for a pitcher who wanted to hit a batter in the head. The sad part is that Marion threw at him. In those days, batters just wore a protective liner, not a full helmet. And that fastball hit Cass right on the temple. It was the hardest I ever saw anyone hit. Either Cass didn't see the ball or he just froze. He never moved. He just went straight down and was bleeding from the nose, the ears, the mouth. Fricano wasn't kicked out of the game. Joost just took him out. There was nothing done to him.

A week later, the Tigers came to town. Cass was from Detroit and was really friendly with a lot of the Tigers. He was a terrific bowler and bowled with a lot of them. So that whole team was angry at Fricano. Well, Marion happened to pitch one game, and the first pitch he threw to the leadoff hitter, Harvey Kuenn, was right behind his ear. A couple of innings later he hit Steve Gromek right in the seat of his pants. Gromek, who was great friends with Michaels, just let the bat fly toward the mound and there was a real brawl, a war. Everyone was down on the ground. I worried that Walt Dropo, the Tigers' big first baseman, would jump onto the pile and kill somebody. I didn't blame the Tigers. Most of us weren't too happy about what Fricano did. Fricano didn't last very long. I don't know if what he did to Michaels played a big part. I think his ineffectiveness was the major reason. He may have been lucky to have gotten out so soon because I feel somebody would have tried to get him sooner or later.

Michaels was in a coma in the hospital for a while. I visited his room. At the time he had lost some of his ability to talk and he stuttered. Chicago gave him another shot in spring training, but he got dizzy and had to quit.

Eddie Joost was always good to me, but he had a couple of run-ins with guys. I got caught between Joost and Gus Zernial because I was rooming with Gus. It was serious between the two. I have always wondered if the trouble was something deeper than Joost's just not liking how Zernial played the outfield. Because Gus always gave 200 percent and was a good guy to have in the lineup on a last-place club with virtually no offense. At one point, Joost asked me to stop rooming with Gus, and what could that request have to do with Gus's defense? I didn't know what Joost's reaction would be, but I told him, "There's no way I'll switch roommates. I want to room with Gus and that's that." And he said, "Well, okay." I never found out why he asked me to switch roommates, and it always bugged me. Maybe he thought Gus was going to turn me against him. Gus was an influence because I was still young, but he never tried to turn me against Eddie.

When I was in Philadelphia, we had a place in a little Italian neighborhood, two or three blocks from the ballpark. We basically stayed inside or just went to a park with the kids for a picnic or something like that. I don't think I ever went downtown. I didn't own a car and couldn't afford to rent one, so we only went places if someone with a car invited us. I never mingled with people in Philadelphia. I developed a bad taste for the city because of the fans. They cheered when you did well, but when they got mean, they were meaner than anybody else. They booed Gus when he was being carried off the field with a broken shoulder—and he was our most popular player! They used to throw beer and mustard at the players' wives from the upper deck. My wife almost had a nervous breakdown because of that. So it was hard just going to the ballpark, as much as I enjoyed playing the game. I preferred playing on the road. I was relieved when the franchise moved to Kansas City.

BOB CAIN:

The Browns traded me to the Athletics after the 1953 season. We had spring training in West Palm Beach. I was coming along really well and had pitched 5 shutout innings against Brooklyn. That was the first time an Athletics pitcher had lasted 5 innings. That night calcium formed in my pitching wrist, and that ruined it for me. It didn't get better and I was sent to Ottawa.

VIC POWER:

I went to my first major league spring training when I joined Philadelphia in Florida. I knew something was strange when the white players checked into the hotel near the ballpark while Bob Trice and I were sent to the "colored section." It was 2 miles away and we'd have to walk both ways because we couldn't take taxis. When we got to the park we discovered we weren't allowed to drink the cold water in the dugouts but had to drink warm water from a fountain behind the centerfield billboard. And we couldn't use the same bathroom as the white players. No one warned me about segregation in the South. No one told me why black players couldn't openly date light-skinned women, or stay in the same hotel as white players, or eat in the same restaurants. I learned English by reading on the team bus while the other players ate in whites-only restaurants. I went into a restaurant in Little Rock, Arkansas, and the waitress said, "We don't serve Negroes," and I said, "That's okay, I don't eat Negroes. I want rice and beans." I would get mad, because they were pushing me. My mother couldn't believe it when I wrote her that a restaurant wouldn't serve a hungry person who had money, or that I got stopped by police for going downtown after 6 P.M.

I got arrested for jaywalking in Orlando for crossing the street on a red light. I explained to the judge, "I'm a Puerto Rican, and on my island, a Negro and a white person go to school together, dance together, and get married. But here I try to go to a restaurant and there's a sign that says: FOR WHITES ONLY. And if I want to go to a bar, or drink from a water fountain, or use a bathroom, I see that sign: FOR WHITES ONLY. So when I saw white people crossing the street when the green light came on, I figured that colored people could only cross when the light was red." He dismissed the case.

No one explained to me about racial problems. They just let me find out for myself. I gained so much respect for Jackie Robinson, Larry Doby, Willie Mays, and the other black players who came before me.

Being from Puerto Rico, where there was no difference between the races, I didn't think I was representing blacks when I played baseball with white players. But black fans cheered for me. Once, in an exhibition game in Mobile, Alabama, the blacks who were sitting in the sun in a segregated section of the ballpark went wild when I hit a ball that knocked down a sign that said: YELLOW TAXIS FOR WHITES ONLY. That gave me a lot of satisfaction.

I became the second black to play for the Athletics. Bob Trice, a tall right-handed pitcher from Georgia, had come up in 1953. Naturally, the team had us room together on the road. I was one of the first Puerto Ricans to play in the majors. That meant a lot to me. It also made me more of a hero in Puerto Rico, though it took time before they knew that Vic Power of the Athletics was the same guy as Victor Pellot in the winter leagues. The first Puerto Rican in the majors had been Hiram Bithorn, a right-handed pitcher who won 18 games for the Cubs in 1943 but didn't pitch much more after returning from the army. I think there were only two other Puerto Ricans in the majors in my rookie year. Ruben Gomez was pitching for the Giants, in his second year. And Luis Marquez, an outfielder–first baseman, played

Vic Power rarely got to play first base in his rookie season in Philadelphia, but he would become the league's best all-around first baseman once the Athletics moved to Kansas City.

for the Cubs and Pirates. He had been in the majors once before, in 1951 with the Boston Braves. Roberto Clemente and Luis Arroyo would be rookies in 1955. And Jim Rivera's parents were Puerto Rican.

Connie Mack was no longer the Athletics' manager or in charge of the organization, but I was fortunate to meet him. He was such a nice old gentleman. I wouldn't have been surprised to learn that he never got mad in his life.

I began my rookie career going 0 for 16 against Mike Garcia, Bob Feller, Early Wynn, and Bob Lemon in Cleveland. If I had still been in the Yankee organization, I probably would have been demoted to the minors. Then we went to Chicago, and I got a bloop single for my first major league hit. The next time up, the pitcher threw at my head. I said, "What's going on here?" Not long after that, another white pitcher told me, "I'm going to stick it in one ear and have it come out your other ear." I said, "That guy's pretty tough!" I figured I'd have to still fight to survive, just like in the minors.

Philadelphia was such a miserable team. Bobby Shantz and Alex Kellner were the only good pitchers, but that year no pitcher had 10 victories. They couldn't strike out anybody, so I was always chasing after balls. I'd get so tired. But I hustled and didn't complain about playing the outfield.

There were some nice guys on Philadelphia. Jim Finigan, our third baseman, was a very friendly man. He was a steady fielder and good contact hitter, but without power. He got by on his intelligence. He was second to Bob Grim in the voting for Rookie of the Year.

I was friends with Elmer Valo. He was from Czechoslovakia, but he was my English teacher on the bench. He learned my accent, and when the umpire made a bad call, Valo yelled out, "You son of a beech!" The umpire would see me in the dugout and throw me out of the game. Any time the umpire made a bad call, I'd have to run into the clubhouse before Valo cursed at him.

I rarely socialized with teammates during my major league career because very few of them liked to go to art museums, shop for clothes, eat at good restaurants, or go listen to classical music or jazz. They wanted to play cards and drink beer. I liked to go out and have a good time, but I wasn't a drinker. Carlos Paula, a Senators' outfielder from Cuba, was drunk every time I saw him, and there were others who would drink before games. A lot of players couldn't get on a plane without getting drunk in the airport bar. Still, I didn't see too many heavy drinkers in the majors.

I was making $12,000 as a rookie. I was supposed to be a Rookie of the Year candidate and was even invited on "The Ed Sullivan Show" to sing some song I didn't know the words to. But I hit only .255. I didn't like that Wally Moses took away my 36-ounce bat and made me use a lighter bat.

BILL WILSON:

I was unhappy with the White Sox because for the second straight year Paul Richards wasn't playing me, even when the team was going bad. Then, in June, we were in New York when Frank Lane told me I had been traded to the Athletics. I was happy because I knew I'd get the chance to play. Joost put me in center, while Vic Power,

Bill Renna, Gus Zernial, and Elmer Valo shared time in left and right field. It was different playing for him than for Richards. He'd get upset, but he got along with his players much better. He didn't hang around with us, though he was still a player, too.

I wasn't a loner. I palled around with Joe De Maestri, who I played against in the minors and was a pretty good player, and Gus Zernial and Bill Renna, who were both roommates during the year. On the plane or train I'd play poker with Sonny Dixon, Al Sima, and a couple of other guys. I knew Dixon and Sima from the minors. We had a good group. Valo was a nice guy. Lou Limmer and Spook Jacobs were especially nice. Spook was a pretty good little player who had gotten hung up in the Dodgers' chain and didn't have a chance to break in. He had great speed and stole 4 bases one game.

This was a partying team that moved around pretty good. There were a lot of single guys, although guys like Finigan didn't party much. Vic Power did. Marion Fricano ran around with Spook Jacobs. Ed Burtschy liked to party. So did Gus Zernial. And we had a little substitute catcher who ran around with a singer. I'd go out and have my beers. There was quite a bit of drinking. They had beer in the clubhouse.

Philadelphia was a tough town to play in. The only people who were halfway decent to us were those we'd run into in restaurants. They were good fans. But when you played in front of the bleacher fans, you saw and heard a lot of crazy people. They threw stuff at both teams. Gus was always a target. I was playing beside Gus when he broke his collarbone and the goddamn fans were booing him. He was lying there saying, "One good thing about this: I'll get to go home." He had some good years there and they were booing him.

Zernial was a pull hitter. He had a long stance and would push his foot up and come right back down with it. His power impressed me. His homers weren't cheap.

CLEVELAND INDIANS

JIM GRANT:

I went to Florida A&M University and majored in English. The scouts who had followed me as a teenager in Lacoochee, Florida, lost track of me and wondered where I'd gone. I finally convinced my mother that English teachers didn't make a lot of money and that I could make good money playing baseball. By this time I was old enough to sign.

I visited an uncle in New Smyrna Beach because it was near Daytona Beach, where Cleveland trained in Indianville. I intended to introduce myself to the Indians, not knowing that their scout Fred Merkle was trying to track me down. One day in February, my high school coach, Hiram James Goodwin, rode by in his big Buick and escorted me to the training camp of Indianapolis, the Indians' Triple A team. Ted Beard, Dave Pope, Billy Harrell, Hank Foiles, Dick Tomanek, Herb Score, Rocky Colavito, Sad Sam Jones, Hank Aguirre, and Joe Altobelli were on that team and they would win the American Association pennant that year. We sat in the stands and watched them work out. I knew I could do what they were doing. Luckily, Hank Greenberg walked by and he decided to keep me around. I got a chance to work out at third base with the Triple A club with the nice striped socks and to talk with the players. I became the gofer for those guys who played poker at night and wanted beer and hot dogs from the little stand at the entrance to Indianville. They'd always let me keep the change and I actually made more money in spring training doing that than when I signed a contract for about $250 a month. I made something like $1,500!

The other players started to filter in. Finally I got a uniform and became a professional. That whole spring I played third base. I used a three-finger glove that I had cherished since my uncle gave it to me as a child. I was confident and played well and thought they should have signed me. But there were 500 players in camp and they kept releasing players every day. Fred Merkle told me that if they gave me the line "Come back next year" as a third baseman, I should announce I could pitch. Sure enough, I was told to come back next year. So I said I could pitch. That sparked their interest. They decided to pitch me that afternoon. Red Ruffing and Spud Chandler, who were both roving minor league coaches, liked me and stacked a "B" team against me, rather than have me pitch against the best hitters in camp. At noon time, when they gave you three vanilla cookies, some milk, and a banana and apple, Ruffing told me, "I know you can do this. When the first guy comes up, I want you to throw one under his chin." So I did that and for the rest of the game not one batter got close to the plate.

By the fifth inning, the word was getting around camp that I was pitching a no-hit shutout. Everybody came over to my field and I had an audience. I threw a 9-inning no-hitter. They said, "That wasn't too bad . . . We'd like to see you throw again." It was at the camp that I got my great nickname Mudcat because I used to dress and speak a little odd. Some players thought I was a welfare case from Mississippi. They started calling me Mississippi Mudcat, Mudhead, Mudface, but after that no-hitter they were calling me Mister.

There was no way the Indians were going to let me get away after that no-hitter. I couldn't go to any of their D teams because they were in the South. Blacks were usually notched above Class D because of the segregation they would have had to endure. So I went to Fargo in Class C. I was the Rookie of the Year.

AL SMITH:
The Yankees had won 5 straight world titles, so at our spring training camp we didn't assume we could beat them. But about two weeks into the season, we realized we were good enough. We had a lot of talent, and except for me and our rookie relievers, Don Mossi and Ray Narleski, our team had a lot of veterans who knew how to play the game. I adapted my style to fit the Indians. Lopez made me a leadoff hitter, so while I still hit with extra-base power, I didn't worry about hitting homers. I liked playing in Municipal Stadium because it had a good background and it was easy to pick up the ball. I stood right on top of the plate, choking up on my 34-inch, 31-ounce bat. I looked for walks. I wanted to get on base because the second hitter was Bobby Avila, who was a .300 hitter. I'd give him a sign that I was going to steal, or he'd move me along with a bunt down the third-base line or a hit-and-run. I had fair speed and knew how to run the bases, always taking advantage of outfielders who were slow, lazy, or had weak arms. I wanted to get into scoring position and let Al Rosen, Larry Doby, or Vic Wertz drive me in. I scored 101 runs.

We won 111 of 154 games, an American League record, and beat the Yankees by 8 games. The Yankees came into Cleveland for a doubleheader in mid-September, and we drew a record crowd of nearly 85,000 fans although the race was pretty much over. We had a strong offense. Avila hit .341 to lead the league in hitting. Doby led the league with 32 homers and 126 RBIs. Rosen hit over .300 with over 100 RBIs, and Wertz, Dave Philley, and Wally Westlake all hit homers and drove in runs. I hit .281 and drove in 50 runs batting leadoff.

Rosen was the best player I ever played with. He was a tremendous fielder and could really swing the bat. He made himself a great player by working hard. I think that he had a clause in his contract giving him bonus money for reaching a certain number of homers or RBIs. I think Bob Feller and some other guys had similar clauses. That was the only way they could make money.

We had a lot of hitting, but pitching is 75 percent of the game and we had the best in baseball. Bob Lemon and Early Wynn led the league with 23 wins each. Mike Garcia won 19 games and led the league in earned run average. If we had scored the runs for him that we did for Wynn and Lemon, Mike could have won 26 games. We'd lose 2–1, 1–0 for him, but if Wynn went out there we'd score 10 runs. Bob Feller could no longer pitch every fourth day, so he and Art Houtteman split time. Houtteman went 15–7 and Feller 13–3. Houtteman worked hard all the time, and when he went to the mound he was all business. Of course, all the Indian pitchers were like that. Wynn, Lemon, and Garcia liked to go the distance, but if a starter got into trouble we had the league's best bullpen with Mossi, a left-hander, and Narleski, a right-hander. They were rookies, but they didn't let the pressure bother them. We also had veteran Hal Newhouser in the pen, and he did a good job, too.

GEORGE KELL (RED SOX):

Feller, Lemon, Garcia, Wynn, Narleski, and Mossi all threw bullets. When you went into Cleveland for a 4-game weekend series, if you didn't manage your times at bat well, you'd come out of there 0 for 15. You had to plan on getting your hits. There was no letup. I'd know who was going to pitch each game before I arrived in Cleveland. That first time at bat I was like a wild man: "I'm going to get a base hit my first time up Friday night. I'm going to get a base hit!" If I didn't, I was even wilder my second time up. Because the quicker you got a hit, the quicker you relaxed. In his prime, Bob Feller was the toughest pitcher I faced, with Bob Lemon a close second. At this point, Lemon was the toughest

right-hander in the league. Garcia and Wynn weren't far behind. Wynn was a mean pitcher. His pet peeve was when a batter hit the ball through the middle. It would make him so mad, he'd die. I hit a lot of balls through the middle—Ty Cobb said that was the way to get out of a slump—and Wynn would scream at me.

FRED HATFIELD (TIGERS):

I broke up a no-hitter in the ninth inning against Early Wynn in 1954. I'm still waiting for him to knock me down. He just kept pitching me in on the fists. Man, he could thread a needle. Everyone had respect for him because he could stare right through you. He never changed expressions. Lemon was like that, too. They knew they were going to beat you. You just hoped to go 0 for 2 instead of 0 for 4. That was pretty good. You wanted a base on balls or to get hit on the ass.

LES MOSS (ORIOLES):

Bob Lemon was the toughest right-hander in the league and had been since after the war. He had good stuff—a fastball, slider, sinker, and curve—and good command. He'd get after you inside a lot, but not like Wynn would. If you hit the ball toward Wynn and either nicked him or made him jump, the next time you were going down. You could bet on it. But I didn't let him intimidate me.

JIM FRIDLEY (ORIOLES):

Wynn wanted to knock you down. I had been his roommate when I was on Cleveland just two years before, but it didn't matter to him that we were friends. I once shortened up as if I were going to bunt and he got infuriated and warned, "I'll knock you on your big ass. Get in and hit like a man!"

VIC POWER (ATHLETICS):

Wynn was the toughest pitcher for me. He was too smart. He'd find a batter's weakness. He'd jam me, high and inside. I read where he said he'd knock down his grandmother if she got a hit off him, and I'm thinking, "I'm not in his family—he might kill me."

I also faced Bob Feller for the first time as a rookie. He was supposedly on his way out. The count was 3–2 and then I fouled off 6 or 7 pitches. I couldn't get around on his fastball. Then he struck me out. I had to laugh thinking how tough he must have been when he was younger.

EDDIE JOOST (ATHLETICS):

Early Wynn was a great, great pitcher—and a mean pitcher who liked to come inside. Yet Bob Lemon was the most intimidating pitcher I faced. He had great natural stuff and he cheated, too. He'd throw spitters, sweatballs. I challenged the ball at the time. He threw a spitter and I called out to the umpire to look at the ball. The catcher, Jim Hegan, smartly dropped the ball before he showed it to the umpire, so that it was covered with dirt. Then Lemon threw another spitter and the umpire started laughing because he could tell Lemon was loading it up. There was nothing wrong with that, and, anyway, I couldn't hit him if he just hung the ball on a string. One day in Cleveland he threw me a fastball that didn't do anything. I hit a line drive off his shin. The ball flew to the dugout and he's lying on the mound in pain, screaming and cussing at me as I run to second laughing: "Finally, finally, I hit the ball!" He got up and started laughing, too.

GUS ZERNIAL (ATHLETICS):

The toughest pitcher I ever faced in the American League was Lemon. Without a doubt. A lot of players said that, even Ted Williams, I believe. If you had to face him, you'd know why.

A. SMITH:

The Indians had several leaders, not just Al Rosen. Feller, Wynn, Garcia, and Lemon were leaders, and other veterans like Dale Mitchell, Hank Majeski, and Jim Hegan were very popular and much admired. Hegan was one of the nicest ballplayers—a gentleman and a scholar. This was a close team. I spent time with my roommate, Larry Doby, and Dave Pope, a good-hitting outfielder from Alabama, who I also roomed with at times. I'd also go out with guys like Avila, who was from Mexico, Lemon, Wynn . . . sometimes Rosen would go with us. Cleveland was a fun city, with people who knew us, good restaurants, and a lively night life. Black and white players went out together. Wynn became my lifelong best friend. We'd eat out all the time. We'd go to fancy restaurants, or we might eat fried chicken, or barbecue, or Mexican food with Mike

Garcia, particularly at spring training in Tucson. Early liked jazz, so in Boston or New York we'd see saxophonist Flip Phillips, who was one of our favorites, and other musicians.

I learned quickly that black players were knocked down all the time. If a white player hit a homer, the white pitcher would wait until a black player came up before throwing a knockdown pitch. Doby, Pope, and myself—and Luke Easter, Harry Simpson, and Dave Hoskins when they were on the Indians in 1953—were often decked. So Wynn, who always spoke his mind, told the other pitchers that "we can't score runs with those guys on the ground." He protected Doby and me by knocking down opposing batters. No one wanted to fool with him. He got our other pitchers to protect our black players, too. This helped unify the team for the successful pennant run.

BALTIMORE ORIOLES

BOB TURLEY:

When the Browns moved to Baltimore, our new city greeted and treated us well. It was a very enthusiastic town that loved baseball. One night, when we'd drawn 40,000, I was pitching a no-hitter against the Indians with 2 outs in the ninth and a 1–0 lead. I had struck out 14. Al Rosen didn't hit the ball good, but it went between short and third for their first hit. On the next pitch, Larry Doby hit a real high fly ball that just went over the fence at the foul pole, only about 305 feet away. The people in Baltimore were more upset than I was.

The trouble is that we were still the St. Louis Browns although "Baltimore" was written on our uniforms. We moved ahead of the Athletics into seventh place, but our own record was the same: 54–100. As the season went on, the welcome wore off and the crowds dwindled. We weren't like the Braves, who were drawing over 2 million people in Milwaukee. Still, we drew over a million fans to Memorial Stadium, more than three times our attendance in St. Louis.

I liked playing for our new manager, Jimmy Dykes. He was a fun-loving guy, but a hell-raiser with umpires. I liked that he inserted me into the rotation and used me only as a starter. I had an excellent year, going 14–15

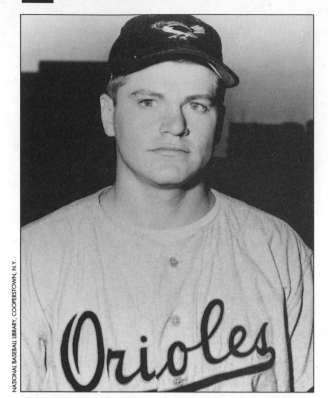

NATIONAL BASEBALL LIBRARY, COOPERSTOWN, N.Y.

"Bullet Bob" Turley won 14 games for the first-year Baltimore Orioles and became coveted by the New York Yankees, who would acquire him in the off-season in an eighteen-player trade.

for a bad ballclub, with a 3.46 ERA. I also led the league with 185 strikeouts, although my league-leading 181 walks probably got more attention. I was voted the team's most valuable player and was given a Cadillac. I got so many pats on the back that I felt like I was back in Aberdeen having a great year. The fans treated me really nice. So I loved my one year in Baltimore, during which time my wife and I lived in Lutherville. But the greatest day of my life was November 18, 1954, when Don Larsen, Billy Hunter, and I were traded to the New York Yankees for Gene Woodling, Willie Miranda, Harry Byrd, Gus Triandos, Jim McDonald, and Hal Smith, in the first part of what would be an 18-player deal.

LES MOSS:

When the Browns left St. Louis, the fans didn't seem too upset. They still had the Cardinals, a much better

team. We were excited because many more fans came to the park in Baltimore. Of course, we knew many fans were coming out just to see the visiting clubs and their star players. We didn't feel like celebrities.

The best thing I saw on these Orioles was three good young pitchers who would end up with the Yankees: Bob Turley, Don Larsen, and Ryne Duren.

Turley was all business. He went out to beat you and for the most part he did. He was a lot like Virgil Trucks, stuff-wise and in how he worked. He was a power pitcher who got the nickname "Bullet Bob." We worked well together because we thought in the same way. I'd call mostly fastballs. I don't think I ever caught him when he lost.

Larsen was a happy-go-lucky guy who loved the quintuples. Nothing could depress him. He wasn't depressed when he went 3–21 in 1954. He would have been the same if he lost 51 games. He shrugged it off when he 2-hit the Yankees but lost 2–0 when Bob Cerv

With the exception of Vern Stephens, who also was traded away and returned, Les Moss was the only member of the 1946 St. Louis Browns to play on the inaugural Baltimore Orioles team.

NATIONAL BASEBALL LIBRARY, COOPERSTOWN, N.Y.

homered off him. He had a great arm and had a good fastball and breaking ball.

Ryne Duren made only 1 appearance for us, but it was obvious he had a major league fastball. That was his bread-and-butter pitch. He was one of the toughest pitchers to catch. Usually a guy is wild high or wild low, but Duren was wild all over. If he ever went 9 innings, a catcher'd be worn out. He'd have benefited from some good major league instruction, but except for a team like the Yankees, no team in the majors had much good instruction.

Otherwise there was not much to be optimistic about. Vern Stephens, who had come back to the team in mid-1953 after years with Boston, led the Orioles with just 8 homers. Other than him, our two best average hitters were outfielder Cal Abrams and first baseman Eddie Waitkus. Cal was just a journeyman who'd do a good job for you, not someone who could make a major contribution. I knew Eddie a long time. I was a batting-practice catcher when he was at Tulsa, before he went to the Cubs. His career was winding down after 8 or 9 years with the Cubs and Phillies. He never talked about being shot, and I never asked him.

Jim Fridley was our left fielder. Big Jim was a big strong son of a gun, and when he made contact he hit the ball a long way.

JIM FRIDLEY:
After the Indians' organization had given up on me, I joined the Browns' organization in 1953 and played at San Antonio in the Texas League. Because I was supposed to have a bad arm, Ryne Duren, my teammate there, changed my nickname from ''Fearless'' to ''Former Fearless.'' I had a big year at San Antonio, batting .293 with 26 homers and 96 RBIs, and was brought up by Baltimore in 1954.

Bob Turley was our best player. He was a clean-cut guy who never drank a beer and was a perfect role model. He lost that no-hitter when Rosen kept fouling off pitches and Clint Courtney kept calling for fastballs. Finally Rosen singled. That was one of our most upsetting defeats, but we lost a lot in similar fashion.

Cal Abrams was a smart, friendly guy and a pretty good hitter. He'd been around for several years but had never realized his full potential. Courtney was a good hitter and fair catcher. He was known for wanting to

fight. Off the field, he didn't drink a lot, but when he did, he'd have trouble. As soon as Waitkus had one drink, he wanted to talk about being shot back in 1949. He'd always say, ''Poor old Eddie, poor old Eddie.'' He insisted he never knew the woman who shot him. He had a hole going in the front and coming out the back. You could put your arm in it. It was grotesque.

Don Larsen couldn't fall asleep and stayed up playing pinball machines. Casey Stengel would later say, ''Larsen would be unbeatable after midnight.''

Les Moss was a real nice guy. It was a real tragedy when his wife was killed in a car crash. Everyone really liked her. Les stayed out a while and then came back. He was as much of a leader as the Orioles had because he had been with the team many years.

I was back in the majors, but it wasn't fun playing part-time on a losing club. The fans were nice considering how bad we were, but many began to think we weren't trying. We tried but just couldn't do anything. Even a proven hitter like Vic Wertz struggled. His average was around .200 and he had trouble homering in Memorial Stadium, so the Orioles traded him to Cleveland, where he thrived. That trade was a sign of what was to come: we had such a bad team that 21 players would be traded. In December, I was included in the second part of an 18-player deal that landed me in the Yankees' organization, at Denver.

RYNE DUREN:
It wasn't until I got into professional baseball that I became aware of what poor control I had. I thought wildness was indicated by bases on balls and I hadn't walked that many guys back home in amateur ball. The umpires had bigger strike zones. Toss alcoholism into the mix, and mine was a pathetic struggle to learn how to pitch. The effects of alcohol on my central nervous system were devastating and kept me in the minors and an adolescent for a long time. A lot of my minor league managers saw my wildness and misbehaving and would get angry at me. They said, ''You dumb son of a bitch, with talent like yours, you should be in the big leagues winning 20 games a year.'' That made it even more frustrating.

Everybody had a gimmick to help me gain control. At Wausau, which was Class D ball and where I learned to chew tobacco, somebody got a green canvas target the size of the strike zone and put it in a big metal frame with real thick lacing around it. They gave me a whole bunch of balls to throw at it. After about 4 or 5 minutes I had all the lacing torn apart.

In the minors, they felt more secure putting me in to pinch-run than to pitch. At a Browns' spring training camp, I had been the fastest runner on the team.

The first time I saw a major league club I was on it, the St. Louis Browns. By the time I pitched in my first game, however, the Browns had become the Baltimore Orioles. I made only 1 appearance in 1954, giving up 2 runs on 3 hits and a walk, and striking out 2 in 2 innings. I had the misfortune of having had my knuckle broken by a pitch just before Baltimore called me up from San Antonio. I wouldn't pitch in the majors again until I was with Kansas City in 1957.

BILLY O'DELL:

I grew up on a farm in Whitmere, South Carolina, and attended Newberry High School, where I got a lot of attention pitching for the baseball team. In those days you were embarrassed to throw anyone a curve, so I threw only my fastball and pitched a lot of no-hitters and averaged about 23 strikeouts a game my senior year—I once fanned 28 in a ballgame because my catcher dropped one third strike. I was a top left-handed prospect, and scouts from all 16 teams approached me. I was tempted to sign, but because of the bonus rule I would have had to stay on a major league team for 2 years if I took $4,000. And I didn't think I was ready for the majors because I weighed only 136 pounds. So I went to Clemson on a baseball and basketball scholarship and majored in textile manufacturing. I left after my junior year—when I was 5′11″ and still a light 154 pounds— and signed with Baltimore in June of 1954. Counting both my bonus and salary for the rest of the season, I think I received about $18,000 or $19,000. I was a bonus baby and would go directly to the majors. I chose Baltimore because they didn't have a whole lot of pitching and I would likely not be relegated to the bench. I figured I would be able to tell in two years if I could be a major leaguer.

I joined the Orioles in Boston. It was exciting walking onto the field and there was Ted Williams taking batting practice. All of a sudden I realized I was in the same league as this guy and would have to get him out.

Harry Brecheen, the pitching coach, had me throwing a day or so after I got there. Williams was standing there talking to him. Harry asked how I threw my fastball and then suggested I try it while holding the seams a bit. I threw a couple and Williams said to Brecheen, "Hey, you leave the kid's fastball alone." I would learn a lot from Brecheen, but he never said another word to me about changing my grip. He had that much respect for Ted Williams.

Brecheen told me that I was going to be a good pitcher and be in the majors a long time. He said that I'd see a lot of people on the way up and should be nice to them because someday I'd see them on the way back down. That thought is what I always tried to live by. I'm proud of the fact that I never forgot who I was. I guess any major league ballplayer feels like a celebrity, but I tried not to let it bother me.

Jimmy Dykes was from the old school and believed you needed a lot of experience to be a big league player, so he didn't use me from June to sometime in August. Then we played Washington in a doubleheader and were behind in the eighth inning of one game. So I went to the mound for the first time in my major league career. The first batter was outfielder Jim Busby, who later became a friend of mine. My first pitch in the majors bounced about halfway between the mound and home plate. Clint Courtney got another ball from the umpire and walked out to the mound. He called everyone "Meat," and he said, "Meat, I've never seen anyone miss home plate that far in my life." He then turned and walked back toward the plate, but stopped halfway there and looked back and added, "But I tell you one thing, I haven't seen many throw it no harder." I walked Busby on 4 straight pitches. Then I got 2 balls on the next hitter and noticed there was activity in our bullpen. I stepped back and reminded myself I could throw strikes. The batter hit into a double play and I struck out the third guy. That is how my major league career began. That was my biggest thrill in baseball. The first time you play is a special moment.

Being in Baltimore with a new team was exciting. I liked the town from the beginning, and the fans really took a liking to me, which made it easier. Dykes wouldn't let me play, and it was tough sitting on the bench. But every time I'd do something, the fans would hoot and holler and give me a lot of encouragement.

They carried me through, because I seriously considered going home. I didn't talk to Dykes about not playing. I was young, and in those days you wouldn't go to a manager and tell him what you wanted to do. So every day I pitched batting practice and ran and kept quiet.

None of the Orioles resented me for being a bonus player. I was the youngest player on the team and the older players took me under their wings and looked after me. The Orioles were a loose team. Players would have a few beers, but there wasn't a lot of heavy drinking. We played hard and talked a lot about baseball. Maybe eight or ten of us went to dinner together on the road. It wasn't a cliquish team. Also, there was no one player who was a leader.

I roomed a great deal by myself that year because I came in late and everyone was paired up. But I did room some with Bob Turley, who was helpful. I was impressed by how hard he threw. I got to know a lot of the other players. Eddie Waitkus was a quiet, nice guy. I never heard him say anything about being shot. Billy Hunter was a lot of fun. He chewed tobacco all the time, talked a lot, and had a deep love of baseball. Vern Stephens wasn't as outgoing as Billy. He was an old-timer who liked to sit around and drink a beer or two and talk baseball. Cal Abrams was a quiet guy. He was almost comical but never tried to be. Les Moss didn't hit very much but he was a good catcher and heckuva guy. He knew a lot about baseball and liked to sit around talking about the game and about the last time we had played. Clint Courtney was a fiery type on and off the field. He and Billy Martin used to fight almost every time we'd play the Yankees. Yet he was a likable fellow. Don Larsen always gave a good effort and wouldn't quit. We didn't score any runs for him and he lost, but he took it all in stride. Jim Fridley was so big and strong that I thought a tank would have to run over him to hurt him. Then one day we were going to have dinner in New York and he stepped out of a taxi and broke his ankle.

BOSTON RED SOX

GEORGE KELL:

By now we were flying more, although we no longer had to travel to St. Louis, which had been the farthest point west. Jackie Jensen, whom we got from the Sena-

tors, didn't want to fly at all. He did fly, but he got deathly sick. Everybody understood. I'm sure he was embarrassed, but it became too much for him. So he'd take the train and always make it to the ballgame.

I think we had the best outfield in baseball with Jensen in right—he would have 25 homers and nearly 120 RBIs that year—Jimmy Piersall in center, and Ted Williams in left. Williams missed the beginning of the year because he broke his collarbone in spring training. But when he came back in May, he debuted by going 8 for 9, with 2 homers in a doubleheader. He would hit .345 for the season, with nearly 30 homers and 90 RBIs in less than 400 at-bats. We didn't get to play together very much during my stay in Boston, but as a veteran ballplayer I ran with him a bit. He was a loner but wanted someone with him if he had to go to a restaurant. So I ate with him a lot. I never saw him wear a tie. He did it his own way.

I always got along with Jimmy Piersall. He lived out where I lived in West Newton, and we'd ride with each other to the park each day. He'd fret and worry because he wasn't hitting. If he went 0 for 4, that's all he'd talk about the next day. He was just a kid, so I explained to him that there were 154 games in a season and that they had to be played one at a time. "You shouldn't worry about the whole season. You need to relax and maybe you'll get a hit tonight." We had a great rapport. Jimmy was an amazing fielder. Unfortunately, he hurt his arm that year in a throwing contest against Willie Mays prior to a Red Sox–Giants charity game in Boston.

I was traded to Chicago in May. But I played a short time with Harry Agganis. This was his rookie year. He replaced Dick Gernert as the Red Sox first baseman and much was expected of him. He was a hometown hero who had starred in baseball and football in high school and at Boston University, and was much adored in Boston. He was the "Golden Greek." Harry had the potential to be a very good ballplayer.

Outside of Detroit, I loved playing in Boston the best. I loved the city and the people, and I sure loved Fenway Park. But I was disappointed in my experience there. What was wrong with the team was what was always wrong with them: Tom Yawkey was too good. He wanted a winner so bad, but thought he had to pamper everybody and be every player's friend. He should have kicked some ass because the players never gave him his money's worth. New England also spoiled the Red Sox. Fans came from everywhere in New England to Fenway Park whether the team did good or bad.

Ted Williams wasn't one of the players who were spoiled and pampered. No, sir. He probably wouldn't say it, because the Red Sox were his whole life, but he also was disappointed that the team didn't win more. He wanted to win. Ted Williams deserved a championship.

WASHINGTON SENATORS

HARMON KILLEBREW:

I was born in 1936 in Payette, Idaho, a small rural town across the river from Oregon. I was planning to go to the University of Oregon on a football scholarship, but I also intended to play baseball because my childhood goal was to be a major leaguer. Some of the articles on me later would imply that I was "discovered" in "the sticks" by the Washington Senators, but it wasn't really like that. By that time I had spoken to scouts from every team but one.

I was recommended to Clark Griffith by Herman Welker, the senator from Idaho. He was a great baseball fan and had seen me play when he came home. I had some contact with him because my sister worked in his law office for a while. The team I wanted to sign with was Boston. For a couple of years, I had spoken to Earl Johnson, who was a former Red Sox player who was now their scout in the Northwest. He would play golf with me and take me out for dinner. He said that when I got an offer from another team I should call him to see if he could better it. However, when I got an offer from Washington, he said the Red Sox couldn't match it. I wish I could have seen myself in Fenway Park for my career.

I was still 17 when I signed with the Senators in June of 1954, right after graduation. I was given a $4,000 bonus and $6,000 salary for the next three years. So I was a bonus baby and had to stay with the parent team for two years. I wanted to go directly to the major leagues and figured it was to my benefit to start out with a bad team like Washington. I knew of that saying: "First in war, first in peace, and last in the American League." I thought I'd get an opportunity to play.

I joined the team on the road in Comiskey Park. I

didn't know what to expect in the majors. I had never even seen a major league stadium, and all of a sudden I'm playing in them with and against major league players I had read about. So everything was strange. Yet while I was shy and quiet, I wasn't wet behind the ears. I had worked from the time I was 12, and after my father died four years later, I had to pretty much take care of myself. I was able to adjust to the majors.

Bucky Harris was a nice guy. He had managed the Yankees to a pennant, yet now he was stuck with a bad team and still was patient and handled the situation pretty well. We finished sixth, which would be our best finish until 1960.

The Senators had a lot of veterans. The leaders were guys like first baseman Mickey Vernon, who first played with the Senators in 1939, third baseman Eddie Yost, and Pete Runnels. Pete was a shortstop when I got there, but later played second and first for us. He was an excellent hitter. We became good friends.

When I signed, I was eager to play immediately. I didn't take into account that Yost was a fixture at third, having been there ever since the mid-'40s. He played every game, scoring over 100 runs and walking way over 100 times, as he always did. I got into only 9 games and batted just 13 times. Because of Yost, I played only at second base, even though I wasn't a second baseman. Yost was helpful to me, although I wouldn't say he took me under his wing. I don't think he considered me much of a threat to his job.

Roy Sievers was our left fielder and an excellent hitter. He had just come over from the Browns after floundering for a few years. He had his first good season since he was a rookie in 1949, hitting about 25 homers and driving in over 100 RBIs for the first time. He replaced Vernon, who was aging, as the star of the team and would remain the star for several years. He was a very friendly guy and we became very good friends.

Sievers, Runnels, Yost, Jim Lemon, me, and some of the others talked baseball all the time, on the train trips and in hotel lobbies. There was a lot of cardplaying, but I didn't play cards or pool or anything like that. I went to a lot of movies. Players would go out together to eat. Word would get out about different spots and they would become our hangouts. In Washington there wasn't much around the ballpark, but a lot of us would go to a ribs place across town. In New York we went to

Eighteen-year-old bonus player Harmon Killebrew batted only 13 times and didn't homer in his rookie season, so few fans of the Washington Senators expected he was beginning a Hall of Fame career that would produce 573 homers.

Mama Leone's, which was a fine restaurant at the time. In Baltimore the players went to the Chesapeake, a great seafood restaurant. However, most players were steak-and-potato types.

My roommate on the road was Johnny Pesky. He had been a star infielder for the Red Sox in the '40s, but the Senators had just acquired him from the Tigers and he was playing his last season. He was a good guy. Johnny had a friend named Russ Tuckey who lived near the Capitol. Russ had been a professional basketball player and a road manager for the Ice Follies, but at the time he was a Pullman conductor. I lived with him for my first year, and he cooked for me and kind of looked after me. The next year I lived in a house with several other ball-players.

One of the guys I enjoyed playing with was Connie Marrero. He was a cute little Cuban pitcher who was about 5'6" or 5'7" and was always smoking Cuban ci-

gars. He was a wily right-hander in his late 30s who threw a lot of off-speed pitches. He had been with the Senators since 1950. This was his last good season. The Senators were known for signing Cuban players, and we also had rookies Camilo Pascual, who would become the ace of the staff, and outfielder Carlos Paula, the Senators' first black player. In 1955, we'd get shortstop Jose Valdivielso, first baseman Julio Becquer, and pitcher Pedro Ramos.

PEDRO RAMOS:

Morristown quit the Mountain States League, so I was sent to Kingsport, Tennessee, about 45 miles away. I went 15–4. I wasn't given any instructions in the minors, not even on how to hold a baseball. I did it the hard way. I just threw hard and threw strikes. I relied on guts; I wasn't afraid of anybody.

There were a lot of beautiful girls in Kingsport. My English was terrible, but they liked my crew cut and blue eyes. Joe Cambria, the scout who signed me, used to tease me: "You're too pretty to be in baseball." I didn't know if that was a compliment. I had a lot of girlfriends. I learned my English taking them to the movies. Sometimes they took me to the drive-in movies.

The whole league collapsed and I finished the season in Hagerstown, Maryland, which was B ball. I went home to Cuba and pitched batting practice to teams there. I was sent a contract for $350 a month, which was big money to me, to report to Charlotte in 1955.

DETROIT TIGERS

FRED HATFIELD:

I had one of my best years, batting a career-high .294 while filling in for Ray Boone at third and Frank Bolling at second. Of course, I'm sure most people didn't notice my hitting because we got good years from Boone, Harvey Kuenn, who led the league in hits, and our 19-year-old rookie outfielder Al Kaline, a bonus player. I thought of Kaline as "a little young Red Ass." He had fire and pride. He matured very quickly. He was a great athlete who held his own as a hitter, had good speed, played good defense, and had a tremendous arm. I think I was the only guy who pinch-hit for him. There was a right-handed pitcher in Fenway, and Freddie

Hutchinson sent me in for Kaline, and I hit a 2-run homer to tie it up. I would never forget that. And I would never let Kaline live it down. I said, "Don't get cocky, kid, or I might pinch-hit for you again." And he'd say, "Hatfield, you pinch-hit for me for the last time." And he was right.

That year, Steve Gromek and several other Tigers got upset when Cass Michaels of the White Sox got beaned by the Athletics' Marion Fricano. Michaels was their friend. Fricano was a mediocre pitcher who always got roughed up and then threw at somebody. We'd tell him that he couldn't throw hard enough to hurt anyone, but then he almost killed Michaels. Pitchers used to intentionally hit guys, but not in the head. They just threw it right behind their ribs.

The Pirates brought the protective helmet into baseball. I think Larry Doby brought it to the American League because he'd been hit on the head. He wore the protective flap on both ears and we all kidded him about it. Some of us used to kid guys in helmets by saying they looked ready to play football. If you played before the rule came in, you didn't have to wear one. I never wore one. I had to have something, so all the time I had this little plastic liner inside my baseball cap, on the sides of my head.

Baseball was a hard game, which is why players wound down after games by going out on the town, perhaps to a nightclub or good restaurant. Of course, we didn't get a whole lot of money for such things. The most meal money we ever got was $8 a day. I might get the Walgreen's "special," or a good steak for $3 or $5. Some of us might go to Gibby's, which was a steak place in Chicago, or to the Dutchman, a piano bar in New York. Every town had a good steak house. But if Cleveland had a night life, I never did find it. There was nothing there except a couple of active hotel bars.

As long as I can remember, there were "ballpark Annies." They'd meet the train or bus, especially if you had young bonus ballplayers, like at Detroit. Five to ten girls were there every time we came to New York or Boston. Everyone knew them because they were the same every time. The young girls were worse than anybody. I remember Hutchinson kicking a girl in the butt in New York, saying, "Don't you have a home to go to?" They'd call your room or sit in the lobby waiting

for you. You almost had to hide out from them. I don't remember a ballplayer ever marrying one. There were two kinds of players: those who liked to play and those who didn't. The opportunity was there. Most of them were smart enough to keep it under their hats. Sportswriters knew ballplayers were just human, and didn't get into their social lives.

When a guy's social life affected his playing, usually the manager or front office got to him and attempted to correct it. He was fined privately. From the time I came into the big leagues, if you were caught with a woman in your room, it was an automatic fine. You were in your room at midnight for a day game the next day. Anybody who thought he was fooling somebody was stupid because the club knew where you were nine nights out of ten. Clubs had private detectives follow some players. That year Phillies' owner Bob Carpenter had to apologize to Granny Hamner for hiring a detective. Managers would send coaches to check on rooms. I didn't think that was an invasion of privacy. They were paying me to play, and if they'd have thought my social life was affecting my play, then they had a right to check.

There were guys who dissipated too much. It probably affected their careers. The manager would have one-on-ones with ballplayers. In my last year in the minors, Pinky Higgins had told me that I had a bad reputation: "You drink and stay up late at night." I was a little wild, having been in the army. I closed a few bars and dance halls. Higgins told me to take care of myself: "If you're going to do it, don't get caught."

CHICAGO WHITE SOX

BILLY PIERCE:

The White Sox never sponsored any family parties or picnics. However, there was a man named Mr. Bruce who had a swimming facility in the Lockport area and usually once a summer we'd all go there for a picnic. Also we'd visit our pitching coach, Ray Berres, once each summer. Berres became the White Sox pitching coach in 1949, the same time I joined the Sox, and he stayed for Paul Richards and our later managers, and was very helpful to pitchers. He taught Harry Dorish his "slip pitch," which dropped off the table and made him hard to hit, and got me to slow down. Berres had a place in Twin Lakes, Wisconsin, and a bunch of us would go up there. And invariably we'd end up playing some kind of ball. We just loved to play. It wasn't just salary.

We thought of ourselves as an unusual team. I remember one player joining us and commenting that we were the first team he'd been on that had no stars. Several of us made All-Star teams, but when this fellow said this, I felt pretty good. We were a mixed group, but we all got along. Nobody was on a pedestal and no one was afraid to approach another player. We all goofed around with each other, kidded each other. My status didn't change as I became more successful. I was still one of the guys. It was the ideal situation. We all knew what we accomplished on the field: those things spoke for themselves. But they didn't interfere with our relationships. We were a team.

That's why when I slipped to 9 wins, I could still be happy that we won 94 games and that Virgil Trucks, Bob Keegan, Jack Harshman, and Sandy Consuegra had good years, winning between 14 and 19 games each. I was limited because I had an adhesion in my arm. I had to throw through the pain, harder and harder until it loosened enough for me to pitch. I'd do that for the rest of my career. Even if I'd won more, it's very unlikely we would have caught the Indians, who won 111 games, or even the Yankees, who won 103. But we were 25 games ahead of the fourth-place Red Sox. This was Richards's last year as our manager. Marty Marion took over in late September when Richards went to Baltimore as manager and GM.

CHICO CARRASQUEL:

Nineteen fifty-four was my best year. Nellie Fox and I led the league in double plays and I scored a career-high 106 runs. Richards wanted me to hit with more power, so he moved me closer to home plate. Until then I had hit a total of 9 homers in 4 seasons. Then I hit 12 homers and drove in a career-high 62 RBIs. I remember the game we beat the Athletics 29–6 in Kansas City. I got 7 RBIs, 3 on a bases-loaded triple that hit the top of the fence.

As a rookie in 1950, I didn't steal any bases, but in 1951, under Richards, I stole 14, double the number I stole in 1954, my next-best total. So then I asked Frank Lane for a raise. He said I should hit more home runs. After hitting those 12 homers in 1954, I went to Lane and reminded him of what he said. But now he said that I didn't steal enough bases!

MINNIE MINOSO:

It was very upsetting when Cass Michaels was beaned by Marion Fricano. Fricano was never a great pitcher, but he got advice—maybe from Jimmy Dykes when he had managed the Athletics—to throw at batters to frighten them. He nearly killed Michaels. He ran him out of the game, taking away his livelihood. I hope God punishes Marion Fricano slowly so he remembers how he hurt Michaels and his family.

GEORGE KELL:

When I came to Chicago in May for Grady Hatton, I saw we had a good ballclub. For one thing, Billy Pierce, my old teammate on Detroit in 1948, was the ace of the staff and was one of the best pitchers in the league. He still got a lot of strikeouts, but he had also harnessed his control. And he was still smart.

But I thought Chicago was one of those clubs that had only one chance to win the pennant, and that if we didn't do it then, we'd go downhill. We had several fairly young key players, like Pierce, Fox, Lollar, Rivera, and Minoso—who had more than 50 RBIs, more than any other Sox—but there weren't many other guys who I thought would be around after a year or two.

Paul Richards and I were already friends because we'd played together at Detroit in 1946. He was an innovator, a manager who had used 5 first basemen in a game Pierce pitched the year before. His reputation for being better with young players than veterans was correct. He once told me, "I wouldn't be a good manager of the Yankees because guys like Mantle and Berra wouldn't listen to me." But I think Richards would have done fine with the Yankees. He was an excellent manager, a disciplinarian whose idol was Douglas MacArthur. I teased him that he probably stood in front of the mirror each morning and said, "I'm Paul Richards and I'm tough."

I played less than 100 games total for Boston and Chicago, and had one of my least-productive years. My average was just in the .270s, after 8 straight .300 seasons. I knew it was just an off year at the plate rather than an indication that I was finished, because my play at third base was still at a high level.

This may have been the best infield I was part of, with Chico Carrasquel at short, Nellie Fox at second, and Ferris Fain at first. They were all outstanding fielders and they could all hit. Fox and Fain both hit over .300. Fain supposedly drank a great deal, but I didn't run with him, so I couldn't be sure. He was a loner. On the field he was high-tempered and extremely competitive. I sometimes spelled him against left-handers. That was the first time I played a lot of first base.

I really enjoyed playing with Nellie Fox. I remembered when he was a teenager and came to spring training at Philadelphia. He was a 5'8" first baseman and it was like throwing to a toy bulldog. Nobody had any idea back then that he was going to be a good ballplayer. Playing with him every day, I got to see just how good he was. Often when you watch a player on another team you think you'd like to play with him, but when you do play on the same team he turns out to be selfish or covers up his deficiencies. Richards said to "beware of those players who act like they don't care. We all care." I discovered that Nellie Fox did care. He wanted to win and knew how to win. He was a great ballplayer. He's the one guy from this era who deserved to make the Hall of Fame but would be overlooked.

AL KOZAR:

I still hoped for one more shot at the majors. I knew my playing days were almost over because I was getting very bad ankles and heel spurs. I could hardly run. I had invested in a tavern and property back in McKees Rocks, Pennsylvania, even before I married, so I was already thinking of going back there. I got a contract from Memphis again, for $850 a month. The other guys were making several times less. So my wife, Merilyn, and I shot down to Memphis, where we had met a couple of years ago at a party—she had been an American Airlines stewardess. Don Gutteridge was the manager and I think he had orders from the top to stick it to me good. He was a loudmouth and told me to sit. I was given an old raggedy uniform. He got furious with me for helping a couple of infielders who asked my advice on how to play second and ordered me not to talk to them. Even my friends on the team wouldn't have a beer

with me because all the players were told to stay away from me. They sent me to Tulsa. I played a couple of games and was so out of shape that the GM there questioned my willingness to play. I told him I wanted to get out of the White Sox organization. I was through at 32. (Seven years later, in 1961, when I was working at Pratt-Whitney doing aircraft work, I would get a letter from the White Sox saying I was officially released and should go get a job on my own!)

NEW YORK YANKEES

GENE WOODLING:

After 5 consecutive pennants and world championships, we finished in second place. People asked if we let up or got depressed. How could we? We won 103 games that year, which was more than in any of our title years. We veterans played hard, and youngsters like first baseman Bill Skowron, third baseman Andy Carey, and pitcher Bob Grim, who won 20 games, gave it everything. Grim was the Rookie of the Year and our top winner. We just fell short because the Indians had such a tremendous season.

This would be my last season with the Yankees. This meant that my arguments with Casey Stengel over platooning would finally be over. I appreciated Casey much more after I left. When I would be getting just one hit a week the next year in Baltimore, he'd tell the writers, "He ain't mad enough to play." There were a lot of field managers as good as Casey, but Casey was better than other managers at understanding his players' attitudes. He figured out how to stir us up so that we were so angry—and I wanted to kill him sometimes—that we'd go out and beat the other team's fanny. He could handle 25 temperamental guys. This was an important part of managing. I couldn't argue with success. I know he made me into a better ballplayer.

Stengel was a leader. All that fun stuff was for the press and fans, but he was a tough man to play for. You didn't horse around with him. He was all business. Which isn't to say he wasn't compassionate. You could go to him with problems. If your children were sick, for instance, he'd send you home immediately. He and Edna didn't have children and he was very sentimental about kids. One spring training we all had our families at the beach and the writers were accusing Casey of running a country club. He let them do it for a week before calling them together and saying, "I thought you guys were smart. You say I'm running a country club because I let them bring their families to Florida. But for some reason I never have to worry about my ballplayers at night. I know where they are. The best protection in the world is their wives and kids." He was shrewd.

I wasn't the type to get sentimental over a town or uniform. Anyway, I knew I'd be seeing my Yankee teammates 22 games a year. (Soon after I got traded to Baltimore, I came up to play in New York. Yogi was catching, Eddie Rommel was the umpire, and I was the batter. I'm trying to concentrate when I hear, "Hey, Gene, did you know Carmen's pregnant?" Rommel busted up. Yogi was serious, not trying to distract me—that was Yogi. I remembered what it was like playing with him and the others every day.)

JOHNNY SAIN:
I wanted to retire and become a Chevrolet dealer. I bought a dealership. But I stayed with the Yankees another year at Casey's request. I made a career-high 45 appearances, all in relief. On most teams in those days, going to the bullpen was the same as being put out to pasture, but it wasn't that way with Casey. Being a relief pitcher was an important role on the Yankees. Reynolds had even relieved on occasion before I came to the Yankees. Unofficially, I saved 22 games, to become the only pitcher to have led one league in victories one year and another league in saves in another year. At one point, the Yankees won 15 straight games in which I pitched.

I liked sitting out in the bullpen for a full game, getting some sun and chatting with the fans around us. I got to know faces and voices. Yankee fans were great. I also got to know them coming and going from the ballpark over the years. I lived in the Concourse Plaza for two years, near Yankee Stadium. I also lived across the George Washington Bridge in New Jersey, in Englewood. I'd ride the bus across 175th Street and then take a couple of subways to the stadium. I met many fans along the way. This was really my last year in New York, although I'd pitch 3 games early in 1955 before Enos Slaughter and I were traded to Kansas City. I think the Yankees would still pay my salary when I played for the A's.

WORLD SERIES

1954

INDIANS VS GIANTS

AL SMITH · INDIANS:
We didn't take the Giants for granted. We had played them in spring training in Tucson, so we knew they had a strong team. They had a good-hitting lineup with Willie Mays, Don Mueller, Hank Thompson, Alvin Dark, Davey Williams, Whitey Lockman, Monte Irvin. And they had a good left-handed hitter on the bench: Dusty Rhodes. But we thought our pitching was better than theirs. Our scouts told us that if we could get by Sal Maglie and Johnny Antonelli, we would be all right. They assumed Ruben Gomez and Don Liddle wouldn't give us trouble, but they were just as tough.

Willie Mays's catch off Vic Wertz with 2 men on in the eighth inning and the score tied was certainly a key play in Game One. If Wertz had pulled the ball 30 to 40 feet, instead of hitting it to deep center, Mays never would have caught it. Personally, I thought Mays had time to run the ball down and turn around to catch it, but Willie liked making dramatic catches like that and caught it while running the other way. We weren't that frustrated by that catch because it didn't end the inning. But we didn't score, and the Giants won the game, 5–2, when Rhodes hit a 3-run pinch homer against Bob Lemon in the tenth inning.

I led off Game Two with a first-pitch homer off Johnny Antonelli. It had never been done before. That was a thrill. But we didn't score again. Rhodes tied the game with a pinch single in the fifth and homered in the seventh, and we lost, 3–1.

Even after losing the first 2 games, we felt we had a shot at winning. But we went back to Cleveland, and Gomez and Liddle beat Garcia and Lemon, 6–2 and 7–4. In Game Three, Rhodes had a 2-run single pinch-hitting for Monte Irvin early in the game to put the Giants up 3–0. So he came through every time in the Series. We knew about Rhodes from our scouts, how he pinch-hit and played the outfield sparingly. We knew he had power, but the homers he hit off us in the Polo Grounds weren't hit that far. They just went down the line and just made it in—we called them Chinese home runs.

Rhodes didn't beat us alone. We beat ourselves. We scored only 9 runs in the 4 games. We couldn't get any hits. Who would have figured that Rosen and Doby wouldn't drive in any runs and that Avila and Doby would hit well below .200? We didn't think the Giants had a better team, but that our loss was just one of those things. We were upset but we thought we had such a good team that we'd come back and win it next year.

JOHNNY ANTONELLI · GIANTS:
It wasn't such a surprise that we won the World Series, only that we won in 4 straight games. In the spring, the Indians were in Tucson and the Giants were in Phoenix and we played many times. We even barnstormed together through Arizona, Texas, and the Southern states, playing every day. We didn't have any problems with them. We matched up well against the Indians, so we were confident.

Willie Mays's catch against Vic Wertz came in the World Series, so it was played up as one of the greatest catches of all time. But we had seen him make more spectacular catches all year long. If you knew Willie Mays and saw him start pounding his glove, you knew he'd catch it. Our team knew he'd catch Wertz's fly long before the average fan did. He was pounding his glove as he was running back. It was a helluva play, yet it was just a typical Willie Mays play. His throw back to the infield as he fell down, preventing them from scoring, was just as good.

I started in the second game against Early Wynn. I was 24 and both excited and nervous. I'd had a bad September, so I didn't know how I'd do. I didn't know why I didn't quit after my first pitch, which Al Smith hit out of the park, but at least after that, I felt I was in a ball game and had to go to work. I was in trouble that whole game and was lucky. I gave up 8 hits and walked 7 more. They left about 15 men on base. I struck out around 9, and it seemed like their shortstop, George Strickland, kept coming up with the bases loaded and would pop up or ground into a double play. So I was lucky. Durocher came to the mound one time, but Westrum and I said I was pitching okay and he left me in. That year I didn't get taken out too often. So I held them scoreless the rest of the game and we scored 2 runs in the fifth inning, 1 on a pinch single by Rhodes, and the other when I hit into a force-out. Then, in the seventh, Rhodes homered. And we won 3–1.

Don Liddle did well in the Series. He was the pitcher when Vic Wertz hit that long fly to Mays in the first game. Then he started and won the fourth and final game. He went into the seventh inning, and then Wilhelm and I finished up for him. We combined on a 6-hitter and won 7–4. I had better stuff that game than the one I started. I struck out 3 of the 5 batters I faced and got the others to hit foul pop-ups. Dale Mitchell ended the game with a pop-up that went no more than 20 feet in the air. I got to finish the World Series and was thrilled to do that.

We played in Cleveland, so had to fly back to New York. There were a lot of people who greeted us at the airport, and then there was a ticker-tape parade of the type only New York could do. We were honored at City Hall by the mayor. This was the New York Giants' first World Championship since 1933, so you can imagine how proud we were and how excited our fans were.

NATIONAL LEAGUE
1955

"I HAD ACCEPTED A $12,500 SALARY FOR 1954 FROM BRANCH RICKEY INSTEAD OF THE $15,000 I HAD ASKED FOR AND DESERVED ONLY BECAUSE HE PROMISED TO TAKE CARE OF ME IF I HAD A GOOD YEAR. I HAD A GOOD YEAR IN '54 AND WHAT DO YOU THINK HE OFFERED ME FOR 1955? $15,000!"

FRANK THOMAS

MILWAUKEE BRAVES

BOB BUHL:
After my terrible 1954 season, I was well rested and came back strong to pitch over 200 innings and have a better ERA than Spahn or Burdette. It was a strange year because we scored a lot more runs and moved up from third to second place, yet had a worse record. Spahn was an automatic to win 20 games, but he won only 17, and Burdette tied me for second best on the staff with 13 wins. It was hard to get wins. I'm not sure why. Henry Aaron had a solid second year, batting .300—as I had told Quinn he would—hitting over 25 homers, and driving in over 100 runs. And Mathews had another 40-homer season. And Crandall had a big homer year. I think we missed Joe Adcock, who was out most of the year after being hit on the wrist by the Giants' Jim Hearn.

We were fortunate to have George Crowe to pick up for Adcock. He was a very quiet, easygoing, intelligent man who had gone to college. He was a big left-handed first baseman who had a lot of power and did a good job for us. However, I didn't think he was an everyday ballplayer because his body couldn't take the wear. He was best coming off the bench or pinch-hitting—he was already one of the best at that and would get even better in later years. He had played in the Negro Leagues and in professional basketball, so he was already over 32 or 33, despite not having had much major league experience. But he looked older than that. He moved even slower than Joe.

I think it was either in 1954 or in '55 that the Braves started flying. The Braves chartered a plane from one of the airlines. We'd fly a turbojet, and when it took off, it sounded like a sewing machine. We knew we had to do it, but it was scary.

ST. LOUIS CARDINALS

DICK SCHOFIELD:
Because I had spent two years with the parent club after receiving bonus money, the Cards were allowed to demote me in 1955. They sent me to Omaha. While I was gone, Eddie Stanky was fired as the manager and was

replaced by Harry Walker. (I wouldn't play for Walker when he was the Cards' manager, so it wouldn't be until I played for him on the Pirates in the 1960s that I discovered why everyone hated him.) Under Stanky and Walker, the Cards finished seventh. They had a good defensive team—especially with the additions of Bill Virdon, the Rookie of the Year, in center and Ken Boyer at third—but while most of the players had decent offensive seasons, only Musial had an outstanding year, hitting about .320 with over 30 homers and 100 RBIs—he also won the All-Star Game with a 12th-inning homer. I think the lineup lost a lot when Joe Cunningham missed the entire season after being injured. The pitching was probably the biggest disappointment. Luis Arroyo, a little rookie southpaw from Puerto Rico with a good screwball, won 11 games, and Harvey Haddix won 12 games, but no one else won in double figures. Vic Raschi was released, and after Brooks Lawrence had a terrible sophomore season, he was traded to Cincinnati.

CHICAGO CUBS

RANDY JACKSON:
I had another good year. Although I was out for a month or so with a hand operation, I hit a career-high 21 homers and drove in 70 runs. I made the All-Star team for the second straight year. It was a thrill that Ernie Banks also was an All-Star. He hit 44 homers to break the record for shortstops and hit a record 5 grand slams. We played side by side all year. I'm sure Banks was making about what I was making, although players didn't know what each other made. The owners brought up other players' salaries, but it's doubtful they were truthful. Anyway, a salary shouldn't be based on what others were making but on what you did the year before.

On the Cubs, no one in management ever expressed appreciation for my contributions. They may have congratulated me when I made the All-Star team, but there was never much emotion expressed up there. I didn't expect anything. Baseball was my first occupation, and as far as I knew, that was the way it was in every job between employers and employees. The employers may speak to you, but they don't come in and say, "Boy, you're great."

Apparently, the Cubs didn't think I was great because in December they traded me to the Dodgers along with Don Elston for third baseman Don Hoak, outfielder Walt Moryn, and pitcher Russ Meyer. Hoak would play only one year for the Cubs and Elston would pitch just 1 game for the Dodgers before returning to the Cubs. The deal was a complete surprise, but I was ecstatic to be going to the Dodgers. If I'd had the chance, I would have thanked the Cubs' management. In fact, I didn't even know what happened until a newspaperman called me. He played the guessing game with me. He said, "You've just been traded, guess where?" I named everybody but the Dodgers. When he told me it was the Dodgers, I said, "You have got to be teasing me!"

FRANK BAUMHOLTZ:
The greatest ballplayers played in my era. Every ballclub had outstanding players—name after name after name. What made this era special was the introduction of great black players. The first wave brought Jackie Robinson, Larry Doby, Roy Campanella, Don Newcombe, Luke Easter, Sam Jethroe, and a few others, and the second wave, in the '50s, brought such players as Willie Mays, Hank Aaron, Junior Gilliam, Vic Power, Roberto Clemente, and Ernie Banks. And the only one with a mean streak was Jackie Robinson. He just wanted to beat everyone so badly.

Banks looked like a future Hall of Famer. By 1955 he was an All-Star shortstop. He was a great ballplayer, a wrist hitter. He also was a super guy. He was shy, but Hank Sauer and I would talk to him every day after the game. We told him not to change his personality. And he never did.

Hank and I had lockers right next to each other. Banks and Sam Jones were nearby. We used to sit and eat what was left of the crackers and salami that Stan Hack would leave in his office, and we'd have an extra beer or two and talk. Most of the guys would dress right away and get out of there.

Sad Sam Jones was a nice, fun-loving guy who, despite his nickname, always had a smile on his face. He always had a toothpick in his mouth, so they also called him "Toothpick." He had a wicked curveball that sent many a batter into the dirt.

Ernie and Gene Baker, another guy I liked very much, were part of the Cubs' changing of the guard. I still hit almost .290, but my playing time was down considerably. By the next year, Hank and I—who had come together to the Cubs back in 1949—and Randy Jackson would be on three other teams. I would be sold to the Phillies in December. It was sad leaving fans who really liked me. I was never booed in Chicago.

HANK SAUER:

I wish I'd kept the letters and contracts the general managers sent me stating I wasn't getting a raise because of this or that. In my years in Chicago, I never felt that I was paid adequately for my contributions. My biggest salary raise came after my MVP season in 1952. My highest salary was $37,500. The only time I was really unhappy, however, was after the '54 season, when I hit a career-high 41 homers, batted .288, and drove in 103 runs, and they sent me a contract with a $1,500 cut in salary. I said, "Are you sure you're sending this to the

So popular with the fans that he was dubbed "The Mayor of Wrigley Field," former National League MVP and homer champion Hank Sauer completed his sterling career with the Chicago Cubs.

right guy? I had a pretty good year." They said, "You had a pretty good year, but we still ended up in seventh place. We could have ended up in seventh without you." But they wouldn't have gotten that many fans without me! I had to wait them out just to get my same salary back.

The Cubs moved up from seventh to sixth place in 1955, and won over 70 games. A lot of that had to do with the emergence of Ernie Banks. We also got good pitching from Bob Rush and Sad Sam Jones. Sam was a big right-hander who had played briefly for the Indians in the early '50s, when they were signing a lot of black players. He lost 20 games but won 14 and led the league in strikeouts. In May he was pitching a no-hitter against the Pirates in the ninth inning. We were ahead 4–0. Then Sam walked the first guy, second guy, and third guy, bringing the tying run to the plate. Stan Hack wanted to take Jones out. I said, "Stan, he's pitching a no-hitter. You can't take him out. They'll run you out of town!" So Hack left him in, and Jones struck out the next 3 batters. That was something. He was the first black to pitch a no-hitter.

I was injured much of the season and finished with very poor statistics. The Cubs felt that age was creeping up on me. Wid Matthews told me, "Hank, we want you to stay in the organization. We want you to play and manage the Los Angeles Angels in the Pacific Coast League and eventually end up managing here." I asked what the alternative was. He said, "St. Louis wants you." I said, "You know, Mr. Matthews, I don't think that I can trust you. I'll go to St. Louis." Those were my exact words. I was disappointed that I had to leave Chicago. I think everybody who ever played in front of Cubs fans—with the exception of Roy Smalley—felt they were wanted. It was a great feeling. The loyalty went both ways. The best part of my career—my most fun and my best days—was with the Cubs.

JIM BROSNAN:

I went back to the minors for one more year and pitched for the Los Angeles Angels. I refined my slider and progressed as a pitcher. Bubba Church, who was now on the Angels with me, said, "There's only one starting pitcher on this team who's going to make it to the big leagues." He said that when I had a .500 record at midseason. I didn't lose another game all year.

BROOKLYN DODGERS

DON NEWCOMBE:

I won my first 10 decisions, and was 14–1 at the All-Star break and 18–1 in early August before losing 1–0 to Sam Jones of the Cubs. I finished at 20–5, although a soreness in my back and arm kept me from pitching much in September or in the World Series. I threw a 1-hitter, in which I faced the minimum 27 batters, and two 2-hitters, and had the best percentage in the league. Only Robin Roberts won more games than me, and he pitched over 300 innings.

Roy Campanella also had a comeback season, winning his third MVP award. He hit over 30 homers and drove in over 100 runs, second only to Duke Snider on the Dodgers, and he led our team in hitting. Actually, I led the team with a .359 batting average, but I was up less than 120 times. I tied a league record for a pitcher with 7 homers and might have tied the major league record of 9 if I could have played more at the end of the season. Alston would use me as a pinch hitter.

Sandy Koufax was a 19-year-old left-handed pitcher from Brooklyn. He couldn't be sent to the minors because of the bonus rule, so he sat on the bench and couldn't pitch because he couldn't get the ball over the plate. He had a helluva time because he was a Jew. Many times players on the Dodgers made comments about "this Jew was sitting on the bench not helping us a fucking bit and we have to be shipped to the minors to make room for him." They said the same thing about us blacks a few years before. Sandy would never forget how Jackie, Roy, and Don took care of him. We related to what he was going through. (When Sandy became "the great Sandy Koufax," some of those same players tried to become Sandy's friends, but he wouldn't let that happen. He never forgot.)

Back in 1945, when I was with the Newark Eagles, my manager, Willie Wells, told me not to pick up a baseball for the first 10 days of training camp. All he wanted me to do was run. He said, "You're big, and your legs will carry you." I won 14 games that year, so what he said stuck with me. I became known for my running. I ran to keep my legs strong—I didn't get tired in the seventh inning, but got stronger. Alston used to compliment me on my strength in the later innings in St. Louis and Cincinnati in the heat. In close games, he'd let me stay in, because I wasn't tired and was a good hitter. We won many games because I knew I had to run.

I was a hard worker. I didn't have control of my fastball or an outstanding curveball until I worked hard. I probably made it because of my work ethic. I'm sure Dodgers like Duke Snider will verify that I was the hardest worker on the team. It was the hard work that again made me one of the toughest pitchers in baseball.

ED ROEBUCK:

Walter Alston had been my manager at Montreal, so he saw what I could do in relief. Alston replaced Chuck Dressen as the Dodgers' manager in 1954, and the next year he wanted me. So finally I was brought up to the Dodgers.

I was in the minors for several years without getting an increase in salary. I thought after doing well in Montreal that I'd finally get one. So when I reached the majors, I asked for a salary increase before I signed a contract. Buzzy Bavasi told me, "If you're still with the team in a month, I'll give you the raise you want." In the first part of the season I was unconscious. So at the All-Star break I went back to Bavasi. But he wouldn't give me the increase. He now told me that they couldn't tear up signed contracts and issue new ones in mid-season because they'd done that with Clyde King in 1952 and he was terrible the second half of the year. So I didn't get the money.

It was so exciting coming to New York in the mid-'50s and playing in Ebbets Field, the Polo Grounds, and Yankee Stadium. There were rivalries between the 3 teams and everyone argued who was better—the Dodgers, Giants, or Yankees? And who was the best center fielder—Snider, Mays, or Mantle? And who was the best shortstop—Reese, Dark, or Rizzuto? And who was the best catcher—Campanella or Berra, the two MVPs in 1955?

I lived in Bay Ridge in Brooklyn. Several of the players lived there and we formed a car pool and drove each other to the ballpark. The players and wives would also have bridge parties. That typified the Dodgers, who were a very unified, closely knit team. Pee Wee Reese was the guy everyone looked up to. He was the leader. But there were other leaders, like Gil Hodges. Hodges

After several excellent years as a starter in the high minors, Ed Roebuck was finally brought up by the Dodgers and made an immediate impact as a reliever.

was quiet and well liked. Of course, guys also looked up to Jackie Robinson and Roy Campanella.

Of all things in my career, I'm most proud of being on that 1955 championship team. We won 98 games, which was 13 games better than the second-place Braves. We started out 22–2! We had five future Hall of Famers—Robinson, Reese, Snider, Campanella, and Koufax—and many other great players, like Hodges, Don Newcombe, Carl Furillo, Clem Labine, Carl Erskine, and Johnny Podres. Jackie, who was splitting time at third with Don Hoak, and Pee Wee, who was still doing a great job playing every day, were probably the only guys past their prime. We were in first place from the first day of the season and led the league in runs, homers, batting average, stolen bases, saves, earned run average, almost everything. We had over 200 homers, and Snider, who had 42, and Campanella, Hodges, and Furillo all had over 25. Snider led the league in RBIs—and, I think, in runs for the third

straight year—and he, Campanella, and Furillo batted over .300. Roy was the league's Most Valuable Player. Newcombe went 20–5, and if there had been a Cy Young award then, he might not have had to wait until 1956 to get one. It was hard to beat us. I can't believe I was a member of that team. And I led it in saves as a rookie.

What made me so effective was my sinkerball. Oddly, I first learned how to throw strikes and then learned how not to throw them. I learned to finesse the plate so that my pitches were in the area where it was hard for batters to tell if they were strikes or balls. I wanted my pitches to look too good to let pass, so the batters would swing.

Walter Alston was pretty quiet, but he was all right as a manager. He didn't have to dream up any special strategy because he was used to having great talent. Having managed me already, he knew what I could do. Podres and Koufax were our only left-handers, so Alston didn't have a southpaw in the bullpen. He used Labine and me, two right-handers, and brought in whoever was hot at the time. Walt used me in certain key situations, especially at the start of the season. I think Clem was one of the best relievers ever—he won 13 games in 1955, a few as a starter—and, looking back, I don't know how I could have ever been sent into a ball game over him. Alston brought me in because I'd always been able to get the ball over the plate at Montreal. I got into a hot streak and he kept using me. Then I got cold in the middle of the year and he barely used me after that, going almost strictly with Labine as we pulled away in the pennant race. Clem led the league with 60 appearances. I was in 47 games, all in relief.

Newcombe was the ace of the staff and Erskine was right behind him. Billy Loes was flaky, but he was smart, cagey, canny. He was different, yet he was accepted as part of the team. He fit right in. We brought up rookies Roger Craig and Don Bessent and they beat the Reds in a doubleheader and went on to have excellent seasons, relieving and spot starting. Johnny Podres was our left-handed starter and was becoming a pitcher we could count on in tough games.

Sandy Koufax had great stuff and pitched shutouts in his first 2 major league victories, but Alston was afraid to put him into games. Typically, he couldn't hit the backstop. I roomed with him down in spring training, and he was really despondent because he had this wealth of talent but wasn't allowed to pitch. They couldn't send him to the minors to learn how to pitch because he was a bonus baby, having received about $20,000 while at the University of Cincinnati.

Karl Spooner was a cocky kid left-hander who came out of Double A, where he'd been striking out 14 or 15 batters a game. He had come to the big leagues at the end of 1954 and did the same thing, pitching 2 consecutive shutouts and striking out 27 batters. He had long arms and batters had difficulty timing his pitches. He was tough. But he hurt his arm and struggled to an 8–6 season in 1955. I think he would have been very close to what Sandy Koufax became if he didn't get hurt. Instead, he never pitched again in the majors.

STAN WILLIAMS:

I went to Class B, Newport News, Virginia, in the Piedmont League. I was somewhat timid, but I was averaging 14.6 strikeouts at the All-Star break, so my confidence went up. I went 18–7 and at one point pitched 45 consecutive scoreless innings. I led the league in 8 or 9 departments and broke Johnny Vander Meer's league strikeout record with 301 in 242 innings. I also tied his single-game record of 20. The catcher didn't need a signal because all I had was a fastball. It had good movement. I didn't try to throw inside; I just threw in the direction of the plate, hard. I would throw three-quarters. Usually, you keep your fingers behind the ball to drive it, but I was actually releasing the ball at times with my fingers on the side, and the ball jumped sideways at times.

NEW YORK GIANTS

JOHNNY ANTONELLI:

My wife and I spent our second year in New York living in the Fort Washington area of the city, around 183rd Street, in a place called the Hudson View Gardens. Sal Maglie, Jim Hearn, and I each sublet apartments overlooking the Hudson River and George Washington Bridge. It didn't take long to get to the Polo Grounds, which was located on East 159th, between Coogan's Bluff and the Harlem River.

The Giants dropped to third place, 18 games behind the Dodgers. Durocher felt that some of our players were getting up there in age and wanted to use them as trade bait to build for the future. But Horace Stoneham was loyal to the players who won the title in 1954 and was reluctant to make deals. It was only when we were out of contention in August that he or his GM, Chub Feeney, sold Maglie to the Indians. That left a rotation of me and Hearn—we both went 14–16—and Ruben Gomez, with other starts being given to Don Liddle and Ray Monzant, a rookie right-hander from Venezuela.

Our offensive star was, of course, Willie Mays. He drove in about 125 runs and slugged 51 homers. He was sensational.

JOHNNY KLIPPSTEIN (REDS):

Willie Mays was the best all-around player I ever saw. By this time, a lot of players felt that way about him. He could do it all. You could get him to chase more bad pitches than Hank Aaron would, but if you threw the ball in the strike zone, he was going to hit it. He was particularly tough with men on base and the game on the line. He'd wait for his pitch even if it took 2 or 3 pitches to get it.

BOB BUHL (BRAVES):

When Willie Mays came to bat, I'd tell him, "I'm going to get you this time." I said I'd throw at his knee and he pleaded, "Don't do that," and I'd say "I owe you one." I never did knock him down because I thought he was a better hitter after you did that.

J. ANTONELLI:

In addition to Mays, Don Mueller hit over .300 and drove in over 80 runs, Alvin Dark had a decent season—and fought with Jackie Robinson for running over Sheldon Jones on a play at first—and Dusty Rhodes had another good year coming off the bench. But most of the remaining veterans struggled, and it became clear that Durocher was right about the need to add youth to the team. There would be almost an entirely new starting lineup in 1956, but Durocher wouldn't manage it because he resigned at the end of the season. New York baseball lost a great deal with his departure.

HAL WOODESHICK:

I had spent two years in the service and pitched for the company team at Fort Bragg. I was now 23 and big—6′3″ and 200 pounds. The Giants assigned me to their Class B team in Danville in the Carolina League. I was the top pitcher in the league. Afterward I should have been moved up to Triple A because of my army time. But the Giants put me on a Double A roster—San Antonio—and I got drafted by Charleston, Detroit's Triple A team.

PHILADELPHIA PHILLIES

ANDY SEMINICK:

I played only a few games for the Reds before they sent me back to the Phillies. Jim Greengrass came with me, and Smoky Burgess went to the Reds, and there were a few other guys involved. I was very happy returning to the Phillies. I had been with them 9 years before my 3 years with the Reds.

Mayo Smith was now the manager. We had played together in the minors. He was a very nice man. There were some different players on the Phillies, but a number of my old teammates were still there and still playing well. Robin Roberts was still the best pitcher in the National League, in my opinion—he twice outdueled Don Newcombe, his chief rival over the years. Roberts set a record for home runs allowed but that didn't mean anything because he led the league with 23 victories and led in innings pitched and most other categories. In May, he gave up a leadoff homer to Grady Hatton of the Reds and then retired the next 27 batters. Ashburn led the league in batting; Ennis was still hitting homers and driving in runs and getting viciously booed by the Phillies' fans; and Willie Jones, Granny Hamner, and Curt Simmons were still part of the Phillies' nucleus. The player who had emerged during my absence was catcher Stan Lopata. He played briefly with the Phillies in 1948, but didn't get significant playing time until 1949. He was learning back then, working with the coaches. While I was in Cincinnati, he came up with a peculiar batting stance, with the deep, twisted crouch, and he had success with it. Stan and I alternated behind the plate and were a productive combo. He hit 22 hom-

ers in about 300 at-bats, and we combined for 33 homers and over 90 RBIs.

One of the new pitchers I got to catch was Saul Rogovin, a big veteran right-hander who came over from the American League for the first time. He was a good guy and funny. He was knowledgeable about pitching and decided that it was best to just throw the ball down the middle and let it go where it wanted to go. So much for pitching philosophy. Saul or somebody else once told me that when he was pitching in the winter leagues, the owner got so mad at him for walking some batters in the first inning that he had some policemen arrest him on the mound and walk him to jail.

There wasn't as much togetherness among the players as there had been, but we still had a pretty good team. We were in first place for much of the season before ending up 77–77.

DEL ENNIS:

When Mayo Smith became the manager, the Phillies initiated a new rule in spring training in Florida that prohibited wives from staying with us in the hotel. The players didn't like that. Nor did we like Smith having someone planted in the elevator who'd have you autograph a baseball when you came in at night, so he'd know who missed curfew. We had to climb nine flights of stairs to miss that. Smith was a bad manager—the worst. He lacked confidence, never stuck up for the team, and didn't do anything positive on the field.

I didn't like playing for Smith, but I had another good season. I batted close to .300 and had 29 homers and 120 RBIs, which was behind only Duke Snider and Willie Mays. I was the starting left fielder in the All-Star Game and got my 1000th run batted in for the Phillies. But, of course, the fans continued to boo me. That's why my wife rarely came to the ballpark. When my son was ten, I took him to a game for the first time. I homered my first 3 times up, driving in all 7 runs in a 7–2 win. But I popped up my fourth time up and they almost booed me out of the ballpark.

Philadelphia was tough on a lot of players, but I received harsher treatment from fans than anyone else. I'd get things thrown at me and I'd be booed just for walking on the field. The other Phillies would tease me about how lucky they were not to be getting the abuse. I hit over 20 homers 8 times and drove in over 100 runs 6 times with the Phillies, yet they booed me. That's because I was from Philadelphia. I'd homer and 20,000 fans would boo and 20,000 would give me an ovation. Northern Philadelphians would cheer. Southern Philadelphians would boo. I think that was a lot of it. It wasn't everybody. I think they booed to stimulate me. I wouldn't let the boos bother me—I just played as hard as I could. When I first went out to the outfield for a Saturday afternoon game, people would try to hit me with sandwiches in wrappers. I would annoy them by taking off the wrappers and eating the sandwiches, telling them, ''Thanks.'' On Sundays a booster club would give cars away, and one time in 1955, when a big, fat guy was heckling me, I planned to visit him after the game when he was waiting to see if he won the car. So I ran up into the stands and threatened him. He wouldn't get out of his seat. From that time on, nobody really bothered me. It helped that I used to have my tough friends from the old neighborhood sit out in the left-field bleachers. The hecklers wouldn't get on me too much with those guys sitting there.

The boo birds weren't the only nuisance. The Philadelphia reporters were the meanest in the country. They spurred the fans against me. The fans would pick up on what they wrote. The writers had their own section on the train, but they mingled with us. Once we were riding on the train toward St. Louis. I was in the same berth with Frank Yeutter, a *Philadelphia Bulletin* writer, and he was drinking beer. He had opened several bottles on the ledge behind the commode. He told me to sit down to chat and I felt something running down my back. It was blood. He had broken off the neck of a bottle and it was stuck in the ledge, and it stabbed me. I needed stitches. That night we played the Cardinals and I couldn't lift my shoulder. We ended up losing on my weak throw to the plate. My wife sent me the *Bulletin* and I read Yeutter's summary of the game. He criticized me for having a weak throwing arm, not mentioning he was the one responsible for it being that way.

Finally, one night in Chicago, I lined all the writers up against the wall and said, ''I'll knock your heads off one at a time if you write one more thing about me.'' I wouldn't take any lip from them. After that, they didn't write anything bad.

There was a German sportswriter named Stan Baumgartner who had pitched for both Philadelphia teams in the 1920s. He was with the *Inquirer* my entire career and he never wrote a good story about me. If I hit a homer and made an error in a game, he'd write only about the error. I didn't know what he had against me. The funny part is that when he was dying in the fall of 1955, he called me up at home and asked me to come to the hospital. When I got to his bedside, he told me, ''Del, if I ever had a son, I would have wanted him to be just like you.'' I just looked at him.

ED BOUCHEE:
After my freshman year at Washington State, I got married on May 17, and I signed a contract the following week with the independent Spokane Indians so I could play in Class A ball instead of lower. They put a clause in there stating that if I was sold to a higher league or to a major league team I'd get 25 percent of what Spokane got for me. It turned out to be a pretty good deal.

It was nice that I got to live at home. On the road I roomed with my longtime friend Jack Spring. We spent a lot of time playing pinochle. The team traveled in three Cadillac limousines with extended jump seats. We had 18 players, plus the manager and the trainer. Three of the older players drove. After my one year in Spokane, during which I batted .319, I got drafted into the army in March of 1953. The guy who gave me the physical was a baseball fan from Spokane, and he put down that I had flat feet. So they put me in the Signal Corps and I was stationed at San Luis Obispo, California. They used to come get me off the rifle range to play baseball.

After two years in the army, I was planning to go back to Spokane but was delighted when the Phillies bought me for $6,000, of which I received $1,500. I was discharged from the service on March 2, and was expected to be at the Phillies' minor league camp at Bennettsville, South Carolina, on March 15. So I drove my wife and baby to Spokane and then drove to Bennettsville with two other former Spokane Indians for spring training. In those days, you were given one-way airfare, so if you drove, you could save some money. I had a two-door 1952 Studebaker Land Cruiser and the three of us drove in four-hour shifts without stopping for 3,200 miles.

My initial reaction to my first camp wasn't good. They were mad at me because in my last year in the service I was a cook and went up to 245 pounds. Don Osborn, my manager at Spokane and now the manager of Schenectady, decided to cure me or kill me. After practice was over, I had to do extra work with him. He'd throw balls 20 feet to either side of me and I'd have to run pick them up. I lost 20 pounds the first week.

Don wanted me at Schenectady in the Eastern League, which was Class A ball. I had an excellent year: I hit .313 and I had 22 home runs, 40 doubles, and 109 RBIs. I didn't know if the Phillies had any plan for me to rise to the majors—the only person I talked to from the organization was the roving hitting coach Eddie Miller, the old shortstop, and he didn't give me much instruction.

PITTSBURGH PIRATES

FRANK THOMAS:

I had accepted a $12,500 salary for 1954 from Branch Rickey instead of the $15,000 I had asked for and deserved only because he promised to take care of me if I had a good year. I had a good '54 season and what do you think he offered me for 1955? $15,000! Rickey used to compare me negatively to Ralph Kiner. I said, "If you're going to compare me, give me the same opportunity. Put back Greenberg Gardens for me and I'll hit you 50 homers because I can tattoo that scoreboard."

I wouldn't sign Rickey's contract. He warned me, "Go ahead and hold out. I'll keep you out of baseball for five years." That's what the attitude of almost all the general managers was. I held out for 17 days, keeping in good shape by working out in Pitt Stadium. Rickey always used to say he'd never divulge anyone's salary in negotiations. Branch Jr., or "the Twig"—his son—and I were the only ones who knew what I was offered and what I wanted. But I turned on the television and a reporter said emphatically, "If Frank Thomas doesn't get a $25,000 contract, he won't sign." It said the same thing in the morning paper. I called the Twig the next day and told him, "Your dad is a liar." I wouldn't negotiate with the Twig, and he told me his father didn't want to talk to me. So I walked into Rickey's office. He brushed all the papers on his desk onto the floor and ranted and raved about how I was doing my negotia-

tions in the *Sun-Telegraph* through reporter Chili Doyle, who was getting information from my father. I told him I had nothing to do with what was in the paper and then I walked out. I was working in my cousin's hardware store when Branch Jr. called me. I told my cousin to get on the other line and listen to the conversation. I got him up to $18,000. I said, "I've got a family to feed and this is hurting me. But if you want an unsatisfied ballplayer, I'll sign for that."

At spring training I walked into the hotel and Branch Rickey walked right past me, ignoring me. I got out to the ballpark. Ryne Duren was pitching. I hit a homer my first time up. The next time up, I beat out a bunt down third. Fred Haney then took me out of the lineup because it was obvious I was in shape. I went through spring training and then all of a sudden I caught the flu and got dysentery. I lost 17 pounds in 3 weeks. I threw up in the clubhouse in front of Haney. He told me to stay in bed a few days and see the doctor and then join the team in New York. Dr. Joseph Finegold was the Pirates' doctor. I told him what was wrong and he said, "There's nothing wrong with you that a few base hits won't cure." I stood up and said, "Am I a human being?" I wouldn't let him treat me. I went home to my family doctor. He wrote Haney exactly what I had. As Fred suggested, I stayed in bed a few days and then joined the team in New York. I had to hold on to the railing when I walked up the steps of the Commodore Hotel. I stayed in a room by myself so no one could catch what I had. The next morning I went to church and then to the ballpark. I told Fred, "I'd play for you if I had a broken leg." He said, "I don't want you to play until you tell me you're ready." The next night we were in Milwaukee. We had men on second and third in the ninth inning and they brought Spahn in. Haney sent me in to pinch-hit, knowing I'd be walked, and then I played the outfield in the ninth. The next day I saw that I was in the lineup, although I was still weak and hadn't told Haney I was ready. I didn't say anything. Next we went to St. Louis. After an extra-inning game, we went to Chicago and didn't get in until about 1 or 2 A.M. At 7 A.M. the phone rings and it's Branch Rickey. He calls me to his room. He says that the writers were saying I was having a bad year because of him. I reminded him about what I said about being an unsatisfied player. He let me know that he wasn't going to be back as general manager in 1956—I was one of the first to know—and then said, "I'll tell you what I'm going to do. I'll tell whoever takes my place not to cut your salary." I said, "If I have a bad year, I'll take the consequences. I don't want any favors from you whatsoever. You know how I feel about you."

I had my one bad year for the Pirates. I hit 25 homers, but my RBIs were down and I hit below .250.

DICK GROAT:

I came back from the service and went to spring training with the Pirates. I never smoked or drank all through high school, college, or the service, but I go to my first spring training and all my peers and all my idols and all the guys I've been looking up to are smoking at lunch and so forth, and that is exactly when I started smoking. Would you believe it? A bad habit I never would be able to shake. A larger percentage of ballplayers smoked in those days. Quite a few guys chewed tobacco. I probably put a chew in my mouth six or seven times a year. That would only be during practice, never in a game, because I was afraid I would swallow it.

Fred Haney had taken over as manager in 1953 and was about to have his third straight last-place finish. Fred was a fun guy, a players' manager, but he was just so frustrated because we were so bad. I once did some stupid running and he said, "You have to be a god-damned college hot dog to run bases like that. That was just a dumb, dumb, dumb thing." Of course, you make those kinds of mistakes when you are a kid in baseball. Haney knew that, but he was just discouraged.

I enjoyed being back in the majors with my teammates. It was good to play again with Bob Friend. He had vastly improved and his luck was changing, too: he led our team with 14 wins and led the entire league in earned run average. I was also back with Roy Face, and got to know outfielder Jerry Lynch, who had come out of the Yankees' system, and Gene Freese, a good-hitting third baseman. Gene and I roomed together. You never knew what he was going to do because he was a nutty guy. (He ended up owning a bar down in New Orleans.)

Bobby Clemente was a rookie in 1955. He had the greatest God-given talent I ever saw in baseball. There wasn't anything he couldn't do. He was a great hitter and exciting player. If he wanted to lead the league in stolen bases, he could have done that. He was a marvelous base runner and had great instincts. He also had a great, great arm. And he had a great body, strong at the top and with a thin waist. When he first came up, after being drafted from the Dodgers, he had trouble adjusting. That's because in Fort Myers, the black and Latin players had to stay in hotels in a completely different area from the rest of us. When we got to Pittsburgh, Bobby still had a language problem. Nobody could speak Spanish. So he was very quiet. I liked him so much. In all the years I would play with Bobby, we never had bad words.

Next to my father, no one influenced my life more than Mr. Branch Rickey. I had tremendous respect for him. He knew my mind. He knew what to say and when to say it to me. I was slumping in 1955, and was getting frustrated, worrying they might think I needed some minor league seasoning. So he called me into his office. He said, "Maybe you should go back to Triple A because you don't have any confidence. Let's face it: you're a young man that's never had any success. You were only the best college basketball player in America, you played on two championship teams at Duke University, you never played in the minor leagues, you led the Pirates in hitting in your rookie year. I can understand why you don't have confidence." I walked out of there thinking about what he said and went on to finish very strongly that season. I never did have to go to the minors.

I played in 151 games and batted .267, with 28 doubles and 51 RBIs. I made too many errors, but I led the league in putouts and chances per game, which meant I was getting to more balls than the other shortstops. So altogether I was satisfied with my comeback.

We were in Philadelphia when the Pistons' coach, Charley Eckman, came by with an NBA contract for more money than I was getting in baseball, even after Mr. Rickey had given me a nice raise. My basketball skills hadn't diminished, because I had played 60 to 70 games a year in the service. I promised I would sign, but only after speaking to Mr. Rickey. He said Mr. Rickey had already consented but I wanted to ask him personally. I saw Mr. Rickey the following Monday. I felt in my heart that he would give me his blessing to play both sports, but he had no sense of humor about it. I always felt that at 24 I could have played both sports well. I used Gene Conley as an example, but Mr. Rickey said, "Conley pitches every fourth day and is just a backup basketball player. You'll play 150 games for us and you would be a starting guard with the Pistons. It's too much." He couldn't force me to quit, but I wasn't going to fight him. So I gave up basketball. I confess that one reason I chose baseball over basketball was that my father didn't like basketball. He loved baseball. He threw out his arm pitching when I was just a boy, and he dreamed of having a son be a major league baseball player. He never missed a game when I was with the Pirates. When Rickey retired in December, I made no attempt to go back to basketball. Joe Brown, who replaced him as GM, wouldn't have had a better sense of humor about it.

BEN WADE:

In January the Cardinals traded me to Pittsburgh for pitcher Paul LaPalme. I didn't mind because Fred Haney was the manager and I knew him from the Hollywood Stars. He was a good manager and likable guy. It was just unfortunate that he was stuck with a last-place club.

However, the Pirates were improving. They had a few good players who were developing, and this was Roberto Clemente's rookie season. I'd played against him in the winter in Puerto Rico. He was a kid but he was already a great player. This was an ideal club for him to break in with because even if he played badly he couldn't hurt anything. There would have been more pressure on him if he had broken in with the Dodgers, who had originally signed him. Although he might have had some added difficulty now because there weren't many blacks breaking in with the Pirates. However, he didn't have any race problems with fans or other teams, because Jackie Robinson had settled all that.

I think Clemente and Dick Groat were the emerging leaders of the Pirates. A lot of people didn't think of Groat as fiery, but he was. Vern Law was another player everyone admired. We all knew he was a Mormon and very religious, but that didn't interfere with his relationships. He was a great guy and got along with everybody. What a competitor he was: he pitched 18 innings to beat the Braves.

I was on the Pirates until July, which was when my major league career ended. I hadn't pitched very much and had lost my only decision, but I thought I did fairly well and my earned run average was around 3.20. I didn't think baseball in the period I played was a difficult occupation. It was something I wanted to do, felt I could do, and loved to do. The pressure was there: you wanted to make the club and not go back to the minors. But there was no more pressure playing baseball than having a regular job and having to work hard enough to keep it.

ELROY FACE:

I returned to the Pirates with my newly learned forkball and did pretty well. My record of 5–7 was about what I had in my rookie season, but my strikeouts were up and my ERA dropped by exactly 3 runs a game. I found that the guys who gave me the most trouble were Richie Ashburn and the others who guarded the plate and

Having added the forkball to his arsenal during a year in the minors, ElRoy Face would become the relief ace of the Pittsburgh Pirates for the next dozen years.

punched the ball. I didn't have trouble with big hitters.

The roster had changed a lot since 1953. We now had Dick Groat at short, Roberto Clemente in right, Dale Long at first, Gene Freese at third, and Jerry Lynch in the outfield, and pitchers Vern Law and Ron Kline had been recalled from the minors. We even had veteran pitcher Max Surkont. I had played with a bunch of the younger players in New Orleans.

We were a last-place team, but everybody got along. During rain delays we played cards. After the game we'd get six to eight guys and go out to a restaurant and have dinner. A lot of times we'd sit in the clubhouse for an hour or two after a game talking about the game. No one was in a big hurry to get out of there.

Fred Haney was in his last year as manager of the Pirates. I enjoyed him. Nobody had any problems with him. He was a prankster. Rookie Lino Donoso, a slim Cuban left-hander, was always in a hurry to get dressed after a game. One day he put his feet in his street shoes and couldn't move. Haney had driven spikes through them. Then Fred gave Lino money to buy himself a new pair and maybe a little extra. After leaving us, Fred would have great success with the Milwaukee Braves.

During the off-season many guys stayed in touch, particularly those who lived in the Pittsburgh area. Groat, Thomas, Ronnie Kline, Bobby Del Greco, an outfielder who would be on the club in the spring, and I played charity basketball games around the city. As you would expect, Groat scored almost all of our points. He was a scoring machine.

CINCINNATI REDS

ART FOWLER:

I lost 4 in a row and I was sitting by my locker, very worried, since this was only my second year. Tebbetts walked up and said, "Are you okay, Art?" "I guess so, Birdie, but I just built me a house, and I'm in debt for a lot of money." He told me, "You're going to pitch every 4 days even if you lose 40 games in a row." That picked me up and I wound up 11–10. Only Nuxhall, who won 17 games, had more victories. I liked to give Birdie complete games. When he would come out to the mound and ask if I was tired, naturally I was going to

say no. I never asked out of the game. But he said, "If you get us to the seventh inning, I'm not going to let you lose this game. I have a guy in the bullpen who's paid to either save or lose the game." He was talking about Hershell Freeman. We all knew Hershell could do the job.

I liked to beat everybody. Pittsburgh couldn't beat me, and I pitched good against the Giants. The Giants had a great team, but the '55 Dodgers were the best team I ever saw. They won their first 10 games and nobody could beat them until they were so far in front that it didn't matter anymore. It was tough pitching against the Dodgers because they had so many great players. Jackie Robinson was the best black player I ever saw. I first saw him in Montreal in 1946, when he couldn't stay in hotels, couldn't go into restaurants to eat, and they'd throw at him. What he went through made him play the way he did. I pitched him close, but I didn't try to hit him. Robinson had slowed down by 1955, and I think Snider and Reese were the keys to the team. The fans were crazy and it was hard to pitch to good hitters in a small park, but I liked being in Ebbets Field.

Birdie Tebbetts was friendly to the players but didn't hang around with us. He was off with his coaches or alone. He never drank until he started managing. We were in Pittsburgh one night and Joe Nuxhall, Gus Bell, Wally Post, and I were in a bar drinking. It was getting to be closing time. We had been due back at the hotel at 1:30. Gus, Nuxhall, and Wally suddenly ran out the back door. I didn't run; I just sat there drinking. Someone came up behind me and said, "Gentleman, I'll buy you a beer." It was Tebbetts. The next day he says he caught 4 players drinking past curfew. He fined Nuxhall, Bell, and Post $100 apiece. He said, "But I ain't gonna fine that motherfucker drunk who was with them because he didn't run." I respected Birdie. Most of the other players felt the same. We thought he did a good job—we finished in fifth place again, but felt we were just a couple of pitchers and players away from contending.

I roomed some with Smoky Burgess after he came over from the Phillies. They put me with him because they figured I wouldn't get into trouble drinking too much. He didn't smoke or drink, and when I drank beer, he'd get on me for it. He drank milk shakes. I loved the guy, but he wouldn't go into a bar, so I ran around with Nuxhall, Post, and Bell. They wouldn't pass up a bar. Roy McMillan would have a couple of beers and go home. He was a good person and might have been the best shortstop I ever saw.

Johnny Temple and Ted Kluszewski ran around together. I liked Temple. He didn't hit any more homers than McMillan, but we had Klu, Post, and Bell for that, and Temple hit .280 to .300 and played good, hard second base. He wanted to win and wasn't adverse to getting into a fight. Klu wasn't as much of a leader. He never said nothing—he just played. The big guy could hit: in 1954 Kluszewski had hit 49 homers and he hit 47 in 1955, and drove in runs almost every game. I liked to hang around him because my salary was just $6,000 and $9,000 in my first two years and he was making $40,000 or $50,000, so I knew he'd buy me two or three beers. That would make my day. Everybody loved Klu. I had a lot of fun with him. I'd be agitating him and he'd grab me by the head and lead me around the clubhouse. I couldn't get loose from him because he was as strong as Hercules. He wouldn't fight because he was afraid he'd hurt someone. His wife was an itty-bitty girl.

Everybody on the team liked me, I think. I also got along with the players I played against. If I got beat and ran into guys from the other team in a bar, I'd buy them drinks. Baseball is for professionals; you can't get mad at your opponents. I even loved the sportswriters. If I did bad, they wrote that, but if there were 30,000 people in the stands, everyone knew I was bad anyway. They had to make a living, too.

JOHNNY KLIPPSTEIN:

I came to Cincinnati knowing that the Reds and the city had good reputations among ballplayers. I was joining a contending team with a great bunch of guys, and Cincinnati was a good place for a ballplayer with a family. Almost everybody had small children and a mortgage. The wives were friendly with one another and there were a lot of family-oriented picnics and parties. Players also often visited the Children's Hospital in Cincinnati, though by and large, charity work by players would become much more prevalent in future decades.

The Reds were a fairly loose team and we had a great time. We had some good beer drinkers. There were a few guys who would outdo Art Fowler. And I didn't

Johnny Klippstein was happy to move from the Cubs to the Reds, a team with much stronger offensive support.

even think Wally Post was such a big drinker. He was a lot of fun and enjoyed life, but a lot of the guys drank more than he did. Now, Ray Jablonski, who just came over from the Cardinals, was a damn good beer drinker. He was in the Steve Bilko category. Ray was a great guy, one of the best. He was known as a good hitter, but had the bad tag of being a "no-field" third baseman. But he was an adequate defensive player.

Fowler was a piece of work. He was a funny guy away from the ballpark, especially when sitting around drinking beers, but when he was pitching he was very serious. You wouldn't think it was the same guy. Art gave 100 percent. He wasn't a big guy and didn't have overpowering stuff, but he could pitch to spots and had a great slider that moved quickly and was hard to pick up. Batters didn't understand how he got them out. But he was tough.

Joe Nuxhall was a fun guy. Once, on a train, I bet him that he couldn't drink 5 bottles of beer in 20 minutes. Somebody had told me that nobody could drink so much from bottles because of all the air. Joe was playing cards and set the beers down and started drinking. He finished all 5 beers in about 10 minutes. I wanted to kill the guy who told me about the air in the bottles.

Smoky Burgess didn't drink at all. He was a quiet guy and frugal—he'd eat only in inexpensive places. He was one of the best hitters I ever saw, especially off the bench. He was just a great pinch hitter. He didn't need batting practice to hit line drives. He had exceptional hand-eye coordination. His friend Hershell Freeman didn't drink either. He was another very nice, quiet, religious, family-oriented person. He and Smoky could have been brothers.

Those two didn't drink, so it wasn't as easy to sit around and talk to them as it was with guys like Lynch, Bell, Post, Fowler, Nuxhall, Jablonski, or my roommate Don Gross. When we were on the road, I started going to the racetrack every off-day, often with Gross. I figured it was better than sitting around drinking beer. I didn't worry about bar fights. Ballplayers would get into fights only if they went into rough places. If they went into nice places, they usually didn't have any problems.

Birdie Tebbetts was a fun guy to play for. He demanded only that you go out and give 100 percent. He handled pitchers fairly well. In 1955 we didn't have a lot of good starters or good set-up men for Freeman, so Tebbetts used me in both roles. It worked out, because I had a much better year than my 4–11 season with the Cubs in '54. I went 9–10, with a 3.39 ERA, which was my career best at that point. I got 14 starts, and of my 3 complete games, 2 were shutouts.

HERSHELL FREEMAN:
The Red Sox sold me to Cincinnati in May. Birdie Tebbetts was instrumental in getting me because when I had pitched for Louisville, I had success against Indianapolis, which he managed. My first day with the Reds, he told me, ''You're going to pitch. You're my short man. Here's the baseball—go get 'em.'' So I immediately felt that I was accepted as part of the ballclub. Birdie knew baseball and how to handle players as individuals. He would give players their plus points and minus points individually, but then said, ''We win and lose as a team.'' He used to say, ''At times each of you will have

to pick up the morning paper and see where you lost. I don't like to read where we lost and you won't either. But if you're going to lose, lose with pride and caring.'' Birdie's door was always open and he'd play golf with us on off-days, but he didn't really socialize with us. However, if we had a party or cookout, he was invited and most times showed up. Then he'd leave early because he felt the players would relax more if he wasn't there.

I didn't really appreciate being a major leaguer until I played for Cincinnati. This was the happiest time for me. Once your ballclub accepts you, you learn to relax. The Reds were a great bunch of guys and the club was like a big family. On an off-day, it was common to see six or eight couples with their kids at some park, having barbecues or whatever. The wives all sat together in a reserved section at the park. They'd come to the game and talk, and on the way home my wife would have to ask me what happened on the field.

On the Reds, the players were very involved in the community. When we had spare moments, most of us loved going to the children's hospital, to the burn wards, to the cripple area. All the players had fan clubs and devoted time to them. The various clubs would have outings and there would be me, Smoky, Wally, Nuxhall, and our families; Ted and Eleanor Kluszewski didn't have kids, but they'd always be at the party. When you had a party, barbecue, or picnic, you invited the whole ballclub. The Reds were more of a group than individuals. If we made guest appearances, rookies and established players got the same money and attention.

I felt very close to Smoky, Roy, Ted, and a lot of other players. We were quite a cross section, but when you walked in and out of that clubhouse, you were a Cincinnati Red. We defended each other that way. We had a lot of pride.

Being a Red and a major league ballplayer never made me feel like a celebrity. I felt I was special to play in the big leagues, but I never wanted to feel I was better than Joe Blow who was out digging ditches. I wanted to be a good ballplayer and make a living playing ball. Notoriety comes to you if you play in the big leagues, particularly if you have a good year or two. I accepted that, but that was as far as it went.

For a couple of years, some sportswriters and management people had been calling the team the ''Redlegs'' because ''Reds'' had other implications in this era. But the players didn't care—we said Reds as much as Redlegs.

After I got over to the Reds, I was doing only relief pitching. Tebbetts had me in there 50 times and I responded well to the frequent work. I went 7–4 and saved 10 or 11 more games, and had my best earned run average, 2.12. Sportswriters would say to me that I never looked bothered coming into tight situations. I'd reply, ''If it bothered me, it would drive me crazy.'' Well, it did bother me, but it was one of those things I controlled and didn't let other people see. Somewhere on that walk from the bullpen to the mound I felt a nervous twinge, but I'd take a deep breath and swallow and go after 'em. I tried to keep a light approach. I remember Birdie coming out once and reminding me that the bases were loaded and no one was out. I said, ''Heck, I thought those guys were extra infielders.'' That let Birdie know I knew what the situation was and that I was relaxed.

I had a regular pattern. When I got to the park, the pitchers would go out and hit and bunt. We'd have our home run derby—I could hit the ball a long way. Then the nonstarters would come out and we'd shag for them. Then the regulars and maybe the starting pitcher would come in, and a coach would throw batting practice while the rest of us would shag. Then, with about 15 minutes left before the game, we'd do wind sprints. Then I'd go into the clubhouse and change sweatshirts. If it was cool weather, I'd have the trainer put baby oil or liniment, usually a mixture, on my shoulder and back. Then I'd put on a sweatshirt and jacket and go out and get ready for the game. I was fortunate that I knew

I'd be in the game only under certain circumstances. I'd sit in the bullpen, maybe with my shoes untied. I didn't worry about the game until about the sixth inning. Then I'd tie my shoes, make sure where my glove was. In the seventh or eighth, I'd wait for Birdie to give the sign. If I knew I was going into the ballgame, I'd get up and throw 10 or 15 lob pitches at half speed. Then I'd throw harder. If Birdie made a circular motion, I had to get ready quicker. I could throw 15 to 20 pitches and be ready to go. That was my routine from the time I was in Birmingham.

Pro baseball players eventually train themselves to hear only who they want to hear in the stands and to blank out everyone else. You can't afford to let every catcall in the world bother you. In the Polo Grounds, there were a couple of people who started riding me as soon as I walked on the field. I'd tip my hat to them and that usually shut 'em up.

My mother would come to a game, and if I got into trouble, no matter what level of baseball I was pitching in, she would leave the stands and go to the concession stand and wait there until I got out of trouble. Then she would return to her seat. After the game, she would give me holy hell for scaring her to death. The truth was that she had a heart condition. My pitching didn't affect it, but she would get so darn nervous. When I was playing at Cincinnati, my parents could pick up the games on radio. If I came in to relieve, my dad would turn the volume down and tell her what was going on. If I got into trouble, he'd lie to her a little bit. I didn't worry about this while I was pitching. My mother knew I was doing what made me happy and she was happy for me.

AMERICAN LEAGUE 1955

"I HAD A BAD BACK AND COULDN'T PLAY EVERY DAY FOR THE ONLY TIME IN MY CAREER. I DIDN'T LIKE THAT FEELING AT ALL AND ABOUT TWO-THIRDS OF THE WAY THROUGH THE SEASON I MADE UP MY MIND NOT TO PLAY ANYMORE. I WAS ONLY 32, BUT I WASN'T A HOMER CHAMPION ANYMORE. ONCE YOU'VE BEEN THERE AND CAN'T TURN IT UP AGAIN, IT'S NOT ANY FUN."

— RALPH KINER

KANSAS CITY ATHLETICS

JOE DE MAESTRI:

I thought it was great that the Athletics moved to Kansas City. The fans who watched us in Municipal Stadium were polite, win or lose. They couldn't have been nicer. They were knowledgeable about baseball because for years they had supported the Yankees' minor league team, the Kansas City Blues. They were so excited to get a major league team, and we had a lot of pride being that team. We had a loose, happy, optimistic club, and I really enjoyed the 1955 season—I even went 6 for 6 one game.

Lou Boudreau was the new Athletics manager, replacing Eddie Joost. When he had played, he'd led the league's shortstops in fielding 8 or 9 times, and he helped me more than anybody. He worked with me on the double play. He got me to shorten up on hitters and used a stopwatch to see how fast I could get the ball out of my glove to first base from second base. I practiced what I learned until it really made a difference. I was able to compete in the majors because I learned how to play the hitters. I think that was the secret for me, because I didn't have great speed like Luis Aparicio. Those guys covered so much ground it was incredible.

We had a pretty good infield. Vic Power played first, and I played between Jim Finigan and Hector Lopez, a rookie from Panama. Hector played some second but mostly he played third, while Jimmy, 1954's third baseman, switched to second. Lopez and I always talked about how many games each of us played. We each played about 125 games that year. He batted .290, with 15 homers, and had about 70 RBIs, so he was a great addition to the team.

I got along great with Finigan, who was a super, fun-loving, cheerful guy. He had a terrific rookie year at Philadelphia, hitting .302. But the Athletics' management didn't think he could maintain his record because of the way he swung. So they tried to change his style and absolutely destroyed him. He wasn't the same ballplayer in 1955. His average plummeted. His move to second base from third wasn't a good decision either.

Vic Power was a terrific hitter. He could handle that bat. And he could certainly handle a first baseman's glove. But he was a very tough first baseman to play with because he timed everything. When you went in that hole and came up throwing, you had to hope you could find the empty base to throw at because Vic wasn't there yet and we didn't have a target. But it never cost us anything. I can honestly say that Vic always got the throw. He played deep, often way over toward second, yet he could still get to that bag. If you had a bad throw, you could rely on Vic catching it. Other first basemen couldn't make the play. He had great hands and was the best at digging balls out of the dirt. There is no question that he saved errors for me. A lot of guys claimed Vic was the best they ever saw. There were a lot of good first basemen, but Vic was unique.

For Bobby Shantz, 1955 was a comeback year. He didn't have a good win-loss record, but he pitched pretty well. He was too quiet to be a leader, but everyone thought the world of him. We looked up to him just because of the way he went out and did his job.

Joe Astroth, our catcher, was more of a leader—but maybe he was more of a clubhouse lawyer than a leader. Actually, what he was, was a talker. Whether voicing an opinion or working with a player, he would talk, talk, talk.

I think a lot of the guys looked up to me at this point. I was the player rep for five years. I would have to go to those winter meetings and then explain what went on to the players and be the intermediary when they voted on different issues. The biggest concern was getting more meal money, which I was successful at. I'm talking about increases of $3 a day to a total of about $12 a day. If something came up, management was able to settle it. They would come at us and say, ''Here. We're going to give you this.'' They said ''give,'' but of course they gave us next to nothing in those days.

What we did get was free beer. Schlitz was a sponsor for Kansas City, and they gave all the players cases of free beer during the year. It wasn't a bad practice because it would just stack up and we'd either give it away or forget it was there. I don't think there was a drinking problem on the team.

However, this was a team that liked to eat. The players ate mostly steak, but it depended on what town we were in. In Washington we'd go to a special Italian restaurant and order pizza or pasta. It wasn't unusual to see fifteen to twenty players walk into the same restaurant. And sometimes the other team would be there. Harvey

Kuenn and I became great friends that way. I'd often go to a little steak house in Detroit down by the Book Cadillac Hotel, where all the teams stayed. If I were alone and Harvey was there, we'd have dinner together. We were both shortstops, so we had a lot to talk about. In Chicago we'd go to an Italian restaurant down by the South Shore, near our hotel. A lot of White Sox players ate there after a game. In Kansas City all the ballplayers went to the Majestic Restaurant, which served both pizza and steak. Those were the types of perks we had as ballplayers.

GUS ZERNIAL:

We moved to Kansas City and the fans treated us well. I got off to a good start and knew I could have a really productive year. But then Lou Boudreau started his platooning. It used to drive me nuts to go into Boston of all places and not play. And balls just flew out of the park in Kansas City, so I wanted to be in the lineup. One day in Boston, I batted and then took my position in left. And here comes Elmer Valo. He said, ''Lou sent me out to play left field.'' I loved Elmer, but he wasn't a great outfielder. I said, ''*You* are coming in for defense?'' I knew what was going on, and I was playing him along, having fun with him. We kept talking in the outfield. In Baltimore I was in the starting lineup and the bases were loaded in the first inning. I stepped into the batter's box and I looked across the plate and there was Enos Slaughter batting left-handed. I asked, ''What are you doing here?'' He said, ''Pinch-hitting for you.'' I said, ''Come on. First inning, bases loaded?'' My forte was driving in runs! I was so mad. I was heading back to the dugout and I was going to say something to Boudreau, but before I could get back, Slaughter doubled and brought home all 3 runs. How could I say anything after that? I was angry at Slaughter for doubling.

We had some pretty good outfielders. Valo hit .364, Slaughter over .320, and Harry Simpson about .300, all playing part-time. We also had Bill Renna and Bill Wilson, two homer hitters. And there was me. I played outfield in only 103 games, pinch-hitting in 17 others. I think I went to bat a little over 400 times. I still drove in 84 runs and hit 30 homers, which was second in the league to Mantle's 37. I would have led the league in homers if I'd played more, and maybe in RBIs, too. Again I was the victim of circumstances. Again, there was no reason not to play me—there were no phenoms on the team.

There was a reason Boudreau and I had problems. My wife was due with our second child. She had terrible difficulty with the birth of our daughter, so I told her I would be with her when the second baby was due. I left the ballclub and was with her when our son was born through a Cesarean. I don't think Boudreau bought my explanation for leaving.

I think I should have insisted that I be shifted to first base in 1954 or 1955. But we had Vic Power, who was an excellent-fielding first baseman. I think we would have been a better club if he'd developed as an outfielder, because he was faster. If I'd played first, maybe the Red Sox would have acquired me. After they traded Walt Dropo, they never had a solid first baseman in the '50s. Would I have loved to have played in Fenway Park in a lineup with Ted Williams, Jackie Jensen, and some of those guys! But I was platooning for the Athletics and, beginning in 1954 and '55, everything was going downhill for me.

VIC POWER:

The Athletics added two black players prior to our first season in Kansas City: Hector Lopez and Harry ''Suitcase'' Simpson. In spring training, they had to stay with Bob Trice and me in the colored sections of the towns we played. They'd pick out the best house in the colored section for us, maybe the house of a school principal. Once I had to stay with a funeral director, sleeping upstairs with the corpses down below. I had trouble adjusting to the greasy foods and grits blacks ate in the South, so I'd have to walk to a supermarket and buy salami, ham, and bananas to take back to my room.

I was popular in Kansas City because I'd already had 2 great years with the Blues in 1952 and 1953. One time we were in Boston and I went to see the Boston Pops. A white couple from Kansas City sat next to me, and at intermission we started talking and they asked about my accent and where I was from. When I said I was from Puerto Rico, they said, ''Gee whiz, the best player on the Athletics is Puerto Rican and we all love him.'' I told them I was that guy, but the woman wouldn't believe me until I pulled out my driver's license. Then she started getting out papers for me to sign for everyone in her neighborhood. You see, as a player they liked me.

But I was living two lives. On the field, I was neither black nor white. But after the game, I was just another colored guy in town. I tried not to let it bother me and to joke about the race problem so I could survive.

My best friend on the Athletics was Cletis Boyer, who was a rookie in 1955. He got $35,000 to sign, which was 3 times what I got as a rookie (and just $3,000 less than the top salary I'd make in the majors). We were just like a couple of kids together. He came from a small town in Missouri, and he'd tell me that if he ever brought me home, I'd be hanged or tarred and feathered. I would have liked to room with Cletis, but in those days black and white players never roomed together. Harry Simpson and my roommate Hector Lopez—Bob Trice was no longer in the majors—got mad at me for befriending Boyer because they thought we blacks should stick together. Simpson called me an Uncle Tom, but I pretended not to know what he meant. Cletis used to tease Simpson by singing, ''Eenie Meenie Minie Moe, I got Simpson by the toe.'' But Simpson wouldn't want to fight Boyer—he'd want to fight me.

I liked playing for Lou Boudreau. He was a beautiful man. He let me go back to my heavy 36-ounce bat and he moved me to first base. Ever since I was a youngster, I caught everything one-handed. So I did this when I played first base in the majors, although no one else caught the ball with one hand in those days. Little League coaches complained about me, and writers and other players accused me of showing off.

FRED HATFIELD (TIGERS):
Vic Power was a hot dog. We always kidded him: ''We'd better play fast or you're going to run out of mustard!''

V. POWER:
I was happy my one-handed fielding was entertaining because I believed in giving fans their money's worth. But I did it only because it gave me more flexibility and range. I played extremely deep so I could cover a lot of ground. I learned about the hitters and I knew where a Ted Williams or Nellie Fox would hit the ball, how hard they would hit it, and how fast they could run. They'd get so mad because I'd catch their grounders and just beat them to first base. I also knew when a player would bunt against me, and I would race from the edge of the

outfield and pounce on the ball. I was always in the game. I didn't have a great arm, but I had a quick release; I wasn't fast, but I was quick and got a tremendous jump. I had great reflexes and great instincts, even a sixth sense. I had finesse—some writer compared me to a ballet dancer. I also was daring: when I caught a grounder with a man on second, I'd often throw to third to beat him there instead of getting the sure out at first. Because I played so deep, I had to convince Joe De Maestri and the other infielders to throw to an empty base rather than wait until I reached the base—they were reluctant to throw with just the base as their target until I proved I would always get there in time and would save any bad throws. I think it was my range that made me better than other good-fielding first basemen. Gil Hodges, Ferris Fain, and some others had great hands and could catch everything, but they didn't even try to get to the balls I ran down.

One reason I liked playing first better than the outfield is that I got to know a lot of players when they reached base. The guys I liked would fool around a bit. For instance, when I held on Billy Martin, he'd put dirt in my back pocket. Ted Williams was the only guy on the Red Sox who liked me. When he'd reach first, he might start a conversation by saying, "Hey, look at that beautiful girl in the stands." "Which one?" "That beautiful black girl behind the column." "Oh, she's beautiful. I'd like to go out with her." "That's my wife." And we'd both laugh.

One game against Boston, Jimmy Piersall got mad when I caught his line drive, and when he got back to the dugout he shouted, "You black son of a bitch!" The next time he got on first, I told Bobby Shantz to throw over to the bag and I gave Piersall a hard tag on the back of the neck. He yelled at me for hitting him so hard, and I told him I was going to kill him and dropped my glove. The umpires ran up and it looked like we were going to fight. Then he took a deep breath and said, "You don't want to kill me. I've got a big family." And everyone started laughing. After that, Jimmy and I got along fine. He'd put dirt in my back pocket, too.

My batting stance was also different. When I stood in the batter's box, I swung the bat in my left hand like a pendulum. The best pitchers threw the ball low, and I wanted to make them think that I was a low-ball hitter

so they'd change their style. Then they would throw the ball at eye level, where I liked it much better. They didn't think I had time to pull my bat up and back and swing so high. But I could do it. I had warning-track power, so I hit line drives instead of trying for home runs. I had good bat control and could hit to all fields. Although I was a free swinger and swung at a lot of pitches out of the strike zone, I rarely struck out.

I liked to play against the Yankees. I was having a much better year than in 1954, so I wanted to show them they made a mistake in trading me. The guy I loved to bat against was Eddie Lopat. He'd throw so slow and I always got a bunch of hits off him. I couldn't wait until his turn came to pitch. The only trouble was that nobody else on the A's could hit him. He pitched only 2 years at the beginning of my career, and during the second year, 1955, the Yankees traded him to Baltimore.

Whitey Ford gave me a lot of trouble. He'd throw three types of curves that would go low, a little higher, and a little higher than that. They weren't strikes, but I'd swing at them anyway. Later, I learned to wait. Then, when he fell behind in the count, he would have to bring the ball up to where I could hit it.

I knew some of the Yankee players from the Kansas City Blues. Elston Howard and I were still friendly, but I thought he was too much of a yes-man. He was like a lot of blacks in those days—like Larry Doby, Monte Irvin, and my good friend Junior Gilliam—who would never speak out about anything. I also knew Bill Skowron and Bob Cerv from the Blues, when they'd homer and I'd get hit in response because I was black. Once, when we were fooling around, they told me to use my glove like a football and try to run by them. I didn't know nothing about football, but I took my glove and tried to run past them. And they hit me in the stomach. They taught me a lesson. I never played football again. One time Bob Cerv kept grabbing my feet in the bus when I was trying to sleep. I finally had to hit him in the face. But we stayed friends.

I played well against the Yankees and the other six teams. I was second or third in hits, doubles, triples, and total bases. I even hit a career-high 19 home runs. I was first among first basemen in putouts, assists, and double plays. I became the first Puerto Rican to play in the All-Star Game, which made me very proud. We played in

Milwaukee, and I had to bat against Don Newcombe. I was a very smart kid and knew he would throw me a fastball. Oh, baby, I was ready for him. So he threw the pitch, only it was a change-up. I was so off balance that my hat flew off and I popped to second.

I was close to Al Kaline in the batting race until the last month. But he was too much. When I'd get 2 hits, he'd get 3; when I got 3, he got 4. So I just said to hell with it and had more fun than he did. When he was sleeping, I was out at a jazz or classical music concert. Kaline hit .340 and I finished second with a .319 average, my career high.

When the Kansas City sportswriters were going to vote on the A's most popular player and give him a new Chrysler, Minnie Minoso and Jim Rivera of the White Sox told me they had bet money I was going to win. Well, they lost their money because the writers gave the car to Enos Slaughter. He was up only about 250 times that year. I didn't like Slaughter in those days, but he was my teammate, so we got along. He was one of the toughest players and had been in a lot of fights. A writer called me up and said, "Vic, you're young. You're gonna win a lot of cars. He's an old man, on his way out."

I never got into an argument with a sportswriter in Kansas City, but those guys had it in for me. They called me a showboat because I caught everything one-handed and had that pendulum swing. But what really bothered them was my conduct off the field. They didn't like that I dated white girls and drove a Cadillac.

BILL WILSON:

There was an attitude change when we moved to Kansas City. There was a new park, a new manager, and new fans. They gave us a parade when we opened the season, and we beat the Tigers, 6–2. I went 3 for 3 with a homer and double, and Alex Kellner got the win. Harry Truman was there, along with Connie Mack. It was sweltering hot in Kansas City, but I liked the town itself. There were good places to eat. Also, the stadium was good and the fans were great and very supportive of the players. Everybody had a group of fans who followed them. Zernial was the biggest name on the team.

Kansas City had other big names, veterans who provided leadership: Bobby Shantz, who had all the guts in the world, and former Yankees Vic Raschi, Enos Slaughter, Ewell Blackwell, and Johnny Sain. I looked up to these guys. They were legends as far as I was concerned.

Our best player in 1955 was Vic Power, who had a much better season than he'd had in Philadelphia. I didn't get to know him that well because he wasn't outspoken and kept pretty much to himself. Everybody knew that Vic had better not go over to the Kansas side because the police were ready to arrest him for driving around with white women.

I got along with Lou Boudreau, but if you didn't do things his way, you were doing them wrong. Three other guys could agree with you and he'd still say you were wrong. I was very competitive and hated to lose, but it worked out because under Boudreau the Athletics weren't a depressed team. We were a very loose ball-

Bill Wilson belted 15 homers in just 273 at-bats for the first-year Kansas City Athletics in 1955, yet he would be demoted to the minors in 1956 and never play in the majors again.

club. On airplanes maybe 15 of us, including Boudreau, would play poker. And in the clubhouse we had free Schlitz. I don't think any players took advantage of it.

The team didn't sponsor any functions. But once Vic Raschi had the whole team out for a barbecue. He lived out by a lake, and Enos Slaughter and I went out on a boat and caught some bass. We had a great time. Nobody played golf. Management frowned on it because they feared the golf swing would mess up your bat swing.

I didn't feel pressure. I just wanted to play more. They didn't seem to notice that I was putting up decent power numbers. I had 15 homers and 12 doubles in just 273 at-bats. If I could have doubled my at-bats I would have hit 30 homers. But no one wanted to give me that opportunity.

JOHNNY SAIN:

In May the Yankees sent me and Enos Slaughter to Kansas City for pitcher Sonny Dixon and cash. Arnold Johnson owned the Athletics but I never saw him. The club was run by Parke Carroll, his vice president and GM. He did a good job, running such a tight operation that the team made money although our games weren't televised. I told Lou Boudreau I'd do whatever he wanted. The first time he brought me in was in the ninth inning against Boston, with the score tied, no outs, the bases loaded, and a 3–0 count on the batter. I got out of that jam. People in Kansas City who heard the game would talk about it for a long time.

Kansas City was great to me and I enjoyed my year there. Vic Raschi, my onetime Yankee teammate, also came to the Athletics during the year, and we roomed together. We finished our careers together. I ended with 139 victories, plus 2 in the World Series. I also had a lifetime batting average of .245, and only Don Newcombe was a better-hitting pitcher during the time I played. I had a good career, and I got out of the game when I was ready.

EWELL BLACKWELL:

I essentially retired in 1953 when I was with the Yankees. I didn't pitch at all in 1954. Then, in 1955, the Yankees included me in a deal with Kansas City. I pitched just a couple of games and 4 innings. That was all. I wanted to get traded so I could get my release. I didn't want to be owned by anybody.

CLEVELAND INDIANS

AL SMITH:

We didn't fear the Yankees anymore. They feared us. In 1955, we should have beaten them again and were out in front by 3 games late in the season. But the Washington Senators knocked us out of the race by winning 2 of 3 in Griffith Stadium and 2 of 3 in Cleveland. We won the season series from the Yankees. I thought we were the better team. But they squeezed by, beating us out by 3 games. We won 93 games.

Bob Feller's career was winding down and he didn't get many starts. That opened a spot for left-hander Herb Score, a nice young rookie who could really throw that ball. I had seen him in spring training and knew he could pitch. He had won over 20 games at Indianapolis by just throwing a 95-mph fastball. He was fortunate to have an outstanding pitching coach, Mel Harder, who taught him to throw a curve. Also, all the great veteran pitchers helped him. He won 16 games and led the league with 245 strikeouts. They were already predicting the Hall of Fame for him.

I had my best year with the Indians. I played 154 games, mostly in left, but I also played about 40 games at third, and even played short and second. I hit .306, with 27 doubles, 22 homers, a league-leading 123 runs, and 77 RBIs. I made the All-Star team—I got to meet Ted Williams!—and wasn't that far behind Yogi Berra in the Most Valuable Player balloting. I also set the Indians record for being hit by pitches. It seemed that blacks were setting just about every team's record for that.

EDDIE JOOST:

Now that my days as player-manager with the Athletics were over, I was contemplating my options. The phone rang one morning and it was Hank Greenberg. He told me not to bother to call any ballclubs to find a position because he wanted me to come to spring training with the Indians. I was happy to do it because they had a very good team. I went down to Florida and told him what kind of money I was looking for. In those days, a free agent could expect to get $10,000 just for signing. He said, ''No problem.'' I'm down there playing really good for Al Lopez. I had the team made. Still I hadn't been given a contract. Finally, Greenberg said he wouldn't give me the $10,000 up front. Lopez offered to give me the money because he thought he could win the pennant again with me at short. But I felt Greenberg was the one who had to pay me. One day Al told me not to put the uniform on because Greenberg wouldn't sign me. So we parted.

RALPH KINER:

Now that I was with the Indians, I wasn't allowed to be the National League player representative anymore, so Robin Roberts took over. Since Allie Reynolds was now out of baseball, he wasn't allowed—according to our original agreement with the owners—to continue to be the American League rep, so Bob Feller took over for him.

I was happy to come to a team that had just won the American League pennant and had won a record 111 games. When I first got to Cleveland, my kids were all in school, so Bob Lemon and I lived downtown at the Cleveland Athletic Club. I had known Lemon for years because he came from Long Beach and I was from Alhambra. When school ended, my wife came with the kids and we rented a nice home in Mayfield, just beyond Shaker Heights.

On the road, I roomed with Al Rosen. I hadn't known him before. He was the leader of the team and the best all-around player I ever played with. All the information I got about pitchers came from Rosen, so I wasn't at a disadvantage. I learned quickly that the American League was a fastball league. There were more curveball pitchers in the National League because of the strike zone. In the American League they called a high strike, whereas in the National League they called a low strike. Still, there wasn't all that much difference between the two leagues.

We had a great group of guys and I made some very good friends on the team. Jim Hegan and Vic Wertz were super guys. I had known Wertz slightly. I knew Bob Feller from having been on his exhibition barnstorming teams. In New York, I'd go to a restaurant that had opera singers at the tables, and I often ran into Feller there. I also dined with Al Lopez, the manager. We went to his favorite Spanish restaurants.

I played in left field, with Al Smith, our best hitter that year, in right and Larry Doby in center—Doby set a league record for errorless games. Cleveland was a great team, the best I played on. It was a thrill to play on a team that won. We should have won the pennant, but we had a lot of aging players whose production sagged a bit—including mine—and the Yankees got hot and beat us at the end. A pennant race was a different experience, but it came too late for me. I had a bad back and couldn't play every day for the only time in my career. I didn't like that feeling at all and about two-thirds of the way through the season I made up my mind not to play anymore. I was only 32, but I wasn't a homer champion anymore. Once you've been there and can't turn it up again, it's not any fun.

GENE WOODLING:

Al Lopez wanted me in the worst way although I hadn't hit a lick at Baltimore. So he traded for me. He was a shrewd manager. As soon as I got to Cleveland, I started hitting like hell. I couldn't explain it. When I was on Cleveland I used a 36-inch, top-heavy 40-ounce bat, the heaviest bat in the league for many years. I was late getting to the batting cage one day and just picked up Early Wynn's bat. I hit good in batting practice with it, and since I was in a slump, I used it in games, too. I used it for the rest of my career.

BALTIMORE ORIOLES

LES MOSS:

There were several American League catchers I admired. The best defensively was Jim Hegan of the Indians. He'd catch a ball and it looked like he was catching a powder puff. He had soft hands and he handled pitchers good, in terms of pitch selection and everything else. You could see he was calling a good game. Sherm Lollar, my onetime teammate, was close to Hegan. Yogi Berra also called a good game. Overall, Berra was the best catcher during my time. There were rules against fraternizing with opposing players before games and I never had dinner with any, so I never really spoke to other catchers, except if I knew them real well. Mostly we said hello and good-bye.

GENE WOODLING:

Before I was traded to the Indians, I played briefly and unsuccessfully for the Orioles. When I had been on the

Yankees, their payroll was pretty high because there were a lot of high-salaried stars. When they sent me to Baltimore, which had no stars, I became the Man. I made a lot more money in Baltimore.

Paul Richards, who replaced Jimmy Dykes as Orioles manager in 1955, got me out of bed to look at a young kid to see if he should sign him. He was a nice young man from Little Rock, Arkansas, who hadn't even played high school ball. He couldn't run, he couldn't throw, he couldn't hit. I never would have signed Brooks Robinson.

At the time, Billy Cox was the third baseman. I got to play briefly with my onetime World Series foe. During the off-season, the Dodgers had traded him and Preacher Roe to the Orioles. Roe retired and Cox didn't seem to have his heart in playing for a new team in a different league. He struggled for a while and then disappeared. He just went home. I don't know if he even told anybody. That was the end of his career.

Cox left on his own, but I got booed out of Baltimore. Since I came from the Yankees, the fans thought I was a DiMaggio. They didn't like it when I got one base hit a week. Paul Richards said, "I'd better get you out of here before they kill you." So he quickly traded me to Cleveland.

BROOKS ROBINSON:

My father was a career fireman in Little Rock, Arkansas, and a good semipro ballplayer. I'd tag along with him and shag flies. I was a big major league baseball fan and kept scrapbooks, cutting out the obituaries of Babe Ruth and Cy Young, and I knew about such players as George Kell, Johnny Vander Meer, and Ewell Blackwell, Dizzy Dean, Bill Dickey, and Lon Warneke, "the Arkansas Humming Bird." For the eighth grade I had to write a booklet called *My Vocation: What I Want to Do When I Grow Up,* and I wrote about being a professional baseball player. I followed in my father's footsteps and went to the same high school and played on the same American Legion team from the age of 14 to 17. It was a good Legion program from which about 15 guys ended up signing professional contracts. I believed I'd make the big leagues. There were a lot of bird dogs who saw me play. I wasn't a secret.

Baltimore knew about me from a fellow by the name of Lindsay Deal, who had played for Paul Richards when he had managed the Atlanta Crackers. Lindsay was a close friend of my parents and went to the same church. He wrote Richards and told him to send someone to look at me. With Richards as manager, the Orioles were in the process of signing a lot of players. So Richards sent scouts to see me play. When I graduated from high school there were about seven or eight major league scouts who talked to me but the Orioles and Reds were the only teams to offer me a major league contract. The Yankees and Tigers wanted to give me the same $4,000, but they wanted to sign me to a minor league contract. I wanted a major league contract because that meant the club could have me for only 3 years before either bringing me up or putting me up for the draft. If I had signed a minor league contract, they would have been able to control me for 6 years before having to make a decision. I was sold on Baltimore because of the major league contract and because Paul Richards told me that if I showed anything in the first couple of years of minor league ball, I'd get the chance to play in the big leagues. I had been offered a basketball scholarship to the University of Arkansas and my parents wanted me to go to college, but they left the decision up to me.

I signed with the Orioles as a second baseman, which is what I played my last two years in Legion ball. At 18, I wasn't seen as a big $30,000 bonus kid with all the talent in the world—just a kid worth a $4,000 investment. At the time I was an outstanding fielder, hit well, had average speed and an average arm. They hoped I'd develop into a major league hitter, and I believed in myself.

I took my first plane ride to Baltimore on the day I graduated from high school. I met Paul Richards for the first time. I spent five or six days there and went on a road trip with the Orioles to Cleveland. I roomed with Hoot Evers, an older guy who was a close friend of George Kell. Then I was assigned to York, Pennsylvania, in Class B. I hit .331 in about 100 games; and had an outstanding year.

Coming from the South, I hadn't played with blacks before. I got kidded some being from Little Rock during that period. I had a few black friends in Little Rock, but not many, and all the schools were segregated in 1955. Strangely, I would never think anything about it when I

An 18-year-old bonus player of whom few people in baseball expected much, Baltimore's Brooks Robinson would become the best third baseman of his time and a future Hall of Famer.

played with blacks on the Orioles and in the minors. There were lots of white guys from the South and black guys, and everyone just played together. It was a real easy adjustment.

At the end of the year I was brought up to the Orioles. I played my first game on September 17, 1955, against the Washington Senators, and I went 2 for 4 and knocked in a run. I then went 0 for 18 and struck out 10 times before the season ended. I wasn't frustrated because I was only 18, but I did realize that guys were way ahead of me and that it would take time for me to learn the ropes.

The Orioles of the mid-'50s weren't a close team because so many guys were coming and going. Richards made a lot of deals. Richards was far beyond anyone else as far as knowing the game of baseball. He had been a catcher but he knew about pitching, hitting, fielding. He was a fantastic manager. However, he was a very cold individual, even to young players. We got along great, but he wouldn't go out of his way to say hello or talk to you or charm you. He was quiet and just stayed around his own group—guys like Harry Brecheen and Luman Harris. On the field, he was all business. He was like God to me. That's the respect I had for him. Our relationship never changed.

RYNE DUREN:

I went to spring training with the Orioles at Miami Beach and then Daytona Beach. Richards called me into his office and said, "Mr. Duren, from now on, I want you to consider yourself a breaking-ball pitcher." He felt I needed another pitch besides my fastball, and thought an off-speed pitch might help my control. As a starter at San Antonio the previous year, I was walking between 5 and 8 batters per 9 innings and throwing 200 pitches a game. So I started to throw curves and sliders. The result was a sore arm.

Richards then sent me out to Freddie Hutchinson at Seattle in the Pacific Coast League. In my first game, I pitched a 1-hitter against the Los Angeles Angels, who had Steve Bilko and Gene Mauch. Mauch had the game's only hit, and it was really an error by the second baseman that was scored a single to keep Mauch's 16-game hitting streak alive. I didn't win another game for Seattle and my elbow was killing me. So Hutchinson sent me back to San Antonio, thinking the warmer weather down there would help. I had some sensational games—one time I struck out 18 batters—but I was still scattering the ball quite a bit.

BOSTON RED SOX

HERSHELL FREEMAN:

I hadn't played for the Red Sox since 1953 and in 1955 made only 2 appearances with them before being sold to Cincinnati in May. I hadn't pitched much for Boston, but I enjoyed my time with them.

I wasn't with Boston in July when first baseman Harry Agganis unexpectedly died while in the hospital with pneumonia. I had played with Harry at both Louisville and Boston. Had he lived to fulfill his baseball life, I think he would have been one of the all-time great players. He was real friendly, easygoing, and so modest that you never would have known that he had any history of fame or had even seen a football. It was a shock throughout baseball when he died. To be hit by something cold-faced like Harry dying—you aren't ready for something like that. One year he's a big strapping athlete, the picture of health, and then, boom, he's gone. Baseball players tried to make the game go forward, and to remember Harry Agganis because he would have pushed the game forward. It was a lot like a policeman or fireman dying, because we had our own fraternity. And it hurt.

FRANK MALZONE:

I went to my first spring training with Boston. It had been seven years, including two in the service, since I signed a professional contract. I figured I'd get some playing time because Pinky Higgins had been promoted to manager of the club. He had been my manager at Louisville in 1954, when we won the Junior World Series and I had a good year. We had a good relationship, but Pinky felt more secure in his first year as Boston's manager going with veterans. He gave Grady Hatton the third-base job and sent me back to Louisville. I had emotions, but I didn't show them or say anything. There was no one to complain to. So I said nothing and returned to Louisville and hit .315. I was recalled by Boston in September and went 7 for 20, ending the year on a bright note.

EDDIE JOOST:

The day after I left the Indians' camp, Joe Cronin, Boston's GM, called because his shortstop, Milt Bolling, just broke his arm. He gave me the money that Cleveland wouldn't pay me. Unfortunately, I didn't play much because early in the season I broke my hand on an inside fastball thrown by the same Harry Byrd I had traded from the Athletics prior to the 1954 season. I didn't even realize I'd been hit until the umpire insisted I go to first. Then I went out to play short and Ted Williams threw me a ball on the fly. I reached up. Down I went. It was a triangular break. I couldn't catch the ball without flinching and I couldn't grip the bat. So I just sat. Mike Higgins told me they'd have someone fill in until I was ready, but by the time I was healed Billy Klaus had won the shortstop job.

We finished fourth, behind the Yankees, Indians, and White Sox, 12 games back. I couldn't really see the reasons for the team's failures during the season. We had a lot of offense: Jackie Jensen led the league with 116 RBIs. Ted Williams missed a lot of games but hit 28 homers and batted much higher than Al Kaline, although he didn't have enough at-bats to win the batting title. First baseman Norm Zauchin hit 27 homers and drove in over 90 runs, including 3 homers and 10 RBIs in one game. And Jimmy Piersall, Sammy White, and a few other guys had very good years. But the pitching was only fair. Mel Parnell, who had always given me difficulty with a moving overhand screwball, was no longer the pitcher he had been. The team's new ace, Frank Sullivan, tied Bob Lemon for the league lead with 18 wins, and Ellis Kinder did a solid job in the bullpen, but our other starters, Willard Nixon, Tom Brewer, George Susce, Jr., and Ike Delock, had only fair seasons, winning between 12 and 9 games each.

Ted Williams was much respected by all his teammates, but I couldn't tell if he was thought of as the leader. What impressed me is how he was just as effective on the road as he was at home, while about two-thirds of Jackie Jensen's production came at Fenway Park. The Sox would point this out to Jensen when he wanted the same money as Williams.

Piersall was an excellent outfielder. He could run and throw and was a pretty good hitter. But his presence unraveled the whole team. He could have been a great player, but he would do irrational yet premeditated things. One day when I'm at short, the umpire has to call time. He points to the outfield and there's no center fielder. Piersall's hiding behind the flagpole, just to get attention.

I'd go out early and work with the kids on the Red Sox. Mike Higgins appreciated this. Cronin saw me doing all this. After the season, he said, "Frisco, I know you can still play but we've got a problem. We just bought the San Francisco minor league team and we want you to manage it." I told him I wanted to play another couple of years in the majors. I was 39 but was still in great shape. He insisted that I do it and talked me into it. Not only would it be a terrible experience, but it meant that 1955 with the Red Sox was the finish to my major league career.

BILL MONBOUQUETTE:

I was born in 1936 in Medford, Massachusetts, just outside of Boston. When I was a kid, it was my dream to be a professional ballplayer, but not necessarily with the Red Sox. I liked Ted Williams, but I used to be a Boston Braves fan and my heroes were Johnny Sain and Warren Spahn. I was a member of the Knothole Gang that would pay 10 cents to sit way up in the left-field pavilion at Braves Field—the players looked like ants. I never stepped into Fenway Park until 1954, when I played in a Hearst All-Star Game with high school kids from the New England area. I was the winning pitcher and was picked as the Most Valuable Player. Then there was a Hearst All-Star Game in New York at the Polo Grounds and I represented New England. I won that game, too. Scouts were watching me all along and I was pursued by the Red Sox, Tigers, and Cubs. There wasn't much money being offered by any team, so I chose the Red Sox because I wanted to play in Boston and it seemed like they would need pitching help. I was signed by Fred Maguire after I graduated in 1955, and in July I started playing in Corning in the PONY League. After a week I was sent to Bluefield in the Appalachian League, only to be reassigned to Corning for 1956. My goal was just to move up a classification every year.

PUMPSIE GREEN:

I was born in Oakland in 1933. I grew up nearby in Richmond, where my mother was a nurse at a convalescent home and my father worked for the city. I had four younger brothers and we were brought up in a church, as were most black people. We were Baptists. I was named Elijah Jerry, but my mother nicknamed me Pumpsie. Credelle and Cornell would grow up to play in the NFL, but I wanted to play professional baseball.

I was 14 when Jackie Robinson broke the major league color barrier. I didn't really think about it because New York and the major leagues were so far away. I played integrated ball in the Bay Area, and the only integration of professional baseball that mattered to me was when such former Negro League players as Piper Davis, Ray Dandridge, and Luke Easter joined the Pacific Coast League, playing on independent teams who owned the players outright. I was a fan of the Oak-

land Oaks of the PCL, and that's who I wanted to play with.

After my second year of playing short and being about the fourth-best player at Contra Costra Junior College, I signed with Oakland in 1954. I was sent to Wenatchee, Washington, Class A ball. Then, in 1955, I went to spring training with Oakland, hoping to realize my dream. But I was sent to Stockton, California, in Class B. I was having a great year when with about two months left in the season the Boston Red Sox bought my contract. So I never got a chance to play with Oakland. I wasn't really disappointed because the next year Oakland moved to Vancouver.

The Red Sox gave me a signing bonus of $3,000 to $4,000 and I was going to get $300 to $400 a month, a typical minor league salary. I was aware that the Red Sox had no black players on the major league level, but I didn't worry that they would never bring me up because I was black. The rumor was that I was going to Montgomery, Alabama, where they had one other black player, pitcher Earl Wilson. I wasn't ready to go to Montgomery, Alabama, in the mid-'50s. Roy Partee, my coach at Stockton, assured me I was going to stay at Stockton until the season's end. So I did.

WASHINGTON SENATORS

HARMON KILLEBREW:

There was always optimism during spring training. No matter who you were, you expected a winning season. Even the Senators. Our new manager, Chuck Dressen, had managed Brooklyn, so he wasn't used to losing. He told us, "I'll steal enough games to put us well into the first division." Instead, we dropped from sixth place to dead last.

Other than Sievers and Vernon, nobody had a very good year on the Senators, including me. At least I got to play slightly more and at third base. Also, I hit my first 4 major league homers. I hit my first home run in a lopsided loss to the Tigers in May. It came at Griffith Stadium against Billy Hoeft, the Tiger left-hander. Frank House was the Detroit catcher, and with a 2–2 count, he said, "Kid, we're going to throw you a fastball.'' What did I know? I was a green kid and wasn't sure if I would get a fastball. But I did get one and hit one of the longest home runs I would ever hit in that park, maybe the longest. When I came around the bases and touched home plate, House said, ''Kid, that's the last time we ever tell you what's coming.'' And he never did it again.

When I came into the league there were no helmets. Our trainer, ''Doc'' Lentz, developed a liner that we wore inside our hats. I stood close to the plate, but I didn't really have to worry about getting hit until I started hitting homers with regularity. Then I would be drilled. When I was knocked down I didn't want to let the pitchers know that it bothered me, so I would just get up and try to smash the ball somewhere, which was the best response I could think of. I would never get into a fight, although we would have a lot of them. I acted only as a peacemaker.

At the time, the play *Damn Yankees* was playing on Broadway, and for a while reporters and fans in Washington called me ''Joe Hardy,'' implying I was another country boy who became a slugger in the majors. I thought that was kind of amusing and didn't take it at all seriously.

I didn't get to know Clark Griffith that well because he died at the end of the season. But I could see he was quite an old character—the ''Old Fox.'' I felt he was pro-player. Calvin Griffith took over after his father's death. He was much different, easier to get to know. We would become friends.

PEDRO RAMOS:

I was invited by the Senators to spring training for the first time, with a real chance to make the team. If I'd been with the Yankees or Dodgers, I might never have made it to the big leagues, so it helped me to be with Washington.

When I arrived in Orlando and checked into the Winter Haven Palmer House, where we used to stay, I knocked on the door of my room and Camilo Pascual opened it. I had met Camilo in Havana before I was invited to spring training. He was surprised to see me. I didn't know anyone else on the team. We roomed together for a while. But Charlie Dressen wanted me to learn English, so he put me with Don Mincher, a powerful first baseman from the South. Don was a friendly

guy. He liked Cuban music, and every time we went back to the hotel he'd want me to play it.

I didn't know who anybody was in the major leagues other than Mickey Mantle, Yogi Berra, and a few others. At one spring training game, all I knew was that we were playing a team in red. It was Cincinnati. The Reds scored 10 to 14 runs and we used a lot of pitchers. When I came in, the bases were loaded and no one was out. This was my cherry in the big leagues. I struck out the first 2 guys and the third guy popped to first base. I got such a big hand that I asked Camilo Pascual what was going on. He said, ''You know who you just faced? Ted Kluszewski, Wally Post, and Gus Bell!'' I was glad I didn't know who they were.

I had a good enough spring to make the team. I got the Senators uniform, and my shirt and pants were too big. I was number 28 at first but wound up with 14. Any time I put on a baseball uniform, I enjoyed myself— every day for every single minute, whether I won or lost. I remember Dressen's saying, ''The day you can't tie your shoes or put your socks on, it's time to quit.'' I liked Charlie. He was a little guy, no more than 5'6'', but he spoke his mind. He had a lot of spirit and a positive outlook.

I was a 20-year-old rookie with a salary of $6,500. Like most of the young players, I looked up to Mickey Vernon. He was a little older, so I respected him. He was also our only .300 hitter. I was told that he hit .300 almost every year.

EDDIE JOOST (RED SOX):
Mickey Vernon was a great unheralded player who spent many years with those terrible Washington teams. He was a good hitter, a good first baseman, and just as nice a person as there was in baseball.

GENE WOODLING (ORIOLES):
Mickey Vernon never got the credit he deserved because he played for the Senators. He had excellent statistics and even they didn't indicate how good he was. He was a Hall of Fame–caliber player and it would be a disgrace when he would later be passed over.

P. RAMOS:
After the season, Vernon would be traded to Boston. Three of the veteran pitchers—Frank Shea, Bob Porter-

Colorful Cuban right-hander Pedro Ramos began his major league career at the age of 20 in 1955 and would be a gallant hurler for the lowly Washington Senators team for the rest of the decade, often leading the league in losses despite pitching well.

field, who was a hard thrower, and Mickey McDermott, a fun guy—were also in their last year with the team. It was obvious that the Senators wanted new blood, particularly on the pitching staff, because they had brought in Chuck Stobbs, Dean Stone, and Pascual in the past couple of years and then added me and Ted Abernathy in 1955.

On other teams, I might have sat on the bench at my age, but Dressen pitched me more than 40 times, mostly in relief. I didn't know who any of the batters were, but I did okay. My record was only 5–11, but my earned run average was below 4.00.

There were a lot of nice guys on the Senators, like Vernon, Shea, Roy Sievers, and Eddie Yost. But my English wasn't good enough yet to really talk to them. My best friend was Pascual. Camilo was a very quiet guy who minded his own business and pitched when he was supposed to pitch. We lived together for a while in Washington in an apartment. He didn't like air conditioning. I liked air conditioning because I couldn't sleep in the hot weather. Otherwise we got along fine. We went out a lot to eat; we went to movies. Camilo was already a tough pitcher in 1955, although his record was bad. He had a good fastball and one of the best breaking balls I've ever seen. Sometimes he was a little wild, but he was a tough competitor when he got in a jam. Anybody can pitch an easy ball game.

DETROIT TIGERS

FRED HATFIELD:

In those days, managers were in complete control. The manager may not have always been right, but he was never wrong. Everybody had respect for the manager— they kept their disrespect a secret and never brought it up at a club meeting. Yet there was a lot of criticism among Tiger players of Bucky Harris when he became manager in 1955, replacing Fred Hutchinson. They thought Bucky was afraid to make moves, leaving pitchers in too long. They thought he was one of those managers who were afraid to come out and be booed. Also, we thought his coaches could have been more useful. I don't remember having any big league coach who did anything except hit fungoes and throw batting practice, and 9 out of 10 were too old to throw. We just figured that the coaches were friends of the manager.

But I didn't really gripe because I played a lot under Harris. I was the starting second baseman and batted over 400 times, with 60 walks. I had 8 homers and 15 doubles, which were my major league highs. The team also improved, going over .500 for the first time since I'd been there. We got good starting pitching from Hoeft, Garver, Gromek, and Frank Lary, a rookie right-hander who won 14 games. Lary also came from Alabama, and we might occasionally jump on a Larry Doby or, in spring training, Jackie Robinson. We did it. We'd yell, "The jig's up" and stuff like that. Nobody said anything. They never reacted to it.

We got terrific seasons from our three big guns. Kuenn hit over .300 and led the league in doubles;

Boone led the league in RBIs; and Kaline drove in over 100 runs and led the league with 200 hits and a .340 average. He was the youngest batting champion because he was just 20.

GEORGE KELL (WHITE SOX):

Al Kaline was the only guy I could compare to Hank Greenberg as a clutch hitter. He was the equal of Mickey Mantle.

JOE DE MAESTRI (ATHLETICS):

Other than Mickey Mantle and Ted Williams, the best hitters in the American League were Al Kaline and Harvey Kuenn. Kaline was probably one of the best of all time. He could do it all. I thought he was another Joe DiMaggio.

F. HATFIELD:

Players were getting younger and younger. Whereas the veterans were witty, the younger guys were pranksters. They tried to pull things on the old coaches. Kaline or Kuenn or Hoeft would nail their shoes to the floor. We'd all play tricks on reporters. Sometimes we'd start a rumor to confuse the guy. Maybe I'd be talking to Kaline or Kuenn and a Boston sportswriter would sit close by to eavesdrop and I'd say something like, ''Ray Boone's going to Boston for so-and-so. I think they'll announce it soon.'' The next day in the paper: ''Boone's coming to Boston!'' We did that every now and then. Sometimes, when the Tigers would be coming into a city and the Senators would be on their way out, some local photographer would come around looking for Chuck Stobbs and my teammates would say, ''Hatfield, go tell him you're Stobbs.'' And he'd take 2 or 3 shots of me. That's how we had our fun.

CHICAGO WHITE SOX

BOB CAIN:

I had returned to my first major league team at the end of the 1954 season but hadn't pitched. But I hoped to get a good opportunity in 1955, especially when Marty Marion replaced Paul Richards as manager. During spring training in West Palm Beach, Marion and his wife had to go somewhere one day and left my wife and me to watch over their two little girls at the motel. They were a little difficult. In the early evening one of the girls called me over, and when I squatted down she took both hands and struck me on both cheeks. I reflexively grabbed her. At that exact moment Marion and his wife drove in and saw me grabbing her arms. Marty held that against me. I pitched 13⅓ scoreless innings for him that spring, yet he cut me from the ballclub. So my major league career ended on a sour note.

GEORGE KELL:

I had great admiration for Marty Marion because he was a gentleman in every respect, but I didn't think he was cut out to be a manager. Even so, we finished only 5 games out in 1955, closer than the Sox had ever been under Richards—although we won 3 fewer games than the previous year. I rebounded with a solid season, hitting .312—my highest average since 1951—and driving in 81 runs—my most since 1950. So I felt somewhat revived.

BILLY PIERCE:

Our starting rotation got a boost when Dick Donovan, a strong, clever right-hander, came to the White Sox. He had spent several years in the Red Sox' and Tigers' organizations, but hadn't pitched much in the majors. Marty Marion put him right into the rotation, where he stayed with me, Jack Harshman, and various other pitchers for several years. Dick had excellent control and was a tough competitor and usually won about 15 or 16 games a year. On the day he pitched, he was the most precise, exacting person in the world. He would sit down on the bench and take the towel from his shoulders, fold it very neatly, and put it beside him. If he walked to the water cooler, you didn't get in his way. He would just brush you aside without acknowledging you. He was about the only guy like that. Strangely, he was very sociable on every other day. I was more loose and even talked to fans when warming up. He couldn't understand and once asked, ''You talk to these people?'' I'd say, ''Well, it relaxes me.'' I noticed that the next time he started, he went out of his way to say hello to somebody. Then he got knocked out in the first inning. He said, ''To hell with your ideas.''

We also got Walt Dropo from the Tigers in a deal for Ferris Fain. Walt was our starting first baseman in 1955 and after that played part-time. He was 6′5″ and strong, so he provided some power and led our team in homers that year, but he was also a deceptively good fielder. The big fellow was very good at getting the ball out of the dirt. He, Fox, Carrasquel, and Kell gave us an excellent infield offensively and defensively. We also had Sherm Lollar behind the plate, and Rivera, Busby, and Minoso in the outfield—with Bob Nieman and Bob Kennedy coming off the bench—so we had a solid offensive and defensive team to go along with me, Donovan, Trucks, and Harshman on the mound. We had become an excellent team and finished just 5 games behind the Yankees and 2 behind the Indians.

This was my best year, although I won more games in other years. Because of the pain in my arm, I didn't get as many starts as I had between 1950 and 1953. Also, I lost four 1–0 games. I won only 15 games, but I

Chicago's Billy Pierce was finally given due recognition in 1955 when he became the only pitcher of the decade to post an ERA below 2.00.

had a 1.97 ERA. That stood out in my career. I was the only starting pitcher in the decade to give up fewer than 2 runs a game. (In fact, I would be the only pitcher to do it between Hal Newhouser in 1946 and Sandy Koufax in 1963.) ERA was very important to pitchers then: it was a good indicator of how well you had been pitching. So while a lot of pitchers in the league won more games than me, I was again the starting pitcher in the All-Star Game. I again faced Robin Roberts. Again the beginning of the game was tense, but this time Mantle hit a 2-run homer, and after our 3-inning stints, I led 4–0. If that score would have held up, I would have gotten credit for the victory.

With recognition came an occasional endorsement. I remember doing a Camels commercial in Tampa, although I'm not sure of the year. It was a two-day shoot in a new ballpark, and both days seemed to go well. Then I got a phone call telling me we had to reshoot what we did on the first day. We hadn't noticed that on the second day someone had planted three palm trees in center field!

CHICO CARRASQUEL:

From 1950 to 1955, my years in Chicago, I was the only Venezuelan in the big leagues, so I was a hero in my native country. I'd go back every year after the season and play winter ball. In 1954 I played in 155 games for the White Sox, one being a tie, and then went to Venezuela and ended up playing almost 300 games overall. Every April I'd look forward to playing 154 games in the majors and to hitting .300, but toward the end of the summer I'd start to feel tired. This happened to many Latin players, and they were accused of being lazy. I was never accused of being lazy because it was obvious that I tried hard and loved baseball. I was loved by the Chicago fans during my 6 years there. I played my best ball for them.

LES MOSS:

In mid-season, the Orioles sent me to the White Sox for Harry Dorish. I was reunited with Marty Marion, who had been player-manager at St. Louis. He was a good man and well respected by the players. There were no player leaders on this team either, but it didn't matter because Marty and his coaches were the leaders. There was a different attitude on the White Sox than on the

Browns and Orioles. We were winning, and winning is the greatest teacher in the world. The White Sox were a relaxed team, full of pranksters. That suited me fine.

Marty wanted me to back up Sherm Lollar. I'd get in there every 3 or 4 games. I batted just over 100 times, my least at-bats since I was a rookie in 1946, but I ended up with my best average, just below .300. I didn't compete with Sherm for playing time—I knew my role. Sherm and I were real good friends, having played together with the Browns in the late '40s. I don't think he had an enemy in the world. He was a good, smart catcher. He should have been a big league manager.

I hung around with Lollar, my roommate Ron Northey, and Dick Donovan. After almost every road game, we'd go out together and have a couple of beers and dinner. Northey was an outstanding pinch hitter and one of the jolliest, most colorful men in baseball. He was about 5'10", but nobody knew what he weighed because he wouldn't get on the scales. He was a lot of fun. We'd be walking along and he'd stop some stranger to ask where some street was at. He didn't give a damn about the street. He'd explain, "I just wanted to see what that guy would say."

BARRY LATMAN:
I grew up in the predominantly Jewish Fairfax section of Los Angeles, and from the age of 10 to 13 I could not play baseball because I had to study Hebrew for my bar mitzvah. I couldn't miss a day because the rabbi would knock on our door on the way home from the synagogue to see if I was all right. My father, who was a furniture auctioneer and real estate broker, promised me that if I wanted to play baseball after I was bar mitzvahed, he would be willing to sponsor a team for me to play on. From the time I was 13, I wanted to be a professional ballplayer, and my father worked with me all the time and encouraged me in every way. I was a good pitcher at Fairfax High—Larry Sherry, who was also Jewish, played second base—and in semipro ball, and was written up in the local sports pages. There were a lot of scouts watching me, from the majors and the Pacific Coast League. I played in the Hearst high school All-Star Game in the Polo Grounds in New York City, representing California. Then, when I was supposed to

just watch the Yankees, Giants, Dodgers, and Pirates, I illegally worked out for them.

But my father wouldn't let me sign a contract until I graduated from college. To appease him, I went to USC on a baseball scholarship. I had a fight with the coach, Rod Dedeaux, because he wanted me to bring my arm up higher and use my height. But I could already throw as hard as anybody. I told my dad they were trying to change my style and he got mad: "They aren't going to change your style. We'll sign a professional contract. To hell with them!"

I signed with the White Sox because of Bob Pease and Hollis Thurston, who had followed me ever since ninth and tenth grades. I could have signed a bonus-baby contract, but I chose to go to the minors. My father said he'd give me 3 years to make the majors, and if I didn't make it, I had to promise to go back to school. So I started with the White Sox in the minor leagues. I continued my education for 2½ years but never graduated. My grandfather threw me out of the family when I signed a baseball contract. My father had wanted to be a professional ballplayer, but he hadn't let him. I'd visit my grandfather later, but he would never ask me what I was doing.

I thought I was going to make the White Sox at spring training that first year in Florida. I pitched in the intrasquad games and even pitched against another major league team. I pitched so well that I couldn't believe it. I thought the White Sox were going to keep me. But they broke camp and left me behind. I was a cocky, confident 19-year-old and thought, "How could they do that?" Now I assumed I'd leave camp with Indianapolis, the Triple A team. Then they left town. I finally left with Waterloo, Iowa, in Class B. I was making the most money on the team, $800 a month.

NEW YORK YANKEES

BOB TURLEY:
I was thrilled to come to the Yankees, leaving a team in Baltimore that scored 2 runs a game for one that scored 5 or 6 runs, and had such a great tradition and reputation that they drew enormous crowds at home and on the road. At first it was scary being with the Yankees and all

their stars, but by the time spring training was over, I was just one of the guys. I kept my home in Baltimore and stayed at the Concourse Plaza Hotel on 161st and the Grand Concourse. A lot of players lived there and it was a friendly group. I had a lot of fun.

There weren't as many arguments on the Yankees as there were on the Browns, and that had been a friendly team. There were so many talented players, veterans and rookies, who kept their mouths shut. There was verbal leadership coming from guys like Hank Bauer, who would remind everyone that they'd have to play hard to make the World Series. Then there was silent leadership from guys who would go out there and bust their asses every day. Mantle was a silent leader. He loved to play baseball and would do his best every day.

Everybody got along. Everybody fit in, including Elston Howard, a catcher-outfielder who became the Yankees' first black player. We all liked Ellie. On the road, we married players would mix with single players. We'd play a lot of bridge, hearts, pinochle. Don Larsen and I were pinochle partners. We had played ball in the minors together and were friends. But we didn't go out together. I would go to dinner or a movie with single guys, but Larsen drank and partied, and that wasn't my style. I wasn't a drinker or a carouser. I was dedicated to what I was doing; I stayed in shape and worked hard.

I'd come to the ballpark early. I wasn't the type of pitcher who wouldn't talk to other players before I went to the mound—I just didn't eat for 4 or 5 hours before I pitched. I thought of myself as a role model, and the Yankees would room a lot of young players with me so some of how I approached the game would rub off. Early on, I roomed with Andy Carey and Bill Skowron. Carey had come up at the end of the 1952 and 1953 seasons and had his first full year in 1954, hitting over .300. He played more in 1955 and his average dropped. He was a pretty good hitter without much power, and a pretty good third baseman, though he didn't get much credit for it. He was a hard-nosed player and a nice guy. He was studying to be a securities accountant.

Skowron was a better hitter. He was a tough out who hit for average, hit homers, and drove in key runs. He was good enough to play every day, but Stengel often platooned him with left-handed-hitting first basemen, Joe Collins and Eddie Robinson. Bill was a Polish guy

who we all called "Moose" because he had a crew cut like Mussolini had. He was a friendly, naïve guy who everyone liked to kid. We all liked Moose.

I pitched as much as I did with the Orioles the year before: a lot. I started 34 games and went 17–13, including a 1-hitter against Chicago. Whitey Ford led the team and the entire league with 18 wins, and Tommy Byrne won 16. Ford was the ace of the staff, or, as we called him, the "Chairman of the Board." He had good breaking stuff and fantastic control and was the best competitor I ever saw in my life. I admired him very much. Byrne and I had been on the Browns together. He was a comical, lovable guy who wanted to have fun but wasn't a drinker or carouser. When he came up with the Yankees in the '40s he was a wild, hard-throwing left-hander. The Yankees scored a lot of runs, so he won 15 games in both 1949 and 1950, but he had trouble winning on the Browns. He was traded away and played in the minors, before the Yankees brought him back. When he returned he threw more sliders, curves, and sinkers. His walks were down and he was a much more effective pitcher in his last few years.

The Yankees were a fun team and we laughed a lot. But when we lost we didn't say a helluva lot. We were respectful of our losing pitcher, and if a guy got 2 or 3 hits he wasn't outwardly happy. Fortunately, we didn't lose very often, particularly late in the season, when we beat out the Indians and White Sox. We played better than .700 ball down the stretch, although Mantle was out much of the time with a hamstring pull. He hit his last homer when I was pitching early in September—and he still led the league. Ford was tough in September and everyone else made a contribution, including Billy Martin, who came back from the army and went on a tear.

EDDIE JOOST (RED SOX):

Billy Martin was just a player, not a star. He became a star in the 1952 World Series when he caught that ball behind the mound to end a Brooklyn rally. He was a journeyman second baseman. His reputation was that he'd fight anybody. I can't understand how a guy weighing 165 pounds dripping wet could walk up to a big guy and knock him down. Sure, he was aggressive and a fighter—I was, too—but I couldn't understand.

Evidently, he had so many facets to him that no one really could explain him completely.

JIM FRIDLEY:
The Yankees didn't bring me up from Double A in 1955. I would have a couple of good years at Denver—in 1956 I would bat .291 with 24 homers and 105 RBIs—but they had a tendency to forget about you if they thought you had a bad arm, which was the reputation I got in Baltimore. Irv Noren batted over .300 and made the All-Star team playing left field for the Yankees, so I got stuck in the minors. In the off-season I worked for many years as a supervisor in a paper mill in Dayton, for Kimberly-Clark. I always reasoned that I needed an outside job. I got a piece of metal stuck permanently in my inner right thigh. I bled a little when it shot into me, but it never bothered me when I played ball.

WORLD SERIES

1955

YANKEES vs DODGERS

BOB TURLEY · YANKEES:

Playing in a World Series was different than I expected. The nerve-racking part was not playing the games but the time between games. There was no hatred between the Yankees and Dodgers. A lot of us had good friends on the Dodgers. We all liked Campanella, Hodges, Snider. . . . There was a mutual respect between the teams. I don't think we thought we were better, especially with Mantle hobbling. We knew how good they were.

We had advance scouting reports. For instance, I was told that I wouldn't have much trouble with Snider because I was a high fastball pitcher and he had trouble getting around on high fastballs. For the most part we were told not to let them hit long flies in cozy Ebbets Field. In Yankee Stadium, we wanted them to hit long flies from right center to left center. I had never been in such a small park as Ebbets Field. There was a lot of excitement there. The fans were yelling and screaming and throwing things at us as we passed by.

Whitey Ford won the first game over Don Newcombe, 6–5. Joe Collins hit 2 homers for us. That's the game in which Jackie Robinson stole home. Yogi tagged him, but the umpire called him safe. Tommy Byrne outpitched Billy Loes in the second game, 4–2. He also got a big hit in the inning we scored all our runs.

I started Game Three against Johnny Podres, but got knocked out in the second inning. In Series games, if you start out shaky, you aren't given time to get into a groove. Campanella had a big game and the Dodgers went on to win, 8–3. We lost the fourth game to Clem Labine, 8–5, when they hit 3 homers. I relieved Bob Grim in Game Five after the Dodgers had hit 3 homers off him, including Snider's third and fourth of the Series—he had a great Series. I pitched the final 2 innings and did okay, but we lost 5–3 to Roger Craig.

We evened the Series in Game Six, by scoring all our 5 runs in the first inning off Karl Spooner. Bill Skowron hit a 2-run homer, and Ford pitched a 4-hitter to win his second game.

The seventh game began as a battle of left-handers, with Tommy Byrne opposing Podres. Gil Hodges drove in 2 runs to back Podres. I shut out the Dodgers in the eighth and ninth innings of Game Seven, in relief of Byrne and Grim. I might have been the winning pitcher if Sandy Amoros hadn't run down Yogi Berra's liner down the line in deep left in the sixth. We had two runners on base and that would have tied the game 2–2. We were sure it was going to fall in. Yogi was a pull hitter, so we couldn't believe Amoros was playing him near the left-field line. That killed our rally, and Podres beat us 2–0 on an 8-hitter—they got only 5 hits off us—and the Dodgers finally won a Subway Series after losing to the Yankees in 1941, 1947, 1949, 1952, and 1953. The Yankees were quiet during that game and afterward. We were always somber when we lost. We congratulated them.

RUBE WALKER · DODGERS:

The Podres game that decided the World Series was a thriller, a super-pitched ball game. Amoros was almost in center field when Berra hit that ball. It kept drifting away, but Sandy made a great catch and McDougald was doubled at first. That stopped them! I never saw Johnny pitch a better game, but he pitched many great games. I wasn't surprised Alston went with him in Game Seven with Newcombe hurting and the Series on the line. He was a tremendous competitor. The game

ended when Elston Howard grounded to Pee Wee—he had lived through all the Dodgers' losses to the Yankees, so he was delighted. Later, at the Bossert Hotel, we all celebrated!

ED ROEBUCK · DODGERS:

What I remember most about the Series was the close relationship between Podres and his father. In the clubhouse after Johnny pitched the shutout to win the final game, they were hugging and crying. I was making about $6,000 or $6,500, and we got World Series shares of $9,700. That's what it meant to me. Actually, who won the World Series didn't mean that much to me. Even the losers' share was more than my salary. Getting to the World Series was it. But it was very emotional for the older players who had lost in past years. Reese, Furillo, Hodges, Robinson, Snider, Newcombe, Erskine, Campanella—that's who got the most out of it. Duke Snider was thrilled to win because the Yankees had beaten great Dodgers teams in the past—all Brooklyn wanted to get rid of the ghosts. In fact, Duke thought the best team he ever played on was the 1952 team, but they didn't win the championship. We did.

NATIONAL LEAGUE 1956

"BROOKS LAWRENCE LATER TOLD ME THAT MONTE WAS THE BLACK PLAYER ALL THE OTHER BLACK PLAYERS LOOKED UP TO. JACKIE ROBINSON WAS ALOOF TO THEM, WHILE IRVIN WAS WILLING TO HELP. SO WHILE THEY IDOLIZED JACKIE, THEY LOVED MONTE. LAWRENCE EXPLAINED, 'I WANT MY IDOLS TO TALK TO ME.'"

JIM BROSNAN

MILWAUKEE BRAVES

BOB BUHL:

I was sad when Charlie Grimm was fired a third of the way through the season because we were playing only slightly above .500. We would have gotten it together because we were too good to keep playing that way. I liked Charlie a lot. He was a good manager and a show-man. He once had flags in his back pocket and made signs with them, waving them to guys on the base paths. Another time, Charlie dug a hole in the ground and buried the lineup card. He'd dig it up to see who would hit next.

Grimm was replaced by Fred Haney, who had managed those terrible Pirates teams. We won our first 11 games for Fred. We played great ball for him and almost won the pennant. Fred was in his late 50s and a real gentleman. He was a good manager who knew baseball in a different way than Grimm. Charlie would say, "Boys, here's a bat, ball, and glove, go out and get 'em." Fred was a smarter manager and figured out more ways to win. But he didn't use me any differently than Grimm did, other than starting me a few games more and cutting back on my relief appearances.

I pitched well against all teams but Cincinnati. I think I beat them once in all the years I faced them. It worked out best when I'd pitch the days before and after we faced them. The Reds' Ted Kluszewski was the toughest hitter in the league for me. He could hit anything I threw up there a long way. Even when I broke his bat, he'd still get a hit.

I didn't mind pitching against the Giants, even after Mays became a great player. But the only fans in baseball who really gave me grief were those in the Polo Grounds. We had to use the runway to the clubhouse and all the hecklers would gather there.

The team I liked to face most was Brooklyn. I even looked forward to facing them in Ebbets Field, which was too small and had tough fans right on top of us, both in and outside the park. I wanted to beat the Dodgers because ever since I was in the league they went first-class and had the best. When we went on trains they'd be flying, and they'd have Vero Beach for spring training and we didn't have diddly. We were envious of them, especially since they kept winning pennants.

I beat the Dodgers 8 out of 9 times in 1956. The Dodgers had a lot of right-handed hitters I had success against. I showed them I was the boss. They knew I would brush them back. I'd pitch Hodges inside and throw him a lot of curves because he wasn't a good curveball hitter. I'd throw Campanella nothing but high inside fastballs because he was muscle-bound and would hit the ball off his fists an awful lot. Maybe I'd waste a slider away on him. I'd pitch Duke Snider—their best left-handed hitter—high and tight. He hated change-ups. I'd just make Reese hit the ball. Carl Furillo was one of the better hitters and would spray the ball around. I tried to keep the ball away from him. They had so many great players. Jackie Robinson was a helluva ballplayer even in 1956, his last season. He still gave 110 percent all the time and would do anything to beat you, like bunting with 2 men out and a man on a third, anything you wouldn't expect. He was a team player and we thought he was the leader of the Dodgers.

The one game I lost to Brooklyn wasn't a funny game to me. I was ahead 1–0 going into the last of the ninth inning in Ebbets Field. I walked Campanella, and Hodges was up. My catcher was Del Rice and we figured Hodges would bunt, so I threw him a high fastball. He hit it into the stands. The next night we played them the last game of the series and Burdette was pitching for us. They had the bases loaded and nobody out in the seventh or eighth inning, and I went into the game. I struck out the first batter and then Jim Gilliam hit into a double play. We scored 3 runs in the next inning and Ernie Johnson saved the game. I got credit for my eighth win against the Dodgers.

We won 92 games in 1956 but still finished 1 game behind the Dodgers. I think we would have won if I hadn't busted my finger in August. I won 18 games although I pitched only twice in September. Spahn went 20–11 and Burdette, who led the league in ERA, went 19–10. So we were a formidable threesome. We wanted to outdo each other, so I would have liked the chance to pitch the full season. I lost only 8, so I was on a pace to win 21 or 22, which would have given me the most wins. We were always competing one way or another. On the field, we'd play pepper, and whoever booted the most would have to buy drinks after the workout. That kept up the entire time I was in Milwaukee. But I wouldn't compete with them with the bat. They were both good hitters and I was probably the worst in baseball. They'd laughed at my hitting. No one remembers that I was a good bunter.

Eddie Mathews would get into some of our off-field competition. He and I would get into one taxi, and Burdette and Spahn would get into another, and we'd race from the Polo Grounds to our Manhattan hotel. Whoever got back first would get dinner bought by the other two that night, so we'd slip the drivers an extra $5 to stay ahead of the other cab. Another thing we did was mark off blocks in New York and try to hunt each other down. If Spahn and Burdette couldn't find Ed and me in a certain amount of time, they'd have to buy dinner. If they found us, we got stuck with the check.

Eddie became increasingly competitive with Henry Aaron on the field, once Aaron began exhibiting more power. They never criticized each other because both produced so much and played so hard. Still, you could see it. Each one felt they could do better than the other and they tried to prove it. Henry was a better hitter than Eddie, but Eddie could hit the ball farther. I don't think there was jealousy between the two. Both were making good money—though they never discussed that, of course—and both were getting a lot of recognition. They were friends although they didn't chum together off the field.

Aaron was a natural. As good as he hit, I think he could have been a little bit better. He could steal bases, but he never stole that many. He could take an extra base, but he never overexerted himself. If we needed it, he would do it, but he wouldn't do it every day. He didn't loaf and he'd catch everything, but he didn't hustle as much as Mays. If Willie could see a double, he'd go for it, where Henry would round first and pull up.

In 1956, Aaron led the league in average, and both he and Mathews hit a lot of homers and drove in over 90 runs. But probably the biggest offensive threat we had that year was Joe Adcock, who returned from his wrist injury. He led the team with 38 homers, one more than Eddie, and was our only player with over 100 RBIs. Because of what Jim Hearn had done to him on an inside pitch in 1955, Joe now thought everyone was trying to knock him down. The truth was that he was 6'4" and had long arms and couldn't move fast enough to get out of the way of pitches. One day in July, Hearn's Giant teammate Ruben Gomez hit him on the arm and Joe started down to first, stopped and said something to Gomez, and started out to the mound. So Gomez threw the ball and hit him again. And Joe took off after him. Here was Big Joe, 220 pounds, and him lumbering after this terrified rabbit. Gomez runs out to the center-field fence and Joe's trying to cut him off at the path and Gomez circles him and comes back and runs into the dugout, through the runway, and into the clubhouse and locks the door and grabs an icepick. And here comes Joe chasing him. They stopped him at the dugout. It was comical, though both men were fined and Gomez was suspended. We'd always laugh at Joe and ask him if he knew what he'd looked like chasing this little guy who could run like a deer. I'd say, "Did you catch him yet, Joe?" Every time we'd face Gomez, we'd say, "Joe, you can catch him now." But after that one time it was forgotten between the two.

Joe was an even-tempered guy who usually got mad only at himself when he wasn't hitting. He and Johnny Logan used to chum together. Big Joe wouldn't hurt a flea, but Logan wasn't like him. He was a real competitor, a fiery guy who would fight at the drop of a hat, teammates or opponents. There were other players his size that he didn't like. He got into it with the Reds' Johnny Temple a few times. (A few years later he even charged Don Drysdale once.) Of course, John was an instigator, and once a fight started and we all got there he would sneak out. Logan was a character. You couldn't understand what he was talking about. He'd start talking about one thing and get lost and suddenly be talking about something else. He was a good man to have on a team. He was a good batter and reliable short-stop. We called him "Yatcha." I remember that he had hundreds of autographed baseballs.

LEW BURDETTE:
I had good seasons from 1953 to 1955, going 15–5, 15–14, and 13–8, but in 1956 I really emerged from Spahn's shadow. I went 19–10, winning only 1 fewer game than Warren, although he pitched 25 more innings, and I led the league with a 2.70 ERA and 6 shutouts. I was a sinker-slider pitcher from the beginning. My fastball was a sinker because I threw sidearm and three-quarters and the ball went down. I had a slider that went the other way. One went down and away and the other went down and in. When I came up, I came in. The

batters were already intimidated because I pitched inside, but I had an additional advantage in that they worried I threw a spitter. Burleigh Grimes, the last legal spitball pitcher, had been a roving pitching coach in the Yankees' minor league system when I was there. I learned a lot from him in Triple A. I asked him to teach me to throw a spitball. He said, "If I teach you how to throw one, you'll get caught and get banned from baseball. But if you make them think you throw it and don't—and don't get caught—they'll be looking for something that isn't there. If your ball moves, they'll complain. When hitters make outs they'll complain because they're all egotistical." I discovered that if I could get one of the first 3 hitters in the first inning to go back to the dugout saying I was cheating, by the fifth inning everybody on the team wanted to see the ball when they batted. If I made any motion to my mouth they became suspicious. So I'd go through my ritual, going to my hat and then crossing my chest. I got so many Catholic medals and sacred heart medals in the mail. I had a whole drawer of mementos which fans sent to me "from one good Catholic to another." I was a Southern Baptist.

Hitters were so funny that I just had a ball on the mound. I'd almost bust out laughing when they'd complain about a spitball after I'd really thrown a bad change of pace, screwball, or slider. Even if they hit a hard liner straight at the center fielder, they went by the mound complaining like the dickens. I'd suck it all up. The umpires didn't believe them. They'd come out and practically undress me. I'd tell them they missed a certain place and they'd get a little ticked.

ST. LOUIS CARDINALS

HANK SAUER:
I was disappointed when I was traded to the Cardinals for outfielder Pete Whisenant just prior to the 1956 season. It was upsetting leaving Chicago, and St. Louis had Wally Moon in right field and Rip Repulski in left and I knew I wouldn't get many at-bats. But I had a pretty good year, and I liked my teammates and the St. Louis fans, who were tough on opponents but cheered all the Cardinals.

Fred Hutchinson, the Cards' new manager, was one

of the best guys I've known in my life. He had a philosophy that I wanted to remember if I became a manager. He never had fun with the everyday player. He had fun only with the guys sitting on the bench. He said, "Hank, if you keep those guys happy, then you'll have a successful ballclub."

I lived in an apartment downtown, but on the road, Stan Musial was my roommate. If you couldn't get along with Musial, you couldn't get along with anybody. We became very close. He was a superstar and a super person. When he was offered $100 for a postgame interview he'd tell me not to go off until he was through because he wanted to use the money to buy dinner—for us and a couple of the young kids he'd invite along. He'd always pick up the tab. After Ted Williams, Musial was the best hitter I ever saw. He had a couple of advantages over Ted. He could outrun Ted. And while Ted was a pull hitter, Stan could hit the ball all over. I'd call him the Hawk because he'd find the open spots in the outfield in which to drop his hits. That year the *Sporting News* voted him its Player of the Decade, ahead of DiMaggio and Williams.

Stan wasn't the leader type. He just did his job and did it well. I'd say Alvin Dark, who came over during the season from the Giants, was as close to being the team leader as anybody. He was a hard-playing, fiery type. Ken Boyer wasn't yet a leader because he was just in his second year and was fairly quiet. But he was already a terrific third baseman and hitter. His numbers weren't much below Musial's.

It was a close team and there were no problems. The big mistake that was made during my year there is that in mid-May we traded Bill Virdon to the Pirates for Bobby Del Greco, another center fielder. What a terrible deal. Virdon would hit over 100 points higher than Del Greco that year—and he was a great fielder, much better than Del Greco. We were in first place at the time of the trade—then the ballclub just went downhill.

I hit .298 for the Cards in about 150 at-bats. In September we were in Cincinnati. The new general manager, Frank Lane—who had last been with the White Sox—told me, "We're going to have to let you go." I said, "Why? I had a pretty good year." He said, "You had a good year but your roommate had a lousy year." Heck, batting in front of me, Musial led the league in RBIs, hit 27 homers, and batted .310. He led the team in

After being the star of the Chicago Cubs for many years, Hank Sauer found himself playing part-time on the Cardinals in 1956, before coming back to prominence with the New York Giants the following season.

all 3 categories. I said, "What's wrong with that?" He insisted Musial had a bad year. Of course, Lane was the guy who would once try to trade Musial—but Gussie Busch prevented it. He was the guy who traded Virdon. Lane didn't stick around long after getting rid of me.

BILL WILSON:
After the 1955 season, I was sold to Toronto in the St. Louis chain. I didn't think of quitting. Frank Lane, who had signed me out of the Coast League for the White Sox years before, sent me a telegram that said if I had a decent year, he'd bring me up. So that was something to look forward to. I didn't have a bad year, but I screwed up my arm and couldn't throw the way I used to. So I knew I wouldn't make it back to the majors. I would

have liked to have played more in the majors, but I didn't regret anything. I had a great time with my teammates and had met a lot of wonderful people traveling around the country.

CHICAGO CUBS

JIM BROSNAN:

I returned to the Cubs in 1956. I suppose I didn't help much because we finished in last place. But, starting 10 games and relieving in 20 more, I went 5–9 with a 3.79 ERA and showed enough to stick in the majors—for good. This was a team that won only 60 games and had only one pitcher win more than 10 games. Bob Rush won 13 games and Sam Jones and Turk Lown were next best with 9 wins each. So I did okay.

One roommate I had was backup infielder Jerry Kindall. He was a religious fanatic and we spent our nights together arguing. I also roomed with Moe Drabowsky after he got out of college and came directly to the Cubs. He would become an expert practical joker as his career progressed—he would order pizza or call overseas from the bullpen phone—but then he was 20 or 21 and the only thing I found unusual about him was that he used 8 to 10 towels a day and threw them on the floor. He was a neatness freak. I thought that was kind of weird. I thought, "Where in the hell have you been brought up, you dumb Polack?" He actually was born in Poland. I asked, "What am I going to dry myself with?" "They have more towels," he replied. "All you gotta do is call 'em and they'll bring 'em." He did this every day.

There weren't many blacks in the Cubs' organization. Ernie Banks and Gene Baker were the first blacks to play for Chicago. Both were very quiet men. In Chicago, white and black players could have socialized together without there being any questions at all, but Banks and Baker didn't mix with the white players. As far as I knew, they didn't ask to. I didn't know that Ernie Banks had any opinions except "Let's play at beautiful Wrigley Field." Within those safe confines, he had all kinds of clichés he'd mutter, never venturing an opinion if he had one. He had an act and he was very good at it.

Monte Irvin came from the Giants to the Cubs in 1956 and played his final season. He did pretty good in limited playing time—his 15 homers were third-best on the team to Banks and Walt Moryn. It's a shame I didn't get to know Irvin, because Brooks Lawrence later told me that Monte was the black player all the other black players looked up to. Jackie Robinson was aloof to them, while Irvin was willing to help. So while they idolized Jackie, they loved Monte. Lawrence explained, "I want my idols to talk to me."

When I was with the Angels I developed an annoying superstition. When I won I'd make sure to drive the same route to the ballpark every day until I lost. Sometimes those routes would take me far out of the way. In Chicago I lived pretty far west of Wrigley Field, and after I won I'd take some awfully long and circuitous routes to the ballpark. I might lose my way. It was almost a relief when I lost a game and could take a quicker route.

BROOKLYN DODGERS

DON NEWCOMBE:

In 1956 I went 27–7 and was voted MVP. That meant that Don Newcombe was the best player in the National League in 1956. That was more important to me than winning the first Cy Young Award, which in 1956 signified that I was the best pitcher in *either* league. I was MVP in a league that had Stan Musial, Robin Roberts, Willie Mays, Jackie Robinson, Roy Campanella, Willie Mays, and Henry Aaron. I was the best.

I had learned from Satchel Paige that major league hitters looked for a ball in a certain spot. Paige wasn't about to give it to them there, and neither was I. I pitched toward batters' weaknesses. Except for Stan Musial and Hank Aaron, they all had weaknesses, even Willie Mays. So by pitching to their weaknesses, I had the advantage and had a good chance to win.

I wouldn't say I had a lot of pleasure playing baseball. It was damn hard work. It wasn't fun pitching on a summer night in St. Louis when it was 95 degrees and 95 percent humidity. It was my job and I worked hard to maintain my position and I did well and made money. But I wouldn't ever say I loved baseball. I wouldn't have played for nothing, and when I heard players say they would, I told them to give me their paychecks. However, I had gratification when I was successful. Winning the MVP was success. That was gratification.

It wasn't enough to be thought of as a good pitcher. I wanted to be thought of as a black man who became successful and did something for his people. I always reminded people that I was about 60 percent Indian, but the fact was I was a black man and proud of it. The same was true of Jackie, Roy, Larry, Satchel, and all the others that came along in that era. What we did should be passed on from generation to generation. It would have appalled me to think that in years to come some black ballplayers who became rich wouldn't even know who Jackie Robinson was.

I did my job and had the chance to reach a standard of living I never would have reached without baseball. I also became famous. Frank Sinatra would stop his show if Jackie, Roy, or I walked into a nightclub—he'd introduce us. Sinatra, Billy Eckstein, Nat King Cole, Duke Ellington, Count Basie, Joe Louis, and Sugar Ray Robinson were all friends of ours. Everywhere we went we sat down front. That was certainly gratifying, but it also meant something that people began to recognize what we were about, and what our responsibility was, especially to black people around the world. One day I met a man named Martin Luther King, Jr., and we became friends. He told me, "You, Jackie, and Roy will never know how much easier you made my job with what you did on the baseball field." Easier! Here was a man who would be billy-clubbed and thrown in jail, and have police dogs bite him, and have hoses directed at him. Yet we made it easier for him!

We had our chapter, our phase, and made our contribution. As Jackie had hoped, things got significantly *better* during our era, and we made it possible. It didn't have to happen. What would have happened to black baseball players if Branch Rickey had not signed Jackie Robinson? Would sports have been that meaningful in the overall integration of America? Who would have been the owner to have changed things? And when? Would Bill Veeck have done it?

Nineteen fifty-six was Jackie Robinson's last year in baseball. I didn't like when he was traded to the Giants in December. I got the feeling he had worn out his welcome with the Dodgers. Look what they traded him for: Dick Littlefield. The Dodgers were changing, and Jackie was getting older and more vociferous. He let you know how he felt. Jackie wasn't going to leave New York, and the Dodgers planned to move to Los Angeles.

I think Walter O'Malley and Buzzy Bavasi had a meeting and decided to trade him. I would have hated to pitch against him in 1957, but he retired instead of joining our chief rivals. He couldn't see himself as anything but a Brooklyn Dodger.

RUBE WALKER:

You couldn't beat being in another pennant race. We had a slow start and trailed Milwaukee until late in the season. We didn't clinch until the last day of the season against Pittsburgh when Newcombe won his 27th game, Duke Snider and Sandy Amoros hit 2 homers each, and Jackie Robinson homered in his final regular-season game. We beat the Braves by 1 game and the Reds by 2 games. The Dodgers were still a great team.

After 6 years with the Dodgers, I was still backing up Campanella and playing about 40 games and batting 140 times a year. And I was still enjoying myself. It was challenging facing tough right-handers like Robin Roberts and, on occasion, a tough left-hander like Warren Spahn. It was even more rewarding working with our great pitchers: veterans like Newcombe, Labine, and Erskine, who no-hit the Giants for his second career no-hitter in 1956, and young pitchers like Roger Craig, Don Drysdale, Ed Roebuck, and Sandy Koufax.

I got a kick helping our pitchers get out the league's toughest hitters. Stan Musial was the best hitter I saw. He hit the ball all over and there was no way to pitch him. Ted Kluszewski was also hard because you could bust him inside and he'd still muscle the ball out of the park. Guys like Aaron, Banks, and Clemente were instant stars. Their bats were so quick. These were homer hitters who weren't muscle men. Pitching to Willie Mays, you'd try to come inside as far as you could and then go away from him. That's how you tried to get almost everybody. Of course, Mays knew what we were trying to do and wasn't the type to be fooled very often.

There were some who said Sandy Koufax would never overcome his wildness. But he wasn't given the chance to pitch. No one would take batting practice against him. It was tough just throwing to a catcher all the time. Other Dodger pitchers had been wild when they came up: Johnny Podres, for instance. In 1955 and 1956 Koufax was nervous. Even Drysdale was nervous when he came up in 1956. But I could see they were both going to make it.

Sal Maglie came over to the Dodgers from the Indians. Everybody was shocked to see him in a Brooklyn uniform and wondered how we'd treat him after the Barber had given us so much grief as a Giant. He had hit most of our players. We got along great. We were happy to get him. All the young pitchers talked to him and learned from him. He pitched against the Giants just like he had pitched against us. Now they were his enemy. At the age of 39, he went 13–5. He threw a no-hitter against the Phillies in the heat of the race and then combined with Labine for a doubleheader sweep of the Pirates on the next-to-last day of the season. He was a major reason we edged the Braves for the pennant. He and Newk carried us for two months.

Players on the Dodgers never talked with each other about their contracts. But every once in a while everyone would complain about a salary offer. I think Buzzy Bavasi occasionally offered low salaries just to see our reactions. I'd get a contract in the mail and take it with me to spring training, and then sit down and talk it over. I figured I would get a small raise every year because I always gave them what they needed from a backup catcher. I played good defense and called a good game. I was consistent.

ED ROEBUCK:

When I talked contract with Buzzy Bavasi, he would point to fake contracts of the other Dodgers. He'd say, "See, Duke Snider makes only $25,000." But Duke was making more. The players had no say. If you talked about a union it was like being a Communist, so nobody talked about unions or other players' contracts. There were inequities—the general managers battered down the players.

I was young and not fully paying attention to much other than my own career, but I could see the aging process taking place on the Dodgers. You could see it first with Jackie and maybe Pee Wee. I think Pee Wee threw a lot better when I first saw him years before at spring training. Don Zimmer, his backup, could have been a star if it weren't for Reese and getting beaned a couple of times. He was a helluva shortstop who might have hit 30 homers a year, but Pee Wee stopped a lot of shortstops from playing.

Jackie Robinson would be traded after the season, and a month later, he quit. Baseball is something. Some-

one that great leaves and you still say, "So what?" Because in the dog-eat-dog world of baseball, there's always someone to take his place.

Alston used Clem Labine and Don Bessent in save situations during the season, but I got a lot of work. My statistics were only slightly better than in 1955, but I pitched well through the entire season instead of just at the beginning. This time I gave up fewer hits than innings and my strikeouts went way up.

I'm proud of the pitch I threw to Joe Adcock in June that he hit on the roof at Ebbets Field. It cleared the 83-foot wall at the 350-foot marker in left field. He was the first player to do it, and I felt I had something to do with it. I got a lot of distance records in most parks for hitting the fungo, and I tried to hit one where he did, but never could.

Winning the pennant meant we would have a rematch with the Yankees. There wasn't real hatred of the Yankees. There was more respect. In fact, I even went to one of their parties. That's how I know they drank on that team.

RANDY JACKSON:

I got my contract in the mail and expected a raise from the Dodgers, the World Champions. But they sent me the same contract I got with the Cubs in 1955. I wrote back Buzzy Bavasi and reminded him that I had a good year in 1955 and made the All-Star team. He wrote back that I hadn't done anything for the Dodgers. But he said he'd give me a $1,000 raise anyway. So what could I do? I didn't know the man from a sack of salt. (I didn't feel I was appreciated in baseball until I got out. The most I would make in the majors was $21,000, in my last year.) The guys I played with on the Dodgers—stars like Campanella, Reese, Snider—were making only $40,000 and they were from a first-place team.

When I was traded to the Dodgers, some of the Chicago media said it was a good move because they got rid of the "phlegmatic" Jackson for the fiery Don Hoak. If that is what they wanted, that was fine. But I got to go to the first-place Dodgers. I was delighted. I could tell the difference in the clubhouse immediately. Everyone there was a winner. When I was with the Cubs going into Brooklyn, we always felt we were a couple of runs behind before we started. Because of the attitude over there and because of the fans, you knew you were play-

When Dodgers owner Walter O'Malley and manager Walter Alston decided to ease outspoken Jackie Robinson out of the organization, they acquired the Cubs' Randy Jackson to share time with him at third base.

ing the best team in the league. When teams played the Dodgers they'd have a defensive frame of mind.

It was a thrill to put on the Dodger uniform. All of a sudden I'm sitting next to these great players I admired, and people were looking at me with the same eyes with which they were looking at them. I had been playing against the Dodgers since 1950, so the players knew me and I was accepted right away, the first day of spring training. I felt they wanted me or they wouldn't have traded for me. They'd take any kind of help they could get from me anyway—no one resented that I was going to be playing Jackie Robinson's position.

Robinson had played third base in 1955, so theoretically I was supposed to replace him at third. I knew that Jackie was on the decline. But he was a *great* player. He was the best all-around player I ever saw, including Willie Mays, Stan Musial, and Ernie Banks. He had the

best instincts and would beat you doing something with the bat, his feet, or glove. By this time it had been several years since he had been razzed about his color. You don't razz great players because it makes them play better. He had a short fuse and yelled at umpires, but that's because he was so fired up. He got wrapped up in a game right away. Jackie and I got along fine and were around each other on road trips, though I never got to really know him on a personal basis. I hardly got to know any of the Dodgers that way. But Jackie was somewhat of a loner. I don't think he ran around much with the other guys.

I didn't run around with any of the Dodgers in Brooklyn. I spent time with my wife and our two young boys in our house in Brooklyn. Some of the guys had been together for so long that they visited each other and did things together. On the road, I ran around with my roommate, Roger Craig. He was a 6′4″ right-handed pitcher who was born in North Carolina. Roger was probably my favorite roommate. He was a smart, funny guy. We decided about movies, where to eat, whether to stay in. He was a good pitcher and won 12 games as a starter, but the Dodgers had such a strong staff that in future years he was either in the bullpen or used as a spot starter. He'd pitch for many years but never win 12 games again.

Nobody walked from their home or apartment to the ballpark, because they'd never get there because of all the autograph seekers. However, we talked to fans before and after games. Brooklyn fans were twice as vocal as other fans. They didn't cause trouble—they just liked to shout at you. As soon as you put the Brooklyn uniform on, the fans accepted you, and as long as you produced they liked you. Fans weren't dangerous. Kids in Brooklyn would sometimes squirt visiting players with ink, but no one died from that. You weren't wary of fans in any city; in Philadelphia they were vicious in what they said, but they wouldn't pull a gun or knife. Giant fans were a little bit on the rowdy side, but compared to Brooklyn fans they were sedate. In the Polo Grounds, it was so big that the sound of the fans kind of died before it reached you. You always thought Yankee fans felt superior to other fans and that their team was in a class by themselves.

The animosity between the Dodgers and Giants was on the same plane as Texas hates Texas A&M and

Georgia hates Georgia Tech. You didn't hate the Giant players; you just didn't like them as a team. You didn't hate Mays or Maglie or Dark, you "hated" the Giants. Maybe the fans did, but not the players. We were glad to get Sal Maglie, the ex-Giant. All of a sudden he was our best friend because he was helping us fight for the pennant. If he changes uniforms, he becomes your buddy.

Being in the pennant race was fun. The Dodger players who had won every year were just as hungry as I was. They wanted to win just as much as the year before. And they wanted to win the World Series again. When you're playing with guys who've been there many times before, it's easier to play. You feel more secure playing with winners. They understand that you do what you do best and not try to do extra. When you try to do more than you can do is when you mess up. These guys knew to play within themselves, and I learned that. Milwaukee came into Brooklyn to play us during the pennant race. You looked into the dugout and you realized that if you hit any of them real easy on the head, they would have cracked. They had never been there before, fighting for a pennant, and they were just sitting on eggshells. The Dodgers were just loosy-goosy because they had been there. I caught that feeling from them and relaxed and had fun. I wasn't the bubbling kind, but I enjoyed the banter of the other players. Gilliam and Campanella were chatty. Every team had chatter on the bench. If you sit there for 2½ hours, you have to do something.

I batted cleanup for a month and half before I got hurt. So while I batted .274, I was restricted to pinch-hitting for much of the year and played third in only slightly more than half our games. But I was in there for some key games. On September 25 I played third base when Sal Maglie no-hit the Phillies, 5–0, to keep us a half game behind the Braves. During the season we had a full house against Philadelphia. Stu Miller was pitching a great game against us, and we were behind, 5–2, in the bottom of the ninth. Reese got on and Snider, who was batting third, hit one over the fence. They took out Miller and brought in a new pitcher to face me. The first pitch was a ball, and the second I hit up in the left-field seats, which tied the game, 5–5. I got an ovation. I floated over the bases. Then Hodges came up and on the first pitch hit one into the seats. And there was pandemonium, with fans trying to get out on the field. We thought we had lost. I had never seen 3 homers to win a game in the last of the ninth. There was extra celebrating after that game. The media came in and took pictures.

I never had anybody in the Dodgers' organization tell me I had to kick dirt on the umpires or slide into a fielder and break his leg or argue. I did my job and no one said anything about it. I hadn't changed my style. I was as emotional as anyone when someone homered or I made an error that let in the winning run.

Walt "Smokey" Alston was much respected by the team. He was undoubtedly the best manager I ever played for. He didn't say a whole lot but he was smart, and you didn't want to challenge him because he was a very strong person physically. I remember two guys getting into a heated argument in the shower. Before they came to blows, Walter walked in and picked up one in one arm and one in the other and said, "We aren't going to have any of this." He wasn't a bubbling personality, but in his own way he praised his players. If Walter came to you and said, "Nice hit," you knew he meant it.

Sandy Koufax and Don Drysdale didn't pitch much when I was there, but you could tell they had potential. They were part of a gradual youth movement that was taking place on the Dodgers. To be honest, I never thought of the aging process taking effect on the team—not with them bringing in old vets like Sal Maglie. I guess I realized it most when Jackie Robinson was traded after the season.

STAN WILLIAMS:
I was just 18 when I went to my first spring training at Vero Beach. I'd been invited to spring training out of Class B ball, which was unusual. It was just to look me over. It was a thrill to see my idols. I could watch the Dodgers play on Sundays. We intermingled with the Dodger players, but we didn't actually mingle. What surprised me about Jackie Robinson was how big a man he was.

I didn't feel like I was anything special. I felt like a member of an army. You used to see guys run by in a green uniform, number 248; red uniform, number 284; orange uniform, number 185. If you ever got under 100, you felt like a prospect. There were so many players and most were pretty good because at that time the minor league teams could afford to keep you around, since they were all making a profit—soon television knocked out the minor leagues because people stayed home and watched major league teams play.

I wasn't a mean pitcher until I was at Newport News. That was something the Dodgers bred into pitchers at all levels. In Dodgertown they used to have "Chalk Talks" whenever it rained. They'd get everybody into a little room and Ray Hathaway would conduct meetings and say, "If your grandmother walks up to the plate with a bat in her hands, knock her on her ass." The Early Wynn school perhaps, but it was the Dodger way of thinking, and the way the game was played in those days. The theory was that when you got ahead of a hitter, you kept him off the outside corner by pitching him in and knocking him back or down. My first year at Newport News is when I tried to implement that idea. But I would aim the ball high and tight, and you can't do that: when you're coming inside, you have to drive the ball and get it where the batters can't get the bat extended. I didn't want to hit them, so I guided several 0–2 pitches inside and gave up homers. Then I just started rearing back and throwing it as hard as I could at their chins and let them get out of the way. I found out that worked a lot better.

Don Drysdale, another big right-hander who learned to pitch that way, got to the big leagues a couple of years earlier than I did. He and I were in spring training in 1956 together and he made the ballclub and I didn't. He was more polished and self-confident. I had a tremendous spring, pitching 17 or 18 scoreless innings, but I didn't know that the reason I was so effective is that no one wanted to get in and hit against me because I was so goddamn wild and threw so hard. According to Campanella, I threw harder than Drysdale or Koufax. All of us threw around 100 mph. But I didn't belong in the majors yet because I was so green.

I began 1956 in Double A, at Fort Worth in the Texas League. I didn't get a penny raise. I accepted that because they didn't give me a cut in 1955 after my bad year in Class D. I was in Double A about a month and should have been demoted to A ball. But the Dodgers used reverse psychology because they didn't want to break my spirit and instead promoted me to Triple A, at St. Paul. It was a good move. I don't know who figured it out. The Dodgers sent me to the American Associa-

tion where the weather was cooler—I had been losing 20 pounds every 4 or 5 innings in Texas—and there were older players who couldn't catch up to my fastball. I ended up 9–7, which wasn't bad for a 19-year-old in Triple A. There was good opposition. The Giants' team had Orlando Cepeda, Jim Davenport, Bob Schmidt, Gail Harris—youth going up and veterans coming down.

At the end of the year I went to winter ball in the Dominican Republic and played for a combined team of Dodgers and Giants. Bob Schmidt, the Giants' catcher, taught me the slider in about 1½ minutes. He just showed me how to hold my thumb and how to release the ball. All of a sudden I had a breaking ball and it made all the difference in the world.

NEW YORK GIANTS

JOHNNY ANTONELLI:

My wife had relatives in Jamaica, Queens, and she wanted us to live near them so she could have them around when I was on the road, so in 1956 we lived in an apartment complex called Jamaica Estates.

That was one of many changes that took place that year. Bill Rigney replaced Leo Durocher as the manager. He was a friendly guy and very knowledgeable. But he had an almost completely revamped team and could lead us to no better than a sixth-place finish. Monte Irvin was finishing his career on the Cubs. Hank Thompson and Jim Hearn were in their last seasons and playing much less. And Davey Williams's major league career was over. During the season, we would trade Alvin Dark, Whitey Lockman, Don Liddle, and Ray Katt to the Cards. We got back Red Schoendienst to play second, outfielder Jackie Brandt, and a few other players. (We'd get Lockman back after the season in a trade for Hoyt Wilhelm.) Brandt, who hit almost .300, did a good job for us, as did Bill White, another rookie. White was a left-handed-hitting first baseman who played exceptional defense. Our new starting shortstop was Daryl Spencer, who had played with the Giants in 1953 before going into the service. He was big for a shortstop and not that graceful, but he was a hard-nosed player and had home run power.

I was now one of the veterans on the team. I was, in

fact, the player rep. I thought that the players' association was very important because it got us an effective pension plan. But I was not a union person. I thought unions were needed to get rid of sweatshops, not to be in baseball.

Ruben Gomez had a bad year, and another starter, Al Worthington, struggled to get wins, so I became a workhorse for Rigney. I pitched over 250 innings and went 20–13, leading the league again with 6 shutouts. I was our only pitcher with more than 7 wins, so it wasn't easy. A good indication of how well I pitched was that I beat Brooklyn 3 times, which was unheard of for a left-hander. And I beat them in 3 different ballparks! I beat them in the Polo Grounds, in Ebbets Field, and in Jersey City, where the Dodgers played about 15 games that year. I won that game 1–0 on a Willie Mays homer.

PHILADELPHIA PHILLIES

DEL ENNIS:

In 1956 I would have had my fifth straight 100 RBI year, but the 5 RBIs I got on Opening Day in Pittsburgh were erased because that game got rained out. So I finished with 26 homers and 95 RBIs. Stan Lopata hit 32 homers and also drove in 95 runs. This was only the third time I didn't lead the team in home runs and, in my 11-year Phillies career, the only time other than 1951 that I wouldn't lead the team outright in RBIs. Meanwhile, Richie Ashburn had used his bottle bat to get a lot of singles. He was my friend, but if he put together a Hall of Fame career at Philadelphia, as many people would contend, then so did I. I knew I would never get a lot of votes because I wasn't friendly to the writers who got the votes. Besides, both Richie and I were at a disadvantage because we played our best years in Philadelphia rather than New York, which had many more writers.

I was just 31 and expected to have several more big years with the Phillies. But it didn't happen because of Roy Hamey. Bob Carpenter had appointed him general manager in 1954. Hamey was a loudmouth. He was tough to me and that's how I was to him. I used to say, "I'll go see Bob. I don't have to talk to you." It was Roy who traded me to the Cardinals while Bob was off on a hunting trip and couldn't object. I was shocked.

ANDY SEMINICK:

I was fouling off pitches that I used to hit. That's how I knew I was losing it. I could see that I would now only be a backup to Stan Lopata, who was five years younger than me to the day. Stan did great playing almost every game—he hit 32 homers. I had 7 homers in around 160 at-bats, but my average was below .200.

FRANK BAUMHOLTZ:

It was strange for me to go to the Phillies in 1956, having spent so many years with the Cubs. They had a couple of good years since their 1950 title season, but they had never challenged for another pennant. Now they seemed to be an aging team that was on a downward turn. The starting lineup was very solid, with guys like Richie Ashburn, Del Ennis, Granny Hamner, Willie Jones, Stan Lopata, and Elmer Valo, and the pitching was good, with Robin Roberts, Curt Simmons, Harvey Haddix, Stu Miller, and Jack Meyer. We had some good players, yet we finished fifth, winning just 71 games. I had reservations about Mayo Smith as a manager—I guess they were more than reservations: he wasn't very good.

I had led the league in pinch hits in 1955, so the Phillies got me to be their top pinch hitter. I again led the league in pinch hits. Unfortunately, Smith used me almost exclusively as a pinch hitter and played me very little in the outfield. I hit well those few times I was in the lineup, but they still went out and got another left-handed-hitting outfielder to play against right-handers.

Ashburn and Ennis played every day in center and left field, so Elmer Valo, who was picked up from the Athletics during the season, and Jim Greengrass shared right. I got out there only a few times, while Valo started against right-handers and Greengrass played against southpaws. Valo kept to himself. I liked Greengrass. He was easygoing and very friendly. He was a good ballplayer who had a couple of big years with the Reds. He didn't hit too well in 1956, which turned out to be his last year in the majors. He was only in his late 20s, but he had a lot of trouble with his legs. If training conditions had been better in those days, he could have prevented some of his injuries and prolonged his career.

Richie Ashburn was a super ballplayer. He hit over .300 and had over 500 putouts in center field, leading the league. I didn't see him other than at the ballpark. I liked Del Ennis. He had a dry sense of humor. He was a good hitter and good left fielder, yet the Philadelphia fans booed him. There were tough fans in Philly. There was one fan who would get on me in both Philadelphia and New York. He was a real loudmouth who'd shout, "Hey, Baumholtz, go get a bushel basket." One day I invited him to come down to the Warwick Hotel to have lunch with me. We talked for hours. From that time on, we were friends and he thought twice about yelling those things at me.

After Ashburn and Ennis, the best hitters on the Phillies were Stan Lopata, who hit in that strange crouch, and Willie "Puddin' Head" Jones. Willie was my roommate, but actually I roomed with his bags. He was a super guy. He loved to have a good time and he had many of them. Now, this was a guy who could drink. I was amazed by his stamina.

Robin Roberts was still the Phillies' ace pitcher. He pitched almost 300 innings and for the fifth straight year led the league in complete games. He refused to come out. Roberts won 19 games, ending his 6-year string with 20 victories and his 4-year string of leading the league in victories. In his prime, Roberts was as good a pitcher as there was in baseball. Even when I had hit him hard, the ball went right at somebody. I had gotten an occasional hit off him, but not 3 or 4 a game. He didn't care if the other team got 15 hits off him, as long as the Phillies stayed 1 run ahead. He'd shut the door in their face.

If Curt Simmons would have had a little better control, he would have been a super pitcher, too. He was very good, winning 15 for us. He had been one of the toughest left-handers I had faced, so I was glad not to face him anymore. He scared me to death sometimes. I did much better against Warren Spahn.

Reliever Jack Meyer had a great rookie season in 1955, but struggled a great deal in 1956. I remember a game when we were leading the Reds in the ninth. They loaded the bases with 2 outs, and Smith brought in Meyer. A pinch hitter, maybe Smoky Burgess or George Crowe, hit the first pitch in the lower deck to beat us by a run. I thought Meyer was going to kill himself when he came into the dugout. He kicked over the water cooler. I don't know how he didn't break his foot.

Dick Farrell was a wild and woolly young prospect who pitched briefly for us. I never saw much of him at night, but I'd hear about him and the guys he'd run around with. He was tough on the mound. He didn't mind throwing at batters.

Another player who came up for the first time was first baseman Ed Bouchee. I saw that he was a good left-handed hitter with pretty good power, and predicted good things from him. He was a sharp, very funny guy—a good person to have on a team.

ED BOUCHEE:

After my good year at Schenectady, I was invited to spring training with the Phillies in Clearwater, all the way from A ball. I deserved to make the team, but they kept Marv Blaylock as their first baseman although he had hit less than .210 with them in 1955. I was sent to the Miami Marlins in the International League. Again Don Osborn was my manager—I was following him around. Bill Veeck was the owner, and he was a great guy who took care of the ballplayers and their families. When the guys were on the road, he and his wife threw parties for the players' wives.

Satchel Paige was with the Marlins. He was a real gentleman. He carried a satchel that contained fifty or sixty different medicines in it, pills and ointments, including a special oil somebody made for him that the trainer rubbed him down with. Satchel told us stories and talked about Josh Gibson, who he insisted was the greatest catcher that ever lived. He liked the way I swung the bat and told me, "Bouchee, you can hit anybody that picks up a baseball."

By now Satchel was mostly a relief pitcher and the fans gave him a rocking chair to sit on in the bullpen. However, he did start every once in a while, particularly 7-inning second games of doubleheaders. One night in August, Veeck threw a huge promotion for charity that drew 55,000 fans to the Orange Bowl. He brought in all kinds of big-name entertainers like Little Anthony and the Imperials. And Satch was going to pitch the game against Columbus. A helicopter dropped him right on the mound at the beginning of the game. Satch pitched well, but we were behind 3–2 late in the game. Then he batted with the bases loaded and doubled to win the game 5–3. That was a great night!

When I was sent down after spring training I was not

really disappointed because I knew I wasn't going to get much chance to play on the Phillies anyway. But I got a bit frustrated as the season progressed and Marv Blaylock didn't improve any. However, it didn't affect my play. I was relaxed on the field and had fun. I hit .293, with 17 homers and 100 RBIs.

I was promoted to the Phillies at the end of the season. I don't even recall who I first played against or my first game. I know I started 4 games and was 6 for 22, with 2 doubles and 5 walks. The main thing I remember is pinch-hitting against Sal Maglie when he no-hit the Phils 5–0 in Brooklyn at the end of September. His fastball had a good tail on it and his slider was breaking a foot and was just running in on batters. I had never seen a ball move so much.

The ballplayers of this era were harder-living guys than the ones who came later—especially the veterans

Hard-hitting Ed Bouchee came up to the Phillies to stay in late 1956, solving the team's first base problem.

whose long careers were winding down. For instance, we had Elmer Valo, an old-style ballplayer who had been around for years. The Phillies acquired him during the 1956 season and traded him before the 1957 season. He was a good hitter and hard-nosed player. He was a good guy but a bit different, as were many of the old-timers. The only time he showered was when he was at the ballpark, I guess. And he wore the same clothes for entire road trips. These types of guys were kind of off by themselves. I don't remember Elmer hanging out with anybody.

PITTSBURGH PIRATES

FRANK THOMAS:

Joe Brown was the new general manager, and he told me, "Mr. Rickey said that I'm not supposed to cut your contract." I said, "Joe, you do what you want to do. I don't want any favors from him. But if you don't cut my salary and I have the best year of my career, I'll sign for whatever you want for 1957." So he didn't cut my salary. Lee Walls played a lot in left, so I played mostly at third base. I felt more in the game in the infield and got to be more of a chatterer. I played in 157 games, including ties, and batted .282, which was third on the team to Bill Virdon and Clemente, and had 25 homers and 80 RBIs, behind only Dale Long. After my good year, Brown came back with the same salary. I said grudgingly, "I'm a man of my word and I'll sign." He said, "No, I'm just kidding. I'll give you a $1,000 raise." He thought I'd think him generous. I said, "If I have another good year in 1957, and you throw it up to me that you already gave this token raise, I'm going to go to the bank and give you the $1,000 back and we'll negotiate for 2 years on my terms."

DICK GROAT:

The Pirates moved up to seventh place in 1956, thanks in large part to Bob Friend winning 17 games and good offensive years by Dale Long, Bill Virdon, who came to us from St. Louis early in the year and batted way over .300, Frank Thomas, Roberto Clemente, and a few others. I batted .273. Long was a good guy who had a great sense of humor and was always kidding around. He had a memorable year. His 8-day homer streak in May of 1956 was the hottest streak I have ever seen. Everything he hit in batting practice was a line drive. He was a strong man. He broke the record by hitting homers against 4 teams. He tied the record with his 6th homer in 6 games against the Phillies' Curt Simmons, who was probably the toughest left-hander in the league against left-handers. The next day he hit a ball that I was sure was going out of the park, but it faded and hit the fence. In his last at-bat, he faced Phillies relief pitcher Ben Flowers. I hated batting against Flowers because he had a pretty good knuckleball and threw it hard. But Long put a major league charge into one of his pitches. He hit it completely over everything. We mobbed him and carried him to the dugout. The next day Long hit his 8th homer against Carl Erskine in Forbes Field. Don Newcombe stopped him the next day, but he was still batting over .400. In fact, as bad as we were, we were in first place at the time. But Long cooled off and we did, too.

I thought it was a frustrating season because our manager, Bobby Bragan, kept saying we had a Triple A infield, with Long at first, Bill Mazeroski at second, me at short, and Frank Thomas at third. If he would have been more encouraging, we would have done better.

By 1956 I knew what I was capable of doing at shortstop. On the basketball court, nobody knew I was slow because my first two steps were so quick. But on the baseball field, it was obvious that I couldn't run a lick. I could never get an infield hit. So that meant, to play shortstop, I had to work and educate myself about every hitter in the National League so I would know what and where he hit. For instance, Stan Musial was a pull hitter in Busch Stadium because that was a short ballpark, but in Pittsburgh, he hit the ball everywhere. I also noted that by the mid-'50s he was slowing down a bit. I know I spent much more time than most infielders studying hitters because I knew I couldn't just wander out to short and make up for bad positioning with blinding speed.

The hardest guy for me to determine where to play was Henry Aaron. At that time Aaron was just like Bobby Clemente: he hit the ball line to line. In 1955 and 1956 I'd play him one way and he'd hit it in the hole. I'd move toward the hole and he'd hit it through the middle. You never knew. Later—to show you how great he was

as a hitter—he would change his whole style of hitting and became a dead pull hitter. He'd still hit .300 but would hit more homers. It would be easier to position myself, but I couldn't play up in the stands.

Bill Virdon became my permanent roommate and we became close, lifelong friends. He was a quiet person and we never argued. We were inseparable on the road and I'd have been lost without him. We did everything together and had great times: movies, dinner. In 1956 the Pirates had three days off in New York City and sportswriters Milt and Artie Richmond invited Bill and me to Grossinger's as their guests. We went up there and started playing golf. We fell in love with the game. (I would end up putting my life savings in a golf course outside of Pittsburgh, with Jerry Lynch as my partner, and Bill invested in a small piece of the business.)

ELROY FACE:
When Dale Long went on his rampage, it brought him nationwide attention. He was even on "The Ed Sullivan Show." He looked so good in batting practice that the other players didn't mind if he was the only one to get batting practice. We'd all stand and watch him. We were in Philadelphia toward the end of the streak and Long was late catching the bus to the park. The driver wanted to pull out, but Nellie King got out and lay down in front of the bus until Long arrived.

Bill Mazeroski was a rookie. There was no question that he was going to be a great second baseman because he had the hands and all the moves. Oddly, he had been a shortstop until Branch Rickey moved him to second in 1955. His arrival meant that we had the nucleus for what would be our 1960 title team: Groat was at short; Clemente was in right for the second year; we acquired Bill Virdon to play center—defensively, he had great speed and instincts and was even better than Willie Mays; Bob Skinner was emerging as our regular left fielder; Bob Friend and Vernon Law were starting; and I was being used strictly in relief. I pitched in 68 games, starting only 3 times. I went 12–13 with 6 saves and a 3.52 ERA, a pretty good year on a seventh-place team.

One game I threw just 5 pitches before Bragan called me in. It didn't take me long to warm up. That's because during batting practice I would field grounders on the left side of the infield and throw across to first base.

Later, it wouldn't take long to warm up because I'd already stretched my arm. Bragan knew this from managing me in 1952 at New Orleans, where he'd pitch me for an inning or two in relief between starts. He pitched me in 9 straight games in 1956, which set a record.

CINCINNATI REDS

ART FOWLER:

I had pitched over 200 innings and was the Reds' second-biggest winner in 1955, but Gabe Paul raised my salary by only $2,500 to $10,500. I again felt underpaid but still pitched well. I went 11–11 in 45 games, pitching half the time in relief and half the time as part of a strong rotation with Joe Nuxhall, Brooks Lawrence, Johnny Klippstein, and my roommate Hal Jeffcoat, who had been an outfielder.

I didn't care if I started or relieved. I just wanted to pitch. My goal was simple: if a guy on my team pitched a good game one night, I wanted to be better than him when I pitched the next day. I was never jealous of nobody, but I just tried to be better. When I pitched badly, I didn't get mad. I hated to lose and sometimes I lost my cool, but I never broke bats or threw helmets. And I never had feuds with opponents who beat me. I knew that wouldn't help anything. I tried to be loose and in the clubhouse agitated my teammates to keep them loose. I never felt pressure. I always thought that when I went into baseball I never had nothing, so I had nothing to lose. I only could gain.

In 1956 all the starters and Hershell Freeman pitched solid baseball and our offense was tremendous. I never hit a home run in my major league career, but I got a ring with the number 221 engraved on it because the Reds tied the homer record that year of the '47 Giants. In one game against Milwaukee the team smashed 8 homers. Frank Robinson hit 38 homers, Post and Kluszewski hit around 35 each, and Bell and catcher Ed Bailey had just under 30. Every time I looked up, the ball was flying out of Crosley Field. We won 91 games and almost won the pennant.

Robinson almost made the Reds in 1955 but got sick. This year he came up and had a great season. He was a super guy who didn't give anybody any trouble. He got along well with the sportswriters. What could they write bad about him? He was an outstanding player. With Bell in center and Post in right, we had a super outfield.

I liked playing with Ed Bailey. He was a good receiver and hitter. He was from Strawberry Plains, Tennessee, and you would think he was plowing with a mule all day. He didn't consider himself a celebrity. We were roommates for a while.

I didn't gamble or play cards in the clubhouse or on trains with other players. The only movies I went to were cowboy movies. I had other things to do. I didn't like to fly. I preferred the train. You've got two cars—you've got a club car where you eat. All the players would be together. We'd drink and talk about the game we just played. We lived and breathed baseball. The media would be there, too. There were no secrets.

I got more friendly on train trips with George Crowe, the big first baseman and pinch-hit specialist. We got him from the Braves for Corky Valentine and Bob Hazle. I'd be in the dining car and George would ask if he could sit with me. I'd say, "Why the hell do you ask for? Sit your ass down here." Attitudes changed after Jackie Robinson broke in. None of the black players had any trouble in the '50s.

JOHNNY KLIPPSTEIN:

George Crowe didn't care about color. If he saw you eating breakfast, he'd come over and sit down with you, which was great because he was a likable, very quiet guy. Other black players might not have felt comfortable doing that. Black and white players got along but were reluctant to do things together away from the ballpark. There was fraternization on the train, but only rarely did they go out together for dinner. I don't know why we didn't socialize, because we liked each other. I do remember when Joe Black went to a party with a bunch of us. Joe was a friendly man. He hadn't been too successful since his great rookie season in Brooklyn in 1952, and was trying to come back with us in 1955 and 1956 after the Dodgers gave up on him. Tebbetts gave a party at the end of every year for the pitchers and catchers. He had fined us during the season for various misplays and used the money to throw a party at which he'd give us dinner and gifts. Joe was the rare black guy on the staff, and he didn't want to go because the party was in Kentucky. We finally talked him into coming and he had a great time. Joe didn't drink, but he ate more than anyone else, including five or six desserts. Man, could he eat.

There were several black players on the Reds at this point, including our top pitcher, Brooks Lawrence, who won 19 games. But only Frank Robinson emerged as a leader. He was a quiet guy, but he was definitely a leader because everyone admired him. He hit 38 homers to set a rookie record. He also hit .290 and led the league in runs scored. For a big man, he was very fast and was a tremendous baserunner. He was one of the greatest competitors I ever saw. He reminded me of Jackie Robinson: he was that tough. He stood on top of the plate and would always get hit on the arm or leg, but he'd never even rub. If you knocked him down, he'd get up and hit the ball out of the park.

If there was another leader on the team, it was our second baseman, Johnny Temple. He was a tiger. He was outgoing and the most outspoken player we had. He would make it known if we weren't hustling, and would get on certain players. He did it to Kluszewski one time—of course, that was the only time. Klu just picked him up with one hand and said, "Shut up!" and put him down. Kluszewski was a stabilizer. Of course, he was too big to argue with. He was great to play with because he was a good competitor and a helluva hitter. We had a lot of sluggers, including Robinson, Post, Bell, and even Ed Bailey, but Kluszewski was the guy we still counted on. In 1956, with all our hitting, he led the team in average and was our only player to drive in over 100 runs.

Wally Post had great power. He hit 40 homers in 1955 and 36 in 1956. He and Bell were both terrific guys. Gus wasn't a great outfielder, didn't have a great arm, and didn't have great power, but he did everything well and was a good ballplayer. He was as steady as they come.

Ed Bailey first played with the Reds in 1953, but didn't become the regular catcher until '56. "Gar"— which was short for Edgar—hit .300 and had 28 homers in fewer than 400 at-bats. When he caught, you could shake him off most of the time. But late one game I was pitching to Hank Aaron with 2 men on. I shook him off about 6 times because I wanted him to call for my slider. Tebbetts finally came out and asked what was going on. Ed said, "He wants to throw a slider." So Tebbetts

asked him why he wouldn't put down that sign. Ed's response was "Because he don't have a slider." Tebbetts said, "Well, he thinks he has a slider. Call for it, or it will cost you money." So I threw a slider to Aaron and he hit a line drive that Temple caught in the web of his glove, jumping as high as he could. Bailey walks into the clubhouse and calls to me, "Hey, wise guy, you still don't have any damn slider." He had a mind of his own, but we got along well.

Not only did we have great hitters in the lineup, but we also had great guys on the bench, including two of baseball's all-time great pinch hitters, Smoky Burgess and George Crowe. (In 1957 we'd add another one, Jerry Lynch!) We also had another good left-handed pinch hitter, Bob Thurman. At the time we had 3 of the best-fielding shortstops in the league: Roy McMillan, Rocky Bridges, and Alex Grammas. So Tebbetts would pinch-hit for a shortstop or two in the sixth or eighth and not hurt our club.

At the beginning of the season, Tebbetts had a pitchers' meeting and told us, "They bum-rapped our staff. All you guys would run through the wall for me and do anything to win. We've got a good pitching staff, so don't believe what you read." That was great to hear. What we didn't know is that two weeks later he called in the hitters and catchers and said, "Boys, you know what kind of pitching staff we have. We've got to score a whole lot of runs." He was a good psychologist because we finished only 2 games behind the Dodgers, despite having a mediocre pitching staff. Like all the pitchers, I benefited from our offense. I pitched a career-high 211 innings, which was only 8 innings less than Lawrence, had career highs with 29 starts, 11 complete games, and 12 victories, losing 11.

My highlight was pitching 7 innings of hitless ball against the Braves on May 26. They had scored a run and Tebbetts took me out for a pinch hitter in the top of the eighth. Everyone was really mad but me. I knew we had to win the game. Hershell Freeman and Joe Black relieved me and the Braves didn't get a hit until there were two outs in the tenth. Then they won in the eleventh. (Not many would remember this game, but oddly, *exactly* 3 years later, in a famous game on May 26, 1959, the Braves would beat the Pirates despite Harvey Haddix no-hitting them for 12 innings!)

HERSHELL FREEMAN:

We turned the Reds' program around and became contenders. When there's just a week to go and you are still in the race with Brooklyn and Milwaukee, that's exciting. I had never been in a race before, so I was eating it up. Everybody was having a good year, not just me. It would have been the greatest thing to have gone to a World Series, but Brooklyn ended up two games ahead of us and Milwaukee one game up. We gave it a good shot, but it wasn't meant to be.

I had my best year in baseball. I appeared in 64 games and pitched over 100 innings. I won 14 games and saved more than that. Not every pitcher can be a reliever. You have to have the type of arm that will respond the next day. I could pitch an inning or two 5, 6, 7, or 8 days in a row. At one point I won both ends of a twinight doubleheader and then won another game the next afternoon.

Although the Reds' batters boomed a National League record 221 homers in 1956, no one overlooked the tremendous contributions of reliever Hershell Freeman, who won 14 games and saved 18 others.

We had a lot of home run hitters who stood close to the plate. If the other team brushed back or knocked down one of my teammates, I retaliated. I had to protect him. I was 6'3" and between 215 and 225 pounds, so batters didn't want me getting after them. I wouldn't let a batter take the plate away from me. If I had to brush a guy back, I'd do it. But I didn't intentionally hit anyone. If I hit him, it would be in the leg. There wasn't a place for pitchers who wanted to throw at batters' heads. You can kill a man with a baseball without any problem. Thank God, I never hit anybody in the head.

I was primarily a fastball pitcher with a three-quarters delivery. I threw up in the 90s and my fastball sank, breaking down and in to a right-handed hitter. It was a heavy pitch. Smoky Burgess said it was like catching a shot put. I also threw a curveball. In 1956 I started messing around with a forkball, which ElRoy Face was throwing for Pittsburgh. I found it easy to pick up because I had big hands that I could almost wrap around a ball. But my out pitch was still my fastball. I was a fast worker. I thought it was cooler in the dugout than standing out in the hot sun. I liked that Smoky was a fast-working catcher. Ed Bailey shared the catching with Smoky and also was great to pitch to. But he liked to talk to everybody and sometimes didn't work as fast as I'd have liked. I wanted to just get it over with.

Smoky was my best friend on the Reds. He was a nice, clean-living person who didn't smoke or drink. Neither of us drank, which is a reason we ran around together all the time. If you saw Smoky on a road trip, I was close by, or vice versa. He was very popular. Smoky never met a stranger. He was easy to talk to and was always willing to give time to a sportswriter or radio or TV people.

Most of the time at Cincinnati, I roomed with Roy McMillan. He was one of the all-time great shortstops. He won a lot of games with his glove, so all he had to do was hit .240 or .250 and it was like he was a .500 hitter. Roy was laid back when he played, but if someone made him mad he wouldn't hesitate to go after him.

His double-play partner, Johnny Temple, was an Eddie Stanky type who would challenge anyone. He even challenged Klu one day in the dugout. Everybody laughed, even Klu. Johnny realized how it sounded and he laughed. He was quite a ballplayer. He was in a lot of almost fights, but any time one broke out, Johnny was there, guaranteed. He was a tough guy.

On occasion I roomed with Klu. He was so big that players joked you could tell where he was staying in the hotel by the way it was leaning. When Klu would come in after a ballgame, he was always carrying one egg-and-ham sandwich he bought for himself and one he bought for me. I might be in bed reading or sacked out. He'd say, "Okay, roomie, here's your sandwich." I might say, "I don't want it, Klu." The next thing you know, my mattress is on the floor and I'm eating the sandwich. You didn't jump up and argue with him, not as big as he was. He was like a big kid. We used to fish together in spring training.

I think Kluszewski was the leader of the team, the captain. Nobody objected to him. He was a big, easygoing guy. He'd been a second-string All-American at Indiana. His teammate Pete Pihos, who later was a receiver for the Eagles, said that "if you ran around him, you were out of bounds."

Rocky Bridges was just a good ol' tobacco-chewing country boy who had just enough ability to play in the majors. He was a good glove man and would never hurt us. I think he slept with tobacco in his mouth. I remember getting up a lot of times and getting on the elevator to go down to breakfast and there was Rocky with his big chew in his mouth. We always accused him of putting tobacco on his cereal. He was a helluva guy.

We had the best outfield in baseball. Wally Post was very easygoing: a good hitter, a good team man, a helluva family man. I was happy to have him behind me because I knew he'd get me a run sooner or later. Gus Bell was one of the all-time great center fielders, a good hitter, a good team man, a good all-around ballplayer. Frank Robinson was an exceptional ballplayer. A pitcher doesn't like a hitter to take the plate away from him, but Robbie would take it away even if it meant getting hit. He got nailed many times, but he'd brush it off and come right back and beat the pitcher. He was young and like a kid, but he settled in real quick. He wasn't a standoffish black and became one of the guys as soon as he came up.

All the black players were part of the team. Bob Thurman, who had been in the Negro Leagues, couldn't break into our outfield, but he was a terrific power hitter who hit a lot of pinch homers. George Crowe was another tremendous pinch hitter, even better than Thurman. He could play first base with the best of them and was a good team man. He had a very good head on his shoulders but wasn't really an outgoing guy, and I think he kept a lot inside that he needed to say. Brooks Lawrence worked as hard as anyone at being a good pitcher and he was our best starter. He usually left the game with a lead—he would have told you that I helped him win a lot of ballgames.

We had a standing rule on the Reds: if a pitcher missed a ball hit through the middle or off the dirt part of the mound, within reason, Birdie would fine him $25, and that would go into a kitty for a party for pitchers at the end of the year. Roy McMillan saved old Hersh a lot of $25 fines—but he wasn't invited. We'd have the party at Russ Olster's across the river. A bunch of us at that time lived in Swifton Village, an apartment complex out toward Hamilton from Crosley Field. They'd say, "Okay, Hersh, you're driving tonight, so we can have a few." You knew guys like Nuxhall and Fowler were going to bend their elbows, but they'd never let it control their baseball lives—if they did, they wouldn't stay around.

Nuxhall was a country boy, even though he was from Ohio. He never changed. He didn't have an enemy in the world, but he'd walk out to that mound and he was a tough pitcher. Fowler had the most remarkable arm I ever saw in my life. He could walk on the field and snap his fingers and be ready to pitch. More than any other pitcher, he hated running with a passion. He said many times, "You don't run that ball across the plate, you throw it across the plate." He was a drinker, but it didn't affect his pitching. If you were out at a party with Art, you knew he'd drink.

In the middle '50s, relief pitchers became part of the makeup of a ballclub. Before that, everyone thought relievers weren't good enough to do anything else. Relief pitching became a special form of pitching. Still, I probably would have made more money if I were a starter with a 14–5 record. At least I felt the Reds were fair to me. On our last road trip, Gabe Paul called my room and told me to come to his room to talk about the next year's contract. Well, you get on the elevator and say to yourself what you'll ask for, probably more than what you expect to get. Gabe says, "You had a helluva year, and I want to offer you so-and-so." And I say, "I think I deserve so-and-so." And you strike a happy medium, everybody shakes hands, and you walk out happy. As far as money goes, I came along 20 or 25 years too soon.

AMERICAN LEAGUE

1956

"I WAS SITTING NEXT TO MANTLE AND SHOWED HIM THAT I COULD PREDICT ALL THE PITCHES. HE SAID, 'GOD ALMIGHTY, LET'S WORK SOMETHING OUT.' SO DURING ALL MY YEARS IN NEW YORK, MICKEY AND I WOULD HAVE ALL KINDS OF SIGNS BASED ON MY WHISTLING TO LET HIM KNOW WHAT WAS COMING. HE LEARNED FROM ME."

BOB TURLEY

Due to lack of playing time, Athletics slugger Gus Zernial had his worst season in 1956, but he would rebound in 1957 for his sixth season with over 25 homers.

KANSAS CITY ATHLETICS

GUS ZERNIAL:

I batted only about 270 times for Lou Boudreau in 1956 and hit just 16 homers. We won only 52 games and finished in last place. It was pretty much a lost season.

Vic Power was one of our few players who had a good season. But he got into trouble in Kansas City. He was a young buck, like we all were at one time. He made a few mistakes and it got out big. Boudreau and the organization handled it pretty well. Vic wasn't a disruptive influence.

JOE DE MAESTRI:

I think Vic was going with a white girl from Kansas at that time. They were seen together quite a bit, and our management was really quite upset about it because it was getting a lot of negative feedback from the law. I can't remember it really bothering anybody on the team. It certainly didn't bother me. I suppose management told Vic either to quit dating her or to go where they wouldn't be seen.

Vic got along with his teammates, but he did have a run-in with Timmy Thompson, who alternated with Hal Smith as the A's catcher in 1956 and 1957. One night in 1956 Thompson went to catch a pop foul and Vic came racing down from first base and barreled right into him. Vic made the catch, of course, and Thompson went flying. Both were tough cookies and they took swings at each other in the dugout. Later, Boudreau called Thompson into his office and chewed him out for starting the fight. Thompson was upset Boudreau didn't also chew out Power. Because of his days in Cleveland when he managed Larry Doby, Luke Easter, and Satchel Paige, Boudreau had a reputation for favoring black players. Which was fine. This incident affirmed that reputation among our players.

VIC POWER:

I couldn't understand why everyone got so upset when I went out with light-skinned women in Kansas City. In Puerto Rico there was no such thing as color. There were many black players like Willie Mays and Roberto Clemente who dated white women, just as there were white players who went out with black women. So it made me mad that they had better reputations than me because they did it secretly. If they went to a motel, they would each get a room and get together later. If I went out with a white girl, I'd just go. We'd sit down and listen to music, in public. I'd drive around in my Cadillac with the top down. I didn't hide that my closest friend in town was a white woman. She appreciated art, which was one of my hobbies, and she liked to watch me play baseball. I had problems with the restaurants in Kansas City that wouldn't serve blacks, so we stopped in front and she went in to get the food. They didn't like that kind of behavior. When Boudreau told the unmarried players they could bring a girl, a friend, to a team picnic, they didn't like it when I brought her.

But no one could complain about my production. Boudreau shifted me back and forth between first, second, and the outfield, yet I still hit .309 and again made the All-Star team. I had 5 hits in a game twice in a month.

CLEVELAND INDIANS

AL SMITH:

I wasn't offered a fair salary after the 1955 season. Hank Greenberg was a nice person, but he was a tough negotiator and he was hard to budge. In those days you'd hear guys talking a bit about their salaries, usually griping because they were getting less than they deserved. When you'd try to get a $10,000 to $12,000 raise, which was a substantial raise then, it was like pulling teeth.

I didn't get the money I wanted, but I had another good year. Unfortunately, Larry Doby had been traded in the off-season and our offense wasn't as good overall as it had been. However, we got a boost from rookie outfielder Rocky Colavito, who hit over 20 homers. I could tell he was going to become a big home run hitter once he played a little more. Rocky was a helluva guy and kept everyone laughing. We had a lot of fun with him and would tease him because he threw the ball so hard and because of his flat feet.

Rocky was good friends with Herb Score, who was another congenial, religious man. Score was even better in 1956 than in his rookie year. He matched Early Wynn and Bob Lemon with 20 wins, and again led the league in strikeouts. At the time I thought Wynn, Lemon and the Tigers' Jim Bunning were the toughest right-handers in the league, and Score was the toughest left-hander.

Colavito and Score were welcome additions to an otherwise veteran Indians team. Everybody liked them. I like to think I was also popular with my teammates. They called me "Fuzzy" because hair would grow so fast on my face. I always needed a shave.

GENE WOODLING:

If anybody ever had angel's wings on him, it was Rocky Colavito. He was a good ballplayer, not great. Other than having a great arm, he didn't have much natural ability and had to work hard at everything he did. I admired him for accomplishing so much.

Al Lopez was a great person, a ballplayer's manager. We had a lot of respect for him when I was on the Yankees. It's too bad he had to finish second behind the Yankees in 1951, 1952, and 1953 before the Indians finally beat us out in 1954. Then I came over to the Indians and we finished second to the Yankees in 1955 and 1956.

CHICO CARRASQUEL:

I was happy to get an opportunity to play in Cleveland. I loved playing for Al Lopez, who had been my manager at the 1955 All-Star Game in Milwaukee. He was a real good man and a real good manager. I appreciated that he spoke to me in Spanish.

The Indians had a lot of talented veterans from the 1954 championship team, as well as Herb Score. They improved themselves by trading for me to play short-

stop and by bringing up Rocky Colavito. Rocky was a young man who had good power and had the best arm in the league. He would get better every year. He was a real friendly boy. Rocky, Bobby Avila, Al Rosen, Jim Hegan, and George Strickland, another shortstop, were my best friends on the team.

I enjoyed my first year with the Indians, beginning at spring training in Tucson. I loved to eat and they had every kind of food there. Coming over from the White Sox after spending my entire career with them turned out to be easier than I thought because the Indians players were so friendly. I also liked my living situation. I lived in a downtown hotel close to Municipal Stadium and everything was nearby, which made it easier than in Chicago, where we'd have to take long, expensive taxi rides. The only sad moment of the year was when my brothers called me from Caracas to tell me that our father had died.

Displaced by Luis Aparicio in Chicago, Chico Carrasquel welcomed the opportunity to be the Cleveland Indians' starting shortstop.

NATIONAL BASEBALL LIBRARY, COOPERSTOWN, N.Y.

BALTIMORE ORIOLES

BROOKS ROBINSON:

In 1956 Richards had all the young guys come to Arizona in the middle of February, two weeks before training camp. He didn't just have three-hour sessions: it was daylight to dawn. Then, when the exhibition season started, we worked out in the morning and got on the bus and went to Tucson or Mesa to play a game, and then returned to our camp and usually had some extra hitting practice. That was Richards's accelerated program to try to get us to the big leagues. His coaches worked harder than anyone.

Bill Krueger and Al Vincent were instructors with the Orioles in spring training, and they worked a lot with me on playing third base. They knew I could catch the ball, but they told me one very helpful thing, which was to get my glove down to the ground as soon as the ball was hit, instead of waiting until just before it reached me. So I worked on that until it became automatic to put the glove right on the ground as soon as the ball was hit. I always had great hand-eye coordination and was blessed with the instinct to be where the ball was hit. What makes some infielders great is that they were born with that instinct. Infielders have to find out how to best get a jump on the ball. You have to find your own way. I did it a little differently than other third basemen. My style would never change. I didn't like to be in a dead-stop position, so I moved a little, like a tennis player waiting for a serve. I didn't commit myself one way or the other, but I'd kind of walk into a play, taking a half step, and when that guy was swinging the bat I liked to have my feet parallel with one another and be in motion. I wasn't fast and didn't have a great arm, yet I compensated by quickly getting my feet in position to throw and getting rid of the ball quicker than anyone else. That's what enabled me to play third.

I also learned just from watching George Kell. As a youngster I admired him, so it was a thrill to play with him when he came to the Orioles in 1956. He took me under his wing and helped me adjust to the big leagues. He even took me to my first stage play in New York. At the time I was making $6,000, the major league minimum. I found out that George made $30,000, and I decided making that kind of money would be my goal because it would make me rich.

GEORGE KELL:
I was reunited with Paul Richards at Baltimore. He and I would play golf every day. He was always being innovative, and in spring training he devised a new bunt strategy. With men on first and second, he didn't want the batter to deaden the ball to third base, which was the customary play, but to bunt it hard past the pitcher toward second. He figured the second baseman would be running to cover either second or first if the first baseman ran toward the plate. In either case, he'd be on the move. Since I was a veteran who made contact and had good bat control, he had me attempt the play. It worked just as he had planned and we ended up with the bases loaded. We didn't have occasion to use Richards's play during the regular season until late in the year. Then I came up in a similar bunting situation with men on first and second. Richards gave me a look and I knew what he was thinking, so I bunted hard toward second. And again we ended up with the bases loaded. Richards was so excited. It was like winning the World Series to him because he had introduced a play to major league baseball and it had worked.

I remember Richards went to the mound one game to take out Billy Loes, and Loes started arguing with him

in front of the crowd. One thing a player doesn't do is show up a manager on the field, especially not Paul Richards. So Richards told Loes not to shower but to come directly to his office after the game. The rest of the players could hear Richards and Loes really going at it, both with raised voices. Suddenly the door flew open and the defeated Loes came out and announced, "He thinks he's God!" Well, Richards was the manager, so he was God on the Orioles.

Richards also had conflict with a few other players. Bob Nieman, a power-hitting outfielder, didn't think Richards played him enough or gave him enough respect. Richards was always criticizing him for making mistakes.

If there was a team leader, it was Gus Triandos. We became very close friends. He was the catcher and probably the best hitter on the team. He was a big, strong power hitter who got everything out of himself. Richards liked him.

When I first saw Brooks Robinson I could see that he could play third base. He had all the moves and the instincts. Many third basemen just grab the ball and can't wait to get rid of it. Even as a youngster, Brooks never hurried his throws. However, I never thought he'd be a good hitter. Pitchers would throw him higher and higher and he'd keep swinging. I said he'd never hit a lick, but I was as wrong as could be. I didn't realize what was inside of him. He was determined to be a good ballplayer. It would be written so many times that I helped him develop into a great third baseman that I would tell Brooks that I liked getting the credit. But it's not true. What I did for Brooks was teach him how a big leaguer is supposed to live. I took him under my wing and took him to good restaurants and we'd have breakfast and talk. I related my experiences as a young ballplayer, and I think that helped him adjust to the major leagues. Brooks and I were raised 90 miles apart, went to the same church, had the same family background, had the same goal of being a big league ballplayer despite having no real chance. In baseball, Brooks Robinson, Al Kaline, and Harmon Killebrew were the three players who were my idea of outstanding Christian gentlemen on and off the field. I admired them so much and they went on to become everything I thought they'd be.

RYNE DUREN:

In the spring I wouldn't throw as hard as I could because subconsciously I was scared of that excruciating pain in my elbow. So the Orioles sent me to Vancouver. Lefty O'Doul was my manager. He reeked of liquor on the bench a few times—a couple of times he didn't even make it to the game—and he had quite a temper—he'd lost his eye in a bar fight. He was a helluva guy anyway, a great kidder and a great teacher. He was kind of a father figure. I was 0–7 when he said, ''You know, Ryne, the reason you don't have any control is because you don't know how to move the ball.'' So he got a catcher and took me out to the mound. After I warmed up, he told me to ''throw a pitch that you consider high and tight to a right-handed hitter.'' So I threw it close to the plate. He said, ''Nah, that's not high and tight. I mean high and tight.'' So he instructed the catcher, Lennie Neal, to put his mitt far to his left so that if I were throwing to a right-handed hitter I'd be aiming for behind his head. So I threw it there. And Lefty said, ''That's not high and tight.'' So I said, ''Where the fuck do you want it?'' and threw the son of a bitch out of the stadium.

He said, ''Yeah, now you're getting it.'' Then he had me ''throw one low and away.'' I threw one way off to the side and into the dirt. And he said, ''That's right, that's low and away.'' So I kept throwing the ball all over the stadium and out of the stadium as he gave new instructions. He said, ''Now you've got it.''

Everybody had been standing around laughing, but now Lefty got dead serious. He said, ''Look in the dirt at where your steps are.'' I could see that I stepped differently when I threw to different locations. Before, I had been stepping the identical way on all pitches. He said, ''I want you to think about pitching inside and outside and getting your body into it so you move in different ways. And when you're warming up, I don't want you to throw strikes. I want you to throw high and low, outside and inside. I want you to develop a sense of touch so that you can tell when you're not throwing right. Then you can bring the ball in.'' He was absolutely right. I became very sensitive about the rest of my body when I pitched, and that helped me develop enough control so that I could pitch in the majors. It took me seven years in the minors for someone to ex-

plain to me how to *pitch*. Then Lefty taught me how to *win*. I said to hell with my pain and started striking out hitters again. I went to 11–11 on a last-place team. But Baltimore still didn't bring me up in 1956. And in the winter they traded me to Kansas City.

BOSTON RED SOX

FRANK MALZONE:

I believe the Red Sox had planned for me to be their starting third baseman in 1956. Unfortunately, that winter I lost my first child, who was just over a year old. She got sick and we took her to the hospital, and they called us the next morning and told us that she died overnight. It hit me and my wife really hard. We went to spring training in Sarasota and pulled into the same place we'd stayed the previous spring and people asked, ''Where's Suzanne?'' We started crying again. I made the team but had a terrible time playing baseball. The first part of the year I might as well not have been there because I couldn't function. I hit .165 and I dropped pop-ups and did everything wrong. Higgins had to give Billy Klaus the third-base job, and after a month and a half of nonproductivity, I was sent back to AAA. This time I went to San Francisco. My wife, our baby son, and I drove out to California. After we were there a week, we met a priest and he talked to us about our situation. He was able to settle my wife down a little bit, and that helped me settle down. And I went on to hit close to .300 and revive my career.

PUMPSIE GREEN:

I went to spring training at the Red Sox minor league camp in De Land, Florida. Earl Wilson and I both wound up at Albany in the Eastern League. I wasn't thinking of the majors at this time. I was just trying to play baseball and have a good year and go as far as I could. I thought I was lucky to even be in a major league organization. I had seen so many guys in high school and college who were better players than me. I used to admire those guys. But none of them became pros.

WASHINGTON SENATORS

HARMON KILLEBREW:

I started out the year with the Senators but pinch-hit more than I played in the field. Since I had been with the Senators for two years to fulfill my bonus-player requirement, they sent me to Charlotte in the Sally League. I thought that was a good idea because I needed to play every day. I had a lot of success, hitting .325, with 16 homers and over 60 RBIs in only about 250 at-bats.

PEDRO RAMOS:

My first year in Washington, I lived on 14th and O and then I moved to what was called Potomac Housing on 25th and K. I adjusted to life in the big leagues and in America. I had a good year on the field, going 12–10 for my only winning season with Washington—Chuck Stubbs, who went 15–15, was our only other pitcher to have more than 6 victories—and I enjoyed myself off the field as well.

In the apartment, Pascual and I did a little cooking Cuban style. Often we'd go to a place called the Blue Moon in downtown Washington. I used to go to a lot of American places to eat. In New York, Camilo and I would go to Cuban restaurants, but I got used to the American food. I got into the habit of eating steaks and salads. Chicken in a basket with potatoes and a glass of milk was 75 cents.

One of my hobbies was listening to music. I liked Cuban music, I liked Mexican music, I liked country and western. I liked piano, and was a fan of Russ Williams and Carmen Caballero. I liked violins. I liked Frank Sinatra. I wasn't crazy about rock and roll and Elvis Presley—although I wore sideburns.

I loved visiting New York City. I'd go to 42nd Street because I liked all the movies and all those people. They had arcades and I'd shoot the rifles. We'd go to a movie at 10 A.M. and then go to another movie. Camilo, Jose Valdivielso, and I would see two or three movies a day.

If you traveled, you had to wear a necktie. At the hotel you didn't have to wear a tie, but you had to have a jacket. Later on they changed it so you'd just have to wear a sweater. It could be comfortable, but it had to be decent. I liked cowboy clothes, cowboy movies—I'd see them ten times each to help me with my English—anything that smelled Western. When we went to Kansas City, Clint Courtney wanted to buy some cows and I went along with him because I loved anything that smelled of country. Then we went to a Western store that sold guns, gun belts, boots, hats, and suits. So I bought everything. I put the guns in my suitcase, but I wore the clothes on that road trip. I had stetson hats, black suits like Hopalong Cassidy, fringed jackets. One day I walked in downtown Washington with my gun belts on. The people didn't know if they were real guns—they were real. I dressed Western when I went to the ballpark, but without guns. I wasn't rowdy. I was just having fun.

I learned that players never went out with the manager. And players couldn't go in the hotel bar because he'd be there. The coaches could do that. I thought it should be the other way around. The players would go out on the street and get drunk and then they'd have to find their way home instead of just falling asleep.

I didn't drink too much, maybe a beer. But I'd be lying if I said I didn't go out with a lot of women. I was a bachelor and dated a lot. Charlie Dressen used to call two or three of us "night riders." Every team had a few. Let's say we'd get to Detroit or Chicago and wouldn't play until the next day. You'd get off the plane and go to a bar and have a drink. If something came along you can scout and sign, let's go. Sometimes you didn't have to look for them: they'd scout you. In Chicago I was in my hotel room and a girl called me and said, "I saw you on the field, I'd like to meet you." So she invited me to meet her in the coffee shop. And I hoped she wouldn't be too ugly. When I got down and saw her, I said, "Man, she can play in the big leagues." I wasn't making that much money, yet had a lot of girls chasing me, which makes me wonder about players once salaries went up. Whatever hotel or ballpark I went, I saw girls looking for somebody. There were phone calls. Some guys were going to play around, some weren't going to play around, no matter what. Not too many married guys fooled around, and if they did, they did it quietly. It was the same with some of the clean-cut single guys. Anyway, I didn't have the time to check out the other players because I was off doing my own thing.

I never saw a fight between a player and someone in a bar. If there was the chance of a fight, I'd just hit the first door I'd see. No one ever bothered me. If I saw a girl with a man, I looked the other way. If he went to the bathroom and I didn't know about him, I asked if she had company. If she said she did, I put several chairs between us. I played carefully, more carefully than I pitched to Mickey Mantle. I picked the right girls because I didn't want problems. There were a lot of girls in town, so why should I pick one that would give me trouble? I liked Jewish girls. I used to go out with a girl in Boston, and her mother told me not to call her anymore because she was Jewish. I didn't know Jewish girls weren't supposed to go out with non-Jewish guys. I said I wouldn't call her anymore, but if she called me I'd still go out with her. She called.

Charlie Dressen always tried to catch guys breaking curfew. But he liked me and would call from his hiding place, "Hurry up, hurry up." I never missed a curfew, a bus, or a plane. If I had to be at the park at 5 P.M., I'd get there at 4 P.M. and be in uniform at 4:30. The only day I would arrive late at the ballpark was Sunday. I was Catholic, in my way, and at the beginning of my career I went to church every Sunday. Not to pray, but I went to church. We were given an extra hour to get to the ballpark.

I didn't like pitching in Kansas City, Detroit, or Baltimore. I didn't like the cities or the ballparks. I liked Fenway Park, though most pitchers didn't like it there because of the short fence. And I liked pitching in Yankee Stadium, although Mickey Mantle almost hit one of my fastballs out of the park on May 30. The count was 2–2 and I didn't want to walk him. I wanted Mantle to hit it, but he hit it too far. I thought it was just a fly ball, but it went 117 feet off the ground and hit the façade, just 18 inches from going out of the Stadium. No one ever came that close. I wasn't mad. I respected him for that. He was so strong. If you were a right-hander like I was, you tried to bust him inside or throw low and away and pray he didn't smash it back to the mound. But occasionally I'd challenge him and he hit a few homers off me. The only difference with that homer was that it was a little longer than the others. I never saw Mickey hit a cheap homer. He could have hit more in another park because I saw him hit so many balls to the monuments about 460 feet from home. In 1953 at Griffith Stadium

he hit a 565-foot homer off Chuck Stobbs. Chuck said he looked up and thought it was going into the Potomac River. And he didn't throw as hard as I did.

DETROIT TIGERS

FRED HATFIELD:

I had played several years, but I was never an established ballplayer. Nobody built a team around me. I felt I could play and thought I was pretty good trade bait if a team didn't want to keep me, so I didn't worry about being traded. I wanted to be on a pennant winner, but I knew a lot of the clubs I was on weren't going to win, especially during those lean years in Detroit. Like a lot of guys, I hoped to get traded to the Yankees, thinking it would be great to get some of that World Series money. I didn't go to the Yankees when the Tigers traded me in May, but at least I went to a better team, the Chicago White Sox.

HAL WOODESHICK:

The Detroit organization was interested in me because I had beaten their Durham team so many times when I pitched for Danville. Frank Skaff, the Durham manager, recommended that I be drafted from the Giants' organization, so I went to Charleston, West Virginia, the Tigers' Triple A team. It was a big jump from B to Triple A. Charlie Metro was the manager, and he didn't think I was worthy of pitching for him after so big a jump. We were playing Denver in the rarified air and they were clobbering us every game. I was laughing in the shower and Metro asked angrily what I thought was so funny. I said, "What the hell can I cry about? I didn't pitch." So he said, "As soon as we get back to Charleston, you're pitching against Denver." So I pitched against Denver and lost 1–0 on a ninth-inning homer. And instead of Metro saying, "Nice game," he said, "If you want to stay in Triple A, you have to pitch like that." A couple of weeks later, Metro was let go. Frank Skaff became the manager and I was moved into the starting rotation with Jim Bunning, Duke Maas, and Gene Host, a left-hander.

Bunning was my roommate. He was a great person. He had something about him, and I could tell he was going to be successful in the majors. Jim would have

After many setbacks, Hal Woodeshick finally got an opportunity to pitch in the majors when he was brought up for a brief period by the Detroit Tigers.

made it to the Tigers sooner, but had been going to college at Xavier and was always late coming to spring training. He had briefly pitched with the Tigers in 1955, but wasn't quite ready. At Charleston I was going great guns and the Tigers were thinking of bringing me up in mid-season. Instead they brought up Bunning, and that's when he really got going, winning 5 of 6 decisions. He became a Hall of Fame–caliber pitcher.

I won 13 games and made the All-Star team, so the Tigers brought me up at the end of the season. The guys who came up for the Tigers lived at a downtown hotel. It was across the street from a pool hall and beer garden, and all the ballplayers used to loaf there. The Tigers were a close, very humble group. Ray Boone, Steve Gromek, and Al Kaline were extremely kind to me and my fiancée. Kaline was a star, a .300 hitter who drove in over 125 runs that year, yet he was just one of the guys. One day at the ballpark he asked me if I'd ever been to a horse race. I told him I hadn't, and soon after he picked me up and took me to the track. That made me feel welcome.

Bucky Harris was the Tigers' manager. He said, "So you're the phenom from Triple A. Well, son, we'll let you pitch against the Yankees to see how good you are." So in my first game I started against the Yankees in Detroit, going against Don Larsen. At the time I threw only a sinking fastball. I didn't get the first 8 guys out and was relieved that the pitcher was coming up, but Larsen hit the ball off the center-field wall. It was a disaster. I pitched one other time, starting 4 days later against the Red Sox with Ted Williams, Jackie Jensen, and Jim Piersall, and I couldn't get them out either. After those 2 games I thought I didn't belong in the big leagues. Kaline, Kuenn, and those guys treated me fantastically. They wanted me to do well and told me to hang in there. A young kid could really get down on himself.

CHICAGO WHITE SOX

BILLY PIERCE:

I had been married in 1949, and in the off-season, we moved back to Highland Park, Michigan. During the season I'd say three-quarters of the White Sox rented apartments in hotels in the Hyde Park area of Chicago, between 53rd and 57th, from the Lake Shore Drive to about a mile west. There were many furnished apartment hotels where players and their families stayed. Most of the time we stayed at either the Flamingo Hotel or the Shoreland Hotel. Players didn't like to rent houses outside of the city because transportation was difficult. The wives got along well together. So when we'd go on the road for ten days to two weeks, they would get together, especially those with young children.

On the road, Nellie Fox and I would stick together year after year. We were very, very close. He wouldn't go to movies with me, but we'd always eat together. Nellie was a meat-and-potatoes man. When some player would say they discovered a great fish place, Nellie would ask if they had steak there before agreeing to go. He was also a big breakfast eater because he came from a rural area of Pennsylvania. He loved ham and eggs. On the field he chewed tobacco, and off the field he smoked cigars. However, if I was going to pitch the next day, he wouldn't smoke cigars in our room. His wife,

Joanne, would complain to me that he would not smoke for me but not for her.

Nellie was a fantastic competitor, on and off the field. Almost every night after a road game, he and I played gin rummy. He could win a bunch of hands, but if he lost one hand he'd get so mad. One time someone gave him some dice. We were about to go eat prior to a game when he suggested we roll the dice a few times for a dollar or so. He got behind and refused to quit. We got to the ballpark on time, but we didn't eat dinner that night.

Nellie was the aggressive leader on the team. He always gave 100 percent and other players were motivated by him. He'd dive for pop flies. If he got hit by a pitch or was racked up at second, he'd come right back for more. He had a lot of confidence and we picked up on that. Even if Herb Score was pitching and Nellie made an out, he'd come back to the dugout and say, "He hasn't got anything. You guys can hit him." He would always be talking on the field, keeping us on our toes, cheering us on. He just loved to play.

That year, Nellie got a new double-play partner. The Sox had traded Chico Carrasquel to Cleveland because rookie Luis Aparicio could take his place. Luis had a bit more range, especially since Chico got a little heavier. I won 20 games for the first time, so I couldn't complain. I felt lucky—it was nice to pitch having great fielders like Chico and Luis at short.

CHICO CARRASQUEL (INDIANS):

I watched Luis Aparicio play in Caracas from the time he was a young boy. His father was one of the greatest shortstops to play in Venezuela. He was called "Luis le Grande." As Luis got older and played professional ball, I saw that he had the talent to play in the major leagues. I was responsible for the White Sox signing him. In 1954 I called Frank Lane from Caracas and told him about Aparicio. Lane said I should bring him to the States. He was assigned to Waterloo, in Class A, and then Memphis. In 1956 he was ready to play in the big leagues. So I got traded to Cleveland to make room for him. I was happy to help him. And he was always grateful and told sportswriters about me. When I was on Cleveland I talked to him almost every day. On my first trip back to Chicago, Luis was waiting for me. He told me, "I want to go home." "Why?" "Because Income Tax took all my money." "Speak to the White Sox. I know they're going to help you." "No, no, no. I want to go home tomorrow." "Luis, you can't go home. You've proved to everybody that you can play in the big leagues. And it's because of you I now play in Cleveland. So you better stay here." That's when Aparicio started to collect his salary without being taxed. The White Sox paid his tax in order to keep him in America.

B. PIERCE:

Larry Doby joined the White Sox in 1956. He hit a 3-run homer for us his first time up. Larry was a good ballplayer. He led our team in homers and RBIs and was a good outfielder. Minoso, Doby, and, say, Dropo, Lollar, or Rivera, gave us a great middle of the order. They'd always pick up Aparicio and Fox.

I was the player rep on the White Sox, and I think it was Minoso and Doby who came up to me one day in spring training. At that time blacks couldn't stay in the same hotels as white players in Florida. I asked how things were going. "Wonderful, Billy, it's great. They gave us a car.... But there's one thing wrong. You've got to get that Chicago reporter out of there." Their only complaint was that a Negro sports reporter was staying there and bugging them with questions. So I'd have to say that by the mid-1950s black players didn't have many problems adjusting to the majors. I never noticed an incident of bad race relations in my career. Players knew that if they didn't get along with their teammates they wouldn't win. It bothers me when black players from that period say they would have wanted to mingle more with white players. Then why didn't they? I never saw an instance of a black player wanting to converse with a white player and being snubbed. I never saw anyone shunned. It may have happened, but I didn't see it.

Marty Marion managed the White Sox to third-place finishes in 1955 and 1956. He did a very good job with us and I didn't know why he didn't stay with us longer, other than that Al Lopez was available.

LES MOSS:

I caught about 50 games, giving Sherm Lollar time off. I got only 30 hits during the year, but 10 were homers. The White Sox had the best pitching staff of any team I'd been on, so I enjoyed catching. I learned a great deal from Ray Berres, who was the best pitching coach around. He worked with pitchers on their mechanics and delivery. He wanted the catchers to make the pitchers keep the ball down because we had good infielders who could scoop up anything hit on the ground.

Dick Donovan was one heck of a pitcher and catching him was fun, although he was extremely intense. He could throw a slider for a strike any time he wanted. Billy Pierce had a good fastball and good breaking stuff. Little Sandy Consuegra was a pretty good pitcher who fooled batters with an array of pitches, including an effective slider, and motions. He had been 16–3 in 1954 and won a lot of games without anybody noticing. He was from Cuba and spoke very little English, so we had a lot of fun with him in jest. We'd call him all kinds of names and he didn't know what we were saying. As long as we smiled, he'd smile, too. He made us laugh, too, especially when doing impressions of everybody from Dick Donovan to Adolf Hitler. I was sorry when he was traded to Baltimore early in the season.

There were a lot of good guys on the team. Nellie Fox was a team man. He was a great competitor but also was a happy-go-lucky guy. Big Walt Dropo was another good guy. He had a lot of dry humor and was a smart guy. Minnie Minoso was one of the funniest guys I was ever around. When he thought an umpire made a bad call, he'd argue in half English and half Spanish and you wouldn't know what the heck he was saying.

Luis Aparicio also had trouble with English, but he was a good guy and player. He had an outstanding arm and great speed. He'd make errors but on balls no one else would get to. He and Fox were a great double-play combination.

Larry Doby was a quiet guy. He still put up big numbers, but by this time his career was winding down. You didn't see him much because he stayed to himself. Dave Philley, the old Texan, was pretty quiet, too. He played pretty much in the field, but Marion also tried to make a pinch hitter out of him. He didn't get any pinch hits all year, but in 1957 he would be an outstanding pinch hitter. He was a tough player, one of the few guys who'd charge the mound after pitchers.

I roomed some with Jungle Jim Rivera. He was a funny guy who'd pull off a prank every now and then, But he'd give 110 percent every time he went on the field. He had been in prison. If he'd played when he was younger, there's no telling how good he could have been. You couldn't help liking him. He wasn't a partygoer and I don't know if he drank. He loved movies in the day and would be in the room every night watching television. We didn't talk all that much baseball. His wardrobe was as long as the wall and mine was the size of the door.

GEORGE KELL:

In May I was part of a 6-player deal that landed me in Baltimore. I was grateful to first have had the opportunity to play with Luis Aparicio. Carrasquel was a terrific shortstop, but Aparicio was a great all-around ballplayer. There was nothing he couldn't do on the ballfield. He could bunt, hit-and-run, steal, hit, and play shortstop as well as anyone I'd ever seen, including Phil Rizzuto. He was a happy-go-lucky guy who just seemed so tickled to be in the big leagues, so it was a joy to play with him. Offensively and defensively, Nellie Fox and Luis Aparicio were the best second baseman and shortstop in the game.

FRED HATFIELD:

When I went from the Tigers to the White Sox, I replaced George Kell, as had happened when I went from Boston to Detroit in 1952. It's tough following an All-Star everywhere you go. But I got a lot of playing time at third base and had a good year, hitting .261.

We had a pretty good team with guys like Pierce, Aparicio, Minoso, Fox, and Donovan. Dick Donovan never spoke a word the day he pitched. He wouldn't recognize anything you said to him. There was nothing you could do to change his routine. I used to tear a piece of paper and lay it where I knew he was going to sit in the dugout. When he'd see it, he'd kick it and clear his space. He never said anything if a player made a nice play behind him, or changed his expression. He thought we were supposed to do good.

Nellie Fox was a great little player. I picked him to lead the league in hits and average each year because he just didn't strike out. If he'd have played in a running era, he would have been an even better hitter. He hit with his hands, and would go wherever the ball was pitched. From the middle of the plate and out, he'd go to left. He foreshadowed Pete Rose as far as hustling, on and off the field. I'd play third base and he'd play second, yet sometimes he'd beat me to the dugout after the inning. He was of Hall of Fame caliber to me.

''Jungle Jim'' was the right nickname for Rivera. Bucky Harris, Detroit's manager, used to call him the ''zipper ripper.'' He was a headfirst, dust-flying type player. When he broke in with the Brownies in 1952, Bill Veeck would give him a few extra hundred dollars for stealing extra bases.

Larry Doby and Minnie Minoso were on the Sox, so I played with blacks for the first time. Years before, I had razzed Doby when he came up to the Indians, but there was no animosity between us. He even asked me to go with him to downtown Washington to see Johnny Mathis perform. We kidded around and I told him I was going to invite him and Minoso down to Mississippi for ''bear'' hunting during the winter. We brushed it off as a joke, but it was a touchy subject with Larry.

Minoso was one of the hardest-playing Latin ballplayers I ever saw. He had his toe broken by a pitch, so he cut out part of his shoe in order to play. He may not have taken batting practice, but when the bell rang he gave you 100 percent. He was a typical wild-swinging Latin player. He was really witty. He told Doby not to go to Mississippi for ''bear'' hunting. He'd tease me, saying, ''I'm coming through Birmingham to see you in my new Cadillac. I'll have two blondes with me and I'll want you to invite all the neighbors over.''

JIM LANDIS:

I had spent two years in the army. The first year I was stationed at Fort Ord. But remember how Billy Martin got into trouble after it was learned that he was playing baseball instead of being assigned to more legitimate duties when he was stationed in Colorado? There was a big government investigation on baseball players getting special treatment. Because of that I spent my second year in Alaska. That hurt my career because while I still played ball, there was no real competition.

When I got out, I went to the Memphis Chicks in Double A. Barry Latman and I roomed together in downtown Memphis, with Al Papai, who was in his mid-30s. Barry and I became good friends. I used to get on him because he had to call his dad every time he pitched. I'd tell him not to call, but Barry would say, ''If I don't call him, it's war, it's war.'' So he'd call after every game whether it was good or bad enough for him to get chewed out.

I really struggled for half a season, but I came on pretty good and did really well in the 1956 ''Dixie Series''—the Southern Association playoffs.

I got married right after the season and honeymooned in Puerto Rico. I played winter ball there and got a lot of good experience. I played with such guys as Vic Power, who was a character and great, hard-playing ballplayer, and Luke Easter. Luke, who was still a star in the minors, was a great person. I loved him. He was an everyday guy who was good for young people. He gave me more encouragement than my manager. He told me, ''You'll be there. Don't worry about it. You'll make it.''

NEW YORK YANKEES

BOB TURLEY:

After the 1955 season, the Yankees management questioned my walk-to-strikeout ratio when we talked contract. I had walked 177 batters and struck out 210, my career high. I said, ''Wait a minute. Who's the best damn pitcher in the league?'' ''Bob Lemon.'' ''Well, add the walks and hits he gave up and see which one of us puts the most men on base.'' I pointed out that even if I walked 3 batters in an inning, I still hadn't given up a run. I had pitched 6 shutouts during the year and Lemon hadn't had any. My earned run average was just 3.06, which was much better than Lemon's. They gave me the raise I wanted.

I didn't want to walk anybody. But management didn't realize that fastball pitchers will always throw more pitches than anybody else. If I made a good pitch, the batter would miss it or foul-tip it. I'd have to pitch again to get him out. I had played with Eddie Lopat in 1955 and had faced him the year before, and it was no mystery why he never walked anybody. Batters would jump off the bench to hit against him and would swing at everything. He had the worst control of any pitcher alive, but he wouldn't walk anybody because no batter could stand up there and let all that slow garbage go by without swinging. When they swung, they hit the ball.

Casey Stengel didn't believe in using a 4-man rotation. He'd have 5, 6, or 7 starters so that we'd all be well rested for September. Most of us had excellent win-loss percentages—we won 97 games and finished 9 games ahead of Cleveland—but we didn't like that Casey used so many starters. We wanted to raise our salaries by winning a lot of games, but we couldn't pitch enough to do that. Only Whitey Ford and Johnny Kucks pitched over 200 innings, and they didn't get the extra starts they needed for 20 wins. In 1954 Bob Grim won 20 games as a rookie, but in 1955 Stengel cut his innings in half and he won only 7 games. Tommy Byrne went 16–5 as a starter in 1955, but was back in the bullpen in 1956 and won just 7 games though he was pitching just as well. I won 17 games in 1955, but pitched more than 100 innings less in 1956 and won only 8 games. I never got as many starts in a season. (The same kind of thing would happen to Kucks after he won 18 games in 1956 and Tom Sturdivant after he won 16 games starting in both '56 and '57. Casey'd also put Duke Maas in the bullpen after he won 14 games in 1959. Ford wouldn't pitch enough to win 20 games until 1961, when Ralph Houk became manager.) All the pitchers would gripe to each other because it messed up our rhythm to go 6 or 7 days between starts. We didn't talk to Casey about it. He talked more to the press than to the players.

One day I was ahead 2 or 3 to nothing against the Senators with 2 outs in the fifth inning. I needed just another out to get credit for a win if I were relieved later. I had walked only 1 and given up only 1 hit. A left-handed batter dunked one over third base for their second hit. And I see Casey coming out of the dugout, waving me out of the damn game and bringing in Tom Morgan. I couldn't believe my eyes. I started walking after him around the mound, asking "Why?" And I added a few choice words. I was really disturbed. I went through the dugout and into the bathroom and tried to flush my uniform down the toilet. Casey avoided me for a month until he came into my compartment on a train. He said, "Now that you've calmed down, I'll tell you why I took you out of that game. I did it because you weren't striking out anyone." I said, "Casey, thank you. Now get the hell out of my room." You see, pitchers in my day didn't want to come out of a game. We needed complete games to make more money.

The batters grumbled, too, because Stengel pla-

tooned most of them. He believed in playing all 25 players on his roster. He kept Mantle, Berra, and Bauer out there every day. But Elston Howard, rookie Norm Siebern, and Bob Cerv were sharing left field; and Bill Skowron was still splitting time at first with Joe Collins. And while Gil McDougald and Billy Martin were the regulars at short and second, Jerry Coleman would often play at those positions, sometimes sending McDougald to second. At various times, all three played third when Casey benched Andy Carey against tough right-handers. One day, while paying a visit to the Yankees, Joe DiMaggio asked, "Bob, if Casey picked any nine of the Yankees and played them, what would happen?" "We'd probably win the pennant," I answered. "Well, so much for his platooning," he said.

It's a good thing Stengel didn't platoon Mickey Mantle in 1956 because he was voted the league's Most Valuable Player for winning the Triple Crown with 52 homers, 130 RBIs, and a .353 average. We didn't think too much about it because there wasn't much focus on that kind of achievement in those days, and Ted Williams had just done it 9 years before. (There would be much more pressure in 1961 because of the media circus while Mantle and Roger Maris tried to break Babe Ruth's home run record.) Mantle was always amazing. He had more talent than anyone I ever saw in my life. They say that if he would have taken better care of himself he would have been a lot better off. I don't know if I agree with that. I'd seen him come to the park as fit as a fiddle at times and having been out on the town all night at other times, and he might have had a better game in the latter condition.

B. PIERCE (WHITE SOX):

I don't really remember Mantle beating me in an extra inning game with his 50th homer of the year. It doesn't surprise me, though, because he had several heroic at-bats against me. I was left-handed, so Mantle batted right-handed against me. He probably had a higher percentage of his homers batting lefty, but I think he was a much better and disciplined hitter from the right side. Batting left-handed against right-handed pitchers he chased high pitches and balls into the dirt. Unfortunately we left-handers had to try to get him out by throwing strikes.

FRED HATFIELD (WHITE SOX):

Pitchers wouldn't throw at Mickey Mantle for drag-bunting. They'd probably thank him for not hitting the ball 500 feet. When Mantle batted in a 1–0 game, I'd play deep on the outfield grass so that he'd try to bunt. That was my own decision. Mantle was one of the strongest men ever to play. I saw him hit back-to-back homers from opposite sides of the plate to the opposite fields. About a month after I left Detroit, he hit 2 balls in one game into the center-field bleachers in Briggs Stadium—no one had done that before! Anywhere he hit the ball, he hit it good.

B. TURLEY:

When I was with the Browns I became intrigued with figuring out what pitchers would throw, depending on how they held their gloves. I kept getting better at it with the Orioles and Yankees. At Yankee Stadium I'd go into the television booth and study pitches when the camera was on them. I eventually could pick up everyone. For instance, Early Wynn was Mr. Perfectionist; everything was slow and deliberate, so he was easy to pick up during his stretch. If the top of the glove went to the top of his nose, he would throw a fastball. If it went just below his nose, he would throw a curve. If his glove was even with his nose, he would throw a slider. And if he kept his glove at waist level, he would throw a knuckleball. We wore him out, and he couldn't understand it was because I was calling his pitches for the Yankee batters. One day on the bench, I was sitting next to Mantle and showed him that I could predict all the pitches. He said, "God almighty, let's work something out." So during all my years in New York, Mickey and I would have all kinds of signs based on my whistling to let him know what was coming. He learned from me.

Billy Martin, Mantle's roommate, liked me because I also would let him know which pitches were coming. He'd talk to me every day about that. A few guys didn't want to know what was coming because it would mess them up. For instance, I would call a pitch for Skowron and he'd swing at it regardless of its location.

The Yankee pitchers would come to me to make sure they weren't giving away pitches. In spring training I'd watch them. Once I told Whitey, "You call all your own pitches." He snapped, "How the hell do you know that?" I said, "Just from watching you pitch." He'd call his own pitches and then Yogi would put fingers down and they didn't mean anything. If he was bent over when he looked in at Yogi, that meant he would throw a fastball—unless he shook his glove, which meant he would throw a curveball. If he was standing upright, that meant he would throw a curve—unless he shook his glove, which meant he would throw a fastball. Whitey said, "Don't tell anybody." I said, "I won't tell anybody because you're my teammate. But if I get traded, you'd better change your style."

WORLD SERIES

1956

YANKEES VS DODGERS

BOB TURLEY · YANKEES:

The Dodgers had an outstanding ballclub again in 1956. They had great hitting and solid defense. I don't think their pitching was as good overall as it had been but they had great pitchers like Don Newcombe, Carl Erskine, and Clem Labine. Sal Maglie won the opener over Whitey Ford, 6–3. He pitched better in Game 5, giving up only 2 runs, but that's when Don Larsen pitched a perfect game.

I was on the bench when Larsen threw his perfect game because I was going to pitch the next day. There was some chatter on the bench during the game but mostly we were quiet. Larsen had started the second game, in which we took an early 6–0 lead, but Casey took him out when the Dodgers rallied in the second inning. That made him really mad, especially since we ended up losing 13–8. Don was a drinker and he went drinking every night after that. On the Yankees, you didn't know if you were pitching until you looked in your locker and discovered that our pitching coach, Jim Turner, had put the ball in your shoe. So Larsen didn't know he was pitching until he came to the Stadium that day. He'd slept only about a half hour the night before so he went to the training room and took a nap until noon, an hour before the game. Don had good stuff that day and there weren't a lot of hard hit balls, but he wasn't dominating. He would get ahead in the count and good defense was played behind him. After Mantle put us ahead in the fourth with a homer, he made a great catch of Hodges's drive to left-center. McDougald and Carey also made some great plays.

The next day, I pitched the best game of my major league career but we didn't score any runs off Clem Labine and I ended up losing in the tenth inning, 1–0. I did everything right, keeping the ball in the park in Ebbets Field. I came close to the World Series strikeout record and I should have had a no-hit, no-run ball game myself. But they got a bad-bounce single to McDougald, and Enos Slaughter misplayed three balls in left field: he lost Labine's hit in the shadows, Gilliam's hit in the sun, and on Robinson's game winning hit in the tenth, he lost the ball in the haze and white shirts and charged in, only to have the ball shoot over his head. That was heartbreaking. We won the Series the next day, 9–0 behind

Johnny Kucks's nicely pitched 3-hitter. Yogi hit 2 homers—Newcombe never could pitch to him.

It was exciting winning my first World Series and celebrating in the clubhouse, yelling and screaming and having fun, and pouring champagne all over each other. Then at the victory party at the Waldorf-Astoria, Stengel came over and said the nicest thing he ever said to me: "I want to tell you something. You pitched the best ball game I ever witnessed in my life. It was better than Larsen's."

RUBE WALKER · DODGERS:

Whitey Ford beat us 5–3 in Game Three, when Enos Slaughter hit a 3-run homer off Roger Craig, and they went up 3 games to 1 when Tom Sturdivant 6-hit us and Mantle and Bauer homered. Then Don Larsen was awesome in his perfect game. You just don't do what he did by throwing your damn glove out there, especially against our lineup. It was amazing. We didn't talk to each other about what he was doing. We didn't even say a word. We didn't have to. We didn't like being his victim, but we had to give him credit—some of the guys would tell me that since we weren't going to beat Larsen that day that they were rooting for him to pull off the first perfect game in World Series history. He didn't use a windup and I reckon that threw off our batters' timing a bit. But I have to say that Babe Pinelli's called

third strike on our final batter, pinch-hitter Dale Mitchell, was actually a ball.

DON NEWCOMBE · DODGERS:

I had a tough World Series thanks to Yogi Berra, who hit a grand slam homer off me in the second game and two 2-run homers off me in Game 7. Because of him I pitched only 4⅔ innings in all and quickly fell behind in the final game. I had success crowding Mickey Mantle and could strike him out, but a guy like Berra who would swing at anything gave me trouble. I always said he would swing at a horse turd and hit it. He always hit me. I tried to knock him down with 2 strikes on him and he knew I would, so when I threw at his head and didn't get it in far enough, he hit the ball over the right-field fence. Every pitch I threw to him I wanted back.

ED ROEBUCK · DODGERS:

I pitched in Games 2, 4, and 7, striking out 5 and giving up only 1 hit in 4⅓ innings. Unfortunately, that hit resulted in the only run I gave up in 6⅓ innings of World Series play over two years. It was a solo homer to Mickey Mantle in Game 4 at Yankee Stadium. Duke was in center. He didn't even turn around, then had a second thought and turned to see how far it would go. It was a tremendous blast. I was proud to be part of it.

NATIONAL LEAGUE 1957

"I DIDN'T THINK THE DODGERS WOULD MOVE. I REALLY THOUGHT O'MALLEY WAS BLUFFING TO GET WHAT HE WANTED IN BROOKLYN. TO ME, THE BROOKLYN DODGERS WERE AN INSTITUTION. IT WAS LIKE MOVING THE WHITE HOUSE OUT OF WASHINGTON, D.C."

ED ROEBUCK

MILWAUKEE BRAVES

BOB BUHL:

We were better than the Dodgers in 1956, but we didn't win the pennant until 1957, the first title for the Milwaukee Braves. The Dodgers, without Jackie Robinson, slipped to third and we beat out the Cardinals by 8 games. We won 95 games and clinched the pennant on an extra-inning homer by Hank Aaron off the Cards' Billy Muffett. Aaron had a great flare for the dramatic. That was a real thrill. He had a great year, batting over .320 and leading the league with 44 homers and 132 RBIs, and was the National League's MVP.

JOHNNY KLIPPSTEIN (REDS):

Hank Aaron was the toughest hitter in the league. Whatever I threw or wherever I threw it, I couldn't tell where he was going to hit it or how hard he was going to hit it. You could make him look bad on a pitch but when you came back with that same pitch an inning later, he might hit it 400 feet. He was uncanny. I'd try to make him chase bad breaking balls and get him out with fastballs that were inside and from the waist up. He liked to get those arms out. He was so loosy-goosy at the plate that I'd joke, "If that guy could relax he'd be a helluva hitter."

B. BUHL:

But there were many stars besides Aaron. Mathews hit over .290 with over 30 homers and 90 RBIs. We picked up Red Schoendienst from the Giants during the season and he was a real key to our championship. We had other good second basemen but they couldn't turn a double play or hit .300 like Red. He was an established ballplayer. And he got along with everybody. With Red at second, Johnny Logan at short, and Mathews at third, we had tremendous infield defense.

Wes Covington was a left-handed-hitting outfielder who hit over 20 homers for us in his second season, although he wasn't in even 100 games. He'd mouth off as if he were mad at someone, but he wasn't. We used to tease him. He'd always get on the bus wearing a fancy hat. And we'd take it when he wasn't looking and burn it. He was a good natured guy and we all liked him. However, he'd have to hit .400 to help a club because he wasn't that good in the left field. Bob Hazle was another part-time outfielder and he did hit over .400. "Hurricane" was a streak hitter and nobody couldn't get him out all year—he was amazing. Everything they threw was hit for a line drive. Frank Torre, who took over at first when Joe Adcock was hurt, also did a good job. He was slow but was a good left-handed batter and an excellent fielder. He'd pal around with Johnny Logan.

Again, the starting pitching came through. I went 18–7 to record the best percentage in the league and give me a 2-year record of 36–13. I had a career-low 2.74 ERA. Burdette won 17 games, and Spahn led the league with 21 wins and was voted the Cy Young Award. I liked watching Spahn pitch because he was a master out there. You never saw the catcher run back to the screen. Everything was just like it was supposed to be. It's not that he wasn't an emotional pitcher. He'd throw his glove or kick it if he lost a close game or got knocked out of a game early. And he'd glare at umps and use his hands to ask where the pitch was, although he never did anything to show them up. It's just that when Spahn was on the mound, everything was under control. If he had a sore arm you wouldn't know it, because he always pitched. Warren and I didn't talk about our pitching styles because he was left-handed. But we'd talk about hitters and how to get them out. Lew and I would talk more. Once you've seen the hitters you have a pretty good idea yourself how to get them out. In 1957, we were getting most hitters out.

ED BOUCHEE (PHILLIES):

The guys you hit good, you didn't worry about. I hit Warren Spahn and Lew Burdette like I owned them. (I bet I hit .340 or .350 average against them for a lifetime.) The main reason is that they threw strikes. Burdette would get so mad if I homered against him that he'd yell at me as I ran around the bases: "Bouchee, you lucky son-of-a-bitch!" And I'd say, "I'm just hitting them where you pitch them." But I couldn't touch Bob Buhl. He had that herky-jerky motion and I couldn't hit him with a paddle.

B. BUHL:

Spahn, Burdette, and I were all competitive so we made sure we did all our work. We all did a lot of running. I'd do at least 10 laps every day back and forth across the field. And during the off-season, I'd run to keep in shape. I'd drink only beer because I felt that I could run and sweat the beer out of my system. I always was told that if you drank the hard stuff it went to your legs. And a pitcher is only as good as his legs.

ST. LOUIS CARDINALS

DICK SCHOFIELD:

Johnny Keane had been my manager at Omaha and if the Cards had hired him at this time to be their manager instead of bringing in Fred Hutchinson, I probably would have been the starting shortstop in 1957. But when Alvin Dark refused to play third base, Hutchinson kept him at short for another year. Eddie Kasko was given the chance to play third and had a good season, and I wasted another year on the bench, batting only 59 times. I don't know why I was recalled. It was really frustrating. Players didn't ask to be traded in those days, but I was noticeably unhappy.

However, I didn't dislike Hutchinson. He was completely different from Stanky. He had some rules, but he treated his players like grownups. He was a decent guy and a good manager. He was also a tough guy no one wanted to mess with. Under Hutchinson, we finished second, eight games behind the Braves. We had pretty good pitching, and a solid lineup, with Stan Musial, who won the batting title, Del Ennis, Wally Moon, and Ken Boyer giving us a strong middle of the order. Wally had a good year, with around 25 homers and a long hitting streak.

Boyer was a super player who was willing to shift to center field from third after we traded Bobby Del Greco. He wasn't yet a team leader because he was still pretty young and trying to take care of himself. He liked to agitate a little bit, but otherwise he didn't say very much.

Our second baseman was Don Blasingame. We had played together in Cuba in 1954 and roomed together at Omaha in 1955, and had become life-long friends. It was nice to see him do so well. He was a popular guy and solid player, who was in the lineup every day, scored over 100 runs, led the league in at-bats, and played excellent defense.

Another one of my good friends, Joe Cunningham,

had come back from his injury in 1956 and showed he could hit .300. But he was still playing parttime because when he had been hurt, Musial had moved permanently to first base, which was Joe's best position. Because of Musial, he never got to play enough and had to move back and forth between first and the outfield. I know that delayed his development.

Larry Jackson won 15 games in 1957 and became the ace of the Cardinals' staff. He was cocky and one of the toughest pitchers in the league. If he was winning 7–0, pretty soon the score would be 7–6, but if he was ahead 1–0, it would stay that way. He was hard for batters to figure out (which I would learn firsthand after I was traded). If he had you at 0 balls and 2 strikes, you'd look for a change-up and he'd throw a slider; if the count was 2–0, you'd look for a slider and he'd throw a change-up. (I would never figure him out.)

Lindy McDaniel also won 15 games. He was a control pitcher who was always around the plate. He gave up a lot of hits but usually managed to pitch out of jams. Because he wasn't really a strikeout pitcher and didn't have a great fastball, Hutchinson converted him to a starter in his second season. In 1957 and '58, McDaniel would start for Hutchinson, but for the rest of his 20-year career, pitching for other managers, he would be strictly a reliever—and one of the best. Lindy was very religious, but otherwise I didn't get to know much about him.

His 18-year-old brother, Von McDaniel, was also very religious. He had just graduated from high school and debuted for the Cards with a 2-hitter against the Dodgers. This got a lot of attention in the press. I didn't think he'd ever lose a game. But all of a sudden he hurt his arm. He went 7–5 as a rookie and that was it: he never won another game.

Murry Dickson was a good guy. He had started out with the Cardinals back in 1939 and had pitched for them until 1949. He returned to the Cardinals from the Phillies during the 1956 season and won 13 games for us at the age of 40. He pitched much less for us in 1957 and won only a few games. He'd throw every day on the sidelines and would have gone into a game every day if you let him. He was a real battler. Boyer was his roommate and he'd tell me, "He drinks coffee all day long and eats once a week."

I roomed with Hoyt Wilhelm for a little while. He didn't even pitch a full season with us before he was traded to the Indians. He wasn't very effective for us. I don't know what the trouble was, but once he left us he returned to form.

Sam Jones won 12 games for us. He was a real character. He said funny things, he looked funny. And he could make some right-handers do some funny things at home plate. He looked the same at 35 as he did when he was 5—I saw a picture of him.

Billy Muffett was a hard-throwing rookie right-hander. He gave up the homer to Hank Aaron that won the pennant for the Braves. That was the first time Milwaukee had won and it was pretty wild in the downtown area that night. People were running all over the streets celebrating.

DEL ENNIS:
After 11 years with the Phillies, I came to St. Louis. It was too far to commute back to Philadelphia, which was my lifelong home, so I took a house. It's funny but that year I got cheered in two cities. I was never booed in St. Louis and when I went back to play in Philadelphia, the fans finally were on my side and cheered me. I would get fan mail saying how much they missed me.

The Cardinals had a pretty good team, with pitchers like Larry Jackson, Lindy McDaniel, Sam Jones, Herm Wehmeier, and Vinegar Bend Mizell, and Stan Musial, me, Ken Boyer, and Wally Moon supplying the power. Don Blasingame and Alvin Dark were a good second-short combination offensively and defensively, and Hal Smith was one of the best defensive catchers.

The Braves clinched the pennant on a home run by Hank Aaron off us. The funny part is that Aaron didn't hit against the Cardinals at all. We had Toothpick Jones, a big colored pitcher. When he wasn't on the mound himself, he'd encourage our pitcher to put the ball in Aaron's ear. He'd call Aaron every name in the book and when Aaron would turn to look at him, he flashed a big toothy grin. Then Aaron would make an out.

St. Louis was owned by Augie Busch, and the team was sponsored by Budweiser. We'd get a free case every week. That's when I started to drink beer. Except for guys like Alvin Dark and the McDaniel brothers, who were deeply religious, St. Louis was a drinking team. After a while the guys had me going to clubs and everything else. I drank enough to last me a lifetime. I didn't really have many close friends on the Cardinals. I thought Lindy McDaniel, Jackson, and Wilhelm were good guys. Alvin Dark always had something to say and I didn't like that too much. He wanted to be the team leader but Musial was the guy everyone looked up to.

Musial could have run the town or been governor. He was my best friend on the team. I no sooner get into St. Louis than Musial has a car for me and everything else. He was glad to have me batting behind him so he would get good pitches. I roomed with him. He asked for me because I was quiet. We spent a lot of time together and we'd go out nights on the road to the best spots, where he'd be treated so well. He never had any money with him. I was his banker and paid all the tabs. After the road trip, we'd come back and he'd peel off the $700–$800 he owed me. He could drink like a fish. When he went out he ordered scotch, not Budweiser. Then he'd get 3 or 4 hits the next day.

Stan was the best hitter I ever saw. He would tell me that he was going to get 3 hits against Warren Spahn. He'd raise 3 fingers when Spahn looked at him. "Yeah?" Spahn laughed. Then Musial got his 3 hits. He didn't have many slumps. He was a tremendous competitor.

Oddly, I got a larger paycheck than he did. He never collected all his money, but had half of it deferred. He played for many years and they owed him $50,000 this year, $50,000 the next year. (Eventually they would owe him $500,000. That's how he became Vice-President of the Cardinals. That must have been his plan.) He got a lot of money from endorsements. He had one from a savings company and another from a motel in Florida, and others, both locally and nationally.

With me batting behind him, Stan's average went up 41 points to .351 and he won his seventh and last batting title and drove in over 100 runs for the last time. We moved up from fourth to second place, largely due to my contributions. I played in the field in only 127 games yet had 105 RBIs. I didn't compete with Musial in RBIs. Unfortunately Musial ended with only 102 RBIs. It turned out that if you beat Musial in RBIs, in St. Louis, you might as well pick up your walking papers. Fred Hutchinson told me, "You know, you don't beat

Musial." Even Stan said that I wouldn't play regularly the next year because I beat him.

TOM CHENEY:

I was in my fifth minor league season. It was still fun because I was relatively young. But the bus leagues were tough. Lots of times you'd ride all night and then have to play. We'd play pool and eat hot dogs. On the road we stayed in mostly decent hotels, but there'd be places like the Mayflower in Jacksonville that were awful. There were hookers and other rough types hanging about, and if you fooled around there, you felt you'd get your throat slit.

We never went by train in the minors. But in Omaha in 1956 and 1957, we flew most of the time. We had a couple of rough times. We took off for Omaha. Nelson Burbrink and Moe Mozzali, a real character, were sitting in the plane and the rain was really coming down. Moe says "Boys, if we don't have two runways we're in a mess. Because there's one runway over there!" And we landed on the infield of the airport. We could hear the pilot and copilot yelling at each other. They never touched the runway. The wives were there to greet us, but we just walked right by them without saying a word.

One night we flew out of Indianapolis into a storm. The Indianapolis ballclub took off behind us, but they turned back. That's the most frightened I ever was. We were blown around like a feather. Just before we went into the storm, I lit a cigarette. I never took a draw of that cigarette. I remember it burning my fingers. Even with seatbelts on, it felt like we were out of our seats. We got into Chicago to change planes. And we balked. Our manager Johnny Keane assured us there was good weather ahead. And Frank Barnes, a good black pitcher, said, "J.K., you ain't lying to us, are you?" So we took off and it was okay. Frank went up to go to the bathroom and the seatbelt sign came on. And he flew out of there pulling up his britches, yelling, "J.K., you told us a damn lie!"

I finally joined the Cardinals in 1957 and got into 4 games. At the time, I could throw hard but my control was off and on, like it would be my entire career. I couldn't tell when warming up how it would be in the game. I was taught that if you were wild to be wild throwing hard and not aim the ball because that's when you get hurt. I never let up. Out of 10 pitches, I'd throw 7 or 8 fastballs. My strikeout pitch was a high fastball. On a 2–2, I figured the hitter was anxious so I usually went with the fastball but I had a good curve. All my career, I much preferred pitching to a left-hander than a right-hander, and I know that's just backward thinking because I was a righty. But my fastball ran. They called it a cut fastball. I could jam a left-hander but had trouble pitching a right-handed hitter inside.

I liked when Hal Smith caught me. He was one of the best catchers in baseball. We were in synch. In a certain situation, I'd shake him off and throw a pitch I had more confidence in. Sometimes Hal or another catcher would override me. At times, it hurt me to go along with the catcher. Your mind is set on one channel, that one pitch. If it was a new catcher, I'd sit with him before the game. But the vets like Smith really knew the hitters and you could depend on them.

My roommate was Hoyt Wilhelm, a nice guy. I always could learn a new pitch by watching another pitcher and I learned the knuckleball from Hoyt. He showed me how he held it while we were playing catch in the outfield. He held it with the tip of his fingers, not the knuckles. Like him, I always hooked my fingers behind the seams where you could pull with your thumb. Mine wasn't as good as his, but it was good at times. Wilhelm was the team's best reliever. The Cards also had a strong starting rotation, with Larry Jackson, Lindy McDaniel, Sad Sam Jones, and Vinegar Bend Mizell. I knew it would be hard to break into that.

I wasn't on the team long enough to have many memories. But I remember Sam Jones being very businesslike on the mound. I remember that Larry Jackson was a smart guy who was our player rep. I remember that Lindy McDaniel always was late to the ballpark on Sunday because he went to church, but no one said anything about it. Mizell and Alvin Dark also went. I was a Baptist but because services didn't start till 11 A.M. on Sunday, I couldn't go as often as I'd have liked.

I liked having the opportunity to play with Stan Musial. It was amazing watching him hit. He had that deep crouch. He was both a smart and great hitter. He would say that he'd get his pitch once every time he went to bat. That was the first time I ever heard that. It was comical that other teams (like Pittsburgh when I joined them in 1960) hoped he got 2 or 3 hits in games before he faced them because they knew if he'd been shut out, he'd break loose against them. What impressed me was that he had such confidence that he didn't feel he had to impress anybody. He gave 100 percent. And he was a terrific person. He'd hang around with players in the clubhouse and have a beer or two as we wound down after a game.

Augie Busch had built a nice facility for players to have sandwiches between games of a doubleheader. I was pitching the second game so I was resting up when Stan Musial came in. He wasn't playing that first game. I overheard him call the accounting office and tell them to hold $25,000 out of his next check for tax purposes. I didn't know that much money existed. I was making $6,000 total that year.

On the road, we had to wear a tie and jacket. Musial wore brightly colored ugly jackets. So did Dick Schofield. He had one that was the Sunday funny papers. He didn't care if they were ugly. He spent a lot of money on clothes. All his sports clothes were loud. I said, "Ducky, you need help."

I was only able to get my feet wet in the majors, pitching 9 innings and walking 15 batters and striking out 10. I would have liked to have pitched more, but my career suffered a setback when I was drafted into the service for two years.

CHICAGO CUBS

JIM BROSNAN:

We won two more games than in 1956 and that was enough for us to tie the Pirates for seventh place. Bob Scheffing, the one-time Cubs catcher, had become the manager. I had been with Bob in Los Angeles so I knew him and liked him. My wife and his wife got along very well, to an embarrassing degree in one respect. We'd carpool and when Bob and I got off the plane either my wife or his wife would be waiting to drive us back to our houses. Of course, the other players would razz me about this special treatment. There were a lot of veterans on the team who were expert needlers.

However, the worst needler wasn't a player, but a

New York Giants fan named Dirty Louie. Every time we went to the Polo Grounds, he was there. He was particularly gross. He smelled like he hadn't had a shower in a month. He obviously spent all his time reading everything in *The Sporting News* and the sports gossip columns because he shouted out all our little secrets in a big booming voice. He could embarrass you with his words and because he was so embarrassing himself it was hard to tolerate. Mays hit a lot of tremendous home runs off me, but I dreaded Louie more.

There are always between 5 and 7 players on a team who fill up the roster and do the shit work. In 1954 I had been strictly a mop-up man. In 1956 and 1957 I mopped up and started occasionally, even less in the second year. I was growing up a little bit. I wasn't so pissed off when I lost or as befuddled when I won. I was now becoming a pitcher. I understood my mistakes and knew what I had to do to get batters out—so I was able to do it more often. I was used more, 41 times in 1957, all but 5 in relief. I was 5–5 with an ERA below 3.40, and I struck out almost 7 batters for every 9 innings I pitched.

The team I did best against was the champion Milwaukee Braves. Guys like Joe Adcock, Eddie Mathews, and Johnny Logan told me they couldn't understand how "you four-eyed son-of-a-bitch can get us out." I had a theory on how to get out Henry Aaron. I'd get behind him and throw changes on the outside corner, or I'd pitch him a foot inside because he gave you that much room. I might walk him if he didn't swing, but he had a hard time getting a solid hit off me.

Our starters didn't get very far, so the bullpen was always trying to bail them out. Me, Turk Lown, and usually Don Elston, Don Kaiser, and Dave Hillman were among the relievers. We developed an *esprit de corps* in the pen that didn't exist in the dugout. It was as if we were a separate team. We wondered why we got along so well when those other sons of bitches couldn't get along enough to make our team better. Excluding the relievers, we had some pretty good talent on the club—Ernie Banks, Dale Long, Walt Moryn, Lee Walls, Bob Rush, Moe Drabowsky, Dick Drott—yet we were a last-place club. The bullpen decided to throw a party and not invite the starters. Bob Rush asked, "If I pitch one game in relief can I come to the party?" Our pitching coach Ray Miller, the bullpen coach, and five

relievers chipped in $20 apiece and we rented a room in a hotel in St. Louis and had one great party.

Lee Walls was my roommate. He was quite gregarious and for years during the off-season, worked as a greeter in Palm Springs. We'd always go to the fanciest restaurants we could find and Lee would smoothly talk us inside without reservations, past the maitre d'. Lee liked to throw around money. Of course, we couldn't afford such places on our meal money, so we didn't do it often. He would always ask me to join him, Walt Moryn, and some other players. Now that I felt that I was part of the team, I was more willing to socialize.

BROOKLYN DODGERS

DON NEWCOMBE:

In this era, you didn't hear about players being alcoholics. But that's what I was. There were some Dodgers who didn't drink—Erskine, Pee Wee, Roy, Gil—but we had other players who drank too much. Ed Roebuck and I were drinking buddies. Johnny Podres, Duke Snider . . . It almost killed Podres, it almost killed me. We all had to come to grips with it.

Drinking took away my desire. I was a hard worker, and during the later stages of my career I'd go to spring training and not even have a bottle of beer. But once the season started, I started drinking again. I'd get drunk after a game and wouldn't go to the ballpark the next day and work out, or I'd just go through the motions. I wasn't there 2–3 hours before the rest of the team, running with my sweatsuit on, as had been my routine. I know it hurt me in 1957, when my record dropped to 11–12.

One always hears about "the pressures of baseball." That's not why players drink. These are trained professionals. Pressure has got to be a brain surgeon operating on a patient, a pilot flying a jet with 400 people on it. There's no pressure on a baseball field. I'm a pitcher, I've got eight guys helping me. All I have to do is use my innate talent, which I had or I wouldn't be out on the mound in the first place. By using my talent and the help of my teammates I could become successful and famous. That's not pressure.

Those other players who drank heavily also drank

Don Newcombe would go with the Dodgers to Los Angeles but, perhaps appropriately, all 123 victories the longtime Dodger ace would have with the team would come in Brooklyn.

before they came to the major leagues. In junior high, high school, even in elementary school, like me. They got it, liked it, and drinking became a bad habit. My father gave me beer—he didn't think it would hurt me, he didn't want me to be a drunk and throw away my baseball career. But I did. That's why I didn't give beer to my sons. (My father didn't get to see me in 1966 on my knees swearing to God—a god he never told me about.)

RUBE WALKER:

It was a shock when we learned we were leaving Brooklyn. There had been rumors for a couple years, but we had never talked about it. I think Walter O'Malley even extended his lease on Ebbets Field. I don't think the Brooklyn fans believed it. They thought, "What the hell

is baseball without Brooklyn?" We felt terrible for the loyal Brooklyn fans but couldn't feel guilty as players because we had to go. I liked Mr. O'Malley from conversations we had in the clubhouse over the years and was sorry to see that he became the villain. The Brooklyn fans hated him after they learned he was moving their team. Maybe if they had built O'Malley a new, bigger stadium in Brooklyn he would have stayed.

ED ROEBUCK:

I had one of my best seasons. Alston again used me as the closer behind Labine, and I won 8 games and saved 8 more. My ERA was 2.71 for 96 innings and I struck out 73. I lost only twice (once in what would be my only major league start in 460 appearances). I made Dodgers history by recording the last Brooklyn victory, an 8–4 win over the Phillies on September 28, 1957.

I didn't think the Dodgers would move. I really thought O'Malley was bluffing to get what he wanted in Brooklyn. To me, the Brooklyn Dodgers were an institution. It was like moving the White House out of Washington, D.C.

I didn't feel guilty about leaving Brooklyn. Most of us were happy to be going to Los Angeles. Of the veterans, Duke Snider was sad to leave Brooklyn yet looked forward to playing in L.A., where he was from. I think Gil Hodges and Carl Furillo thought it was horrible because they were Easterners. Gil lived in Brooklyn and his wife was from there, so it was tough on them. Of course, it was roughest on the Dodgers fans. But the players were not the ones to blame.

STAN WILLIAMS:

After having learned the slider in winter ball, I went from 9–7 to 19–7 in my second year at St. Paul. I led the league in strikeouts and finished second in ERA. I hadn't been hearing from the Dodgers themselves and the thought of talking to the home office was just out of the question. I felt like a pawn. In fact, I went from Class D to AAA without getting a raise. I then told them I was going to take my six months of military service, and they gave me a raise so I wouldn't go. Finally, the Dodgers recalled my contract and told me to join the club after my season at St. Paul. However, we won our last 4 games and another team lost its last 4 games and we made the last spot in the playoffs. So the Dodgers called back and told me to stay with my team in the playoffs, and I won a couple of games. That was my one chance to play in Brooklyn but I never made it. I would have liked to have played there in Ebbets Field.

RANDY JACKSON:

It was different in the clubhouse in 1957 because we weren't winning or in contention. We were trying too hard, probably. But the Dodgers remained close. I hurt my knee against the Pirates when I stepped on first base and Frank Thomas jumped into the air and came down on top of me and bent it backward. They kept me in the hospital for a week. They couldn't decide whether to operate or not. Finally they just put it in a cast. That was enough to get me out of shape. I batted only about 130 times and my average was under .200.

It was in the summer that we learned that Brooklyn was moving to Los Angeles. That meant Duke Snider hit the last Dodgers' homer in Ebbets Field—it gave him 40 homers for the fifth consecutive year—and I hit the last Brooklyn Dodgers' homer, in Philadelphia, in our next to last game. But it had no special meaning to me at the time.

Many times over the years I would hear people say that they stopped being baseball fans when the Dodgers left Brooklyn.

NEW YORK GIANTS

JOHNNY ANTONELLI:

In 1957, my wife and I lived in Flushing, Queens. That was tough because it meant I had to drive against traffic on the Grand Central Parkway at 4:30 in the afternoon. Most of the ballplayers lived in Hastings-on-the-Hudson or Westchester. But they wouldn't live there long because this was the Giants' last year in New York. I loved playing ball in New York for 4 years. It helped that I had the good fortune of pitching in the Polo Grounds where the fans were knowledgeable, supportive, and friendly. I have been told I pitched the last game in the Polo Grounds, losing to the Pirates, 9–1. Afterward the sparse crowd ripped apart the stadium for souvenirs. But I don't remember pitching that game.

Leaving New York was sad. There were rumors about a move to the West Coast, of a new stadium being built in Manhattan, and of the team being sold to Bill Terry. But in August we were all surprised when the organization voted to move to San Francisco. I was a player rep but didn't anticipate the move at all. I wasn't taken into management's confidence. I thought that New York City deserved major league teams in both leagues, and I couldn't believe both the Dodgers and Giants would leave. I just couldn't believe it. It was such a letdown.

HANK SAUER:

The Giants got me from the Cards because they wanted someone who could bat behind Willie Mays so they would stop pitching around him. In 1956, he had hit under .300 with only 84 RBIs. Bill Rigney batted me clean-up and Mays hit third. I had 26 homers in just 378 at bats and Mays hit .333 with 35 homers and 97 RBIs, so the plan worked fine. I got the Comeback Player of the Year Award.

Willie Mays was a great kid and great all-around player. There wasn't anything he couldn't do well. Seeing him day after day, he was exactly like I'd thought he was. I never heard him moan about anything. He loved to laugh and kid around in the clubhouse. When he walked in you'd hear his familiar high-pitched laughing and his ''Say, hey.'' How the fans loved him, especially the kids—he loved to sign autographs and used to play stickball with them in the streets. I played next to him in the outfield. I told him, ''I'll take everything from me to the foul line and you take everything from me to center field.'' Of course, he laughed. He laughed more than he did anything in the world.

The team finished sixth, 16 games under .500. We had some good hitters, but a few of them had off-years. And other than Ruben Gomez, who won 15, and Johnny Antonelli, our pitching was a little weak.

I lived about 20 miles away from the park. I didn't think I'd enjoy New York because it was hot in the summer and cold in the spring. But I did. My wife had always stayed in California during the season to look after our children, rather than joining me in Chicago or St. Louis, but she came to be with me in New York. We had team parties and got the families together, and of course, there was so much to appreciate in the city itself. I also enjoyed playing in the Polo Grounds. Before, as an opposing player, the fans would get on me, trying to upset me. I never let it bother me because they did it to everyone. When I became a Giant, they were great to me.

I feared baseball was changing when we moved out of New York and left for San Francisco. It was tough leaving the Polo Grounds. I felt there was a big letdown, prior to the new ballparks being built in the early '60s. An era was ending and I thought that was very sad.

PHILADELPHIA PHILLIES

ANDY SEMINICK:

When Del Ennis was traded, it signaled that the Phillies were going to start moving out the older players and completely dismantle our 1950 title team. I was the next to go, early in the 1957 season. I was expecting it because Stan Lopata had proven himself as an everyday

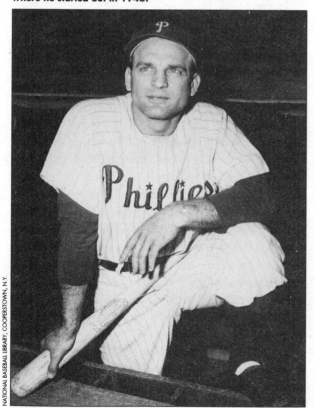

Andy Seminick's solid fifteen-year career ended in Philadelphia, where he started out in 1943.

player and I would get rusty on the sidelines. So my playing career came to an end when I was 36, after 15 years in the majors. I never did have to go back and work in the coal mines.

FRANK BAUMHOLTZ:

Early in the year, we worked out after a heavy rain and I couldn't take the cold wind. I wound up in the hospital for a month with violent spasms. I decided that at 38, it was time to retire. In those days if you were over 30 you were considered past your prime.

I wouldn't trade the 10 years I spent in the big leagues for any amount of money. I enjoyed every second of my career. I met some of the finest people in major league baseball. During that era, there was more joy and satisfaction and exhilaration, more heartaches and sadness—more of everything than could be experienced in any other business. I realized all my dreams and dreams are very important to athletes.

ED BOUCHEE:

I went to spring training at Clearwater. It was a good feeling that the veterans were rooting for me. I didn't speak very much to Mayo Smith, but I talked a great deal to his hitting coach, Wally Moses. I had been hitting with the straight stance at camp and wasn't making good contact and was getting jammed a lot. So Wally said, "Why don't you open up and put that weight on the back foot? You'll see that ball better and you can get around on that inside pitch." So he worked on me and worked on me. Then he said, "What I want you to do is just lift the back heel off the ground, which is what you see a lot guys doing now in the big leagues. That will make you keep your weight back." With the open stance I had more hip action and my hands were quicker. We went to Orlando for a spring training game and I took batting practice against one of our left-handers. "All right," Wally said, "I'm gonna have him throw you nothing but curveballs." I hit four in a row out of the ballpark. He said, "I think we've got it."

Otherwise I stayed the same, back in the batter's box, using a 35-inch, 33-ounce bat. I walked a lot because I swung only at pitches that were in my strike zone. I had confidence because I knew I was a good hitter. I hit curveballs and knuckleballs as well as fastballs. I didn't get the ball in the air a lot, but hit hard line drives. I just went up there and hit the living crap out of the ball. It was a God-given talent.

Smith told me I was going to make the Phillies. About 8 of us from Miami made the team. I was going to be the starting first baseman. So my wife and I rented a townhouse in northeast Philadelphia. I started off real good and the fans got behind me 100 percent, which is fortunate in Philadelphia. They saw that I was a hard-nosed player. I got hit by pitches, and I was a hard slider who would knock over catchers if they blocked the plate or infielders if they were trying to turn the double play. I'd even throw rolling blocks—they were illegal but umpires didn't call them.

Once in the lineup, I wasn't going to let anyone take me out. I played 154 games as a rookie. In those days you played hurt. (In Miami, I had sliced a long gash in my knee and didn't even know it. So they took me down to the first aid at Miami Stadium and they stitched me up with a dull needle and no Novocaine.) You didn't want anybody taking your job so if you got cut, or sprained your ankle, or got hit by a pitch, you played. I led the league in getting hit by pitched balls in 1957. I took it as a compliment. They just tried to pitch me inside all the time, throwing sliders in on me. Pitching inside was part of the game. Robin Roberts was one of the few guys who didn't throw brushback pitches. I asked, "What do you do when you get in trouble?" He said, "I just throw harder."

To be in the majors on any team in 1957 when there were only 16 teams and 400 players was a real honor. So I was proud to be a Phillie. I came in as an era drew to an end in Philadelphia, although I was too content playing every day to notice it. Del Ennis had been traded away after the 1956 season but some of the other aged Whiz Kids were still around for a while: Richie Ashburn, Robin Roberts, Curt Simmons, Andy Seminick, Granny Hamner, Puddin'head Jones, Stan Lopata. Robin was the leader in the clubhouse and Granny was an on-field leader. They had a lot of pride and it rubbed off on the rest of us. Ashburn was a leader in that he got on base and ignited our offense. He also led the league's outfielders in putouts, chances, and assists. Richie was also a good clubhouse presence in that he had a sharp wit and was a gung-ho, rah-rah guy.

HERSHELL FREEMAN (REDS):

I thought Richie Ashburn was the best leadoff man in the National League. He was a slap hitter. He'd try to hit the ball on the ground to the left side because he could run as well as anyone. If it took over two bounces, he was safe. He was also a fine center fielder. He didn't have the strongest arm but he covered a lot of ground.

E. BOUCHEE:

The Phillies were a unified team, with the young guys being accepted by the veterans. I liked when we'd sit around and talk baseball. Mostly we'd talk about hitting, but I loved talking with Roberts and Simmons about pitching. They were eager to talk. On the road, the guys saw a lot of movies and played a lot of cards. Not much poker, but a lot of gin and pinochle. I played with Roberts, Ashburn, Hamner, and Jack Sanford, who played a lot of gin. We played for a quarter of a cent a point.

Hamner was our racetrack guy. He loved the horses, just loved them. I didn't go to the racetrack because I didn't like to bet on anything that has someone riding on its back. I preferred the dogtrack in Florida. The other thing I did to pass time was to read a lot of books that were based on history. A few other players read.

A lot of the Phillies and Eagles hung out together. I was good friends with Bobby Walston, the tight end and place kicker. Stan Lopata was a very good friend of linebacker Chuck Bednarik. In fact they lived next door.

Some players did charity work. People would ask me to go and visit a kid in a hospital or something like that. It wasn't organized back then. They'd call the team and the team would ask who wanted to participate.

I batted third behind Ashburn and Hamner, and in front of guys like Willie Jones, Rip Repulski, Harry Anderson, and Stan Lopata. Jones was a good guy. He had the worst set of feet you'd ever want to see. I had never seen feet so ugly. They looked as if somebody took a sledge hammer and broke all his toes. Those toes were sticking up. Whenever Sad Sam Jones was pitching for St. Louis, Willie would say to Mayo Smith, "Skip, my dogs are just killing me. It must be the weather. I don't think I can go today." Willie hated facing Sad Sam because his curveball started behind Willie's back and looked like it would hit him. Also, Sam had about six different-speed curveballs and Willie couldn't hit any of them.

Anderson also came up in 1957 and played left field. He was 6'3" and had power. He struck out a lot but he hit 17 or 18 homers in just 400 at-bats, so he and I gave the Phillies two strong, young left-handed hitters. When he came into the league he was a notorious low-ball hitter so he never saw a ball below his waist. By pitching him up, they made him a good high-ball hitter. (So in 1958, he would hit over 20 homers and raise his average over 30 points to .300.)

I led the team with 76 RBIs, hit 17 homers and batted .293. I also led the league's first basemen in assists. I was a decent fielder and caught what I got to. The errors I made were usually the result of bad judgment—rookie mistakes. *The Sporting News* chose me and Sanford co-Rookie of the Year, which was a highlight of my career.

Jack was twenty-nine in his rookie year. He went 19–8 and led the league in strikeouts. He was a very good pitcher and tough competitor. You hit one off of him and you had better be looking for a lot of chin music the rest of the game.

Sanford won the most games on our team, but Roberts was still pitching the most innings. He was still the ace and the most respected pitcher on our staff, but by now he usually lost more games than he won, often leading the league. In 1957, he went 10–22. Roberts was still very aggressive on the mound. He was just a fastball pitcher but had the control of Satchel Paige. You'd hold your glove out and he'd hit it nine out of ten times. The Phillies tried for years to get him to throw a curveball (but he wouldn't do it until he went to Baltimore in 1962 and revived his career).

At his best, Curt Simmons was the toughest left-hander in the league. He had a herky-jerky motion and batters would see a fastball that seemed to be coming down the middle of the plate suddenly veer toward their bellies. Left-handers hated him because balls just tailed into them and sawed off their bats. He also had a wicked curve, which made him even more effective. A batter would be waiting for the fastball and suddenly there was a curve on the outside corner. He developed four different speeds for curveballs.

Mayo Smith didn't have complete control over the younger players and I don't think he properly handled young, hard-throwing pitchers like Don Cardwell and

Turk Farrell. Farrell went 10–2 as a rookie reliever but he and Cardwell could have contributed a lot more to the team if given the chance. They never could get into a rhythm and never knew what their roles were. Smith let Roberts, Simmons, and Harvey Haddix go on their own more than the other guys.

Smith was a so-so manager who was much too iffy. If I had a problem, Smith would be helpful but I talked more to Wally Moses than him. Mayo wouldn't talk to you unless you went up to him. He wouldn't come over and say, "Hey, you had a great game yesterday. Keep it up." Young players needed that occasionally.

One guy who really helped the younger players was Andy Seminick. After he quit playing, he would be the Phillies' catching coach for years. He always talked to you and would come over and give you advice when he saw you doing something wrong. He was from the old school and believed in helping everyone. Even when he was losing playing time to young Joe Lonnett, Lopata's backup, he helped Joe. There was no real competition. He wanted everyone else to do well and he made sure that attitude existed on the Phillies as a team.

Some of the veterans resented the Dalton Gang, comprised of young pitchers Turk Farrell, Seth Morehead, and Jim Owens, who wouldn't really stick with the team until 1959. I don't know if they were actually disruptive but they were always in the office of the general manager. I was used to their actions because Farrell, Morehead, and Owens ran around together in Miami when I was there. Were they wild? Nah. I remember staying in a hotel room in Plant City, Florida, that shared a bathroom with Farrell and Morehead. I'm in there on the throne one day reading a newspaper and Farrell takes out his .45 and starts shooting through the door. You've never seen somebody hit the floor so fast in your life. Farrell claimed he always carried that gun with him. Were they wild? I'll never forget one night in Milwaukee. All the teams used to stay at the Schrader Hotel and right across the street was a big joint called Fazio's. One night we're in there after a game and Farrell picks up the juke box—picks it up!—and starts to dance with it. The owner told him to put it down or he was going to call the cops. So Turk put it down and went into the washroom and proceeded to rip all the mirrors and towel holders off the bathroom walls. The Phillies got a bill for that. On the mound, Farrell was a tremendous competitor. If you took a good swing at his pitch, you knew he was going to come up and in on you. And he could throw hard. He'd get out there and just lose all sense. That's why I thought he could have been a great pitcher. I don't know if Farrell was a new breed of player or part of a dying breed.

The Phillies had a lot of old-breed players so they never shied away from fights. I saw a few when I came up. We had some great fights with Cincinnati. I didn't mind because Ted Kluszewski would walk over and grab me by the arm—and you knew how big that sucker was—and say, "Come on, Ed. Let's go stand over by first base. We got our man. We don't want to go out there and get spiked and stepped on." And we'd walk over to first base and stand.

Other than low salaries, what the Phillies griped most about was travel conditions. The Dodgers had their own plane but almost all of the time, the Phillies still took trains. In 1958, we would start flying to the coast. There was a suitcase players used that was made especially for trains. A guy in St. Louis made them special for all the ballplayers when they came into town. It was a big three-suiter, about three feet by two feet and probably a foot high. It was hard as a rock so that they could toss it around. Most ballplayers had them because a lot of times you were gone for ten or twelve days and you had to take a lot of things. The airlines wouldn't let us use them later because they were too big. A lot of times when we'd play a Sunday afternoon double-header in Cincinnati the train wouldn't pull out until eleven o'clock at night. We had to check out of the hotel that morning, so what in the heck were we going to do after the game? Go to dinner with the guys and then go to a movie? Hang out at the railroad station? At least we weren't carrying our own suitcases. In the morning, they loaded them on a truck and took them to the park, where later they loaded all the playing gear onto the same truck and took it all to the train. Despite the hassles, I preferred train travel. There was a camaraderie among the players that was lost once plane travel began. I also got to know the sports writers who traveled with us. The Philly writers were a pretty decent bunch of guys. So were our announcers, Gene Kelly and his sidekick By Saam. Kelly was about 6'7". They'd have all our games on the radio and between 50 and 60 on TV.

PITTSBURGH PIRATES

DICK GROAT:

Back in 1952, I tried for a spell to force my arms away from my body when I hit. I ended up with a stance in which my arms were square and I had a swing just like Ralph Kiner's but without his power. I hit that way through 1956. I went home the winter of 1956–1957 and I started thinking to myself, "Why are my hands way up here when I'm eventually going to move them down anyway?" So I dropped my arms to where they would remain for the rest of my career. I remember thinking that since Branch Rickey had said I could hit .300, there was no reason why I couldn't do it. And I hit .315.

If someone expressed confidence in me, I felt an obligation to prove him right. When Danny Murtaugh, who was a coach, replaced Bobby Bragan as manager with about 50 games to go in 1957, the first thing he said was, "Mazeroski and Groat are my second base–shortstop combination" and he made it known that he had faith in me. So I did my best to prove him right. I respected Danny and if he believed in my talent, I saw no reason why I shouldn't believe in myself.

As the pitching staff got better, I improved as a shortstop. I would listen to Law, Friend, and the others at pregame meetings when they would say how they wanted to pitch certain hitters. They had matured so now they were able to pitch exactly as they intended. What they said influenced my positioning. And from what I had learned about where to play hitters I had the confidence to go to the mound and say, "Remember that this guy is a great fastball hitter. You have to throw this way and we'll play him that way, or you pitch him that way and we'll play him this way."

We finished in a last-place tie, but under Murtaugh we were slightly over .500, so we were encouraged. Our pitching was much better. Friend won 14 games, Vern Law went 10–8 with an ERA under 3.00, and Ron Kline, Bob Purkey, and Roy Face all did good jobs. Clemente had an off season and hit only about .250, but almost everyone else in our lineup had a good batting average. Bob Skinner, Dee Fondy, and myself hit over .300; Frank Thomas, Bill Mazeroski, and Gene Freese weren't much below that. Our problem was that no one but Thomas drove in runs that year. I thought we needed someone to replace Dale Long, but I looked around at Clemente, Skinner, and a couple of others and saw we already had guys who could supply the missing power.

FRANK THOMAS:

I was in 151 games in 1957, playing half the time at first, where I had never played before, and the rest at third and in left. The reason I didn't have a permanent position was that we had good players at those positions—Dee Fondy, who we picked up during the season for Dale Long, Gene Freese, and Bob Skinner. The moving around didn't hurt my hitting. I batted .290 and led the Pirates with 23 homers and 89 RBIs. Joe Brown gave me a good raise to $25,000 for the 1958 season.

ELROY FACE:

I got my last start in 1957. In the ninth inning, the game was tied but I developed a blister. I was relieved by Ron Kline who came in and lost the game. I was supposed to get my second start of the season on the day Danny Murtaugh replaced Bobby Bragan as manager. Danny scratched me and put me in the bullpen. When we came off the road trip and my wife picked me up, Danny told her, "Make sure he gets his rest because he's going to do a lot of pitching." He made me strictly a relief pitcher. I wouldn't start another game in my career. I didn't mind because I pitched more often and if I came in with a couple of men on base and got them out I knew I had accomplished something. I enjoyed relief pitching. I would take pride in my 12-year consecutive-game relief streak.

Murtaugh knew baseball and used proper psychology to handle each player. He got the most out of us. As long as you did your job, he left you alone. Some guys he'd kick on the butt and some he'd pat on the back. One year Stan Musial beat me with a homer in the tenth inning in St. Louis to end my 21-inning scoreless streak. After the game, Danny Murtaugh came by my locker, looked me in the eye and said, "Relief pitcher, my ass." I couldn't get mad at Murtaugh because that was his way of making me feel better.

Like all managers, Danny had a curfew, but he wouldn't check on us every night. If we were going bad, he'd give us an occasional call. He caught only two guys in all the years. And that was only because they

took the elevator up without checking for messages—Murtaugh had left them a message to call him when they got in, but they didn't call. When he had managed me at New Orleans in 1954, he sat outside the hotel one night and as each of us returned he fined us $50. He said, "Someone dumped a laundry bag full of water on me tonight. I'm fining everyone who wasn't here. That way I'll catch the guy who did it."

Danny pitched me in almost 60 games in 1957, covering 90-plus innings. I went 4–6 with 10 saves—though they weren't counting saves then—and an ERA of just above 3.00. These were good statistics considering we were a cellar club. I was the finisher, but Luis Arroyo, a left-hander from Puerto Rico, got as much work as I did. He had pitched for us in 1956, after coming over from the Cardinals. He had a great screwball even then (but he wasn't nearly as effective as he'd be with the Yankees in the early sixties). We didn't learn from each other. He didn't learn the forkball and I didn't learn the screwball. The most we did was talk about how to set up particular hitters.

Among the relievers I admired were the Dodgers' Ed Roebuck, the Reds' Hershell Freeman, and the Cardinals' Lindy McDaniel, although he was starting at the time. McDaniel came to me in one of these two years and asked me to show him how to throw a forkball. He worked on it and used it effectively when he went back to relieving.

CINCINNATI REDS

ART FOWLER:

I thought we had a good chance to win the pennant in 1957, especially when we got Don Hoak to play third base. But we won only 80 games and dropped to fourth place. Kluszewski hurt his back and was missed even though George Crowe hit 30 homers and had a helluva year in his place. Most of the other guys had pretty good years, but not quite as good as in 1956. I had my troubles. I went 3–0 but I gave up a lot of hits and had a high ERA and was taken out of the starting rotation for most of the year. Coaches didn't really help pitchers in those days and the other pitchers didn't help you when you were struggling. There was too much competition for jobs. However, the pitchers were friends. Nuxhall and I were very close. And Hal Jeffcoat and I were always together. After the game we'd go out to eat and have a couple of beers. But it was up to me to figure out why I wasn't pitching well.

JOHNNY KLIPPSTEIN:

I had lost a no-hitter in 1956 when Tebbetts removed me from the game after 7 innings; and in 1957, I lost another one. Only this time I was responsible. I gave up a hit to Hurricane Hazle of the Braves in the eighth inning of a game in September. That was the second 1-hitter of my career—Pee Wee Reese had broken up a no-hit bid of mine a few years back in the ninth inning.

I started that game against the Braves, but the majority of my appearances during the year were in relief. Brooks Lawrence, who won 15 or 16 games, Joe Nuxhall, and Hal Jeffcoat were the primary starters, with Don Gross and me getting spot starts. Both of us also helped out Hershell Freeman and Tom Acker in the bullpen, where I seemed to do better. I was 3–2 in relief, while going only 5–9 as a starter. I credit Tebbetts for being the one to move me to the bullpen for a purpose, not as a demotion. I had already considered that I might be able to prolong my career as a reliever.

It was always a comfort pitching for the Reds because they probably had the best defensive team in the league. It was hard to hit the ball past Roy McMillan or Johnny Temple. And our infield was further improved when we acquired Don Hoak. He led the league's third basemen in most fielding categories, as well as having a solid year at the plate. Like Temple, Hoak was a tiger. He liked to fight but I didn't see him win too many. He was a better talker.

Pitchers didn't get mad at fielders for making errors, only for loafing. In one of my years with the Reds, I made a mistake in a game at the Polo Grounds. Gus Bell, my good buddy, was playing center field and Wally Post was playing right. It was a 4–2 game going into the eighth or ninth inning. A fly to right-center fell in between them and the winning runs scored. It was one of those "You take it—I've got it" plays. Tebbetts came out to the mound and I grumbled "I could have caught that ball in my jock," and he got all over me. He said, "You've made about eight mistakes since you've been on the mound today. Those guys are out there hustling . . ." We ended up winning the game and I made

sure to tell Gus and Wally exactly what I said and apologize. I knew I was wrong.

Pete Whisenant came to the Reds from the Cubs in 1957. He was a tall, strong outfielder from North Carolina. He was different from anybody. You talk about tough. He'd fight very quickly. Anywhere. He didn't like the idea that on New York sidewalks, people would walk straight at you and never move to the side. So he and a couple of other players would walk shoulder-to-shoulder and not give an inch, knocking people all over the place. If anyone said anything he was ready. Despite this, Pete was a good-natured guy and everybody liked him. He wasn't the greatest hitter in the world, but he'd bust his tail for you in the field.

Whisenant fit in well with the Reds, a team that always had a lot of characters and guys who liked to have a good time. Tebbetts didn't want to be too strict about curfews, but treated us like men. So in one of those years, he told us that if we were going to miss curfew because some family member was in town that we should leave a note in his box. He said, "I want to know about it because if a writer says he saw a player out late, I want to be able to say that he had my permission." Well, that plan lasted about a month. A couple of players stayed out all the time, claiming they had all kinds of "cousins."

HERSHELL FREEMAN:

The Reds had a disappointing year in 1957, despite excellent years from George Crowe, Frank Robinson, Brooks Lawrence, and a few others. Our fans stuffed the ballot box and voted 7 or 8 guys onto the starting All-Star team. So the commissioner, Ford Frick, stepped in and replaced Crowe, Post, and Bell with Musial, Aaron, and Mays. Our new third baseman, Don Hoak, had an outstanding season. He was the most fiery competitor I ever played with. He would have eaten nails if he thought it would help the ballclub. He'd fight his mother to win.

We weren't in a pennant race, so I was used to the same degree as back in 1955. I didn't pitch as well, but even so my record was 7–2, giving me a 3-year 28–11 record for the Reds. Essentially my career with the Reds was over, although I would pitch in 3 games for them in 1958 before being traded to the Cubs. I had hoped to finish my career with them.

Looking back, I'd say baseball was harder then. There were more players and more farm clubs and only the very best players made it to the big leagues. The outstanding players from my day would have been outstanding in any era. Every day, you'd face a Hall of Fame–type player. Willie Mays was the best all-around player I ever saw. He could hit, run, and throw. I used to crowd Willie because you'd have to take the arms away from all good power hitters. Mays would tell me: "Hersh, don't throw too close to me. You throw too hard and you know you could hurt Willie."

Hank Aaron and Roberto Clemente were the hardest guys for me to pitch to. You might make them look bad on one pitch, but they would hit that same pitch the next time up. They had such good wrist action that they could throw the bat at the ball and make contact. Clemente was a little tougher for me. I could make him look sick on a fast ball up and in, and he'd throw the bat at the next pitch and hit it nine miles. You couldn't have a pattern with him.

If you got Stan Musial out, it was a rarity. We tried to pitch him away in St. Louis so he'd hit it to the deep part of the ballpark. In Cincinnati, we threw it over and felt lucky if no one was on base.

I was never scared of any ballplayer. After you've been in the big leagues for awhile, you think that they're just other major leaguers with just a bit more talent than the average man. Stan Musial, with all his notoriety and accomplishments, was one of the friendliest, everyday common people you'd ever want to be around. In his own mind, he was just another ballplayer. Guys who thought like that wouldn't be so evident in future eras.

JIM O'TOOLE:

I signed with the Reds in December, a month before my 21st birthday. I was the son of a policeman and grew up in the South Side of Chicago, in a tough neighborhood with Irish, Italian, Polish, and everybody else. I wasn't a bad kid, but was tough enough to get the nickname "Rocky"—I was always fighting. At 13, I fought in the Golden Gloves, knocking out guys 25 pounds heavier than me. My dad taught me to do that. I led a restricted, disciplined life because of my father. I got into as much trouble as other kids but was smart enough not to get caught.

When I was 12, I played softball in Moran Park—"Windy City Ball." I didn't play any hardball until I was 14. When I was 16 I was a pitcher in summer ball with guys who were 19 and 20 and I had no trouble getting them out. I was a big baseball fan and loved to see Billy Pierce and Whitey Ford, other left-handers. I knew in my heart that I could be a major league pitcher. But no one else knew about me until I was a senior and struck out 18 in a 7-inning summer league game against the city champs. Then scouts offered me contracts. I said no. I had met the gal I would marry and she wanted me to go to college. I also was interested in an education. I went to Wilson Junior College and then to the University of Wisconsin.

I pitched in Mitchell, South Dakota, in the Basin League, which had future major leaguers like Frank Howard, Dick Radatz, Ron Perranoski, Dick Howser, Bob Gibson, and Don Schwall. I got paid $500 a month, supposedly for a job I worked about five hours a week. The first year I was so wild they released me and I was replaced by Gibson. I didn't want to go home and face my dad so I thumbed down the road and joined the team in Madison, South Dakota. The first game I pitched was against Gibson and I beat him 3–1. That turned my life around. I vowed that I would beat him to the big leagues. Which I would.

After I had more success in the Basin League, teams were wining and dining my dad. In September of 1957, Don Schwall and I started traveling around the country together, working out with the Red Sox, Phillies, Athletics, Reds. I chose the Reds because they had great hitting but little pitching, and their manager was Birdie Tebbetts who, with his Irish blarney and way with people, reminded me of my father. I signed for $50,000 but I didn't read between the lines. It turned out that only $12,000 was a bonus and the rest of the money was going to be salary over three years.

AMERICAN LEAGUE 1957

"THE FIRST GAME I EVER APPEARED IN WAS AT FENWAY PARK AND THE FIRST BATTER I FACED WAS TED WILLIAMS, WHO HIT .388 THAT YEAR. I THREW THREE STRAIGHT STRIKES AND NESTOR CHYLAK CALLED THREE STRAIGHT BALLS. I STARTED HOLLERING AND SCREAMING AT HIM. HE SAID, 'MR. WILLIAMS WILL TELL YOU WHEN YOU THROW A STRIKE.'"

BARRY LATMAN

KANSAS CITY ATHLETICS

GUS ZERNIAL:

I played more in 1957, especially after Harry Craft replaced Lou Boudreau as manager. I still batted only 437 times, but I hit 27 homers, my last big homer year. It was also my final year with the Athletics. I think I had a very good career with them, winning one homer title and finishing second three times.

Hank Sauer, who played many years on bad Cubs teams, and I had similar careers in that we were the only players to provide homers and RBIs on not very successful teams. We also had reputations for not being able to field, although I think we held our own. We used to think a "dream" outfield would be Hank, me, and Ralph Kiner. Hank would joke, "Yeah, and I'd probably be the center fielder." Hank and I didn't have Hall of Fame careers, but we both had records that would keep our names alive in the towns we played.

Hank was a good friend of mine. During the off-season in California, we would play handball, jog, take steam baths, and play catch and pepper, so when I got to spring training, I never had to lose weight. My playing weight was about 220. Hank weighed less. He had a 10-pound nose. We kidded him about that. When we played ball, we called him "Horn" and said, "Here comes The Nose." He was never offended. Hank also played golf with Peanuts Lowrey and Gene Mauch. I wouldn't get in on their little bets, but Hank was so good that he inspired me to play, hoping I could play like him.

JOE DE MAESTRI:

It was hard being married as a young ballplayer and when the kids came along, it really got tough. Probably tougher for my wife than it was for me, because at least I was with the guys. When I was alone in Kansas City each spring I stayed at the Sans Souci Hotel. Meanwhile, my wife was in California waiting for the kids to finish school. When they joined me, we lived in a house out in Shawnee, Kansas. We met many people who we stayed in touch with over the years.

I was very fortunate to have made a lot of friends in Kansas City because in 1957, when I was having a good year and made the All-Star team, they gave me a night.

It was quite an experience. A close friend of mine organized it. He had a son whose head was too big for his body and went to special schools. So he'd ask me to go to these schools to talk to the kids. He was very appreciative and pushed for a night for me. I visited the schools on my own. There wasn't much organized charity work then. There was the Jimmy Fund of Ted Williams up in Boston. Williams had buddies on other teams that he'd take with him to hospitals. But I can't remember any teams sponsoring anything like that.

In 1957, I led American League shortstops in fielding percentage, making only 13 errors. (I would do the same in 1958.) Fielding was second nature to me and I always felt relaxed. My only problem was that I enjoyed fielding so much that was all that I ever worked on. I thought, "Well, this is the part that's going to keep me here." Consequently, my hitting never really improved. I usually hit about .240 with 6 homers and about 37 or 38 RBIs. I was always tired at the end of the year and really struggled at the plate, but I was always hot at the beginning of the year. That's because I came to training camp in great shape to make sure I could beat out anybody after my job. I worked out during the off-season.

I did a couple of endorsements while in Kansas City. I got about $50 total to do an ad for some kind of pizza. Gus and I also did a radio commercial for some brand of coffee. We got about $50 for that, too. To pick up extra money but still have free time in the off-season, I worked as a salesman for my father's beer and wine business.

VIC POWER:

At first I lived in the colored section in Kansas City. Later, after not finding an apartment, I stayed in a hotel in the white section. I didn't have problems where I lived, but I did have trouble on the streets. I'd be driving my Cadillac 25 mph, and the police would pull me over and I'd have to give them the name of the dealer where I'd bought it. When I'd tell them "I'm Vic Power, the ballplayer," they'd say, "Okay, we were just making a routine investigation." The editor of the black paper in Kansas City wrote that he saw 50 policemen when driving by the ballpark but when he saw a man beating a screaming woman two blocks past there were no cops around because they were back at the ballpark "waiting for Vic Power so they could make a routine investiga-

tion." One time a policeman said he thought I stole my car. I got mad because I had just received a certificate for being the best-dressed player in the major leagues and I was well dressed in a hat and tie. I told him, "You look more like a thief than me."

I got married at home and brought my wife to Kansas City. She was a light-skinned Puerto Rican with dyed blond hair, and the police would always pull us over. They'd ask rude questions about her race and get angry when she didn't answer. When I tried to tell them she didn't speak English, they'd snap, "We didn't ask you!"

There was a camaraderie among blacks throughout the league. We'd get together when our teams played each other. Of course, Minnie Minoso, who was in Chicago, and the other Latin blacks would talk because we all spoke Spanish. Some managers didn't like their Latin players speaking Spanish because they were afraid they were talking behind their backs.

MINNIE MINOSO (WHITE SOX):

Latin players on the different teams usually became friends. But the only Latin player you'd automatically consider your friend was Vic Power. When I'd come to Kansas City, he'd say, in Spanish, "Hey, buddy, come to my house and have rice and beans with me." So he'd take me to his house and I met his wife, a nice lady, and baby, and he'd cook for us all. He was a good friend. He lived an open life. If he'd have an errand to do, he'd say, "You're my brother. Take care of my family till I'm back." He made me feel at home. I saw him with his family and thought that's the type of life I wanted.

V. POWER:

In 1957, I started calling Minoso "Mau Mau" and he had no idea I was referring to those black terrorists in Kenya who were in the news. In New York, I'd call Elston Howard "Mau Mau." Soon, all the blacks in the league were jokingly calling each other "Mau Mau." Then, in fun, the white players started calling the black players "Mau Mau." The Copacabana incident? I was told Whitey Ford, Mickey Mantle, Hank Bauer, and Johnny Kucks were celebrating Billy Martin's birthday and had been drinking and Billy Martin or someone at the table jokingly called Sammy Davis, Jr., who was performing, a "Mau Mau." The people at the next table may have heard that and then called him some worse names and there was a fight that spilled into the men's room.

ART FOWLER (REDS):
Billy Martin later told me that Hank Bauer and some others started a fight and Billy tried to stop it.

V. POWER:
It was a tough year. I slumped to .259, Zernial led the team with less than 70 RBIs, and Tom Morgan and Virgil Trucks led the pitchers with just 9 victories each, although we had some pretty good pitchers in Ned Garver, Ralph Terry, and Alex Kellner. Boudreau got fired and Harry Craft replaced him as manager. Craft was a nice, intelligent man, but he was too much like a D.I., an army man. When Hector Lopez dropped a ball, Craft made him shag flies for an hour. I was getting dressed after a long doubleheader when Craft made us all go back on the field for batting practice because we got only 2 hits in the second game. So I had to go take batting practice although I got both our hits!

RYNE DUREN:
During the winter, Baltimore traded me to Kansas City. I pitched fairly well in spring training and made the team. Jim Pisoni was my best friend on the team. We had come up together through the Browns' farm system and had been traded together to the Athletics. I'd also run with Johnny Groth, who was a good drinker.

It was great pitching for Lou Boudreau. He was a good baseball man and pretty engaging. He tried to make the game interesting. I got along with Harry Craft, Boudreau's lieutenant and eventual successor, but I didn't like Spud Chandler, his pitching coach. Spud had won 20 games twice for the Yankees in the forties. He would tell me that if he had my stuff he'd have won thirty games, inferring I was dumb and he was smart.

I pitched pretty well but didn't get much run support. The first game I started in the major leagues was against the Yankees. I drove in our only run on a 2-out drag bunt against Tom Sturdivant, but they beat us 2–1. After the game, Bauer, their leadoff hitter, and McDougald commented that I threw too hard for married men to hit against. Billy Martin was down in the lineup. I threw him a fastball that ate him up inside and sawed off the bat in his hands. He fell to the

ground and watched the ball trickle back to me. I picked it up and threw him out. Martin got up, wiped the dirt off and walked back to the dugout where everyone was dying laughing. He yelled at me, "I'll get you, you four-eyed son-of-a-bitch!" The next time the Yankees were in town, I was surprised that Boudreau sent me in to relieve. It was June 15, trade-deadline day. I knocked down Berra and he hollered, "You'd better not do that again." I said, "Go back to your tree!" I walked back into the clubhouse and Parke Carroll wanted to speak to me. He had traded me to the Yankees along with Pisoni, Suitcase Simpson, and Milt Graff. The deal brought Billy Martin to the Athletics, along with Ralph Terry, Woodie Held, and Bob Martyn. Martin had just been involved in the Copacabana incident and New York wanted to get rid of him. Boudreau told me that he hadn't wanted the trade because he considered me the best pitcher on the team.

CLEVELAND INDIANS

AL SMITH:
I got married in 1956 and we lived in Wade Park, 20 minutes east of the ballpark. It was good to settle down and raise a family. I think it made me a better man. Now, I mostly spent time with the married players, while the bachelors went their own ways. On off-days, Early Wynn and his wife would visit, and we'd go out back and have drinks. All the wives would sit together at the ball park and, when the Indians were out of town, many spent time together elsewhere. They'd work with charities like the Red Cross or help with underprivileged children.

Kerby Farrell replaced Al Lopez as manager. He tried to get too much out of his players. Our team had changed and we were no better than a .500 team and some of the guys weren't capable of what he expected of them. But he was a funny guy and we got along well.

I moved to third base and Gene Woodling played left. We had a good outfield because Rocky Colavito continued to improve and we brought up a promising rookie: Roger Maris. He was very quiet. I couldn't tell if he'd hit many homers but I could see he could swing the bat with a lot of power. He was left-handed.

Surprisingly, the Indians' weakness was pitching.

Early had an off year and Mike Garcia, although he had a decent record, and Bob Lemon were almost finished. Worst of all, of course, is what happened to Herb Score, who was just 23.

In May, I was playing third base against the Yankees when Herb was hit by Gil McDougald's line drive. When Herb threw the ball he always fell toward the hitter, moving downward. McDougald's drive came right back at him and hit him in the eye. I picked up the ball and there was silence in the stadium. I started running toward Herb, who had collapsed on the mound. They started hollering, "Throw the ball to first!" I almost threw it in the stands but I got McDougald out. When I reached the mound, blood was pouring out Score's nose, mouth, and ears. It was sickening. He looked like a boxer had just demolished him. But he never lost consciousness. He kept asking for Mike Garcia, his good friend.

CHICO CARRASQUEL:

Herb Score was a real nice boy. He wanted to be the best and by 1957, he was the best pitcher in the American League. Joe Cronin of the Red Sox offered to buy his contract for $1 million, but Hank Greenberg turned him down. When he got hurt, I was playing shortstop, Bobby Avila was on second, Al Smith was on third, Vic Wertz was on first, and Jim Hegan was the catcher. We all went to the mound where Herbie was lying. I remember that everything was silent. It was so upsetting.

I liked Roger Maris. He was a likable guy, a good family man. We spent a lot of time talking on the road and became good friends. He talked a lot about baseball. This was his rookie season and in one game, he got 2 home runs. He was so happy. He said, "Chico, one of these years I'm going to hit 20 to 25 home runs!"

GENE WOODLING:

I played in left, Roger Maris was in center, and Rocky Colavito was in right. Maris was a serious guy who didn't laugh, which is why he would get unfair press later in his career. I didn't really see his potential. But I liked him.

I was playing when Score was hit by McDougald's line drive. He really got whacked. It was unbelievable. The guy who felt worse than anyone was McDougald. He would feel terrible for years and years. Herb came

out of it in great style. He hated when people implied that this was what ruined his career. He didn't want pity. What happened is that he later hurt his arm and that ruined his career.

Playing for Kerby Farrell, I had the best statistical year of my career, batting .321 with 19 homers and 77 RBIs, all career highs at this point. He was around so long in the minors that some guys took advantage of him. I thought he was a good man.

I became the American League player rep in 1957, the year a new five-year pension plan went into effect. Robin Roberts was the National League rep. I wasn't a nice guy. I was very blunt because I wanted results. General managers promised you the moon—but I said pay us now and we'll worry about the future. They judged all ballplayers as dummies. I wasn't dumb. I kept after them. Baseball didn't really like me but I didn't care.

We never talked strike or unionizing. We just wanted a fair pension. I used to try to educate the players. They'd complain about minor things like faulty showerheads. I'd say if that was the type of complaints we'd bring to the owners, they'd gladly change the showerheads and say, "Look, we already gave you that."

Most people wouldn't even remember I was a player rep. I didn't do it for fame, but because I was asked by other players. I didn't expect any pats on the back because I would benefit also. There were three or four general meetings every year. The winter meetings and the All-Star break were the times we tried to get results. The owners didn't want to give you anything. They were using our money, putting it in a central fund, and I said that had to stop, period.

Everything was verbal until that time. Which was illegal. You can't set up a pension plan verbally in this country. But for 10 years we trusted people. Our money was in a central fund. It was a sad situation. Our knowledge was limited so we brought in New York lawyers, and they weren't as good as I would have liked.

I wasn't an outcast or a clubhouse lawyer. I just wasn't liked by a lot of owners and general managers for the simple reason that I was fighting for the right things. There's nothing harder than being honest—you get into all kinds of trouble. They told me they were going to try to get me out of baseball. A fair response? I stuck out my neck knowing that if I didn't play ball I'd still make a good living in the business world, and even make more money. The funny thing is that as long as you hit, you stay, and if you don't hit you'll go home anyway. They made me mad enough to hit and stick around for several more years.

BALTIMORE ORIOLES

BROOKS ROBINSON:

I made the Orioles' roster in spring training. But I had a knee operation right after the season started and was out for two months. Then I spent some time in the minors before coming back. George Kell was still the Orioles' starting third baseman and was having a solid final season, but I got to play in almost 50 games. I played with a very good infield.

First baseman Bob Boyd, who was one of the first black players I played with, was called "El Ropo" because he hit the darnedest line drives you ever saw. He was a good fielder and hitter—he hit .318 that year, the best on the team. Second baseman Billy Gardner was a leader by example. He was the MVP for the Orioles that year, when he played 154 games and led the league in at-bats and doubles and led second basemen in fielding percentage. He was a terrific player, who got by on blood and guts.

Willie Miranda was one of the first guys I met when I came to the Orioles. He was from Cuba but his English was pretty good. He never hit much but he was a terrific shortstop with a lot of range and a great arm. He could go in the hole and throw guys out better than anyone I ever saw, including Luis Aparicio. He had a glove that he used almost his entire career. It was so old that he resorted to putting tongue depressors and cotton in the fingers to keep them stiff. He gave me that idea: When a glove I really liked was getting old and loose, I'd stick tongue depressors up the thumb so I could use it longer. Willie was a great guy. After the season, I would play against him in winter ball.

GEORGE KELL:

When I played, the *Game of the Week* was the only nationally televised game there was. There wasn't the same coverage so we didn't have the pressure of playing on television every game. Even All-Star Games took place at three in the afternoon, not in prime time. Locally, the Orioles telecast less than half their games. (Unfortunately, expanded television coverage would negatively affect the talent in the majors by bringing about the demise of the minor leagues and causing expansion in the early sixties.)

In 1957, I played in my last All-Star Game. The American League won, 6–5, when Minnie Minoso made a game-saving running catch off Gil Hodges with 2 outs in the ninth. What I remember most was Willie Mays hitting a sharp grounder to my left. I came up with it and had to whirl to throw him out by a step. The Indians' Vic Wertz was the first baseman and when we came into the dugout, he said, "That's what I like. You throw strikes." It was a real thrill and honor to play in All-Star Games and I would never be able to understand how anyone would turn down an invitation for any reason. I was chosen for 10 All-Star Games and went to them all, even the two times I was injured and couldn't play. I just wanted to be there.

I told Paul Richards that I decided to quit at the end of the season. But I almost didn't make it that far. In September I was beaned for the first time in my career. I was hit by Steve Gromek in Detroit and they had to carry me off the field. I didn't lose consciousness but I didn't really know what was going on. Almost two weeks to the day, we were in Chicago for the second game of a Sunday doubleheader. We had a lot of injuries or I wouldn't have been playing both games. It was extremely hot and my mind wasn't on the game. I was relaxed at the plate and on the first pitch, Dick Donovan hit me right on the side of the head. I could have gotten out of the way, but I just wasn't ready. I went down like a ton of bricks. I remember Paul saying, "I want him taken to the hospital." I stayed two nights. Paul visited and asked what I wanted to do. I told him that since the season was ending I wanted to go home for the duration. However, I did as he suggested, which was to go home for a couple of days and then rejoin the team on Friday. I was sitting in the clubhouse and Paul told me I was playing that night. I said, "You're kidding!" He said, "No, you need to play." So he played me the rest of the year. He didn't want me to finish my career sitting on the bench.

BILLY O'DELL:

I was in the service in 1955, stationed in Fort McPherson in Georgia, and when I got out in 1956 I got to pitch only 8 innings at the end of the season. So it wasn't until 1957 that I resumed my career. When I had joined Baltimore in 1954, there was no real leader on the team, but now there was George Kell and Hal "Skinny" Brown, a pitcher. Everyone looked up to them and if you had a few problems, you could go to them. George was quick to help with your fielding or hitting, and Skinny was the same way with pitchers. I roomed with Skinny for a couple of years and he gave me a lot of good advice about playing baseball and about being a major leaguer.

Gus Triandos, who had become the Orioles' catcher in my absence, was considered a leader by some players, but I thought he was a bit quiet. Gus was a great guy in every way and a good hitter and catcher. He was regarded as the slowest runner in the game, but he was so big and took such long strides that it seemed he was slower than he was.

Paul Richards was strict, wanting things done his way. He completely changed everything on the team. To him, baseball was pitching and defense. He made me a reliever. Between starts I couldn't sit still, so I'd go down to the bullpen. Richards told me that if I was going to throw every day anyway that he'd like to put me in games for an inning or two. So I both started and pitched in relief. I made 15 starts and relieved 20 times. My overall record was just 4–10 but I had a 2.69 ERA, which was my best with the Orioles, and struck out 97 batters and walked only 39 in 140 innings. So it was a pretty good year.

Against the Yankees, Richards would conceal who his starter was so Stengel, who platooned, couldn't fix his lineup. I warmed up underneath the stands before one game. Richards started Ray Moore, a righty, and Stengel countered with his left-handed batters. Richards let Moore pitch to only the first batter, and then brought me into the game. The first batter had doubled and Moore told me, "If that guy scores, I'll kill you." He did score and Ray was the losing pitcher.

Brooks Robinson was a real gentleman and that wouldn't ever change. Kell helped him a lot at third. He became a great fielder yet he'd still work on it. He'd

Left-hander Billy O'Dell had joined Baltimore in 1954, but he didn't get to pitch much until 1957, when his poor record belied his excellent earned-run average.

catch grounders just as long as you were willing to hit them to him. He also worked hard on his hitting. No one worked any harder.

Billy Loes had come over from the Dodgers in 1956. He was still a pretty good pitcher and could get by with a lot of stuff less intelligent pitchers couldn't. He was flaky, though not a prankster, and Richards took him with a grain of salt. He was sort of quiet but if you asked him something, he'd tell you exactly what he felt. He was no phony. The players liked him but he was a loner. If you wanted to go eat with him, it would be okay with him but he wouldn't ask first. He wasn't outgoing at all.

BOSTON RED SOX

FRANK MALZONE:

At my third Red Sox spring training camp, Higgins didn't play me in the first couple of weeks of exhibition games. I came home and told my wife that I had to decide whether to quit or not. We talked and decided to stick it out through the spring. Boston went to San Francisco to play an exhibition game in Seals Stadium, where I'd played the previous year. I didn't even bother checking the day's lineup. I was on the field taking ground balls when my good buddy, catcher Pete Daley, told me I was playing. I batted sixth and went 1 for 4. I played every inning of every remaining game during spring training. I didn't know why they decided to live or die with me at third base.

Frank Malzone finally stuck with the Red Sox in 1957 and became a fixture as he batted .292, drove in a career-high 102 runs, and won a major-league Gold Glove with his play at third base.

I opened the season with the Red Sox and played every inning of the entire schedule. Billy Klaus shifted to short. We had a good ballclub, one that was built for power. We went for big innings and home runs by everyone in the lineup. Williams, Jensen, Gernert, Piersall, me . . . Williams, Gernert, Gene Mauch—who played some at second base—and I tied a league record with 4 homers in an inning. We didn't feel it was absolutely necessary to have speed. The Yankees didn't need speed to win. The pitching, led by Frank Sullivan, Tom Brewer, and Willard Nixon, was shaky, but that's to be expected in Fenway Park—once a few weak fly balls hit the wall for doubles, pitchers become tentative and get hurt.

At 38 or 39, Ted Williams led the league with an amazing .388, his best average since his .406 in 1941. He also had 38 homers, his highest total since 1949. He had two 3-homer games and in one stretch in September got on base 16 times in a row.

HANK SAUER (GIANTS):

I had been around 20 years and Ted Williams was the greatest hitter I ever saw. I saw him only in All-Star Games and during spring training but the reason I rated him above Stan Musial, who I considered the best all-around player, is that I never saw him hit the ball easy. Williams had more power than Musial and hit everything right on the nose, even as he approached forty.

F. MALZONE:

I had a solid year, playing good defense and providing the power they had been lacking at third base. I hit .292 with 15 homers, and finished fifth in the league in total bases, third in doubles with 31, and tied Jackie Jensen for third in RBIs with 103.

One game I had 4 hits and had another bat coming. I was just going to swing away. But Mickey Vernon, who truly was a prize to play with, walked past me at the bat-rack and said, "Get the fifth one." I didn't get it but I tried. From that day on I realized what he was talking about—you don't want to waste opportunities because someday you'll regret not having done what you could have.

One highlight of my career was to play in my first All-Star Game. Another was to win the first Gold Glove given to a third baseman. The Gold Glove was started that year. It was called the Major League Gold Glove that year and was given to only one major league player at each position. It was a thrill and honor being one of only nine players who received them. The other recipients were Sherm Lollar as the catcher, Gil Hodges at first base, Nellie Fox at second, Roy McMillan at shortstop, Al Kaline in right, Willie Mays in center, Minnie Minoso in left, and pitcher Bobby Shantz. (I'd always kid Brooks Robinson that he never got one that said Major League.)

In those days, the New York press controlled everything. If the New York sportswriters wanted something done, they could get it their way. They were the ones who made sure Joe DiMaggio was MVP over Ted Williams in the 1940s. All year I was regarded as a rookie, but in the last month, the New York press managed to get my classification changed so that Yankee shortstop Tony Kubek would win the Rookie of the Year award. My name was taken off the ballot and Tony won. I didn't think too much about it then, but years later I realized I would have liked to have always been known for having been a Rookie of the Year. I would have gotten more prestige.

The Yankees won the pennant, as they did almost every year. They had a great ballclub. They won with good pitching and the late inning homer, and by not making mistakes and giving you a second shot. We tried to do the same, but it never worked out.

I saw immediately that there was a big rivalry between the Red Sox and Yankees. It was there in the DiMaggio-Williams days and stemmed all the way back to when Boston sold Babe Ruth to the Yankees. The media from both towns contributed to the rivalry, making every game seem vital and trying to build feuds between managers and between players—Williams's new rival in the MVP voting was Mickey Mantle, who got the award over Ted despite not having as good a year. We weren't the same as the Dodgers-Giants rivalry because we weren't in the same city and the players on our two teams didn't dislike one another. There weren't even any major fights in the years I played, just knockdown pitches that everyone expected. If a guy threw it under my chin and didn't hit me, it was no big deal. The rivalry also was heightened because in each park there were the same number of Boston and New York fans. That made it great. Our games were the highlights of the season. There was more action, more involvement, more fans. The exciting atmosphere got my adrenaline running and I couldn't wait to get to the ballpark.

BILL MONBOUQUETTE:

In my second year in professional baseball, I played the first month in Albany, which was A-ball, and was then dispatched to Greensboro in the Carolina League. This was my fourth team. At this time I noticed that there still weren't many blacks in the Red Sox system, but I didn't think it was because the organization didn't want blacks to play for them in the big leagues.

I grew up in a black neighborhood and when I went into pro ball I couldn't understand the horrible treatment of blacks. White players from the South were always insulting black players. In the South, blacks couldn't drink from the same water fountains, go to the same bathrooms, or stay in the same hotels as white players. I couldn't understand it. It bothered me that we dropped off the black players at rundown black hotels and continued on to our much plusher hotels. It bothered me that they had to sit in the bus and wait for us to bring food back from the restaurants we ate in. I remember getting on a public bus in Ocala, Florida, and being told to move from the back of the bus because that's where blacks were supposed to sit.

I had been exposed to the Red Sox players during the previous years because after the minor league season was over I'd gone home and thrown batting practice to the parent club. I wanted to get my feet wet and find out what pro ball was all about.

I don't recall being taught Red Sox pride or tradition, but Boston had a good farm system that prepared you for the majors. The guys who helped you most were the managers because there were no coaches. But I did get some attention from Johnny Murphy, the Sox farm director, and Charlie Wagner, who was a roving pitching coach and had pitched for Boston in the late '30s and early '40s. The most instrumental guys for developing players were Joe Cronin, the general manager, and Bobby Doerr, who traveled around checking up on minor leaguers. Doerr saw me strike out 14 batters yet suffer a tough loss in Greensboro when it was about 107 degrees. He told me, ''If you keep pitching like that you'll be in the majors soon.'' He gave me confidence.

WASHINGTON SENATORS

HARMON KILLEBREW:

I started the season with Chattanooga in the Southern Association. The manager was Cal Ermer, who had a great baseball mind and helped me more than anyone. The most important thing he taught me was how to play third base. He also worked with me on hitting. As a kid I was different than typical right-handed batters because I hit low fastballs better than high fastballs. I learned to hit the high fastball. Cal actually pitched to me himself most of the time, before batting practice. We had good results: I hit 29 homers and drove in 101 runs.

My stay with the Senators that year was brief. I played in only 9 games. Cookie Lavagetto replaced Chuck Dressen as the Senators' manager early in the season. He was in his mid-forties and had been a coach for Dressen. In fact, Dressen had me room with Cookie for a little while in 1955 to teach me about baseball. He was an excellent coach and knew a lot about the fundamentals of baseball, but managing players—and the Senators weren't a hard team to handle—put a strain on Cookie that I don't think he was prepared for.

PEDRO RAMOS:

After I had a winning record with a seventh-place team in 1956 at the age of 21, I asked for a $1,000 raise to $7,500. I negotiated directly with Calvin Griffith. He cried how the team didn't make much money. He told me that I would get a $500 raise and if I didn't like that I could stay in Cuba and cut sugar cane. It was unbelievable. We were like slaves. If it had been years later I would have said, "Mr. Griffith, I'm going to spend this year in Cuba with the pretty Cuban girls and next year I'll be a free agent. You can go to hell." But then I had to sign his contract. I was disappointed. All the players considered Griffith to be cheap. It was tough to get money out of him. But I couldn't say he treated me different than the white players. As a matter of fact I was like one of the family. I would babysit for his grandchildren, Bruce and Mike. I'd play with them around the pool and take them to movies.

1957 was a terrible year for the Senators, maybe our worst. We won just 55 games and finished in last place. I was 12–16 and no other pitcher won more than 8

games. Stobbs went 8–20 and Pascual 8–17. We had no offense other than Roy Sievers. He batted .300 and led the league with 42 homers and 114 RBIs, 50 more RBIs than Jim Lemon, who was second on our team. All the players looked up to Sievers after Mickey Vernon was traded. He was a good man and I admired him. I also loved the way he swung the bat.

We were doing so badly that Griffith fired Charlie Dressen early in the season and hired Cookie Lavagetto. He was a good baseball man. If you couldn't play for him, you couldn't play for anybody. He laid the rules on the table and you went by them, no problem. He told you straight what he thought, in a nice way. The one time I complained was when he fined me $5 for stealing the only base of my career.

I didn't really hear players complain about being on a losing team. I lost so many tough games in Washington that I wanted to cry for. 2–1 losses that would have been 3–2 wins if I were on the Yankees. I was mad but I didn't show my emotions. Lavagetto would say, "Pedro, you did a good job and tomorrow's another day." So I looked toward the next time.

I just loved to pitch. When I got on the mound, I didn't even know how many people were in the stands. That's why fans never bothered me in opposing cities. If they did boo me, I never heard them. Even if they cheered, I didn't look up past four or five rows. I didn't care which ballpark I pitched in. I didn't care if the mound was high or low. I didn't talk to the groundskeepers to fix the field for me, as many pitchers did. I just concentrated on pitching. I went hitter by hitter, inning by inning. The umpires used to tell me they liked calling my games because I pitched quickly. I didn't give a batter too much time to think. I knew what I was going to throw. My best pitch every time.

When I was pitching, I didn't want anyone to talk to me. I wanted to concentrate. I didn't like catchers to come to the mound. Clint Courtney, who was a funny guy who'd drink a lot of beer and talk about cows, didn't bother coming to the mound because all he wanted was fastballs. That was no problem. Except for the day he wanted me to hit Ted Williams. I didn't want to do it. He motioned for the knockdown pitch and I shook him off. Ten times! Then he walked to the mound. He said, "You goddamn, yellow Cuban bastard." Courtney and me were pretty good friends, otherwise I would have told him to get the hell away from me. He said, ''Do it!'' I said, ''All right, get back there, I'm going to hit him.'' I didn't want to do it because I didn't want to hurt him. You don't hurt a Williams—you need players like that in baseball. I had a lot of respect for him. If I could get him out, why should I hit him? I don't think it's fair. But anyway, I hit him. I busted him right on the arm. The next time up, I fired one in there and he hit one over the scoreboard. I told Courtney, ''See, you woke him up!''

Ted Williams was the best hitter I ever faced. He didn't swing at bad pitches so you had to throw him strikes. I struck him out only once in my life. I remember when Ted Abernathy, who threw underhanded, struck out Williams twice in a game in Boston. He went by me to drink some water and he said, ''Pete, I got the Big Man twice.'' I said, ''You better shut up, because the Big Man has to come up at least one more time.'' Oh, man, in the eighth inning the bases were loaded and the Big Man came up. Abernathy got two quick strikes, but then I could hear Williams christen his bat: he rapped the ball all the way into the bleachers. Lavagetto took Abernathy out and I reminded him of what I said. I can't repeat what Abernathy said.

Abernathy was a dandy. A family man, minded his own business, easygoing. We roomed together for a while and got along great. He threw underhanded and threw good but he gave up a lot of hits and walks. (He would spend most of his time in the minors until the mid-sixties when he was switched to the bullpen and became a top-notch reliever.)

JIM FRIDLEY (MINORS):

Other than the left-handed Herb Score, who was intimidating to all batters, Ted Abernathy was the toughest pitcher against right-handers I faced in the '50s, in the majors or minors. He'd give me fits. Most curve balls sink, but Abernathy threw underhanded and his ball shot up. Batting against him was like swatting flies.

DETROIT TIGERS

HAL WOODESHICK:

In the winter of 1956 I had gotten married. I ate well. And since I couldn't pitch in winter ball because there

were arguments over my contract, I didn't get any exercise. So I came to the Tigers' spring training weighing 250 pounds, having put on 45 pounds. I couldn't get anyone out. The year turned out to be a washout. Instead of pitching for the Tigers, I had to go back to Charleston, only this time I couldn't get anyone out there, either. The Tigers were mad at me so they sent me to Augusta, Georgia, where it was over 100 degrees every day and I could get my weight down. After a while I started pitching well, but the Tigers didn't bring me up. I was no longer in their plans.

COOT VEAL:

My minor league career was long. Six years. I played in strictly bus leagues. I saw a lot of the United States. A 600-mile trip was nothing. For a couple of years, it was a lot of fun because I was so young and enthusiastic. When our kids got older, it got tougher moving about. We moved every summer. I always hit about .280 in the minors and did a good job at shortstop. I wasn't fast but I was quick and hustled and could steal a base. I made the All-Star team in the Southern Association. I was improving. But it was a question of being on the right team at the right time. I'd get discouraged when I'd hear through the grapevine that the Tigers were fixing to call me up and then I wouldn't be, or that a trade was in the works and that didn't happen. I came within a whisker, they told me, of going to the Yankees in 1957, before Tony Kubek moved up from Richmond.

CHICAGO WHITE SOX

MINNIE MINOSO:

Between 1951 and 1957, I hit over .300 five times, scored over 100 runs four times, drove in more than 100 runs three times, and led the American League in both triples and stolen bases three times. I even led the league in being hit by the pitch—I did it for the team. (I had my head fractured by pitches—Bob Grim hit me in 1955 and I was out two weeks.) I made the All-Star team five times. In 1957, I won the first of three Gold Gloves. I batted .310 and had 103 RBIs, more than 20 RBIs more than any teammate, but after one year playing for Al Lopez, I was traded with Fred Hatfield back to the Indians for Early Wynn and Al Smith. Lopez had been my manager when I was traded from Cleveland in 1951. (And he'd trade me again in 1961.) It seemed that every time I was traded, Al Lopez was the manager who got rid of me. I'm not the kind of guy who says anything so I wouldn't make a public statement about Lopez. (Maybe someday, I will explore it.)

LES MOSS:

Everybody liked Al Lopez. He was the best manager I played for. He knew baseball and got more out of a ballclub than anyone and he did it easily. He knew pitchers well, he knew catchers because he had been one, he knew baseball. I loved playing for him.

BILLY PIERCE:

The White Sox kept a nucleus over the years but still made a lot of trades, even after Frank Lane was no longer the GM because of his feud with Chuck Comiskey. We pretty much had the same players up the middle and in the outfield, but for many years we kept getting players shuffled in to play first and third. There were new guys at those positions almost every year. When I joined the team there was Charlie Kress at first and Floyd Baker at third. The next year it was Eddie Robinson and Hank Majeski. Then Bob Dillinger replaced Majeski. The year after that, it was Robinson and Hector Rodriguez, a rookie from Cuba who Frank Lane traded after he made a big error, along with the losing pitcher, Chuck Stobbs. Then we had Ferris Fain and Bob Elliott. Following them, there was 6'7" Ron Jackson, who played parttime, Walt Dropo, Earl Torgeson, and Ray Boone at first, and George Kell, Fred Hatfield, and Bubba Phillips at third. This pattern would continue.

We also changed managers a lot. Al Lopez became our manager in 1957, coming over from Cleveland to replace Marty Marion. Whereas Paul Richards, Marion's predecessor, had been a teacher, Lopez expected us to know how to play the game. Richards got along with the younger players and rookies better than Lopez. Al liked veterans more. They both paid a lot of attention to pitching and developed strong staffs, with Ray Berres as their pitching coach. Al played a little more percentage baseball than Richards so he'd bunt a man to second in a situation Richards might just have the guy try to steal. Like Richards, Lopez was a top-flight manager.

He finally got us over the hump and into second place, behind only the Yankees. I pitched well for him. Jim Bunning and I were the only pitchers in the league to win 20 games. And for the second straight year, I led the league in complete games.

We were in first place until late June, but then the Yankees pulled ahead and won by 8 games. There was frustration that we couldn't win the pennant over the years, but we realized there was a lot of talent in the league. There were four other good ballclubs, discounting the Athletics who faded after the early '50s. New York had pitching, hitting, and defense. Cleveland had great pitching and some hitting, Boston had great hitting but inconsistent pitching, and Detroit had good hitting and a few good starters but not much pitching depth. The five of us were good, tough, solid teams. We just waited for our time to come, while management tried to make improvements.

We improved in the outfield in 1957 when we brought up Jim Landis. He played right field that year, but what a great center fielder he would become. He would also develop into a good clutch hitter. Jim was a super guy and he became good friends with Nellie and me.

JIM LANDIS:

When I came to spring training, I had good feelings right away. They had liked what I had done in Memphis in 1956, and told me I was the right fielder and that it was my position to lose. I didn't know if I was ready but I was on cloud nine. I had a slow start in spring training but then surprised myself by hitting a few home runs. Things started going well and I clinched the job.

My first game in the major leagues was the thrill of all thrills: Opening Day 1957. I was so flabbergasted that I didn't know where I was half the time. And in that frame of mind, I had to face Herb Score in his prime (before he got hurt). I grounded out weakly, flied weakly to right, and struck out. It was still beautiful.

Larry Doby was in his last year as our regular center fielder. So I played right field as a rookie. I had never played there before and it was entirely different than center because the ball would sink and sail away from you. I had to learn different coverages. I didn't work with Doby at all. Again it was entirely with John Mostil.

The 1957 White Sox were a great, unified team. We

Jim Landis was sent down to the minors in his rookie season but would return the following year and become a clutch-hitting, Gold Glove center fielder for the White Sox.

National Baseball Library, Cooperstown, N.Y.

won a lot more than we should have because we had a unique bunch of guys. Some of the veterans were unbelievably friendly to young players. Nellie Fox, Sherm Lollar, and Billy Pierce were fabulous. They made me feel part of the team without forcing the issue.

I saw a lot of team pride. We didn't take any guff from any other team, including the Yankees. We had a few fights with them. That year Larry Doby decked Art Ditmar after he threw at his head. That started a fight. Enos Slaughter comes running in from the outfield and he and Walt Dropo—who was all class—got into it. Slaughter had his shirt ripped off, and it got to be a pretty good hassle with 12 to 15 guys going to town. I had a pulled hamstring so there was no way I was going to get in the middle. Billy Martin often started fights. He was sneaky. Once he instigated a brawl, he would back out of the action.

Al Lopez welcomed me to the team. I usually called him Mr. Lopez, not Skip, because he exuded class. He was very helpful in my career. He'd say to writers,

"Leave this kid alone and he'll be fine." I was broken-hearted when he told me that I was being sent down. But I knew that my performance justified my demotion. After more than 90 games, I was hitting below .220 and had about 15 RBIs. Lopez said, "I'm sending you down to get a little more experience." He said he wasn't worried about me and that I was his center fielder the next year. So I knew I'd be back.

FRED HATFIELD:
Every player got fan mail in the '50s. I always answered mail and sent back autographs and pictures. Just about every ballpark had one fan who was always there, trying to get you to autograph a ball or something or just shake your hand. Every city had its Pete or Jack or Bill or Grandpa. New York had some elderly lady who was always in the hotel lobby getting autographs. Chicago had a woman behind the dugout who asked for our autographs and heckled visiting players.

People knew you everywhere you went. At the time, baseball was much bigger than the other sports and attracted all the best athletes. It was the All-American sport. I looked forward to playing on television so I'd be seen all over the country. They'd see me in Tallahassee and remind me when I came back in the winter. I'd feel like a star. However, on my next visit some guy from home would ask, "Are you still chasing that baseball around, Junior?" That put me back into reality.

1957 was the last year I got any significant playing time, although it was way down from the previous year. I was used frequently as a pinch-hitter and didn't do that well. My average dropped to .202. Early in my career, I was aggressive, probably too much so, but I got smarter over the years and knew how pitchers would work me, and I became more selective. Still, when I got my pitch I now fouled it off. I was a fastball-cripple hitter. A fastball right down the middle of the plate was my pitch. As I always said, I had trouble hitting a pitched ball, but otherwise I was a good hitter.

BARRY LATMAN:
I had done well at Waterloo in 1955 and Memphis in 1956, but I struggled at Indianapolis, Chicago's Triple A team. The manager was also my catcher and he'd get pissed off at me and we'd argue. After my fifth straight loss, he told me he was sending me back down to

Memphis. Then I got a telephone call the next day from Chuck Comiskey, the owner of the White Sox, telling me to come up to the parent club. I just assumed it was a joke, laughed and hung up the phone. So he had to call me back and say, "I'm not kidding. This is Chuck Comiskey and if you're not up here in four hours, you're really going to have some trouble!" So I made the majors by losing five straight games. They wanted me to come up to see what I was doing wrong.

I came up at the end of the season. I roomed with a guy who didn't play baseball, a fraternity brother from USC, who was in Chicago that year. Most of the players lived on the South Side but I lived on the North Side.

The first game I ever appeared in was at Fenway Park and the first batter I faced was Ted Williams, who hit .388 that year. I threw three straight strikes and Nestor Chylak called three straight balls. I started hollering

Brought up at 21 by the White Sox, Barry Latman would pitch well for the White Sox through 1959, yet wouldn't get enough work from Al Lopez to realize his potential.

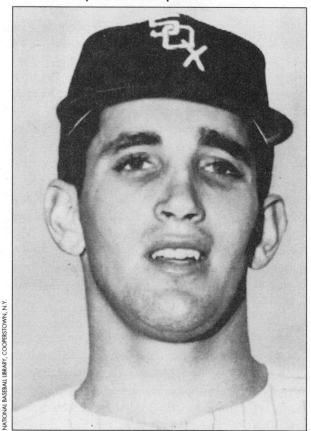

and screaming at him. He said, "Mr. Williams will tell you when you throw a strike." Lollar came out and made sure I kept my composure. I threw the next ball down the middle and Williams walked. And I was taken out. The next day Ted came up to me and told me I threw four straight strikes. I'm surprised he didn't swing, but I guess he wanted to see what I had. Then we took a train down to New York for a game the next day. My father came to New York and there were 19 family members in the stands. I was brought in to face my second big-league batter: Mickey Mantle, who hit .365 that year. I got him out and got out of the inning. Al Lopez called me over and asked, "What was your first pitch?" "Fast ball." "What was your second pitch?" "Curve ball." "What was your third pitch?" "Fast ball." "What was your fourth pitch?" "Curve ball." "You need some more pitches, kid."

Lopez never welcomed me. He was a very aloof manager who had his group of favorites and that was it. He was good with established pitchers, but I was much younger than the others on the staff. What Lopez wanted from me was passed along by Ray Berres, his great pitching coach. I was strictly a fastball pitcher and at spring training Ray and Ted Lyons had taught me how to throw a breaking ball. My curve was lousy at first but it started to improve. Once I made the majors, Berres taught me to throw a slider. He showed me how to put different amounts of finger pressure on the seams to make the ball move. My fastball moved upward—it had a hop to it. Now I could make it slide either way. Dick Donovan helped me a lot, too. I liked him. He was the first pitcher to show me how to get on top of the slider. That was Dick's money pitch.

I was a fast worker and still threw 60% to 70% fastballs. My out pitch changed with each hitter, but more and more it became the slider Berres and Donovan taught me. I wanted batters to swing at that because they were expecting my fastball and would either miss it or not hit it solidly. I didn't try for strikeouts. The more I pitched, the more the umpires called strikes. They were influenced by experience. My favorite homeplate umpire would be Ed Runge. Over the years, I pitched well when he was umpiring.

I'm glad I got to spend a brief time playing with Minnie Minoso, because he wouldn't be on the team in 1958 or 1959. I got to know him a lot better than Larry Doby, who only spoke to me a couple of times. Minoso was a great, fun guy. Pitchers had to throw inside to him, but if you got it too far inside, you'd hit him because he froze. Some pitchers honestly slipped and hit him. Minnie would never back up, he wouldn't give in.

NEW YORK YANKEES

BOB TURLEY:

When I first pitched in the majors, I just reared back and threw a fastball at over 90 miles an hour, and then threw the next one harder. I didn't really learn how to pitch until 1957. I had a very good year, going 13–6 with a career-low 2.71 ERA. Eddie Lopat, surprisingly, is the one who taught me the most. He had become the manager of Richmond, the Yankees' International League team. He said the key was to make batters hit the ball before it reached the plate or after it passed the plate, but never over it. To do this, I had to change speeds and keep them off-balance. So I'd have Elston and Yogi call more curves, changes, and sliders in out situations. They called my game, but I never threw a pitch I didn't want to. Howard was better defensively than Yogi, but Yogi wasn't far behind. Joe Garagiola would make Yogi seem like a comical character, but Yogi was a very serious player who knew baseball and pitching really well. He and Elston allowed me to try control rather than trying to strike out everyone. I cared about strike-outs only with a guy on third and less than 2 outs. The rest of the time, I worked on getting batters to hit the ball where I pitched it. I wanted them to hit it on the ground because we had excellent infielders like Martin and McDougald, and their successors at second and short, Bobby Richardson and Tony Kubek.

Bobby Richardson was a nice, religious young man who came from South Carolina. He was just 21 or 22 and Casey Stengel wouldn't let him play every day. Even after Martin was traded Bobby had to share second with Jerry Coleman, who was in his last year, and Gil McDougald. He was already a great fielder, with quickness and instincts. He was also a much underrated hitter—he'd bat in front of the pitcher—who would improve with more playing time (especially after Ralph Houk replaced Stengel in 1961). He'd become a good leadoff hitter eventually although you couldn't walk him because he'd swing at everything. He was a smart player, never too emotional. Tony Kubek was equally smart and laid-back, which is probably why they became friends and such a steady double-play combination. Tony was 6′3″, about 5 or 6 inches taller than Bobby, and batted left-handed. Like Bobby, he usually made contact and could hit to all fields. He had more power, though he was an ideal second batter—at times, he would lead off with Bobby second. It was obvious that he was going to become the Yankees' starting shortstop, but in 1957 he played as much in the outfield, and he even played some third base. He wasn't a flamboyant shortstop like Aparicio, but he was excellent. He hit nearly .300 and was voted the American League's Rookie of the Year. Both Bobby and Tony were winning ballplayers and upstanding individuals, different from the old-breed of Yankees. The Yankees hired detectives to keep an eye on their wilder players—the ones assigned to Bobby and Tony got bored watching them drink milkshakes.

There were certain players who liked to go out and drink beer and have fun. I'm not saying they were married or were after girls, but only that they wanted some excitement. At that time, women were very attracted to the Yankees and it was very easy for players to get dates. For some guys, the nightlife became a problem. I saw some guys who couldn't separate their outside lives from baseball. They'd be tired when they came to the park.

Oddly, when I lived in New York, I didn't take in the nightlife at all. That would happen after my career was over. In 1957, it paid to stay out of nightclubs because a bunch of players got in trouble because of that fight at the Copacabana. They thought Billy was a bad influence on Mantle so they sent him to Kansas City right after that. Then Mickey roomed with Whitey Ford. After a while, they roomed by themselves.

Still there continued to be a lot of camaraderie on the team. I liked the train and plane trips with the card-playing and socializing. After a game, a lot of guys would stick around, especially on the road. There was no spread in the Yankee clubhouse, but we could order sandwiches. Some would eat, others would drink beer. We'd talk baseball and everything else a bunch of guys would talk about. Then I'd go back to the hotel and go to bed.

RYNE DUREN:

Billy Martin was a favorite of Casey Stengel's, but the Yankees wanted to move him after the Copacabana incident so they sent him to the A's. The Yankees were really after Harry Simpson and sent Jim Pisoni and me to Denver in the American Association. That really bothered me because I thought I was a big leaguer. I went to Denver and immediately threw the only no-hitter in Denver history. Ralph Houk was the manager of Denver. We got along pretty well. He even bailed me and Norm Siebern out of jail in Louisville. I had gotten drunk with Siebern and Pisoni and apparently insulted some guy's wife. Later the guy caught up with Siebern and me in a coffee shop and began taunting me. He was setting me up for his friend who came at me with a blackjack. I needed 22 stitches and got thrown in the slammer for disorderly conduct and resisting arrest. I don't know what they charged Siebern with, but he was in jail with me. So Houk had to come down to get us out, which was okay since it turned out another of our players was in there anyway.

I went 13–2 but still the Yankees didn't bring me up in September. Instead they picked up Sal Maglie on waivers from the Dodgers to win a couple of games down the stretch.

WORLD SERIES

1957

YANKEES vs BRAVES

BOB TURLEY · YANKEES:

Lew Burdette was the star and story of the World Series, beating us three times. He gave up only 2 runs while pitching 3 complete games, two shutouts. We won the first game, 3–1, when Ford beat Spahn, but then Burdette bested Bobby Shantz, 4–2. I started Game 3 against Buhl and had a 3–1 lead in the second when Stengel replaced me with Larsen for no good reason. We won 12–3 and Larsen got credit for the win. The Braves won Game 4 on a 2-run homer by Mathews in the tenth inning off Grim. I pitched the final inning of Game 5, in which Burdette beat Ford, 1–0, putting them one game up. Then I started Game 6 against Buhl. I gave up homers to Frank Torre and Hank Aaron but only 2 other hits and won 3–2 on homers by Berra and Bauer. Hank's went off the foul pole. That was my first World Series victory. In the future Aaron, who became a good friend of mine, would recall how long his home run was off of me, but he wouldn't mention that I also struck him out. I had more success against the Braves than the Dodgers. They were surprised that I had a good curve ball to go with my fastball. We lost Game 7 to Burdette, 5–0. He was on a roll because not many pitchers could beat us three games in a row, especially in the World Series. We were surprised that we lost but we took it in stride and looked ahead to next year.

BOB BUHL · BRAVES:

Hank Aaron hit 3 homers, Eddie Mathews had a big homer in Game 4 and a big double in Game 7, and Lew Burdette was invincible. That's why we won the World Series. Lew excelled for reasons I don't know. Only 2 runs in 27 innings against the Yankees? The Yankees were an impatient fastball-hitting team and he kept them off balance with all his motions and his sinkers and sliders. He'd always make the big pitch. They had the bases loaded in the ninth inning of Game 7 when he got Moose Skowron to ground out to Eddie at third, ending the Series. Lew wasn't even scheduled to pitch that game but Spahn got sick.

The night before the seventh game, we roomed together in New York because Spahn and Eddie had their wives in town. We didn't talk about the upcoming game. We just watched television and had room service. Lew could make coffee nervous. Spahn would always be calm, and I didn't get too excited or would be excited and not show it. But Lew was fidgety all the time. I made him go to bed before midnight.

LEW BURDETTE · BRAVES:

In the Series, I pitched as I always did. I didn't pitch any different. Maybe I had better control and threw the ball where I wanted to. And the Yankees cooperated beautifully. It was just one of those things: whenever I needed something I got it. If I needed a double-play grounder, a Yankee would hit it right at an infielder. In my first two starts, Wes Covington, of all people, helped me with great catches. Going into the last game, I had confidence. I had pitched before with two days rest and it didn't bother me. That made me even finer as far as control was concerned. We had a 4-run rally early in the game, Crandall later homered, and everything else fell into line. They got only 7 hits and didn't really have a threat until the last inning. In a short series, any team can beat a winner, even the best team in history. They had to have only four bad days. Even in the 1–0 game against Ford, Game 5, something had to happen, something had to give. And Jerry Coleman misjudged Eddie Mathews's speed and backed up on a grounder in the sixth inning. Mathews beat it out. He got to second and scored on Adcock's single up the middle. That's the only break we needed. We won that game and went on to dethrone the Yankees. I won 3 games and was voted the Series MVP, and the Braves were the world champions. That was an unmatchable thrill. We were the first non-New York team to win the title since 1948.

NATIONAL
LEAGUE
1958

"I LIKED TO HAVE FUN, BUT I WAS A SERIOUS, FOCUSED PLAYER. IN MY DAY, PALYERS WERE DEDICATED TO THEIR TEAMS, TOOK PRIDE IN THEMSELVES. WE WERE MOTIVATED BY OUR COMPETITIVE NATURES AND OUR LOVE OF THE GAME. I COULDN'T WAIT TO GO TO THE PARK."

ELROY FACE

MILWAUKEE BRAVES

BOB BUHL:

I had arm problems in 1957 but it wasn't from throwing the ball. I couldn't even lift my arm to put on a jacket. The Braves sent me to the Mayo Clinic, Johns Hopkins, and all over the country trying to find out what was wrong. I received shots in the back with cortisone and Novocaine and was subjected to all kinds of tests. One doctor wanted to operate and take a tendon out of my shoulder, but another pitcher who had that done told me he couldn't use his arm since because he had lost control. One doctor said I'd have to learn to pitch left-handed. These were professional doctors! I happened to be living in an apartment that was owned by a dentist and he asked me to come to his office. He turned on an electrical device and went through every tooth, checking nerves. He found two teeth that had no nerves and said that the poison from those teeth could be settling in my arm at the spot I used the most. His brother, another dentist, pulled the teeth. He put two false teeth in and gave me medicine to take the poison out of my system. Two weeks later I was pitching with no pain! I was very fortunate. A dentist saved my career.

I pitched in only 11 games during the year and had only 5 wins. Luckily my absence didn't prevent the team from winning another pennant. Spahn led the league with 22 wins, and became the first southpaw to win 20 games 9 times, Burdette won 20 games, and we got a few wins from Bob Rush, who we acquired from the Cubs, Juan Pizarro, and rookies Carlton Willey and Joey Jay.

Pizarro had a lot of talent. But he was a moody guy. When he wanted to pitch he was good, but when he didn't want to, he wasn't. Joey Jay was the first ex–Little Leaguer to make the majors. I liked Big Jumbo. We used to call him "Kid" because he was one of the bonus babies. We would carry him for two years. He wasn't a consistent pitcher so I helped Joey come up with a slider. (After he was traded to Cincinnati, he would credit me with helping him. He became a really good pitcher with the Reds.)

LEW BURDETTE:

I won 20 games for the first time, led the league in won-lost percentage, and had a 2.91 ERA. Warren won 22 games, but with Buhl out with a bad arm, no other pitcher won more than 10 games on the team. So to repeat as the pennant-winner we had to rely more on the offense. Aaron and Mathews came through as usual and each hit over 30 homers. Mathews was a very good hitter. He had a short stroke for a power hitter and pulled the ball most of the time. He worked hard on his fielding and became a darn good third baseman and all-around ballplayer.

Hank never showed any emotion. The most he would do was clear his throat every once in a while. He was fantastic. He was the best line drive hitter I ever saw. He could have been a .400 hitter if he didn't try to beat Eddie in homers. There was definite competition between the two. Mathews had won the homer title and Hank kept trying to match him. He became a consistent homer hitter, but I think he would have homered just as often by hitting line drives—to all fields. But he wanted to get more loft on the ball. He had great forearms and wrists. He could be fooled completely and be way out on his front foot and the bat would still be back and he'd just roll his wrists and hit the ball out of the ballpark. He had control over his body. Aaron was the best all-around ballplayer I ever saw—better than Mantle or Mays. Mays was great, but Aaron did everything he did without the flair. Whatever Mays did, his hat was going to fly off and his arms would flail about. But Willie would pick the ball up in the outfield and throw it into the seats sometimes, while Hank always made perfect throws. He was just nonchalant.

ST. LOUIS CARDINALS

DICK SCHOFIELD:

I was unhappy with my playing time on the Cardinals. But I liked St. Louis and the fans treated me good. I also got along with the sportswriters for the *Globe-Democrat* and *Post-Dispatch,* guys like Jack Herman and Bob Broeg. And of course it was great to be a teammate of Stan Musial. He had his salary upped to $100,000 that year, the most in the National League. I was in the on-deck circle on May 13 when Musial got his 3,000th hit,

a pinch double off Moe Drabowsky in Chicago. That was a thrill. Stan was excited, too.

We had acquired Curt Flood from the Reds to play center field. He had his own program and didn't run with the team too much. But at eight o'clock, he could play as good as anyone. He was a great center fielder. His addition meant that Ken Boyer could return to third base. Hutchinson then shifted Eddie Kasko to short, so instead of Alvin Dark and me battling for that position, we were both traded. Dark went to the Cubs and I went to the Pirates. I was traded a month after Dark, on June 15, at the trading deadline. I was in the parking lot talking to my wife and parents and the clubhouse man came and got me. I was totally surprised. I think Hutchinson liked me okay but he got cash and back-up infielders Gene Freese and Johnny O'Brien for me. Freese, who was a nutty guy, said, "They traded two hamburgers for a hot dog."

DEL ENNIS:

The Cardinals made few changes from the previous year. About the only new pitcher I remember was Jim Brosnan, who did a pretty good job for us. Brosnan didn't talk much at all. He was independent, a loner, and had his book in the back of his mind. Players didn't not like him but they were wary of him. They didn't know what he'd say or do.

Curt Flood was inserted as the everyday center fielder. Another rookie, Gene Green, got a lot of playing time, sharing catching duties with Hal Smith, but more often he and I were platooning in the outfield with Wally Moon and Joe Cunningham. As I had been warned by Musial and Hutchinson, my playing time was drastically reduced because the organization didn't like that I had more RBIs than Musial the previous year. Stan *was* The Man in St. Louis. I liked Hutchinson—he was a bull and a good manager—but I should have been playing every day. I didn't complain, but I didn't like it. I wasn't surprised that the Cardinals dropped to sixth place and Fred was replaced by Stan Hack before the end of the year.

JIM BROSNAN:

Beginning in 1948, I had worked in the off-season for Arthur Meyerhoff's advertising agency in Chicago. I did a little bit of everything, including telemarketing surveys. Meyerhoff wanted me to become a fulltime accountant for him once I got baseball out of my system. He was more serious about my job than I was. He was on the board of directors of the Cubs, so it didn't hurt my career to have him mention my name every once in a while. Several years after I started working there, Bob Boyle, who was something like an associate editor of *Sports Illustrated* when it started, came by the agency. He wanted to know if there were any ballplayers in town in the middle of winter who could give an opinion of P.K. Wrigley and since I was in the same building they sent Boyle to talk to me. We hit it off immediately. He was looking for material for *Sports Illustrated* so he asked me if I'd ever written anything. I mentioned the diary I began before I went into the army, and he asked, ''Have you ever thought about writing anything on baseball?'' I said, ''Nothing particularly exciting has ever happened to me in baseball. Or dramatic. Or worth my time writing about it.'' And he said, ''Well, if anything happens, let me know.'' I'll be damned if I'm not traded by the Cubs to the Cardinals in late May. And the day after, I get a call from Boyle, who says, ''Well, something happened to you. How about writing about it?'' So I wrote an article—a journal covering two weeks from the date I was traded until I started a game and shut out the Giants. Boyle loved it, and *Sports Illustrated* printed it. And they ordered another piece.

Fred Hutchinson had wanted me. He had been the manager of Seattle in the Coast League when I pitched for the Angels. I beat his team five times and he remembered that. I did well the rest of the season for the Cardinals, splitting my time between starting and relieving. I won 8 of 12 decisions and saved another 7 games. I had a better year than Hutchinson, who was replaced by coach Stan Hack at the end of the season.

I came from a poor organization to one that was overly organized. Everyone was a Cardinal. If we weren't Cardinal-bred but had come from another organization, we quickly learned how to act like a Cardinal. There was definitely a Cardinals' tradition.

Of course, the symbol of the Cardinals was Stan Musial. I got along with Stan, as everyone did. Most of the guys called him Stash, a derivation of Stanislaus. He wasn't a leader other than by example. He wasn't a teacher, he wasn't a rah-rah cheerleader on the field or the bench. He stood out because he was so much better at what he did than anybody else. Professionals demand only one thing—consistency. Musial was consistently better than anybody else for the years in which he played. In 1958, he batted .337 at the age of 37. Ken Boyer and Joe Cunningham, playing parttime, were the only other .300 hitters on the team but they didn't come close to Stan. Nobody resented that he was making so much more money than the rest of us.

Stan was very arrogant about his hitting. He believed he could hit a ball on the nose every time he swung the bat. Of course, nobody can do that. He told me that in his best year, he hit the ball hard three out of four times every game and couldn't understand why he didn't hit .500. He also said he could tell me how to pitch every hitter in the league, but I wasn't sure that was true. He had great discipline. He would get upset with himself in situations when he knew he should do certain things and didn't do them. Like not pulling the ball when there was a man on second with nobody out. He would do almost imperceptible things to show, ''Gee, I'm upset with myself,'' like striking the barrel of the bat once on the ground—not enough to break it—or kicking his foot. Nothing more than that.

BOB BUHL (BRAVES):

When I faced Stan Musial, I tried to fool him so he'd only get two bases. Actually, I had good luck against him for some reason. I usually threw either my sinker, which would go down and away from him, or a high inside fastball that would ride into him. I also used my slider and changeup on occasion.

JOHNNY KLIPPSTEIN (DODGERS):

All hitters say they never guess what pitch is coming, which is baloney. They qualify that by saying that ''once in a while, I'll look for a particular pitch.'' Well, Musial didn't look for a fastball, curve, slider, or changeup. He didn't care what it was. He looked for a ball that was either inside or outside, and if you threw it to one side of the plate when he was waiting for a pitch on the other corner he wouldn't swing at it. However, even if you made the perfect pitch on the outside corner and he was waiting for it, he'd hit the darnedest line drive base hit. And if he was looking for an inside pitch, you could throw it there with good stuff on it and he'd jerk it down the right-field line or over the fence. You couldn't jam him or make him look bad.

J. BROSNAN:

In St. Louis, I stayed at the George Washington Hotel, a 30-minute, 25-cent streetcar ride to Busch Stadium. On the road, Lindy McDaniel was my mismatched roommate. We had nothing in common. He didn't drink, he had no sense of humor. He was exactly like Jerry Kindall, my onetime Cubs roommate. Almost every team had a couple of very religious players, but Jerry, Lindy, and his younger brother Von were among the few who proselytized. Lindy and I would argue religion until 2:30 in the morning. Lindy never won but he never gave up. I was well versed in religion, having been raised a Catholic and haven taken philosophy when I attended Xavier University one semester in 1947. So I'd heard arguments from both sides, including the Jesuitical arguments about creation. At that time, I had abandoned any kind of religion (although my kids would bring me back into it years later).

The Cardinals had a lot of card players. There were poker players who played in the back room of the clubhouse and there was a group of bridge players. Bridge was the only card game I liked. Larry Jackson and I partnered a lot. During the Cards' postseason trip to Japan, Larry and I partnered on the trip from Tokyo to Osaka. We played the guide, a warrant officer, and a sergeant who broadcast the games for shortwave radio. We didn't win a hand. Not in 5½ hours. I never had such bad cards. I was sure they were cheating because they couldn't stop giggling. At first Jackson was pissed off but then he started to giggle too. We were playing for only a penny a point or something so we lost only a few bucks.

I got to know Sam Jones, the Cards' other top starter, on the flight back from Japan. For some reason, he wanted to talk and sat next to me on the plane. We talked for eighteen hours, including the four hours we drank together in Honolulu. He was much brighter than I ever thought he was. I hadn't gotten to know him during the season—he never had the time. But now he talked about growing up in Fairmont, West Virginia, and how tough it was and what it was to grow up black. Sam was almost a fair-skinned black. He had red hair. I would have liked to have gotten to know Sam better in

the coming year, but in March, Bing Devine traded him to San Francisco for Bill White.

CHICAGO CUBS

JIM BROSNAN:

I began the year not on the Cards but on the Cubs. I came to spring training in great physical condition, having been one of the first guinea pigs at the University of Illinois Fitness Center. I had been on a rigorous training regimen. I took a test that indicated I had the hamstrings of a little girl. So I was told to build up my upper legs and also use my strong back when I pitched so that I'd get good leverage and power on my throws.

The Cubs' biggest winners in 1957, Moe Drabowsky and Dick Drott, who'd won 15 as a rookie, were unavailable Opening Day—I think they were serving their 6-months military hitches—and Bob Rush had the flu. So I was the Opening Day pitcher in St. Louis. That seemed to get me somewhat of a cachet, and afterward I was much more accepted by the players. I had grown up in the Cubs organization. I'd finally "joined the club," to use their term. I was being sociable and getting along with everybody. I had just built a house in nearby Morton Grove. In December, before I closed on it, I went to John Holland, the Cubs' general manager, and asked if I was going to stick with the team for a while. As I expected, he answered, "We're planning on you being one of our starting pitchers. You are going to be around for a while." Well, I was around for six weeks of the season before Holland traded me to the Cardinals for Alvin Dark. My record in early 1958 was just 3–4, but I was pitching well. So I was really shocked and very unhappy to be traded.

We were in Pittsburgh and I had sort of a tearful "I'm going to miss you" goodbye with my roommate Lee Walls. Two weeks later I was pitching for the Cardinals against the Cubs and Walls came up. He was part of the strongest Cubs offense in years—he, Long, Moryn, and Bobby Thomson would hit 20 homers and Ernie Banks would lead the league with 47 homers and over 120 RBIs and be voted the MVP. So I couldn't take it easy on anybody. I tried to get the ball up and in and unintentionally drilled Lee in the back. When he was going down to first he had an expression that asked, "How can you do this? Broz, you're attacking *me*!"

HERSHELL FREEMAN:

I was disappointed to leave the Reds, but when I was traded to the Cubs I figured that was part of baseball. It was an experience playing for them. We had a menagerie. Players showed up at the ballpark, said let's get nine innings in, and—win or lose—we'll go do this or that afterward. They didn't have a winning attitude, which didn't fit well with me at all. I don't like to lose at anything.

My career ended quickly. It was bursitis, or a torn rotator cuff. I'd drive home and my wife would rub liniment on it. It felt like someone would stick an icepick in my shoulder, pull it out, and stick it back in. It hurt that much. The Cubs asked me to go down to Fort Worth, Texas, as a pitcher-coach. I'd pitch and then need to relieve the pressure. The Cubs wanted me to go to Denver the next year but I hung it up.

DICK ELLSWORTH:

I don't want this to sound presumptuous but my making the majors at 18 didn't surprise me. I programmed my life from the time I was 16 years old. I was going to become a major league baseball player at a very early age. It was the same with my personal life: once I met my wife-to-be in high school, I knew she was going to be my wife and bear my kids.

I was born in Lusk, Wyoming, in 1940, but from the time I was five, I lived in Fresno, California, which had been a hotbed for baseball since the late teens. Little League was formed in Fresno when I was 11, but I decided not to leave a neighborhood playground league. A few years later I pitched for my junior high and high school teams. I was left-handed and at that time I was primarily a fastball pitcher but I could also depend on my curve. I threw so hard that my only concern was to throw strikes. I was written up in the local papers, and, I learned after the fact, was scouted by the majors starting in the ninth grade.

Pat Corrales, Jim Maloney, and I were on the same high school team. Jim was our shortstop and pitched only when we had scheduling problems. Our coach, Ollie Bidwell, ran our team as if it were a professional club. We had spring training every year, we had a three-man starting rotation. He taught me more about baseball than anybody. He didn't talk to you about the good things you did, which he presumed you'd do, he'd talk about your mistakes. It didn't make any difference if you threw a 2-hit shutout because you were striving for a no-hitter. There was a lot of pressure on us. I was playing four or five times a week. My whole adolescence was devoted to baseball. Twelve months out of the year. I was not part of the social scene in high school. I didn't date anybody until my senior year and the girl I dated I ended up marrying.

My three-year record in high school and American Legion was 105–5, which explains why 10 or 15 scouts were at virtually all our games. I was so straightlaced that none of them ventured to go outside the rules with me. I signed a major league contract in June of 1958. All things being equal financially, I signed with the Chicago Cubs because my parents and I were impressed by how the scouting staff conducted itself at ball games and when visiting our home. Gene Handley was the Cubs' West Coast scout who had watched me on a regular basis and Ray Hayworth came out to Fresno at about the time I graduated to talk about a contract. They made no false promises about making the majors. I was promised only that I would be be on the spring training roster in 1959. I was given the minimum major league salary of $7,500 a year, plus a handsome bonus.

So I joined the Cubs in 1958. I pitched the Cubs' annual midyear exhibition game against the White Sox and did quite well. Then I started a game in Cincinnati. In the third inning, I was taken out with the bases loaded. I'll never forget that Glen Hobbie relieved me and Gus Bell hit a grand-slam home run off him. So I got charged with 3 earned runs and wound up with an enormous earned run average. That was the only game I pitched that season. Still I knew there would be a tomorrow.

After the exhibition game, I knew that I was only going to be with the Cubs four or five weeks that summer. Baseball had just eliminated the bonus-player rule requiring I spend two years on the bench. So I just observed our team from the sidelines—watching pitchers like Hobbie, Dick Drott, Don Elston, and Moe Drabowsky, and seeing Ernie Banks conclude his MVP season. I also traveled with the team, taking those long flights in those piston-engine planes, the DC-7s. I remember the card games that went on in the lounge area.

I actually roomed with the pitching coach, Freddie Fitzsimmons, so he could get to know what made me tick and I could get to know him. Freddie was concerned that I may be tipping my breaking ball from a stretch position. So in the hotel room at night, I'd stand in front of the mirror with a baseball in my hand and he'd show me how to position my glove and what to do with my elbows. I was being tutored with the understanding that I was going to be sent to the minors to gain some experience.

After the season, I came home and attended Fresno City College.

LOS ANGELES DODGERS

RUBE WALKER:

Roy Campanella's car accident, which left him a paraplegic, was one of those things you didn't believe. It happened at the end of January, early in the morning. I had just talked to him. He said he was going to drive to L.A. and then go to spring training in Florida. He wanted to know if I was going to drive to L.A. I think his car was being serviced and they lent him a car. It was icy and apparently the car skidded into a tree. They say he didn't even hit it hard.

VIC POWER (ATHLETICS):

It was shocking when Roy Campanella was in that car accident. He was one of my heroes, one of the people who was baseball to me. Everybody loved him. We'd play baseball and think that was the most important thing and then something would happen that shook us up: Harry Agganis dying, Vic Wertz getting polio, Herb Score getting hit in the eye, Cass Michaels being beaned, Red Schoendienst getting tuberculosis in 1959, and Roy Campanella being in a car accident that ended his career and put him in a wheelchair . . . just like that.

FRANK THOMAS (PIRATES):

I liked Campy. Everyone did. You know what my most vivid memory was? I would foul-tip balls and they would strike his fingers and he'd snap at me, "Hit the ball!"

LEW BURDETTE (BRAVES):

Roy's accident was a real shock. It made all the players realize what thin ice we're all on. Many people thought that there was some hostility between the two of us. It went back to 1953 when Roy charged me one time with the bat. I had knocked him down three times and struck him out. He swung so hard on the last one, bless his heart, that he fell down again. He was a stocky person and bounced like a rubber ball. I couldn't help but crack a smile and he saw me and a few words later he ran toward me with the bat.

But I thought Roy was a super guy. He told me I was the first opposition player who came to see him after his automobile accident. I read in the paper that Roy went back to his liquor store. I was on my way to the Polo Grounds to pitch the second game of a doubleheader. I told the cabbie to take me by his store. A tall guy was inside and I asked if Roy was there. He called to Roy, "Lew Burdette's here to see you." And I could hear Roy's high-pitched voice, "You gotta be shittin' me!" That was funny. He said, "You're the last person I thought would be coming by to see me. But I want you to know, you're the first one to stop by."

R. WALKER:

It was eerie: soon after, Jim Gilliam and then Duke Snider, Don Zimmer, and Johnny Podres were in minor car accidents. The loss of Campanella was a terrible psychological blow to the team and I'm sure it contributed to our losing record and seventh-place finish as much as our disorientation being in a new city.

It was tough leaving Brooklyn, but we got excited once we were in Los Angeles. However, it was a shock playing in the Los Angeles Coliseum, with that very short left field and a right field that was too long for me or anyone else who batted left-handed. Even Duke was frustrated, and he could go the other way with power. Hodges and Charlie Neal were our only batters with over 20 homers and Furillo was our only player with over 65 RBIs. We didn't have the closeness that we had in Brooklyn, but I don't think players in any other city ever experienced that with fans. Once in a while, we'd still get angry letters from Brooklyn fans about our front office. The fans in Los Angeles were knowledgeable, and those that weren't learned by listening to Vin Scully, the longtime Dodger announcer.

The team might have been changing all along, but I didn't really notice it until we got to Los Angeles. Campy was gone, Newcombe would soon be traded, Erskine and Reese were almost through. Don Zimmer had finally taken over short from Pee Wee, Johnny Roseboro became our catcher, Neal bumped Gilliam from second to third, and Drysdale, Koufax, and rookie Stan Williams had joined Podres in the rotation. Just five years before it was Podres who was our young pitcher and now he was the veteran.

I wasn't really happy in L.A. I felt my career was winding down. After 1958, I began a new career as a manager in the minor leagues.

DON NEWCOMBE:

It was more than upsetting to move to Los Angeles and not have Roy Campanella on the team. Over my entire career, he had been my steadying influence, the player I looked up to. What can I say about his car accident? There are no words that can express how I badly I felt. Yet he carried on. The adversity that man overcame in his life is amazing.

In 1958 I started the season 0–6. My arm was bad. The doctors were shooting 13 needles into my arm and it wasn't doing any good. So the Dodgers concluded my career was over and, despite my long history with the organization, traded me to Cincinnati.

ED ROEBUCK:

I was young so I thought it was a great thing being a pioneer out west. They gave us a big parade the morning of our first game in Los Angeles. I figured there would be a lot of perks, like free cars. It turned out we didn't get right-out perks, just advantages. It was exciting that we drew large crowds to the Coliseum. What really surprised me is that there wasn't much media coverage when we got to Los Angeles. There wasn't much television and reporters had paid more attention to us back in Brooklyn. They wrote about the Hollywood celebrities instead. Fortunately, we didn't make the gossip columns. As it had been in Brooklyn, the media didn't get into our personal lives. They saw a lot of stuff happening that they didn't write about.

I never got hurt pitching. I got hurt not pitching. I used to pitch in the summer and then in winter ball. One year in Montreal I was 18–15, then went to Cuba and

was 14–7, then barnstormed until spring training. After two years in the big leagues, American players were no longer allowed to play winter ball. So I stayed in Brooklyn and didn't throw in the winter. That's when my problems started. I went to spring training in 1958 and had a helluva time. And it just got worse. Because of the inactivity, scar tissue had formed. I pitched only 44 innings.

RANDY JACKSON:

It was weird, weird, weird playing in the Coliseum. It was such a big place. We may have had twice as many people as we had in Brooklyn but we couldn't hear them. They were so spread out and it was real open and it was such a long distance to the stands in certain spots. In Brooklyn, the people were almost sitting on the bench. So it was different. You felt you were in spring training. But it was nice that we were heroes to these fans and it was fun looking in the stands for celebrities.

STAN WILLIAMS:

I had never played in Brooklyn, so all I experienced was changing my hat in spring training from one with a *B* to one with *LA*. Once I arrived in Dodgertown, I was accepted as one of the Dodgers. I remember that the first night I was there, Carl Erskine and Duke Snider took me out to dinner and I went home and wrote about 15 letters to my friends to tell them about it. That was such a great thing. They were like the President to me. In those days you had a lot of respect for the big leaguers—it wasn't yet the time when young players would come up and say, "Move over, old-timer, I'm taking your job."

Don Newcombe took me under his wing conditioning-wise. He said, "You're a big man like myself. You're going to have to work awfully hard to stay in shape. Come on, I'm going to make sure you get there." And he used to run me in and out of the palm trees and up and down the hills. He'd keep me out half an hour after everyone else. I'd think this old-timer isn't going to outdo me. We had contests where we'd throw the ball, run and bend over and pick it up. He'd do 268 of those and I'd do 269.

This time I figured I had a chance to make the ballclub. But after pitching just 5 innings, I found a dreaded pillowcase in my locker. That meant for me to put my belongings in the pillowcase and take them to the minor

As a 21-year-old rookie on the Dodgers' first team in Los Angeles, 6'5" Stan Williams joined Don Drysdale, Sandy Koufax, and Johnny Podres in the rotation.

leaguers' clubhouse. I was upset about it because I had a great year at St. Paul and didn't think it was fair that I be sent back. Since I was being sent back after a good year, I worried what would happen if I went back and had a bad year.

I pitched Opening Day in Charleston, West Virginia, 14 innings of 0–0 ball against Don Lee. Our manager wouldn't let me go any further and said the organization would kill him already for letting me go that far. So I left with a man on base in the fifteenth and the relief pitcher gave up an RBI triple to the first batter and I was the loser. The next game I lost 2–1 on two unearned runs. So I figured my luck was running bad.

About a month later, I was still in St. Paul, and my wife was six or seven months pregnant. We'd just bought a new station wagon and rented a house from a ballplayer who was sent somewhere else. Then the Dodgers called me at 2 A.M. and said they wanted me to leave for Chicago at 7:30 the next morning because they needed me to pitch that day. I almost didn't want to go.

But I packed up and went to Chicago. It turned out they started Clem Labine instead of me. It was the only road trip I remember in which you hit the same town twice. We started in Chicago, and then went to St. Louis, Philadelphia, and Pittsburgh, and then came back to Chicago. An outfielder was brought up with me and when we got to St. Louis, he was sent up to pinch hit and struck out on three pitches, and the third pitch he chased. They sent him back to the minors after the game. I said, "My god, it's tough up here." I knew that they were waiting till they got back close to St. Paul, so they could pitch me once and if I failed, send me back there. So I had to do my job when my time came. We went back to Chicago and on our last day in town it was freezing cold, so they pitched me instead of Drysdale. From the time I came up I had fooled around with a no-wind-up delivery, like Don Larsen used. I thought it would improve my control, which was my major problem. So I decided to use that against the Cubs. I beat them 1–0 on only 94 pitches. Alvin Dark and Dick Drott, the opposing pitcher, got the only 2 hits off me. That was my debut. The next day I bought as many papers as I could. After that no one could send me down. The other players were happy for me. The team was way down in the standings so they needed to make changes.

My play wasn't negatively affected by pressure, but I couldn't relax and say I was established. I was always fighting for the next opportunity to go out there, for the chance to stay in the big leagues. I remember going out and pitching a shutout and saying, "Boy, that ought to keep me here for another month or so." The pressure forced me to do well and kept my concentration where it had to be. After I felt more secure, my wife came out from Minnesota. We lived in Baldwin Hills, which was a 10-minute drive to the Coliseum.

It really wasn't until I was in the majors that I realized that the Dodgers' minor league system was as good as its reputation. When I needed to know something, it was there. I gained a lot of knowledge about every phase of the game and how to play correct fundamental baseball, which was what the Dodgers believed in. It had sunk in. Of all the time I was in the Dodger organization, I learned much more from my peers than pitching coaches. Our pitching coach with the Dodgers was an ex-catcher, Joe Becker, and the only thing he taught was how to run at the end of a fungo. He never talked about how to pitch a batter. But I learned from the Carl Erskines and Don Newcombes.

Newk, Erskine, Koufax, Drysdale, Podres, Labine, Hodges, Furillo, Gilliam, Neal, Zimmer, Snider, and Reese came out to Los Angeles from Brooklyn. It was the old Dodger team except for Jackie Robinson and Campy. I think all the Dodgers from Brooklyn enjoyed it out in L.A., although I'm sure they lost money because of the endorsements that they had back East. L.A. was so green and so new that there were zero dollars to be made along those lines. But it was a new experience and everyone had fun.

Vin Scully, the Dodgers' announcer—he had come with the team from Brooklyn—had to teach the people what baseball was all about, and everyone took a radio to the park to listen to him explain what they were seeing. Then they could pretend they knew something about the game. We were excited to see actors and entertainers in the stands. Ransom Jackson would call our attention to all the celebrities sitting behind the dugout, like Lauren Bacall and Nat King Cole. He was quite a comedian and one day, he looked up and announced, ''There's Lana!'' Everybody jumped up because we wanted to see Lana Turner, who was pretty big in those days. Everybody looked but couldn't see her. ''Where, Randy?'' ''Right there in the fifth row.'' ''Where???'' ''Right there in the fifth row—Lana Schwartz.''

The Coliseum was a weird place to play ball. Everybody sitting off to one side would think a ball hit 100 feet foul to the other side was a home run. They couldn't tell because of the angle. It was 251 feet to left field and 4 miles to right field. Only 10 or 11 homers were hit to center or right all year. The short left field could hurt me when I threw a ball past a left-handed hitter, who could swing late and bloop a short fly to left that turned into a home run over the 42-foot screen. You beat him, yet he beat you. For some reason, I wouldn't give up that many home runs there. A few flukes but not that many. I guess it was because I was a line-drive pitcher. The only left-handed hitters who had an easy time homering to left were guys like the Cardinals' Wally Moon who were inside-out hitters and could loft the ball over the screen. That's why we would get Moon from the Cards in December.

We had great players but they were at the end of their era. We weren't that good offensively. Charlie Neal, one of our young players, tied Hodges for most homers on the team with only 22—Gil did set the NL record with his fourteenth career grand slam. Neal's 65 RBIs was second to Furillo, who had about 80. But we knew how to scrape together a run and how to play the game. We were very good defensively and had great pitching, which went hand in hand.

I was the least used of a rotation with Don Drysdale, Sandy Koufax, and Johnny Podres. I went 9–7, winning only four less than our leader, Podres, although I pitched far fewer innings than the others. Podres was a tremendous pitcher and great competitor. And he threw hard. But 92 mph didn't seem that fast compared to Drysdale, Koufax, and myself, when we were all around 100 mph. Koufax was just another pitcher then. He had great stuff but hadn't honed the mental part of pitching into the physical part, and really wouldn't do that for another few years. His 11–11 record was considered a breakthrough because it was his first season with more than 5 wins.

HANK SAUER (GIANTS):

The toughest pitchers I ever faced were Koufax and Drysdale, even though they hadn't peaked yet. When Sandy came up he threw hard, had a good curve and changeup, but never could get anything over. When he began to get all three pitches over in 1958, he became so much tougher. If you looked for one pitch and he threw another, you couldn't handle it. If you guessed right, you had better do something with it. If you got a hit off Drysdale, he'd knock you down the next time up. He'd as soon knock you down as look at you. He was intimidating because he was big and could throw hard. But when you got to know him, he was a real nice guy. That's the way it was in baseball.

JOHNNY KLIPPSTEIN:

When I came over from the Reds in the deal for Don Newcombe, Walter Alston asked me if I wanted to pitch short relief. I said I'd give it a shot. He used me in 45 games over the rest of the year and I learned I could throw quite often. That was the biggest break I could have had because I'd stick around for another nine years as a reliever. I walked too many batters to be a successful starter. As a reliever, I worked more often and gained better control—I got more confidence in my breaking pitches and batters couldn't always expect the fastball when I needed a strike.

I was used to the Los Angeles Coliseum because the Reds had played there earlier in the year. The first time I went to the mound in the Coliseum, I took my warm-up pitches and looked over my right shoulder and did a double-take. The fence seemed to be right behind the infield. Even with the 42-foot screen, it was a pitcher's nightmare. We were always very conscious of that fence.

Alston was one of the best managers I ever played for. He didn't talk much but when he said something he demanded respect. He wasn't opposed to inviting you into his office, physically or politely. He was a tough, very strong guy and I heard that he had some physical confrontations with players in the past.

Many of the Dodgers starters were getting older. Snider, Reese, Hodges, and Furillo were either nearing the ends of their careers or their productive years. I saw Hodges in an incredible slump. He was 0 for a lot. I know it was killing him but when he'd strike out he wouldn't reveal any emotion and he'd go out to first base and do a good job. He was an even-tempered, classy man. Snider was popular among his teammates but he was more of an individualist than a leader type like Hodges, Pee Wee, or Johnny Roseboro.

Roseboro was Campanella's successor on the Dodgers and the only starting black catcher in the National League. He was an excellent receiver with quick hands and feet and was the best in baseball at blocking the plate. He was tough. He also was a good left-handed hitter with a fair amount of power.

We had other young players. Jim Gilliam was still young. He was a great ballplayer. He was a hustler, knew how to play, liked to win. Charlie Neal was a good second baseman and also had power. Gino Cimoli had a lot of talent, including a great throwing arm. He was content being a parttime outfielder and pinch hitter. Norm Larker was a promising left-handed hitting rookie first baseman.

The Dodgers were real nice to me, but I was an older guy who had been around a while and could mix in and find my way. Overall, there wasn't much socializing on the team, considering that it was known for its unity. Players didn't even hang around in the Dodger club-house after a game and talk baseball. In 25 minutes everyone was gone. This wasn't a club where players and their wives would get together for dinner. Ransom Jackson, Don Zimmer, Furillo, and I lived in the same area so we'd carpool to the ballpark. However, few people got together off the field. The only time we'd get together was on a road trip. Even so, since flying had replaced train travel, players broke into twos and threes rather than groups. Zimmer was a horse-racing fan, so we'd go to the track together. He was ready to go anytime. Johnny Podres also loved horse racing.

I buddied around mostly with Sandy Koufax and Carl Furillo. They were somewhat removed from the main group. So if anyone new came to the club those were the guys he took to because the other players seemed to be occupied. Furillo told me that there had always been real cliques on the Dodgers. He also was unhappy with management, and they'd have a bad salary dispute in 1959.

Big Frank Howard was brought up by the Dodgers at the end of 1958 when we were in Wrigley Field. He had played football at Ohio State and was 6'7" and about 250 pounds. He was frightening looking and the strongest guy I ever saw in baseball—including Ted Kluszewski—but he was mild and meek and called everybody Mister. He hovered over everyone but would say, "Okay, Mr. Reese," or "Okay, Mr. Hodges." Alston started him in right field against the Cubs, but he came up with a charley horse in about the fifth inning and had to be taken out. So Hodges and Reese jokingly got on him, "This is your first time in the big leagues and you only stayed out there four innings. We don't do that in the big leagues." Frank thought they were serious and said apologetically, "I didn't want to come out, but my leg really hurt." But they kept after him for a couple of innings. When Pee Wee left the dugout to bat, Gil went over to Frank and said, "Look, we've been putting you on. When Pee Wee comes in next inning I want you to grab him and pick him up and put him against the wall, and tell him 'If you ever open your mouth to me again, I'll put you right through that wall.'" Frank said, "Oh, Mr. Hodges, I couldn't do that to Mr. Reese." But all the guys talked him into it. Well, here comes Pee Wee. He walks by Frank and mutters, "I don't know about you, Frank." Suddenly Frank grabs him by the shirt and puts him up against the wall, and says, "Mr. Reese, don't you ever say another word or . . ." Pee Wee's eyes were as big as golf balls and he was pleading, "Put me down, Frank." He thought Frank was going to kill him. The bench was in stitches.

VIC POWER (INDIANS):

I managed Frank Howard in Puerto Rico before he played for the Dodgers. He had some power—he hit one homer over the center-field fence that was probably the longest ball ever hit in Puerto Rico. He was a great guy. He'd say, "Wherever you want me to play, I'm ready." I played him at first but the fans wanted to see me play there so I'd put him in the outfield. But he was slow and had no range. So I made him into a relief pitcher. He pitched against Orlando Cepeda and Roberto Clemente and they were scared of him because he was ten feet tall and threw hard. He won those games, but the Dodgers wrote me not to let him pitch anymore.

SAN FRANCISCO GIANTS

HANK SAUER:

The Giants moved to San Francisco and opened up at Seals Stadium, while they made plans to build a new stadium. We had a capacity of only 22,900, but there were more there for our opener, a day game against the Los Angeles Dodgers. It was the first game on the West Coast. We beat Don Drysdale 8–0 behind Ruben Gomez, and Daryl Spencer hit our first homer. Orlando Cepeda, who was a big, powerful rookie first baseman from Puerto Rico, also homered. The next night, they beat us behind Johnny Podres, as Duke Snider hit a couple of homers.

A few days later, I hit the first homer in the Los Angeles Coliseum against the Dodgers. In fact, I hit 2 homers that game. It never dawned on me that this was anything significant. We lost the game 6–5 when the umpires ruled that rookie Jim Davenport failed to touch third on Willie Kirkland's triple when scoring the tying run in the ninth inning. There were over 78,000 fans at that game—a record for the National League—which made me realize that the Dodgers stood to have much more financial success than the Giants in our new cities. But San Francisco welcomed our team and despite our small seating capacity, we filled it up and drew over a

million people. The fans were knowledgeable because they had always had Pacific Coast League baseball.

A week later, back in Seals Stadium, I hit a couple of homers against the Cardinals—the second a 2-run game-winner in the ninth—to become the first National Leaguer to homer in 12 parks.

I was glad Bill Rigney was still our manager. I liked him and thought he did a good job. He was the kind of guy who wouldn't take much from anybody but he was easy to play for, especially if you were one of the youngsters on the team. We had six good rookies: Cepeda, Davenport—who was a marvelous third baseman and an instant leader—catcher Bob Schmidt, and outfielders, Leon Wagner, Willie Kirkland, and Felipe Alou. What's amazing is that all these guys could already hit.

It was unfortunate that Willie Mays wasn't as popular in San Francisco as he had been in New York. Willie batted .347, which was only a couple of points behind Richie Ashburn for the batting title. They both got 3 hits on the final day. He had over 200 hits and about 30 homers, and led the league in runs and stolen bases. He had an excellent year, yet the fans expected that he would never make an out. I think he resented that the fans never cheered him the way they had in New York and other places. They never treated him like the superstar that he was. Supposedly, they were still partial to San Francisco-native Joe DiMaggio as baseball's great center fielder. The fans instead took to Cepeda, who had never played in New York so could be regarded as one of their own. "The Baby Bull" was a tremendous right-handed hitter. He batted over .300 and had 25 homers and 95 RBIs. He was voted Rookie of the Year and it was apparent that he could become a great player.

JOHNNY ANTONELLI:

The Giants and Dodgers began a new era in 1958, making major league baseball a coast-to-coast operation. I loved San Francisco, but I wasn't thrilled to move from the spacious Polo Grounds to tiny Seals Stadium, where it was freezing and had swirling winds. The Dodgers had their own problems playing in the overly large Los Angeles Coliseum. Neither of us were in stadiums conducive to baseball.

NATIONAL BASEBALL LIBRARY, COOPERSTOWN, N.Y.

After four seasons in New York, Johnny Antonelli continued to be the ace of the Giants staff in their first year in San Francisco.

Fortunately, the Giants-Dodgers rivalry continued after we moved to California. The difference was that we wouldn't see the same faces in both ballparks like we did at the Polo Grounds and Ebbets Field. Also, in 1958, we dominated the Dodgers like we never had back in the East, winning 16 of the 22 games. We had an excellent team and were in first place at the end of July before a slump dropped us to third. We averaged about 5 runs a game and had 9 players, including 5 rookies, who had more than 10 homers. In one game, we trailed 11–1 going into the bottom of the ninth and lost 11–10, ending the game with the bases loaded. I had a pinch double that inning. A few months later, I became the first pitcher to homer in Seals Stadium. This team had so many talented hitters that we couldn't make room for them all and one by one over the next two years, we traded Bill White, Jackie Brandt, Leon Wagner, and Willie Kirkland—players other teams might have considered untouchables. Along with Mays, who was now the veteran on the team, the Giants would build around young players Orlando Cepeda, Jim Davenport, Felipe

Alou, and Willie McCovey, who would be brought up in 1959. These players were our untouchables.

Felipe Alou was a rookie outfielder from the Dominican Republic. He was a solid player with tremendous potential. He would hit for average, hit homers, and drive in clutch runs. I liked him a lot. He was a quiet guy who wouldn't bother anybody.

I think the problems the Giants were said to have were the result of our having Latin players who primarily spoke Spanish and had trouble communicating with the American players. The Latin blacks and American blacks had nothing in common. The Latin players were close. Cepeda and Alou were good friends. Ray Monzant, a pitcher from Venezuela, became part of that group. That may have given some an impression there were cliques on the team, but I was never aware of it.

I got along really well with Bill Rigney and knew he had confidence in me. I had a good first season in San Francisco, leading the staff in most pitching categories. I pitched in over 240 innings and went 16–13 with a 3.28 ERA. Ruben Gomez, Al Worthington, and 19-year-old Mike McCormick, another lefty and my roommate, each won only 10 or 11 games, and our other starter, Stu Miller, had a losing record although he led the league in earned run average. The feeling on the Giants was that if we added a couple of big winners to our staff to go along with our hitting we could win the pennant.

PHILADELPHIA PHILLIES

ED BOUCHEE:

My stats were down in 1958 because I missed over 60 games. Dave Philley, who was primarily an outfielder, and Pancho Herrera, who played some for Willie Jones at third, each filled in at first. Philley was something else. He thought there was only one way to play—as hard as you can from the get go. And I believed him. He hit .300 for us. He led the league in pinch hits and set a major league record by getting 8 in a row. By the time he batted in late innings he had the pitcher figured out. After any pitcher went two innings he could tell you every pitch that was coming. He'd sit on the bench and would whistle if a fastball was coming. If it was an off-speed pitch, he would do nothing. The other teams would pick up what was going on after an inning or two of whistling, so he tried to teach guys to read pitchers. I learned from him and could tell by the way a pitcher gripped the ball and the position of his fingers and wrist. Sometimes it didn't help.

Frank "Pancho" Herrera was a very good friend of mine. We had played together in 1955 at Schenectady and in 1956 at Miami. He was a big, happy-go-lucky outfielder-infielder who would have played twenty-four hours a day. Frank and Chico Fernandez, who also was from Cuba, didn't room with the rest of the Phillies when we were in the South. To me, this arrangement was strange because I was raised with blacks and Orientals out in Spokane. We grew up together, we played together, we ate together. When I went to the South for the first time, I was really surprised by what was going on.

I didn't really notice a difficulty in white-black or white-Latino relationships among the players. The difficulty was that the American blacks and the Latinos didn't like one another and didn't group together. Even though you were a black Latino, you were still a Latino.

The Phillies had a few guys who did well: Richie Ashburn got 3 hits on the last day to lead the league with a .350 average and way over 200 hits—he also had about 100 walks so he was always on base. Harry Anderson drove in nearly 100 runs and batted over .300, and Willie Jones and Wally Post had fair seasons. And Robin Roberts won 17 games. But we fell into last place. Halfway through the season, Mayo Smith was fired and Eddie Sawyer was brought back. He had managed the Whiz Kids to the pennant in 1950, so they thought he might do a good job with all the young players the Phillies were bringing in. He was a quiet, very congenial guy who spent more time with the players than Smith. Sawyer was always complimenting people, especially in spring training.

Despite our bad season, the team remained unified and we had fun together. Back in those days, they didn't have sports bars or that kind of thing. However, there were hangouts where the players would gather. Through the grapevine, people would find out that players would stop at a certain place for dinner or a few beers. Some of the Phillies were drinkers, but it wasn't a partying team.

Wally Post, who we got from the Reds, could drink his beer, I tell you. He drank only beer. We were in Mil-

waukee one time and a Saturday afternoon game was rained out. There was a little bar right down the street, about ten feet wide, called The New Yorker. So Wally and I went down there at noon. I had a couple of beers and he said, "Come on, have some more." I said, "To hell with you. I'm gonna go get something to eat and then I'm gonna go to the movies." So I come back there at eight o'clock at night and walked into the bar and he was still sitting on the same stool! Man, he'd work out before a game and he'd be completely wet. His shoes would be soaked. That's how much he'd sweat, just to get that beer out of him.

There was too much drinking. Way too much. I didn't drink that much when I played (but that led to my drinking a great deal after I retired and I would become one of many former players to join AA).

PITTSBURGH PIRATES

DICK GROAT:

We needed more power so Joe Brown got Ted Kluszewski from the Reds for Dee Fondy, in a deal of first basemen. He was strong as an ox but was a good man to have on a ballclub because he was congenial, easygoing, well-respected, and a really good player. He never said anything but went out there and did his job. He hit almost .300, but it turned out his power was gone so the Pirates brought up Dick Stuart.

Stuart was a 6'4", muscular right-handed hitter who had slugged 66 homers in the Western League in 1956. He crushed homers over the center field fence at Forbes Field. He had awesome power. Years later when he went to other teams a lot of the players didn't like him— but on the Pirates all 24 of his teammates loved him. He was a fun guy from the word go. And he did a great job for us. We didn't worry about his strikeouts because he hit a lot of homers and drove in runs, just like we wanted. Hitting is what his game was all about. His defensive troubles at first base weren't only the result of his not being able to catch the ball. He had trouble concentrating. If he'd strike out to end an inning, he would go out to first and be standing there asking himself, "Why did I swing at that curve ball?" as the leadoff hitter shot a grounder right by him.

It's lucky we had Bill Mazeroski on the right side of

the infield to pick up some of the balls that Stuart couldn't reach. Of course, he did the same thing for me around second. That's why he led the league in assists. Without doubt, Mazeroski was the greatest defensive second baseman in the history of baseball. My wife could have led the league in double-plays playing short next to Mazeroski. He was that good. I think by 1958, when we started to win, he was beginning to be appreciated. He was also a very good hitter. Maz was just starting out on a great career that would, without question, be worthy of induction in the Hall of Fame.

The Pirates were primarily Mr. Rickey's team. He had signed Friend, Skinner, Law, Stuart, Thomas, me. He had drafted Face and Clemente. He had traded for Virdon. We were all force-fed at an early age. I always loved it, but it was still very difficult for a team to do well with so many players learning in the majors. Then, out of a clear blue sky in 1958, we finished second. Our record was 84–70. When does a bad team become a very good team? It happened very quickly for us. We were tied for last place on July 27 and there was a good chance we'd finish in the cellar for the second straight year. Then we beat the Dodgers in a doubleheader in Pittsburgh. From that point on, the team was outstanding. We never threw to the wrong base, we never made a base-running blunder, we played solid defense. Our pitching matured: Bob Friend led the league with 22 wins, Vern Law won another 14 for his best year so far, and ElRoy Face became baseball's most dominant reliever. Skinner and I hit .300. Clemente, Virdon, and Skinner were exceptional in the outfield. And the infield kept improving.

FRANK THOMAS:

I loved spending half the season at home while playing in Pittsburgh. We lived in the south hills of the city, in Green Tree. My wife and I wanted a big family and we would eventually have four sons and four daughters.

Being on the road and away from my family never got easier. But I liked that it gave me a chance to answer mail and get to know the players better. We talked to our roommates. We talked to reporters. We talked to everyone on the train. We talked baseball all the time. My good friends on the team were my roommate Vernon Law, Bob Friend, Bill Mazeroski, Roy Face, Roberto Clemente, Bob Skinner. I'd agitate Friend all the time.

He was a nervous type and I'd get on him to take his mind off what he had to do on the mound. I'd get him so mad that he took it out on the opposition. I was one of the greatest agitators in baseball. But I did it all in fun, never to hurt anybody. Dick Groat was the real leader of the team, but I think I also provided leadership.

Mazeroski was too quiet to be a leader. But what a great second baseman he was. I hadn't really appreciated him until 1957 when I played alongside him at first base. In the outfield and at third, I couldn't tell. But now I knew that the ball never made it all the way into his small glove. He was that quick with his release. That's why he was nicknamed "No Hands." Maz was also a solid hitter. He had good power and hit 19 homers, batting .275. (Yet the batting coach, George Sisler, would change him into a Punch-and-Judy hitter, like he tried to do to me. I was too stubborn to change but Sisler made Maz hit the ball to all fields and he would never hit that many homers again or have that high an average. I think they screwed him up.)

I liked Roberto Clemente and thought he was already a great player, but his play was at times erratic. I thought he hurt the club by showing off his strong arm. He'd throw over the cutoff man's head and we'd lose games because of that. Roberto would shine when we played the Giants because he wanted to prove he was just as good as Willie Mays.

HANK SAUER (GIANTS):

After Stan Musial, Clemente was the best all-around ballplayer I ever saw. I placed him slightly above Willie Mays. Could Clemente ever throw! Even better than Mays. He was more accurate.

VIC POWER (INDIANS):

Roberto Clemente was three years younger than me and started playing in Puerto Rico several years after me, long after I was established. We became friends and would go out together. At one time in the mid-fifties, I managed him at Caguas, but mostly he played for other teams. I had a better career than him in the winter leagues. He won a batting title but he didn't play too much because he had a sore back. We did play together in Cuba, in a Caribbean Series. He became a hero in Puerto Rico mostly because of his play in America and Puerto Ricans would read the paper to find out about

Clemente, Orlando Cepeda, and me. We were in different leagues in the majors, but we remained close. Roberto was a very proud ballplayer who hated to lose. He was a great hitter but he also could run and field and make circus catches. Of course, the American sportswriters called him a showboat, as they did me. Why didn't they ever call a white player a showboat?

F. THOMAS:

They don't come any better than center fielder Billy Virdon. He'd have guys hit him grounders and flies before every game. You could see the improvement. He made himself into a great outfielder. He was also a steady left-handed hitter who could bat leadoff yet provide extra-base power. I think Billy could have been an even better hitter. He hit way over .300 when he first played for us in 1956, but after that he hit in the .250s or .260s. I don't know why.

ElRoy Face was the best relief pitcher in the league. He had a great heart and would do everything for you. On the mound, he was fearless. He always challenged batters.

Ted Kluszewski was the Pirates' first baseman, after 10 years on the Reds. He got our only hit against the Cubs' Moe Drabowsky. He no longer hit many home runs, but he still hit the hardest ball I ever saw. It was in Philadelphia and struck the pitcher in the chest. I thought it killed him, that it went right through to his heart. Ted wouldn't wear sleeves so he could show off his muscles and scare pitchers. So I'd tease him about his "chicken wings." Ted was a gentle giant. He wasn't a fighter and neither was I. We tried to break up fights because we didn't like seeing anybody get hurt.

I had the best year of my career. I batted over .280, hit 35 homers and drove in 109 runs. Hitting 3 homers in a game against the Reds was one of the highlights of my career. On September 3, however, the Reds' Tom Acker broke the bat in my hands and struck my thumb. I kept playing although I was in pain. I hit only 3 more homers for the rest of the year. I went to Dr. Finegold. I should have gone to an orthopedic surgeon. Finegold operated on me in his office. It kept hurting but he assured me I was okay.

I talked contract with Joe Brown. He offered me a $10,000 raise up to $35,000. I said, "I've played here six years and have never received large raises from Branch Rickey or you. But after last year, when I played a large part in the Pirates' second-place finish, I'd like another $5,000 from you." He wanted to split the difference, but I wasn't keen on forgetting about that extra $2,500 that could have gone for things for my kids. He said, "I've never had a ballplayer say this is what I want and that's it. Well, I can't give you what you want." I said, "If that's the case, I'm not signing." I walked out of there and told my wife that I wasn't going to be a Pirate much longer. That's how cold my conversation with Brown was.

I told Brown to tell me if I was traded before he told the media so I could prepare myself for reporters. Meanwhile, I went to Germany with Joe Garagiola, umpire Nestor Chylak, and some others to give baseball clinics at our air force bases. I get a phone call early one morning and the radio man asks how I feel about being traded to Cincinnati for Smoky Burgess, Don Hoak, and Harvey Haddix. I was burning up. Thank God, Joe Garagiola was my roommate because he told me to put my hand over the phone and not burn my bridges behind me.

I was upset to be traded away from the town I lived in. And I would miss the fans, though most didn't appreciate me until after I was gone—when I returned to Forbes Field I would get ovations. I felt the Pirates were about ready to play in the World Series. (They would prove I was right in 1960. I always say my claim to fame was that I was traded for the guys who helped bring the pennant to Pittsburgh.)

ELROY FACE:

I didn't consider myself flaky, like typical relief pitchers. I liked to have fun, but I was a serious, focused player. In my day, players were dedicated to their teams, took pride in themselves. We were motivated by our competitive natures and our love of the game. I couldn't wait to go to the park.

I was laid-back and a bit shy, not outspoken. On the mound, I had a lot of confidence in my talent and that gave the impression that I was a bit cocky—though I wasn't. I was often asked how I could stand the pressure of going into a game in late innings with men on base and a one-run lead. I always felt the pressure was on the batter. I had eight guys helping me and he was all alone. He not only had to hit the ball, but hit it where someone wouldn't catch it. My philosophy was to throw strikes and let them hit the ball and have my teammates do their jobs. I never felt scared on the mound. However, I had times when I felt I had good stuff but was jinxed because they'd hit the ball off the end of the bat and get hits. Other times I wouldn't have good stuff and they'd hit line drives right at somebody. I've gone to the mound without any stuff and somehow gotten them out with nothing. So I didn't worry.

One spring we were down in Florida playing the Washington Senators on Easter Sunday. We had to leave Pompano Beach and be back at our Fort Myers camp that evening because some of the players and wives were going to have a party. So we wanted the game to end and didn't care who won. It was a tie game in the ninth when I came in to relieve. I just laid the ball in there. But no one on the Senators could get a hit. I was striking guys out. I was out there three or four innings. I finally went and took a shower and they called the game because of darkness.

In 1958 I really came into my own because now that our team was a contender I could accumulate wins and saves. This year when Friend, Law, Kline or rookies George Witt and Curt Raydon left games, they had leads and I was in save situations. In 57 appearances, I went 5–2, winning my last 5 decisions, and had 20 saves. I rarely blew a lead, which is why some people thought this was my finest year of all, although I'd be much more publicized in 1959 and 1960.

By now I had four pitches: a 90 mph fastball, a curve, the forkball which I picked up in 1954 at New Orleans, and a decent slider, which I developed in 1957 and 1958. Because I had good control, I threw all pitches on all counts. I'd throw harder stuff to a breaking-ball hitter and more breaking stuff to a fastball hitter. I didn't have a real pattern. If a guy had me timed on the fastball, I might throw my slider at the same speed and the little bit of movement took the ball to the end of the bat instead of the sweet part. If my forkball was working I might throw it 70 percent of the time. Even if my forkball didn't work, I'd throw it around 30 percent of the time to keep batters honest. There was no such thing as a good forkball hitter. Some batters would swing a foot over it. I was hurt by hanging curves and sliders but not with the forkball, if it broke properly.

I didn't throw inside much. Back in the minors, I was

having a really good year but one day was being hit hard by a team. So I proceeded to intentionally hit four batters in a row. The last batter just got his hand up or it would have hit him in the face. At that moment, I thought about this guy's wife and kids and how I almost ruined his career. So from that time on I never threw at a batter intentionally.

DICK SCHOFIELD:

When the Cardinals sent me and cash to Pittsburgh for Gene Freese and Johnny O'Brien at the June 15 trading deadline, I thought the world had come to an end. Nobody wanted to play on the Pirates then. They were a last place team and Forbes Field was a tough park. When I had visited with the Cardinals I hadn't enjoyed my visits to Pittsburgh. Besides, the Pirates had Dick Groat at shortstop, which meant I would remain a backup. If I'd been traded to a few other teams, I would have started immediately. That killed me. I deserved to play and have a chance to get a higher salary. I was making only about $10,000–$12,000.

I kind of hoped Pittsburgh got me because they intended to shift Groat to another position, but he stayed put and I became a utility player. I had played only shortstop with the Cardinals, but Danny Murtaugh also played me at second, third, and even a few times in the outfield.

I had played against Murtaugh in the minors. Also he was from Chester, Pennsylvania, where my dad was from, and they had known each other. He was an easygoing guy, but he was tough and revealed an Irish temper when dealing with umpires. He was good to play for and treated me well. I think he was the right man to manage this team. I also liked Joe Brown, the general manager. He was around a lot and went on many road trips with us. He and Murtaugh were pretty close.

I don't think the team was that unified when I got there. There were a few cliques. There were four guys in one place, four guys someplace else. The guys who had been there for a while tended to hang together. Fortunately, as time went on that seemed to ease up a little bit.

As the season progressed, the team got better in every area. We surprised everyone by finishing second, 8 games behind the Braves. By this time, I was feeling better about being on the Pirates.

CINCINNATI REDS

JIM O'TOOLE:

I went to spring training in Tampa with the Reds. It was actually a mini-camp that took place a month earlier than the regular spring training. It was full of young pitchers like Jay Hook and myself, with Dutch Dotterer, Ed Bailey, and Pete Whisenant catching us. Birdie Tebbetts taught us what baseball was all about. We'd sit in a room with a little fire going and he'd go through every rule in the book and tell us what it was like to play in the big leagues. I remember him saying, "Don't throw anything on a 2–2 pitch that you wouldn't throw 3–2." Then he'd say, "When you go out to drink, buy your own drink and don't buy anyone else a drink or you'll be obligated to let him buy you one." He said, "If the curfew is at twelve you'd better make sure your ass is in bed." Birdie talked of Reds' pride and how Cincinnati was the only team to play for in the big leagues. He told us how he didn't smoke or drink when he played ball but took care of his body. "If you make the sacrifices now, you can be in the big leagues a lot quicker than the guys having a good time in the minors."

The bonus rule was no longer in effect, so I was sent to the minors. It was encouraging when Birdie told me they were sending me to Double A instead of the low minors, as was typical. He told me I had enough poise to pitch in Nashville.

I had the confidence, cockiness, and drive to feel I would be in the majors soon. Once I got by my first game in the minors, in which I walked about nine in three innings, I harnessed my control. I never walked more than four in my life after that. I pitched 280 innings that year, with 200 strikeouts and 23 complete games, and went 20–7 and started the All-Star Game. The Reds didn't talk to me all year, but in September they brought me up. By this time, Tebbetts had resigned and had been replaced by Jimmy Dykes.

I pitched one major league game. My debut was against the world champion Milwaukee Braves. Lew Burdette was going for his 20th victory. I had my family there in Milwaukee. I was a nervous wreck while warming up. And I was scared to death facing Hank Aaron and Eddie Mathews in my first game, but I got them out almost every time, or walked them. I gave up only 4 hits

Twenty-one-year-old left-hander Jim O'Toole made his first appearance in 1958, beginning a nine-year stint as one of the Cincinnati Reds' most dependable and toughest pitchers.

in 7 innings but lost 2–1. Frank Robinson was at third instead of Don Hoak and he let a ball go through his legs to let the winning run in. I was satisfied with my performance. After that game *Parade* magazine flew me to New York and I was on *The Ed Sullivan Show* telling Whitey Ford, Bob Turley, Yogi Berra, and Mickey Mantle how to pitch against the Braves in the upcoming World Series. I was overwhelmed—I couldn't believe how everything was happening so fast.

I was proud to be a Cincinnati Red. Here I was, the son of a Chicago policeman, on the Reds. Everyone in my life told me as a kid, "Jim, I know you have ambitions about being a big league ballplayer, but you're not going to be any different than my son—you'll be a policeman or work for the city." I'd look them in the eye and say, "I don't know what your son will be but I am going to make it to the big leagues.'' I had that determination.

As a young player, I was in awe of the old Reds like Gus Bell, Johnny Temple, Roy McMillan, and Smoky Burgess. Burgess always had a bad stomach, or asthma, or something else bothering him. But he was the greatest hitter off the bench I ever saw in my life. He didn't like to catch—he just wanted to hit. Burgess would be traded to Pittsburgh prior to the next season. We had another record-breaking pinch-hitter to replace him: Jerry Lynch. This was a team in transition and I was part of a crop of younger players who were replacing all those older Reds.

ART FOWLER:

After four years, my Reds career was over. Gabe Paul demoted me to Seattle. Then he traded me, Steve Bilko, and Johnny Klippstein to the Dodgers. I had to prove they were wrong. So I went to the Dodgers' team in Spokane and led the league with 16 wins, 17 complete games, 249 innings pitched, and 5 shutouts. I wasn't washed up.

JOHNNY KLIPPSTEIN:

Before my trade to the Dodgers for Don Newcombe, I pitched pretty well for the Reds, going 3–2 in a dozen appearances. Other than Bob Purkey and Joe Nuxhall, we didn't have strong pitching and I thought they could have used me. But the team had made a few changes already, trading Ted Kluszewski and Wally Post, and it seemed they wanted to make more changes to fix such mistakes. The team was on its way to a losing season, and not long after my trade, they changed managers.

DON NEWCOMBE:

The Dodgers had traded me because they couldn't find anything wrong with my arm. But when I got to Cincinnati, the trainer, not a doctor, found a knot in the back of my neck. He got rid of that and I won 7 games. I could still pitch.

FRED HATFIELD:

After playing just a handful of games with the Cleveland Indians, they waived me out of the American League. It was a big disappointment. I was picked up by the Reds, but I batted just once for them before being demoted to the Pacific Coast League, where I'd play until 1960. I was better than a lot of major league players but couldn't find a place to play either in 1958 or 1960. At least, my major league career ended without me getting a cut in pay. Every year in the big leagues I got a little more money. That's how I always knew I was doing something right.

JIM FRIDLEY:

It had been four years since I had last played in the major leagues with the first Baltimore Orioles team. In the interim I had some good years in the minors with Denver and the Los Angeles Angels. In 1956, I had 24 homers and 105 RBIs at Denver. When I joined the Cincinnati Reds in 1958, there were about a dozen outfielders, so I knew I wasn't going to be there for long. But I could see that this was a class team. Frank Robinson was the star player. He was a likable, classy guy. Johnny Temple was a good competitor, but he was like Ferris Fain in that he was would lose control of his emotions if he drank. Smoky Burgess was a quiet guy. He didn't look like a ballplayer because he had a potbelly. I believed Roy McMillan was the quiet leader, while Don Hoak was the hellraiser. I couldn't stand being with Hoak in the dugout because all he did was curse. It would get on my nerves. Jimmy Dykes finally told him he had had enough of his cursing.

I batted only 9 times and got 2 hits, both doubles. This was my last time in the majors. It didn't seem to matter that when I played in the minors that year for Nashville, I drove in 101 runs and led the Southern Association with a .348 average. Major league teams were no longer interested. (I would have several more good seasons in the minors before finishing my career in 1961. I also had many experiences. I was with Tommy Lasorda in the Dodgers chain and the three worst fights I ever saw were initiated by him. Each time someone homered off him, he smashed the next batter with a pitch.)

Looking back, I didn't play as much as I should have. By the time I quit I was very experienced and knowledgeable but it had taken too long to get that way. I had never gotten over my reputation for having a bad arm, so I was allowed to waste years in the minors when major league teams could have used me. Still, I felt fortunate I had played when not many players made it to the majors. Baseball had been good to me.

AMERICAN LEAGUE
1958

"WHEN THEY'D SAY I THREW A SPITTER, I'D SAY IT WAS MY 'CUBAN PALMBALL.' I NEVER THREW A PALMBALL. NOW I CAN SAY THAT I DID WET IT A LITTLE BIT. JIM BUNNING USED TO PUT GREASE IN HIS PANTS, WHITEY FORD USED TO MARK AND SCUFF THE BALL. A LOT OF PITCHERS DID THINGS TO THE BALL. SO I DECIDED THAT IF I COULD GET AWAY WITH THAT, I WAS GOING TO DO IT."

PEDRO RAMOS

KANSAS CITY ATHLETICS

JOE DE MAESTRI:

I think that the attitude on the team was that Vic Power never considered himself black. I don't mean that to be negative. We'd take the bus in Florida during spring training, and we'd stop at a gas station where there were both WHITES ONLY and COLORED bathrooms. And Vic had no qualms about walking into the WHITES ONLY bathroom. Some guy would have to stop him. Because they used to watch him. Boy! You'd come out of those gas stations and they had some young redneck watching the place.

At Lake Okeechobee in 1958, Vic refused to go to the COLORED bathroom at a gas station. Then he paid for a Coke but walked out without paying the deposit. As he was getting on the bus, the redneck attendant, who was about 18, demanded the deposit. So Vic reached into his pocket and just threw the nickel at him. About 20 minutes later a state trooper stopped us. He got on the bus and started looking at the players. I was sure it had to do with one of us throwing a beer bottle out the window. He says, "I'm looking for a colored fellow." We had a pitcher from New York named Bob Davis who was studying to be a lawyer and he got up and said, "What seems to be the problem, officer?" "Well," the trooper said, "this fellow back at the station said that this fellow threw some money at him or something." Davis calmed down the guy a bit and he eventually got off and told us to take off. So we did. We thought it was all over and we continued to drive toward West Palm Beach. But once it turned dark about six patrol cars overtook us. These guys were in T-shirts with holsters and .45s. They came in and said, "Everybody out." So we got herded out and were made to stand with our hands on the bus. We were all terrified because they were talking to everybody just like they were talking to Vic. It wasn't a case of just Vic by this time, but all of us.

Meanwhile the kid from the gas station points at Vic and says, "That's the guy. I want him." Whereupon Davis says, "Vic, keep it shut. Don't say a word." The cops wanted to take him away and if that had happened we probably wouldn't have seen him again. I mean, these guys were real tough-looking suckers. Somehow we were able to give them money for Vic's "bail." A cop asked for $250, but I don't think we had that much money between all of us. So we gave what we had. Vic was supposed to go back to stand trial.

When we arrived in West Palm Beach, we told our manager Harry Craft, "We had a problem." The Athletics always had an attorney at spring training and we talked to him about what happened and he made some phone calls. That's the last I heard of it.

VIC POWER:

The Lake Okeechobee incident was the worst experience I had in baseball. The way I remember it is that the Athletics were returning from Fort Myers to West Palm Beach and we stopped at a gas station for "piss call." All the players got off the bus to use the bathroom, but the attendant wouldn't let me go in because I was black. I had to go so badly but couldn't go behind the bus with that guy watching me. So I bought a Coke from his soda machine and planned to use the empty bottle. When it was time to get on the bus, the guy ordered me to return the bottle although I hadn't finished the Coke. I offered him a quarter deposit but he insisted I give him the bottle. So I pushed it at him. He then ran and called the sheriff and told him to arrest "that black bastard in the back of the bus." But the players wouldn't let him on. The sheriff talked to the attendant and then told me I could have the bottle for a $500 deposit. I had to borrow money from my teammates so we could leave. I was so afraid that I never used the bottle. So I paid $500 for a Coke. But I was lucky. After that, the team left me home when we went to small towns to play. I thought that was nice, but I wish they had forced the issue more.

Overall, spring training became a little easier for black players. Every year we'd get more rights. One year we could stay in the hotel with whites but we couldn't eat in the restaurant, use the pool, or look at white women. Then we could eat in the restaurant. Then we could swim in the pool. But we were always told not to look at white women.

In 1958, Bill Tuttle joined the A's from the Tigers. He was an outfielder from Illinois. This was the first time I had a teammate who I could sense didn't like blacks.

I was hitting over .300 again in 1958 and had a 22-game hit streak when Woodie Held and I were traded to the Cleveland Indians for Roger Maris, Dick Toma-

neck, and Preston Ward. I didn't have a bad reaction. I was happy to be going to a good team.

CLEVELAND INDIANS

MUDCAT GRANT:

In my rookie season, I was inserted into a good rotation with Cal McLish, Gary Bell, and Ray Narleski. I pitched over 200 innings, won 10 games, and never returned to the minors. I preferred beginning my major league career with Cleveland rather than the Yankees or Red Sox because the Indians and Dodgers had been the ringleaders in signing black players. As a young boy, Jackie Robinson had been my main hero until the Indians signed Larry Doby. I liked that name! Those guys inspired me to want to be a major league ballplayer. Now the Indians made me the only black starting pitcher in the American League. The only other black starters were Don Newcombe and Brooks Lawrence of the Reds and one of my heroes, the Cardinals' Sad Sam Jones. On the Cubs, Sam became the first black to pitch a no-hitter after staying out all night.

I got to play with my greatest hero, Larry Doby. The most I ever learned about the game was from him. He taught me everything from how to dress and mix colors to how to become part of the community. Larry made sure he went out into his community and spoke to people. He knew people by name everywhere from Kansas City to Washington, D.C. Larry would say we're going to some barbershop in Cleveland or restaurant in Chicago or some friend's apartment in Detroit. When I first went to Washington, D.C., he introduced me to Adam Clayton Powell. He also introduced me to Sarah Vaughan, Miles Davis, Count Basie, and Billie Holiday. I had listened to their music on 78s and here was Larry casually introducing me to them. We'd sit down and talk about everything under the sun—all day long. Larry was quiet to people who didn't know him and never said too much or ventured an opinion. But he'd open up to those he knew well. I knew of his disappointments because I'd ask him. We all heard the bullshit from people who said that when Larry first came up, they did this and did that for him. I asked, "Larry, did they really do that for you?" And he'd say, "Hell, no." But he'd never tell anybody else. He'd let the story go on.

A personable, outspoken right-hander from Lacoochee, Florida, Jim "Mudcat" Grant reached the Cleveland Indians in 1958 and would become the American League's first successful black starting pitcher.

Of course, Larry couldn't really teach me much about pitching. But I already knew something about that. You know who gave me the best advice? Satchel Paige. I met him in about 1955, when we both were in the minors, and had some great conversations with him. I asked him what he thought was the most important thing about being a pitcher. He told me, "Young man, you gotta have a titty pitch. If you don't have a titty pitch, you can't win." I asked, "What is a titty pitch?" I thought he was putting me on, getting ready to say something about sex. He ran his hand across his chest and said, "A titty pitch is right here." Of course, he was right about the need to pitch inside to win in the big leagues. He just had a different way of putting it.

MINNIE MINOSO:

In December I had been traded back to the Indians for Early Wynn and my good friend Al Smith, who I had known since the Negro Leagues. I was disappointed to leave Chicago but I was a professional ballplayer so I immediately gave everything I had to make my new team win. I batted over .300 and hit 24 homers, which was the most in my career.

It had been a long time since I was on Cleveland, but I was friends with many players on the team. Larry Doby also was traded back to Cleveland in the winter, so this was the third time we played together. I also got to play again with Chico Carrasquel, who had been my best friend in Chicago. Then the Indians got Vic Power from Kansas City. This was the first time we got to play together.

BILLY MORAN:

I hadn't heard from Cleveland during my two years in the army. In 1957, I had resumed my minor league career, going to San Diego, the Indians' team in the Pacific Coast League. Then Bobby Bragan asked me to play for him in Cuba, where he shifted me to second because the Indians already had George Strickland and Billy Harrell at short. That winter, the Indians' new GM, Frank Lane, hired Bragan to replace Kerby Farrell as the Indians' manager in 1958 and I made the team in spring training. Bragan wanted me to play for him, but I'm not sure Lane thought I was ready.

I wasn't the player I had been. If you were a shortstop or second baseman you were slotted to bat leadoff, second, or eighth. Eddie Stanky, who was then an Indians coach, tried to make a leadoff hitter out of me because I could run. But he got me so messed up that it took me two or three years to get out of it. He made me choke up, stand close to the plate, take a lot of pitches, and foul off strikes in order to walk. It was bad advice. He wanted me to hit like he once did, but I had more talent than him. And I wasn't as little, though they referred to me as "Little Billy"—I was 5'11" and weighed 185. I didn't have a home run swing, but I was a Harvey Kuenn–type hitter who hit line drives and hard grounders to all fields, a lot of tweeners for extra bases. Because of what Stanky taught me, I was confused about hitting and struggled. The Indians had a lot of coaches, but none really took an interest in me. Then I got the flu and never got back my full strength. Bobby Avila went back to second and did a good job for the rest of the year while I played sporadically. Bragan was gone by the middle of the year and Joe Gordon replaced him.

Al Rosen's last year had been 1956 and the team

lacked leadership in his absence. But Strickland, Avila, Wertz, and Garcia were still there and Minoso and Doby had come back and we had a good clubhouse. Gary Bell, who was my teammate at San Diego, Mudcat Grant, and I were rookies. The three of us would join in the poker games, but otherwise only Gary felt comfortable with all the veterans. Mudcat and I were reserved, and since our opinion was never asked for kept our mouths shut and observed. But Bell quickly became the life of the clubhouse, stirring up everything. He could get away with anything.

Mike Garcia was a super guy who took me under his wing. He had midget racecars and he'd take me to see them. Anytime he'd go somewhere, he'd take me with him. Bobby Avila also was nice, but he was wary of me taking his job—though I did that for only a month. We were never rivals and always good friends, but he didn't exactly take me and show me how to do things either. I didn't have a mentor.

Billy Moran had a rough rookie season in 1958 with the Cleveland Indians after coaches altered his batting style and decided to shift him back and forth between second and short.

I got to know Larry Doby some and liked him. I know he had problems in the Cleveland organization before I was there. The poop on Larry was that he always had a chip on his shoulder because he was black. I heard all these stories before I got there and he turned out to be really friendly toward me.

Frank Lane loved Minnie Minoso and it was a point of irritation for some of the guys that he was noticeably his favorite. Minoso couldn't do anything wrong as far as Lane was concerned. Not that he did much wrong. He was a tough player. I didn't get to know him well because he was a superstar and I was a rookie. He knew if he stood on top of the plate he was going to get drilled, so he accepted it. He got mad just once. I think we were in Kansas City. A pitcher hit him the first time up. And the next time up, he knocked him down. Then he knocked him down again in the same at bat. Minnie didn't say anything. The next time up, he let the bat fly at the pitcher and the pitcher jumped as the bat went right where his knees had been. Minnie walked past the pitcher's mound and got his bat around second base. He then walked back past the pitcher's mound and got back in the batter's box. He never said a word but his message got across. That's the only time I saw him retaliate in any way. Boy, he would get hit and he'd never say anything or rub anything. Of course, he had an upper body that was out of sight. He had skinny legs but was big from the waist up.

Rocky Colavito had become the star of the team by 1958. This was his first big season. He hit 41 homers, drove in over 100 runs, and batted over .300. I liked that he always hustled, although he couldn't run a lick. He'd kid himself about his flat feet. Surprisingly, he wasn't awesome strengthwise but was built like Joe DiMaggio, just a big rawboned guy who could swing the bat. He was extremely likeable. I know he married a woman he dated in Reading, Pennsylvania, in 1953, a year before I played there. Several guys married Reading girls in the Cleveland organization. Rocky was devoted to his wife, Carmen, who was a beautiful girl. Her family had a mushroom farm, and he used to go back in the winter and tend the farm.

Don Mossi was the nicest guy in the world but he was not a pretty fellow. People made fun of his big ears and his nose. We used to always say he looked like a cab coming down the street with the front doors open. If our team didn't do it, the other teams would do it. He took the ribbing and even made fun of himself. You couldn't make him mad. On the other hand, Ray Narleski wasn't a good-tempered person. He was sensitive and seemed to want to get mad. Cleveland wasn't a good place for a thin-skinned player. The fans weren't as tough as those in Philadelphia, but if you screwed up they could be hard on you. Fortunately, Narleski usually did a good job, whether coming out of the bullpen or starting, which he was doing with increasing frequency.

Roger Maris was a great player already. I couldn't see him as a 30-homer-a-year player, but he was a super outfielder, could run well, had a good arm, and was a very good hitter. I don't understand why Cleveland didn't want to keep him. Of course, Frank Lane would trade away Colavito in another year.

The Indians got Vic Power in the deal for Maris in the middle of the season. Nobody could play first base better. He was also an offensive threat. He hit to all fields and always made contact. He had a big old bat. Vic was a smiling, jovial person and didn't cause trouble in the clubhouse.

At that time, there was still the black and white thing. The first time we went to Kansas City, the black players had to stay in different train cars and we stayed in hotels on different sides of the river. The only time we saw them was at the ballpark. Kansas City was the only place like that. Even in Florida, we all stayed at barracks in Daytona Beach.

There wasn't much partying by the full team, but about seven or eight couples would get together almost every homestand for a silly party. It was the young guys. There was never a Minoso, Doby, Garcia, or Avila there. However, the Vernons and Wilhelms would occasionally join us. There would be socializing between couples. For instance my wife and I would go out to dinner with Gary and Barbara Bell and with Russ Nixon and his wife, or we'd have a dinner party at one of our homes.

I didn't go to bars with some of the players because I was a rookie and didn't want to get caught by the manager. Anyway, I wasn't much of a boozer and didn't know what to do in a bar. During the second half of the season I spent time with my roommate, Billy Hunter, who had come over from Kansas City. He'd go to bed early and put a wad of tobacco in his mouth. He'd chew

it all night long, even when he was asleep. He'd chew tobacco all the time. He must have had a cast-iron stomach.

Clubhouse meetings were generally called so we could get our butts chewed out. Usually the whole team got it. Bragan was pretty good about not singling out individuals in front of everyone else. He'd take them in his office rather than showing them up. But there was a lot of tension playing for Bragan. He wanted to fine players for everything. But things didn't seem to get better when Lane fired Bragan and brought in Joe Gordon. Especially for me. He didn't know what I could do, so he didn't play me much.

Lane was good for show, to get people to come to the ballpark, to raise interest. I liked him because he was always fair to me, but he didn't make sure that players in the system were developed. He was impatient and would impulsively get rid of promising or key players, and managers. So there was no stability or direction.

The Indians were still hoping to duplicate 1954, but players were gone and it never got back to that level. 1958 was a year of transition and we didn't have a real good year. I found nothing remarkable about playing with Cleveland except being on a field playing Boston. Here I am playing second base and Ted Williams is hitting. That was awesome.

HAL WOODESHICK:
Beginning in 1957 my wife and I lived in the off-season in Charleston, West Virginia, where I played ball. I worked at an industrial supplies company, learning how to be a businessman. In February, I was there when I found out that the Tigers had traded me to the Indians for Hank Aguirre.

I had a good spring and made the team. We played exhibition games against the Giants in Texas, and then both teams came north by train. We played poker, stopped in a small town for a game, had dinner, and then got back on the train and played cards again. Willie Mays always played.

I was happy to come back to Cleveland, but then Bobby Bragan wouldn't give me a chance to pitch. I was assigned to San Diego. I lost my first 2 games and then won 9 in a row before the All-Star break. I asked to go home to see my wife and baby in Pittsburgh. When I was there I got a call from a radio station that told me I had been brought up by the Indians. I called San Diego and was told that I hadn't been called up and should fly back to California. Ralph Kiner, who was the general manager, called me into his office before a big Sunday doubleheader. He said, "You're going up to Cleveland but you're still going to pitch a game today." So I pitched and won one game of the doubleheader and Bob Lemon, whose major league career was over, pitched the other game. Then catcher Earl Averill, the son of the Hall of Famer, and I went up to the Indians. Bragan had been fired and the new manager, Joe Gordon, wanted us.

Gordon and Mel Harder, his pitching coach, were super to me. And Eddie Stanky was a good coach. I don't care what anyone else says about Eddie—I can say only nice things about him. I got a lot of encouragement and good advice and did a good job. Starting and relieving, I went 6–6 with a 3.64 ERA.

I don't know if there was any real leadership on the team, but we didn't need it because the players all stuck together. There were no problems on that team between black and white players. We ate, went to the movies, and played cards together. Poker was big with the Indians. I think almost everyone played except Rocky Colavito and Herb Score. They were too dedicated to baseball to play cards with the rest of us. But they were good people. There were a lot of good guys on the team. Larry Doby and Minnie Minoso were super people. Gary Bell was a hilarious guy. He was crazy and the guys called him "Ding Dong."

VIC POWER:

After I learned the A's had traded me to the Indians, Frank Lane promised me $3,000 if I could make it to Cleveland in time for a series against the Yankees. So I started packing like crazy. But it took me three days to drive there and I never got any money. I learned that Lane always gave players an extra incentive. For instance, if a pitcher got 2 hits in a game, Lane might give him money to buy a new suit. Minnie Minoso would get a Cadillac each year for hitting .300. I liked Lane and thought he was good for baseball.

Although I didn't get the extra money, I was glad to be on Cleveland. I hit .317 for the rest of the year and finished at .312, which was fifth in the league in batting and only 16 points behind the winner, Ted Williams. At one point, Williams, Pete Runnels, and I were neck-and-neck for the batting title and they had us pose for a picture together. I dropped off a little after that—I played winter ball and always got tired at the end of the major league season. But this was one of my best years. I finished third in the league in hits behind Nellie Fox and Frank Malzone, third in runs, second in doubles with 37 to Harvey Kuenn's 39, and led the league with 10 triples. I also won the first of seven consecutive Gold Gloves for my play at first base. This was the first year the award was given in both leagues.

The one who had a bad reaction to the trade was Roger Maris, who went to the Athletics. Maybe he didn't like going to Kansas City or maybe he didn't like being traded for a black player, but I could tell he was mad at me. When he reached base, he'd never talk to me like other players would. One time when I was playing second for the Indians, Maris slid very hard with his spikes high and caught me in the ribs. I warned him that the next time he slid like that I was going to give him an eye for an eye. I had seen how Jackie Robinson would jump over a sliding runner and land on top of him with his spikes, and that's what I planned for Maris. And the next time he slid hard into the base, I jumped up into the air. But he slid past the base and I realized that I was about to come down directly on his face. It would have looked like an accident if I came straight down, but I quickly split my legs and landed with my spikes on both sides of his face. I didn't hurt him, but I did teach him a lesson.

At first I lived in the colored section of Cleveland, but eventually I moved into an area that had more white people. I had a bad driving experience with police in Cleveland that reminded me of Kansas City. I came to a stop sign, stopped and looked both ways. Then I continued on. A policeman pulled me over and said I didn't stop at the corner. I started to tell him I had, but he said, "Don't argue with me!" and gave me a ticket. That made me realize that the police in America could do anything they wanted as far as black people were concerned.

In August, I stole home twice in one game against Detroit, which tied a major league record that was last accomplished in the 1920s. My first steal tied the game 9–9 in the eighth inning and my second won it 10–9 in the tenth inning. I surprised the Tigers because I stole only one other base all year. But I could have stolen more bases if that was the style then. In Puerto Rico I set a record by getting on first and then stealing second, third, and home in two different games. I stole home against Detroit because their pitchers used to throw at me all the time. My strategy on the first steal was to go and come back to third, go and come back. Finally I took off. On my second steal, I just ran because I didn't want to call attention to myself. Neither play was close. If they had been, I probably would have been called out. Black players didn't get many close calls. I know I didn't.

The reason I usually swung at the first pitch and at so many bad pitches was that some of the umpires called anything a strike on me. In the winter leagues I was a patient hitter, but not in the majors with umpires like Ed Runge and Jim Honochick calling everything against me. (Moe Drabowsky later confided that an umpire told him that all he had to do was pitch the ball to me and he'd call it a strike—not because I was black but because I was Vic Power.) One time against Boston, the plate umpire called a strike on an obvious ball so I called time and stepped out of the box to argue. The umpire told the pitcher to throw the ball so he could call a strike. He threw it and I jumped back into the batter's box and tripled. There was a big argument because the Red Sox were mad at the umpire.

RANDY JACKSON:

I have no idea why Cleveland wanted me. We had a strange mix of players that didn't jell that year. We were a bunch of individuals who came from different teams and didn't have any loyalty to the Indians. We just happened to be playing in Cleveland. So the fans most adored Rocky Colavito, who had come up in the system. He hit the ball a long way and the fans came to the park to see him do it.

It was fun being in the American League for a while, but I didn't really feel comfortable, and I wasn't productive in my three months there. I was facing new pitchers and going into different parks. Hitting in Fenway Park was the strangest. I couldn't figure it out. You wanted to hit it over the Green Monster because it was easy to do, but if you tried to do it it was too hard. Still you had to go that way because if you hit the ball to center or right, the outfielders had fun catching it.

I saw Ted Williams play for the first time in Fenway Park. It was just beautiful to watch him hit the ball. We came in on a Friday. I went in as a late-inning pinch hitter and homered over the left-center-field fence, which was the deepest part of Fenway. So the next day, Joe Gordon inserted me in the lineup at third base. In the bottom of the first, we employed Lou Boudreau's ''Williams shift'' and I moved to the shortstop position when he batted. I was thinking, ''Here I am standing out here for the first time in my life playing against Ted Williams and watching him hit.'' I knew he wasn't going to hit it toward me because he didn't hit that way. So I was stunned when he hit a one-hopper off my shins. And talk about hurt! Nothing ever hurt so much. In two seconds I had a welt the size of a football on my shin.

BALTIMORE ORIOLES

BILLY O'DELL:

I had my best season with the Orioles, going 14–11 with a 2.97 ERA and 137 strikeouts. It was really exciting to pitch in the All-Star Game in Baltimore. I was young and hadn't played all that much baseball so I didn't expect to get into the game. Bob Turley started and Early Wynn pitched. I was surprised when Casey Stengel wanted me to pitch the last three innings. I threw three perfect innings and we won 4–3 on Gil McDougald's single. That was one of the greatest thrills I had in baseball. I got to see Mays and Musial and be lucky enough to get them out.

Richards relied on me more, pitching me in 41 games, 25 games as a starter. I was part of a pretty good four-man rotation with Jack Harshman, Arnold Portocarrero, who won 15 games, and Milt Pappas, a rookie. It was the best group of pitchers that the franchise had in years. The Orioles also got a big lift from veteran outfielder Gene Woodling. Gene was a likable, somewhat reserved guy and we benefited from his experience. It meant a lot to our young players to have a teammate who had those great years with the Yankees when they won world titles. Plus he could still hit.

GENE WOODLING:

After I hit a career-best .321 at Cleveland in 1957, Richards traded back for me. Nobody else would have had

NATIONAL BASEBALL LIBRARY, COOPERSTOWN, N.Y.

Gene Woodling got a second chance to play in Baltimore and showed the Oriole fans why he was considered such a good player on the Yankees and Indians.

the guts to bring me back to Baltimore after I was booed so much in 1955. Especially since I was already 35 and wasn't the most popular man in baseball because of my work for the pension plan. He was probably the only guy who would employ me. He believed in me strongly and told me not to worry that others were trying to run me out of the game.

Of course, I had to deliver on the field or he would have let me go, regardless. Fortunately, I did the job, batting .276 with 15 homers and a fair number of RBIs. All you had to do was show up and play hard for Paul. That I was able to come back and do well in Baltimore after being booed out of town made me extremely popular in the city. I didn't care about bad publicity but this time in Baltimore I didn't even have problems with the press.

Billy Loes was on this team and was an unusual guy. He once had the bases loaded and threw the ball out of the stadium. That upset Richards.

Brooks Robinson became the Orioles third baseman. He had made it despite my negative opinion of him several years before. The kid was amazing. Nobody played third like that. And he was a nice young man. I was one of the veterans on the team and assumed a leadership role. I looked after Brooks and the other young players, and you didn't fool with my boys.

BROOKS ROBINSON:
1958 was my first full year in the big leagues. I played 145 games but I hit only .238 and didn't distinguish myself as a major leaguer. Maybe my high point was going in for defense in the last couple of innings when Hoyt Wilhelm threw a 1–0 no-hitter against the Yankees in September. That was exciting. To tell the truth, I was scared to death. It was drizzling and the grass was wet and I worried that I'd screw it up. But that didn't happen. Going in for defense is the worst job in baseball because all you can really do is screw up. At least when you screwed up in those days, it probably wasn't on television. There wasn't much television coverage and it was a real happening when we were going to play on the *Game of the Week*. I knew people would be watching back in Arkansas.

As a kid in Little Rock, I used to see Gus Triandos play for Birmingham in the Southern Association. And now he was the Orioles' catcher and star player. He was the best catcher I ever played with overall. In 1958, he hit 30 homers, including one off Don Larsen that helped Wilhelm win that no-hitter. And he led the team in RBIs. He wasn't really a leader type. He was an easygoing, jovial, funny guy who just went about his business. A helluva guy. But they always booed him. He was the slowest guy I ever played with and when you're big and slow they're on your ass all the time. He was very sensitive to the boos. And what made him even more sensitive is that he had to catch Hoyt Wilhelm after we acquired him that year. He dreaded that knuckler.

I always got along with the Baltimore fans and around this time, a girl named Mary Lou La Martina wrote me about starting a fan club. She would send out letters to the kids in the fan club and handle much of my fan mail. We became longtime friends.

BOSTON RED SOX

FRANK MALZONE:

I rented a home in Needham. It was a duplex we shared with another Italian couple we got to know real well. It was a comfortable situation and I didn't look forward to road trips. On the road, ballplayers slept a lot. We didn't need that much sleep, but young men tend to sleep much of their lives away. Most of us would go to movies to break the monotony. Only Williams didn't go to movies because he thought they hurt your eyes. On trains, we played a little cards, talked baseball, got to know each other. We mingled and sat together in the lounge car. On planes, you'd sit in your seat and talk to maybe one guy. That didn't help team unity. My best friends on the Red Sox were Jackie Jensen, Pete Runnels, and Pete Daley. But I never had problems getting along with everybody.

If I was considered a leader, it was only because of the way I played. If there was a leader on the Red Sox, it was Sammy White, the catcher. He didn't show much with the bat, but he knew the game and had a lot of enthusiasm. He was a great receiver and knew how to handle pitchers.

Ted was more of a teacher than a leader, but he was the loudest guy in the clubhouse. You always would hear him, growling, "Let's go, team!" or "Clubbie, get me . . ." He was temperamental and had a winning attitude. Jimmy Piersall was quite popular with the players, as he was with the fans. But he wasn't a leader. He tried to be, but he was so highstrung no one wanted to listen to him. Jensen could have been a leader but he was having personal problems and problems because of his fear of flying. Jensen was a great guy, a former Rose Bowl hero. He was quiet, keeping to himself almost as much as Ted. But he wasn't as loud in the clubhouse. Jackie and I were similar-type hitters so we talked a lot about hitting and how different pitchers worked us.

Runnels was my roommate and we also talked a lot of baseball, although he was left-handed. He was a hard-nosed player and an outstanding hitter who batted over .300 all five years he played with the Red Sox. In 1958, he was battling Ted for the batting title. We were in Washington at the end of the year. He said, "What do you think my chances are?" I said, "Go out and get a couple hits and you'll win the title." Pete batted second and Ted hit behind him. The first time up, Pete gets a base hit to right field. Then Ted comes up. A base hit to right field. Then Pete doubles to right center. Ted comes up. A double down the right-field line. Pete says to me, "I don't think he's going to let me win this batting title." I said, "I don't think so either." Pete popped up the next time up and Ted homered. Ted went on to beat out Pete, .328 to .322.

Fans rode Ted just to get a reaction. They wanted to rile him up so he would take out his anger on the opposing team. They loved Ted. There were several incidents of him spitting after being booed—and being fined by the Sox front office for that—but I think he knew the fans were just trying to agitate him. Still, I'm not sure how he really felt about them or anything else. Ted was so recognizable that he couldn't go out with the rest of us, so I couldn't get to know him that well. We knew him as "The Player." I thought of him as a tremendous competitor, a teacher who would try to help his teammates against certain pitchers and who would call me a "dumb dago" for swinging at first pitches. He was around forty, but still took pride in doing his job, including fielding. He'd say, "I can play left field as well as anybody, especially in this park." He was right.

AL SMITH (WHITE SOX):

I liked Ted Williams because he was always willing to talk and it didn't matter that I was on the other team. If I was in a slump, he'd try to help. He'd always say to hit the ball through the middle.

JIM LANDIS (WHITE SOX):

Ted Williams awed me. Once he hit 2 homers at Comiskey and I got embarrassed because I ran toward right center thinking I could catch them. But both balls had such backspin that they took off and went into the upper deck. Billy Pierce used to holler at him when he wouldn't swing at pitches just off the plate. Billy would say, "I made the perfect pitch and he wouldn't swing at it." He was a fabulous hitter. He could pull anybody and so hard. He could hit even the best pitchers, sometimes better than the average pitchers. He pounded Pierce at his best and Herb Score in his prime. He could go 10 for 20 against the best pitchers in the game. He figured the best pitchers had certain systems and he studied them more. .500 pitchers were more erratic and harder to figure out.

F. MALZONE:

I think the Boston press was so hard on him in order to motivate him to say something they could use. Their tactic worked because Ted never held back. He was highstrung and the writers all appreciated him because he gave them copy.

I had a good relationship with the Boston press. They only got on me for not popping off and blowing my own horn. They appreciated me as a ballplayer but not as an interview subject. I'd say, "I'm telling you what happened during the game. What more do you want?"

I had another good year, making another All-Star team. I scored the winning run for the American League on a Gil McDougald single in the sixth inning that broke a 3–3 tie. We didn't play those games for fun. We went all out because it meant a lot to beat the National League. When you play in All-Star Games, you play with the best—Al Kaline, Mickey Mantle, and Yogi Berra. And you play against Willie Mays, Hank Aaron, Ernie Banks, and Stan Musial. There's no way such individuals would ever not play hard or play their best. So I played as they did.

I batted a career-high .295, with 15 homers and 87 RBIs, and led the league with 627 at-bats in 155 games. I also led the league in several defensive categories and won the American League Gold Glove for third basemen. Jensen hit 35 homers and led the league with over 120 RBIs and was voted the American League's Most Valuable Player. Williams and Runnels were 1–2 in average and Williams hit over 25 homers and drove in a lot of runs. But all we could manage was third place, 13 behind the Yankees.

We didn't have the best ballclub, although each year we felt that we did. In spring training, Williams, Jensen, Runnels, and some of us others thought that if we all played the way we were capable of and we got a big year from talented pitchers like Tom Brewer, Frank Sullivan, and Willard Nixon then we could stay with the Yankees. We thought we had the personnel to match them. But we could never put it all together. The pitchers were inconsistent and never had good years at the same time—even in 1958, when Delock, Brewer, and Sullivan pitched well, none of them had even 15 victories. And overall we made too many errors and fielding mistakes—which the Yankees just didn't do. Also I think management was partly to blame. Tom Yawkey and Joe Cronin, who would resign as our GM to be the league president in 1959, didn't make enough deals. We were one of the many teams who stood pat year after year even though the Yankees, the only team that was winning, always brought in young players and made big deals for veterans to help in the pennant drives. The Red Sox finally tried to do things like that but they got different results.

BILL MONBOUQUETTE:

At the beginning of the season, I was promoted to Minneapolis, the Red Sox AAA team, and a couple of months later made it to the big leagues. My first game in the majors was a start against Detroit in Boston. That was the first time my mother saw me pitch in a professional game. I was the first hometown Red Sox pitcher in many years so the fans were really rooting for me, even giving me a standing ovation when I warmed up. Still, I was nervous. We made 2 or 3 errors in the first inning and they scored 3 runs. I went 5 innings and they scored 5 runs. The big hit was by Billy Martin. The next time up I knocked him down. After he made an out he ran by the mound and said, "You owed me that, rook."

Unlike in the minors, if you made a mistake in the majors you didn't get away with it. There were too many good hitters. Sal Maglie used to say, "You're not entitled to mistakes." You get away with mistakes every once in a while, but you have to pitch well to succeed in the big leagues. Throw strikes, pitch ahead, work fast—that's how you win.

I had a good fastball, slider, change, and curve. On some days I struck out a lot of batters but I preferred not throwing a lot of pitches to get a batter out, especially at Fenway where batters didn't go to the plate taking pitches. I wanted them to make outs swinging at first and second pitches outside the strike zone. I never believed that you should *pitch* inside—you should *throw* inside. When I threw inside it was always a ball. I didn't jam hitters, they jammed themselves. When they saw a ball coming inside at Fenway their eyes lit up. Even as a rookie I wasn't leery about throwing inside—it didn't matter if I hit the batter because it was his job to get out of the way. It was always in the back of my mind that a batter would pull the ball at Fenway so of course I made adjustments, particularly late in a close game.

I was a very feisty pitcher, one of the last who would charge off the mound and get into the umpire's face to argue a call. I even did this as a rookie and Sammy White would have to pull me away before I got kicked out of the game. When we came back from a road trip I found a note in my locker to come see Joe Cronin, the general manager. After telling me that I should call him Joe and not Mr. Cronin, he lit into me: "You are the worst S.O.B. I have ever seen in my life. You can't charge off the mound to argue with an umpire." He told me that what I was doing was going to take me back to Minneapolis. So I changed.

Still I was awful on the day I pitched. I'd tell everyone, "Get away from me." However, I didn't mind when Sammy White came to the mound to calm me down. I got along with the umpires. Ed Runge was the best umpire as far as pitchers were concerned. Nestor Chylak was good. He'd say to me, "Take it easy, Frenchie. I can see your neck turning red and your veins are getting big. Relax, relax."

I don't know if this was a close team but we'd get together off the field every so often. Lou Berberet, who was Sammy White's backup receiver, would hold a cookout or something. Most of the players were married and they'd bring their wives. I'd bring a date. Such events were usually organized by the players, although the club would sometimes have a family picnic during spring training.

The Red Sox still traveled mostly by train. Other than Jackie Jensen, not too many guys liked to travel by train. I could never sleep because of all the rocking. But train travel was a good way for us rookies to get to know our teammates. The guys played cards or gathered in the dining cars—the food was great.

My roommate was Ted Bowsfield, a rookie right-hander from Canada. We had been friends in the minors and hung around together. We were too young to hang around with the veterans. We'd share the abuse. As rookies, sometimes on the road we didn't even get lockers and would have to hang our clothes on nails. We didn't dare say anything.

Ted Williams was a veteran who always treated me

NATIONAL BASEBALL LIBRARY, COOPERSTOWN, N.Y.

A fiery competitor even as a rookie, Bill Monbouquette would become the Boston Red Sox' ace starter by the early '60s.

good. I first met him in 1955 when I threw batting practice. When I came up in 1958 and walked through the door, he announced, "This is the guy who used to come in and throw batting practice. He can throw strikes." Ted was the leader on the team although he wasn't a vocal leader. We all looked up to him for the way he played and how hard he worked. He signed for a record $135,000 that season. If anyone deserved it, it was Ted.

Jimmy Piersall was well liked by his teammates and not disruptive. He was the best center fielder in baseball, better than Mays or Mantle. He played shallow and covered so much ground. When Boston traded him at the end of the year, it was a big mistake which we never got over, especially since Williams and Jensen had only a couple of years left. I think the problem with the Red Sox was defense, and other than Frank Malzone at third and Piersall in center, we were below average. We lost because we were always giving teams extra outs. Certainly the solution wasn't to send Piersall to Cleveland.

Malzone was a great third baseman and solid hitter. We were good friends. Before I'd pitch a game, I'd ask, "How are you feeling, Frank?" And he'd say, "Why do you ask? Do you think I should play deeper?"

Everyone liked Tom Yawkey. He'd walk around the clubhouse slapping everyone on the back. But forget that notion we were a country club team. There were no teams like that in baseball. We probably got the tag simply because we didn't win.

PUMPSIE GREEN:

There was no pressure on me in the Red Sox system. I was confident because I didn't skip two or three minor league levels at a time, but moved up gradually. I always was comfortable because I kept seeing the same players on the way up.

I had learned the most from Gene Corr, my high school and college coach, until I was managed by "The Genius" in 1958. Gene Mauch was my manager at Minneapolis, the Red Sox Triple A team. I was playing shortstop and he was playing second base and he'd tell me things and I would tell him if I agreed or disagreed. I was a student of the game and he taught me how to play baseball. So I had success at Minneapolis. We finished in fourth place but still won the playoffs, in four straight over powerful Montreal. At this point I was thinking of making the Red Sox. I wasn't concerned that they wouldn't bring me up because of my color. I knew I would be the first black on the Red Sox if they did bring me up. I couldn't get around it. Earl Wilson was another prospect to be Boston's first black.

WASHINGTON SENATORS

HARMON KILLEBREW:

I started out the season with Washington but after pinch-hitting twice, I was sent back to the minors. We didn't have a Triple A team at the time, so I was sent to Indianapolis, the White Sox' American Association team. Boy, that was a good league and having not played regularly for a while, it was like starting spring training all over again. I had more errors than I had hits. So the Senators told me they were sending me back to Chattanooga. I didn't know why I had to go prove myself again at Chattanooga after having had such a good year there in 1957. So I was at the crossroads of my baseball career. I decided to go to Chattanooga and had another good year, batting over .300 with good power numbers. Then Washington brought me up at the end of the season and I never went to the minors again.

I was confident in my ability but I had to prove it to other people. I never got discouraged and wished I had signed with a team other than the Senators. It wasn't an unhappy time for me. I never complained about my lack of playing time and being sent three times to the minors. I needed to develop and in the Senators system I had an opportunity to learn.

When the 1955 season ended, I had married a girl I had known since the seventh grade. In those days, a lot of guys were getting married young. I was only 19 years old and it was too young to get married. There was an added strain because I was trying to establish my career. It was a tough life for young ballplayers and their wives, more so for the wives who didn't know a lot of people and worried about being uprooted. We lived in Idaho during the off-season, but it was difficult during all the seasons I was being shipped back and forth between the Senators and the minors. It was a relief to finally make the team and rent an apartment in Alexandria, Virginia. But I wasn't feeling secure yet.

PEDRO RAMOS:

In Cuba, everyone looked up to me and Camilo when we returned in the off-season. If we said anything, they listened to us. We were called on to help with charities. In America, it was different. We were from Cuba and didn't speak good English. So we listened and weren't outspoken. I was content to be one of the guys rather than a leader. I was easygoing and everybody liked me. When the guys sat around, I sat with them as we talked about baseball, movies, girls—who's going to get it, who got it, what you got, whether it was good or bad.

The Senators improved slightly in 1958, although we finished far behind the seventh-place club. Sievers and Lemon had good seasons and the guy who played between them in the outfield was the league's Rookie of the Year, Albie Pearson. He was a 5'5" left-handed batter who hit for a decent average. He was a nice enough guy, although he had a big mouth for a little guy. But we didn't get mad at him. He played hard and was a pretty good little ballplayer. He probably would have been better if he were bigger.

Again I was the Senators' top winner with 14 victories, but my 18 losses was the most in the league. Our only other pitcher to win 10 games was Dick Hyde, who was an outstanding relief pitcher. We didn't go around together but we sat around and laughed a lot. He wore glasses and we called him ''Snake'' because of what he had down below the belt. Hyde threw underhanded, like Ted Abernathy. Until he hurt his back he was hard to hit. ''Snake'' was a sneaky pitcher.

I guess I'd have to say I was a sneaky pitcher, too. Most of the time I was too honest and just threw a fastball ball down the middle when I had two strikes—which is why I usually led the league in yielding homers—but in time I wised up. Opposing managers and players always accused me of throwing spitballs. When they'd say I threw a spitter, I'd say it was my ''Cuban palmball.'' I never threw a palmball. Now I can say that I did wet it a little bit. Jim Bunning used to put grease in his pants, Whitey Ford used to mark and scuff the ball. A lot of pitchers did things to the ball. So I decided that if I could get away with that, I was going to do it. My curve wasn't that effective, so I needed another pitch to help me get by in tough situations when I didn't want to use my heater. I needed a ball that would sink so I could get double-play grounders instead of 2-run homers. I heard from other pitchers that if you just wet the tips of the fingers, the ball would move. So I started working on the side with it and started developing a pretty good ''Cuban palmball.'' I did throw some and was never caught.

DETROIT TIGERS

GUS ZERNIAL:

After almost seven years with the Athletics, I was traded to the Tigers in November 1957, in an enormous deal that involved 13 players. Billy Martin, Tom Morgan, Mickey McDermott, and a couple of other players were traded with me. The Tigers were my favorite team as a kid and now my dream had come true to play with them. I hit .323 and had a pretty good year, though I batted only about 125 times. Oddly, I was a better hitter now than I had been at any time in my career, but I didn't get the opportunity because we had a tremendous

outfield with Al Kaline, Harvey Kuenn, and Charlie Maxwell.

Al Kaline was a great player. He wasn't as dynamic a hitter as Mantle but he was on that level. He led the league in hitting only once and never led in homers or RBIs, but he batted .300 with a lot of extra base hits, was a tremendous clutch hitter, and was the best right fielder in baseball. In those years, Kaline was as complete a player as Joe DiMaggio. I really admired his consistency. Although he wasn't a take-charge guy, he led just by the way he played the game. He was valuable to us in many ways.

Harvey Kuenn was also a super player, though a completely different type than Kaline. Like Kaline, he was a lock to hit .300, but he didn't have as much power. He hit line drives into the gaps and led the league in doubles in both years I was with the Tigers. As was the case with Kaline, he led, but not verbally.

After seven seasons with the Athletics, during which time he was one of the American League's top power hitters, Gus Zernial got to finish his career with the Detroit Tigers, the team he dreamed of playing with as a youngster.

In all the years, I didn't think I was on a team that had a chance to win the pennant except for one year with the A's and that first year with Detroit, when we had that great outfield, a solid second base–shortstop combination in Frank Bolling and Billy Martin, and an impressive rotation with Frank Lary, Jim Bunning, Billy Hoeft, and Paul Foytack. But we got off to a bad start under Jack Tighe. We did better after he was replaced by Bill Norman, but we still managed just a .500 record and fifth-place finish. I was disappointed in our record, but overall that year was an enjoyable experience.

COOT VEAL:

I was playing for Birmingham and in June we were in Little Rock. A bunch of players went to an afternoon movie. I was paged and told to come to the hotel. My dad was in pretty bad health, so I started running from the movie theater. My manager was standing outside waving, telling me to calm down. He said, "You're going up to the Tigers." I said, "You've got to be kidding." I left on a bus to Memphis and then caught a plane. We started banking. The pilot announced problems with the motor and after six years in the minors, I said, "It's not meant to be." But I did make it to Detroit and took a bus to the ballpark. The radio was on and Jim Bunning was pitching and Ted Williams was playing. I was sitting there dreaming that tomorrow night I'd be out there with those two guys. Williams won that game with a tenth-inning homer.

The following night I was out there playing shortstop. I got to the park early, of course. My knees were shaking. I batted eighth and the first time up I got a hit down the third base line off Ike Delock and drove in a run. That was a thrill.

Bill Norman, who had replaced Jack Tighe as manager a few days earlier, brought me up to Detroit. I had played with him at Augusta for two years and at Charleston, West Virginia. He was a big, boisterous man, who talked loud but carried a little stick. He was hard to get know but if you did, you liked him.

The first two guys I met were Al Kaline and Harvey Kuenn. Al was friendly, but Harvey was the nicest person I ever met in baseball. Kaline was as moody as he could be in those days, and didn't have a whole lot to say to anybody. Harvey was just the opposite and if

Perseverance paid off for Coot Veal because after six years in the minors he was brought up by the Tigers to play short.

there was a leader on the team, it was him. They were both tremendous offensive players.

I didn't know where Norman planned to play me because the Tigers had just picked up Billy Martin to play short. But he put me at short and moved Martin to third. I had admired Martin when he was with the Yankees and I saw him on television. But he wasn't playing second anymore and didn't impress me as much. He made too many statements about the organization and players. He remarked that it was a country club. He wanted it to be more Yankee-like, and more serious because he knew what it took to be a winner. Other than Billy, no one knew what it was like to win in the big leagues so he tried to be our leader. But management didn't take kindly to his comments and he was soon exiled to Cleveland.

I played in almost 60 ballgames, and hit .256 and led the league's shortstops in fielding. Frank Bolling and I were both good fielders and made a good double-play combination. I was making just the major league minimum of $7,500, but this was my best time in baseball, playing on the field with guys like Kaline, Kuenn, Charlie Maxwell, Bolling, Jim Bunning, who no-hit the Red Sox in July, and Frank Lary, who beat the Yankees seven times. I played every day and thought I did well. I made the Rookie All-Star team.

CHICAGO WHITE SOX

LES MOSS:

I started flying in the late fifties when I was with the White Sox. The Sox had their own plane, a DC-6, and it was scary. But that's not the reason I quit playing early in 1958. My shoulder wore out and my elbow was worse. There was a calcium buildup and they operated and moved the nerve over. At 35, I just hurt too much to play anymore.

AL SMITH:

In December of 1957, Early Wynn and I were traded from the Indians to the White Sox with Minnie Minoso going to Cleveland. Minnie was popular with the Chicago fans after being there so many years, so when I replaced him in left field I was booed. That made it a bit difficult, but that's not why my production was low. I had chipped a bone in my ankle in the last game of the '57 season, sliding into home. It would bother me all year, but the Sox didn't inform the fans or sportswriters.

The White Sox were a good veteran team that brought in a few young players each year. In 1958, we finished in second place, 10 games behind the Yankees, and I saw that we had the talent to challenge them the next year.

JIM LANDIS:

As Lopez had promised, I was the White Sox center fielder from the beginning of the season. Lopez stressed that the center fielder was boss. If I yelled, it was my ball, no ifs, ands, or buts. Nellie Fox was such a bull that he believed everything in shallow center was his. So we took a while to communicate there. There were a couple of balls that dropped because we fought over them. I'd get chewed out by Lopez for letting a second baseman take balls that I could reach. He'd chew Nellie out, too.

It took a while before I had enough confidence to move Nellie out of the way. Then things worked better.

I didn't watch other center fielders. I really felt that my teachers did as good a job on me as possible. I don't know what else I could have done. Mantle played deeper than me, which he got accustomed to doing in spacious Yankee Stadium. I played deeper there too because I sure hated to run into the gaps. Our styles were different. I didn't study Piersall either, though he was a good outfielder.

I was known for playing shallower than most center fielders. I had confidence going back on a ball and felt I could cheat a bit. It was a learning experience. I was on my own but on rare occasions, our coach, Tony Cuccinello, waved a flag at me to get over. I learned that positioning had a lot to do with who was pitching, how hard he was throwing, what he was throwing, and where he was throwing. I didn't communicate with the pitcher or catcher when we were in the field. The shortstop and second baseman did most of that and once in a great while they would signal me. But I'd watch them and pick up clues from where they positioned themselves.

Against power hitters like Mantle and Colavito, I'd cheat into the gaps. But for most hitters, I'd play straight-away. Billy Pierce threw so hard that for some left-handed batters, I actually played in left-center. With Early Wynn on the mound, I'd play the hitters more to pull, because he couldn't throw as hard as Pierce. And Wynn had a pitching system: if you looked closely, you'd see that two out of three pitches were up and inside. He was great at getting batters to swing at balls. Dick Donovan was the hardest to gauge. You couldn't cheat too much with him pitching so I played straight-away. He threw sinkers and sliders, many of which were just out of the strike zone.

All our pitchers were great to play behind, but Early Wynn was particularly good because even when you messed up, he'd tell you, "Hey, let's go out and get a bite to eat. I'm treating." Wynn might have been mean on the mound to opposing batters but he was always great to his teammates. Many of the guys called him "Sea Lion" because he was chubby. How mean was he on the mound? The meanest. His reputation was true. In an exhibition game, Joe Cunningham took a vicious cut and missed a Wynn pitch. Al Smith, who had come over with Wynn from Cleveland, told me to watch out for

Wynn's next pitch. Sure enough Wynn drilled Cunningham—just for taking a vicious cut, not even hitting the ball, in an exhibition game! That's how mean Early was. I said, ''Oh, my god!''

Lopez always had his door open. A player could go to him with problems but more often he'd call you in and try to straighten things out, saying what you could be doing better. He wouldn't bring up what you were doing wrong at a clubhouse meeting. Lopez was the one of the best psychologists. He knew how to handle players as individuals, always. Sometimes I tried too hard and when it didn't work out, I'd really get down. I wasn't temperamental, so I would let things eat me up inside when I was going bad. Mostly it had to do with my hitting. Lopez never got on me verbally, loudly, drastically. I remember he sat me down in the exhibition season for three days. That was his way to wake me up.

Usually when players had problems they'd go to each other for advice. Most often someone would come to you if they detected you had a problem. Nellie Fox, Sherm Lollar, and Billy Pierce were tremendous leaders. They didn't even have to talk to be leaders.

In late June, Billy pitched 8⅔ innings of perfect baseball against the Senators and he had two strikes on Ed Fitz Gerald, the catcher for Washington. Fitz Gerald hit a knubber that landed on the chalk line in right field to spoil the perfect game. We went into the clubhouse and I looked at Billy and there was no way in the world you could tell what happened. He just got showered like he did every day and went home to be with his family. That's strong, silent leadership.

I remember when Bob Cerv broke up a double play by knocking Nellie all the way to the outfield grass—I'm not exaggerating. Nellie played about five more innings. We went out to dinner and he just couldn't move. But Nellie had a long consecutive-game streak going and the next day, he was in the lineup for about five innings before he had to come out. That's the kind of leader we looked up to.

Nellie led our team with a .300 average, and he and Aparicio led the league in several fielding categories. He also set a record by not striking out in 98 consecutive games. There is no doubt that he was a Hall of Fame–caliber player. That's why he was an All-Star second baseman year after year. His ability was there for everyone to see but I wish more sportswriters would have realized his other traits. He wasn't outspoken or controversial enough to get the writers' attention. He was just laid-back, went out and played the game, never verbally abused anyone. His character was ideal for a ballclub.

Nellie and I ran a lot together and had a great deal of fun. We went back to his home in the area around St. Thomas and Chambersburg, Pennsylvania. It was just the opposite of what you'd expect when a hero returns home. Instead of him waiting for people to call attention to him, he was the one honking his horn and waving at Joe Blow. That meant more to me than anything else because I really got to see what a good guy he was.

Married players hung out together. Nellie, Pierce, Lollar, and myself would go out to dinner a lot. Back of the stockyards area, those steak places downtown, Rush Street, Bill Smitz had a great fish place. We'd know certain people who ran nice restaurants and as many as six or seven couples would go there for a good time. Everybody but Billy drank, everybody had their belts. Nellie and I could have maybe two or three bourbons. Some guys were beer drinkers. Once in a while I'd go to nightclubs with Nellie. He loved country and western music and we saw some of the best, like Ferlin Husky. In Chicago, Billy, Nellie, and I would see entertainment at the various hotels. Tony Bennett, Louis Prima and Keely Smith, you name it. Lopez had a curfew and it was strictly enforced. I couldn't blame him.

This was an active team with not many guys who read anything outside of the sports page. On trains, we played lots of cards, mostly poker and hearts, which was popular in those days. We went to movies—any movies. We went bowling and got a lot of kicks out of it. We'd get into L.A. at about 6 o'clock and go bowl about six games. My roommate Sammy Esposito, a good guy, would come along. Nellie averaged in the 190s and you couldn't beat him. A few times, we went to the racetrack. I remember going at different times with Esposito, Torgeson, and maybe Walt Dropo. The tracks were usually too far out of town. During the season, not too many people fished. Even golf was pretty much a taboo during the season. They didn't just object to the golf swing but to us getting tired from being out in the sun all day long.

The two black players I palled around with were Earl Battey and Al Smith. Earl and I were really good friends when I first started out in 1957. He'd been up with the Sox for the previous two years, but that was the first season he played a lot. Then in 1958, Al came over from the Indians. I was sorry the fans were so bad to him—the Sox fans were usually great fans—but he was taking the place of a town hero, Minnie Minoso. Al was great to play with and a great person. I'd drink with him, and Sammy and I played poker with him. Earl and Al would take me to colored nightclubs and to be honest, in those days it was a little scary. We saw Billie Holiday and I was thrilled to death.

We had a great time, but we were always ready to play hard in every game. There were a lot of tough competitors on the team. I liked to think I played hard. I think I always played scared. That sounds silly but I had to develop my confidence and it took a while. I revered the game and idolized people I was now playing with and against. I was in awe and it was hard for me to tell myself that I was as good as they were. I got sent out my first year with the White Sox and I know that had a lot to do with it. Pressure didn't bother me. Pressure was entirely different. I did better in pressure circumstances. My improvement had to do with confidence.

I was so glad I had a good second year. I hit .277 with 15 homers and 64 RBIs, and stole 17 bases. At one point, I had a 14-game hitting streak and the next day I tied a modern major league record by striking out 5 times facing Baltimore's Connie Johnson—God, he had a sinful curve and vicious fastball! It was hilarious at the time. Then I came back with a 9-game hitting streak. As a rookie, I might not have gotten another hit all year long.

BARRY LATMAN:
The first time I broke camp with the White Sox was in 1958. But I spent the year going back and forth between the Sox and Indianapolis. In the majors, I went 3–0, winning 2 of my 3 starts and shutting out Kansas City. I gave up only 27 hits in 47 or 48 innings and my ERA was 0.76. At the end of the season, I was told what the Sox wanted me to work on for the beginning of next season. It was then that I knew I had made it as a major leaguer.

NEW YORK YANKEES

BOB TURLEY:
I continued to improve and in 1958 I had my best season as the Yankees won another pennant. I was 21–7 with 6 shutouts and a 2.97 ERA. I led the league with 19 complete games. Players always had media attention in New York because there were so many newspapers, but now I'd be on the cover of magazines. The Cy Young Award was already an important honor and was given only to one pitcher for both leagues. Don Newcombe had won it in 1956 and Warren Spahn in 1957, and in 1958 I became the first American Leaguer to win it. I beat out Spahn. There was no ceremony at all. The next year, someone would have the award at the ballpark. They would hand it to me beside the dugout, a picture would be taken, and that was it.

Bob Turley won the Cy Young Award in 1958 by leading the league with 21 wins, but injuries and Casey Stengel's reluctance to give him a comparable amount of work kept him from winning more than 9 games in subsequent years.

NATIONAL BASEBALL LIBRARY, COOPERSTOWN, N.Y.

RYNE DUREN:

I had to work my ass off in spring training and watch my behavior because the Yankees were still reluctant to bring me up. I made the team as a relief pitcher, but then Casey didn't want to use me in save situations. Ralph Houk, who was now a Yankee coach, knew I was a poor fielder because he'd managed me at Denver. I asked him one night if we could go out early so he could hit shots back to me on the mound. Against Baltimore I came in with men on first and third and one out in the ninth and Jim Marshall drilled a grounder right back at me that stuck in my glove and I turned it into a double play. So I got my first save with my glove, not my fastball. After that Casey used me when the game was on the line and I saved a league-leading 20 games and won 6 more. I had a 2.02 ERA and struck out 87 batters in 75 innings. *The Sporting News* selected me as Rookie Pitcher of the Year. It was an exciting season because we won the pennant by 10 games over the White Sox.

I pitched in the pennant-clincher in Kansas City. Afterward we did a lot of drinking at the victory dinner and on the train to Detroit. Of course I got drunk and shoved Houk's cigar into his mouth, which didn't make him too happy. He swung his hand at me and struck me pretty good with one of his World Series rings and cut my head. I was too drunk to remember what happened but I was told I went after Houk and Don Larsen had to pull me off him and take me back to my Pullman car. This incident was written up by Leonard Shecter of the *New York Post* and made national headlines. You would think I would have been so embarrassed that I would have changed my behavior. But instead of learning a lesson, I chose to ignore what happened.

Bob Turley wanted the mound at Yankee Stadium to be flat and since he was the top gun of the staff in 1958, the groundskeepers kept it that way. I preferred it to be sloped. My theory was to throw the first warmup pitch hard and then adjust to how the mound felt. One day, I threw the first pitch and my foot hit the ground and I thought my knee was going to hit me in the chin. The ball went up on the screen. The fans got a big kick out of it and the sportswriters played it up. So now and then I would throw my first warmup pitch onto the screen. Frank Crosetti encouraged me to do it because he said it put a little extra fear in the opponents. I never felt it did that, but maybe it did.

There was no doubt that batters were scared of me, especially on days when I was throwing at my best. Some hitters would take swings after the ball went by just so their at-bats were quicker. I'd always kid the A's Joe De Maestri about three feeble swings he took one at-bat, telling him, "You looked like Zorro." If anybody ever threw at 100 mph, I'm sure I did. Yogi, Whitey, and Tony Kubek and other guys who had seen lots of pitchers told me that they had never seen anyone throw so hard.

It was an exaggeration that I once hit the guy in the on-deck circle with a wild pitch. The player in question was Jimmy Piersall. He was doing like Ted Williams when Williams was on-deck, standing five or six feet from the plate and studying and timing the pitches. I wouldn't hit Williams, but I threw the ball near Piersall. He fell down and started hollering and I said, "You've got yourself confused with a hitter."

Elston Howard was by far the best mechanical catcher in baseball at the time. Reporters didn't write about it but he was a better catcher than Berra. He was big, had soft hands, and beautifully handled the low fastball and other sinking pitches—he didn't just stab at them, but brought them back into the strike zone so we'd get strike calls. Elston also had a fast release, which helped me with baserunners, because I didn't get my pitches away quickly. Yogi would admit that Howard caught me better. Yogi didn't like catching me because his hand would puff up and he'd have to box the low pitches Howard caught. Yogi also was slow getting rid of the ball. One day I told Elston, "You know, you catch me so much better than Yogi. If you'd come into the game with me, I'd feel a lot more confident." He agreed, but when I suggested that he go tell Stengel that he'd like to be my catcher, he said, "Are you kidding?" So I said I'd ask Stengel. Not that I went in there that much on my own, but Casey's door was always open to me. He'd invite me in and tell me how great I was doing. He'd take me out of the hotel lobby and take me out to dinner. So it didn't bother me to go tell him what was on my mind. I said, "Casey, you know Ellie catches me so much better than Yogi and has such a better arm. Is there any chance that Ellie can catch me and Yogi can either move to the outfield or come out of the game?" He nodded the entire time I spoke. Then he said, "Mr. Duren, I couldn't agree with you more, but who's going to tell Mr. Berra." This was one of those times when I realized that Berra had a helluva lot to do with making decisions about the team, including who played. He had a great baseball mind and was powerful enough so Casey didn't want to piss him off. I said, "I'll ask him." Casey asked, "You'd do that?" "Sure." So I went out to Yogi in the outfield during warmups and went through the whole thing with him, reminding him about his complaining about my sinking fastball. He said, "I don't give a shit. I don't like to catch you anyway."

Stengel made some pretty gutsy moves and even jerked Mantle's ass out of a game for not remembering how many outs there were and being doubled up. But he would never do that to Berra.

There was a lot of leadership on the Yankees. Berra had the most power among the players and Casey deferred to him. Bauer and McDougald were hard-nosed, straight-talking guys. Our coaches, Frank Crosetti and Jim Turner, were disciplinarians. Mantle and Whitey were the fun guys. Turner told me to stay away from them. Whitey usually picked the night he pitched to go out and raise a little hell. When it came down to late September and we were fighting for the pennant, he was different. I wasn't. I could end up totally out of control—that never happened to Whitey, though he was affected by alcohol.

Mantle was an awesome talent and that in itself gave him some leadership. But I thought of him as just one of the boys. He had a great sense of young players' feelings and made sure that they felt comfortable around him. He had a great sense of humor and was a great kidder. Yet he was bear-down and serious during a game. I think Mickey got awful down on himself and was moody a lot of times, kicking the water cooler and those kinds of things. I don't think he liked Stengel too much. But he played hard for him.

The ballplayers were tough guys. We banded together and there was tremendous camaraderie. The common enemy was the front office, the establishment, whereas the common enemy of players in the future would be the stress and isolation that comes from being millionaires. We were hungry ballplayers. I think we lived kind of recklessly, at least us borderline players. We figured we could make as much money when the season was over. I had to work in the off-season, in a clothing store selling men's furnishings. After the 1958 season I was a little bit on the banquet circuit, but that paid only $100 at most for a night. If we got a small endorsement, we thought it was great. I did a Remington Rollectric commercial and got about $300 total. I did a Viceroy commercial for a little money. Every year Topps baseball cards gave us about $250 or the choice of a present from a catalogue.

Baseball was a hard game. You not only had to produce statistically each game, but also to make sure you didn't have mental lapses. There was a lot of stress, especially for the borderline players. There were only 16 teams and there were a lot of guys who could take your job.

WORLD SERIES

1958

YANKEES
VS
BRAVES

RYNE DUREN · YANKEES:

The Yankees had won their fourth straight pennant, so most of my teammates had experienced a World Series, but this would be my first time. It was an edgy-nervous time. The Series was a rematch with the Braves and all the guys really bore down to make sure the Yankees didn't lose again.

Spahn beat Whitey Ford and me in Game 1 and pitched a 2-hit shutout against Ford in Game 4; Burdette won Game 2, and they led us 3 games to 1. Yet we rallied to beat them. That hadn't happened since 1925. We had the better team. The Braves were a pretty easy team for me to pitch against because most of them were free swingers. I don't think Eddie Mathews fouled the ball off me.

I lost Game 1, 4–3, on 3 singles by Adcock, Crandall, and Bruton in the tenth inning, but otherwise had a terrific Series, saving Don Larsen's 4–0 victory in Game 3, and winning Game 6. I ended up with a 1.91 ERA and 14 strikeouts in 9⅓ innings. Turley won 2 games and saved another, Hank Bauer had 4 homers and 8 RBIs, and Skowron, McDougald, and Mantle had big homers, but in all honesty, I think the key to our winning the Series was the job Stengel got out of me in the sixth game, when we were down 3 games to 2. In relief of Ford and Ditmar, I held the Braves scoreless for more than four innings, striking out 9. Then in the tenth inning, McDougald homered to break a 2–2 tie and singles by Howard, Berra, and Skowron scored our fourth run. We ended up winning 4–3. I just couldn't get the last out in the bottom of the tenth and Turley came on with the tying and winning runs on to get the save. That was a tense game and at one point I gave the homeplate umpire, Charlie Berry, the choke sign. Berry didn't see it, but Ford Frick would fine me $250. After the game I was interviewed in the locker room by Jack Lescoulie for the next morning's *Today* show. I was looking forward to seeing myself but they had to cut the segment because Yogi Berra had been walking around buck naked in the background scratching his rear end.

The final game matched Don Larsen and Lew Burdette. I was ready if needed, but Turley did a great job in long relief. The game was played in Milwaukee, which was just 90 minutes from my home, so we had a family celebration.

BOB TURLEY · YANKEES:

We were down 3 games to 1, when I pitched the fifth game of the Series. I won 7–0, on a 5-hitter, beating Lew Burdette. That was his first loss to us after 3 wins in the 1957 Series and a win in the second game of the 1958 Series. I had been knocked out in Game 2 in the first inning and got the loss despite having pretty good stuff, but making up for that game never really crossed my mind. I wasn't any more determined than usual. In Game 6, I relieved Ryne Duren with 2 outs in the tenth inning and pitched out of a jam for a 4–3 win. The next day we played Game 7, and Stengel brought me in for Larsen in the third inning, with us ahead 2–1. I went the rest of the way. They tied the score in the sixth inning, but we got 4 runs off Burdette with 2 outs in the 8th on Elston Howard's single and Bill Skowron's 3-run homer and won 6–2. Being on the mound for the final out in the World Series was the most exciting moment of my career. I could hardly walk off the mound I was so damn tired. It was as if I had pitched two entire ball games in four days.

The day after the Series, Burdette, Eddie Mathews, and I flew to Hawaii. The Cardinals were on tour, and the promoters hired us to come over and play for an Ha-waiian team against them. Despite our exhaustion, Lew and I pitched the whole game and lost 1–0.

BOB BUHL · BRAVES:

As soon as we won the 1957 World Series, I was looking forward to the next World Series because I thought we would run away with it again. We should have. We had the Yankees down 3 games to 1 and lost. We knew we should have won. We figured we'd come back and win the next year. But we didn't because the team would mistakenly change managers and move personnel around.

LEW BURDETTE · BRAVES:

I won the second game of the Series, but lost in my other two starts, including the seventh game. It was disappointing to lose that Series. After scoring 13 runs in the second game, we couldn't score any more. We were shut out twice. You know we didn't score when I had the biggest hit for our team—a three-run homer in Game 2—and both Spahn and I had one more RBI than Hank Aaron and the same as Eddie Mathews. Eddie had a miserable Series. We thought we were going to blow them away.

NATIONAL LEAGUE 1959

"MCMILLAN WAS THE KING OF KINGS, THE GREATEST SHORTSTOP I EVER SAW. HE HAD GREAT HANDS AND ALWAYS POSITIONED HIMSELF IN FRONT OF THE BALL. HE WAS A REAL BATTLER AND I LIKED THE WAY HE STAYED ON THE BAG TO MAKE SURE HE GOT THE OUT, EVEN IF IT MEANT BEING HIT BY THE RUNNER. HE HAD KNOTS ALL OVER HIS LEGS."

JIM O'TOOLE

MILWAUKEE BRAVES

LEW BURDETTE:

I had my second straight 20-win season, tying Warren Spahn and the Giants' Sam Jones for the league lead with 21 victories, and leading the league with 39 starts and 4 shutouts. I also led the league in hits allowed but because I walked so few batters I wasn't hurt that often. If you get a reputation of not walking many batters and you hit your spots at least 80 percent of the time, a hitter will swing at bad pitches, even if the count is 1–0, 2–1, and even 3–1. He thinks you'll throw a fastball down the middle and is geared up to go downtown with it. If you deceive them by throwing a sinker or slider that looks like a strike but breaks down knee high, they'll go for bad pitches. The whole Philadelphia ballclub did that for years until Joe Koppe went over there from our team in 1959 and told them what he'd overheard us saying. He told them not to swing at Spahn or Burdette and to make them throw strikes. I'd throw any pitch on any count because you can't narrow yourself to being a one-pitch pitcher.

My most unusual win came when I hooked up against the Pirates' Harvey Haddix on May 26. That's when Harvey chose to throw a 12-inning perfect game. I had the displeasure of making the final out in the third, sixth, ninth, and twelfth innings. Haddix was just methodical. Everything worked good for him. I was adequate. I think I scattered 12 singles in 13 innings. I gave up two hits in only one inning. I got three double plays to get out of jams. I wasn't out there too long and didn't throw too many balls. After 10 innings, Fred Haney asked if I wanted out. I asked, "What for? I'm not tired. I'd like to hang with it." I don't know what would have happened if Don Hoak hadn't thrown the ball low to Rocky Nelson at first in the bottom of the thirteenth. They gave Hoak the error but Rocky could have stretched and caught the ball. He opted to backhand it and trap it close to the bag and it ran up his arm. That's what lost the game for Haddix. Mathews then bunted Mantilla to second and Haddix intentionally walked Aaron to get to Adcock and set up a double play. Adcock hit the ball out of the ballpark. They had just brought in the fences in County Stadium and they had two cyclone fences, one 15 to 20 feet behind the other.

One of the National League's most consistently effective pitchers since 1953, Lew Burdette won a career-high 21 games in 1959, tying for the league lead.

Aaron knew that Mantilla was going to score. He saw the ball hit a fence and thought it was the front fence and assumed the ball was still in play. So once he touched second to prevent the force, he just turned and came across the mound. But the ball had hit the second fence and should have been a homer, and Adcock kept on going. The minute Joe touched third he was automatically out for passing Aaron. Warren Giles, the league president, made a decision and called it a 1–0 ballgame, which sounded better than 3–0.

There were no superemotions in our dugout, except I was happy. I called Harvey that night in the visiting clubhouse. I told him, "I realize I got what I wanted, a win, but I'd really give it up because you pitched the greatest game that's ever been pitched in the history of baseball. It was a damned shame you had to lose." And he said, "That's nice of you to say that, Lew." I said, "How long have we known each other, Harvey? 12

years now?" He said, "Yeah, we played against each other in the minors, our paths have crossed a few times, we've had beers together and talked a lot of baseball." I said, "Yeah, I thought you knew better than to bunch your damn hits . . ." And he hung up on me. The next day he had about 50 writers in the dugout with him, and he called me over to tell them what I did to him over the phone.

BOB BUHL:
Haddix's 12-inning perfect game against Lew Burdette was really extraordinary because we called every pitch that he threw because his catcher, Smoky Burgess, was tipping them off. Burgess was chubby and couldn't squat all the way down. We'd see his fingers below his legs—just like we would when Ed Bailey caught for the Reds. We'd yell from the bench what he was calling. But Harvey was doing such a good job of putting on and taking off speed that the hitters couldn't time him until Adcock reached him in the thirteenth inning.

It seemed like old times with the Braves and Dodgers battling for the National League pennant. Actually the Giants were ahead of us both for much of the season until the Dodgers swept them in late September and dropped them into third, where they stayed. The Dodgers moved ahead of us by a game with two games left, but then they lost to the Cubs and Warren Spahn beat the Phillies, 3–2, for his 267th career win, which was a new league record for lefties. However, on the final day, the Dodgers clinched a tie in an afternoon game at Wrigley Field, meaning we'd have to beat the Phillies that night in Milwaukee. Fred Haney would put a baseball by the locker of the pitcher who would start for him. Haney wanted Juan Pizarro to go for us that night. Pizarro saw the ball and took it to Haney and said, "Why me?" So Haney took the ball and gave it to me. Of course, I thought it was my turn to pitch anyway. We knew the Dodgers had won and we had to win to tie them. I beat Philadelphia, 5–2. Other than my first win in the majors, that was the most exciting moment of my career.

Our win meant that we had to begin a 2-out-of-3 playoff series with Los Angeles. Spahn rarely pitched against the Dodgers because he didn't have good luck against them, and Burdette had pitched the game before Spahn, so that meant Carlton Willey would pitch the first playoff game. Willey pitched in the rain in Milwaukee and they beat us 3–2. Then they rallied for a ninth inning tie against Burdette in the next game, and eventually won 6–5 in 12 innings to eliminate us.

That was a disappointing defeat, but we should have won the pennant prior to a playoff because we had a better team. Spahn and Burdette each had 21 wins and I came back from the bad arm to go 15–9, pitching about 90 fewer innings than them. Offensively, Aaron and Mathews had their usual great years. Ernie Banks led the league in RBIs with over 140, but Hank and Eddie led in everything else. Hank won the batting crown, hitting over .350, and had 39 homers and over 120 RBIs, and Ed led the league with 46 homers. Eddie finished second to Banks in the MVP vote. But I'm sure it hurt us that Red Schoendienst missed almost the entire season with a bout of tuberculosis. We could have won anyway if an umpire didn't miss a call in the Los Angeles Coliseum in mid-September. In about the sixth or seventh inning, Adcock hit one up into the tower on the other side of the screen and it ricocheted back down and landed on the playing field. And the umpire who was looking at it called it a ground rule double. We eventually lost by a run. We complained to the umpires and protested the game but nothing ever happened.

ST. LOUIS CARDINALS

JIM BROSNAN:

After the Cardinals returned from Japan during the off-season, I did a third piece for *Sports Illustrated* on the guy who organized the trip, a very fascinating billionaire from Hawaii. They didn't print that piece and I went to New York to find out why. Bob Kramer was given the task of explaining to me that I went wrong when I didn't employ the journalistic style I used in my first two essays. Bob Boyle of *SI* suggested that while I was in town I go see his friend Evan Thomas, Norman Thomas's son, down at Harper and Row, where he was the man in charge. Thomas was a baseball fanatic. So I walked over to visit Thomas and a half hour later I left with a contract for what would become my first book, *The Long Season.*

This was in February 1959. The next month I went to spring training with the Cardinals in Charleston, South

Carolina, and started to keep a record of what was going on with the team. And with the new manager Solly Hemus, his coaches Johnny Keane and Harry "the Hat" Walker, and all the people who later claimed I made fun of them in *The Long Season.* Well, in a way, I did make fun of them. Hemus had no idea how to manage, Walker was an egomaniac who didn't know how to teach hitting, and Keane wasted his time hitting fungoes when it was apparent he should have been managing instead of Hemus—which I'm sure Hemus knew. They were pompous asses and deserved whatever treatment I gave them. Considering what I could have written, I was extremely gentle. I wasn't trying to attack them or the Cardinal organization. For instance, I didn't attack Augie Busch or his policy to give players free beer once a week. (Of course, when *The Long Season* was published in 1960, Bing Devine, the Cardinals general manager, took the company line and declared me a traitor.)

I hadn't called anybody to get permission. It didn't even occur to me since this was a personal journal about my experiences. I'd received no negative feedback on my articles in *Sports Illustrated.* I had a line about "Hobie Landrith's bats all seem to have holes in them," that made Hobie a bit upset, but he was a small guy so it didn't come to anything. Otherwise those pieces were about me and not so much about other players. In a book, I would have to talk about other people, describe who they were and what they said and how I thought about them and how they thought about me . . . But I still believed I had the freedom to do what I was doing without letting anybody know, because this was *my* story.

I roomed with Alex Kellner. He was in the last year of his career, and his only year with the Cardinals. He was a likable guy, who supposedly roped mountain lions as a hobby. He was addicted to television westerns and I wasn't one to argue with him.

I got to know Bill White, who had been with the Giants. Curt Flood and George Crowe—a great pinch hitter—were occasionally in the lineup, but Bill was the only black who was an everyday player that year. He was a .300 hitter, and because he was left-handed had the potential to hit a lot of homers in Busch Stadium. He played left field for us because Musial—who was having his only poor year, dropping into the .250s—was now playing first. Bill was very bright and very articulate. Having not known blacks when growing up in Cincinnati or in the Cubs organization, I appreciated getting to know someone like him.

Solly Hemus, who was leading the Cards to a seventh-place finish, didn't have much use for me and pitched me infrequently in important situations. At times I was almost a bystander. Then in June, I was traded to the Reds for Hal Jeffcoat.

TIM McCARVER:

I was born in Memphis, Tennessee, in 1941. We were a Catholic family in a predominantly Protestant town. My father was a policeman, first a patrolman and then a lieutenant, and then left the force to became a private detective. Meanwhile, my mother raised five children. I had three brothers and a sister, and oddly it was my sister, Marilyn, who helped me develop as an athlete. While my parents encouraged me and my brothers ignored me, Marilyn played both tackle football and baseball with me. She was the one who turned this right-handed kid into a left-handed hitter. I joked that she also taught me to be a low-ball hitter by rolling the ball to me when I was very young. When I turned 8, I played on a Little League team nicknamed "the Candy Kids" and at 10, I was on the Bemis Bag Company team. That's when I first started catching. Throughout my youth I played other positions, and even pitched, but I was a catcher.

During my youth I played a lot of sandlot ball and a two-boy street game called "cork ball" in which the ball was made of a cork, tape, and a penny. I pretended to be my heroes, Monte Irvin, Hank Aaron, and, from my beloved Cardinals, Rip Repulski and Jabbo Jablonski. I also pretended to be Cardinals broadcaster Harry Caray announcing our games.

In high school at Christian Brothers, I played baseball, football, and basketball and was on the track team. Football was my first love and I was sorely tempted by the scholarships Kentucky, Tennessee, Alabama, and Notre Dame were dangling in front of me. But I opted for a professional baseball career.

The first time I realized I had professional talent in baseball was when I was a sophomore in high school and scouts started hanging around. They never talked about my signing but they'd talk to my parents and friends and parents of friends. When I was a junior there

The St. Louis Cardinals' large financial investment in 18-year-old Tim McCarver would pay off in the '60s when he would become the most versatile catcher in the franchise's history.

was an article in the local paper by a sports reporter who thought I should pursue a professional career instead of going to college. He wrote "The price tag continues to go up." Of the teams that pursued me, the Giants, Yankees, and Cardinals were the ones in the running. I thought I would sign with the Yankees because their scout, Hall of Fame catcher Bill Dickey, was really after me. He upped the Yankees' bid to pass that of the Giants, but it turned out I got the highest offer from my favorite team, the St. Louis Cardinals. The two men who courted me were scout Buddy Lewis—who claimed he signed the barefoot Vinegar Bend Mizell at a swimming hole—and farm director Walter Shannon. On June 15, 1959, I signed with the Cardinals for

$75,000, which to me was a fortune, more than my father had made in his entire career. That money was spread over five years. The Cards explained it was for tax purposes. When I learned more about handling money, I realized it was for *their* tax purposes.

The bonus rule was no longer in effect, so the Cardinals didn't have to keep me on the major league roster for two years. They sent me to Keokuk, Iowa, in the Class D Midwest League. This was a jolting period in my life. I had always been better than those I played with but suddenly the caliber of play went up dramatically. Now I was playing with guys in their early 20s. Unlike me, their bodies had already formed. The pitching was a lot better, the runners were a lot faster. Yet I was prepared for professional ball and hit .360 at Keokuk and moved up to Rochester in AAA and hit .357 in 17 games.

In September I was brought up by the Cards and found myself wearing a major league uniform. It was quite a thrill, especially because I was so young. So was sitting on the same bench with Stan Musial. I also got to see Ken Boyer in the midst of a torrid 29-game hitting streak. He was finally stopped by Glen Hobbie—and I had the satisfaction of getting my first major league hit off Hobbie, an infield hit at Wrigley Field. Hal Smith was a fair hitter and great defensive catcher so I didn't get to see much action. I had only 24 official at-bats in 1959, and got only 4 hits. But I did start a couple of games and got a couple of hits against Phillies rookie Ed Keegan. So that was a nice way of breaking in.

Bob Gibson and Marshall Bridges also started out that year. Bridges, who was a left-handed reliever from Jackson, Mississippi, actually had a more impressive debut, winning 6 out of 9 decisions and striking out one batter per inning. But he was already 28. Gibson went 3–5 but he was just 23 and everyone saw that he had tremendous potential. He was really a hard thrower and a fierce competitor. Another rookie pitcher was Dick Ricketts, who was about 6'7". He went 1–6 and never pitched in the majors again (but his brother Dave, a catcher, would play on the Cards starting in 1963).

Jeoff Long, a pitcher—and later an outfielder and first baseman—had signed for $85,000, and he and I were brought up by the Cardinals at the same time. We were called "The Gold Dust Twins." I was from Tennessee and he was from Kentucky and we were born a

week apart, so we naturally hung around together. Although underage, Jeoff and I decided to go to the Grand Burlesque Theater in St. Louis, and we saw our first strip show. One of the dancers was a woman named Kim Riviera. I couldn't believe this woman. She had better moves than the other dancers and was absolutely gorgeous. The next night at the park, all Jeoff and I could talk about was Kim Riviera. All the veterans were looking at us and laughing. A week later Don Blasingame called me at the George Washington Hotel and invited me and Jeoff over for dinner on a Saturday night. Blazer and Joe Cunningham, who were both single, had an apartment in Gaslight Square above a Greek restaurant called Smokey Joe's Cafe. Jeoff and I were thrilled to be invited to dinner by good major league ballplayers. In fact that year Cunningham batted .345, which was second in the league to Hank Aaron's .355. When we got there, I noticed that the table was set for five. A half hour later, Don goes into the bedroom and emerges with Kim Riviera! He was dating her! So Jeoff and I sat there at dinner with dumbfounded looks and our acne and crewcuts and $12 ban-lon shirts—which were top-of-the-line shirts in our wardrobes. And we dined with Kim Riviera! I *never* got over this. It was one of the great things that *ever* happened to me.

I was so naive in those days. Bob Grim, the former Yankee pitcher who spent a little time on the Cardinals, told me about putting sour cream and chives on baked potatoes. I didn't even know what sour cream and chives were. I did know what a potato was. Bob would take me to try food I'd never had before. And it was then that I started to develop an interest in restaurants.

TOM CHENEY:

I played baseball in the service for two years. We had a stacked team made up of pros, and we got special treatment. I also learned to play golf. I played so much that when I got out of the army I was a scratch golfer. That's not something you want to talk about too much.

I got out of the service in 1959. I had saved up my leave time so I got out 30 days early and joined the Cardinals. Bing Devine was the general manager and when I walked in, he said that I had to sign a new contract. He said, "How does eighty-five sound?" And I asked, "Do you mean $850 a month?" He said, "$8,500 for the year." I said, "That sounds great." I had gotten

$6,000 when I left. When I was in the service, my wife got an allotment, but my paycheck was $27 a month.

I was in just 11 games, with 2 starts. I was rusty and was hit pretty hard, and when batters didn't get hits off me I either walked them or struck them out. That winter the Cards sent me to Havana, Cuba, to work on control. Mike Gonzales, an old-time major league catcher from Cuba, owned the team and worked with me. My wife and 8-month-old daughter came with me. We got $350 a month in expenses to go along with my $1,500-a-month salary. It was a life of luxury. We had a nice home, with a maid from the Virgin Islands, and had access to the yacht club and country club. We played just four games a week. One afternoon in December, Ray Katt came over to my house and told me Bing Devine had just traded me and outfielder Gino Cimoli to Pittsburgh for pitcher Ron Kline. I thought of all the years I had spent in the Cardinals organization and how when I was on the brink of making it in the majors, they traded me. But I wasn't bitter.

CHICAGO CUBS

DICK ELLSWORTH:

I went to my first spring training with the Cubs in Mesa, Arizona. They were really impressed that I knew the fundamentals and didn't have to be taught the drills. I had learned all my fundamentals as a pitcher in high school and didn't learn any with the Cubs. In fact, I could have written their manual.

I spent the entire season with Fort Worth in the American Association. My manager was Lu Klein (who would become one of Chicago's revolving coaches in 1961 and 1962). After the season, I came home and was married.

LOS ANGELES DODGERS

ED ROEBUCK:

I was told I'd never pitch again. Luckily, Kenny Myers, who was a Dodgers scout and great teacher, knew something about training. He'd have me throw against a fence and then take my arm and stretch it, just really tear it. Every day, he would ask me if it was better. He was responsible for bringing me back. I had to go to St. Paul

for the year. I started all 28 games I pitched and threw almost 200 innings. I won 13 games and had an ERA under 3.00. I was ready to return to L.A. and get a big league salary again.

JOHNNY KLIPPSTEIN:

Sandy Koufax was a loner and fairly introverted but he was a real nice guy. He and I would fish together in spring training, often with Carl Furillo. That's how I got to know him because during the season we didn't spend much time together. He was a noncommittal, private person who didn't really reveal his feelings about baseball or anything else. He had a sense of humor in that he would appreciate what was funny, but joking around wasn't part of his routine. In 1958 and 1959, Sandy finally got to pitch a fair amount and realize some of his potential. In June, he struck out 16 Phillies and in August he tied Bob Feller's major league record by striking out 18 Giants in the Coliseum. I was struck by how he changed from being a guy who would get mad at himself and blow up on the mound to someone who was very composed.

Maury Wills had been in the minors since 1951, when the Dodgers brought him up midway through the season to be our regular shortstop. He impressed everybody with his speed and hustle but wasn't a base stealer yet. He was somewhat on the cocky side. At times, he would get a bit mouthy and pop-off, but it was all talk. Once Charlie Neal invited him to go under the stands and settle their dispute, but Maury didn't go. He knew Charlie would have whipped him. But Maury was a good ballplayer and he sure could run. Still I couldn't tell he'd become such an impact player in the next couple of years.

Wally Moon, who had been acquired from the Cardinals for Gino Cimoli, was an impact player that year. He was a left-handed hitter but he had an inside-out swing and had a knack for lifting balls into the left-field screen. Only Hodges and Snider hit more homers for us.

I was there for ''Roy Campanella Night'' on May 7. Before an exhibition game against the Yankees, Pee Wee wheeled Roy onto the field in front of more than 93,000 people, which was an attendance record. Then they turned out the lights and everybody lit a match. It was unbelievable. Roy wasn't only a great ballplayer, but he was also a good person. What happened to him had an effect on everybody in baseball. It was sad to see anyone so vital and so strong suddenly be in a wheel-chair.

At the time, the L.A. Dodgers and San Francisco Giants hadn't yet reestablished the rivalry they had on the East Coast. But there was some bad blood between the Braves and Dodgers. We had a rivalry. The Braves had finished second to the Brooklyn Dodgers in 1955 and 1956, when they lost out by one game. Then the Braves won the pennants in both 1957 and 1958. My biggest memory of our left-field fence is when the um-pires took a homer away from Joe Adcock near the end of the year. It hit where two fences butted together but one was a little higher. I think the rule was that if it was hit to the right of the smaller portion of the fence it was a home run, but if it was to the left of that it was a dou-ble—and that's how it was ruled. I honestly couldn't tell what it was. The Braves were irate. I had to think that so many Braves came onto the field that they must have seen it pretty good. If that had been a homer they would have won and most likely there wouldn't have been a playoff series.

I hurt my back in August and pitched sparingly the rest of the season. I finished at 4–0, but had a much higher ERA than I would have liked. Our ace pitcher was Don Drysdale, who pitched over 40 games and won 17. He led the league in strikeouts. Batters were rarely afraid of pitchers who came inside, but Drysdale put some fear in right-handed batters. Stan Williams was a little different. He might throw one inside occasionally. He would get a little wild at times and get himself in trouble—much like I would—but he was a good pitcher. He threw hard, had good stuff, and was a real competitor.

STAN WILLIAMS:
I pitched a few more innings than in my rookie season but Alston started me less and relieved me more and I won only 5 games. Roger Craig and left-hander Danny McDevitt got a lot of starts and did good jobs. We also got great relief pitching from Larry Sherry and Clem Labine. Ed Roebuck was hurt, so the Dodgers brought up Sherry to pitch middle relief in the pennant race. He also started a few games. He was a Los Angeles product who had a hard fastball and an effective slider. He was only 24 but he was a tremendous competitor.

Our offense was much improved. Veterans like Snider, Furillo and Hodges gave it one last shot. Wally Moon came over from the Cards to hit a bunch of hom-ers into the left-field screen and join Snider and Hodges in providing the leadership that was missing now that Reese had retired. He was a solid left-fielder. Don Dem-eter played a good center field—Duke played more than Furillo in right—and hit a few homers. We got good all-around play from Charlie Neal, Jim Gilliam, and rookie shortstop Maury Wills, who put Don Zimmer back on the bench. We also had good left-handed hitters Norm Larker and Ron Fairly coming off the bench. They could play first base and the outfield.

We weren't a great team, but we won the pennant with what was then the lowest number of wins in the history of the game. We won just 86 games out of 154. We had won one key game from the Braves in which Adcock hit a ball that wedged between the two poles on the screen, over one pole and under the other one. And they called it a ground rule double, which was the right call to me because the ball didn't leave the ballpark.

Our victory total went up to 88 games when we took both games from Milwaukee in the playoffs. We played the first game in Milwaukee and Larry Sherry won it with over seven innings of shutout ball in relief of McDevitt, 3–2, and Johnny Roseboro hit a homer.

I got the win that put us in the World Series. I was the sixth pitcher in the second game, in Los Angeles. Lew Burdette started for the Braves and we trailed going into the ninth inning, 5–2. We knew that if we lost we'd have to face Bob Buhl in the final game, and Buhl owned the Dodgers. So it was looking bleak. Then we rallied for 3 runs to tie the score. Drysdale, Podres, Koufax, and La-bine had pitched, so there were no other pitchers avail-able. So I went out in the tenth inning and pitched the last three innings. I threw only one breaking ball, a slider to Hank Aaron. His eyes got as big as saucers and he tomahawked the ball and it went straight up into the air and came straight down in front of the screen for an out. I didn't want to make another mistake so I went strictly with the hard fastball. Early in the game, Norm Larker had thrown a cross body block trying to break up a double play, and Johnny Logan was hurt and came out, with Felix Mantilla shifting from second to short. In the last of the twelfth, with runners on first and second, Carl Furillo hit a 2-out grounder off Bob Rush, which

Mantilla made a great stop on. He should have held on to it because he was off balance, but he threw it past Frank Torre at first and Hodges scored the winning run. When Furillo hit the ball, I was already up and heading for the mound to pitch the next inning. I was in disbelief that the game was suddenly over and the Dodgers had won the pennant.

ART FOWLER:

After winning 16 games at Spokane in 1958, I went to Cuba to play in the Winter Leagues with Alamanderos. They gave me money and expenses. Bobby Bragan, who managed Spokane, knew a guy called "Macho" and he asked me to come down there. I met Bob Allison, Rocky Nelson, Dick Brown, Jim Baxes, Carlos Paula, Sandy Amoros, and Willie Miranda. We went to Venezuela and won the Little World Series. We were supposed to get $10,000 per person and on the plane they gave us the money, but it was only about $1,000 apiece. What could we say?

In 1959, the Dodgers brought me up and Walter Alston put me in the bullpen to relieve guys like Sandy Koufax, Don Drysdale, and Johnny Podres. I relieved Koufax one game after he walked the bases loaded while leading the Giants 2–0 in Seals Stadium. Leon Wagner hit a grandslammer off me and we lost, 4–2. I told Koufax, "I got you out of that jam quick, didn't I?"

Drysdale was a superduper. He never missed a turn. We were in St. Louis one Saturday and Drysdale was knocked out in the first inning and I relieved him. They beat me up worse than Drysdale. So they took me out of the game, too. I joined Don in the clubhouse and we drank a couple of beers while the game continued. We were staying at the Chase Hotel, so both of us later went to the hotel bar. The bartender was talking to two guys who had been to the ball game. One said, "I've never seen anything so disgusting. We went to see Drysdale pitch and he stunk. The guy they put in next was worse." I had to hold Drysdale back. He wanted to kill those guys. I said, "We were that bad, so don't worry about it."

The Dodgers fans didn't know baseball back then. They just wanted to be where the celebrities were. But they were great fans. I remember when a record 93,000 of them came out to the Coliseum for "Roy Campanella Night." The Dodgers were paying tribute to Campy

prior to an exhibition game we lost to the Yankees. His family and Dodger friends were around him, and then they turned off the lights and everyone struck a match. Gorgeous! It was very moving. Campanella was a good guy. (The next spring, when Roy came to Vero Beach in his wheelchair, he rolled up to me and said, "I can still hit you, buddy." I said, "I understand.")

Every day, I used to play pepper for about an hour, and then I'd run about 8 or 10 laps. I didn't do a lot of running. When a Dodgers coach wanted us to run 40 laps, I told Walter Alston that I couldn't do it: "I throw the ball, I'm not a runner."

I pitched in 36 games right off the bat, including 12 in a row—I was tired at the end of that. But I got sent back to Spokane. When the Dodgers won the pennant and World Series, they voted me a full share. I was surprised. (But I wouldn't get my ring until Peter O'Malley sent me one 30 years later!)

SAN FRANCISCO GIANTS

HANK SAUER:

There was no animosity between players on the Giants, including Mays and Cepeda. In Cepeda's second year he had a slightly better average than Mays and had 105 RBIs to Mays's 104, but Willie again outhomered him, 34 to 27. But they got got along fine and I didn't see anything more than friendly competition between the two. But I think Cepeda did have trouble when Willie McCovey came up in 1959. Cepeda didn't dislike McCovey but resented that the Giants wanted McCovey to play first and Orlando to move to left field. Cepeda only wanted to play first base. But Cepeda could run a lot better than McCovey, who was 6'4" and quite large. Cepeda was a big guy himself, about 6'2", but he was built differently and would fool you with his speed. He would win races in spring training against fast runners.

I lived at the Whitcombe Hotel on Broadway in downtown San Francisco. I enjoyed the city and had good friends on the team. (In time, I'd play golf with Willie Mays, Willie McCovey, and Jim Davenport.) However, I think the team was closer in New York. Players didn't run around too much together, even on the road. We didn't have the team parties or family get-togethers in San Francisco. The players started to separate once we moved. That was another sign that baseball was changing. Looking back I thought that the biggest change was that from 1958 or 1959 on, players started to become loners and cliques formed on teams. There was nothing like that during my entire career. As for the level of play, I thought that it hadn't changed much over the years—it may even have improved.

I batted only 15 times during the season, which was my last. I was over 40 and was ready to retire. After my long big league career with the Reds, Cubs, Cardinals, and New York and San Francisco Giants, I just wanted to be remembered as a good ballplayer who hit in the clutch and did his job and did it well. It was also very, very important that I always be known as a nice guy.

JOHNNY ANTONELLI:

During the off-season, the Giants acquired Jack Sanford from the Phillies for Ruben Gomez and Sad Sam Jones from the Cardinals for Bill White and Ray Jablonski. We now had a very strong pitching nucleus. Rigney relied on essentially only five pitchers. Sanford and I pitched almost exclusively as starters, but he used Jones and Mike McCormick as starters and in the bullpen to support his ace, Stu Miller, who now was exclusively a reliever. Jones pitched in 50 games and McCormick almost that many. We all pitched well. I had a career-high 38 starts and 282 innings. I went 19–10 with a 3.10 ERA and was a co-league leader with 4 shutouts, the third time I led the league in that category. Jones also had 4 shutouts. He led the league in ERA and tied for the lead in wins with 21.

Unfortunately, Mays and Cepeda were about the only guys in the lineup whose hitting didn't decline from the previous year. The young players did well but weren't ready for a full year's run at the pennant. The offense didn't really get a jolt until we brought up Willie McCovey from Phoenix at the end of July. He debuted by going 4 for 4 with two triples against Robin Roberts, and started us on a hot streak that brought us back into contention. For a time we were even in first place, before we went into a tailspin in late September and finished 3 games behind the Dodgers and Braves. He hit over .350 and was voted Rookie of the Year.

Cepeda and McCovey became the hometown heroes over Willie Mays. They were great ballplayers and likable people, but it's too bad that the fans would support them at the expense of Mays. Actually I didn't hear the fans boo Mays too much because I was having my own problems at the time. I made a statement about the city's climate and was almost run out of town.

I had troubles with the press. The fans read the articles and I was booed unmercifully. They didn't boo me because of my pitching but because of what they read. And what they read was misquoted. I never said anything bad about the city, just about Seals Stadium. The Dodgers were in town for an important series and I was pitching against Don Drysdale. The score was 1–1 late in the game. I had retired 17 straight batters when they got a man on. Then Charlie Neal hit a ball that our shortstop called for and our left fielder Jackie Brandt started in for. Then the jet stream took it over the left-field fence for a home run and we lost 3–1. We were fighting for a pennant so that wasn't the happiest of situations. I walked into the clubhouse and a reporter wanted to know what pitch Neal had "pummeled" over the fence. Pummeled? That made it sound like Neal had clouted a 490-foot homer. So I took offense and asked him to leave the clubhouse, telling him to stick the ballpark in the usual area. Unfortunately, he was out for sensationalism and wrote vindictively that I said, "You can stick *San Francisco . . .*" I got pretty good headlines for a while, and the fans started booing me and telling me to "Go back to Rochester where it's snowing!" I wasn't thin-skinned on the road and I hadn't minded being booed in Los Angeles, but it was disappointing to be booed in San Francisco when I'd had such a good record with the team.

PHILADELPHIA PHILLIES

ED BOUCHEE:

I got my only endorsements from MacGregor for shoes and gloves, which they sent me every year. The best thing they ever gave me in return was a set of golf clubs (that would last 33 years). I wanted a trapper model glove but they would send me an old-style glove, which was essentially a solid piece with a hole in it. I'd stick their gloves in my locker and go out and buy a Spalding. And MacGregor complained, "What are you wearing that for?" I said, "When are you going to make me one like the one I ask you to make? I've told you many times. Yet you won't invite me to the factory so I can tell the glovemaker exactly what I want.'' I always gave the gloves away. They were shit.

I loved to warm up pitchers because that is how I broke in my first baseman's gloves. A glove would take a year to break in just by taking infield practice and playing in a game. But by warming up the pitcher in the bullpen or along the side of the field, you get that pocket set in there real good real quick.

Topps gave us a choice of merchandise in exchange for using us on their cards. I think we had five or six different choices. Maybe a dining room set or some kind of camera or golf clubs. The players thought they were getting reamed. But we had nobody to complain to.

The Phillies again finished in last place, but I played a full season and had a season comparable to my rookie year. I led the team with a .285 batting average, and my 15 homers trailed only Gene Freese and Wally Post on the team, and my 74 RBIs was second to Post. I led the league's first basemen in putouts, assists and chances per game.

Our team was changing so rapidly that I was the only starting infielder on the team who had been a regular in 1958. Freese replaced Willie Jones at third, Joe Koppe replaced Chico Fernandez at short, and Sparky Anderson replaced Granny Hamner and Solly Hemus at second. Sparky was awfully quiet. He hadn't been much of a hitter in the minor leagues and was just thankful to play in the big leagues in 1959. He hit less than .220 and would never play in the majors again.

John Quinn had quit the Braves to become our GM and he was dismantling the team. Stan Lopata had been traded to Milwaukee before the season and Willie and Granny were both traded to the Indians during the season. Richie Ashburn would be dealt to the Cubs at the end of the year, and Simmons, who wasn't pitching much, would be sent to St. Louis early in 1960. That would leave only Robin Roberts from the 1950 championship team. Roberts was still our big winner. But he got good support from Jim Owens and Gene Conley, whom we acquired from the Braves. Both won a dozen games for us. Owens rejoined Turk Farrell's Dalton Gang. Conley was quiet, a big, tall drink of water. We got along because we had common roots.

PITTSBURGH PIRATES

DICK GROAT:

We found the last pieces to our championship puzzle in January when Joe Brown made a big deal with Cincinnati. He traded Frank Thomas and we got Don Hoak to play third, Smoky Burgess to catch and pinch-hit, and Harvey Haddix to join the starting rotation. That solidified our team. It would take us a year to learn to play together, but in 1960 we would be ready for a title run.

I loved Hoak. He had a great baseball mind and was a marvelous competitor. He was an excellent base runner and he never made mistakes in the field. Like me, he studied hitters and knew how to play everybody in the National League. He not only hit in the .290s but led the league's third basemen in putouts, assists, and chances. How fortunate I was to play between Mazeroski and Hoak. That's why I led the league's second basemen in putouts, double plays, and chances.

Burgess, who was very quiet, and Vernon Law roomed together. Smoky and the Deacon. Smoky was an unbelievable hitter and not that bad a receiver. When he caught, lots of players said they could see his signals. That's what they said after he caught Haddix's incredible perfect game. When I heard that, it made me laugh. The announcers were always talking about seeing signs from second base. Give me a break. It doesn't happen. A runner at second doesn't have time to figure out the signals because they change the signal sequence every inning. A runner isn't going to gamble on telling one of his teammates that he picked up a signal he thinks is for a curve or fastball. I never had a sign called for me in my career. The only thing you can tell your batter is where the catcher moves after giving a sign so he'll know if the pitch is supposed to be inside or outside.

After his 22-win season, Bob Friend struggled and lost 19 games. Law became our ace, with an 18–9 record. Haddix and Ronny Kline also pitched well, winning in double figures. Surprisingly, ElRoy Face tied Law as the team's biggest winner and he lost only once. 18–1! He had the best percentage in baseball history! Face had been great in 1958, but this was the year he was really recognized as the premier relief pitcher in baseball. He wasn't built high off the ground but when Danny brought him out of that left-field bullpen, he lifted you that far off the ground. You just knew he was going to do something, somehow. He did so many little things, like picking off runners at second base. That's a difficult play and he was the best in the league at it. He was also a great fielder. There was nothing he couldn't do. You needed a strikeout, he'd get it. You needed a double-play, he'd get the grounder. I'm not talking about one year, I'm talking about over his whole career—which definitely should have qualified him for the Hall of Fame. It was great fun to watch him in 1959. We figured that if Face was in there, it would work out. Even if he blew a lead, we'd come back and win for him. He was amazing. He also was a hell of a guy with a great sense of humor. I called him Sam Spade. I said, ''Don't break curfew because ElRoy will find you.''

ELROY FACE:
I never took ball games home with me. If my wife didn't know what the score was, she couldn't tell by my demeanor if we'd won or lost. If she didn't read the paper or go to the ballpark, she wouldn't have known I was having a good year in 1959. I was proud of my accomplishments but wasn't an excitable type. After my record 22-game win streak ended against the Dodgers in September, dropping my record in '59 to 17–1, I went into the clubhouse between games of the doubleheader. There were about 15 writers waiting for me. One of them said, ''How does it feel to lose?'' My answer was, ''I'll just have to start another streak.'' And they all left. That was the end of the interview.

1959 wasn't my best season. I won 18 games but had only 10 saves, and in other years I would have more than 28 combined wins and saves and make more of a contribution. If we'd done better than a fourth-place finish, I might have felt differently—of course, then I might have had more saves. I had a good earned run average of 2.70, but I had my share of luck. The team had five or six come-from-behind wins that gave me victories instead of losses. I could easily have gone something like 12–7.

I never went in before the seventh inning. Many times I'd be asleep in the clubhouse or lying there listening to Bob Prince call the game on the radio when they'd come and get me. I wouldn't come in only in save situations. Relief pitchers weren't used like that in those days. I would come into close games, even if we

NATIONAL BASEBALL LIBRARY, COOPERSTOWN, N.Y.

Once a bench warmer at St. Louis, Dick Schofield became a backup to shortstop Dick Groat and second baseman Bill Mazeroski in Pittsburgh and would have to wait until 1963 before he finally got his chance to start.

were behind. I'd face right-handed and left-handed batters. I would be my own setup man and pitch several innings if necessary. When I walked from the bullpen to the mound, I would think about the situation and by the time I reached the mound I knew exactly what I wanted to do.

Hank Foiles was a good defensive catcher for the Pirates from 1956 to 1959 and Murtaugh would often insert him when I came in to relieve. (In the next couple of years, he'd put in Bob Oldis, who also was pretty good to work with.) But I didn't like to get used to one catcher. Essentially I'd call my own game and shake off anything I didn't want to throw. If the catcher put down the same sign after I shook him off twice, then I'd know Murtaugh was calling the pitch.

Although we had a disappointing year, everyone realized that the preseason acquisition of Don Hoak, Harvey Haddix, and Smoky Burgess had given us the players that made us a solid team that could contend for a title. Hoak became my roommate and added a lot of fire. He was an emotional player and was really upset after his throwing error in the thirteenth inning ruined Haddix's perfect game.

I had received a lot of publicity in 1959, and I pitched in the All-Star Game for the first time. Yet I didn't feel I was a celebrity. But I got special attention in Pittsburgh. For instance, I was maitre d' at a downtown restaurant in 1959, greeting people for lunch three hours a day. It was always nice to pick up some money to supplement our baseball salaries—I belonged to the carpenter's union and in the off-seasons did 10 to 12 game rooms, including one for Mazeroski.

DICK SCHOFIELD:
Unfortunately I didn't get many starts during the year, but I played shortstop when Harvey Haddix pitched 12 perfect innings against the Braves. That was a bizarre, pressure-packed game. Harvey had such great stuff and seemed to get 2 strikes on every batter. You'd look at the scoreboard and there'd be 2 outs and 2 strikes and he wasn't going to let anybody get a hit off him with 2 men out. It was just a shame that we couldn't score for him.

CINCINNATI REDS

DON NEWCOMBE:
In 1959, I proved that my 7–7 record with the Reds in 1958 had not been a fluke. I pitched over 220 innings and went 13–8, the best record of any Reds starter. I had the 23rd and 24th shutouts of my career. I had regained my form once the Reds trainer had gotten rid of the knot in my neck. I had 20 victories since then. However, I was drinking and not taking care of myself and wouldn't be so effective in 1960. In late July, the Reds would send me to the Cleveland Indians, my final major league team.

DEL ENNIS:
The Cardinals had traded me to the Reds prior to the season. I went to their spring training camp in Tampa. Throughout my career, I had bad springs because I suffered from rose fever, but this time I was on fire. I hit about a dozen homers and drove in over 30 runs. But on Opening Day, the Reds' new manager Mayo Smith—who had traded me when he managed the Phillies—told me I was going to be platooned. I said, "What do you mean? Either play me every day or trade me." He did the latter. I was traded to the Chicago White Sox.

JIM O'TOOLE:
I made the team and played for Mayo Smith for half a season. Smith was too easygoing and it was obvious to the players that Gabe Paul, the GM, was making the decisions instead of Smith. I didn't agree with Paul's decision to go with all the old pitchers, like Don Newcombe, Brooks Lawrence, and Joe Nuxhall, while I didn't get much of a chance. I thought I'd be one of the starters but instead I pitched every 10 days. You can't do that when you're young. I had a bad year in 1959, winning just 5 of 13 decisions and having a high ERA.

When Fred Hutchinson took over from Smith, his reputation preceded him. We knew Fred was tough because both Jim Brosnan and Eddie Kasko had played for him in St. Louis. We were glad when he came because we had talent but needed discipline. Everybody respected him and was scared to death of him. You didn't want to be alone in the room with him because he'd kick the shit out of you. When he came to the mound, all you'd dare say was, "Yes, sir." He'd look you right in the eye and when he said you had to do something you'd do it.

I didn't know what to expect when I came to the big leagues. Most of it turned out to be fantastic. You travel, you stay in the best hotels, you get to meet the best people. In Cincinnati everyone knew who we were. The downside was that we were prey to anyone after our wallets or anything else. People were always telling players how to invest their money. Players would invest in oil and stuff like that. I put a couple of thousand into something that didn't pan out.

It was good to be married. That was the only way to do it. Being single and playing ball? Forget it! There are too many temptations. I was surprised at the number of women who chased after ballplayers. If you wanted, you could have a girl in every town. Most of the guys on the Reds were happily married and we tended to hang out together so no one got into trouble.

We took some trains but mostly we flew commercial and charter flights. I loved flying. The quicker the better. The only trouble was that the Reds would cut corners. They'd want to save a half a day's meal money, so instead of having us fly out of Cincinnati at night following a game to be in, say, Philadelphia for a game the following night, they fly'd us out the next day at noon. We'd get in only a few hours before the next game, probably feeling jet lag, and they'd get pissed off when we lost. Pitchers in particular wanted rest. That was to save $5 a man. The Reds were a cheap team, like Pittsburgh and a few others.

I roomed with Eddie Kasko. On the field he was all business but off the field he was a funny guy and we got along well. He was a heady player and smooth shortstop and was taking over for Roy McMillan. McMillan was the king of kings, the greatest shortstop I ever saw. He had great hands and always positioned himself in front of the ball. He was a real battler and I liked the way he stayed on the bag to make sure he got the out, even if it meant being hit by the runner. He had knots all over his legs.

Probably our most outspoken player was Jerry Lynch. He was our most frequently-used left fielder, although against left-handers, Frank Thomas would play out there and Lynch would be saved to pinch hit. Pete Whisenant also would speak up but it takes an everyday player to be a leader.

Gus Bell was a leader of sorts because he was our player rep. I admired him a lot. He could still hit in the .290s and drive in over 100 runs. The silent leader of the Reds was Frank Robinson. He wasn't outspoken or the type of guy who would call a meeting to give a pep talk, but he led with his bat, arm, legs, and competitiveness. In 1959, he hit over .300, socked around 35 homers and drove in 125 runs. He was some player.

Vada Pinson was a great, great ballplayer. He was a terrific left-handed hitter who batted .300 with power. This was his first full season and he had over 200 hits, of which about 70 or 80 were for extra bases, and he scored over 130 runs. He really could get around the bases. He led the league in several categories and some people were already saying he was going to be a Hall of Fame player. His trouble was that he was too laidback. I think if he had more heart, he could have been the best player in baseball.

Frank Thomas was a great player with the Pirates but when he came to the Reds, he got jammed on the hands and wasn't worth a damn. We called him "the big donkey." He was an antagonizer who always wanted to get your goat. I'd want to punch him many times when he'd say, "Hey, rookie." But I decided I'd better not.

Don Newcombe had lost a little on his fastball and was depending on whatever else he could come up with. I thought he threw a spitter. He had a good year, but Hutchinson would get rid of him during the 1960 season, maybe because he would drink and get loud. He was a hard worker. He'd put his rubber jacket on and run. I figured he was so big that he had to do that—just like Joe Nuxhall, who ran because he had trouble with his weight. Nobody had to tell me to run. That was drilled home to me in rookie camp. Your arm was only as good as your legs. A lot of pitchers hated to run but I loved it.

Cot Deal was the pitching coach of the Reds. I was told to keep the ball down and get ahead of the hitter. That's the way I had to pitch, especially in Crosley Field where straight-away center was only 380 feet and right center was 360 feet. I didn't give up many homers, maybe 7 or 8 a year. Being left-handed, I was supposed to have an easier time against left-handed batters, but when I first came up, I had problems getting ahead of them and would have to come in with too good a pitch. Fortunately, there weren't many good left-handed hitters in the league at this time. The Braves had Eddie Mathews, the homer champion, and he and Pinson were the toughest left-handed hitters that year. Willie McCovey was tough, especially on right-handers, but he came up at the end of the year and I didn't have to face him much. I pitched to Stan Musial only a few times and he was having an off season. L.A. had mostly right-handers—and for some reason, Duke Snider never batted against me.

I was cocky and didn't let anybody push me around like they did Claude Osteen, another left-hander who was just turning 20. He'd throw what the catcher wanted instead of his best pitches and get hit hard. It would take him several years and trades to different teams before he'd finally make it. It's stupid to throw the catcher's pitch instead of your own. It took me half a year and a few home runs to learn. I had a lot of problems with Ed Bailey. He'd come to the mound and say, "Listen, kid, I've been up here five years, you throw my pitch." Then I'd shake him off and he'd say, "Throw what the hell you want." So I did.

FRANK THOMAS:

Before I signed a contract, I informed Gabe Paul that I had a bad hand that wasn't healing. He told me not to worry. I asked for $40,000. He said, "I think you're being fair but if you make that kind of money you have to be that type of ballplayer this year." I signed. 1959 turned out to be the worst year of my career. You don't drop from 35 homers and 109 RBIs to 12 homers and 47 RBIs unless there is something radically wrong. My hand was very, very sore. I had tears in my eyes every time I put any pressure on it and when I hit the ball on my fists it really jarred it. I tried everything to take the pressure off, but nothing worked. I never asked to be taken out of the lineup, but Mayo Smith and later Fred Hutchinson had me on the bench a lot of the time. I'd mostly alternate with Willie Jones at third, but I played some in left and at first. I couldn't even get my average up to .230. I'd later kid that I would call home collect and no one would accept the charges, or that my kids were burning my bubble gum cards. The Reds fans treated me pretty good considering the big trade that was made. There were some boos from people who thought I was going to help the team win the pennant. But they didn't know about my hand. It was a shame I couldn't produce and add my bat to those of Frank Robinson and Gus Bell, who each drove in well over 100 runs.

Robinson and Bell got a lot of support anyway. Vada Pinson led the team in hitting and had 20 homers. He was a good athlete who could run and had real quick wrists. Johnny Temple hit over .300. He stayed to himself and was hard to get to know, but on the field, he always gave 100 percent. I didn't get to know Brooks Lawrence well, but he was a good pitcher with a good slider. He had been moved to the bullpen and did a good job for us. Jim Brosnan was another good reliever. He had been my cousin when I batted against him in previous years. I didn't get to know him well. I also didn't get to know Jim O'Toole but I saw that he was a talented young left-hander who tried very hard to do well.

Don Newcombe was a veteran pitcher who still worked really hard. He used to pitch batting practice for an hour and then run for an hour. He really used to sweat. I didn't realize he was an alcoholic. George Crowe was his roommate and didn't know he was an alcoholic. Don was a super guy and still a fine pitcher.

After the season, the Cubs were interested in acquiring me. But they wanted me to go to their doctor. He put me to sleep and operated on my hand. He later said, "I think there are going to be a lot of red faces in Pittsburgh and Cincinnati. I don't know how you did as well as you did." It turned out I had tumors growing around my nerve.

JIM BROSNAN:

When I came over from the Cards in early June, I couldn't tell that the Reds were putting together the nucleus for a team that would win the pennant in just two years. We were a sixth-place team with a losing record and a manager whose days were numbered. Mayo Smith was a kind, gentle man and I couldn't figure out how he ever got to be a big league manager. He wasn't the type. He didn't have any idea how to control his ballclub. Players talked about him behind his back. Ed Bailey, never one to hold back, told Smith to his face, "You don't know shit!" whenever Smith came to the mound to say how he wanted a batter pitched to.

Fred Hutchinson had been my first manager at St. Louis. I think when the Reds told him he would soon replace Smith, he asked Gabe Paul to trade for me. I did most of my pitching for Hutch, going 8–3 in a half year with the Reds. He pitched me mostly in relief and I hoped that wouldn't be the trend in 1960.

Brooks Lawrence and I used to have long discussions in the Reds bullpen about jazz and the black experience. He was one of the few players who talked politics. (After he got out of baseball he would get a political job in Springfield, Ohio.)

I wasn't in the bullpen the entire game. I was usually in the dugout bullshitting with Pete Whisenant. He'd beaver shoot and tell me what he saw. Crosley Field was a tiny ballpark and players didn't need binoculars. All Pete did was turn around and the women were right there in the box seats. Pete also would talk about Costa Rica, where he would eventually live. It's not that we weren't also paying attention to the game. One second, he could be talking about a woman or Costa Rica, and the next he was yelling something to the batter, pitcher, catcher, or umpire. He was a great cheerleader.

Don Newcombe was another unusual guy, but not at all like Whisenant. He was hard to get to know because he had his own agenda. After a game, he didn't hang around with other players. When he got to the ballpark he started to work. Newk was one of the hardest working ballplayers I ever saw. I didn't know he was alcoholic. Except for one time when we flew from Cincinnati to St. Louis. He was supposed to pitch that night. Newcombe hated to fly and—I'm not sure if this is true—he was given permission by Hutchinson to take a bottle of vodka and bottle of grape juice on the plane to relax him. He had it in a brown paper bag. We hit a storm front in our DC-3. We went south toward Memphis but we couldn't get around the storm. A forty-minute flight took over two hours. And about twenty minutes outside of St. Louis we were hit by lightning and it shaved off about a foot of the stabilizer. When we got off the plane we stood there staring at it. Except for Newk, who couldn't see anything because he drank the whole bottle of vodka. He didn't pitch that night.

One side benefit I had being on the Reds in 1959 is that two of my teammates were probably the two guys I had the hardest time pitching to. Frank Thomas once got 9 straight hits off me, 6 for extra bases. Whatever I threw him—a fastball, slider, or change, inside or away—he was looking for it. He said, "I know what you are going to throw." Without me to bat against in 1959, his power numbers were down. Willie Jones also gave me fits. Puddin'head would look terribly fooled on one pitch and then really smash it the second time I threw it to him, as if he expected it. I was happy when we got him halfway through the season. Those tough Phillie fans had often booed him, but now when he went into Philadelphia as a Red they gave him a standing ovation.

AMERICAN LEAGUE

1959

"WHEN I WAS PLAYING, BEING THE

FIRST BLACK ON THE RED SOX

WASN'T NEARLY AS BIG A SOURCE

OF PRIDE AS IT WOULD BE ONCE I

WAS OUT OF THE GAME. AT THE

TIME I NEVER PUT MUCH STOCK IN

IT, OR THOUGHT ABOUT IT. LATER I

UNDERSTOOD MY PLACE IN

HISTORY."

PUMPSIE GREEN

KANSAS CITY ATHLETICS

JOE DE MAESTRI:

In my five years in Kansas City, the biggest thing that happened is that we once won 11 or 12 games in a row. Parke Carroll wanted to give everybody a watch or some damn thing for that, but it never came about. Other than a golf tournament and a couple of picnics, the organization didn't really reward us for our efforts. Maybe if we had become a winning team, it would have been different. But we just weren't strong enough to maintain anything positive. After finishing sixth in 1955, we dropped to eighth in 1956, and then finished seventh in 1957, 1958, and 1959.

Joe De Maestri played his seventh and last season in Kansas City before finally getting the opportunity to play on a championship team, the 1960 and 1961 New York Yankees.

We were called the stepchild of the Yankees, but we weren't insulted. The players could care less. The truth was that nobody else was willing to trade with them because they were afraid of making them stronger. So they just went to the team that needed the most help and grabbed somebody that could help them for a while and gave us somebody that could help us for a while. None of us gave it a second thought about our trading with them. Then on December 11, 1959, I was traded with Roger Maris and first baseman Kent Hadley to the New York Yankees for Hank Bauer, Norm Siebern, Marv Throneberry, and Don Larsen.

CLEVELAND INDIANS

MUDCAT GRANT:

Nineteen fifty-nine was the Indians' only good season when I was there. For a change, we were winning on a continual basis. We weren't the best team in the league, but we had a good attitude and got on such a long roll that we almost won the damn thing, coming up only 5 games behind the White Sox. If Joe Gordon had been a little better manager, we might have won it.

I don't think we had a field leader, but there were many dependable players. For instance, you could depend on Rocky Colavito to hit homers and drive in key runs. Tito Francona had a helluva year, hitting .363. Minnie Minoso hit over .300 and drove in over 90 runs. Vic Power was a tough, clutch player at bat and in the field, where he was the best. Sometimes when we thought we had lost, Minnie or Vic would do something that was unbelievable and we'd get some new energy. And we had a lot of good slot players like Francona, Jim Baxes, Jimmy Piersall, and Billy Martin. They played a lot, filling in at different positions. Martin played second and third, and though Gordon didn't like him, he was good for the ballclub because he was a fighter and knew how to win from his years with the Yankees. Our pitching was good. Cal McLish was 19–8, Gary Bell was 16–11, Jim Perry won 12 games, and I won 10 games for the second straight year.

The Indians were as close to being unified as a team could be in those days. We were like a family, although there were walls between black and white teammates. We had a lot of star black players, but it didn't make any difference how good they were. Jackie Robinson and Larry Doby had been stars, but how close could they get to their white teammates in the late '40s? I think there was respect for a black star on the one hand and disrespect on the other. As long as we played well, we got respect, but when the game was over, it was a different story: we went one way and almost everyone else went another way.

The feeling among many people is that after Jackie Robinson and Larry Doby integrated baseball, it was easy for the black players who followed. That's bullshit. Major league baseball, from the beginning, was slow to react to the problems of black players, and that never changed. Except when baseball brought in Jackie Robinson and Larry Doby, it went along with the slow, general transition in society instead of taking the initiative. A lot of us who came along after Jackie and Larry broke in were justifiably angry at our treatment. We had to go along with much that was humiliating. For instance, because I was black, it was generally accepted by the powers that be that I wasn't smart enough to both pitch and call my own game—it was infuriating that the white manager and his white catcher called my games. The reason I didn't succumb to my anger is that I understood that racism is inbred. People don't just become bigots. It has to be taught.

I got angry the whole time I was in the game. But, as I'm sure was the case with Don Newcombe, you can only take your anger to a certain level or you can't compete. You have to be able to kick out your anger until after the game. I think Don really loved to play the game and pitch. But racism is constant. It's like a bad headache or bad backache—I don't say leg ache because you can survive with that, but a constant headache and backache are hard to endure. That's what racism is: it's all around you. It was a constant struggle all the time, so we could have been angry all the time. White people would think we were complaining if we brought up anything negative. But they didn't have to deal with the constant pain and aggravation of being dehumanized.

That there was prejudice resulted in a bond among the players of color on the Indians. That happened on other clubs as well. There was always a bond between blacks and Latin players of color. However, a white-skinned Latin player may have wanted all the advantages he could get, so he may have gone by the rules set down for white players and become part of a white-player clique. That's why there was often trouble between blacks and light-skinned Latin players. It was up to individual light-skinned Latins which way they wanted to slide.

Vic Power, a black Latin player, came to the Indians in the middle of the 1958 season from Kansas City. At times we were roommates, and we became great friends. I was always interested in various cultures, so I was interested in learning from him about Puerto Rico, including the customs, the food, and the music. Vic wouldn't subdue his actions. He demanded independence and freedom. He was outspoken. Of course, those in management would feel less easy with Vic than with me because they assumed I would know better that blacks should adhere to the "rules" we had here in America. But a black Puerto Rican wouldn't necessarily follow the rules, because he was used to freedom. They didn't know how much they could get Vic to do before the powder keg exploded. If Vic came to a place that had a door that said WHITE, a manager would think, "What am I going to do if he goes in there?" You can't insult the man because he's a foreigner.

We American blacks loved when the black Latin players did things that weren't expected of black ball-players. For instance, it cheered all of us when they wouldn't allow "Colored" to be written on their passports. Vic would argue, "I'm Puerto Rican, not colored." Minnie Minoso would say "I'm Cuban. Don't put no colored stuff on my passport!" Minoso was very outspoken. And he was even darker than Vic. In this country, if there was a hotel where we couldn't stay in the South or in Kansas City or Baltimore, Vic and Minnie stayed with the rest of the blacks but they objected as much as they could. There were places we couldn't go. In Baltimore, they eventually let us stay in the same hotel as the white players, but we couldn't go with them to the nightclubs right across the street. Guys like Vic and Minnie knew that was part of what they had to accept if they wanted to play major league baseball, but they expressed their anger.

Every team was cliquish. Vic Power and I were good friends. That was a clique. Rocky Colavito and Herb Score were good friends. That was a clique. That doesn't mean two cliques can't get together. Colavito and Score were wonderful men, beautiful people, and I

honestly believe that if we had invited them to go somewhere with us, they would have come. But I know some of the other cliques wouldn't have done it.

Gary Bell, a white pitcher, became one of the best friends I'll ever have. He had been raised in Texas, where whites and blacks didn't socialize, and admitted he was influenced by that. He might say, "Mudcat, if I saw you with a white girl, I may not like it—I don't know why, but I wouldn't like it." I'd ask, "Would you go with a black girl?" "Yeah!" That was Gary Bell. He was your friend. If there was a clique of white players who didn't like us because we were black, Gary would tell us not to mess with them. If they'd say accusingly, "Gary, you were with those black guys," he'd respond, "Damn right, what are you going to do about it?" He was right out front, and everybody respected him for his independence, for doing what he wanted, and for having the friends he wanted to have. He was one of the few white players who went to the Apollo Theater or Howard Theater or into black-owned restaurants. He was one of the few who would consider rooming with a black teammate. In those days, teams didn't have black and white road roommates, so at times we'd get a third hotel room and stay together there. I'm sure management got on Gary for associating with blacks, but after a while they had to give up because he couldn't be influenced.

Larry Doby was no longer on the team, so I hung out mostly with Vic, Gary, and a couple of other guys. (In future years, pitchers Barry Latman and Bob Allen would be with us.) After a game, some of us might go see a show—maybe Lionel Hampton. I became friends with many show business people. And we'd visit the homes of fans who were great cooks—in Cleveland, Kansas City, Washington, everywhere. If they didn't cook, they'd take us to people who did cook. There were all kinds of fans who were wonderful people. We knew we were celebrities, yet we didn't feel or act like celebrities because even the most famous people we knew didn't act like celebrities. We learned from them to try to be part of the community.

I lived for several years in downtown Cleveland (before I finally built a house in Shaker Heights) and tried to meet as many people as I could. I got to be friends with a lot of them, just typical working people. Cleveland could be a bit dull, but I thought it was a great town. It was no different than any other town in that it had its side for whites and its side for blacks and it had suburbs where blacks, Christian whites, and Jews lived together. I liked that it was a family city, and that it was an old baseball town with a lot of good fans.

VIC POWER:

Mudcat Grant was my best roommate because we had a lot in common. He would dress up, he liked music, and if I invited him to my sister's house to eat rice and beans, he would be happy to come. He also got along with white players as well as black players. I was very independent, but Mudcat and I would spend time together. Minnie Minoso was a good ballplayer and friend, but he wasn't as good a roommate. He liked girls and he liked to dance, so he was never in the room.

Gary Bell was a beautiful guy and we were close. He was a funny guy. I told Gary that I'd stop off to see him when driving through Texas. He joked, "Don't forget that you have to come in by the kitchen." I asked him why whites didn't like colored people in America. He said, "Vic, it's been like this for a hundred years and we're gonna keep it that way."

Rocky Colavito was a nice guy and very religious. He'd ask me what I ate on Friday, and when I told him I had a big steak, he'd tell me I was supposed to eat fish. He'd get mad at me for sleeping late on Sunday instead of going to church. He was one of the leaders on the team. I felt that if Rocky used his power, the pitcher had control, and I had my glove, the Indians would win. You could count on him for homers. One game in June, he hit 4 consecutive homers in Baltimore to tie the record. Each homer went farther than the one before it. He had some power. He led the American League that year with 42 home runs. In 1958, after I stole home to win that game against Detroit, a sportswriter didn't congratulate me—he reminded me that Colavito was at bat and could have homered.

We had a good team. I hit .289 and led the league's first basemen in all the fielding categories. Billy Martin was the second baseman, and we didn't let anything get through the right side of the infield. Woodie Held, a nice, quiet guy who came from the Athletics with me, was erratic at short but hit about 30 homers. George Strickland, the veteran, was at third most of the time. We had a good outfield with Colavito in right, Jimmy

Piersall in center, and Minnie Minoso in left. And Tito Francona had a great year playing in the outfield and at first base, when I moved to second or third. They couldn't get him out. Our catcher was Russ Nixon, a smart player and good receiver.

Jimmy Piersall became our centerfielder in 1959 and really helped the team. He gave me his book *Fear Strikes Out,* and it was a very sad story. We became close friends. I also got along with Billy Martin. Back in 1954, when he was on the Yankees and I was on the A's, I worried about playing against him because I had read that he fought with black players on the Dodgers. I told myself to be ready for him. But the first time I played against the Yankees, he came over and we shook hands. Maybe he knew that I came up through the Yankee organization. We always got along beautifully.

Cal McLish was our biggest winner. He was a crafty veteran. For some reason, Frank Lane traded him after the year, and we needed him. We also had good young starters in Bell, Mudcat, and Perry. Herb Score and Mike Garcia were also on the team. They were all friendly guys. Score was trying to make a comeback, but he couldn't throw strikes. Everyone felt sorry for him. I used to talk to him about baseball, but not about the accident because we didn't want to remind him.

I liked Joe Gordon. Maybe he wasn't the best manager, but he was funny and easygoing. Under him, we finished just 5 games behind the White Sox. Unfortunately, I made the out against Chicago that eliminated us from the pennant race. Gerry Staley was the pitcher and I never hit the ball so hard, right over the middle of the diamond. But Luis Aparicio came up with it, tagged second, and threw to first to double me up. And we lost.

BILLY MORAN:

Cleveland had a strange mix the previous year, with Minnie Minoso, Gary Bell, Mudcat Grant, Vic Power, Cal McLish, Don Mossi, Larry Doby, Rocky Colavito, Ransom Jackson, and Billy Hunter, but it got even stranger in 1959 when we added players like Jimmy Piersall, Billy Martin, and Granny Hamner. But they had a winning attitude and I thought this was a pretty good nucleus for a pennant-contending team.

Joe Gordon wanted to do everything differently from Bobby Bragan. Bragan wanted to make all the decisions, to hit-and-run, bunt, steal. Gordon cared only about hitting. So he played Woodie Held at shortstop and Tito Francona at first and in the outfield. They were hitters. Francona just wore out pitchers that year, and Gordon jumped on his coattails. Tito gave Gordon credit for telling him to swing down on the ball. Gordon also told other players to do that, but only Francona burned it up.

Woodie Held was a strong kid who could hit the ball a ton and run well. He hit homers and struck out. He also made a lot of errors at short. Woodie wasn't smooth enough to be much of an infielder and was at that position only because Gordon wanted his bat in the lineup. I thought he'd have been better off playing center field like Mantle, who was a converted shortstop.

Held couldn't be moved to center once the Indians acquired Piersall, which meant I wouldn't get a shot at short. Second base was out because the Indians traded for Billy Martin. So I had no position and was demoted to San Diego. The only thing that encouraged me was that Frank Lane gave me a raise. Later, Martin got hit in the face, so they called me back up. But I batted only 17 times all season. They wanted to win the pennant with veterans and almost did it. But I wasn't part of their plans.

HAL WOODESHICK:

I won 16 games total in 1958, 10 at San Diego and 6 with the Indians, but Frank Lane sent me a contract for the minimum again. I thought I deserved a raise. He said that if I didn't sign the contract he'd send me back to the minors. I went to spring training with his contract signed, yet he sent me back to the minors anyway, despite the good job I'd done. I didn't get a shot to pitch even one game for the Indians. Lane told me that he wanted to give a kid pitcher a chance because he had been getting everyone out in spring training. That kid was Jim Perry, and he went on to win over 200 games.

So I opened the season for Toronto in Havana, Cuba, when Fidel Castro took over. There were machine guns all over the place. I shut out the Havana Sugarcanes and the Miami Marlins a few days later. A sportswriter wrote, "What is this guy doing in the minor leagues?" So I sent that article to Frank Lane. Then I won my next game, to go to 3–0. I was hoping I'd be recalled by Lane, but meanwhile my manager, Dixie Walker, told me to go home to Pittsburgh and get my wife and baby

and meet the team in Toronto. There was a party before our home opener, which I was scheduled to pitch. Jack Kent Cooke, our owner, showed me a telegram he got from Frank Lane. Cooke said, "It looks like we're going to have you all year." Soon Lane traded me to the Washington Senators.

BALTIMORE ORIOLES

BILLY O'DELL:

My wife and I were still living in South Carolina, but we rented a home in Baltimore during the baseball season. Baltimore was a pleasant city and my baseball home and I enjoyed my years there. I was treated fairly in terms of salary by the Orioles. I played every year for what I wanted. I never asked for more. They would send a contract and then we would talk back and forth until we were both satisfied.

I didn't mind pitching for Paul Richards, but we did have some problems. In 1959 he didn't start me against Kansas City because he was holding me back for the Yankees, and he didn't want me to pitch at Fenway Park because of the short left-field wall. We talked one day about how he was using me. I told him I just wanted a chance to pitch when my turn came. I was tired of trying to beat the Yankees, Chicago, and Detroit for a living—I also wanted a chance like everyone else to pitch against the other teams and improve my record for salary negotiations. The conversation got pretty heated. I think that was one of the reasons I was traded.

For a left-hander, I wasn't strong enough against left-handed hitters. My ball went away from lefties and in to righties, and sometimes I thought I got out right-handed hitters easier. But Sherm Lollar hit me the hardest of anyone. And his big White Sox teammate Walt Dropo, who was also right-handed, gave me problems. Everyone else got him out with change-ups, but I'd throw one to him and he'd hit it half a mile. Mickey Mantle batted right-handed against me. I had pretty good luck against him by keeping the ball inside. He was one of the best clutch players ever to play the game. I didn't pitch too much against Ted Williams, but I had pretty good luck against him. He was by far the greatest hitter I ever saw. You talked about Ted Williams and then you talked about the rest of the guys.

The Baltimore Orioles' Billy "Digger" O'Dell had developed into one of the American League's best left-handers by 1959, but in 1960 he'd be pitching in the National League with San Francisco.

I liked pitching in Yankee Stadium. In other parks, I had trouble when batters hit me to right-center and center—and they all seemed to hit me that way—but Yankee Stadium was roomy in the middle of the field. I didn't beat the Yankees a lot, but I pitched pretty well against them. In fact, Stengel always tried to trade for me.

However, the Yankees weren't the team that acquired me. One night in November, our general manager, Lee McPhail, called to say that I had been traded to the San Francisco Giants. At the time, I was really disappointed,

BROOKS ROBINSON:
I had an army obligation. My choice was to be drafted for two years or spend sixth months' active duty in the Arkansas National Guard and then be in the Army Reserve for 5½ years. I chose the National Guard and got out just when the season started in 1959. I was on the Orioles for about a month, not playing too much but working my way into shape. I thought Baltimore was going to send out another third baseman and keep me, but they sent me to Vancouver in the Pacific Coast League. I was shocked. That was the only time I was

ever frustrated in baseball. My ego was really hurt. I thought of all my friends back in Arkansas talking about me being sent down. Yet it turned out to be the best thing that could have happened to me.

When I left, Richards said, "Look, you go out and play, and at the All-Star break we're going to bring you back." However, I knew that a lot of players had been told such things by managers but once they were out of there were forgotten about. Most guys weren't brought back. However, I did very well at Vancouver and was brought back at the All-Star break. And it was like night and day. I could hit! I had more confidence and also I had gotten stronger physically, so I was no longer overmatched. I batted .284.

I got to play next to Chico Carrasquel. Like most veterans, he was more than happy to help me. He'd been around a long time, so I was more than willing to listen to him and I could gauge where I was supposed to play by seeing where he played.

Billy Loes was both an effective starter and reliever for us in the late '50s. He was one of the craziest guys I ever met. We called him "Cuckoo." He was very likable, but he was very quiet and marched to his own beat. His famous philosophy was to win less than 20 games every year because if you won 20 once and didn't do it again, they'd cut your salary. Billy would go out to the bullpen, take off his hat, and put suntan lotion on his face. I remember him sleeping through an exhibition game in Memphis—they just let him sleep. He gave me a lot of laughs. If anyone could piss off Paul Richards, it was Billy. He would do a lot of back-talking, but Paul put up with it because Loes was a good pitcher and won games. I don't think Paul considered him a bad influence.

Gene Woodling was a terrific pro. He'd always say, "Don't get gay when you're full of bull." Only he didn't really say it that way—he'd say, "Don't get gay when you're full of shit, Robinson." In other words, he was telling me not to think I had this game beat because that's when it will come up and knock you down.

GENE WOODLING:

I consider 1959 my best year in baseball. My stats were slightly higher with the Indians in 1957—.321 with 78 RBIs to .300 with 77 RBIs—but I got more key hits and won more ball games. I even made the All-Star team.

CHICO CARRASQUEL:

I finished my career in Baltimore, again playing for Paul Richards. I played all 4 infield positions, but mostly at short. It was Brooks Robinson's second year as the Orioles' starting third baseman. I couldn't tell he was going to become a great fielder, except that he was a hard worker. Every day he'd catch a lot of ground balls, and he'd listen to anybody.

This was my worst season in the majors. I batted only .223. I had to quit after the season because of my legs. I had an operation on my left leg. That allowed me to play a few years in Venezuela, but at first base.

BOSTON RED SOX

PUMPSIE GREEN:

I joined the Red Sox at spring training in Scottsdale, Arizona. This was my first major league spring training, and I was treated well by Jackie Jensen, Ted Williams, Frank Malzone, Gene Stephens, Sammy White, Bill Monbouquette, and the other guys. It was a friendly group and I had no problems. I didn't impose myself on anybody.

Nobody talked to me about talking to the media, and they came after me. They paid more attention to me than anyone else. Sometimes that was hard. Oddly, they seldom brought up black-white issues. Mostly they just talked about general things. I never met anyone from the NAACP.

Having just played in Panama during the winter, I was on a level above the guys who hadn't played since the previous fall. I had a great spring. I'm pretty sure I led the Red Sox in every category, including home runs. They couldn't get me out. One sportswriter said, "It looks like you made the team, kid." When the spring was over, I was the first to go. Pinky Higgins, the manager, called me over after a game and told me I was going back to Minneapolis. He didn't give me an explanation and I didn't ask for one. That's when all the hoopla started. The NAACP got involved because the Red Sox still didn't have a black player. I was gone by that time, so I don't know what happened. Nobody ever talked to me about it. I divorced myself from the controversy, but of course it flashed through my mind. I couldn't wipe it out completely.

I went back to Minneapolis. Gene Mauch talked briefly to me about what had happened and assured me that I would make it to the majors if I continued to work hard. I went back to concentrating on baseball. Minneapolis was a powerhouse. We led our league by 10 or 12 games in July. That's when I was brought up to the majors, about ten days before Earl Wilson, and Boston became the final team to integrate. My first game was in Chicago. I got there that afternoon and was in the lineup that night against Early Wynn. My biggest thrill in the majors was my first time up in Fenway Park. I felt comfortable at the plate because the pitcher was the A's John Tsitouris and I had batted against him in the minors. I tripled off the left-field wall.

Fenway Park was an exciting place to play. Yankee Stadium wasn't one of my favorite places to play, but being there, especially the first time, was thrilling. Mickey Mantle and the whole Yankee club could impress you. But we weren't intimidated by them. We had great players of our own, like Ted Williams, Jackie Jensen, and Pete Runnels. We had good games against them and seemed to play our best against them.

Pete Runnels really impressed me. He was a left-handed singles hitter who hit everything the other way. The other teams played him to hit the other way, but he still hit .300.

Ted Williams, of course, was a left-handed batter who pulled the ball. He had the only bad year of his career in 1959, but that didn't depress him. I never saw him too upset, even when he'd strike out a couple of times, which was infrequent. He'd curse a lot and then go about his business. He was a very independent person, so a lot of people didn't really get to know him. If you wanted to know anything about hitting, Ted would sit you down and have an hour seminar. I appreciated it.

I was the only switch-hitter in the Boston lineup. But I batted just .233. As usual, my strong suit was my field-

When Pumpsie Green was brought up by the Boston Red Sox in 1959, this meant the overdue completion of a full sixteen-team integration that had begun when Jackie Robinson played with the Brooklyn Dodgers in 1947.

COURTESY OF THE BOSTON RED SOX

ing. I played about 45 games, only at second base. I never felt I had made it with the Red Sox. I never got that feeling I had at Minneapolis, where I knew the job was mine and I could handle it. Almost every game I played, I felt like I was trying out. I *never* felt comfortable. It had nothing to do with the way I was sent down the first time. Maybe it was self-imposed. If I had felt more at ease, I might have done a better job. Unfortunately, I was given only one opportunity, and three or four days in a row in the lineup isn't really a fair opportunity. You put too much pressure on yourself realizing that "if I don't do well, I'm back on the bench—or back in the minors." I was also aware that major league teams rarely kept black players who were not starters. If you didn't play, you were outta there. That was the constant pressure I felt. I was married and had a son, but that didn't really add to the pressure because they were back home in California, while I rented an apartment in Dorchester.

Billy Jurges took over as manager from Pinky Higgins during the season. I couldn't really expect much encouragement from him because he was sort of in the position I was in: he was a rookie manager trying to make it. He wasn't as confident in his job as Higgins, who was a fixture in the Red Sox organization. Billy was a little jumpy.

I wasn't unhappy with the Red Sox. I wouldn't let myself be. I had made it to the major leagues, and I knew a bunch of people who wish they had. I felt lucky and at peace with myself. The Red Sox fans treated me just like everyone else. If I did a good job, they gave me a hand; if I didn't, it would go the other way. I never got hate mail.

When I was playing, being the first black on the Red Sox wasn't nearly as big a source of pride as it would be once I was out of the game. At the time I never put much stock in it, or thought about it. Later I understood my place in history. I don't know if I would have been better off in another organization with more black players. But as it turned out, I became increasingly proud to have been with the Red Sox as their first black.

BILL MONBOUQUETTE:

Pumpsie Green was an amiable, quiet guy, and I think the media made it uncomfortable for him by making what was happening bigger than it should have been. The fans were warm to Pumpsie and Earl Wilson. I never saw them have trouble.

Billy Jurges replaced Pinky Higgins as manager halfway through the season. I liked him very much. Higgins had me in the bullpen, and Jurges was the guy who made me a starting pitcher. He got the idea when I shut down a team by pitching 6 or 7 innings in relief. That game was on CBS, and Jackie Jensen had been given a watch because he had a big day. He gave me the watch, saying I deserved it more.

Jensen and I were good friends. He was a very tense individual. I don't think he and Williams were competitive, although they kidded each other. They were good friends. Unlike Williams, Jackie would get on guys, urging them to play better. Jackie wanted to do well himself and had a lot of productive years, including his 1958 MVP season. He drove in over 100 runs 5 of 6 years and won the RBI title 3 times, including in 1958 and 1959. He was a tremendous athlete who had good enough speed to lead the league once in stolen bases. He was known for baseball and football—he had a 70-yard touchdown run for Ohio State in the Rose Bowl—but he could do a lot of sports. I'd get mad when he was criticized for hitting into so many double plays. If you hit the ball as hard as he did, that was bound to happen.

I entered a pitching rotation that included Tom Brewer, Frank Sullivan, Jerry Casale, and Ike Delock. Casale and Delock were probably our best pitchers in 1959, but Brewer and Sullivan were better pitchers and had been fairly productive for several years. Brewer had all kinds of stuff, including a good fastball and nasty curveball. He was a great athlete who could run like an antelope.

Sullivan wasn't overpowering, so he'd try to get ahead in the count and get his breaking ball over. His best years had passed, but he still had good stuff and guts. He'd say, "I'm in the twilight of a mediocre career." Another of his lines was "When you can't hit, run, or throw, there's only one thing you can do—holler." He was one of the characters on the team who was very witty and kept the guys laughing. After Higgins was fired, we got on a plane that had to turn around on the runway because of a bomb scare. And Sully said, "I

didn't think Pinky would go this far." When we'd come home from a disastrous road trip, he'd say, "When we get off the plane, spread out so they don't get us all at once."

FRANK MALZONE:
When Pumpsie Green and Earl Wilson integrated the Red Sox, I had no idea it had significance. I didn't realize they were the first black players until a reporter told me. Having grown up in the Bronx, I had played with blacks long before I got to the big leagues.

I had another solid season. I batted .280, scored a career-high 90 runs, went up to 19 homers and 92 RBIs, and won another Gold Glove. I was again selected to the All-Star team. The second All-Star Game was played in the Los Angeles Coliseum, and the American League got all its homers from Italians—Yogi Berra, Rocky Colavito, and me—and won, 5–3. I would always tease Don Drysdale, "I told you not to hang that curveball."

Jackie Jensen also had a good year, hitting 28 homers and winning his second consecutive RBI title. But after third-place finishes in my first two years, the Red Sox dropped to fifth. It was obvious that we were fading from being a contending team. Piersall had been traded in the off-season to the Indians, Jackie was having so many problems with flying that he was going to temporarily retire in 1960, and Ted dropped in to the .250s, the only time in his career he was under .300. You didn't realize he was hitting so low because he hit everything hard. But the year was a downer for him, as it was for the team as a whole.

WASHINGTON SENATORS

HARMON KILLEBREW:
The Senators were still a last-place team in 1959 and even lost 18 in a row, but I didn't think the players were frustrated because there were signs of improvement. We had a very good offense and I was part of it, playing regularly at third. Roy Sievers hit over 20 homers, Jim Lemon and Bob Allison hit 30 or more, and I hit 42, tying Rocky Colavito for the league lead, and drove in 105 runs. They called us the "Fearsome Foursome." The four of us were very close friends.

Jim Lemon had become the Senators' starting left fielder in 1956, after a couple of years as a reserve, and he and Sievers had carried the offense since then. Jim could hit the long ball and drive in a lot of runs. In one game against Cleveland he hit 2 homers and drove in 6 runs in 1 inning, tying a record. He was one of our best baserunners, and I don't think anyone ever accused him of being a bad outfielder. He just wasn't smooth because he was 6'4" and gangly.

Bob Allison played briefly with the Senators in 1958 and then broke into the lineup in 1959, the same year I got my chance. He had a fine rookie season. He played center field that year but would then move to right field. We became roommates, and that would last 10 years. We had great years together, never competing against each other. Bob was a personable, outgoing guy and a great physical specimen.

My first All-Star Game was in 1959 in Pittsburgh. We lost 5–4 on hits by Aaron and Mays in the bottom of the eighth. I didn't get a hit, but it was quite a thrill. My fondest memory was having Casey Stengel be my manager. I don't know if he knew who I was. He didn't call anybody by their names. All-Star Games were very important to me. I took them very seriously and think most players did. It was a big honor to represent your team and the league.

I liked playing in Washington and not just when I started having good years. The fans were kind to me from the beginning. And where else would Presidents, Cabinet members, and congressmen come out to the ballpark? Eisenhower was a baseball fan, and in 1959 he came to the park and called me over to his seat. He asked me to autograph a ball for his grandson David. That kind of thing was extraordinarily exciting.

PEDRO RAMOS:

I'd often lead the league in starts, so since I was on Washington it wasn't surprising that I'd also lead the league in losses, including 1959, when I lost 19, against 13 wins. As I said, I'd also lead the league in homers because I challenged batters with my fastball. Sometimes I'd come in close and they couldn't get out of the way, which is why a couple of times I led the league in hit batsmen. The only time I threw at someone in retaliation is the day that I hit Mickey Mantle. A Yankee pitcher—either Bob Turley or Ralph Terry—knocked

me down once and also knocked down three of my guys, including Bob Allison. Allison came to the bench and said, "Ramos, do something about it." I said, "The first guy who steps up, I'll knock him down." I didn't know the first guy up was Mickey. I had to do it anyway. So I went for the hip. He went to first base without saying anything. The next day, when I was at the batting cage, Mickey came around. He said, "I'm going to drag one to first, and then when you cover first, I'm going to open your chest like a fish." I said, "Mickey, you got a base hit because I ain't going to be there." I think he was joking, but just in case, I took him serious. He never did bunt but I'd rather he bunted than swing.

I didn't throw at batters. Even if a batter homered off me, I wouldn't take it out on him the next time up. And I didn't try to get the next guy. That year Billy Martin homered off me in Cleveland. The next hitter was Jimmy Piersall. I just wanted to pitch him inside like I always did. He thought I was trying to hit him. He pointed the bat at me and told me that if I did it again, he was coming after me. Then I did knock him down good. I was aiming for the left shoulder and the ball went a little up and over his head. He charged me with a bat. Meanwhile my catcher, J. W. Porter, threw the ball back to me. And I yelled at Piersall, "You'd better stop with that bat because I got the potato back and I can nail you from here." So he dropped the bat and came after me with his fists. So we had a little rumble there. Everybody was out there. Their manager, Joe Gordon, was trying to get to me from the side.

I never thought of running from Piersall, but I'm sure I could have beaten him in a footrace. I thought I was one of the fastest runners in the majors. I raced Carlos Paula, Don Hoak, Richie Ashburn, and some other guys and never lost. I beat Richie so bad that he stopped and said he pulled a leg muscle. Clint Courtney was my promoter. We'd travel by train with another team in the spring and he'd go from one car to another asking, "Who wants to race my horse?" The races were 100-yard dashes. We'd bet $5 to $10 and the whole team would get together and bet. I made $20 on one race and $75 on another. The other races were just for fun. Most would take place in spring training.

In 1959 Zoilo Versalles, a speedy shortstop from Cuba, was a rookie and Lavagetto said, "Ramos, Versalles said he can beat you." I said, "No way." So we decided to race across the field. We walked to the other side to race back to where the team stood. Versalles asked me to let him win because he was a rookie. I said I'd keep up with him and then let him go ahead at the end. So that's the way we did it and he beat me. Then he started jumping around, bragging he'd beaten me. I reminded him I'd let him win, but he said it wasn't so. We were talking in Spanish. So we went back and did it again. I put some dirt in his eyes. He should have stayed quiet. We would always joke about that.

At this time, Cubans still played ball in the United States in the summer, and I would return there to pitch in the Cuban Winter League. And there would still be an International League team there until 1960. I had never heard of Fidel Castro until the revolution. I didn't know about politics, but I never was for him, not even at the beginning. When I learned that Batista left and Castro came in, I was surprised. I didn't understand why hundreds of thousands of people went into the streets to cheer for Castro. Why would they follow a guy like that? Castro loved baseball, but it was a lot of crap about him once being a good ballplayer. He wasn't known as a good-looking prospect, although he tried out for the majors. I saw him throw out the first pitch at a Cuban game when he was in his 30s. He threw about 20 pitches before he threw 1 strike.

HAL WOODESHICK:

After being stuck at Toledo in the Cleveland organization, I was thrilled to be traded to the Senators. They were still a last-place team but had some talent and were improving. I wasn't there the entire season, but Lavagetto put me in over 30 games and I had some pretty good outings.

My wife and I lived on 16th Street at the Woodner, an apartment hotel. It was close to the zoo, and she would take our small daughter there while I was on road trips. She became friends with Shirley MacLaine, who took her daughter to the zoo while she was entertaining in Washington. Many stars came to Washington to perform. Jerry Lewis loved baseball, and he'd work out with the Senators when he was in Washington. He liked to play first base, and every time after he'd left, Roy Sievers discovered that his first baseman's mitt was missing.

Already much traveled in the minors and majors, 6'3" Hal Woodeshick would have moderate success in 1959 and 1960 with the Washington Senators.

DETROIT TIGERS

GUS ZERNIAL:

My second year with Detroit wasn't as fulfilling because I knew I was on my way out. Jimmy Dykes became my manager again that year, and he sat with me and said, "Gus, we have to face the end." I didn't think it was the end for me because I could still play. But I accepted it.

COOT VEAL:

I expected to be a full-time player, but the Tigers brought in Jimmy Dykes to manage. Dykes was a fine gentleman, but in 1958 he had been with Cincinnati in the other league and didn't know me from Adam. He had a chance to get Rocky Bridges, a veteran, from the Senators to play shortstop. So I sat. I never regretted anything about pro baseball except not being given the chance to be a starting shortstop for one full year. I always felt I could do the job if given the opportunity to play, and if I didn't feel that way, I had no reason to be there.

I played in the field only about 70 games and didn't have many more at-bats than that. I didn't complain. I didn't want to voice opinions. Heck, all I wanted was to play baseball. When I played I was more demonstrative. I'd fly off the handle real easy and get thrown out of ballgames for arguing with umpires about balls and strikes and plays at seconds. Back then, umpires took a lot more until you used profanity and got too personal. You had to use it to get thrown out of a ballgame. I did stick around long enough to hit my only major league homer—I kept the ball.

We didn't assume the Yankees were going to win the pennant. We had a good team. We had Kuenn leading the league with a .353 average, Kaline batting way over .300 and hitting homers and driving in runs, and Charlie Maxwell hitting over 30 homers. We knew we could beat the Yankees when we played them. As long as Frank Lary was pitching, we knew we'd win at least one game of a series. Paul Foytack and Jim Bunning could also beat them. Bunning was a great pitcher, different from anyone else I'd seen. He was a sidearmer who fell all over the mound. He was tall and all arms and legs.

But beating the Yankees wasn't enough because we had trouble beating Kansas City and Washington, and other teams under .500. I think it had to do with attendance. The Yankees would come in and we'd have 45,000 for each game, but we were likely to have only 5,000 for the Athletics or Senators. The louder the fans, the better we'd play.

My best friend on the team was Larry Osborne. He was a left-handed-hitting first baseman, another good ol' boy from Georgia. For about 6 of my 13 years in pro ball, Bo was my roommate, including a couple of years in Detroit. We did a lot together and our wives were really good friends. There were different guys who hung around together, but it wasn't cliquish. It was a team of individuals, but we all got along. A few guys drank a lot. I didn't drink—I chewed tobacco. I spent most of my time at the movies while on the road, or playing pinochle or hearts. Some guys played poker, but not the guys who didn't have money to lose. I'd pal around with Larry and 4 or 5 other guys. Bunning, Kaline, and J. W. Porter would play golf with Larry and me. I don't remember parties thrown by the team.

All the players had fan clubs that we'd visit every once in a while. We'd talk to them about the club and sign autographs. But I don't think there was any sense of community. Everyone lived in the suburbs. I lived in Ferndale in one year, then Garden City another. In the off-season, my wife and I went back to Macon, and I worked as a surveyor.

The Tigers stayed in first-class hotels on the road. There was no dress code, but we always made sure to be presentable in public. We had to use our own discretion and dress like major leaguers. We were given meal money. I believe it was $18 a day, which was from $8 to $14 more than I got in the minors, depending on the league.

At first I liked flying. But it got frightening because I read of all the planes that went down. It got so I would sweat during takeoffs and landing. Most players just started playing cards—I started sweating.

CHICAGO WHITE SOX

BILLY PIERCE:

How did we win the pennant? Sherm Lollar and Al Smith were our only home run threats in 1959, and I'm sure they didn't hit 40 homers between them. We were last in the league, with less than 100 homers. Nellie Fox was second in RBIs on the Sox with only around 70, and our leader, Lollar, didn't have many more than that. And Nellie was our only .300 hitter, and our only everyday player over .275. So how did we win the pennant? We ran, we had great defense, and we had good pitching. We won something like 35 of 50 1-run games. A lot of guys contributed. Fox probably contributed most, which is why he won the league's MVP award, beating out Aparicio and Wynn. He had a high average, drove in those runs, and was our top hustler and cheerleader. In addition, Nellie was a key part of our running game with Aparicio—who was the league's stolen base champion—Landis, and Rivera, and was part of our outstanding up-the-middle defense with Lollar, Aparicio, and Landis.

RYNE DUREN (YANKEES):

Nellie Fox was the toughest guy in the league for me to face: foul ball, foul ball, foul ball, foul ball, base hit or walk.

B. PIERCE:

Bob Shaw, who had never done much with Detroit or Chicago after we acquired him in 1958, raised his point of delivery under Ray Berres's tutelage and came out of nowhere to go 18–6. We needed Shaw to come through because Dick Donovan's wins were down. I added 14 victories and Barry Latman did a good job for us when he got the opportunity. Also we had two dependable right-handed relievers in Gerry Staley, who had been a successful starter in the National League before he came to the American League in the mid-'50s, and Turk Lown, who had been a good reliever with the Cubs until we picked him up in 1959. Staley's out pitch was a sinker. Berres got Lown to stop throwing his blooper and just throw hard. If we needed a double play Staley came in, but Lown came in if we needed a strikeout.

But the key to our pitching was Early Wynn. That son of a gun was an amazing competitor! He was 39 years old, yet he led the league in starts, innings pitched, and wins. He won 22 games, including 5 shutouts, and without him we would have won the pennant. He was justifiably voted the major leagues' Cy Young winner. He hit well, too!

Al Smith had come to the White Sox with Wynn in 1958 from the Indians for Minnie Minoso. Frank Lane, our former GM, was now the GM at Cleveland and was still making big trades. Minnie was such a favorite with the Chicago fans that they booed Al when he took Minnie's place. Al struggled with his hitting for a couple of years, and he had a rough time with the fans. Bill Veeck, who became the majority owner before the '59 season, wanted the fans to give Al a chance, so he even held an "Al Smith Night," at which everyone who was named Smith or Schmidt or who had a name like Smith got in for free. Eventually, Al started to hit and the fans took to him. He would have some good years for us at bat and in left field. His home run against the Indians clinched

the pennant. That was a big one. Of course, the moment almost everyone would remember was when a fan's beer fell on his head during the 1959 World Series—he was good-natured about it.

AL SMITH:

I was glad to be in another pennant race. The surprise is that the team we had to beat turned out to be Cleveland, my former team, and not the Yankees, who had a bad year. For much of the season it seemed like we couldn't lose. Aparicio would get on and steal or advance to second or third when Fox sacrificed or hit the ball to right field on a hit and run. If Aparicio got on we'd bring him in. Then Wynn, Pierce, or Shaw would close the door. We didn't score a lot of runs, but teams didn't score

Even an "Al Smith Night"—during which he had his worst game of the year—failed to help Al Smith shake a lengthy batting slump, but he finally won over White Sox fans by hitting a pennant-winning homer in 1959 and batting a career-high .315 in 1960.

many against us either. Not many of our players had experienced a pennant race before—but Early and I had done it with the Indians in 1954, also playing for Al Lopez. So maybe some of the younger guys looked up to us. My average was lower than I would have liked, but I won a lot of games with homers or big clutch hits. I know I got my biggest hit when it counted most, in the game we clinched the pennant by beating the Indians. Early started that game and I broke a 2–2 tie with a home run off Mudcat Grant, and that put us ahead to stay. That was a great thrill.

On our team good defense was essential for us to win most of the low-scoring games we played. Our infield was solid with Aparicio and Fox and I think we had a good outfield offensively and defensively. I played in left, Jim Rivera and Jim McAnany played in right, and my buddy Jim Landis played center. Landis could really go get the ball. He had tremendous speed and great instincts and we knew that if the ball was in the air from right-center to left-center he was going to catch it.

JIM LANDIS:

There were many reasons that we won the pennant. It helped that New York had a bad year—we finally won the season series from them. Another reason is that everybody continued to get along so well. There were arguments, of course, but nothing serious. Al Lopez ran things so well, catering to us in certain ways, that there was no reason to fight. It certainly helped that Early Wynn had a Cy Young year and Nellie Fox was the MVP. Nellie did everything possible with his bat—on Opening Day, he got 5 hits and won the game with a fourteenth-inning homer. And he and Aparicio were the game's best double-play combination. Nothing got through them. Oddly, Nellie and Luis were just business friends. They were hardly around each other off the field.

Aparicio's speed ignited many rallies—in many cases it was the entire rally. He had been leading the league every year by stealing between 20 and 30 bases, but Lopez let him loose and suddenly he stole 56 bases, an extraordinary number in those days. Luis had his own way to steal that I couldn't learn from. He told me that he watched pitchers' eyes. I'd stand on first and I couldn't pick up a pitcher's eyes. I don't know how he did it, but he was successful.

I think it helped our team to have a dependable utility infielder waiting on the bench, allowing Aparicio or third baseman Bubba Phillips to get an occasional rest. Sammy Esposito was my main roommate for many years on the White Sox. He had been a basketball player at the University of Indiana. Luis beat him out for the shortstop job, and he sat on the bench and didn't really develop. It's hard to tell what he could have done playing every day. Considering everything, he did a good job. When you're on a good ballclub, when you come in the crucial innings you had better field that ground ball. Sammy did.

The additions of Ted Kluszewski, Barry Latman, and Jim McAnany picked up the team. It was special playing with Kluszewski because of the tremendous career he had with Cincinnati. He was an everyday guy, not cocky at all. I was a kidder, and he liked that. I was a blade and would stand next to him and flex. He'd laugh. Barry Latman was a gutsy pitcher, a real competitor. There were a couple of times when Lopez needed a pitcher and Barry would say, "Gimme the ball." And he would pitch a terrific game. He threw hard. Jim McAnany had been a great minor league player. He hit over .400 in the minors but had bad eyes: that's why his career would be so short.

Jim Rivera was an unsung hero. I think he was a leader in a more vibrant way than Lollar, Fox, or Pierce. He was a rah-rah guy and kept everybody loose. Dick Donovan was a very intense pitcher. He had certain things he did in the dugout. He would come in and fold a towel in a certain way. It had to be perfect. Rivera would run over and mess up that towel. Dick would come right back and refold it. When Jim would be interviewed by a sportswriter, he'd have a bat in his hand, and while he answered questions he'd swing the bat, pounding away on the reporter's knee. The guy would just sit there listening to Rivera's story. We were in the middle of a pennant race and lost a doubleheader to Washington of all teams. We were distressed. We get onto the team bus and we start hearing little explosions. Rivera had filled the aisles with little caps that went pop when you stepped on them. Lopez came on the bus and some were still popping. We all broke up. Lopez admired Rivera. Lopez was mellow but understood the club needed someone like Jungle Jim.

Bob Shaw was another unsung hero. We considered

him an oddball, but in the sense that he was good for the ballclub. He was the type who would stand in a corner in his street clothes doing his full windup. He'd be talking and then all of a sudden he'd get the urge to wind up. Maybe that's what made him a good pitcher. (I wonder how much of an oddball he really was: he invested his money in land in Florida and became a millionaire.)

We won the pennant despite not having much of an offense. One game, Wynn 1-hit the Red Sox but needed his own homer to win the game, 1–0. In one game against Kansas City, we scored 11 runs in 1 inning although we got only 1 hit, a single by Johnny Callison. We got 5 bases-loaded walks and a bases-loaded hit batsman. I had the privilege of making 2 outs that inning.

BARRY LATMAN:

I was never on a team that talked about winning the pennant during spring training. That's when teams just tried to prepare for the season. There was a good attitude on the White Sox. When we realized we could beat the Yankees in 1959, our excitement really went up. We went into Yankee Stadium and won 2 out of 3, and Lopez said that we had a helluva shot at winning the pennant. I think the whole league was surprised. Until you win a pennant and realize how hard it is to do, you don't understand. It's unreal. 1959 was unreal. The White Sox hadn't won in 30 years, so every place we'd go, all anybody was talking about was the pennant race. Every time we'd come back to Chicago, there would be 5,000 to 10,000 people at the airport. We felt like celebrities.

We were a fun team. Nothing meant so much that we would stop having a good time. Winning the pennant was great, but so what? It wasn't like life or death and we played it that way. It was on the road where I'd see how unified we were. We'd go out to eat, mostly steak and lobster places, and delicatessens. There was definitely drinking after every game in the clubhouse while we discussed the game, but this wasn't really a drinking team.

Norm Cash, a left-handed first baseman from Texas, was my roommate. He was a super guy. My other good friends were catcher Earl Battey, who had been my first roommate with the Sox—we were the rare black-white roommates—another catcher, John Romano, and outfielder Jim McAnany, a top prospect.

Lopez had curfews. But the older players would always know because he'd tell them, and they'd tell the rest of us. We thought, "That asshole's having another curfew, but he won't catch us out tonight." Actually, it was smart of Lopez because he could keep the whole team in that way.

I got along with Donovan, Pierce, and all the other pitchers. I gladly accepted their help. Early Wynn tried to help me, but he was a different kind of pitcher than I was. Unlike Pierce, who threw very hard, Early had lost his fastball and was throwing high stuff and everything else wrong—and winning. He was the first one to throw a backup slider. His slider went high and tight on purpose—I'd have to make a mistake to throw it there. Wynn was mean on the mound and took charge by throwing inside to get his share of the plate. That was my style, too. You couldn't talk to Wynn on the day he was pitching. In fact, you never talked to any pitcher when he was getting his rubdown in the last half hour. Another thing you couldn't do was touch Dick Donovan's glove.

Sherm Lollar would take charge of meetings and on the field. I'd look up to him. Guys like Al Smith, Bubba Phillips, and Sammy Esposito were quiet and would just take their positions. All the pitchers would listen to Lollar, including Wynn. Battey and Romano had to get all their signs from Lopez, but Lollar was on his own and called a good game.

Nellie Fox was a good hitter, great ballplayer, and great guy. I don't think he was as much of a leader as Sherm Lollar. Fox was loud, but Lollar was the quiet leader. Fox's main thing was getting on base. He wasn't the greatest defensive ballplayer. He had trouble with the double play because his arm had weakened.

Luis Aparicio was magnificent. There has never been a better shortstop. Until you played with the guy, you couldn't imagine how good he was. All you wanted to do was have the batter hit the ball on the ground and Aparicio would get to it and throw him out. I thought he and Fox were friends, though I never saw them together outside the ballpark.

How could you not like Jungle Jim Rivera? He would say he went to "college" and he meant the army brig. He was charged with raping a colonel's daughter on the base. He always said he didn't do it and was cleared. He was just a nice guy, who was loud and lots of fun. His nickname fit the wild way he played.

We had team meetings at the beginning of every home stand on how we would pitch every batter and how we would defense them. I used to keep a book on how I pitched guys and I'd go over that. Going into games, we pitchers realized that the team had little offense and there was the good chance we could pitch well and lose.

When I was scheduled to pitch a day game, I would eat a full breakfast but no lunch. For a night game, I'd have a light breakfast and a big lunch around one o'clock, and then not eat again until the game was over. For a night game I'd get to the ballpark around four o'clock, and take batting practice.

I had a good season, starting 21 games and making almost as many relief appearances. I won 8 of 13 decisions, all as a starter, and posted a 3.75 ERA. I didn't pitch any differently because I was in a pennant race. I didn't suddenly get superstitious, although I still wouldn't touch the white chalk line on the base paths on days I pitched. Once in Yankee Stadium someone yelled my name and I tripped over the line and fell over.

Ironically, my grandfather, who threw me out of the family for becoming a ballplayer, let me back when he saw me pitch on national television from Yankee Stadium one Saturday. He then called me in the clubhouse. It didn't matter that I was a baseball player, because only bums did that, but since I was on national television and he could show his grandson to his friends, it was okay with him what I was doing. From then on, he'd call me up and ask, ''Are you coming down to see me this weekend? Someone wants to meet you.'' Then he was happy.

DEL ENNIS:

The day I joined the White Sox marked my first day in the American League. I walked into the clubhouse between games of a Sunday doubleheader. I was back to drinking Coke only, as I had done before I was on the Cardinals. I looked around and saw that one white player had a bottle of scotch over on one side, and some colored players were drinking gin. I wondered, ''What am I getting into here?'' The White Sox turned out to be the worst drinking team I played on, by far. Many of the

Having been in the National League since 1946, Del Ennis finished his impressive career with a brief, unhappy stint on the White Sox.

guys would drink all the time, and some were unbearable.

Chicago was too wild for me. I roomed with Earl Torgeson, who was my teammate on the Phillies in the early '50s. We stayed at the Piccadilly Hotel. The first night, some guy was running around firing a gun. For dinner, Earl and I went to the Blue Note, a nightclub where colored people went. Earl drank a few martinis, and the next thing I know, he's saying very loudly, ''I hate niggers!''

I liked Al Lopez and thought he was a good manager, I thought Nellie Fox was a terrific guy and great player, and liked that Billy Pierce was a tough, hard-throwing pitcher who'd go right after batters. But I couldn't handle the drinking, the wildness of the city, or the flying back and forth to my home in Philadelphia. So I left before the Sox won the pennant. In June, I quit baseball.

GARY PETERS:

I was born in Grove City, Pennsylvania, in 1937. I really started playing ball when I was 13 or 14 in industrial and mill leagues, with my father. We'd get about $5 for gas money. I was a first baseman and pitched occasionally. I was left-handed and could throw fairly hard. I tried out with Chicago as soon as I graduated from high school. The White Sox signed me for $175 a month and gave me a few thousand dollars, which I used to attend Grove City College—I began majoring in engineering but finished up in math. I was playing college basketball in the winter and professional baseball in the summer. I spent several half seasons in the minors—starting out in places like Dubuque, Iowa, and Holdrege, Nebraska— just so I could go back to college. I wanted to make sure that if I didn't make it in pro ball I'd have something else to do. I first attended the White Sox spring training camp in 1958, but the first full year I played was 1959, when I went to Indianapolis, their Triple A team. By that time I was no longer an outfielder but a starting pitcher.

All I had was a sinking fastball. I didn't learn a slider until I got to Indianapolis and had no breaking ball until I got to the big leagues. Sox pitching coach Ray Berres, a pitching guru, had already worked with me a little bit and told me I had a good arm and told me what to learn. He was important in getting me to the big leagues. He talked about balance and keeping my weight back and getting my arm and body in synch as I threw the ball. The White Sox were a defensive ballclub, so they wanted us to work as fast as we were comfortable working so the fielders wouldn't get flat-footed. We had a lot of games that were less than 2 hours. We were ready to throw when we got the ball back from the catcher.

I had a good year at Indianapolis in 1959, going 13– 11. And in September I was brought up to the Sox for the first time. They were in Boston, and my first roommate was Early Wynn, who was on his way to winning the Cy Young Award. He was rooming by himself and they stuck me in with him.

We then went to Washington, where I think the Sox scored 4 runs and swept a 3-game series. I was impressed with the pitching and defense. And it was exciting watching Nellie Fox, Sherm Lollar, and Luis Aparicio, who was the best I ever saw at shortstop. I had played that winter with Aparicio's club in Maracaibo,

Venezuela. I could see that he and Fox were very different, but they were good friends. Nellie and Billy Pierce were roommates, and I thought they were the leaders on the White Sox. They set examples both on and off the field and influenced everybody.

I was there when Chicago clinched the pennant against the Indians in Cleveland. We won 4–2. Al Smith homered and our relief ace, Gerry Staley, got Vic Power to hit into a game-ending bases-loaded double play with his sinker. I wasn't eligible for the Series, but I made the trip to L.A. and pitched batting practice. It was very exciting. That was the only Series I would be involved in. L.A. beat them and they were upset. Afterward I got to know pitcher Ray Moore. He had just bought a new pickup and was headed for Maryland. He dropped me off in western Pennsylvania, where my wife and family were.

NEW YORK YANKEES

BOB TURLEY:

Despite my Cy Young season in 1958, Stengel relied on me less in 1959. It was still his style to drastically cut winning pitchers' innings the following year. Both Whitey Ford and Art Ditmar pitched about 50 innings more than me, and Duke Maas pitched almost as much. It really wasn't a very satisfying year for any of us, because there were no big winners. Ford had the most wins, 16. He won one game, 1–0, when Bill Skowron homered in the fourteenth inning against the Senators— that was supposedly the longest game ever won 1–0 on a homer. My highlight was my second 1-hitter, against Washington. I lost my no-hit bid in the ninth when Julio Becquer's fly to left dropped in front of Norm Siebern.

RYNE DUREN:

The Yankees had a rare off year and fell to third, 15 games behind the White Sox and 10 behind the Indians. In May we were in last place for the first time since before the war. We had a power shortage in that Mantle led the Yankees in RBIs with just 75. We really missed Bill Skowron, who had his arm broken when Coot Veal ran into him at first. Moose, not Mickey, was the guy who won close games for us. However, I had another terrific season, with 14 saves, a 1.88 ERA, and 96 strikeouts in 76 innings. There was one stretch covering 18 games in which I was unscored upon for 36 innings. My ERA at the time we were eliminated from pennant contention was 0.69. Then I was running to get to one of my frequent after-game golf dates with Mickey. I ran across the field instead of through the tunnels, and a young fan threw a block into me and I fell and broke a bone in my wrist. (Years later I got a letter from him—he had become a policeman and also was an alcoholic—and he apologized to me. But it wasn't his fault.)

Despite our bad year, there was a winning attitude in New York. You thought more of the team and less of yourself. But it should be stressed that we tried to do well for each other rather than the Yankee organization. That's because all the players hated George Weiss. They didn't dislike George Webb or Dan Topping, although they did you a favor if they just said hello. Players just despised Weiss. He was cheap and aloof. We all felt exploited and frustrated. That's the way I felt when Weiss sent me a contract on Christmas Eve at four o'clock with a $4,000 cut, from $16,000 down to $12,000. After the year I had, I wasn't going to sign that contract.

WORLD SERIES

1959

WHITE SOX vs DODGERS

BILLY PIERCE · WHITE SOX:

The White Sox hadn't won a world championship since 1917, so we were excited to get the chance. I thought we were a better-rounded team than the Dodgers, position by position. We exploded in the first game, when Kluszewski hit 2 of his 3 Series homers, and were on the verge of a comeback in the second game when Lollar was waved around third on Al Smith's double and was thrown out at home with no one out in the eighth. After that, we didn't hit and they won in 6 games. We couldn't do anything against Dodgers reliever Larry Sherry. Everything he threw we hit at somebody. He did nothing wrong.

Before the Series, Lopez never told me what my role was going to be. Never a word was spoken. I did know that he was going to pitch Early Wynn as much as he could, after Wynn's great season. Al started him 3 times in the 6 games. He and Gerry Staley combined to shut out the Dodgers in Game One, 11–0, but he got knocked out in the third inning of Game Four and the fourth inning of Game Six, 2 of our losses. Bob Shaw pitched well but lost Game Two, 4–3. Then Bob started Game Five and beat Sandy Koufax 1–0, before a World Series record 92,000 fans in the Coliseum. Jim Rivera made a great game-saving catch in deep right-center and Dick Donovan got the save that game. Donovan started Game Three and was locked in a scoreless tie with Don Drysdale until Furillo had a pinch-hit single with the bases loaded in the seventh inning and they went on to win, 3–1.

I pitched only in relief, in the final 3 games, and gave up no runs in 4 innings. I thought I was going to start the sixth game. It was in Chicago, so Lopez didn't have to worry about a left-hander pitching in the Los Angeles Coliseum with that short fence in left. But Al went with Early. If I'd say I wasn't unhappy that after all my years in Chicago I wasn't given a chance to start a game in our first Series, I'd be a fool. At the time, the Chicago press questioned Al's decision. It was one of those things where one man calls the shots and no one else can do anything about it. (I would get over it because I would get my opportunity with the San Francisco Giants in 1962.)

AL SMITH · WHITE SOX:

I was surprised that Al Lopez didn't start Billy Pierce. We all knew why Lopez didn't pitch him, but we never told anyone and I won't say now. I will say that I thought he should have pitched. He'd been pitching all year, hadn't he?

The World Series was disappointing because we thought we should have beaten the Dodgers. Larry Sherry and Charlie Neal had an exceptional series against us. Neal hit a homer in the second game to center field. I just backed up against the wall to see if I could jump and catch it. But it went into the first row and a fan who went for the ball knocked his beer on my head. He didn't pour it on me on purpose. There was a famous picture in the *Chicago Tribune* of the beer pouring on me. The other players didn't laugh about what happened to me. I laughed about it.

BARRY LATMAN · WHITE SOX:

I don't have too many memories of the World Series because I didn't get into it. I warmed up 3 times. I was going to start Game Four, but Lopez came to me on the plane back to Chicago and said, "If I start you and I lose, I can be second-guessed. If I start Wynn and lose, no one will say a word. So guess who's going to start?" So that was it. I was disappointed. It really pissed me off not to get in the Series at all. The only consolation is that Lopez didn't start Billy Pierce either.

We played real well, then we got blown out of the damn thing. It was one of those things that can happen in a short series. I don't think they were better than us. I think over the course of the year we could have beaten them. But they won 4 out of 6 games.

JIM LANDIS · WHITE SOX:

The 1959 World Series should have been the thrill of my career. But at the time I had 2 little kids and we brought them out to California. They cried most of the night and I didn't get much sleep. I'm not making alibis because I had a decent series. Lopez told reporters he was happy with my performance. But I couldn't enjoy the Series.

The best thing memory-wise was that I faced Don Drysdale and Sandy Koufax before they became great pitchers. I also faced Johnny Podres, and he acciden-

tally hit me on the head. I was worried because I had no idea where I was.

I think we were more intense than during the regular season. The fun stuff was missing, like Jungle Jim Rivera, who was always loosy-goosy, doing things in the dugout. But maybe you were supposed to be more intense in the Series—I didn't know. I was nervous and the Coliseum was the toughest park to see in, fielding and hitting. I don't know how anyone went 3 for 4 in that ballpark. There was no blocked-off area, so it was really hard to pick up the ball. All you could see was shirts in the stands. I lost one fly ball as soon as it hit the bat. It hit me on the toe.

Larry Sherry was fabulous for the Dodgers. He just came in and shut the door. Chuck Essegian—I don't care if he didn't do anything much the rest of his career, but you have to give him credit for what he did. His 2 pinch homers went a long way—they weren't cheap.

JOHNNY KLIPPSTEIN · DODGERS:

It was a real thrill to play in the Series against the White Sox. Going into the Series, I thought if we could score 4 or 5 runs in a game, our pitching could hold them below that because they didn't have much power. With the exception of the first game, that was pretty much true.

My back was still bothering me, but I did get into one game, the first game in which the White Sox ran away, 11–0. I pitched a couple of innings of shutout ball, giving up 1 hit, and striking out 2. It was enjoyable.

My main memories were the 2 homers in Game Two by Charlie Neal, who had a helluva Series, and the relief pitching of Larry Sherry, who did nothing wrong in saving Games Two and Three for Podres and Drysdale and winning games Four and Six. Every time he came in, we didn't need any more pitchers because he'd shut down Chicago. Larry was a good pitcher all year round, so he didn't surprise me. The surprise of the Series was that they didn't start Billy Pierce against us.

STAN WILLIAMS · DODGERS:

After we lost the first game 11–0, in Chicago, Don Zimmer came into the clubhouse and said, "Boys, the Go-Go Sox are dead. They've got no chance." Everybody laughed though we'd just got bombed. We knew what he was saying was true. We had looked at them as a ballclub and knew we were better. It's just that the first game of the World Series was anticlimactic after the playoffs, which were an all-or-nothing type of thing. Now we were playing for 60 or 40 percent of the big money when before we might have had nothing if we'd lost. There was a letdown after we beat the Braves, and we immediately got on a plane, flew to Chicago, and were right in the World Series. We relaxed one game and got our butts kicked. Then we came back and won 4 of the next 5. I made my only appearance in the game we lost, Game Five. Bob Shaw beat us 1–0. I pitched 2 shutout innings in relief of Koufax.

Larry Sherry won 2 games and saved the other 2, and had an ERA of 0.71. The Sox just couldn't figure out his slider. He relieved Podres in Game Six in the fourth inning and went 5⅔ shutout innings. We won 9–3. All the other games were close. A lot of our guys contributed. Hodges hit around .390; Charlie Neal hit a little below that, with 6 RBIs, and 2 homers in Game Two; and Chuck Essegian hit a couple of big homers. But there was no doubt that Sherry was the star and deserved the MVP.

NATIONAL LEAGUE 1960

"I BELIEVED WE HAD TO SET GOOD EXAMPLES FOR KIDS. I DIDN'T DO A VERY GOOD JOB OF IT BECAUSE I SMOKED AND HAD A FEW BEERS, BUT THAT WAS THE END OF IT. KIDS COULD HAVE DONE WORSE LOOKING UP TO GUYS LIKE BILL MAZEROSKI AND BILL VIRDON AND SOME OTHERS ON THIS TEAM."

DICK GROAT

MILWAUKEE BRAVES

BOB BUHL:

I had my last big season with the Braves, winning 16 and losing 9. Spahn had 21 wins—including his first no-hitter, against Philadelphia—and Burdette got 19. When I was starting 28, 30, 33 games, Spahn and Burdette were starting 38 games. That was my big argument with management. They always questioned why I didn't win 20 games, and I'd say, "I don't have the baseball as much as them." At contract time they'd question me until I told them to look at my record against first-division ballclubs. When they'd do that they'd say, "Okay, how much do you want?" Because I had the best record against first-division ballclubs. Yet Spahn was making $60,000 to $75,000 and the most I ever made was $38,000.

We didn't understand why Fred Haney was fired because nobody could have done more with a team than he did with us. But Charlie Dressen came in and did a satisfactory job, leading us to a second-place finish behind the Pirates. Dressen had his pet players, but we got along. Eddie Mathews, Spahn, Burdette, and I teased him all the time. He was always trying to catch someone out past curfew, so we set him up. At the Coconut Grove in Los Angeles, we'd stay in bungalows. One night, Eddie and I were staying on one end of the place and Burdette and Spahn were on the other end. Eddie and I ran into the darkness. Dressen gave chase. We sneaked in the back door and Dressen knocked on our front door and asked if we were the ones outside. No, we said. Meanwhile, Burdette turned on the sprinklers and Dressen got soaked when he went back out. He started cussing. Then Burdette and Spahn ran through the darkness into their room, and Dressen ran down there to see who they were. By the time he got back, Eddie and I had turned the sprinklers back on and he got soaked again. He stood there dripping and just shook his head.

I can't remember anybody being fined in all the years I was with Milwaukee, even for breaking curfews. As long as the team was going good, they let things go. If we'd go into a losing streak, they'd make sure the players were in their rooms. We had spot room checks, or somebody'd be sitting down in the hotel lobby to see who was coming in. Dressen had a lot of room checks.

The ballplayers weren't dumb. If we were playing badly, we'd be in our rooms and get our rest.

Mathews, Spahn, Burdette, and I didn't miss curfew. We didn't make a big deal of going out and drinking so much that we wouldn't know what was going on. We'd have a few beers and eat, and if we wanted another beer we'd have it in the room. We played sober. When we were together we never had problems. We'd go to a nice restaurant, and if someone caused trouble, the waiter would ask him to leave.

Spahn and Burdette weren't fighters, but Eddie was a tough guy. The two of us got into a few squabbles. We weren't looking for trouble and fought only if someone harassed us. If someone brought up something about the game, we'd turn around and say, ''Feller, I know I had a bad day. Just drop it.'' If he kept going on and on, you'd get up and say, ''Okay, would you like to go outside and get this over with?'' If he'd say yes, then fine, we'd go off. If this guy had someone with him, Eddie made sure to come along. We'd probably settle it in the elevator on the way down. As long as it was one-on-one it was fine, but if they tried to gang up on one of us, it didn't work out for them because Eddie was always there and I was there for Eddie. It worked pretty good for us. Everybody wanted to see how good we were. Even when I'd go home after a season, everybody would want to challenge me. It got to the point where I just wanted to get it over with and go about my business. Just because we were ballplayers, guys who were jealous harassed us.

LEW BURDETTE:

Buhl and Mathews were a rougher pair than Spahn and me. Mathews would rather fight than eat when he was hungry, and Buhl was almost like that. There were people who challenged them. Those people lost. In St. Louis at the Chase Hotel, they were going down to their room and four tough guys made the mistake of getting on the elevator with them. Buhl and Mathews got off on their floor and went to bed and the elevator continued down. When the elevator opened in the lobby, there were four guys lying in a heap. They liked to fight, but I never saw them pick a fight. It's just that there was always a smart aleck in the crowd.

Spahn, Buhl, Mathews and I had a lot of fun together over the years. I'll tell how I remember the sprinkler in-cident in Los Angeles with Charlie Dressen. Spahn and I had adjoining cabanas with Buhl and Mathews, and Charlie had a cabana at the end of a long walkway. I looked through the shades and saw Charlie hiding in the bushes. Charlie would rather catch a player missing curfew than win a ball game. One guy was sneaking in late. Charlie jumped out of the bushes, but the player ran away with Charlie on his tail. When Charlie came back, the automatic sprinklers came on and he didn't know which way to run to. At least, we called them ''automatic.'' I'm not saying what happened or who did what. He just walked slowly back to his cabin. That was fun.

Charlie was all right. I took him fishing the following spring training. On the coast, he called Spahn, Buhl, Mathews, and me the four worst offenders on the ballclub. We joked around about it. Then we came back to Milwaukee and they had camera day and we posed with our hats turned over to the side and had gloves on our belts and Mathews had baseballs on his shoulders and Spahn was giving what he called his ''manager's look'' with his mouth open. We had the photo blown up and signed it ''the four worst offenders'' and put it in Charlie's locker. (After he died, his wife said, ''You guys thought Charlie didn't like you. That picture was framed and was on the wall of his bar at home. He was really proud of that picture.'')

Dressen may have pretended not to like us, but he must have appreciated what the four of us did for him on the field that year. Eddie had about 40 homers and 125 RBIs—he was just below Aaron in both categories—and Spahn, Buhl, and I were all big winners. I went 19–13. In August I had a string of 32⅔ scoreless innings that included a 1–0 no-hitter against the Phillies. Tony Gonzalez was their only baserunner. He got hit by a pitch and then was erased on a double play, so I faced the minimum 27 batters.

ST. LOUIS CARDINALS

TIM McCARVER:

The Cardinals still had an exceptional farm system. They had about 24 teams, 5 Class D teams. At spring training, there were 300 guys and they'd give you a number like 109A, which they'd pin on the uniform. Guys were released right and left. There's no question that the large bonus I was paid was to my benefit. They looked at me differently.

The teams that had been around for many years taught tradition. I was taught to have pride in being a Cardinal, part of a winning tradition, and to believe I was part of a big family. The problem was that guys bought into "being part of the family" and then were unprepared to be traded or released. It was disillusioning. It was a one-way family which they could dissolve anytime by getting rid of you.

In the Cardinals' system, the catchers' first concern was to handle pitchers. Second, they had to learn mechanics behind the plate. Third, it was offense. That's the proper order. Our offensive skills weren't geared for Busch Stadium, but for all ballparks. It was only 310 feet down the right-field line, yet I wasn't taught to be a pull hitter, but to hit to all fields and utilize my speed because that was the Cardinals' style. The Cardinals only led the league in homers 5 times in their history, despite having power hitters like Ducky Medwick, Johnny Mize, and Stan Musial. They prided themselves more on their base-running, a more adventurous form of baseball that puts extra pressure on opponents.

Each year I would go to spring training and learn more about what was required to be a major league catcher and then be sent down to the minor leagues to try what I learned. I would play only briefly in the majors. In 1960, for instance, I got into only 10 games with the Cards, catching only 5 times, and batting only 10 times, 4 of them as a pinch hitter. So I really wasn't part of the team that jumped from seventh to third place, but I was there long enough to admire the performances of guys like Ken Boyer, who played great third base and batted over .300, with 32 homers, and Stan Musial, of course. Musial had an off season by his standards but still batted .275, with 17 homers, in about 330 at-bats. After the year, he instructed the Cardinals to cut his salary from $100,000 to $80,000. Bill White had a good year at the plate and at first, and Boyer at third, Julian Javier at second, and Curt Flood in the outfield also contributed defensively. The Cards had good pitching, with Ernie Broglio and Larry Jackson from the right side and Curt Simmons and Ray Sadecki from the left. Lindy McDaniel was the first great reliever I caught. We didn't joke around—even when warming up he was stoical and deep in thought. Only the Pirates' ElRoy Face compared to McDaniel as a reliever that year. McDaniel won 12 games, third most on the team, and saved 12 more. He and Mike Fornieles of the Red Sox were chosen by *The Sporting News* as its first Firemen of the Year.

Broglio won 21 games to tie Warren Spahn for the league lead. He had everything: a nasty curve and tailing fastball. He threw hard and heavy. Jackson was the Cardinals' ace starter before the emergence of Bob Gibson. His nickname was "Cocky" because he carried himself with confidence, class, and charm. He was a fine pitcher who threw 2 types of fastballs, a curve, and a slider. He was tough and not at all adverse to throwing a knockdown pitch.

If a guy was going well, Solly Hemus would give him a couple of hundred bucks and tell him to take a few guys out on the town. He could be a classy guy. Yet while he loved veterans, he was cold to younger players, probably because he felt his job was on the line. He didn't like Curt Flood: he didn't think Curt could play in the outfield. So the Cardinals traded about 5 prospects for Don Landrum. But Landrum had a long hitless streak and proved he wasn't the answer. (Landrum would eventually be traded to the Cubs, and once Hemus was no longer manager, Flood would become a star center fielder.)

Solly also didn't like Bob Gibson. I don't think it was a black and white thing. He complained, "Bob throws every pitch at the same speed." That's like saying an atomic bomb explodes at the same velocity every time, so you can't use it. Bob wasn't worried about being traded because the Cards were paying him $1,000 a month to stop playing basketball with the Harlem Globetrotters during the winter. However, they sent him down. He threw 2 shutouts for Rochester and was brought back, never to be sent out again.

Gibson was a tough man who would always test you. One day in spring training, we were riding the bus to Bradenton. I bought an orange drink, and Gibson said, "Hey, Tim, can I have a swallow of that?" I looked at him and looked at my drink, and said, "I'll save you some." Bob said, "I thought you'd say that." I didn't consider myself prejudiced because I had come from Memphis, a town that was very prejudiced against blacks, Jews, and us Catholics. But Bob had made me reveal some prejudice, even if it was nonmalicious. I'd never had a drink after a black person before—in Memphis, there were separate water fountains. Bob made his point. Our relationship evolved. And it was difficult, as were all relationships with him. Bob could be intimidating because he had no tolerance for small talk. None. There was no "How's the family, did you have a nice winter?" conversation. He was very cerebral and outspoken. Bob showed his anger more than Curt Flood or Bill White. Yet while Bill and Curt were serious when they made statements, Gibson exhibited an acute sense of humor. It was on the mound that Gibson got totally serious. He was the toughest competitor I ever played with or against. Better than anybody else, he channeled his anger into his pitches.

Certainly there was justifiable anger at the root of things. Bill, Curt, and Bob all exhibited anger. Bill on a broader stage than the others: he went to the press. He was angry that black players would have to stay in black neighborhoods during spring training instead of in the hotels with the white players. They were being treated horribly. In either 1960 or 1961 Bill took a big stand in Florida, stating that black players were being treated like animals, and advocating that all the players stay together. So things changed. With Bob Gibson, Curt Flood, and Bill White, there were three defiant and outspoken black players on one team. They forced the issue.

CHICAGO CUBS

FRANK THOMAS:

After my hand operation, I had a fair season with the Cubs. My average was only slightly higher than it had been with the Reds, but I hit 21 homers and drove in about 65 runs in only about 480 at-bats. I was second to Banks in homers, but all of a sudden Lou Boudreau—who replaced Charlie Grimm early in the season—stopped using me as a regular. They brought up Ron Santo to play third, and George Altman and then Billy Williams played left. I went up to Boudreau and asked if I was going to play only against left-handers from then on. He insisted it was the front office's decision, but when I asked if I could call the front office, he admitted it was his decision. So I lost all respect for him. I decided to spend the rest of the season at the end of the bench, looking the other way and not saying a word. I knew this would get to him, because I had always been a rah-rah cheerleader when I didn't play. Then one day two of our outfielders collided in Wrigley Field. Boudreau pointed at me and said, "Don't *you* want to play?" That's showing up a ballplayer. I went out and played. When I came back to the dugout, I went over to him and said, "Don't you ever do that to me again. I never showed you up, and if you ever do that to me again, we are going to come to blows." A few days later we were in L.A., and before he sent me in to pinch-hit, he said, "Come by a little early tomorrow morning. John Holland and I want to talk to you." So I came down. Holland, our general manager, asked me, "What seems to be the problem?" "There's no problem, John—I just want to play. If I can't play on *this* ball-club, there's something wrong." There was a check on the table for $1,000. Holland explained that it was for me if I would coach the young kids on the team, and said that if I changed my attitude he'd double it at the end of the year. I told him I didn't want it. He stuck it in my pocket. Two weeks before the season ended, Holland gave me a check for $2,000. So that made the sum $3,000. It was supposed to seem like a bonus, but I knew how things worked. I told him, "If my contract for the coming year includes a cut in salary, you are going to hear from me." Sure enough, they cut me $8,000. I sat down and wrote a 10-page letter telling Holland how I felt he was trying to buy me and appease me. When he got the letter, he told me to fly into Chicago. He offered to take back the $3,000 and not cut my salary. I agreed. I gained tremendous respect for him. He was fair, someone I could talk to.

Richie Ashburn and I roomed together. We ran together in spring training and he would run, run, run, run. He still had speed and could hit. I was still telling anyone that if they held the ball across the seams I could catch the hardest balls they threw. Richie took up the challenge and I caught him. Then Richie got Willie Mays to bet $100 that I couldn't catch his throw. After I caught it, Mays went to Ashburn and said, "Let's make that $10." Either way, he never paid. The hardest to catch was Don Zimmer. He drew a line 60′6″ from me and then ran up to it and threw a spitter. The ball moved, but I still caught it. He threw his glove up in the air in disbelief.

Ernie Banks was a super guy. My kids loved him. Could he ever hit! He had just had back-to-back MVP seasons despite playing for a bad ballclub. He had his fourth straight year with over 40 homers and way over 100 RBIs. Ron Santo was a good ballplayer as a rookie. He got his first hit off Bob Friend of the Pirates and kept going. He was a much more aggressive ballplayer than Ernie. Of course, no one was more relaxed than Ernie.

I didn't get to know Dick Ellsworth. He was just a young kid who worked hard and tried to be a good pitcher.

DICK ELLSWORTH:

I returned to the Cubs in May and was immediately placed in the starting rotation. I finished the season with a 7–10 record. I was probably lucky that I started with the Cubs because they had a dire need for left-handed starters. At the same time, I felt I was a good enough talent to make any team's rotation. But I do know that I got to Chicago quickly, at age 20, because there was a hole to be filled. None of the players resented my quick rise because we had a common purpose.

The life of a major leaguer was different from what I presumed only in one area: I had never really considered the media. In high school we had only one or two local writers at our games. In the majors there was a contingent, an army of media, all the time. They covered all 154 ball games, at home and on the road. You were very aware of them. I learned early on that reporters had jobs to do and that you needed to give every question a good honest answer because they were going to write down what you'd say—and sometimes they'd also write what you didn't say. So answers required time and thought. I had good relationships with such Chicago reporters as Jerome Holtzman, Richard Dozer, and Jim Enright. I think the other Cubs also got along with the Chicago press. I didn't think they were too personal. I felt that the Chicago media was fair. If anything, they were tolerant of our lack of success, which I sensed was out of respect to the Wrigley family. During those same years, the media in other cities could be unfairly critical.

Still just 20, former high school sensation Dick Ellsworth moved into the Cubs' starting rotation, where he remained through 1966.

Baseball on the field wasn't any different in the majors than it had been in high school. Nine guys went out to play on each team, and we played with the same ball, same bat, and, I even think, same pressure. There was enthusiasm on the field in professional baseball, although there wasn't nearly as much enthusiasm on the bench in terms of rah-rah encouragement. I don't think the Cubs lacked enthusiasm. We had a young pitching staff with Don Cardwell, Glen Hobbie, Bob Anderson, and me; and we had young infielders Ed Bouchee, Jerry Kindall, and Ron Santo to go along with Ernie Banks, our veteran. I was always on the quiet side, but I was attentive and into every game whether I was pitching or not.

I felt fortunate that the Cubs always added a few seasoned veterans in the twilights of their careers. In 1958 we added Bobby Thomson, and in 1960 we got such players as Richie Ashburn, Don Zimmer, Jim Hegan, and Frank Thomas—guys who commanded a great deal of respect. Richie had just come over from the Phillies. He was at the tail end of his career, but he still covered a lot of ground in center field, batted around .300, and scored about 100 runs. He was a tremendous leadoff hitter who led the league in walks. I admired him a great deal. He was a great teammate because he was willing to help anybody. I'd go to him to talk about hitters, about how some pitcher threw to some batter, and related topics. He also helped Billy Williams, another left-handed hitter, when he came up at the end of the year. Not many players knew as much as Richie about the various aspects of baseball.

Ron Santo was just 20 when he took over the Cubs' third-base job. He and I kind of came up together. We went to our first spring training in 1959 in Mesa. He came up to the Cubs in June of 1960, a month after me. We became roommates for four years. We really got along well. We went to movies together, waited for each other to have breakfast, ate dinner together, had snacks together after the game, and talked a lot of baseball.

I went home after the season and my wife had a baby. I decided I was going to learn something about the retail business, so I started working with a sporting goods company. Since I was no longer going to school, that was going to be my education.

ED BOUCHEE:

The first game that Don Cardwell pitched after we came from the Phillies in May was a 4–0 no-hitter against the Cardinals. He got the last out when Walt Moryn made a diving catch on a ball hit by Joe Cunningham. That was the only time I played behind a pitcher who hurled a no-hitter. I tied the record for total chances in a game, with 17 putouts and an assist. It was a real thrill for Cardwell and I was happy for him. He was a likable, quiet, tall right-hander from North Carolina. We'd played together since 1955, and I saw that he had real talent. Catching his ball was like catching a brick: it was that heavy. I thought he should have had a much better record, but he didn't have much success in Philadelphia. It wasn't until he got to Chicago that he got a real opportunity. He would struggle in 1960 but win 15 games in 1961. He wouldn't have the career he should have had with his stuff, but he lasted for years—which is what could happen if you could throw hard.

Lou Boudreau had just become manager. He came out of the Cubs' broadcast booth to replace Charlie Grimm less than 20 games into the season, with Grimm replacing him as a broadcaster. Boudreau thought he knew a lot about the game, but I didn't think he did. I don't think he could handle pitchers for beans. I shouldn't really say anything about the guy, but I just didn't like him as a manager. They make a trade for me, and then he plays me half the time? What the hell good is that?

I didn't like sitting on the bench, but that's where the riding took place. There were certain guys that you liked to ride. For instance, everybody rode Pirates' third baseman Don Hoak. Yosh Kawano, our equipment manager, would sit in the dugout and shout, "Hey, Hoak! Whaddaya got on the bottom of your shoes? 'Eat at Joe's in Chattanooga, Tennessee'?" Hoak used to get so irritated. Then Yosh would get started and the whole team would get on Hoak. It was good-natured fun. You've got to do things to keep the guys loose on the bench. I wasn't a razzer, though. I tended to business and urged on my teammates.

Another ex-Phillie, Richie Ashburn, came to the Cubs a few months before the season. The only reason he was happy to be on the Cubs was because he was closer to Nebraska and could root for the Big Red. He was a big University of Nebraska fan, because that is where he was originally from. Richie was just one of those happy-go-lucky guys politicking his way through baseball. He never bothered anybody. We were friends from Philadelphia, and that wouldn't change.

LOS ANGELES DODGERS

ED ROEBUCK:

My arm was sound, so I returned to the Dodgers and went 8–3, with 8 saves. Larry Sherry had become the Dodgers' ace reliever, so Clem Labine was dealt to Detroit at the trading deadline. The Dodgers' starting pitching was outstanding, with Drysdale, Podres, Williams, and Koufax, but it should be noted how many relief appearances Larry and I made. I was in 58 games and he was in 57. Sherry was an excellent reliever—he, Drysdale, and Williams were the Dodgers' "headhunters."

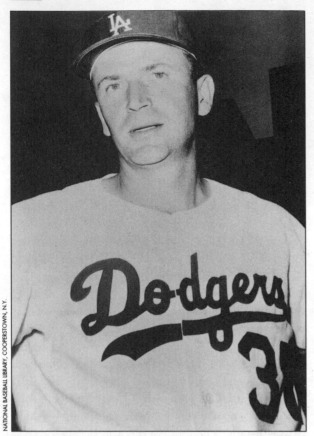

NATIONAL BASEBALL LIBRARY, COOPERSTOWN, N.Y.

Despite arm problems, Ed Roebuck began a three-year stretch in which he'd go 20–5.

The Dodgers slipped to fourth place despite the strong pitching. We tied Pittsburgh for giving up the least runs, but we had trouble scoring ourselves. We were going through a transition, easing out veterans like Snider and Hodges, and building the offense around younger players like Maury Wills, Frank Howard, Norm Larker, Tommy Davis, and Willie Davis. Maury played his first full season and led the league with 50 stolen bases, Howard hit over 20 homers and was voted Rookie of the Year, Larker hit just a couple of points behind Dick Groat in the National League batting race and led our team in RBIs. Tommy Davis didn't get to play a whole lot but showed he could be a good hitter. And Willie Davis played only briefly. Kenny Myers, who had helped me with my bad arm, signed Willie, a left-handed batter from Arkansas. He was a 20-year-old rookie and we couldn't believe how fast he ran from first to third and chased down flies in the outfield. He

was faster than Wills. We knew he was Duke Snider's successor in center field.

STAN WILLIAMS:

My reputation was *mean*. That's what I wanted. Off the field, I was a big teddy bear, but Drysdale, Larry Sherry, and I used to joke about our mean reputations. But I don't think it was accurate to call us "headhunters," because rather than trying to bean somebody we were just knockdown pitchers. There was a fine line between where you could and couldn't throw the ball. If you threw the ball in front of the hitter, at his chin or something, and knocked him on his ass, it was good for a laugh and what you were trying to accomplish. But you never threw the ball behind hitters because they reflexively went backward and down and would be hit.

I went through every phase of pitching. I went from being a one-pitch fastball pitcher to a wild, all-over-the-place pitcher. Then I learned how to harness my power for better control. Then I picked up my slider. As the years went by, I learned to throw any pitch at any time. I had 2 or 3 different types of curveballs and change-ups, a screwball, whatever it took. I didn't know anything about scuffing the ball. I wish I had. At times I'd get my fingers wet and throw a spitter. A small percentage of pitchers threw spitters. It was just another way of getting an edge. If I threw 60 spitters in a season, which was probably the most I threw, I probably got 55 strike-outs—that's how effective it was. Somebody taught it to me somewhere along the line.

In 1960 I wasn't a starter at the beginning of the season, but I went into the rotation when Roger Craig broke his collarbone on a collision at home with the Reds' Vada Pinson. I began implementing a pitching plan and everything started coming together. I was 8–1 at the All-Star break and made the All-Star team, and by the beginning of August I was about 12–3 with around a 2.25 ERA. Then one day I pitched against Lew Burdette in Milwaukee and hurt my arm. And that was it. It took me a long time to get back my form. I finished the season at 14–10, with a 3.00 ERA, and with 175 strikeouts in a little over 200 innings.

Norm Sherry, Larry's brother, and I thought alike, so I liked having him as my catcher. It helped having a catcher who would go along with you if you didn't want to throw a pitch. All I had to do was stare at him and he'd know what I wanted to throw instead. Johnny Roseboro was also an excellent catcher, but he didn't like catching—he wanted to be an outfielder.

Both Norm and Johnny were among the leaders on the team, as were guys like Hodges, Snider, and Moon. Everybody felt comfortable in a leadership role. We policed ourselves. I remember pitching in an away game against the first-place Pirates at a time we couldn't afford mistakes. I locked up with Vernon Law and it was 0–0 late in the game. Our defense was set up for Dick Groat, a right-handed hitter, to go the other way, but I stupidly threw him a slow curveball, the only pitch he could possibly pull. Groat pulled a 7-hopper over third that went for a triple, and he ended up scoring the game's only run. When I came into the dugout, Wally and two or three others jumped on me something fierce. Moon said what later-day ballplayers might take offense to. But I knew he was right and had the right to say what he did. That's how we felt on the team, which is why we got along so well.

SAN FRANCISCO GIANTS

JOHNNY ANTONELLI:
I got along with Horace Stoneham, but in all the years I didn't really get to know him. He wasn't an owner who visited the clubhouse too often. He lived in Arizona, and we'd see him more in spring training sitting up in the stands or talking to someone on the field. I rarely spoke to him. I did contract negotiations with the Giants' GM, Chub Feeney, Stoneham's nephew. The Giants weren't known as a generous team, but I enjoyed pitching for them and playing for Stoneham.

I also liked living in the Bay Area. A few of the players lived in Daly City, which was very close to the ballpark, but most of us lived farther south. I lived in San Mateo and then Redwood City, lovely areas. Mike McCormick lived in Palo Alto and he'd drive me and infielder Joey Amalfitano to and from the park every day. I didn't do much socializing with players outside the ballpark, so I don't know what other guys did.

I loved San Francisco, but its weather wasn't conducive to good baseball in either Seals Stadium or Candlestick Park, where we moved in 1960. There's something wrong if Willie Mays is out in center using a hand warmer. When you're out there for 15 days in a row wearing long underwear, neckbands, and heavy shirts, with your eyes watering and teeth chattering because of the wind and cold, you aren't going to play your best. And the jet stream would do tricky things to fly balls. It was a shame San Francisco was cheated of seeing top-notch baseball on an everyday basis.

My misquoted words about the weather in 1959 were still haunting me. I was still being booed by the fans who thought I insulted the city rather than the ballpark. It didn't help that the team was doing worse than expected, which cost Bill Rigney his job, and I was having trouble getting wins. 66-year-old coach Tom Sheehan, who finished the season for Rigney, inserted newcomer Billy O'Dell into the rotation with Jones, Sanford, and McCormick, and moved me to the bullpen with Stu Miller. I didn't do badly out there, considering this was the first time since 1950 that I was used mostly in relief. But I wasn't enjoying myself because of the unsupportive fans and media. Normally I avoided controversy, but before you knew it, I was saying things I probably shouldn't have said. There's no question that was the reason for my demise in San Francisco and swift departure. In December, after 7 years with the Giants, I was traded with Willie Kirkland to Cleveland for Harvey Kuenn.

BILLY O'DELL:
I wasn't happy to be traded to the Giants, but once I got out to San Francisco I enjoyed it a great deal. The Giants had a great organization—the best, in my opinion. Horace Stoneham really loved baseball and took care of his players. I got what I wanted in terms of salary. Bill Rigney was a fine guy and a good manager, so I was upset when he was let go about 60 games into the season. I told him that the reason he got fired was that he traded for me. In truth, I didn't understand it because we were 8 games over .500 at the time, and on a winning streak. We played less than .500 for the rest of the season under our interim manager, Tom Sheehan.

It wasn't hard to adjust to a new league. I was a fastball-slider pitcher in the American League. In the National League I mastered the curveball and learned to throw a heckuva change. There was supposed to be a different strike zone, but there wasn't a nickel's worth of difference. However, there were some different hitters. Hank Aaron hit me pretty good. He'd either hit it out of the ballpark or, even if he didn't hit it well, get a base hit. (He would hit 6 or 7 homers off me.) I think Aaron was comparable to Mays, although he wasn't as publicized because he had never played in New York. In addition to his hitting, he was a good outfielder with a strong, accurate arm and he could steal a base whenever he wanted—you couldn't throw him out. Roberto Clemente was a super ballplayer, but I had more success against him than against Aaron. He stood far away from the plate and I kept the ball in on him and had good luck. Frank Howard was the other guy I had trouble with, even as a rookie. Everyone got him out but me.

I lived in San Mateo, about 30 miles south of San Francisco. It was a small town at the time, which made it easier for me. It was completely different from San Francisco. Even the temperature was different. Many players lived in the area—if not in San Mateo, then probably in San Jose.

I roomed on the road with Mike McCormick, another lefty. We spent a lot of time together and became close friends. We were compatible and would go out to dinner, take in a movie. We had some mutual friends in some towns. 90 percent of the typical player's friends were in baseball, but if you played long enough, you met people from outside baseball and made good friends.

Mike was a good pitcher who threw over 250 innings that year and led the league in earned run average. He and I were the left-handers in the rotation, while Johnny Antonelli moved to the bullpen and did a great job. I also went back and forth between starting and relieving, as I had done on the Orioles, so I got into over 40 games and pitched over 200 innings. I won only 8 games while losing 13, but my ERA was just 3.20. My ERA had always been under 3.00 in Baltimore, but I learned to expect a higher ERA because I did half my pitching in Candlestick Park, where the winds carried the ball all over the field and sometimes over the fence. I never did as well in Candlestick as in visiting parks.

Sad Sam Jones won 18 games for us. He was a good, tough pitcher, a workhorse with a great big curve. Off the field, he was an easygoing fellow, and a loner. Jack Sanford, our other right-handed starter, also stayed to himself. He had his own ideas about pitching, and they

must have been pretty good, since he was very successful. He won only 12 games for us in 1960, but he led the league in shutouts. He could be very intimidating.

The rotation improved dramatically when the Giants brought up Juan Marichal, a slim, 22-year-old right-hander from the Dominican Republic. He threw a super 1-hitter in his first start, against the Phillies, striking out 12. He would go 6–2 as a rookie with a low ERA. There was no doubt he would be a great pitcher. He had a good fastball, breaking ball, everything. And he had that unusual delivery with a high kick. He was quiet but wasn't as much of a loner as some of the guys on the club. He had a bit of a temper but wasn't as mean on the mound as someone like Sanford.

Our offense wasn't as strong in 1960 as it had been in the past. Willie Mays and Orlando Cepeda both had outstanding seasons, but right fielder Willie Kirkland was the only other guy who was consistently productive. Willie McCovey hit some homers and drove in runs when he was in the lineup, but he sat a lot, including games against tough left-handers. I don't know if this was because he couldn't yet hit left-handers or because Cepeda wanted a chance to play first base. McCovey was an even-tempered guy and, as far as I know, never complained about his lack of playing time or being sent down for part of the season. I think he should have been in there because he was a good hitter and good fielder.

McCovey wasn't yet a leader in the clubhouse. He just went out and did his job. Jim Davenport was one of our leaders. He was level-headed and a good thinker. Our other leader was Mays, yet he wasn't as outgoing as many superstars. He was a quiet guy. You'd have to look around sometimes to see if he was there. What Mays had done already in his career, and how he still worked hard to accomplish more, was what inspired the other players and made him a leader. He would still take batting practice and shag fly balls. He'd even take infield practice because he always wanted to be a shortstop. He could have been. Mays could do anything. Even then, if you needed a base stolen, he'd steal it. He was a laid-back guy with no temper at all. We admired that even if he struck out 3 times in a row, he wouldn't get down on himself.

On the other hand, if Cepeda had a bad day, he would sulk. I think there was some unstated competition between Willie and Orlando. There was competition for press attention for a while, but that smoothed over and they were friends. I didn't notice Mays getting unfair treatment from the fans. Orlando had a quick smile, but the fans seemed to like Mays just as much. If they got on Willie, it might have been just to push him to some new heroic feats. They always cheered him when he came through—they didn't mind when he proved them wrong. I'm sure they all recognized he was a great player.

PHILADELPHIA PHILLIES

ED BOUCHEE:

The majors were no different than I expected except for all the politics. Salaries weren't published back then, but I talked to other players, so I had an idea of what I should be getting. But everybody had trouble negotiating with our GM, John Quinn. He was so stingy it was unreal. After my good '59 season, he sent me a contract for a $1,000 raise. I said that he should double what I made. He waited about a month and then sent me a pointed letter and a new contract. I had no choice but to sign it. We had no power, none whatsoever. No union, no agents, nothing to help us.

After 2 last-place finishes, Eddie Sawyer quit after 1 game of the 1960 season. We came north, lost on Opening Day, and that was it. I'm sure it wasn't just because of his players but because of his frustration with the front office. It was a real shock to me.

Gene Mauch replaced Sawyer. Mauch had been a successful minor league manager at Minneapolis and knew baseball as well as anyone. I liked him. When he came in, he had a talk with the players and explained his philosophy. He was one of those managers who would play for one run rather than a big inning.

In the spring we were about to buy a house. That's when I found out I was traded with Don Cardwell and Sparky Anderson to the Chicago Cubs for Tony Taylor and Cal Neeman. I didn't really know why I was traded. I didn't think I had it coming. Maybe Gene Mauch felt that Frank Herrera could do the job at first base, but all Pancho would do was hit an occasional homer and set a league record for strikeouts because he tried to hit many

more—he had to, because no one else hit at all on the Phillies, as they stayed in last place. The more likely reason for the trade was that the Phillies needed a better second baseman than Anderson and they had a chance to get Taylor. Getting traded from Philadelphia was my biggest regret in baseball. But there was nothing I could do about it.

PITTSBURGH PIRATES

DICK GROAT:

We won the Pirates' first pennant since 1927! It was wonderful. We set a team attendance record as we won 95 games and beat out the Braves by 7 games. I led the league with a .325 average and was the Most Valuable Player, which made me very proud. One game against Milwaukee, I went 6 for 6. But it was a case of everyone having a great season. Don Hoak finished second in the balloting because he drove in about 80 runs, played great defense, had about 80 RBIs and was a driving force on the team. Bobby Clemente hit .314, which was third in the league, and led our team with over 90 RBIs. Bob Skinner drove in a lot of clutch runs. Dick Stuart hit over 20 homers and drove in runs. Virdon, Mazeroski, and Burgess and bench players like Gino Cimoli, Hal Smith, and Rocky Nelson all made tremendous contributions. Law and Friend were finally good in the same season. Law won 20 games and was voted the Cy Young Award and Friend won 18 games, and Harvey Haddix and Vinegar Bend Mizell were strong third and fourth starters. Roy Face, who was great once again, and Fred Green came through almost every time they relieved.

Amazingly, Mizell was about our only new acquisition despite our fourth-place finish in 1959. He was enough. We got him from the Cardinals and he won 13 games. He was a good guy, a very solid person, who was extremely serious about everything. He would eventually become a congressman, but as a ballplayer he wasn't political. Players didn't really talk politics.

Interestingly, we had only one player who was recognized as a superstar, Clemente, and two others who were unrecognized superstars, Mazeroski and Face. The rest of us were all just solid baseball players. Bobby bolstered our confidence when competing against the Braves because he gave us a player on the level of Henry Aaron. I already thought Bobby was the greatest talent in baseball and had his best years ahead of him.

There is something unique about winning ballclubs, especially in those days. We all had roommates, yet we all palled around together. You could go out and have a beer after a game with anyone on the team. There were no cliques. We were a very, very close-knit team, which helped us win, and winning made us even closer. We'd stay close for the rest of our lives.

This club enjoyed going out and having a couple of beers. Or we'd sit in the clubhouse drinking beer provided by Iron City, our sponsor. But we weren't a big-drinking team or a heavy card-playing club. Forget poker. That was a no-no. Danny had a cut-and-dry rule against poker: he said gambling made for hard feelings. So we played a lot of hearts and gin, but not for a lot of money. I played bridge with ElRoy. Danny played a lot of gin with our longtime traveling secretary Bob Rice, a beautiful man who just loved gin. You knew the guys who were going to be goofy and kept tabs on them. Sometimes two or three of us would get in a cab and go get them out of trouble, before somebody had them drawn and quartered. Those things would happen, and that was part of being a team. Ballplayers were targets, especially if they were well known, so you had to be very, very careful. I believed we had to set good examples for kids. I didn't do a very good job of it because I smoked and had a few beers, but that was the end of it. Kids could have done worse looking up to guys like Bill Mazeroski and Bill Virdon and some others on this team.

I was chosen captain and I tried to lead by example. I constantly advanced runners and took strikes to protect runners and the batters behind me. I showed that a batter could do all the right things for the team and still hit .300. Something like that becomes contagious.

Danny Murtaugh was a great leader our title year. He got the best out of all 25 players, which is the key to good managing. He handled people exceptionally well and played the game, right down the line. Whether I played in or deep was his decision, but otherwise Danny left me alone. For instance, in all the years he managed me, he never knew my hit-and-run sign or when I was going to put it on. He never asked. No one knew my

sign except for the baserunner, usually Billy Virdon. Under Murtaugh, Bill led off and I batted second the whole time.

On September 6 we were in a big series against the Braves and Lew Burdette was pitching against us. One inning, Eddie Mathews was playing way off third. As usual, I took the first pitch; it was a ball. I knew Burdette was going to lay the next one in and I decided to reach out quickly and pull the ball down the line for a double. So I reached out, only he didn't throw a strike. He threw a fastball a little inside. I absolutely froze and got my wrist broken. I never had any resentment toward Lew because it wasn't even a brushback pitch. We later laughed about it. The only thing is that he would fib that the pitch was a slider when I knew it was a fastball.

LEW BURDETTE (BRAVES):
Groat thought I was going to throw him a slider and reached out. I threw him an inside fastball and it hit him right on the wrist. He always said that pitch might have been a strike. So Groat's season ended with him leading the league in hitting. I would kid him, saying, "I won the batting title for you."

D. GROAT:
Ducky Schofield took my place down the stretch. He was, in my opinion, as fine a utility infielder that ever played this game. He could play second, short, and third and could play all of the positions very well. He could give you two or three weeks of great play at any one of those positions. I wasn't sure if he was physically strong enough to play every day and keep his average up. But he was valuable to the Pirates all year, and in September he came in and hit a ton and played great shortstop.

DICK SCHOFIELD:
Everybody had a nickname on this team: Groat was "the chicken," Mazeroski was "the whale," Hoak was "the tiger," Skinner was "the dog," I was "the duck," and I think we called Stuart "the donkey." There was a lot of agitating and a lot of laughter. We'd get on someone new every day and stay on him. I also took a great deal of agitating—probably because I deserved it. Hoak loved to agitate me. He'd call me "Midget," and every day he'd make up a story about me. He'd lie like a dog

about me and just laugh. Hoak was different. I actually think he had a problem. He wanted to be so tough and acted tough, but he wasn't like that—he never won a fight in his life. But he could play. Dick Groat was the team captain, but Hoak was also a leader. Groat was a quiet leader, while Hoak had a lot to say.

By 1960, the Pirates had become a very close, loose team. We had a lot of fun together, on and off the field. I roomed with Joe Gibbon, a hard-throwing rookie left-hander from Mississippi. He was 7 or 8 inches taller than me. Gibbon, Hoak, Haddix, Virdon, Skinner, Mazeroski, Cimoli, and Tom Cheney were some of my friends on the team. There weren't many arguments.

Mazeroski was one of the nicest guys I ever played with. Plus, no one was better at second base. You can only get so good. It was a joy to play next to him. Virdon was another very likable guy, who was a tough competitor. I think he was one of our leaders. He could play center as well as anybody. He never made mistakes. If he'd hit a few more homers he'd have been an all-star.

Skinner was quiet. He liked to just sit back and laugh at things and do a little agitating. He was a good guy. He was also a very good hitter and a decent left fielder. Cimoli kept everybody loose. He'd joke around on the team bus, telling Murtaugh what everybody did the night before. Murtaugh didn't want to hear it, but when you win, everything's a big joke.

When Tom Cheney and I were together at Omaha we became friends and our wives became friends. He'd always make fun of my clothes. I used to get Palm Beach clothes out of Cincinnati. What did that Southern cracker know about clothes? Skinhead had a great arm and threw a great curve, but when he came to Pittsburgh he was still trying to stick in the majors. He was always nervous. He'd light one cigarette right after another. I would be glad Tom had success after he left Pittsburgh because he was a good guy.

Dick Stuart was pretty much a loner, but he was the kind of guy you couldn't help but like. Every once in a while he'd do stupid things, but he was a super guy and fun to have on the team. He'd say and do funny things, and you couldn't embarrass him. (Years later, he was wondering why his son was only my size and he teased me by asking, "Where was you at?") We all got irritated with his fielding at times—he led the league in errors that year and didn't save too many of our bad throws. But he was a lot better hitter than people gave him credit for. He had tremendous power and blasted tape-measure homers over the center-field fence at Forbes Field. He hit 23 homers and drove in over 80 runs in 1960 while batting less than 450 times.

Roberto Clemente was off by himself even more than Stuart. You didn't see him away from the park. A lot of things bothered him. I'd say he was paranoid. Maybe he thought some of the players didn't like him, or that a pitcher was trying to hit him, or that the sportswriters were out to get him, or he wasn't getting the proper recognition. That might have bothered some of the guys a bit. He wasn't always included in the agitating. As a player, Clemente was as good as you could get. He was a great hitter, baserunner, fielder, and thrower. He had a fantastic arm and led the league's outfielders in assists in 1960. In fact, he led the league several times—in 1961 he'd throw out 27 runners!—before runners wised up and stopped challenging him. He could hit the ball hard between the first and second basemen as good as anybody and he'd get 50 singles a year like that. I'm sure he would have tried for more homers if he didn't play in Forbes Field. If he had ever played in a smaller park, like Wrigley Field, he would have had a ton of homers.

Smoky Burgess could hit a fastball on January first. He liked to pick his spots and catch when he wanted to, but he could hit as well as anyone in baseball. He was religious and was good friends with Vernon Law, his roommate. Smoky felt comfortable about agitating us because he knew he never did anything wrong. Of course, I took the brunt of a lot of nonsense from him.

Bob Friend was somewhat religious, though not like Burgess. He was "nervous in the service." He worried about everything. Law was much calmer. He was well respected, a leader by example. When he went out there, we knew we had a good chance to win. You could get on Deac pretty good. Guys would call him "Dirty Deacon" and names like that and he didn't mind. He was very religious but never stuck it in anyone's face. We'd find ourselves not cussing in front of him just out of respect. One time a Phillies pitcher undressed a couple of our hitters with inside fastballs, so Murtaugh said, "Okay, Deac, you've got to knock this first guy down." And Deac said, "I don't do that." "Well," said Murtaugh, "if you don't do that, I'm going to fine you." So he picked up his glove and as he was walking from the dugout he said, "Those who live by the sword shall die by the sword." Then he knocked down the batter.

ElRoy Face would throw about 4 or 5 warm-up pitches and come in and crank it up. He had a lot of guts and would challenge everybody. He was certainly one of the greatest relief pitchers ever. I think he was better in 1960 than when he went 18–1 in 1959.

Everybody had confidence in each other. We had a team that would win in late innings. If we were ahead or tied in the seventh, eighth, or ninth innings, we'd win it. If we were behind, we'd probably come back to win. I'm not sure we had the best team, but we had the right attitude. We knew we weren't going to be beaten. There were a few key comebacks. We had a couple of big rallies against the Reds. In one game, Skinner had an inside-the-park homer in the ninth inning. We beat Cal McLish of the Reds about 7 times that year. Once Don Newcombe was scheduled to pitch for the Reds, but umpire Dusty Boggess threw him out during an argument for having sleeves of different lengths. So McLish started the game and Virdon hit his first pitch for a homer and we beat him 1–0. I think we beat Don Drysdale twice in a doubleheader, once as a starter and the other time as a reliever.

Many guys outside the nucleus had fantastic seasons. It was a real team effort. When Groat got his wrist broken, I stepped in and got 3 hits in the first game. I hit .406 that month and ended up batting .333, 99 points higher than in 1959. Everything fell into place for me. I think my teammates would have said that I played hard and battled all the time and I was always wanting to play. Guys respected me because they knew if I was put into the game, they were going to get an effort out of me. They could rely on me.

Nineteen sixty was the most exciting year I ever experienced in baseball. It got more exciting every game. You couldn't walk down the street in Pittsburgh because half the people who passed by would say hello. They came out of the woodwork. It turned out that Pittsburgh was a great town to play in. Pittsburgh came alive. When we returned home after clinching the pennant, the buildings were lit up downtown and they had a torchlight parade.

ELROY FACE:
As a reliever, I wasn't given the same consideration during salary negotiations that I would have been given had I been a starter. But after going 18–1 in 1959, I got a $10,000 raise, which made me happy. I think I had a better year than in 1959. I went 10–8, with 24 saves (plus 3 more in the World Series) compared to 18 wins and 10 saves. I pitched better.

Going into spring training, we all felt we had a good chance to win the pennant. We had a good club with the type of players who just never gave up. The players on the bench rooted for the guys who kept them on the bench. Murtaugh was the same manager he'd always been. He never panicked. There were several games that stood out. The Cardinals came in for a big series in late July and we beat them 4 out of 5 and were never out of first place after that. We were down to Cincinnati 5–0 in the ninth inning with 2 out and no one on base and scored 6 runs to beat them. Against the Dodgers we tied a game with 3 runs in the ninth when we had 2 outs and no one on base, and then beat them in the tenth. We never lost 4 games in a row. Every time we lost 3 in a row, Vernon Law would win. He could throw 4 fastballs in a row and still be tough to hit because all 4 came in at different speeds. He won 20 games that year and was the Cy Young winner. He and Friend won the two All-Star Games. I was in the first game for my third straight appearance.

The only injury we had was when Dick Groat broke his wrist. And Dick Schofield replaced him and hit over .400. Schofield was a great utility player, a good man on the bench and in the clubhouse. He wore bright jackets, as did Pirates announcer Bob Prince. I did occasionally. So did Cimoli, who kept the guys loose. Bob Oldis was a clown, but I don't remember what he wore.

Don Hoak had only 80 percent major league ability, but he made himself into a complete ballplayer by giving 120 percent on the field. He got 7 stitches in his toes after slipping on a ladder getting out of a swimming pool, yet he still went out and played every day. Between innings he'd disappear into the runway and grab his leg because he was hurting so bad. Out on the field, he never limped, so Murtaugh didn't know anything was wrong. After every game, there'd be blood in his shoes because he needed to be restitched. Groat was the captain and a leader, but Hoak was the guy who got on your butt. He'd go to the pitchers and say, "If you don't want to pitch, there's a guy in the bullpen who wants to come in here." He wouldn't let a pitcher get down on himself and take himself out of the game.

Groat didn't have a lot of range, but he was very smart. He played the position really well so the ball was always hit to him. Maz did have a lot of range, and there were times when he'd run all the way over to the first-base line to get a ball that Stuart let go by. He'd throw the guy out on what should have been Stuart's ball. When I'd come in from the bullpen, Stuart would be over at first kicking dust. He'd slide over into my path and tell me not to throw the ball to him on a pickoff attempt because he'd already had enough trouble with his fielding. Once there was a grounder hit to Dick Groat, who threw to first. Stuart had turned around to argue with the umpire and the ball went whizzing past his ear from behind. The other players would yell at Stuart, but he didn't really care. We all liked him. I'd drive to the park with him from the North Hills section.

I considered myself an all-around ballplayer and always took pride in my hitting and fielding. I went 7 for 17 in 1960 for a .412 average. I started switch-hitting. The first time I batted from the left side was against Don Newcombe of the Reds. He had a high kick, so I laid down a bunt and beat it out. He didn't like that. Of course, I didn't like when he stole home against me a few years before.

I never won a Gold Glove, but I think I fielded as well as Harvey Haddix and Bobby Shantz, who were considered the best fielding pitchers. I had good reflexes on balls hit back to me and got off the mound quickly. I loved picking off runners. I'd run a daylight play with Dick Groat at second, and we caught a lot of guys. Sometimes Stuart or Rocky Nelson would be playing behind a runner at first and I'd put my hands together. That was the signal for us both to start counting for when I'd throw to first. I had a very good move because I was well balanced on my pivot. The way I stood, I didn't have to look over my shoulder to see the runner on first but could see him just by glancing. Then I'd balance myself on my back foot and turn and throw to first with power. When I threw to second, the balance would be on my front foot. Picking off runners was a highlight of my 1960 season. I once came in with men on first and second and picked off the runner on second

and then picked off the runner at first. That was fun. One of my favorite moments of the season came against the Cardinals in that crucial 5-game series. They had the tying run on second, and pitcher Curt Simmons went in to pinch-run. I picked him off.

TOM CHENEY:

When I got to Pittsburgh, I discovered I wasn't just on a great team but got to play with a great bunch of guys. It wasn't cliquish at all. Other than Vern Law, Vinegar Bend Mizell, and Smoky Burgess, who were all terrific guys, any 5 to 10 of us would go out together after games. Stars and nonstars, it didn't matter. Or maybe we'd just sit around together in the clubhouse after a game, have a beer, and unwind. Some players were card players. Some listened to rock 'n' roll. I liked country music. So did Face, Harvey Haddix, and Hal Smith— they'd play guitars and sing. That would get a reaction. I can't remember Deacon Law listening to music. There weren't many readers. Bob Friend was interested in the stock market. Jim Umbricht, a young right-hander, was a crossword puzzle fanatic. Some of us would play golf together. ElRoy Face and I would go fishing.

Face was "something else"—that's the only way I can describe him. He was great. He was never given enough credit. One of his best assets was that he could throw just 5 warm-up pitches and be ready to go into a ball game and throw hard. He had a good slider that few people talked about because of his great forkball. He could hit a gnat flying with that forkball. I never learned the forkball, although I probably could have because my hands were big enough. The only guy in baseball besides Face who could throw a good forkball was Red Sox outfielder Gary Geiger, who had been a pitcher with me in the Cardinals' organization.

We pitchers always argued about our hitting. Vern Law was a fun guy who joined in. He didn't carry his religion on his shoulder. Very few pitchers are good hitters, so we looked forward to competing with each other at batting practice. We only got a chance to take batting practice at home and we never missed it.

Pittsburgh had good starters in Friend, Law, Haddix, and Mizell, so I didn't pitch much and spent time at Columbus. I was in only 11 games, 8 as a starter. Yet this team was so tight that I was voted a full World Series share. They accepted me.

COURTESY OF TOM CHENEY/© 1990 TV SPORTS MAILBAG

Once a Georgia farm boy, Tom Cheney got to play only briefly with the Pittsburgh Pirates, but fortunately it was in their 1960 championship season and he got to appear in the World Series.

I was 2–2 and beat Cincinnati twice. I shut them out on a 4-hitter—that was my first really well pitched game. Bob Oldis caught the last part of that game. He was a great defensive catcher and said, "Throw whatever you want and I'll catch it. We don't need any signs." Bob didn't catch very much but he really sparked the club because he had a great attitude. Just being on the club was what mattered.

Along with Stan Musial, Roberto Clemente was the best player I played with. He could do it all. He had a great year at bat, but what really amazed me was his arm. He was in a different class than Mays, Colavito, all of them. I saw him make hard throws like no one I have ever seen, and he was accurate. Dick Groat and Bill Mazeroski were bruised all over their arms, legs, and chest from his throws into second. He threw so hard that he'd throw a ball that one-hopped from near first base to home and still handcuffed the catcher. I was friends with Clemente, but he was more of a loner than the other blacks on the team, Gene Baker, Earl Francis, and Bennie Daniels. He brooded, he had his pouting periods, he was temperamental, and at times he looked like he was dogging it.

BOB BUHL (BRAVES):

Roberto Clemente was a hustler all the way except if he hit a grounder or easy fly. If he saw a base hit or extra-base hit, he ran all out. I didn't have much trouble with him because he liked the ball away and I pitched inside.

T. CHENEY:

Clemente wanted to be the top dog all the time. Possibly, he didn't feel he was given enough recognition. Robbie always felt that if a pitch came too close, the pitcher was throwing at him, and he'd want us to retaliate. But all we saw were purpose pitches, not beanballs. If they knocked him down every time, sure we were going to protect him.

LEW BURDETTE (BRAVES):

Clemente always hit the ball to right off me. He'd stretch his arms and hit the ball the other way. If I pitched him inside, there was the danger he'd move into the ball and be hit. I got accused of throwing at him on a ball that I swear wasn't an inch inside. I got fined $50 for that.

T. CHENEY:

This club had so many clutch players, not just Clemente. It didn't matter who was up. Murtaugh could just point. It could have been Dick Groat, who led the league in hitting. Or it could have been Dick Schofield, a good player who came in when Groat got hurt, and carried the ballclub. He was a good, gutsy ballplayer. You talk about hotheaded—Lord, he'd throw bats, he'd throw helmets! Or Murtaugh could have pointed to Rocky Nelson, a left-handed-hitting first baseman who batted .300 and hit a few homers while spelling Dick Stuart against tough right-handers. Or Bob Skinner, who had a great swing and was one of the best left-handed hitters I ever saw. Or Hal Smith, another left-handed batter who might have led our team in homers and RBIs if he didn't have to split catching duties with Burgess.

Smoky was the best pinch hitter I ever saw. He was a good hitter when he started, too. It was unbelievable to watch him day in and day out. Smoky was a very quiet, gentle person. Don Hoak used to get on him, but Smoky would just sit there like a teddy bear and grin. We played an exhibition game in Denver and it was freezing. They had to shovel snow off the ground. They had us 4–3 in the ninth but we had a man on second. Smoky was sitting there all bundled up in heavy clothing, and Murtaugh told him to get a bat. Hoak told him, "Fat man, don't swing, just take 3 pitches and we can go home." But on the first damn pitch, Smoky lined a base hit to tie the game and we had to go 14 innings. They always said he could get out of bed Christmas morning and single. I've never seen anything like it. He could hit liners or seeing-eye balls that dribbled through the infield.

If there was one guy who defined the character of the team, it was Don Hoak. Dick Groat was the captain and was a helluva person, but Hoak drove that ballclub. I remember Hoak winning a game for us in the eleventh inning. Nobody knew that he went to our club doctor, Dr. Finegold. He was playing with Dr. Finegold's grandchildren and his foot slipped while climbing out of the pool and he split his toe wide open. He had Finegold sew up his toe. He came early and put his shoes on. When he got the winning double in the eleventh inning he had blood running out of his shoes. Hoak had guts. A normal guy would have never played, but he never missed a game.

Dick Stuart could joke about himself and take ribbing. We called him a crazy fool. He had that don't-give-a-damn attitude. But I know he cared. I remember against the Dodgers I threw a ball over to first and he came walking toward the mound saying, "Don't throw so hard over here, you'll make me look bad." He was serious. He cracked me up, but he made me so mad I wanted to kill him. I really think he was scared to have the ball hit toward him, and it affected him, although he tried not to show it. Dick loved to hit. He hit 3 homers in Forbes Field one game—only Ralph Kiner had done that. Once in Cincinnati, Cal McLish was pitching and we were down by 1 run. Stuart was waiting to be used as pinch hitter if someone got on. He said, "McLish is going to throw that slow curve up there on the second pitch and I'm going to hit it on top of the laundry over the fence." McLish threw a slider away, then came in with the slow curve on the second pitch and Stuart jerked it on top of the damn laundry to win the ball game. He was a good hitter.

I beat Cincinnati. Everyone on our team beat Cincinnati. I was friends with Gordy Coleman, who became the Reds' first baseman in 1960. We had played together in the service. Gordy came in one day and made a reference about the Reds' manager, Freddie Hutchinson. I knew Freddie had a terrible temper and wasn't the type who could tolerate so many losses to the Pirates. Gordy said, "I know you're going to beat us, but for heaven's sakes make it look good."

CINCINNATI REDS

JIM O'TOOLE:

Hutchinson moved me into the starting rotation with Bob Purkey, Jay Hook, and Cal McLish. I started 31 games and pitched almost 200 innings. I went 12–12 for a sixth-place team, finishing behind only Purkey's 17 wins. My ERA went down to 3.80, and after having more walks than strikeouts in 1959, I had almost twice as many strikeouts in 1960. So I felt I was making swift improvement and Hutchinson was gaining confidence in me.

Nobody ever got too close to Hutch, but it was obvious that he didn't like players who got to the park late, ones who wouldn't play hurt. He didn't like Frank Robinson very much. Robinson was a fantastic player and was the only guy I knew who didn't need batting practice and could come out swinging from his ass. But Frank always had tape on his arms and whined and complained. They all liked to be babied a lot. Hutch didn't like that. There was a bit of battle of wills between the two that was divisive on our club. Hutch always won. I remember a series in 1960 in which Robinson just sat and sulked for 3 days and we played without him.

We had picked up Billy Martin in the off-season and I loved him. He had the Napoleon complex many little guys have and always seemed to be in a fight. Someone always wanted to knock him down and he'd always retaliate. But he got along with everyone on our team. He and McLish would go out with a few of us and we never had any problems. The guys I'd hang out with most were Joe Nuxhall and Purkey. Purkey was a very intelligent pitcher who'd pitch a lot of innings and win 16 or 17 games a year, and sometimes more. He was 8 or 9 years older than me.

I got along with Jim Brosnan, but I think most of the players felt negatively toward him. He was a real loner, more than most pitchers were. But he did a good job for us year after year and saved me quite a few games. I usually didn't mind him coming in for me.

JIM BROSNAN:

When *The Long Season* was published, I started getting a lot more attention than was usually accorded a pitcher with my lifetime record. The book was selling and there was debate about whether or not I had gone too far. Gabe Paul, who was in his last year as Reds' GM in 1960 and was still the guy who signed my contracts, questioned the propriety of one incident in which my former teammate Ernie Broglio and I suggested giving each other one good fastball when we batted against each other in one game. Paul said, "That's sort of collusion. It's not acceptable in baseball." As it turned out, and as I explained, when Broglio came up, I was in a situation in which I had to strike him out. He never got any easy fastball. I threw him 3 curveballs and got him out. And when I came up, that's all I got, too. So it never really occurred. But the suggestion that maybe a player would do that was what Paul was warning against. He did not say that I couldn't write anymore about baseball. I wouldn't have stopped even if he told me to.

Fred Hutchinson converted me to a full-time reliever in 1960—against my desire. I finished a couple of games for him and, according to his instructions, went all out for just a couple of innings. I got the side out, and that convinced him. He told me on an off-day and made sure I didn't object by ordering a lot of liquor and telling me to help myself. He pointed out how I always tired in late innings when I started. He said that he wanted me to finish games for him. At that time, there were no such terms as "saves" or "closer." I'd come in whenever the game was close, whether we were ahead, tied, or behind.

Becoming a reliever was well suited to me. I had been one of the slowest workers in the history of the game. I'd often stand with my back to the catcher, and also to the fans, and meditate about the times I'd faced every batter in every type of situation. In the minors the press and fans got on me for making the games too long. As a reliever, I could stop thinking. I no longer felt caught up in the pressure of a situation and the anxiety of stopping someone from scoring. I had to just do it, so my adrenaline stayed high. I'd just say, "I'm going to throw strikes and get the son of a bitch out. And I'm going to use only 4 pitches." Most often it took more pitches, but that was my plan.

Bill Henry and I thought of ourselves as a lefty-righty tandem. Supposedly he would get out left-handed batters and I would get out right-handed batters. But because of pinch hitters, our success was due to his ability to get out right-handed batters by hitting the outside corner and my ability to get out left-handed hitters with a slider up and in. When they left a left-handed batter in against Henry, he'd eat them up. Eddie Mathews never got so much as a loud foul off him. He'd strike out Mathews on 3 pitches. In 1960 I was 7–2 with a 2.36 ERA and 12 saves, while Henry was 1–5 with a higher ERA but more saves. What is strange is that we never said anything to each other either in the bullpen or after one of us did anything in a particular game. "Gabby" just didn't talk. It's hard to talk to a guy who doesn't talk, but we did work well together.

My roommate was Billy Martin, who played second for us only in 1960. He was a very nice man. He was happily married to Gretchen at the time. That was a pretty good year for him, except for the game in which he thought Jim Brewer, a rookie with the Cubs, was throwing at him and went out to the mound and broke his jaw with a punch. That eventually cost Billy $30,000. He'd accusingly say to me, "How can you drink gin? And how can you drink so much of that shit?" I'd had only three martinis—which was heavy for me—but that was an awful lot to him. Billy thought he could drink, but after a couple of drinks he was drunk. Unfortunately, he ran around with groups that drank a lot and he'd try to keep up. There was a lot of drinking in baseball but it was of the 4-or-5-drink variety and there weren't a lot of falling-down drunks.

My former Cubs roommate Lee Walls and I were reunited for a while in 1960 before he was traded again. He backed up Wally Post in left. We'd still head out at night for a lot of fancy restaurants so he could try to smoothtalk us inside—like Tony's in San Francisco. Among the restaurants I'd go to with Lee or on my own were Stan Musial's place, Stan and Bigie's, in St. Louis; Danny's in Pittsburgh; and Caproni's, Tony's—for veal marsala—and the Barn, a barbecue place, in Cincinnati. I usually didn't go where other players went. I was never a big meat eater, so I would go to restaurants that had fish of some sort. Most ballplayers were meat eaters, though some would have an occasional lobster.

I was friends with Jay Hook, a smart guy. He pitched over 200 innings and won 11 games, behind only Bob Purkey and Jim O'Toole on our team. Of the 3 talented young pitchers on the Reds—Hook, Jim Maloney, and O'Toole—I predicted that Hook was going to be the best. Which proves my eye for talent.

AMERICAN LEAGUE 1960

"I WAS A FRINGE PLAYER, SO I NEVER WAS COMFORTABLE ENOUGH TO MOVE MY FAMILY TO DETROIT. MY WIFE THOUGHT I WAS THE MOST NEGATIVE PERSON IN THE WORLD. I WASN'T COCKY. I WASN'T OUTGOING OR OUTSPOKEN, AND I NEVER TRIED TO STIR UP ANYTHING. I JUST WANTED AN OPPORTUNITY TO PLAY AND PROVE MYSELF."

COOT VEAL

CLEVELAND INDIANS

MUDCAT GRANT:
Frank Lane had put together an excellent team that almost won the pennant in 1959, and then he proceeded to dismantle it. He traded Minnie Minoso to the White Sox and Cal McLish and Billy Martin to the Reds after the 1959 season. Then he made it even worse with his celebrated trade of homer champion Rocky Colavito, who was our most popular player, to the Tigers for batting champion Harvey Kuenn two days before the two teams played on Opening Day. I don't know what Lane was thinking about. There was no way we could make up for the loss of 200 RBIs and a 19-game winner. We got Johnny Temple from Cincinnati and he wasn't a bad ballplayer, but he wasn't worth McLish and Martin and had only a couple of years left. And though Kuenn was a great ballplayer, he wasn't an RBI man.

Not surprisingly, we dropped from first to fifth in the league in runs scored and slumped to fourth place, 21 games behind New York. The pitchers didn't get enough support. It was Lane's fault, but his solution was a mid-season trade of his manager, Joe Gordon, for the Tigers' manager, Jimmy Dykes.

VIC POWER:
Minnie Minoso was traded back to Chicago after the 1959 season in a deal that brought us catcher Johnny Romano and third baseman Bubba Phillips. So when I didn't room with Mudcat, I now roomed with Walter Bond, a likable guy from Tennessee. He was about 6'7" and very strong. He would snore and I'd throw pillows at him to wake him up. He'd sit up and look around and not know what happened. I once recorded his snoring and played it over the loudspeaker in the clubhouse.

We had a lot of players coming and going, but the biggest mistake was trading Colavito. We didn't have anyone who could take his place. I even batted cleanup a lot of the time. I had 84 RBIs, which was my career-best, but I wish someone else on the team had more because we needed it. We had a lot of good hitters but no RBI men, and so our pitching slumped, with the exception of Jim Perry.

I thought it was strange when Frank Lane traded managers. Gordon liked my style and used me at almost every position in the batting order and played me all over the infield. That year I made the All-Star team as a utility infielder—he knew I could play second, short, and third, where I never made an error.

Jimmy Dykes wasn't like Gordon. He was like an army sergeant. He was the only manager I didn't get along with. Once, at a rest stop, I thought it was okay to order some food, but Dykes got furious because we'd stopped only to use the bathroom. And we started yelling at each other. He always tried to intimidate me. He once fined me for missing midnight curfew when all I did was step outside the hotel at 3 A.M. to watch a lunar eclipse. Once he fined a few of us for trying to sneak in at 1 A.M. after bowling. He was usually easy to sneak past because he was an old man and would fall asleep in the lobby, but that night he got the elevator boy to flatter us into autographing a baseball so he could see who got in late.

Dykes did help me once with some good advice. I was getting upset that when I caught one-handed—which I did at every position I played—Mickey Mantle or someone else would scream that I was a "hot dog," "clown," or "son of a bitch." I told Jimmy that I was going to try to catch everything with two hands so people wouldn't be mad at me. He then told me something I never forgot: "Don't argue with success." He explained that the only reason those guys hated my style was that I beat them with it. So because of Dykes I kept using one hand, although sportswriters called me a showboat and opposing players and fans cursed me. My psychology was: I'm not going to be the way people want me to be.

Once Mel Allen, the Yankee broadcaster, asked me to catch a ball with two hands in a game against the Yankees. He said he wanted to announce before the game that I promised to do it. So I did it and he was so excited on the air, announcing, "Vic Power caught the ball with two hands!"

All the Yankees respected my talent, but some didn't like my style of play. Mantle didn't like me. He thought he deserved special treament because he was Mickey Mantle, and when I picked him off first, he didn't think I was supposed to do that. And when I took an extra base on him because I had read he had a bad hand, he cursed me for taking advantage of him. I told Mantle I didn't like that he made all that money and wouldn't run out

Vic Power drove in a career-high 84 runs for the Cleveland Indians in 1960 as he tried to make up for the loss of traded slugger Rocky Colavito.

grounders. So I pretended to accidentally miss first with my foot. Then all the Yankees would yell for Mantle to race down the line and he'd have to do it—only to see me tag the base just before he got there. Oh, that made him mad. There were two photographs taken that showed Mantle and me at first base. In the first he was lying on the ground injured because something cracked or pulled when he was running to first and I was leaning over trying to help him; in the second, I was lying on the ground injured after he ran into me and he was standing on the bag, looking the other way.

Hank Bauer, who was traded to Kansas City in 1960, had been the toughest Yankee. He was an ex-Marine and would scare you. He would deliberately step on my heel when he crossed first base. He broke six pairs of my shoes!

Yogi Berra was a good guy, but he was tricky. When I came up to bat, Yogi Berra would ask me about my family, and by the time I finished answering, I'd have 3 strikes.

I loved Casey Stengel. He told me that he wished I had been a Yankee, because I hit my best against the Yankees. I drove him crazy by doing anything it took to win: I'd bunt, sacrifice, hit-and-run, go for the long ball. I used to hit his pitchers pretty good, so they'd throw at me. That would just make me more aggressive, so he'd shout, "Don't wake him up!" He also knew I was a bad-ball hitter, so he'd tell his pitchers, "Just throw strikes!"

Casey was my friend, but I had problems with Chicago's Al Lopez, although I thought he was a great manager. Minoso had told me that Lopez had trouble with black players. He also didn't like Latin players and wouldn't let them speak Spanish. Both times Lopez managed Minoso, he traded him. Now Bill Veeck had brought back Minoso to Chicago—but Lopez would get rid of him after two years. Veeck wanted me, too, but Lopez didn't. When I became a teammate of Mike Garcia on the Indians in 1958, I asked him why he used to throw at my shins all the time when Lopez was his manager. He told me that Lopez instructed him never to throw at black players' heads because they had good reflexes. In my career, I was hit on the head and in my face, but the most frightened I ever got was in 1960 when I was hit in the back by Dick Donovan, who was pitching for Lopez. It was so painful. I stayed in the game and later homered, but I was so mad. I called Lopez some names and challenged him to come out.

I didn't realize that Lopez was going to be my All-Star team manager a couple of weeks later. I told a sportswriter, "I'll bet I don't play." The night before the game in Kansas City, I flew out of Cleveland to catch a connecting flight the next day in Chicago. In Chicago, I ate at a Puerto Rican place at around 4 A.M., and it was chilly. I caught a cold. We flew into Kansas City and it was about 100 degrees. By game time I had a bad fever. Lopez told me that after introductions, I should just go into the clubhouse for the game. So I went inside and took off all my clothes and listened to the game on the radio. But around the sixth inning, with 2 men on base, Lopez sent the trainer to get me to pinch-hit. I was so scared because I wasn't dressed and was too sick to play. The next day there was a big headline in the Chicago papers: "Vic Power Didn't Want to Play in the All-Star Game Because He Had a Bet." I had to fly to New York and talk to Ford Frick, the commissioner. I explained that my bet wasn't serious, but just like "I bet I have more hair on my head than you." Frick was losing his hair and he laughed at my joke. The next day there was another big headline. It didn't say, "Vic Power Is Clear." It said, "The Boy Is Clear." You see: that's my story.

My hobby was photography, and I had the best baseball photo collection because I'd take my camera to All-Star Games and everywhere else. I'd also have my picture taken with such people as Ty Cobb, Connie Mack, and Satchel Paige. I had a picture of me with Fidel Castro that was taken in Cuba. I also posed with John Kennedy when he was in Detroit for a convention and stayed at the same hotel as the players.

MINNIE MINOSO (WHITE SOX):
Vic Power was one of the best photographers I have ever seen. No other baseball player ever took such beautiful pictures. I told him he could become a millionaire if he became a professional photographer.

V. POWER:
I got to play with Don Newcombe for the only time. That was exciting because he was one of the pioneers. He was the first great black pitcher in the major leagues. Supposedly, he drank a lot, but I didn't notice. We weren't together for very long. I still remembered him for fooling me in my first All-Star at-bat in 1955.

DON NEWCOMBE:
I played with Vic Power briefly on Cleveland, but my biggest memory of him was when he was on Kansas City and the Dodgers played against them in an exhibition game. Vic was running to second base and didn't slide, or slid late, and our shortstop, Don Zimmer, hit him right between the eyes on a throw to first. Zimmer could throw a ball as hard as anybody. Zimmer said, "I don't know how he's alive. It must be that he was so close to me when I hit him. A little farther away and I would have killed him."

I finished my major league career with the Indians, appearing in about 20 games and winning a couple. I was only 34, but the alcohol had taken its toll. I think it shortened my major league career by about 6 or 7 years. As it was, I had three 20-win seasons and had won 149 games—and had a .623 percentage—despite beginning my career in the Negro Leagues, being kept in the minors 2 or 3 years too long, and losing 2 more prime years to the military. I was Rookie of the Year, the Cy Young Award winner, and the MVP, the only player to win all three awards. I also batted .271 lifetime.

I regret that I didn't take better care of myself in the latter part of my career because I would like to have made the Hall of Fame, where I think I belong. My career might not have been extensive enough, but it's ironic that if I had the exact same statistics just playing in the Negro Leagues, I would likely have qualified. Even so, I even think there should be a special division in the Hall for MVP winners, which is supposed to be the most meaningful award in baseball.

JOHNNY KLIPPSTEIN:

I joined the Indians about a week before the season started. A few days after that, Frank Lane traded Rocky Colavito. Rocky was Cleveland's most popular player, and when the Indians and Tigers opened the season against each other in Cleveland, the stands were packed with unhappy people. After that they stopped coming to games, because Colavito was playing in another city. I never could figure out Cleveland. It was more of a football town. We were only a couple of games out around the All-Star break yet drew only 25,000 to a doubleheader against the Yankees.

I debuted in the American League and I had one of my best years. I pitched only in relief and had an ERA under 3.00. They didn't have a saves stat in those days, but I had the most in the league with 14. I got a lot of work. When Jimmy Dykes became manager, I pitched several games in a brief period and my arm went dead. Jimmy asked me if I could pitch if he needed me. I told him honestly that I couldn't—the only time in my career when I refused to take the ball. He understood. He wasn't a bad guy.

The Indians were a loose team. There were a lot of cardplayers, a few beer drinkers, guys who wanted to have fun. My best friends on the team were Gary Bell, Dick Stigman, and Johnny Romano.

Mudcat Grant and Gary Bell had a strong friendship. They used to kibitz each other unbelievably. It was ra-

cial stuff, and we wondered how they could say such strong, insulting things to each other and get away with it. If they said such things in later years, someone would have had to die.

Vic Power was a good guy and a helluva hitter and first baseman. But he should have been more careful about his language. One game, Ohio State's revered football coach Woody Hayes was at Municipal Stadium with his wife, as guests of the ballclub. Vic Power didn't know this. Vic booted a ball for one of the only times in his career and Woody got on him, inning after inning. In about the fifth inning, Vic walked past and told Woody in graphic terms that he'd had sex with Woody's wife the night before, etc., etc. When the game ended, one of Cleveland's vice presidents came to the clubhouse and asked Vic if he knew who he had insulted. Vic said he didn't care. Then he was told, "That was Woody Hayes, our honored guest."

I didn't know Don Newcombe was an alcoholic. The only thing I noticed was that after 2 innings he was soaking wet. But I didn't associate it with drinking. I usually could look at a guy's face and tell if someone drank, but, at the same time, I didn't really know what an alcoholic was.

Jimmy Piersall was always interesting. My main memory of him was in Detroit when he took some insect repellent out to center field and was spraying the bugs out there while the pitcher was winding up. I remember him tipping his cap to Tiger manager Jimmy Dykes after hitting a home run, and Dykes didn't forget that when he came to the Indians to manage during the season. Piersall had a lot of children, so he put in his contract where he could go home on Mondays when we didn't play. He'd want to get home, so he'd often get thrown out of games on Sundays and leave early. We had a meeting, and Dykes told Piersall that even if he got kicked out of a Sunday game, he had to be in the clubhouse when the game was over. He also told Jimmy that if he broke any more helmets or destroyed any more uniforms he would be charged for them.

Barry Latman was a good guy. He was a high-fastball pitcher, and when he was on, he was great. The only home run I ever saw Ted Williams hit down the left-field line was off Barry.

I was glad to get the opportunity to pitch to Williams before he retired at the end of the year. He batted 5 times against me and didn't have one bad swing. I got him out the first 4 times. Then in the second game of a doubleheader in Cleveland he pinch-hit against me. I made up my mind to throw him all breaking balls and change-ups, except for a first-pitch fastball for a strike. He hit the first pitch out of the ballpark. Sometimes the hitter is a helluva lot smarter than the pitcher.

BARRY LATMAN:
The day after the Indians traded Rocky Colavito to the Tigers, they traded his best friend, Herb Score, another crowd favorite, to the White Sox for me. This was the day before the season started, and I was angered by the trade, but I made it to Cleveland that day. After drawing a big crowd on Opening Day, which we lost to the Tigers in 15 innings, the Indians didn't get many fans for about 2 months. Then in July, when we were leading the league, we attracted fans. That lasted for 2 months, and then nobody came anymore. By that time we were out of the race.

I didn't get to know Frank Lane. I just knew he was fair to me in terms of salary and did things just to create controversy, like trading Colavito for Kuenn and later swapping managers. Dykes was a good manager. He was older and knew how to push the right buttons. He didn't get in your way and bother you. You just played the game for him and didn't see him until the next day.

The Indians were a fun-type team with a lot of drinking and palling around together. Gary Bell made it a close team. He was my roommate, and I had a great time with him. He was funny on the bus, or sitting in the outfield bullshitting. He had a quick wit and was deadly with one-liners. We both got along great with Mudcat Grant, who was a helluva pitcher and the go-between between black and white players. He was friends with Vic Power. Vic was pretty much of a loner and some guys thought him standoffish, but he was a good guy once you got to know him. He was also the greatest first baseman who ever played. He told me not to worry where he was when I fielded a ball: "You throw it and I'll get there." And the son of a gun would do it.

I didn't like Jimmy Piersall. He was disruptive. He liked Vic, but that was about it. He went his own way and you never saw him after a game and never talked to him. He wasn't weird. He just exploited his own reputation for being crazy when he hadn't been sick for years.

I got tired of hearing about it. I was pitching in Yankee Stadium in 1960 or 1961 when people in the stands rushed out at Piersall. I turned around and there was Piersall kicking somebody in the ass. I just laughed.

Our best pitcher that year was Jim Perry, a quiet Southern type. He tied for the league lead with 18 wins. I was in the rotation with him, Grant, and Bell, and my good buddy Dick Stigman would get an occasional start. I thought we all pitched pretty well, but Perry was the only guy to get any wins.

BALTIMORE ORIOLES

BROOKS ROBINSON:
From 1957, off and on, a couple of other players and I rented a three-bedroom house from a lady on Chestnut Avenue, three blocks from Memorial Stadium. Ron Hansen and Chuck Estrada, who had been my roommates at Vancouver in 1959, lived with me all of 1960, until I got married. We were all single, though there were married players who rented there and had their wives stay when they were in town. We were having a ball, playing regularly in the big leagues and having good seasons, and making a run for the pennant. We didn't feel any pressure to do anything. It was a good life. On the road, I roomed with Ronny, who became my best friend in baseball. He was a terrific guy and we liked the same things. He broke in strongly, winning the Rookie of the Year award. Ron hit 22 homers, which was a lot for a shortstop.

I also had my first big year. I hit .294 with 88 RBIs and 50 extra-base hits, and made the All-Star team for the first time, as a backup to Frank Malzone. The team moved up from sixth place to second, and I finished third to Roger Maris and Mickey Mantle in the MVP vote, which was amazing. So I was flying high. When we started playing well was the first time I felt lucky to have signed with the Orioles. However, in hindsight, I figured I was lucky to have joined Baltimore at the beginning of its history and to have had the chance to experience the initial bad times and first years of success. Of the players on the 1955 team I first joined, only Gus Triandos and Gene Woodling, who played for Cleveland from mid-1955 through 1957, were on the 1960 Orioles.

Paul Richards had outstanding scouts and they were always finding good young players, particularly pitchers like Milt Pappas, Chuck Estrada, Steve Barber, Jack Fisher, and Jerry Walker. They were called the "Kiddie Korps." These guys all came in at the time I started to click. Pappas, Barber, the left-hander, Estrada, and Fisher threw as hard as any four guys I ever saw on one team. Yet they had different styles. Pappas, who was in the rotation the earliest, in 1958, had only a fastball and slider, but he had good control and was pretty steady—you could count on him to win about 15 games a year. In 1964, he'd throw 7 shutouts, 3 in a row. Barber could throw up to 95 mph but I thought of him as a sinkerball pitcher. He had below-average control. Steve would lead the league with 8 shutouts and win 18 games in 1961 and would become the Orioles' first 20-game winner in 1963. Estrada was the hardest worker of the pitchers, yet still had control problems. As a rookie in 1960, he tied for the league lead in wins with 18, but after leading the league in losses in 1962, he would be shifted to the bullpen. Fisher had average control. His problem was that he gave up too many hits. Ted Williams hit his final home run off him in 1960, and Roger Maris would hit his 60th homer off him in 1961.

We had a pretty good mesh of young players and veterans like Triandos, Woodling, and Hoyt Wilhelm. Gus was getting his first chance to win. He had come up through the Yankee organization with the thought he'd be the catcher on a championship team, but then he found himself on horrible Orioles teams instead. In 1958 and 1959 he had big home run years, but he hurt his hand in '59 and wasn't the same player. But he was having a decent year at the plate and was enjoying our success as much as the younger guys. Richards also helped him and our other catchers by devising an enormous oversized mitt to catch Wilhelm's knuckler. This was soon after both Gus and Joe Ginsberg set a record with 3 passed balls in one inning because of that knuckler. Gus still hated every minute catching Hoyt. I think it took 5 years off his career.

As a starter, Wilhelm had won 15 games for us in 1959 and led the league in earned run average. Hoyt got a few starts in 1960, but this year Richards converted him permanently into a relief pitcher to make room for the Kiddie Korps. He was kind of the odd man out. Of course, he became a great reliever.

We got Jackie Brandt from the Giants after the 1959 season for Billy O'Dell and Billy Loes. He was a good center fielder with a strong arm and some pop in his bat. He was funny and a real nice guy, but he was strange. He'd perplex Richards even more than Loes did. He had an answer for everything. He was the type who would drive an extra 15 miles to a Howard Johnson's and then order vanilla ice cream. On a 3–2 count, batters don't normally look for change-ups, but once Jackie came back to the dugout after striking out looking, saying, "I got just the pitch I was looking for—the change-up." We asked why he didn't swing and he said, "I was looking for it low and it was high." I think he tried to drive Richards crazy. Brandt had some baseball talent, but I think Richards liked him because he was a very good golfer.

In 1960 we just had fun and didn't feel pressure being in a pennant race. Yet it turned out to be very disappointing. New York came into Baltimore on Labor Day, 2 games ahead of us, and we swept a 3-game series. They left 1 game behind. Soon we went up to New York to play 4 games and we lost them all. They ran off about 14 wins in a row and we finished second. We were young, so we were able to shake it off. The slogan for the next year was "It could be done in '61." We wouldn't do it, but that's what we thought about.

In 1960 I won my first of 16 straight Gold Glove awards, which was very exciting. Had I improved? I do think my arm got stronger from throwing so much. I was now better known for picking up a topped ball and throwing the batter out at first. You can work on that. There are a few tricks to the trade. If the ball is stopped or coming to a stop, you can bare-hand the ball. If it's a slow roller, you try to pick it up with both the gloved hand and bare hand so you can throw on your next step. The other thing is to get a decent angle to throw so you don't have to throw all the way across your body. As I gained more experience, I was given carte blanche on positioning most of the time. Richards played pretty much by the book. For instance, I'd move close to the line in the late innings to protect against the double. But things would depend on who was pitching, who was hitting, who was running. The same was true with whether I played in or deep. The guys who were the hardest to defense hit the ball my way and could run fast. Al Kaline and Minnie Minoso were difficult because you couldn't play them as deep as you would a slower power hitter like Harmon Killebrew.

In 1955 I played winter baseball in South America. In the 1956 off-season I went back to college at Little Rock University, as a business major. In 1957 I played winter ball in Cuba. In 1958 I went to college. In 1959 I went in the army. In 1960 I got married.

GENE WOODLING:

I had some of my best years after I passed 35. I had some good years with the Yankees and Indians, but I think my best years were the three I spent in Baltimore, ending in 1960. At 38, I played 124 games in the outfield and hit .283, just a point below what would be my career average. Oddly, on the expansion Senators the next year, my average would go up 30 points!

BOSTON RED SOX

FRANK MALZONE:

This was Ted Williams's last year, and it was fitting that he rebounded to hit over .300 again and hit 29 homers in just over 300 at-bats. He was excited when he homered in his final at-bat against Baltimore's Jack Fisher. The wind was blowing in from right field at Fenway Park that day and it was hard to hit one out. He hit 2 other balls that game that went too high and died in the outfield. Then he hit a line drive that he knew was gone. He gave that familiar skip-hop of his and took that professional run around the bases. He figured that Pinky Higgins, who was back managing after replacing his replacement, Billy Jurges, at mid-season, would just let him go to the clubhouse. But Hig sent him back to left field and then replaced him with a sub, Carroll Hardy, so that the fans would have a chance to give Ted an ovation. He ran in and tipped his hat to the fans, and then disappeared into the runway. He didn't come out again to acknowledge the fans. By the time we came in to congratulate him he was halfway to the clubhouse. We didn't make it into a big deal. Ted didn't want that.

Despite Ted's super final season, Vic Wertz driving in over 100 runs, and Pete Runnels winning his first batting title, the Red Sox dropped to seventh place, the team's worst finish in many years. Pitching was our worst problem—Bill Monbouquette was our only starter with a winning record—but we also missed Jackie Jensen, who stayed out the year rather than fly. My stats were down slightly, but I had a fair year with 14 homers and 79 RBIs. By this time I had evolved into a pull hitter to take advantage of Fenway Park.

I didn't win the Gold Glove in 1960, as Brooks Robinson claimed it permanently. I fielded well, but I made an occasional error. Luckily, the fans left me alone. I was well liked in the Boston area. Considering I never played on a pennant winner, I received much recognition from New England fans and press. Playing in several All-Star Games helped. The way I did the job made me the type of player Boston fans liked, and I never had to worry about going on the field and hearing the boo birds.

Don Buddin was the guy who caught it more than anybody. He was on the Red Sox for about 5 years and was booed all the time for making errors at short. Buddin told me it didn't bother him, but I know I wouldn't have wanted to be booed just for stepping on the field. By this time we were drawing only 15,000 to 20,000 fans and you could hear every heckler. They used to give it to him pretty good, and I used to stand on third thinking, "I'm glad it's you, Don." Eventually they ran him out of Boston. I felt sorry for him.

New England fans loved the Red Sox, and even the elite would come to watch us play. When John Kennedy was a Massachusetts senator, he and Bobby came to a game at Fenway Park. They sat right in front of the boxes with the players' wives. My wife was just two rows behind them, thinking John wasn't a bad-looking guy. The score was tied late in the ballgame and I came up. My wife later told me that she overheard John tell Bobby, "If this guy doesn't do it, we're not going to win, so we might as well go home." I hit one off the wall and we won the ball game. John turned to Bobby and said, "See, I told you."

BILL MONBOUQUETTE:

I officially became the ace of the staff, as Higgins pitched me in over 200 innings and against all the other top pitchers, like Whitey Ford in New York, Jim Bunning and Frank Lary in Detroit, Bud Daley in Kansas

City, and Billy Pierce and Early Wynn in Chicago. I went 14–11 and made my first All-Star team.

I started the first All-Star Game at Municipal Stadium in Kansas City. We lost 5–3 and I was the losing pitcher. I didn't pitch well. When people asked me what went wrong, I'd joke, "Yogi was putting down the wrong signs." Of course, what happened is that I threw a fastball over the plate to Ernie Banks and hung a curve to Del Crandall and they deposited them in the parking lot behind the left-field fence. It was still a thrill. We had a second game two days later in New York, and I cherished the camaraderie between the players on the plane trip. That first game was a bummer for me and I was sitting in the lobby of the hotel thinking about what went wrong when Stan Musial came over and said, "We're going to eat, come along." I always admired Stan because he wasn't just a great player but was also a very nice man. He was on the National League team but he still was that kind to me. He even treated everyone to dinner. That was the kind of thing I'd never forget.

I was in the bullpen when Ted Williams homered in his last at-bat, his 521st homer. We all knew that he was going to finish his career that game in Boston instead of going with the team for the final 3 games in New York. He hit 3 balls that game that the wind held up. It was blowing in real hard. So we watched what we knew would be his last time at bat. Ted got hold of a pitch and hit a screamer. And we're going, "Wow! Holy Christ! What a way to end a career!" The ball flew toward the bullpen and hit the overhanging roof. I could have caught it, but I didn't even think of doing that. I was too awed. I turned to one of the other players and said, "Only Ted Williams could do that."

PUMPSIE GREEN:

We weren't having winning years, but the players weren't depressed. We played ball and had fun, although it wasn't a party atmosphere. A few guys ran together, mostly roommates, but a lot of the guys went their own ways. Earl Wilson and I were roommates each time he was brought up to the majors. Naturally. In those days, if a team had 3 blacks and 2 were roommates, the third one would be sent back to the minors. It was two by two. Earl and I hung around together. We did a lot of cardplaying and saw a lot of movies, espe-

cially in New York. I didn't hang out with anybody on the Red Sox except for Earl.

For the most part, I didn't mix with the white players. I didn't eat with them or sleep with them. We were separate. The only interaction we had was on the ballfield. But I did go out a couple of times with Frank Malzone and Pete Runnels, who were as fine gentlemen as you ever wanted to meet. One time in Kansas City, Ted and I were joking around before a game, and I bet him a dinner I would have a better day. Sure enough, he took me out to dinner.

Ted was interesting to watch at the end of his career. Even then he was probably the greatest hitter who ever stepped up to home plate. He was probably even better than his reputation. He was Ted Williams, the "best hitter in baseball." And if you didn't believe me, you could have asked him and he would have told you the same thing. He could concentrate so much harder than the average person. If the average player was going to bat 4 times in a game and got hits his first 3 times up, he'd be satisfied even if he failed the fourth time up. He'd relax after the third hit. Ted was his most vicious his fourth time up. That's what set him apart. I wasn't surprised when he homered in his last time at bat. He could do almost anything he wanted to do. That was Ted Williams.

WASHINGTON SENATORS

HARMON KILLEBREW:

I struck out a lot—and would even set a record one year—but it didn't bother or embarrass me. I never changed my batting stance. I stood close to the plate and was a pull hitter, so managers often put a shift on me. Lou Boudreau was the first to do that to me when he was managing Kansas City in the mid-'50s. I think I could have been a .300 hitter, but I decided early on that I was helping the club more driving in a lot of runs than going for a high average. In 1959 I hit only .242 but I drove in 105 runs. In 1960 my average went up to .276, and though I was hurt and batted 100 less times, I still hit 31 homers and drove in 80 runs. What helped the most is that I cut down on my swing to make it more compact.

There was no point where I said, "I'm now an established major leaguer," but after a couple of good years, I felt respected. Still, it always bothered me that I had a rep for being a bad fielder. When you come into the league they categorize you as good or bad and never alter that. At an early age I was not a good third baseman. However, I worked hard and became good, although I would never get the recognition. Maybe that's because in 1960 Cookie Lavagetto started moving me between third and first. When I played third, left-handed hitters Julio Becquer and rookie Don Mincher played first, and when I played first, Reno Bertoia played third. Shifting back and forth was hard mostly because it was hard to use different gloves.

Griffith Stadium was a nice old stadium. It was kind of like Fenway and Briggs Stadium in that the fans were close to the field. In those days the crowds were so small that faces seemed familiar. The old story went: "Somebody called the park and asked, 'What time's the game?' and the operator said, 'Well, what time can you get here?' " I really think the fans were supportive considering we weren't a winning ballclub. After the 1960 season I was home in Idaho when I found out that the Senators were moving to Minnesota. So we never even had the chance to say good-bye to Washington.

PEDRO RAMOS:

I got married in 1960 to a nice girl from Cuba, a beauty queen. I was just 25. After I married her, I felt like a caged tiger. I was too young to know the responsibility of being married. I was still going out, but not as much.

Early in my career, I thought I could get everyone out with my fastball. If I'd been smarter, I would have monkeyed around instead of always challenging batters when I got ahead. I became a better pitcher when I learned the sinker. I still threw hard, in the 90s, but I had another strikeout pitch. I developed a good sinker by throwing the spitter. Then I didn't need to throw the spitball anymore. But they still thought that everything that moved was my spitball. I held the sinker in the same position and threw it with a three-quarters motion, and it moved pretty good. Once I struck out J. C. Martin on a sinker and he complained to Ed Runge that it was a spitball. And Runge checked my uniform and made me change.

I participated in the only all-Cuban triple play with Jose Valdivielso and Julio Becquer. I should remember exactly what happened, but I don't. But I think it was one of the team's best fielding plays all season. Our problem was defense. It didn't matter what kind of pitchers we had because if we gave up 3 earned runs our defense added 3 unearned runs. I told Jim Lemon, "If I won as many games as balls you drop in left field, I'd be the best pitcher in the American League." He said, "You goddamn Cuban, I'll kill you." Lemon was a great hitter—he had 38 homers and 100 RBIs that year—but not much of a fielder. I remember one game in Washington I was leading the Yankees 3–0 with 2 outs in the ninth. Yogi hit a grounder between first and second, and though it was the second baseman's ball, the first baseman went after it. I break a little late and the guy beats it out. Two outs, man on, so what? Then Mickey hit a grounder through my legs. Then Skowron hit a grounder right at our shortstop, Jose Valdivielso, right between his legs. So it was 3–1, with runners on the corners and Elston Howard up as a pinch hitter. He hit a line drive to left. Lemon ran in and tried to catch it underhanded, and the ball hit his knee. He chased it to the foul line. Somehow he got the ball back to Valdivielso near third base, and Jose got the ball and threw it right into the stands. You talk about bad defense. It was unbelievable. If I would have pitched with the Yankees, I would have won 18 to 19 games a year.

I don't remember being the last Washington Senators pitcher, on October 2, 1960, against Baltimore. But I lost in the typical way, 2–1.

I was friends with Vice President Richard Nixon. He suggested that I become a U.S. citizen. Once, before I pitched on Opening Day, he sent me a telegram wishing me luck. And I lost. After that he sent me another telegram that said, "You can't win them all." When he ran for President in 1960, I sent him a telegram to wish him luck. When he lost, I sent him another telegram that said, "You can't win them all."

HAL WOODESHICK:

For the first time in the majors, I began a season with the team I finished with in the previous season. And for the first time I stayed an entire season in the majors. Consequently, I pitched more than I had before, starting and relieving in more than 40 games and pitching 115 innings. I thought I did a fair job with Ray Moore and Tex Clevenger in the bullpen.

The team continued to improve, moving out of the cellar into fifth place in its last year in Washington. Although he didn't make a real contribution in 1960, Jim Kaat was brought up. He became my roommate. We were well matched because we were both tall left-handers. We called him "Kitty Kat." He struggled, but he was just 21, and I knew he'd do well once he had some experience. He had talent and was a very smart and confident pitcher.

Living in Washington wasn't bad, but Griffith Stadium was an old park in a slum area. My wife didn't go to many games because it was dangerous, both driving to the park and sitting in it. She came to one game with Pete Whisenant's wife. Pete made an error in the outfield and some fans responded by pouring beer on his wife's head. It got nasty there—especially during one Sunday doubleheader against the Yankees when they were scoring 100 runs and it was 100 degrees and the fans were drinking beer. I remember some fans ripping out seats from the stands.

Pete Whisenant was a character. One time in early August we were scheduled to play a night game against the White Sox in Chicago. That afternoon Harmon, Bob Allison, Pete, and I went over to see the Cubs play at Wrigley Field against the Reds. We spoke to Billy Martin before the game in the Reds' clubhouse, and he said he was fed up with getting knocked on his ass every time up now that he was in the National League. He swore, "Somebody's going to pay." That game Jim Brewer pitched too close to him and he went out to the mound and broke Brewer's jaw. After the rumble on the field, the four of us went into the locker room. The phone was ringing, and Pete picked up the phone and told the reporter on the other end that he was Billy Martin. The writer asked, "Did you mean to hit him?" And Pete said, "Yeah, and I would have liked to have hit him again!" After that we worried we'd have to testify in court at Martin's trial that it had been Pete and not Billy on the phone that day.

The Senators always got into fights. We'd be way behind and then one of our pitchers would throw way inside and that would do it. We'd all have to run onto the field and pull everyone apart. Camilo Pascual started a lot of those fights because he pitched inside all the time. One of our coaches, Clyde McCullough, the former catcher, said, "I'm getting tired of getting the hell kicked out of me trying to stop these fights. We ought to form a circle and let the suckers stay in there."

DETROIT TIGERS

COOT VEAL:

Detroit was a good team, but it was the wrong team for me. I needed to have been with the Yankees or another power-hitting team who could carry a low-hitting, good-fielding shortstop. The Tigers tried to give Kaline and Maxwell some power support before the season by trading Harvey Kuenn for Rocky Colavito. Harvey had grown up playing in Detroit and had been a good player for several years. Of course, Colavito was a good player, too, but if you get rid of your own it creates a little ill feeling. People in Detroit were upset by the deal, just as they were upset in Cleveland.

Sportswriter Joe Falls was very critical of Colavito and other individuals, and the team as a whole. He'd keep track of the runs Rocky did *not* drive in. A lot of guys disliked him, and finally he was barred from the clubhouse. He may have been right in his criticism. The press had no reason to talk to me except to ask about someone else, so I had good relations with them—including Joe Falls.

Detroit's frequent managerial changes may have had to do with why the team didn't finish high despite having good talent. We never had a manager who could teach us how to be winners. Jimmy Dykes and his replacement, Joe Gordon, couldn't do it. Gordon knew me a bit because he was a hitting instructor in 1953 at spring training. But by this time Chico Fernandez was the Tigers' shortstop, having come over from Philadelphia. He wasn't a bad player, but he led the league in errors.

That year I roomed with Charlie Maxwell. "Paw Paw" was funny, down-to-earth. He was easy to get along with and easy to know. The right-field porch in Detroit wasn't hard to reach for left-handed hitters, so he had a lot of big games there. I don't know why he hit so many of his homers on Sunday. Maybe it was because we played doubleheaders, and if you gave Charlie between 8 and 10 at-bats in a day, especially in Briggs Stadium, there was a good chance he'd hit a homer or two.

The Tigers picked up another left-handed power hitter when they got Norm Cash to play first base. Chicago had just traded him to Cleveland and we got him before the season. He was a young pull hitter with a pretty swing, so I could tell immediately that he was going to have productive years in our ballpark. With Cash and Colavito, the Tigers were finally going to have the power that they had sorely missed. But I wasn't going to be on the team.

I had fun in Detroit, but there were always pressures because I wasn't a .300 hitter or a power hitter. I always felt there was someone behind me ready to take my place. For that reason, if I had a minor injury, I wouldn't ask out of the lineup. I was a fringe player, so I never was confident enough to permanently move my family to Detroit. My wife thought I was the most negative person in the world. I wasn't cocky. I wasn't outgoing or outspoken, and I never tried to stir up anything. I just wanted an opportunity to play and prove myself. Unfortunately, I never got it in Detroit.

CHICAGO WHITE SOX

BARRY LATMAN:

I wasn't with the White Sox long enough to warm up to Al Lopez. I was sent to the Indians for Herb Score before the 1960 season. I was madder than hell when I was traded. My father had passed away in 1959, and my mother and my youngest sister had bought a house in Gary, Indiana, to be near me in Chicago. Then, on the day before our season opener, I was getting a haircut when it came across the air that I had been traded that morning. That's how I found out. I was very perturbed.

MINNIE MINOSO:

Bill Veeck had wanted me back on the White Sox as soon as he acquired the team in 1959. After the season, he got me in a 7-player deal. I was welcomed back to Chicago after two years in Cleveland. I hit 2 home runs in the first game, the first with the bases loaded and the

After two years in Cleveland, the ageless Minnie Minoso returned to the White Sox in 1960, hitting 2 of his eventual 20 homers on his first day back, driving in 105 runs, and leading the league with 184 hits.

other with one on in the bottom of the ninth to win the game, 10–8. It was a festive day.

I felt that I was back home and had one of my best years. I batted .311, had 20 home runs, drove in 105 runs, the second-most in my career, and led the league with 184 hits. They said I was old, but I played all 154 games.

AL SMITH:

I was friends with Minnie Minoso. He played on the New York Cubans in the Negro National League when I was on the Cleveland Buckeyes. We played against each other in the 1947 Negro World Series. Then we were roommates on San Diego in the Coast League in 1950. We stayed friends, even after we were traded for each other in 1957. He was always a happy-go-lucky guy. If anything bothered him, he kept it inside. He just loved to go to the park and play baseball. He played left field and I moved to right. We did good together. I found my stroke and hit .315 and Minnie hit .311—after Pete Runnels's .320, we were second and third in the league.

Bill Veeck installed an exploding scoreboard in Comiskey Park and I was our first player to set off the fireworks and music with a homer. It came off Jim Bunning, and Nellie Fox wasn't too happy about it. Nellie usually batted behind Aparicio but that day he batted after me and he knew he was going down because Bunning wasn't too happy with my homer or the exploding scoreboard.

JIM LANDIS:

During the off-season my wife and I returned to Richmond, California, where, in my first couple of years in the big leagues, I worked in a bathtub factory to make ends meet. Luckily, my job wasn't hard. I just shifted the tubs from one line to another by using some kind of instrument. During the season we lived on Chicago's South Side at 51st and Hyde Park. If I had a night game, I might not get home until 1 A.M. I'd get up with my kids to play with them instead of sleeping late. So, as the season progressed, I got more tired than the single guys. It was a tougher life for my wife in that when I went on the road, she stayed home with the kids.

After the World Series, a new regime came in. Hank Greenberg came back into our system as a GM. I thought I had a great year in 1959, so I wasn't going to sign the contract I was offered. All I wanted was $2,000 more. Greenberg coaxed me into coming to Florida to sign. When I got there he more or less said, "Sign or else." I either had to pay my way back home to California or sign. I thought that was one of the dirtiest things that ever happened to me. I lost a little heart for the White Sox because of that treatment. Most clubs were stingy in those days, but the White Sox were a little bit stingier.

Players never talked about each other's salaries. Most players didn't have salary gripes. The only time it got comical is when we cut up our World Series shares

at the end of the year. People would complain that guys who played only half a year were getting too much. There would be a big debate. Fox was always trying to get players full shares if they made contributions. He'd say, "You goddamn guys, don't you realize it's only about $30 out of your pocket?" Nellie made $60,000— he deserved it.

I don't think we were treated like celebrities. There wasn't a lot of sponsorship, we weren't seen on television, we weren't promoted. We got only $200 to pose for baseball cards. Cards weren't a real big deal. I got very few endorsements. I had a great one with Camel cigarettes. Then the government got after athletes doing cigarette commercials. Nellie had about three or four good endorsements. He had that one for Red Fox Chewing Tobacco.

Nellie would yell every once in a while that the Cubs got more ink than us. But we had to worry about our own league—why worry about the Cubs? I didn't think there was a rivalry between the White Sox and Cubs. I think the media was fair to the White Sox. Jerome Holtzman was a great booster of mine. Most reporters were pretty good. At the time sportwriters wrote about baseball as a game. They didn't go beyond what was needed.

The Cubs fans were more vocal, but I thought White Sox fans were great, knowledgeable baseball fans. We were recognized on the street and it was fun to sign autographs. The Sox were strict about when you could sign autographs at the ballpark. You'd get fined if you did it at the wrong time, or even talked to fans. It felt great having a fan club. A couple of girls, who were about 12 or 13, asked permission to form a club for me. Of course I said yes. I'd go meet the members every once in a while and answer baseball questions. They kept scrapbooks of my career.

The White Sox became the first team to have names on the backs of uniforms. And we made more important changes. A lot of our young guys, like Johnny Callison and Norm Cash, were dealt away because the team wanted more power, and later it turned out Callison and Cash had power. I was upset. Nellie and Sherm Lollar were even more upset that they broke up something that was pretty good and gave away our promising youth at the same time. I felt confident that I wouldn't be traded. My average went down a bit in 1960 but I had 10 homers and 25 doubles, and scored a career-high 89 runs and stole a career-high 23 bases. Plus, I won my first Gold Glove.

When Herb Score came to the White Sox for Barry Latman, we got to know each other while barnstorming in exhibition games. We hit it off real well. There was no one classier than Herb. To have gone through what he did and to have taken it so well impressed me. Lopez and Ray Berres worked night and day with the poor kid, trying to find his old delivery. He could throw as hard as he once did on occasion, but he had no consistency. I never thought of Herb in terms of religion. He'd have his drink and his swearwords. He was an everyday good person. I didn't even look at him as a church person—which I hope he was.

I thought we had a good chance to win another pennant, and we were even in first place as late as the middle of August. But then we fell slightly behind the Yankees and Orioles. We had a key game against Baltimore at the end of August that we should have won but lost because of the umpires. We were behind by two runs in the eighth or ninth inning and Ted Kluszewski hit a 3-run pinch homer off Milt Pappas. But while he was rounding the bases, the umpires announced that they had called time out because a couple of our players were warming up in the wrong place. So we lost two games in the standings and never recovered.

BILLY PIERCE:
The club hoped that we'd repeat as American League champions, so it went after some veterans. We got great years from both the returning Minnie Minoso and first baseman Roy Sievers, and third baseman Gene Freese hit pretty well. But we finished a disappointing third. In the process we got rid of much of the team's future. Most of our young prospects were traded away, like Norm Cash, Johnny Romano, Johnny Callison, and Earl Battey. We were really surprised about Battey because we thought he was going to be Sherm Lollar's successor. Cash could have solved our first-base problems. He was a good hitter—you couldn't get a fastball by him. A lot of us were second-guessing management.

I went 14–7 that year, while Wynn, Shaw, Frank Baumann, and reliever Gerry Staley tied for second in wins with 13. Baumann, a left-hander we picked up from Boston, led the league in earned run average.

NEW YORK YANKEES

BOB TURLEY:
The Yankees came back to win the pennant. Roger Maris was a great addition. He was the league's RBI leader and MVP, just nosing out Mantle, who edged him in the homer race. We got good years from a lot of guys, including the starting pitchers: Whitey Ford, me, Art Ditmar, Ralph Terry, and Jim Coates.

JIM LANDIS (WHITE SOX):
The Yankee pitchers were sneaky. Bob Turley would throw inside but not out of meanness. But Jim Coates was a bugger.

MINNIE MINOSO (WHITE SOX):
I don't want to name the pitchers who threw at me on purpose . . . but if you guessed Jim Coates, I wouldn't say you were wrong.

JOHNNY KLIPPSTEIN (INDIANS):
Coates was one of the few pitchers who would deliberately throw at a batter's head. I couldn't condone that. Pitchers tried to get him but never got him good. I wouldn't have felt sorry for him.

VIC POWER (INDIANS):
Jim Coates was a bad guy. He used to throw at me all the time. But I got back at him—I hit 4 home runs off him, and I knew he wouldn't forget because they occurred on holidays.

B. TURLEY:
I still didn't get as much work as I wanted, though I pitched about 20 more innings and wound up with a 9–3 record.

It wasn't really surprising that Stengel was let go after the 1960 season. The club had a policy that you had to retire at 70. George Weiss, the general manager, also retired although he was a little younger. I respected Weiss tremendously because he knew how to run a ballclub. I couldn't say I liked him because I didn't get to know him. Nobody did.

JOE DE MAESTRI:

I went to spring training with the Yankees. Putting on a Yankee uniform for the first time was like "What am I doing here?" This was the team to be with. I looked around and there was Mickey Mantle, Yogi Berra, Whitey Ford, Bill Skowron, and my locker happened to be right next to Gil McDougald's and Yogi Berra's. Of course, we knew each other because of all my years with the A's. They made me feel part of the team. They also told me words I'd never forget: "Joe, remember one thing. When you walk on that field, you are screwing around with my money." You talk about pride.

I know Mickey had the highest salary at $100,000 or maybe $110,000. I think Whitey and Yogi were in the $50,000 to $60,000 range. I don't think there was resentment. In those days hardly anyone made a lot of money. On the Yankees, if you were dissatisfied with your contract they'd tell you, "Don't worry, you're going to pick up World Series money in October."

I thoroughly enjoyed playing for Casey Stengel, especially after playing against him and hearing so much about him. The man was a tremendous psychologist because he could get you to play when you were hurt. He knew he could do that with Mantle. After Mickey had a tough night or something, Casey would walk over to him with his head down and say, "Well, I guess you don't want to play today," and walk away. And Mickey would follow him right into the office, telling him, "You put me in that lineup, Casey. You put me in that lineup." And Casey'd say, "If you want me to." I definitely think Mantle, Maris, and Berra respected him. He treated everybody the right way. There were no favorites with Casey, no special rules for guys like Ford and Mantle.

My roommate on the road was Bill Skowron, a helluva guy. In New York, before my wife came east, I lived with Tony Kubek at the Stadium Motor Lodge at 161st Street, right by Yankee Stadium. We used to walk to the park because we didn't have a car. I was Kubek's backup. Our fielding was about the same, but he was a much better hitter, so I didn't play very much in the first half of the season. But I was in a lot of games in the second half. When we got ahead, Casey sent me in for defense and usually moved Tony to left to replace Berra or Howard—Tony would have been a great outfielder if that had been his position. Often Casey would wait for Yogi to bat before I came in. Howard would catch at the end of the game, replacing Berra or Blanchard. So games would end up with Howard catching, me playing short, and Tony in left.

I was lucky because when I spelled Kubek at short I played between Bobby Richardson and Clete Boyer. Bobby was the best second baseman in the league. He was so quick. As a hitter, Bobby could handle a bat as good as anybody I ever saw. Depending on where the ball was pitched, he'd either flip his wrist or just reach out with the bat and he'd have a hit. He was a threat because he always could hit the ball somewhere, often with extra-base power. He made a great leadoff man, batting in front of Kubek, although sometimes Kubek led off and Richardson batted second. They both had such great bat control and hit the ball all over, so that they were impossible to defense. They were always on base for our sluggers.

Cletis Boyer was a laid-back player yet a hardworking player. That probably doesn't make any sense, but he went out and played hard yet did it without going out of his way. He was such a great third baseman. He was always making diving stops or charging topped balls and throwing out speedy runners. I just loved to watch that guy.

BROOKS ROBINSON (ORIOLES):

In terms of catching the ball and throwing, Clete Boyer was the best defensive third baseman I played against.

J. DE MAESTRI:

Boyer batted eighth but was a pretty good hitter at times. He hit a lot of homers for someone that low in the order. While Mickey, Whitey, and Yogi were probably the leaders of the team, none of them wanted that role, and Cletis was more outspoken than any of them in the clubhouse. He spoke out in a positive way.

In the clubhouse, Mantle was pretty much a class-clown type. He never acted like a star. He always made the young guys feel comfortable, including Roger Maris and me. He was great. Of course, I had gotten to know him a bit over the years, mostly when he'd pull into second with a double against the Athletics. Mickey had torn apart the Athletics over the years, but I didn't realize just how great he was until I watched him play every day. He was incredible, especially when you consider what he went through physically. He had osteomyelitis. Unfortunately, some of his physical problems were his own fault. He didn't train and didn't take good care of himself. He just assumed that he would die at an early age of Hodgkin's disease, as had his father and others on his father's side. So he lived it up at night. He'd wrap those knees every single day and then go out and do the job. Amazingly, he could still run and hit despite the pain. He would never take himself out of the lineup unless somebody just said, "Hey, you can't play anymore." He was truly a marvel to watch.

JIM LANDIS (WHITE SOX):

I was awed by Mickey Mantle. I had friends on the Yankees like Bill Skowron, Johnny Blanchard, and Elston Howard, and sometimes I'd go into their clubhouse in Yankee Stadium before I got dressed. I would see Mantle get wrapped up before every game from the top of his legs down to his ankles. Blanchard would tell me, "Sometimes you don't realize what kind of pain he is in." You'd notice every once in a while when he was hitting left-handed that he'd hop off his leg when it hurt—yet he still hit a home run. What he could do on the field while being in that condition was amazing. He stole bases on a bad leg. And he could still hit anybody. Batting right-handed, he tried to pull left-handers, so I played him deeper and in the hole more. In Chicago, I once was playing him about 380 feet out. I heard his bat break clear out in center. The ball went over the fence. That was power.

BROOKS ROBINSON (ORIOLES):

Ted Williams was the best hitter I saw, but Mickey Mantle was the best player in the American League to play against day in and day out. Mantle was a right-center and left-center hitter and I didn't get a lot of grounders from him.

J. DE MAESTRI:

Of the teams I played on, the Yankees were the team that drank the most. We certainly weren't discouraged from drinking—Ballantine sponsored our games and Mel Allen called a Yankee homer a "Ballantine blast." Mickey, Whitey, and some others could go out and drink all night and still come out and play ball.

Whitey used to tell great stories about how he and Mickey would arrive in a new city and have detectives hired by the team waiting for them at the hotel. They would get in a cab, drive around the block, and go back into the hotel in order to lose them. One night they were out having a couple of drinks. They knew who the guys were who were sitting three or four tables away, and they finally picked up their drinks and went to sit with them. They were going to be together all night anyway, so they might as well drink together. I never went drinking with them—just to dinner. In fact, those two guys would take out ten, fifteen guys and treat.

Roger Maris and I had become good friends when we were teammates in Kansas City. A lot of guys had trouble getting to know him because he was an introvert, but we spent a great deal of time together and became very close. He was one guy that needed a lot of comfort, and New York wasn't the ideal spot for him. But I'm sure he was happy when he was traded from Kansas City to New York. He had some success on the A's, but he was pitched around with men on base. In New York, with him batting third and Mantle and Berra hitting behind him, he got good pitches all the time. So I wasn't really surprised at his instant success in New York. People tend to forget he was the league's MVP in 1960. He led the league in RBIs and slugging percentage, and despite his missing a lot of games, his 39 homers were just 1 behind Mantle's league-leading total. Also, people were impressed by what a great right fielder he was. He saved us so many times down the stretch with his defense. Since he was so strong and stocky, it surprised people how fast he was. He would always run down long flies or cut off sure extra-base hits and hold runners to singles. His arm was a gun. He'd throw runners out going from first to third, and no one in the park could believe it. His defense was overshadowed by his hitting, but everyone on the Yankees was aware how good he was.

Ryne Duren was also a teammate of mine at Kansas City, but he had been there only briefly before he was traded to the Yankees. Then he became the scariest guy in the league for me to bat against. So I was glad I was now his teammate on New York. He told me, "You used to stand on top of the dirt without digging your cleats in so you could get out of the way." I'd reply, "Hell, I'm not stupid." During the World Series, Ryne came in to pitch when Elston Howard was catching. I think Clemente was the hitter. Howard had a sign for a spitter—Whitey had a great spitter because he sweated so much—but Ellie didn't call for it and wasn't expecting it. Ryne threw it on his own, and you could see the spit fly off the ball as it shot 20 feet into the air and wound up on the screen. Howard never even stood up. That was the maddest I ever saw Ellie. He chewed out Duren something terrible after the inning was over: "Don't you ever throw one of those when I'm not looking for it." Duren was a super guy. He was sharp and very knowledgeable. God, he could throw.

RYNE DUREN:

I finally got a $1,500 raise. The New York press was responsible. They took Weiss the average figure for top relievers and showed him that I was making too little. Weiss told me that was the dirtiest thing anyone ever did to him.

I still could throw fairly well after my wrist injury—I

The most intimidating pitcher in baseball: the fireballing, nearsighted, alcoholic Ryne Duren, relief specialist for the New York Yankees.

struck out 67 in 49 innings—but I could tell I'd lost just a bit. My arm had been in a cast for 7 or 8 weeks and I wasn't at full strength. Consequently, I had a mediocre season with only 3 wins and 9 saves. But batters were still nervous when they batted against me. Maybe it was because I always pitched with dark glasses. Sometimes the glare off the white shirts behind the batter would get to me. I was just trying to protect myself and see as well as I could. My eyes weren't good to begin with, and lots of times I was hung over and my eyes were light-sensitive. Nobody protested.

VIC POWER (INDIANS):

One time Casey brought in Duren, who wore dark glasses and was an alcoholic. He threw the first warm-up pitch into the stands and my legs started shaking. After some more wild warm-up throws, I nervously got into the batter's box. Then Duren started squinting under those glasses, trying to make out Berra's sign. Then he took off his glasses and cleaned them off. My anxiety increased. Finally he threw a fastball behind my back. I got off the ground and took my bat and walked over to the Yankee bench, where everyone was laughing, including Casey. I told Casey, "Listen, old man, if he hits me, I'm not going to fight him, I'm going to fight you!" Of course, I didn't really want to fight him. I was just so nervous I had to say something. Casey just kept laughing.

R. DUREN:

I wasn't a headhunter, but the bravado was necessary for me to be effective. If I wanted to hit someone because his team was throwing at our batters, I'd throw the ball behind his butt and let him back into it. I had good enough control not to hit batters . . . except for Jim Landis. Landis was a good friend of mine in winter ball, and I got to know him and his family quite well. I was always afraid of hurting someone, but for some reason I kept hitting him. It scared me to death. When he'd come up, I'd think so much about not hitting him that I couldn't keep my eyes off him, instead of looking at the catcher. One time I hit Landis on the helmet and knocked it clear back to the screen. I thought I had killed him. Landis went down, but was all right. Casey took me out of the game and Gene Freese, the on-deck batter, later told me that he applauded Casey for doing him that favor. Gene then grounded into a double play and just laughed like hell because he didn't face me.

JIM LANDIS (WHITE SOX):

Duren hit me on the head about 4 times. My bells rung. I don't know why it happened. We had played in winter ball together; we fished together. He would even apologize to me. I'd forget my normal batting stance and move to the corner of the batter's box, as far away as I could get. He'd say, "Jim, I'm serious. I'm not trying to hit you. It just seems to happen." I said, "Quit it, please." Once after Duren beaned me, our relief pitcher was ordered by Lopez to retaliate against the first batter he faced. He didn't, and, boy, did Lopez chew out his fanny! Lopez was saying, "I told you—fair is fair! . . ."

R. DUREN:

Despite my unsatisfying season, I was glad that the Yankees came back to win 97 games and beat out the Orioles by 8 games. Roger Maris had come to us from Kansas City and had a Most Valuable Player campaign, leading the league in RBIs and slugging 39 homers. Roger was a terrific ballplayer and a helluva guy who we all liked very much. A star in New York in that era felt a lot of pressure and Roger was the only guy big enough to take some of the pressure off Mickey. I think Mickey played under a tremendous amount of stress. And I'd guess he was one of us who tried to manage stress with alcohol, mostly on a subconscious level. I never saw Mantle drunk before a big game, but he overdrank now and then, as he later admitted. I don't know if, in his mind, he thought his drinking was controllable.

The Yankees weren't a standoffish team. Once you put on the pinstripes, you were accepted by everyone. There were small cliques, but nobody closed you out. You could go to dinner with Mantle or Ford or Bauer or Skowron or Kubek, Richardson, and Shantz. Maybe I'd have dinner with Kubek and Richardson and then go have a few drinks with some of the other guys. For instance, I'd run a lot with Johnny Blanchard and Duke Maas, my best friends on the team.

We didn't feel like celebrities, maybe because most of us weren't paid like celebrities. I'd go to places like Danny's Hideaway on the East Side and Danny would pick up the tab. We'd go to Frankie and Johnny's on 48th Street, where a lot of the show biz people went. Harold's Club was right across the street. That's where I met the grand old Irish actor Thomas Mitchell. There were also prominent families around who wanted to take you out to dinner. That was a pretty important thing in those days.

There were a few gals in the picture. Here and there you might have what we referred to as "a cousin." Baseball Annies and "gangbangers" were always around, but they had bad reputations and weren't the women I met. I met women on my own, not those who hung around the hotels and ballparks—and bullpens— trying to pick up ballplayers. There were women who hung around bars and they were available to all men, not just ballplayers. The ballplayers, like other men, were drawn to bars that had good-looking women. We were just like other men—except that many of us were married. I was so much into the drinking that every once in a while I'd pick up a girl and then choose to sit at a bar and drink all night instead of taking her home. It's not that we tried to pick up bar girls every night. We didn't. I might have had a couple of drinks before dinner and felt very happy just going to a movie with some of the other guys.

Peformance was the permission to do what we wanted. As long as Mantle and Whitey could drink and have success, there was no reason for management to clamp down on anyone's drinking. I drank because I drank, because everyone around me drank. Sure, I'd drink a lot after a bad game—but I think my poor performance was a justification for drinking. The truth is that once the addict takes a drink, the judgment leaves. I never drank prior to a game. That would have proved that I had a problem, and I wanted to deny it.

That winter I was out one night with Mickey in Dallas. I drank him drink for drink and outdrank him and drove him home. My feeling was that this proved I didn't have any problems. That also was part of my denial. Nobody told me I was an alcoholic. Players didn't talk about such things. But after an incident in Washington, D.C., Mantle and Ford told me I shouldn't drink. They thought I was a different type of drinker from the others. After an incident I might tell myself that I'd swear off drinking, and I might not drink for a while. I thought my drinking was affecting my pitching, but no one else said anything.

Alcohol changed my personality a little bit. Sometimes I'd be an angry drunk, but not always. I was unpredictable. But like most alcoholics, I didn't drink like the other people drank. By the time my teammates saw me, they thought I'd had two drinks, when in reality I probably was having my seventh and eighth drinks. My alcoholism put me alone a lot. I would think less about pitching than about how to fit in with the rest of the players. Because for any adolescent, which I still was, that's the most important thing in your life.

The pressure of playing baseball on a professional level plus booze kept a lot of players adolescents. Almost everybody had their drinks. Most drank in social situations and there was little moderation. Everybody in the majors who was any drinker at all was, ignorantly, an alcohol abuser. I had no idea I was an abuser and had entered a dangerous area. I wasn't the only one who woke up with hangovers and couldn't remember the night before. I went drinking with many Yankees. But after a while they stayed away from me because I'd get too drunk. There were little innuendos in the press about my drinking. But the sportswriters had loyalty toward me because we'd go drinking together. Some were dear friends of mine. As a group, I'd say they had a higher rate of alcoholism than the players.

We all thought drinking was part of a ballplayer's social life. We drank ignorantly. The Yankees didn't drink more than any other team. It's just that the Yankees were more noteworthy. What Casey and other managers tried to do was manage the personalities as they showed up in the ballpark and get rid of those who were too much trouble. Stengel never said anything about my drinking or anyone else's. (Years later, Casey would tell me that he knew there was a lot of drinking on the Yankees, but he thought it useless to ask players if they had problems. "They might admit to having a couple of drinks," he said, "but what they wouldn't tell me is that they were as big as pisspots.")

WORLD SERIES

1960

YANKEES VS PIRATES

JOE DE MAESTRI · YANKEES:

We respected the Pirates. They had a good pitching staff with Friend, Law, Haddix, and Face. They had Clemente, Groat, Hoak, Virdon, Skinner, Mazeroski, and that great pinch hitter Smoky Burgess. They had a hell of a ballclub. It wasn't a case of us not knowing who the hell we were going to play. We scored many more runs, we had many more total bases, Richardson drove in a record number of runs, Ford shut them out twice. When we won, we destroyed them. We did everything right in that Series except win the final game.

I roomed with Yogi in Pittsburgh. We sat up all night before Game Seven, and he said, "Now, here's what's going to happen tomorrow. We're going to do this and do that and they're going to bring in ElRoy Face. And I'm going to hit a home run." And that's what happened. He hit a 3-run homer off Face that put us ahead. Face was making remarks on TV and the whole bit, really knocking the club. That really got to the guys more than anything. Yogi says, "I know he is going to come in tomorrow, and I know what I'm going to do." By God, he did it. Unfortunately, we didn't win, as Yogi also predicted. Face ended up looking like the genius.

We thought we had the final game locked up, but it got away from us. I was supposed to come in to play short in the bottom of the eighth inning, with Kubek replacing Berra in left. But I was held back because Yogi was due up. In Forbes Field, you warmed up down the side near the dugout. I had stopped throwing and was standing past the third-base coach's box watching the Pirates bat. With one on, Virdon hit that hard grounder that shot up and hit Tony in the throat. Boy, he went down like a ton of bricks. I tell you, I thought the guy was going to die because he couldn't breathe. His throat started swelling. I came in to replace him and they took him to the hospital. Soon the Pirates scored 2 runs on singles by Groat and Clemente, who beat Skowron to first. Then Hal Smith hit a 3-run homer off Coates to put them ahead 9–7. That homer completely shocked me. Still, we came back to tie the game in the top of the ninth. Mickey's base-running prevented a double play and kept the rally going.

Of course, I'll never forget what happened in the bottom of the ninth. Ralph Terry threw the first pitch of the inning right down the middle to Bill Mazeroski. He didn't swing, but Casey went to the mound to talk to Terry. He turned around and he was coming back toward the dugout. He was walking right toward me and was about 3 feet from the dugout when he heard Mazeroski lay into Terry's second pitch, the *same* pitch. Casey never looked at the ball, but just made a left turn and walked toward the clubhouse. He didn't have to look. Mazeroski really crunched that ball—it cleared the wall in left center and that was a long, long way. It was a devastating loss. I know Mickey cried. Other guys did, too.

Casey Stengel wasn't rehired for 1961. The Yankees said it was because he was 71 and had reached the retirement age for the organization, but I'm sure our loss to the Pirates had something to do with it.

BOB TURLEY · YANKEES:

We didn't blame Ralph Terry for the Mazeroski homer. The guy who gave up the big hit was Jim Coates, who gave up Hal Smith's 3-run homer in the eighth to put them ahead. He shouldn't have been in there when we had Ryne Duren and Luis Arroyo sitting down in the bullpen. I'm sure that contributed to Stengel being fired.

RYNE DUREN · YANKEES:

Stengel brought in Jim Coates before me and it backfired. Stengel later told me, ''I only made one mistake in baseball and that's bringing in the other guy when I should have brought you in.'' The real story of that game was not the homer Terry gave up to Mazeroski but the 3-run homer Coates gave up to Hal Smith. Coates gave Smith 3 high fastballs, and Smith had him timed. If Stengel was going to have a pitcher throw fastballs, then he should have had Smith try to hit mine. In Games One and Five, I'd struck out 5 batters in 4 innings. Besides, Stengel brought in Coates too soon. He should have left in Bobby Shantz to face Bob Skinner. It should have been a left-hander against a left-hander. More important, it was a bunt situation and you don't take out the best-fielding pitcher in baseball and replace him with one of the worst. Skinner was able to move up the runners. One out later, Clemente hit a slow grounder down the first-base line. Coates didn't get off the mound quick enough and Clemente beat Skowron to first. Then

Smith followed with his homer. The loss to the Pirates in the World Series was devastating to me.

DICK GROAT · PIRATES:

I was coming off a broken wrist and I was forced to catch almost everything with my bare hand in the entire World Series. I didn't want Danny Murtaugh to know this because I had to play.

Since we hadn't played the Yankees all season, we relied on scouting reports, which said they were the most notorious high-ball-hitting team we had played. They were right, but our pitching staff couldn't get the ball down for love or money. It was incredible. Bobby Richardson, who was a dead high-ball hitter, had a field day. He got 11 hits and drove in a record 12 runs. We couldn't get him out. And we couldn't get a lot of their other guys out either. They hit about .340 that Series and outscored us 55 to 27.

The Yankees killed us 16–3, 10–0, and 12–0. There was no contest. But when we were young players, Mr. Rickey told us, ''You can always win or lose by long numbers. But the great teams always win the close games.'' And we won every close game in the Series. When the Yankees would lose a close game to us, their players would have to go to the locker room and say, ''Jesus! If I had done this or done that or if I'd gotten a hit . . .'' We never fell into that second-guessing trap and got down on ourselves because we got blown out in all the losses. When we fell far behind in Game Two, Danny took me out so I could put my hand in the whirlpool. After the game, a bunch of guys came in. Instead of being depressed, they were excited by the gigantic 3-run homer Mickey Mantle hit off Joe Gibbon. Virdon was the first to reach me and he said, ''Roomie, you missed the granddaddy of them all! You wouldn't believe it! Mantle hit one over that iron gate, 30 feet above the wall! It was a rocket!'' About seven guys told me the same thing. No one complained about what went wrong that game. We had won Game One on the pitching of Law and Face and Mazeroski's 2-run homer, so we felt pretty good, having split the first 2 games.

Whitey Ford shut us out and now we are down 2 games to 1. Then we got great pitching performances from Law, Haddix, and Face to win Game Four, 3–2, and Game Five, 5–2, and we come back to Pittsburgh up

3–2. Then Whitey came in and shut us out again. We didn't worry. We had come behind from the seventh inning on about 35 or 40 times that year, so we didn't think we could lose. Every game we were in, we got the big hit when we needed it.

But the seventh game didn't go by the book. There were a lot of weird happenings. It was an intense game. The Yankees had us by 3 runs going into the eighth inning. And Bobby Shantz had shut us down for 3 innings. Gino Cimoli pinch-hit leading off and hit a flare for a single. Then Shantz got Virdon to hit a tailor-made double-play ball to short, but the ball shot up and struck Kubek in the neck. So we had 2 runners on and no outs. I was the tying run at the plate, facing Bobby Shantz, who had great control and knew how to pitch. I wanted to hit the ball the other way, but Bobby was the hardest pitcher in baseball for me to do that against. He kept running the ball inside and taking something off, and the best I could do was foul off a few pitches. For one of the few times in my career, I stepped out of the batter's box and I found myself sweating. I said to myself, "I'm just shitting myself. I'd better just go up there and hit the ball hard and forget about going to right field." So here comes the pitch and I hit a shot to left, our first line drive off Shantz. Cimoli scored, Virdon went to second, and I became the tying run on first.

Bob Skinner, a left-hander, was the next batter. It was then that Casey Stengel made a huge mistake. Sportswriters could have had a field day with him if they understood what was going on, but they never questioned his decision to take out Shantz, the best defensive pitcher in baseball and a left-hander, and bring in a right-hander, Jim Coates. Until my single, we hadn't hit one hard ball off Shantz. And Skinner was going to bunt, without question, and Shantz was great at defensing bunts and forcing the runner at third. One thing about Danny Murtaugh was that he never went away from the book. The Yankees had scouting reports from Mayo Smith and Bill Skiff, who had been traveling with us for two months. They knew what we ate for breakfast, so they certainly knew Murtaugh would have Skinner bunt. So against Coates, Skinner bunted us to second and third. Then Rocky Nelson hits a fly ball that wasn't deep enough for us to advance. So there were 2 outs and we were still 2 runs behind and Stengel's decision hadn't backfired yet. But then Bobby Clemente hit a high chopper to Bill Skowron, and he looked up and saw that Coates forgot to cover first base. Clemente beat it out. Now we were behind by one run, with the left-handed-hitting Hal Smith facing the right-handed Coates. Hal hit a 3-run homer and we went up by 2 runs! The Yankees had semi-beaten themselves.

The Yankees did tie the score in the top of the ninth thanks to some clever base-running by Mantle. When Mazeroski came to bat to lead off the bottom of the ninth, I was at the very end of the dugout at the bat box. I had just put on my helmet because I was the fourth hitter in the inning. When he hit Ralph Terry's pitch, all I could think of was "Get off the wall and get extra bases." I didn't think it had a chance to go out in Forbes Field. There was dead silence. The crowd swelled, but there was no sound in the dugout. Nobody said anything. Everybody was just kind of hypnotized, and when it went over, we just exploded out of the dugout.

Winning the World Series was a great feeling, especially for me. To play on a world championship team in your hometown? How lucky can you be? Especially after being a Pirates fan my whole life and then joining them when they were the worst baseball team in history. It was such a boost for a town that hadn't had a winner in any sport for a long time. The Pirates hadn't won a World Series in 35 years, which is why I think this team would always be the most special of the Pirates' championship teams. Everything was shut down and you couldn't go anyplace, and everybody was racing into town. Yet only about 3 windows were broken, nobody was beaten up, no cars were burned, no property was destroyed. Most of the cost for the cleanup went to remove confetti. Pittsburgh, then a baseball town, had the happiest celebration in the world.

When that ball hit Tony Kubek at shortstop, I thought, "This could be me." It could have been anybody. That's the rub of the green. I had to return to Presbyterian Hospital the day after the Series and have x-rays taken of my wrist to see if I had done any more damage. After I'd finished, I went up to see how Tony was doing. He was ready to check out. The funny thing is that when I walked into his room, he had no idea who I was. He had only talked to me when I wore my cap and he didn't know I was bald.

ELROY FACE · PIRATES:

I looked forward to challenging some of those big Yankee hitters. I saved the first game for Law, but Elston Howard touched me for a 2-run homer in the ninth. I struck out Maris and Mantle with forkballs the first time I faced them, and I pitched good baseball for 2⅔ innings in both Games Four and Five, saving wins for Vern Law and Harvey Haddix. I came into Game Four with a 3–2 lead in the seventh inning and got 8 straight outs. Bob Prince was announcing that I was throwing one forkball after another but I was mostly busting sliders off the fists of the Yankee left-handers, like Dale Long and Johnny Blanchard. The one good hit off me was by Bill Skowron, a right-handed batter, but Virdon saved me with a great over-the-shoulder catch. In Game Five I kept the Yankees hitless with more sliders, pitching from out of the sun into the shadows. But Mantle got a big hit off me in the last game of the World Series. And Berra hit a 3-run homer off me into the right-field screen. That was a mistake slider that I wanted to grab back before it reached the plate. I was a little tired by the end.

I didn't see Mazeroski's homer. I was in the clubhouse listening on the radio. Then all the players rushed in. I wasn't surprised that he homered. People forget he had power and had 19 homers in 1958. He had homered off Coates in Game One to put that game out of reach.

There was a big celebration at the Webster Hall Hotel in downtown Pittsburgh. I was thrilled, but not surprised we beat the Yankees. We were confident we could win. We knew we could win close games because we'd done that all season long.

DICK SCHOFIELD · PIRATES:

Of course, it was exciting being in the World Series and playing in Yankee Stadium and going against Mantle, Maris, Berra, and the rest of that great team. The Yankees were fantastic, probably a better team than us. They beat us badly 3 times, but in that year, if we'd have played them 99 times, we'd have won 45 times. We knew we were going to win. We were even more confident than the Yankees.

My first time up I walked, and the next time up I got a hit off Bob Turley. But I batted only twice more. I was disappointed I wasn't playing after hitting .400 in Sep-

tember. Groat's wrist healed awful quick and Murtaugh reinserted him at short. I wanted to play bad. At the time, I thought Murtaugh's decision was completely wrong. But later I understood why Murtaugh played Groat—after his MVP year and after playing so many years on bad Pittsburgh teams, he deserved to play. I'm sure Murtaugh realized that we both deserved to play and didn't know what to do about us.

I was playing shortstop in Pittsburgh in the second game. The Yankees had a couple of men on base and Mantle hit a fly to the outfield. I thought I was going to get a relay from Virdon. But Mantle had crushed the ball. It looked like a 2-iron going over the center-field fence. It was awesome, and he had a couple of others that were ungodly. I think he put Freddie Green in shock for about two years.

So many bizarre things happened in Game Seven. There was so much drama. But since so many guys on our team did things to help us win, it wasn't surprising when Mazeroski homered to win the game, even though a right-hander homering off Ralph Terry was an unlikely prospect. It happened so fast that none of us on the bench had time to think about who might homer for us to win the game. All of a sudden, Berra went back to the wall and ran out of room. Then we were all jumping up and down and running to home plate. I think the Yankees were shocked that we beat them.

In the clubhouse, everyone was just milling around. Then we went to the Webster Hall Hotel and had a big celebration. The wives and families were there. There was food and drink. The town went nuts. 1960 was a tough year to top.

TOM CHENEY · PIRATES:

Against the Yankees, we were in a whole lot of trouble all the way down the Yankee lineup. They said don't let certain guys beat you, but what's the difference when you let the guy behind him beat you? Any 9 guys they put up there were capable of beating you. We couldn't match up our lineup against theirs, so we talked at length that we had to beat them on defense and pitching, in low-scoring games. And other than the seventh game, that's how we won our games. As Gino Cimoli said, "They set the records and we got the money."

I pitched in relief in all 3 games we were blown out.

In 4 innings, I gave up 4 hits and only 2 runs, and struck out 6, but I helped some of the guys who pitched before me increase their ERAs. I had the misfortune of pitching to Bobby Richardson with men on base. I'd throw the ball over his head and he'd crush it.

Bob Friend, who started Game Two and Game Six, had a great sinker, but the balls the Yankees hit had eyes. That second game got out of hand right quick. Friend had a terrible series. But Harvey Haddix and Vern Law were great and Roy Face saved 3 games.

Game Seven was a thriller. We were lucky because we beat them at their own game, a high-scoring game. After it got tied up and Ralph Terry pitched the bottom of the ninth, Bill Mazeroski led off. He was strictly a high-fastball hitter. The first pitch was a letter-high slider and Maz took it. I was in the bullpen but I could tell. All the color drained out of my face. It was right in his wheelhouse. I couldn't believe it. I would always tell him that I wanted to punch him for taking it. Maz claimed, "I was baiting him." Terry came right back with the same pitch and Maz jerked it. Everybody knew it was gone when he hit it. By the time he reached home plate, it had been torn up and he had scratches and claw marks all over where people had grabbed him.

I was elated when I saw that homer. Tensions had built up so much. Even though I wasn't involved too much, I was as tight as a guitar string. Everyone else was, too. I had thought we'd lost, but then Hal Smith hit that 3-run homer in the eighth. Hal Smith made the statement about Mazeroski's homer, "Hell, yes, I'm jealous. I was supposed to be the hero."

The game was over about 4 P.M. My wife didn't come because we were leaving the next day for Georgia. It was 2 A.M. before I could get a cab to take me home. People parked cars wherever they stopped, often right in the middle of the street. The police couldn't do anything about it, so they just joined the people who went into bars to celebrate.

NATIONAL LEAGUE 1961

"WE LIKED IT BECAUSE IT WAS A DUMP. I REMEMBER SEEING ALL 9 PITCHERS LINED UP THERE. AND ONE CATCHER. EACH YEAR, THE BAR GOT A LITTLE NICER. BUT IT GOT TOO NICE, SO WE FOUND ANOTHER DUMP TO GO TO INSTEAD."

STAN WILLIAMS

MILWAUKEE BRAVES

LEW BURDETTE:

We used to like West Coast trips because we enjoyed San Francisco. Warren and I would always go over to Lefty O'Doul's. Lefty had been my manager on the San Francisco Seals and he'd come in and buy us beers and sandwiches and tell Spahn a story he got a big kick out of. When I played for Lefty, he had managed the Seals for many years and his word was law. O'Doul would inch up to the dugout steps and say, "Hit him in the belly!" So I had to do it. One Sunday morning I read in the paper that I had tied O'Doul's league record for hit batsmen, which he'd set in something like 1922. I didn't say anything about it and I was pitching that day when he shouted, "Hit him in the belly!" He didn't care if the batter heard him. And I shook my head no. He came out to the mound and questioned my refusal. I said, "I read an interesting article in the paper this morning." I told him I didn't want to beat him, just tie him. He said, "Dammit, at least come close!" Lefty loved that story.

In San Francisco, we'd play golf when we had an afternoon off. Once we went golfing with a guy who supplied all the meat to the best restaurants in the area. Bob Buhl, who had an odd baseball stroke to say the least, swung at the ball on the first tee and the guy told him he could get him a job for $50,000 a year in a slaughterhouse. He said, "You've got the greatest steer-killing stroke I've ever seen in my life." Buhl almost walked off the course. We didn't really tease Buhl about his hitting. We all knew he couldn't hit, but he was a good bunter. He could fake a bunt and chop down on the ball pretty good if he choked up on the bat.

BOB BUHL:

The Braves seemed to be heading for pennant contention in August when we won 10 straight games. Then we were beaten by the Phillies, ending their record 23-game losing streak, and we didn't do much after that. With about a month to go in the season, it was apparent that we weren't going to win the pennant, so Chuck Dressen was fired and replaced by Birdie Tebbetts. He used me differently than my previous managers in that he wanted me to pitch only in relief. I ended up with only 9 wins and pitched about 75 or 80 innings less than

Bob Buhl wasn't washed up despite winning only 9 games in his final full season with the Braves, and would revive his career in 1962 with the Cubs.

Spahn and Burdette. Birdie and I didn't see eye to eye.

As usual, Spahn led the league in wins, with 21, as well as in ERA. And Burdette added 18 wins. We also got the expected offensive from Aaron, Mathews, and Adcock, and this year we got Frank Thomas to play left field. He was a good ballplayer, a hustler who wanted to win. Frank used to laugh when I'd break the bat off in his hands. He was a good-natured guy and didn't mind when we kidded him. After all, he was a guy who caught throws bare-handed. Strange.

FRANK THOMAS:

On May 9, I rode a bus with the rest of the Cubs from Chicago to Milwaukee. At that time I was told I was changing uniforms. I walked into the Milwaukee clubhouse and Charlie Dressen told me, "You're my left fielder." We had a great team: Joe Adcock at first, Frank Bolling at second, Roy McMillan at short—I

didn't realize he was an amazing fielder until I saw him every day—Eddie Mathews at third, Joe Torre behind the plate because Del Crandall was injured, Lee Maye in right, Hank Aaron in center, me in left, and Warren Spahn, Lew Burdette, and Bob Buhl pitching. Despite those three guys, pitching was our weak area. We didn't have anyone in the bullpen other than Don McMahon.

Hank Aaron was the greatest hitter I ever played with. I would have taken him over Roberto Clemente because he could beat you in more ways. That year he batted about .330 and had 34 homers and 120 RBIs, and that was a typical year for him. We had a lot of power. Mathews and Adcock also hit over 30 homers and I added 25 in about 140 fewer at-bats. On June 8 against Cincinnati, the four of us homered consecutively, the first time that had been done. Mathews and Aaron homered off Jim Maloney and then Adcock and I homered off Marshall Bridges. The team went on to hit 14 homers over 3 games. Then, about a week later, Aaron, Adcock, and I hit consecutive homers against the Dodgers.

Warren Spahn had just turned 40 when he no-hit the Giants back in April. Supposedly, he almost had another no-hitter in his next start but lost it on a misplay by left fielder Mel Roach. Roach was traded for me a few days later. I had the locker next to Spahn when he won his 300th game in August, beating the Cubs, 2–1. Spahn was a great pitcher and correctly had a lot of pride in himself. I got along with him, but wished he wouldn't promise to do me favors and then not do them. He only made sure things were done for him.

I was doing well for the Braves, so a month after the trade, John McHale, the GM, tells me he wants to sign me for 1962. I said I'd sign before I left for the winter. Two weeks before the season was over, he called me back in. I said, "Let me ask you one question before signing. What are your intentions for me next season? Because if you may trade me, please don't let me sign. Let me dicker with the new club I'm going to." His exact words were "We're counting on you heavily to be our regular left fielder." So I signed. In November I was off hunting when my wife called and told me I'd been dealt to the expansion New York Mets for cash and a player to be named later. McHale never returned my calls. He wasn't even man enough to own up to what he did after the conversation we had. I lost a lot of respect for him. But that's the way baseball treated players. That's why I would never begrudge players in later eras for getting the upper hand and getting as much money as they could. General managers treated players like slaves. They made money off us and that was their only consideration. At spring training the next year with the Mets, we had an exhibition game against the Braves and I went up to McHale and said sarcastically, "Thanks."

JOHNNY ANTONELLI:

On Independence Day, I was sold to the Braves and finished my career with the team I started with in 1948. I was in only 9 games but I got 1 victory, which was the 126th of my career. Things hadn't changed so much since 1953. As had happened then, Spahn won over 20 games, Burdette and Buhl pitched well, and Mathews and Adcock hit a lot of homers and drove in runs. Of course, the big difference is that the Braves now also had Henry Aaron.

In October I was sold to the New York Mets for their initial season, but I officially retired. I never liked traveling and didn't enjoy road trips. When I quit at an early age, that was one of the reasons.

ST. LOUIS CARDINALS

TIM MCCARVER:

The ballplayers in my era were more educated than the previous generation, but they were equally tough. There was still an eye-for-an-eye brand of baseball. Because there were one-year contracts, it was played with much drive and tenacity. There was a lot of camaraderie among players—we talked baseball, played cards, went places together. Very rarely did guys go out on their own. There was a lot of drinking—probably too much. Ballplayers were supposed to play ball and guzzle beer. And for single men like myself, dating was important.

It was hard spending all my time for 8 months around grown men, some married, some single. Then in the fall, I would go back to college at Memphis State and for one semester I'd be back with people in my age group. I can imagine they were unsettled by how much I had grown up in those first few years. I had gone past them and it was difficult making the social adjustment. It was hard to keep a balance. There was an innocent life and one not so innocent. One of my friends told me, "I'm happy for you and a bit envious of you for what you have experienced. But it's a shame that you miss the college times. It's as if you're missing a vital part of your life."

In 1959, 1960, and 1961 I spent brief time with the Cardinals, a kid among adults. Bob Nieman called me "Bush" for 2 years and I became offended if other players didn't call me that. I thought that was a compliment. Nieman would sidle up to me and say, "I nicknamed Brooks Robinson 'Bush' and look where he is today." That made me feel good. Once Nieman criticized my open stance, saying, "You make contact, but you don't put any punch into it." And Bill White took up for me: "You keep getting on the kid, and all he does is go back to the minors and hit .300 every year." I thought, "Thanks, Bill." It was nice he noticed me. Nobody on the Cards rode me in a bitter, truculent way. Guys like Walt "Moose" Moryn and Kenny Boyer couldn't have been friendlier. I even dated Kenny's sister-in-law and he had me over for barbecues and stuff like that. I really felt I was one of the guys although I was definitely the kid.

You have to experience failure before you can move on to be successful. I first experienced failure in 1961. I split my middle finger on my throwing hand while I was playing on the Miami Islanders in Puerto Rico. Then we moved to Charleston, West Virginia, and took the original Miami nickname, the Marlins. We were the Charleston Marlins although there were no Marlins within 1,500 miles of us. I had a miserable year. They were knocking the bat out of my hands. Left-handed George Crowe, who had set the National League record the previous year with his 12th pinch homer, was released by the Cardinals at this time and had his salary immediately terminated. When he was asked by the Cards if he wanted to be a minor league hitting coach, he naturally accepted so he could make the extra money. He came to Charleston and closed my stance, moved my hands to the end of the bat, and started me hitting against my front side. Under his tutelage, I changed to a batting style that would allow me to have success at a major league level. I may have been successful without George's help, but not nearly so much.

Because of all the money the Cards invested in me, I was given every opportunity to make the majors. When I had the bad year in 1961, they were inclined to give me every benefit of the doubt. A nonprospect would have been released, but I was recalled.

Solly Hemus was fired halfway through the season and replaced by Johnny Keane, who had spent something like 30 years in the minors. He was a devout Catholic who went into the priesthood when he was younger. He was more of a father figure than Hemus and nurtured young players. My introduction to Keane was at a club meeting. Keane didn't like left-handed pitcher Maury McDermott, who was trying a comeback with the Cardinals. "Mickey" began his career as a teenager with the Red Sox back in 1948. Being Irish, he was popular with the Boston faithful, not only for his pitching but for his nightclub singing. He still liked to get out on the town, as was proven in San Francisco, when he was never in his room during the Cards' nightly bed checks. On Sunday morning, Keane called a meeting. After talking over a few things, he pointed his finger at McDermott. "Maury," he began, "you came to spring training this year without even cab fare and the Cardinals gave you a contract. And to show your appreciation, all you've done is fuck around all year. We've been checking your room since Thursday night. We don't know if you even checked in. We don't know where you've been staying. We don't care." All the players were embarrassed being witness to this. Most of us were looking at the ground. Mickey challenged Keane: "Johnny, if you feel that way, I'll just take my uniform off and go home." On cue, Johnny pulled a pink slip out of his pocket. "That's exactly what you'll do," he told the stunned McDermott. "You're released." Keane did this openly to get rid of a player he didn't like and for effect to show us he was a strict disciplinarian, but he did it in the cruelest way possible. It was horrible. It scared me to death. I just got there and I saw a manager fired and a player released. I wondered what this baseball business was all about.

I got to like Keane because he gave me a chance to play—I caught about 20 games for him and batted 67 times, even hitting my first major league homer. So I was willing to abide by his rules. He got along pretty well with everybody. The Cards had played 8 games under .500 for Hemus, but played good ball for Keane and wound up 6 games over .500 and in fifth place. Both Boyer and Flood hit over .320 and Bill White batted .285 and drove in 90 runs. Not long after Keane arrived,

Bill tied Ty Cobb's record by getting 14 hits in back-to-back doubleheaders against the Cubs, going 14 for 18 in our 2 sweeps. Oddly, Cobb died on the first day.

I remember when Johnny stood up to Bob Gibson. Bob had his first productive year, pitching over 200 innings and winning 13 games, which was just 1 less than the team leaders, Larry Jackson and Ray Sadecki. But one game he gave up a homer on a 0–2 slider and Johnny was furious, telling him, "Dammit, I told you about those 0–2 pitches a thousand times." Gibson countered, "If I'd have struck him out, you wouldn't have said anything. All you've been doing to me is bitch, bitch, bitch. If you don't like it, you go out there and try to get those guys out." Johnny followed him right up the runway to the cooler and they were screaming at each other. Long after that, Bob confided, "I wouldn't have admitted it then, but Johnny was right."

CHICAGO CUBS

DICK ELLSWORTH:

My wife and I bought a house in Morton Grove, a suburb northwest of Chicago. The players were scattered around. I rode by myself to the ballpark every day. I'd eat a big breakfast in the morning, even when I pitched, and leave the house at 8:45 or 9:00 A.M. I was at the ballpark at 9 or 9:15. The absolute luxury of playing day baseball in Wrigley afforded me the time to see my family in the morning and have dinner with them every evening and play with the baby. It was great. Only Cubs players could enjoy that normal family life. Most of the players were married, and there were several occasions when families would get together. There were barbecue parties at one of our houses. Being married and having a child when I was just starting out in baseball wasn't so difficult for *me*. Selfishly, I spent the majority of my time at baseball. It was more difficult for my wife, who at a very young age found herself alone half the time making family decisions. Thank God, we survived it. When I lost, I was tough on myself and everybody around me. My wife would always remind me what a miserable person I was to be around after I lost. I couldn't wait to get to the ballpark the next day to get ready for my next opportunity. I think everybody felt that way.

We were a pretty close team. On the road, we were together a lot. At the hotel, there were always groups of guys going out to dinner. I didn't sense there were any cliques. You were free to move from group to group. You might go with a group going to a movie, to a restaurant, or to a racetrack. You were welcomed by everybody.

Players didn't discuss their salaries openly, but we talked privately among ourselves. We trusted each other. So when it came time to negotiate your salary, you had a real good sense what other guys in your position were making.

There was no griping about the front office other than when it decided not to have a manager in 1961, and instead initiated a revolving coaching system that had Vedie Himsl, Harry Craft, Elvin Tappe, and Lou Klein taking turns as "head coach." Players griped that there was no leadership in the dugout. At first I didn't like it because it wasn't traditional—then I became really disenchanted when it didn't work. It was supposed to work because it was a "brain trust" and everybody was going to contribute to it. Instead, it became counterproductive because there were jealousies among the coaches and not much cohesiveness. I went 10–11—only Don Cardwell, with 15 victories, won more games—but I really didn't feel I was getting proper instruction or direction.

ED BOUCHEE:

It had been terrible under Lou Boudreau, but it got even worse with the collection of coaches instead of one manager. Every few weeks they'd have a new head coach. It was weird. They assured us there was no competition between coaches, but I couldn't see how there wasn't. Nobody knew who was playing until after you got to the ballpark and they had their meeting. They had the ballplayers so screwed up because nobody knew what was going on. The only guys who didn't grumble about it were those who knew they were going to start, like Ron Santo, Billy Williams, Ernie Banks, and George Altman. The rest of the spots were up for grabs. The year was a complete waste.

There was no leadership on the team. Nothing. Ernie Banks was very quiet. He was a good person to have around because he kept everybody loose, but he'd just go out there and want to play two games every day. Ron Santo was too young to be a leader, as far as I was con-

cerned. At the time, I really didn't see any leadership qualities in him.

Billy Williams, the league's Rookie of the Year, led by what he did. He was a great performer and had the quickest bat in baseball. What a swing! It was so smooth. He hit 25 homers, drove in about 85 runs, and never went into a slump. He didn't have a lot of speed, but he stole a base every now and then and was a little above average as a left fielder. Banks, Altman, and Santo had stats that were as good as or better than Billy's, but he was already the best hitter on the team. He was the best player I ever played with.

After batting in the .240s in my 2 years of part-time play with the Cubs, I felt that I might be traded in the off-season. I guessed they might want to switch Banks to first base because he was slowing down. I wasn't surprised to be included in the expansion draft.

LOS ANGELES DODGERS

ED ROEBUCK:

I had arm problems again and pitched only 5 games. My spot in the bullpen was taken by rookie left-hander Ron Perranoski. He came from the Cubs and also had a sinker. I could have been selected in the expansion draft after the season. However, neither the New York Mets, who selected Gil Hodges, Don Zimmer, and Roger Craig, nor the Houston Astros, who picked Bob Lillis, Norm Larker, and Turk Farrell, drafted me. In 1959 I preferred being with another organization and pitching in the majors and getting around $15,000 than to possibly going back to St. Paul and making $6,000. I told this to Pete Reiser, who knew I could pitch because he managed me on a good Dominican team with Felipe Alou and Frank Howard. Pete told me that the Dodgers had instructed him to stop pitching me in winter ball because they wanted to protect me in the minor league draft. As it turned out, the Dodgers left me off their 40-man roster, but I wasn't drafted because Al Campanis had passed along the word that I couldn't relieve anymore. They thought up all this little trickery.

I think Kenny Myers and catcher Norm Sherry helped Sandy Koufax learn control. They convinced him to ease up a bit on his fastball because no one could get around on it anyway. He improved year after year, and in 1961 really came around. He won 18 games to tie Podres for the team lead and won his first strikeout title, setting a National League record with 269. Stan Williams and Don Drysdale finished second and third in the league.

ED BOUCHEE (CUBS):

By 1961 the toughest pitchers to face were Sandy Koufax, Don Drysdale, and Bob Gibson, in that order. They were young eat-your-lunch pitchers, who were all about to peak. Koufax was the best pitcher I ever faced. Oddly, we called every pitch he threw. When Koufax threw a fastball, his hands would be way over his head during his windup. When his hands went way back, we knew it would be a curveball. Still we couldn't hit him. I hit left-handers pretty good, but Koufax? Who hit Koufax? I think I got 4 or 5 hits off him my whole career. When Koufax first came up, you didn't want to get in the box against him. You hoped he knew where his pitches were going, but he didn't. Then Joe Becker, the pitching coach for the Dodgers, finally convinced him just to take a little bit off the ball so he had better control. His fastball was so fast that he could afford to let up just a little and throw 95 mph instead of 100 mph. But his fastball isn't what made him a great pitcher. His curveball just dropped right off the table. I enjoyed batting against him because of the challenge. I remember in 1958, when the Dodgers played in the Coliseum, I hit one just as far as I could possibly hit a ball into right field. I guess it was about 440 feet to that fence out there. It was just a double, but it was off Koufax and I wouldn't forget it.

STAN WILLIAMS:

Sandy Koufax finally learned to *pitch* in 1961. In just a couple more years he would become the greatest pitcher who ever lived. Sandy's emergence, following Drysdale's, was part of the change that was taking place on the Dodgers. I thought I was establishing myself, too. I set personal records with 15 wins and 205 strikeouts. I also had my most starts and innings pitched.

Offensively, the Sniders and Hodgeses were giving way to Maury Wills, Frank Howard, and Willie and Tommy Davis. In fact, Snider was out for a while after Bob Gibson broke his elbow following his 370th homer.

Howard—the Jolly Giant—had been 1960's Rookie of the Year, but he wasn't a very good hitter yet. He hadn't yet learned how to lay back and wait for the ball to come to him. If he hit the ball, it would go out in any direction, but he just didn't connect that often. About this time, Stu Miller struck him out 13 consecutive times with all that motion of his. Then one day against Miller, Howard one-handed a homer off the flagpole.

Tommy Davis was just 22 and was quickly becoming a really fine hitter. He was a big man but could run like hell. In the 60-yard dash, he was just a step behind Wills. Willie Davis was the fastest runner. By the time you looked, he was out of sight. They had races in Vero Beach in which Maury, Tommy, Willie, and another guy ran. In the first 10 yards, Maury would have an 8-yard lead over Willie, but Willie would catch him in the next 30 yards, and leave him behind. Willie had the longest stride of anyone. On a triple, it looked like he touched the ground only 3 or 4 times between bases. If he had been able to get out of the box as fast as Wills, he would have been something else. Coaches couldn't stop him when he was going at full speed. They'd put their arms up and he'd zoom right by them.

The Dodgers were like a family, the closest team I ever played on. There was no problem with color or creed; we were all friends. When we went on the road, all the wives got together and played bridge and spent time together. Meanwhile, all the players would go out as a group, almost as if we were a bunch of brothers. We played a lot of bridge, played a lot of poker in the rooms. After a game we'd get together and drink beer and rehash the game, and then a few of us would go eat somewhere. I think we inherited the Dodger togetherness from the older players and continued it from group to group as the roster evolved. We took pride in being accepted by our peers and strove for that.

I had a few fishing and hunting buddies on the Dodgers. A bunch of us went to Lake Mead. Norm Larker was a great fisherman and sportsman. Roebuck went although he didn't seem to be into it. Walter Alston and Bob Lillis loved hunting and fishing. Lillis, Larker, and I had been in Triple A ball together, and back then I'd take them home to Colorado, where one of my brothers was ready to take us to the hills for hiking and fishing.

The pitchers always were close. We had a bar we

went to in Milwaukee called the New Yorker. It was a block from the hotel. We liked it because it was a dump. I remember seeing all 9 pitchers lined up there. And one catcher. Each year, the bar got a little nicer. But it got too nice, so we found another dump to go to instead. Our whole group would go to bars in each city and re-hash the ball game and talk about how to pitch batters. We'd learn a lot from those sessions, plus just have a good time and key down from the ball game. Around midnight we'd send the next day's pitcher back to the hotel. We were leisurely drinkers on the Dodgers. We had a couple of guys who snorted it down pretty good sometimes, but it wasn't to the point where they were hurting themselves or the ballclub.

We had a good bunch of guys. Roger Craig was a comedian. He was always good for a laugh—though he didn't like to take it as well as he could give it. Eddie Roebuck was humorous in his own way. Eddie, Norm Larker, Turk Farrell—who was on the Dodgers for part of the '61 season—and I drove back and forth to the Long Beach area, and Eddie's big thing was to cover his eyes on the freeway when he was driving 65 mph. We would stop at the neighborhood bar and get Larker in trouble with his wife by keeping him out too late. She'd get mad as hell. One day she hit him in the head with a bowl full of potatoes.

We had our laughs, but we were very serious on the field. We didn't play for money. We fought for the chance to go back out there the next time, more than worrying about next year. We knew that if you had a bad outing, you might not get a next time because management could demote you the next day if they wanted, and you might never get back. So we had to fight for our existence.

SAN FRANCISCO GIANTS

BILLY O'DELL:

Onetime New York Giants shortstop Alvin Dark became the San Francisco Giants' manager in 1961. We got him from Chicago in a trade and he retired as a player. We moved up from fifth place to third, finishing 8 games behind the Reds. We got good results because Dark gave more playing time to Willie McCovey and Felipe Alou, who took over right field from the departed Willie Kirkland. Willie Mays and Orlando Cepeda had fantastic years. Mays, who had just become the majors' highest-paid player, hit 40 homers and drove in over 120 runs. And Orlando did even better, leading the league in both categories. He had over 140 RBIs. In a game that Lew Burdette started for the Braves, Willie hit 4 homers and drove in 8 runs. He also had a 3-homer game against Philadelphia.

LEW BURDETTE (BRAVES):

When I pitched to Mays, I tried the element of surprise. He'd give himself away sometimes. Before you let the ball loose, you could sometimes see his front shoulder start outside. I could wait that long and then, instead of going outside, I'd jam him. I had good enough control that Willie gave me credit and didn't try to pull me all the time. He'd hit the ball up the middle, and it was hard to get him out. He was smart enough to adjust.

Orlando Cepeda was the toughest hitter I ever faced. He stood way back in the box. If I threw a slider, he'd step in and hit it to right-center. If I threw him a sinker inside, he'd step straight ahead and pull it. With power both ways. Then catcher Sammy White came over to the Braves in 1961. Sammy asked me, "Could the Baby Bull hit the ball any better off you if he called the pitches himself?" So when Cepeda came up the next time, Sammy told him I wanted him to call the pitches. Cepeda said, "Oh, no, can't do that, can't do that, no, man." He didn't want to know what was coming. The umpire had to force him into the box. Sammy yelled to me, "He won't call them, so you have to call them." I said, "Okay, slider on the outside corner." He took it. Strike one. I said, "The same thing. A slider on the outside corner." Strike two. I said, "Fastball right down the middle. We'll see how far he can hit it." I threw it down the middle and he popped it up to me with a weak swing. For 3½ years after that, I would tell him every pitch that was coming, and he never hit the ball out of the infield. He had been the only guy who hit me well on that ballclub.

B. O'DELL:

I went 7–5, pitching mostly in relief. McCormick, Sanford, and Marichal each won 13 games as starters.

Oddly, our biggest winner was reliever Stu Miller, who won 14 games and saved a lot more. He did a great job. He was the winner of the All-Star Game that was played in Candlestick Park, although he balked in a run when he got blown off the mound. He was a change-up pitcher—and he'd change up on his change-ups. It was almost comical sometimes watching batters try to hit Miller. They'd swing before it got there—it was a combination of his change-up and the way he delivered it. Stu was a subdued pitcher who never got excited about anything. The ball game would be getting tense, and I'd look down at the end of the bench and Stu was working crossword puzzles.

TIM MCCARVER (CARDINALS):

Stu Miller threw a 75 mph fastball, and his change-up was a little bit slower. What made his change-up so hard to hit was that he'd jerk his head before throwing it and that would mess up the batter's timing. It was like trying to hit a feather.

B. O'DELL:

I liked Dark and thought he did a great job as manager. I thought he worked well with pitchers. I didn't always agree with him, but he always thought out everything and had a reason for his decisions. You couldn't fault him for that.

There were a lot of Spanish guys on the team. Cepeda, Marichal, Felipe Alou and his brother Matty, shortstop Jose Pagan, who came from Puerto Rico, and others. There was some controversy about the way Dark treated them, but I think the press started that. I never saw Alvin treat anyone differently or without respect.

Alvin was a believer, but he never forced his religion upon anyone. But if you asked him about it, he'd be willing to share it with you. We talked a lot about it. I had a religious background and there were a lot of guys who were very involved with religion. For instance, there were a lot of Catholics on the Giants, including the Latin players. Many of us would go to church together on Sunday before a ball game. I was a Methodist at that time, but we usually ended up going to Baptist churches because they had services at all hours. Nobody was really tied down on denomination.

PITTSBURGH PIRATES

DICK GROAT:

After winning the World Series, some of the Pirates did banquets and a few got endorsements. I did Camels commercials. There was an unposed picture taken of me and Arnold Palmer by *Sports Illustrated* after I had just won the MVP and Arnold Palmer had won Golfer of the Year. He was doing L&M commercials. We both had unlit Camels in our mouths. At the time, we were at a country club playing doubles against Palmer's father and another old goat named Mr. Curry and they were just kicking our asses. We were intently watching Mr. Curry hit another great tee shot and we weren't even conscious that they were snapping all these pictures of us looking stunned and miserable. They whipped us good.

We opened our title defense against the Giants and Dodgers for two 3-game series, and afterward we figured out that the first 3 men in our lineup—Virdon, me, and Skinner—were either hit or knocked down 13 times. We weren't mad. We expected that was going to happen. We expected to have a tough time trying to repeat because all the teams would be ready for us. Then Vern Law hurt his arm, and our pitching staff was no longer strong enough for a pennant winner. Friend led the team with only 14 wins. Joe Gibbon and Harvey Haddix won in double figures and Face had another great year, but they didn't have enough support. Offensively, Clemente proved me correct by leading the league with a .351 average and providing power as well, and Dick Stuart had a great year with 35 homers, almost 120 RBIs, and a .300 average. But most of the other guys didn't match their 1960 seasons. I actually had 5 more RBIs despite playing less, but my average dropped 50 points.

ELROY FACE:

Back in high school, I was laid up after breaking my leg playing football, and so I started fooling around with my brother's guitar, learning to play some chords. I liked music. During the summer, my dad was a square dance caller—he won a championship in the New England states in 1949—and when I first started playing ball, I'd take over for the winter. When I came back from the service, I played a little piano in a square dance band. I also played guitar. On the Pirates, Harvey Haddix, Hal Smith, and I would take out our guitars after a game and sing country songs. After winning the 1960 World Series, Hal and I did two shows at the Holiday House in Pittsburgh. We recorded a live album there. We were on "The Perry Como Show" and performed in some movie houses in Pittsburgh and Gary, Greensburg, Morgantown, Mercer. A little three-piece band accompanied us. I did songs like "Bouquet of Roses," "Five Foot Two." I also recorded a single in 1961. But I wasn't serious about a recording career.

On the Pirates, we made appearances around the area, but didn't get the press you'd get out of New York, Chicago, or St. Louis because the closest wire services were in Columbus or Philadelphia. Because we weren't well known, we didn't get many endorsements, even after winning the Series. Hal and I did two national spots: a Camels commercial and a One-A-Day vitamin commercial for "The Saturday Night Fights." And Maz and I did a local spot for Iron City Brewery.

We all had pride, having been on that 1960 title team. Nobody wanted to be traded, although we might have received more publicity elsewhere. Anyway, in those days, if you were traded you took your contract with you and got no new signing bonus from your new team. You'd even have to rent a place in your new city on top of paying the mortgage on the house you may have owned in the first city. Since traded players were burdened with additional expenses, no one wanted to be traded.

After my 1960 season I got $42,500, which was the top salary on the team. That was before Clemente's salary escalated. I had an off season in 1961, going 6–12 with an ERA around 3.80. But I had 17 saves to again lead the league. I expected to receive the same salary for 1962 or get a small increase.

TOM CHENEY:
I didn't leave Pittsburgh on the best of terms. I talked to my dad on a Wednesday night. He was farming and I thought in good health. He wasn't 52 years old. They called me on Thursday night and told me he was dead. A heart attack. The family doctor had been treating him for something else. I flew home immediately. It was approaching the cutdown date for rosters, and I knew it

was between me and pitcher George Witt to go. So I called Joe Brown and said, "Joe, fill me in. I know it's cutdown date. My wife is down here. Do I have to bring her back to Pittsburgh so we can move?" He said, "No sir. You take care of business and fly back." So I spent 5 days getting my mother and brother somewhat settled. Then I flew back and drove straight to the ballpark and dressed. Murtaugh asked me to throw batting practice. In the meantime, Brown sent word for me to come up to his office. He said, "We're sending you out to Columbus." When he said that, I cursed him terribly, calling him everything a man can be called. He finally said, "I'm sorry, it was just something we had to do." Which caused me to lay into him again. I went to the clubhouse and dressed, and got out of there. I could have handled the truth, but don't lie to me. That was the worst thing that ever happened to me in baseball. So I had to arrange for my wife to come back up north to help with the move. I never forgave Brown. I told him that "the best thing you can do for me is to get me out of this whole organization, because I'll never play for *you* again." I meant it. I pitched a few games in Columbus before I was traded to the expansion team in Washington.

CINCINNATI REDS

JIM O'TOOLE:
After spring training, I didn't think we were a championship team. I remember after we lost a bunch of games on the coast and after a doubleheader loss to the Dodgers in the Coliseum, Hutch ordered us back on the field for batting practice. This was punishment for playing shitty. That night there was a bed check. I got in just in time because I was due to pitch the next day against Chicago. Gene Freese, our new third baseman, came in right behind me, but he went to the hotel bar instead of going to his room. Players weren't allowed in there— that was the domain of the manager and coaches—but he figured no one would see him. But Hutch was in there and Gene ended up buying him a drink. Gene didn't know that they had just called his room and that his roommate, Gordy Coleman, tried to cover for him by saying he was asleep. Hutch caught 13 guys out of 25 and fined them $100 each. That straightened us out.

Hutch was the main reason we won the pennant. He

brought us all together. But it helped when we had a players-only meeting and spoke our piece about each other, getting stuff off our chests. For instance, some of the guys pointed out that I was overreacting to errors—I'd throw my glove or curse the fielder. After that I bit my lip when someone blew one.

We played together as a team and everyone played well. I matured as a pitcher and won 19 games. Joey Jay matured and won 21 games; Bob Purkey won 16. The three of us pitched about 250 innings each. Jim Brosnan and Bill Henry were an effective righty-lefty relief tandem. We had good defense up the middle with Vada Pinson in center, Eddie Kasko at short, Don Blasingame at second, and 4 different catchers—Ed Bailey, who was traded to the Giants early in the season, Jerry Zimmerman, Darrell Johnson, and Johnny Edwards, our future starter. Pinson and Robinson had tremendous years. Pinson hit .343, which was second in the league to Clemente, and Robinson hit over .320, and was among the league's homer and RBIs leaders—he was voted the National League's Most Valuable Player. There were other guys who provided power. Freese and Coleman each hit about 25 homers. Gordy, a fun guy who kept you laughing, was a great hitter, but the only left-hander he could hit was Warren Spahn. He wasn't the best defensive first baseman. If Gordy didn't catch a grounder directly on the bag, the pitcher knew he had to get over there for his throw. We also had Wally Post, Gus Bell, and Jerry Lynch, who drove in over 100 runs between them while alternating in left field and pinch-hitting. Lynch was a whale of a pinch-hitter. He hit .400 with home run power. They used to say: "Lynch in the pinch." He had a lot of homers and RBIs in not very many at-bats.

I palled around with Kasko, Blasingame, Freese, Coleman, Ray Shore, who was the bullpen coach, Lynch, Edwards, Jay, Purkey, Joe Nuxhall, and Jim Maloney. After a game we'd go to a small bar, grab a sandwich, take three coins out of our pockets, and sit there playing a game in which we guessed how many coins were in all our closed fists. It was an elimination game in which the last guy got stuck buying a round of drinks. We sat around, drank beer, and had a lot of laughs. We usually talked about things other than baseball, and it was relaxing. We didn't get into trouble. People often challenged ballplayers, but when three or four of us

One of the main reasons Cincinnati won the pennant in 1961, Jim O'Toole won a career-high 19 games and led the Reds' staff in earned-run average.

took up the challenge they wouldn't want any part of us. We'd get back to the hotel 2½ hours after the game.

The day I pitched, win or lose, I'd go have a few drinks with the guys and maybe stay out a little longer because I couldn't sleep because I was so stiff and tense. If I won, it was somewhat easier, but if I lost, whatever I did wrong would stick in my brain. The next day would consist of a lot of running. The second day I'd run and get on the mound and throw 10 or 15 minutes. Then I'd rest the third day except for running. The day before I pitched again, I might run 5 or 6 laps instead of the usual 20 so I wouldn't tire myself out.

I had a fastball and slider, and I got to where I could throw an overhand curve and a three-quarters curve and take the speed off. I pitched 80 percent of the time in-side into right-handed hitters rather than nibbling the outside corner. When I got ahead, I threw hard inside to Mays, Aaron, and Clemente. I don't mean the inside corner, but 6 inches inside. They hit balls, not strikes. If I threw them a strike, it was a hit. It was a joy to jam right-handed hitters. It wasn't until 1961 when I could hit that outside corner with my fastball. Once I could move in and out, I became more effective. The guy who helped me most was Darrell Johnson, who came from the Phillies during the season. He was coaching at that time, but they put him back behind the plate. I was 6–7 at the All-Star break, and he caught me the second half of the season and I went 13–2, including 5 wins in Sep-tember. I didn't give up a homer during that time. John-son made me throw the slider in and the fastball away. He gave me the target and all of a sudden I was hitting it.

On the mound, I never laughed. I didn't want to talk to anybody or have anybody talk to me. A catcher might come out and tell me if something was wrong mechani-cally, but I usually already knew. Between innings I sat by myself and didn't say anything. I wanted to concen-trate on what I had to do to win the game. I just wanted to get batters out. I was a fast worker.

I think the turning point of the season was when we shut out the Dodgers in a doubleheader in mid-August before more than 70,000 fans. Purkey and I handcuffed them, 6–0 and 8–0. My win was the only complete game by a left-hander in the Coliseum that year, includ-ing Koufax. That was one of the best games I pitched in my life. After handling the Dodgers the way we did, we knew we could win the pennant. We finished 4 games ahead of them.

In late September we beat the Cubs in a day game in Chicago and then clinched the pennant when the Pirates beat the Dodgers that night in Pittsburgh. We were scheduled to go straight on to Pittsburgh for a game the next day, but instead they flew us back to Cincinnati and we went by bus to a rally at Fountain Square. 10,000 people were there and it was havoc. We ended up stay-ing at a downtown hotel and had a huge victory celebra-tion with a cocktail party, dinner, and dancing to a band. Hutch congratulated us all and even got up there and started singing. It was a fun, fun thing. Once in a life-time.

JIM BROSNAN:

Only two people got really mad at me because of *The Long Season:* Solly Hemus, who had been my manager on the Cardinals, and Gino Cimoli, who had been my teammate. I had written that Cimoli had gotten a bad break on a fly ball and then jaked it, costing me a game. My 1961 Reds roommate, Howie Nunn, a relief pitcher, was close to Cimoli from their days together on the Cards. He said, "You know, if Cimoli ever sees you, he'll kill you because you embarrassed him in your book." I replied, "I didn't know Cimoli learned how to read." Howie thought that was funny, so he went and told Cimoli and then reported back that Cimoli was even more upset. One day in Cincinnati, Howie told me to meet him at the Rendezvous, a popular rathskeller. He said, "I've got a friend who wants to meet you." I figured it was some broad. But Howie walks in with Gino Cimoli. The Cardinals were in town to play us. After some angry stares, it was apparent that neither Gino nor I wanted to fight. After three or four drinks we were laughing about the whole thing.

In 1961, when I was writing my second book, which would be titled *Pennant Race,* everyone knew what I was up to but no one said anything. Nobody asked why I didn't ask permission to write about the ballclub. After *Pennant Race* came out, Bill DeWitt, who was now run-ning the Reds, pointed to a clause in the player's con-tract that stipulated the club would have to clear any-thing a player wrote. Of course, DeWitt knew what I was doing or should have known because everybody else with the Reds certainly knew. I came right out and said so. Players would come by and give me stuff to use—or, as they more often put it, "Just stick this in your fucking book!" Most often they'd give me mate-rial that was too strong or too offensive to print. I never detected that the players mistrusted me.

After the 1960 season I had gone to Germany for a baseball clinic with Jim Bunning, Eddie Yost, and an umpire, and I bought a dozen berets, which I wore all through the 1961 season. Those berets probably contrib-uted to my "flaky" image, if I had one. Also being an egghead and being nicknamed "Professor" contributed to how I was perceived. I also smoked a pipe and carried a tape recorder so that I could play classical music in the hotel room on the road. Of course, such things made some people think I was snobbish.

There was a limit to how much I could fit in. I was a good cook, but I wasn't going to discuss fine cuisine with another player. I wasn't going to ask any of the players to go with me to see Vladimir Horowitz in concert. I wasn't going to ask Bill Henry to come over and listen to Mahler. I never met anybody in baseball who liked classical music to the extent that I did. If they saw the ecstasy on my face they would have wondered what was wrong with me. I read, but I wasn't going to be discussing gambling as Dostoyevski wrote about it with any of my teammates. However, I did run into a few readers. Joey Jay read a lot. Fred Hutchinson was a bright guy and a big reader. He loved John O'Hara and John Cheever. I recommended a few books to him.

While controversy swirled about his book writing, Jim Brosnan helped the Reds win the National League pennant with his superior relief pitching.

I was not a very gregarious person. I was recognized as pretty much of a loner. On the road, I really didn't socialize with the players or go out drinking with them. I wasn't part of a clique or social group. However, I would stick around after a game with the other guys. This year DeWitt allowed beer in the clubhouse—a popular decision with the players.

I was friends with Pete Whisenant, who rejoined the team down the stretch.

HAL WOODESHICK (TIGERS):
I was told that Whisenant, my former friend and teammate on the Senators, ended up being Hutchinson's bodyguard at Cincinnati. Fred tipped the bottle when he got upset and Pete took care of him.

ED BOUCHEE (CUBS):
Whisenant was one of the wildest guys in baseball. He was quite a nice guy, so I don't know if he got that way just from competing. I don't know what it takes for a player to go off the deep end like he would.

J. BROSNAN:
Lynch was our left-handed pinch hitter and Whisenant was one of our right-handed hitters off the bench. He'd also play defense in place of Wally Post or Gus Bell in left. Pete was still a strange guy. He lived in Evansville, Indiana, during the off-season and worked for the vending machine company there. The vending machine company in Evansville was run by the mob, and we'd kid him about that. He'd protest, "Where did you hear that? What do you mean, the Mafia? There's no such thing as the Mafia." He would never admit that he worked for the mob, but when his friends would come to the ballpark, there wasn't any doubt who they were and what they were like. (Pete got out of baseball after the season, and eventually got into the pornographic clothes business. And he would go from town to town selling marital aids and see-through bras and that sort of thing. Remember candy panties?)

The most sociable I'd get was to go out with pitchers Joey Jay and Bob Purkey and our wives. We'd do that on the few occasions my wife came to the ballpark. Jay, Purkey, and I also played bridge together. That was the only card game I liked. When I was sociable and not in a general funk about one thing or another, I could have as much fun as anybody. We were in a pennant-winning season, and I was having a lot of fun.

Jay, Purkey, and Jim O'Toole all had terrific years doing the brunt of the starting pitching, while Ken Hunt and Jim Maloney were good spot starters. Bill Henry and I were even more effective than in 1960. I won 10 games and we each saved 16. We had a very strong offense with Frank Robinson, Gordy Coleman, Wally Post, and Gene Freese all hitting 20 homers. Robinson hit 37 and drove in about 125 runs. Vada Pinson hit over .340 and Robinson hit over .320 and was voted the Most Valuable Player in the league.

TIM McCARVER (CARDINALS):

Frank Robinson was one of the most intimidating batters I ever caught behind. He stood on top of the plate and dared you to come inside.

STAN WILLIAMS (DODGERS):

I never really cared for Frank Robinson, but I had great respect for his talent and determination. No one was more mentally tough than him. If you knocked him on his ass three times in a row and came anywhere near the plate the fourth time, he'd hit it a country mile. You didn't want to wake him up. But it was hard not to because he stood right on the plate and leaned over, so you had no choice but to pitch him in. There was always a good chance you'd knock him down. Then he became more dangerous.

J. BROSNAN:

Prior to the season, Robinson was arrested for carrying a gun. I didn't blame him. I grew up in Cincinnati. If a black lived in this racist town, particularly in the Avondale area, where rednecks and blacks mixed together, then he had reason to fear for his life. Robinson had seen plenty of black guys beaten up or killed.

The black players on the Reds—Robinson, Pinson, Marshall Bridges—felt left out. In *Pennant Race,* I wrote how we should have included them. But they never asked to join the white players and it never occurred to me to ask them. (Robinson didn't make it clear until years later that he was pissed off that he and Pinson weren't included in the social grouping.) To begin with, I wasn't part of a social group or one who got people together for the evening. After the pennant-clinching game in Chicago, we flew back to Cincinnati and there was a small get-together for players at the Rendezvous, which was very popular with players—white players. I had never seen a black man inside. A couple of us were on our way to the gathering and Frank and Vada were in the elevator, so I suggested they come along. It seemed appropriate that they be part of our celebration. I thought, "Well, here's a damn good chance to integrate the bar. Who in the hell is going to turn away Frank Robinson and Vada Pinson?" And, as it turned out, no one did. The restaurant manager was summoned when we walked in, but he recognized us and told us to all come in. It wasn't particularly crowded that night, and Frank and Vada seemed comfortable. They drank Cokes, not liquor, and I picked up the tab. They stayed about 45 minutes before leaving.

AMERICAN LEAGUE
1961

"I DON'T KNOW HOW STALLARD FELT, BUT IT DIDN'T MATTER TO THE REST OF THE RED SOX IF WE WON OR LOST THAT GAME, AND WE KNEW THAT HOMER MEANT SO MUCH TO MARIS. WHEN HE CAME AROUND THIRD BASE, I WAS UNCERTAIN WHETHER TO SHAKE HIS HAND. I DECIDED THAT WAS UNPROFESSIONAL AND JUST SAID, 'NICE GOING, ROGER.' HE GAVE ME A LITTLE SMILE AND KEPT RUNNING."

FRANK MALZONE

LOS ANGELES ANGELS

RYNE DUREN:

By May, Luis Arroyo had emerged as the Yankees' relief ace, so they sent me and rookie first baseman–outfielder Lee Thomas to the expansion Los Angeles Angels. Playing for the Angels management was completely different from playing for the Yankees. They didn't have any unrealistic expectations about our new team. Bill Rigney was the manager and he was a great guy. He was a lot of fun and kept everyone relaxed in the clubhouse. Our GM, Fred Haney, was also always kidding around with the players. And Gene Autry was a wonderful owner. He'd sit around and visit with the players, just like one of the guys. He cared about us. When my wife came out to Los Angeles, just after we lost a baby, there was Mrs. Autry and her domestic help greeting her and making her feel at home.

Originally, the Angels were Peck's Bad Boys and castoffs. There were such familiar players as Ted Kluszewski, Steve Bilko, Eddie Yost, Rocky Bridges, Albie Pearson, Ron Kline, Tom Morgan, and Leon Wagner. We turned out to have a decent team. We finished far ahead of Kansas City and Washington and won 70 games (which would turn out to be a record for an expansion team). We played in cozy Wrigley Field and 5 guys hit over 20 homers: Wagner, Bilko, Ken Hunt, Thomas, and Earl Averill. We also had some good starters with Kenny McBride, Ted Bowsfield, and Eli Grba, the first pick in the expansion draft. I even got 14 starts, by far the most of my career. I had started only 8 times before that. My ERA was high, but I got career highs with 104 innings pitched and 115 strikeouts. Ten days after I came to the Angels, I tied a major league record by striking out 4 White Sox in one inning—one third strike got by my catcher, Del Rice. Three or four weeks later I tied an American League record by striking out 7 consecutive Red Sox. But I think the highlight of my year was pitching against the Yankees when they came to Wrigley Field. Mantle smashed one over the light tower off me, but I struck out 12 batters in 7 innings and put us ahead with a 2-run single against Bob Turley. We won 5–4 and that was one of the team's most satisfying victories.

I was roommates with Art Fowler, an affable, funny guy. We'd pal around together. He was a drinker, too. We got along fine except the night he got drunk and was going to stick me with a knife over some gal or something. I certainly didn't hold that against him. That's just what happens to the mind when you're drunk.

ART FOWLER:

In 1961 I was 56 days from having 5 years in the big leagues and qualifying for the pension when I flew from Vero Beach to Atlanta to try out for the new Los Angeles Angels. Ironically, Bill Rigney, the Angels' manager, was the shortstop on the Giants when I tried out for them in 1946. I knew they were going to buy me. But I walked the first 4 batters and they said no. So I went to Omaha and won 5 and then they brought me up.

Still exhibiting startling control as he approached 40, Art Fowler became a successful relief pitcher for the new, surprisingly competitive Los Angeles Angels.

I paid $3 a day for a room, with a swimming pool, in Inglewood. Football players would come into the bar around where I lived. On the road, Rigney roomed me with Ryne Duren. Duren was a super person, but after a month I went to Rigney and told him Duren was too much. He didn't drink too much, but it took only three drinks and he was drunk. Still, I loved the guy.

We had a good time on the Angels. Everyone was always playing jokes on each other. I razzed every player I played with. Rigney was such a nice guy that I'd even razz him. I told the other guys I could give him a hotfoot. So at a clubhouse meeting, I crawled toward him, hoping to sneak up on him. But everyone was looking at me and he caught me. He spit on me and said, "The meeting's over." I was on the floor like an idiot.

BILLY MORAN:

I started 1961 with Toronto and played with them until June. I went back to doing things like I did before Cleveland messed me up. I was back in the box, and no longer choking up and trying to punch the ball. Everything worked. I was selected for the International League All-Star Game. But I didn't play, because I got traded to the Los Angeles Angels.

I loved playing for the Angels and Bill Rigney, who knew how to handle players. Although I had been the All-Star shortstop in the minors, Rigney put me at second with Joe Koppe, my buddy, at short. It was strange, but Koppe and I formed a good double-play combination. I hit a respectable .260, but I wasn't satisfied. The perfect indication of how my season went offensively was that I once started both ends of a doubleheader and never got to bat. In both games, Rigney pinch-hit for me on my first time up. Phil Collier, a San Diego sportswriter who was covering the Angels, would just shake his head because every time I came to bat with runners in scoring position, Rigney would pinch-hit for me. *Every* time. I'd play 2 innings, 5 innings. I had always loved to hit with men on base, so I was really frustrated and angry. But I didn't show it. I didn't go to the clubhouse after I was lifted, but stayed on the bench to cheer the other players. At least I proved to myself that I could hit major league pitching.

KANSAS CITY ATHLETICS

VIC POWER (INDIANS):

I was glad I was no longer on the Athletics because they never improved after I left in 1958. Then Charlie Finley, an insurance man, became the owner after the 1960 season, after Arnold Johnson passed away, and it got really confusing. Frank Lane quit as general manager of the Indians to take that job for Finley. Then they replaced Bob Elliott as manager with my former manager Joe Gordon, who Lane had traded in 1960 to the Tigers. But then the team got off to a bad start and Gordon was fired and replaced by Hank Bauer. Then Finley got tired of Lane, too, and fired him. Or maybe Lane quit because Finley was interfering too much, or was too cheap, or both. I know Finley wouldn't allow any more trades with the Yankees.

The A's had a few good players—first baseman Norm Siebern, the former Yankee, was a good power hitter, and second baseman Jerry Lumpe and shortstop Dick Howser were good all-around players and good guys—but overall they were like an expansion team, with a lot of players no one else wanted. They got excited when they signed Lew Krausse, an 18-year-old high school sensation, and he pitched a 3-hit shutout in his debut. But it would be a few years before he was ready to pitch in the majors. Their 2 top winners in 1961, Norm Bass and Jim Archer, never did well again. For the next few years, the Athletics would be near or in the cellar, and Charlie Finley would keep hiring new managers, like Eddie Lopat and Mel McGaha.

Finley was a showman and we never knew what to expect when we came to Kansas City. He had an electric rabbit that would deliver the lineup card to umpires. He also had a real mule that he'd pay players to ride. But it was too big and I wouldn't get on it. Jimmy Piersall would ride it. Sometimes he'd sit on it backward and you couldn't tell if he was coming or going.

CLEVELAND INDIANS

MUDCAT GRANT:

Jimmy Piersall didn't hang out with the other players. The man had about 8 kids and was doing something else

apparently. Still, I got to know him pretty well. Some players thought he was using a crazy act to hide himself, but I thought he was pretty open. He wasn't at all pretentious or elusive. If he did something you didn't like, you could tell him and he'd say, "Did I do that? Oh, man." He'd be sorry, but the next day he'd go do the same thing. Some people didn't like what he did in his three years with Cleveland, such as when he fought with Jim Bunning and other pitchers, or when he charged and threatened umpires, or when he fought with fans in Yankee Stadium. Or when he rested behind the monuments at Yankee Stadium. But it was hot that day, and the relief pitchers were taking a week to get to the mound. So when we were ready to resume the game, there was no center fielder. Umpire John Rice had to walk all the way out to deep center to get him to come back onto the field. Jimmy was an excitable player, so

Mudcat Grant had his best season with the Indians by winning 15 games.

fans got a kick getting on him, and throwing everything from stones to batteries at him.

What people, including those in Cleveland's front office, tended to ignore about Jimmy was that he was a *great* ballplayer. He could play center field as well as anyone in baseball, he could hit, and he knew the game itself. In 1961 guys like Willie Kirkland, Woodie Held, John Romano, and Tito Francona hit a lot more homers, but Piersall was our best hitter. He helped me win some games. He batted .322 and was justifiably upset that he was passed over for the All-Star team as Mantle's backup. So many things went on during the year and in the two previous years that the Indians traded him to the Washington Senators for the 1962 season.

VIC POWER:

I enjoyed playing with Jimmy Piersall more than anyone because he would do something different every day—and that kept me relaxed. He did so many things in the 3 years we spent together in Cleveland that I can't remember what happened when. But one time Jimmy got into an argument with an umpire and took a water pistol from his pocket and shot water into the umpire's face—that was awful. He once asked for time when batting and ran into the clubhouse. He came back with something concealed in his hand. When the ball was pitched, he coated it with mosquito spray! There was smoke all over and we were all laughing. Another time Jimmy hit a home run against Jim Bunning in a big game in front of 40,000 people. Instead of running, he just bowed to the crowd. Suddenly he took off around the bases and slid into home as if he were beating out an inside-the-park homer. Then he just lay there sleeping. That caused a big fight. We had to run out there to save him.

One day they let about 8,000 kids into the ballpark for free and they sat in the stands together. When Jimmy was in the outfield, they'd yell for him to come over and sign autographs. So Jimmy waved for them to come to him and they climbed over the fence and raced into the outfield, where he signed autographs during the middle of the game.

Once in Yankee Stadium some tough guys started calling Piersall names and he challenged one to fight. A bunch of them ran onto the field after him. They started kicking him. So I ran out from first and Johnny Temple ran out from second to rescue him. Temple was a tough guy and he really hit those guys. Piersall wasn't a fighter—he'd just throw tantrums like a little boy.

One time when we played against the Red Sox, the umpire kicked out Piersall for running back and forth in center to distract Ted Williams at the plate. Jimmy charged in from the outfield and I thought he was going to jump on the umpire. I had to leap on his back and push him to the ground so he wouldn't get suspended.

Another time, Jimmy took a home run ball that bounced back onto the field in Comiskey Park and threw it at Bill Veeck's expensive new scoreboard, which was blaring music and explosive noises. And it broke!

He said he wasn't crazy anymore, but he still was sick and I tried to protect him. Joe Cronin, the president of the American League, kept sending him telegrams telling him to behave, and he was sent home a couple of times.

Jimmy had a great season in 1961 and I had an off year. But then we both got traded: he went to the Senators and I went to the Minnesota Twins. It was written in some papers that I was traded because I was a "clubhouse lawyer." How could I be a clubhouse lawyer when I couldn't even speak English and nobody could understand me because of my accent? Once I was talking on the radio about American League pitchers and saying "some of the pitches," and they shut off the program because they thought I said, "son of a bitches." I didn't like having a bad reputation and didn't think I deserved it. It didn't help that I would fight anytime—players didn't like me for this, but they respected me. But I never was drunk. I never came late to the ballpark. I never missed a sign. I played hard every day. I was a funny guy in the clubhouse. I never caused problems. I respected the manager, general manager, and owner. I didn't try to challenge the system.

I never had contract disputes. I would tell general managers to pay me what they thought I was worth. I went and played my game and didn't worry about money. The most I got was $38,000, from Frank Lane. I know that other players got more money, and that some guys like Gabe Paul, who replaced Lane as the Indians' general manager, tricked me. But I figured they'd be in trouble once they tried to get into heaven.

BARRY LATMAN:

I had my best year in the majors, pitching in 45 games and going 13–5. Only Mudcat Grant, who had 15 victories, won more games on the staff. As usual, our team was up and down. Typically, we were good at the beginning and faded away. The trouble with the Indians is that we didn't think we could beat the Yankees, so we didn't really care about the pennant race. We didn't have a good, winning attitude. Unfortunately, our losses cost Jimmy Dykes his job as manager.

JOHNNY ANTONELLI:

In December of 1960 Willie Kirkland and I had been traded by the Giants for Harvey Kuenn. As the Indians hoped, Kirkland provided some of the power they lost when they had traded Rocky Colavito for Kuenn a year earlier. They got me to be a spot starter and long reliever. I was still young, but I was planning to retire after the season, which I thought I would spend in the American League. But I wasn't really effective and my stay in the American League didn't last long. After I went 0–4, the Indians sent me back to the Braves, where I finished my career.

BALTIMORE ORIOLES

BROOKS ROBINSON:

Nineteen sixty-one was a strange year in that Paul Richards put me in the leadoff spot. I played 163 games in the American League's first expansion season, and batted a league-leading 668 times, an Orioles record.

That year, Jim Gentile had—if anyone really analyzed it—the best batting season in Orioles history. However, since Roger Maris and Mickey Mantle were having such big years for the Yankees and another first baseman, Norm Cash, was leading the league in hitting for the Tigers, no one even knew about Gentile. But he batted over .300, hit 46 homers, and drove in over 140 runs! He was third in the MVP race. He hit 5 grand slams, including 2 in consecutive innings in a game in May against Minnesota! They came off Pedro Ramos and Paul Giel, who had been an All-American halfback at the University of Minnesota. I was on first base both times. That was truly amazing. But he was having a sen-sational kind of year. I think he resented that he wasn't getting enough attention.

Gentile was pretty much a self-destructive guy, or he might still be playing. He was his own worst enemy. In 1956 I had played against him in the Texas League when I was on San Antonio and he was on Fort Worth, in the Dodger organization. It was my second year and I hit .270 with 14 home runs and drove in about 70 runs and he hit around .300 with about 40 homers and more than 100 RBIs. The next year I went to the big leagues, but because he was in the Dodgers' system, he went to another minor league team. He was stuck in the minors for about 8 years, and I think he was always bitter about that. He didn't really get to play in the majors until he joined the Orioles in 1960, when he was 25 or 26. (Jim would have a couple of big years for us. But then his average and RBIs would go down, and after the 1963 season he would be traded to Kansas City for Norm Siebern.)

This was Paul Richards's last year as our manager. Actually his coach, Lum Harris, became our manager in September when Richards resigned to become the GM of the new Houston franchise. Going into 1961, I thought we had a chance to win the pennant. We won 95 games in the new 162-game schedule. However, both the Yankees and Tigers won over 100. We didn't feel that we weren't getting the proper attention. The Yankees were just the class of the league and they had Mantle and Maris chasing Babe Ruth. They were our big rivals, and even when we had bad teams we played them pretty much to a standstill. We always had great battles, and it was a real challenge to play against them.

BOSTON RED SOX

FRANK MALZONE:

Carl Yastrzemski was a much ballyhooed rookie in 1961. He replaced Ted Williams in left and had received Ted's endorsement. Ted liked his swing and his attitude. Carl was quiet in the clubhouse, although he would evolve into a leader once he began hitting with power and not just for average. That year both Carl and I hit .266 and I edged him for the team RBI lead, 87 to 80. Although he once had been a great RBI man, Jackie

Jensen struggled in his comeback year and retired again. Two other rookies—Chuck Schilling, a fine-fielding, hustling second baseman, and right-hander Don Schwall—were as valuable as Carl. In fact, Schwall led our staff with 15 victories and was voted Rookie of the Year.

Tracy Stallard was another, left-handed, rookie. He was about 6′5″ and pitched mostly in relief, walking and striking out a lot of batters. His one memorable moment came in the final game of the season when he gave up Roger Maris's 61st homer in Yankee Stadium. It was as electrifying a moment as it could be, considering he hit it against us. I liked Roger and was happy when he hit that homer. Of course, I wasn't Tracy Stallard. I don't know how Stallard felt, but it didn't matter to the rest of the Red Sox if we won or lost that game, and we knew that homer meant so much to Maris. When he came around third base, I was uncertain whether to shake his hand. I decided that was unprofessional and just said, "Nice going, Roger." He gave me a little smile and kept running.

BILL MONBOUQUETTE:

Carl Yastrzemski was an obvious talent at the plate and in left field as Williams's replacement. He had a great arm and beautiful swing. Everything looked pretty. I couldn't tell if he would develop more power. At the time, he hit most often to left field rather than pulling the ball to right with power. That year the great left-handed swing was Roger Maris's. Maris pulled the ball with power, but Carl couldn't do that yet. I didn't think Carl would become the player he did. I was one of the veteran players who got on him for not hustling. I said, "Don't give the fans reason to boo you or they won't ever stop." I knew what happened to Don Buddin. Carl started running out more balls, but it took him a little time.

On May 12, 1961, I beat the Senators 2–1 and set a Boston record with 17 strikeouts. I think I struck out Willie Tasby 4 times and pitcher Pete Burnside 3 times. Guys like Gene Woodling, Billy Klaus, and Danny O'Connell were able to just foul off 2-strike pitches. I really felt I could have struck out up to 22 batters and broken all records. Yet I had a chance to lose that game.

I could be a feisty guy. I'd fight at the drop of a hat.

We would have brawls when I retaliated after an opposing pitcher threw at one of our hitters. I backed up my teammates—I learned to do that in the minors. The only time I had a guy come at me with a bat was against Cleveland after I retaliated. Cleveland had a lot of hard throwers who threw at our batters. In those days, umpires wouldn't discourage you from knocking down a guy. If he was slow getting up, the umpire might even hurry him along. In those days, nobody danced around the base paths or took too much time going around after homering. They'd get drilled. We didn't show each other up in those days. It was a fraternity.

We fought with the Indians, but of course, our main rivalry was with the Yankees. We'd come inside, even on the star players like Mantle, Maris, and Berra after they homered. They respected you for it. They'd come back at our guys. But it was clean play and we didn't have many fights. The Boston–New York rivalry was great. That's because there were Boston fans in New York and New York fans in Boston. The Yankees were pounding everybody in those years and we were having lean times, but the rivalry remained intact. I never missed my turn against them and had pretty good results.

Maris hit 2 of his 61 homers off me, both in July. It was hard to pitch to him with Mantle on deck. One night game in Fenway, Maris hit one up over the exit sign and then Mantle hit the next pitch over another exit sign. The Yankees had great thunder. In one game against us at Fenway Park, Maris, Mantle, and Skowron each hit a couple of homers. When Maris hit his 61st homer against us I was glad for him on a personal basis. Tracy was a happy-go-lucky guy who wasn't the type to get really upset by Maris's homer. He got some lasting notoriety for giving it up.

PUMPSIE GREEN:

There wasn't a whole lot to remember about the year except that Pinky Higgins played me less. He did that although I had my best year for Boston, batting .260, with 6 homers and 12 doubles, in about 220 at-bats. And he played me at short almost every time he put me in the field. Higgins was a low-key guy, so he didn't explain to me how he was using me. This was the first time since I'd been there that he managed the whole year.

WASHINGTON SENATORS

JOHNNY KLIPPSTEIN:

I was drafted by the new Washington Senators in 1961. Having been born and raised in the area, I was happy to have one opportunity to play regularly in Griffith Stadium, where I watched games as a kid. Regrettably, we had a terrible team that lost 100 games and finished last, and I had a terrible year, which I didn't like doing in front of all the people I grew up with. I didn't know what was wrong. It got so bad that I went up to the manager, Mickey Vernon, in the middle of the year, prior to the trading deadline, to get his assurance that I could bring my family to Washington from Chicago. He said okay and we took an apartment on the northwest side of the city.

For some reason Mickey didn't pitch me very much, but I still thought he was a great guy. Vernon was almost too nice to manage. There would be a card game in the clubhouse and he would say, "When you finish that hand, we'll have our meeting." That's just a bit too accommodating for a manager.

Of course, Vernon was stuck with an odd mix of players, so it wasn't easy figuring out how to handle them. There were guys who had never made it, former stars who were on their way out—like Gene Woodling and Dick Donovan—and a lot of mediocre players. I would hang around with Woodling, Billy Klaus, Danny O'Connell, and Marty Kutyna, a pitcher who had come over from Kansas City. There weren't many places to go in Washington, but we'd find some local tavern. That was a funny crew. Klaus and Woodling would agitate each other every day of the week.

Dale Long was a fun guy. Fred Baxter was the clubhouse man in Griffith Stadium. He had been there for ages. He kept candy bars and gum in a metal cabinet that he'd lock up so players couldn't steal from it. One day Long told him, "We're going to take batting practice now. If that lock is not off that cabinet when we come back, I'm going to knock it off with my bat." When we returned, the lock was still on, so Long grabbed a bat and beat that cabinet to death. That's the last time Fred locked up the candy.

Coot Veal was a good guy, and I think he was a good ballplayer. He wasn't a great hitter, but he was a fine shortstop who liked to play and was very serious about his business.

The only rising star we had on the Senators was Chuck Hinton. He was a 27-year-old rookie outfielder who finally got his chance because of expansion. He was a good hitter, one of the few players who developed on the Senators. In 1962 he would hit over .300.

What angered hitters most is when one of their pitchers wouldn't retaliate when they got knocked down. A pitcher has got to protect his hitters. But an interesting situation came up in a game I pitched against Kansas City, the team we tied for last place. Joe Nuxhall was on the mound for the Athletics, and he knocked down Willie Tasby, our center fielder. The bat went one way and the helmet went the other. Willie started jawing with Joe, and Joe knocked him down again. Willie took two steps out and Joe, who was a tough guy, told him to come the rest of the way. Willie didn't go out there, but at the end of the inning Willie came to me and said, "You've got to take care of me. You've got to knock somebody down." That's when Woodling came over to him and said, "Don't tell Johnny to do your work. That guy invited you out there and you didn't go." That was the end of that.

GENE WOODLING:

Everybody in the league liked me so much and wanted to keep me around, so they made expansion teams. I went to Washington in 1961. Mickey Vernon was the manager and he was a great person, but there was nothing the poor guy could do with the conglomeration of players he had. For instance, he had Gene Green catching. Gene, who was a real character but no catcher, would swipe at the ball and it would be back at the screen. It's little wonder we didn't draw people and lost 100 games. I hit over .300 but I didn't particularly enjoy myself.

COOT VEAL:

I was the first infielder drafted by the Senators, so I thought I was going to have a real good chance to play for them in 1961. I won the starting job and looked forward to the season. We had a lot of veterans like Dale Long, Gene Woodling, and Dick Donovan, and after a

NATIONAL BASEBALL LIBRARY, COOPERSTOWN, N.Y.

Coot Veal was the Opening Day shortstop and first batter for the expansion Washington Senators.

good spring, we were pretty optimistic. We didn't expect to win the pennant, but we didn't think we'd finish tied for last.

When we got to Washington, my wife and I rented an apartment in Silver Springs, Maryland. I was the only player on the team out in that area, but we enjoyed it. Considering that we had just been assembled, the Senators were a close-knit team. I was good friends with utility man Harry Bright and second baseman Chuck Cottier, who came over from the Tigers. We played a lot of golf together. Some organizations told their players not to play golf because it messed up their batting swings.

My chance to play every day in the major leagues was ruined when I suffered a groin injury when Earl Battey, the Twins' catcher, bowled into me two nights in a row when breaking up the double play. I never could get back to being a regular and had to split time with Jim Mahoney and Bob Johnson.

I wasn't impressed with Mickey Vernon as a man-

ager. He was a nice fellow, but he had a big ego. He had been a great hitter and had his own philosophy about hitting. Unfortunately, if you couldn't hit his way, then it was too bad. And I couldn't hit his way. When I wasn't getting enough playing time, I went to Vernon's office to find out what the deal was. I spoke up for the first time in my career. I told him if he wasn't going to play me, then he should trade me. He said he'd work on it, but they didn't trade me until November.

TOM CHENEY:
In June the Pirates' organization traded me to the Senators for pitcher Tom Sturdivant. I think the trade was in the works before Pittsburgh had demoted me to Columbus because Mickey Vernon had been a Pittsburgh coach and liked what he'd seen of me.

It was depressing on the Senators. The fans didn't really welcome us. We tried to drum up support with a couple of autograph sessions in shopping centers and a few promotions, but there really weren't many enthusiastic baseball fans around. The stands were pretty empty except when the Yankees came to town. They didn't even come out to see the Twins return to play us.

HARMON KILLEBREW (TWINS):
I regretted that after we moved from Washington and became a good ballclub in Minnesota, the fans in Washington weren't able to see and root for us. When we came back as the Twins to play against the expansion Washington Senators, the fans in Griffith Stadium threw eggs at us.

T. CHENEY:
I can't remember President Kennedy coming to a game other than on Opening Day. But Vice President Johnson did come and the players got to meet him.

I looked forward to pitching for the Senators because I thought it was a good opportunity to establish myself and reach my potential. But we had a bad team and I had a terrible remainder of the season, going 1–4, with an astronomical ERA. An injury kept me from pitching enough. I was out because of Gene Green. Pete Daley did a lot of our catching and was good defensively, but Green, who was primarily an outfielder, caught a few games. We were playing the Angels, and Albie Pearson was on first. After I pitched to Green, I heard someone yell that Pearson was stealing and I got down on one knee and turned to see if Green's throw beat him to second base. Green's throw hit me right in the side. On my next pitch, I barely reached the plate. I had a floating rib and it was six weeks before I pitched again.

Most of the other players had also come from winning teams, so it was hard for all of us to adjust. Nevertheless, it was a friendly team. My best friend was Harry Bright, who had played with me on the Pirates. I liked Coot Veal, who also came from Georgia—we'd tease him that he was the rare guy who could hit a ball and have his bat go backward. Chuck Cottier and I used to play a lot of gin together on the plane. Four or five guys would play poker on flights. I wasn't a moviegoer, but a bunch of guys were always going to the cinema.

DETROIT TIGERS

HAL WOODESHICK:

I began the season with Washington, with Mickey Vernon as the manager. I was doing pretty good early on. Meanwhile, the Tigers were challenging the New York Yankees for the pennant, in a race that would continue until the Yankees pulled away in early September. Detroit was interested in me because I was about 7–2 lifetime against the Yankees. I was called a "Yankee Killer," like Frank Lary. So Detroit traded Chuck Cottier to Washington for me so I could beat the Yankees.

I was glad to return to the Tigers because I thought they had a good chance to win the pennant. This was a much better team than the one I'd played with at the end of 1956. Harvey Kuenn was gone, but Kaline was still there and was still hitting .300, and they now also had Rocky Colavito to hit 45 homers. Billy Bruton, who was a good all-around veteran ballplayer, had come over from the Braves to play center, and they had put together a talented young infield with Norm Cash at first, Jake Wood at second, Chico Fernandez at short, and Steve Boros at third. Everybody was having a good year. In fact, Cash would hit about 40 homers and his .361 would lead the league in batting. He was something else. Cash was a good guy and a friend of actor Dan Blocker. When we were in California to play the Angels, he took a bunch of us onto the "Bonanza" set

and we were treated like celebrities. That was a lot of fun for us. Ballplayers always liked to mingle with actors.

The Tigers had strong pitching. The starters were Frank Lary, Jim Bunning, former starter Don Mossi, and Paul Foytack; Phil Regan was a good spot starter; and we had left-handed Hank Aguirre and right-handed Terry Fox in relief. I admired our starters so much. They were all tremendous competitors who went out and did it. Lary was a helluva pitcher and had a great year beating the Yankees several times. Bunning was a mean pitcher, moving the ball in and out. Along with Kaline, I'd say Bunning and Lary were the leaders of the team. They rooted for each other but at the same time were competitive with each other. But that's the way it is with athletes. I was competitive with my little daughter when we played cards. Only Don Mossi was happy on the mound.

BROOKS ROBINSON (ORIOLES):
The toughest pitcher for me was Frank Lary. He was intimidating, with a lot of fastballs that ran inside and quick-breaking pitches away. I just never could hit him. Other guys had trouble too, especially on the Yankees. He won 23 games in 1961, second to Whitey Ford.

FRANK MALZONE (RED SOX):
Frank Lary was tough on me, but Jim Bunning was worse. He could really loosen you up. He no-hit the Red Sox back in 1958. My hits off him were weak liners or ground balls that squirted through the infield. I could never connect and really hurt him. My only solace was that he liked to strike batters out—he led the league in both 1959 and 1960 with over 200 strikeouts—but said that Pete Runnels and me were the two toughest batters for him to fan.

PUMPSIE GREEN (RED SOX):
The guy I liked to hit against was Jim Bunning. I didn't care what he threw or where he threw it, I could hit it. It just worked liked that. He just couldn't get me out. One game in 1962 when there wasn't a walk situation, he would give me an intentional walk to pitch to Pete Runnels, who at the time was the league's leading hitter. That's what I had on him.

H. WOODESHICK:

I had a bad outing in my first appearance for Detroit. And from then on, I was in Bob Scheffing's doghouse. He was the Tigers' new manager and he pitched me only 12 times. Then the Tigers sent me back to the minors, to Denver. That day the Tigers were playing Washington, so I went over to their clubhouse and told Mickey Vernon I had been demoted. He said, "How the hell did you get through waivers? If we had seen your name, we'd have reclaimed you." "I'm glad to hear that," I said, "because now I'm not going." So I went home to Charleston, West Virginia. Detroit contacted me and asked why I hadn't reported to Denver. I said, "I'm not going to Denver. You pulled a fast one on me. You didn't put me on waivers, but hid me. Washington would have taken me. I'm not going to report to Denver. If you can make a deal with Charleston, I'll stay here and pitch." Charleston had a St. Louis Cardinals farm team at the time—Timmy McCarver was the catcher and Joe Schultz was the manager. So Charleston sent a player to Denver for me. And I pitched for Charleston for the rest of the year, although the Tigers still owned my contract. The Tigers held on to me because when National League expansion came at the end of the season, they were planning to sell me to the new Houston Colt .45s for $75,000, the price for a drafted player. The waiver price was only $20,000, so they didn't want to lose me that way and come out $55,000 short. So they tried to hide me. It wasn't kosher.

MINNESOTA TWINS

HARMON KILLEBREW:

I was very apprehensive about moving to Minnesota. I didn't know what to expect other than that Bloomington was going to be a much colder place to play than Washington. But it all worked out. My wife and I rented a home in Bloomington. We had two sons by this time (with 3 daughters to come later), and the area was an ideal place for a family. We made many friends in and out of baseball. Midwestern people in general are very friendly and our fans from the Minneapolis-St. Paul area were extremely supportive of the team. They were knowledgeable about the game because minor league baseball had gone on there for years.

Out of massive Griffith Stadium now that the original Washington Senators had become the Minnesota Twins, Harmon Killebrew became an even greater slugger: he would slam 46 homers in the Twins' inaugural season and then lead the league in homers in each of the next three years.

One benefit to moving was that there were many companies in the area who wanted players to go to work for them. I happened to get hooked up immediately with a television station. So, in my first year, I hosted a pre-game show, which was unusual for an active player. (I would do this for 12 years.) I figured this might help me develop into a broadcaster when my career was over. I hadn't had any real media experience and doing the show revealed a different side of me. I was forced to develop a more outgoing personality. (Previously, I did appear on the syndicated television show "Home Run Derby," in homer-hitting contests against Rocky Colavito and other players. They were funny. There was a moderator who would talk to us at the beginning and ends of the shows and when our opponents would bat, and our responses would be "Yes," "Uh, huh," and

"Oh, I think so." We had no vocabulary.)

Camilo Pascual and Jim Lemon were the only guys who came to Minnesota with me who were on the 1954 Senators team I first played on—Pedro Ramos and Julio Becquer had joined the Senators a year later. Camilo would be in Minnesota with me long after Lemon, Ramos, and Becquer left. Camilo and I had always been good friends though I spoke *poquito* Spanish. I saw him develop into a marvelous pitcher, probably the best I ever played with. He was one of the best curveball pitchers I ever saw and threw them with a lot of different speeds.

My first year in Minnesota was made better because I had an excellent season. Bloomington Stadium was a hitter's park and I hit a career-high .288 with 46 homers and 122 RBIs. My slugging percentage was over .600 for the only time in my career. Bill Tuttle played a lot at third base, so I played the great majority of games at first. I was on the right side of the diamond with Billy Martin, who played second for the Twins that year. We knew each other really well and were good friends. Billy provided us with leadership and a good clubhouse presence.

Sam Mele replaced Cookie Lavagetto halfway through the season. He developed as a manager as the team improved (and would have his best year managing in 1965, when we finally won the pennant). Mele had the knack of keeping everyone happy, particularly players on the bench. That's not an easy thing to do.

PEDRO RAMOS:
Our new home was totally different from Washington. The fans were great. We had a new ballpark. A Dodge company gave everyone a car to drive. Minnesota was open country, so it was a different atmosphere.

I had been the last Senators pitcher and I became the first Twins pitcher. I went on to start 33 more games, relieve 8 times, and pitch a total of 264 innings. This was following a 1960 season in which I pitched 274 innings in the majors and then 234 innings in the Cuban winter league. I was considered a rubber-armed pitcher. In those days, we had three days' rest and the fourth day we pitched. If I would have pitched every fifth day, I would have been stronger and a better pitcher. But Camilo Pascual, Jim Kaat, Jack Kralick, and I were out there every four days. It used to be, here's the ball, go

nine. For the fourth straight year I led the league in losses, this time going 11–20, but I gave the manager the most innings on the staff, struck out a career-high 174 batters, and had an ERA of less than 4.00. So I was valuable to the team.

Eddie Lopat, the onetime Yankee, was my pitching coach. He knew how to pitch and was the first guy to really talk to me about setting up hitters. He made sense when he told me, "No matter how hard you throw, someone will catch up to your fastball." Another coach I was close to was Sam Mele. When Cookie Lavagetto was fired because we were losing too often, Mele replaced him. Sam called me in and said, "Pedro, you've been a good friend and we'll stay good friends. But now I'm manager and can't associate with you as much. I hope you understand." I did.

The Twins had a good group to build a championship team around. Harmon Killebrew was the star player. He was a quiet man but he hit the ball deep. Bob Allison was a big strong guy, a pop-off sometimes, but nice. Earl Battey was an easygoing guy who played as hard as he could. He was a good catcher, with soft hands, and was a good hitter with more power than most receivers. Center fielder Lenny Green was a good leadoff hitter. He was a funny little guy. Zoilo Versalles was a bit of a showboat but a nice man. He made a lot of errors by making foolish throws, but he was a pretty good ballplayer. He had speed, good range, and, though he was a wild swinger, had a pretty good bat. He was nicknamed Zorro. Jim Kaat was a good left-hander and a likable person. Camilo and I were still good friends, friends for life. As a pitcher, he was becoming better every year. I could see the team improving.

I was single again and moved into an apartment in Bloomington. I had an Irish friend in my building who would go to every Twins game, and afterward we'd get together and hang out, maybe cooking and listening to music. If I had a date, he'd go his own way. There were a lot of pretty girls here, too.

After the season I married a Cuban girl. She was Miss Cuba in 1960. She was in Cuba and I was in Minnesota and we met and got married over the phone. I expected her to join me at the Twins' spring training camp. Instead, she met me at the Indians' camp because I was traded right before the season to Cleveland for Vic Power and pitcher Dick Stigman. I didn't want to go to

Cleveland, but in those days you went wherever they sent you.

CHICAGO WHITE SOX

MINNIE MINOSO:

I was upset when Bill Veeck had to sell the team because of his bad leg. He had a different style than all other owners. I had known him well since the late 1940s, when he signed me to play for the Indians. It wasn't like a boss and employee—we were on the same level. We were close friends. After he was gone, I wasn't as welcome in Chicago. I was traded in November to St. Louis for Joe Cunningham.

BILLY PIERCE:

In mid-season Bill Veeck was ailing, so he sold his stock in the team to Arthur Allyn, who was a minority partner. Veeck hadn't been as outrageous an owner with us as he had been with the St. Louis Browns. He had a couple of promotions—once, in 1959, he had Eddie Gaedel and a couple of other midgets portray spacemen who landed on the field in a helicopter and threatened Nellie and Luis. But probably the most memorable thing he did with us was install an exploding scoreboard in Comiskey Park that would go off when one of our players homered. Our fans loved it—opposing players hated it.

Nineteen sixty-one was an exciting year for everyone in baseball because of what Roger Maris and Mickey Mantle were doing with the Yankees. We knew history was being made. Maris was a fine ballplayer. His defense was much underrated. And though he didn't hit for average, he had good power. What impressed me is that left-handers didn't bother him. He was left-handed but stayed in against us. We couldn't overmatch him with inside stuff, because he was a pull hitter with a quick bat. I think Mantle was more respected and got worse pitches to hit, while Maris would surprise us with his talent. Maris hit quite a few homers against us, including 4 against 4 different pitchers in a July doubleheader. Maris hit only 2 homers off me in 1961, but they both came in a 2–1 game. That was the seventh straight game he had homered and gave him 48 in mid-August, so we thought he had a real shot to catch Ruth.

I won only 10 games, my lowest total since my off year in 1954. And my ERA was 3.80, my highest since 1950. I had a feeling I was going to be traded. I was the player rep on the White Sox, so I was at the winter meetings in November of 1961. I talked to our new general manager, Ed Short. I said, "Eddie, if I'm traded, I don't want to hear it on the radio." Two days later he called me to say Don Larsen and I had been traded to San Francisco for knuckleballer Eddie Fisher, Dom Zanni, and two other players. It made it easier that I was going to the Giants because my son's reaction was "Hot dog, now I can meet Willie Mays!" The next day at the meetings, Harvey Kuenn, the Giants' player rep, brought me in to be his assistant, so I already felt part of my new team.

JIM LANDIS:

I had loved Chuck Comiskey. He was a player's owner and treated us so well. He loved baseball and had a lot of respect for the fans. So did Bill Veeck. Then the new era began and Chicago's new owner, Arthur Allyn, would "barnstorm" ballplayers around the city—to corporations and clubs—to promote the selling of tickets. He actually said that he didn't mind finishing second or third if he drew more people. I thought winning was the name of the game in professional sports, but he was more interested in profit. I stayed home rather than work for him.

Despite the turmoil in the front office, I had my best offensive year. I had career highs with a .283 average, 22 homers, 8 triples, 151 hits, and 85 RBIs. I began to think of myself as a dependable hitter, particularly in the clutch. My style hadn't really changed. I still stood fairly deep in the box. I tried to take the first pitch because I led off a lot even though we had Aparicio. Even hitting third, which Lopez had me do quite often, I usually waited for the pitcher to throw a strike before swinging because that was the style of our ballclub. That year there were guys who could drive in runs. Al Smith, Roy Sievers, and Minnie Minoso all had over 80 RBIs, and Floyd Robinson, a young right fielder, was tremendous in the clutch as well as being a .300 hitter.

AL SMITH:

When I went to the White Sox in 1958, I negotiated my contract with Chuck Comiskey. Then Bill Veeck became the owner and Hank Greenberg was his general manager. They had signed me back in 1948 for the Cleveland Indians. Veeck was a good, honest man, and during his ownership I worked for the ticket office in the off-season, visiting companies and pitching ticket plans. After Veeck took ill and sold the team, Hank Greenberg stayed on only for a while as the GM. Then I had to deal with the new GM, Ed Short. He was a traveling secretary when I came to the White Sox. We didn't get along. Nobody liked him. I'd say he was a drunkard. Veeck had promised me a bonus if I had another good year in 1961. I batted .278, and had 28 homers and 93 runs batted in, both career highs, so I expected the bonus. Veeck even told Short that he had promised me extra money. Short told Veeck that he'd give me the money, but I would find out that getting a fair amount of money from Short wouldn't be so easy.

NEW YORK YANKEES

RYNE DUREN:

I missed Casey Stengel. He was a smart manager and always gave me encouragement. I pitched in only 4 games for our new manager, Ralph Houk, before I was sent packing to the Los Angeles Angels. There's no doubt that my drinking hastened my exit from New York. Like Casey, Houk wanted to get rid of the players who screwed up too much, especially if they weren't producing as they once had. Like Casey, Houk never sat me down and told me to curtail my drinking. That wouldn't have made a difference because if an addict drinks less he's still drinking too much. Houk didn't like me because of a couple of incidents and believed that there would be more. He was correct about me.

BOB TURLEY:

Nineteen sixty-one was a circus-type year because of Maris and Mantle and all the media. We had a great team that breezed to the pennant, winning 109 games. Everybody had a good year, except me. When Ralph Houk became manager I could have been part of a regular rotation, but I just couldn't produce for him. I got only 12 starts and pitched only about 70 innings, and I went just 3–5. Part of that was because I had bone chips in my arm and needed surgery.

Johnny Sain, Houk's pitching coach, did a good job with the pitchers. He had been a change-up–curveball pitcher, so his style worked better with some of the other pitchers. He had a good philosophy and helped pitchers like Whitey Ford, Roland Sheldon, and a couple of my roommates, Ralph Terry and Bill Stafford. Ford won 25 games, Terry came into his own, and Stafford and Sheldon were surprises, also winning in double figures. Sheldon was good until the next year when he wanted to throw only his fastball.

Luis Arroyo also did an incredible job for us coming out of the bullpen and throwing that screwball from the left side that no one could hit—he won 15 games and saved wins for all the starters. Luis was happy-go-lucky, the nicest guy in the world. This would be his one outstanding season.

JOE DE MAESTRI:

Casey was replaced by Ralph Houk, who ran a much tighter ship. He was called "the Major." Whereas Casey took it easy until about the fifth or sixth inning, Houk was always in the game. Having played many years for the Yankees, Houk really liked his players, and even if you went out there and did something stupid and got kicked out of the game, he'd fight for you. Everybody liked him because of that. He was a player's manager.

The 1961 team was close and had enormous pride. Even more than the previous year, the players were determined not to lose. I admired that. We won 109 games. Oddly, there was a pennant race because Detroit won 101 games. The Tigers were a real contender until they came in for a big series in early September. We drew about 60,000 fans to each game. Skowron's 2-out hit in the ninth won the first game, 1–0, and we went on to sweep them. The Yankees were just not going to get beat in 1961.

When Roger and Mickey came to bat, everyone on the bench stopped and waited for something to happen. They must have hit a few back-to-back homers that year. The score would be close and then boom-boom and we'd be far out in front. They just did it every night. It was really getting tense coming down the stretch when they each passed 50 homers. The Mantle-Maris thing was played up by the media as a rivalry. I think the media and New York fans wanted Mickey to be the one to break Ruth's record of 60 homers. Commissioner Ford Frick didn't want anybody to break the record of his old friend so he suddenly came up with the idea of putting an asterisk next to a new homer record if it was accomplished in more than 154 games. That was unfair and put even more pressure on Roger, making it almost seem like he was cheating if he broke the record in 162 games—as if he had been the one who expanded the schedule. It didn't make any difference to the ballplayers who passed Ruth, and Mickey and Roger were such good friends I don't think it made any difference to them who did it.

Eventually, Roger was overwhelmed by the New York media. It put so much pressure on him that it's amazing what he accomplished. There would be fifty reporters standing around his locker. Roger's problem was that he tried to answer every question, not with a "yes," "no," or "maybe," but with a long dissertation. He would fall into that trap and just freeze up. Mickey used to laugh because they weren't bothering him anymore even though he was only a few homers behind Roger. One night in Chicago, Roger struck out 3 times—I think they were all called third strikes—and he had more reporters around him after the game than if he'd hit 3 homers.

COOT VEAL (SENATORS):

It was strange to hear that Roger was getting a bad reputation for being surly. I had been with Whitey Ford and Roger at my apartment in Detroit and he was just the nicest guy you'd ever want to meet. What the press was writing about him was unfair.

JIM LANDIS (WHITE SOX):

I hated to hear that Roger was being written up as "a loner," just because he ate by himself every once in a while. Because there were too many guys who liked him and went out with him. We had broken in together and we were certainly friendly.

J. DE MAESTRI:

If Mickey had stayed healthy and been able to play in the last few weeks of the season, I think both of them would have passed Ruth. But he finished with 54 homers and Roger was on his own. Roger might have hit 61

homers earlier with Mickey batting behind him, and pushing him with homers of his own, and diverting some of the overwhelming media attention. As it was, Roger hit his 59th homer in our 154th game, against Baltimore's Milt Pappas. His 60th came in our 159th game, off the Orioles' Jack Fisher in the Stadium. That tied Ruth. He got his 61st in the most dramatic way, in the 162nd game against Boston's Tracy Stallard, into the right-field seats in the Stadium. Actually it was our 163rd game because we'd had one tie. What a relief and what a thrill that was for Roger and all of us. He was a modest man, but all the players urged him out of the dugout to acknowledge the fans' ovation. He smiled shyly and waved his cap at them. We all congratulated Roger, but as far as I know there was no celebration that night for him.

Was Roger Maris a Hall of Fame–caliber player? He was in 1960 and 1961. You just don't have a better year than he did in 1961.

TOM CHENEY (SENATORS):

Roger Maris hit his 54th homer off me. But it was a situation where I didn't want to walk him. He wasn't going to beat me that way. I had pitched against Roger when he was at Indianapolis and I was at Omaha in the American Association, so I knew how to pitch him. His success didn't surprise me in Yankee Stadium. Hitting that many, yes, but he was strictly a pull hitter and had that short porch in right field to shoot for. Roger couldn't handle the ball too well away from him, but in 1961, if he got the ball from the center of the plate in, he didn't miss it. He didn't miss my pitch.

J. DE MAESTRI:

Because Mantle and Maris got so much coverage, one tends to forget that there were other guys in the lineup hitting home runs. That's why we set a team record with 240 homers. Moose Skowron hit 28 round-trippers, and our 3 catchers, Yogi Berra, Elston Howard, and Johnny Blanchard, each hit over 20. When you put Blanchard, a strong left-handed batter, into the lineup that year, he homered at almost the same rate as Mantle and Maris.

Whitey Ford won over 20 games for the first time, pitching for Ralph Houk and Johnny Sain. In fact, he went an incredible 25–4 and won the Cy Young Award.

JIM LANDIS (WHITE SOX):

Whitey Ford was the best overall pitcher, as opposed to thrower, that I faced. He was very sharp and mixed up his pitches well. He could throw hard and throw to spots. On certain nights he could throw it as hard as anyone. I always had to try to think along with him, actually just to "stay with him, stay with him, stay with him." You had to concentrate against him.

J. DE MAESTRI:

It shouldn't be overlooked what a good job Houk and Sain did with the staff. Outside of Ford, we didn't have pitchers who could frighten anybody. Yet Ralph Terry went 16–3, Bill Stafford went 14–9, and Rollie Sheldon came out of nowhere to go 11–5. Any time any of them got into trouble, Luis Arroyo bailed them out. If we lost a couple in a row, Whitey would pitch and we'd be off on a 5- or 6-game winning streak. Even Whitey would take himself out of games, which I admired. He led the league in starts and innings pitched, but had very few complete games. He'd go 7 strong innings, have a lead, and say, "That's it."

And Luis would come in. He was tough. He had that screwball that absolutely dropped off the table. The only guy that I can remember hitting him that year was Kansas City's Norm Siebern, a left-hander. Luis pitched in a lot of games for us, winning 15 and saving 29 other games. He was just amazing to watch.

Although 1961 was a momentous season for the Yankees—this was considered their best team since the days of Ruth and Gehrig—it was the first time I ever got discouraged in baseball. Ralph Houk knew that I was going to retire at the end of the year, so he used me sparingly. I got into only 30 games, so while there was the pennant race and the Maris-Mantle home run race, the year got very long. But that was only one year in what I considered a wonderful career. I had done what I wanted to do, so I was very satisfied.

WORLD SERIES

1961

YANKEES vs REDS

JOE DE MAESTRI · YANKEES:

I didn't play in my first World Series. Mickey Mantle tried to play, and the stitches on his leg ripped open and he started bleeding, just like somebody threw a can of paint on him. But the Yankees didn't need either of us, I guess, because Cincinnati was really no match for us, other than Frank Robinson. It was a dull, quick, easy series. There wasn't anybody on our team who didn't know we'd win.

JIM O'TOOLE · REDS:

I don't think anyone knew what to expect in the World Series. We just wanted to go out and play like we did all year. The games we pitched would normally have been good enough to win. I gave up just 2 runs in the first game, but lost 2–0 to Whitey Ford. I lost but pitching against my idol and the Yankees in that game was the highlight of my career. Joey Jay pitched a 4-hitter to best Ralph Terry in the second game, 6–2. Bob Purkey pitched a 6-hitter in Game Three but gave up solo homers to Johnny Blanchard in the eighth and Roger Maris in the ninth, and we lost, 3–2. In Game Four, I was again losing 2–0 to Ford, so they took me out and we ended up losing 7–0. Then we got bombed in Game Five, 13–5.

With Mantle out of there with an injury, we thought we had a chance, especially since Roger Maris had only 2 hits. But they got clutch homers from Maris, Blanchard, Elston Howard, and Bill Skowron. Bobby Richardson had 9 hits in the 5 games, Cletis Boyer made plays at third I hadn't seen all year, and Whitey Ford was a genius out there, manicuring the corners. I had a 3.00 ERA for the Series and still lost both games because Ford broke Babe Ruth's record for consecutive scoreless innings. Whitey showed me how good you had to be. He was the difference.

It was a challenge to pitch to Roger Maris after he hit 61 homers that year. I just kept the ball away from him and had pretty good luck. It was more special facing Mickey Mantle one time. He got an infield hit off Eddie Kasko's glove and then had to come out because his leg was bothering him.

But we couldn't hit. Frank Robinson and Vada Pinson had been our keys all year, but they couldn't do anything. Robinson hit a 3-run homer in Game Five, but it was too late. Pinson hit less than .100. But good pitching will take care of good hitting.

The Yankees weren't cocky and didn't do anything to show us up. They just went about their business and kicked the shit out of us. I think the 1961 Yankees were the greatest team of the era.

JIM BROSNAN, REDS:

I ended *Pennant Race* before we played the Yankees in the World Series. I was asked to include the Series but refused. We were crushed. We didn't belong on the same field with the 1961 Yankees, one of the greatest teams of all time. Mantle, Maris, Berra, Ford, Richardson, Howard, Kubek, Arroyo, Boyer, Skowron. . . . The first 3 games were close. Ford shut us out in the first game and Howard and Skowron homered off O'Toole for the only runs of the game. I pitched one scoreless inning. Joey Jay, who won 21 games during the season, then pitched a 4-hitter, and we won 6–2. We were ahead 2–1 behind Bob Purkey in Game Three when Blanchard tied it with a pinch homer in the eighth and Maris won it for them, 3–2, in the ninth. That was a heartbreaking loss from which we didn't recover. They bombed us in the next 2 games. They hit me hard in Game Four. We had done more than we hoped by winning the pennant in a league where there were two or three teams just as good as we were. We didn't think we could beat the Yankees, so we decided to just have fun. The World Series was a party for us. On that basis, it was enjoyable.

NATIONAL LEAGUE 1962

"WHAT I THOUGHT MADE MUSIAL SO GREAT WAS THAT HE COULD HIT THE BEST CURVEBALL. HITTING THE CURVEBALL IS WHAT SEPARATES THE MAJOR LEAGUE HITTERS FROM THE FAILURES. THINK OF THE YOUNG PROSPECT WHO WROTE HOME: 'GET MY ROOM READY, MOM. THEY STARTED THROWING THE CURVEBALL.' MUSIAL NEVER WROTE THAT LETTER."

ED BOUCHEE

MILWAUKEE BRAVES

BOB BUHL:

I was still having a lot of fun off the field. Eddie and I were rooming in the Sheraton West in Los Angeles, when Bob Uecker, our rookie catcher, came down and mentioned our fireplace. Mathews always had a bat with him to swing in the room, so we started a fire using the bat for wood. It turned out there was no chimney—it was a false fireplace! The smoke was going down the hall and the fire department had to be called. Nothing happened.

I had stopped having fun on the field. Early in the season, it was apparent that Birdie Tebbetts was going to keep me in relief. I knew I could still be as effective a starter as Spahn and Burdette, but he preferred using the younger Bob Shaw, Bob Hendley, and Tony Cloninger. His intention was to get rid of some of the veterans the fans liked. When we were flying from Atlanta to Philadelphia, I told Birdie that it made no sense for me to remain with the club. The next morning, Birdie told me he'd traded me to the Cubs for Jackie Cruz. I thanked him. So I flew out to the Coast and joined the Cubs. It wasn't traumatic. I knew I'd see Eddie, Warren, Lew, Adcock, Crandall and the other Braves again. Ironically, I got along a lot better with Birdie after I was traded.

ST. LOUIS CARDINALS

TIM McCARVER:

The Cards got strong offensive years from Curt Flood, Ken Boyer, Bill White—who hit .324 with over 100 RBIs—and Stan Musial—who rebounded to hit .330 and set the all-time National League records for hits and RBIs. At 41, he also became the oldest player to hit 3 homers in a game and tied the major league record with 4 consecutive homers. Amazing.

STAN WILLIAMS (DODGERS):

I was a Stan Musial fan and kept track of his hits every day. The first time I faced him, I struck him out and didn't know whether to feel good or bad about it. He got me back—they all do if you see them long enough. I re-

member Musial outwaiting me one day at the Coliseum. I was ahead 2–0 in the eighth inning, and for the only time in the game the Cardinals had 2 men on base. Musial went up there looking for an outside ball that he could shoot to left for a 3-run homer. Norm Sherry was my catcher, and he signaled for a fastball low and in and I threw it there for strike one. Musial didn't offer at it. Sherry signaled for the same pitch and I shook my head because you don't want to throw Musial the same pitch twice in a row. Norm came back with it, meaning he had a good reason for doing it. So I threw it again and he took it again. Strike two. Norm gave the same signal and again I shook my head, thinking no way would I throw the same pitch for a third time. Finally, Norm begrudgingly signaled for an outside pitch and Musial just stepped out, flipped the bat as pretty as can be, and hit a nice little short fly ball . . . over the left-field fence for a 3-run homer that won the game. I had outdumbed him. Those are the kinds of things you remember. When a Musial beats you, you can't feel that bad because he was a very talented individual. I preferred him on my side. He pinch-hit for me and homered in the second 1960 All-Star Game. That was a thrill.

ED BOUCHEE (METS):

I saw Stan Musial only at the end of his career, and he was still a great hitter. He had a lot of power for someone who wasn't that big. What I thought made Musial so great was that he could hit the best curveball. Hitting the curveball is what separates the major league hitters from the failures. Think of the young prospect who wrote home: "Get my room ready, Mom. They started throwing the curveball." Musial never wrote that letter.

T. McCARVER:

The Cardinals got good pitching from their starters. Larry Jackson led the team with 16 wins and the improving Bob Gibson won 15. Ernie Broglio, Curt Simmons, and Ray Washburn all won in double figures. The Cards again finished 6 games over .500 for Johnny Keane, finishing in sixth place in the expanded 10-team National League. But I spent the entire year with the Atlanta Crackers. I had a pretty good year and hit .275. My manager was Joe Schultz, who was one of my biggest backers. The organization had fired him during the playoffs. Then we went on to win the Little World Se-

ries, and the Cardinals reconsidered and rehired him to be a coach in the majors.

HOUSTON COLT .45S

HAL WOODESHICK:

The Colt .45s got a nice greeting when we were introduced in Houston. We had a team of players who hadn't gotten opportunities to play much elsewhere, like first baseman Norm Larker and third baseman Bob Aspromonte from the Dodgers; shortstop Bob Lillis from the Dodgers and Cardinals; catcher Hal Smith and outfielder Roman Mejias from the Pirates; outfielder Carl Warwick from the Cardinals; second baseman Joey Amalfitano from the Giants; and outfielder Al Spangler from the Braves. Pitcher Ken Johnson had been on the

Hal Woodeshick joined the expansion Houston Colt .45s in 1962 and a year later would become one of the National League's most dominating relief pitchers.

A's and Reds; and Turk Farrell had been on the Phillies and Dodgers. Everyone wanted the chance to prove themselves. The fans of Houston treated us so well. We were given cowboy hats and suits to wear on road trips so when we'd arrive in some town everyone knew we were the Colt .45s. Larker refused to dress up, and our manager, Harry Craft, had to keep fining him. I was so happy to be in the big leagues that I didn't care how they wanted to dress me up.

Craft was the right man to manage the new team. You couldn't ask for a finer or more straightforward person. I loved Paul Richards, the general manager. At spring training he worked with the pitchers and everyone else, and after that he was always around. Richards was popular with the players, but he was responsible for setting up the intense competition that kept Houston from being a close team. You had to fight for yourself because there were people after your job. Richards told us that if we didn't produce, we were gone. So everyone was on edge.

My wife and I lived in an apartment in the southwest part of town. It was interesting that the various apartment complexes around the city would each take in only a few ballplayers because there was a good chance players would be sent out and break rental agreements.

I was a starting pitcher in 1962 along with Farrell, Johnson, Bob Bruce and, occasionally, Jim Golden. Bobby Shantz was our Opening Day pitcher but was soon dealt to St. Louis. I won only 5 and lost 16. Bruce was the only starter to have a winning record, finishing at 10–9. Farrell pitched well but lost 20 games. Roman Mejias, a Cuban outfielder who had floundered for the Pirates since the mid-'50s, was our best hitter. He had two 3-run homers in our 11–2 Opening Day win against the Cubs, behind Shantz. He had a great year, hitting about 25 homers. But after the season he was traded to Boston.

Colt Stadium, which would be the team's home until the Astrodome was completed, was a small park with a capacity of only 32,000, but it favored pitchers because the fences were way back. It was hard to homer there because it was 360 feet down the lines and 420 feet to center. It was so hot in Houston and we had no dome, so we started playing our home games at night. (Players and umpires fainted out there, so in 1963 Houston would be the first city to have night games on Sunday.)

The problem was that the mosquitoes were worse at night. We'd get to the ballpark and watch it rain every day between 4 and 5 in the afternoon. Then the groundskeepers would go through the stands with an insecticide fogger to kill the mosquitoes. The ballplayers would have to be sprayed before every game. If we didn't have the stuff on our bodies, they would eat us up in the bullpen.

DICK SCHOFIELD (PIRATES):

Playing in Colt Stadium was different from anything I'd experienced. The infield was terrible, the heat was murder, and the mosquitoes were bigger than me. It was nasty.

H. WOODESHICK:

We played hard, tight games against everybody, but usually without success. Naturally, the Colts and New York Mets, the other new team, had a rivalry. We were both terrible, but they were even more lousy than we were. The team we had the most trouble with was the Phillies, who shot up from being a last-place team to having a winning record. They beat us 17 straight times. They weren't so easy to pitch against because their outfielders Don Demeter, Johnny Callison, and Tony Gonzalez were .300 hitters, and they had Roy Sievers at first. Also, Tony Taylor and Bobby Wine were a good double-play combination, and their best young pitcher, Art Mahaffey, had a lot of luck against us. But I'd say our main rivalry was with the Cubs. That's probably because we had a good record against them and beat them out for eighth place in our first year, which caused them embarrassment.

Toward the end of the year, my back went out on me and they stuck me in Methodist Hospital for 12 days. I was given two spinal taps, and when I got out of the hospital I could hardly move. My wife drove us back to Pennsylvania, where my mother took me to a chiropractor. I saw him twice for $2.50 a visit. For $5, he fixed my back.

CHICAGO CUBS

DICK ELLSWORTH:

Much to my chagrin, the Cubs continued to employ their system of 8 revolving coaches, with Elvin Tappe,

Lou Klein, and Charlie Metro spending the most time directing the club. The Cubs were at the tail end of a very dark period, and went 59–103, finishing in ninth place. Even the expansion Houston team won more than us. We just floundered. I was completely lost, winning 9 and losing 20. I felt gypped of two years of my baseball life, when I was 21 and 22. The Cubs management was counterproductive at a time I needed good quality management and leadership.

I was never steeped with anything like Cubs tradition, Cubs loyalty, the Cubs way of doing things. We weren't taught Cubs pride. There was nothing on the walls of the clubhouse; there was really no Cubs history any of us hung on to and were inspired by. At the time I didn't realize what we missed was the Dodgers blue or Yankees pinstripes type aura. I'd say that the Cubs fans and media loved the Cubs more than the players did. The problem was that the Cubs hadn't won for so long that no one felt or talked about a sense of achievement or pride. We didn't feel that we had to win or play a particular brand of baseball in order to uphold a tradition. I think it would have helped.

The organization itself never threw parties for us in Chicago. There was always one team function in Arizona that was sponsored by the Cubs: that was a dinner at Mr. Wrigley's place in Scottsdale. The Cubs should have done more to promote the family feeling, even if other organizations weren't doing it, because teams get better production from players when there is a sense of trust between players and management.

The team unity we felt was provided by the players themselves. Ron Santo was a leader. He was always eager to accept responsibility and represent the team. In a nonegotistical way, he was very proud and possessive and never shied away from the spokesman's role. One might think Ernie Banks would have that role on the team. However, I never felt Ernie was the leader of the Cubs. I sensed that he didn't want to be. He was comfortable in his role, which was to play every day and drive in a lot of runs. Behind the doors of the clubhouse, Ernie was a very quiet, private individual who commanded a lot of respect. I was just two lockers away from him all those years, yet I never heard Ernie criticize anyone or openly express disgust at something bad that had happened. But I could see that he took defeat as hard as anyone.

I was extremely happy when we brought up Kenny Hubbs to play second base. He was a spark plug who provided instant leadership and solidified our team. With Hubbs joining Banks, Santo, and shortstop Andre Rodgers in the infield, and with George Altman, Lou Brock, and Billy Williams in the outfield, and with our pitchers, I thought we were finally putting together a solid nucleus for a winning team. Kenny made a difference. From the day he showed up, he was a great player and we knew he was going to be one of a kind. He was a good, improving hitter and a terrific fielder. When he was Rookie of the Year, he set a major league record for consecutive errorless games. There wasn't anything he couldn't do that he said he could do. In the clubhouse, on the plane, on the road, he kept everybody loose. He had a great sense of humor. He was just a good, outward kid with a very promising future. We expected him to be our second baseman for at least a decade.

BOB BUHL:

The Cubs' organization was completely different from the Braves'. That was the time the team used several coaches instead of a manager and each had a different idea and the ballplayers were lost. We even had the majors' first black coach, Buck O'Neil.

Everyone was unhappy, but no one complained. Banks was quiet and didn't want to get involved in the coaching problems. He went his own way. He was just a ballplayer. He hit an awful lot of homers, 37, despite being beaned by the Reds' Moe Drabowsky. Of course, he played in Wrigley Field, so he had an advantage.

Billy Williams wouldn't say much either. He was just coming into his own and batted nearly .300, with over 20 homers and 90 runs batted in. And he would improve each year. Banks was so popular in Chicago that at first he overshadowed Williams. It took fans a while to realize just how good Billy was.

Ron Santo was another young player with a lot of talent. He was a fiery guy. He was so hot-tempered that he'd even fight himself. He didn't do as good as he thought he should. He wanted to be better than his ability, and he couldn't do it. He drove in over 80 runs, but his average was low and he didn't hit many homers. But after a couple of years you could count on him to hit 30 homers, bat around .300, and drive in at least 95 runs.

Ken Hubbs was a good second baseman and would

have gotten better. He was a real good, religious kid. Lou Brock had a lot of raw talent. He had terrific speed and surprising power. In fact, he hit a ball into the center-field bleachers in the Polo Grounds, the only major leaguer to do it other than Joe Adcock in 1953— so I had seen them both. The Braves followed us into the Polo Grounds the next day, and Henry Aaron became the third player to reach the center-field bleachers!

The Cubs were a young club, and I was older than most of the players. There wasn't nearly as much drinking on this club as there had been on Milwaukee, probably because in Chicago there was a lot more to do. Being a ballplayer in Chicago got you a lot of things. If you wanted tickets to a show, you could get them. When you went to restaurants, you got real good service. We were also treated well by the fans. The Cubs had loyal fans who didn't care if you lost, which is good because we lost 103 games in 1962. They came to the ballpark to have a good time. Everything was a lot closer in Wrigley Field, and the fans had you circled.

As I told Birdie Tebbetts before he traded me from Milwaukee, I could still pitch and be an effective starter. I led the Cubs in innings pitched, earned run average, and wins, with 12. However, I was still hopeless as a hitter, going 0 for 70 during the year. I enjoyed hitting—I just didn't make contact too often. I was better in high school than in pro ball because they didn't throw many curveballs. I couldn't hit a curve. I wish I could have hit better because I would have stayed in games longer. I worked on my hitting as much as the pitchers were allowed to, going to the ballpark early and getting in 15 to 20 minutes. Of course, we'd see if we could hit the ball out of the park. I can't remember any pitcher I could hit. There were no pitchers in my book.

LOS ANGELES DODGERS

ED ROEBUCK:
I guess Walter O'Malley had known what he was doing because the Dodgers had become amazingly popular in Los Angeles. In 1962, when we were in a tight pennant race with the Giants, we drew something like 2,750,000 fans to Dodger Stadium, which broke the major league attendance record of the '48 Indians. The fans fell in love with our brand of baseball, which featured strong pitching, speed, and defense.

Don Drysdale pitched over 300 innings for us in '62 and won 25 games and was the National League strikeout champion, ahead of Sandy Koufax. He was voted the Cy Young Award. Don was a real gutsy pitcher, a real knock-'em-down fighter. Like Drysdale, Koufax became a workhorse. He went 14–7 and could have won 10 more games if he wasn't out with a circulatory problem—pitching put a strain on his arm and back. He won his first of 5 consecutive earned run average titles, and at the end of June he threw his first no-hitter, beating the Mets 5–0. A couple of months earlier, he tied Bob Feller's major league record with 18 strikeouts against the Cubs. As good as the starting pitching was with Drysdale, Koufax, Williams, and Podres—who didn't throw as hard but tied a league record by striking out 8 consecutive Phillies—Alston went to his bullpen more than one would think. My arm was sound and I pitched in 64 games and 119 innings, Ron Perranoski was in 70 games and pitched over 100 innings, and Larry Sherry was in 58 games and pitched 90 innings. We saved 40 games between us.

The Dodgers pitchers didn't resent that the offense didn't score runs. Until late September we did score runs in 1962. Frank Howard drove in about 120 of them; Tommy Davis scored 120 runs, and drove in over 150; Maury Wills scored 130 runs; and Willie Davis scored over 100. There was leadership among the offensive players. Snider and Gilliam were still there, and Wills and Tommy Davis led by example.

Wills was a good shortstop and terrific leadoff hitter and definitely the igniter for our offense. He changed the game of baseball, and I think that made him deserving of the Hall of Fame. In the '50s, Pee Wee and Jackie had stolen bases, but only in moderation. Nobody stole many bases. Fifteen stolen bases led the American League in 1950 and in several years during the decade the league leaders didn't have many more than that. Maury came along the hard way. He spent about 8 years in the minors, and he had to learn how to also hit left-handed so he could better utilize his speed. Then he changed everything. When Maury stole 104 bases to break Ty Cobb's major record of 96, and scored 130 runs, that qualified him to be the league's MVP. His steals were very important to our success. But I'd have to say his running was a bit of a distraction. I know it bothered Gilliam, who had to bat behind him. There's that old saying: "If you hit behind a base stealer, you'll always get a good pitch." But that doesn't take into account that pitchers would throw over to first 15 times or that they would quick-pitch Jim. He went so deep in the count so often that it's amazing how few times he struck out and how many times he walked.

In 1962 I was in an 80-game span without a loss that started in 1960. I was 10–0 but then lost twice in September, which made me feel awful because we were in a neck-and-neck pennant race with the Giants, another very good team.

The Dodgers and Giants each won 101 games, forcing a 3-game playoff series. I relieved in the first 2 games, and then, in the third game, Walt brought me in for Podres in the sixth inning with 2 on and no one out. And I was still pitching in the ninth inning. There was no such thing then as being a setup man. We got beat in the ninth. That was terrible. That was pressure. You don't get paid for playing those playoffs, and if you lose, you don't get into the World Series. Jesus, I was tired. I just wanted to get it over with. It seemed like the season was endless.

STAN WILLIAMS:

Our offense consisted of Wills walking or topping the ball for an infield single, and then stealing second and going to third when the catcher threw the ball into center field. The next guy would pop up, the next guy would strike out, and then Tommy Davis would get a 2-out RBI single. That's how it worked. Wills and Tommy Davis were our offense. It was amazing watching Tommy drive in runs every night, especially with our type of team. I think he beat Bob Gibson 1–0 three times during the year with a homer. Davis drove in 153 runs—he also led the league with 230 hits and a .346 average. But he finished only third in the MVP race, behind Wills and Mays. (The funny thing is that Tommy would lead the league in batting average the following year, too, but he was never talked about as a great hitter or received the accolades he deserved—because he did that in the years when there were some great players.)

I had another good season, winning 14 games, 1 behind Podres and the same as Koufax. Drysdale won 25

games, which wasn't easy with our offense. We ended the season with a nonscoring streak of over 20 innings. We couldn't win the pennant clincher. Then we went to the playoffs, which started in San Francisco, and got shut out by Billy Pierce, 8–0. Koufax was the loser.

BILLY PIERCE (GIANTS):

Being a left-hander, I could appreciate other left-handers. Sandy Koufax was a tremendous pitcher. With Spahn aging, Sandy would soon be considered the best southpaw in the league. So it was satisfying that our records were comparable that year and it was a thrill to beat him in the playoffs. He had a great, moving fastball and a very good curveball. He had conquered his wildness. It's funny that he was quiet on the mound, yet he was an aggressive pitcher who challenged batters. He wouldn't try to nip corners—he went right at batters.

S. WILLIAMS:

We came to L.A. for the second game and Drysdale went against Jack Sanford, who would be second to him in the Cy Young race. Both were pitching on only two days' rest. Sanford pitched the first 5 or 6 innings and had a 5–0 lead. They took him out to save him for the World Series, and we came back against the relievers and won 8–7, ending our scoreless streak at 35 innings. I pitched the final 1⅔ innings and got the win. I became the only pitcher in history to win 2 playoff games, having also won the second game of the '59 playoffs against the Braves.

But I'm more remembered for walking home a run in the third game against the Giants. There were so many extenuating circumstances leading up to that. It was rare for me to be out there in that situation. With about two or three weeks to go in the regular season, I pitched a home game against Chicago and beat them 4–0, with no walks and 12 strikeouts. Four days later, I pitched against the Cubs in Chicago and gave up a grand slam in the first inning, and we lost 4–3. Alston took me out of the rotation, and I didn't pitch again until the playoffs. And all of a sudden we're in the playoffs and I'm pitching two days in a row.

I finished and got the win in the second game. The following day, Podres started against Juan Marichal. They scored 2 runs in the third, but Tommy Davis hit a

2-run homer and Wills got 4 singles and 2 stolen bases and we went into the ninth inning with a 4–2 lead. Roebuck had relieved in the sixth and done a tremendous job. Then the ninth inning was a comedy of errors. The Giants got the bases loaded on a single and 2 walks, the first to McCovey, who Roebuck never liked to face anyway. Then Mays hit a bullet that Eddie grabbed, but it tore through his web and went behind the mound, and everyone was safe. That made the score 4–3, and the bases were still loaded, with 1 out, and Orlando Cepeda and Ed Bailey were due up. I was warming up with Perranoski, our left-handed stopper. Alston called me in to pitch to the right-handed Cepeda. I told Ron, "I'll get Cepeda and you get Bailey." We figured Alston would bring him in to pitch to the left-handed Bailey, and Dark would have no right-handed pinch hitter to go to except rookie catcher John Orsino. Unfortunately, Cepeda hit a fly to right that scored the tying run and sent Felipe Alou to third. Then Alston left me in to pitch to Bailey. Roseboro and I chose to go after him with high fastballs. I threw ball one, and then he swung at a high fastball and the ball went off the top of Roseboro's glove and Mays scampered to second—only Willie could have done that. So with runners on second and third and 1 out, the orders came out for me to put Bailey on intentionally. I called Roseboro to the mound and told him I'd much rather pitch to Bailey, who had about a .130 lifetime average off me, than the on-deck batter, Jim Davenport, who was a tough out for me. It was such an important decision that we wanted to call Alston out to the mound. But we couldn't find him because he'd gone up the runway! So we had to follow Alston's order and walk Bailey to load the bases. That brought up Davenport. John asked me how we should pitch him and I said low and away. We started him low and away and missed with two pitches. They were close, but it was a 2–0 count. All of a sudden the realization hit me that there was no place to put him. So I suddenly felt the pressure. I walked off the mound, gathered myself, came back, and threw a strike. Then I threw 2 more balls—they weren't far off the plate, but they were balls. Davenport had a good eye. The Giants went ahead 5–4, Perranoski came in, and the Giants scored once more on the game's seventh error, by Larry Burright, for a final score of 6–4.

It never bothered me that much because I gave it all I had and it didn't work out. Had I let up and thrown a half-assed fastball and the guy had gotten a base hit, I never would have forgiven myself. But I walked him at 100 mph, giving it my best shot. It was the best I could do. If I was booed, I wouldn't have known it. Letting down my teammates was much worse than worrying what the fans and media were thinking.

On the way home, my wife and I stopped and played Putt Putt golf.

In the years to come, everyone always wanted to snipe about 1962, and I would just laugh it off. But it was unfair to be remembered for that when you never gave up a run in postseason play. It makes it seem I was a choker when the pressure was on the line, when just the opposite was true. In my entire career of playoff, World Series, and All Star games, I never allowed a run, other than that run in 1962, and that was charged against Ed Roebuck—I hated to do that to my buddy, but it was true. I was always able to rise to the occasion in money situations—which is probably why I was out there in the first place. Alston thought I could get the job done. I had done it the day before after not having pitched for two weeks. If that appearance had gone wrong, people could have been upset with Alston for putting me in. It could have been the same thing the second day. If it works or not results in whether you're a hero or a goat.

I know the team wasn't happy with the whole situation. Most people thought Drysdale should have been in the ball game instead of me. Don had won 25 games that year and was available. But Don had gotten knocked out in the game before, and he wasn't warming up.

The Dodgers called me in the winter of 1962, right after we moved into our new home. They said I'd been traded to New York. Then they went on talking about how much they appreciated the job I'd done for them. Finally I said, "Hey, hey, hey. New York who? The Mets or the Yankees?" Back then there was a big difference. He said the Yankees, so I didn't feel quite as bad. I would have liked to have stayed with the Dodgers. It was embarrassing to be expendable after having come up through the organization. But it was flattering to be wanted by the great Yankees and to be traded for such a fine player as Moose Skowron. There was no way to fight it. I did feel I was being used as a scapegoat for our loss in the playoffs, which I had something to do with but not in its entirety. Someone had to take the rap. I think the other reason I was traded is that I hurt my arm in 1960 and it was getting progressively worse. (The bad arm would last 6½ years, until something popped and it felt fine again, letting me play until 1972.)

SAN FRANCISCO GIANTS

BILLY O'DELL:

Nineteen sixty-two was a heck of a season. I was back as a starter and won a career-high 19 games despite struggling at Candlestick Park, and pitched a career-high 281 innings. Jack Sanford went 24–7, Juan Marichal won 18 games, and the newly acquired Billy Pierce won 16, including game after game at Candlestick. We had a lot of lumber. Willie Mays was phenomenal, leading the league with 49 homers and driving in over 140 runs, and Cepeda had another great year with 35 homers and well over 100 RBIs. Felipe Alou also drove in about 100 runs. And several players hit above .300, or just below, including Harvey Kuenn. Harvey, who came to the Giants in 1961, was a great guy and as consistent a hitter as there could be. He got his hit every day. He was a super ballplayer, and though he didn't get a lot of credit, I think he contributed to our pennant as much as anybody.

We had so many guys having great years that it looked like we were going to win it early in the season, then we fell far behind, then we came back to win it. September was very exciting. Mays even collapsed from nervous exhaustion. We ran out of pitchers. Marichal had hurt his back, and Billy Pierce could pitch only every fifth or sixth day, leaving only me and Jack Sanford. In the last two weeks of the season, I believe I pitched on Tuesday, Thursday, Sunday, Tuesday, Thursday, and Sunday. We were 4 behind the Dodgers with 7 games to play, and at one point Dark told me that if we lost another game or the Dodgers won another game, he was going to let me go home because I had pitched enough. But we kept winning and they kept losing, and we ended up catching the Dodgers on the last day of the season. I started the final game against Houston and was relieved by Stu Miller. Mays's homer in the

eighth inning off Turk Farrell gave us a 2–1 victory. Then we listened to the Cardinals beat the Dodgers, 1–0, on a ninth-inning homer off Johnny Podres by Gene Oliver.

The playoffs with the Dodgers were exactly like the season. We won the first game 8–0 behind Pierce, then had the second game won 5–0 but lost it, 8–7, and they had us beat 4–2 in the third game when we messed around with 2 outs in the ninth and won 6–4. I was sure that either Drysdale or Koufax would be brought in. It surprised me when I saw Stan Williams coming out of the bullpen instead. Maybe Alston was saving them for the first 2 games in the World Series. Williams was a tough pitcher, but if Alston had the chance to use the 2 best pitchers in baseball and didn't, then it was a big mistake.

BILLY PIERCE:

I was 35 when I joined the Giants in 1962. In spring training I got absolutely nobody out. I had an earned run average of over 16 runs a game! We went to Utah for the last game of spring training. I came in to pitch relief to end the game and got 3 guys in a row out for the first time all spring. And Al Dark says to me, "You've found it. You're going to be my pitcher for the home opener in San Francisco." As it turned out, I won my first 8 decisions during the regular season. Then I lost a game that I was losing just 1–0 when I got spiked and had to be taken out. Candlestick Park was a wonderful place! I had never seen such a *beautiful* park in my life. Of course, my opinion was probably influenced by my success: I won 13 games in a row there in 1962. I couldn't explain why. But the ball carried to right field, so I pitched to right-handers inside and left-handers outside, making all batters hit the ball the other way.

I was also helped by having Mays, McCovey, Cepeda, Kuenn, and Felipe Alou knocking in runs for me, and having Jose Pagan at short, Jim Davenport at third, and Mays in center catching everything. I was finally pitching for a team that had a tremendous offense, but I didn't change my style. I pitched with everything I had all the time, although I knew it was probable I'd get more runs to work with than I had with the White Sox. I didn't believe in pacing myself.

When I played for the Giants, I lived in San Mateo,

as did many of the players. Willie had his home there and lived there the whole year round. We didn't go into San Francisco that often, but occasionally we'd go eat at Ernie's.

The Giants got along pretty well. Billy O'Dell, Harvey Kuenn, and I were from the American League, but we didn't really become good friends until we were on the Giants. I also became good friends with my roommate, Bob Bolin, a tall, hard-throwing right-hander from South Carolina. There were three factions on this team: white players, Negroes, and Spanish players. Alvin Dark had a tough situation, but he handled it and it worked out fine. There was razzing on the team, but it never went too far.

The Giants were a good ballclub. Willie Mays was the superstar, and Orlando Cepeda and Willie McCovey were just a little behind him. The Baby Bull was a very good player. He hit for power and had a high batting average. He was extremely consistent. McCovey was still a part-time player, but it was obvious he'd be great because he hit a lot of long home runs and always came through in the clutch. He was our best hitter against Don Drysdale—he always homered against him. In fact, I got my 200th career victory when Willie hit a 3-run pinch homer off Drysdale. McCovey was one guy Don couldn't intimidate by coming in tight. As big and fearsome as he was at the plate, Willie was very easy to get along with. Cepeda would have his bad days, but I had no problems with him either.

Mays was friendly with everybody on the team, but I don't think he associated with too many guys off the field. But I remember him inviting us to his place, and everything was white-gold. Mays and Cepeda were friends, but they were competitive. I think the press made it hard by getting down on one player while the other was doing good. The fans rooted for Cepeda over Mays, but after two or three years, they realized how good Mays was and rooted for him, too. Cepeda was a terrific player, but there were very few like Mays in baseball history. In 1962 he was second in the MVP balloting to Maury Wills. He hit nearly 50 homers and drove in over 140 runs—no one had ever done anything like that when I was with the White Sox. The one thing that surprised me about Mays was his fielding. I knew he could run down anything, but I didn't know about his

After a brilliant career with the White Sox, Billy Pierce had one more outstanding season in 1962, when he helped the San Francisco Giants win the pennant by being invincible in Candlestick Park—earning him the World Series starts that Al Lopez had denied him in 1959 with Chicago.

anticipation. A batter would hit a fly to an unexpected part of the field and I'd turn around, thinking it was a gapper, and see Mays standing there ready to catch it. He had remarkable instincts both in the field and on the bases. When he was on first, he'd see a pop fly and know instantly if it would fall in, so he'd end up on third while a wait-and-see runner would have stopped at second. I always believed that the greatest players—Mays, Mantle, DiMaggio, Fox, Aaron, Clemente—knew when to take that extra base, without halting on second to see if the ball would drop. Mays knew.

The Giants had an excellent staff. Jack Sanford pitched great ball, winning 24 games, including 14 in a row. In one doubleheader against the Cubs, Jack and I both threw 3-hit shutouts. Billy O'Dell didn't get as much attention, but he pitched tremendous ball. Juan

Marichal was only establishing himself at this time, but you could see he had great stuff. I went 16–6, and my .727 winning percentage was the best of my career. Our relief ace, Stu Miller, was amazing. He'd jerk his head and throw the ball and have these big guys swinging helplessly. He had the greatest change-up in the world, without any question. Bobby Bolin, my roommate, could throw like the devil and went 7–3. And Don Larsen, the veteran, helped out in the bullpen. We also got an occasional lift from our top minor league pitching prospect, Gaylord Perry, who debuted that year and won 3 or 4 games while he was up with us. Gaylord was Jim Perry's younger brother and could really throw the ball.

Both the Giants and Dodgers won 101 games. One reason was the expanded 162-game schedule and another is that we got to play against the new Houston Colt .45s and New York Mets. We pitchers looked forward to those games. However, Houston was the hottest, most humid place in the world to play. Besides, they had giant mosquitoes. It was brutal in Houston, while playing in New York was fun. Under Paul Richards, their GM, the Colts played a tight game, while the Mets under their manager Casey Stengel played loose games and would get beaten by higher scores.

The pennant race with the Dodgers was nerve-racking all season and included many come-from-behind wins. In September we seemed almost out of it but got hot when the Dodgers slumped, and made a final run. I don't know where I was when Willie Mays collapsed from nervous exhaustion. It was at Crosley Field, but I missed it. Luckily, it wasn't major. He stayed home about a day and came right back. Oddly, after it happened, nobody really discussed it.

The most exciting games of my career were the playoffs against the Dodgers. They were great. I started the first game at Candlestick against Sandy Koufax and pitched a 3-hitter. Mays hit his 48th and 49th homers, and Cepeda and Davenport also homered, and we won 8–0. We were ahead 5–0 in the second game but ended up losing 8–7. The third game went back and forth, and we ended up scoring 4 runs in the top of the ninth for a 6–4 lead. I was fortunate to pitch in the third game in relief of Juan Marichal and Don Larsen. It was the biggest thrill of my life getting those batters 1–2–3— Maury Wills, Jim Gilliam, and pinch hitter Lee Walls—

and clinching the pennant. Pandemonium broke loose, and people were throwing seat cushions all over the place. I went inside the clubhouse—Richard Nixon was in there—and came out on the field about an hour later, and it was absolutely quiet and empty. The difference of one hour made such an impression on me. I would never forget that feeling.

NEW YORK METS

FRANK THOMAS:

When I arrived at spring training to play for the new New York Mets, I found a lot of other players with high expectations. Other than center fielder Jim Hickman, catcher Chris Cannizzaro, utility player Rod Kanehl, and some of the pitchers, we had a veteran ballclub,

Frank Thomas was the player who gave the expansion 40–120 New York Mets their largest dose of respectability, as he smashed 34 homers and drove in 94 runs.

with many players from winning traditions. We had Gil Hodges at first, Charlie Neal at second, Elio Chacon at short, Felix Mantilla at third, Richie Ashburn in right, and me in left. We also had Don Zimmer at the beginning of the year and Gene Woodling later in the year. Ex-Dodger Roger Craig was getting the chance to be our top starter. We all had pride in our abilities and expected to have a fair record. We never expected to have a horrendous year and lose 120 games. I think we lost about 50 games by 1 run, and we often blew games in the seventh, eighth, or ninth inning. We had good righty-lefty starters in Craig and Al Jackson, but we had no closer. We lost our first 9 games before Jay Hook 5-hit the Pirates. Losing just became contagious. We lost 17 in a row at one point, and all the pitchers had long losing streaks. Craig Anderson lost his last 16 decisions. Going to the ballpark, you wondered how you would lose that day. We'd lose on errors, balks, throws to the wrong base, bad base-running, every conceivable way. Fortunately, the fans of New York were so happy to have a National League team after the departure of the Dodgers and Giants in 1957—and to have Casey Stengel back managing in town after the Yankees fired him in 1960—that they took us to heart and forgave us everything. No team got more enthusiastic support.

DICK SCHOFIELD (PIRATES):

Playing the Mets was kind of funny. Casey Stengel would be in the other dugout sleeping, and since they had drafted a lot of old guys, we thought we should beat them every game. When we didn't, it was frustrating.

F. THOMAS:

It was an experience playing for Casey Stengel, a great guy. He was good for New York. He took the pressure off the ballplayers by giving the media his Stengelese. When he spoke to us, he was perfectly clear. I loved to sit and listen to him. I always said he forgot more baseball than I'd ever know. He would use reverse psychology to motivate players, letting them overhear his gripes about their play in order to light a fire under them. Sometimes it would backfire with a young kid. Jim Hickman, who was a 6'3" youngster from Tennessee, had trouble with Casey's criticism. He was my roommate, and I'd always tell him that Stengel really felt that

he had great potential and was just trying to bring the best out of him.

We picked up Marv Throneberry during the season and he soon felt he was kind of a scapegoat for the Mets' bad play. For instance, no one would let him forget being called out for missing 2 bases on what should have been a triple. He wasn't as bad as his reputation. He tried, and it hurt him that the media portrayed him as a joke. However, he played up to the media by giving himself the nickname "Marvelous Marv." Jay Hook, who was a smart pitcher who had come over from the Reds and lost 19 games, was a draftsman, so Marv asked him to print that for him to put over his locker. The writers came in and saw "Marvelous Marv" above his locker and started calling him that.

As the losses mounted, Casey and his coaches Rogers Hornsby and Solly Hemus never changed their attitudes. A lot of players hadn't gotten along with Hornsby over the years, but I liked him. He was always nice to me and willing to talk. I'd pick his brain.

I had fun on the Mets. I happened to have a good year. I played 156 games and hit 34 homers and drove in 94 runs batting cleanup. In one 3-game period, I hit 6 homers, hitting 2 homers each game. I just missed hitting another and setting the major league record. That was exciting. I was the Mets' power hitter, so I was brushed back a lot—I even set a record by being hit twice in 1 inning. Because of my star status, I hoped I'd make a lot of money in New York through endorsements. I made about $2,000. . . .

ED BOUCHEE:

After the 1961 season I was purchased by the Mets. Each team had to put up so many guys in an expansion-draft pool, and the Mets and Houston had to pay that team $75,000 for most of the players they took. I was happy to be picked because I thought I'd get to play every day with the Mets. But when I went to spring training, it was shit.

George Weiss was the general manager of the Mets, and he was the guy I got my contract from. They hated him when he was with the Yankees, and they hated him with the Mets, too.

Casey Stengel shouldn't have been managing that team. He was worthless. Worthless! A manager who falls asleep on the bench every day—and this is no ex-

While Mets manager Casey Stengel played older veterans who drew New York fans to the Polo Grounds, the younger Ed Bouchee languished on the bench and was finally sent down to the minors, prematurely ending his career.

aggeration—should not be managing in the majors. Stengel couldn't even remember his players' names—we had two Bob Millers, and he called one of them Nelson to tell them apart. He was there for no other reason than to attract fans. How could he play Gil Hodges, a one-legged first baseman who you had to shoot up with Novocaine, just because he had a name in the New York area and would draw people? How can you play a cripple? I was the guy that should have been playing first base. Gil knew. I told him, "You shouldn't be playing, Gil. Shit! You can hardly walk." And he agreed. At the beginning of the season I pinch-hit 5 times. I hit 2 home runs and a single. I drove in 7 runs. I started the next game against Pittsburgh and went 2 for 4, with a home run. I went 1 for 4 in the next game against Pittsburgh. I never played again! So don't give me no bullshit about Stengel being a good manager! It's all politics.

In May I got demoted to Syracuse. I got down there and hit about 10 home runs in a month, 3 in one game. The Mets called me back up, but Stengel didn't play me again for three weeks. So we go into St. Louis for a Sunday afternoon doubleheader. I pinch-hit in both games and hit doubles, and I go into the clubhouse afterward and Casey says, "We're sending you back to Syracuse." I blew up. I told Casey what I thought of him. He didn't say anything.

I resented the portrayal of the 1962 Mets as a comedy act. But it was a circus. When was the last time you saw a team win 40 and lose 120? We almost had four 20-game losers. Roger Craig and Al Jackson lost over 20, Jay Hook lost 19, and Craig Anderson lost 17. Have you ever heard of that before? The Mets scored runs, but they gave up a lot. A walk, a hit, an error, and they beat us. We didn't have a good-fielding team.

I don't really think there were good things about being on that Mets team. I'm not even sure the Mets fans were as great as they were cracked up to be. I just remember that they liked to boo.

But I didn't hate the players. We got along well. There was no division between old and young players and no infighting between those who played and those who didn't. We were all in the boat together. Richie Ashburn was there, hitting over .300 as usual. I had been with Richie since Moby Dick was a minnow. All my big league career I'd been with him. Catcher Sammy Taylor was a real good friend of mine. He had been on the Cubs, too. Infielders Felix Mantilla and Elio Chacon were good guys. And I liked Marv Throneberry, who was a fun guy and a dedicated player.

Rod Kanehl was Casey's darling. He saw Kanehl hurdle an outfield fence in spring training to go chase after a home run, and he said, "Oh, he's got to be on my team." Another player the media teased was Clarence Coleman. Choo Choo wasn't too bright but he was a fair catcher and fair hitter and had a lot of speed for a catcher.

GENE WOODLING:

I had been with the first-year Washington Senators that had lost 100 games in 1961 and then played a third of Washington's second season, in which they'd lose 101 games. When I arrived in New York in mid-June, after being sold to the first-year New York Mets, some reporter asked me, "How does it feel to now play for a loser?" I thought he was kidding me. I asked, "Where in the world do you think I just left?" Of course, compared to the 1962 Mets, those Senators had been winners. The Mets set a record for futility by losing 120 games. Casey said that we were all going into the Hall of Fame, not as individuals but as a team.

The Mets had much better personnel than the Senators. But on expansion teams everyone is either too young or too old. We had some good hitters like Richie Ashburn, Frank Thomas, Charlie Neal, and Felix Mantilla and scored our share of runs, but we lost because of our fielding and pitching.

We didn't resent how the press wrote about us because we drew large crowds everywhere we went. People couldn't believe we could play as bad as they heard. We went into Cincinnati's Crosley Field after a Dodgers series had drawn just 5,000 a game and we drew 30,000 fans each game. At home we'd pack the Polo Grounds. We'd just keep losing and drawing fans. I liked playing in front of New York fans again. They didn't boo us because they understood what we were up against. Guys like Kanehl and Throneberry were crowd favorites simply because they played bad.

And we had Choo Choo Coleman, a catcher who could fly. I felt sorry for him. He had the misfortune of coming out of a poor area of Florida and not getting much education. He'd painted highway signs down in Florida. Charlie Neal did a good job taking care of him because otherwise Choo Choo would have been lost in New York, literally. The sorriest thing I ever saw was Casey trying to teach Choo Choo how to count on his fingers. He had to paint them. I almost busted out.

Casey told the reporters, "Woodling used to fuss with me to play him more with the Yankees. Well, he can play all he wants over here." Like Gil Hodges, I played about half-time and had a pretty good season. I hit .276, with 10 homers and 40 RBIs, in less than 400 at-bats.

I played almost 80 games in the outfield in my final season, meaning that in my 17 years in the majors I played nowhere else but the outfield. I was out there 1,569 times chasing down pitchers' mistakes. Fortunately, I never got hurt. I never missed a game for a reason other than that the manager didn't write down my name. At the age of 40, it was time to retire. Counting the service years, I was a 20-year man according to the pension plan.

The hardest thing about being a ballplayer had been raising a family. We moved three times a year for 22 years, and my wife had to raise the children because I was gone seven months every year. You had better have a good partner for something like that. Most ballplayers back in our day married girls from home. I was married in 1942 and had known Betty since we were about five years old.

I had worked in the off-season and entered the business world to set myself up for after my career and make triple what I did in baseball. I realized baseball was short-lived, that my career could be over in a day. I also knew that when you took the uniform off, you were going to be remembered for only a short period of time unless you were DiMaggio, Williams, or Mantle—and I wasn't that.

I thanked the good Lord every day for making me a ballplayer because it gave me everything. But when it was all over, I discovered it was a very cold business. You maintained those friendships you built with players from your era, but no one else. When I was the player rep, I should have insisted that the players and owners put everything in writing. But I just didn't think that ballplayers would be the ones to give retired players a hard time. We hadn't trusted the owners or general managers—who were the biggest liars imaginable—but we trusted ballplayers. That turned out to be a mistake because the new players who came in didn't care about the men who played before them. (If things had been in writing, it would have tied their hands, and retired players or their widows would get what they were entitled to. Sadly, once a player got out of the game, he became an outcast and a pain to those greedy new players who cared only about their own pensions. He found that he wouldn't be able to get necessary and accurate information about entitlements from the new people in charge, and that he had lost his voice in how the pension plan should be run.)

PITTSBURGH PIRATES

DICK GROAT:

I was very proud to start the 1962 All-Star Games. The Reds' Fred Hutchinson was our manager, and the first game was played in Washington. Don Drysdale started against Jim Bunning, and Juan Marichal beat Camilo Pascual. In the sixth inning we were in a scoreless tie when Stan Musial pinch-hit and got a base hit. Maury Wills pinch-ran and swiped second base. I wanted to move the ball to right field. There was nobody out, and Pascual and I kept battling and battling and battling. Finally he threw me a curve and I hit it to the right of second base into center field for a base hit that scored our first run. Bobby Clemente got a key hit that inning and another late in the game, and the two of us scored the other National League runs. It was a real good ball game, which we won 3–1. The American League beat us 9–4 in the second game, in Wrigley Field at the end of July. They got homers from Rocky Colavito, Leon Wagner, and Pete Runnels. That would be their last victory in many years.

In 1962 I came back to bat .294, with 199 hits, 34 doubles, and 61 RBIs. Also, Mazeroski and I led the league's second basemen and shortstops in most fielding categories. I had a good year. So did Maz, Clemente, Skinner, Burgess, Face, Friend, who won 18, young 15-game-winner Al McBean, and a few others. Even Vern Law came back to have a decent season. Yet the team finished fourth. I had good market value, so I felt I was expendable. Joe Brown had been the general manager when we won the title in 1960, but I thought he felt that veteran Pirates like me were primarily Mr. Rickey's, and hadn't much loyalty toward us. If I was to be traded, I wanted to go to a good National League team because I didn't want to learn all the pitchers and hitters in the American League. I preferred the Giants, Dodgers, and Cardinals, who supposedly treated their players exceptionally well. I didn't want to go to Philadelphia because the fans were a tough breed. I'd seen them chew up Del Ennis although he had some great years for them. One day in November, two days before the Pirates traded Dick Stuart to the Red Sox, Joe called

me when I was playing golf at the Edgewater Country Club. I said, "I guess this is it." He said, "Yes, you've been traded." I said, "I hope it's to the Cardinals." He said, "Well, that's where you went." I said, "Thank you very much," and hung up. Somebody asked, "Who were you traded for?" and I said, "I have no idea." As it turned out, Brown traded me for pitcher Don Cardwell and Julio Gotay, a young shortstop. The trade broke my heart. But I didn't have an ax to grind. The Pirates had treated me very well.

ELROY FACE:

The Pirates cut me $5,000 in salary after my 1961 season. Despite my losing record and relatively high ERA, I had led the league in saves, so I didn't think that big a cut was justified. But I didn't say anything. I just went out and pitched. I won 8 games, saved a league-leading 28 games, had a 1.88 ERA, and won the Fireman Award as the top reliever in the league. And Joe Brown wanted to give me only a $2,500 raise. I refused to sign. That's the only time I argued salary.

I knew I would get no support from Pirates' owner John Galbraith. That year he threw a cocktail party in Cincinnati for his real estate business associates. He had his players mingle with these people. So Ronny Brand and I were standing together when Mr. Galbraith came over. He said to Ronny, who had been with the Pirates one year, "When you get out of the game, you've got a job in the organization." I'd been with the Pirates since 1953, and he didn't say anything to me. (Any of the players who would get jobs with the organization after retirement were people Joe Brown brought to Pittsburgh. The players Rickey had brought in prior to Brown's arrival—me, Ronnie Kline, Bob Friend, etc.— wouldn't get offers. Years later, after I'd been out of baseball, I called Mr. Galbraith and asked for complimentary tickets to Hollywood Park racetrack because he was the part owner. He told me, "There are a lot of tickets. You won't have trouble getting them." I had played 15 years for the man.)

On a brighter note, Willie Stargell joined the Pirates for a brief time in 1962. He was a big, muscular left-handed power hitter from Oklahoma. He idolized Clemente, and the two of them became close. Willie wasn't a fatherly type yet, not at the age of 21. However, he was a joker, so he fit right in with our team.

DICK SCHOFIELD:

In the first year of expansion, we won 93 games, but we finished behind the Giants, Dodgers, and Reds, who all had super years. We might have done better, but when Vern Law, whose bad arm knocked us out of the pennant race in 1961, came back, he wasn't the pitcher he had been. He didn't have that old zip.

At least I came back from a bad 1961 season, raising my average almost 100 points to .288. My good showing assured the Pirates' organization that I could be a solid starter if given the opportunity.

COOT VEAL:

I had been sold to Pittsburgh in November of 1961. I roomed with Bill Virdon, who was the nicest person in the world and one of several leaders on the team. There were many other guys who had leadership qualities: Roberto Clemente, Dick Groat, Don Hoak, Vernon Law, even Smoky Burgess. Clemente led with his play. There wasn't a better player than Roberto Clemente. Clemente, Mantle, and Kaline were the best all-around players I ever saw, and I think Clemente was the best.

I thought coming to the Pirates was a good break for me. Danny Murtaugh told me that Don Hoak was getting up in age and might no longer be an everyday player, so the Pirates were thinking strongly of moving Groat to third and trying me out at short. But Hoak had a good year and Groat stayed at short. I didn't need any explanation for why I didn't play when we had a player of Groat's caliber at short. And Murtaugh used Dick Schofield as his backup. I batted only once and lasted just a month before Murtaugh told me I was being sent down to Columbus.

I still didn't think of quitting because my skills hadn't diminished. So I went to Columbus, where the manager was Larry Shepard. Infielder Gene Alley almost quit because of Shepard. (A few years down the road, he'd have to play short for him on Pittsburgh.) I couldn't play for Shepard either. I couldn't say I was demoralized, but I wasn't on one of my ups.

CINCINNATI REDS

JIM O'TOOLE:

I lived in the Cincinnati area, in Anderson Township, and always worked in the off-season. One year I sold insurance—but not to other players. Another year I worked as a PR man for a hotel. And I did a few other things. Some players just fished during the off-season. In my spare time I would go to Children's Hospital. I also gave a lot of speeches to kids' groups and the Little League. I had a fan club, which I enjoyed. The girls who ran it would always send me stuff to autograph, and I was happy to do it.

I think the players on the Reds would have described me as a fun-loving guy, a family man, a cocky pitcher who was usually able to back it up. I didn't feel pressure. I always liked the challenge, which was lucky because I often ended up facing Koufax and Gibson. I always liked to finish what I started. I had a temper like Hutch's, and I never wanted to relinquish the ball. We had a couple of incidents, one in Dodger Stadium in 1962 when he tried to take the ball from me after miscues by me and Kasko. I told him I was finishing the game. Our bullpen hadn't gotten anybody out for a week. Before I knew it, we were cursing each other. We almost had a fistfight, and the players pulled me off the field. I was in the clubhouse having a few beers and blowing my stack while we ended up winning 3–2 after Snider hit a couple of foul balls out of the park off Jim Brosnan. Everyone thought I'd get fined. After the game I went to Hutch to apologize. He said, ''Get the hell out of here—I'd have done the same thing.'' So I really loved him. He'd let you say your piece, and he liked guys who would fight a little bit. He didn't fine me.

We won 98 games, 5 more than we did in 1961. Purkey won 23 games, Jay won 21 again, and I won 16. Frank Robinson had an even better year than in 1961. He hit over .340, drove in about 135 runs, and had 39 homers and over 50 doubles. And Vada Pinson and Gordy Coleman had good years. But we still finished in third place behind the Giants and Dodgers. It hurt that we lost Gene Freese when he fractured his ankle in spring training. But our downfall came because we had trouble with the expansion teams. We lost a couple of doubleheaders to the Mets in the Polo Grounds. We beat them every game at home but won only twice in New York. Against the Mets, all you had to do was get the ball over to win, yet we kept blowing games. They had some good old-timers but were pretty much like a triple-A club. Hutch just about went nuts when we lost a doubleheader to them. He told us to be out of the clubhouse in 15 minutes because if anyone was still there by the time he walked in, they were in deep shit. So everyone ran up those stairs, got dressed without showering, and—boom!—was gone. I'd never seen him so mad. He was totally right. We played like a bunch of women.

It was terrible playing in the Polo Grounds. Everything looked on top of you because the fences were so close down the lines. It was a circus atmosphere, and the Mets fans were bad. When you walked up the runway in center field, they would spit and throw things at you.

The Colt .45s had a couple of good pitchers and a couple of good hitters in Carl Warwick and Roman Mejias, but they lacked talent. They played in a terrible stadium with bad lights and mosquitoes as big as half-dollars that would suck the blood out of your legs. It was hot and miserable, and I'd lose 10 to 15 pounds every time I pitched. Unlike in New York, the fans weren't very supportive of their team.

JOHNNY KLIPPSTEIN:

I returned to the National League and was again with the Reds. They were different than they had been when I played for them in the '50s. They were an older group. I enjoyed my first tenure more, but we had a great bunch of guys. Gordy Coleman was born in Rockville, Maryland, only about 12 miles from where I grew up. He was a laid-back guy with a funny twang, somewhat of a country boy. He was a good hitter, who had over 25 homers, and really not that bad a first baseman. Vada Pinson was a good guy and good ballplayer. He hit over 20 homers and drove in 100 runs. He was aggressive, but not as much as Robinson. Jim O'Toole was a great guy. He'd go out there every fourth day and rarely pitched a bad game. He was left-handed and somewhat flaky. Jim Maloney was a loosy-goosy guy. He was a hard-throwing right-hander with great stuff. He was a gambler on the mound, who would take chances that batters couldn't hit certain pitches in certain situations.

I roomed with Jerry Lynch a little bit. We had played together when he joined the Reds in 1957, and he was real likable. He was a fiery guy, a cheerleader on the bench. Of course, Jerry was a tremendous pinch hitter who hit a lot of late-inning home runs for Hutchinson. One night when I had just joined the ballclub, we were sitting and having a drink on an off-day in Cincinnati. It was about 20 minutes before the midnight curfew. And in walks Hutchinson, who sits down at another table for a nightcap. I didn't know him at all then. I said, "Jerry, we've got to get out of here." He said, "Hutch doesn't want us to leave." Jerry wrote him a note that said, "The Klipper and I know not what we do. We may be a few minutes late." We sat there for about another hour. Hutch left before we did and never said a word. That's the kind of guy he was. He knew we were just having a few beers and talking and that we weren't out carousing. I really liked Hutchinson.

Hutch hated bases on balls more than anything. When I'd get behind a guy 3–0 I'd sometimes hear him growl like a bear. The maddest I ever saw him was when Jim Brosnan pitched against the Cardinals with a 3–1 lead and 2 men on. The Cards sent up left-handed pinch hitter Carl Sawatski. Hutch had left-hander Bill Henry warming up in the bullpen. He went to the mound to make the change, but Brosnan must have talked him into letting him pitch to Sawatski. Hutch hadn't even gotten back to the bench when Sawatski hits it into the stands. We didn't score in the bottom of the ninth and lost. I walked into the clubhouse behind Hutch. Around the corner was his office, and in back of his office were these glass windows which you couldn't see through. He goes to kick a bag of baseballs and slips and falls on his butt on the wooden floor. He was swearing like crazy. He got back up and kicked the bag of baseballs and hurt his foot. Then he grabbed the bag of balls and limped into his office and threw it through the glass window to where all the fans were filing out. They were surprised. He wasn't mad at Brosnan. He wasn't mad at anybody but himself.

Back when we were playing ball I wasn't really friends with Brosnan. He was a loner. He would sit around the lobby and knit. That seemed kind of odd. Personally, I didn't see anything wrong with his writing—players were entitled to do anything they wanted to fill up all the time between games. But some of the other players didn't like it.

I still pitched inside. The only guy I wouldn't come in on was Dodgers' infielder Daryl Spencer because he would pretty much freeze on inside pitches. I didn't think anything of it when I hit batters in the ribs. They hit me with line drives. Hank Aaron hit me high in the leg, and I was grateful it didn't hit me somewhere else. Joe Torre hit me above the elbow, and if it had been 3 inches lower, my career would have been over.

The Reds had excellent starters and relievers, but Hutchinson gave me a lot of work. I was in 40 games, even starting 7 times. My record was 7–6. Oddly, my bat figured in the game I remember the most fondly. We were in Houston, and it was so hot that all you had to do was wiggle your finger to break into a sweat. I relieved Bob Purkey in the eleventh inning of a scoreless tie. Hutchinson was going to pinch-hit for me in the top of the thirteenth. Joe Gaines was in the on-deck circle. But we got 2 outs, so Hutch sent me up instead of Gaines. Gaines returned to the dugout and talked me into using his little 34-inch, 33-ounce bat. Don McMahon hung a slider and I hit it out of the park for a 1–0 win. That was one of the highlights of my career.

JIM BROSNAN:
I didn't knit . . . but I would have liked to.

Pennant Race came out in 1963, but Solly Hemus was one guy who was still mad about *The Long Season*. He had been fired as Cardinals manager and was coaching for the New York Mets in 1962. He still harbored a grudge. I came into a game, and he's on my ass from the time I got on the mound until the last out. Profane insults. He even reminded me of the time I got sick in Japan. Everything you could think of. But these were the '62 Mets, and I didn't have to pay attention to what I was doing to strike them out.

Pitching against the Mets was one of my pleasures in the 1962 season. Again I enjoyed myself, although we fell to third place. We had another very good team and won 98 of the 162 games. My stats were down slightly, as were Bill Henry's, but I thought we did a good job. We each won 4 games, I saved 13, and Henry saved 11. However, I don't think the front office was pleased with me. It wasn't so much for my pitching as it was for my writing.

AMERICAN LEAGUE 1962

"BILKO WOULD GO IN THE BATHROOM AND TURN ON THE HOT WATER TO STEAM UP THE PLACE. THEN HE'D CLIMB INTO THE BATHTUB WITH A CASE OF BEER RIGHT BESIDE HIM. THEN HE'D SWEAT AND DRINK THE CASE OF BEER. THAT WAS HIS ROUTINE FOR GETTING INTO SHAPE."

BILLY MORAN

LOS ANGELES ANGELS

RYNE DUREN:

In 1962 we played our home games at Dodger Stadium, and we hit many less homers. Ted Kluszewski had retired and only Leon Wagner and Lee Thomas had a high number. But we had a more balanced lineup and had some solid starters with Dean Chance, Ken McBride, Bo Belinsky, Don Lee, Eli Grba, and Ted Bowsfield. We were in first place on July 4 and might have won the pennant if it weren't for a late-season slump. It was amazing what we could pull off. Many times Rigney had to improvise. In Los Angeles they had big spreads in the clubhouse between games of double-headers. Once Bowsfield was scheduled to pitch the second game against Boston. While he was out there cranking up, I was in the clubhouse really stuffing myself. It turned out that his arm was so goddamn sore that he couldn't pitch. So Rigney came in and said, "Boys, I need a pitcher and bad. Do I have any volunteers?" Nobody raised his hand. He said, "Duren, you just volunteered." I was pitching so I went into the bathroom and stuck my fingers down my throat and threw up. Then I went out and warmed up a little bit and then went back to the bathroom and made myself throw up again. I shut out the Red Sox for 4 or 5 innings, and then Art Fowler came out and shut them out the rest of the way.

Fowler and I were dependable in relief. We played a doubleheader in which the second game was tied in extra innings and it was getting really late. Rigney told the rest of the team, "Just hold them until midnight, boys, because we've got a couple of sons of bitches who can really go about then."

All of the Hollywood celebrities would come into the Angels' clubhouse. Jonathan Winters put on a show one night in the clubhouse, and by the time he got through, every one of us was lying on the floor laughing. They fell off their chairs when he started to mock my stiff Frankenstein-like manners on the mound. Winters had seen me react to an umpire who had missed a call by letting the ball Bob Rodgers threw back to the mound hit me in the chest. So he mocked that.

The Angels had a lot of guys who wanted to have a good time. After Belinsky, who was a rookie left-hander, pitched the Angels' first no-hitter against the Orioles in early May, Walter Winchell, the famous columnist, took him to a lot of parties and introduced him to a lot of women. I got turned off a bit by that. Many of the players used to go to a place called the House of Surface, where there were a lot of gals around. At this point in my life, I didn't like hanging around bars so much. I lived in a pretty nice area of Inglewood and would pretty much stay there. I had a particular friend who was widowed, and I'd spend a lot of time with her.

ART FOWLER:

We didn't really hang out with movie stars. They were good people, but a different breed. I never felt like a celebrity. Bo Belinsky was different. After his no-hitter, he became the media darling. In spring training I could tell Belinsky was different. He had a dog running with him in the outfield. I'd never seen that before. Then when we moved to Chavez Ravine, he walked around with a little poodle. I think it belonged to one of the women he was running around with. I saw him with actress Mamie Van Doren down in Palm Springs. They got a world of publicity. I think they were engaged. She was a sweet person. You never knew about Belinsky. He was supposed to be a pool hustler. He couldn't play pool worth a shit. But he wasn't a bad person.

The Angels were a super group. Supposedly we were too old to compete, but we had a lot of guys who could play. Leon Wagner was a big innocent oaf, a great guy who hit 37 homers and drove in over 100 runs. Billy Moran was a good son of a bitch. They had a sign on the Angels' bus that read "A Bus Named Desire" for us old guys who supposedly couldn't play no more. Couldn't play? We almost won the pennant. Ken McBride won about 10 games in a row. I'd already been in 48 games when I got hit in the head. We were in first place deep into the season. On the day that Marilyn Monroe was found dead, I was shagging fly balls during batting practice when Eddie Sadowski hit a line drive that knocked my eye out. That was the best hit he ever got. I thought I was dead. That ended my season, and I could never hit well after that. We'd have won the pennant if Ken McBride and I didn't get hurt.

BILLY MORAN:

I had a real good spring, and Rigney didn't pinch-hit for me anymore. I hit 17 homers and drove in 74 runs batting second, behind our speedy little center fielder, Albie Pearson, who was always on base. I never reminded Rigney of the previous year, but I wanted to a time or two.

When I made the All-Star team, I looked around and saw Hank Aaron, Willie Mays, and the others and I said, "What the hell am I doing here?" In truth, I had earned it. I would never have made it if the players hadn't been given the vote. If it had been a fan popularity contest, as it had been before, Bobby Richardson would have made it every year because he was a Yankee. I posed for a photo with Maris and Mantle, which was a thrill, but they probably would have preferred Richardson, their teammate, as the starting second baseman.

It was an exciting season. We were a game and a half

Finally given a chance to play regularly, Billy Moran became an All-Star second baseman in 1962, nearly leading the upstart Angels to a pennant.

behind the Yankees with two weeks left to play. We went to New York and split and then went to Minnesota and beat them 2 out of 3. I remember talking to Albie after that series in Minnesota. I was batting around .298, and I said I just gotta hang in and get a couple of extra hits to get to .300. Then we went home and the air came out of the balloon. We stopped scoring and didn't win a game for 2 weeks. We all went into the dumper at the same time. I ended up hitting .282.

One thing that happened was Rigney replacing Joe Koppe with Jim Fregosi at short. I thought that was poor judgment, even though Fregosi was the better hitter.

BARRY LATMAN (INDIANS):

The toughest hitter for me was Joe Koppe. There was no explanation for it, but he got a hit off me every time up.

B. MORAN:

Joe and I worked well together, while Fregosi was impossible to play second with. He'd hide the ball before throwing, and I couldn't find it. Koppe was a .240 hitter, but he was playing great shortstop and we were turning a lot of double plays. Guys like Ted Bowsfield, Ken McBride, and Bo Belinsky were ground-ball pitchers, so infield defense was important. Bringing in Fregosi took away our rhythm. Fregosi was only 20 and Joe was an experienced major leaguer.

I loved Los Angeles. The whole town was friendly, and I made many friends who weren't involved in baseball. The Angels were the Dodgers' stepchildren, but the people treated us like stars. Actors like Cary Grant, Doris Day, Bing Crosby, Phil Silvers, Angie Dickinson, would come see us play at Dodger Stadium. Some would come into the clubhouse.

We had our own celebrity in Bo Belinsky. He got a reputation that I don't think he deserved. He liked the ladies, but he never drank or smoked. I didn't think he was disruptive. Bo was just a kid from New Jersey who didn't mind saying what he thought. At first he did his job and was pretty much a loner. It was Walter Winchell who turned him into a partygoer. He then started dating movie stars and eventually formed a twosome with Dean Chance. When he pitched, he pitched. He wasn't a great pitcher, just a good left-hander. He got an inflated reputation after his no-hitter and 5–0 start as a rookie.

Dean Chance *was* a great pitcher, much better than

Belinsky. He even ended up having a better rookie season than Belinsky in 1962, winning 14 games to Belinsky's 10. Dean had the most raw talent I ever saw. He was awkward-looking, but he could throw the ball through a wall. The only thing wrong with Dean was he got so inspired by all the attention spitters were getting in the majors at the time that occasionally he loaded up and threw one. He didn't need it because his ball was all over the place anyway. He ate the Yankees for lunch. Mantle, Maris, Skowron, and the rest were the best baseball team ever assembled, but he'd go through them like a dose of salt. Dean would just blow them away.

Ken McBride also could beat the Yankees. He could eat up that team because he'd throw junk and they had no patience for him.

We had good pitching, good hitting, and good defense. The only weakness we had on defense was Leon Wagner, who didn't sparkle in left field. But he could hit and drive in runs under pressure.

Lee Thomas had a career season, like many of us did. He hit .290, with over 25 homers and 100 RBIs. He was a very good hitter. Back in 1961 he had tied some records by getting 9 hits and 19 total bases in a double-header.

We had a great clubhouse. The leaders on the team were Leon Wagner, catcher Bob Rodgers, and Earl Averill, a catcher-outfielder. The guys voted me team MVP, so maybe I was a leader, too, but I never was a vocal, rah-rah guy. I think guys respected me, and we had a lot of fun together.

The real leader of the team was Rigney. He was responsible for the relaxed atmosphere. He was always on an even keel. He wanted us to have fun, so he left us alone and never fined anybody. He made it easy on himself by keeping a set lineup. Wagner, Pearson, Thomas, and I all played 160 games. Rodgers even caught 150 games. Rigney also did a great job of juggling his starters and relievers Art Fowler, Ryne Duren, Tom Morgan, and Dan Osinski.

We got Osinski in July from the Athletics for Ted Bowsfield, and he became our bullpen ace. His best pitch was a forkball, like the one ElRoy Face threw. He was a battler and picked us up in some games.

Art Fowler was a good pitcher. He was a great guy who laughed all the time. He was pretty good with the ladies, and he liked to drink. They couldn't have given him blood tests because he used to take two greenies when he got to the ballpark every day and then he'd go out there and pitch an inning or two. He did great things for us. Art was not young at that time. All he'd do was throw a little fastball and hold it a little off-center and it would sail. He had such great control that he could throw it through knotholes. We played Washington and we were 1 run up, and he came in with the bases loaded and no one out in the eighth. He strikes one out, pops one up, and strikes out the next guy. He did it very efficiently.

We had some bad boozers on that team. Ryne Duren was bad when he drank. No one went out with Duren. Late in the season, we were in Cleveland and staying at the Biltmore downtown. My roomie, Joe Koppe, was spending the night at his home in Detroit, so Duren got put in with me. That was the damnedest night. Ryne comes in and wakes me at about 1:30 A.M. He was drunker than the Lord. He couldn't hit the floor with his hat. He says, "Can I have your World Series tickets?" I said, "Sure, sure, sure . . . what the hell . . . I'm not going." Then I started dozing off when he started yelling into the phone, cussing somebody out in Texas. He tried to call Whitey Ford and Mickey Mantle. He finally called up some woman outside of Dallas and started cussing her out. It wasn't his wife. That went on for about an hour. Finally he hung up and lay down on his bed. I sighed, "Oh, good." As soon as I dozed off, I was woken up again because he started yelling in his sleep, cursing out somebody named Blue, "You son of a bitch, I'm going to kill you, Blue!" His eyes were closed. I shook him and he quieted down. I got back into bed, but as soon as I fell asleep again, he started screaming. That was it. I moved to a different room.

Later on that road trip, Duren bothered Eli Grba, who was a big, strong kid. Grba and Kenny Hunt used to room together. They were pretty good drinkers, too. Ryne knocked on their door after they got into bed. Grba got up with his boxer shorts on. Duren came in and started raising hell, asking for World Series tickets. Grba said he wanted to keep his tickets. Duren started raving, so Grba just knocked him out with one punch. He picked him up off the floor, put him over his shoulder, and took him back to his room and threw him on his bed. The next day Duren came downstairs with this enormous shiner. He came over to the table where Grba,

Hunt, Koppe, and I were eating and says, "I don't know what I did last night but somebody knocked the hell out of me." I don't know if he ever found out who did it.

When Ryne was sober, he was a nice fellow. It wasn't like he drank a bottle of gin. Two martinis and he didn't know where the hell he was. It was weird. It was considered a problem. He had fights with everyone, but he never won one because he couldn't see. There was no counseling in those days, and all his drinking was tolerated because he would go out to the mound and throw BBs. I loved watching him pitch. He never pitched a damn inning for us when the first pitch didn't go on the screen. Then he'd kind of laugh. He had those thick dark glasses on, and the word was he couldn't see. He would intimidate batters. All those things I heard about him hitting guys in the on-deck circle in the minor leagues—I don't doubt it. But then when he wanted to, he'd throw it through a knothole.

There were a lot of boozers on the Angels. Joe Koppe drank a lot. Steve Bilko drank his beer. Bilko was huge. He was big in the legs and hips and just square all the way up, with calves as big as my waist. He and Koppe would room together in spring training. Bilko would go in the bathroom and turn on the hot water to steam up the place. Then he'd climb into the bathtub with a case of beer right beside him. Then he'd sweat and drink the case of beer. That was his routine for getting into shape. We'd laugh at him all the time. But he was one of my favorite people. He wasn't dangerous when he was drunk. He was a big old easygoing guy with no temper.

Rodgers and Fregosi didn't drink much, but they were chasing broads all the time. Chasing women was popular in baseball at the time. Jim Bouton, who was a rookie with the Yankees in 1962, told the truth when he later wrote about this era in his book *Ball Four*. He wrote about players using binoculars for "beaver-shooting" in ballparks. Well, I remember players carrying around drills to make holes in walls to spy on women in the adjoining hotel rooms.

CLEVELAND INDIANS

MUDCAT GRANT:
When I joined the Indians in 1958, there had been only 4 black starting pitchers in baseball, and I had been the

only one in the American League. Major league base-ball was still uncomfortable with black pitchers—just as black quarterbacks weren't welcome in the NFL—and black catchers as well, for that matter, but the situation had improved slightly. In the National League, there was Bob Gibson on the Cardinals, Al McBean on the Pirates, and Al Jackson on the Mets; and in the American League, there were three or four blacks who got starts, including me on the Indians and Earl Wilson on the Red Sox; as well as much-used black relievers like John Wyatt on the A's and Marshall Bridges on the Yankees. Baseball was slow to change, but I was encouraged.

BARRY LATMAN:

I got married in 1962 and we lived in Shaker Heights. This was a Jewish area, and there weren't other players living there. Married players would hang out together, as would our wives. We'd have barbecues. The players didn't play bridge, but the wives might. Other than the annual father-and-child games, the teams didn't sponsor any family functions. There was an autograph day, but that was strictly for the players, and management didn't want the wives around. They weren't allowed on the buses. They weren't allowed anyplace. My wife came to Washington when we played the Senators, and it was such a big deal when I attempted to get a private room for us. My wife ended up staying with my family instead of at the hotel.

Just as it had been with the White Sox, we'd wind down every night after a game in the clubhouse. That was the best part of the game. Everyone hung around but Pedro Ramos, who usually left 15 minutes after the game. The rest of us, including the coaches, would sit there and drink and talk over the game.

Pedro joined the team that year. He wanted to challenge everyone to a race. He, Gary Bell, Woodie Held, and I would go out after a game. When Pedro wanted to be with us, he'd stay. If not, he was gone.

Mel McGaha was our new manager, and he thought we were having too much fun. He put in a curfew every night and all that horseshit. It didn't make any difference.

PEDRO RAMOS:

Mel McGaha was a first-year manager and I was a first-year pitcher with the Indians. Maybe that's why we got along. He didn't say too much, but he was a pretty good man. I had only one little incident with him. We were in Chavez Ravine to play the Angels, and prior to the game I was standing by the batting cage with the extra men, like I had done with my other teams. I loved to hit. Mel questioned why I was there. I reminded him I was a good hitter and said I could hit one out right-handed and left-handed. (I was a switch-hitter, although, at Washington, Charlie Dressen had made me bat only left-handed to take advantage of my speed.) Mel was curious—or skeptical—and let me hit, and I homered both ways. But he still didn't give me much chance to take batting practice. That was frustrating. I guess Mel knew we had a lot of guys who could hit the ball out of the park. We had 9 men who would hit over 10 homers that year—Willie Kirkland, Chuck Essegian, John Romano, Woodie Held, Gene Green, Al Luplow, Tito

Now with the Cleveland Indians, Pedro Ramos pitched over 200 innings for the sixth consecutive season and, with 10 wins, had a double-digit victory total for his seventh consecutive and last time, as relief pitching would be in his future.

Francona, Bubba Phillips, and Jerry Kindall. We even tied a record for the most homers in 5 or 6 games. But I showed Mel because one game I pitched a 3-hit shutout and hit 2 home runs, 1 a grand slammer.

We had a lot of good arms. Dick Donovan, Jim Perry, Barry Latman, Mudcat Grant, Gary Bell, Sam McDowell, and I were all used as starters. Donovan was our best pitcher that year, winning 20 games. Perry was second with 12 wins, and Bell and I won 10 each. Donovan was a nice, pretty quiet guy, but he'd lose his cool if anybody touched his glove when he was pitching. I handed it to him once and he snapped at me. Latman could really bring it up there. McDowell was a 6′5″ rookie left-hander with a blazing fastball and so much wildness that batters were scared of him. We all thought that if he learned better control he was going to be a big winner. Mudcat had some arm problems and had an off year, but he was a good pitcher and a good friend. He was a funny guy.

I palled around with Latman and Bell. Latman was Jewish, Bell was Texan. Bell was a fun guy, crazy in a nice way. The three of us would go out with Bob Allen, a good left-handed reliever, and catcher Doc Edwards, who was my roommate and a good guy. Sometimes Mudcat would be with Bell. We'd go out to eat, maybe to drink. Maybe Bell and me would look for some stuff, some girls. We didn't stay up too late, but we went out and ate and had a drink. The Indians drank more than any team I was on.

BALTIMORE ORIOLES

BROOKS ROBINSON:
Despite a 5-game sweep of the Yankees in August, we finished 8 games under .500 for our new manager, Billy Hitchcock. Still it was very satisfying to hit over .300 for the first time. I was barely over, at .303, which was just behind Russ Snyder's .305 as the team's best. My 23 homers were my highest to this point, and I drove in 86 runs, finishing second on the team to Gentile's 33 homers and 87 RBIs. In May I had bases-loaded homers in consecutive games, getting 8 RBIs right there. The Orioles kept turning out tremendous young talent. This year, Boog Powell broke in as a 20-year-old outfielder. At 6′4″ and 230 pounds, he was extremely strong, and it

was obvious he was going to hit with power once he got more experience. It wouldn't take long. He was a great guy and a lot of fun. We always got on Boog.

Dave McNally was a 19-year-old lefty who threw a 2-hit shutout in his first major league game. He was a terrific guy, and we became very close friends. Dave was very quiet, and when he was pitching it didn't matter if he struck out the side or they scored 6 runs off him, he'd just come into the dugout and sit down without expressing any emotion. He couldn't be bothered to talk to anyone, including the manager.

Ronny Hansen had been unable to regain his form after his great rookie year. He was still young, but he had back problems and had been slowed down by a couple of operations. At the end of the year he was traded to the White Sox in the deal that brought us Luis Aparicio. That was a shock to him, and I was sorry to see him go.

BOSTON RED SOX

FRANK MALZONE:
I had one of my finest years in baseball. I lifted my average 17 points to .283, drove in 95 runs, and had a career-high 21 homers. Carl Yastrzemski's 94 RBIs and 19 homers were second-best on the team. Pete Runnels won another batting title, with a .326 average, and we got good production from guys like right fielder Lu Clinton and shortstop Eddie Bressoud, but we finished eighth of the 10 teams because only Kansas City had a higher earned run average. Which isn't to say some of our pitchers didn't have good seasons.

Earl Wilson became the Red Sox' first black pitcher in 1959, but 1962 was his first full season. He was a good friend of mine and my son's favorite pitcher. Earl could pitch and he could hit a few homers. He was about 6′3″ and well built and was a fierce, imposing man on that mound. That he came inside and was wild made him particularly tough.

BROOKS ROBINSON (ORIOLES):
After Frank Lary, Earl Wilson was the guy I hated to face. Like Lary, he'd keep jamming me on the wrists with fastballs and quick-breaking pitches. What added to my discomfort is that he was wilder than Lary.

F. MALZONE:

That year Earl won 12 games, including a no-hitter against the Angels. This was the first Red Sox no-hitter since Mel Parnell did it in 1956, and the first I'd played behind. It was very exciting.

A month after Wilson's no-hitter, Bill Monbouquette no-hit the White Sox, 1–0, besting Early Wynn. Bill was another good, tough pitcher. He won 15 games that year, tying him with Gene Conley. Conley came over before the 1961 season, having pitched for Milwaukee and Philadelphia. He was the type I wouldn't want to get mad. He usually had a little smile on his face, but when it wasn't there, I'd be a little concerned. After all, he was 6'8" and about 250 pounds. He also played pro basketball with the Celtics and Knicks and perhaps that affected his dedication. He was no better than a .500 pitcher for us. I felt that with his stuff he should have won more ball games.

Dick Radatz was a rookie who immediately established himself as the most dominant reliever in baseball. He replaced Mike Fornieles as our stopper. He overpowered everybody. He struck out everybody. When he'd reach the mound, I'd say, "Dick, would you mind if I sat on the bench?" He was 6'6" tall and very intimidating when he unleashed his fastball. He had a slow windup but then let loose and no one could catch up to him. He wanted to win so bad. He was one of the first pitchers to show emotion after getting the last out. He'd shoot his fist up to the sky as if to say, *"I did it!"* He was well liked and respected by the other players. He wasn't a flaky reliever but a down-to-earth family man.

BILL MONBOUQUETTE:

Dick Radatz immediately became a star. With all my heart, I believe he was the best reliever there ever was. Dick could pitch 5 innings one day and then pitch the next day. If he had been used differently, where he pitched only an inning or two a game, I know he could have saved between 80 and 100 games a year. That sounds farfetched but I believe it. One game, I was leading the Yankees 1–0, but I loaded the bases with no one out in the ninth. Then Dick came in and struck out, in succession, Maris, Berra, and Blanchard. Maris and Blanchard I could see, but Berra was, along with Nellie Fox and Bobby Richardson, the toughest guy in the

league to fan. That's why Dick was called "the Monster." Here was a huge guy throwing the ball 97 mph and hitting spots. If he threw the ball under a batter's chin, that batter had better not give Dick a look. He was one of the guys who got salaries up for relievers. I don't think he ever wanted to be a starter. He started in the minors until Johnny Pesky put him in the pen, and it suited his talents. Then in the majors he roomed with Mike Fornieles and learned a lot about relieving, like mixing sliders and fastballs. I liked Dick a lot. He was a great, fun guy who enjoyed life to the fullest.

My personal career highlight came in Chicago on August 1, when I no-hit the White Sox and Early Wynn, 1–0. That prevented Wynn from getting his 300th win that year. When I had my good stuff I knew it when warming up. I could tell I was on that day. I pitched every fourth day during my career but because of the All-Star break my routine had been disrupted. As a result, I had something extra. I didn't want to waste it, so I stopped and got a towel-off because I sweated a lot. Then I came back and warmed up more. I didn't have my slider for about 5 innings, but fortunately I had one of those nasty downer curves working along with a fastball that was really jumping. It was one of those nights when everyone was behind my fastball. That was the best game I ever pitched. Mike Higgins told me, "I've never seen anyone alive throw the ball harder than you did tonight."

Usually Higgins and I didn't see eye to eye. That year, I asked if he'd move me up to pitch a game against Baltimore. I wasn't ducking the Tigers, our next opponents, because I always did well against them. Higgins let me pitch and I got knocked out in the first inning. That night at the hotel, I got into the elevator with him and Rudy York, the hitting coach. He'd had a lot to drink and he said, "Who do you think you are, telling me when you can pitch?" I said, "Mike, I didn't tell you when I was going to pitch. I asked you if I could pitch. You could have said no." The next thing you know, we were shoving and swinging at each other. Then we stopped fighting because the writers in the lobby had heard the commotion and were ready with their pencils. We walked in opposite directions. Later I saw Higgins stuck in the hotel's revolving door and had to help him out and put him in a cab.

PUMPSIE GREEN:

Pinky Higgins cut my playing time, so I was primarily a pinch hitter. I played in the field so little that fans probably weren't sure I was on the team until they thought I'd walked out. For the last time, let me explain what happened with me and Gene Conley. Conley was a nice person, but I never went out with him. We were both down after a game, and I wasn't playing. We had a couple of beers and then a couple of more beers. We were crying in our beer. We didn't plan anything. The only thing I did was stay in New York the entire night and not accompany the team to Washington. I called my wife and said, ''Don't get upset if you hear anything because I'll be in Washington tomorrow.'' She told me it was okay. I went to Washington the next day. I was fined as expected and the case was closed. Then this Israel thing came up. It was reported that Conley and I wanted to hop a plane to Israel. I didn't go to the airport with him to go to Israel. The media came after me and I didn't know what to say. I said, ''I'm going to where? I certainly would have chosen a different place than Israel!'' The reporters had their own answers. I don't know if this incident hastened my departure from Boston. It seems more likely Boston intended to deal me anyway, because black players were rarely employed as utility men and occasional pinch hitters.

WASHINGTON SENATORS

GENE WOODLING:

The Senators had traded Gene Green and Dick Donovan to the Indians for Jimmy Piersall. I was 40, so I told him, ''You can run all over the outfield and take every ball you want. But any you miss you're going to chase down.'' Piersall was a good ballplayer. He was no kookier than I was. A lot of guys resented his actions, but he didn't bother me. I pointed out that he brought people to the ballpark. We got along well.

We had moved out of Griffith Stadium to District of Columbia Stadium, but it didn't help. I was sold to the Mets in June, but was around long enough to see that Washington was on its way to having a season that was as bad as its first year. Probably the only bright spots were Chuck Hinton and Tom Cheney, who pitched good ball for us.

TOM CHENEY:

Sid Hudson, who had pitched for the old Senators and Red Sox, was Mickey Vernon's pitching coach at Washington, and he wanted everyone to pitch like him. He was a sidearm, sinkerball pitcher. I depended on my high fastball because if I could get a batter to swing at anything from the belt up, I had him where I wanted him. I threw over the top and three-quarters, but Hudson wanted me to go lower. When I tried to throw a sinker on the sidelines, I felt it pulling on my arm when I dragged it across. I didn't argue with him but went out and pitched like I knew how to. Vernon never said anything. He was just an easygoing prince of a guy.

If I had been my own pitching coach, I would have kicked myself in the fanny. Because I was always analyzing everything and was unable to relax. They gave me little pills to help relax my nerves. I took them before the game three or four times, but then I stopped because I didn't think they helped. They didn't talk about psychiatrists in those days. My problem was that I was paranoid about the first inning, when I usually had trouble. I tended to overthrow in the first inning and was wild. I wasn't smart enough then to figure it out. Maybe I didn't warm up long enough. If I got past the third or fourth inning, I was usually home free and got increasingly stronger.

On September 12 I set a major league record by striking out 21 players in 16 innings in the Baltimore Memorial Coliseum. I struck out everybody but Boog Powell. It was one of those times in life when just everything worked. I felt good warming up. George Susce was our bullpen catcher. He called everybody ''Good Kid.'' After warming up, I walked by him on the way to the dugout, and he said, ''Good Kid, if you don't pitch a no-hitter tonight, it's your own fault.'' After 9 innings I had 13 strikeouts. They would have had to fight me to have taken me out. We were paid for our complete games back then, though if you got a lot of complete games, come contract time they brought up your ERA instead. Vernon came to me in the twelfth inning to take me out, but I wouldn't let him do it. I said I wanted to win or lose it. He never mentioned my coming out again. He couldn't believe that the further I went, the stronger I got, and that I was strongest in the sixteenth inning. I had no idea how many pitches I'd thrown. It was 228! During the game, I realized that something strange was happening. There were only about 6,000 fans, but they were behind me, and that gave me a nice feeling. After they announced I had tied Bob Feller's and Sandy Koufax's record for a major league game with my 18th strikeout, they gave me an ovation. And they cheered on every strike. I remember Dick Williams squatting and backing up on a pitch right down the middle. He was the last guy, a pinch hitter, my 21st strikeout. Fortunately, we had gone ahead 2–1 on a homer by first baseman Bud Zipfel off Dick Hall in the top of the sixteenth because this was the last inning before a curfew would have been called. Photographers and newsmen came into the locker room. I hadn't felt tired when pitching, but 3 minutes later I felt completely drained. (I believe records are meant to be broken, but no one has broken mine.)

I had my best year in baseball, going 7–9 for a last-place team, with a 3.17 ERA. I pitched over 170 innings—52 innings had been my highest total—and my control improved as a result. I walked 97 batters and struck out 147.

I had no trouble with umpires. They were better back then. Ed Herlihy was a good umpire, although he was hotheaded and you couldn't say anything to him. Nestor Chylak and Ed Runge were good umpires. You could question them if you didn't show them up. If they called a ball and you motioned it was somewhere else, they might nod their heads in agreement. I was never thrown out of a game for arguing.

I wasn't happy we got Jimmy Piersall. I think he hurt the team—you can only raise cain with the umpires so much before they'll take it out on you and everyone else. Piersall was a showboat. As they said, he was crazy . . . like a fox. He made money out of his goofy act. He'd run at the mouth, but he didn't direct his foolishness toward me after I told him that I could put something on him that would really make him crazy. None of the players ran around with him, but it didn't matter because he had friends in every town. In September, Piersall went after a heckler in Baltimore prior to the game and was arrested. The next day he was acquitted but then knocked himself unconscious in a revolving door at a hotel.

Don Rudolph came to the Senators from the Indians for Willie Tasby. He was the typical flaky left-handed pitcher and moved into the rotation with me, Dave Sten-

house—who led our team with 11 wins as a rookie—Claude Osteen, and Bennie Daniels. Rudolph was married to Patty Waggin, the stripper. He got razzed a lot about that, but you know, she was a sweet woman, and what she did was an art.

JOHNNY KLIPPSTEIN (REDS):

I didn't get to know Don Rudolph because he was on the White Sox a couple of years after I was on the Cubs, and on the Reds and Senators a year after I had left both those teams. But I'd hear stories about him and his stripper wife, Patty Waggin. Bob Will, who was a Cubs outfielder when Rudolph lived in Chicago, said Rudolph would take a bunch of guys to see his wife dance.

MINNESOTA TWINS

HARMON KILLEBREW:

It was interesting how we evolved from a last-place team at Washington into a good ball club at Minnesota by 1962. The team began to dramatically improve in 1959 when Bob Allison and I were inserted into the lineup and Camilo Pascual finally became a winning pitcher. Then, before the 1960 season, we traded Roy Sievers to the White Sox and received both Earl Battey, who was a terrific catcher, and Don Mincher, who played first and provided a lot of power off the bench. Lenny Green became our leadoff hitter and played excellent center field. He was a nice little fellow with good speed. In 1961, in Minnesota, Jim Kaat and Jack Kralick became solid starting pitchers and Zoilo Versalles became our shortstop. He was temperamental but had a lot of talent. That year Sam Mele replaced Cookie Lavagetto as manager. Then, in 1962, we got Vic Power from the Indians to play first base, and two young players developed in a hurry: third baseman Rich Rollins and second baseman Bernie Allen, the ex–Purdue quarterback. In 1961 we had finished just seventh of ten teams, but in 1962 we moved all the way up to second, finishing only 5 games behind the Yankees.

Vic Power could catch the ball at first base better than anybody I ever saw. He was a magician. So I couldn't play there. And with Rollins at third, I became the Twins' left fielder for several years.

A lot of players had terrific years. Pascual won 20

games for the first time, Kaat won 18, Allison drove in over 100 runs, and Rollins about that. I led the league with 48 homers and 126 RBIs. We hit a lot of homers. In fact, Allison and I each hit grand slams in the first inning in a game against Cleveland. That set a record. I also became the first person to hit the ball over the roof in Tiger Stadium. It came off Jim Bunning on a very warm evening when there was no wind. I have no idea why it went so far or high. If there ever was a time I surprised myself, that was it.

VIC POWER:

I was glad to be with another team that had a chance to win the pennant. Other than in 1959 with the Indians, I hadn't been in a pennant race. It was a good race, but the Yankees were just a little stronger. Our starting lineup was as good as theirs—although some of our guys weren't as experienced—and our starting pitchers, Camilo Pascual, Jim Kaat, Jack Kralick, and Dick Stigman, all did a good job, but we wouldn't have a reliable reliever until Bill Dailey in 1963.

I batted second behind Lenny Green. Lenny and I tied a record by hitting back-to-back homers to lead off one game. We utilized the hit-and-run a lot because he had good speed and I could hit to right and didn't strike out very much. Over the season I hit .290 and hit 16 homers. Sam Mele liked the way I played. He said that I stabilized his young infield. Zoilo Versalles at shortstop, Rich Rollins at third, and Bernie Allen at second had erratic arms and I saved them a lot of errors. They estimated that I saved Versalles 47 errors alone. The defense was so good that we were voted the best infield in the league. I was voted the Most Valuable Player on the team.

Camilo Pascual thanked me for helping him win 20 games for the first time in his career. He had the best curve in the business and he had a good fastball, but the only years he would win 20 games were the 2 I would spend in Minnesota, anchoring the infield. I liked playing with Camilo. He was a superstitious guy, and he wouldn't let his picture be taken on a day he was going to pitch. In the winter, Camilo lived in Miami and he told me that a sportswriter called him there, long distance, at 7 A.M. The writer asked, "Do you speak English?" And Pascual answered, "Not at 7 A.M.," and hung up.

Zoilo Versalles was crazy and I sensed that Bob Allison didn't like blacks, but I got along with all the other players. Harmon Killebrew was a beautiful guy. The Twins had 8 players who hit over 10 homers and 2 others hit 9, but no one hit them farther than Harmon. Oh, baby, he hit some long homers!

Earl Battey was a good friend. I liked playing with him because he was a very good hitter with good power, he called a good game, and he was an excellent defensive catcher with soft hands. I liked infielder Johnny Goryl, Don Mincher, who was my backup at first, and Dick Stigman, who came with me from Cleveland. I liked Jimmy Kaat very much. He was a smart guy and a talented pitcher. He was a Gold Glove fielder, so they couldn't hit the ball past us.

Jack Kralick was a nice guy. He pitched a no-hitter against Kansas City that August. I caught the final pop-up. For a long time afterward, I got letters from fans that said they almost had heart attacks because I used only one hand. But I never dropped a ball.

The Minnesota writers asked me if I liked them better than the ones in Cleveland. I said, "I like you guys better because in Cleveland they stabbed me in the back and here I get stabbed in the front."

CHICAGO WHITE SOX

AL SMITH:

As it turned out, Ed Short gave me the money Bill Veeck had promised as a bonus if I had a good 1961 season. But instead of it being a bonus for 1961, he made that money the amount of the raise I got for the 1962 season. So I didn't make any extra money. Short and I really got into it over that. I was angry but had another good year for the White Sox, batting .292 with over 80 RBI. Then, in January, Short traded me and Luis Aparicio to the Orioles. I would *never* have anything to do with the White Sox organization after that.

JIM LANDIS:

The White Sox had changed by 1962. Billy Pierce had just been sent to the Giants and Minnie Minoso had been traded to St. Louis. Jim Rivera, Bob Shaw, and our former relief ace Gerry Staley had gone to Kansas during the 1961 season—Rivera's career was now over and

Shaw was on Milwaukee. Sherm Lollar was only a part-time catcher now, and guys like Aparicio, Smith, Wynn, and Turk Lown were playing their last year for the team. Our top right-handed starter was Ray Herbert, who came from Kansas City in 1961. He won 20 games for us. Our top left-hander was former Brave Juan Pizarro, a Puerto Rican pitcher with a lot of talent. Our new bullpen stopper was Eddie Fisher, a knuckleballer we got in the Pierce trade. We had several new players in our lineup, including first baseman Joe Cunningham—who was a fine hitter and fielder—right fielder Mike Hershberger—who was a good ballplayer with quite an arm—catcher Cam Carreon, and left fielder Floyd Robinson. Robinson was a 5′9″ left-handed batter who was the best clutch hitter the White Sox had during all my years there. In 1962 he hit only 11 homers yet drove in 109 runs. That amazed me. He always got a piece of the ball and brought the runner in. He was a .300 hitter and had a lot of doubles and triples.

I still had players to spend time with. Nellie was still there, but I also ran with Hershberger, Carreon, and Fisher. Frank Baumann joined our bowling group. Bob Roselli, another catcher, went with me to the track a couple of times.

I had 15 homers and drove in over 60 runs, but my average dropped to below .230. Although I would continue to be a good clutch hitter, my average would never be over .240 again. The only thing I could say was that I always was a slow starter. I could hit .185 for a month and a half. I don't know why. The Sox thought I was bothered by the cold weather, but I didn't buy that. In more than a few seasons I hit over .300 after that.

GARY PETERS:

I think I got a lot of time in the pension on the ''coffee breaks'' that I had with the White Sox. In 1959, 1960, and 1961, I'd win 12 or 13 games in parts of minor league seasons and then be brought up in the fall. In 1962 I was up with Chicago in the spring. I had about 5 months in the big leagues through 1962, but I didn't lose my rookie status because you had to be there something like 45 or 60 days consecutively. I made only 12 appearances and never was given a start in those 4 years. Between 1959 and 1962, the Sox had such starters as Billy Pierce, Dick Donovan, Early Wynn, Bob Shaw, and Ray Herbert. It was hard to crack that staff. Al Lopez

felt he couldn't take a chance on me with his team in contention. It was getting a little frustrating.

I think every player who wasn't brought up after a few years in the minors thought that he should be allowed to go to a different team. In those days you were a captive of the organization you were in, and though we accepted it, we didn't think it was fair and grumbled amongst ourselves. The owners were all-powerful and the players, especially the minor leaguers, couldn't conceive how to change things. If I had been with some organization that needed pitching, like Kansas City, I would have gotten to the big leagues sooner. Of course, there were guys sitting on the bench in the big leagues who could have been regulars and making a lot more money on different teams. But clubs would keep them.

Until I got to Triple A, I didn't see any real competition between players to make the big leagues. But once you're one notch below the majors, you know you have to get somebody's job to make it. The Sox had tons of other left-handers, but there was no animosity or competition. I felt I had to wait for the White Sox to either make room for me by removing a pitcher from their roster or move me elsewhere.

I felt like I hit a plateau in Triple A and was working on the things Ray Berres was telling me. I was improving my mechanics and building my confidence. After the 1962 season at Indianapolis, I went to play winter ball in Puerto Rico to work on my curveball. Ironically, my slider got real good. I also learned to relax down there and became more natural on the mound. I felt I was ready.

NEW YORK YANKEES

BOB TURLEY:

The Yankees again won the pennant in 1962, by 5 games over the Twins. We again got great years from Maris and Mantle. Maris was down from his 1961 season but still led our team with 33 homers and 100 RBIs. Mantle would have had more but he was injured for much of the year—he came back with a big pinch homer. They got a lot of support from Howard, Skowron, Richardson, and Tom Tresh, who played short while Kubek was in the service. Mickey was the league's MVP.

COURTESY OF BOB TURLEY

Now pitching with increasing frequency, Bob Turley's Yankee days came to an end after eight eventful years.

I still couldn't make much of a contribution though I was one of 4 pitchers to combine on an extra-inning 1-hitter. I pitched even less than the year before and went 3–3. Otherwise, we got good pitching. Ford won 17 and Stafford 14 or 15, but our ace was Ralph Terry, who was a good friend of mine. He was really easygoing, kind of like Don Larsen. I saw him improve over the years. When he was young we called him "Tom Edison" because he came up with so many pitches. He cut down on what he threw and became more effective. He had great control and a good fastball, curve, and slider. He became a terrific pitcher in 1961, when he went 16–3, and in 1962 he went 23–12 and won the Cy Young Award.

In October I was pitching in Puerto Rico to see how my arm felt. I got a telegram from Roy Hamey, the general manager. He's the one who refused to give Maris a big raise after he hit 61 homers. His telegram said I had been sold to the Angels. There was no note, no personal call, no nothing after 8 years with the Yankees. That was the most upsetting thing of my life. The Yankees had indicated that I would be part of their organization, which a lot of teams didn't tell player reps. I didn't want to quit because I felt I still could pitch. But I was very disappointed.

WORLD SERIES

1962

YANKEES vs GIANTS

BOB TURLEY · YANKEES;

Ralph Terry won Games Five and Seven against the Giants. The Series ended when Willie McCovey lined Terry's pitch to Richardson, preserving a 1–0 lead. It was hit well but it wasn't a screamer. It went right to Richardson and it wasn't a hard play. Ralph was my friend, so I was really happy he came back after the Mazeroski homer in the Seventh game of the 1960 Series. This time he won it for us.

BILLY O'DELL · GIANTS:

We started the World Series the day after winning the playoffs from the Dodgers. Our attitude going into the Series was good, although we knew our pitching was ragtag at that point. We thought pitching would be a problem, but it turned out better than expected. I had relieved in the second game of the playoffs and was given the starting assignment in the first game of the World Series. Dark knew I had success against the Yankees while in the American League. I pitched 6 pretty good innings, but I gave up a tie-breaking solo homer to Clete Boyer in the seventh inning and we went on to lose, 6–2.

We thought we had a chance to win the Series in Game Seven. I relieved in the eighth inning with the bases loaded and nobody out. I got Maris to hit into a force play at home and Elston Howard to hit into a double play. Then I got them out in the ninth. I thought we were going to win it in the bottom of the ninth. We had McCovey hitting and the tying run, Matty Alou, at third and the winning run, Willie Mays, at second, and he could score on any kind of a hit. I'll always see it: McCovey hit the ball awful hard—it couldn't have been hit any harder—but it went right to Richardson at second and he made a good play on it. I would have been the winning pitcher.

We wanted very much to win, but we were satisfied with the year we had. So we weren't too downhearted. There was no parade in the city, but the ballclub had a big dinner for us that night in the stadium and we celebrated the season.

BILLY PIERCE · GIANTS:

The Yankees had almost the same team that they had in 1961, when they were one of the greatest teams ever. Only Yogi Berra wasn't playing much now, and Tom

Tresh was in the lineup. But we didn't really have the time to think about their team. We weren't prepared to play. We didn't even have tickets for our wives. That's because we were 4 games behind the Dodgers with a week left in the season. Then we had playoffs. So now we were racing around trying to get tickets when our minds should have been on the first game. We lost 6–2 to Whitey Ford.

Jack Sanford pitched a 3-hitter to beat Ralph Terry in Game Two, 2–0. I started against Bill Stafford in Game Three in New York. It was scoreless until the seventh, when Roger Maris got a 2-run single off me. We ended up losing 3–2. We won Game Four, 7–3, when our second baseman Chuck Hiller hit the first National League grand slam in Series history. That was a pleasant surprise for everyone, including Chuck. In Game Five, Sanford lost to Terry, 5–3, when Tom Tresh hit a 3-run homer in the eighth inning.

We came back to San Francisco trailing 3 games to 2. Then it rained 3 or 4 days in a row. We kept warming up and sitting down. It finally stopped and they dried the field with the air from a helicopter. In Game Six, I went against Ford. This was an extremely tense situation because if we lost we were eliminated. Maris reached me again, this time with a solo homer, but I gave up only 2 other hits and won, 5–2, to even the Series. That was a thrilling victory for me. You can't beat a win in the World Series. I'd waited a long time for it.

Game Seven was tremendous. Sanford went against Terry. During the season, Sanford had won 24 games and Terry had won 23, and they had split their first two meetings in the Series. We were losing 1–0 in the ninth inning. Because I had such good luck in San Francisco, Alvin Dark asked me to warm up. So I was warming up and watching the ball game. With Matty Alou on first, Mays doubled to right field. Roger Maris made a great play in right, cutting off Mays's double to hold Alou at third. That was the key play though few people gave Maris enough credit for it. That brought up McCovey. I couldn't figure out why Houk let Terry pitch to him, a right-hander against a left-hander. The first ball Willie hit was a shot foul. Then he hit the bullet to Bobby Richardson. For a second my heart stopped and then he caught it. And that was it.

NATIONAL LEAGUE 1963

"MAUCH HAD TURNED A TERRIBLE TEAM INTO A CONTENDER IN JUST A COUPLE OF YEARS, BUT HE WOULDN'T BE SATISFIED UNTIL HE WON THE PENNANT. SO HE DROVE HIS PLAYERS A BIT. HE DIDN'T WANT US TO TALK ABOUT ANYTHING BUT BASEBALL. HE DIDN'T WANT US TO TALK ABOUT GOD OR HORSE RACING OR ANYTHING ELSE."

JOHNNY KLIPPSTEIN

MILWAUKEE BRAVES

LEW BURDETTE:
In some ways the Braves hadn't changed since our championship years. Spahn was on his way to a 23-win season, Mathews was still hitting a lot of homers, and Henry Aaron was still the game's best hitter. He would bat about .320 and lead the league with 44 homers and 130 RBIs.

TIM McCARVER (CARDINALS):
According to Lew Burdette, in early summer he and Warren Spahn would pick up Hank Aaron's bat, which he had used since the spring, and the dents were only two widths of the ball. It shows that Aaron hit the ball almost every time with the sweet part of the bat. He kept his hands back so he could hit change-ups. And like Stan Musial, he lifted his back foot off the ground and his weight shifted to his other side. Once Aaron got into the batter's box he rarely stepped out.

STAN WILLIAMS (YANKEES):
I felt lucky to be out of the National League because I didn't have to pitch to Henry Aaron anymore. He was the best hitter I ever faced. About 1960 or 1961 there was a poll of pitchers, and the majority of them said Aaron was the toughest. And we weren't talking about power even, because in those days there were several players who hit 40 homers a year. Most hitters had a weakness that you worked toward when it came time to get them out. I pitched against him for 5 years and never discovered his weakness. He hit balls over his head, off the ground, inside, outside. He had great reflexes, quickness, strength. He was a line-drive hitter, so how he hit all those homers I'll never know.

L. BURDETTE:
However, the old championship Braves were being broken up one player at a time in the early '60s. Bruton, Logan, Covington, Adcock, and Buhl were already gone, and Crandall and I were going to be next. Del lasted until the end of the year, but on June 15 I was traded to the Cards for Gene Oliver and Bob Sadowski.

Years later, a writer called me "a goofy hillbilly

from a hick town in West Virginia.'' Just because I played with Milwaukee instead of the Yankees, it might have made a big difference in how I was perceived. The 3 wins in the 1957 World Series wasn't the only thing good that ever happened to me. I was a starting pitcher for 9½ to 10 years for the Braves and won 179 games for them. That's 18 a year. But the World Series would be the only thing anyone talked about. I was consistent, and managers could rely on me. (Sandy Koufax would never beat me. I would hit 3 game-winning homers off him. Spahn would never beat me. In fact, against Spahn and Sandy Koufax, the two best left-handers of the entire era, I would go 11–0!) I was a pretty good pitcher.

ST. LOUIS CARDINALS

DICK GROAT:

Because the Cardinals needed a shortstop, I had the good fortune to play for the finest organization in all professional sports. The Cardinals treated players better, they treated your kids and family better, they paid you better, they made travel better. The Cardinals were a fairly close team when I got there and became very close. Guys like Bill White, Ken Boyer, Curt Flood, Tim McCarver, Bob Gibson, and I were tremendous competitors. White, Flood and I hit over .300; Boyer and White each hit around 25 homers and drove in over 100 runs; White, Javier, Boyer, Flood, and McCarver were superb defensively. Bob Gibson and Ernie Broglio each won 18 games and Curt Simmons won 15. And we had Stan Musial. This was a solid team.

I went to St. Louis with the intention of showing Pirates general manager Joe Brown that he made a very bad mistake trading me. And in 1963 I had the best year of my career, a better year than in 1960. I hit the ball with more authority. I was leading the league in batting average when Don Drysdale hit me on the thumb in Dodger Stadium. I couldn't hold the bat, but the ballclub was going pretty good and I kept on playing. I went 0 for 28. Still I finished at .319, tying Henry Aaron for third in the batting race behind Tommy Davis and Bobby Clemente. I led the league with 43 doubles, drove in a career-high 73 runs, and had a career-high 201 hits. I was the biggest vote getter in either league

for the All-Star Game, and I finished second to Sandy Koufax in the MVP voting. This was after Joe Brown had said, ''We could never win another pennant with Dick Groat in there.'' It was a matter of pride.

Ken Boyer, Julian Javier, Bill White, and I were the starting infield for the National League. It was the only time that 4 players from one team made up the infield. We were really proud of that because we were chosen by our peers, not the fans. The game was played in Cleveland and Willie Mays had a big game, scoring 2 runs, driving in 2 runs, and making a great catch. That was Stan Musial's 24th and last All-Star Game.

Playing between Boyer and Javier was as good as playing between Don Hoak and Bill Mazeroski at Pittsburgh. After Maz, Javier was the best-fielding second baseman in baseball. Boyer was the captain of the Cardinals and everyone looked up to him on the field and off. He looked after his teammates. In fact, Kenny found a home for my wife and me. After that, we would socialize a great deal with Kenny and his wife, Kathleen, and on the road, Kenny and I palled around.

Bill White could do it all. He was a marvelous left-handed batter who hit for power and average and was the best-fielding first baseman in the league. I never saw a player work so hard, which he had to do to compensate for injuries. He was a very special person, an intelligent, sentimental guy.

White and Boyer were our leaders. But there were many guys with strong personalities on that team, who either motivated the others or led by example. For instance, we all looked up to Stan Musial.

Curt Flood was a super guy with the greatest sense of humor. I loved being around him. We were both very superstitious, so we warmed up together before every game. We were both having good years, so we didn't want to leave each other. Curt could flat out play center field and could really handle a bat. He changed his style and became a truly great hitter. He would pay me one of the greatest compliments in his book when he said I helped teach him how to hit. He was already a .300 hitter, so I guess what I taught him is that you could make sacrifices at the plate for the team and still bat .300. (Curt was a fantastic artist. In fact, he did it professionally in the off-season. He had an art shop in St. Louis. At the time, I wouldn't have thought Curt would be the type to challenge the reserve clause. None of us then really thought about free agency—personally, I had no bitches. But Curt had ties to the city and ballclub and wouldn't want to leave in a trade.)

Flood was the leadoff hitter and I batted second, in front of Stan Musial. I can't say enough about Musial. He *was* the Cardinals. The team had a family picnic every year at Grant's Farm, which was owned by the Busches. It was great for our kids because they could swim in a pond and see all kinds of wild animals—buffaloes, elk, deer—by riding around in a train. In 1963 the picnic was held on an unbelievably hot day in August. We were waiting for the big outdoor cookout to begin when several television trucks started coming in. I knew something was going to happen. It was then that Stan Musial announced he would retire at the end of the

The Pirates traded Dick Groat, their shortstop since 1952, because they sensed his career was on the downswing, but Groat responded with his best year, batting .319 with a career-high 73 RBIs for the St. Louis Cardinals.

season, after 22 years. At the time we were in sixth place. All of a sudden Musial turned on the blowers. I couldn't believe how hard he hit the ball until the end of the season. He was unreal.

Don Cardwell hit me in the ribs in Pittsburgh and I was out for 3 games. Don Drysdale once hit me on top of the helmet, and Juan Marichal hit me on the back of the helmet, but Cardwell was the only guy I felt hit me on purpose. I had been traded for him, and I guess the media got to him about how good I was going while the Pirates had dropped way down in the standings. I missed the rest of the series, and when we got back to St. Louis on a Sunday night, they started shooting cortisone into me. I got up the next day and got another shot. I went out to the ballpark and felt pretty good. I discovered I could field grounders, throw, and swing the bat, so I told Johnny Keane, "I'm ready to play again." I'll never forget this as long as I live. The one thing I hadn't done was run. I didn't have any idea that it was going to hurt that much. Glen Hobbie started against us. With one out in the first, I doubled down the right-field line. When I started, I said, "Oh, Jesus!" I just got to second base, trying to get that thing straightened around. Then, on the first pitch, Musial drilled a liner up the middle for a base hit. So I had to run again and come around to score. The next time up, I singled, and just as I got to first base, Musial hit a frozen rope to right field. I'm running like hell. I was never so happy to see an umpire wave his hand that I could come around to score. I never saw a man hit the ball like Musial did after he announced his retirement. He was 42 at the time. Musial sparked our team to a terrific streak. We almost won the pennant, and gave the Dodgers a good scare.

Bob Gibson was a great pitcher, on the same level as Sandy Koufax. In terms of longevity, Warren Spahn was the greatest pitcher of my era, but the best pitchers I saw were Gibson and Koufax, who were a bit ahead of Juan Marichal, Jim Maloney, and Don Drysdale. Bob was a great athlete who had played basketball with the Harlem Globetrotters. Not only could he pitch, but he was a terrific hitter and fast runner. Gibby had some games where I'd just stand at shortstop and be awed. He could be completely overpowering. He'd devise a game plan and pitch exactly that way. Gibby always had a great sense of humor and he and I were real good friends. Gibson and I both loved bridge and were always partners. We took on anybody, only the more we played, the better we got, and it was hard to get anybody to play with us. The meanness of Bob Gibson? I never saw it. Never. In fact, in those days, he didn't want to knock down batters. He threw so hard, he didn't need to pitch that way.

TIM McCARVER:

Minnie Minoso was on the Cardinals in spring training before being dealt to the Senators in early April. He was a great guy. He had a bad year as a part-time player with the Cards in 1962—early in the season, he ran into a wall and fractured his skull and broke his wrist—so he got so furious at himself after going 0 for 4 that he walked under a cold shower with all his clothes on, including his hat and his spikes. That was a sight.

I had a terrible spring. I had just come out of the army reserve and was trying too hard. Balls would get by me that weren't even in the dirt. My options to the minor leagues had run out, so the Cards had to keep me. They used me sparingly at first. Then I went 3 for 4 in a game against Earl Francis of Pittsburgh, and that opened their eyes. There was an article in the paper that said I recalled former Cardinals' catcher Bill DeLancey. The next day the reporters were asking me, a 20-year-old, to compare myself to DeLancey. I had never heard of the guy. I later discovered he was a part-time left-handed catcher who played about 200 games total in the '30s. Should I have said, ''I have always tried to model myself after him''?

Gene Oliver began the season as the starting catcher. He was a good hitter but had a weak throwing arm. Carl Sawatski was going to retire at the end of the year. So the position was up for grabs. Johnny Keane came up to me one day and said, ''You can hit left-handed pitchers, can't you?'' It was as if I could hit them, if I said I could hit them. So I said, ''Gosh, I've hit them all my life.'' He tucked that away and then traded Oliver to the Braves for Lew Burdette, giving me the Cards' catching job.

We were a veteran team and clearly the weak point was behind the plate. It helped me that there weren't many other young players on the club. Charlie James, who split time with Stan Musial in left, was just 25, but he had played semiregularly for a couple of years already. Infielder Dal Maxvill wasn't a regular and out-

fielder Mike Shannon wouldn't join the team until mid-season (and wouldn't be a regular until 1964). So really, I was the only young player who got significant playing time. I was inserted almost invisibly into the lineup, without pressure to succeed immediately, buffered by a lot of star players.

They weren't expecting me to do as well as I did. I batted .289, which trailed Dick Groat, Bill White, and Curt Flood but was slightly ahead of Ken Boyer. Of course, Boyer drove in 111 runs, more than doubling my total. I caught 126 games, including something like 95 games in a row—and that included about 8 double-headers. Many of those games were in St. Louis, where it would get so hot that the trainer would give us 5 or 6 salt tablets some afternoons—before we learned they weren't good for you. But I wanted to play every day and loved it.

The Cardinals hadn't won since 1946, but they always contended and were considered a winning ballclub. I didn't sense the organization was desperate to win, and management never put that pressure on me. The desperation may have been going on in the bigger picture, but I was unaware of it, maybe because I was young and naïve. The Cardinals under Johnny Keane had done well in 1961 and 1962, but I don't think we were yet considered a championship-caliber team.

The other players expected me to do my job, and never got on me in a bad way. I accepted advice they gave and never got angry at them. I was angry at myself when I made an out because I felt I was letting the team down. Plus, I was in a dilemma because I had always been able to hit the ball hard consistently. That was the biggest adjustment I had to make. Keane and Vern Benson, our third-base coach, took me aside every once in a while to calm me down after I hit a weak little dribbler on a pitch I thought I should have smashed. I got out of it by maturing.

Boyer was a terrific guy and our steadying influence as we got involved in our first pennant race. Years after guys played with Kenny, they would still refer to him in an endearing way as ''Captain.'' He and Bill White were our best all-around players in that they hit for average, hit homers, drove in runs, and were superb fielders. Kenny would say, ''Hey, go'head, come here.'' One night I asked, ''Kenny, are you telling me to 'go ahead'?'' ''No. I'm calling you a goathead.'' That was because of the shape of my head and neck. ''Goat-head,'' ''Melonhead,'' and ''Buckethead'' were terms of endearment.

Dick Groat was another leader, but he was much more acerbic than Kenny. He was an antagonist. He was a tough competitor and would teach you in no uncertain terms how to play the game. You had to play it his way, ''the right way.'' Dick would keep me level after a game. I might be gabbing away and Dick would ask how many hits I got that night. ''Three.'' ''Is that why you're chirping like that?'' I wouldn't stop chirping, but I'd realize I was doing it because I had done well—his point was that I should be more level.

We had an extremely close team. After a game, a group of players might go to a fish restaurant called the Nantucket Cove. More often we'd go to Rosino's, a great little Italian restaurant in St. Louis, which had the best homemade pizza I ever tasted. We'd stack the table with food. You couldn't believe how much we ate, particularly on a day when we might have had only a cup of soup between games of a doubleheader. Because of the St. Louis heat and our flannel uniforms, we might have lost 14 pounds during the day. On Sundays, the owner would put beer in an ice pitcher and we'd drink out of cups. That was one way of getting past St. Louis's blue laws, which outlawed drinking on Sundays. All we did was talk baseball. We'd talk until midnight and then go home and collapse. Then we'd have a game the next day and at 3 o'clock it would begin again.

Since we were prevented from drinking in town on Sundays, Dick Groat and Ernie Broglio would take me to a place called the Stoplight in East St. Louis. That was the first place I had a frozen daiquiri. We'd eat chicken and potatoes and lima beans. It was a continuation of the clubhouse, when we'd start talking and arguing about baseball.

That year, Curt Simmons and I stayed at the George Washington Hotel on King's Highway in St. Louis for $9 a day, the ballplayers' rate. And we'd drive to the park together. Curt was a tough competitor—he didn't retire in the '50s after cutting off part of his big toe with a lawnmower—yet he'd never intentionally throw at a batter, not ever. He was from the Robin Roberts school of pitching. He said, ''The reason I don't throw at guys is that I don't want to put them on base. It's that simple.'' Simmons revived his career in St. Louis, winning

10 games in 1962 and then 15 games in 1963, his most since 1956 when he and Roberts were the aces of the Phillies. Gibson and Broglio won 18 games each, but Simmons had the best ERA on the team. Gibson was throwing hard all season—he sent Jim Ray Hart to the hospital with a broken collarbone. As soon as Hart got out, he had to go back in because Simmons accidentally beaned him. Fortunately, Simmons didn't throw as hard as Gibson.

We were drifting along, having a good year but seemingly out of contention, when suddenly in September we won 19 of 20 games. That put us only 1 game behind the Dodgers. They were playing good, too, having won 13 of 18. The Dodgers came in for a 3-game series and I was welcomed to big-time pressure. We had to face Johnny Podres, who had the best circle change I ever saw, Sandy Koufax, and hard-throwing Peter Richert, three left-handers. They beat us 3–1, and then 4–0 on a Koufax 4-hitter. We scored 5 runs in 2 innings off Richert in the third game, but their relief pitching didn't let us score any more runs. Ron Perranoski relieved for them beginning in the eighth inning. We still led 5–4 with 1 out and nobody on in the top of the ninth when Dick Nen, who had just stepped off a plane from Spokane, hit an unlikely homer against Ron Taylor to tie the game. It was his only hit in 8 at-bats for the Dodgers that year (and he wouldn't play in the majors again until 1965 when he surfaced with Washington). In the bottom of the eleventh, Dick Groat led off against Perranoski with a triple. But he died at third. Then we lost in the thirteenth inning. If we'd won that game, we would have been only 2 back and still in the race. That loss blew us out. But the expectations for our team rose.

This was Stan Musial's 22nd and final season. On September 29 the Cards held a Stan Musial Day and he got his 2 final hits, bringing his total to 3,630, then the National League record. Remarkably, that gave him 1,815 hits at home and 1,815 hits on the road. His second hit drove in a run and he was removed for a pinch runner to an ovation from the crowd. It was quite moving.

Stan was one of the nicest guys in baseball. But I rarely went out with him when I was young. He was a guy who wouldn't help you as a hitter unless you asked him. He didn't make the offer. One day he pulled me aside and said, ''Tim, I want to talk to you about your hitting.'' I was so flattered that he was finally going to talk to me about my hitting. He said, ''We've been watching you and we think you . . . oughtta hurry up a little in the batter's box. You're taking too long.'' What a bummer that was.

Stan was one of the most relaxed players you'll ever see. His rest was very important to him and he could sleep anywhere. He could relax because he was born under a lucky star. He'd play poker and draw inside straights. He'd need a 6 for a 4-5-6-7-8 straight and he'd hit it. If he had 4 hearts and needed one more for a flush, he'd get it. He'd win all the time and have no clue how to play. Everybody in the game would be a better player, yet he'd win. That was Stan. We used to joke that it wasn't safe to fly if Stan wasn't on the plane with us because no plane would go down if Stan was on it. Then one day when we were in Philadelphia, Stan took a train to New York for a speaking engagement, planning to rejoin the team later in the day. The plane took off without Stan and the left engine went out and we had to return to the airport. We were sweating. We looked around and noticed that Stan wasn't with us and we said, ''No wonder.'' After that, it was no longer a joke and half the team would look behind them to make sure that Stan was on the plane before allowing it to take off.

In late September, Stan had his number 6 retired. His playing career was over and he became a Cardinals vice president. Stan was a walking icon and was so revered that we would feel he was part of the team in 1964 when we finally won the pennant. We would think that it was his lucky aura that helped us prevail.

HOUSTON COLT .45S

HAL WOODESHICK:

Paul Richards didn't realize a chiropractor had cured my back problems, so he took me off the Houston roster and assigned me to Oklahoma City. He thought I couldn't pitch. I didn't want to go to the minors again and was convinced to go to Japan by Jack Bloomberg. He and Joe Stanka were the first Americans to play over there in the early '60s. Don Newcombe and Larry Doby had gone in 1962. Jack told me he could get me a big contract in Japan if I could get out of my Houston contract. So I called Richards and asked out of my contract,

but he told me, ''If you're physically able to pitch, we're not going to let you go.''

I was invited to spring training without a contract and tried to prove I belonged. One day I was playing catch with Rusty Staub, who was a 19-year-old rookie first baseman, and he showed me how to throw a slider. All of a sudden I developed a good slider. I had been getting by with just a fastball and slow curve, and that hadn't been enough. The slider was the perfect third pitch for me because I could throw it for strikes easier than my fastball, which moved a lot. It was the pitch that helped me convert to being a reliever. I had a good spring, and one day when I was playing poker with some of the guys, Richards summoned me to his room to tell me I was back on the Houston roster. So I signed with Houston and from then on, I was their number one relief pitcher.

Don McMahon helped me become a good reliever. He taught me how to prepare to go into a game and stressed that I had to go in and throw strikes without being intimidated by anybody. Don had a lot of experience because he had been a successful reliever with the Braves since they won the World Series title in 1957. He did a great job for us in the bullpen in 1962, but in 1963 he slipped a bit and would be traded at the end of the season—but not before Harry Craft gave him his only 2 starts of what would be an 18-year career. Beginning in 1963, I was the only effective reliever on Houston. Craft would use me against right-handers and left-handers. He'd say for me to go in and not even look at who was at the plate.

For a young team we had good starters in Turk Farrell, Ken Johnson, Bob Bruce, and Don Nottebart, who gave us our first no-hitter against the Phillies in May. But I got a lot of work. I was in 55 games and pitched 114 innings, striking out 94 batters and giving up only 75 hits. My ERA was 1.97 and I won 11 games, of which about 6 were in extra innings. At one point we played 4 games in Milwaukee in 3 days. I won in relief on Friday, saved a game on Saturday, saved the first game of a doubleheader on Sunday, and then pitched 5 innings of the second game and won that. On Monday, in Pittsburgh, I came in in the bottom of the ninth inning and pitched 8 scoreless innings before winning in the seventeenth. Back then, we just pitched.

The highlight of my career was being selected to the

All-Star team. That was terrific enough, and then our manager, Alvin Dark, told me I was going to pitch a couple of innings. That was an unbelievable thing. With the National League ahead 4–3, I pitched scoreless sixth and seventh innings and struck out Harmon Killebrew, Bob Allison, and Joe Pepitone. We went on to win 5–3.

Rusty Staub was a great young ballplayer, but he had a problem at first base. Twice I threw over there to keep a runner close and he let the ball get by. One time he was looking home and my throw went zinging by his head. It went behind him and he still hadn't turned around. Richards called me into his office and told me not to throw to first unless I first gave Rusty a signal. He said, "Don't embarrass him. He's young and it will mess up his mind." Rusty had a shaky rookie year, but he was so young and it was obvious that he would be a terrific hitter.

Late in the season, Richards told me he wanted to sign me for 1964 before I went home. He said to return in a couple of days with a salary figure. I was making $12,500, and when I saw him again the figure I had in mind was double that. But I told him, "I think you'll be fair. What do *you* have in mind?" He said, "A $1,500 raise." I said, "Yeah, that's *fair,* Paul." I told him what I wanted. He said, "You want $25,000! You only had one good year!" We ended up compromising and I got something above $22,000.

CHICAGO CUBS

DICK ELLSWORTH:

The Cubs had terminated their rotating coaches experiment and, with Bob Kennedy managing the team by himself, we went 82–80 in 1963. We had good starters in veterans Larry Jackson and Bob Buhl, and Glen Hobbie and me, and excellent relievers Lindy McDaniel and Don Elston. We also had a good double-play combination in Kenny Hubbs and Andre Rodgers; good young outfielders in Lou Brock, Ellis Burton, and Billy Williams; and a a strong offense led by Ernie Banks, Ron Santo, and Williams—Brock had potential to be a good hitter but hadn't developed yet. Our entire team played solid baseball and we felt we could beat anybody.

The improvement of the club helped me improve. I also developed a slider in spring training. I wasn't over-

powering velocity-wise, but my fastball was effective because it tailed and sank a lot. However, because it had so much movement, it was hard to throw inside to right-handed hitters. The ball would sail back across the plate, so I couldn't get it inside unless I threw it directly at the batter. The slider was the pitch that let me come inside. And that helped me go from a 9–20 record and 5.09 ERA in 1962 to 22–10 with a 2.11 ERA in 1963.

The whole team seemed more relaxed. Larry Jackson's presence helped. The card games really started when Jackson was traded from the Cards. He was a bridge and gin player. Jackson, Don Elston, and Don Landrum would play together, and various other guys would join in. It added to the camaraderie.

BOB BUHL:

Larry Jackson was a very tough competitor and sort of a leader because he had a winning attitude. He was only a couple of years younger than me and became my road roommate when he joined the Cubs. I chummed with him most of the time. I also chummed with outfielder Don Landrum. We had an apartment together in Chicago. Dick Ellsworth also chummed around with us every now and then. He was a good guy and a smart, talented pitcher. He had a great year in 1963, but ran into arm trouble after that.

After the 1962 season, I had asked John Holland for a raise. He said that he couldn't give me a raise but that he'd give me 2 percent of my salary for every game we'd win over .500. I said, "You gotta be out of your mind after losing 103 games! We aren't going to be over .500." So he agreed to give me a couple of thousand raise and said that it would hold true about the 2 percent. We were in first place in June, and in July we were about 10 games over .500 and playing good ball. I thought I might make a lot of extra money. As it turned out, we slumped but still ended up 2 games over .500. I reminded John he owed me some money. So he wrote a check out to me. It was a good organization to play for.

Bob Kennedy was a good man. He was a fair but strict manager. He made us run out everything and hustle, and play the game the way it was supposed to be played. He was a major reason our team improved so much.

When I was going through my hitless streak I didn't feel any pressure, because sooner or later a squirrel has to find an acorn, doesn't he? I wasn't excited when I got my hit against Pittsburgh in May in the game where I gave up Willie Stargell's first home run. My hit came after 87 outs in a row. Everybody knew I couldn't get a real hit. The infielder was backing up and caught his spikes and fell down and the ball fell. That was the only reason I got a hit. I laughed. They called time to give me the damn ball. I was embarrassed, but I had to take it. I had good humor about my hitting.

LOS ANGELES DODGERS

ED ROEBUCK:

Everyone had a bad taste in his mouth for having blown the pennant in 1962. But we came back strong in 1963. Maury Wills, Frank Howard, Tommy Davis—who would win his second straight batting title—and left-handed first baseman Ron Fairly led the way offensively, and we had great up-the-middle defense with Roseboro, Gilliam and Wills, and Willie Davis. Wills continued to be our driving force.

TIM McCARVER (CARDINALS):

Maury Wills wasn't as fast as all the base-running specialists for whom he paved the way. But he was smart. He introduced the art and science of stealing bases. I can't remember throwing him out. When I'd call a pitchout, he never ran. He was a little guy who slid late and very, very hard. No one was better at sliding into a base. He had a sixth sense that told him how to be safe. If he knew it would be a close play, he'd slide into the glove and kick the ball out, or he'd avoid the tag and reach the corner of a base with his hand. Wills was made a more effective baserunner because Jim Gilliam batted behind him. Gilliam was one of the most underrated players of the era. He could do everything well—bat, field, the intangibles. He knew how to play the game.

DICK GROAT (CARDINALS):

Maury Wills was an excellent-hitting switch-hitter, a great baserunner, and an excellent shortstop. He and Willie Davis ignited the rallies. Their speed was just awesome. Frank Howard or Tommy Davis hit a lot of homers, but usually the Dodgers won when Don Drysdale or Sandy Koufax shut you out and Maury and Willie stole a base or two and came around on a wild pitch or hit by Tommy Davis, and they'd win 1–0. That's how they won the pennant in 1963.

E. ROEBUCK:

Once again, we got great starting pitching from Drysdale and Koufax. Drysdale threw hard for over 300 innings again, won 19 games, and struck out about 250 batters.

DICK GROAT (CARDINALS):

Don Drysdale was a mean pitcher. I can say sincerely that everybody in the league wanted to beat him because of that. You really battled when he was pitching. In 1962, when he won 25 games and was voted the Cy Young Award, it was the first time he won 20. The inside of the plate was his, but that year he didn't knock as many guys down as he would later on. He had marvelous control. He wasn't that mean then, but he changed after that. I hated to face him. He'd come from the side, and you had to force yourself not to open up.

E. ROEBUCK:

Sandy was healthy and became a workhorse. Like Drysdale, he would pitch over 300 innings. He was amazing. He went 25–5, had an ERA in the 1.80s, threw 11 shutouts, which was a record for lefties, and struck out over 300 batters for a National League record. He won his first of 3 Cy Young Awards and was now unquestionably the best pitcher in baseball. There was such a talent gap between Koufax and the next best pitchers—it must have been like that with Babe Ruth and his peer group. Marichal also won 25 games, but when they faced each other in May, Sandy won 8–0 by pitching his second no-hitter. Watching him pitch, you wondered why he wouldn't hurl more than 4 no-hitters in his career. Sandy didn't fool around trying to neutralize batters. He didn't go to 3–2 counts. He'd get the batter on 3 pitches. He was a modest guy and real intelligent, and he seemed embarrassed by his success. He didn't change at all as a person, and continued to get along with everybody. As good as he was as a pitcher, he became even better after I left.

DICK GROAT (CARDINALS):

Although I didn't wear him out, I never minded facing Koufax. His control was so good that he could have pitched inside, but it didn't make any difference. You could see the ball so well, but you just didn't hit it. His ball had that extra little hop and I'd either foul it off or miss it. For a guy that threw that hard, he had a great curveball and a great change-up. He knew how to pitch. He just didn't go out there and throw.

TIM McCARVER (CARDINALS):

Sandy Koufax came over the top, so he wasn't as frightening as left-handers like Joe Gibbon and Fred Green. But he didn't need to intimidate anybody. When Koufax got ahead of you on the count, your at-bat was over. If his first pitch was strike one, you might as well return to the dugout. If his first pitch was ball one, you had a chance. If he went 2–0, you could expect him to bring the fastball down. There was not a hitter alive who Koufax thought could catch up to his fastball. The key was to let him continue to think like that. You'd think along with him. With Sandy, you knew what was coming on almost every pitch. A batter could guess with him easier than any pitcher. That you still couldn't hit him was a credit to his greatness.

E. ROEBUCK:

I wasn't pitching as much as in other years because Alston was relying mostly on Ron Perranoski, who had become the best reliever in baseball. So in August I went to Buzzy Bavasi and said, "Look, I'm not pitching here and Hodges is managing over in Washington. Get me out of here. I can't take this place anymore." Buzzy said, "Aw, you're part of the family. I'm never going to trade you." He owed me money because the previous year I asked for $25,000, but he said he already had my contract made out for $20,000. He said, "Let's split the difference. Sign this contract and I'll give you another $2,500 in spring training." I said, "Put it in the contract so if I get traded, the other team will know about the $2,500 and pay me." He said, "You're never going to be traded. You'll be in this organization forever. Don't worry." So I go in to see him. Buzzy said, "Whatever happened to that happy-go-lucky kid?" I said "Bull-shit. Give me that money you owe me." He said he'd get his secretary to make out a check right away. He

said, "Just promise me, you'll always be my friend." I said okay. So I go home and get a call at 8 A.M. the next morning from Red Patterson, the assistant GM, saying I'd just been traded to Washington. The only thing I regretted was that I wouldn't play with the Dodgers when they swept the Yankees in the World Series.

SAN FRANCISCO GIANTS

BILLY O'DELL:

After our great 1962 season, we slipped to third place behind the Dodgers and Cardinals. This was despite great seasons from Mays and Cepeda, and Willie McCovey finally emerging from their shadows and leading the league with 44 homers. Sanford won 16 games and I went 14–10. We pitched pretty well but nothing like Juan Marichal, who pitched about 320 innings and went 25–8. He no-hit Houston 1–0, becoming the first Latin to throw a no-hitter. That was the first Giants' no-hitter since Carl Hubbell's in the late 1920s. And he beat Warren Spahn in one game, 1–0, on a home run by Mays in the bottom of the sixteenth inning. He and Spahn both went the distance. By this time you could call Marichal a *great* pitcher. If he had been as tough as a Drysdale or Gibson, he might never have lost a game. Only Koufax was as good as Marichal. Sandy just threw so hard. He had a great curve but mostly he just overpowered you. I pitched a lot against him. It seems like every time I'd go into L.A., my turn would come at the same time as his.

I wasn't mean, but I'd get after hitters. I pitched in a hurry and threw strikes. I was a good pitcher under pressure, which is why I had success as a reliever. I let the catcher call the game, but I'd shake him off when I wanted to throw an important pitch. At least one writer suggested that I didn't pay attention to signals, but that wasn't accurate. What happened is that one year Ed Bailey and I didn't use real signals. Bailey would put down fingers that didn't mean anything and I'd just throw what I wanted. He was a good enough receiver to catch anything I threw without anticipating it. He just gave me a target. We had good luck and continued doing this until Alvin Dark found out about it. He made us stop because he didn't want us to have a passed ball during a critical part of the game. I got along well with my receivers, particularly Bailey. The Giants would trade him after the season to let the younger Tom Haller catch every day. I think the team lost a lot with his departure. He was a happy-go-lucky fellow who kept everybody hopping. He was a prankster, jokester, storyteller, court jester. Not only was he a good hitter and receiver, but he also was probably the only really funny guy on the team.

BILLY PIERCE:

In 1963, everything went wrong. I won the first game at Candlestick and won 2 games the rest of the year. I was just 3–6 as a starter, so, of course, Dark had to take me out of the rotation. I became a reliever, and though I recorded a few saves, my bullpen record was 0–5. I ended the season with 3 wins and 11 losses, and my ERA was over 4.00 for the first time since 1948.

NEW YORK METS

FRANK THOMAS:

In the Mets' second season, we picked up Duke Snider from the Dodgers and brought up a couple of good young players, second baseman Ron Hunt, who was a very tough competitor, and outfielder–first baseman Ed Kranepool, a big 18-year-old local kid.

We also acquired Jimmy Piersall, who I always considered a strange character. I saw him run into the stands in the minor leagues. He was off his rocker then and it was sad. On the Mets, he ran around the bases backward after hitting his 100th career homer against the Phillies' Dallas Green. He made them change the rule. The players thought it was funny. But Green didn't, and neither did the Mets' front office, which soon traded him to the Angels.

Despite a few positive changes, Richie Ashburn had retired and we weren't all that improved. Writers would call and ask how it felt to be on such a terrible team. I'd tell them that we had pride in ourselves. We went out there every day with the idea that we would win. I just took everything in stride and wasn't any different if I was going good or going bad. I believed in the power of positive thinking.

The guys I felt sorry for were Roger Craig and Al Jackson. Craig was a crafty right-hander who hadn't been able to break into the Dodgers' rotation, so he came to the Mets and pitched good ball but lost 24 games in 1962 and 22 games in 1963. He lost 18 in a row at one point before Jim Hickman's grand slam got him off the hook. He was a funny guy, but that was enough to test his sense of humor. Jackson was a little lefty out of the Cardinals' organization. He had great stuff but lost 20 games the first year and 17 the next. Neither guy would have lost 20 games with any other team, but they couldn't get a break. They had to pitch shutouts to win. They were very intelligent and students of the game, and I correctly predicted that they would remain in baseball after their playing careers were over. Craig was lucky to be traded to the Cardinals after the 1963 season, but Jackson had to stick around a few more years.

The truth was I enjoyed playing for the Mets. They were good for baseball. The fans were the greatest alive. The media may have mocked the Mets as a team and picked on Marv Throneberry, but Stengel diverted so much attention to himself that in general they treated the players pretty well. And the organization was first-rate. I liked that the Mets were family-oriented, not only in regard to fans but in regard to their players. The family was always included. For instance, the team would hold a picnic at Grossinger's for the whole family. We lived in Tarrytown, New York, and in Woodbury, Long Island, and really enjoyed the whole New York experience. I would be recognized on the street, prominent people would take me out to dinner, I could even go to the clothing factories and get suits at half price and clothes for my kids at discount prices. There were a lot of advantages to playing for the New York Mets.

ED BOUCHEE:

The Mets didn't even bring me up during the year. They were acquiring over-the-hill players like Duke Snider but paying no attention to younger guys who could help them. I spent the entire season with the Mets farm team in Buffalo. We had the phenom pitchers they had just signed, young players who were being shuttled between the majors and minors, and old guys that didn't make it. There were guys like Ed Kranepool, Marv Throneberry, myself, Chris Cannizzaro. We had a ball. It was the best summer I had in baseball. Still, I knew I was quitting.

PUMPSIE GREEN:

It was a disappointment being traded by Boston to the Mets in 1963. When I first came over, I thought I had a chance to be a regular, but I soon realized that wasn't the case. Ron Hunt, who would be the team's first All-Star, was given the second-base job. In my years with Boston I had played only second base and shortstop, yet with the Mets I played only at third base. Stengel may not have known who I was. I tried to do the best I could—you play the hand you are dealt. Ironically, I had my highest batting average with the Mets, hitting .278. But I never was given the chance to make a real contribution.

The Mets were almost like a zoo, with players coming and going. I never did know what was going on. I don't know why they got me. I don't think they had a plan for me or anyone else. They just put 9 men on the field. If you got 3 hits you played the next game; if you didn't, you were gone. It was Grand Central Station.

There were a lot of fans coming to games, but when you're losing every game and you have apprehension that you'll be on the next bus out of town, there can't be that much excitement. Everyone was doing the best they could, but it was hard to be happy when you were jockeying for position. The players weren't so bad, but it was hard to play in that atmosphere. The fans would wait for us to mess up and we would. We knew we'd lose. We cared if we lost, particularly the pitchers. The most fun we had was beating the Giants. They were a great team, but when they returned to New York we kicked their behinds. We could battle them. We also battled the Dodgers, but it was harder beating Koufax, Drysdale, and their other great pitchers.

Casey Stengel was enjoyable to be with if you could understand what he was talking about. Sometimes I did, sometimes I didn't A few of the players snickered at him, but in general I couldn't tell if they felt respect or fear. A lot of young players were confused.

Choo Choo Coleman, who was one of the team's odd assortment of young players, was sort of like Casey Stengel. No one knew what he was talking about either. We'd laugh at Choo Choo, and he'd laugh at us. He was a funny guy. Usually he wouldn't say a word—if he said anything, you couldn't understand him anyway.

I didn't even finish the season with the Mets. They assigned me to Buffalo. So my major league career was

NATIONAL BASEBALL LIBRARY, COOPERSTOWN, N.Y.

Pumpsie Green had the misfortune to play his last major league season with the disorganized New York Mets in 1963.

over. It was a short career, but going in I realized that most major leaguers played only a brief time. So I was satisfied. When it was over, I wanted to get out and get on with my life.

PHILADELPHIA PHILLIES

JOHNNY KLIPPSTEIN:

The Reds traded me to the Phillies in late March. The Phillies were a very loose team, but our manager, Gene Mauch, was very serious. Mauch had turned a terrible team into a contender in just a couple of years, but he wouldn't be satisfied until he won the pennant. So he drove his players a bit. He didn't want us to talk about anything but baseball. He didn't want us to talk about God or horse racing or anything else. He'd walk down the bench and ask us questions about the game. He'd even ask what the counts were on certain hitters earlier in the game. I liked Mauch, but I thought he took the game away from the players too much. When he managed against the Giants' Alvin Dark, they would each use 22 or 23 players, trying to outsmart each other, rather than just letting us play the game.

However, I'd say the only real drawback to playing with the Phillies was that their fans were the worst in baseball. Back in the '50s, they would cheer Del Ennis, Stan Lopata, or Granny Hamner, and the next day they would boo them. Things hadn't changed. They should have been more loyal because it was hard to play in front of them.

By this time I had become more of a breaking-ball pitcher. I threw many more change-ups, curves, and sliders. I still had a good fastball but didn't throw it as much. I was better because I could mix up my pitches and I did well for the Phillies. I won 5 games and saved 8 others, and struck out 86 batters in 112 innings. My ERA of 1.93 was the best of my career.

We picked up Ryne Duren during the season and he also did a good job in relief. We drove to the ballpark together and I even roomed with him for a while, yet I didn't know he was an alcoholic. He was kind of a loner, and when you ran into him, you didn't know where he'd been or how many drinks he'd had. I did know he drank a lot—he'd phone all over the world from our room. He was a very interesting guy and we got along very well, but Ryne could be a Jekyll and Hyde. Once we almost came to blows. We were in a bar that we went to after games for a few beers and a free sandwich. Ryne probably had about 5 quick drinks and he came over to me and said, "I bet I can whip you." I said, "I don't think you can." We started to walk outside to settle it. But Cal McLish, who along with rookie Ray Culp was our best starter that year, was sitting at the bar and he stopped Ryne. Cal, who had been pitching in the majors since the mid-'40s, was a fatherly figure, a settler of affairs. He said, "Ryne, what kind of guy are you? You want to fight with a guy on your own club? Just a minute ago you were telling me what a great guy he is. Get your butt over there and sit down." So Ryne sat down. About 15 minutes passed and all of a sudden Ryne jumped over the bar after the bartender.

What could have been going through his mind? They threw him out of the bar and never let him come back.

JIM BROSNAN (REDS):
I saw Ryne Duren in action when he destroyed a bar after losing a game in spring training.

RYNE DUREN:
In March the Angels sold me to Philadelphia, so I came to the National League for the first time. The Phillies had been a last-place club just 2 years before, but they were making swift progress under Gene Mauch. After a poor 1961 season in which they set a record for consecutive losses, Mauch had led them to a winning record in 1962, and in 1963 we did even better, moving up to fourth place.

I liked Mauch. You could talk to him and he'd challenge you a bit. One day I walked into his office and asked him what percentage good pitching was to a winning team. He said 75 percent or more. So I said, "Then why do we come to the park every day and spend all our energy for two hours on batting practice. Why don't teams have pitching practice? We might spend a week or two without ever getting on the mound and then we don't pitch so well. So what about holding some pitching practice?" He said, "We could hold pitching practice, but do you think anybody would want to hit against *you*?" So we approached the rest of the team. I said, "The reason Gene doesn't think pitching practice would work is that none of you would want to hit against me. I don't think we have any lily-livers in here. Who will come out and hit against me?" Nobody's hand went up. But soon Roy Sievers put up his hand and said, "I'll bat against you, you four-eyed son of a bitch. I'm not scared of you." I gave him credit for that because I'd hit him a couple of times. After Roy stepped forward, all the other players did the same. So the next day, Mauch held a mock game in which I faced Jack Hamilton. Mauch stood behind the batting cage and called the balls and strikes. The batters would hit the ball but not run them out, so Mauch would indicate where they ended up. There were some bets on that game. I beat Hamilton 1–0 in 5 innings, and it helped me get untracked.

I didn't drink for 4 or 5 months. And my record

showed it. I was 6–2, after being 2–9 the year before. My ERA was 3.30, my best since 1959.

PITTSBURGH PIRATES

ELROY FACE:

Most of the players on the Pirates liked Joe Brown, but I didn't see eye to eye with him—especially after I had a terrific 1962 season and he offered to restore only half of the $5,000 he cut the previous spring from my 1961 salary. I felt somewhat betrayed by him. I wouldn't sign unless I got all $5,000 back. I called him to tell him I'd be in Florida if he wanted to negotiate. He said, ''Well, I'll give you what you want, but I'll be tough on you from now on.'' So I got my $5,000 back. But, because of what he said, our relationship was further strained. Oddly, he later denied saying anything and couldn't understand what was bothering me.

The Pirates were making a lot of personnel changes. Brown had traded Dick Groat to the Cardinals, Don Hoak to the Phillies, and Dick Stuart to the Red Sox, and Bob Skinner would be traded early in the season to the Reds. In their places, we had a lot of young players who weren't quite ready to take over the load. Willie Stargell played left, Donn Clendenon—a powerful right-handed hitter and good defensive player—played first, and Bob Bailey played third. Also, Dick Schofield finally became a starting shortstop, and Jim Pagliaroni came over from Boston to be our starting catcher, with Smoky Burgess moving to the bench. Smoky and Jerry Lynch, who set a pinch-hit homer record that year, were a great duo off the bench. Because of the youth and the changes, the Pirates struggled and finished ahead of only Houston and the New York Mets. We won 19 games fewer than in 1962. Most of our pitchers had rough times winning. Friend had an ERA of around 2.30, yet won only one game more than he lost. I was just 3–9, but had a 3.23 ERA and 16 saves, which trailed only Lindy McDaniel and Ron Perranoski in the National League.

DICK SCHOFIELD:

Dick Groat was traded to the Cardinals after the 1962 season, and I finally became a regular in 1963. I played about 120 games at short and about 20 more at second. My fielding was fine: I led the league's shortstops in chances per game and, despite missing a lot of games, was only 5 double plays behind the league leader, as Mazeroski and I proved to be a good combination. However, my batting average was only .246. To be honest, I was having trouble with hamstring pulls due to not playing enough games all those years. The long haul caught up with me. It made me mad. I should have been a regular a long time before.

It was an experience playing every day. There were certain players who were hard to defense. The left-handed batters who could hit the ball my way and could run were tough. Maury Wills, when he batted left-handed, Lou Brock, and Willie Davis were about the hardest to throw out on a slow grounder. Brock really got to first quickly. Coming into second, Wills slid hard and late. Yet he'd bitch if you tagged him hard. Ron Hunt, the Mets' rookie second baseman, would slide into second and get you. He was a tough player. He didn't mind being in a collision or getting hit by a fastball. Wally Moon slid hard into second with his hands up in the air so he could block throws. Mostly it was outfielders who would slide hard into second because they knew there was no way to retaliate against them with slides.

I thought we were going to have a better team than we did. We added a few great young players: Willie Stargell, Donn Clendenon, Bob Bailey, Manny Mota, and Gene Alley. But they didn't produce immediately and our pitching was a little light. Friend, Law, Gibbon, and Face were still effective, Al McBean was coming around, and we had picked up Don Cardwell, but young pitchers like Bob Veale, Tommie Sisk, and Steve Blass had yet to develop in the system.

CINCINNATI REDS

JIM O'TOOLE:

We slipped to fifth place in 1963, but we still had a good team. Purkey and Jay didn't win a lot of games, but I won 17, Joe Nuxhall, who had returned from the American League in 1962, won 15, and Jim Maloney really came into his own with 23 wins. Maloney had such a great fastball and curve that he was unhittable if he got them both over. He tied a record with 8 consecutive strikeouts against the Braves. He was as good as Koufax. He was one of the real characters on the team. He was a crazy guy who'd do stupid stuff like stand around the clubhouse or sit on the plane with his zipper open and his thing hanging out, or he'd do disgusting things that made you want to puke from watching him.

It was exciting to be the National League's starting pitcher in the 1963 All-Star Game. I went against Ken McBride and pitched the first 2 innings of a 5–3 victory. We got only 6 singles. Willie Mays was our star—he had 2 hits, 2 RBIs, and 2 runs and made a spectacular catch against the fence.

Pete Rose and outfielder Tommy Harper broke in together in 1963. Harper had a lot of speed and was talented, but Rose was a great player. He went about his business on the field like nobody I'd ever seen. Pete was a hometown kid and he had to prove himself to us. Don Blasingame had his best year in 1962 and he should never have lost his second-base job. As a pitcher, I didn't like that Rose couldn't make the double play like Blasingame. But there was no way Hutchinson could get him out of there. In late April, Blasingame was traded to the Giants and Rose went on to be Rookie of the Year. He did the job.

Rose was a cocky guy but not outspoken. Nobody really cared for him much off the field. I was tough on him. I didn't like that he talked like a hillbilly. He wasn't very educated. He hung around with the colored players. His constant hustle annoyed people. But that was Pete. He stuck to his way and it all worked out. He was different. We didn't see him that much. As soon as the game ended, he'd shower and meet the girls who were waiting for him. Very seldom did he go back on the bus to the hotel. Most rookies made sure they were on the bus, but he was like a veteran and went his own way. Like most single guys, he'd go off with women and then relate his antics the next day on the bus.

JIM BROSNAN:

I didn't notice Pete Rose at first. In spring training I would get to the ballpark, do my work, and get back to the beach where I was living. The only reason I noticed him at all was that he wore his pants so tight and so long. I had never seen anyone do that except for Frank Robinson. Rose chased women no matter what they looked like. There was a stripper in Pittsburgh who was famous for being a "star-fucker." She didn't want any part of him because he wasn't a star. But he was the only one on the club she could get. She was a pig. Still, Pete would brag about it. And she brought along a blonde who was even more gross than she was. And here was Pete, who looked like a little brat, standing between these two broads. He went out with both of them. No one was jealous. I was hoping that this would so repulse and embarrass Fred Hutchinson that he would get rid of this kid and let my locker mate, Don Blasingame, continue being our second baseman. But Hutchinson always ignored such things.

BILLY MORAN (ANGELS):

Johnny Temple, who would finish his career with the Reds in 1964, said that Fred Hutchinson told him to make sure of two things: that Pete Rose didn't hang around with the black players and that Rose learned how to use a fork when he ate.

J. BROSNAN:

Despite Rose, in those days, women were not so important in a player's life as Jim Bouton would make out in his book *Ball Four*. Most players were straight arrows. Which doesn't mean that binocular salesmen didn't do a brisk business during spring training.

I knew Bill DeWitt was trying to get rid of me. He didn't like my writing and we had other differences. For one thing, I held out because he was trying to cut my salary by $3,000. The Reds didn't win the pennant in 1962, so he felt he was justified, but the team actually won 5 more games and I had a good year. I had an offer from CBS to do a half-hour television show for which I would be miked during spring training and describe what was going on. The great linebacker Sam Huff had done that for a television documentary on football. But DeWitt refused to give CBS permission. So he screwed me not only out of $3,000 in salary but out of another $4,000. I signed his contract but told him what I thought of him. He pulled out the player's contract and pointed out that I had to get his clearance before I published anything else. About a month later, I was traded to the White Sox.

So I wasn't around when and if Hutchinson told Rose not to pal around with Frank Robinson and Vada Pinson. If he did so, my guess is that he was following orders from above. Fred wasn't the type to pay attention to anything a player did off the field that didn't affect his performance. And Rose was playing great.

I also wasn't around in September when Vada Pinson punched sportswriter Earl Lawson. I thought Lawson had a lot of guts. He was a little bitty guy and he knew damn well when he wrote that Vada Pinson would hit .350 if he would only bunt once in a while instead of going for homers that Vada was going to resent the hell out of it. And when Vada said, "I ought to punch you right in the face," little Earl said, "Well, just try it." And he did. Pinson floored him. If it were up to Lawson, I don't think that story would have come out. He was a tough little guy.

AMERICAN LEAGUE 1963

"IT WAS A TOUGH LIFE BEING A BALLPLAYER. YOU WERE ALWAYS UNDER PRESSURE EVEN IF YOU WEREN'T IN A PENNANT RACE. YOUR WHOLE LIFE WAS DETERMINED BY HOW YOU DID. YOU NEVER FORGOT THAT IF YOU DIDN'T DO THE JOB, THERE WAS SOMEONE IN THE MINORS WHO WAS WAITING FOR YOU TO FAIL OR BE INJURED."

TOM CHENEY

LOS ANGELES ANGELS

BILLY MORAN:

After our terrific 1962 season, we were optimistic about our chances in 1963. I had about the same stats—my .275 was 12th in the league—and Albie Pearson raised his average about 40 points, to over .300. Leon Wagner belted over 25 homers and had 90 RBIs, and Ken McBride and Dean Chance won 13 games each. We all did okay, but most of the other players had off seasons. For instance, Lee Thomas dropped to .220, with fewer than 10 homers, and Bo Belinsky was just 2–9. So we had a dismal season, finishing in ninth place.

Fregosi and I still didn't work well together. We had a reputation for being a good combination, but we weren't. He had pretty good hands and could throw, but I still had trouble finding the ball on double plays. I never missed it, but I always had to hold back to make sure I caught the ball before I could throw it and complete the double play. I could never cheat, so I got roughed up by sliding runners.

The Mets sent Jimmy Piersall to the Angels late in the season after he ran backward around the bases after hitting his 100th homer. I had played with him on the Indians. I still thought he was the most disruptive guy to have on a team and didn't enjoy playing with him. I didn't really like him. He was a good player, as good a center fielder as anybody, but he didn't care about the team and was always showing off. We approached things differently. But I must say that I wish I could have promoted myself more, especially when it would have helped me toward the end of my career.

BOB TURLEY:

I didn't have a good record with the Angels in my brief stay at the beginning of the season. But I had a lot of fun. Bill Rigney was one of the nicest managers I had come across. And Gene Autry was a great owner to play for. I lived in a motel of his on Sunset Boulevard. I made friends with a lot of the players, including Bob Rodgers, Dean Chance, and Bo Belinsky. I didn't socialize with Chance or Belinsky because they were too wild for me, but I liked them both. We had a good team with good starting pitchers, but when the relief pitchers came in, it was like pouring gasoline on a fire.

CLEVELAND INDIANS

MUDCAT GRANT:

I was injury-free in 1963 and rebounded to have one of my best seasons. I pitched almost 230 innings and won 13 games, my second-highest total on the Indians. My ERA was my best on the Indians, and I had a career-best 157 strikeouts. But the team didn't show any improvement under our new manager, Birdie Tebbetts. Managers in Cleveland never lasted very long. Between 1958 and 1963, I had 6 managers, including Mel Harder for 1 game. And I didn't think any of them were any good. Tebbetts hadn't much success managing in the National League, and he didn't impress me with the Indians, although he was certainly as bright as any of my previous managers. The best thing I can say about Tebbetts is that he understood what problems black players would have in the majors.

BARRY LATMAN:

Birdie Tebbetts was our third manager in 3 years, but for the third straight year we finished just below .500. We didn't have much offense. Our rookie third baseman, Max Alvis, led our team with fewer than 70 RBIs. I had some good outings, but I finished below .500 for the second straight year, going 7–12, with a high earned run average. There had been a time when I tore things apart after getting battered on the mound. But I had been cured of that. I walked into the clubhouse after a bad outing and there was the clubhouse man just throwing my things all over, saying, "I'm beating you to it, you son of a bitch." He taught me a lesson.

I became the player rep in 1963. The guys were pretty easy to deal with, and if there was ever a problem I'd go to Mudcat Grant, who had a good relationship with everybody. What I saw is that the players wanted a union. They were less interested in a pension plan than just getting salaries that were big enough to live on. Players didn't grumble about salaries to each other, but it was a major concern. No one knew exactly what the other guy was making, except that it couldn't have been very much unless you were a Mickey Mantle or Willie Mays and making around $100,000. Almost everyone had to have part-time jobs—I sold draperies and was a

Completing a four-year stint with the Cleveland Indians, Barry Latman struck out a career-high 133 batters in just 149⅓ innings.

food broker at different times. One of the gripes among players on the Indians was that we didn't get any money for appearing on the team's postgame radio show, while visiting players were getting $25 for coming on. So we struck. Until our general manager Gabe Paul said, "That's it, boys. You're going on the show tomorrow." So we did, without getting the money.

I negotiated directly with Paul about my own salary. You couldn't bring any kind of help into the room. He would just say, "You're not worth this. What did you do?" His favorite statement was "We have a big pie and there are only 25 pieces to that pie." And he'd say how certain players should make $30,000 because they had been around a long time, thus explaining how your share was so low. He had your salary marked down every year before the season started and that was it. I held out every year until spring training, but could get him to budge only $500 to $1,000. I wasn't angry. I didn't have the great years to support my demands.

PEDRO RAMOS:

I really wanted to race with Mickey Mantle, who had a reputation for being fast. He bet me $1,000 that he could beat me. I didn't make the kind of money he did, so I didn't want to risk losing $1,000. I didn't have as much pride as Mickey about running, so I didn't mind losing the race, just the money. So I went to Gabe Paul and told him about the race. Gabe said for me to tell Mickey that he'd put $2,000 on my legs. So I went back to Mickey, but he didn't want to do it anymore. He didn't need the money and didn't want to chance hurting himself. More than that, he didn't want to be beaten by a pitcher, or as he kidded me, "a damn Cuban." So that was the end of the whole thing. I don't know if I could have beaten him, but it would have been a good race.

I pitched pretty well during the season, going 9–8, with a 3.12 ERA. Mudcat and Jack Kralick led the staff with 13 wins each. We had acquired Kralick from the Twins for Jim Perry and he did a good job for us. We had several other newcomers who helped out. Ted Abernathy, who had been my roommate on the Senators a few years before, returned to the majors and was an outstanding reliever for us, one of the best in the league. Max Alvis was a good defensive third baseman and led our team with 22 homers. Another rookie was our lead-off hitter, Victor Davalillo. He was a 5'7" left-handed hitter from Venezuela. He had a brother named "Yo-Yo." Vic was a good defensive center fielder with a helluva arm. He hit .290 and, for a little man, had good power. He could also run, though I don't know if he could have beaten me. His one trouble is that he did some drinking and sometimes was a little sick when he came to the park. But he still played pretty hard.

After his great career with the Braves, Joe Adcock spent one year with us. Tebbetts used him as a part-time first baseman and pinch hitter, playing him when Fred Whitfield rested. He was a tough country guy from Louisiana, but he was friendly. He'd always be talking about cows, so we called him "the Cow Man."

Early Wynn was another veteran who played for us in 1963. He had been released the previous year by the White Sox after having won 299 games. Rather than retiring, he came back to the Indians to try to win 1 more game because he figured he needed 300 wins to get into the Hall of Fame. His arm was worn out, but he still knew how to pitch and did a good job for us. But he couldn't get that 1 victory. He wanted it so bad he could taste it. Finally, in July, he started against the Athletics and left with a lead after 5 tough innings. Jerry Walker pitched shutout ball the rest of the way and Wynn got his 300th victory! That was the last victory of his career.

Back in May, the Indians sent my friend and roommate Doc Edwards to the Athletics for shortstop Dick Howser and catcher Jose Azcue. Howser was "Mr. Baseball." He talked a lot about the game and learned a lot because at first he didn't play every day. I could see he was managerial material. He was a good little hitter and defensive shortstop. Azcue did a good job hitting and behind the plate. I told Tebbetts that I wanted him to catch me. I didn't like working with Johnny Romano because he let Tebbetts call every pitch. I liked to call my own ball game so if I lost, it was my fault.

I didn't like Tebbetts. One night in Los Angeles, a few of us were trying to get back to the hotel before the 1 A.M. curfew. We just made it. We all got into the elevator, but it wouldn't go up. Who should walk into the elevator but Tebbetts. We all looked at our watches and it was 1 A.M. But Tebbetts's watch had it being 5 minutes after 1, so he fined all of us.

After the season, I played in the Polo Grounds at the Hispanic All-Star Game. I was the losing pitcher, but it was a wonderful experience. Everybody was there and I got to play with National Leaguers like Roberto Clemente and Juan Marichal. And that was the only time I ever was in that old stadium. It looked like a telephone booth.

BALTIMORE ORIOLES

BROOKS ROBINSON:

Billy Hitchcock, the one-time infielder, managed the Orioles in 1962, when we dropped to seventh place, and 1963, when we moved back up to fourth. Billy was the nicest guy you ever wanted to meet, but we didn't play very well under him. It was discouraging because I had thought the Orioles were on the verge of catching up to the Yankees.

The major addition the Orioles made in 1963 was getting Luis Aparicio from the White Sox. Luis was just a sensational player offensively and defensively. He was the era's best-fielding shortstop. He had so much range that I could cheat more to the line than I did with Hansen. Luis had led the league in stolen bases all 7 years he had been with the White Sox, and he led the league his first year with the Orioles, stealing 40 bases. I don't know if he had a special technique—he just stole because he took a big lead, got a great jump, and had outstanding speed.

We also got starter Mike McCormick and reliever Stu Miller in December of 1962 in a deal that sent Jack Fisher to the Giants. McCormick had several good years with the Giants before having arm problems in 1962. Unfortunately, he didn't have much success with us, although he'd revive his career in the late '60s.

Stu Miller wasn't a flaky relief pitcher but a pretty serious man who liked to be left alone. I liked him. He was a nice man. On the mound he was great. There were a few phenomenons that would come along every now and then, and Stu Miller was one of them. No one was like him. Relief pitchers usually threw hard, but he got you on that unusual change-up—batters knew it was coming but could do nothing. He could make hitters look funnier than any other pitcher.

HARMON KILLEBREW (TWINS):

I didn't consider any pitcher totally awesome. But the guy who gave me the most trouble was the Orioles' little relief pitcher. Stu Miller threw a lot of slow curveballs and change-ups and I couldn't hit him. His motion was what was deceptive. It wasn't just his head jerking but also his hips and shoulder. He was really tough.

B. ROBINSON:

Another good relief pitcher we had was 6'6" Dick Hall. He had come to the Orioles in 1961 and was an excellent reliever for us for several years. In 1963 he had a streak of getting out 28 consecutive batters. In 1964 he would win 9 out of 10 and have an ERA under 2.00. He wasn't a flaky reliever—in fact, he worked as a CPA in Baltimore. He was a student of the game. When he got to the mound he'd wet his finger and stick it in the air and adjust his little slider to the way the wind was blowing. He had perfect control and just pitched away, away, away all the time. I first saw him in 1959 when I was at Vancouver and broke up his no-hitter with a little looper over the second baseman. He never let me forget that.

AL SMITH:

I was 35 when Luis Aparicio and I came over to Baltimore from Chicago. I played a little less than I had with either Cleveland or Chicago, so while my average was decent, my production was down. That was the first time I pinch-hit a lot. The Orioles weren't a bad team, and we finished 10 games over .500. However, we weren't as unified as my past teams.

I'd calm a teammate down if he threw a bat or something but I was a quiet guy who never wanted to be a leader. Brooks Robinson was a leader. I liked playing with him. He was a great guy and his glove was like a suction cup.

BOSTON RED SOX

FRANK MALZONE:

I hit over .290, Carl Yastrzemski won the batting title, Dick Stuart led the league in RBIs and hit over 40 homers, and Bill Monbouquette became the first pitcher since I came to Boston to win 20 games. Yet we again won only 76 games and moved up only from eighth to seventh place. It was tough playing. You start playing too much for your own stats, thinking about next year's salary.

Not that they paid us very much in those days. The Red Sox were known as one of the most generous teams, but I thought about working in the off-season because I could have used the money. In the winters I spent in Boston, I did go to a lot of banquets and a lot of Sunday breakfasts.

Tom Yawkey was known to be fair with salaries, but he didn't mingle with players as much as was made out. I saw very little of him. Once in a while he'd come in and ask how guys were doing, but that's the extent of it. He didn't throw any parties or anything for his players. That "country club" label they placed on the Red Sox was bullshit. Someone just trumped that up. After I'd been with the club a few years I wondered what the hell they were talking about. We worked as hard as any team.

BILL MONBOUQUETTE:

Pinky Higgins became Red Sox general manager and Johnny Pesky took over as manager. I liked Pesky. He pitched me a little more than Higgins—almost 270 innings—and I won 20 games for the first time.

So I was very popular in Boston that year. I always thought the Fenway fans were the most knowledgeable in baseball. I did get booed on occasion when I didn't do the job, but I expected that. Overall, they treated me great. One guy who didn't boo anybody was Cardinal Cushing. He was a big baseball fan. He not only came to games but would come into the clubhouse. He knew all the players.

John Kennedy also was a fan. I met him when he was a senator and then again when he was President. Everyone on the team loved him. He was from Massachusetts and one of us. It was so upsetting when he was killed. I was married in 1963 and we were browsing in a furniture store on November 22 when we heard he had been shot.

BOB TURLEY:

I signed with the Red Sox late in the season. As usual, they had a lot of good hitters, but they were a team that always could use an extra pitcher.

The Red Sox were a terrible organization. It was the first time I had seen a team that didn't care about winning. The moves they made hurt the team. The owner, Tom Yawkey, was a recovered alcoholic, and the general manager, Pinky Higgins, had a drinking problem. The manager, Johnny Pesky, was the nicest man in the world, yet third base coach Billy Herman, who also was a likable guy, didn't like Pesky and was trying to get him fired—he would succeed in 1964.

I was good friends with a lot of the Red Sox, especially Bill Monbouquette and Frank Malzone. But a lot of the other guys were coddled athletes. A pitcher might lose 2 games in a row and Yawkey would give him a raise. The Red Sox always had a "country club" tag and I thought it was appropriate.

Boston got some good starting pitching from Earl Wilson, Dave Morehead, and Jack Lamabe, but Monbouquette was the only starter to have an outstanding year. However, Dick Radatz, Boston's relief ace, was something special. He was a big guy with a loose arm, and his ball would really pop. It's a shame he didn't take better care of himself. He wasn't a womanizer but he was a carouser.

After being elected the Yankees rep, and then the

American League rep, I was now the major league rep—which alternated between American League and National League reps. In those days, players wanted anything that would give us more money. I remember one meeting in 1962 or 1963, with Pirates owner John Galbraith, Dodgers owner Walter O'Malley, and Boston owner Tom Yawkey. I proposed that the owners set aside 20 percent of the clubs' incomes for player salaries. Oh, man, you should have seen them react to that. Yawkey had his briefcase open and he was explaining why that was impossible. A couple of owners got up and stormed out. They would have been better off taking it.

I pitched only about 10 games with the Red Sox to go along with the 20 or so I'd pitched earlier with the Angels. I won only 3 games, but I pitched almost 130 innings, which was the most since 1960. I accepted when Boston asked me to be a pitcher–pitching coach the next year.

WASHINGTON SENATORS

TOM CHENEY:

Like almost all of the Senators, I lived outside of Washington. For the first two years, my wife and I lived in Arlington, Virginia. Then we moved to an apartment complex in Maryland, where six or seven of the players lived. We rented a two-bedroom apartment for about $500 a month. It wasn't a homey-type place. Players didn't have too much of a home life. You played a ball game and you didn't get home until it was midnight or 1 A.M. Your kids were asleep and maybe your wife was, too. My wife would wait up and we'd eat at 1:30 or 2 A.M. Then I'd sleep till late morning. At 3:30 in the afternoon, I went back to the ballpark for another night game. We had to devote so much time to baseball that other than once going to the Smithsonian, I didn't see the sights of Washington. Also, my salary wasn't such that I could shop in the expensive clothing stores. I remember Brooks Robinson of the Orioles found a place for players to buy mohair suits for $100.

It was a tough life being a ballplayer. You were always under pressure even if you weren't in a pennant race. Your whole life was determined by how you did. You never forgot that if you didn't do the job, there was someone in the minors who was waiting for you to fail

Tom Cheney finally found his niche with the Washington Senators, where as the ace of their staff in 1962 and 1963 he won 15 games, had an ERA around 3.00, and set a single-game strikeout record with 21, in a 16-inning victory over Baltimore.

or be injured. I guess that was always in the back of my mind because when I was in the minors I was hoping something would happen to somebody in the majors so I could get an opportunity. I never worried about injuries, but I had so much competitiveness instilled in me that I always felt "I've got to do it." Luckily, my wife was understanding.

By this time, Harry Bright had moved on, but Chuck Cottier was still there and I had become good friends with Don Lock, who hit 27 homers and led the team in RBIs. Lock, Jim King, who hit over 20 homers, and Chuck Hinton gave us a good starting outfield. We also picked up Minnie Minoso. He was a great guy who would never say anything critical because he didn't want to hurt anyone's feelings. But it must have been frustrating for him to have to play on a losing club. He knew he was over the hill, yet he played hard.

Catcher Don Leppert was a friend. He was a comical

guy who had been a teammate on Omaha. He hated to catch my knuckleball. One night in Detroit, he said "Skins"—which everyone called me because I was bald—"I'll give you a choice of any plug I have in my tackle box if you don't throw a knuckleball tonight." I said, "I can't hardly make that deal—I may need to throw it." During the game I had one strike on Billy Bruton and Leppert called for a curveball, fastball, and slider, but I kept shaking him off. He wouldn't call the knuckleball. Finally he said, "Go ahead and throw it, you S.O.B." So I threw the best one I'd ever thrown. Bruton swung as it broke straight down. He missed it and fell flat on his back and Leppert got hit on the big toe. I turned my back. And Leppert was yelling, "That's right, you S.O.B., laugh!" Bruton was lying there dying of laughter.

By 1963 I was probably the ace of the staff, along with left-hander Claude Osteen. In 1962 I had led the team with a 3.17 ERA; this year I was doing even better. Unfortunately, the Senators were headed for their worst record yet. So Mickey Vernon lost his job and Gil Hodges took his place.

Gil was trying to make a name for himself at Washington. But he had a bad team and was frustrated. I wasn't his favorite person and he wasn't mine. We didn't get along. Our troubles increased at a clubhouse meeting when we got into a big argument over how to pitch the Yankees' Tony Kubek. Gil wanted me to jam him. I had played against Kubek all the way through the minor leagues and told Gil I wanted to pitch him away. Gil said I couldn't do that. I said I'd done it for years, longer than Gil had seen him, and since I'd gotten good results, this was the way I was going to continue to pitch him. If you have confidence that you can get a guy out a certain way, you can't go against your own thinking. A manager may say he'll take responsibility for your pitching his way, but he won't go to bat for you when you go in and talk contract. Saying the manager told you to pitch a certain way isn't worth two hoots in hell. A good manager wouldn't demand him to pitch a certain way. I wouldn't let Hodges or anyone else tell me how to pitch.

I hurt my arm against Baltimore. I knew something had happened. I threw a pitch and it felt like someone had a knife and ripped me down the forearm. All pitchers have small aches and pains every time they pitch, but this was different. They treated me with cortisone. There was nothing anyone could do. I kept trying to pitch but couldn't take the pain for more than 4 or 5 innings. By that time my elbow would start swelling. I could have gone up to 3 innings without much trouble, but Hodges wouldn't send me to the bullpen. He said that he wanted me to start.

ED ROEBUCK:

When I joined the Senators from the Dodgers, it came to pass exactly like I feared regarding the verbal agreement I had made with Buzzy Bavasi about money. My contract that winter came from the Senators' general manager, George Selkirk, the same guy who in the '30s replaced Babe Ruth in the Yankees' outfield. He was really from the old days. Selkirk looked at my $20,000 contract and instead of giving me the extra $2,500 Bavasi promised, said, "I can't believe you're making all that money." So he sent me a contract with the allowable 25 percent salary cut, cutting me back to $15,000. I told Buzzy what had happened. He complained about Selkirk and said he'd write to the commissioner, Ford Frick, and get it all straightened out. I never heard a thing about it. I had no choice but to sign Selkirk's contract.

Still, I liked pitching for Washington. I idolized Gil Hodges and did a pretty good job for him. He was in the learning stages of managing and you could tell he was going to be good. His team was made up of rejects from other teams and Gil saw the worst. Some of us drank too much, some of us chased women too much, some of us gambled too much. He was trying to be too easy with us. Later, he probably said, "If this is the way it's going to be, I'm not going to be one of the boys."

Don Rudolph, who you'd expect to be the wildest player on the team, turned out to be the exact opposite of the type of guy you would think would be married to a stripper. He was no hotshot, but just a regular, sane guy.

DETROIT TIGERS

COOT VEAL:

The Pirates traded me back to the Detroit organization. I was assigned to Denver. I broke my finger, but I played

through that and had a good year. So I was recalled by the Tigers. Charlie Dressen replaced Bob Scheffing as manager in mid-June. I was happy to be back in Detroit, but it was like I'd never left. We still weren't a pennant contender and I still didn't get to play.

Since I had left, the Tigers had added veterans like Billy Bruton, Gus Triandos, and Bubba Phillips. And there were some young players who were getting a lot of playing time, like second baseman Jake Wood, catcher Bill Freehan, and left-handed pitcher Mickey Lolich. The most unusual of the new group was rookie pitcher Bill Faul. He had problems and would sometimes go wild on the mound. So he went to a psychiatrist and was hypnotized to see if he could be calmed down and just concentrate on his pitching. But it didn't seem to work. He had good stuff but was in a different world. He wasn't dangerous, just different. Players stayed away from him.

TIM McCARVER (CARDINALS):

Bill Faul was regarded as one of the weirdest guys in baseball. That's because he was into self-hypnosis and biting the heads off dead frogs.

C. VEAL:

For the most part, the current players had been on the Tigers when I last played for them in 1960: Kaline, Bunning, Colavito, Cash, Lary, Mossi, Aguirre, and Regan were still around. The Tigers' starting shortstop was now Dick McAuliffe, who had played for the Tigers in 1960. He had been called "Iron Hands" when he had played second back then. I didn't think he ever could hit because of his twisted batting stance, but he had become a good hitter. Which is why I sat on the bench in what turned out to be my last year in the major leagues. In 1964 I would play in Jacksonville.

MINNESOTA TWINS

HARMON KILLEBREW:

I led the league again in homers, with 45, and in slugging. The entire team continued to hit homers, including our great little rookie center fielder Jimmie Hall, who had 33. We hit 8 in one game against Washington. I tied an American League record with 4 in a doubleheader with the Red Sox. We also got great relief pitching from right-hander Bill Dailey, who was almost as good as Dick Radatz that year. We won 91 games for the second straight year, but the Yankees were even stronger and we finished 13 games behind. The White Sox slipped past us into second place.

What made it great to come to the park each day was that the team was very, very close. We still sat around and talked baseball in the clubhouse. We had some food and some guys would drink beer. And on the road, we went out to eat together. For recreation, I still went to movies, as did a lot of other players to pass the time. In the off-season, I was always a sportsman, and when I went back home to Idaho (and then Oregon), I did a lot of hunting and fishing.

VIC POWER:

I was motivated by Gold Gloves, All-Star Games, pennant races, high batting averages. I didn't play for money but because I loved the game. But I think most ballplayers stayed in the game as long as they did because of the money. Because when you weren't on the field playing, it got tiring.

It was very hard to be a married ballplayer. You were away from your house, your wife and kids, your friends. You'd be on the road for two weeks and when you got home your kids didn't recognize you and your wife didn't trust you. Some ballplayers would get in trouble. A player might tell his wife about another married player who had given in to temptation, and his wife would spread the word until the wife who was cheated on found out. I remember some big trouble. In America, a lot of women liked ballplayers. They would follow us around. In places like Philadelphia and Minnesota, you'd see girls in the ballpark or the hotels, or waiting for you where you parked your car. Or you'd go to a bar and there would be all kinds of girls. Young girls were the worst. They'd call your room from the hotel lobby and say they were doing a report on baseball for their school and wanted to interview you. You'd say, "Okay, I'll meet you downstairs." And they'd say, "No, I can come up." You'd offer them soda or a glass of milk and they'd say, "No, I want a beer." Young girls! You had to be careful. We all knew about Eddie Waitkus. I had been married since the mid-'50s and I knew enough to stay clear of those women who chased ballplayers. But for some guys the temptation was too much.

Tony Oliva joined the Twins at the end of the 1962 and 1963 seasons. He was the most natural hitter I ever saw. He was healthy then and fast, but I could see he might have leg problems in his future because he had a tendency to slide even when he didn't have to. He didn't take good care of his body. Tony barely spoke English and I took him under my wing. Tony would follow me everywhere and do everything I did. If I bought a red shirt, he bought an identical red shirt. Whatever I ordered on the menu, he ordered the same. He would have eaten snake. He wasn't too sophisticated. When I told him we'd be facing Whitey Ford, he asked if Whitey was a black guy. He thought the White Sox' Floyd Robinson was Jackie Robinson. He couldn't read English, so when he saw his name in the paper, he'd ask me to translate. I loved to tease him, so I'd say Fidel Castro had passed a law saying all Cuban ballplayers, including Oliva, would have to pay him 50 percent of their salaries—and Tony would get so upset. I taught Tony

In his second year with the Minnesota Twins, Vic Power had his last season as an everyday first baseman.

NATIONAL BASEBALL LIBRARY, COOPERSTOWN, N.Y.

how to drive, but he was hopeless, as bad as my wife. When I had to renew my own license I took them both to take their driving tests—I flunked and they both passed. I was afraid to go home with them.

On October 12 Tony played in an All-Star Game of Latin major leaguers that a New York sportswriter and I organized. We didn't ask the Commissioner for permission, we just did it. It was the last game ever played in the Polo Grounds. We drew 18,000 people and all the players got $2,000. I just called everyone up and they accepted. We had Roberto Clemente, Orlando Cepeda, Julio Becquer, Diego Segui, Felix Mantilla, Hector Lopez, Felipe Alou, Pedro Ramos, Zoilo Versalles, Al McBean, Roman Mejias, Juan Marichal, Manny Mota, Minnie Minoso, Julian Javier, Luis Aparicio, and all the big guys. It was a historic game—too bad not many people remember it.

CHICAGO WHITE SOX

GARY PETERS:

I had seen guys quit in the minors, some because they felt they were never going to be brought up, some because they tired of the travel, and some because of the escalating pressure as they moved upward. I enjoyed it or I would have gotten out and taught school or something like that. Still, I felt that if I didn't make the big leagues in 1963, I was going to get out. I wasn't going to Triple A again. I had a good spring in 1963 and made the team. However, the White Sox planned to either send me down—in which case, I would have quit—or sell me to Kansas City. Charlie Finley had been the A's owner since 1961 and he was trying to stockpile young pitchers. Luckily, Juan Pizarro got sick and I started. My first start was in Kansas City and I think if I'd pitched a bad game it would have been my last with the White Sox. It was just before cutdown day, a month into the season. I don't remember the final score, but I won and hit a homer, and Jim Brosnan saved the game for me. It was the turning point of my career. In 1963 I first signed a major league contract.

I had a lot of confidence and just wanted an opportunity. But I surprised myself. I won 11 in a row. The more I pitched, the more I gained in confidence. I was in a groove. I ended up with 19 wins against 8 losses and

led the league with a 2.33 ERA. I lost my one attempt to win my 20th game. My pal Pete Ward, our third baseman, also had a great rookie year. He hit 22 homers and led the team in RBIs. We were both in the running for Rookie of the Year and were teasing each other a lot. After I won, he'd always ask if I were taking care of *his* trophy.

I was happy to play for Al Lopez, who was a good manager. He knew how to handle the press and knew the game. He was a catcher, so he was a defense-and-pitching-oriented manager. He was hard on the players and screamed at them if they did something wrong. I think he was the reason a lot of our players overachieved.

The veterans went out of their way to help us young players. Nellie Fox and Sherm Lollar were my best friends among the older guys. Sherm would answer all my questions about where to live and whatever. Nellie would give me advice about contracts. I got to know Nellie really well. He also grew up in Pennsylvania, and we were both deer hunters. That summer we would go out and watch a country and western band every once in a while. By this time Nellie didn't have much speed and his arm had suffered to the point he was throwing rainbows from second base, but he still was so sound fundamentally, and a fiery player and a chatterer. He was still bunting and hardly ever striking out. He was the best kind of guy to have on a club, and I looked up to him more than anybody.

Nobody acted like a star, so there was much camaraderie. There was a lot of joking around in the clubhouse even though we played close games. There were no fights. I can't even remember anybody getting mad at anybody else, which was unusual. There was a lot of socializing between players and there was always a mix. Most teams were more divided. For instance, the Yankees had their good boys and their bad boys. The White Sox were really unified. There were guys I spent more time with because we had common interests, like fishing, but I'd go out to dinner with lots of the guys.

When we went out to dinner, there was never a question of what we were going to eat. We were going to eat a steak or prime rib. We'd very seldom eat in the hotel during road trips. That was the domain of the coaches and managers. With Chicago, we wouldn't even go to

Finally given a chance to break into the White Sox staff, Gary Peters responded by winning 19 games and being voted Rookie of the Year, launching what would be a standout career.

the hotel cocktail lounge because the manager, coaches, and writers were in there. The White Sox might even have had a rule that we couldn't go there. We didn't really look for restaurants. When we found one we liked, we just kept going back.

A lot of players signed right out of high school, but the level of education of the individual players didn't matter. It was more what you could do on the ballfield. Most everybody read some. Jim Brosnan, who was a loner, read a lot. I read a little bit, mostly in the plane because I couldn't sleep and didn't want to play poker or hearts with the other guys.

The White Sox weren't much of a drinking team. We might have a drink before and after dinner, but that was about it. You couldn't drink all night and still play. We drank a lot less than other teams. No team drank more than the Braves. The Yankees had some drinkers. All ballplayers drank too much because of the nature of the

life. There was a lot of idleness. That's why I hated travel so much.

I would take tie-flying kits on the road, and then I got to carrying a collapsible fishing pole. Outdoor writers knew the best fishing holes, so I'd arrange fishing trips with them as soon as I came to a visiting town, such as Minneapolis and Kansas City.

I got along with umpires from the start, so I would never be thrown out of a game. One of my first games was in Detroit and Ed Runge was umpiring. I threw a ball that I thought was on the outside corner. He called it a ball. I took a couple of steps toward him and he came tearing out there and said, "When you've been around a couple of years, you'll know that when you throw the ball anywhere in that strike zone, I'll call it a strike. Don't show me up again." I never did. He was a pitcher's umpire. If he saw the ball on the black, he'd call it. There were batters' umpires and those who umpired according to who the batter was. If the umpires respected a player with good eyes, they would call it a ball if the player took a marginal pitch—especially if it meant something. These are things I learned.

It was an exciting year for me, but the Yankees ran away with the pennant, beating us by 10 games. They had a great year, winning 104 games. We never played well against them. Whitey Ford won 24 games that year and many of those were against us.

By the time the season was over, I was pretty tired. I had played winter ball, then gone right to spring training and pitched a lot. I felt worn out. I was looking forward to the 1963 winter to relax and just stay in shape.

JIM LANDIS:

Gary Peters was fabulous. I almost had to cry for him because his easy temperament almost kept him out of the big leagues. Nothing bothered him. He'd come to spring training with golf clubs, fishing gear, and a boomerang. He was known for throwing his boomerang at the park in Indianapolis. You wouldn't think he wanted to be a big league ballplayer. But don't kid yourself. There was no bigger battler. You gotta be loose and love life because otherwise the game will tear you apart. It made him stronger on the mound. Once he had the chance, he showed his ability.

Pete Ward was really an intense, hard, tough ballplayer. He also was a character. We'd start a road trip and his shirt was already wrinkled, as if it had been in his suitcase for a week. And he'd have mustard on his tie. He started a road trip looking like he was finishing one.

I felt sorry for Dave Nicholson, who came to us with Hoyt Wilhelm, and Ron Hansen for Luis Aparicio and Al Smith. He hit over 20 homers for us but set a major league record by striking out 175 times, including 7 times in one doubleheader. He was raw power and tried and tried to become a good hitter. He worked hard but really struggled. He could hit one on the roof and then miss the ball for a week. It was a shame because he really wanted to do good. He wasn't a sulker, but he was mad and depressed.

I had batted against Hoyt Wilhelm when he was on Baltimore. I would laugh because all you'd hear from Gus Triandos behind the plate was cussing. His knuckler was nearly impossible to hit. The only hit I ever got off him was rained out! Hoyt was a tremendous person, very easygoing, happy. Gary Peters and I used to have fun with him. Hoyt always put his head against his shoulder—it may have been because of a bad eye but I was told he had some minor nerve disorder. He'd be tilting his head, so we'd put our heads on our shoulders, too, and say, "Come on, Hoyt, let's go out to eat."

JIM BROSNAN:

Early in the season, I was traded to the White Sox from the Reds. I drove my family to our home in Chicago and then flew to meet my new team in Kansas City. Ed Short, my new general manager, met me at the plane. The first two things he said were "Good to see you" and "You can't write here either." At the time, I wasn't planning on anything specific, but I considered myself a writer and wouldn't stop on his say-so.

Al Lopez didn't say twenty words to me. His coaches Ray Berres and Tony Cuccinello ran the show and communicated with the players.

The White Sox had a pretty good club. There was a group I could fit in with consisting of Dave DeBusschere, the pro basketball player, Nellie Fox, Jim Landis, and Sherm Lollar. They were all friendly.

I was in the bullpen with Hoyt Wilhelm. We were two completely different pitchers but each had success. Hoyt slumped that year, but he knew if he had his stuff nobody could hit him. He expected to get the side out

every time. I felt the same when I had my good stuff, but I didn't have it that often with the White Sox. I discovered that there was a definite difference in the strike zone in the American League. I couldn't get my outside slider called a strike, so if batters laid off it, they'd get a ball call. As the year went on, I became more and more inconsistent. I'd have a couple of good days and then one very bad one. I realized that my enthusiasm for the game was waning and that it was time to retire.

Baseball in my era was often a stodgy game. There wasn't enough running until guys like Luis Aparicio, Maury Wills, Willie Davis, and Lou Brock came along. And the average pitcher didn't have nearly the kind of stuff the average pitcher would have in subsequent eras. The game would be played better than it was then. But it wouldn't have the same personalities or camaraderie—and this comes from a loner—as there was back then. And baseball would become much less fun to play.

NEW YORK YANKEES

STAN WILLIAMS:

I joined the Yankees in 1963. My first day in spring training, relief pitcher Marshall Bridges got shot. Some gal shot him in a bar, but "Sheriff" didn't know it and kept drinking.

The Yankees were a real good, solid all-around ballclub. But there wasn't the Yankee power of the past. Our greatest asset was defense, with Clete Boyer at third, Tony Kubek at short, Bobby Richardson at second, and Joe Pepitone at first. There was no way you could drive a ball through that infield. And Ellie Howard, the league's MVP, would pounce on anything in front of the plate. Pitching for a club like that, especially with a sinker, was great.

I had great respect for Mickey Mantle. He was like a 15-year-old kid with a grin on the side of his mouth, always having fun. Then he put the uniform on to play and he became the most serious guy in the world. If Mickey struck out, nobody would say a word to him until he made some kind of comment himself, because he took it real hard. Then he'd just relax and make a joke or call himself a dummy, and guys could get all over him. Mickey missed almost two months with a foot

Traded by the Dodgers after his 1-inning failure in the 1962 National League playoffs, Stan Williams had a fine season with the Yankees, helping them win the American League pennant.

injury, but he returned with a home run and kept hitting. He was that kind of competitor.

Whitey Ford led the league with 24 wins. He was always an outstanding pitcher. He had tremendous knowledge of pitching itself and of how to pitch the opposition. Plus, he had great control and was a great competitor. He had only average major league stuff except he could pitch. He had 3 curves, which he released at 3 different points. His ball faded away from right-handed batters.

Bobby Richardson was a very religious guy, but he never let his lifestyle interfere with his play or his friendships with his teammates. He didn't preach to us. Bobby was a very, very steady ballplayer. Unassuming. He just did his job extremely well in the field, where he won Gold Gloves, and at the plate.

TOM CHENEY (SENATORS):

The one guy I didn't want to see at the plate was Bobby Richardson. I could not get him out. Beats the hell out of me why he wore my fanny out. He wasn't a flashy guy, but he was a terrific ballplayer and he hit about .280 or .290. He was the first guy who'd come up for the Yankees, and I knew damn well I couldn't get him out. Maybe that's a defeatist attitude, but after he hit me so many times I knew what to expect. I'd almost walk him. He was a free swinger and that's what aggravated me. I preferred seeing Mickey Mantle. He could be pitched to: slow and off-speed stuff, take something off the curve, and Mantle would beat it into the ground. But I had no pattern for Richardson.

GARY PETERS (WHITE SOX):

Richardson was the hardest guy for me to strike out. He was kind of a right-handed Nellie Fox. You could throw just what you wanted to, right where you wanted to, and he'd still get a hit. He was just a good contact hitter and gave me trouble. Richardson was one of the guys who hit homers off me who weren't supposed to hit homers off anybody.

S. WILLIAMS:

Roger Maris was one of my running buddies and a dear friend, a good man I loved dearly. He was somewhat introverted and wasn't an easy guy to get to know, but once you got to know him, he was a friend for life. He and Mantle were very close. He was a small-town boy who was kind of in awe about what had happened to him in New York. Back in 1961, he was going out two hours early and stayed two hours late trying to accommodate the press. And somebody misquoted him and made him feel like a real ass, and so, instead of telling that one guy not to talk to him anymore, Roger said, "To hell with all the press." And once he said that, people took offense and started getting on him. He wasn't really booed when I was there. But he flipped someone the bird once in Minnesota and heard about it.

There were people who always tried to agitate him. I remember having dinner with him, Hal Reniff, Hector Lopez, and Clete Boyer after a ball game at a little second-floor restaurant in Chicago. Some guy came up to Roger and started bad-mouthing him while he was trying to eat dinner. Roger kept trying to shrug him off and then told him to let us have dinner now that he'd had his say. But the guy was just looking for trouble. We got on the elevator and the guy followed us down and kept taunting him. He wanted Roger to punch him or something. I had a bad day on the mound and had heard enough. I just grabbed the guy by the throat and slammed him against the wall and told him not to say another word—and he didn't. He didn't even know who I was. Ballplayers get baited a lot. Roger handled it a lot better than I did.

I had played Triple A against Roger when he was known for his speed more than anything else. We didn't think of him as a power hitter then. I remember he beat us one game with an inside-the-park home run in Indianapolis, and he beat me in a game, 1–0, with a 2-out 2-strike bunt with a man on third. He could do it all. He was a good fielder, he could throw, he could run. And he had one of the prettiest, short swings. He was having only an average year at the plate in 1963—Howard, Pepitone, and Tresh all outhomered him—but that didn't affect his outfield play.

Clete Boyer was another of my running buddies. Yogi was a great guy, too, but he had to go home to Carmen every night. This was his last year as a Yankee player and he wasn't in the lineup much, leaving the catching to Howard and Johnny Blanchard.

The Yankees were like the Dodgers in that everyone got along. Jim Bouton was the only guy on the team Mickey didn't care for. Bouton kind of got too big for his britches. I got along with him and he was my roommate for a while. He was into pitching then, not writing. He had a tremendous year, winning 21 games. Whatever you want to say about him, he was a tough competitor. That's why he was called "Bulldog." I remember when he threw a high fastball and the batter hit it off Bouton's chin and drove him right off the mound.

I enjoyed being with the Yankees, but my arm had gotten progressively worse. There were times when I couldn't raise my arm, so I started throwing from the hip. I had to improvise and I developed a real good sinker. I was part of the rotation with Ford, Terry, Bouton, and Al Downing, an amiable, quiet man who was the Yankees' first successful black starting pitcher. We all had winning records. I went 9–8, with a 3.20 ERA, but I don't think I had a very good year. It could have been much better, but there was one stretch in which I lost 4 or 5 consecutive 1-run games. Minnesota, which had an offensive powerhouse, came into New York after scoring 27 runs in 2 games in Boston, and I shut them out through 9 innings but the score was tied 0–0. I could very well have ended up 14–3.

WORLD SERIES

1963

YANKEES vs DODGERS

STAN WILLIAMS · YANKEES:

I'm not sure we didn't have a better team than the Dodgers, yet they swept us in the World Series. Koufax set the stage for the entire Series in the first game and just took all the confidence away from the Yankee hitters. He was just so sharp and struck out 15, breaking Carl Erskine's Series record. His 15th came against Harry "Not Too" Bright. Tony Kubek, who hardly ever struck out, looked like Molly Putz swinging at the ball. Tom Tresh hit a 2-run homer for us in the eighth, but the game was out of reach already and we lost 5–2. We were overpowered. Sandy confirmed for a national television audience that he was the greatest pitcher who ever lived.

In that game, I pitched 3 innings and struck out 5 and gave up only a 2-strike single to Tommy Davis over second. I had pitched in 2 World Series and had relieved Sandy Koufax and, now, Whitey Ford. As well as I pitched in Game One, I didn't even get another chance to warm up again. It was that kind of a Series.

We played exceptional baseball, too, especially the pitching side of it. But we scored only 4 runs off Koufax, Podres, and Drysdale. Podres pitched the second game for the Dodgers against Al Downing and won 4–1, with Perranoski in relief. Drysdale pitched a 3-hitter to beat Bouton in Game Three, 1–0, with their run coming in the first inning on Tommy Davis's single. Whitey lost the last game despite pitching a 2-hitter. He gave up a homer to Frank Howard, but Mantle homered off Koufax to tie it. It was 1–1 in the seventh when Joe Pepitone lost Clete Boyer's throw in the white shirts behind third base, and Gilliam raced all the way to third and scored the winning run on Willie Davis's sacrifice fly. Pepitone ended the game by hitting a long fly off Sandy that came down right at the bullpen fence. That would have tied the game.

NATIONAL LEAGUE 1964

"THAT SUNDAY MORNING, I WENT TO ST. LOUIS CATHEDRAL. IT WAS JUST ME AND GOD THAT MORNING. I OFFERED THE TYPICAL HUMAN PRAYER, SAYING, 'I MAY NOT HAVE THIS CHANCE AGAIN. JUST THIS ONE TIME, CAN YOU HELP. . . .' IF THAT KIND OF PRAYER IS ANSWERED, YOU TEND TO FORGET ABOUT IT A YEAR LATER. BUT AT THE TIME, I PRAYED AS HARD AS I COULD."

TIM MCCARVER

ST. LOUIS CARDINALS

LEW BURDETTE:
All my fishing buddies on the Cards in 1963—Stan Musial, Red Schoendienst, and Carl Sawatski—had retired. Besides, I hadn't really found my groove with the Cardinals. I had been 6–5 with the Braves before the trade, but was only 3–8 for St. Louis, pitching irregularly. Then, in 1964, I was in only 8 games by June, winning my only decision. So I wasn't surprised or disappointed when the Cards sent me to the Cubs for pitcher Glen Hobbie.

DICK GROAT:
My former Pirates buddy Bob Skinner joined the Cards in the middle of the '64 season. I roomed with Skins, and at other times he, Boyer, and I roomed together. Everybody got along just great. The guys were as funny as they were competitive, and we had constant fun on the buses and planes and in the clubhouse. So many guys had great senses of humor: Tim McCarver, Ray Sadecki, Bob Gibson, Curt Flood. Of course, Bob Uecker was incredibly funny. That's why it was such an enjoyable season.

Uecker joined the team in 1964 from the Braves and backed up McCarver. On the buses, everybody would be talking, and then one by one we noticed that he was in the back doing some impersonation. And it got quieter and quieter until all you could hear was Ueck doing Harry Caray. He'd do Caray's familiar voice and then add a smart remark and everybody would be roaring with laughter. He'd make Harry livid.

We improved a big notch when we got Lou Brock in a mid-season trade with the Cubs. I already knew that he had a great set of legs and blinding speed, and I now noticed that he had a great, strong body, with large shoulders and thin waist. One day I backed into left to catch a pop fly and just as I caught it, he ran into me. It was like standing in front of a Mack truck. I was lucky that I was so relaxed, because I was able to walk away without any problems. Lou was a super guy and a tremendous competitor, but I hadn't realized what a great offensive player he was because he was just a kid. He hit almost .350 with us and finished with 200 hits and over 40 stolen bases. What a lift he gave us.

We had some great competitors on this team. Nobody wanted a rest. You couldn't get Curt Flood out of the lineup despite a badly swollen ankle that he'd have to tape up. He played 162 games and led the league in at-bats and hits. Ken Boyer, who was voted MVP in the league, also played every game, leading the league in RBIs. Bill White played 160 games and I missed only 1 game. Bill had a shoulder so bad that he couldn't lift it, but he wouldn't take any time off and still hit .300 and drove in 100 runs. Brock ground it out every day and was tremendous. Javier missed only a handful of games and had a fine year at the plate and at second base. McCarver caught almost every game in hot St. Louis, yet hit close to .290. Gibson, Simmons, and Sadecki took the ball every fourth day and were extremely effective: Bob won 19, Curt 18, and Ray was a 20-game winner. In long careers neither Curt nor Ray ever won that many games in a season.

As Simmons used to say, "You gotta have a closer." You have to have somebody that can close the deal. Barney Schultz was the ace of the Cardinal bullpen and he came through down the stretch. He didn't come up until late in the season, but then he was magnificent. He gave batters fits with his knuckleball.

Mike Shannon came up and did a good job for us in right field, switching off with Charlie James. He was goofy and you didn't know what he was going to do. When he first came up, someone hit a ball down the right-field line. He could have caught it but instead played it off the wall, thinking he was going to throw the batter out at second base with his great arm. But the guy slid in safely. "Hey, Mike, play the game straight. No tricks. Just get the ball. Don't be baiting guys in the major leagues. They know how to run bases." All those kids. You could tell them anything when they came up and they would listen to you. And they all became great players.

Johnny Keane pretty much let us play. However, he was the only manager—or coach—I had any problems with in my career. We just differed on how the game should be played. But he never benched me or took me out of a game because of our differences.

I got off to a bad start in 1964 but I still came back and hit .294. I was the starting shortstop in the All-Star Game. Bill White and Ken Boyer also started. The game was played in New York at Shea Stadium, the new

home of the Mets. Don Drysdale started against the Angels' Dean Chance, and it was an exciting game. Billy Williams and Boyer homered for us, but we trailed 4–3 going into the bottom of the ninth. Then Mays singled, stole second, and scored on Orlando Cepeda's blooper to tie the game. Then Johnny Callison of the Phillies hit a 3-run homer off Dick Radatz and we won 7–4. So I was on the National League squad that started the long winning streak against the American League. And I took pride in that. (To be honest, seeing All-Star Games is what makes me the most nostalgic. They were very special to me, especially since the players were the ones who voted me onto those teams. It was a great experience.)

I thought the 1964 Cardinals were a carbon copy of the 1960 Pirates. We were contact hitters, line-drive hitters. We scrambled, every game. We employed the hit-and-run, moved men on second to third when there were no outs, went from first to third on singles. We knew when to bunt, we knew when to take a strike, we knew which base to throw to. We had many players who didn't need managers because they were managerial material themselves. We were a competitive team that made few mistakes. We were also a very close team. If anything, because of Brock and Flood, the Cardinals had more speed than the 1960 Pirates.

Everybody talked about the collapse of the Phillies in 1964, and I agree that there was at least a semicollapse. But don't forget how good we played down the stretch. The Phillies must have thought they were entitled to lose a game now and then, but every time they lost, we won. And they lost a lot. The pennant drive was filled with pressure. We had a tough time getting the coffee and eggs down in the morning, there was so much tension. We swept the Pirates 5 in a row in Pittsburgh and had moved to just 1½ games behind the Phillies with 6 games left. They were coming in to play us at Busch Stadium Monday, Tuesday, and Wednesday. We were all happy after the Pirates series and the plane trip home was very lighthearted. The minute we landed at Lambert Field in St. Louis, we saw that the place was packed with Cardinals fans. That's the first time everybody reacted: "Oh, shit! We are in this up to our asses."

About ten or twelve of us stayed at the Bel-Aire Hotel during that Phillies series. Most of our wives had gone home to put the children in school. I was rooming with Bob Skinner. Curt Simmons, Tim McCarver, and seven or eight other guys were on the same floor. We're playing the Phillies Monday night. Baseball players are notorious for not getting up in the morning, especially when playing night games. I never woke up in the morning. But on Monday morning I got up to go to the bathroom and saw that it was about a quarter to six. When I came out of the bathroom, Skinner was sitting there. I asked, "What are you doing up?" He said, "Well, I wanted to get coffee. See if they are out in the hallway with the coffee yet." I opened the door and about four or five other doors opened at the same time and out stepped the other Cardinals to get coffee. We were running on nervous energy. A week before, those doors wouldn't have opened until ten or eleven o'clock.

Chris Short, who started the first game, was the Phillies pitcher we were scared to death of. Chris was a tough lefty and we were primarily a left-handed-hitting team with Brock, White, and McCarver. Short gave us fits earlier in the year. When we beat him we felt we had a chance to sweep them. I think we beat Dennis Bennett the next night. In the final game, Jim Bunning was dazzling everybody and struck out 3 of the first 4 batters he faced. I singled to the right and then McCarver, who wore out Bunning, hit his first offering over the wall. We went on to get the sweep. Then there were 3 games left, and now they were behind us by 1½ games. Then the Mets came in and they were the team we figured to beat, that we had better beat. But little Al Jackson beat Gibson, 1–0. Then they won the next game. We realized that there were no short cuts, even if we played the Mets. Fortunately, we won the final game with Gibson in relief and took the pennant by 1 game over the Phillies and Reds.

TIM MCCARVER:

I couldn't tell if baseball had been diluted by expansion. I had played only briefly between 1959 and 1961, and had been in the minors when the National League expanded in 1962. In those days, I didn't even think of dilution . . . or pollution.

I also didn't think of a players' union. Other players talked about the pension plan, but I was ignorant, probably because I was just beginning my career and wasn't interested in already thinking about retirement. Ken Boyer, our player rep, would tell us we had $2-a-day

more meal money, up from $8 to $10. When it was $8 a day, most teams took out $4 if we had a meal on the plane. The Cardinals did this, and they were considered one of the most generous organizations.

Television wasn't coming in in a big way yet. Radio was more important. Our definition of media in those days was newspapers. Those were the guys we had to deal with on a regular basis. We always thought it was an unusual event when we were on television. We were athletes, not celebrities. Anyway, we played in St. Louis, not in New York. We knew New York was different and that athletes were treated differently there.

Since we were in St. Louis, Bob Gibson didn't get the same amount of press as Sandy Koufax and Don Drysdale in Los Angeles, but by now he was generally regarded as one of the great pitchers in the game. Certainly no pitcher was more frightening to face. I think Gibson became more intimidating by 1963 and 1964. It's true that there were other mean pitchers in the league. Drysdale, of course. Juan Marichal would knock you down. He was the toughest right-hander for me. He'd sting you if you bunted on him. Turk Farrell would throw at your throat and knock you down. The Reds' John Tsitouris was like that. Jim Bunning would drill you in a second. But Gibson was more intimidating than any pitcher. And he was intimidating to everyone.

Gibson never frightened me. He was intimidating, yet he had that sense of humor. However, we went at it pretty good when we worked together. Once Clemente bounced a ball through the right side to drive in 2 runs. Gibson was backing up home, and when he walked past me he said, "Goddammit, you've got more than one finger, don't you?" I said, "You've got a head, too. You could shake me off." Soon we were screaming at each other halfway between home and the pitcher's mound. I'm ready to drop my mitt because I think Bob's going to swing at me. It was embarrassing. That night I couldn't sleep because I was so mad at him for showing me up. I'd had my feelings hurt. The next day, Bob approached me soon after I walked into the clubhouse. He wasn't the type to say he was sorry. But he said something that was so funny that I laughed and we went out into the outfield and started talking as if nothing had happened. He was so blatantly honest.

Gibson and I were pretty much in sync. He'd tell me bitingly, "Just put down the first thing that comes to your mind. And if I don't like it, I'll just shake you off.'' He'd let me call pitches—8 out of 10 would be fastballs in '63 and '64 because his curve and change were terrible. His fastball served as several pitches because it came to the plate and exploded and you wouldn't know where it would go.

What Gibson really hated was my coming to the mound. That was his office, and you didn't go anywhere near it. If batters who made outs would run across the mound on their way back to their dugouts, he'd stare them down and hit them the next time up. You didn't get on his turf. When I'd go out to the mound, he'd say angrily, ''All you know about pitching is that it's hard to hit.'' I said, ''What am I supposed to do, Hoot? Johnny wants me to come out and slow you down, and you tell me to get back behind the plate.''

Dick Groat had gone to Duke and Gibson had gone to Creighton and they were intelligent men. Yet they'd have these childish spats on the field where Dick would question Bob's pitch selection and Bob would fire back, ''If you think I threw the wrong pitches, you throw the pitches.'' Then Dick would back off. Then they'd be friends over a bridge game. They were bridge partners and shrewd players. They would play against Bill White and Ken Boyer. Before the game was over they'd be screaming at one another. That dissent which was out in the open helped fuse the relationships of the blacks and whites on the Cardinals as we went after the title. This was at the end of a period when there was strict bonding of players according to their color. But it was getting away from that. In the early and mid-'60s, the Cardinals were the first team to fuse blacks and whites into a unit. That was largely because of the forcefulness and dignity of Gibson, Flood, and White.

Flood was Gibson's roommate and they were very close. Flood was a great fielder, a consistent .300 hitter—he got 8 hits in an August doubleheader—and a team player. He was a terrific ballplayer and a talented artist. Like Gibson, he was extremely smart and funny. There was a serious side to him, too. He refused to be treated like chattel. (He would make his stand years later against the reserve clause—it was completely consistent with his character.)

Some of us who were living in St. Louis without our families stayed at the Bel-Aire Hotel. My roommate was Bob Uecker, and we paid $12 each to share a room. Bob was a great swimmer and every day he'd go down to the hotel pool, even when it was cool in April. He'd work on his tan. Curt Simmons started calling him ''the Lifeguard.'' Bob was eerily serious when he sat in the hotel room, just staring at the television set. Maybe this was his way of dealing with career pressures and a shaky marriage. Outside of the room, he was a different person, an incredible comedian and mimic. All the players congregated around him on the bus and he made us ache with laughter with his stories and many wild characterizations. All year long, he was supportive of me off the field and a fine backup catcher. He was a big, tough man and was excellent defensively. Offensively, he was weak because he couldn't hit the high fastball, yet, oddly, the only guy he could hit was Sandy Koufax. But his major contribution was to keep everyone laughing all year long, to relieve the pressure. Here's a guy who would carry around a picture of some ugly woman in his wallet and tell people who wanted to talk about family that this was his wife.

At the trading deadline, the Cardinals traded Ernie Broglio, Bobby Shantz, and Doug Clemens to the Cubs for Lou Brock, Jack Spring, and Paul Toth. The Cards were interested in Brock because of his speed and didn't know they were getting such a dynamic package. Playing left field every day, he hit .348 for the rest of the season. He wound up with 200 hits, double figures in doubles, triples, and homers, 111 runs, and 43 stolen bases. The Cardinals were the perfect organization for him because he was allowed to run any time he wanted. His acceleration after 2 steps was remarkable. Since he was left-handed, he could beat out almost anything hit on the ground. He was one of those guys who looked like he was running even when he was walking back to the dugout—when he walked, his feet seemed 3 or 4 inches above ground.

This deal would be considered a steal because Broglio never produced for the Cubs. The reason Ernie had a rough time was that he had an elbow problem. Not many people know this, but he was damaged goods when he went to the Cubs. I don't think the Cubs knew enough about his condition. It shouldn't be forgotten that he was a great talent.

Ray Sadecki made up for the loss of Broglio, winning 20 games. On the mound, Sadecki was business-like, but off the field, he had a delightful sense of humor. He and Uecker were the two jokers on the team, and often they were in cahoots, sometimes with me as the third party. I remember hearing a stewardess scream after a perfectly executed prank by the three of us, involving the mask of a Neanderthal man (''Tom''), some attached clothes, a cigarette, and the toilet in an airplane.

I had a good season, batting .288, just 1 point below my 1963 average. Only this time everybody else in the starting lineup but Julian Javier and right fielder Mike Shannon, who batted only around 250 times, had higher averages. Brock, Flood, and White—who had 102 RBIs—hit over .300, and Boyer and Groat batted in the .290s. Boyer also led the team with 24 homers and led the league with 119 RBIs, earning him the National League MVP Award.

Although Javier batted under .250, he was essential to our pennant effort. He wasn't underrated by the guys who played with him. He was a great player who never got his due. I even rated him above Mazeroski at second. Unlike Mazeroski, he couldn't be taken out by a runner on the double play.

We were 11½ games out on August 23 and didn't move out of fourth place until the beginning of September. The key to the Cardinals' winning the pennant was, to be honest, Philadelphia's collapse. The Phillies led by 6½ games with just 12 games left to play. All they needed was 2 more wins. I think everyone on the team thought we had no chance. We went into Pittsburgh and we were fortunate to miss both tough 18-game winner Bob Veale and the Pirates' longtime ace Bob Friend. Dick Groat said, ''Friend has 18 losses, and any time he sees 20 losses staring him in the face, there ain't no way he's pitching. He'll figure it out so the maximum he can lose is 19.'' Groat had played with Friend when he lost 19 games in both 1959 and 1961. I was happier to miss Veale, a hard-throwing left-hander. He led the league in strikeouts that year, ahead of Gibson, Drysdale, and Koufax. He was awfully intimidating because he was so big. For effect, he'd stand off to the side of the mound and wipe his Coke-bottle glasses with a big red bandanna he carried in his back pocket. And he'd look at home plate and squint. Lou Brock suggested that I not

look at him because I'd end up bailing out at the plate. So when he started wiping his glasses, I'd walk back toward my dugout and get pine tar or something and wait until he was ready to go.

We swept all 5 games from Pittsburgh, including 2 doubleheaders. Meanwhile, the Phillies lost 7 games in a row, to fall out of first place, behind the Reds. Then they came in to play us in a 3-game series. We realized we had to sweep them. And that's what happened. In the final game, Simmons beat Bunning, 8–5. At the same time the Reds lost a heartbreaker to the Pirates, 1–0, in 16 innings. When they left town, the Phillies had lost 10 straight and were in third place and we had won 8 straight and were in first, a game in front of the Reds.

Why did the Phillies collapse? I'm sure it was a combination of things. Gene Mauch said his team was the best team for 150 games, which I think best sums up that year. Some people blamed Mauch for going down the stretch with just two starters, Jim Bunning and Chris Short. Mauch later made a comment that became famous: ''When I went out to the mound, I saw fear in my pitchers' eyes.'' You could feel that fear playing against them. They had everything to lose and nothing to gain, and it was just the opposite for everybody they played.

Going into the last game of the season, the Cards and Reds were tied for first and the Phillies were just 1 game back. The fourth-place Giants had just been eliminated after 160 games. Both the Cards and Reds had a chance to win the pennant outright if they won and the other team lost. However, if the Mets beat us and the Phils beat the Reds, there would be the first 3-way tie in baseball history. The Mets may have been a last-place team but they beat us the first 2 games of our 3-game series. After Al Jackson outdueled Gibson on Friday night, they beat us 15–5 on Saturday, when we made 5 errors, 2 of them mine. Meanwhile the Phillies and Reds split the first 2 games of their 3-game series. We were tight because the pressure was now on us to defend first place.

That Sunday morning, I went to St. Louis Cathedral. It was just me and God that morning. I offered the typical human prayer, saying, ''I may not have this chance again. Just this one time, can you help. . . .'' If that kind of prayer is answered, you tend to forget about it a year later. But at the time, I prayed as hard as I could. I was fervent because I wanted to win and knew I might never have the opportunity to be in another World Series.

So I went to the ballpark and learned that the Mets' intended starter, Tracy Stallard, had broken his wrist—I think he fell off a barstool, but with Tracy there were a lot of things that could have happened. So he was replaced by Galen Cisco, who was not as good a pitcher. We hit him around pretty good. I scored the first run of the game. Bill White and I both had big days, Gibson pitched great in relief despite having had no rest, and we won 11–5. That eliminated Philadelphia. Meanwhile, the Phillies blasted the Reds 10–0, and we ended up a game ahead of both teams. In the last inning of our game, our broadcaster Harry Caray brought the microphone down from the booth and was with Mr. Busch near the dugout. I caught the last ball of the game in front of Ken Boyer. I could hear Harry broadcasting, "The Cardinals win the pennant! The Cardinals win the pennant! The Cardinals win the pennant!" It was part exuberance, part Russ Hodges calling Bobby Thomson's homer in 1951. As he broke into an interview with Mr. Busch, someone snatched my hat. It made me so angry, but that passed in 5 minutes. Then we got off the field and away from the fans who flooded it. Soon we came back out onto the open ramp that led to the clubhouse from the dugout. We stood there and looked up at all these adoring faces around and above us. The aisles were just covered with people.

We returned to the clubhouse, deliriously happy because we knew how unlikely our winning the pennant had been. Bing Devine, whom Busch had fired as GM in August, was there, and we felt bad for him because it was obvious he didn't know what his role in the celebration should be. And there was Bob Uecker dancing naked amid broken glass from a dropped champagne bottle, doing the bop to that old standard "Pass the Biscuits, Miranda." It was bizarre. Next we went to a victory celebration at Stan Musial's restaurant. We noticed that Ron Taylor was missing, and we started asking, "Where's Twitchy?"—he was called Sergeant Twitch. A guard went back to the stadium and found him in his uniform, passed out under his dress clothes with his feet out. He had hyperventilated. The guard put him under the shower and revived him and he joined us at the party. It was a strange day.

I wasn't surprised that Johnny Keane quit after the

World Series. During the season, Leo Durocher had secretly signed a contract to manage the Cardinals in 1965. But we unexpectedly won the World Championship under Keane, and Augie Busch was forced to offer Keane a long-term contract. But Keane quit in defiance—and would become manager of the Yankees after Yogi Berra was fired as their manager for losing to us. To appease the Cardinals' fans, the team would offer the manager's job to Red Schoendienst, a popular Cardinal player for many years, instead of giving it to the outsider, Durocher. (Meanwhile, Keane would go to the Yankees and try to impose his rules on those star players. He was strung too tightly, and eventually the game killed him.)

HOUSTON COLT .45S

HAL WOODESHICK:

Tragedy struck our team just before the season started when pitcher Jim Umbricht died of cancer. Jim was a real likeable guy and had done a good job in the bullpen in 1962 and 1963. We missed him.

We hadn't made much progress by our third year. We were a losing club that would end up in ninth place, which is why Richards replaced Harry Craft with Lum Harris as manager near the end of the season. We weren't often featured on the "Game of the Week." Offensively, we hadn't improved at all, although the team had hope for the future because of Staub and 19-year-old outfielder Jimmy Wynn, a converted shortstop who wasn't very tall but had tremendous power and talent. It was our pitching that kept us competitive. I relieved in 61 games and led the league with 23 saves, Bob Bruce won 15 games, and Ken Johnson and Turk Farrell were consistently effective. Early in the season, Johnson pitched a no-hitter against the Reds but lost 1–0 on Nellie Fox's error on a ball hit by Pete Rose. I think that might actually have been a hit. We used to call him "Mother" Johnson. He was an all-right guy, just a different type of person. Johnson was for Johnson.

Dick Farrell was a great pitcher for us. In both 1963 and 1964 he had winning records though we were still a new club. He was an intimidating pitcher who threw a hard inside fastball and got a lot of strikeouts. Off the mound, he was popular with teammates and popular with the press. He was the type who would spend double whatever our meal money was.

The Dalton Gang was comprised of Turk Farrell, Jim Owens, and another guy from Louisiana who never played on Houston. Farrell and Owens had been friends coming up in the Phillies' system. Farrell was on the original Houston team and Owens joined the team in 1964. They both would have given you the shirts off their backs or last nickels in their pockets. I never saw them cause any trouble. The only thing I'd witness was one or the other pouring a bucket of ice cubes on a player when he was on the toilet, or setting off a lot of firecrackers. They might have had orders from Richards not to be bad influences on the young kids.

I didn't know we had the reputation for being a wild team. And I wouldn't agree with that tag. Houston wasn't a drinking team or a partying team. Richards didn't take that garbage.

My good friends on the team were Al Spangler and Bob Bruce, who had been a teammate on the Tigers in 1961. We played lots of poker, were always going to movies, and went out together to eat—steak and eggs. Jim Owens was the guy I'd go to the track with. When we'd arrive in Cincinnati for a night game, we'd go to River Downs for five or six races in the afternoon. In New York, we'd go to the Big A. We went in Boston and everywhere else. We didn't get into trouble because we were always at the racetrack.

Nellie Fox came over from the White Sox in 1964 to finish his career with us. He was a fine, fine person. Pete Runnels, another Texan, also ended his career in Houston, playing with us in 1963 and 1964. Johnny Temple had been with us in 1963. We old guys were a different breed from the new guys. We loved the game so much that we never gave up. We played through lean years until our talents developed. I had been released 3 times, but kept coming back. We didn't play just for the money, but our attitude was to play well in order to make money to support our families. None of us had big salaries.

I'm not talking about Staub or Wynn, but some of the young guys didn't care about baseball, just the money. When I came in years before, the veterans were very special to me. But some of the new guys didn't care about guys like Fox, Runnels, Temple, or me. At the time, Richards was giving out bonuses to anybody who

could walk, and he paid a pitching prospect named Larry Yellen about $75,000, more than 3 times my salary. Yellen was so cocky and thought he had it all. But he couldn't pitch. He lasted two or three months and never pitched in the majors again. Richards just threw away his money. I think Yellen didn't have the right attitude or desire to become a good major leaguer. We old-timers did.

CHICAGO CUBS

BOB BUHL:

I had another good season, winning 15 games. Larry Jackson won 24 games. Even Warren Spahn never won that many. Dick Ellsworth won 14 games, the third most on our staff. The fourth man in our rotation was Lew

Discarded by the Braves in 1962, veteran Bob Buhl was still going strong in 1964 with the Cubs, winning 15 games at the age of 36.

Burdette. We picked him up from the Cardinals and he won a few games for us. It was fun being reunited. He chummed around with Jackson, Don Landrum, and me.

The Cubs had a fair season, but we all felt the loss of Kenny Hubbs. His death in February was a real shock. He flew a small plane and hadn't had many hours in the air. It was said that he shouldn't have been flying.

DICK ELLSWORTH:
In mid-February I was in Fresno visiting my family when a sportswriter friend called and said that he'd read over the wire that Kenny was missing and presumed to have been in an airplane crash in Utah. I went down to the paper, and his death was confirmed. I was a pall-bearer at the funeral in southern California. The timing couldn't have been worse. He was a bright hope, somebody we were expecting to upgrade the quality of the ballclub. We selfishly knew that he was someone who could help us win ball games. In just two years he had become the symbol of the team—"Hubbs of the Cubs"—and his death deflated the team. It had a real emotional impact on us, because we lost somebody we really loved and because he had been such an important cog in the wheel of our ballclub.

We fell under .500 and dropped to eighth place. It could have been worse, but Ron Santo, Billy Williams, and Ernie Banks had very good years, and Larry Jackson led the league in victories. Buhl won 15 games and Lew Burdette came over and pitched well. I had a good record the first half of the season. Making the All-Star team was a thrill. But I developed bad tendinitis from the slider and couldn't pitch in the All-Star Game. The second half of the season was disastrous for me and I finished at 14–18.

Every year in spring training there was a sense of optimism that we were a better ballclub and were going to do much better. My attitude remained positive in that I thought I'd win whenever I pitched. I'm sure the other pitchers felt the same. I don't know how the everyday players felt when we got into late August and were 15 to 20 games out of first, but I never sensed that anybody on that ballclub gave up. Ernie, Billy, and Ron—like Kenny Hubbs had been—were great competitors. I always felt those guys were giving everything they could.

The Cubs were considered a good organization to play for, one that paid you fairly and didn't demand too much. I felt that we were perceived by the rest of the players around the majors as being pretty middle-of-the-road in terms of salary. This was the feedback I got from them. Primarily, we played for the fans, not for management. They were the ones who gauged our abilities and degrees of success. I think the Cubs players realized the fans loved them. The Chicago Cubs were the biggest things in that entire city. The Cubs owned Chicago.

I think that this was the tail end of an era, the last of baseball as it always had been. The play itself was at a high level and there were many tremendous players. We didn't call guys stars in those days simply based upon how much money they made. A star was just a terrific ballplayer. All the players just loved the game of baseball, and we couldn't wait to get to the ballpark. We wanted to play and were very protective of the uniforms that we wore. We weren't critical of how they fit or how we looked in them—we were just appreciative and proud to wear them. That may sound corny, but that's how we all felt in our hearts.

You were always looking over your shoulder, worried that someone was ready to take your job away from you. It was pressure only in that you paid attention to doing your best all the time. You worked hard, you coveted your job. You had a one-year contract, and if you were in disfavor with management you could soon be in the minors or in a different organization. Nobody really wanted to be traded and leave their parent organization. When you were traded, your heart was broken. If you didn't have the right attitude, playing under such conditions could be frightening and confusing. Bob Buhl, who joined the team in 1962, and Lew Burdette, who came over in 1964, were great influences on me and the whole ballclub, not only because of their fierce competitiveness, but because of their refreshing attitude about the game on a daily basis. They helped me learn to approach baseball with a businesslike manner. I matured quite a bit being around them.

Oddly, the recognition I would receive after I retired from baseball—the baseball cards, the autographs, the letters—would never mean anything to me. I loved *playing* major league baseball. I truly felt it was an honor to play.

SAN FRANCISCO GIANTS

BILLY O'DELL:

The Giants weren't really a close ballclub. Everybody went different ways. But I don't think that's what hurt us. Many of our guys played winter ball and they'd come to spring training in good condition and we'd always burn up the Cactus League while other teams were getting into shape. We weren't so much better than the other teams—we just looked better in the spring. Then everybody expected us to do big things during the year, and we didn't quite live up to it.

In 1964 we dropped to fourth place although we opened the season with 5 homers against Milwaukee and were in the pennant race until early October with the Phillies, Reds, and Cards. We got our customary big year from Willie Mays, who led the league with 47 homers and was our one player with over 100 RBIs, a few ahead of Cepeda. He just never had a bad season.

TIM MCCARVER (CARDINALS):

There were a lot of great players during this period, but Willie Mays was the best. He was an amazing hitter, who hit with power to all fields and hit any pitch. Mays and the Reds' Gordy Coleman were the only two guys you didn't throw curveballs to. Mays, in particular, was a notorious off-speed hitter. Dick Groat would order me, "Don't throw him curveballs." I said, "Dick, you can throw any pitch at any time." He was stubborn: "Don't throw him curveballs. Period." One day Mays had hit a homer off our starting pitcher, and now he was facing Bobby Shantz in middle relief. Shantz only threw curveballs. And Mays hit 2 more homers off him. After the game, Dick said to me, "What did I tell you?" I protested: "But Shantz can't throw a fastball." "I don't care!" he persisted. "Don't throw him curveballs!"

Jim Bunning of the Phillies would tell me, "You know the one thing about Willie Mays is that you have to keep him a little uncomfortable at the plate." The Reds' Bob Purkey also would keep Mays uncomfortable by knocking him down a couple of times. But I never thought of throwing at Mays as a means to getting him out. I had seen Mays get off the ground, dust himself off, and launch the next pitch over the center-field fence. That made me uncomfortable.

B. O'DELL:

Orlando Cepeda and young third baseman Jim Ray Hart each hit over 30 homers, which made up a bit for McCovey's off year. Juan Marichal had another 20-win season, but the next biggest winner had only 12 victories. That was our top pitching prospect, right-hander Gaylord Perry, who pitched over 200 innings. Perry was a hard thrower with a good sinker. He should have been a winning pitcher a long time before he was, but at the beginning he'd get 2 strikes on a hitter and get cute with a little change or curve—and he'd get beat.

Since we didn't have any big winners besides Marichal, Dark used all kinds of guys to try to pick up victories: Jack Sanford, Bob Bolin, rookie Ron Herbel, and veteran Bob Shaw and young Bob Hendley, the 2 pitchers we got from the Braves for Felipe Alou. Hendley, a left-hander, won 10 games for us. I won 8 games, pitching 85 innings. I spent most of the time in the bullpen with Shaw. The Giants even imported left-handed reliever Masonari Murakami from Japan, and nobody could hit him.

I didn't have arm problems until 1964, and then it wasn't bad. I don't think that had much to do with why the Giants traded me at the end of the season to Milwaukee. I had enjoyed my 5 years in San Francisco and left knowing that I had pitched well.

BILLY PIERCE:

I would have liked to have been a factor in the 1964 pennant race, but I didn't pitch much, not even 50 innings. I started only once. Ironically, in my final major league season I went 3–0, the same record I had in 1948, when I was 19, and got my first 3 decisions with the Detroit Tigers. I didn't improve a damn bit!

NEW YORK METS

FRANK THOMAS:

The Mets had made only slight improvements by their third year, although Ron Hunt had developed into their first All-Star–caliber player. We still played hard but came up short. For instance, we lost a 23-inning game to the Giants at Shea Stadium, our new park in Flushing, that lasted a record 7 hours and 22 minutes. It was part of a doubleheader that lasted just short of 10 hours, and people flew from New York to San Francisco and turned on their TVs and the game was still on. I batted 10 times. Del Crandall won it with a pinch 2-run double. We even pulled off a triple play. Ed Kranepool had just been brought up after playing games in Buffalo and played both games. My playing time diminished that season so that younger players like Kranepool could get a deserved opportunity. Kranepool was playing first, and George Altman, who had come over from the Cubs, was in left. So I was expendable and a good prospect for a pennant contender. That's why the Phillies acquired me in August, ending my happy years with the Mets.

ED BOUCHEE:

When I was on the field I would think "I love this game." But there was too much politics off the field. The politics of baseball was depressing. I was the best first baseman in the Mets' organization, but they sent me to the minors and kept me there. It wasn't all fun and games. After the Mets sent me a contract in 1964, I told them, "No. I'm going to quit. Could you give me my release? I'd like to go to Japan." They wouldn't give me my release. I couldn't play in Japan, so I just quit baseball. I was only 30. (You know when the Mets gave me my release? They sent a scout to my house outside Chicago in 1971! He had a form and said, "We want you to sign this." I told the scout, "Stick it up your ass and get out of here!")

COOT VEAL:

After playing the 1964 season at Jacksonville, I was traded to the Mets. I said I'd play only if they guaranteed I'd go directly to the Mets or stay a full season in Buffalo at a certain salary. They said they couldn't do it. So I said, "That's it." When I got out of baseball, I got out of baseball. I didn't want anything more to do with it.

Not that my memories were bad. Playing major league baseball was the fulfillment of a dream that my dad and I had from the time I was born. Perhaps it was not fulfilled as much as I'd have liked. I regretted that I didn't get to play as much as I think I should have and didn't play 5 total years in the majors to qualify for the pension plan. Also, it's too bad I played in an era when ownership made all the money and players had low salaries—although I was not in favor of unions of any

kind. However, I felt so fortunate to have played in the big leagues at a time there were few teams and a lot stronger competition. Only a small percentage of players made it.

PHILADELPHIA PHILLIES

JOHNNY KLIPPSTEIN:

Gene Mauch's plan to put together a pennant-winning team seemed to come to fruition in 1964, when for most of the season the Phillies were the class of the league. The keys to this team were starting pitchers Jim Bunning and Chris Short and reliever Jack Baldschun, who had one of the best screwballs I ever saw.

Bunning had come over from Detroit and had a great season, winning 19 games and being among the league leaders in starts, innings, strikeouts, shutouts, and earned run average. He was a tough pitcher. He threw hard and his ball moved. On Father's Day, exactly 2 weeks after Sandy Koufax no-hit us, Jim pitched a perfect game against the Mets. That was the first regular-season perfect game since 1922 and made him the first pitcher to throw no-hitters in both leagues. So it was a big deal. Bunning was smart and educated and very serious about baseball and everything else. He was chosen our player rep.

Chris Short had to win over Mauch because at first he didn't want to pitch inside. Then he changed his philosophy and became a great pitcher who gave up few runs. He had good stuff and won 17 games.

We also had a strong everyday lineup. Right fielder Johnny Callison was a great fielder and hitter who would lead the team in homers and RBIs and finish second to Ken Boyer in the league's MVP balloting. Clay Dalrymple did a good job behind the plate, Tony Taylor was a solid second baseman, Bobby Wine and Ruben Amaro were tremendous shortstops with strong arms. Left fielder Wes Covington was only an adequate fielder but a good hitter. Center fielder Tony Gonzalez had set a consecutive-game errorless streak and was a very good hitter.

BOB BUHL (CUBS):

I didn't hit anyone on purpose. But some guys couldn't get out of the way. I think I hit Tony Gonzalez in the head 3 times. Gonzalez was the guy who spoiled Lew Burdette's perfect game in 1960 by getting hit. He was a left-handed batter and should have had no problem getting out of the way. I don't know if he couldn't see or just froze when the ball would come in and sail. He just wouldn't duck his head, and I'd hit him on the helmet. The last time I knocked him down, he was unconscious and blood was coming out of his nose. That was scary. Hell, I didn't want to hurt anybody, put them in the hospital. After something like that, you have to tell yourself to pitch the same way.

J. KLIPPSTEIN:

Richie Allen was our third baseman. He played a little in 1963, but this was his rookie year. He swung about a 50-ounce bat, which was unheard of—most guys couldn't swing a 38-ounce bat. So I figured he'd hit about .240 with 25 homers. But he could hit over .300. He could do everything. He could run—he led the league in runs and triples—and was adequate at third. Richie was friendlier with his teammates than he was with everyone else. Still, he was a loner. He often went alone to the racetrack. Richie was moody and on some days didn't want to talk to anyone. Sometimes he would break helmets. You couldn't figure out what was wrong with him. Gene Mauch handled him pretty good, letting him get away with things that he wouldn't allow other players to do.

I was having another good year for the Phillies in 1964, and was excited at our prospects for playing in the World Series. But in late June I was sold to the Minnesota Twins.

RYNE DUREN:

My 1963 season had been encouraging, but at this point my elbow was bothering me and I didn't expect to salvage my career in a meaningful way. However, I wanted to pitch as long as I was doing well. I did all right in a couple of relief appearances for the Phils in the spring, and then was sold to Cincinnati.

ED ROEBUCK:

I moved from Washington to Philadelphia in April of 1964. I asked Gene Mauch if he intended to send me to the minors because he already had Jack Baldschun in the bullpen. But he wanted me. Mauch had seen me pitch in a benefit game in Los Angeles and was convinced that my arm was okay. He was interested in me because I had come from the Dodgers, a winning team, had experience pitching in the National League, and was a reliever.

Baldschun was an excellent relief pitcher whose out pitch was a screwball. I saw him go 3–0 on a hitter with the bases loaded and none out and get out of it. He was amazing. But he always went deep in the count, and this really upset Mauch. Gene just wanted pitchers to go after the hitter 1–2–3 and if he hit it, he hit it. When I came to the Phillies, he told me, "I don't care if they hit balls over the roof against you. Just don't walk anybody!" And I didn't. The first time I relieved, it was for Jim Bunning against the Braves, with the bases loaded and 1 out, and I threw a double-play ball to Joe Torre to end the game. The first 13 times I came in, not one baserunner advanced. I began as a closer, but as the season progressed, I became more of a setup man and Baldschun became the sole closer. Mauch often brought me in early to protect a lead and treated that inning as if it were the eighth or ninth. I think he used me wisely, because I had a great year. I made 60 appearances for them, won 5 games and saved 12, and had an ERA of 2.21, the best of my career. I think I was a big factor in the Phillies' run for the pennant.

Some people didn't like Mauch because of his arrogance and his unwillingness to answer stupid questions. But I thought he was one of the best managers. I thought he was unfairly criticized for starting Bunning and Short too often because that didn't have any bearing on what happened. First of all, Short could pitch with 2 days' rest without losing effectiveness. He had one of the strongest arms I ever saw—if he wasn't on the mound, he'd be throwing somewhere else anyway. Bunning and Short just didn't win down the stretch, sometimes because they didn't pitch as well and sometimes because we didn't score runs for them. In truth, we all chipped in to our collapse. Mauch was in a quandary in September because neither Baldschun nor I was pitching well. Bobby Shantz, who came over from the Cubs in August, was the only reliever pitching effectively, but he was suffering with arm problems and couldn't go on successive days.

That said, I think we lost because we weren't really a pennant-winning team. Gene was able to whip us into a frenzy to get us out front, like a horse getting out of the gate fast and trying to hang on against better horses. He would tear up the clubhouse to motivate us. However, toward the end of the year, Mauch wanted us to do it on our own, and he stopped ripping up the furniture. A lot of our players didn't believe that we could win. They'd just go out expecting to get beat. I don't think the players blamed Mauch for our slump, but I think they were waiting for one of his tirades to jump-start us. But all he kept saying was "They're taking your money away from you, boys. You'd better go get 'em." It was just an unfortunate situation. Frank Thomas's injury hurt us, and both our hitting and pitching fell off. But I think we just weren't good enough. It really depressed me not to win the pennant. I had been with the Dodgers in 1962 when the Giants caught us down the stretch and beat us in the playoffs, and just 2 years later the Phillies blew a 6½-game lead with just 12 to play.

There was leadership on the Phillies: Richie Allen, Johnny Callison, Tony Taylor. But most of the leadership was through example. Jim Bunning could have been more of a leader. He sort of had an attitude that was "How come we're in first place?" instead of "Gee, it's great we're in first place."

Richie Allen had a hard time in the minors at Little Rock. Ray Culp and a couple of other guys who played with him said the people there were merciless to him. But he stuck it out and made the majors. He was an amazing talent. He had poor eyesight, which is why he struck out so much. But he was a great hitter and baserunner, and had a great throwing arm. Richie was a beautiful guy and everyone loved him. But I wouldn't have liked to manage him. He was a free spirit. Richie would show up late for batting practice. One day Gene was looking all over for him and asked Tony Taylor if he'd seen him. Tony was quick to say, "I don't hang around with him!" Richie came waltzing in about five minutes before the "Star-Spangled Banner" and went out and had a great game.

Taylor was one of my best friends. He was a great guy and as much of a leader as anyone on the team. Callison was a quiet leader. Everyone respected him. He was sort of Gene Mauch's pet, and rather than resenting that, everyone was pleased about it. Johnny and Richie would get together in the clubhouse, and as soon as they started jiving each other everyone else gathered around. They had a good relationship.

Except for a few of us, most of the players had come up in the Phillies' excellent farm system. This contributed to the closeness of the team. So did the drinking. Players drank because of a combination of factors: pressure, free time, camaraderie, and money. Some drank because they had problems. I roomed on the road with Ryne Duren for a while. He drank. He once tried to call up Princess Grace in Monaco.

After Duren was sold to Cincinnati, I roomed with Baldschun. We were good friends. I went apartment-hunting as soon as Mauch assured me I was staying with the team, and moved to northeast Philadelphia in an apartment complex where there were about five other players and coaches. I'd end my career with the Phillies in 1966.

I felt fortunate to have been in the game so long. But it wasn't easy. You're so busy trying to stay in the majors from one year to the next, you can't really appreciate what you've done. We were under a lot of pressure. Even if you're a star, you have to go prove it the next day. You have to have confidence in your talent to carry on year after year. I had that. Still, there was always the possibility of injuries. And you knew that eventually you'd have to quit at an early age. Being frequently absent from the family on road trips could cause strains—although this also could be beneficial to marriages at times. It was a tough, tough life. What made it toughest is that you knew that in a very short time you would have to get out of it and go pick up that work bucket. I think that is more frightening than anything else a player goes through. I always thought of that. Yet I didn't prepare for retirement. The transition to real life when you're just 35 sucks.

FRANK THOMAS:
The Phillies acquired me from the Mets in August. And I had a great month, hitting clutch homers and driving in runs. We moved from a ½-game lead to a 6½-game lead. There's no doubt in my mind that if I remained healthy, the Phillies would have made it to the World Series. But I broke my thumb diving into second base. I played the rest of the game and got 2 more hits. I went back to the Warwick Hotel and slept with my hand in

Frank Thomas carried the Phillies' offense after joining them during the season, and his injury was a major reason they were unable to hold on to their large lead in the pennant race.

ice all night. It was completely swollen in the morning and I knew something was wrong. I went to the doctor, and he discovered a hairline fracture. I told him not to tell anybody: "I've had the World Series handed to me. Don't take that away from me." I wanted him to just give me Novocaine. But he wouldn't do it. He made a cast for my hand. I could hit with it, but I had to tell Gene Mauch I couldn't throw. After that he had no use for me. If you didn't play regularly for Mauch, he didn't talk to you. That's the kind of guy he was. John Herrnstein had been doing a good job at first base, but when I came over, Mauch put him on the bench and ignored him. A lot of players hated Mauch for stuff like that.

It was difficult just to sit and watch as the Phillies lost their big lead. The worst loss was when the Reds' rookie infielder Chico Ruiz stole home to beat us. Other than my injury, the key to the collapse was Mauch pitching Bunning and Short too often. They were both great that year. Bunning was the only guy I ever saw fool Henry Aaron, throwing a pitch where the bottom dropped out—it didn't matter that Henry was still able to stroke it to left for a double. When Bunning or Short had four days' rest, they'd win. Mauch could have started Art Mahaffey, Ray Culp, even Jack Baldschun. But he got to the point where he really wanted to win it with his 2 stars. And that failed.

I think Richie Allen could have been the greatest player ever. He struck out about 140 times in 1964, and if he would have just made contact instead of trying to hit 500-foot homers, he could have hit .400. And he would have hit just as many homers because he could hit a ball out of any park without a full swing. At that time, he was the type of guy who liked to agitate but couldn't take it himself. But we got along in 1964. (The fight we had the next year was unfortunate and the media played it up too much and the ballclub and Mauch handled it poorly, putting me on waivers for something that wasn't my fault. Years later, I would play with Richie in an old-timers' game. I would extend my hand and he would hug me, saying, "We're brothers.")

VIC POWER:

The Phillies acquired me because Frank Thomas broke his thumb. I wasn't sure if I joined the team too late to be eligible, but at the time I thought I had a chance to appear in my first World Series. The Phillies were in first place and had a good team, with such players as Johnny Callison, Jim Bunning, Chris Short, Tony Gonzalez, Richie Allen, Tony Taylor, Ruben Amaro, Cookie Rojas, Tony Taylor, Ed Roebuck, Art Mahaffey, Jack Baldschun, and Alex Johnson. Johnson was a terrific hitter and nice guy, but no one would leave him alone. They kept giving him deodorant and he'd get furious.

Every day down the stretch we'd lose a close game. Our pitchers were too tired. I could tell Gene Mauch was nervous because he even asked me, "What are we gonna do?" He wasn't very professional. And I couldn't help. We were playing the Dodgers and Willie Davis was up. I was positioned where I wanted, but Mauch thought he'd bunt and kept calling me in, closer to the plate. Davis swung away and smashed the ball at me and it struck my finger. I was useless the rest of the season. It was so disappointing. That was my last opportunity to make the World Series.

PITTSBURGH PIRATES

ELROY FACE:

The Pirates improved in 1964, moving up to seventh place and close to .500. Clemente led the league with over 200 hits and in batting average, and Stargell, Clendenon, and a few of the young hitters got better. We got good starting pitching from Bob Veale, Friend—though he lost 18 games—Joe Gibbon, a healthier Vern Law, and rookie right-hander Steve Blass, who had a lot of talent. It's a good thing that Al McBean did such an outstanding job in the bullpen, winning 8 and saving over 20 games, because I had my least productive season. I had arm problems and won

ElRoy Face had a rare off-season in 1964, his eleventh with the Pirates, but he would rebound with several more effective years as a reliever and add to his Hall of Fame–worthy credentials.

just 3 and saved only 4, with an ERA over 5.00. (I would recover during the 1965 season and go on to break Walter Johnson's record with 802 appearances for one club.)

On the Pirates, we all knew we didn't get the publicity that we'd get on other teams. It didn't really bother us too much at the time, but we didn't realize then that it would affect how we would be remembered. Bill Mazeroski was probably the greatest second baseman who ever put on a uniform, yet he wouldn't come close to getting into the Hall of Fame. If he'd played on the Yankees, where all those writers would have seen him play every day and promoted him, he would have been voted in for sure. I also believe that if I'd have played for the Yankees, I would have made the Hall of Fame.

DICK SCHOFIELD:

I hit just .246 for the second straight year as a regular shortstop, but the team itself improved. One reason is that Willie Stargell started to put up bigger numbers. He was up only about 420 times, yet hit over 20 homers and had nearly 80 RBIs.

I did all right in my 2 years at shortstop with the Pirates, particularly in the field. But when Gene Alley was ready to play, I became expendable. He might have played third, but then they wouldn't have known what to do with Bob Bailey. (Early in 1965, I'd be Alley's backup for our new manager, Harry Walker—I would hate him, like everybody else did—and then be traded to San Francisco. I would play until 1971 with several teams.)

Baseball had changed since I came to the majors in that there were so many more blacks playing. In Pittsburgh we had a bunch of black players. There were more Latin players from Cuba, Venezuela, and Puerto Rico. The style of player changed in that the Enos Slaughter and Ferris Fain old-school type had been completely phased out by the early '60s—although Pete Rose was a throwback. I don't think there were so many guys looking for trouble. Guys were more into playing the game. I don't think the quality of baseball declined, even with expansion. I think pitching improved. Every team suddenly had one or two *name* relief pitchers, which was unheard of in 1953. Teams also had extremely intimidating starting pitchers. The toughest was Sandy Koufax, but I preferred facing him to Juan Marichal or Bob Gibson. I didn't like to hit against Marichal because he threw 14 different pitches I couldn't hit. Gibson was meaner and threw high fastballs and let small guys like me hit them weakly to left.

I wanted to be a ballplayer and I would do it for 19 years. There was much that was difficult. There was pressure every time you went out between the white lines. You had to spend too much time away from your family. You had to find places to live and place your kids in schools. The older you got, the harder the travel became. Jumping on that iron bird every three days got to be tedious. Yet being a baseball player was also a lot of fun. You got to meet many great people. And you were treated good. At times you felt like a celebrity—that's when people made you feel more important than you really were. People looked up to baseball players.

CINCINNATI REDS

JIM O'TOOLE:

Fred Hutchinson was diagnosed as having cancer in the winter of 1963. When he came to spring training in 1964, he moved about on a golf cart. He went from 220 pounds to 180, 170, and by the middle of the summer he was extremely frail. He'd go home and our coach Dick Sisler would take over the team. We knew he was dying and it was devastating. We wanted to win the pennant for him. I went 17–7 with a career-best 2.66 ERA. Maloney won 15 and Purkey and Jay each won 11. Offensively, we had Robinson, Rose, Pinson, and Deron Johnson, who took over at first base. Deron was a gamer who loved to play baseball. Everybody thought the world of him. He and Nuxhall were roommates and a fun twosome.

We had a pretty good year, and when the Phillies lost 10 straight near the end of the season, we moved into first place. Then we couldn't beat the damn Pirates. They used their aces against us. They beat us 1–0 in 16 innings on a squeeze play—there were 36 strikeouts that game—and then Bob Friend beat us 2–0. Then I came back against the Phillies and had a 3–0 lead in the eighth. Leo Cardenas was the eighth-place hitter and they pitched around him to get to me. He was barely grazed by a pitch yet went out toward the mound with a bat, as if they wanted to hit a guy who was 0 for his last

30. Both benches emptied and all that bullshit. It woke up the Phillies when they had been ready to go home. Cardenas was a sulker, and now he sulked because he didn't think we backed him up enough. When the ball was being thrown around the infield, he refused to take a throw. Frank Thomas pinch-hit for Chris Short and I broke his bat. The ball went on a pop to short and Cardenas wouldn't move back to catch it. Pete Rose ran behind him and almost caught it, but it fell in. I almost went after Cardenas right there on the field. I was so upset that I walked the next guy and was taken out of the game. Billy McCool came in and struck out Johnny Callison. But instead of taking him out and bringing in our ace, Sammy Ellis, Sisler let McCool pitch to Richie Allen. Allen tripled, making it 3–2, and soon after, Alex Johnson doubled and we lost 4–3. After the game, I grabbed Cardenas and threw him against the wall and was ready to pound his head a few times, but was pulled off him. Chico was so scared that he came after me with an ice pick, saying, "I keel you!" Joey Jay grabbed him from behind and he ran off.

So the race went down to the last day. We had to beat the Phillies in order to tie the Cardinals. Maloney had pitched 3 days before, but you couldn't talk him into pitching that game. He wanted to go in the playoff. So we flipped a coin and John Tsitouris pitched. We lost 10–0 to Jim Bunning.

Dick Sisler had no idea what to do that last week. If Hutch had been healthy, we'd have won. Cardenas's ass would have been on the bench. He knew how to handle Cardenas.

RYNE DUREN:

The Phillies sold me to the Reds in early May and I did a good job in the bullpen with Sammy Ellis, Billy McCool, and Bill Henry. My ERA for the year was just over 3.00 and I walked only 16 batters in 46⅔ innings, while striking out 44—I'd never had such good control.

The Reds were the rowdiest bunch I played with. I saw and participated in much wilder stuff than with the Yankees or Angels, two teams that were much better known for such things. I remember in Houston when we were in a closed pool late after hours and tore each other's clothes off—someone had to get towels so we could climb out. Then there was the incident in Chicago when the airplane was delayed and the Reds' traveling secretary kept buying us drinks. We got rolling pretty good and then started buying our own. A bunch of us got in the back of a Delta flight and started raising hell, tore each other's shirts off, scared the shit out of the other passengers. Delta banned us from then on.

There were a lot of big guys on this team: me, Deron Johnson, Joe Nuxhall, Marty Keough, Johnny Edwards. We were all up in a hotel room playing cards and I took a big pitcher of beer and threw it on Deron, Nuxhall, and Keough. I was in my shorts, and the sons of bitches pushed me out the window and held me—with wet hands!—upside down by my legs. I was 16 flights up! I was saying, "Drop me. It's all right with me."

The Reds had a bunch of good starting pitchers—O'Toole, Maloney, Purkey, Jay, Nuxhall, and Tsitouris—and relievers, and that was fortunate because the Reds didn't have as good an offensive team as they had in past years. Frank Robinson was our only .300 hitter and only he, Johnson, and Pinson had more than 20 homers. He had about 95 RBIs and that was good enough to lead the team. Robinson was the best competitor I ever saw. I think after he got knocked down he must have hit about .500 with a lot of home runs. He was a good team man, but he might have been a bit too radical to have been a leader. He was anti–front office.

This was Pete Rose's second year and he wasn't yet a great hitter. He was still a kid. The excessiveness was already there. Nobody hustled like he did. He just had a different mindset than anyone else. He was around the other guys, but his mind was in another world. I'd say that he had a sociopathic profile.

Fred Hutchinson was dying and was so pale and thin. He wasn't even showing up at the end, and Dick Sisler was managing. The Phillies collapsed in September and we had the pennant won. I won a home game against St. Louis in which we came from behind, and then we hit the road and won 9 straight. We came back home on a Sunday night in first place and there were 10,000 people greeting us at the airport. On Tuesday we played Pittsburgh and there were only 8,000 people at the ballpark. We couldn't believe it. Big Bob Veale beat us 1–0 in 16 innings, beating Jim Maloney. It was the damnedest game. We had men on third, inning after inning.

We went down to the end of the season battling the Phillies and Cardinals for the pennant. On the next-to-last day, we had the Phillies beaten 2–0. Then Gene Mauch had Chris Short throw at our shortstop, Leo Cardenas. Cardenas wanted to fight him. We tried to calm down Cardenas, telling him to forget it because the pennant was at stake. Leo didn't speak much English and didn't comprehend what we were saying. He assumed that none of us liked him and wouldn't stick up for him. So in the next inning, the eighth, a Phillie hit a pop-up to short that should have been the third out. But Cardenas intentionally let it drop. A run scored and the batter reached first. Then Richie Allen tripled and we ended up getting beaten. Jim O'Toole was the pitcher and he wanted to kill Cardenas after the game. I remember it being a long screwdriver that Leo picked up and tried to stab O'Toole with. That loss dropped us into a tie with St. Louis. The next day I packed to go to the ballpark on Sunday. Afterward I could have gone to one of three places: St. Louis for a playoff, New York for the World Series, or home. I ended up going home.

My alcoholism was progressing. I would pitch only one more year, dividing time between the Phillies and Washington Senators. I would go to the Phillies after the Reds released me in the spring following some crazy incidents in Mexico—others will have to give the details because I didn't remember them in the morning. Pete Rose told me I broke down his door. The joke was that any time they saw something beat up or knocked down, they assumed "Rinold must be here."

AMERICAN LEAGUE 1964

"MY CAREER HAD ALREADY SURPRISED ME. CONSIDERING THE TOOLS I HAD, I GOT MORE OUT OF MY CAREER THAN I DESERVED. I DIDN'T DREAM ABOUT THE HALL OF FAME WHEN I SIGNED A CONTRACT. I JUST LOVED THE GAME."

BROOKS ROBINSON

LOS ANGELES ANGELS

ART FOWLER:

During the summer of 1964, I turned 42. I could still throw the ball 90 mph and had good control, but I knew my major league pitching career was over, and went home to South Carolina. Soon Minnesota called and asked if I wanted to be their pitching coach at Denver.

BARRY LATMAN:

In December, Joe Adcock and I had been traded to the Angels for Leon Wagner. Wagner had been the team's star since its debut in 1961, and Fred Haney traded him over Bill Rigney's objections. Rigney was really upset and told me the first day in camp, "I don't want you, I want Wagner back." It wasn't my fault. When I pitched well, he didn't use me. He just didn't want any part of me.

Most guys lived in Orange County, but I was living in the Valley, in the Dodgers' area. And most of the fans were down there, too. It was different pitching where I grew up and played high school ball, and I felt extra pressure. But it could have been great if I got to pitch enough to have had a good season. I finished with just a 6–10 record, although I had a decent ERA.

Gene Autry was a wonderful owner and the players were great. I became good friends with Jim Fregosi, who was becoming the star of the team, and Bob Rodgers, an outstanding catcher. They were part of Rigney's clique, along with Bobby Knoop and, perhaps, Lee Thomas. There were other cliques on the team, but everyone got along.

I was close to Art Fowler. He was like Gary Bell had been on the Indians, a popular, outspoken guy full of funny one-liners. He could still throw strikes, so I was sorry to see him go. I also liked Ken McBride, who was a good pitcher with a helluva curve. He was a battler. Unfortunately, he had a bad year in 1964. Joe Adcock was older than the rest of us. He led the team in homers, with a few more than Fregosi, but he was just about finished. He'd talk about his racehorses in Louisiana more than baseball or anything else.

Dean Chance was a great guy. He and Bo Belinsky were best friends. Belinsky got suspended and assigned to Hawaii after a run-in with a sportswriter, but I'd say Dean was the real bad one and Bo just followed along. Bo got the publicity about women and partying because he was single, while the reporters didn't write about Dean's exploits because he was married. I was living at home, so all I knew I read in the papers. Chance was a helluva pitcher who threw hard and inside. Nobody could hit him that year.

Fred Newman was the only other pitcher to win in double figures. Our only .300 hitter was outfielder Willie Smith, who also pitched. So it is surprising that we did as well as we did. We came close to winning the pennant, and any time that happens, it's fun.

We were playing a game yet making much more money than the average person, although not outrageous sums. Nobody flaunted their salaries, no one resented us for being ballplayers. Baseball was fun despite my feeling insecure my entire career. I knew I had to pitch well or I was gone. I was always reminded of my tenuous position, and I'm not even talking about during salary negotiations. Some coach would always remind you of somebody pitching well down in the minors. I was always the youngest and in the most vulnerable position. So I played under pressure. But that kept me going. And I continued to love baseball. I loved my entire career.

(Ballplayers felt like celebrities, even outside of Los Angeles. It would take me about ten years after I finished playing in 1967 to come back down and realize I was just a normal person. It's terrible—it's the hardest comedown in the world.)

VIC POWER:

When I was dealt by the Angels to the Phillies in September, I was semiprepared: after three houses and three trades, I had known better than to buy a house in Los Angeles. I lived in an apartment in Hollywood. That's when the hippies were coming in. And I saw the Beatles at the Hollywood Bowl. There weren't too many sports fans, as far as I could tell. I'd say I was a player and people would think I was a musician. But I enjoyed my time there after being traded from Minnesota.

Bill Rigney was a beautiful man and good manager. He didn't play me every day, but I was getting older. He

used me often as a late-inning defensive replacement. He also played me frequently at third and a few times at second. We had a good team and for a time were in the pennant race.

I loved Gene Autry. We used to stay at the Melody Ranch in Palm Springs. Late at night, he'd get drunk at the bar and want to sing in Spanish, so he'd tell the bartender, "Call Vic Power." They'd wake me up to come sing with Gene Autry.

That year, Gene Autry made a college player rich. He gave the biggest bonus in history—$200,000—to Rick Reichardt, a tall outfielder from Wisconsin. He was a nice young man with all the tools. But he cost what they paid Mickey Mantle and Willie Mays combined! Baseball was changing!

I was reunited with Jimmy Piersall. I also spent a lot of time with Bo Belinsky and Dean Chance. I got to go to their parties. Bo was a playboy who was always dating some beautiful woman. There was one party when Bo hadn't shown up yet and one of his girlfriends was drunk and waiting for him in a dark bedroom. A player would knock on the door. She'd call out, "Who is it?" He'd answer, "Bo Belinsky." And she'd say, "Come in." So he went inside. About ten players knocked on the door and claimed to be Bo Belinsky and she invited them all in. Bo never did come to that party. Bo was pitching well for us, but then he had trouble with a sportswriter and was demoted to Hawaii. (He'd return to the majors, but not with the Angels.)

Until I saw Chance, Bobby Shantz was the best pitcher I ever played behind. Chance was the Angels' first 20-game winner and had over 200 strikeouts. Dean would say, "Get me one run and I'll win." And he always did it. He won 5 games 1–0 and threw 11 shutouts! His earned run average was 1.65! He was amazing. He was the major league's Cy Young winner.

In July, I had an argument with umpire Jim Honochick after a close play at second base. I always chewed bubble gum to help me relax, and when we were arguing, my gum flew out of my mouth and hit him in the face. I got accused of spitting on him and was fined and suspended 10 games. But I didn't do it. I learned that if you want to argue, throw out your gum.

The Angels rented the Dodger plane. It was a beautiful private plane with a library, tables for cardplaying, even a few beds. Flying was much easier than taking trains, but it became tiring, too. I felt myself wearing down.

In September, the Angels were out of the race, so they traded me to the Philadelphia Phillies, who needed a first baseman after Frank Thomas hurt his thumb. Actually, I was pretty much loaned to them for the pennant drive because the Angels bought me back in November for my twelfth, and final, season.

BILLY MORAN:

I don't know what my reputation was. Years later, the Twins' Tony Oliva would say, "I remember you—a *pesky* little player." In a certain sense I was pesky. I was certainly a student of the game who talked baseball all the time to learn how to get the advantage over more talented players. I also considered myself a clutch hitter, who had a lot of tying and winning hits in 1962 and 1963. I loved to hit with men on base and was a better hitter then. I had even batted cleanup some in 1963.

I was a dependable fielder. I had led the league in putouts and chances per game in 1962 and putouts, chances per game, and assists in 1963. Unfortunately, I didn't play second base in 1964. In the spring, Rigney came to me and said, "We have a guy in Hawaii, Bobby Knoop, who we'd like to play second. And we'd like you to move to third." In those days, when you were 30, they looked to replace you no matter what you were doing. I told Rigney I had played second base for so long that I couldn't throw anymore, but I wanted to help the team, so I said okay. I should have objected and said I had to stay at second. I could have gotten Rigney to play Knoop at third base, and then I could have stayed in L.A. for a couple more years. That was the worst mistake I made. I didn't play much at third in spring training, and when the season began I felt out of place and my arm was weak. I had about 10 errors in a month. The experiment lasted until the middle of June. Then I got traded back to Cleveland in a 3-team deal that brought Vic Power and Lenny Green to California from Minnesota. I was really disappointed.

I had never negotiated a contract with Gene Autry. But I knew him because he was always around and involved with the games. When my son Steve was three, he got hit with a rock that damaged his eye. Then, in

1963, a kid hit him in the eye with a stiff paint brush and he had an abrasion, and they had to take it out and put in a prosthesis. Leonard Firestone, who along with Bob Reynolds was Autry's partner on the Angels, got the best eye doctor in the country to perform the surgery on Steve. The surgery was scheduled right after the trade. I was no longer with the Angels, but Mr. Firestone paid for it all. I never got a bill. Every time I'd see Gene Autry he'd ask about Steve.

CLEVELAND INDIANS

BILLY MORAN:

When I went to Gabe Paul on the Saturday after I was acquired from the Angels, I told him I had to be in L.A. Monday for my son's eye surgery. He said, "I don't know if you can do that. We've got doubleheaders. . . ." I said, "Gabe, I don't care if you've got a quadruple-header. I'm going to be with my son." They were coming to L.A. Tuesday anyway. That was so bush league.

I asked him what the Indians planned to do with me. Supposedly he got me to play second, but they already had Chico Salmon, Larry Brown, and Woodie Held to play there. Paul said, "I don't know yet." Saturday night, I sat on the bench but pinch-hit in the eighth inning and had a hard line single to right. I didn't get to bat again for 2 weeks, when I pinch-hit again. Several weeks later, I started 3 games against Boston and had a big series. I didn't play again for three weeks. So the writing was on the wall: I wouldn't play at all.

Gabe Paul? He knew as little about talent as anybody I ever knew in baseball. How he stayed on top for so long is a mystery because he never won anything. I didn't like him. Birdie Tebbetts was my manager. I didn't like him either. Tebbetts tried to bluff you. He was a big bag of wind.

Sam Mele, the manager of Minnesota, wanted to get me over there, but Cleveland wouldn't deal me. After the year, Paul wanted to cut my salary and I wanted to quit. But I lacked 13 days to qualify for the pension plan, so I had to come back for one more year in 1965. There would be a whole new set of problems.

MUDCAT GRANT:

There were rumors about my being traded, so I asked about it because I wanted to buy a house in Shaker Heights. They assured me I wasn't going anywhere. I bought my house. On June 15 Gabe Paul traded me to the Twins.

AL SMITH:

I returned to the Indians in 1964. It was a totally different experience and a bit upsetting because they weren't a very good team anymore. But I liked playing with guys like Gary Bell, Luis Tiant, Pedro Ramos, Leon Wagner, and Mudcat Grant.

Bell was a funny man. He loved to play tricks on you. He'd also squirt everyone with a water pistol. He enjoyed getting on Tiant. I played against Luis Senior on the New York Cubans in the Negro Leagues. Luis was a good pitcher, but his daddy was even better. Leon Wagner was Cleveland's best hitter, by far. The Indians didn't have anybody else who could hit 30 homers and drive in 100 runs. We called Leon "Jaws" because he had enormous cheekbones.

PEDRO RAMOS:

Leon had a good sense of humor. I liked him a lot. I also liked Tiant and Sonny Siebert, two clever, hard-throwing rookie right-handers. Luis and I had known each other a little in Cuba, but we didn't become friends until he was brought up by Cleveland. He debuted with a 4-hit shutout over the Yankees. Luis was pretty quiet, but he had his funny moments and guys would get on him because of his high-pitched voice and laugh and cigar smoking.

Left-hander Tommy John was another rookie. He was also a friendly, quiet guy, though not so funny. At that time, he was a hard thrower, before learning how to pitch. Sam McDowell and the three rookies were all pitching well, and I assumed they would form a solid rotation for the rest of the decade. I thought that veterans like Dick Donovan, Mudcat Grant, and I should move elsewhere while the team built around youth. Fortunately, the Indians were thinking the same way.

Even at the beginning of the season, I asked the Indians to trade me because I didn't want to play for Birdie Tebbetts anymore. I didn't like a manager who'd tell his players, "I'm number one. That's why I wear number 1. Things are going to be done my way." There weren't three guys on Cleveland who liked Tebbetts. He suffered a heart attack just before the season started, but he returned in July and hadn't changed. If he hadn't been manager, I might have enjoyed my stay in Cleveland more.

BALTIMORE ORIOLES

BROOKS ROBINSON:

I never thought I'd live year round in Baltimore, but I did once I got married. My wife was from Canada, near Detroit, and I didn't want to go there and she didn't want to live in Little Rock, so we compromised on Baltimore. The most difficult part of being a ballplayer was being on the road all the time. But that was part of the job and my wife understood that. What made it even more difficult is that for a couple of years after our marriage, I worked for the Orioles in the off-season in public relations. That meant I was out almost every night making appearances. I got to know a lot of people in the community.

Baltimore was basically a football town. The Colts were the NFL champions in 1958 and 1959, and everyone in town loved them. Baseball didn't cause as much excitement, especially since we hadn't won a title yet. I knew all the football players well. After a home football game, we'd have a couple of Colts come over for dinner or we might go to Johnny Unitas's restaurant. Of course, after baseball games we'd go to Eddie and Brooks Robinson's Gorsuch House, on Gorsuch Avenue near the ballpark. We served steaks and seafood, because Baltimore was a seafood town and many sports people went there. Eddie Robinson, the veteran first baseman who had coached for Paul Richards, had an earlier partner in the restaurant, but when they had a falling out I became his partner. (There were actually about five of us who became partners for about fifteen years.)

By 1964 a strong rivalry had developed between the Yankees and Orioles. We had the pitching to beat them, so we always played tough series. This was the first year the Yankees really could have been had. We should

NATIONAL BASEBALL LIBRARY, COOPERSTOWN, N.Y.

Baltimore's Brooks Robinson would win 16 consecutive Gold Gloves at third base, but in 1964 it was his bat along with his glove that won him the Most Valuable Player award.

have won the pennant, but we lost Boog Powell in the last month with a broken wrist. They ended up beating the White Sox by 1 game and us by 2 games. They were still winning pennants, but they were no longer the dominant team they had been in 1961—that was the best team I ever played against. Either they had come back to the pack or the rest of the teams had caught up to them.

Hank Bauer managed us in 1964. I liked playing for him because he would just write your name in the lineup and say, "Go play, boys." He wrote the same names in there every day. And he got good production from many of us.

For instance, it all came together for Boog Powell. He had hit 25 homers the year before, but now he hit 39 and drove in 99 runs although he missed most of September. Luis Aparicio stole a career-high 57 bases. Right fielder Sam Bowens hit over 20 homers. And second baseman Jerry Adair, Aparicio, and I led the league at our positions in fielding.

Nineteen sixty-four was an incredible season for me. I don't have any answers for why it happened. I just got into a groove and never fell out of it. I batted fourth most of the year and drove in 118 runs, which was 30 more than my previous high in 1960. I also hit 28 homers, which was 5 more than I hit in 1962. Being voted the 1964 MVP, although we didn't win the pennant, was unbelievable. Since I was a baseball historian, it was more special because I could look back and see the other guys who had won. That was certainly the highlight of my career at that point. I had been noticed in the early '60s, but now I really received national attention. I got endorsements from Coca-Cola, Gillette, Vitalis, just about all of them.

We got terrific pitching from many guys, including rookie Wally Bunker, who went 19–5, Milt Pappas, who was 16–7, and Robin Roberts, who won 13 games. The Orioles purchased Roberts from the Phillies after the 1961 season. He seemed to be washed up because he went only 1–10 that season and was trying to hold on. He wasn't overpowering anymore, but he was able to adjust and win ball games. He had 3 excellent seasons for us. It was exciting having a legend from the other league come over. He was a strong influence in the clubhouse. He was very smart, articulate, and easy to speak to. We learned a lot from him, not only about playing baseball but about the inner workings of the game. He would talk about what we should think about when we were getting ready to retire, like pensions and medical plans.

There wasn't a lot of griping about not having free agency. That's the way it was, and we played under those rules. At that time I kind of thought I'd play forever, which is how most of the young guys felt. But the longer I played, the more freedom I wanted, and I began to think about such things as free agency and a players' union. But I wasn't outspoken. I wasn't a leader type in those years, just easygoing and able to get along with everybody.

My career had already surprised me. Considering the tools I had, I got more out of my career than I deserved. I didn't dream about the Hall of Fame when I signed a contract. I just loved the game.

BOSTON RED SOX

FRANK MALZONE:

Tony Conigliaro was just 19 when he joined the Red Sox. He was competitive from day one. In his first game, he homered over the wall in Fenway, which was some way for a hometown kid to break in. He was hardworking and brash enough to make his feelings known. He tried to create a winning atmosphere. One day a few guys on the bench laughed when a player made an error and Tony jumped on them: "No wonder you guys haven't been winning the last few years." That quieted down everyone. I smiled because I thought he was the type who could ignite the ballclub. As a rookie, Tony batted .290 and in just over 400 at-bats hit 24 homers, a record for a teenager. I thought he was destined to set a lot of records in our ballpark. He didn't just hit line drives that would hit the wall—he hit fly balls that would go over it. I figured that once Yastrzemski developed power, the two of them could carry the Sox.

GARY PETERS (WHITE SOX):

Carl Yastrzemski was a great hitter who hit anything in the strike zone hard. Years later I told him he hit me better in his autobiography than he did in reality. He got a few hits off me, but I had good luck with him because I had a good slider that was particularly hard on left-handers. You'd have to throw inside every once in a while, so Carl couldn't reach the outside corner. I'd

Playing his last of eight seasons as Boston's everyday third baseman, Frank Malzone continued to excel in the field as well as produce at the plate.

knock him down a few times. . . . Still, we went fishing together.

F. MALZONE:

This was my last year as a full-time player, although I would play another couple of years, the first with Boston. I would go on to play a total of 1,370 games in the field, all at third base. I felt fortunate that I had been part of some very strong batting lineups that included Ted Williams, Jackie Jensen, Pete Runnels, Carl Yastrzemski, and Tony Conigliaro. When I looked back at the Boston pitchers I played behind, I'm surprised we didn't do better. We had some good hurlers: Tom Brewer, Frank Sullivan, Willard Nixon, Ike DeLock, Don Schwall, Earl Wilson, Bill Monbouquette, Mike Fornieles, and Dick Radatz. Yet we always had trouble winning. Without pennant races, I'm sorry to say that you began to think more of your personal stats, to help you in your fight for your salary or job. In earlier years, though the Yankees dominated then, too, we were competitive and I needed no other motivation to play hard than just putting on my major league uniform and going out on the field.

I always enjoyed the life of a professional ballplayer, playing in front of fans I felt close to. I didn't feel like a showman or celebrity; I just felt it was my lot in life to do this. I can't speak for other guys, but I took pride in my job, going in day in and day out.

BILL MONBOUQUETTE:

I expected a good raise because I was the first Boston pitcher to win 20 games since Mel Parnell in 1953. Higgins offered me only $3,000 more. That hurt me. At the night of the annual Boston sportswriters' dinner, he said, "You didn't even have the decency to return your contract." I said, "How can you expect decency when you send a contract like that?" I told him I wouldn't sign it. He told me to come by his office soon after and we'd settle our differences. So I went over and he handed me the same contract. I slammed it down. And before you know it, we were wrestling and throwing punches again. I eventually got the raise I wanted before spring training started, but it wasn't a comfortable situation.

I worked out at Tufts before each year. Tony Conigliaro came by one day. He had just played one year in the minors. I loved what I saw. He had a quick, beautiful swing, and the ball jumped off his bat. I knew we had something special. He came to spring training and made the ballclub. He was a really good kid.

At the time, our only genuine power hitter was Dick Stuart, who came to the Red Sox in 1963 from the Pirates. He was a good-natured, fun-loving guy. We all knew about his fielding problems—he was nicknamed "Dr. Strangeglove" after the movie—and we tried not to let batters hit the ball down the first-base line. One time I was pitching and turned around and saw a paper plane sailing toward him during a game. He caught it and got a standing ovation. But Dick was a good, powerful hitter who had a couple of huge years in 1963 and 1964. He hit 75 homers in those 2 years, many that were really smashed, and drove in well over 200 runs. He had a terrific swing, and it was even exciting to watch him strike out.

I had become good friends with Earl Wilson, who

pitched almost as many innings as I did. We'd hang out together, though he lived in Boston and I still lived in Medford. He had moved into the rotation in 1962, and won 11 or 12 games for us the next few years. He was a feisty guy, too, a big, strong pitcher who was 6'3" and had a physique like Jim Brown's. He could throw hard. One time in spring training, Earl and I were sitting in the dugout watching a pitching prospect with a name like "Petula" throwing batting practice. "Petula" apparently had hurt his arm, although our suspicions were that he was a hypochondriac. That day the hitters didn't have any chance against him. He was throwing the ball close to 100 mph. Afterward he came over and Johnny Murphy asked him, "How do you feel?" And "Petula" said, "Aw, I can't get anything on the ball today." Earl and I looked at each other in disbelief. We thought "Petula" was destined for the Hall of Fame.

The players of my time were hard-nosed, dedicated guys who loved the game and didn't play solely for the money. In those days, guys got cuts in salaries and just kicked themselves in the pants and vowed to do better. There was nothing bad about being a ballplayer. There's nothing wrong with dreaming and nothing wrong with fulfilling a dream. Probably 90 percent of the population didn't like what they did for a living. I loved what I did. Baseball was my life and I owed it everything I had. It was everything I hoped it would be and much more.

BOB TURLEY:

I got into great shape for spring training in 1964, thinking I'd pitch and be the pitching coach. But I stopped pitching so I could concentrate on the coaching. One prospect who really caught my eye was Jerry Stephenson, a 20-year-old right-hander who threw like Dean Chance. Nobody could get a hit off him, and he struck everyone out. I wanted to bring him north, but Mike Higgins wouldn't let me because Stephenson didn't have any experience. We argued, and he said he'd bring up Stephenson if he did well for 30 days. I had to tell the poor kid that he was going back to the minors, but I promised that if he did well he'd be back in a month. A month passed and he was 4–0 with an 0.89 ERA, but Higgins wouldn't bring him back. Stephenson got so frustrated that he jumped the team and went home. Then he hurt his arm and was never much good after that. I thought that was a disgusting episode. It wasn't worth ending my pitching career to be part of something like that.

AL SMITH:

At the end of the season, I came over to Boston to finish my career. Pinky Higgins thought I could help the team. But the Red Sox finished badly and ended up in eighth place, ahead of only the Senators and Athletics. With about 2 games to go, Billy Herman, the third-base coach, replaced Johnny Pesky as manager.

I could tell that Tony Conigliaro and Carl Yastrzemski were going to be great ballplayers. Tony already displayed a lot of power, and Carl already hit for a high average. I knew they'd both improve. Of the two, I talked more to Carl, who was a very friendly guy.

Boston had a lot of players who hit homers, especially in Fenway Park, but Dick Stuart was the only guy who drove in runs that year. And he couldn't field. Boston had such little run production that Bill Monbouquette and Earl Wilson had trouble winning and the team's top winner turned out to be Dick Radatz, who won 16 games. There were a few good relief pitchers in the American League at this time, including Hoyt Wilhelm on Chicago, Stu Miller on Baltimore, Bob Lee on Los Angeles, Al Worthington on Minnesota, and Don McMahon on Cleveland, but Radatz was the most feared. He'd strike out more than one batter an inning. He'd throw hard—you just had to be ready. Oddly, I never had too much trouble hitting him because I was a fastball hitter.

I'd been around, so I knew almost everyone on the team. It wasn't at all difficult being a black player on Boston. I was with the Red Sox for just a month and a half before the season ended. It was a good way to end my career.

WASHINGTON SENATORS

TOM CHENEY:

No other team would take a chance on a guy with a bad arm, so I couldn't hope to be traded by the Senators. So I was stuck with Gil Hodges. The last game I pitched in 1964 was against Kansas City. He kept me out there much too long. I stayed out there throwing until tears were coming out of my eyes. I finished the game and won it. They scored a few runs, but I had a good lead. Afterward I was sitting in front of my locker. Hodges walked by and said, "Thattaway to go." I said, "Yeah, you son of a bitch, that was the last game I'll ever pitch." I tried a comeback in 1966, but I didn't have it.

I didn't like how my baseball career ended, particularly because I was so young. I won only 19 games total. But I realized how fortunate I was to have made it to the majors. Not many make it. And how many guys who played for many years didn't get to play in the World Series or win a title? I also cherished the togetherness of players in an era when we didn't make enough money for money to matter. So I got about as much out of the game as a person could ask for.

MINNESOTA TWINS

HARMON KILLEBREW:

I was the captain of the Twins and in my own unassertive way tried to be a leader through my actions on the field. I never had to be the only leader on the team because we a lot of smart leader types. From the Washington days, we still had Earl Battey, Don Mincher, and Jim Kaat. We got Jim Perry from the Indians during the 1963 season, and then in the middle of the 1964 season we got Jim "Mudcat" Grant from the Indians. There was always an excellent relationship between black and white players on the Twins. Black players like Battey and Grant always felt comfortable to speak their minds. Certainly Mudcat wasn't a laid-back type. He was a great addition to the team on and off the field. I think we got him because he always beat us pitching for Cleveland.

The other major addition to our team was Tony Oliva. He played a little in 1962 and 1963, but his rookie year was 1964, when he led the league in batting. He was one of the greatest hitters I ever saw, maybe the best off-speed hitter ever. If you threw him a change, he'd kill you. He'd hit the ball all over the ballpark with power. Many times he didn't even know who the pitcher was. He had great reactions and just saw the ball and hit it.

Oliva gave us still another guy who could hit 30

homers a season. In one game against the Athletics, Tony, Bob Allison, Jimmie Hall, and I hit consecutive homers. My personal hightlight was a homer I hit off Baltimore's Milt Pappas in Memorial Stadium. It went 471 feet and they said it was the longest measured home run ever hit there. Who knows if there were longer un-measured homers.

The Twins had an off season, dropping to fourth place, but we got good years from Oliva, Allison, Kaat, Versalles, and many of the other players. I led the league again with 49 homers, drove in 111 runs, and batted .270, so I was very satisfied with my year.

GARY PETERS (WHITE SOX):

Harmon Killebrew was the toughest guy I pitched to in the big leagues. I had a bad time keeping him from hit-ting the ball hard, and he slugged a lot of homers off me. I would throw a sinker low and away and he was strong enough to pull it or hit it over the fence to the opposite field. He could do that in Minnesota or Chicago. Whitey Ford told me that the best way to pitch him was to throw a lot of junk inside and let him hit that foul and get 2 strikes, and then throw him a bad pitch and hope he'd swing. So I had the best luck with him when I gave him nothing to hit.

H. KILLEBREW:

I had goals every year, but they weren't ones I ex-pressed outwardly. I'd want a certain number of homers and RBIs and to cut down on strikeouts. My walks went up, but that was never a goal—I just learned to have pa-tience and cut down my strike zone. My only disap-pointment is that I didn't hit 50 homers, which is a mag-ical number. I hit 48 homers in 1962 and 49 in 1964, but I didn't reach 50. (In 1969, my best year, I really hit 50 homers, but an umpire in Boston didn't realize that a ball I hit went *over* the center-field wall before bounc-ing back onto the field.)

VIC POWER:

I began the year in Minnesota, before moving on to Los Angeles and Philadelphia. As I said, I bought a house there. I hated shoveling snow in Minnesota, so I told Tony Oliva that Ted Williams became such a good hit-ter because he spent a lot of time shoveling snow. On the morning of the next big snow, I looked out my win-dow and Tony was outside with a shovel. He shoveled our sidewalk and driveway all winter. He led the league in hitting as a rookie in 1964 and always believed it was because he shoveled snow.

One time I caught him walking through a hotel lobby with an ugly date. I said, "Tony, this is the big leagues—you can't go out with women who look like Willie Mays." He explained, "Every time I go out with her, I go 5 for 5." I said, "Okay, you go out with her, but you gotta use the fire escape." Soon after, I intro-duced Tony to the woman he would marry.

Oliva was such a great hitter that they gave him the right-field job, moved Bob Allison from right to first, and in early June traded me and Lenny Green to the Los Angeles Angels. Everyone knew I was a better player than Allison, but he had more power and was a little younger. The trade really frustrated me. I liked being on the Twins and living in Minnesota, where the people were very kind to me. When I had bought a house in Kansas City, I was traded the next year. I had waited until my third year in Cleveland before buying a house, and then I was traded. And now, when I bought a house in Minnesota, I was traded. I got so mad. I never saw that house again. I ended up divorced. You can see why players didn't like the reserve clause.

I would play only one more year, with the Angels. When they wanted to sell my contract to Japan in the spring of 1966, I would retire to pursue an acting career in Los Angeles and then return home to Puerto Rico, to manage, play ball, and eventually scout and run base-ball clinics. It was time to get out of the majors. I said before that I was born in 1931 and that's what my base-ball record always said, but I can now say that I was actually born in 1927. You see, when I was born my fa-ther didn't go immediately into the city to register me. Rather than being fined for not registering me in time, he kept my birth quiet. When I had a brother born four years later, my father registered us as twins. So I was always four years older than the records said, in school and in baseball. When I got out of the major leagues I wasn't 34, but 38. I admitted this only when I applied for my pension.

Of my accomplishments, I was most proud of the seven Gold Gloves, seven All-Star Game appearances, and being the first Puerto Rican to play in an All-Star Game. I got to travel and meet all kinds of people in and out of baseball: John Kennedy, Fidel Castro, Ty Cobb, Satchel Paige, Connie Mack, Jackie Robinson, Jimmy Piersall, Bo Belinsky. I got to play with the best players: Ted Williams, who was the greatest hitter ever, Bob Feller, Stan Musial, Sandy Koufax, Willie Mays, Brooks Robinson, Don Newcombe, Luis Aparicio, Nellie Fox, Henry Aaron, Roberto Clemente, Camilo Pascual, Mickey Vernon, Rocky Colavito, Harmon Killebrew. I got to see the Boston Pops in Boston, Tito Puente at the Palladium in New York, Lionel Hampton, Stan Getz, Duke Ellington, Count Basie, the Beatles, even Billie Holiday. Baseball was never everything. I combined work with pleasure.

MUDCAT GRANT:

It didn't hurt me going to the Twins in mid-June because they were coming into their own as a great power-hitting team, and were only a year away from winning the pennant. I hung out with Earl Battey, who was a great guy, Don Mincher, and former Indians Dick Stigman, Jerry Kindall, and Jim Perry. We knew a lot of the same people and had a lot of fun together. I got along well with Harmon Killebrew, and Tony Oliva was one of the best people you'll ever find. The Twins had good pitching but there was room for me in the starting rotation. I did okay, winning 11 and losing 9, but I gave no one any hint that I would win 21 games the next year.

JOHNNY KLIPPSTEIN:

In those days the players bought their own shoes and sanitary socks and the team paid for everything else. And most guys had contracts for gloves or shoes with Rawlings or another company. The clubhouse man took care of your cleaning and drying. Players didn't really gripe about being underpaid. It's amazing. They probably knew that they could make more money if there was a union or they had agents and lawyers representing them, but they were so used to negotiating for themselves that they preferred it. I had sat down with the

After spending his entire career in the Indians' organization, Mudcat Grant was traded to Minnesota in 1964, one year before he would be the American League's top winner and lead the Twins to a pennant.

likes of Buzzy Bavasi and Gabe Paul and Calvin Griffith, and they were all tough to deal with. They wanted to sign you as cheaply as possible and more or less told you that if you didn't like it, they'd find somebody else to play. In my current relieving days, I generally felt that I should have received bigger raises.

I came to Minnesota in late June and pitched in 33 games, all in relief. I think I did a good job, although I didn't have stats that would mean anything during salary negotiations. It was a good opportunity for me, and I enjoyed myself. The Twins were a family-oriented team, and the players and wives would get together socially and have parties. Griffith was always coming up with something at the park to take care of the wives. They had a large room there if someone needed anything or wanted to come early or have a party or have drinks after a game. It was a nice atmosphere.

The Twins were a terrific bunch of guys and very close. Killebrew and Bob Allison were great guys and *great* players. Rich Rollins and Bernie Allen were great guys and *good* players. Tony Oliva was one of the finest people I ever played with. He was also one of the best hitters I ever saw. He was amazing. As the Rookie of the Year, he led the league with a .323 average and had 32 homers and over 40 doubles. He didn't care who was pitching or what he threw, and was a remarkable 2-strike hitter. Zoilo Versailles had a few problems. He was very high-strung, very moody and thin-skinned. He was pretty much a loner. Eart Battey was a super person. I liked pitching to him. He could settle down any pitcher. I thought he was like a granddaddy.

Mudcat Grant, who joined the Twins from Cleveland two weeks before I got there, was a great athlete. In 1960, when we had played together on Cleveland, he was only a fair pitcher. But when he came over to Minnesota he developed into one of the best pitchers in the league. Camilo Pascual was a first-class guy and already a great pitcher. He had a great attitude and worked hard. Jim Kaat was a wonderful guy. We would go to the racetrack together. He was very smart and was very outgoing, and a hard worker, so he was a natural leader. He could do everything on the field—hit, run, field, and pitch. Kaat was the guy the A's Bert Campaneris faced his first time up in the majors and homered off on the first pitch—Campaneris hit another homer that game besides to tie another record.

Sam Mele, the manager, was a quiet man who never had much to say. He reminded me of Walter Alston in how he ran a club.

The Yankees had charisma. When you played in their stadium, you felt lonely out there. You felt you were playing against the world. They were an aloof team, much like the old Brooklyn Dodgers—only I'd rather have played with the Dodgers. The Yankees were impressed by themselves. Maybe they should have been because for many years they were in a class by themselves. But after the 1964 season we figured the Twins would be legitimate challengers the next year, and this turned out to be true. We weren't cocky, but we sensed that if we played hard and well, we could beat anyone—including the Yankees.

CHICAGO WHITE SOX

GARY PETERS:

I don't recall the team congratulating me for being Rookie of the Year in 1963. I don't think they gave me a bonus for winning the award. With Chicago, you had to fight for every dollar. I had to negotiate on my record, not the award. I got to go to a few dinners here and there, including the annual White Sox writers' dinner, but that was about it. Nellie Fox told me that the White Sox weren't known for high salaries and were liable to try to sign me for the same salary I had as a rookie. The first contract they sent me wasn't with much of a raise. The White Sox weren't like Boston, where the owner was a fan and baseball was his hobby. The White Sox were run by businessmen. The general manager, Ed Short, was trying to keep salaries down. Our payroll was low.

There was more pressure on me in my second year. Once you win, you're expected to win again, plus you've got a position you want to protect from guys coming up from the minors. But I had confidence. I knew the hitters and umpires a little better my sophomore year; plus, I started all year beginning with Opening Day.

The pitchers on the White Sox learned a lot from each other. That was encouraged by Ray Berres, who had a lot to do with our staff's having the league's best earned run average—a low 2.72. Somebody would be working in the bullpen on some pitch or delivery and I'd have him explain the feeling he had when he released it. And I'd explain my pitches and technique to the others. On the Sox, most of us were sinker-slider pitchers. We threw sliders low and away and sinkers on the inside and once in a while threw a running fastball inside to keep guys off the plate. Our goal was to get them to hit the ball on the ground, not get strikeouts. Ron Hansen wasn't as fast as an Aparicio or Versalles, but he led the league's shortstops in putouts, assists, and double plays. In my first two years, I threw fastballs, sliders, and sinkers predominantly and an occasional straight change, and I added a slow curve in 1964. I threw mostly at knee level, and tried to induce batters to hit balls out of the strike zone. I struck out left-handers with sliders, but a lot of games I would get 20 outs on ground balls.

Joel Horlen was a good pitcher, with a good curveball. His ERA was 1.88 for the year, just a little above Dean Chance's. He had excellent control and really battled in low-scoring games. Juan Pizarro was a fastball pitcher. J. C. Martin caught him a lot. Sometimes, after 3 or 4 innings, J.C. would tell him to forget the breaking ball. He had so much action on his fastball that it didn't matter if batters knew he was going to throw it. John Buzhardt was our fourth starter, though he didn't pitch as much as the rest of us down the stretch when Lopez went to a 3-man rotation. He had all the pitches and a good attitude.

Hoyt Wilhelm was great coming out of the bullpen. He threw the best knuckler I ever saw. Eddie Fisher, our other main reliever, threw a lot harder knuckler than Hoyt Wilhelm did, but it didn't compare. You couldn't touch Hoyt's, much less catch it. If you were playing catch with him and he started throwing knucklers, you'd just leave because he'd hit you with one. The catchers who knew Hoyt would put on the equipment when they warmed him up, which they never did for anybody else because there was no reason. There was a catcher, Jim Napier, who came to the big camp for the first time. Somebody told Napier to run down and warm up Hoyt. He said he didn't need a mask. After Hoyt got warmed up, the third or fourth knuckleball broke Napier's nose. He never caught him again without the mask.

The White Sox used you as a short man in the bullpen on the second day after you started. The standard training procedure was that the day after you pitched, you'd run as much as you could, and the day after that, you might throw batting practice, and the day after that, you threw a little bit, and the next day you started again. That was how everybody did it.

I pitched a little differently in every park, emphasizing different pitches. Our team was tailored for Comiskey Park. Since we had all sinkerball pitchers, they kept the area in front of home plate wet to slow down the ball. We had pretty big dimensions and the ball didn't carry good because the wind would come underneath that upper deck, especially if it was blowing off the lake. One day Jim Fregosi got hold of one of my pitches and went into his home run trot and the wind was blowing in so hard that the left fielder caught it on the warning track. He couldn't believe it. He'd always say,

"That ball should have been on the roof," and I'd counter, "You hit it on your fists."

In Boston, right-handed batters would be standing on top of the plate to pull the ball. They thought I'd try to throw them a sinker on the outside corner, which was my natural pitch. It was a hard pitch to pull unless the batter was on top of the plate. With them on the plate, I'd instead throw a lot of running fastballs up and in, bad pitches for them to hit. We'd call them "runners." I broke a lot of bats. I had pretty good luck in Fenway Park. I never had trouble with the big hitters like Dick Stuart and Tony Conigliaro. There was just a little more of a guessing game there and usually I won because the batters got anxious.

The Angels played at Dodger Stadium, where the infield was tailored for the Dodger speedsters, Maury Wills and Willie Davis. It was hard and a ground ball would bounce so high that they could beat it out for a base hit. That infield was tough on ground-ball pitchers like me. In some ballparks you pitched away because there was more room in right and right-center. Tiger Stadium had a big center field, and if right-handers hit the ball, our great center fielder, Jim Landis, would track it down. Of course, Yankee Stadium was like that, too.

I tailored my pitching for each ballpark but never changed my style of pitching. I stayed a sinker-slider pitcher with an occasional curveball. I had luck against right-handers because of my sinker. However, I had trouble against Minnesota because their right-handed hitters, Killebrew, Allison, and Versalles, had a lot of patience. I had more luck against Kansas City because, other than Rocky Colavito, who they acquired from Detroit in 1964, their right-handed batters—Ed Charles, Nelson Mathews, Bert Campaneris—were free swingers. Plus they had a lot of left-handed hitters like Jim Gentile, Billy Bryan, and Manny Jimenez.

If someone homered off me, I didn't usually brush him back next time up. I'd more likely do it if they threw at someone on my team. Nobody had to tell me to do that. No manager ever told me to hit anyone. The catcher would give a sign for a fastball inside. Over the years I'd throw at Campaneris, the A's speedy rookie, when he'd lead off. I'd throw at his ankles. He could never hit me well because he worried I'd hit his legs, his bread and butter. There was no use knocking down guys like Kaline or Killebrew because you'd wake them up or get them mad. If you made good pitches to Mickey Mantle, you could get him out. He was a lot better high-ball hitter as a right-hander, and I was a low-ball pitcher, so I had good luck against him. He was a hard swinger and, except for Killebrew, I preferred pitching to that kind of guy.

I was a good-hitting pitcher and Earl Wilson of Boston was a good-hitting pitcher. He homered off me and I homered off him. So we had a rivalry. I also had a pitching rivalry with Whitey Ford in 1963 and 1964. I could beat the Yankees, but not when I pitched against Ford. He'd beat me 1–0 and 2–1. I couldn't wait for him to retire because we couldn't score off him. I also started a rivalry with rookie Mel Stottlemyre, who would replace Ford as the Yankees' ace. It would really develop more later in my career. We'd have a drink after a game. Socializing on the field between opposing players was frowned upon, and rightly so.

Anyway, I had a lot of friends on the Sox. I roomed with Horlen for many years in the minors and majors. We were very compatible. He was from Texas, and we would hunt and fish together in the winter. A bunch of us would go on hunting trips: Joel, me, Eddie Fisher, Dave Nicholson, and Jerry McNertney. Al Weis even went once. He was from New York and had never shot anything. We went to Colorado to hunt deer and elk and to Nebraska for pheasant. We did it for several years.

Pete Ward and Juan Pizarro were funny guys. Hoyt Wilhelm was always playing jokes or making ridiculous bets. Don Gutteridge, one of the coaches, was a fun guy. So was Joe Cunningham, who was with us in 1963 and at the beginning of 1964. It was just as well that Joe was only playing first because it had been comedic to watch him in the outfield misjudging fly balls. He'd catch most of them, but he'd run 20 feet to catch one that was hit right to him.

Our new first baseman, Tom McCraw, was a good team man. He was a great fielder and a good hitter. Dave Nicholson was a great hunter and outdoorsman but not as good a baseball player. He was a very strong fastball hitter but struck out a lot on curveballs. Like most guys, he was just happy to be in the big leagues no matter how he did. John Buzhardt was a quiet country guy from Prosperity, South Carolina. Infielder Don Bu-

ford was a battler. He and Al Weis would switch off at second base. They were both switch hitters, but Don had more power and hit a lot of line drives into the gaps.

Ron Hansen was a friendly guy and an all-around shortstop, the first of the big shortstops. He couldn't compare to Aparicio in the field, but he was a dependable shortstop and had a good arm and good range. I think he got some negative reaction from the fans for replacing Aparicio, who was a crowd favorite in Chicago. Ron would make the plays—he just wasn't as flamboyant as Luis. He'd also hit 20 homers, which made him a slugger on this team.

Left fielder Floyd Robinson was a good low-ball hitter. He hit a lot of line drives for extra bases. His fielding was adequate because on our team we couldn't afford to have bad fielders. Right fielder Mike Hershberger was known for his great arm, but he also was a pretty good hitter. Jim Landis was a tremendous center fielder. He also wasn't a bad hitter. Jim came through in the clutch.

Off the field, we didn't really feel we were celebrities. We thought movie stars who came into our clubhouse in Los Angeles were celebrities. I signed autographs at the ballpark, but I could walk around Chicago. They knew me, but no one would bother me.

The Chicago fans were great. I had no problems with them. I figured they were partly paying my salary, so they had the right to boo me if I pitched badly. They were positive most of my career, especially at the beginning. We had a lot of commuter-suburban fans while the Cubbies had more city fans. I'm sure we had so many doubleheaders so that families could come from Joliet or wherever and spend a whole day at the ballpark. I think the hardcore White Sox fans were more knowledgeable than Cubs fans. Because of the nature of our team they knew baseball a little better. We didn't hit homers, so they were more aware of the defensive intricacies than the average fan and they liked low-scoring games. They knew about nuances, like the hit-and-run and moving up runners, while the Cub fans just wanted to see the ball go out of the ballpark. I think the White Sox fans had to learn more about baseball.

I would have preferred playing in a small town, but I got used to Chicago and liked the people and the organization. And I liked where we lived, which was in the

South Side of Chicago in the Hyde Park area—in the Piccadilly Hotel and the Del Prado. It was good for my kids because there was the park and museums, and we had a membership to a pool. At one time we stayed out in Schiller Park but the drive was too long and I wouldn't get home until about 1 A.M. after a night game. Jim Landis, Camilo Carreon, and a few others lived out there. Joel Horlen, Ron Hansen, Johnny Buzhardt, and some others lived in the Hillside area.

I did a lot of interviews but probably wasn't a very interesting subject. I had gotten to the big leagues through perseverance, and that story doesn't sell papers. I think the Chicago writers were a pretty good bunch of guys. In other competitive markets they had more of a tendency to misquote you, or make ill-informed guesses, or eavesdrop or do other things writers shouldn't do. The Chicago writers like Jerome Holtzman and Warren Brown were from the old school. They were knowledgeable and pretty much stuck to the facts. They didn't try to dig and find something bad, as did other writers.

We were part of an exciting pennant race in 1964 with the Yankees and Orioles. Horlen, Pizarro, and I started a lot of games pitching every third day. That was one of the best grooves I got into. You would think the arm wouldn't heal so quickly. I think we were 2 games behind with about 13 games left. We won something like 10 or 11 out of 13 and the Yankees won 10 out of 12, so we gained 1 game and ended up losing by just 1 game. It went down to the final Sunday. The Yankees played in Cleveland. I remember thinking Sam McDowell would beat them, but he didn't.

I ended up 20–8, with a 2.50 ERA; Pizzaro won 19 games with a slightly higher ERA; and Horlen won 13. Wilhelm, in relief, won 12 games and had an ERA below 2.00. Buzhardt, Fisher, Herbert, and Don Mossi also pitched very effectively. I vaguely remember winning my 20th game. It was bigger to the fans. It wasn't really such a big thing then, except it helped in regard to salary. There's the same difference between winning 20 or 21 as winning 19 or 20, but management doesn't think of it that way. They saw a line there I didn't pay much attention to. It was good to be a 20-game winner, but it was also good being a 19-game winner the year before.

JIM LANDIS:

In 1964 I won my last Gold Glove. I was proud to have won 5 Gold Gloves in succession. I was fortunate that I didn't make too many errors in the field, so it didn't bother me when I did make one. Except those few times I dropped easy fly balls—because they were automatic. Like Brooks Robinson and Luis Aparicio, I got most of my errors on tough chances.

During my years with Chicago, the only team besides the Yankees we worried about going into a new season was Cleveland. And that was only for a couple of years. The same with the Orioles. You *always* worried about the Yankees. I sometimes felt we were somewhat overmatched, but we were taught in our system that pitching and defense win ball games. We were just as good as the Yankees in those departments, so I thought we always had a shot going into April. Other than Mickey Mantle, the Yankees didn't awe me because of their ability, but I was impressed that they always won. We had shots. We won it in 1959 and we could have won it in 1964, when we had 98 victories and finished only 1 game behind the Yankees. I think they had a great ballclub and I didn't have as warm feelings for any opposing team's players as I did with the Yankees. I loved Elston Howard and joked around with Berra, and Kubek and Richardson—the three of us broke in together. Ford and I got to be fairly close and Mantle was an all-around fine person.

Our ace in the hole was always Al Lopez. Over the years, he remained accessible to players and sportswriters. He tried to make everyone happy, and I think it finally got to be too much. He was such a generous person all those years, and it finally got him. It is sad to say, because I always idolized Lopez, but for the last couple of years we thought he was physically sick . . . his stomach. He became more temperamental. Until the '60s, when things ran smoothly, he didn't have to lose his temper with us. I think this was because in those early days the players had more love for the game. The dollar hadn't taken over and players were more willing to put their bodies on the line. Beginning in the 1960s, the Sox players worried about themselves more as individuals. It moved away from strong unity, not drastically but gradually. I think Lopez had a hard time with this change.

Nellie, Billy, and Sherm were no longer on the White

Sox. I was looked up to more and more, as an elder statesman. I was chosen the player rep. I didn't like that too much. In those days, player reps were always in trouble because they were spokesmen. I got into trouble. The players were griping that WGN in Chicago wouldn't pay them $50 for guest appearances. They didn't ask for anything for appearing on small radio stations. After Opening Day, Ed Short, the GM, came in and I made my speech to him, voicing what the players had voted on. And I ended up not playing for a while. That's the honest-to-God truth. That hurt pretty much. Management knew I wasn't speaking for myself but they wanted to make me an example. After that I was pretty much in the doghouse. Mike Hershberger and Fred Talbot got into the doghouse with me and we were all traded after the season to Kansas City.

Up to a certain point I was very loyal to the White Sox and it was ''Thank you, thank you for letting me play on your team.'' But there were a few things that happened along the way that resulted in my not being upset when I was traded. The makeup of the team changed and the front office got—and this is the word that I want to use—stinkier. Maybe it was time to go.

MINNIE MINOSO:

I had played for the White Sox from 1951 to 1957, when Frank Lane traded me back to the Indians. I was Bill Veeck's favorite player and his good friend so he brought me back to Chicago in 1960, after he bought the team from the Comiskey family. He had been the one to sign me to my first major league contract with the Indians in 1948. After Veeck had to sell the team because he was sick with his leg, the players he picked up were let go, including me. I was traded to St. Louis after the 1961 season. I played there in 1962 and with the Washington Senators in 1963. I was unhappy that I had go somewhere else to play again. But I took pride in being a professional ballplayer and played as hard for my new teams as I had with Chicago. Soon after I went to St. Louis I ran into a wall against the Dodgers and fractured my skull and broke my wrist. I didn't play as much after that.

In the spring the White Sox brought me back from Washington. I was happy to sign another contract with the White Sox and return once more. The fans were happy to see me back. I was used mostly as a pinch hit-

ter. I got my last home run against Kansas City. It was in a game Dave Nicholson hit a ball on the roof at Comiskey Park. It was a pinch homer with two men on base. I got a big ovation. I could still hit but Chicago wanted to go with youth, so I retired. In future years I would remain with the White Sox, coaching, helping with promotions, doing everything to help. Chicago was my home and the White Sox were my family. (Everyone thought my playing career was over but they'd later have designated hitters and once each decade I would want to remind everyone I could still hit, no matter what age.)

NEW YORK YANKEES

STAN WILLIAMS:

I pitched in only 21 games and finished only 1 of my 10 starts because my arm was giving me trouble. Then I hurt my leg on the last day of the season. I blocked

Fittingly, Minnie Minoso became a Chicago White Sox for the third time and finished—or so everyone thought at the time—his marvelous career.

home plate against Al Luplow, the former football player, in extra innings against Cleveland, although the game didn't matter to either team. Nobody cared who won or lost but me because I was out there pitching and trying to get just my second win of the year. I caught a throw a little way up the line and Luplow flew through the air and his knees went into my thigh. I pitched a couple of more innings and lost anyway. But when I came out of the shower I discovered I couldn't lift my leg off the ground. That almost ended my major league career. I wouldn't pitch for the Yankees again.

PEDRO RAMOS:

I was traded by the Indians to the Yankees in early September for Ralph Terry, Bud Daley, and cash. I always wanted to play with the Yankees but had hoped it would have happened before I passed the midpoint of my career. When I joined them in Kansas City they were in a losing streak and had fallen a few games behind. I would have thought they wouldn't have much hope—but I had never been on a championship team before. I was sitting by my locker hearing various players say, "We're not out of it yet. Let's win this thing." Several spoke up. Clete Boyer, Roger Maris, Bobby Richardson, Elston Howard . . . Mickey wouldn't say anything, but everyone looked up to him and Maris. If Mantle would go through a wall, everyone would follow him.

I would say the players respected Yogi Berra as their new manager—Ralph Houk was now in the front office—but in a way he was still one of the guys. Sometimes you can be one of the guys if you're a manager and sometimes you can't. He was in a tough position. It was hard for him to discipline players who had been his teammates. Before I got there, he had to knock a harmonica out of Phil Linz's hand for playing on the team bus after a loss. That was a silly business.

When I joined the Yankees, I asked what time curfew was. They didn't have one. I kept one myself—two hours after the game on the road—because I wanted to get a good night's sleep. I lived with my second wife and walked from the hotel to Yankee Stadium and then straight home after the game. I was a better husband the second time than the first.

Whitey Ford and Mickey Mantle would go together. I don't know what they did. I guess they'd drink. I don't know about women. I never saw them with women. That was private. I found a girl crying one day in the runway of a hotel in Los Angeles because she wanted to go out with Mickey, and he wouldn't let her in the room. I don't know how she found his room and got upstairs, but she did. I asked Mickey, "How can you let her go by, so easy? She's so beautiful." He said, "Too young. That's a problem. I don't want her."

The Yankees had a lot of different types of players, but they were a close, fun, talented club. Mickey and I were friends, not that we were in love. He didn't hold a grudge for my having hit him a few years back. He still hit 35 homers and drove in over 100 runs, but his legs were giving him more trouble and there was a good chance I could have beaten him in a footrace at this time. Roger Maris was a quiet guy, a country guy. He minded his own business, and if you left him alone he didn't bother you either. He did his job. I never saw him joke with anybody. I think he was unhappy in New York because the fans booed him for not hitting 61 homers again. He hit over 25 but that wasn't good enough.

Joe Pepitone, who replaced Moose Skowron at first, was another powerful left-handed hitter who had the perfect swing for Yankee Stadium. He hit a lot of homers and had 100 RBIs. He was also a fun guy and funny. Everyone liked him because he made the clubhouse less tense. He loved to have a good time, but we didn't run around together. Some of those guys were like lone rangers, especially in New York.

Bobby Richardson was "God's Man." That's what we called him because he was so religious. Everything was okay by that man. He was a nice person who read my fan mail for me. One time he got a letter and said, "Wait a minute, Pete, I can't read you this one." So I went to Elston Howard and asked him to read it. He started reading it and said, "No wonder, this is a very nasty letter."

Elston was a very good hitter and the best defensive catcher I ever saw. He showed me a lot of tricks. He taught me to use 2 pitchouts in a row, even 3. That worked for me. He handled me pretty good. He was a polite gentleman who tried to help everyone the best he could.

Clete Boyer was a pretty likable guy and a helluva third baseman, the best I saw other than Brooks Robinson. Tom Tresh was a good guy and a pretty good ballplayer. He played left field because Tony Kubek was at short. Kubek wasn't hitting as well as he had, but he was still a solid ballplayer and a good man to have on a club. He was another quiet man who did his job and minded his own business. Phil Linz was his backup shortstop. Linz liked to have a drink and have fun. He was a fair ballplayer. Hector Lopez had been a steady player for the Yankees for several years, playing left field or coming off the bench. He was a quiet guy who did the best he could.

Jim Bouton had a big mouth. But he could pitch. He was our top winner in 1964, with 18 victories. Al Downing was a left-hander with good stuff. He was a quiet gentleman, much like Elston Howard. Steve Hamilton was a 6'6" left-hander who pitched with me, Pete Mikkelsen, and Hal Reniff out of the bullpen. He was a helluva guy. He liked to do funny things and use all kinds of motions on the mound.

Whitey Ford liked to have fun and joke around, but he was a pretty quiet guy. He had been around many years, but he was still a smart, talented pitcher. In 1964 Ford went 17–6. He always had such a good winning percentage. Whitey was good at scratching the ball. We used to call his pitch a "mudball." That was my palm-ball. Whitey showed me one day how he did it and said he bet I couldn't hit it. That was true. He used to throw it at half speed. Whitey told me that I had such good con-trol that it was bad. He said I threw too many strikes and said I could have been a better pitcher over the years if I'd moved the ball around once I got ahead on the count. With my control, I could have done that. I was too honest a pitcher and too often challenged a hitter. With the Yankees, if I got ahead on my fastball or rinky-dinky curve, then I used the sinker. I didn't try for the strikeout with the high and hard fastball anymore. I threw from the belt down and was happy if the batter just made bad contact. Now I relied on my sinker and the results were much better.

My first game was in relief in Kansas City. They had men on first and third with one out. I came in to pitch to a right-handed hitter. But Bill Bryan, a left-hander, pinch-hit. He had always hit me good. I pitched him low and away and hoped he hit a ground ball. And he hit one to my right. I looked back and saw Kubek catch the ball and flip it over to Richardson and he completed the double play, and I got excited, thinking, "Man, these aren't the Washington Senators. Nobody's going to beat me here." In that month I got 7 saves and 1 win, lost none, and the Yankees won by 1 game. That was exciting. But I helped the Yankees win the pennant and then wasn't allowed to participate in the World Series because they got me too late for me to be eligible. That was hard. At least I got to play on the Yankees' last pennant-winner of the era.

WORLD SERIES

1964

YANKEES VS CARDINALS

STAN WILLIAMS · YANKEES:

I shouldn't have been eligible for the World Series because of my leg injury in the last game of the season. Maybe they could have put Pedro Ramos in my place. I told Yogi I couldn't pitch in the Series and told him to replace me. But they decided not to in case I came around. Maybe they figured they didn't need me anyway. So I dragged my leg down to the bullpen every day and watched the game.

The Series with the Cardinals went back and forth. Ford got hit hard in Game One and didn't pitch again. Bouton won both games he started. And Berra gave 3 starts to Mel Stottlemyre, who had come up from Triple A during the season and gone 9–3. Gibson beat him in the decisive seventh game.

DICK GROAT · CARDINALS:

The Yankees weren't as strong as the 1960 team because Mickey Mantle's shoulder was killing him. He played only because he was such an integral part of the club. In our first victory, Mantle played right field in the very short Busch Stadium. Lou Brock had reached first against Whitey Ford and I hit a line drive between first and second. Mickey got to the ball at about the time Brock was at second, but when Brock raced toward third, the best Mickey could do was lob the ball to second base. He couldn't throw. But I admired him so much for being out there with that bad shoulder and his bad knees. He was one of the greatest competitors I ever saw in baseball.

In Game Three, Curt Simmons and Jim Bouton hooked up in a 1–1 game. Keane brought in Barney Schultz to pitch the bottom of the ninth inning, and Mickey put a major league charge into it and hit one off of this planet. A third-decker. So they beat us 2–1 and took a 2–1 lead in the Series. Stottlemyre had beaten Gibson, 8–3, in Game Two.

Game Four was the key game. We had to win it, but Sadecki fell behind 3–0 in the first inning. Keane brought in Roger Craig with men on first and second. He had the best pickoff move in the league besides ElRoy Face. And we picked off Mantle at second. That may have been the biggest play of the Series because it prevented them from scoring again. Craig and Ron Taylor shut out the Yankees on 2 hits for 8⅔ innings. And in the top of the fifth, Ken Boyer hit a grand slam homer off Al Downing, which was enough for us to win 4–3. That was the turning point in the Series. If we'd lost, we were out of it.

In Game Five, Bob Gibson overpowered the Yankees. He had them shut out 2–0 going into the bottom of the ninth. I was having the best defensive series I had in my whole life, which was fortunate because I couldn't do anything at the plate. But then I almost cost us a ball game. Mickey dragged a bunt toward shortstop. I stupidly didn't remember he was running on bad legs, and charged the ball as fast as I could, and made an error on an in-between hop. Then Tom Tresh hit a 2-run homer to tie the game. I didn't feel great. But Timmy McCarver bailed me out. He hit a 3-run homer off Pete Mikkelsen in the tenth inning, and we won, 5–2. Thank God!

Bob Gibson was great in the Series, which wasn't unexpected. He was a big-game pitcher. The relievers let him down in Game Two, but he came back to win Game Five, going all 10 innings, and he also won Game Seven, gutting it out although he was tired. He gave up 5 runs in that game, but not until we had already scored 6. He went the distance for a 7–5 win and we were World Champions!

TIM McCARVER · ST. LOUIS:

If Bob Uecker had not been on the Cardinals, then it's questionable whether we could have beaten the Yankees. He kept everything so funny that we never had the chance to think of what a monumental event we were taking part in, against the New York Yankees of all teams. He didn't play but he kept us all loose. I still remember him merrily fielding grounders with a trombone he borrowed from a band that played at Busch Stadium prior to the first game. He was actually charged for damage to the instrument, and Augie Busch wouldn't pick up the bill.

There was no way the World Series could be anything like the pennant race. We knew that going in. We split the first 2 games in St. Louis. We came from behind in the opener, tying the game on a Mike Shannon homer off Whitey Ford that broke the U in Mr. Busch's BUDWEISER sign, and eventually winning 9–5. We lost the second game to Mel Stottlemyre, 8–3. The Yankees broke it open with 4 runs in the ninth after Gibson had been removed for a pinch hitter. Our relief ace, Barney Schultz, would have a rough Series.

The 3 games in New York were phenomenal. Did Mantle ever hit that ball off Schultz's knuckler to win Game Three! It landed in the highest tier, somewhere in the darkness. Ken Boyer won Game Four for us, 4–3, with a grand slam in the fifth inning off Al Downing. We got fabulous relief pitching by Roger Craig and Ron Taylor. In Game Five, Gibson dueled Stottlemyre. We went ahead 2–0 in the fifth and it appeared that was the way the game would end because Gibson was so dominating. He struck out 13. But the Yankees unexpectedly tied the game on a 2-run homer by Tom Tresh in the bottom of the ninth. In the top of the tenth, we got runners on first and third with 1 out against Pete Mikkelsen and I came up to hit. Mikkelsen's best pitches were his palm ball and sinkerball, but on a 3–2 count he threw me a fat fastball up in the strike zone. I didn't think I hit it that good, but in Yankee Stadium you didn't have to hit it that hard to get it out in right. I remember touching first, but after that I could no longer feel my legs as I circled the diamond. I had to look down to make sure my feet were touching the bases. Gibson shut the Yankees down in the bottom half of the inning for a 5–2 win, and at that point I sensed we were going to win the Championship. My homer was one of a number of keys in the Series.

The Yankees came back to win Game Six in St. Louis, 8–3. Jim Bouton won his second game of the Series and Pepitone hit a grand slam and Mantle and Maris hit solo homers.

In the seventh game, Gibson went against Stottlemyre for the third time. We got homers from Brock and Boyer and took a 6–0 lead after 4 innings and held on for a 7–5 victory. Gibson gave up solo homers to Clete Boyer and Phil Linz in the ninth inning that made the final score close. Johnny Keane told the press at the end of the game that he had no intention of taking out Gibson because he "owed it to his heart."

After the World Series, Bob and I went on "The Ed Sullivan Show." We got $500 and were ecstatic: "$500 for just one day?" Ed came backstage before the show. He called me "Irishman." On the show, he made a comment and I improvised, "Yes, sir, Mr. Sullivan."

When I had time to think about what we had accomplished, I realized that dethroning the Yankees was incredibly rewarding. They weren't the New York Yankees of the '50s or even 1961, but they still had the name and the tradition. They still had Mantle, Maris, Ford, Richardson—who set a Series record with 13 hits—Pepitone, Kubek, Boyer, Tresh, Howard, and other great players. Just because we beat them, I didn't think that their dynasty was over. But I was wrong. . . .

INDEX

Note: Page numbers in *italics* refer to photographs.

INDEX